WHERE TO FIND BUSINESS INFORMATION

WHERE TO FIND BUSINESS INFORMATION

EDITORIAL STAFF

The Hudson Group, Inc.

JOAN LIZZIO   Managing Editor

BRENDA DARCEY   Senior Editor
MARGARET HUFFMAN   Senior Editor

Editorial Assistants

Christopher Carruth   Paul Lizzio
Hayden Carruth   Cynthia Lord
Mary Egner   Dorcas Malott
Raymond V. Hand, Jr.   Ellen Slater
Karen Lizzio   Carol Sweeney

AEIOU, Inc.

Cynthia Crippen and Felice Levy   Editorial Directors
Nancy Newfield   Editor

WHERE TO FIND BUSINESS INFORMATION

Second Edition

A WORLDWIDE GUIDE FOR EVERYONE WHO NEEDS THE ANSWERS TO BUSINESS QUESTIONS

DAVID M. BROWNSTONE

GORTON CARRUTH

A Hudson Group Book

A WILEY-INTERSCIENCE PUBLICATION
JOHN WILEY & SONS
New York • Chichester • Brisbane • Toronto • Singapore

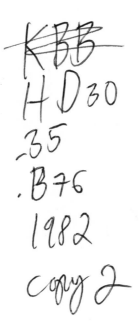
Library of Congress Cataloging in Publication Data:

Brownstone, David M.
    Where to find business information.

    "A Hudson Group book."
    "A Wiley-Interscience publication."
    Includes index.
    1. Industrial management—Information services.
2. Business—Information services. 3. Industrial
management—Bibliography. 4. Business—Bibliography.
I. Carruth, Gorton. II. Title.

HD30.35.B76 1982 016.33 81-16439
ISBN 0-471-08736-X AACR2

Printed in the United States of America

10 9 8 7 6 5 4 3 2 1

PREFACE

This Second Edition of *Where to Find Business Information* represents a stem-to-stern revision of the First Edition. Each of the original entries was scrutinized: names, addresses, telephone numbers, and prices were revised from the latest available information supplied by individual publishers. Many of the descriptive annotations were made more accurate. Furthermore, the index was overhauled: in some areas new subject headings were supplied to make the index easier to use, and every term was checked for accuracy and appropriateness. The coverage of newspapers and data bases was expanded. New periodicals and books were added; outdated and defunct publications were deleted. In every area this Second Edition is more current and useful.

We have been gratified by the professional reviews and the many helpful letters that have offered friendly criticism and useful new information. We were especially pleased that our colleagues in the publishing industry selected *Where to Find Business Information* as 1979's most outstanding book in the area of Business and Management. Our thanks, then, to everyone who has helped us produce a better book.

DAVID M. BROWNSTONE
GORTON CARRUTH

January 1982

PREFACE
TO THE
FIRST EDITION

Today's manager needs a readily available, inexpensive, and easy-to-use "key" to the kind of information required to run modern business more successfully. This essential business information, because of instantaneous electronic communication, vast computer storage, and very rapid publication, has become so extensive and is found in so many different places throughout the world that managers hardly know where to turn to find it. We have compiled this book, therefore, not only with a real sense of urgency (the information "explosion," after all, expands exponentially), but especially with a genuine belief in its usefulness for managers themselves and for all people, such as librarians, accountants, attorneys, and other professional men and women, who serve the business community.

We have designed *Where to Find Business Information* to show precisely and quickly where current business information is located and how to get it. We have described briefly what kind of information each source contains and told how much it costs. We have listed a wide variety of publications—more than 5000—appearing in English throughout the world. We have covered all subjects of interest to the world of business.

We wish to emphasize the word *current.* Unlike conventional bibliographies, which cover old books and long-dead magazines stored away in libraries, this directory includes only those sources of business information that are up-to-date and now being published. We have concentrated especially on periodic publications and services, such as magazines, newsletters, continuously revised loose-leaf services, computerized data bases, printouts, and microforms. We have excluded those dictionaries, encyclopedias, and textbooks that are not frequently revised by their publishers. The vast library, moreover, of out-of-print books, some of them no doubt classics in their day, does not consume in our book the much needed space we have set aside for current publications.

We also wish to draw attention to the *scope* of *Where to Find Business Information.* Its coverage is unique in at least two respects: (1) it is thoroughly international, listing English-language publications from all countries of the world; and (2) it is far-ranging in the variety of publications it describes. English is, after all, the language of commerce, and there are noteworthy publications from such far distant places as Hong Kong and Geneva, Sydney and Toronto, Tel Aviv and New York, and London and Johannesburg. But business persons throughout the world look especially to North America, not only for technical help and financial resources, but also for markets, and we have therefore been particularly diligent in locating useful American and Canadian publications of the widest scope.

The kinds of publications we have selected include:

1. Current business, financial, and related information services in print. These periodically updated compilations, often loose-leaf, cover areas in which information accretes rapidly and must be disseminated quickly. Examples are the Commerce Clearing House services worldwide, the Bureau of National Affairs services in the United States, the De Boo Canadian service, and the Moody and Standard and Poor financial services.

2. Major newsletters covering business information. These tend to be more interpretive than the information services, though they contain valuable current information. Examples are the Business International letters and many trade association letters.

3. Trade periodicals. Every major industry is serviced by one or more periodicals focusing on the special needs of that industry. Examples include *Publishers Weekly* and *Retail Memo.*

4. General business periodicals. These include such well-known newspapers and magazines as the *Financial Times* and *Fortune.* Included in this category are periodicals of a more general nature that contain strong business information sections; an example would be *The New York Times.*

5. Computerized data bases, such as the United States Department of Commerce National Technical Information Service.

6. Published books focusing upon the recording of current business information, with special emphasis on yearbooks and directories.

7. Governmental business information output, including international, national, state, provincial, and some important local sources. Examples are some of the United Nations, United States Treasury, and United States Department of Commerce publications.

We have organized *Where to Find Business Information* with an eye to efficiency. In this regard a real innovation is the placement of its chief index first—ahead of all else. We call this index the "Source Finder." It lists in alphabetical order more than 2500 subjects covered by business publications and it is, with its generous use of cross-references, the indispensable "starting point" for the proper and efficient use of the directory. Most of the subjects are in turn sorted by geographical subheads—more than 2000 of them—which direct the user to specific sources of information about various regions, countries, states, and cities of the world. This highly detailed "Source Finder" pro-

vides a quick, easy-to-use entry to the exact information source the business person needs.

Second, we have provided a separate section listing each publisher and its titles. There are more than 1500 worldwide publishers listed in the "Publishers' Index" and they are represented by over 5000 sources of business information. It is here, in the second index of the book, that the user can see at a glance the scores of titles published by, for example, McGraw-Hill in New York, Commerce Clearing House in Toronto, or Her Majesty's Printing Office in London.

Third, last, and the heart of the book, is the "Sources of Business Information," arranged alphabetically by title. Each title has been assigned its own number, which is utilized by the "Source Finder" and the "Publishers' Index." Since there are nearly always several entries to a page, this special number permits the user to locate immediately the title wanted.

If you have the name of a specific business information source, and want to find out more about it, go directly to "Sources of Business Information." Caution—you may not have the name quite right, and may need to find the source through the "Source Finder" or the "Publisher's Index."

If you have only the name of the publisher, go directly to the "Publisher's Index," which will refer you to "Sources of Business Information." Caution here as well —you may not have the name quite right, or have the wrong publisher, and may need to find the source through the "Source Finder."

If you have neither source name nor publisher, go directly to the "Source Finder," and look for the sources you need under the appropriate subject headings. They will lead you directly to the full descriptions carried in "Sources of Business Information."

We would like to illustrate each of these three sections more graphically:*

*The sample that follows comes from the First Edition and therefore titles and page numbers are different from those in this edition.

SECTION I: Source Finder

Subject title.

IMPORTS AND EXPORTS. *See also*
Foreign Trade

Important cross-references here.

Arabian Year Book 295
Business International (BI) Data 697
Commodity Imports 1028
Confederation of British Industry (CBI)
Overseas Reports 1103
Export Administration Report 1819
Exporter's Financial and Marketing
Handbook, 1975 1823
Export Shipping Manual 1851
Foreign Market Reports Index 2134
Manufacturer's Agent 3107
Market Share Reports 3142
Multinational Business Yearbook and
Marketing Guide 3334
Thapar's First International Import and
Export Directory of the
World 4605
Verified Directory of
Manufacturers' Representatives,
1977 edition 4847
Whaley Eaton Foreign Letter 4959
Yearbook of International Trade Statistics
5094

Titles of sources are arranged alphabetically.

Africa

Foreign Trade Statistics for Africa Series A
Direction of Trade 2140
Foreign Trade Statistics for Africa Series B
Trade by Commodity 2141
Research Reports 4092

American Nations

Carribean Year Book, 1977–78 864
Latin America Commodities Report 2972
Research Reports 4092

Full titles, with necessary dates and parts, are given.

Australia

Australian Directory of Exports 394
Australian Exports, Country by
Commodity 400
Australian Imports, Country by
Commodity 404
Australian Trading News 420
Balance of Payments 451
Exports of Major Commodities by Country
1852
Imports 2443
Imports Cleared for Home Consumption:
Part 1, Chapters 1–67 of Customs Tariff
2445
Imports Cleared for Home Consumption:
Part 2, Chapters 68–99 of Customs
Tariff 2446
Overseas Trade, Part 1: Exports and
Imports 3661

Overseas Trade, Part 2: Comparative and
Summary Tables 3662
Overseas Trade (Preliminary), Part 1:
Exports 3663
Overseas Trade (Preliminary), Part 2:
Imports 3664
Overseas Trade Statistics, Part 1: Exports
3666
Tariff Brief 4530

Sources of general, "across-the-board" interest come first.

Belgium

Belgian American Trade Review 520
BRU Export Finance Service 631

California

California International Trade 737

Cambodia

Business China 674

Canada

Action Canada France 45
Bank of Canada Review 485
British Columbia Market News 605
Canada United Kingdom Trade News 770
Canadian International Trade Classification
Numeric Index. E and F 810
Export and Import Permits Act
Handbook 1820
Export News Bulletin 1829
Exports by Commodities 1830
Exports by Countries 1831
Exports Merchandise Trade. Imports
Merchandise Trade 1852
External Trade Report 1976 1864
Importfile 2442
Imports by Commodities 2444
Review & Digest Bulletin 4119
Summary of External Trade 4492
Trade and Industry Bulletin 4649
Trade of Canada Commodity
Classification E and F 4667

Title numbers give exact location of entry in Section III, "Sources of Business Information."

China, People's Republic of

Business China 674

Geographical subtitles help locate precise source needed.

Colorado

Colorado Foreign Trade Directory 987

Europe

Consumer Europe 1153
European Marketing Data & Statistics
1785
Kelly's Manufacturers & Merchants
Directory 2907
Research Reports 4092

SECTION II: Publishers' Index

IPC BUSINESS PRESS LTD
205 E 42nd St
New York, NY 10017

Applied Ergonomics 286
Applied Mathematics Modelling 287
Composites 1068
Computer-Aided Design 1071
Cryogenics 1265
Energy Policy 1687
Food Policy 2094
Fuel 2195
Fuel Abstracts and Current Titles 2196
Futures 2204
Iron and Steel International 2786
Marine Policy 3121
Microprocessors 3214
Non-Destructive Testing (NDT)
    International 3530
Optics and Laser Technology 3632
Policy Publications Review 3795
Polymer 3807
Resources Policy 4097
Science and Public Policy 4196
Telecommunications Policy 4583
Tropical Agriculture 4722
Utrasonics 4738
Underwater Information Bulletin 4740
Welding and Metal Fabrication 4944

All appropriate sources of business information are listed for each publisher.

IRAN

IMPERIAL EMBASSY OF IRAN
Economic Section
5530 Wisconsin Ave
Washington, DC 20015

Iran Economic News 2779

**IRAN AMERICAN CHAMBER OF
COMMERCE, INC**
555 5th Ave, Suite 500
New York, NY 10017

Iran American Interchange 2778

City, state, and national governments are listed as publishers.

IRELAND

CENTRAL STATISTICS OFFICE
Earlsfort Terrace
Dublin 2, Ireland

External Trade Statistics 1866
Irish Statistical Bulletin 2781
Statistical Abstract of Ireland 4419
Trade Statistics of Ireland 4676

Titles are arranged in alphabetical order.

IRISH CONGRESS OF TRADE
Unions Research Serv
19 Ragland Rd
Ballsbridge
Dublin 4, Ireland

Trade Union Information 4679

IRISH EXPORT BOARD
Strand Rd
Sandymount
Dublin 4, Ireland

Export 1817
Irish Export Directory 2780

Publishers are listed in alphabetical order.

PETER ISAACSON PUBLICATIONS
46–49 Porter Street
Prahran, Vic 3181, Australia

Australian Directory of Exports 394
Australian Hospital 402
Australian Hospitals and Health
    Services Yearbook 403
Aviation News/Airmarket 440
Datascope 1344
Graphix 2260
Hospitality 2393
Hotel, Motel, and Travel Directory 2400
Metal and Engineering Industry Yearbook
    3196
New DP Index 3436
Pacific Computer Weekly 3679
Travelweek 4705
Visa Information Guide 4859

Title numbers give exact location of entry in Section III, "Sources of Business Information."

ISRAEL DISCOUNT BANK LTD
511 5th Ave
New York, NY 10017

Business Review and Economic News
    from Israel 720

ITALY

ITALIAN EMBASSY
Commercial Office
1601 Fuller St NW
Washington, DC 20009

Italian Trade Topics 2792
Italy: An Economic Profile 2793

Addresses suitable for ordering are given.

**ITALY AMERICAN CHAMBER OF
COMMERCE, INC**
350 5th Ave, Suite 3015
New York, NY 10001

United States Italy Trade Directory 4808

SECTION III: Sources of Business Information

Title numbers correspond with reference in "Source Finder" and in "Publishers' Index."

4131
RHM Convertible Survey
RHM Assoc, Inc, 417 Northern Blvd, Great Neck, NY 11021. Telephone (516) 487-8811.

Weekly report. Offers convertible bond and convertible preferred stock investment advice. Tables and charts. Price $125.00 per year.

4132
RHM Survey of Warrants. Options and Low-Price Stocks
RHM Assoc, Inc, 417 Northern Blvd, Great Neck, NY 11021. Telephone (516) 487-8811.

Weekly report. Provides investment advice on warrants, call and put options, and low-price stocks. Tables and charts. Price $120.00 per year.

Current prices are given.

4133
Rhodes Report
Eric F Rhodes, editor, Educational Service Bureau, Inc, 610 Madison St, Alexandria, VA 22314. Telephone (703) 683-5080.

Magazine issued eight times per year. Covers career opportunities in education, including nationwide openings at all levels, scholarships, and grants. Price $15.00 per year.

4134
Risk Management
Risk and Insurance Management Society, Inc. 205 E 42 St, New York, NY 10017. Telephone (212) 557-3222.

Monthly magazine. Features articles and news on insurance risk management. Price $15.00 per year.

4135
Road Accidents
Her Majesty's Stationery Office, PO Box 569, London, England SE1 9NH. Telephone (44)(01)928-1321.

Annual report on British road accidents. Price £2.00.

Foreign addresses and telephone numbers are given.

4136
Road Maps of Industry
Conference Board, Inc, 845 3rd Ave, New York, NY 10022. Telephone (212) 759-0900.

Semimonthly report. Presents graphic summaries on various economic and management facts of general interest. Price available on request.

4137
Road Transport Service Bulletin
Statistics Canada, Publications Distribution, Ottawa, Ont, Canada K1A OT6. Telephone (613) 992-2959.

Semimonthly service. Provides statistical summary information on Canadian motor vehicle transport industries, warehouses, urban transit systems, and motor vehicles. Includes data on traffic accidents, roads, and toll facilities. Price $2.80 per year.

Titles are arranged alphabetically for easy locating.

4138
Robert's Dictionary of Industrial Relations 1971 edition
Harold S Roberts, Bureau of National Affairs, Inc, 1231 25th St, NW Washington, DC, 20037. Telephone (202) 223-3500.

Book. Covers government regulations, labor laws, and Supreme Court decisions affecting industrial relations. Defines terms. Price $15.00. ISBN 0-87179-135-8.

When available ISBN and ISSN numbers are given.

4139
Rocky Mountain Journal
Front Range Record, Inc, 1459 S Holly St, Denver, CO 80222. Telephone (303) 757-3311.

Weekly newspaper. Delivers Denver area business information. Notes real estate activity, building permits, new corporations, and oil well starts. Price $25.00 per year.

Descriptions include type and frequency of publication.

4140
Rocky Mountain Mineral Law Institute
Matthew Bender & Co, 235 E 45th St, New York, NY 10017. Telephone (212) 661-5050.

Annual book on proceedings of Rocky Mountain Mineral Law Institute. Features articles on mining, oil, gas, water, and public lands. Price $50.00 per year.

4141
Roofing Siding Insulation.
Incorporating Solar Contractor
Harcourt Brace Jovanovich Publications, 757 3rd Ave, New York, NY 10017. Order from Harcourt Brace Jovanovich Publications, 1 E 1st St, Duluth, MN 55802. Telephone (218) 727-8511.

Special ordering addresses and telephone numbers are given.

Because of this directory's emphasis on *current* business information, some of the contents of this book will naturally undergo rapid change, especially the prices of products and services. Many publishers are reluctant to provide price lists except to immediate customers. In the case of some weekly and monthly loose-leaf services and many computer information banks, prices change almost monthly. The American price of many foreign publications will change with the fluctuating fortunes of the dollar on international money markets. Postage costs, both domestic and international, affect the price of a book or periodical. We strongly recommend that the price given in this directory be used chiefly as guidelines and that they be checked before an order is placed.

Newsletters, which are often published by an individual or a small team of experts, rather than by a large, permanent organization, spring up or disappear rapidly, and it is wise to double-check their addresses and most recent prices before sending money. It is not unreasonable, especially in the case of newsletters and expensive periodic information services, such as daily, weekly, or monthly loose-leaf publications, to ask for sample material before placing an order.

Since a busy executive is often eager to get information quickly, we have included a telephone number for nearly all publishers, even those whose offices are overseas.* The exceptions are often for the newsletters, which are sometimes written and published in a private home; their publishers preserve their privacy by refusing to give telephone numbers or street addresses. Telephone numbers are often direct lines to the sales departments of a large publisher; when a central switchboard is reached, however, simply ask for the sales manager or the sales department.

Some institutions, such as professional societies, and some publishers, such as those that restrict their circulations to a particular market, may want to know a customer's credentials before shipping sample material or accepting an order. We have been astonished from time to time at how difficult it is to get some publishers to sell their products! Over the telephone, persistence and emphasis is sometimes required, and valuable time is frequently saved by first writing an inquiry under a business letterhead and then, if necessary, following it up with a telephone call.

Sometimes we have given two addresses for a publisher, that of its headquarters or main editorial offices and that of its sales or order fulfillment departments. Sometimes a single address is for only its sales department. At any rate, do not count on using the addresses provided in this book for correspondence with an editor or writer. For such purposes, use the address given on the title page or in the masthead of most business books and periodicals.

Please note that we have not separately listed several overarching databases as specific sources of Business Information, such as The New York Times Information Bank and Lockheed's Dialog, as these sources are so comprehensive as to make it inappropriate to cite and index them in this work. The relevant components of these databases are of course covered herein.

We reserve to this final paragraph a few words about the underlying philosophy guiding our selection. We have chosen those sources of business information that seem to us the most complete for their subject or discipline, that are frequently up-dated or revised, that emanate from a reputable source, and that will be of general use to managers, executives, and professional people serving the business community. We avoided choosing those dictionaries, encyclopedias, and other reference books (of which there are a great many) that a library needs for occasional consulting but are seldom required in the day-to-day activity of running a business. We have also considered geographic coverage; we wanted to include informational sources that are useful throughout the English-speaking world. Thus, given all these considerations, we were highly selective—in spite of the more than 5000 titles herein described—and we certainly omitted some that will be missed by their publishers or by those familiar with them. Some omissions resulted from a publishing deadline. Some omissions, of course, will turn out to have been completely unintentional. For these we apologize and offer to make amends in the next edition of *Where to Find Business Information.*

DAVID M. BROWNSTONE
GORTON CARRUTH

May 1979

*For instructions on placing overseas calls, see your telephone directory or contact your telephone company.

CONTENTS

WHERE TO FIND BUSINESS INFORMATION

SOURCE FINDER

Australia

Advertising News 69

Great Britain

Advertiser's Annual 65
Brad Advertiser & Agency List 581

AERONAUTICS AND SPACE. *See also* Airplanes. Missiles

Abstract Newsletters, Biomedical Technology & Human Factors Engineering 2.06
Abstract Newsletters, NASA Earth Resources Survey Program 2.23
Aerospace Daily 75
Aerospace Facts & Figures 76
AN, AND, & MS Standards 216.01
Aviation Europe 437.01
Aviation News/Airmarket 440
Aviation Week & Space Technology 441
Aviation Week & Space Technology, Marketing Directory Issue 442
Computer Network of Databases 1081
Defense Industry Organization Service 1355.01
DMS Aerospace Agencies 1475
DMS Aerospace Companies 1475.01
DMS Aerospace Intelligence 1475.02
DMS Civil Aircraft 1475.05
DMS Code Name Handbook 1475.06
DMS Missiles/Spacecraft 1475.25
Identified Sources of Supply 2433.01
Metric Standards 3204.01
National Aeronautics and Space Administration (NASA) Activities 3356
National Aerospace Standards 3356.01
Quarterly Summary of Pacific Northwest Industries 3976
Renegotiation/Management Letter 4060
Standards and Specifications Information Bulletin 4378.01
World Aviation Directory 5042

Far East

White's Air Directory and Who's Who in New Zealand Aviation 4969.01

New Zealand

White's Air Directory and Who's Who in New Zealand Aviation 4969.01

AERONAUTICS AND SPACE, COMMERCIAL VENTURES

Aviation Week & Space Technology 441

Aviation Week & Space Technology, Marketing Directory Issue 442
DMS Aerospace Companies 1475.01

United States

Space Letter 4352

AERONAUTICS AND SPACE, MILITARY VENTURES

Aviation Europe 437.01
Aviation Week & Space Technology 441
Aviation Week & Space Technology, Marketing Directory Issue 442
DMS Aerospace Agencies 1475
DMS Missiles/Spacecraft 1475.25

United States

Aerospace Facts & Figures 76
Space Letter 4352

AERONAUTICS AND SPACE, VEHICLES

Aviation Week & Space Technology 441
Aviation Week & Space Technology, Marketing Directory Issue 442
Backlog of Orders for Aerospace Companies MQ-37D 446
DMS Missiles & Satellites (Europe) 1475.24
Mil-Hdbk-5C Handbook 3228.01

AERONAUTICS AND SPACE ADMINISTRATION, NATIONAL (NASA) (US)

Abstract Newsletters, NASA Earth Resources Survey Program 2.23
DMS Operation & Maintenance 1475.28
National Aeronautics and Space Administration (NASA) Activities 3356
Space Letter 4352

AEROSOLS

Manufacturing Chemist & Aerosol News 3113

Great Britain

Manufacturing Chemist Aerosol Review 3112

AEROSPACE INDUSTRIES. *See* Aeronautics and Space

AFFIRMATIVE ACTION.

Affirmative Action Compliance Manual for Federal Contractors 76.01

AFRICA. *See also* region and country names

Africa 77
Africa Guide 1981 78
Africa Research Bulletin 81
Africa South of the Sahara 82
African Business 79.01
African Textiles 79.03
Courier—European Communities—Africa, the Caribbean and the Pacific 1239
Current African Directories 1269
Economic Bulletin for Africa 1543
Modern Africa 3252
New African Development 3432
Statistics—Africa 4448

AFRICA, NORTH

Middle East and North Africa 3217
Trade and Credit: Problems and Resolutions in the Middle East and North Africa, in Asia and the Pacific and in Latin America 4646.01

AFRICA, SUB-SAHARA

African Business & Trade 79.02

AFRICA, WEST

West African Farming & Food Processing 4948.01
West African Technical Review 4949

AFRICAN TRADE CENTRE

African Trade/Commerce Africain 80

AGED AND AGING. *See also* Housing, Vacation and Retirement Homes. Labor, Older Workers. Nursing and Rest Homes. Pension Plans. Retired People

Aging and Work 88.01
Current Literature on Aging 1278
Perspective on Aging 3753

AGED AND AGING, GOVERNMENT REGULATIONS

Perspective on Aging 3753
Suggested State Legislation 1980 4490

AGE DISCRIMINATION IN EMPLOYMENT ACT OF 1967 (US)

Federal Wage-Hour Handbook for Banks 1976

AGRIBUSINESS

C. Brewer Today   588

AGRICULTURE.   *See also*
Agribusiness. Agronomy. Commodities and Commodity Exchanges. Fertilizers. Food. Grain. Horticulture. Irrigation. Ornamental Crops. Pesticides and Pests. Rural Areas. Seeds (Crop). Product names, eg, Fruits and Vegetables

Agricultural Engineering Abstracts   98
Agricultural Outlook   102
Agricultural Statistics   106
Agro Service International   116
Bacon's Publicity Checker   448
Canadian Farm Economics   792
Consumer Magazine & Farm
    Publication Rates & Data   1156
Direct Mail List Rates and Data   1401
Doane's Agricultural Report   1476
Economic Planning   1563
Farm Industry News   1900
Farmline   1901.01
Food & Agriculture Organization of the
    United Nations (FAO) Production
    Yearbook   2077
Food Policy   2094
Foreign Agriculture   2110
Foreign Agriculture Circulars   2111
Irrigation Age   2789
Journal of Agricultural Science   2821
Monthly Bulletin of Agricultural
    Economics and Statistics   3278
Outlook and Situation Reports
    3653.01
Oxford Agrarian Studies   3672
Print Media Production Data   3850
Selected Business Ventures   4252
State of Food and Agriculture   4402
Statistical Yearbook   4444
Trends   4716
United Nations Industrial Development
    Organization Guides to Information
    Sources. UNIDO/LIB/SER.D/8—
    Information Sources on the
    Agricultural Implements and
    Machinery Industry   4775
Weekly Weather and Crop Bulletin
    4943
World Agricultural Economics & Rural
    Sociology Abstracts   5036
World Agricultural Situation   5038
World Farming   5064

Africa

Africa South of the Sahara   82
Agricultural Economics Bulletin for
    Africa   96
Economic Bulletin for Africa   1543

Modern Africa   3252
West African Farming & Food
    Processing   4948.01

Arkansas

Arkansas USA   321.01

Australia

Primary Industry Newsletter   3841
World Agricultural Report   5037

California

Economic Outlook: California Report
    1558

Canada

Spectrum   4359.01
Field Crop Reporting Series   1984
Handbook of Agricultural Statistics,
    Part I: Field Crops   2318
Saskatchewan Monthly Statistical
    Review   4182

China, People's Republic of

Soviet-Eastern Europe-China Business
    & Trade   4351

Colorado

Business Economic Outlook Forum
    678

Europe

Agro Service International   116
Soviet-Eastern Europe-China Business
    & Trade   4351

European Economic Community

Basic Statistics   514.01
Bulletin of the European Communities
    646
Common Market News   1038
European Trends   1787.01
Green Europe: Newsletter on the
    Common Agricultural Policy
    2264.01
Yearbook of Agricultural Statistics
    5090.01

Far East

Asian Agricultural Survey   326

Great Britain

Agricultural Statistics: England &
    Wales   107
Agricultural Statistics: United Kingdom
    110
Agriculture Abroad   112

Guam

State and County Data, Vol I   4385

Hawaii

Hawaii Annual Economic Review
    2347

Illinois

Illinois Agricultural Statistics   2436

Iowa

Wallaces' Farmer   4875

Iran

Iran Economic News   2779

Ireland, Republic of

Agriculture Abroad   112
Statistical Abstract of Ireland   4419

Ireland, Northern

Statistical Review of Farming in
    Northern Ireland   4440

Mexico

Agriculture Abroad   112

Minnesota

Farmer   1896

New Mexico

Economy   1577

New South Wales

Commodity Bulletin   1025

New York State

Central New York Business Review
    890

New Zealand

New Zealand Agricultural Statistics
    3491

North Dakota

Farmer   1896
North Dakota Crop and Livestock
    Statistics   3536

Scotland

Agricultural Statistics, Scotland   109

South Dakota

Farmer 1896

South (US)

Southern Journal of Agricultural Economics 4349

Third World

Ceres: Food and Agriculture Organization (FAO) Review on Development 894

Tropical Areas

Tropical Agriculture 4722

Union of Soviet Socialist Republics (USSR)

Agriculture Abroad 112
Soviet-Eastern Europe-China Business & Trade 4351

United States

Agriculture and Commodities Service 111
Agriculture Abroad 112
Amer Journal of Agricultural Economics 194
Business & Capital Reporter 658
Census of Agriculture Preliminary Reports for Counties, States, and the United States, 1978 874
Farmer 1896
Food Institute Reports: Report on Food Markets; Washington Food Report; Weekly Digest 2089
From the State Capitals: Agriculture and Food Products 2169
Guide to Trade and Securities Statistics 2305
Handbook of Agricultural Charts 2317

Wales

Agricultural Statistics: England & Wales 107

AGRICULTURE, ADVERTISING

Agri Marketing 115

AGRICULTURE, COOPERATIVES

Agricultural Co-Operative Bulletin 95
American Cooperation 167

Canada

Co-Operative Consumer 1193

United States

Annual Report of the Farm Credit Administration 255
Farmer Cooperatives 1897

AGRICULTURE, DEBT

Farm Credit Corporation Statistics 1894.01
Statistical Release (Agricultural Credit Conditions Survey) 4439
World Agricultural Economics & Rural Sociology Abstracts 5036

AGRICULTURE, EQUIPMENT. See also Machinery. Tractors

Agri Marketing 115
Farm Industry News 1900
Farm Machines and Equipment MA-35A 1902
Food and Agriculture Organization of the United Nations (FAO) Trade Yearbook 2078
Implement & Tractor 2442
National Electronic Injury Surveillance System (NEISS) Data Highlights 3373
United Nations Industrial Development Organization Guides to Information Sources. UNIDO/LIB/SER.D/8— Information Sources on the Agricultural Implements and Machinery Industry 4775
What's New in Farming 4962
World Farming 5064

United States

Census of Agriculture Preliminary Reports for Counties, States, and the United States, 1978 874

AGRICULTURE, EXPERIMENTAL PROJECTS

Experimental Agriculture 1814

AGRICULTURE, FEED CROPS. See also Grain

Feedstuffs 1980
Beef 517
Outlook and Situation Reports 3653.01

AGRICULTURE, FINANCES. See also Banking and Finance, Agricultural Banking

Agricultural Finance Outlook 99
Agricultural Finance Review 100
Agri Finance 114

Canadian Farm Economics 792
Economic Indicators of the Farm Sector: Income and Balance Sheet 1552.01
Farmline 1901.01
Outlook and Situation Reports 3653.01
Oxford Agrarian Studies 3672
Review of Marketing and Agricultural Economics 4125
Tropical Agriculture 4722
World Agricultural Economics & Rural Sociology Abstracts 5036

Australia

Quarterly Review of the Rural Economy 3971.01

Canada

Farm Cash Receipts 1894
Farm Credit Corporation Statistics 1894.01

European Economic Community

Economic & Social Committee of the European Communities. Bulletin 1537

Illinois

Illinois Agricultural Statistics 2436

New South Wales

Review of Marketing and Agricultural Economics 4125

North Dakota

North Dakota Crop and Livestock Statistics 3536

South (US)

Southern Journal of Agricultural Economics 4349

Union of Soviet Socialist Republics (USSR)

Problems of Economics 3857

United States

Annual Report of the Farm Credit Administration 255
Census of Agriculture Preliminary Reports for Counties, States, and the United States, 1978 874

Farm Real Estate Market
Developments   1903
Statistical Release (Agricultural Credit
Conditions Survey)   4439

AGRICULTURE, GOVERNMENT PROGRAMS AND REGULATIONS

Agri Finance   114
Food Policy   2094
Food Research Institute Studies   2097
Foreign Agricultural Trade of the
United States   2108
Foreign Agriculture   2110
Kiplinger Agricultural Letter   2912.02

AGRICULTURE, IMPORTS AND EXPORTS

Food and Agriculture Organization of
the United Nations (FAO) Trade
Yearbook   2078
Foreign Agriculture   2110
Outlook and Situation Reports
3653.01
Outlook for U.S. Agricultural Exports
3654
Weekly Roundup of World Production
and Trade   4939
World Agricultural Economics & Rural
Sociology Abstracts   5036

Australia

Crops   1260

United States

Foreign Agricultural Trade of the
United States   2108
Guide to Trade and Securities Statistics
2305
What's New in Farming   4962

AGRICULTURE, INSURANCE

Agricultural Finance Review   100

AGRICULTURE, LABOR

Oxford Agrarian Studies   3672

Florida

In-Season Farm Labor Report ES-223
2587

North Dakota

North Dakota Crop and Livestock
Statistics   3536

AGRICULTURE, LAND

Outlook and Situation Reports
3653.01
Tax Sheltered Investments   4570

United States

Farm Real Estate Market
Developments   1903

AGRICULTURE, MARKETING

Agri Marketing   115
Doane's Agricultural Report   1476
Review of Marketing and Agricultural
Economics   4125
World Agricultural Economics & Rural
Sociology Abstracts   5036

European Economic Community

Agra Europe   89
Agricultural Markets: Prices (Two
Series)   101
Green Europe   2264

Illinois

Illinois Economic Data Sheets   2438

Northwest (US)

Ag Marketer   88.02

New South Wales (Australia)

Review of Marketing and Agricultural
Economics   4125
Weekly Marketing Notes   4935.01

AGRICULTURE, PRICES

Agricultural Price Report   103
Developments in Price Spreads for
Farm Foods   1375.02
Kiplinger Agricultural Letter   2912.02
Outlook and Situation Reports
3653.01

Australia

Australia Journal of Agricultural
Economics   406

Canada

Handbook of Agricultural Statistics,
Part I: Field Crops   2318
Industry Price Indexes   2563

South Dakota

South Dakota Crop and Livestock
Reporter   4344

United States

Foreign Agricultural Trade of the
United States   2108
Guide to Trade and Securities Statistics
2305

AGRICULTURE, PRODUCTION

Doane's Agricultural Report   1476
Economic Indicators of the Farm
Sector: Production and Efficiency
Statistics   1552.02
Weekly Roundup of World Production
and Trade   4939
World Agricultural Economics & Rural
Sociology Abstracts   5036
World Agriculture Supply and Demand
Estimates   5038.01

Canada

Farm Credit Corporation Statistics
1894.01
Field Crop Reporting Series   1984
Handbook of Agricultural Statistics,
Part I: Field Crops   2318
Saskatchewan's Financial & Economic
Position   4183

European Economic Community

Agricultural Production (Two Series)
104
Green Europe   2264

Florida

Florida Statistical Abstract   2069

Illinois

Illinois Agricultural Statistics   2436

South Dakota

South Dakota Crop and Livestock
Reporter   4344

AGRICULTURE, RESEARCH ON

Abstract Newsletters, Agriculture &
Food   2.04
Auber Bibliography   346.01
Illinois Research   2439

AGRICULTURE, SHIPPING

Food & Agriculture Organization of the
United Nations (FAO) Production
Yearbook   2077
Food and Agriculture Organization of
the United Nations (FAO) Trade
Yearbook   2078

AGRICULTURE, TAXATION

Agricultural Finance Review   100
Agri Finance   114
Doane's Agricultural Report   1476
Farmer's Tax Report   1898
Internal Revenue Service Publications
2649

AGRICULTURE, TECHNOLOGY

Food Policy   2094

AGRICULTURE, TRADE.   *See*
Agriculture, Imports and Exports

AGRICULTURE, WAGES AND HOURS

Farm Wages in Canada   1906
Food & Agriculture Organization of the
United Nations (FAO) Production
Yearbook   2077

AGRICULTURE, WASTES

United Nations Industrial Development
Organization (UNIDO) Guides to
Information Sources.
UNIDO/LIB/SER.D/Rev.1—
Information Sources on
Bioconversion of Agricultural Wastes
4767.01
United Nations Industrial Development
Organization (UNIDO) Guides to
Information Sources.
UNIDO/LIB/SER.D/Rev.1—
Information Sources on the
Utilization of Agricultural Residues
for the Production of Panels, Pulp
and Paper   4767.15

AGRONOMY

Agro Service International   116
Canadian Farm Economics   792
Economic Planning   1563
Farm Economics   1895
Oxford Agrarian Studies   3672
Review of Marketing and Agricultural
Economics   4125
Tropical Agriculture   4722

Australia

Australian Journal of Agricultural
Economics   406

South (US)

Southern Journal of Agricultural
Economics   4349

United States

Amer Journal of Agricultural
Economics   194
Handbook of Agricultural Charts
2317
Palmetto Economics   3689

New South Wales

Review of Marketing and Agricultural
Economics   4125

AGRONOMY, RESEARCH ON

Agricultural Economics Research   97
Illinois Agricultural Economics   2435

AID.   *See* International Development,
Agency for (US)

AIR CONDITIONING.   *See also*
Research and Development, Air
Conditioning and Heating

Air Conditioning & Refrigeration
Business   120
Australian Refrigeration,
Air-Conditioning and Heating
413.01
Contractor   1187
Heating & Air Conditioning Journal
2366
Heating/Piping/Air Conditioning
2368
Heating–Plumbing Air Conditioning
2369
Solar Heating and Cooling Magazine
4326.04

AIR CONDITIONING, GOVERNMENT REGULATIONS

Advertising Substantiation Program   72

AIR CUSHION VEHICLES

Lloyd's Weekly Casualty Reports
3034

AIR FORCE.   *See* Armament and
Defense

AIR FREIGHT

Airtrade   127
Aviation Week & Space Technology
441
Aviation Week & Space Technology,
Marketing Directory Issue   442
Decisions of the Air Transport
Committee   1353
International Freighting Weekly   2683
Routes Yearbook   4144

Canada

Decisions of the Air Transport
Committee   1353

New England

Boston Marine Guide   577

United States

United States Airborne Exports and
General Imports FT986   4793

AIRLINES.   *See also* Airplanes.
Airports. Transportation

Air Transport   128
Air Transport World   129
Business & Commercial Aviation   659
Business Traveller   725
Handbook of Airline Statistics   2322
Lloyd's Law Reports   3032.03
Travel Weekly   4706
World Air Transport Statistics   5039
World Aviation Directory   5042

Canada

International Air Charter Statistics
2655
Transcontinental and Regional Air
Carrier Operations   4687

Far East

White's Air Directory and Who's Who
in New Zealand Aviation   4969.01

Great Britain

Civil Aviation Authority Monthly
Statistics   952
Travel Trade Directory   4702

New Zealand

White's Air Directory and Who's Who
in New Zealand Aviation   4969.01

United States

Hawkins Civil Aeronautics Board
Service   2349

AIRLINES, FINANCES

Air Transport   128
Handbook of Airline Statistics   2322

AIRLINES, GOVERNMENT REGULATIONS

World Aviation Directory   5042

United States

Aviation Cases   436
Aviation Law Reports   438

AIRLINES, INSURANCE

Aviation Cases   436
Aviation Law Reports   438

AIRPLANES.   *See also* Airlines.
Airports, Gliders. Helicopters.
Navigation, Air. Transportation

Abstract Newsletters, Transportation
  2.28
Aviation Daily   437
Aviation Week & Space Technology
  441
Aviation Week & Space Technology,
  Marketing Directory Issue   442
Business & Commercial Aviation   659
DMS Civil Aircraft   1475.05
DMS World Aircraft Forecast   1475.35
Flying   2072
Flying Annual & Buyers' Guide   2073
Reference Book of Transportation
  4041
World Air Transport Statistics   5039

Australia

Aviation News/Airmarket   440
Trans-Tasman   4699

Canada

Decisions of the Air Transport
  Committee   1353
Handbook of Air Carrier Legislation
  2321.01

Europe

Aviation Europe   437.01

Great Britain

Civil Aviation Authority Monthly
  Statistics   952

New Zealand

Trans-Tasman   4699

United States

Backlog of Orders for Aerospace
  Companies MQ–37D   446

AIRPLANES, ACCIDENTS AND SAFETY

Aviation Monthly   439
Federal Aviation Administration (FAA)
  General Aviation News   1912

Flying   2072
Lloyd's Weekly Casualty Reports
  3034
National Transportation Safety Board
  Service   3409

AIRPLANES, CHARTER

International Air Charter Statistics
  2655

Canada

Decisions of the Air Transport
  Committee   1353

United States

Aviation Cases   436
Aviation Law Reports   438

AIRPLANES, GOVERNMENT REGULATIONS

Aviation Cases   436
Aviation Law Reports   438
World Aviation Directory   5042

AIRPLANES, IMPORTS AND EXPORTS

Complete Aircraft and Aircraft
  Engines. M37G   1064

AIRPLANES, INSURANCE

Aviation Cases   436
Aviation Law Reports   438

AIRPLANES, MILITARY

Aviation Europe   437.01
Aviation News/Airmarket   440
Aviation Week & Space Technology
  441
Aviation Week & Space Technology,
  Marketing Directory Issue   442
DMS Military Aircraft   1475.20
DMS World Aircraft Forecast   1475.35

AIRPLANES, PARTS AND EQUIPMENT

Complete Aircraft and Aircraft Engines
  M37G   1064
Flying   2072
Flying Annual & Buyers' Guide   2073
World Aviation Directory   5042

Far East

White's Air Directory and Who's Who
  in New Zealand Aviation   4969.01

New Zealand

White's Air Directory and Who's Who
  in New Zealand Aviation   4969.01

AIRPLANES, PASSENGER

Aviation Week & Space Technology,
  Marketing Directory Issue   442
Metropolitan   3205

Australia

Aviation News/Airmarket   440

Canada

Air Passenger Origin & Destination,
  Canada–US Report   123
Air Passenger Origin & Destination,
  Domestic Report   124

United States

Air Passenger Origin & Destination,
  Canada–US Report   123
Complete Aircraft and Aircraft Engines
  M37G   1064

AIRPLANES, PERSONNEL

Federal Aviation Administration (FAA)
  General Aviation News   1912

AIRPLANES, SPECIALIZED

Business Flying   683
Federal Aviation Administration (FAA)
  General Aviation News   1912

AIR POLLUTION

Pollution Abstracts   3803
Transportation Planning and
  Technology   4693

Canada

Canadian Environmental Control
  Newsletter   791
Eco/Log Week   1533

United States

Abstract Newsletters, Environmental
  Pollution & Control   2.15
Air Pollution Control   125
Pollution Control Guide   3804

AIRPORTS

Airport Services Management   126

Canada

Air Carrier Traffic at Canadian
  Airports   119

Great Britain

Civil Aviation Authority Monthly
Statistics 952

United States

From the State Capitals: Airport
Construction and Financing 2170

AIRPORTS, GOVERNMENT REGULATIONS

From the State Capitals: Airport
Construction and Financing 2170

AIR TRANSPORT ASSOCIATION, INTERNATIONAL

World Air Transport Statistics 5039

AIR TRANSPORT COMMITTEE (CANADA)

Decisions of the Air Transport
Committee 1353

ALABAMA

Alabama Business 133
Alabama Development News 134
Alabama Directory of Mining and
Manufacturing, 1980–1981 edition
134.07
Alabama Mining & Manufacturing
Directory, 1980–81 136
Alabama: State Industrial Directory,
1980 136.01
From State Capitals 2169–2191
State and Local Taxes 4386
State Legislative Reporting Service
4396
State Tax Reports 4413

ALASKA

Alaska Business News Letter 137
Alaska Economic Trends 138
Alaska Industry 139
Alaska—Occupational Employment
Forecast 141
Alaska: Petroleum & Industrial
Directory, 1980 141.01
Alaska Review of Social & Economic
Conditions 142
From the State Capitals 2169–2191
Government 1975—Occupational
Employment Statistics 2246
Labor Market Information Directory
2938
State and Local Taxes 4386
State Legislative Reporting Service
4396

State Tax Reports 4413
Statistical Quarterly 4437
Trade and Regulated Industries
Occupational Employment Statistics
4650
Unfilled Job Openings Report 4746

ALBERTA PROVINCE (CANADA).
See Canada.

ALCOHOL (NONBEVERAGE)

Bottom Line 579

ALCOHOLIC BEVERAGES. *See*
Alcoholism. Liquor

ALCOHOLISM

Bottom Line 579
Monday Morning Report 3266.01

ALGERIA

Developing Business in the Middle East
and North Africa 1371

ALLOYS. *See also* Metal Products.
Metals and Metallurgy

Mil-Hdbk-5C Handbook 3228.01

ALUMINUM

Aluminum Data 150
Aluminum Ingot and Mill Products
M33-2 151
Aluminum Statistical Review 152
World Aluminum Abstracts 5040

AMERICAN FEDERATION of LABOR-CONGRESS of INDUSTRIAL ORGANIZATIONS (AFL-C1O)

AALC Reporter 79

AMERICAN NATIONS AND WESTERN HEMISPHERE POSSESSIONS. *See also* country names

Business Latin America 700
Caribbean Business News 863
Caribbean Regional Report 863.01
Caribbean Year Book, 1977–78 864
Courier—European Communities—
Africa, the Caribbean, and the Pacific
1239
Economic & Social Progress in Latin
America: Annual Report 1538
FFO/Latin America (FFO/LA) 1982
Hanson's Latin American Letter 2341

Informational and Technical
Publications of the General
Secretariat of the Organization of
American States (OAS) 2569
Inter-American Economic Affairs
2641
Latin America & Caribbean, 1981
2969.01
Latin American Index 2975
Latin America Weekly Report 2976.02
Mexico and Central America Regional
Report 3206.02
Southern Cone Regional Report
4347.01
Statistics—America 4449
Trade and Credit: Problems and
Resolutions in the Middle East and
North Africa, in Asia and the Pacific
and in Latin America 4646.01

AMERICAN STATES, ORGANIZATION OF (OAS)

Estadistica 1744

AMERICAN STOCK EXCHANGE (AMEX)

American Exchange Stock Reports
173
Amer Stock Exchange Guide 208
Chartcraft Weekly Service 912
Daily Graphs American Stock
Exchange/O.T.C. 1297
Dow Jones Investor's Handbook 1500
Moody's Industrial Manual and News
Reports 3314
Stock Guide 4466
Trade Levels Option Report 4656
Trade Levels Report 4657

AMUSEMENTS. *See* Entertainment.
Recreation

ANIMALS. *See also* Fur Goods. Pet
Food. Pet Shops. Pets. Types of
animals, eg, Sheep. Veterinary Medicine

Agricultural Engineering Abstracts 98

ANIMALS, RESEARCH ON

Abstracts on Health Effects of
Environmental Pollutants (HEEP) 4

ANNUITIES. *See* Insurance,
Annuities

ANTHROPOLOGY

Economic Development & Cultural
Change 1548

ANTITRUST ACTIONS AND LAWS

Antitrust Bulletin 272
Antitrust Laws and Trade Regulation 273
Business International Washington (BIW) 699.01
Guide to Legislation on Restrictive Business Practices 2299
Journal of Reprints for Antitrust Law and Economics 2880
Law and Business of Licensing 2977

United States

Acts 46
Antitrust & Trade Regulation Report 271
Law and Business of Licensing 2977
Trade Cases 4653
Trade Regulation Reports 4671

APARTMENT HOUSES. *See* Housing, Multifamily. Housing, Rentals.

APPAREL. *See also* Footwear. Fur Goods. Knitting and Knitgoods. Hosiery. Retailing

Body Fashions/Intimate Apparel Incorporating Hosiery and Underwear 569
Men's Apparel M23B 3189
Sportswear Graphics 4365
Textile Institute and Industry 4599
United Nations Industrial Development Organization Guides to Information Sources. UNIDO/LIB/SER. D/12—Information Sources on the Clothing Industry 4779
Women's Misses', and Juniors' Apparel M23H 5015

Africa

Africa Woman 83
African Textiles 79.03

Australia

Clothing Industry News 967.01
Men's Wear 3189.02

Europe

West European Living Costs 1977 4952

Great Britain

British Clothing Manufacturer 599.01
Drapers Record 1505.02
Men's Wear 3189.01

Hong Kong

Apparel Magazine 282.01
Hong Kong Trader 2388

South (US)

Apparel South 282.01

APPAREL, BUYERS

British Clothing Manufacturer 599.01
Buying Offices and Accounts 729
Major Mass Market Merchandisers 3063
Nationwide Men's & Boys' Wear 3416

APPAREL, FINANCES

Apparel Trades Book 283

APPLIANCES, HOME. *See* Home Furnishings. Types, eg, Electrical Appliances. Gas Appliances

APPRAISERS

Appraisal Institute Magazine (AIM) 290
Appraisal Journal 291
Appraisal Manual 291.01
Appraiser 292
Bibliography of Appraisal Literature 548
Directory of Designated Members 1426.01
Real Estate Appraiser and Analyst 4011
Valuation 4838

APPRENTICESHIPS. *See* Labor, Training

ARAB COUNTRIES. *See* Middle East

ARBITRATION. *See also* Labor–Management Relations

Arbitration Journal 299
International Commercial Arbitration 2667
Lawyers' Arbitration Letter and Digest of Court Decisions 2989
News and Views from the American Arbitration Association 3462
Summary of Labor Arbitration Awards 4493

Great Britain

Industrial Tribunal Reports 2555

New York State

New York No-Fault Arbitration Reports 3478

ARBITRATION, LAWS ON. *See also* Specific laws

Commercial Arbitration Yearbook 998
Lawyers' Arbitration Letter and Digest of Court Decisions 2989

ARBITRATION ASSOCIATION, AMERICAN

News and Views from the American Arbitration Association 3462

ARCHITECTURE. *See also* Buildings. Design, Commercial. Housing

Architectural Record 300
Building and Environment 633
Dodge Construction Systems Costs 1480
Housing 2407.01
Progressive Architecture 3895

Canada

Canadian Architect 775
Solar Age 4326

Great Britain

Building Design 636

ARCHIVES AND RECORDS. *See also* Government, Publications. Information Retrieval. Libraries. Microfilm and Microfiche

International Guide to Library, Archival and Information Science Associations 2684

ARCTIC and ANTARCTIC

Arctic Alternatives 301

AREA PLANNING AND DEVELOPMENT. *See also* Land Use Planning. Rural Areas. Urban Areas. Zoning

Downtown Idea Exchange 1505
Geo Abstracts 2217.01
Law of Zoning and Planning 2987
Progress in Planning 3894
Regional Studies 4049
Site Selection Handbook 4290
Socio-Economic Planning Sciences 4324

Urban Land   4832
Urban Studies   4833

Canada

Northern Perspectives   3540

Illinois

Chicagoland Development   936

Nebraska

Nebraska Now   3424

New York State

Central New York Business Review
   890
Orange Rockland Westchester Business
   Review   3636

United States

Community Development Digest   1049
Environmental Comment   1721
From the State Capitals: Housing and
   Redevelopment   2174
Housing & Development Reporter
   2410

Westchester County (New York)

Orange Rockland Westchester Business
   Review   3636

West Indies

West Indies Chronicle   4953

Union of Soviet Socialist Republics
(USSR)

Problems of Economics   3857

ARGENTINA

Latin American Services   2976.01

ARIZONA

Annual Planning Information   253
Arizona: Manufacturers Directory, 1980
   313
Arizona Progress   315
Arizona Purchasor   316
Arizona Review   317
Arizona's Economy   317.01
Arizona: State Industrial Directory,
   1981   317.02
Arizona Statistical Abstract   317.03
From State Capitals   2169–2191
Job Openings: Indicator of
   Occupational Demand   2811

Phoenix Business Journal   3765.05
State and Local Taxes   4386
State Legislative Reporting Service
   4396
State Tax Report   4413
Statistical Abstract of Arizona   4418

ARKANSAS

Arkansas Economic Report   319
Arkansas: Manufacturers Directory,
   1980   320
Arkansas: State Industrial Directory,
   1981   320.01
Arkansas. The Great Location in the
   Sunbelt   321
Arkansas USA   321.01
Basics of Plant Location in Arkansas
   514
Directory of Arkansas Manufacturers
   1409
Financial Trend   2032
From State Capitals   2169–2191
Inside Arkansas   2588
State and Local Taxes   4386
State Legislative Reporting Service
   4396
State Tax Reports   4413

ARMAMENT AND DEFENSE.   See
also Aeronautics and Space, Military
Ventures. Airplanes, Military. Atomic
Power and Weapons. Research and
Development, Military. Tanks

Defense & Economy World Report
   1354.02
DMS Code Name Handbook   1475.06
DMS Defense Budget Intelligence
   1475.10
DMS Defense Market   1475.11
DMS Defense Procurement Budget
   Handbook   1475.12
DMS International Defense Intelligence
   1475.18

American Nations

DMS South America/Australasia
   1475.32

Australia

DMS South America/Australasia
   1475.32

Great Britain

Defense Statistics   1354.01

United States

Directory of Defense Electronic
   Products and Services: US Suppliers
   1426
DMS Aerospace Intelligence   1475.02
DMS Agency Profile   1475.03
DMS Defense RDT & E Budget
   Handbook   1473.13
DMS Electronic Warfare   1475.15
DMS Military Simulators   1475.23
DMS Rapid Deployment Force
   1475.30
Federal Organization Service
   Military/Civil Charts   1933
Military Research Letter   3229
Renegotiation/Management Letter
   4060

ARMAMENT AND DEFENSE,
CONTRACTS

Cost Accounting Standards Guide
   1225

Africa

DMS Middle East/Africa   1475.19

Europe

DMS NATO/Europe   1475.26
DMS NATO Weapons   1475.27

Middle East

DMS Middle East/Africa   1475.19

United States

Board of Contract Appeals Decisions
   567
Contract Appeals Decisions   1186
Defense Industry Organization Service
   1355.01
Defense Week   1355.02
DMS Aerospace Companies   1475.01
DMS "AN" Equipment   1475.04
DMS Company Profile   1475.07
DMS Contracting Intelligence   1475.08
DMS Contract Quarterly (Agency CQ,
   Company CQ, County CQ,
   Production CQ, RDT&E & Service
   CQ)   1475.09
DMS Electronic Systems   1475.14
DMS Foreign Military Sales CQ
   1475.16
DMS Ships/Vehicles/Ordnance
   1475.31
Government Contracts Reports   2239
Identified Sources of Supply   2433.01
Military and Federal Standards and
   Specifications   3228.02
Missile/Ordnance Letter   3244

Renegotiation/Management Letter
4060
Standards and Specifications
Information Bulletin   4378.01
Underwater Letter   4741

ARMAMENT AND DEFENSE, EQUAL OPPORTUNITY

Race Relations & Industry   3983

ARMED SERVICES.   *See* Armament and Defense

ARMY.   *See* Armament and Defense

ART.   *See also* Graphics

American Art Directory   155.01
Art Direction   322
Catalog of Copyright Entries   868
Forecaster   2107
Informational and Technical
Publications of the General
Secretariat of the Organization of
American States (OAS)   2569
Journal of Technical Writing and
Communication   2888
World of Learning   5072

ART, COMMERCIAL

Color Research and Application   991

Italy

Pubblicita in Italia   3920

ARTISANS GUILDS

World Guide to Trade Associations
5067

ARTS AND HUMANITIES.   *See also*
Copyrights. Types, eg, Musical Arts

Aslib Directory, Volume 2   333.01
Comsearch Printouts   1092
Dialog   1375.03
Valuation   4838

Africa

Africa   77

American Nations

Informational and Technical
Publications of the General
Secretariat of the Organization of
American States (OAS)   2569

California

Orange County Illustrated   3635

Canada

Metropolitan Toronto Board of Trade.
Journal   3206
Perspective Canada   3752

Great Britain

Leisure, Recreation and Tourism
Abstracts   3004.01

Nebraska

Nebraska Now   3424

South Africa

South Africa Yearbook   4337

United States

Comsearch Printouts   1092

Venezuela

Venezuela Up-to-Date   4845

ASIA.   *See* Far East, South and Southeast Asia and Pacific Areas. Region and country names

ASIAN DEVELOPMENT BANK

Annual Report   254
Key Indicators of Developing Member
Countries of Asian Development
Bank (ADB)   2910

ASSOCIATION EXECUTIVES, AMERICAN SOCIETY OF

Who's Who in Association Management
4979

ASSOCIATIONS (PROFESSIONAL, SCIENTIFIC, TECHNICAL, AND TRADE).   *See also* Institutions and Agencies. Names

Association & Society Manager
Magazine   335
Association Management   339
Dictionary of Economics   1378
Energy Executive Directory   1680.01
McGraw-Hill Dictionary of Modern
Economics: A Handbook of Terms
and Organizations   3160
O'Dwyer's Directory of Corporate
Communications   3573
Public Affairs Report   3922
Who's Who in Association Management
4979

World Guide to Trade Associations
5067

Belgium

United States–Belgium Trade Directory,
1980–81 edition   4794.01

Europe

Directory of European Associations
1428

Great Britain

Directory of British Associations   1412

Ireland, Republic of

Directory of British Associations   1412

United States

Business Organizations with Tax
Planning   715
Encyclopedia of Associations, 11th
edition   1670

ASTRONAUTICS.   *See* Aeronautics and Space

ATHLETICS.   *See* Sports

ATLASES.   *See* Maps, Charts, and Atlases

ATOMIC POWER AND WEAPONS.
See also Arms Control. Hazardous
Cargoes. Radiation. Uranium. Uses, eg,
Electric Light and Power

Alternative Energy: Trends & Forecasts
149.01
Energy Developments   1679
Fusion Power Reports   2203.01
Nuclear Waste News   3554.01
Nucleonics Week   3555

United States

Abstract Newsletters, Government
Inventions for Licensing   2.16

ATOMIC POWER AND WEAPONS, GOVERNMENT REGULATIONS

Nuclear Law Bulletin   3553
Nuclear Regulation Reports   3554
Nucleonics   3555

ATOMIC POWER AND WEAPONS, NUCLEAR FUEL

Nuclearfuel   3552

AUDIOVISUAL AIDS

Audio Visual Communications 346.02
Audiovisual Market Place 347
Educational Marketer 1592
Media and Methods 3165
National Information Center for
  Educational Media (NICEM)
  Newsletter. 3385
Speechwriter's Newsletter 4361.05
Total Information Package for 1980–82
  4643
Videocassette & CATV Newsletter
  4854

AUDIT BUREAU OF CIRCULATIONS

Audit Bureau of Circulations Factbook
  348
Audit Bureau of Circulations (ABC)
  News Bulletin 349

AUDITING. *See* Accounting and Auditing

AUDITORS, INSTITUTE OF INTERNAL

Internos 2744.01

AUSTRALIA

Annual Industrial Review 249.01
Annual Mining Review 249.01
Australia and New Zealand (ANZ)
  Bank Business Indicators 380
Australian Dept. of the Treasury.
  Round-Up of Economic Statistics
  392
Australian National Economic &
  Legislative Report 413
Australian Trading News 420
Canberra Comments 849
Consumer Price Index 1161
Enterprise 1713
Executive Briefing 1797
Far East and Australasia 1892
Foreign Investment 2117.01
Handbook for Industrialists 2313
Statistical Yearbook for Asia and the
  Pacific 4445
Statistics—Asia & Australasia 4450
Trans-Tasman 4699
Western Australia Manufacturers
  Directory 4950
Wool 5018
Work and People 5021

AUSTRALIAN INDUSTRY, CONFEDERATION OF

Confederation of Australian Industry
  (CAI) News 1098

AUSTRALIAN TRADE PRACTICES ACT

Australian Trade Practices Reports
  419

AUTOMATION. *See also*

Computer-Aided Management
Techniques. Office Systems. Word
Processing.

American Federation of Information
  Processing Societies Office
  Automation Conference 175.01
Autotransaction Industry Report
  435.01
Digital Systems for Industrial
  Automation 1396.01
Officemation Management 3579.02
Officemation Product Reports 3579.03

AUTOMOBILE ACCIDENTS. *See*

Traffic Safety, Accidents

AUTOMOBILES. *See also* Gasoline and Service Stations. Traffic

Automobile Facts and Figures 426
Automobile International 427
Automotive Fleet 429
Automotive Industries 430
Automotive Industries/International
  431
Car Dealer "Insider" 859
Commercial Car Journal 1000
Motor Business 3325.01
Motor Report International 3328
Reference Book of Transportation
  4041
Safe Driver 4157
Solidarity 4327
Ward's Automotive Yearbook 4882
World Automotive Market 5041.01

Canada

Automotive News 434
Eco/Log Week 1533
Facts and Figures of the Automotive
  Industry 1871
Ward's Automotive Yearbook 4882

Great Britain

Motor Report International 3328
Number of Road Vehicles, New
  Registrations 3556

India

Commerce Yearbook of Road
  Transport 996.04

Michigan

Michigan Manufacturer & Financial
  Record 3209

United States

Automotive News 434
Consumer Information Catalog 1154
Interstate Commerce Commission
  Annual Report 2745

AUTOMOBILES, GOVERNMENT REGULATIONS

Canada

Decisions and Orders of the Motor
  Vehicle Committee 1349

United States

Advertising Substantiation Program 72
AN, AND, & MS Standards 216.01
Federal Carriers Reports 1916
From the State Capitals; Motor Vehicle
  Regulation 2182
State Motor Carrier Guide 4401

AUTOMOBILES, IMPORTS AND EXPORTS

World Automotive Market 5041.01

AUTOMOBILES, INSPECTION AND EQUIPMENT REGULATIONS

From the State Capitals; Motor Vehicle
  Regulation 2182

AUTOMOBILES, INSURANCE

Best's Casualty Loss Reserve
  Development 525
From the State Capitals; Motor Vehicle
  Regulation 2182
Law of Liability Insurance 2983
New York No-Fault Arbitration
  Reports 3478

AUTOMOBILES, PARTS AND ACCESSORIES

Automotive Marketer 432
Automotive Marketing 433
Home & Auto 2383
World Automotive Market 5041.01

Canada

Automotive Marketer 432

Great Britain

Automotive/Spares & Accessories
  434.01
Autotrade 435

Euromarket News   1764
European Directory of Business
   Information Sources & Services
   1773
European Investment Bank. Annual
   Report   1780
Europe's 5000 Largest Companies
   1792
Organization for Economic Cooperation
   and Development (OECD) Financial
   Statistics   3643
Polk's World Bank Directory
   International Edition   3800
Predicasts F&S Index Europe Annual
   3828.02
Times 1000   4622

European Economic Community

Intelligence Digest Business Trends
   2638

Far East

Asian Wall Street   329
Polk's World Bank Directory
   International Edition   3800
Quarterly Bulletin of Statistics for Asia
   and the Pacific   3959

Florida

Florida Banker   2065
This Week   4608

France

French-American News   2165.01

Great Britain

Bankers Almanac and Year Book   466
Bank of England Annual Report and
   Accounts   487
Bank of England Quarterly Bulletin
   488
Bank Sorting Code Numbers   502
Barclays Review   508
Financial Market Surveys   2007
Financial Statistics: Explanatory
   Handbook   2021
Financial Times Newspaper   2026
Investors Review and Financial World
   2775
Journal of the Institute of Bankers
   2893
Lloyds Bank Economic Bulletin   3031
Lloyds Bank Review   3032
Management Information Manual
   3081
Midland Bank Review   3227
Times 1000   4622

Hawaii

Pacific Banker and Business   3676

Idaho

Pacific Banker and Business   3676

Illinois

Illinois Banker   2437

India

Commerce   994

Ireland, Republic of

Business and Finance   661
Central Bank of Ireland. Quarterly
   Bulletins and Annual Report   889
Times 1000   4622

Israel

Business Review and Economic News
   from Israel   720

Japan

Focus Japan   2074
Japan External Trade Organization
   (JETRO) Business Information Series
   2801
Japan Stock Journal   2803.01
Organization for Economic Cooperation
   and Development (OECD) Financial
   Statistics   3643
Times 1000   4622

Kansas

Corporate Report, Kansas City   1212
Kansas Economic Indicators   2904

Korea (South)

Korean Trade Directory   2921

Louisiana

Financial Trend   2032

Massachusetts

Banker & Tradesman   465
New England Economic Review   3441
Western Massachusetts Commercial
   News   4951

Mexico

Mexletter   3207
Polk's World Bank Directory North
   American Edition   3801

Michigan

Michigan Manufacturer & Financial
   Record   3209

Middle East

Businesman's Guide to the Arab World
   709
Middle East and North Africa   3217

Missouri

Corporate Report, Kansas City   1212

Montana

Pacific Banker and Business   3676

Nebraska

Business in Nebraska   694

Nevada

Pacific Banker and Business   3676

New Mexico

Financial Trend   2032

New South Wales

Handbook for Industrialists   2313

New York State

Capital District Business Review   854

New Zealand

Australia and New Zealand (ANZ)
   Bank Business Indicators   380
Australian Business Law Review   388
Economic Review   1569
Etruscan   1758
Life and Business in New Zealand
   3011
New Zealand Economist   3500
New Zealand Financial Times   3503

Oklahoma

Financial Trend   2032

Oregon

Pacific Banker and Business   3676

Organization for Economic Cooperation and Development

Financial Market Trends   2008

Puerto Rico

Carribbean Business   862
Puerto Rico Business Review   3943
Spotlite   4365.01

Scotland

Scottish Bankers   4204

South Africa

Times 1000   4622

Texas

Bankers Digest   467
Financial Trend   2032
Texas Banking Red Book   4595

United States

American Banker   157
Amer Institute of Banking Leaders
  Letter   186
Bank Directory of the Ninth Federal
  Reserve District   463
Bank Fact Book   474
Bank Pooled Funds   498
Commercial West   1011
Consensus of Insiders   1119
Directory of Business and Financial
  Services   1414
Directory of the Mutual Savings Banks
  of the United States   1460
Economic Outlook: US Report   1560
Economic Perspectives   1562
Federal Deposit Insurance Corp Annual
  Report   1919
Federal Reserve Bank of Dallas Annual
  Report   1935
Federal Reserve Bank of New York
  Annual Report   1936
Federal Reserve Bank of Philadelphia
  Business Review   1938
Federal Reserve Bank of Richmond
  Economic Review   1940
Federal Reserve Bank of San Francisco
  Business and Financial Letter   1951
Fed in Print   1977
Financial Letter   2004.01
French-American News   2165.01
Installment Lending Directory   2592
Leaders Letter   2995
Modern Banking Forms   3254
New England Economic Review   3441
Organization for Economic Cooperation
  and Development (OECD) Financial
  Statistics   3643
Polk's World Bank Directory North
  American Edition   3801
Predicasts Forecasts   3828.08
Public Periodic Releases   3926
State Banking Law Service   4387
State and Area Forecasting Service
  4383.01
This Week   4608
Times 1000   4622
United States Banker   4794
Update   4827

Vickers Guide to Bank Trust Guide
  4849
Voice of the Federal Reserve Bank of
  Dallas   4866
Washington Banktrends   4884
Washington Financial Reports   4887

Utah

Pacific Banker and Business   3676
Statistical Abstract of Utah   4422

Virgin Islands

Caribbean Business   862

Washington (State)

Pacific Banker and Business   3676
Seafirst Magazine   4213

**BANKING AND FINANCE,
ACCOUNTING AND AUDITING**

Bank Auditing & Accounting Report
  459
Journal of Bank Research   2824
Magazine of Bank Administration
  3057
Proceedings of the 1972 National
  Operations and Automation
  Conference—"The Common
  Denominator—Management"   3858

**BANKING AND FINANCE,
ADVERTISING**

Bank Marketing Report   484
Best Financial Advertising   522.02
Financial Advertising Report   1991

**BANKING AND FINANCE,
AGRICULTURAL**

Agricultural Banker   94

**BANKING AND FINANCE, BANK
BRANCHING**

International Banking Report   2657
Polk's Daily Bank Information Service
  3798
Polk's World Bank Directory
  International Edition   3800
State Banking Law Service   4387

American Nations

Polk's World Bank Directory North
  American Edition   3801

Canada

Polk's World Bank Directory North
  American Edition   3801

Mexico

Polk's World Bank Directory North
  American Edition   3801

United States

Polk's World Bank Directory North
  American Edition   3801

**BANKING AND FINANCE, BANK
FAILURES**

Federal Deposit Insurance Corp Annual
  Report   1919
Polk's Daily Bank Information Service
  3798

**BANKING AND FINANCE, BANK
ROBBERIES**

Bank Protection Manual, 1974 edition
  499
Bank Security Report   501

BANKING AND FINANCE, BLACKS

Black Enterprise   560

BANKING AND FINANCE. *See*
Capital Markets

Securities Week   4237

**BANKING AND FINANCE,
CHECKING ACCOUNTS**

Bank Operations Report   495

Canada

Cheques Cashed   934

United States

Nacha Quarterly Update   3354
Proceedings of the 1972 National
  Operations and Automation
  Conference—"The Common
  Denominator—Management"   3858

**BANKING AND FINANCE,
CLEARING HOUSES**

World Banking Survey   5045

**BANKING AND FINANCE,
COMMERCIAL BANKS**

Banking   475
Journal of Contemporary Business
  2842
New York State Banker   3480
Northwestern Banker   3545
Washington Banktrends   4884

United States

Bank Installment Lending Newsletter 479
Bank Loan Officers Report   481
Payment Systems Newsletter   3708
Trust Assets of Insured Commercial Banks   4726
United States Federal Deposit Insurance Corporation Bank Operating Statistics   4801

BANKING AND FINANCE, COMMUNITY BANKS

Community Bank Series on Operations and Automation   1048
Condition Report of Weekly Reporting Commercial Banks—Eleventh Federal Reserve District   1096
Construction Lending Handbook   1133
Federal Reserve Bank of San Francisco Western Economic Indicators   1954
Journal of Commercial Bank Lending 2838

BANKING AND FINANCE, COMMUNITY RELATIONS

Urban and Community Economic Development   4830

BANKING AND FINANCE, CONSORTIUMS

International Banking Report   2657

BANKING AND FINANCE, CUSTOMER RELATIONS

Bank Teller's Report   506

BANKING AND FINANCE, DIRECTORS AND OFFICERS

Bankers Digest   467
Texas Banking Red Book   4595

BANKING AND FINANCE, EDUCATION

Bankers School Directory, 1977–78 edition   472
Florida Banker   2065
Journal of Financial Education   2856

BANKING AND FINANCE, ELECTRONIC FUNDS TRANSFER SYSTEMS (EFTS)

Bank Automation Newsletter   460
Bank Operations Report   495
Payment Systems Action Report   3707
Payment Systems Newsletter   3708

Savings Bank Journal   4189
State Banking Law Service   4387

BANKING AND FINANCE, FORMS

Modern Banking Forms   3254

BANKING AND FINANCE, FRAUDS, SWINDLING AND EMBEZZLEMENT

Bank Insurance & Protection Bulletin 480
Bank Security Report   501
Business Crime: Criminal Liability of the Business Community   676.01

BANKING AND FINANCE, GOVERNMENT REGULATIONS, LAWS AND PROGRAMS

AP–Dow Jones Bankers Report   277
Bank Officer's Handbook of Commercial Banking Law   490
Central Banking Legislation: A Collection of Central Bank, Monetary, and Banking Laws   888
Forex Service   2145
Illinois Banker   2437
Investing, Licensing, and Trading Conditions Abroad   2755
National Assn of Mutual Savings Banks' Annual Report   3359
New York State Banker   3480
Savings Bank Journal   4189

Australia

Bankers' Magazine of Australasia   470

Florida

Florida Banker   2065

New Zealand

Bankers' Magazine of Australasia   470

Texas

Bankers Digest   467

United States

Agricultural Banker   94
American Banker   157
Banker's Letter of the Law   468
Bank Executive's Report   473
Bank Fact Book   474
Banking Law Journal   477
Bank Installment Lending Newsletter 479
Bank Loan Officers Report   481
Bank Marketing Newsletter   483

Bank Protection Manual, 1974 edition 499
Bank Tax Report   505
Capital   851
Control of Banking   1189
Federal Banking Law Reports   1914
Federal Deposit Insurance Corporation —Law, Regulations, and Related Acts   1920
From the State Capitals: Small Loans, Sales, Finance Banking   2185
Issues in Bank Regulation   2791
Munn's Encyclopedia of Banking and Finance, 7th edition   3342
State Banking Law Service   4387
Washington Weekly Report   4897

BANKING AND FINANCE, INSURANCE

Bank Insurance & Protection Bulletin 480
Changes Among Operating Banks & Branches   904
Digest of Bank Insurance, 1973 edition 1384
Federal Banking Law Reports   1914
Federal Deposit Insurance Corp Annual Report   1919
Federal Deposit Insurance Corporation —Law, Regulations, and Related Acts   1920
United States Federal Deposit Insurance Corporation Bank Operating Statistics   4801

BANKING AND FINANCE, INTERNATIONAL

Action Canada France   45
Business International Money Report 699
Community Markets   1050
Euromoney   1765
Financing Foreign Operations   2035
Foreign Credit Insurance Assn (FCIA) 2112
Foreign Market Reports   2134
Institutional Investor International Edition   2602
International Banking Report   2657
International Banktrends   2657.01
Trends in International Banking and Capital Markets   4717

BANKING AND FINANCE, MANAGEMENT

Bank Auditing & Accounting Report 459
Bank Board Letter   461
Bank Director's Report   462

Bankers Magazine   469
Bank Executive's Report   473
Bank Operations Report   495
Credit Executive   1246
Journal of Bank Research   2824
Magazine of Bank Administration
  3057

BANKING AND FINANCE, MARKETING

Bank Marketing   482
Bank Marketing Report   484

BANKING AND FINANCE, MERGERS

American Banker   157
International Banking Report   2657
Polk's Daily Bank Information Service
  3798

BANKING AND FINANCE, MUTUAL SAVINGS BANKS

Directory of the Mutual Savings Banks
  of the United States   1460
Mutual Savings Bank Guide to Federal
  Income Tax Law   3352
Mutual Savings Bank Report   3353
National Assn of Mutual Savings
  Banks' Annual Report   3359
National Fact Book of the Mutual
  Savings Bank Industry   3374
Savings Bank Journal   4189

BANKING AND FINANCE, NATIONAL BANKS

Bank of England. Report   489
Control of Banking   1189
Federal Aid to Financing   1911
State Banking Law Service   4387

BANKING AND FINANCE, PERSONNEL

Bank Director   461.01
Bank Personnel Report   497
Bank Teller's Report   506
Digest of Executive Opportunities
  1389
Financial Executive   1998
Financial Executive's Handbook, 1970
  1999
International Banking Report   2657
Magazine of Bank Administration
  3057
Polk's Daily Bank Information Service
  3798
Reference Book of Corporate
  Managements   4039

State Banking Law Service   4387
Survey of Bank Officers Salaries   4506
Survey of Bank Personnel Policies and
  Practices   4507

Florida

Florida Banker   2065

Texas

Texas Banking Red Book   4595

United States

Bank Personnel News   496

BANKING AND FINANCE, SAVINGS BANKS. *See also* Banking and Finance, Mutual Savings Banks

E E/Epargne Europe   1598
Federal Aids to Financing   1911
Payment Systems Newsletter   3708
Washington Banktrends   4884

BANKING AND FINANCE, STATE-CHARTERED BANKS

Control of Banking   1189
Federal Aid to Financing   1911
Spectrum Three; Bank Stock Holdings
  Survey   4361
State Banking Law Service   4387

BANKING AND FINANCE, TAXATION

Bank Tax Report   505
Guidebook to North Carolina Taxes
  2279
Magazine of Bank Administration
  3057

BANKING AND FINANCE, TECHNOLOGY. *See also* Banking and Finance, Electronic Funds Transfer Systems

Bank Auditing & Accounting Report
  459
Bank Automation Newsletter   460
Bank Operations Report   495
Bank Security Report   501
Bank Systems & Equipment   503
Community Bank Series on Operations
  and Automation   1048
Journal of Bank Research   2824
Nacha Quarterly Update   3354
Proceedings of the 1972 National
  Operations and Automation

Conference—"The Common
  Denominator—Management"   3858
Results of the 1972 National
  Automation Survey   4101
Savings Bank Journal   4189
Thruput   4617

BANKING AND FINANCE, WOMEN

Business & Professional Woman   663
National Association of Bank Women
  (NABW) Journal   3357

BANK OF CANADA

Bank of Canada Weekly Financial
  Statistics   486

BANK OF ENGLAND

Bank of England Annual Report and
  Accounts   487
Bank of England. Report   489

BANK OF NEW SOUTH WALES

Etruscan   1758

BANK PROTECTION ACT (US)

Bank Protection Manual, 1974 edition
  499

BANKRUPTCIES, BUSINESS

Business Failure Record   682

Australia

Australian Bankruptcy Bulletin   386

Canada

Record Survey of Predecessor and
  Defunct Companies   4517.01

Colorado

Rocky Mountain Journal   4139

Illinois

Illinois Economic Data Sheets   2438

United States

Bankruptcy Law Reports   500

BAR ASSOCIATION, CANADIAN

Canadian Institute of Chartered
  Accounts/Canadian Bar Association
  (CICA/CBA) Recommendation on
  the Income Tax Act   804

BATHROOMS

Domestic Heating   1492
Kitchen Business   2918

BATTERIES AND FUEL CELLS

Advanced Battery Technology   61

BEARER SECURITIES.   *See* Stocks and Bonds

BEAUTIFICATION PROGRAMS

Downtown Idea Exchange   1505

BEAUTY AND GROOMING AIDS.
See also Cosmetics and Toiletries

Africa Woman   83

BEDS, BEDDING, AND MATTRESSES

Mattresses, Foundations, and Sleep
    Furniture M25E   3157
Sheets, Pillowcases, and Towels.
    MQ-23X   4273

BEEF.   *See* Meat

BEER AND BREWING INDUSTRY

Brewing Industry in the US: Brewers
    Almanac   590
Food and Drink   2079
Thomson's Liquor Guide   4613
United Nations Industrial Development
    Organization (UNIDO) Guides to
    Information Sources.
    UNIDO/LIB/SER.D/1/Rev.1—
    Information Sources on the Beer and
    Wine Industry   4767.05

BEES.   *See also* Honey

Honey Production   2385

BEHAVIORAL SCIENCES.   *See also*
Human Relations. Mental Health.
Motivational Research

Abstract Newsletters, Behavior &
    Society   2.05
Behavioral Sciences Newsletter   519
Current Contents: Social and
    Behavioral Sciences   1273

BELGIUM

United States-Belgium Trade Directory,
    1980–81 edition   4794.01

BETTER BUSINESS BUREAUS

News & Views   3461

BETTING.   *See* Gambling

BEVERAGES.   *See also* types, eg,
Liquor

Food Engineering   2085
Leisure Beverage "Insider"   3004
Process and Chemical Engineering
    3859
Target Twenty   4529
United Nations Industrial Development
    Organization Guides to Information
    Sources. UNIDO/LIB/SER.D/15—
    Information Sources on the
    Non-alcoholic Beverage Industry
    4782

BEVERAGES, IMPORTS AND EXPORTS

Food and Drink   2079

BIBLIOGRAPHIES

Auber Bibliography   346.01

BILLBOARDS.   *See* Advertising,
Outdoor

BIOGRAPHIES

Association of Executive Recruiting
    Consultants: 1980 Directory   340.01
Defense Week   1355.02
Hambro Euromoney Directory   2311
International Who's Who   2742
International Year Book and
    Statesmen's Who's Who   2744
O'Dwyer's Directory of Public
    Relations Executives   3573.01
Who's Who 1980–81, 132nd Edition
    4975.02
Who's Who in Engineering, 4th edition,
    1980   4983
Who's Who in the World   4997
World Who's Who in Science   5085

Saudi Arabia

Who's Who in Saudi Arabia   4991

United States

Register of Corporations, Directors and
    Executives   4051
Who's Who in America   4977
Who's Who in American Law   4978
Who's Who in the East   4992
Who's Who in Finance and Industry
    4985
Who's Who in the Midwest   4993
Who's Who in South and Southwest
    4995

Who's Who of the West   4996
Who's Who of American Women
    4998

BIOLOGY.   *See also* Ergonomics.
Marine Biology

Abstract Newsletters, Biomedical
    Technology & Human Factors
    Engineering   2.06
Abstract Newsletters, Government
    Inventions for Licensing   2.16
Abstract Newsletters, Medicine &
    Biology   2.22
Biological Abstracts (BA)   554
Biological Abstracts/RRM   554.01
Biotechnology and Bioengineering   557
International Journal of Systems
    Science   2697

BIOMETRIC SOCIETY

Statisticians and Others in Allied
    Professions   4447

BIOPOLYMERS

Polymer   3807

BLACK LUNG DISEASE

Benefits Review Board-Black Lung
    Reporter   522

BLACKS.   *See also* subjects, eg,
Labor, Blacks

Black Enterprise   560
Gibson Report   2225
Index to Black Newspapers   2500
Race Relations & Industry   3983

BLUE COLLAR WORKERS

European Compensation Survey   1771

BLUE LAWS.   *See* Sunday Sales

BOARDS OF TRADE

Metropolitan Toronto Board of Trade.
    Journal   3206
Sounding Board   4331

BOLIVIA

Andean Group Regional Report
    222.01
Latin American Services   2976.01

BOND INTEREST.   *See* Stocks and
Bonds, Bond Interest

CARPETS AND RUGS

Carpet & Rug Industry   864.02
Carpet and Rugs. MQ-22Q   865

CASE STUDIES. *Note:* material covers actual case studies in various fields

Advertising Techniques   73
Area Development   303
Banking Law Journal   477
Bank Installment Lending Newsletter   479
Business Law Cases for Australians   701
Columbia Journal of World Business   992
East/West Technology Digest   1527
Environment Reporter   1730
Fair Employment Practices (FEP) Guidelines   1878
Industrial Development Handbook   2515
Industrial Participation   2535
Interfaces   2643
Januz Direct Marketing Letter   2795
Journal of Advertising Research   2820
Journal of Organizational Communication   2871
Journal of the Operational Research Society   2896
Marketing   3127
Public Relations News   3932
Safety Management   4158
Timber Tax Journal   4618
Training   4684
White Collar Managemen t   4967
World of Work Report   5073

CASSETTES. *See* Recordings (Disc and Tape)

CASTINGS, IRON AND STEEL

Iron and Steel Castings M33A   2785

CASTINGS, NONFERROUS

Nonferrous Castings. M33E   3531

CASUALTIES AND LOSS. *See also* Accidents and Safety. Insurance, Casualty

Fire and Loss Statistics for the United Kingdom   2041

CATALOGS AND DIRECTORIES. *See also* subjects

Brad Directories & Annuals   583
Current African Directories   1269
Current European Directories   1275

Guide to American Directories, 9th edition   2286
Mail Order Business Directory, 1975 edition   3059
Trade Directories of the World   4654

CATERING COMPANIES

Catering Trades   871
Hotel & Catering Equipment & Supplies   2399
Hotel, Restaurant & Catering Supplies   2401

CATTLE. *See also* Dairy Products. Meat

Beef   517
Beef Buying Guide   518
Chicago Mercantile Exchange Yearbook   937
Livestock Market News Reports   3030
Tax Sheltered Investments   4570

Australia

Livestock   3026.01

Canada

Report on Livestock Surveys: Cattle, Sheep   4070

CEMENT

United Nations Industrial Development Organization Guides to Information Sources. UNIDO/LIB/SER.D/2— Information Sources on the Cement and Concrete Industry   4769

CEMETERIES. *See* Death. Funeral Homes and Directors

CENSUS, BUREAU OF THE (US)

Bureau of the Census Catalog   651
Bureau of the Census Catalog of Publications, 1790–1972   652
Census of Population   876.01
Census Retrieval System   880
Data on Selected Racial Groups Available from Bureau of the Census, No. 40, Revised May, 1977   1338
Data User News   1344.01
Data User News   1345
Directory of Data Files, Bureau of the Census   1424
Directory of Federal Statistics for Local Areas: A Guide to Sources, 1976   1430
Reference Manual on Population and Housing Statistics from the Census Bureau, 1977   4042

Statistical Abstract of the United States   4421
United States Census Report   4794.03

CENSUS REPORTS. *See* Census, Bureau of the (US). Population. Surveys and Polls, Census. Vital Statistics

CENTRAL AMERICA. *See* American Nations and Western Hemisphere Possessions

CENTRAL BANK OF IRELAND

Central Bank of Ireland. Quarterly Bulletin and Annual Report   889

CERAMICS AND POTTERY

Ceramic Data Book   891
Ceramic Industries Journals   892
Ceramic Industry   893
United Nations Industrial Development Organization Guides to Information Sources. UNIDO/LIB/SER.D/17— Information Sources on the Ceramics Industry   4784
Abstract Newsletters, Materials Science   2.21

CERTIFIED PUBLIC ACCOUNTANTS, AMERICAN INSTITUTE OF

Amer Institute of CPAs Professional Standards   187
Amer Institute of CPAs Professional Standards—Accounting   188
Amer Institute of CPAs Professional Standards—Auditing, Management Advisory Services, Tax Practice   189
Amer Institute of CPAs Professional Standards—Ethics & Bylaws   190

CERTIFIED PUBLIC ACCOUNTANTS, WEST VIRGINIA SOCIETY OF

West Virginia CPA   4954

CERTIFIED PUBLIC ACCOUNTANTS, WISCONSIN INSTITUTE OF

Wisconsin CPA   5007

CHAMBERS OF COMMERCE

Atlantic Anglo American Trade News   343.01
Commercial Arbitration Yearbook   998
International Report   2726

Public Affairs Report   3922
World Guide to Trade Associations
   5067

Africa

African Trade/Commerce Africain   80

Belgium

United States–Belgium Trade Directory,
   1980–81 edition   4794.01

Brazil

Brazilian–American Business
   Review/Directory   585

Canada

Canada–United Kingdom Year Book
   771

Great Britain

Canada–United Kingdom Year Book
   771
Commerce International   996

Hawaii

Legislative Action Bulletin   2997
Voice of Business   4864

New Zealand

New Zealand Commerce   3497

Scotland

Industrial Index to Glasgow and West
   of Scotland   2531
Journal of the Glasgow Chamber of
   Commerce   2891

United States

Amcham Overseas Report   154
Association Taxation   342
Congressional Action   1111
Financial Management Handbook for
   Associations   2006

CHARTERED ACCOUNTANTS OF SCOTLAND, INSTITUTE OF

Institute of Chartered Accountants of
   Scotland Official Directory   2597

CHARTS.   *See* Maps, Charts, and
Atlases

CHECK FRAUDS.   *See* Banking and
Finance, Frauds

CHECKING ACCOUNTS.   *See*
Banking and Finance, Checking
Accounts

CHEESE.   *See* Dairy Products

CHEMICAL INDUSTRY.   *See also* Chemistry. Petrochemistry and Petrochemicals

Achievement   39
Central Patents Index, 1981   890.01
Chemical Abstracts   918.01
Chemical and Engineering News   920
Chemical Economics Handbook   921
Chemical Economics Newsletter   922
Chemical/Energy New Product
   Directory, 1980   922.01
Chemical Engineering   923
ChemicalHorizons North American
   Report   925
Chemical Horizons Overseas Report
   925.01
Chemical Industry Notes   925.02
Chemical Marketing Reporter   926
Chemical Week   929
Chemical Week—Buyers' Guide Issue
   930
Chemical Week Newswire Service   931
Inorganic Chemicals M28A   2581
Manufacturing Chemist & Aerosol
   News   3113
Process Engineering   3860
Selected Business Ventures   4252

Australia

Process and Chemical Engineering
   3859

Canada

Canadian Chemical Processing   784
Corpus Chemical Report   1224.01

Far East

Japan Chemical Annual   2795.01
Japan Chemical Week   2795.03

Great Britain

Achievement   39

India

Chemical Age of India   919.01
Indian Chemical Directory   2503.03

Japan

Japan Chemical Annual   2795.01
Japan Chemical Directory   2795.02
Japan Chemical Week   2795.03

United States

Abstract Newsletters, Chemistry   2.09
Chemical Regulation Reporter   928
Directory of Chemical Producers USA
   1417
Imports of Benzenoid Chemicals and
   Products   2474

CHEMICAL INDUSTRY, CONSTRUCTION

Chemical Age   919
Chemical Engineering   923

CHEMICAL INDUSTRY, EQUIPMENT, FACILITIES, AND MATERIALS

Chemical Engineering—Equipment
   Buyers' Guide Issue   924
Chemical Week   929
Chemical Week—Buyers' Guide Issue
   930
Cost Forecasting Service   1227

CHEMICAL INDUSTRY, GOVERNMENT REGULATIONS

Chemical and Engineering News   920
Chemical Regulation Reporter   928

CHEMISTRY.   *See also* Chemical
Industry

Solid State Abstracts Journal   4328

CHEWING GUM.   *See* Gum

CHICAGO.   *See* Illinois

CHICAGO BOARD OPTIONS EXCHANGE

Chicago Board Options Exchange
   Guide   935
Trade Levels Option Report   4656

CHICAGO MERCANTILE EXCHANGE

Chicago Mercantile Exchange Yearbook
   937

CHICKEN.   *See* Eggs. Poultry

CHILD LABOR.   *See* Labor, Child
Labor

CHILE

Latin American Services   2976.01

CHINA BUSINESS REVIEW

CBR Index and Microfiche   872.01

CHINA, PEOPLE'S REPUBLIC OF

CBR Index and Microfiche   872.01
China Business Report   940.01
China Letter   942
Information Peking (Beijing)   2573.02
Soviet-Eastern Europe-China Business
 & Trade   4351

CHOCOLATE

Confectionery Including Chocolate
 Products. M20C   1097

CHRISTIAN SCIENCE MONITOR

National Newspaper Index   3396.01

CHURCHES.   *See* Religious Edifices

CIGARETTES.   *See* Tobacco

CIGARS.   *See* Tobacco

CINEMA.   *See* Motion Pictures

CIRCUSES AND CARNIVALS

Amusement Business   212

CITICORP

Citicorp Report   950

CITRUS FRUITS

Food Industry Studies   2088

CIVIL AERONAUTICS BOARD (CAB) (US)

Hawkins Civil Aeronautics Board
 Service   2349
National Transportation Safety Board
 Service   3409

CIVIL ENGINEERING.   *See* Engineering, Civil

CIVIL SERVICE PROGRAMS

Civil Service Statistics   954
From the State Capitals: Personnel
 Management   2183

CLAY.   *See* Brick and Tile

CLAYTON ACT (US)

Antitrust Laws & Trade Regulation
 273

CLEANING AND MAINTENANCE

BMCIS   566.01
Cleaning Maintenance & Big Building
 Management   958
DMS Operation & Maintenance
 1475.28
Modern Cleaning & Maintenance
 3255.01
United Nations Industrial Organization
 (UNIDO) Guides to Information
 Sources. UNIDO/LIB/SER.D/Rev.1
 —Information Sources on Industrial
 Maintenance and Repair   4767.02

CLEARING HOUSES.   *See* Banking
and Finance, Clearing Houses

CLIMATE.   *See* Weather

CLOSED-CIRCUIT SYSTEMS

Multicast   3331

CLOSELY HELD CORPORATIONS.
See Corporations, Closely Held

CLOSURES.   *See also* subjects

Closures for Containers. M34H   967

CLOTHING.   *See* Apparel

CLOTHING AND TEXTILE WORKERS UNION, AMALGAMATED (ACTWU) (US)

Labor Unity   2945

COAL

Bunker Fuels. FT810   648
Coal Age   968
Coal Age—Annual Buyers' Guide   969
Coal Daily   970
Coal Data   970.01
Coal Mine Directory   971
Coal Service   971.02
Coal Week   972
Coal Week International   973
Fuel   2195
Illinois Economic Data Sheets   2438
International Coal Report   2666
Keystone Coal Industry Manual   2911
Keystone News-Bulletin   2912

Australia

Australian Mining   411

Canada

Miscellaneous Petroleum and Coal
 Products Industries   3243

Europe

Annual Bulletin of Coal Statistics for
 Europe   237
Coal: Monthly Bulletin   971.01

European Economic Community

Coal   967.02
Euro-Abstracts: Scientific and Technical
 Publications and Patents, Sections I
 and II. Section I: Euratom and EEC
 Research. Section II: Coal and Steel
 1759

United States

Coal Information   970.02
Mining Lease Reports   3239.01

COASTAL AREAS

Coastal Zone Management Journal
 974
Marine Policy   3121

COATINGS.   *See* Adhesives, Sealants,
and Coatings

COCOA

United Nations Industrial Development
 Organization (UNIDO) Guides to
 Information Sources.
 UNIDO/LIB/SER.D/Rev.1—
 Information Sources on the Coffee,
 Cocoa, Tea and Spices Industry
 4767.06

CODES

DMS Code Name Handbook   1475.06

COFFEE

Green Coffee: Inventories, Imports, and
 Roastings. BG41   2263
United Nations Industrial Development
 Organization (UNIDO) Guides to
 Information Sources.
 UNIDO/LIB/SER.D/Rev.1—
 Information on the Coffee, Cocoa,
 Tea and Spices Industry   4767.06

COINS.   *See* Currency

COKE.   *See* Coal

COLLECTIONS AND COLLECTORS.   *See also* subjects

Forecaster   2107
Money Strategies   3273

COLLECTIVE BARGAINING. *See* Labor–Management Relations. Subjects, eg, Education

COLLEGES AND UNIVERSITIES. *See also* Research (Basic), Colleges and Universities. Scholarships and Grants. Fields of study

College and University Reports 980
World of Learning 5072

Canada

Optimum 3633

Great Britain

Education Year Book 1981 1597

United States

From the State Capitals: Institutional Building 2176
Vickers Guide to College Endowment Portfolios 4850

COLLEGES AND UNIVERSITIES, CAREER OPPORTUNITIES FOR GRADUATES

Guidepost 2285
Journal of College Placement 2833

Great Britain

First Destination of University Graduates 2045

United States

College Placement Annual 981
Directory of Career Planning and Placement Offices 1416
Directory of College Recruiting Personnel 1417.01
Journal of College Placement 2833
Recruiting Trends 4038
Salary Survey 4164

COLLEGES AND UNIVERSITIES, GRADUATE AND PROFESSIONAL SCHOOLS. *See also* specific fields, eg, Managers and Management, Education

American Assembly of Collegiate Schools of Business Newsline 156
Executive Woman 1811
World of Learning 5072

COLLEGES AND UNIVERSITIES, VOCATIONAL TRAINING

International Labour Documentation 2698

COLLEGE STORES. *See* Retailing, College Stores

COLLEGE STORES, NATIONAL ASSOCIATION OF

College Store Journal 983

COLOMBIA

Andean Group Regional Report 222.01
Latin American Services 2976.01

COLOR

Color Research and Application 991

COLORADO

Business Economic Outlook Forum 678
Colorado Business Review 984
Colorado City Retail Sales by Standard Industrial Classification 985
Colorado: Manufacturers Directory, 1980–81 987
Directory of Colorado Manufacturers 1418
From State Capitals 2169-2191
Rocky Mountain Journal 4139
State and Local Taxes 4386
State Legislative Reporting Service 4396
State Tax Reports 4413

COMMERCE, DEPARTMENT OF (US)

Commerce Publications Update 996.02

COMMERCE AND INDUSTRY. *See also* Banking and Finance. Bankruptcies Corporations. Crime, Business. Entrepreneurs and Small Businesses. Foreign Investments. Industrial headings. Labor Managers and Management. Manufacturers and Manufacturing. Multinational Companies. Partnerships. Research and Development, Industrial. Specific fields, eg, Retailing

ABI/INFORM 2.01
Accountant 18
Across the Board 43
Akron Business & Economic Review 132
Alabama Business 133
American Industrial Development Council Journal 181
AP–Dow Jones Economic Report 278
Baker Library. Core Collection, an Author & Subject Guide 449

Ball State Business Review 454
Ball State Journal for Business Educators 454.01
Baylor Business Studies 516
Business America 656
Business & Public Affairs 665
Business & Society Review 667
Business Economics 679
Business History Review 686
Business in Brief 690
Business Index 690.01
Business Information Service Financial Times 692.01
Business Information Sources 693
Business International 696
Business Law Review 703
Business Studies 723
Business Week 727
Color Research and Application 991
Columbia Journal of World Business 992
Commerce International 996
Confederation of British Industry (CBI) Members Bulletin 1102
Confederation of British Industry (CBI) Overseas Reports 1103
Croner's Reference Book for World Traders 1257
Current Business Picture 1271
Custom Market Extract Reports 1286
Dialog 1375.03
Dictionary of Economics and Business 1379
Direct Mail List Rates and Data 1401
Directory Information Service 1406
Discount Merchandiser 1464
Dow Jones—Irwin Business Almanac 1501
Dun & Bradstreet Standard Register 1515
DunsWorld Letter 1520
Economic Analysis & Policy 1535
Economic Review 1571
Encyclopedia of Business Information Sources, 3rd edition 1671
Enterprise 1714
European Directory of Business Information Sources & Services 1773
Facts on File Weekly News Digest 1874
Financial Digest 1997
Financial Indicators and Corporate Financing Plans 2003
Financial Times International Business Yearbook 2025
Forbes 2103
Foreign Economic Trends 2116
Financial Weekly 2033.01
Foreign Market Reports Index 2134
Fortune 2150

Fraser Opinion Letter 2161
Harvard Business Review 2345
Impact 2441
Industrial Photography 2535.01
Industrial World/Industrial World en
 Español 2556
Information Guide for Doing Business
 in Countries Abroad 2571
Intelligence Digest Business Trends
 2638
International Business Intelligence
 2662
International Businessman's Who's
 Who, 1980 edition 2663
International Country Risk Guide
 2670
International Economic Indicators and
 Competitive Trends 2675
International Series 2727.01
Investment and Taxation Monograph
 2760.01
Investment Bulletin 2761
Investment and Business Opportunity
 News 2760
Journal of Business 2827
Journal of Business Law 2831
Journal of Commerce and Commercial
 2836
Journal of Contemporary Business
 2842
Journal of Industrial Economics 2861
Licensing in Foreign and Domestic
 Operations 3010
Looking Ahead and Projection
 Headlights 3046
Management Contents 3076
Marketing Economics Key Plants,
 1979–80 3129
Mid-Atlantic Journal of Business
 3215.01
Monthly Letter 3292
MSU Business Topics 3330
Nation's Business 3414
New York Times 3487
NOW Machine 3551
Predicasts F&S Index International
 3828.03
Predicasts F&S Index International
 Annual 3828.04
Predicasts Source Directory 3829
PTS Abstract Services 3915
PTS Statistical Service 3919
Publications by the Faculty of the
 Harvard Business School 3923
Quarterly Economic Reviews Service
 3962.01
Recent Additions to Baker Library
 4033.01
Research Index 4088
Review of Business 4120

Select Information Exchange (SIE)
 Guide to Business & Investment
 Books, 1974 edition 4255
Service to Business & Industry 4268
Sophisticated Investor 4330
Sound of the Economy 4332
Southern Economic Journal 4348
Statistics Sources, 4th edition, 1974
 4459
Tax and Trade Guide Series 4535
Three Banks Review 4616
Time 4619
Trends 4716
United Nations Industrial Development
 Organization Guides to Information
 Sources. UNIDO/LIB/SER. D/6—
 Information Sources on Industrial
 Quality Control 4773
United States News and World Report
 4812
Value Line OTC Special Situations
 Service 4841
VNR Dictionary of Business and
 Finance 4862.01
Wall Street Journal 4878
Wall Street Journal Index 4879
Wall Street Review of Books 4881
What's New in Industry 4963.01
Working Papers in Baker Library: A
 Quarterly Checklist 5024
World Business Weekly 5046.01
World's Largest Industrial Enterprises
 5078.02
Worldcasts 5047
World Trade Centers Association
 (WTCA) News 5083
Yearbook of Industrial Statistics
 5090.2

Africa

Africa 77
Africa South of the Sahara 82
African Business 79.01
Current African Directories 1269
Economic Bulletin for Africa 1543
Investment Africa 2758
Modern Africa 3252
New African Development 3432
Pittsburgh Business Review 3774

Alabama

Alabama: State Industrial Directory,
 1980 136.01

Alaska

Alaska Business News Letter 137
Alaska Economic Trends 138
Alaska Industry 139
Alaska: Petroleum & Industrial
 Directory, 1980 141.01

American Nations

Business Latin America 700
Caribbean Business 863
Caribbean Year Book, 1977–78 864
International Market Guide—Latin
 America 2706
Latin America & Caribbean 1981
 2969.01

Arizona

Arizona Business 311
Arizona Business & Industry 312
Arizona Review 317
Arizona: State Industrial Directory,
 1981 317.02
Phoenix Business Journal 3765.05

Arkansas

Arkansas Economic Report 319
Arkansas: State Industrial Directory,
 1981 320.01
Financial Trend 2032
Inside Arkansas 2588

Australia

Annual Industrial Review 249.01
Australian Accountant 383
Australian Business Law Review 388
Australian Directory of Exports 394
Australian Economy: Economic
 Advisory Service 396
Australia Newsletter 399
Australian Key Business Directory
 407
Australian Trade Practices Reports
 419
Australian Trading News 420
Canberra Comments 849
Confederation of Australian Industry
 (CAI) News 1098
Economic Analysis & Policy 1535
Enterprise 1713
Executive Briefing 1797
Guide to Investment 2296
Handbook for Industrialists 2313
Impact 2441
National Bank of Australasia. National
 Bank Monthly Summary 3364
Primary Industry Survey 3842
Report on Production Trends 4072
Times 1000 4622
Trans-Tasman 4699

Belgium

Belgian American Trade Review 520
United States-Belgium Trade Directory,
 1980–81 edition 4794.01

Brazil

Brazilian–American Business
Review/Directory   585
Doing Business in Brazil   1483.01

Bulgaria

Economic News of Bulgaria   1556.01

California

California International Trade Register,
1980–81   737.01
California: State Industrial Directory,
1981   738.05
Journal of Commerce Review   2837
Kiplinger California Letter   2913
Los Angeles Business Journal   3046.01
Orange County Business   3634
San Diego Business Journal   4179
San Francisco Business Journal   4180
South Bay Economic Review   4342
Union-Tribune Annual Review of San
Diego Business Activity   4753
Union-Tribune Index   4754
Wells Fargo Bank Business Review
4947

Cambodia

Business China   674

Canada

Atlantic Report   345
Bank of Montreal Business Review
492
Bank of Nova Scotia. Monthly Review
494
Blue Book of Canadian Business   562
British Columbia Business Bulletin
599.02
British Columbia Industry and Small
Business News   602.01
Canada Commerce   744
Canada Report   761
Canada: Scott's Atlantic Industrial
Directory, 2nd edition, 1979–80
762.01
Canada: Scott's Ontario Industrial
Directory, 12th edition, 1981–82
762.02
Canada: Scott's Quebec Industrial
Directory, 10th edition, 1980–81
762.03
Canada: Scott's Trade Directory, Metro
Toronto, 1st edition, 1980–81
762.04
Canada: Scott's Trade Directory,
Toronto Vicinity, 1st edition,
1980–81   762.05

Canada: Scott's Western Canada
Industrial Directory, 5th edition,
1980–81   762.06
Canada–United Kingdom Trade News
770
Canada–United Kingdom Year Book
771
Canadian Business   778
Canadian Business Index   778.01
Canadian Business Management
Developments   780
Canadian Business Review   781
Canadian Key Business Directory   811
Canadian Manager   815
Daily Commercial News and
Construction Record   1294
Directory of Business and Financial
Services   1414
Edmonton Report on Business and
Travel Development   1588
Financial Post Newspaper   2014
Financial Times of Canada   2027
Globe and Mail "Report on Business"
2231
Journal of Commerce   2834
Journal of Commerce   2835
Metropolitan Toronto Board of Trade.
Journal   3206
National Bank of Canada, Economic
Review   3364.01
New Equipment News   3445
Ontario Business News   3620
Quarterly Canadian Forecast   3960
Sounding Board   4331
Survey of Business Attitudes   4509
Times 1000   4622
Wholesale Trade   4971

China, People's Republic of

Business China   674
CBR Index Microfiche   872.01
China Business Report   940.01
China Business Review   941
China Letter   942
Chinese Economic Studies   944
Soviet-Eastern Europe-China Business
& Trade   4351

Colorado

Colorado Business Review   984
Colorado Regional Profiles   988
Rocky Mountain Journal   4139

Connecticut

Commercial Record   1009
Connecticut Business and Industry
Assn (CBIA) News   1116
Connecticut: State Industrial Directory,
1981   1117.03

Cyprus

Owen's Commerce & Travel and
International Register   3670

Delaware

Delaware: State Industrial Directory,
1980   1355.03

Dominican Republic

Caribbean Business   862

Egypt

Developing Business in the Middle East
and North Africa   1371
Egypt/North Africa   1598.02

Europe

AP–Dow Jones Eurofinancial Report
279
Bacon's International Publicity Checker
447
Basic Statistics   514.01
Business Europe
Common Market News   1038
Doing Business in Europe   1486
Doing Business with Eastern Europe
1489
Eastern Europe   1523
European Directory of Business
Information Sources & Services
1773
European Industrial & Commercial
Review   1777
Europe's 5000 Largest Companies
1792
Europe's 5000 Largest Companies
Directory, 1980   1792.01
Financial Times of Canada   2027
Industrial Short-Term Trends   2551.02
Intelligence Digest BUSINESS TRENDS
2638
International Market Guide—
Continental Europe   2705
Predicasts F&S Index Europe   3828.01
Predicasts F&S Index Europe Annual
3828.02
Soviet-Eastern Europe-China Business
& Trade   4351
Visión—The Inter-American Magazine
4860
Times 1000   4622

Far East

Asian Business Quarterly   324.01
Asia & Pacific 1981   324.02
Asian Business   326.02
Asian Wall Street Journal   329
Business Asia   668

Economic Bulletin for Asia and the
  Pacific   1544
Far Eastern Technical Review   1892.01
Industrial Development News Asia and
  the Pacific   2516
Modern Asia   3253
Owen's Commerce & Travel and
  International Register   3670
Small Industry Bulletin for Asia and
  the Pacific   4304

Finland

Finnish–American Chamber of
  Commerce Newsletter   2040

Florida

Florida/Industries Directory, 1981
  2067.01
Florida/State Industrial Directory, 1981
  2068.01
Kiplinger Florida Letter   2915
Miami Business Journal   3208

France

French–American Commerce   2165

Georgia

Atlanta Business Chronicle   343
Georgia Business   2218
Georgia State Industrial Directory,
  1980   2219.01

Germany (West)

German American Trade News   2221

Gibraltar

Owen's Commerce & Travel and
  International Register   3670

Great Britain

Aslib Directory, Volume 1   333
Business News   713
Canada–United Kingdom Trade News
  770
Commerce International   996
Confederation of British Industry (CBI)
  Members Bulletin   1102
Cumbria Weekly Digest   1266
Estates Times   1755
Government & Municipal Contractors
  2236
Input–Output Tables   2584
Kelly's Post Office London Directory
  2908
Kelly's Regional Directory of British
  Industry and Services   2908.01
Labour Research Department Fact
  Service   2956

Manchester Business School Review
  3096
National Westminster Bank Quarterly
  Review   3413
Procurement Weekly   3861
Quarterly Trade Statistics of the United
  Kingdom   3978
Sell's Directory   4260
Times 1000   4622

Guam

Economic Censuses of Outlying Areas,
  1977, OAC 77   1547.01

Hawaii

All About Business in Hawaii   145
Bank of Hawaii Monthly Review   491
First Hawaiian Bank Economic
  Indicators   2047
Hawaii Facts and Figures   2348
Pacific Business News   3677

Hong Kong

Hong Kong Enterprise   2387
Hong Kong Trader   2388

Illinois

Chicago: Geographic Edition, 1981
  935.01
Chicagoland Development   936
Commerce   993
Illinois Economic Data Sheets   2438

India

Commerce   994
Embassy of India Commercial Bulletin
  1640
India News   2504

Indiana

Indiana Business Magazine   2503
Indiana Industrial Directory, 1981
  2503.01
Indiana State Industrial Directory, 1981
  2503.02

Indonesia

Indonesia Letter   2506

Iraq

Developing Business in the Middle East
  and North Africa   1371

Ireland, Republic of

Business and Finance   661
Confederation of Irish Industry
  (CII)/ESRI Business Forecast   1107

Ireland International Reference Manual
  2779.02
Republic of Ireland Reference Book
  4078
Thom's Commercial Directory   4612
Times 1000   4622
Trade Union Information   4679

Israel

Business Review and Economic News
  from Israel   720

Japan

Doing Business in Japan   1486.01
Focus Japan   2074
Japan Economic Journal   2796.01
Japan Economic Yearbook   2797
Japanese Breakthroughs   2797.01
Japan International Reference Manual
  2802.02
Japan Letter   2803
Japan Stock Journal   2803.01
Oriental Economist   3648
Times 1000   4622

Kansas

Corporate Report, Kansas City   1212
Kansas State Industrial Directory, 1981
  2904.02

Kentucky

Kentucky State Industrial Directory,
  1981   2908.03

Korea (North)

Business China   674

Laos

Business China   674

Louisiana

Financial Trend   2032
Louisiana Business Review   3047
Louisiana Economy   3048
Lousiana State Industrial Directory,
  1981   3048.02

Maine

Maine Business Indicators   3060
Maine State Industrial Directory, 1981
  3061.01

Malta

Owen's Commerce & Travel and
  International Register   3670

Maryland

District of Columbia   1469.01
Maryland: State Industrial Directory,
   1980   3146.02
Maryland Statistical Abstract, 1980
   edition   3147
University of Baltimore Business
   Review   4823

Massachusetts

Industry   2558
Massachusetts Business & Economic
   Report   3148
Massachusetts: State Industrial
   Directory, 1981   3149.04
Western Massachusetts Commercial
   News   4951

Mexico

Mexican–American Review   3206.01
Rubio's Mexican Financial Journal
   4151

Michigan

Michigan Manufacturer & Financial
   Record   3209
Michigan: State Industrial Directory,
   1981   3210

Middle East

Aramtek Mideast Review   297
Developing Business in the Middle East
   and North Africa   1371
Middle East   3216
Middle East Review 1981   3219.01
Middle East Week   3222
Mideast Business Exchange   3225
Near East Business   3422
Owen's Commerce & Travel and
   International Register   3670

Minnesota

Minnesota   3240
Minnesota: State Industrial Directory,
   1980   3240.02

Mississippi

Mississippi: State Industrial Directory,
   1981   3246.01

Missouri

Corporate Report, Kansas City   1212
Missouri Corporate Planner   3248
Missouri: State Industrial Directory,
   1981   3250.01

Mongolia

Business China   674

Montana

Montana Business Quarterly   3276
Montana: State Industrial Directory,
   1981   3276.02

Nebraska

Business in Nebraska   694
Nebraska Now   3424
Nebraska: State Industrial Directory,
   1981   3425

Nevada

Nevada: Industrial Directory, 1981
   3430.01
Nevada Review of Business &
   Economics   3431
Nevada: State Industrial Directory,
   1980   3431.01

New England

New England Business Magazine   3439

New Hampshire

New Hampshire: State Industrial
   Directory, 1980–81   3448

New Jersey

Jersey Business Review   2806
New Jersey Business   3450
New Jersey: Directory of
   Manufacturers, 1981–82   3450.01
New Jersey: State Industrial Directory,
   1980   3453.01

New Mexico

Financial Trend   2032
New Mexico: State Industrial Directory,
   1981   3455.01

New York City

Annual Summary of Business Statistics,
   New York State   265
Quarterly Summary of Business
   Statistics, New York State   3975
Review of Business   4120

New York State

Annual Summary of Business Statistics,
   New York State   265
Business Trends in New York State
   726
Capital District Business Review   854
Capital Journal   857.01

Central New York Business Review
   890
New York State Business Fact Book
   Part 1: Business & Manufacturing
   3481
New York: State Industrial Directory,
   1980   3483.01
Omnibus   3619.01
Orange Rockland Westchester Business
   Review   3636

New Zealand

Australia and New Zealand Bank
   Business Indicators   380
Australian Business Law Review   388
Economic News Bulletin   1555
Handbook for Investors—New Zealand
   2314
Life and Business in New Zealand
   3011
National Business Review   3365
New Zealand Business Who's Who
   3495
New Zealand Commerce   3497
New Zealand Economist   3500
New Zealand Industrial Production
   3507
New Zealand Trade Report   3513.01
Overseas Investment and Business in
   New Zealand   3659
Quarterly Survey of Business Opinion
   3977
Report of the New Zealand Dept of
   Trade & Industry   4066
Trans-Tasman   4699

Nigeria

Federal Ministry of Industries Annual
   Report   1932
Handbook of Commerce and Industry
   in Nigeria   2325
Nigeria Newsletter   3517.01

North Carolina

North Carolina Review of Business &
   Economics   3535
North Carolina: State Industrial
   Directory, 1980   3535.01

North Dakota

North Dakota: State Industrial
   Directory, 1981   3536.02

Norway

Norwegian–American Commerce   3548

Ohio

Development News Notes   1375.01
Ohio Developer   3593.01

Ohio: Industrial Directory, 1981
3593.02

Oklahoma

Financial Trend   2032
Oklahoma Business Bulletin   3614
Oklahoma Now!   3618
Oklahoma: State Industrial Directory,
1981   3618.01

Oregon

Oregon: State Industrial Directory,
1980   3638

Pacific Northwest

Marple's Business Newsletter   3144
Quarterly Summary of Pacific
Northwest Industries   3976

Pennsylvania

Pennsylvania Business Survey   3715
Pennsylvania Industrial Directory
3717
Pennsylvania: State Industrial
Directory, 1980   3717.02

Puerto Rico

Caribbean Business   862
Economic Censuses of Outlying Areas,
1977, OAC 77   1547.01
Puerto Rico Business Review   3943
Puerto Rico: Official Industrial & Trade
Directory, 1980   3943.01

Rhode Island

Rhode Island: State Industrial
Directory, 1981–82   4133

Saudi Arabia

Developing Business in the Middle East
and North Africa   1371
Saudi Arabia Newsletter   4183.02

Scotland

Industrial Index to Glasgow and West
of Scotland   2531
Journal of the Glasgow Chamber of
Commerce   2891
Scottish National Register of Classified
Trades   4206

South Africa

Financial Mail   2004.01
South African Market Guide   4339
Times 1000   4622

South Carolina

Business and Economic Review   660
South Carolina: Industrial Directory,
1981   4342.01
South Carolina: State Industrial
Directory, 1980   4342.02

South Dakota

South Dakota Business Review   4343
South Dakota: State Industrial
Directory, 1981   4345.02

Spain

Spain–US   4353

Switzerland

Economic Survey of Switzerland   1572

Tennessee

Survey of Business   4508
Tennessee: Business and Industrial
Review   4592
Tennessee: State Industrial Directory,
1981   4593.01

Texas

Business Information for Dallas   691
Dallas/Fort Worth Business   1314.01
Financial Trend   2032
Houston Business Journal   2417
Texas Ideas Newsletter   4597

Third World

United Nations Industrial Development
Organization Newsletter   4789

Union of Soviet Socialist Republics
(USSR)

Business China   674
Soviet-Eastern Europe-China Business
& Trade   4351

United States

Business and Economic Review   660
Business Executives' Expectations
681.01
Business in Brief   690
Business Organizations with Tax
Planning   715
Business Report   719
Business Week   727
Census of Manufacturers, 1977   876
County Business Patterns, 1974.
CBP-74   1237
Daily Report for Executives   1305

Directory of Business and Financial
Services   1414
Doing Business in the United States
1488
Dow Jones News/Retrieval   1502
Down to Business   1504.01
Economic Perspectives   1562
Federal Reserve Bank of Philadelphia
Business Review   1938
Federal Reserve Bank of Richmond
Economic Review   1940
Federal Reserve Bank of San Francisco
Western Economic Indicators   1954
Federal Reserve Bank Reviews. Selected
Subjects   1955
Fed in Print   1977
Financial Times of Canada   2027
Foreign Economic Trends and Their
Implications for the US   2117
Guide to Trade and Securities Statistics
2305
Kiplinger Washington Letter   2917
Middle Market Directory   3224
Million Dollar Directory   3230
News Front/Business Trends Databank
3465.01
Predicasts   3828
Rand McNally Commercial Atlas &
Marketing Guide   4000
Research Reports   4093
Review of Regional Economics &
Business   4127
Select Information Exchange (SIE)
Guide to Business & Investment
Books   4255
Sophisticated Investor   4330
Standard Industrial Classification
Manual, 1972   4374
State Sales Guides   4406
Statistical Abstract of the United States
4421
Statistical Service   4442
Survey of Business   4508
Times 1000   4622
United States Industrial Outlook   4807
Update   4827
Viewpoint   4857
Washington Report   4889
Whaley–Eaton American Letter   4958

Utah

Statistical Abstract of Utah   4422
Utah Economic and Business Review
4835
Utah: State Industrial Directory,
1980–81   4835.02

Vermont

Vermont: State Industrial Directory,
1981   4847.01

Vietnam

Business China   674

Virginia

Virginia: Industrial Directory, 1980–81
4858.01
Virginia: State Industrial Directory,
1981   4858.02

Virgin Islands

Caribbean Business   862
Economic Censuses of Outlying Areas,
1977 OAC 77   1547.01

Wales

Business News   713
Progress Wales   3897

Washington (DC)

District of Columbia   1469.01
Maryland: State Industrial Directory,
1980   3146.02

Washington (State)

Seattle Business Journal   4218
Washington: State Industrial Directory,
1981   4894.01

West Indies

Caribbean Year Book, 1977–78   864

West Virginia

West Virginia Economic Profile   4955
West Virginia: State Industrial
Directory, 1980–81   4957.01

Wisconsin

Wisconsin State Industrial Directory,
1981   5008.02

Yugoslavia

Business News   714

COMMERCE AND INDUSTRY, ACQUISITIONS AND MERGERS

Announcements of Mergers and
Acquisitions   233
International Licensing   2702

California

Journal of Commerce Review   2837

Great Britain

Acquisitions & Mergers of Companies
41

New England

New England Business Magazine   3442

United States

Standard Research Consultants (SRC)
Quarterly Reports   4378

COMMERCE AND INDUSTRY, BLACKS

Black Enterprise   560
Purchasing People in Major
Corporations   3954
Race Relations & Industry   3983
Survey of Minority-Owned Business
Enterprises, 1977, MB77   4516.01
Try Us: National Minority Business
Directory   4731

COMMERCE AND INDUSTRY, COMMUNITY RELATIONS

Business & Society   666
Business & Society Review   667
Public Affairs Report   3922

COMMERCE AND INDUSTRY, EDUCATION

American Assembly of Collegiate
Schools of Business Newsline &
Bulletin   156
Ball State Business Review   454
Ball State Journal for Business
Educators   454.01
Business Education Forum   680
Dictionary of Economics and Business
1379
Journal of Business Communication
2828
Management Advisory Services Manual,
1977   3071
Short Courses and Seminars   4284
Training and Development Journal
4685

Great Britain

Business Graduate   685
Confederation of British Industry (CBI)
Education and Training Bulletin
1100

North Carolina

North Carolina Industrial Data File
3534

COMMERCE AND INDUSTRY, EQUIPMENT

Administrative Digest   56
Applied Ergonomics   286

Business Systems & Equipment   724
Industrial Equipment News   2520
Industrial Property   2537
Industrial Purchasing Agent   2538

Canada

Canadian Industrial Equipment News
801
New Equipment News   3445
Private and Public Investment in
Canada Outlook   3851

United States

Survey of Current Business   4514

COMMERCE AND INDUSTRY, ETHICS

Government Regulation of Business
Ethics: International Payoffs   2251

COMMERCE AND INDUSTRY, FINANCES. *See also* Financial Planning

Annual Statement Studies   261
Business Economics   679
Business Failure Record   682
Business Information Reports   692
Compustat   1070
Credit and Financial Management
1245
Dun & Bradstreet Reference Book
1514
Dun & Bradstreet Standard Register
1515
Financial World   2034
Fraser Opinion Letter   2161
Industrial Development Handbook
2515
Journal of Business Finance and
Accounting   2830
Journal of Industrial Economics   2861
Journal of Reprints for Antitrust Law
and Economics   2880
Statistical Bulletin   4425

American Nations

International Market Guide—Latin
America   2706

Arkansas

Basics of Plant Location in Arkansas
514

Australia

Australian Key Business Directory
407

COMMERCE AND INDUSTRY, FOREIGN FACILITIES

Canada

Canadian Key Business Directory   811
Doing Business in Canada   1484
Fixed Capital Flows and Stocks   2056
Private and Public Investment in
  Canada Outlook   3851

Europe

International Market Guide—
  Continental Europe   2705

Great Britain

Company Finance   1053
National Income and Expenditure
  "Blue Book"   3382

Ireland, Republic of

Republic of Ireland Reference Book
  4078

New York City Metropolitan Area

Review of Business   4120

New Zealand

Mercantile Gazette of New Zealand
  3190

North Carolina

North Carolina Industrial Data File
  3534

South Africa

South African Market Guide   4339

United States

Census of Manufacturers, 1977   876
Middle Market Directory   3224
Million Dollar Directory   3230

COMMERCE AND INDUSTRY, FOREIGN FACILITIES

American Industrial Properties Report
  (AIPR) Worldwide Guide for
  Foreign Investment   184
News from the Hill   3464
Overseas Assignment Directory Service
  3655
Swiss–American Chamber of
  Commerce. Yearbook   4522

COMMERCE AND INDUSTRY, FOREIGN INVESTMENTS

Information Guide for Doing Business
  in Countries Abroad   2571

Canada

Action Canada France   45

France

Action Canada France   45

Great Britain

Anglo American Trade Directory   224

Japan

Japan External Trade Organization
  (JETRO) Business Information Series
  2801
Japan Trade and Industry News   2804

United States

Anglo American Trade Directory   224
News from the Hill   3464

COMMERCE AND INDUSTRY, GOVERNMENT REGULATIONS, LAW AND PROGRAMS

Bank Officer's Handbook of
  Commercial Banking Law   490
Business International   696
Business Lawyer   704
Businessman & The Law   707
Commercial Laws of the World   1005
Compendium of Commerical Finance
  Law   1060
Digest of Commercial Laws of the
  World   1386
Enterprise   1714
Gallagher Report   2206
Government Regulation of Business
  Ethics: International Payoffs   2251
Industrial Property   2537
Industrial Property Reports from
  Socialist Countries   2537.01
Journal of Business Law   2831
Lloyd's Maritime & Commercial Law
  Quarterly   3033.01
Robert's Dictionary of Industrial
  Relations, 1971 edition   4138
Trade Secrets and Know-How
  throughout the World   4675
World Law of Competition   5068.01
You and the Law   5101

Australia

Australian Corporate Affairs Reports
  391
Australian Director   393
Australian Trade Practices Reports
  419
Business Law Cases for Australians
  701
Guide to Investment   2296

Brazil

Doing Business in Brazil   1483.01

Canada

British Columbia Industry and Small
  Business News   602.01
Business Law Reports Volume 1   702
Canadian Business Law Journal   779
Doing Business in Canada   1484
Establishing A Business   1742
Ottawa Letter   3650

Connecticut

Connecticut Business and Industry
  Assn (CBIA) News   1116

Europe

Commercial Laws of Europe   1004.01
Common Market Reports   1039
EEC Competition Law Reporter
  1597.02
Eurolaw Commercial Intelligence   1762
European Commercial Cases   1769
European Law Digest   1782
Journal of Business Law   2831

Great Britain

Industrial Cases Reports   2511
Journal of Business Law   2831

Hawaii

Legislative Action Bulletin   2997
Starting a Business in Hawaii   4381

Japan

Doing Business in Japan   1486.01
Focus Japan   2074

Louisiana

Louisiana Business Review   3047

Mexico

Commerical Laws (Mexican)   1004

Middle East

Commercial Laws of the Middle East
  1004.02

Scotland

Journal of the Glasgow Chamber of
  Commerce   2891

Texas

Brief Guide to Business Regulations
  and Services in Texas   592.01

United States

Acts 46
Advance Session Laws 64
American Business Law Journal 165
Business Law Review 703
Daily Report for Executives 1305
Doing Business in the United States
 1488
Economic Regulation of Business and
 Industry 1565
Federal Trade Commission Annual
 Report 1973
Federal Trade Commission Decisions
 1974
Kiplinger Washington Letter 2917
Munn's Encyclopedia of Banking and
 Finance, 7th edition 3342
News from the Hill 3464
Review of Regional Economics &
 Business 4127
Starting a Business in Hawaii 4381
Trade Cases 4653
Trade Practice Rules 4668
Trade Regulation Reports 4671
Trade Regulation Rules 4672
Warranty Watch 4883
Whaley–Eaton American Letter 4958

COMMERCE AND INDUSTRY, HISTORY

American Business Activity from 1790
 to Today 164
Business History Review 686

COMMERCE AND INDUSTRY, INDUSTRIAL DEVELOPMENT

Bulletin 643.01
Development Digest 1373
Embassy of India Commercial Bulletin
 1640
Industrial Development 2513
Industrial Development Abstracts
 2514
Industrial Planning and Programming
 Series 2536
Site Selection Handbook 4290
Training for Industry Series 4686
World Development 5055

Alabama

Alabama Development News 134

Canada

Northern Perspectives 3540

Europe (West)

New Products & Processes From
 Western Europe 3458.01

Germany (West)

German American Trade News 2221

Michigan

Michigan Plant Location Directory,
 1980–81 3209.02

Texas

Texas Industrial Update 4597.01
Texas Means Business 4597.03

Third World

International Licensing 2702
United Nations Industrial Development
 Organization Newsletter 4789

United States

From the State Capitals: Industrial
 Development 2175

COMMERCE AND INDUSTRY, MINORITIES. *See also* Commerce and Industry, Blacks

Abstract Newsletters, Business and
 Economics 2.08
Access 7
Commerce: Journal of Minority
 Business 996.01
Guide to Obtaining Minority Business
 Directories 2299.01
Journal of Small Business Management
 2884
Minority Business Information Institute
 (MBII) Newsletter 3241
Race Relations & Industry 3983

COMMERCE AND INDUSTRY, NATIONALIZATION OF INDUSTRY

Canada–United Kingdom Trade News
 770

COMMERCE AND INDUSTRY, NEW VENTURES

Brief Guide to Business Regulations
 and Services in Texas 592.01
Florida Economic Indicators 2066
Illinois Economic Data Sheets 2438
Japanese Breakthroughs 2797.01
Minnesota 3240
New Product–New Business Digest
 3458
New Plants 3457.01
Rocky Mountain Journal 4139
Sales Management and Sales
 Engineering 4172
Selected Business Ventures 4252

Site Report 4289.01
Starting a Business in Hawaii 4381

Great Britain

Sales Management and Sales
 Engineering 4172

COMMERCE AND INDUSTRY, PLANTS AND SITES. *See also* Industrial Parks

American Industrial Properties Report
 183
Chilton's Market/Plant Data Bank
 939
Industrial Development 2513
Industrial Development Handbook
 2515
Industrial Property 2537
Journal of Industrial Economics 2861
Journal of Regional Science 2879
Minnesota 3240
New Plants 3457.01
Plant Location 3780
United Nations Industrial Development
 Organization (UNIDO) Guides to
 Information Sources.
 UNIDO/LIB/SER.D/Rev.1—
 Information Sources on Industrial
 Maintenance and Repair 4767.02

Michigan

Michigan Plant Location Directory
 1980–81 3209.02

Oklahoma

Oklahoma Now! 3618

United States

Abstract Newsletters, Industrial &
 Mechanical Engineering 2.18
New Plants 3457.01
Prepared Sites 3835.01
Site Report 4289.01
Survey of Current Business 4514

Washington (State)

Announced New Plants & Expansions
 in the State of Washington 231

COMMERCE AND INDUSTRY, PRODUCTION. *See also* Quality Control

Business International (BI) Data 697
Indicators of Industrial Activity
 2505.01
Journal of Operations & Production
 Management 2870.01
Monthly Bulletin of Statistics 3283

COMMODITIES AND COMMODITY EXCHANGES, FUTURES

COMMODITIES AND COMMODITY EXCHANGES, IMPORTS AND EXPORTS

Third World

COMMODITY EXCHANGE ACT (US)

COMMODITY EXCHANGE AUTHORITY (US)

COMMODITY FUTURES TRADING COMMISSION (US)

COMMON MARKET. *See* European
Economic Community (EEC) (Common
Market)

COMMON STOCKS. *See* Stocks and
Bonds, Common Stocks

COMMUNICATIONS COMMISSION, FEDERAL (FCC) (US)

COMMUNICATIONS SYSTEMS.

See also Organizational
Communications. Telecommunications
Types, eg, Television and Radio

Applied Science & Technology Index (ASTI)   288

Alaska

Australia

Canada

Europe

Far East

Great Britain

Japan

United States

COMMUNICATIONS SYSTEMS, LAWS ON. *See also* specific laws

COMMUNITY ACTION AGENCIES (US)

COMMUNITY BANKS. *See* Banking and Finance, Community Banks

COMMUNITY DEVELOPMENT BLOCK GRANT PROGRAM

Community Development Digest   1049

COMMUNITY RELATIONS. *See* Commerce and Industry, Community Relations

COMPARISON SHOPPING

Consumer Reports   1171

COMPOSITE MATERIALS. *See also* Research and Development, Composite Materials

Composites   1068

COMPREHENSIVE EMPLOYMENT AND TRAINING ACT (US)

Education and Work   1593
Employment and Training Reporter   1654
Manpower and Vocational Education Weekly   3098

COMPUTER-AIDED ACCOUNTING SYSTEMS

Financial/Retail Systems Reports   2018.01
Information Industry & Technology Service   2573
Management Advisory Services Guidelines Series   3070
National Public Accountant   3401
Retail Roundup   4109

COMPUTER-AIDED BANKING

Autotransaction Industry Report   435.01
Bank Automation Newsletter   460
Bank Systems & Equipment   503
Community Bank Series on Operations and Automation   1048
Financial/Retail Systems Reports   2018.01
Information Industry & Technology Service   2573
Nacha Quarterly Update   3354
Proceedings of the 1972 National Operations and Automation Conference—"The Common Denominator—Management"   3858
Results of the 1972 National Automation Survey   4101
Thruput   4617

COMPUTER-AIDED DESIGN

Computer-Aided Design   1071

COMPUTER-AIDED EDUCATION

Journal of Educational Technology Systems   2850

COMPUTER-AIDED INFORMATION SYSTEMS

Computer-Readable Data Bases: A Directory and Data Sourcebook, 1979 edition   1081.02
Information Industry Market Place: An International Directory of Information Products and Services   2573.01
Journal of the American Society for Information Science   2888.01

COMPUTER-AIDED INSURANCE SYSTEMS

Insurance Agency Computer Power   2609

COMPUTER-AIDED LABORATORY FUNCTIONS

Lab World   2959

COMPUTER-AIDED MANAGEMENT TECHNIQUES.
See also Office Systems

Computer Data   1074
Decision Line   1348
Decision Sciences   1352
Digital Systems for Industrial Automation   1396.01
Financial/Retail Systems Reports   2018.01
Information & Management   2568.01
Information Industry & Technology Service   2573
Journal of Applied Systems Analysis   2823.01
Officemation Management   3579.02

COMPUTER-AIDED MARKETING

Financial/Retail Systems Reports   2018.01
Friday Report   2167

COMPUTER-AIDED PRODUCT DEVELOPMENT

Small Business Computer News   4300

COMPUTER-AIDED PUBLISHING

IDP Report   2433.02

COMPUTER-AIDED RESEARCH

Tax Research Techniques   4568

COMPUTER-AIDED TRADE

World Trade Information Center   5083.01

COMPUTERS. *See also* Automation. Microprocessors. Applications, eg, Computer-Aided Design. Information Retrieval

ACM Guide to Computing Literature Annual   40
ACM Transactions on Database Systems   40.01
ADP Network Services   60
American Federation of Information Processing Societies Conference Proceedings   175
Anbar Management Publications Accounting and Data Processing Abstracts   217
Auerbach Applications Software Reports   350
Auerbach Computer Programming Management   356
Auerbach Data Center Operations Management   358
Auerbach Data Communications Management   359
Auerbach Data Processing Management   363
Auerbach Software Reports   375
Auerbach Standard EDP Reports   376
Auerbach Systems Software Reports   378
Ball State Business Review   454
Communications of the ACM   1043
Computer and Information Systems Abstracts Journal   1072
Computer Business News   1073
Computer Decisions   1075
Computer Dictionary and Handbook, 3rd edition   1076
Computer Law and Tax Report   1079
Computer Output Program   1081.01
Computer Report   1082
Computers and Industrial Engineering   1084
Computers & Operations Research   1086
Computers and People   1087
Computer Times   1088
Computerworld   1089
Computer Yearbook   1090
Computing Reviews   1091
Computing Surveys   1091.01
Condensed Computer Encyclopedia   1094

Louisiana

Louisiana Business Review 3047
Louisiana Economic Indicators 3047.01

Massachusetts

Western Massachusetts Commercial News 4951

Michigan

Michigan Manufacturer & Financial Record 3209

Middle East

ICW's Mideast Construction Business Report 2431.05

New Jersey

Building and Realty Record 634

New York City Metropolitan Area

Realty 4030

New Zealand

Information Releases 2573.03
New Zealand Building and Construction Statistics 3494
New Zealand Census of Building and Construction 3496

Pennsylvania

Building and Realty Record 634

Puerto Rico

Economic Censuses of Outlying Areas, 1977, OAC 77 1547.01

United States

Abstract Newsletters, Building Industry Technology 2.07
Blue Reports 565
Dodge Bulletins 1478
Dodge Construction Potentials Bulletin 1479
Dodge/Scan Microfilm System 1483
Economic Week 1575
Federal Reserve Bank of San Francisco Western Economic Indicators 1954
Industrial Series, CC77-1-1 to 28 2564
Realty 4030
What's New in Building 4961

Utah

Utah Construction Report 4834

Virgin Islands

Economic Censuses of Outlying Areas, 1977, OAC 77 1547.01

Washington (DC) Metropolitan Area

Blue Reports 565

CONSTRUCTION, CONTRACTS

Construction Briefings 1125.01
Dodge Bulletins 1478
Dodge/Scan Microfilm System 1483
Forms and Agreements for Architects, Engineers, and Contractors 2146
ICW's Africa Construction Business Report 2431.02
ICW's Asia Construction Business Report 2431.03
ICW's Latin America Construction Business Report 2431.04
ICW's Mideast Construction Business Report 2431.05
International Construction Week 2669

CONSTRUCTION, EQUIPMENT, MATERIALS, AND PLANTS

ABS 2.02
Abstract Newsletters, Civil Engineering 2.10
Associated Equipment Distributors Edition of Construction Equipment Buyers Guide 334
Australia Newsletter 399
Building Construction Cost Data 635
Building Materials 639
Building Products News 641
Building Supply News 642
Commercial Bulletin 999
Construction Equipment 1127
Construction Equipment Distribution (CED) 1128
Construction Equipment News 1129
Construction Machinery. MA-35D 1134
Construction Machinery. MQ-35D 1135
Construction Plant & Equipment 1139
Cost Forecasting Service 1227
Cost-of-Doing-Business Survey 1228
Dodge/Scan Microfilm System 1483
Ebasco Cost Newsletter 1529
Engineering News-Record 1711
Housing and Construction Statistics 2409
ICW's Africa Construction Business Report 2431.02
ICW's Asia Contruction Business Report 2431.03
ICW's Latin America Construction Business Report 2431.04

ICW's Mideast Construction Business Report 2431.05
International Construction Week 2669
National Home Center News 3379.01
Rental Compilation 4061
Serial Number Field Guide 4262
Serial Number Location Guide for Construction Equipment 4263
Truck & Off-Highway Industries 4722.01
United Nations Industrial Development Organization Guides to Information Sources. UNIDO/LIB/SER D/9— Information Sources on the Building Board Industry Based on Wood and Other Fibrous Materials 4776
What's New in Building 4961

United States

Industrial Series, CC77-1-1 to 28 2564

CONSTRUCTION, FINANCES

Building Construction Cost Data 635
Cost Forecasting Service 1227
Dodge Building Cost Calculator and Valuation Guide 1477
Dodge Construction Systems Costs 1480
Dodge Digest of Building Costs and Specifications 1481
Ebasco Cost Newsletter 1529
Engineering News-Record 1711
Forms and Agreements for Architects, Engineers, and Contractors 2146
Housing 2407.01
International Construction Week 2669
Mechanical & Electrical Cost Data 3164.02
National Real Estate Investor 3402.01

Africa

ICW's Africa Construction Business Report 2431.02

American Nations

ICW's Latin America Construction Business Report 2431.04

Australia

Australian Building and Construction News 387

Canada

Construction Price Statistics 1140

Far East

ICW's Asia Construction Business Report 2431.03

43

Great Britain

Housing and Construction Statistics 2409
Laxton's Building Price Book   2992

Middle East

ICW's Mideast Construction Business Report   2431.05

New York City Metropolitan Area

Realty   4030

United States

Bank Loan Officers Report   481
Consolidated Ledger Abstract   1121
Construction Lending Handbook   1133
Realty   4030
Industrial Series CC77-1-1 to 28   2564

CONSTRUCTION, LABOR

Building Construction Cost Data   635
Construction News   1137
Cost Forecasting Service   1227
Dimensions   1397
Ebasco Cost Newsletter   1529
Engineering News-Record   1711
International Construction Week   2669
Mechanical & Electrical Cost Data 3164.02

Canada

Construction in Canada   1130

Great Britain

Construction News   1137
Laxton's Building Price Book   2992

United States

Construction Labor Report   1132
Industrial Series, CC77-1-1 to 28   2564
United States Housing Markets   4804

CONSTRUCTION, LAWS ON. *See also* specific laws

Construction Contractor   1126

Great Britain

BMCIS   566.01

New York City Metropolitan Area

Realty   4030

United States

Realty   4030

CONSULTING AND CONSULTANTS. *See also* Management Consultants. Fields of activity

Association of Executive Recruiting Consultants: 1980 Directory   340.01
Consultants and Consulting Organizations Directory, 3rd edition 1144
Directory of Evaluation Consultants 1428.01
Directory of Members   1446
New Consultants, 3rd Edition   3435
Who's Who in Consulting, 2nd edition 4982

CONSUMER CREDIT ASSOCIATION, INTERNATIONAL

Credit World   1253

CONSUMER CREDIT PROTECTION ACT (US)

Acts   46

CONSUMER MARKET. *Note:* Material covers buying and spending habits and efforts to reach consumers. *See also* Consumer Protection

Advanced Retail Marketing   62.01
Consumer Attitudes and Buying Plans 1150
Consumer Research Service   1171.01
Co-op Consumers   1191.02
Direct Mail List Rates and Data   1401
Guide to Consumer Markets   2291
Hardware Age   2343

Canada

Canadian Consumer   786
Market Research Handbook   3138
Survey of Consumer Buying Intentions 4513

Europe

Consumer Europe   1153
Marketing in Europe   3130.02

Great Britain

Advertising Magazine   68.01
General Household Survey   2210
Mintel   3242

Japan

Japan External Trade Organization (JETRO) Marketing Series   2802

United States

Consumer Information Catalog   1154

CONSUMER MARKET, SPENDING

Statistical Bulletin   4425

Great Britain

Annual Abstract of Statistics   234
Economic Trends   1573
Family Expenditure Survey   1883
National Income and Expenditure "Blue Book"   3382

Ireland, Northern

Family Expenditure Survey, Northern Ireland   1884

CONSUMER PRODUCT SAFETY ACT (US)

Consumer Product Safety Guide   1168
Product Safety & Liability Reporter 3876
Products Liability   3878

CONSUMER PROTECTION. *See also* Product Testing and Rating. Specific products, services, and industries

America Buys   154.01
American Council on Consumer Interests. Journal of Consumer Affairs, Newsletter, Consumer Education Forum   168
Caveat Emptor/Consumers Bulletin 872
Consumer Action Update   1147.01
Consumer Newsweekly   1160
Consumer Reports   1171
Consumers Digest   1172
Consumers Digest Guide to Discount Buying   1173
Consumer Sourcebook, 1st edition 1175
Consumers' Research   1177
Consumers Union News Digest   1178
Co-op Consumers   1191.02
Executive Action Report   1796
Journal of Consumer Affairs   2840
Law of Advertising   2979
Money   3267
News & Views   3461
Of Consuming Interest   3576

Australia

Choice   945
Handbook for Industrialists   2313
Insurance Record of Australia and New Zealand   2635

Copper Controlled Materials ITA 9008
1199.01
Copper Data   1200

COPYING MACHINES

Information and Records Management
2570

COPYRIGHTS

Bureau of National Affairs (BNA)
  Patent, Trademark, & Copyright
  Journal   649
Catalog of Copyright Entries   868
Copyright   1201
Copyright Management   1201.01
Intellectual Property Management:
  Law/Business/Strategy   2637
Licensing in Foreign and Domestic
  Operations   3010
United States Patents Quarterly   4814

COPYRIGHTS, LAWS ON.   *See also*
specific laws

Bowker Annual of Library and Book
  Trade Information   580
Copyright Protection in the Americas
  1201.02
Intellectual Property Management:
  Law/Business/Strategy   2637

Canada

Canadian Patent Reporter   826

Great Britain

Fleet Street Patent Law Reports   2062

United States

Bureau of National Affairs (BNA)
  Patent, Trademark, & Copyright
  Journal   649
Copyright Revision Act of 1976   1202
United States Patents Quarterly   4814

CORPORATE BONDS.   *See* Stocks
and Bonds, Corporate Bonds

CORPORATE TAXES.   *See* Taxation,
Corporate

CORPORATION ACT (CANADA)

Canada Corporation Act Bulletin   745

CORPORATIONS.   *See also*
  Bankruptcies, Business. Entrepreneurs
  and Small Businesses. Managers and
  Management. Multinational
  Companies. Professional
  Corporations. Stocks and Bonds

AP–Dow Jones Economic Report   278
AP–Dow Jones Financial Wire   280
Chief Executive   937.01
Compmark Data Services   1067
Credit and Financial Management
  1245
Directors and Boards   1404
Discount Merchandiser   1464
Dow Jones International Banking Wire
  1497
Dow Jones International News Wire
  1499
Dun & Bradstreet Standard Register
  1515
International Market Guide—
  Continental Europe   2705
Long Range Planning   3044
Management Decision   3077
Managerial Planning   3095
Mergers & Acquisitions   3195
Moody's Investors Fact Sheets
  3314.01
Omega   3619
Optimum   3633
Planning Ideas   3777.01
Sound of the Economy   4332
Value Line Investment Survey   4840
World Guide to Abbreviations of
  Organizations, 5th edition   5065
World's Largest Industrial Enterprises
  5078.02

American Nations

International Market Guide—Latin
  America   2706

Australia

Australian Director   393
Australian Key Business Directory
  407
Extel Australian Company Service
  1856
Extel Overseas Companies Services
  1863
Foreign Kompass Register. Australia
  2120

Brazil

United States–Brazil Business Listing
  4794.02

Canada

Business Law Reports Volume I   702
Business Who's Who, 1974   728
Canada Corporation Act Bulletin   745
Canadian Key Business Directory   811
Financial Post Corporation Service
  2011

Fraser's Canadian Trade Directory
  2162
Optium/A Forum for Management
  3633
Register of Corporations, Directors, and
  Executives   4051

Colorado

Rocky Mountain Journal   4139

Europe

The Brussels Report   632
Europe's 5000 Largest Companies
  1791
Extel European Company Service
  1859
Extel Overseas Companies Services
  1863

Great Britain

Director   1403
Guide to Key British Enterprises   2298
United Kingdom—Guide to Key
  British Enterprises I   4757
United Kingdom Guide to Key British
  Enterprises II   4758
United Kingdom Kompass Register
  4759

Hong Kong

Hong Kong Cable   2386

Ireland, Republic of

Republic of Ireland Reference Book
  4078

Japan

Japan Company Handbook   2796
Who Owns Whom: Australasia & Far
  East   4972

New Zealand

Management   3068
New Zealand Company Directory &
  Executive   3498

Scotland

Journal of the Glasgow Chamber of
  Commerce   2891

Texas

Houston Public Companies Directory
  2418

United States

Babson's Investment & Barometer
  Letter   444

Business Organizations with Tax
Planning   715
Copmark Data Services   1067
Corporate Examiner   1206
Corporate Foundation Profiles   1208.01
Corporate Report, Kansas City   1212
Corporate Report Fact Book   1213
Defense Week   1355.02
Dow Jones News/Retrieval   1502
Extel North American Company
Service   1862
Extel Overseas Companies Services
1863
Financial Trend's Corporate Directory
Service   2033
Kess Tax Practice Report   2909
Market Chronicle   3126
Middle Market Directory   3224
Million Dollar Directory   3230
Multinational Marketing and
Employment Directory   3336
News Front/Business Trends Databank
3465.01
News Front/Business Trends Directory
3465.02
Predicasts F&S Index of Corporate
Change   3828.05
Predicasts F&S Index United States
Annual   3828.07
Register of Corporations, Directors, and
Executives   4051
Standard Directory of Advertisers
4371
State Sales Guides   4406
United States–Brazil Business Listing
4794.02
Walker's Manual of Western
Corporations   4874

CORPORATIONS, ACQUISITIONS AND MERGERS

Business & Acquisition Newsletter   657
Committee on Uniform Security
Identification Procedures (CUSIP):
Digest of Changes in CUSIP   1017
Euromarket News   1764
International Licensing   2702
Journal of Accounting, Auditing and
Finance   2817.02
Mergers & Acquisitions   3195
Predicasts F&S Index United States
Annual   3828.07

Great Britain

Acquisitions & Mergers of Companies
41

United States

Corporate Acquisitions & Mergers
1203

Million Dollar Directory   3230
Predicasts F&S Index of Corporate
Change   3828.05
Predicasts F&S Index United States
3828.06

CORPORATIONS, CLOSELY HELD

How to Take Money Out of a Closely
Held Corporation   2425
Tax Desk Book for the Closely-Held
Corporation   4546
Tax, Financial and Estate Planning for
the Owner of a Closely-Held
Corporation   4553.01

CORPORATIONS, DIRECTORS AND OFFICERS

Directors and Boards   1404
International Businessman's Who's
Who   2663

Canada

Canadian Book of Corporate
Management   777
Canadian Corporate Secretary's Guide
786.01
Register of Corporations, Directors, and
Executives   4051

Great Britain

Business Who's Who, 1974   728
Directory of Directors   1427

United States

Financial Trend's Corporate Directory
Service   2033
Million Dollar Directory   3230
Register of Corporations, Directors and
Executives   4051

CORPORATIONS, DIVESTITURES

Mergers & Acquistions   3195

CORPORATIONS, FACILITIES AND SITES

Area Development   303
Site Selection Handbook   4290

CORPORATIONS, FINANCES

Accounting Trends & Techniques   38
Analytics   214
AP–Dow Jones Economic Report   278
Business Information Reports   692
Compustat   1070
Corporate Accounting Reporter
1202.01
Corporate Controllers and Treasurers
Report   1204.01

Corporate Financing Week   1208
Corporate Report Fact Book   1213
Corporate Treasurer's and Controller's
Encyclopedia   1215
Corporation Service   1221
Disclosure Record   1463
Dun & Bradstreet Reference Book
1514
Dun & Bradstreet Standard Register
1515
Financial Management Letter   2006.01
Financial World   2034
Fitch Commercial Paper Reports   2050
Fortune Double 500 Directory   2151
Institutional Investor International
Edition   2602
Investment Dealers' Digest   2762
Journal of Accounting, Auditing and
Finance   2817.02
Journal of Business Finance and
Accounting   2830
Journal of Futures Markets   2858
Moody's Commercial Paper Reports
3311
Moody's Investors Fact Sheets
3314.01
Value Line Investment Survey   4840

American Nations

International Market Guide—Latin
America   2706

Arkansas

Financial Trend   2032

Australia

Australian Key Business Directory
407
Company Review Service   1054
Extel Australian Company Service
1856
Extel Overseas Companies Services
1863
Jobson's Year Book   2814

Canada

Blue Book of CBS Stock Reports   563
Canadian Business Service Investment
Reporter   782
Canadian Key Business Directory   811
Corporate Insurance in Canada   1209
Corporation Financial Statistics   1216
Financial Post Investment Databank
2012.01
Fixed Capital Flows and Stocks   2056
Industrial Corporations, Financial
Statistics   2512
Investor's Digest of Canada   2772

Europe

Extel European Company Service
1859
Extel Overseas Companies Services
1863
International Market Guide—
Continental Europe   2705

Great Britain

British Company Service   610
Extel Handbook of Market Leaders
1860
National Income and Expenditure
"Blue Book"   3382
Unquoted Companies Service   4825

Ireland, Republic of

British Company Service   610
Republic of Ireland Reference Book
4078
Unquoted Companies Service   4825

Japan

Japan Company Handbook   2796

Louisiana

Financial Trend   2032

New Mexico

Financial Trend   2032

New Zealand

Jobson's Year Book   2814
New Zealand Financial Times   3503

Oklahoma

Financial Trend   2032

South Africa

Johannesburg Stock Exchange Monthly
Bulletin   2815

Texas

Financial Trend   2032

United States

American Exchange Stock Reports
173
Analysts Handbook   215
Corporate Report Fact Book   1213
Corporation Law & Tax Report   1219
Federal Trade Commission. Quarterly
Financial Report for Manufacturing,
Mining, & Trade Corporations   1975
Financial Trend's Corporate Directory
Service   2033

Industry Surveys   2565
Internal Revenue Service Statistics of
Income: Corporate Income Tax
Returns   2650
Journal of Corporate Taxation   2843
Middle Market Directory   3224
Millon Dollar Directory   3230
Moody's Handbook of Common Stocks
3313
Moody's Over-the-Counter (OTC)
Industrials Manual and News
Reports   3317
Northwest Investment Review   3546
Northwest Stock Guide   3547
Securities & Exchange Commission
Docket   4227
Standard Corporation Records   4370
Subchapter S: Planning & Operation
4482
Survey of Current Business   4514
Tax Desk Book for the Closely Held
Corporation   4546

CORPORATIONS, FORMS

Corporation Forms   1217

CORPORATIONS, GOVERNMENT REGULATIONS, LAWS AND PROGRAMS

Corporate Counsel's Annual   1205
Investment and Taxation Monograph
2760.01
Multinational Business   3333
World Accounting Report   5034

Canada

Alberta Corporation Manual   143
British Columbia Corporation Manual
600
Canada Corporation Act Bulletin   745
Canada Corporation Manual   746
Canada Corporations Law Reports
747
Ontario Corporation Manual   3621
Ontario Corporations Law Guide   3622
Quebec Corporation Manual   3979

Europe

Company Law in Europe, 3rd edition
1053.01

United States

Business International Washington
(BIW)   699.01
Corporate Acquisitions & Mergers
1203
Corporate Controllers and Treasurers
Report   1204.01
Corporate Practice Series   1211

Corporation Law & Tax Report   1219
Corporation Law Guide   1220
Corporation Management Edition
1221.01
Directory of Companies Filing Annual
Reports with the US Securities &
Exchange Commission   1419
Going Public   2232
Securities & Exchange Commission
Docket   4227

CORPORATIONS, INVESTOR AND PUBLIC RELATIONS

Corporate Communications Reports
1204
Investor Relations Newsletter   2769
O'Dwyer's Directory of Corporate
Communications   3573

CORPORATIONS, PROFESSIONAL. *See* Professional Corporations

CORPORATIONS, REORGANIZATION

Securities & Exchange Commission
Docket   4227

CORPORATIONS, SOCIAL ISSUES

American Art Directory   155.01
Business & Society   666
Report on Company Contributions
4068

CORPORATIONS, SUBCHAPTERS

Subchapter S: Planning & Operation
4482

CORPORATIONS, SUBSIDIARIES

Canada

Who Owns Whom: North America
4974

Europe

Who Owns Whom: Continental Europe
4973

Far East

Who Owns Whom: Australasia & Far
East   4972

Great Britain

Guide to Key British Enterprises   2298
Who Owns Whom: United Kingdom &
Republic of Ireland   4975

United States

Agricultural Banker   94
Bank Fact Book   474
Business & Capital Reporter   658
Consumer and Commercial Credit
   1149
Credit and Capital Markets   1244
Financial Letter   2004.01
Public Periodic Releases   3926
Reporting on Governments   4063
Statistical Indicator Reports   4428
Statistical Release (Agricultural Credit
   Conditions Survey)   4439

CREDIT, CAPITAL MARKETS.   *See* Capital Markets

CREDIT, COLLECTION

Executive's Credit and Collections
   Letter   1807.02
Regency International Directory   4045

CREDIT, COMMERCIAL

Compendium of Commercial Finance
   Law   1060
Credit and Financial Management
   1245
Journal of the Asset-Based Financial
   Services Industry   2889.01

New York City Metropolitan Area

Review of Business   4120

United States

Bank Loan Officers Report   481
Consumer and Commercial Credit
   1149
Uniform Commercial Code Law
   Journal   4750
Uniform Commercial Code Law Letter
   4751

CREDIT, CONSUMER

Credit   1242
Credit World   1253
Finance Facts   1989
Finance Facts Yearbook   1990

United States

Consumer and Commercial Credit
   1149
Consumer Credit and Truth-in-Lending
   Compliance Report   1151
Consumer Trends   1178.01
From the State Capitals: Merchandising
   2180

Uniform Commercial Code Law
   Journal   4750
Uniform Commercial Code Law Letter
   4751

CREDIT, GOVERNMENT REGULATIONS, LAWS AND PROGRAMS.   *See also* Credit, Truth-in-Lending

Consumer Credit and Truth-in-Lending
   Compliance Report   1151
Creditalk   1243
Credit World   1253
Investing, Licensing, and Trading
   Conditions Abroad   2755
Lending Law Forum   3005

Great Britain

Credit Management   1247

United States

American Bankers Assn Bank
   Installment Lender's Report   159
Bank Installment Lending Newsletter
   479
Consumer and Commercial Credit
   1149
Consumer Credit Guide   1152
From the State Capitals: Small Loans,
   Sales, Finance Banking   2185
How and Where to Get Capital:
   Dollars in Your Future   2419
Secured Transactions Guide   4221
Uniform Commercial Code Law
   Journal   4750
Uniform Commercial Code Law Letter
   4751

CREDIT, INSTALLMENT.   *See also* Retailing, Installment Sales

Delinquency Rates on Bank Installment
   Loans   1356

United States

American Bankers Assn Bank
   Installment Lender's Report   159
Bank Installment Lending Newsletter
   479
Consumer Credit Guide   1152
From the State Capitals: Small Loans,
   Sales, Finance Banking   2185
Installment Lending Directory   2592

CREDIT, INTERNATIONAL CREDIT MARKETS

Directory of Euromarket Borrowers
   1427.01
East Asian Economic Service   1522.01
Euromoney   1765

Euromoney Syndication Guide
   1766.01
Foreign Credit Insurance Assn (FCIA)
   News   2112
(FCIB) International Bulletin   2113
Journal of Monetary Economics
   2868.02
Latin American Services   2976.01

CREDIT, MANAGEMENT

Credit Executive   1246
Credit Review   1248
Credo   1254
Dun & Bradstreet Handbook of Credits
   and Collections   1512
Executive's Credit and Collections
   Letter   1807.02

Australia

Credit Review   1248
Credo   1254

CREDIT, RATINGS

Moody's Bank and Finance Manual
   and News Reports   3308
Moody's Commercial Paper Reports
   3311
Moody's Industrial Manual and News
   Reports   3314
Moody's Municipal Credit Reports
   3316
Moody's Over-the-Counter (OTC)
   Industrials Manual and News
   Reports   3317
Moody's Public Utility Manual and
   News Reports   3318

CREDIT, SMALL LOANS

From the State Capitals: Small Loans,
   Sales, Finance Banking   2185

CREDIT, TRUTH-IN-LENDING

Consumer Credit and Truth-in-Lending
   Compliance Report   1151
Consumer Credit Guide   1152
Uniform Commercial Code Law Letter
   4751

CREDIT, WOMEN

Business & Professional Woman   663

CREDIT CARDS

American Bankers Assn Bank Card
   Newsletter   158
Consumer Credit Guide   1152
Installment Lending Directory   2592
Magazine of Bank Administration
   3057

Payment Systems Action Report 3707
Report on Credit Unions 4069

CREDIT MANAGEMENT, INSTITUTE OF (GB)

Credit Management 1247

CREDIT UNION ADMINISTRATION, NATIONAL (US)

Items of Current Interest 2793.01
National Credit Union Administration
  (NCUA) Annual Report 3369

CREDIT UNIONS

Credit Union Commentary 1248.01
Credit Union 1249
Credit Union Magazine 1250
Credit Union Manager Newsletter
  1251
Report on Credit Unions 4069
Washington Banktrends 4884
World Council of Credit Unions
  Newsletter 5050
World Reporter 5077

California

California Credit Union League
  (CCUL) Digest 735

Canada

Alberta Corporation Manual 143
British Columbia Corporation Manual
  600
Ontario Corporation Manual 3621

United States

Credit Union Statistics 1252
Items of Current Interest 2793.01
National Credit Union Administration
  (NCUA) Annual Report 3369
NCUA Review 3421
Payment Systems Newsletter 3708
Regulatory News Release 4058
United States Banker 4794
Washington Financial Reports 4887

CRIME. *See also* Prisons. Specific
crimes, eg, Robberies and Thefts

Great Britain

Criminal Statistics, England and Wales
  1255

Wales

Criminal Statistics, England and Wales
  1255

CRIME, BUSINESS

Business Crime: Criminal Liability of
  the Business Community 676.01

CRUDE OIL. *See* Oil (Petroleum)
and Gasoline, Crude

CRUISES. *See* Ships and Shipping,
Cruises

CRYOGENICS

Cryogenics 1265

CULTURE. *See* Arts and Humanities.
Specific fields, eg, Musical Arts

CURRENCY. *See also* Banking and
Finance. Evaluation Theory.
International Monetary Fund

Banker 464
Bank of England Quarterly Bulletin
  488
Committee for Monetary Research &
  Education (CMRE) Money Tracts
  1013
Currency Forecasting Service 1268.02
Economic Inquiry 1553
Finance and Development 1988
Financial Market Trends 2008
Forecaster 2107
Foreign Letter 2120
Green's Commodity Market Comments
  2266
Indicator Digest 2505
Institute of Public Affairs Review
  2600
Institutional Investor International
  Edition 2602
International Country Risk Guide
  2670
Journal of Monetary Economics
  2868.02
Journal of Money, Credit, & Banking
  2869
Lynch International Investment Survey
  3051
Overseas Development Institute (ODI)
  Review 3657
Pick's Currency Yearbook 3769
Royal Mint Annual Report 4147
Rundt' s Weekly Intelligence 4153
Staff Papers 4369
Wall Street Journal 4878
World's Monetary Stocks of Gold,
  Silver, and Coins—On a Calendar
  Year Basis 5079

Africa

Surveys of African Economies 4521

Australia

Institute of Public Affairs Review
  2600

Canada

Bank of Canada Review 485
Customs Tariff Complete Service 1289
Financial Flow Accounts 2001

Europe

Euromarket News 1764

Far East

Economic & Social Survey of Asia &
  the Pacific 1540

Great Britain

Bank of England Quarterly Bulletin
  488
Britain & Overseas 596
Financial Statistics 2020

Ireland, Republic of

Central Bank of Ireland Quarterly
  Bulletins and Annual Report 889

Massachusetts

New England Economic Review 3441

Switzerland

Swiss–American Chamber of
  Commerce. Yearbook 4522

United States

Citibank Monthly Economic Letter
  949
Federal Reserve Bank of Philadelphia
  Business Review 1938
Goldsmith–Nagan Bond & Money
  Market Letter 2235
Income Investor 2484
New England Economic Review 3441
Public Periodic Releases 3926
Treasury Bulletin 4708

CURRENCY, EUROCURRENCY

AP–Dow Jones Bankers Report 277
Borrowing in International Capital
  Markets 576
Currency Risk and the Corporation
  1268.03
Euromarket Letter 1763
Euromoney 1765
Euromoney Currency Report 1766
Euromoney Syndication Guide
  1766.01
Financial Market Trends 2008

Chile

Latin American Services 2976.01

Colombia

Latin American Services 2976.01

Ecuador

Latin American Services 2976.01

Far East

Federal Reserve Bank of San Francisco.
Pacific Basin Economic Indicators
1953

Mexico

Latin American Services 2976.01

Peru

Latin American Services 2976.01

United States

Bank Fact Book 474

Uruguay

Latin American Services 2976.01

Venezuela

Latin American Services 2976.01

CUSIP. *See* Stocks and Bonds,
CUSIP

CUSTOMER RELATIONS. *See also*
subjects, eg, Banking and Finance,
Customer Relations

Sales Manager's Building 4174

CUSTOMS, BUREAU OF (US)

Customs Regulations of the United
States 1288

CUSTOMS (DUTIES). *See* Tariffs
and Quotas

CUSTOMS TARIFF ACT (CANADA)

Customs Tariff Complete Service 1289

DAIRY PRODUCTS

Agra Europe Preserved Milk 92
Dairy Products Report 1313
Food Industry Studies 2088
Foreign Agriculture Circulars 2111
Outlook and Situation Reports
3653.01

United Nations Industrial Development
Organization (UNIDO) Guides to
Information Sources.
UNIDO/LIB/SER.D/Rev.1—
Information Sources on the Dairy
Product Manufacturing Industry
4767.07
Urner Barry's Price-Current 4833.01

Canada

Dairy Review 1314
Handbook of Agricultural Statistics,
Part VII: Dairy Statistics, 1920–68
2321

Great Britain

Livestock Farming 3028

North Dakota

North Dakota Crop and Livestock
Statistics 3536

South Dakota

South Dakota Crop and Livestock
Reporter 4344

United States

Dairy Industry Newsletter 1310
Dairy Market News Reports 1312
From the State Capitals: Milk Control
2181

DAIRY PRODUCTS, PRICES

Monthly Price Review 3294
Restaurant Buyers Guide 4098
Weekly Insiders Dairy and Egg Letter
4933

**DAIRY PRODUCTS, RESEARCH
ON**

Journal of Dairy Research 2844

DATA ENTRY. *See* Computers

DATA PROCESSING. *See*
Computers. Information Retrieval.
Applications, eg, Computer-Aided
Design

DEATH. *See also* Cryogenics. Funeral
Homes and Directors

Journal of the Institute of Actuaries
2892
Population and Vital Statistics Report
3809
Statistical Bulletin 4426

DEBT. *See* Bankruptcies, Business.
Credit. Subjects, eg, Government, Debt

DECEPTIVE ADVERTISING. *See*
Advertising, Deceptive

**DECISION SCIENCES, AMERICAN
INSTITUTE FOR**

Decision Line 1348

DECORATIVE ACCESSORIES

Housewares Incorporating Gifts and
Fancy Goods 2405

DEFENSE, DEPARTMENT OF (US)

Defense Week 1355.02
DMS Defense Budget Intelligence
1475.10
DMS Defense Market 1475.11
DMS Defense Procurement Budget
Handbook 1475.12
DMS Defense RDT&E Budget
Handbook 1475.13
DMS Operation & Maintenance
1475.28
United States Waterborne Exports and
General Exports FT985 4822

DEFENSE CONTRACTS. *See*
Armament and Defense, Contracts

DELAWARE

Central Atlantic States: Manufacturers
Directory, 1981 886
Delaware: State Industrial Directory,
1980 1355.03
From the State Capitals 2169–2191
State and Local Taxes 4386
State Legislative Reporting Service
4396
State Tax Reports 4413

DEMOGRAPHIC MATERIAL. *See*
Population. Surveys and Polls, Census.
Vital Statistics

DENTISTS. *See also* Oral Prosthetic
Devices

Abstract Newsletters, Medicine &
Biology 2.22
Dental Laboratory Review 1359
Dental Management 1360

DENTISTS, EQUIPMENT

Dental Industry News 1358

DEPARTMENT STORES. *See*
Retailing, Department Stores

DESIGN. *See also* Computer-Aided
Design. Construction, Design. Subjects

Communications News   1042
Engineering & Contract Record   1703

DESIGN, COMMERCIAL

Building Design & Construction   637
Chicagoland Development   936
Computer-Aided Design   1071
Contract   1185
Corporate Design Systems   1205.01
Engineering News-Record—Directory
    of Design Firms   1712
Material Handling Engineering   3152
Power—Electric Utility Generation
    Planbook   3818
Product Design & Development   3863
Stores   4476
Visual Merchandising   4862

DESIGN, INDUSTRIAL

Canadian Patent Reporter   826
Design Engineering/UK   1369
Design Engineering/USA   1369.01
Eureka   1758.01

DETECTIVES. *See* Investigators and
Detectives

DETERGENTS. *See* Soaps and
Detergents

DEVELOPING NATIONS. *See*
Third World

DIAMONDS

Forecaster   2107

DIESEL MERCHANT SHIPS. *See*
Ships and Shipping, Diesel Merchant
Ships

DIET. *See* Food, Nutrition

DIPLOMATS. *See* Foreign Service

DIRECT MAIL. *See* Advertising,
Direct Mail

DIRECTORS, INSTITUTE OF (GB)

Director   1403

DIRECTORS AND OFFICERS. *See*
Banking and Finance, Directors and
Officers. Corporations, Directors and
Officers

**DIRECT RESPONSE
ADVERTISING.** *See* Advertising,
Direct Response

DISABILITY INSURANCE. *See*
Insurance, Disability

DISARMAMENT. *See* Arms Control

DISCOUNT SALES. *See* Retailing,
Discount Houses

DISCRIMINATION. *See* Subjects

DISPLAY ADVERTISING. *See*
Advertising, Display

DISTRIBUTION. *See* Manufacturers
and Manufacturing, Distribution

DIVIDENDS. *See* Stocks and Bonds,
Dividends

DOCUMENTATION

Journal of Documentation   2844.02

DOW JONES AVERAGE. *See*
Stocks and Bonds

DOWNTOWN REVITALIZATION.
See Urban Areas

DRAPERIES. *See* Curtains and
Draperies

DRILLING STARTS. *See* Gas
(Illuminating and Fuel), Drilling Starts.
Oil (Petroleum and Gasoline), Drilling
Starts

DROP SHIPPING

Drop Shipping News   1505.04
Drop Shipping Source Directory of
    Major Consumer Product Lines
    1506

DRUG ABUSE AND TRAFFIC

Security Management   4243

DRUGS AND DRUG TRADE

Abstract Newsletters, Medicine &
    Biology   2.22
American Druggist   169
Animal Health International   225

Annual Survey Report—Ethical
    Pharmaceutical Industry Operations
    270
Chain Store Age, Executive Edition
    900
Chemists' and Druggists' Supplies and
    Toiletries   933
Drug and Cosmetic Catalog   1507
Drug and Cosmetic Industry   1508
Drug License Opportunities   1508.01
Drug Product Liability   1509
Drug Store News   1509.01
Drug Topics   1510
IMS Monitor Report   2476.01
Manufacturing Chemist & Aerosol
    News   3113
Medical Marketing and Media   3181
New Product Card Index   3457.02
Nielsen Researcher   3517
Pharmaceutical Marketletter   3764.01
Pharmaceutical News Index   3764.02
Pharma Prospects   3764.03
Prescription Drug Industry Factbook
    3836
Product Marketing   3875
Scrip World Pharmaceutical News
    4212
United Nations Industrial Development
    Organization Guides to Information
    Sources. UNIDO/LIB/SER D/20—
    Information Sources on the
    Pharmaceutical Industry   4787
World Directory of Pharmaceutical
    Manufacturers   5058.01
World Health Environmental Surveys
    5067.01
World License Review   5068.02
World Pharmaceutical Introductions
    5073.03

**DRUGS AND DRUG TRADE,
GOVERNMENT REGULATIONS,
LAWS AND PROGRAMS**

Advertising Substantiation Program   72
Drug and Cosmetic Industry   1508
Medical Marketing and Media   3181
Pharmaceutical Marketletter   3764.01
Scrip World Pharmaceutical News
    4212

Canada

Food and Drug Act and Regulations
    (Departmental
    Consolidation)/Complete Service
    2080

Europe

Scrip World Pharmaceutical News
    4212

United States

Food Drug Cosmetic Law Reports
2084
Pharmaceutical News Index   3764.02

DUPLICATING MACHINES. *See*
Copying Machines

DURABLE GOODS. *See also* types,
eg, Automobiles, Housing

Consumer Attitudes and Buying Plans
1150

DUTIES. *See* Tariffs and Quotes

EARNINGS. *See* Stocks and Bonds,
Earnings

EARS AND HEARING

Advertising Substantiation Program   72
Protection   3904

EARTH, THE

Abstract Newsletters, NASA Earth
Resources Survey Program   2.24
Earth Surface Processes and Landforms
1522

EARTHQUAKES

Earthquake Engineering & Structural
Dynamics   2845

EAST GERMANY. *See* Germany
(East)

ECOLOGY. *See* Environment.
Environmental Protection

**ECONOMIC ASSOCIATION,
AMERICAN**

American Economic Review   170

**ECONOMIC COOPERATION AND
DEVELOPMENT, ORGANIZATION
FOR (OECD)**

Organization for Economic Cooperation
and Development (OECD) Observer
3644

**ECONOMIC POLICY, NEW
JERSEY OFFICE OF**

New Jersey Economic Policy Council
Annual Report   3452

ECONOMICS. *Note*: Material carried
here is on economic theory and
practice. *See* Economies for specific
economic conditions, worldwide and in
individual geographic regions. *See also*
Evaluation Theory. Social Economics

ABI/INFORM   2.01
Abundance   5
Akron Business & Economic Review
132
American Economic Review   170
American Economist   171
AP–Dow Jones Economic Report   278
Association for Comparative Economic
Studies Bulletin   338
Atlantic Economic Journal   344
Baker Library. Core Collection, an
Author & Subject Guide   449
Ball State Business Review   454
Baylor Business Studies   516
Business & Public Affairs   665
Business Economics   679
Cambridge Studies in Applied
Econometrics   740
Challenge   902
Committee For Monetary Research &
Education (CMRE) Money Tracts
1013
Contents of Recent Economic Journals
1183
Contents Pages in Management   1184
Dictionary of Economics   1378
Dictionary of Economics and Business
1379
Dow Jones–Irwin Business Almanac
1501
Econometrica   1534
Economic Analysis & Policy   1535
Economic Development & Cultural
Change   1548
Economic Education Bulletin   1550
Economic Inquiry   1553
Economic Journal   1554
Economic Planning   1563
Economic Review   1571
Economic Road Maps   1571.01
Federal Reserve Bank of San Francisco
Economic Review   1952
Fortune   2150
Futures   2204
History of Political Economy   2375
International Journal of Systems
Science   2697
Job Openings for Economists   2810
Journal of Behavioral Economics   2825
Journal of Economic Affairs   2845.01
Journal of Economic Issues   2846
Journal of Economic Literature   2847
Journal of International Law &
Economics   2864

Journal of Political Economy   2873
Lloyds Bank Review   3032
Long Range Planning   3044
McGraw-Hill Dictionary of Modern
Economics: A Handbook of Terms
and Organizations   3160
Mid-Atlantic Journal of Business
3215.01
National Institute of Economic Social
Research Annual Report   3387
New England Business Magazine   3439
New York Times   3487
Oxford Economic Papers   3674
Politics and Money   3797
Progress in Planning   3894
Publications by the Faculty of the
Harvard Business School   3923
Review of Business   4120
Service to Business & Industry   4268
Wall Street Review of Books   4881
Working Papers in Baker Library: A
Quarterly Checklist   5024

Africa

Survey of Economic Conditions in
Africa   4515

American Nations

Latin American Economy—Economic
Survey of Latin America   2974

Australasia

Statistical Yearbook for Asia and the
Pacific   4445

China, People's Republic of

Chinese Economic Studies   944

Europe

Economic Bulletin for Europe   1546

Far East

Economic Bulletin for Asia and the Far
East   1544

Great Britain

Abundance   5

Japan

Chinese Economic Studies   944
Japanese Economic Studies   2798

*Union of Soviet Socialist Republics
(USSR)*

Problems of Economics   3857

ECONOMICS, ECONOMETRIC MODELS

BI/Metrics 553.01
Economics Letters 1571.02
Journal of Econometrics 2845

ECONOMICS, RESEARCH ON

Abstract Newsletters, Business & Economics 2.08
Akron Business & Economic Review 132
American Economist 171
Amer Journal of Economics & Sociology 195
Association for Comparative Economic Studies Bulletin 338
Atlantic Economic Journal 344
Auber Bibliography 346.01
Brookings Papers on Economic Activity 629.01
Bulletin of Economic Research 644
Carnegie-Rochester Conference Series on Public Policy 864.01
Economic Analysis & Policy 1535
Economic Inquiry 1553
Economics Letters 1571.02
Economic Titles/Abstracts 1572.01
European Economic Review 1774
Executive Bulletin 1798
Federal Reserve Bank of Minneapolis Quarterly Review 1935.01
History of Political Economy 2375
Journal of Accounting and Economics 2817.01
Journal of Behavioral Economics 2825
Journal of Economics and Business 2848
Journal of Development Economics 2844.01
Journal of Economic Behavior and Organization 2845.02
Journal of Economic Dynamics and Control 2845.03
Journal of Financial Economics 2855.01
Journal of International Economics 2863.01
Journal of Mathematical Economics 2868.01
Journal of Monetary Economics 2868.02
Journal of Policy Modeling 2872.02
Journal of Public Economics 2875.01
Key to Economic Science and Managerial Sciences 2912.01
National Instititute of Economic Social Research Annual Report 3387
Nebraska Journal of Economics Business 3423
New England Journal of Business and Economics 3443

Oxford Bulletin of Economics & Statistics 3673
Quarterly Journal of Economics 3964
Regional Science and Urban Economics 4047
Research Reports 4091.02
Review of Business 4120
Review of Economics and Statistics 4120.01
Review of Economic Studies 4121
Southern Economic Journal 4348
Third World Quarterly 4606.01
World Economy 5062.01

ECONOMIES. *See also* Economics. Inflation and Recession. Gross National Product. National Product, Net

Abecor Country Report 2
AP–Dow Jones Economic Report 278
AP–Dow Jones Financial Wire 280
Australian Economic Review 395
Australian Stock Exchange Journal 416
Bank of England Quarterly Bulletin 488
Barclays Review 508
Business in Brief 690
Business International (BI) Data 697
Business Periodicals Index 716
Business Week 727
Central Bank of Ireland Quarterly Bulletins and Annual Report 889
Citibank Monthly Economic Letter 949
Committee for Economic Development Newsletter 1012
Committee for Monetary Research & Education (CMRE) Money Tracts 1013
Currency Forecasting Service 1268.02
Current Business Picture 1271
Development Forum 1374
Development Forum: Business Edition 1375
Dow Jones–Irwin Business Almanac 1501
DunsWorld Letter 1520
Economic Analysis & Policy 1535
Economic Outlook: Global Report 1559
Economic Report 1567
Economist 1576
Facts on File Weekly News Digest 1874
Federal Reserve Bank of New York Annual Report 1936
Federal Reserve Bank of San Francisco Business and Financial Letter 1951
Federal Reserve Bank of San Francisco Economic Review 1952
Finance and Development 1988

Financial Times Newspaper 2026
First Chicago World Report 2044
Fleet Street Letter 2061
Food Research Institute Studies 2097
Forecaster 2107
Foreign Credit Insurance Assn (FCIA) 2112
Foreign Economic Trends 2116
Foreign Economic Trends and Their Implications for the US 2117
Fraser Opinion Letter 2161
French-American News 2165.01
Grindlays Bank Economic Reports 2267
ICC World Economic Yearbook, 1980 2431.01
Holt Executive Advisory 2379
Industrial Development 2513
Institute of Public Affairs Review 2600
Institutional Investor International Edition 2602
Intelligence Digest Business Trends 2638
International Development Review 2671
International Journal of Social Economics 2696
International Monetary Fund Survey 2709
International Monetary Fund Annual Report of the Executive Directors 2710
Job Openings for Economists 2810
Journal of Development Economics 2844.01
Journal of Industrial Economics 2861
Journal of Regional Science 2879
Keesing's Contemporary Archives 2905
Lloyds Bank Review 3032
Lynch International Investment Survey 3051
Midas 3215
Money Manager 3271
Monthly Bulletin of Statistics 3283
Monthly Letter 3292
National Bank of Canada, Economic Review 3364.01
National Forecast 3377
National Westminster Bank Quarterly Review 3413
New International Realities 3449
Organization for Economic Cooperation and Development (OECD) Observer 3644
Oxford Economic Papers 3674
Petroleum Economist 3758
Economic Report 3962
Quarterly Economic Reviews Service 3962.01
Quarterly Journal of Economics 3964

Rundt's Weekly Intelligence 4153
Socio-Economic Planning Sciences
    4324
Sound of the Economy 4332
Stateman's Year-Book, 1980–81 edition
    4408
Statistical Bulletin 4425
Statistical Yearbook 4444
Tax Management International Journal
    4560
Three Banks Review 4616
Time 4619
Trade and Economic Development
    4647
Transdex 4687.01
United States News and World Report
    4812
World Bank Atlas, 15th edition 5044
Worldbusiness Perspectives 5046
World Business Weekly 5046.01
Worldcasts 5047
World Economic Service 5060
World Economic Survey 5061
World Economy 5062
World Economy 5062.01
World Index of Economic Forecasts,
    2nd edition 5067.02
World Tables 1980 5080
Yearbook of National Accounts
    Statistics 5096

Africa

Africa 77
Africa Research Bulletin 81
Africa Guide 1981 78
African Business 79.01
African Business & Trade 79.02
New African Development 3432
Statistical and Economic Information
    Bulletin for Africa 4424
Surveys of African Economies 4521
Trade and Credit: Problems and
    Resolutions in the Middle East and
    North Africa, in Asia and the Pacific
    and in Latin America 4646.01

Alabama

Alabama Business 133
Alabama Development News 134
Alabama Economic Abstract 135

Alaska

Alaska Economic Trends 138
Alaska Review of Social & Economic
    Conditions 142

Algeria

Developing Business in the Middle East
    and North Africa 1371

American Nations

Abecor Country Reports 2
Andean Group Regional Report
    222.01
Caribbean Basin Economic Survey 861
Caribbean Business News 863
Economic & Social Progress in Latin
    America: Annual Report 1538
Economic Bulletin for Latin America
    1547
Hanson's Latin American Letter 2341
Informational and Technical
    Publication of the General Secretariat
    of the Organization of American
    States (OAS) 2569
Inter-American Development Bank
    News 2640
Inter-American Economic Affairs
    2641
Latin America & Caribbean 1981
    2969.01
Latin American Index 2975
Latin America Weekly Report 2976.02
Noticias 3549
Southern Cone Regional Report
    4347.01
Trade and Credit: Problems and
    Resolutions in the Middle East and
    North Africa, in Asia and the Pacific
    and in Latin America 4646.01

Argentina

Latin American Service 2976.01

Arizona

Arizona Planning Information 253
Arizona: An Economic Profile 310
Arizona Business 311
Arizona Progress 315
Arizona Purchasor 316
Arizona Review 317
Arizona's Economy 317.01
Statistical Abstract 4418

Arkansas

Arkansas Economic Report 319
Arkansas. The Great Location in the
    Sunbelt 321

Australia

Abecor Country Reports 2
Australian Council of Trade Unions
    Bulletin 390
Australian Dept of the Treasury.
    Round-Up of Economic Statistics
    392
Australian Director 393
Australian Economic Review 395

Australian Economy: Economic
    Advisory Service 396
Australia Newsletter 399
Australian Investment and Economic
    Newsletter 405
Australian National Economic &
    Legislative Report 413
Australian Stock Exchange Journal
    416
Bank of New South Wales Review
    493
Canberra Comments 849
Confederation of Australian Industry
    (CAI) News 1098
East Asian Economic Service 1522.01
Economic Analysis & Policy 1535
Economic Review 1569
Executive Briefing 1797
Far East and Australasia 1892
Guide to Investment 2296
Institute of Public Affairs Review
    2600
Midas 3215
National Bank of Australasia. National
    Bank Monthly Summary 3364
Trans-Tasman 4699
Trends 4716

Belgium

Belgian–American Trade Review 520

Bolivia

Latin American Service 2976.01

Brazil

Brazilian–American Business
    Review/Directory 585
Brazil Regional Report 586
Latin American Service 2976.01

Bulgaria

Economic News of Bulgaria 1556.01

California

Economic Outlook: California Report
    1558
Northern Coastal California—Economic
    Trends in the Seventies 3537
Quarterly Economic Report 3962
Security Pacific National Bank Monthly
    Summary of Business Conditions,
    Central Valley Counties of California
    4245
Security Pacific National Bank Monthly
    Summary of Business Conditions,
    Northern Coastal Counties of
    California 4247
Security Pacific National Bank Monthly
    Summary of Business Conditions,
    Southern California 4246

Financial Times Newspaper   2026
Fleet Street Letter   2061
Investment Analyst   2759
Lloyds Bank Economic Bulletin   3031
Lloyds Bank Review   3032
Monthly Summary of Business
   Conditions in the United Kingdom
   3302
National Westminster Bank Quarterly
   Review   3413

Guyana

Caribbean Basin Economic Survey   861

Hawaii

All About Business in Hawaii   145
Economy of Hawaii   1579
First Hawaiian Bank Business Outlook
   Forum   2046
Hawaii Annual Economic Review
   2347
State of Hawaii Data Book   4403

Hong Kong

East Asian Economic Service   1522.01

Illinois

Commerce   993
Illinois Economic Data Sheets   2438

India

Commerce   994
East Asian Economic Service   1522.01
India News   2504

Indonesia

Indonesia Letter   2506

Iran

Iran Service   2779.01

Iraq

Developing Business in the Middle East
   and North Africa   1371

Ireland, Northern

Atlas of Ireland   346
Social and Economic Trends in
   Northern Ireland   4311

Ireland, Republic of

Atlas of Ireland   346
Business and Finance   661
Central Bank of Ireland Quarterly
   Bulletins and Annual Report   889
Confederation of Irish Industry (CII)
   Economic Trends   1106
Irish Statistical Bulletin   2781
Statistical Abstract of Ireland   4419

Israel

Business Review and Economic News
   from Israel   720

Italy

Economic News from Italy   1556
Italy: An Economic Profile   2793

Japan

Focus Japan   2074
Japan Economic Journal   2796.01
Japan Economic Yearbook   2797
Japanese Economic Service   2797.02
Japan Letters   2803
Oriental Economist   3648

Korea (South)

Korean Trade News   2922

Kansas

Kansas Economic Indicators   2904

Louisiana

Louisana Business Review   3047
Louisiana Economic Indicators
   3047.01
Louisana Economy   3048
Louisiana State Industrial Directory,
   1981   3048.02

Maine

Maine Business Indicators   3060

Maryland

University of Baltimore Business
   Review   4823

Massachusetts

Industry   2558
Massachusetts Business & Economic
   Report   3148
New England Economic Review   3441

Mexico

Caribbean Basin Economic Survey   861
Latin American Service   2976.01
Mexican–American Review   3206.01
Mexletter   3207

Michigan

Michigan Manufacturer & Financial
   Record   3209

Middle East

Middle East Review 1981   3219.01
Middle East Week   3222
Mideast Business Exchange   3225

Trade and Credit: Problems and
   Resolutions in the Middle East and
   North Africa, in Asia and the Pacific
   and in Latin America   4646.01

Montana

Montana Business Quarterly   3276

Nebraska

Business in Nebraska   694

Nevada

Nevada Review of Business &
   Economics   3431

New England

New England Business Magazine   3439
New England Journal of Business &
   Economics   3443

New Jersey

New Jersey Economic Outlook   3451
New Jersey Economic Policy Council
   Annual Report   3452

New Mexico

Economy   1577
New Mexico Business   3454

New York City

Annual Summary of Business Statistics,
   New York State   265

New York State

Annual Summary of Business Statistics,
   New York State   265
Long Island Business Newsweekly and
   Reference Series   3042
Quarterly Summary of Business
   Statistics, New York State   3975

New Zealand

Bank of New South Wales Review
   493
Business Indicators   690.02
Economic News Bulletin   1555
Economic Review   1569
Information Releases   2573.03
Life and Business in New Zealand
   3011
National Business Review   3365
New Zealand Balance of Payments
   3493
New Zealand Economist   3500
New Zealand National Income &
   Expenditure   3510
New Zealand Prices, Wages, & Labour
   3512

Report of the New Zealand Dept of
Trans-Tasman 4699
Trade & Industry 4066

Nigeria

Economic & Financial Review 1536
Nigeria Newsletter 3517.01

North Carolina

North Carolina Review of Business &
Economics 3535

Ohio

Development News Notes 1375.01
Ohio Developer 3593.01

Oklahoma

Oklahoma Business Bulletin 3614
Oklahoma Now! 3618
Statistical Abstract of Oklahoma 4420

Oregon

County Economic Indicators 1238

Pacific Northwest

Marple's Business Newsletter 3144
Quarterly Summary of Pacific
Northwest Industries 3976

Peru

Latin American Service 2976.01

Philippines

East Asian Economic Service 1522.01
Journal of Philippine Development
2872.01
Philippine Development 3765.01
Philippine Letter 3765.03
Philippine Statistical Yearbook
3765.04

Puerto Rico

Puerto Rico Business Review 3943
Spotlite 4365.01

Saudi Arabia

Developing Business in the Middle East
and North Africa 1371

Scotland

Scottish Economic Bulletin 4205

South Africa

Financial Mail 2004.02
South Africa Yearbook 4337

South Carolina

Business and Economic Review 660
Directory of Labor Market Information
1439

South Dakota

South Dakota Business Interview 4343

South Korea

East Asian Economic Service 1522.01

Surinam

Caribbean Basin Economic Survey 861

Switzerland

Economic Survey of Switzerland 1572

Taiwan

East Asian Economic Service 1522.01

Tennessee

Survey of Business 4508

Texas

Kiplinger Texas Letter 2916.01
Texas Facts 4596.01
Texas Industrial Update 4597.01
Texas Means Business 4597.03

Third World

Annual Aid Review 236
Ceres: Food and Agriculture
Organization (FAO) Review on
Development 894
International Development Review
2671
Overseas Development Institute (ODI)
Review 3657
South—The Third World Magazine
4349.01
Third World Quarterly 4606.01

Union of Soviet Socialist Republics (USSR)

Problems of Economics 3857

United States

American Journal of Agricultural
Economics 194
Annual Statistical Supplement, Social
Security Bulletin 263
Babson's Washington Forecast Letter
445
Bicentennial Statistics 550

Blue Chip Economic Indicators 563.01
Brookings Papers on Economic Activity
629.01
Business and Economic Review 660
Business Executives' Expectations
681.01
Business in Brief 690
Business Week 727
Citibank Monthly Economic Letter
949
Committee for Economic Development
Newsletter 1012
Daily Report for Executives 1305
Economic Outlook: US Report 1560
Economic Perspectives 1562
Economic Review 1570
Economic Week 1575
Enterprise 1714
Federal Reserve Bank of Minneapolis
Quarterly Review 1935.01
Federal Reserve Bank of New York
Annual Report 1936
Federal Reserve Bank of New York
Quarterly Review 1937
Federal Reserve Bank of Philadelphia
Business Review 1938
Fed in Print 1977
Financial Letter 2004.01
First Hawaiian Bank Business Outlook
Forum 2046
French–American Commerce 2165
French–American News 2165.01
Handbook of Agricultural Charts
2317
Holt Investment Advisory 2381
Income Investor 2484
Industry Forecast 2561
Lanston Letter 2966
Looking Ahead and Projection
Highlights 3046
Nevada Review of Business &
Economics 3431
New England Business Magazine 3439
New England Economic Review 3441
New Jersey Economic Outlook 3451
Newsbank Library 3462.01
Peter Dag Investment Letter 3753.02
Predicasts Basebook 3828
Public Periodic Releases 3926
Quarterly Economic Report 3962
Rand McNally Commercial Atlas &
Marketing Guide 4000
Reporting on Governments 4063
Research Reports 4091.01
Research Reports 4093
Review of Regional Economics &
Business 4127
Savings and Loan News 4187
Statistical Abstract of the United States
4421
Survey of Business 4508

Survey of Buying Power Data Service 4511

Survey of Current Business 4514

Tax Review 4569

Texas Facts 4596.01

This Week 4608

Transfer Payments by Major Source 4688

United States Economic Service 4796.01

United States Regional Forecasts 4815

Washington Report 4889

Whaley–Eaton American Letter 4958

Uruguay

Latin American Service 2976.01

Utah

Statistical Abstract of Utah 4422

Statistical Review of Government in Utah 4441

Utah Economic and Business Review 4835

Venezuela

Caribbean Basin Economic Survey 861

Latin American Service 2976.01

Venezuela Up-to-Date 4845

Wales

Welsh Economic Trends 4948

Washington (State)

Washington State Economy: Review and Outlook 4893

West Indies

Caribbean and West Indies Chronicle 860

West Virginia

West Virginia Economic Profile 4955

Yugoslavia

Business News 714

ECONOMIES, ECONOMIC INDICATORS

Economic Education Bulletin 1550

European Economy—Economic Survey of Europe 1775

International Economic Indicators and Competitive Trends 2675

International Economic Scoreboard 2675.01

Main Economics Indicators 3061

Statistical Bulletin 4425

World Economic and Social Indicators 5059

World Tables 1980 5080

Africa

Survey of Economic Conditions in Africa 4515

Alabama

Alabama Business 133

Alabama Economic Abstract 135

American Nations

Economic Bulletin for Latin America 1547

Arkansas

Arkansas Business and Economic Review 318

Australia

Australia and New Zealand (ANZ) Bank Business Indicators 380

Executive Briefing 1797

California

Forecast 2106

Canada

British Columbia Business Bulletin 599.02

Canada's Business Climate 762

Canadian Industrial Relations & Personnel Developments 802

Canadian Statistical Review 835

Edmonton Economic Report 1587

Quarterly Canadian Forecast 3960

Quarterly Canadian Forecast (QCF) Historical Supplement 3961

Quarterly Provincial Forecast 3968

Saskatchewan Economic Review 4181

Europe

Eurostatistics 1792.02

Statistical Indicators of Short Term Economic Changes in ECE Countries 4429

Far East

Asean Business Quarterly 324.01

Key Indicators of Developing Member Countries of Asian Development Bank (ADB) 2910

Great Britain

British Business 598

CSO Macro-Economic Databank 1265.01

Economic Trends 1573

National Income and Expenditure "Blue Book" 3382

Kansas

Kansas Economic Indicators 2904

Louisiana

Louisiana Economic Indicators 3047.01

Massachusetts

Massachusetts Business & Economic Report 3148

Nebraska

Business in Nebraska 694

New England

New England Economic Indicators 3440

New York State

Business Trends in New York State 726

New Zealand

Australia and New Zealand Bank (ANZ) Business Indicators 380

Information Releases 2573.03

Nigeria

Economic Indicators 1552

North Carolina

North Carolina Review of Business & Economics 3535

Oklahoma

Oklahoma Economic Indicators 3616

Philippines

Philippine Economic Indicators 3765.02

South Africa

Financial Mail 2004.01

South Carolina

Business and Economic Review 660

EEC. *See* European Economic Community (EEC) (Common Market)

EEO. *See* Equal Employment Opportunity Office (EEO) (US)

EFFICIENCY

Execu-Time   1794.02

EGGS

Chicago Mercantile Exchange Yearbook   937
Outlook and Situation Reports   3653.01
Urner Barry's Price-Current   4833.01

Canada

Production and Stocks of Eggs and Poultry   3866.01

South Dakota

South Dakota Crop and Livestock Reporter   4344

United States

Monthly Price Review   3294
Poultry Market News Reports   3813
Restaurant Buyers Guide   4098
Weekly Insiders Dairy and Egg Letter   4933

EGYPT

Developing Business in the Middle East and North Africa   1371
Egypt/North Africa   1598.02

ELASTOMERS.   *See also* Rubber

Abstract Newsletters, Materials Sciences   2.21
Elastomerics   1599
Polymer   3807

ELECTION COMMISSION, FEDERAL (US)

Federal Election Campaign Financing Guide   1921

ELECTIONS

Campaign Contributions and Lobbying Laws   740.01
Campaign Practices Reference Service   741
Campaign Practices Reports   742
Federal Election Campaign Financing Guide   1921

ELECTRIC LIGHT AND POWER.
See also Atomic Power and Weapons. Electric Light and Power Companies. Electrical Appliances. Electrical Construction. Electrical Equipment and Supplies

Alternative Energy: Trends & Forecasts   149.01
Annual Bulletin of Electric Energy Statistics for Europe   238
Electrical World (Magazine)   1609
Electric Letter   1613
Electric Perspectives   1614
Mechanical & Electrical Cost Data   3164.02
Power—Electric Utility Generation Planbook   3818
Rate Service Newsletter   4006

Australia

Electrical Engineer   1602

Canada

Electric Power Statistics   1617

European Communities

Electrical Energy: Monthly Bulletin   1601.01

Far East

Electric Power in Asia and the Pacific   1616

New York City

New York City Business Fact Book Part 1: Business & Manufacturing   3474

United States

Edison Electric Institute (EEI) Pocketbook of Electric Utility Industry Statistics   1583
Edison Electric Institute (EEI) Statistical Year Book   1584
Electrical Week   1605
Electrical World   1608
Fuel Price Analysis   2197
Year-End Summary of the Electric Power Situation   5100

ELECTRIC LIGHT AND POWER, ENVIRONMENTAL CONTROL

Electrical Week   1605

ELECTRIC VEHICLES

Electric Vehicle News   1617.01
Electric Vehicle Progress   1617.02

ELECTRICAL APPLIANCES.   *See also* Electrical Equipment and Supplies. Types, eg, Fans

Appliance Magazine   284
Appliance Manufacturer   285
Electric Housewares and Fans: 1976. MA-36E   1610
Mart   3144.01
Mingay's Price Service—Appliance Edition   3236
Mingay's Retailer & Merchandiser   3238
Radio & Electric Retailing   3986
Underwriters Laboratories Standards for Safety   4741.01

ELECTRICAL APPLIANCES, HEALTH HAZARDS AND SAFETY

National Electronic Injury Surveillance System (NEISS) Data Highlights   3373

ELECTRICAL APPLIANCES, IMPORTS AND EXPORTS

Export/El Exportador   1821

ELECTRICAL EQUIPMENT AND SUPPLIES

Electrical Construction and Maintenance   1600
Electrical Construction and Maintenance (Annual)   1601
Electrical Marketing Newsletter   1604
Electrical Patents Index   1604.01
Electrical Wholesaling   1606
Electrical Wholesaling (Magazine)   1607
Housewares   2404
Mingay's Electrical Supplies Guide   3235
National Electrical Manufacturers Association Standards Publications   3372
Year-End Summary of the Electric Power Situation   5100

ELECTRONIC FUNDS TRANSFER SYSTEMS.   *See* Banking and Finance, Electronic Funds Transfer Systems (EFTS)

ELECTRONIC SURVEILLANCE.
See Wiretapping and Other Forms of Surveillance

ELECTRONICS. *See also*

Aeronautics and Aerospace. Computers. Engineering, Electronics. Other fields of use

Defense Industry Organization Service 1355.01
DMS Electronic Systems 1475.14
DMS Electronic Warfare 1475.15
Electronic Component News 1620
Electronic Design's Gold Book 1620.01
Electronic Distributing 1621
Electronic Engineering 1622
Electronic Market Data Book 1629
Electronic Market Trends 1630
Electronic New Product Directory, 1978–79 1630.01
Electronic News Financial Fact Book & Directory 1631
Electronics 1632
Electronics & Communications 1633
Electronics & Communications Abstracts Journal 1634
Electronics—Buyers' Guide 1635
Electronics Times 1637
Graphix 2260
International Journal of Electronics 2691
Journal of Electronic Engineering 2850.01
Journal of the Electronics Industry 2889.03
Outlook 3652
Science Research Abstracts Journal, Parts A&B 4197
Selected Business Ventures 4252
Technology Growth Markets and Opportunities 4581.01
United Nations Industrial Development Organization (UNIDO) Guides to Information Sources. UNIDO/LIB/SER.D/Rev.1— Information Sources on the Electronics Industry 4767.08
What's New in Electronics 4961.01
Worldwide Guide to Medical Electronics Marketing Representation, 1977 5088

Australia

Australian Electronics Engineering 397

Far East

Asia Electronics Union 324.03
Electronics Buyers' Guide 1634.01

Hong Kong

Electronics Buyers' Guide 1634.01

Japan

Electronics Buyers' Guide 1634.01
Japan Fact Book 2802.01

United States

Directory of Defense Electronic Products and Services: US Suppliers 1426
DMS "AN" Equipment 1475.04
Weekly Television Digest with Consumer Electronics 4940.01

ELECTRONICS, IMPORTS AND EXPORTS

Electronic Industries Association. Quarterly Statistical Report. US Exports (by Country) of Electronic Products Within Scope of the EIA Consumer Group 1623.01
Electronic Market Data Book 1629
Electronic Market Trends 1630
Electronics Foreign Trade 1636
Journal of the Electronics Industry 2889.03

Far East

Asia Electronics Union 324.03

United States

Electronic Industries Association. Monthly Statistical Report. US Imports (by Country) of Electronic Products Within Scope of the EIA Consumer Electronics Group 1623
Electronic Industries Association. Quarterly Statistical Report. US Imports and Exports (by Country) of Electronic Products Within Scope of the EIA Communications Division 1624
Electronic Industries Association. Quarterly Statistical Report. US Imports and Exports (by Country) of Electronic Products Within Scope of the EIA Industrial Electronics Division 1625
Electronic Industries Association. Quarterly Statistical Report. US Imports and Exports (by Country) of Electronic Products Within Scope of the EIA Parts Division 1626
Electronic Industries Association. Quarterly Statistical Report. US Imports and Exports (by Country) of Electronic Products Within Scope of the EIA Solid State Products Division 1627

Electronic Industries Association. Quarterly Statistical Report. US Imports and Exports (by Country) of Electronic Products Within Scope of the EIA Tube Division 1628

ELECTRONICS, MANAGEMENT

Electronic Business 1619

ELECTRONICS, MARKETING

Electronic Distributing 1621
Mainly Marketing 3062
Mart 3144.01
Outlook 3652

ELECTRONICS, PERSONNEL

Electronic Market Data Book 1629
Outlook 3652

ELECTRONICS, RESEARCH ON

Electrical Patents Index 1604.01
Electronics & Communications Abstracts Journal 1634

Australia

Australian Electronics Engineering 397

United States

Abstract Newsletters, Electrotechnology 2.13
Abstract Newsletters, Government Inventions for Licensing 2.16

EMBASSIES. *See* Foreign Service

EMBEZZLEMENT. *See* subjects, eg, Banking and Finance, Frauds

EMIGRATION. *See* Immigration and Emigration

EMPLOYEE BENEFIT PLANS, INTERNATIONAL FOUNDATION OF

International Foundation of Employee Benefit Plans Digest 2682
Textbook for Employee Benefit Plan Trustees, Administrators, and Advisors 4598

EMPLOYEE BENEFITS. *See* Labor, Employee Benefits. Managers and Management, Employee Benefits. Pension Plans. Other specific types, eg, Insurance, Health

EMPLOYEE RETIREMENT INCOME SECURITY ACT (ERISA)

EMPLOYEES. *See* Labor. Personnel Management. Subjects

EMPLOYEES ASSOCIATIONS

EMPLOYMENT AGENCIES AND COUNSELING SERVICES. *See also*

Colleges and Universities, Career Opportunities for Graduates. Managers and Management, Executive Recruiting. Vocational Guidance.

United States

EMPLOYMENT AND TRAINING ADMINISTRATION (US)

EMPLOYMENT BENEFITS. *See*

Labor, Employee Benefits

EMPLOYMENT PROTECTION ACT (GB)

EMPLOYMENT STANDARDS ADMINISTRATION (US)

EMPLOYMENT TAXES. *See*

Taxation, Employment Taxes

ENCYCLOPEDIAS

ENERGY. *Note:* Energy conservation

is covered under Energy, Programs. *See also* Fuel. Private Utilities. Public Utilities. Research and Development, Energy. Types and sources, eg, Electric Light and Power. Oil (Petroleum) and Gasoline

American Nations

Arizona

Arkansas

Australia

Canada

Europe

ENERGY, ALTERNATE

Annual Bulletin of Gas Statistics for
  Europe 239
Energy Statistics 1696
Yearbook 1978 1697
European Energy Report 1775.01
European Marketing Data & Statistics,
  1981 1785
Europe Energy 1788

European Communities

Energy Statistics (Three Series) 1696

Far East

Asia Research Bulletin 331

Great Britain

Achievement 39
Annual Abstract of Statistics 234
Digest of United Kingdom Energy
  Statistics 1394
Energy Trends 1700

Hawaii

Hawaii Annual Economic Review
  2347

Louisiana

Financial Trend 2032

New Mexico

Financial Trend 2032

North Carolina

North Carolina Industrial Data File
  3534

Oklahoma

Financial Trend 2032

Texas

Financial Trend 2032

United States

Abstract Newsletters, Problem Solving
  Information for State & Local
  Government 2.27
Capital Energy Letter 855
Coal Data 970.01
Corporate Examiner 1206
Energy Analects 1676
Energy Controls 1677
Energy Executive Directory 1680.01
Energy Users Report 1701
Federal Contract Opportunities:
  Energy/Environment 1917.01
Federal Power Service 1934

ENERGY, ALTERNATE. *See*
Energy, Programs. Types, eg, Energy,
Solar

ENERGY, COAL. *See* Coal

ENERGY, CONVERSION

Conservation and Recycling 1120
Energy Info 1682
Energy Policy 1687
Fuel 2195
Maritime and Construction Aspects of
  Ocean Thermal Energy Conversion
  (OTEC) Plant Ships 3122

ENERGY, DEPARTMENT OF (US)

DMS Operation & Maintenance
  1475.28
National Geothermal Service 3377.01

ENERGY, ENGINEERING. *See*
Engineering, Energy

ENERGY, FINANCES

Energy Developments 1679
Energy Policy 1687
Energy Research Bureau 1691
Petroleum Economist 3758
Quarterly Energy Reviews 3962.02

ENERGY, GEOTHERMAL

Mining Lease Reports 3239.01

ENERGY, HEALTH HAZARDS
AND SAFETY

Communicators Directory, 1980 edition
  1046

ENERGY, GOVERNMENT
REGULATIONS AND LAWS

Capital Energy Letter 855
Energy Controls 1677
Energy Daily 1678
Energy Index 1681
Energy Information 1682.01
Energy Sources 1695
Energy Update 1700.01
Federal Petroleum Regulatory
  Newsletter 1933.01
Federal Power Service 1934
Oil & Gas Price Regulation Analyst
  3598.01
Platt's OHA Digest 3783.03
Platt's Oilgram Legislative Service
  3784

ENERGY, PROGRAMS

Abstract Newsletters, Energy 2.14
Alternative Energy: Trends & Forecasts
  149.01
Conservation and Recycling 1120
Energy Daily 1678
Energy Directory Update 1680
Energy Management 1686.01
Energy Research Programs, 1980 1692
Energy Sources 1695
Heating/Piping/Air Conditioning
  2368
International Journal of Energy
  Research 2692
Oil, Gas & Petrochemical Equipment
  3604
Petroleum Economist 3758
Power 3817
State-Owned Energy Enterprises 4404

Canada

Energy Analects 1676

United States

Consumer Information Catalog 1154
Energy Analects 1676
Energy Controls 1677
Energy Executive Directory 1680.01
Energy Management 1686
Energy Users Report 1701

ENERGY, RESEARCH ON. *See*
Research and Development, Energy

ENERGY, SOLAR

Alternative Energy: Trends & Forecasts
  149.01
Communicators Directory, 1980 edition
  1046
Practical Solar 3822.01
Roofing Siding Insulation.
  Incorporating Solar Contractor 4141
Solar Age 4326
Solar Energy Digest 4326.01
Solar Energy Intelligence Report
  4326.02
Solar Engineering Magazine 4326.03
Solar Heating and Cooling Magazine
  4326.04
World Solar Markets 5079.01

ENERGY, STEAM

Power 3817

ENERGY, SUPPLY

Annual Bulletin of Electric Energy
  Statistics for Europe 238

Annual Bulletin of General Energy
    Statistics for Europe   240
Quarterly Energy Reviews   3962.02
World Energy Supplies   5063

Europe

Annual Bulletin of Coal Statistics for
    Europe   237
Annual Bulletin of Gas Statistics for
    Europe   239

United States

Coal Data   970.01
Energy Users Report   1701

ENERGY, TECHNOLOGY.   *See also*
subhead Conversion. Engineering,
Energy

Energy Report   1690
Energy Users Report   1701

ENERGY, THERMAL

Maritime and Construction Aspects of
    Ocean Thermal Energy Conversion
    (OTEC) Plant Ships   3122

ENERGY ADMINISTRATION,
FEDERAL (US)

Energy Management   1686

ENERGY CONSERVATION.   *See*
Energy, Programs

ENGINEERING.   *See also*   Civil
Engineering. Other fields

Applied Science & Technology Index
    (ASTI)   288
Australia's International Engineering
    Exhibitions AIEE   422
College Recruiting Report   982
Computer-Aided Design   1071
Engineering Index   1710
Engineering News-Record   1711
International Journal for Numerical
    Methods in Engineering   2689
ISMEC   2790
Non-Destructive Testing (NDT)
    International   3530
Scientific, Engineering, Technical
    Manpower Comments   4201
Who's Who in Engineering, 4th edition,
    1980   4983

Australia

Australia's International Engineering
    Exhibitions AIEE   422
Metal and Engineering Industry
    Yearbook   3196

Canada

Daily Commercial News Progress
    Report   1295
Engineering & Contract Record   1703
Engineering Digest   1709

Great Britain

Achievement   39
Consulting Engineers' Who's Who and
    Yearbook, 1980   1147
Engineer   1702

India

Engineering & Metal's Review   1704
Handbook of Statistics, 1980   2337.01

Michigan

Michigan Manufacturer & Financial
    Record   3209

United States

Abstract Newsletters, Civil Engineering
    2.10
American City & County   166
United States Ocean Shipping
    Technology Forecast and Assessment,
    Final Report   4813

ENGINEERING, CHEMICAL

Chemical Abstracts   918.01
Chemical Engineering   923

ENGINEERING, CONSULTING

Canadian Consulting Engineer   785
Consulting Engineer   1146

ENGINEERING, DESIGN

Engineering News-Record—Directory
    of Design Firms   1712
Eureka   1758.01

ENGINEERING, ELECTRONICS

Journal of Electronic Engineering
    2850.01

ENGINEERING, ENERGY

Power   3817
Power Engineering   3819
Solar Age   4326
Solar Engineering Magazine   4326.03

ENGINEERING, HEALTH
HAZARDS AND SAFETY

Industrial Health Foundation
    Engineering Series   2525

ENGINEERING, INDUSTRIAL

Abstract Newsletters, Industrial &
    Mechanical Engineering   2.18
Computers and Industrial Engineering
    1084
Engineering Digest   1709
Industrial Engineering   2519

ENGINEERING,
MANUFACTURING

Industrial Maintenance and Plant
    Operation   2532
Machinery & Production Engineering
    3053

ENGINEERING, MECHANICAL

ISMEC   2790

ENGINEERING, PERSONNEL

Consultion Engineers' Who's Who and
    Year Book 1980   1147
Executive Compensation Service Top
    Management Report   1802.01
Scientific, Engineering, Technical
    Manpower Comments   4201

ENGINEERING, RESEARCH ON

Abstract Newsletters, Civil Engineering
    2.10
Abstract Newsletters, Industrial &
    Mechanical Engineering   2.18

ENGINES.   *See also* fields of use

Abstract Newsletters, Energy   2.14
DMS Gas Turbine Engines/Gas
    Turbine Markets   1475.17
DMS Turbine Intelligence   1475.34

ENGINES, INTERNAL
COMBUSTION

Abstracts from Technical and Patent
    Publications   3

ENGLAND.   *See* Great Britain

ENTERTAINMENT.   *See also*
Recreation. Types, eg, Television and
Radio

Amusement Business   212
Managing the Leisure Facility   3095.03
Orange County Illustrated   3635

ENTREPRENEURS AND SMALL BUSINESSES. *See also* Commerce and Industry, Minority Businesses. Partnerships. Taxation, Small Business. Types of businesses

American Journal of Small Business 196
Anbar Management Publications Smaller Business Management Abstracts 220.01
Business Ideas Letter 688
In Business 2476.03
Journal of Contemporary Business 2842
Journal of Small Business Management 2884
Leadership & Organization Development 2994.01
Management Accounting 3069
Management Aids 3072
National Federation of Independent Business (NFIB) Quarterly Economic Report for Small Business 3375
Salesman's Opportunity Magazine 4175
Small Business Administration Annual Report 4298
Small Business Bibliographies 4299
Small Business Management Series 4301
Small Business Reporter 4302
Starting and Managing Series 4382
Voice of Small Business 4865

Canada

British Columbia Industry and Small Business News 602.01

Great Britain

Daltons Weekly 1315

Ireland, Republic of

Thom's Commercial Directory 4612

United States

American Journal of Small Business 196
Employment by Type and Broad Industrial Source 1657
Small Business Report 4301.01
Source Guide for Borrowing Capital 4334

ENTREPRENEURS AND SMALL BUSINESSES, COMPUTER APPLICATIONS

Packaged Software Reports 3680
Small Business Computer News 4300

ENTREPRENEURS AND SMALL BUSINESSES, FINANCES

In Business 2476.03
Small Business Reporter 4302

ENTREPRENEURS AND SMALL BUSINESSES, GOVERNMENT REGULATIONS, LAW AND PROGRAMS

National Association of Small Business Investment Companies (NASBIC) News 3362
Voice of Small Business 4865

ENTREPRENEURS AND SMALL BUSINESSES, TAXATION. *See* Taxation, Small Business

ENVIRONMENT. *Note:* Material carried here is general. For efforts to improve and preserve the environment, *see* Beautification Programs. Environmental Protection. *See also* Natural Resources. Research and Development, Environment

Development Forum 1374
Ecology USA 1533.01
Enterprise 1714
Environmental Health Letter 1722

Canada

Canada 743

Hawaii

State of Hawaii Data Book 4403

Tropical Areas

Tropical Agriculture 4722

ENVIRONMENTAL POLICY ACT OF 1969 (US)

Environmental Impact Handbook 1723

ENVIRONMENTAL PROTECTION. *See also* Air Pollution. Beautification Programs. Environmental Organizations. Water Pollution

Abstract Newsletters, Urban and Regional Technology & Development, Urban Technology 2.29
Abstracts on Health Effects of Environmental Pollutants (HEEP) 4
Air/Water Pollution Report 131
Chemical Week 929
Clean Water Report 959

Energy Sources 1695
Envirofiche 1718
Enviroline 1719
Environment Abstracts 1720
Environmental Health Letter 1722
Environment Index 1726
Environment Report 1729
Executive Action Report 1796
Final Environmental Impact Statement of Maritime Administration Tanker Construction Program 1986
International Environment Reporter 2677.01
International Journal of Social Economics 2696
Journal of Environmental Systems 2852
Journal of Regional Science 2879
Land Economics 2961
Mineral Facts and Problems 3231
Noise Control Report 3528
Pollution Abstracts 3803
Pollution Engineering 3805
Power 3817
Progress in Planning 3894
Resources Policy 4097
Sludge Newsletter 4297
33 Metal Producing 4607
Toxic Substances Sourcebook 4644
World Environmental Directory 5063.01

Australia

Handbook for Industrialists 2313
Process and Chemical Engineering 3859

Canada

Canadian Environmental Control Newsletter 791
Eco/Log Week 1533

Europe

Bulletin of the European Communities 646
Europe Environment 1789

Great Britain

Building Design 636

Massachusetts

Industry 2558

North Carolina

North Carolina Industrial Data File 3534

United States

Abstract Newsletters, Environmental Pollution & Control 2.15
Abstract Newsletters, Industrial & Mechanical Engineering 2.18
Environmental Impact Handbook 1723
Environment Reporter 1730
Washington Environmental Protection Report 4886

ENVIRONMENTAL PROTECTION, GOVERNMENT REGULATIONS, LAWS AND PROGRAMS

API/NFPA Environmental Report 282
Environmentat Regulation Analyst 1724
Environment Report 1729
International Environment Reporter 2677.01
Journal of Environmental Systems 2852
Land Use & Environment Law Review 2961.01
Pollution Engineering 3805

Canada

Eco/Log Canadian Pollution Legislation 1532

United States

API/NFPA Environmental Report 282
Babson's Washington Forecast Letter 445
Chemical Week Pesticides Register 932
EIS 1598.03
Environmental Comment 1721
Environmental Impact Handbook 1723
Environment Regulation Handbook 1728
Environment Reporter 1730
Federal Contract Opportunities: Energy/Environment 1917.01
Statefiche 4390
Urban Affairs Reports 4829
Washington Environmental Protection Report 4886
Washington Report 4890

ENVIRONMENTAL PROTECTION, RESEARCH AND TECHNOLOGY

Abstract Newsletters, Environmental Pollution & Control 2.15
Pollution 3802

ENVIRONMENTAL PROTECTION AGENCY (EPA) (US)

Chemical Week Pesticides Register 932
Environmental Regulation Analyst 1724
Pollution Control Guide 3804
Sewage Treatment Construction Grants Manual 4271

EQUAL CREDIT OPPORTUNITY ACT (US)

Consumer Credit and Truth-in-Lending Compliance Report 1151

EQUAL EMPLOYMENT OPPORTUNITY, OFFICE OF (EEO) (US)

The Equal Employment News 1731
Equal Employment Opportunity Today 1735
Fair Employment Report 1879

EQUAL EMPLOYMENT OPPORTUNITY COMMISSION (EEOC) (US)

Employee Relations Bulletin 1646
Equal Employment Opportunity Commission (EEOC)—Affirmative Action Manuals 1732
Equal Employment Opportunity Commission (EEOC) Compliance Manual 1733

EQUAL OPPORTUNITY EMPLOYMENT. See Labor, Equal Employment Opportunity

EQUAL PAY ACT OF 1963 (US)

Federal Wage-Hour Handbook for Banks 1976

EQUIPMENT LEASING

Rent All 4062
Tax-Sheltered Investments 4570

ERGONOMICS

Applied Ergonomics 286
Cambridge Studies in Applied Econometrics 740

ERISA PLANS. See Employee Retirement Income Security Act

ESTATES. See Wills and Estates

ESTATE TAXES. See Taxation, Estate and Gift Taxes

ETHICS AND MORALS. See fields of activities

EURATOM

Euro-Abstracts: Scientific and Technical Publications and Patents, Sections I and II. Section I: Euratom and EEC Research. Section II: Coal and Steel 1759

EUROBONDS. See Stocks and Bonds, Eurobonds

EUROCURRENCY. See Currency, Eurocurrency

EUROPE

Company Law in Europe, 3rd edition 1053.01
Current European Directories 1275
Europe's 5000 Largest Companies Directory, 1980 1792.01
Predicasts F&S Index Europe Annual 3828.02
Statistics—Europe 4452

EUROPE (EAST)

Doing Business with Eastern Europe 1489
Soviet-Eastern Europe-China Business & Trade 4351

EUROPE (WEST)

Europa Year Book 1767
New Products & Processes From Western Europe 3458.01

EUROPEAN COAL AND STEEL COMMUNITY

Coal: Monthly Bulletin 971.01
Euro-Abstracts: Scientific and Technical Publications and Patents, Sections I and II. Section I: Euratom and EEC Research. Section II: Coal and Steel 1759
Iron and Steel: Monthly Statistics 2787

EUROPEAN COMMUNITIES

Basic Statistics 514.01
Economic and Social Committee of the European Communities. Bulletin 153
Electrical Energy: Monthly Bulletin 1601.01

Energy Statistics (Three Series)   1696
European Economy   1774.02
Hydrocarbons: Monthly Bulletin   2431
Unemployement: Monthly Bulletin
   4745.01

EUROPEAN ECONOMIC COMMUNITY (EEC) (COMMON MARKET)

Agricultural Markets: Prices (Two
   Series)   101
Agricultural Production (Two Series)
   104
Britain and Overseas   596
British Industry and Services in the
   Common Market   614
The Brussels Report   632
Bulletin of the European Communities
   646
Business Europe   681
Commercial Laws of Europe   1004.01
Common Market News   1038
Common Market Reports   1039
Community Markets   1050
Company Secretary's Review   1055
Courier—European Communities—
   Africa, the Caribbean, and the Pacific
   1239
Directory of Euromarket Borrowers
   1427.01
Economic & Social Committee of the
   European Communities. Bulletin
   1537
EEC/ASIA Report   1597.01
EEC Competition Law Report
   1597.02
Energy Statistics   1696
Euro-Abstracts: Scientific and Technical
   Publications and Patents, Section I
   and II. Section I: Euratom and EEC
   Research. Section II: Coal and Steel
   1759
Euromoney   1765
Europa Transport: Observation of the
   Transport Markets (Three Series)
   1766.02
European Economic Service   1774.01
European Industrial Relations Review
   1778
European Law Letter   1783
European Report   1786
European Trends   1787.01
Eurostatistics (Bulletin of General
   Statistics)   1792.03
Fisheries: Quantity and Value of
   Landings   2048
Green Europe: Newsletter on the
   Common Agricultural Policy
   2264.01
Industrial Short-Term Trends   2551.02

Journal of Common Market Studies
   2839
Official Journal of the European
   Communities   3585.01
Pig-irons and Steel: Basis Prices   3771
Purchase Prices of the Means of
   Production   3948.01
Report of the Results of the Business
   Surveys Carried Out Among
   Management in the Community
   4067
Reports of Cases Before the Court
   4075
Management in the Community
   4100.01
Statistical Office of the European
   Communities. Balances of Payments
   Geographic Breakdown   4433
Statistical Office of the European
   Communities. Basic Statistic of the
   Community, 18th edition, 1980
   4433.01
Statistical Office of the European
   Communities. Monthly External
   Trade Bulletin   4434
Statistics of Foreign Trade, Series C:
   Annual Tables by Commodity
   4453.02
Transnational Economic and Monetary
   Law: Transactions and Contracts
   4690
Yearbook, 1974–1978   5090

EUROPEAN ECONOMIC COMMUNITY, COUNCIL OF MINISTERS

Community Markets   1050

EUROPEAN ECONOMIC COMMUNITY, COURT OF JUSTICE

Common Market Law Reports   1037
Community Markets   1050
Reports of Cases Before the Court
   4075

EUROPEAN ECONOMIC COMMUNITY, EUROPEAN COMMISSION

Community Markets   1050
E E/Epargne Europe   1598

EUROPEAN ECONOMIC COMMUNITY, INVESTMENT BANK

Community Markets   1050
European Investment Bank. Annual
   Report   1780

EVALUATION THEORY

Directory of Evaluation Consultants
   1428.01
Evaluation Studies Review Annual
   1793

EXCHANGE RATES.   *See* Currency,
Exchange Rates

EXCISE TAXES.   *See* Taxation,
Excise Taxes

EXECUTIVE RECRUITMENT.   *See*
Managers and Management, Executive
Recruiting

EXECUTIVE TRAINING
PROGRAMS.   *See* Managers and
Management, Education

EXECUTIVES.   *See* Corporations.
Managers and Management

EXPATRIATES

Journal of International Business
   Studies   2863

EXPLOSIVES

Dangerous Properties of Industrial
   Materials Report   1316.01

EXPORT-IMPORT BANK OF THE UNITED STATES

Export-Import Bank of the United
   States   1826

EXPORTS AND IMPORTS PERMIT ACT (CANADA)

Export and Import Permits Act
   Handbook   1820

EXPORTS OF GOODS AND
SERVICES.   *See* Imports and Exports

EXPOSITIONS.   *See* Trade Fairs

EYES AND EYESIGHT

Protection   3904
Review of Optometry   4126

FABRICS.   *See* Textiles

FACTORIES.   *See* Commerce and
Industry, Plants and Sites.
Manufacturers and Manufacturing,
Plants and Equipment

FERTILIZERS

Doane's Agricultural Report   1476
Farm Industry News   1900
Green Markets   2265
Inorganic Fertilizer Materials and
   Related Acids M28B   2582
Outlook and Situation Reports
   3653.01
United Nations Industrial Development
   Organization Guides to Information
   Sources. UNIDO/LIB/SER D/21—
   Information Sources on the Fertilizer
   Industry   4788

FERTILIZERS, AMMONIA AND CHEMICAL

Fertilizer Industry Series   1981
Green Markets   2265

FERTILIZERS, NITROGEN, PHOSPHATE AND POTASH

Green Markets   2265

FIBERBOARD

United Nations Industrial Development
   Organization Guides to Information
   Sources. UNIDO/LIB/SER D/9—
   Information Sources on the Building
   Board Industry Based on Wood and
   Other Fibrous Materials   4776
Yearbooks of Forest Products Statistics
   5099

FIBERS.   *See also* Fiberboard

Chemical Horizons North American
   Report   925
Chemical Horizons Overseas Report
   925.01
Clemson University Textile Marketing
   Letter   961
Fiber Producer   1983
General Imports of Cotton, Wool, and
   Manmade Fiber Manufacturers
   2211
Journal of the Textile Institute   2897
Polymer   3807
Textile Organon   4602
United Nations Industrial Development
   Organization Guides to Information
   Sources. UNIDO/LIB/SER D/9—
   Information Sources on the Building
   Board Industry Based on Wood and
   Other Fibrous Materials   4776
Worldcasts   5047
World Commodity Report   5048

FILING SYSTEMS.   *See* Archives
and Records. Information Retrieval

FILM.   *See* Photography and
Photographic Film

FILMS.   *See* Motion Pictures

FINANCE ACT (REPUBLIC OF IRELAND)

Tolley's Taxation in the Republic of
   Ireland 1977/78   4636

FINANCE.   *See also* Banking and
Finance. Credit. Government, Finances.
Investments (General). Subjects, eg,
Construction, Finances

Journal of Finance   2854
Journal of Financial & Quantitative
   Analysis   2855
Working Woman   5025

Canada

Globe and Mail "Report on Business"
   2231

United States

Moody's Industrial Manual and News
   Reports   3314

FINANCE, PERSONAL.   *See also*
Cost of Living. Credit, Consumer.
Financial Planning, Personal.
Investments (General)

Finance Facts   1989
Finance Facts Yearbook   1990
MONEY BEGETS MONEY: A Guide
   to Personal Finance   3268
Seafirst Magazine   4213

Great Britain

Money Management   3269

Union of Soviet Socialist Republics (USSR)

Problems of Economics   3857

United States

Changing Times   907
Economic Education Bulletin   1550
Successful Personal Money
   Management 1977   4488

FINANCE COMPANIES

Compendium of Commercial Finance
   Law   1060

Fitch Corporate Bond Ratings Book
   2051
Journal of the Asset-Based Financial
   Services Industry   2889.01
Moody's Bank and Finance Manual
   and News Reports   3308

American Nations

Polk's World Bank Directory North
   American Edition   3801

Canada

Polk's World Bank Directory North
   American Edition   3801

Mexico

Polk's World Bank Directory North
   American Edition   3801

United States

Polk's World Bank Directory North
   American Edition   3801

FINANCIAL ANALYSIS.   *Note:*
Contains material on theory and
application in areas of investments

Analyst's Service   216
Chartcraft Weekly Service   912
Dunn & Hargitt Market Guide   1517
Financial Analyst's Handbook   1994
Financial Analysts Journal   1995
Financial World   2034
Forbes Special Situation Survey   2104
Industry Surveys   2565
Investors Intelligence   2773
Investors Research Service   2774
Journal of Portfolio Management   2874
Junior Growth Stocks   2902
Nelson's Directory of Securities
   Research Information   3428
Outlook   3653
Technical Trends   4579
Wall Street Advisor   4876

Great Britain

Investors Chronicle News Letter   2771

United States

Babson's Investment & Barometer
   Letter   444
Financial Analysts Federation
   Membership Directory   1993
Investment Quality Trends   2766

FINANCIAL ANALYSTS FEDERATION

Financial Analysts Federation
   Membership Directory   1993

FINANCIAL INSTITUTIONS. *See* Banking and Finance. Credit Unions. Federal Reserve System. Finance Companies. Savings and Loan Associations. Specific Banks

FINANCIAL MANAGEMENT. *See* Financial Planning

FINANCIAL PLANNING

Financial Management Letter   2006.01
Journal of Financial & Quantitative Analysis   2855
Money Management and Unitholder 3270

FINANCIAL PLANNING, PERSONAL. *See also* Cost of Living. Finance, Personal. Families, Finances

Journal of Financial & Quantitative Analysis   2855
Powell Alert   3814

FINANCIAL REPORTS. *Note:* Contains general material

Disclosure Record   1463
International Accounting Standards 2654
Professional Engagement Manual   3887

FINANCIAL TIMES (PUBLICATION) (GB)

Business Information Service Financial Times   692.01
Guide to Financial Times Statistics 2293

FINDERS FEES

Finderhood Report   2036

FIRE EQUIPMENT

Security/Fire Equipment Manufacturers' Directory   4240.01

FIRES. *See also* Insurance, Fire, Flammability

Industrial Safety   2551

FISH AND FISH PRODUCTS

Security Letter   4242
Yearbooks of Fishery Statistics   5098

Alaska

Alaska Business News Letter   137
Alaska Industry   139

Canada

Journal of the Fisheries Research Board of Canada   2890

Europe

Agra Europe Eurofish Report   90
Fisheries: Quantity and Value of Landings   2048

Great Britain

Sea Fisheries Statistical Tables   4214

Pacific Northwest

Quarterly Summary of Pacific Northwest Industries   3976

Scotland

Scottish Sea Fisheries Statistical Tables 4207

United States

Meat, Poultry and Seafood Digest 3164.01
Restaurant Buyers Guide   4098
Seafood Price—Current   4215

FISHERIES. *See* Fish and Fish Products

FISHING. *See* Fish and Fish Products

FLAMMABILITY

Dangerous Properties of Industrial Materials Report   1316.01

FLOOR COVERINGS. *See* Carpets and Rugs

FLOORING

Flooring   2064

FLORIDA

Apparel South   282.02
Dimensions   1398
Florida/Industries Directory, 1981 2067.01
Florida Outlook   2068
Florida/State Industrial Directory, 1981 2068.01
From the State Capitals   2169–2191
Kiplinger Florida Letter   2915
Miami Business Journal   3208
State and Local Taxes   4386
State Legislative Reporting Service 4396
State Tax Reports   4413

FLOUR. *See also* Grain

Flour Milling Products. M20A   2070
Grain Trade of Canada   2256
Milling, Feed & Fertilizer   3229.01

FOOD. *See also* Agriculture. Catering Companies. Hunger. Kitchens. Restaurants. Supermarkets. Vitamins. Types of food, eg, Fruits and Vegetables

Agricultural Outlook   102
Agro Service International   116
British Journal of Nutrition   617
Co-op Consumer   1191.02
Food & Agriculture Organization of the United Nations (FAO) Production Yearbook   2077
Food and Drink   2079
Food and Nutrition   2082
Food Engineering   2085
Food Engineering International   2086
Food Industry Newsletter   2087
Food Industry Studies   2088
Food Manufacture   2091
Food Promotions   2096
Food Research Institute Studies   2097
Monthly Bulletin of Agricultural Economics and Statistics   3278
Monthly Bulletin of Statistics   3283
Progressive Grocer   3896
Snack Food Blue Book   4309
State of Food and Agriculture   4402
Supermarket Business   4497
Target Twenty   4529
Thomas Grocery Register   4610

Australia

Food Manufacturing News   2092
Hospitality   2393
Process and Chemical Engineering 3859

Great Britain

Household Food Consumption and Expenditure (National Food Survey) 2403

Ireland, Republic of

Food Processing in Ireland   2095

United States

Abstract Newsletters, Agriculture & Food   2.04
Consumer Information Catalog 1154
Food Institute Reports: Report on Food Markets; Washington Food Report; Weekly Digest   2089

FOOD, CANNED

Progressive Grocer Market Scope, 1980
3896.02
Thomas Grocery Register   4610

FOOD, CANNED

Canned Food: Stocks, Pack, Shipments
850

FOOD, COOPERATIVES

Coop Marketing & Management   1197

FOOD, FROZEN FOODS

Quick Frozen Foods   3981
Quick Frozen Foods Directory of
Frozen Food Processors   3982
Restaurant Buyers Guide   4098
Seafood Price—Current   4215
Trade Practice Rules   4668

FOOD, GOVERNMENT REGULATIONS, LAWS AND PROGRAMS

Food Policy   2094
Kiplinger Agricultural Letter   2912.02

Canada

Food and Drug Act and Regulations
(Departmental
Consolidation)/Complete Service
2080
National Food Review   3376

United States

Food Institute Reports: Report on Food
Markets; Washington Food Report;
Weekly Digest   2089
From the State Capitals: Agriculture
and Food Products   2169
Trade Practice Rules   4668

FOOD, INSTITUTIONAL

Food Management   2090
Foodservice Equipment Dealer   2098
Institutions/VFM   2603
Nation's Restaurant News   3414.01

FOOD, MARKETING OF

C-Store Business   1265.01
Food Industry Newsletter   2087
Food Manufacture   2091
Food Manufacturing News   2092
From the State Capitals: Agriculture
and Food Products   2169
National Food Review   3376
Nielsen Researcher   3517
Nutrition Action   3558.01
Progressive Grocer Marketing
Guidebook, 1981   3896.01

Progressive Grocer Market Scope, 1980
3896.02
Target Twenty   4529

FOOD, NUTRITION

Abstract Newsletters, Medicine &
Biology   2.22
British Journal of Nutrition   617
Consumer Information Catalog   1154
National Food Review   3376
Nutrition Action   3558.01

FOOD, PACKAGING

Almanac of the Canning, Freezing,
Preserving Industries   149
Food Industry Studies   2088
Food Manufacture   2091
Food Plant Ideas   2093
Frozen Food Pack Statistics   2192

FOOD, PRICES

Food Policy   2094
Foreign Agriculture   2110
Developments in Price Spreads from
Farm Foods   1375.02
Restaurant Buyers Guide   4098

Europe

West European Living Costs 1977
4952

FOOD, RETAILING. See Food, Marketing

FOOD, SAFETY

National Food Review   3776

FOOD, SHIPPING

Food & Agriculture Organization of the
United Nations (FAO) Production
Yearbook   2077

FOOD, SNACK FOODS

Snack Food   4308
Snack Food Blue Book   4309

FOOD, WAREHOUSING

Food Industry Newsletter   2087
Thomas Grocery Register   4610

FOOD, WHOLESALE

Progressive Grocer Marketing
Guidebook, 1981   3896.01
Thomas Grocery Register   4610

FOOTWEAR

Drapers Record   1505.02
Footwear Manual   2101
Footwear Statistics   2102
Nationwide Directory of Sporting
Goods Buyers   3415
Shoes and Slippers. M31A   4281

FORECASTS (ECONOMIC, POLITICAL, SOCIAL). Note: Covers all material containing forecasts and predictions

Agricultural Finance Outlook   99
Alternative Energy: Trends & Forecasts
149.01
Arizona Energy Inventory: 1977, a
Report on the State's Energy Position
& Outlook to 1985   313
Babson's Investment & Barometer
Letter   444
BI/Metrics   553.01
Blue Chip Economic Indicators   563.01
Business Economic Outlook Forum
678
Business Executives' Expectations
681.01
Business International   696
Business International (BI) Data   697
Coal Service   971.02
Cost Forecasting Service   1227
Credit and Capital Markets   1244
Currency Forecasting Service   1268.02
Current Business Picture   1271
DMS World Aircraft Forecast   1475.35
Drilling Service   1505.03
Earnings Forecaster   1521
Economic Education Bulletin   1550
Economic Outlook: California Report
1558
Economic Outlook: Global Report
1559
Energy Service   1694
Euromoney Currency Report   1766
Exchange Rate Outlook (ERO)
1794.01
Financial Indicators and Corporate
Financing Plans   2003
Financial World   2034
Florida Outlook   2068
Forecast   2106
Forecaster   2107
Futures   2204
ICC World Economic Yearbook, 1980
2431.01
Industry Forecast   2561
International Reports   2727
Johnson's Investment   2816
Journal of Futures Markets   2858
Labor Market Trends   2940.01
Latin American Service   2976.01

Manpower Planning 3100
Market Share Reports 3142
Massachusetts Business & Economic
   Report 3148
National Forecast 3377
Nation's Business 3414
New International Realities 3449
New Jersey Economic Outlook 3451
Organization for Economic
   Co-operation and Development
   (OECD) Economic Outlook 3641
Outlook for US Agricultural Exports
   3654
Quarterly Economic Reviews Service
   3962.01
Sales and Marketing Management
   Survey of Buying Power (Part II)
   4167
Services and Software Information
   Program 4267
Smart Money 4307
State of Food and Agriculture 4402
Steel Service 4461
Technological Forecasting and Social
   Change 4580
Trade Levels Report 4657
Transportation Planning and
   Technology 4693
Transportation Service 4694
Worldcasts 5047
World Index of Economic Forecasts,
   2nd edition 5067.02

Alaska

Alaska—Occupational Employment
   Forecast 141

Australia

Australian Economic Review 395

California

Northern Coastal California—Economic
   Trends in the Seventies 3537
Southern California—Economic Trends
   in the Seventies 4347

Canada

British Columbia Economic Activity,
   1980 Review and Outlook 601.01
Canada's Business Climate 762
Canadian State and Area Forecasting
   Service 814
Quarterly Canadian Forecast 3960

Europe

European Economic Service 1774.01

Far East

Asean Business Quarterly 324.01

Great Britain

Economic Outlook 1557
Population Projections 3810

Hawaii

Economy of Hawaii 1579

Ireland, Republic of

Food Processing in Ireland 2095

Japan

Japan Company Handbook 2796
Japan Economic Yearbook 2797
Japanese Economic Service 2797.02

United States

Agriculture and Commodities Service
   111
Chemical Services 928.01
Economic Outlook: US Report 1560
Forest Products Service 2144
Insurance Service 2636
Peter Dag Investment Letter 3753.02
Probe 3856
Standard New York Stock Exchange
   (NYSE) Stock Reports 4375
Survey of Buying Power Forecasting
   Service 4511.01
Survey of Buying Power Part II 4512
United States Economic Service
   4796.01
United States Ocean Shipping
   Technology Forecast and Assessment
   Final Report 4813

Washington (State)

Washington State Economy: Review
   and Outlook 4893

FORECLOSURES

Rocky Mountain Journal 4139

FOREIGN AID. *See also* Credit,
International Monetary System

Agency for International Development
   Research and Development Abstracts
   86
Annual Aid Review 236
Arab Aid: Who Gets It, For What, and
   How 295
Development Digest 1373
EEC/ASIA Report 1597.01

Proposed Foreign Aid Program,
   Summary Presentation to Congress
   3903

**FOREIGN DIPLOMATIC CORPS
AND CONSULAR OFFICES.** *See*
Foreign Service

FOREIGN FACILITIES. *See*
Commerce and Industry, Foreign
Facilities

FOREIGN INVESTMENTS. *See also*
Commerce and Industry, Foreign
Investments. Manufacturers and
Manufacturing, Foreign Investments.
Taxation, Foreign Investments

American Bulletin of International
   Technology Transfer 163
American Industrial Properties Report
   (AIPR) Worldwide Guide for
   Foreign Investment 184
Arab Investors: Who They Are, What
   They Buy, and Where 296
Banker 464
Business International Washington
   (BIW) 699.01
Business Studies 723
Financial Tactics and Terms for the
   Sophisticated International Investor,
   1974 2022
Financing Foreign Operations 2035
Global Investment Flows 2230.01
International Business Intelligence
   2662
International Executive 2678
Journal of International Business
   Studies 2863
Private Investors Abroad 3854

Africa

Investment Africa 2758
Trade and Credit: Problems and
   Resolutions in the Middle East and
   North Africa, in Asia and the Pacific
   and in Latin America 4646.01

Algeria

Developing Business in the Middle East
   and North Africa 1371

American Nations

Caribbean Regional Report 863.01
FFO/Latin America (FFO/LA) 1982
Noticias 3549
Trade and Credit: Problems and
   Resolutions in the Middle East and
   North Africa, in Asia and the Pacific
   and in Latin America 4646.01

Arkansas

Arkansas USA   321.01

Australia

Guide to Investment   2296

Belgium

United States–Belgium Trade Directory,
1980–81 edition   4794.01

Bulgaria

Business Eastern Europe   677

Cambodia

Business China   674

Canada

Canada's International Investment
Position   763

China, People's Republic of

Business China   674

Czechoslovakia

Business Eastern Europe   677

Egypt

Developing Business in the Middle East
and North Africa   1371

Europe

Breve   587
Business Europe   681
Doing Business in Europe   1486

European Economic Community

EEC/ASIA Report   1597.01

Far East

ASEAN Briefing   324
Business Asia   668
EEC/ASIA Report   1597.01
Trade and Credit: Problems and
Resolutions in the Middle East and
North Africa, in Asia and the Pacific
and in Latin America   4646.01

France

French–American News   2165.01

Germany (East)

Business Eastern Europe   677

Great Britain

British–Israel Trade Journal   615
Who Owns Whom: United Kingdom &
Republic of Ireland   4975

Hungary

Business Eastern Europe   677

Indonesia

Indonesia Letter   2506

Iran

Developing Business in the Middle East
and North Africa   1371

Iraq

Developing Business in the Middle East
and North Africa   1371

Ireland

Who Owns Whom: United Kingdom &
Republic of Ireland   4975

Israel

British–Israel Trade Journal   615

Italy

United States–Italy Trade Directory
4808

Japan

Canada Japan Trade Council
Newsletter   756
Japan Trade and Industry News   2804
Who Owns Whom: Australasia & Far
East   4972

Korea (North)

Business China   674

Laos

Business China   674

Mexico

Doing Business in Mexico   1487

Middle East

Arab Investors: Who They Are, What
They Buy, and Where   296
Middle East Week   3222
Trade and Credit: Problems and
Resolutions in the Middle East and
North Africa, in Asia and the Pacific
and in Latin America   4646.01

Mongolia

Business China   674

New Jersey

New Jersey International Report   3453

New Zealand

Handbook for Investors—New Zealand
2314
Life and Business in New Zealand
3011
Overseas Investment and Business in
New Zealand   3659

Philippines

Philippine Letter   3765.03

Poland

Business Eastern Europe   677

Rumania

Business Eastern Europe   677

Saudi Arabia

Developing Business in the Middle East
and North Africa   1371

Spain

Spain–US   4353

*Union of Soviet Socialist Republics
(USSR)*

Business China   674
Business Eastern Europe   677

United States

Amcham Overseas Report   154
Announcements of Foreign Investment
in US Manufacturing Industries   232
Consensus of Insiders   1119
Doing Business in Mexico   1487
Foreign Direct Investment in the
United States, 1974 edition   2115
French–American News   2165.01
United States–Belgium Trade Directory,
1980–81 edition   4794.01
United States Direct Investment
Abroad, 1966   4796
Who Own Whom: North America
4974

Vietnam

Business China   674

Yugoslavia

Business Eastern Europe   677
Business News   714

FOREIGN INVESTMENTS, GOVERNMENT REGULATIONS, LAWS AND PROGRAMS

Forex Service   2145
International Report   2726
Investment and Taxation Monograph
   2760.01
Investment Laws of the World   2763

Canada

Foreign Investment in Canada   2118

Japan

Japan Letter   2803

United States

Doing Business in Canada   1484
Doing Business in Mexico   1487
Whaley–Eaton Foreign Letter   4959

FOREIGN RELATIONS. *See*
International Relations

FOREIGN SECURITIES. *See* Stocks
and Bonds, Foreign Securities

FOREIGN SERVICE

The Ambassador's Directory   153.02
Official Congressional Directory   3583

FOREIGN TRADE. *See also* Balance
of Payments. Imports and Exports.
Import–Export Companies. Trade Fairs

Atlantic Economic   344
Australian Economic Review   395
Banker   464
Barron's   509
Basic Instruments and Selected
   Documents (BISD)   513
Croner's Reference Book for World
   Traders   1257
Direction of Trade   1400
Economic Report   1567
Export Administration Regulations
   1818
Finance and Development   1988
Financing Foreign Operations   2035
Foreign Credit Insurance Assn (FCIA)
   2112
Foreign Market Reports Index   2134
Foreign Tax and Trade Briefs   2137
Guide to Trade and Securities Statistics
   2305

GATT Activities   2209
International Banktrends   2657.01
International Commercial Financing
   Intelligence   2668
International Monetary Fund Annual
   Report of the Executive Directors
   2710
International Report   2726
International Trade   2736
International Trade News Letter   2740
Journal of Commerce and Commercial
   2836
Journal of International Economics
   2863.01
Journal of World Trade Law   2901
Key to Economic Science and
   Managerial Sciences   2912.01
Minnesota   3240
OECD Import–Export Microtables
   3575.01
Organization for Economic
   Co-operation and Development
   (OECD) Economic Outlook   3641
Rundt's Weekly Intelligence   4153
Shipping and Trade News   4275
Statistics of Foreign Trade, Monthly
   Bulletin   4453
Statistics of Foreign Trade, Series B:
   Annual Tables by Reporting Country
   4453.01
Tape Subscriptions to IFS, DOT, BOP,
   and GFS   4528
Tax-Free Trade Zones of the World
   4553.02
Trade Directories of the World   4654
United Nations Conference on Trade
   and Development Guide to
   Publications   4765
Whaley–Eaton Foreign Letter   4959
World Marketing   5069
World Trade Annual   5082
World Trade Centers Association
   5083
World Trade Information Center
   5083.01
Yearbook of International Trade
   Statistics   5094

Africa

Foreign Trade Statistics for Africa—
   Series A—Direction of Trade   2140
Foreign Trade Statistics for Africa—
   Series B—Trade by Commodity
   2141
Surveys of African Economies   4521
Trade and Credit: Problems and
   Resolutions in the Middle East and
   North Africa, in Asia and the Pacific
   and in Latin America   4646.01

American Nations

Caribbean Business News   863
Caribbean Year Book, 1977–78   864
Trade and Credit: Problems and
   Resolutions in the Middle East and
   North Africa, in Asia and the Pacific
   and in Latin America   4646.01

Argentina

Latin American Service   2976.01

Australia

Australian Economic Review   395
Australia Newsletter   399

Belgium

Belgian–American Trade Review   520

Bolivia

Latin American Service   2976.01

Brazil

Brazilian–American Business
   Review/Directory   585
Latin American Service   2976.01

Bulgaria

List of Bulgarian Foreign Trade
   Organizations   3025

California

California International Trade   737
California International Trade Register,
   1980–81   737.01

Canada

Bank of Canada Review   485
Canada Commerce   744

Chile

Latin American Service   2976.01

China, People's Republic of

China Business Report   940.01
China Business Review   941
China Letter   942
China Trade and Economic Newsletter
   943
Soviet-Eastern Europe-China Business
   & Trade   4351

Colombia

Latin American Service   2976.01

Cuba

East–West Trade Council. Newsletter
1528

Ecuador

Latin American Service   2976.01

Egypt

Egypt/North Africa   1598.02

Europe

Europe's 5000 Largest Companies
Directory, 1980   1792.01
Monthly External Trade Bulletin
3290.01

European Economic Community

EEC/ASIA Report   1597.01

Europe, East

Doing Business with Eastern Europe
1489
East–West Trade Council. Newsletter
1528
Soviet-Eastern Europe-China Business
& Trade   4351

Far East

ASEAN Briefing   324
Asia Letter   325
Asian Business   326.02
Asian Wall Street Journal   329
Asia Research Bulletin   331
Basic Facts, Developing Member
Countries (DMCs) of Asian
Development Bank (ADB)   512
EEC/ASIA Report   1597.01
Trade and Credit: Problems and
Resolutions in the Middle East and
North Africa, in Asia and the Pacific
and in Latin America   4646.01

Great Britain

Achievement   39
Britain & Overseas   596
Business Monitors Miscellaneous Series
712
Overseas Trade Analysed in Terms of
Industries   3660
Quarterly Trade Statistics of the United
Kingdom   3978
Statistics of Trade through United
Kingdom Ports   4455
Trade Promotions Guide   4669

Hong Kong

Hong Kong Cable   2386
Hong Kong Trader   2388

India

Embassy of India Commercial Bulletin
1640

Iran

Iran Economic News   2779

Ireland, Republic of

Statistical Abstract of Ireland   4419

Italy

Italian Trade Topics   2792

Japan

Canada Japan Trade Council
Newsletter   756
Focus Japan   2074
Japan Economic Journal   2796.01
Japan External Trade Organization
(JETRO) Business Information Series
2801
Japan External Trade Organization
(JETRO) Marketing Series   2802
Shipping and Trade News   4275

Mexico

Latin American Service   2976.01
Mexican–American Review   3206.01

Middle East

Mideast Business Exchange   3225
Trade and Credit: Problems and
Resolutions in the Middle East and
North Africa, in Asia and the Pacific
and Latin America   4646.01

New Zealand

Information Releases   2573.03
New Zealand Commerce   3497
New Zealand Economist   3500

Nigeria

Nigeria Newsletter   3517.01
Trade Report   4673

Oregon

International Trade Directory   2739

Peru

Latin American Service   2976.01

Philippines

Philippine Letter   3765.03

Puerto Rico

Puerto Rico: Official Industrial & Trade
Directory, 1980   3943.01

Saudi Arabia

Saudi Arabia Newsletter   4183.02

Switzerland

Swiss–American Chamber of
Commerce. Yearbook   4522

Third World

Commodity Trade and Price Trends,
1980 edition   1031

Union of Soviet Socialist Republics (USSR)

East–West Trade Council. Newsletter
1528
Soviet-Eastern Europe-China Business
& Trade   4351

United States

Amcham Overseas Report   154
Breve   587
China Business Review   941
Domestic and International
Transportation of US Foreign Trade,
1976   1491
East–West Trade Council. Newsletter
1528
Foreign Economic Trends   2116
International Trade Commission
Annual Report   2737
International Trade Commission
Quarterly Report to the Congress &
the East–West Foreign Trade Board
on Trade Between the US & the
Nonmarket Economy Countries
2738
Norwegian–American Commerce   3548
Noticias   3549
Operation of the Trade Agreements
Program   3628
Survey of Current Business   4514

Uruguay

Latin American Service   2976.01

Washington (State)

Washington State Foreign Trade Trends
4894

Routes Yearbook 4144
Transportation Service 4694

Canada

Canada–United Kingdom Trade News
770
Canadian Transportation and
Distribution Management 842
Dangerous Goods Shipping Regulations
1316
Inventories, Shipments, and Orders in
Manufacturing Industries 2754
Products Shipped by Canadian
Manufacturers 3880

Great Britain

Canada–United Kingdom Trade News
770
Export Services 1832
International Freighting Management
2682.01

New England

Boston Marine Guide 577

United States

Domestic and International
Transportation of US Foreign Trade,
1976 1491
Federal Carriers Reports 1916
Custom House Guide 1285
Research Review 4095

FREIGHT FORWARDING, LAW

Canada

Dangerous Goods Shipping Regulations
1316

Europe

Croner's Road Transport Operation
1258

Great Britain

Croner's Road Transport Operation
1258

United States

Federal Carriers Reports 1916
Research Review 4095

FREIGHT FORWARDING, TAXATION

Custom House Guide 1285
Research Review 4095

FRINGE BENEFITS. *See* Labor,
Employee Benefits. Managers and
Management, Employee Benefits.
Pension Plan. Other specific types

FROZEN FOODS. *See* Food, Frozen
Foods

FRUITS AND VEGETABLES. *See
also* Citrus Fruits

Chicago Mercantile Exchange Yearbook
937
Outlook and Situation Reports
3653.01
World Commodity Report 5048

Australia

Weekly Market Review 4936

Canada

Fruit and Vegetable Production 2193

European Economic Community

Agricultural Markets: Prices (Two
Series) 101

United States

Fresh Fruit and Vegetable and
Ornamental Crops Market News
Reports 2166
Restaurant Buyers Guide 4098

FTC. *See* Trade Commission, Federal
(FTC) (US)

FUEL. *See also* Research and
Development, Fuel. Types, eg, Gas
(Illuminating and Fuel). Fields of use

Mineral Facts and Problems 3231
Mineral Industry Surveys 3232

Australia

Handbook for Industrialists 2313

United States

Electrical Week 1605
Fuel Price Analysis 2197

FUEL, SYNFUEL

Alternative Energy: Trends & Forecasts
149.01
International Journal of Energy
Research 2692

FUND RAISING

Fund Raising Institute (FRI) Monthly
Portfolio 2199

Fund Raising Management 2200
Fundraising Weekly 2200.01

FUNERAL HOMES AND DIRECTORS

Funeral Service "Insider." 2201

FUR GOODS

Fur Review 2203

FURNITURE. *See* Home Furnishings

FUTURES TRADING. *See*
Commodities and Commodity
Exchanges, Futures

GAMBLING

Betting and Gaming Bulletin 546
Security Management 4243

GAO. *See* Accounting Office, General
(GAO) (US)

GARDENING EQUIPMENT. *See
also* Horticulture

Consumer Information Catalog 1154
Lawn & Garden Marketing 2978.01

GAS APPLIANCES

Appliance Magazine 284
Appliance Manufacturer 285
Drilling Service 1505.03
Mingay's Price Service—Appliance
Edition 3236
Mingay's Retailer & Merchandiser
3238

GASES, INDUSTRIAL

Industrial Gases M28C 2522

GAS (ILLUMINATING AND FUEL).
See also Gases, Industrial. Liquefied
Natural Gas. Liquefied Petroleum Gas.
Methane Gas. Pipelines

Annual Survey of Oil and Gas.
MA-13K 269
Chilton's Oil and Gas Energy 940
Construction News 1137
Gas Facts: A Statistical Record of the
Gas Utility Industry 2208
International Oil and Gas Field
Records 2716
International Petroleum Encyclopedia
2720
Japanese Newsletter 2800
Law of Pooling and Unitization—
Voluntary, Compulsory 2985
LP-Gas Industry Market Facts 3050

Manual of Oil and Gas Terms,
   Annotated   3103
Oil & Gas Journal   3595
Oil and Gas Law   3596
Pipeline & Gas Journal   3772
Rate Service Newsletter   4006
Rocky Mountain Mineral Law Institute
   4140
Walter Skinner's Oil and Gas
   International Year Book   4294
Tax Sheltered Investments   4570
World Production and Reserve
   Statistics   5074

Alaska

Alaska Industry   139

California

Oil in California   3605

Canada

Brown's Directory   630
Canadian Oil Register   825
Canadian Petroleum   827
Crude Petroleum and Natural Gas
   Production   1262
Daily Oil Bulletin   1303
Financial Post Survey of Mines and
   Energy Resources   2015
Oil and Gas Reporter   3599

Europe

Annual Bulletin of Gas Statistics for
   Europe   239

Great Britain

Construction News   1137
North Sea Letter   3543
Oilman   3606

Nevada

Oil in California   3605

New York City

New York City Business Fact Book
   Part 1: Business & Manufacturing
   3474

Texas

Oil in Texas   3605.01

United States

Brown's Directory   630
Crude Petroleum and Natural Gas.
   M:T58   1263
Fuel Price Analysis   2197
National Wildcat Monthly   3413.01

Oil and Gas Reporter   3599
Oil in the Mid-Continent   3605.02
Oil in the Rockies   3605.03
United States Oil and Gas Production
   News   4813.01

GAS (ILLUMINATING AND FUEL), DRILLING STARTS

Chilton's Oil and Gas Energy   940
Daily Oil Bulletin   1303
Oil & Gas Journal   3595
Oil, Gas, & Petrochem Equipment
   3604
Petroleum Engineer International   3759
Profile—A Continuing Study of Oil and
   Gas Programs   3891
Rocky Mountain Journal   4139

GAS (ILLUMINATING AND FUEL), EXPLORATION

Annual Survey of Oil and Gas.
   MA-13K   269

Belgium

Oil and Gas, The North Sea
   Exploitation   3601

Canada

National Exploration Daily   3373.01

Denmark

Oil and Gas, The North Sea
   Exploitation   3601

Great Britain

Oil and Gas, The North Sea
   Exploitation   3601

Netherlands

Oil and Gas, The North Sea
   Exploitation   3601

Norway

Oil and Gas, The North Sea
   Exploitation   3601

Sweden

Oil and Gas, The North Sea
   Exploitation   3601

United States

National Exploration Daily   3373.01

GAS (ILLUMINATING AND FUEL), GOVERNMENT REGULATIONS

Annual Institute on Oil and Gas Law
   and Taxation   250

Belgium

Oil and Gas, The North Sea
   Exploitation   3601

Denmark

Oil and Gas, The North Sea
   Exploitation   3601

Great Britain

Oil and Gas, The North Sea
   Exploitation   3601

Netherlands

Oil and Gas, The North Sea
   Exploitation   3601

Norway

Oil and Gas, The North Sea
   Exploitation   3601

Sweden

Oil and Gas, The North Sea
   Exploitation   3601

United States

Law of Federal Oil and Gas Leases
   2982
Law of Oil and Gas Leases   2984
Oil & Gas Price Regulation Analyst
   3598.01
United States Oil and Gas Production
   News   4813.01

GAS (ILLUMINATING AND FUEL), LEASING

Law of Federal Oil and Gas Leases
   2982
Law of Oil and Gas Leases   2984
Oil and Gas Law: Abridged Edition
   3597
Oil and Gas Lease Reports   3598
Oil in California   3605
Oil in the Mid-Continent   3605.02
Oil in the Rockies   3605.03

GAS (ILLUMINATING AND FUEL), OFFSHORE

Construction News Magazine   1138
International Petroleum Encyclopedia
   2720
Offshore   3590
Offshore Rig Newsletter   3592
Oil, Gas, & Petrochem Equipment
   3604
Petroleum Engineer International   3759

Belgium

Oil and Gas, The North Sea
Exploitation 3601

Denmark

Oil and Gas, The North Sea
Exploitation 3601

Great Britain

Oil and Gas, The North Sea
Exploitation 3601

Netherlands

Oil and Gas, The North Sea
Exploitation 3601

North Sea

North Sea Letter 3543
Offshore 3590

Sweden

Oil and Gas, The North Sea
Exploitation 3601

Texas

Oil in Texas 3605.01

GAS (ILLUMINATING AND FUEL), PERSONNEL

Walter Skinner's Who's Who in World
Oil and Gas 4295

GAS (ILLUMINATING AND FUEL), TAXATION

Annual Institute on Oil and Gas Law
and Taxation 250
Federal Taxation of Oil and Gas
Transactions 1964
Oil & Gas Tax Quarterly 3600

GASOLINE. *See* Oil (Petroleum) and
Gasoline

GATT. *See* Tariffs and Trade, General
Agreement on

GENERAL SERVICES ADMINISTRATION (GSA) (US)

Business Service Centers 721

GEOGRAPHY. *See also* Maps,
Charts and Atlases

American Nations

Caribbean Year Book, 1977–78 864

Arkansas

Arkansas. The Great Location in the
Sunbelt 321

Australia

Far East and Australasia 1892

Far East

Far East and Australasia 1892

United States

Rand McNally Commercial Atlas &
Marketing Guide 4000

West Indies

Caribbean Year Book, 1977–78 864

GEOLOGY. *See also* Rocks

Abstract Newsletters, Natural
Resources & Earth Sciences 2.24
Earth Surface Processes and Landforms
1522
Geo Abstracts 2217.01
International Journal for Numerical
Methods in Engineering 2689

GEORGIA

Apparel South 282.02
Atlanta Business Chronicle 343
From the State Capitals 2169-2191
Georgia Manufacturers Directory
2218.01
Georgia State Industrial Directory,
1980 2219.01
State and Local Taxes 4386
State Legislative Reporting Service
4396
State Tax Reports 4413

GIFTS. *See also* Taxation, Estate and
Gift Taxes

Gifts & Housewares Buyers 2226
Gifts & Tablewares 2227
Housewares Incorporating Gifts and
Fancy Goods 2405
Housewares Promotions 2407

GLASS. *See also* Containers and
Packaging

Ceramic Industry 893
Flat Glass. MQ-32A 2058
Glass Containers 2229
Glass Containers M32G 2230
United Nations Industrial Development
Organization Guides to Information
Sources. UNIDO/LIB/SER D/16—

Information Sources on the Glass
Industry 4783

GLIDERS

Federal Aviation Administration (FAA)
General Aviation News 1912

GOLD

American Board of Trade Spot and
Forward Markets 160
Chartcraft Commodity Survice 910
International Monetary Market
Yearbook 2713
International Reports 2727
Johnson Survey 2816.01
Pick's Currency Yearbook 3769
Powell Gold Industry Guide &
International Mining Analyst 3815
Powell Monetary Analyst 3816
Selected Interest and Exchange Rates
4253
World's Monetary Stocks of Gold,
Silver, and Coins—on a Calendar
Year Basis 5079

Europe

NOW Machine 3551

South Africa

International Gold Digest 2683.01

United States

Gold Data 2233

GOVERNMENT. *See also* Elections.
Subjects. Country, city, state, and
municipality names

AP–Dow Jones Economic Report 278
AP–Dow Jones Financial Wire 280
Committee for Economic Development
Newsletter 1012
Currency Forecasting Service 1268.02
Directory Information Service 1406
Dow Jones International News Wire
1499
Economic Development & Cultural
Change 1548
Economist 1576
Facts on File Weekly News Digest
1874
Foreign Letter 2120
Government Product News 2248.01
Holt Executive Advisory 2379
Information Industry & Technology
Service 2573
Institute of Public Affairs (IPA) Review
2600

International Year Book and
  Statesmen's Who's Who   2744
Journal of Policy Modeling   2872.02
Journal of Political Economy   2873
Nation's Business   3414
New International Realities   3449
New York Times   3487
Petroleum Economist   3758
Politics and Money   3797
Quarterly Economic Reviews Service
  3962.01
Sound of the Economy   4332
Statesman's Year-Book, 1980–81 edition
  4408
Time   4619
Transdex   4687.01
US News and World Report   4812

Africa

Africa   77
Africa Guide 1981   78
Africa Research Bulletin   81
Africa South of the Sahara   82
Middle East and North Africa   3217
New African Development   3432

American Nations

Andean Group Regional Report
  222.01
Caribbean Regional Report   863.01
Caribbean Business News   863
Caribbean Year Book, 1977–78   864
Latin America & Caribbean 1981
  2969.01
Latin American Commodities Report
  2972
Latin American Index   2975
Latin America Weekly Report   2976.02
Mexico and Central America Regional
  Report   3206.02
Noticias   3549
Southern Cone Regional Report
  4347.01

Arizona

Statistical Abstract of Arizona   4418

Arkansas

Arkansas. The Great Location in the
  Sunbelt   321

Australia

Institute of Public Affairs (IPA) Review
  2600

Brazil

Brazil Regional Report   586

Canada

Almanac and Directory 1981   148.01
Canada   743
Canada Gazette/Part III   751
Canada Report   761
Canadian News Facts   820
Corpus Almanac of Canada   1224
Financial Times of Canada   2027
Government of Canada Telephone
  Directory/National Capital Region
  2247
Metropolitan Toronto Board of Trade.
  Journal   3206
North   3533
Optium/A Forum for Management
  3633
Public Sector   3935

China, People's Republic of

China Letter   942

Egypt

Developing Business in the Middle East
  and North Africa   1371
Egypt/North Africa   1598.02

Europe

Breve   587
Doing Business with Eastern Europe
  1489
European Report   1786
Financial Times of Canada   2027
Predicasts F&S Index Europe Annual
  3828.02

European Economic Community

Bulletin of the European Communities
  646
Common Market News   1038

Far East

ASEAN Briefing   324
Asia Letter   325
Asia & Pacific 1981   324.02
Asia Research Bulletin   331

Florida

Dimensions   1398

Georgia

Georgia Statistical Abstract   2220

Great Britain

Company Secretary's Review   1055
Economist   1576
Fleet Street Letter   2061

Leisure, Recreation and Tourism
  Abstracts   3004.01
Management Information Manual
  3081
Statistical News   4430

Hawaii

All About Business in Hawaii   145

India

India News   2504

Indonesia

Indonesia Letter   2506

Iran

Developing Business in the Middle East
  and North Africa   1371
Iran Service   2779.01

Iraq

Developing Business in the Middle East
  and North Africa   1371

Ireland, Republic of

Ireland International Reference Manual
  2779.02

Italy

Economic News from Italy   1556

Japan

Japan Economic Journal   2796.01
Japan International Reference Manual
  2802.02
Japan Letter   2803
Oriental Economist   3648

Mexico

Mexico and Central America Regional
  Report   3206.02

Middle East

Businessman's Guide to the Arab
  World   709
Middle East   3216
Middle East and North Africa   3217
Middle East Review 1981   3219.01
Middle East Week   3222

Montana

Montana Business Quarterly   3276

New York State

Capital Journal   857.01

Omnibus   3619.01
Orange Rockland Westchester Business
   Review   3636

New Zealand

Capital Letter   857.02
Department of Statistics Annual Report
   of the Government Statistician   1363
Life and Business in New Zealand
   3011
National Business Review   3365
New Zealand Trade Report   3513.01

Nigeria

Nigeria Newsletter   3517.01

Philippines, Republic of

Philippine Development   3765.01
Philippine Letter   3765.03

Puerto Rico

Spotlite   4365.01

Saudi Arabia

Developing Business in the Middle East
   and North Africa   1371
Saudi Arabia Newsletter   4183.02

South Africa

Financial Mail   2004.02
South Africa Yearbook   4337

Third World

South-The Third World Magazine
   4349.01

United States

Bicentennial Statistics   550
Census of Governments, 1977   874.01
Financial Times of Canada   2027
Government Data Systems   2239.01
Newsbank Library   3462.01
Official Congressional Directory   3583
Savings and Loan News   4187
Statistical Service   4442
United States Government Manual
   4803

Utah

Statistical Review of Government in
   Utah   4441

Venezuela

Venezeula Up-to-Date   4845

West Indies

Caribbean Year Book, 1977–78   864
West Indies Chronicle   4953

GOVERNMENT, ADMINISTRATION

Tax Review   4569

Canada

Optimum   3633

United States

Abstract Newsletters, Administration
   and Management   2.03
Government Employee Relations
   Report   2240
Government Manager   2245

GOVERNMENT, ADVISORY ORGANIZATIONS

Business Service Centers   721
Encyclopedia of Governmental
   Advisory Organizations, 2nd edition
   1673
New Governmental Advisory
   Organizations, 2nd edition   3447

GOVERNMENT, AWARDS

Labor Arbitration in Government
   2925

GOVERNMENT, BUILDINGS

Great Britain

Kelly's Post Office London Directory
   2908

United States

Blue Reports   565

Washington (DC) Metropolitan Area

Blue Reports   565

GOVERNMENT, BUSINESS RELATIONS

American Nations

Caribbean Regional Report   863.01

Canada

Ottawa Letter   3650

Japan

Focus Japan   2074

Oregon

Directory of Oregon State Services to
   Business   1453

United States

Business Service Centers   721

GOVERNMENT, CHIEF EXECUTIVE

United States

Defense Week   1355.02

GOVERNMENT, CONGRESS (US)

CIS/Index   948.01
CIS/Microfiche Library   948.02
Congress Daily   1110.01
Congress in Print   1110.02
Congressional Action   1111
Congressional Index   1114
Congressional Insight   1114.01
Congressional Legislative Reporting
   1115
Congressional Monitor   1115.01
Congressional Record Scanner   1115.02
Congressional Yellow Book   1115.03
CQ Alamanc, 1980   1241
Defense Week   1355.02
Official Congressional Directory   3583
Washington Information Directory,
   1980–81   4887.02

GOVERNMENT, CONTRACTS

Great Britain

Government & Municipal Contractors
   2236

United States

Affirmative Action Compliance Manual
   for Federal Contractors   76.01
Briefing Papers   593
Briefing Papers Collection   594
Business Service Centers   721
Commerce Business Daily   995
Communiqué   1047
Comptroller General's Procurement
   Decisions   1069
Directory of Government Production
   Prime Contractors   1434
Extraordinary Contractual Relief
   Reporter   1867
Federal Contract Opportunities:
   Energy/Environment   1917.01
Federal Contracts Reports   2239
Government Contractor   2238
Government Contracts Reports   2239
Government Prime Contracts Monthly
   2248

State Executive Directory   4389.01
State Government News   4392
State Headlines   4393
State Legislative Leadership,
   Committees and Staff   4395
State Legislative Reporting Service
   4396
State Slate: A Guide to Legislative
   Procedures and Lawmakers   4407
Statistical Reference Index   4438
Suggested State Legislation, 1980   4490

Wales

Local Government Financial Statistics,
   England and Wales   3038

GOVERNMENT, SURPLUS PROPERTY

Commerce Business Daily   995

GOVERNMENT BONDS. *See*
Stocks and Bonds, Government Bonds

GRAIN. *See also* Agriculture, Feed
Crops. Flour

Feed Industry Red Book   1978
Feed Industry Review   1979
Financial Facts About the Meat
   Packing Industry   2000
Foreign Agriculture Circulars   2111
Grain Age   2253
Law and Policy of Intergovernmental
   Primary Commodity Agreements
   2978
United Nations Industrial Development
   Organization Guides to Information
   Sources. UNIDO/LIB/SER D/13—
   Information Sources on the Animal
   Feed Industry   4780
World Commodity Report   5048

Canada

Grain Trade of Canada   2256

North Dakota

North Dakota Crop and Livestock
   Statistics   3536

South Dakota

South Dakota Crop and Livestock
   Reporter   4344

United States

Feedstuffs   1980
Grain Market News Reports   2254

GRANTS. *See* Scholarships and
Grants

GRAPHICS. *See also* Prints and
Printing

Art Direction   322
British Printer   620
Direct Advertising   1399
Letterheads, Volumes I to III   3006.01
Modern Publicity   3263
Print   3847
Sportswear Graphics   4365
Trademarks/7   4663.01
United Nations Industrial Development
   Organization Guides to Information
   Sources. UNIDO/LIB/SER D/14—
   Informaton Sources on the Printing
   and Graphics Industry   4781
World of Logotypes, Volumes I & II
   5072.01

GREAT BRITAIN. *See also*
Commonwealth of Nations. Ireland,
Northern. Scotland. Wales

Acquisitions & Mergers of Companies
   41
Agricultural Statistics: England &
   Wales   107
Agricultural Statistics: United Kingdom
   110
Annual Abstract of Statistics   234
Annual Digest of Port Statistics,
   Volumes I and II   244
Annual Estimates of the Population of
   England and Wales and Local
   Authority Areas   245
Bank of England. Report   489
Betting and Gaming Bulletin   546
Bill of Entry Service   552
Britain in Context   596.01
British-Israel Trade Journal   615
British Labour Statistics. Year Book
   618
Business Monitor, Production Series
   710
Business Monitors Miscellaneous Series
   712
Catering Trades   871
Cinemas   946
Civil Aviation Authority Monthly
   Statistics   952
Civil Service Statistics   954
Company Finance   1053
Computer Management—United
   Kingdom   1080
Control of Immigration: Statistics
   1190
Criminal Statistics, England and Wales
   1255
Cumbria Weekly Digest   1266

Department of Employment Research
   1362
Digest of United Kingdom Energy
   Statistics   1394
Economic Trends   1573
Economic Trends Annual Supplement
   1574
Education Statistics for the UK   1596
Facts in Focus   1873
Family Expenditure Survey   1883
Financial Statement and Budget Report
   2019
Financial Statistics   2020
Financial Statistics: Explanatory
   Handbook   2021
Fire and Loss Statistics for the United
   Kingdom   2041
First Destination of University
   Graduates   2045
General Household Survey   2210
Guide to Official Statistics   2300
Historical Directory of Trade Unions
   2373.01
Household Food Consumption and
   Expenditure (National Food Survey)
   2403
Housing and Construction Statistics
   2409
Industrial Tribunal Reports   2555
Inland Revenue Statistics   2579
Input–Output Tables   2584
Input–Output Tables for the United
   Kingdom   2585
Insurance Business Statistics   2613
Insurance Companies and Private
   Pension Funds   2615
Kelly's Regional Directory of British
   Industry and Services   2908.01
Leisure, Recreation and Tourism
   Abstracts   3004.01
Lloyds Bank Economic Bulletin   3031
Management Information Manual
   3081
Media Reporter   3178
Monthly Digest Annual Supplement
   3288
Monthly Digest of Statistics   3289
National Income and Expenditure
   "Blue Book"   3382
New Earnings Survey   3437
Number of Road Vehicles, New
   Registrations   3556
Population Trends   3811
Price Index Numbers for Current Cost
   Accounting   3838
Quarterly Trade Statistics of the United
   Kingdom   3978
Railway Accidents   3994
Registry of Ships   4056
Report of the Commissioners of Her
   Majesty's Customs and Excise   4064

Report of the Commissioners of Her Majesty's (HM) Inland Revenue 4065
Report on the Census of Production 4074
Retail Intelligence 4106
Retail Trade 4113
Road Accidents 4135
Sea Fisheries Statistical Tables 4214
Social Security Statistics 4319
Social Trends 4321
Statistics of Trade through United Kingdom Ports 4455
Survey of Personal Income 4517
Times Rates of Wages and Hours of Work 4620
Trade Promotions Guide 4669
Trade Union Handbook, 2nd edition 4677
Transport Statistics, Great Britain 1964–74 4698
United Kingdom Mineral 4760
United Kingdom News Contact Directory 4760.01

GROCERIES. *See* Food. Supermarkets

GROSS NATIONAL PRODUCT

Predicasts Basebook 3828
Statistical Bulletin 4425
World Bank Atlas, 15th edition 5044
World Economic and Social Indicators 5059
Yearbook of National Accounts Statistics 5096

Canada

National Income & Expenditure Accounts 3381
System of National Accounts—National Income and Expenditure Accounts 4526

Far East

Basic Facts, Developing Member Countries (DMCs) of Asian Development Bank (ADB) 512
Federal Reserve Bank of San Francisco. Pacific Basin Economic Indicators 1953

Japan

Japan Economic Yearbook 2797

United States

National Income and Product Accounts 3383
Survey of Current Business 4514

GROUP COUNSELING. *See* subjects

GROUP INSURANCE. *See* Insurance, Group Plans

GROWTH STOCKS. *See* Stocks and Bonds, Growth Stocks

GUM

Naval Stores Market News Reports 3420

HAIR SPRAY. *See* Beauty and Grooming Aids. Cosmetics and Toiletries

HANDICAPPED

Australian Hospitals and Health Services Yearbook 403

HARDWARE. *See* Computers

HARDWARE SUPPLIES

Hardware Age 2343
Housewares Promotions 2407
National Hardware Wholesalers Guide 3377.02
Southern Hardware 4348.01

HARVARD UNIVERSITY

Baker Library. Core Collection, an Author & Subject Guide 449
Current Periodical Publications in Baker Library 1279
Harvard Business Review 2345
Publications by the Faculty of the Harvard Business School 3923
Working Papers in Baker Library: A Quarterly Checklist 5024

HAWAII

All About Business in Hawaii 145
Bank of Hawaii Monthly Review 491
Construction in Hawaii 1131
Dangerous Goods Shipping Regulations 1316
Dangerous Properties of Industrial Materials Report 1316.01
Directory of Shopping Centers in Hawaii 1456
Eco/Log Week 1533
Economy of Hawaii 1579
From the State Capitals 2169-2191
Hawaii Annual Economic Review 2347
Hawaii Facts and Figures 2348
Hawaii: Manufacturers Directory, 1981–82 2348.01

Legislative Action Bulletin 2997
Starting a Business in Hawaii 4381
State and Local Taxes 4386
State Legislative Reporting Service 4396
State of Hawaii Data Book 4403
State Tax Reports 4413
Voice of Business 4864
Who's Who in Government 4986

HAZARDOUS CARGOS. *See also* methods of transportation

Dangerous Goods Shipping Regulations 1316
Hazardous Products Act and Regulations/Office Consolidation 2353
Hazardous Waste News 2353.01
Regulations for Transportation of Dangerous Commodities by Rail 4057
Solid Wastes Management 4329.01
State Regulation Report: Toxic Substances & Hazardous Waste 4405.01
Toxic Materials Transport 4643.03

HAZARDOUS PRODUCTS ACT (CANADA)

Hazardous Products Act and Regulations/Office Consolidation 2353

HAZARDS, INDUSTRIAL. *See* Industrial Hazards

HEALTH ACT, FEDERAL (US)

Best's Safety Directory 541

HEALTH CARE. *See* Insurance, Health. Hospitals. Medicine and Health

HEALTH, EDUCATION, AND WELFARE, DEPARTMENT OF (HEW) (US)

Employment and Training Report of the President 1655

HEALTH HAZARDS. *See* Accidents and Safety. Specific products and fields of activity, eg, Recreation, Health Hazards and Safety

HEALTH INSURANCE. *See* Insurance, Health

HEARING AIDS. *See* Ears and Hearing

HEATING. *See also* Insulation. Research and Development, Air Conditioning and Heating

Australian Refrigeration, Air-Conditioning and Heating 413.01
Contractor 1187
Domestic Heating 1492
Heating & Air Conditioning Journal 2366
Heating & Ventilating Engineer 2367
Heating/Piping/Air Conditioning 2368
Heating–Plumbing Air Conditioning 2369
Solar Heating and Cooling Magazine 4326.04

HELICOPTERS

DMS Civil Aircraft 1475.05
DMS Military Aircraft 1475.20
DMS World Helicopter Forecast 1475.36
Federal Aviation Administration (FAA) General Aviation News 1912

HEW. *See* Health, Education, and Welfare, Department of (HEW) (US)

HIGHWAY SAFETY. *See* Traffic Safety

HIGHWAYS AND EXPRESSWAYS

Abstract Newsletters, Civil Engineering 2.10
From the State Capitals: Highway Financing and Construction 2173
Kiplinger Florida Letter 2915
Research Review 4095

HISTORIC BUILDINGS AND LANDMARKS

Dodge Building Cost Calculator and Valuation Guide 1477

HISTORY. *See also* specific subjects and geographic areas

Economic Development & Cultural Change 1548

Africa

Africa South of the Sahara 82

American Nations

Caribbean Year Book, 1977–78 864

Australia

Far East and Australasia 1892

Far East

Far East and Australasia 1892

North Carolina

North Carolina Industrial Data File 3534

United States

Bicentennial Statistics 550

West Indies

Caribbean Year Book 1977–78 864

HOBBY AND CRAFT ITEMS

Model Retailer 3251
Playthings 3788
Toys Hobbies and Crafts 4645

HOGS. *See* Pigs

HOLDING COMPANIES. *See also* Stocks and Bonds, Holding Companies

American Nations

Polk's World Bank Directory North American Edition 3801

Canada

Polk's World Bank Directory North American Edition 3801

Mexico

Polk's World Bank Directory North American Edition 3801

United States

Polk's World Bank Directory North American Edition 3801
Washington Financial Reports 4887

HOLIDAYS AND VACATIONS. *See* Housing, Vacation, and Retirement Homes. Travel and Resorts

HOME APPLIANCES. *See* Home Furnishings. Types, eg, Electrical Appliances. Gas Appliances

HOME ECONOMICS

What's New In Home Economics 4963

HOME ENTERTAINMENT ELECTRONIC EQUIPMENT

Electronic Technician Dealer 1638
Videocassette & CATV Newsletter 4854

HOME FURNISHINGS. *See also* Beds, Bedding, and Mattresses. Carpets and Rugs. Curtains and Draperies. Lamps and Lighting

Appliance Magazine 284
Appliance Manufacturer 285
Contract 1185
Gift & Housewares Buyers 2226
Happi 2341.01
Home & Auto 2383
Housewares 2404
Housewares Promotions 2407
Mart 3144.01
Mingay's Price Service—Appliance Edition 3236
Mingay's Retailer & Merchandiser 3238
National Electronic Injury Surveillance Systems (NEISS) Data Highlights 3373
Professional Furniture Merchant 3888
Trade Practice Rules 4668
United Nations Industrial Development Organization Guides to Information Sources. UNIDO/LIB/SER.D/4— Information Sources on the Furniture and Joinery Industry 4771

HOME FURNISHINGS, IMPORTS AND EXPORTS

Housewares Incorporating Gifts and Fancy Goods 2405

HOME LOAN BANK BOARD, FEDERAL (US)

Federal Home Loan Bank Board Journal 1926
Savings and Home Financing Source Book 4184

HOME REPAIRS AND ALTERATIONS

Building Conservation 634.01
Repair and Remodeling Cost Data 4062.01
Residential Alterations and Repairs. C50 4096

HONEY

Honey Production 2385

HONG KONG

Apparel Magazine 282.01
Hong Kong Cable 2386
Hong Kong Enterprise 2387
Hong Kong Trader 2388
Toys Magazine 4645.01

HORSE RACING

Managing the Leisure Facility   3095.03

HORTICULTURE.   *See also*
Gardening Equipment. Landscaping.
Ornamental Crops. Plants and Trees.
Seeds (Crop)

Agricultural Engineering Abstracts   98
Green Europe   2264
Lawn & Garden Marketing   2978.01

HOSIERY

Directory of Wool, Hosiery & Fabrics
   1462.01
Hosiery Statistics   2389
Trade Practice Rules   4668

HOSPITALS.   *See also* Medicine and
Health. Nurses and Nursing. Physicians
and Surgeons

Cross-Reference   1261
Hospitals   2396
Hospital Week   2398

Australia

Australian Hospital   402
Australian Hospitals and Health
   Services Yearbook   403

Canada

Health Care   2356.02

Great Britain

Health and Personal Social Services
   Statistics for England   2354

United States

American Hospital Association Guide
   to the Health Care Field   178
Fitch Hospital and Other Non-profit
   Institutional Ratings   2053
From the State Capitals: Institutional
   Building   2176
Hospital Statistics: Data from the
   American Hospital Association
   Annual Survey   2397
National Hospital Economic Activity
   3380
Trustee   4728

Wales

Health and Personal Social Services
   Statistics for Wales   2355

HOSPITALS, FINANCES

Fitch Hospital and Other Non-profit
   Institutional Ratings   2053

Hospital Statistics: Data from the
   American Hospital Association
   Annual Survey   2397
National Hospital Economic Activity
   3380
Trustee   4728

HOSPITALS, LAW ON.   *See also*
specific laws

Hospital Medical Staff   2395
Hospital Week   2398

HOSPITALS, STAFF

Cross-Reference   1261
Hospital Medical Staff   2395

HOSPITALS, VOLUNTEER PROGRAMS

Volunteer Leader   4868

HOTELS AND MOTELS

Business Travel Costs Worldwide
   724.01
Financial Times World Hotel Directory
   2030
Hotel, Restaurant and Catering
   Supplies   2401
Institutions/VFM   2603
Lodging Hospitality   3040
Motel/Hotel "Insider"   3323
Multinational Executive Travel
   Companion   3335
Travel Weekly   4706
Trend of Business in the Lodging
   Industry   4715
Trends in the Hotel Industry   4718
World Travel Directory   5084

Australia

Hospitality   2393
Hotel, Motel, and Travel Directory
   2400

Canada

Trend of Business in Hotels (Canada)
   4714

Far East

Hotel, Motel, and Travel Directory
   2400

Great Britain

Daltons Weekly   1315
Hotel & Catering Equipment &
   Supplies   2399
Leisure, Recreation and Tourism
   Abstracts   3004.01
Travel Trade Directory   4702

New York City

Registry of Manhattan Office Spaces
   4055

HOTELS AND MOTELS, RATES

Europe (West)

West European Living Costs 1977
   4952

HOUSE ORGANS.   *See* Periodicals

HOUSEHOLD EQUIPMENT.   *See*
Home Furnishings

HOUSING.   *See also* Buildings,
Residential. Construction. Home
Repairs and Alterations. Mortgages

Downtown Idea Exchange   1505
Housing   2407.01
Institute for Social Research Newsletter
   2594
Journal of Regional Science   2879
Journal of Urban Analysis   2900
Lawyers Title News   2991
National Assn of Mutual Savings
   Banks' Annual Report   3359
Professional Builder   3883

Alabama

Alabama Economic Abstract   135

Europe

Annual Bulletin of Housing and
   Building Statistics for Europe   241

Florida

Florida Outlook   2068
Florida Statistical Abstract   2069

Great Britain

Housing and Construction Statistics
   2409
Property Journal   3901

Illinois

Chicagoland Development   936

Louisiana

Louisiana Economy   3048

New York City

New York City Business Fact Book
   Part 2: Population & Housing   3475

New York State

New York State Business Fact Book
   Part 2: Population & Housing   3482

New Zealand

Life and Business in New Zealand
3011

United States

Community Development Digest   1049
Consumer Information Catalog   1154
Economic Briefs   1541
Federal Home Loan Bank Board
Journal   1926
From the State Capitals: Housing and
Redevelopment   2174
Housing Affairs Letter   2408
Housing & Development Reporter
2410
Housing Completions   2412
Housing Market Report   2413
Housing Vacancies H111   2416
Jenkins Mobile Industry News Letter
2805
Real Estate Newsletter   4023.01
Reference Manual on Population and
Housing Statistics from the Census
Bureau, 1977   4042
Savings and Home Financing Source
Book   4184 ·
Savings and Loan Fact Book   4185
SREA Briefs   4368.01
United States Housing Markets   4804

HOUSING, CONDOMINIUMS

Condominium Lenders Guide   1096.01
Digest of State Land Sales Regulation
1392
Rental House & Condo Investor
4061.01

HOUSING, EQUAL OPPORTUNITY

Equal Opportunity in Housing   1736

HOUSING, GOVERNMENT REGULATIONS AND PROGRAMS

Community Development Digest   1049
From the State Capitals: Housing and
Redevelopment   2174
Housing Affairs Letter   2408
Housing & Development   2410
Jenkins Mobile Industry News Letter
2805
SREA Briefs   4368.01
Urban Affairs Reports   4829

Canada

Digest of State Land Sales Regulation
1392

United States

Digest of State Land Sales Regulation
1392

HOUSING, HOUSING STARTS

Housing Starts C20   2415
New Residential Construction in
Selected Standard Metropolitan
Statistical Areas C21   3460

California

California Construction Trends   733

United States

Construction Reports Housing Starts
1141
Economic Briefs   1541
Housing Completions   2412
Housing Units Authorized by Building
Permits and Public Contracts
2415.01
United States Housing Markets   4804

HOUSING, MANAGERS

Managing Housing Letter   3095.01

HOUSING, MOBILE HOMES

Jenkins Mobile Industry News Letter
2805
Manufactured Housing Newsletter
3106

HOUSING, MULTIFAMILY

Apartment Management Report   274
Apartment Owners & Managers Assn
of America Newsletter   275
Housing Starts C20   2415
Market Absorption of Apartments
H-130   3125
Multihousing News   3332

HOUSING, PREFABRICATED

Manufactured Housing Newsletter
3106

HOUSING, PRICES

Existing Home Sales Series   1813
Price Index of New One-Family Houses
Sold C27   3839

Europe (West)

West European Living Costs   4952

Great Britain

Housing and Construction Statistics
2409

HOUSING, PUBLIC

From the State Capitals: Housing and
Redevelopment   2174

HOUSING, RENTALS

Housing Vacancies   2416
Market Absorption of Apartments.
H-130   3125
Rental House & Condo Investor
4061.01
United States Housing Markets   4804

HOUSING, SALES

Economic Briefs   1541
Existing Home Sales Series   1813
New One-Family Houses Sold and For
Sale C25   3457
United States Housing Markets   4804

HOUSING, VACANCY RATE

Economic Briefs   1541
United States Housing Markets   4804

HOUSING, VACATION AND RETIREMENT HOMES

Fitch Hospital and Other Non-profit
Institutional Ratings   2053
Homes Overseas   2384

HUMAN RELATIONS

Abstract Newsletters, Behavior &
Society   2.05
Executive's Personal Development
Letter   1808
Manage   3067
Personnel Management Abstracts   3746
Training   4684

HUMAN RELATIONS, MINORITIES

Journal of Non-White Concerns in
Personnel and Guidance   2870

HUMAN RESOURCES MANAGEMENT. *See* Human Relations

HUMAN RIGHTS

European Human Rights Reports
1776
Legislative Review   3001

HUMANITIES. *See* Arts and Humanities

HYDROCARBONS

Hydrocarbons: Monthly Bulletin   2431

HYDRO ENERGY. *See* Energy, Hydro

HYDROGRAPHY (US)

Abstract Newsletters, Ocean
Technology & Engineering   2.25

HYDROLOGY

Earth Surface Processes and Landforms
1522
Hydraulics & Pneumatics   2430

IBRD. *See* International Bank for
Reconstruction and Development
(IBRD) (World Bank)

ICC. *See* Interstate Commerce
Commission (ICC) (US)

ICSID. *See* International Centre for
Settlement of Investment Disputes

IDAHO

From the State Capitals   2169-2191
Idaho: Manufacturing Directory,
1978–79   2431.06
Idaho Statistical Abstract, 1980, 3rd
edition   2432
State and Local Taxes   4386
State Legislative Reporting Service
4396
State Tax Reports   4413

IFC. *See* International Finance
Corporation

ILLINOIS

Chicago: Geographic Edition, 1981
935.01
From the State Capitals   2169-2191
Illinois Economic Data Sheets   2438
Illinois Manufacturers Directory, 1981
2438.01
Illinois Services Directory, 1980–81
2438.02
State and Local Taxes   4386
State Legislative Reporting Service
4396
State Tax Reports   4413

ILLINOIS, UNIVERSITY Of

Illinois Agricultural Economics   2435
Illinois Research   2439

IMF. *See* International Monetary
Fund

IMMIGRATION AND EMIGRATION

International Tax Haven Directory
2731

Canada

Canada Manpower and Immigration
Review   758

Great Britain

Control of Immigration: Statistics
1190

New Zealand

Life and Business in New Zealand
3011

Switzerland

Swiss–American Chamber of
Commerce. Yearbook   4522

IMPORT–EXPORT COMPANIES.

See also Imports and Exports. Foreign
Trade

Eximbank Record   1812
Trade Names Dictionary   4665

Australia

Australian Directory of Exports   394

Great Britain

Export Services   1832
Sell's British Exporters   4258

Korea (South)

Korean Trade Directory   2921

Puerto Rico

Official Industrial Directory for Puerto
Rico   3585

United States

United States–Italy Trade Directory
4808

IMPORTS AND EXPORTS.   *See also*
Foreign Trade

Business International (BI) Data   697
Confederation of British Industry (CBI)
Overseas Reports   1103
Export Administration Report   1819
Export Shipping Manual   1851
Foreign Market Reports Index   2134
Manufacturers' Agent   3107
Market Share Reports   3142

Random Lengths Export   4002.01
Statistics of Foreign Trade, Series C:
Annual Table by Commodity
4453.02
Thapar's First International Import and
Export Directory of the World   4605
Verified Directory of Manufacturers'
Representatives, 1977 edition   4847
Whaley–Eaton Foreign Letter   4959
Yearbook of Internaional Trade
Statistics   5094

Africa

Foreign Trade Statistics for Africa—
Series A—Direction of Trade   2140
Foreign Trade Statistics for Africa—
Series B—Trade by Commodity
2141
Research Reports   4092

American Nations

Caribbean Year Book, 1977–78   864
Latin America Commodities Report
2972
Research Reports   4092

Australia

Australian Directory of Exports   394
Australian Trading News   420
Exports, Australia   1828
Imports   2443
Imports Cleared for Home
Consumption   2445
Tariff Brief   4530

Belgium

Belgian American Trade Review   520
BRU Export Finance Service   631
United States–Belgium Trade Directory,
1980–81 edition   4794.01

California

California International Trade   737
California International Trade Register,
1980–81   737.01

Cambodia

Business China   674

Canada

Action Canada France   45
Bank of Canada Review   485
British Columbia Export/Import
Opportunities   601.02
Canada–United Kingdom Trade News
770

Summary of US Export Administration
Regulations   4494
Summary of US Export and Import
Merchandise Trade   4495
United States Airborne Exports and
General Imports FT986   4793
United States–Belgium Trade Directory,
1980–81 edition   4794.01
United States Exports—Domestic
Merchandise SIC-Based Products by
World Areas FT610   4798
United States Exports Commodity by
Country   4798
United States Export Weekly   4800
United States General Imports Schedule
A Commodity by Country FT135
4802
United States–Italy Trade Directory
4808
United States Trade—Puerto Rico and
United States Possessions FT800
4821
United States Waterborne Exports and
General Imports FT985   4822

Vietnam

Business China   674

West Indies

Caribbean Year Book, 1977–78   864

Yugoslavia

Business News   714

IMPORTS AND EXPORTS, FINANCE

Chase World Guide for Exporters and
Export Credit Reports   918
Export Times   1854
Foreign Credit Insurance Assn (FCIA)
News   2112

Belgium

BRU Export Finance Service   631

France

BRU Export Finance Service   631

Germany (West)

BRU Export Finance Service   631

Great Britain

BRU Export Finance Service   631
Export Services   1832

Italy

BRU Export Finance Service   631

Japan

BRU Export Finance Service   631

Netherlands

BRU Export Finance Service   631

South Africa

BRU Export Finance Service   631

United States

BRU Export Finance Service   631

IMPORTS AND EXPORTS, GOVERNMENT REGULATIONS

Exporters' Encyclopaedia—World
Marketing Guide   1822
International Trade News Letter   2740

Canada

Export and Import Permits Act
Handbook   1820
Importweek   2475

Great Britain

Croner's Reference Book for Exporters
1256

Japan

Japan External Trade Organization
(JETRO) Marketing Series   2802

United States

Business International Washington
(BIW)   699.01
CECON Trade News   873
Export Administration Regulations
1818
International Trade Reporter's Import
Weekly   2740.01
United States Export Weekly   4800

IMPORTS OF GOODS AND SERVICES.   See Imports and Exports. Foreign Trade

INCENTIVE SALES.   See Sales and Salespeople, Incentive Sales

INCOME.   See also Taxation, Income Tax

Institute for Social Research Newsletter
2594

International Journal of Social
Economics   2696
Review of Income and Wealth   4123
Yearbook of National Accounts
Statistics   5096

Alabama

Alabama Economic Abstract   135

Arizona

Arizona Statistical Abstract   317.03

California

Economic Outlook: California Report
1558
Union-Tribune Annual Review of San
Diego Business Activity   4753
Union-Tribune Index   4754

Canada

Canada Tax Service   769
Income After Tax, Distribution by Size
in Canada   2480
Income Distributions by Size in Canada
2481
Income Distributions by Size in
Canada, Preliminary Estimates   2482
Market Research Handbook   3138
National Income & Expenditure
Accounts   3381
Perspectives Canada III   3753.01
Saskatchewan's Financial & Economic
Position   4183
Survey of Buying Power   4510
System of National Accounts—National
Income and Expenditure Accounts
4526

Florida

Florida Statistical Abstract   2069

Hawaii

First Hawaiian Bank Economic
Indicators   2047

Great Britain

British Economy in Figures   611
Economic Trends   1573
Family Expenditure Survey   1883
Inland Revenue Statistics   2579
National Income and Expenditure
"Blue Book"   3382
Social Trends   4321
Survey of Personal Income   4517

Louisiana

Louisiana Economy   3048

Australia

East Asian Economic Service   1522.01
Midas   3215

Bolivia

Latin American Service   2976.01

Brazil

Latin American Service   2976.01

California

Economic Outlook: California Report
1558

Chile

Latin American Service   2976.01

Colombia

Latin American Service   2976.01

Ecuador

Latin American Service   2976.01

Far East

East Asian Economic Service   1522.01

Great Britain

Britain and Overseas   596

Mexico

Latin American Service   2976.01

Peru

Latin American Service   2976.01

United States

Citibank Monthly Economic Letter
949
Economic Outlook: US Report   1560
Lanston Letter   2966
Monthly Tax Features   3303

Venezuela

Latin American Service   2976.01

Uruguay

Latin American Service   2976.01

INFORMATION RETRIEVAL. *See
also* Automation. Computer-Aided
Information Systems

ABI/INFORM   2.01
Abstract Newsletters, Administration
and Management   2.03

Access Reports-Privacy   9.02
ADP Network Services   60
The Annual Review of Information
Science and Technology/Volume
15,1980   258
Bulletin of the American Society for
Information Science   645.01
Canadian Office   822
Computer Network of Databases   1081
Computers and People   1087
Data Management   1335
Directory of Special Libraries and
Information Centers   1457
Electric Data Processing, EDP Industry
Report   1590
Encyclopedia Americana, International
edition   1668
Encyclopedia of Information Systems
and Services, 2nd edition   1674
Energy Information Locator   1684
IDP Report   2433.02
Information & Management   2568.01
Information and Records Management
2570
Information Hotline   2572
Information Industry & Technology
Service   2573
Information Industry Market Place: An
International Directory of
Information Products and Services
2573.01
Information Society   2575
Infosystems   2576
International Guide to Library,
Archival, and Information Science
Associations   2684
Journal of Documentation   2844.02
Journal of Purchasing & Materials
Management   2876
Journal of Systems/Management   2886
Journal of the American Society for the
Information Science   2888.01
Management Accounting   3069
Modern Office Procedures   3257
New Encyclopedia Britannica, 15th
edition   3438
Omega   3619
Online   3619.02
Online Bibliographic Databases: An
International Directory   3619.03
Predicasts Terminal System   3830
Prestel   3837
Proceedings of the 1972 National
Operations and Automation
Conference—"The Common
Denominator—Management"   3858
SDC Search Service   4212.01
Stores   4476
Telecommunications Policy   4583
Washington Information Directory,
1980–81   4887.02

INLAND SHIPPING. *See* Ships and
Shipping, Inland

INSECTICIDES. *See* Pesticides and
Pests

INSIDER TRADING. *See* Stocks and
Bonds, Insider Trading

**INSTITUTE OF DIRECTORS
(AUSTRALIA)**

Australian Director   393

INSTITUTIONAL INVESTORS. *See*
Stocks and Bonds, Institutional
Investors Investments, Management

INSTITUTIONS AND AGENCIES.
See also Foundations. Names

World Guide to Abbreviations of
Organizations, 5th edition   5065
Yearbook of International
Organizations   5093

**INSTITUTIONS AND AGENCIES,
NONPROFIT.** *See also* Foundations

Association Taxation   342
Fitch Hospital and Other Non-profit
Institutional Ratings   2053
Fund Raising Management   2200
Fundraising Weekly   2200.01
Law of Associations: An Operating
Legal Manual for Executives and
Counsel   2980
Tax-Exempt Organizations   4552

**INSTRUMENTS AND CONTROL
SYSTEMS**

Control & Instrumentation   1187.01
Control Equipment Master   1188
Instruments and Control Systems   2606
International Journal of Control   2690
Update   4826

INSULATION

Insulation   2607
Roofing Siding Insulation.
Incorporating Solar Contractor   4141

INSURANCE. *See also* Actuaries.
Actuarial Methods. Insurance Agents
and Brokers. Insurance Companies.
Labor, Employee Benefits, Labor,
Workmen's Compensation. Social
Security. Subjects subhead Insurance

Advanced Underwriting Service   63
Best's Directory of Recommended
Insurance Attorneys   526.01

Chartered Property & Casualty
  Underwriters (CPCU) Annals   916
Computer Network of Databases   1081
Dictionary of Insurance   1380
Equifax News   1737
Estate Planner's Letter   1747
European Directory of Business
  Information Sources & Services
  1773
Financial Times World Insurance Year
  Book   2031
Foreign Credit Insurance Assn (FCIA)
  2112
Institutional Investor   2601
Insurance Forum   2622
Insurance Guide   2623
Insurance Industry Newsletter   2624
Insurance Literature   2630
Insurance Marketing   2632
Insurance Periodicals Index   2633
Insurance Record   2634
International Insurance Monitor   2685
Journal of Risk and Insurance   2882
John Liner Letter   3020
Lloyd's List   3032.03
Money Management Unitholder   3270
Mutual Insurance Bulletin   3351
Policy, Form, & Manual Analysis
  Service   3793
Tax Letter Service   4558
Weekly Underwriter   4942

Australia

Australian Business Law Review   388
Cover Note   1240
Insurance and Other Private Finance
  2611
Insurance Record of Australia and New
  Zealand   2635

California

California Services Register, 1981
  738.04

Canada

Almanac and Directory 1981   148.01
Canadian Insurance   806
Hines Insurance Adjusters   2372
Hines Insurance Counsel   2373
Insurance Institute of Canada Annual
  Report   2626
Underwriting Results in Canada   4742

Europe

European Directory of Business
  Information Sources & Services
  1773

Great Britain

Chartered Insurance Institute (CII)
  Journal   914
Insurance Business Statistics   2613
Money Management   3269
Money Management and Unitholder
  3270
Policy Holder Insurance Journal   3794

Korea (South)

Korean Trade Directory   2921

Middle East

Businessman's Guide to the Arab
  World   709

New Zealand

Australian Business Law Review   388
Insurance Record of Australia and New
  Zealand   2635
New Zealand Insurance Statistics   3508

United States

Adjusters' Reference Guide   53
Hines Insurance Adjusters   2372
Hines Insurance Counsel   2373
Insurance Update   2636.01
Proceedings of the NAIC   3857.01
Standard—Northeast's Insurance
  Weekly   4376
United States Banker   4794

INSURANCE, ACCIDENT

Insurance Law Reports: Life, Health,
  and Accident   2629

INSURANCE, ANNUITIES

Best's Retirement Income Guide
  538.01

INSURANCE, BUSINESS

Best's Underwriting Guide   543
Business Insurance   695
Canadian Risk Management and
  Business Insurance   830
Corporate Insurance in Canada   1209
DLB Advanced Sales Reference Service
  1473
International Commercial Financing
  Intelligence   2668
Security Letter   4242
Tax Letter Service   4558

INSURANCE, CASUALTY

Best's Casualty Loss Reserve
  Development   525
Best's Insurance Management Reports:
  Property–Casualty Edition   529

Best's Insurance Report:
  Property–Casualty   531
Best's Key Rating Guide   533
Best's Reproductions of Convention
  Statements   538
Best's Review: Property–Casualty
  Insurance Edition   540
Best's Underwriting Newsletter   544
Fire, Casualty, & Surety Bulletins
  2042
From the State Capitals: Insurance
  Regulation   2177
General Insurance Guide   2213
Insurance Advocate   2608
Insurance Law Reports: Fire and
  Casualty   2628
Insurance Service   2636
Journal of American Insurance   2822
National Underwriter   3411
Rough Notes   4142
Stone and Cox General Insurance
  Register   4473

INSURANCE, CLAIMS ADJUSTING

Best's Directory of Recommended
  Insurance Adjusters   526
Best's Directory of Recommended
  Insurance Attorneys   526.01
Canadian Independent Adjuster   800

INSURANCE COMPANIES, FINANCES

Best's Casualty Loss Reserve
  Development   525

INSURANCE, DISABILITY

Health Insurance Underwriter   2361
Payroll Guide   3710
Unemployment Insurance Reports
  4744

INSURANCE, FINANCES

Best's Flitcraft Compendium   527
Best's Insurance Management Reports
  529
Consensus of Insiders   1119
Insurance Advocate   2608
Insurance Company Funds   2616
Probe   3856
Vickers Guide to Insurance Company
  Portfolios—Common Stocks   4851

INSURANCE, FIRE

Best's Aggregates & Average   524
Fire and Loss Statistics for the United
  Kingdom   2041
Fire, Casualty, & Surety Bulletins
  2042

From the State Capitals: Insurance
Regulation 2177
Insurance Advocate 2608
Insurance Law Reports: Fire and
Casualty 2628
Mutual Insurance Bulletin 3351

INSURANCE, GOVERNMENT REGULATIONS, LAWS AND PROGRAMS. *See also* Medicaid. Medicare. Social Security

Best's Directory of Recommended
Insurance Adjusters 526
Best's Directory of Recommended
Insurance Attorneys 526.01
DLB Advanced Sales Reference Service
1473
Insurance Advocate 2608
Insurance Casebook 2614
Insurance Counsel Journal 2617
Insurance Law Reports: Life, Health,
and Accident 2629
Law of Liability Insurance 2983
Probe 3856
Product Liability International 3874
World Insurance Report 5068

Canada

Canadian Insurance Law Reports 807
Canadian Insurance Law Service 808

Great Britain

Insurance Record 2634
Lloyd's Law Reports 3032.02
Policy Holder Insurance Journal 3794

United States

Automobile Insurance 428
Federal Aids to Financing 1911
From the State Capitals: Insurance
Regulation 2177
Insurance Department Service 2618
Insurance Law Reports: Fire and
Casualty 2628
Insurance Law Reports: Life, Health,
and Accident 2629
Unemployment Insurance Reports
4744
Weekly Underwriter 4942

INSURANCE, GROUP PLANS

Employee Benefit Plan Review (EBPR)
Research Reports 1644

INSURANCE, HEALTH. *See also* Medicaid. Medicare

Best's Insurance Management Reports
528

Best's Insurance Report 530
Best's Review: Life/Health Insurance
Edition 539
Chartered Life Underwriters (CLU)
Journal 915
Executive Compensation Letter 1799
From the State Capitals: Insurance
Regulation 2177
General Insurance Guide 2213
Health Insurance Underwriter 2361
Insurance Advocate 2608
Insurance Industry Newsletter 2624
Insurance Law Reports: Life, Health,
and Accident 2629
Insurance Sales 2635.01
National Health Insurance Reports
3378
National Underwriter 3411
National Underwriter: Life & Health
Insurance Edition 3412
Source Book of Health Insurance Data
4333
Textbook for Employee Benefit Plan
Trustees, Administrators, and
Advisors 4598
Who Writes What 5000

INSURANCE, LIABILITY

Agent's & Buyer's Guide 87
Business Insurance 695
Canadian Risk Management and
Business Insurance 830
Insurance Facts 2620
Insurance Industry Newsletter 2624
Journal of Insurance 2862
Law of Liability Insurance 2983
Product Liability International 3874
World Insurance Report 5068

INSURANCE, LIFE

Best's Agents Guide to Life Insurance
Companies 523
Best's Aggregates & Average 524
Best's Insurance Management Reports
528
Best's Insurance Report Life–Health
530
Best's Review: Life/Health Insurance
Edition 539
Canadian Insurance 806
Chartered Life Underwriters (CLU)
Journal 915
DLB Advanced Sales Reference Service
1473
Economic Education Bulletin 1550
Federal Aids to Financing 1911
In Focus 2566.01
Insurance Advocate 2608
Insurance Industry Newsletter 2624
Insurance Sales 2635.01

Journal of the Institute of Actuaries
2892
Life Financial Reports 3013
Life Insurance Fact Book 3014
Life Rates & Data 3017
Market Builder Magazine 3125.01
National Underwriter 3411
National Underwriter: Life & Health
Insurance Edition 3412
Policy Statistics Service 3796
Stone and Cox Life Insurance Tables
4474
Tax Facts on Life Insurance 4553
Who Writes What 5000

Canada

Canadian Insurance 806
Choosing Life 945.01
Stone and Cox Life Insurance Tables
4474

Great Britain

Savings Market 4190

United States

Best's Settlement Options Manual 542
From the State Capitals: Insurance
Regulation 2177
Insurance Law Reports: Life, Health,
and Accident 2629
Insurance Service 2636
Probe 3856

INSURANCE, MARINE

Best's Aggregates & Averages 524
Commerce Yearbook of Ports, Shipping
& Shipbuilding 996.03
Fairplay International Shipping Weekly
1880
Fire, Casualty, & Surety Bulletins
2042
Insurance Facts 2620

INSURANCE, NO-FAULT

Law of Liability Insurance 2983
New York No-Fault Arbitration
Reports 3478

INSURANCE, PROPERTY

Agent's & Buyer's Guide 87
Best's Casualty Loss Reserve
Development 525
Best's Insurance Management Reports:
Property–Casualty Edition 529
Best's Insurance Report:
Property–Casualty 531
Best's Key Rating Guide 533

Best's Reproductions of Convention
　　Statements　538
Best's Review: Property–Casualty
　　Insurance Edition　540
Best's Underwriting Newsletter　544
Business Insurance　695
Canadian Risk Management and
　　Business Insurance　830
General Insurance Guide　2213
Insurance Facts　2620
Insurance Industry Newsletter　2624
Insurance Service　2636
Journal of American Insurance　2822
Journal of Insurance　2862
National Underwriter　3411
Rough Notes　4142
Stone and Cox General Insurance
　　Register　4473
World Insurance Report　5068

INSURANCE, REINSURANCE

Canadian Insurance　806
Re Report　4078.01
World Insurance Report　5068

INSURANCE, RISK MANAGEMENT

Best's Underwriting Guide　543
Canadian Risk Management and
　　Business Insurance　830
International Country Risk Guide
　　2670
Risk Management　4134
Weekly Underwriter　4942
Who's Who in Insurance　4988
Who's Who in Risk Management
　　4990

INSURANCE, TAXATION

Canadian Insurance　806
DLB Advanced Sales Reference Service
　　1473
Guidebook to Massachusetts Taxes
　　2275
Insurance Guide　2623
Life Insurance Planning　3016
Tax Facts on Life Insurance　4553

INSURANCE, UNDERWRITING

Best's Aggregates & Averages　524
Best's Underwriting Guide　543
Best's Underwriting Newsletter　544
Canadian Underwriter　845
Provincial Results (Underwriting)
　　3908
Underwriting Results in Canada　4742

INSURANCE AGENTS AND BROKERS

DLB Agent's Service　1474
Insurance Brokers' Monthly and
　　Insurance Advisor　2612
Insurance Forum　2622
Insurance Guide　2623
Insurance Industry Newsletter　2624
Producer News　3862
Standard—Northeast's Insurance
　　Weekly　4376
Who's Who Among Professional
　　Insurance Agents　4976
Who's Who in Insurance　4988

New York City Metropolitan Area

Telephone Tickler　4587

New Zealand

Insurance Directory of New Zealand
　　2619

INSURANCE ASSOCIATION, BRITISH

Insurance Record　2634

INSURANCE COMMISSIONERS, NATIONAL ASSN OF

Financial Review of Alien Insurers
　　2018.01
Proceedings of the NAIC　3857.01

INSURANCE COMPANIES

Best's Agents Guide to Life Insurance
　　Companies　523
Best's Key Rating Guide　533
Federal Aids to Financing　1911
Financial Review of Alien Insurers
　　2018.02
Fire, Casualty, & Surety Bulletins
　　2042
Insurance Almanac　2610
Insurance Industry Newsletter　2624
Life Financial Reports　3013
Who's Who Among Professional
　　Insurance Agents　4976

Canada

Corporate Insurance in Canada　1209
Stone and Cox General Insurance
　　Register　4473

Europe

Europe's 5,000 Largest Companies
　　1792

Great Britain

Insurance Companies and Private
　　Pension Funds　2615

New York City Metropolitan Area

Telephone Tickler　4587

New Zealand

Insurance Directory of New Zealand
　　2619

INSURANCE COMPANIES, FINANCES

Best's Agents Guide to Life Insurance
　　Companies　523
Best's Flitcraft Compendium　527
Best's Insurance Report: Life–Health
　　530
Best's Insurance Report:
　　Property–Casualty　531
Best's Insurance Securities Research
　　Series　532
Best's Key Rating Guide　533
Best's Market Guide　535
Best's Reproductions of Convention
　　Statements　538
Best's Settlement Options Manual　542
Federal Taxation of Life Insurance
　　Companies　1963
Insurance Company Funds　2616
Life Financial Reports　3013
Moody's Bank and Finance Manual
　　and News Reports　3308
Stone and Cox General Insurance
　　Register　4473
Vickers Guide to Insurance Company
　　Portfolios—Common Stocks　4851
Vickers Guide to Insurance Company
　　Portfolios—Corporate Bonds　4852

INSURANCE COUNSEL, INTERNATIONAL ASSOCIATION OF

Insurance Counsel Journal　2617

INSURANCE INSTITUTE OF CANADA

Insurance Institute of Canada Annual
　　Report　2626

INTER-AMERICAN DEVELOPMENT BANK

Inter-American Development Bank
　　Annual Report　2639
Inter-American Development Bank
　　News　2640

INTEREST RATES

AP–Dow Jones Bankers Report   277
Business International (BI) Data   697
Business International Money Report
   699
Dow Jones International Banking Wire
   1497
International Reports   2727
Public Periodic Releases   3926
Report on Credit Unions   4069
Sound of the Economy   4332

Australia

East Asian Economic Service   1522.01
Bankers' Magazine of Australasia   470

Canada

Bank of Canada Weekly Financial
   Statistics   486

Europe

Euromarket Letter   1763
Monthly Summary of Business
   Conditions in the United Kingdom
   3302

Far East

East Asian Economic Service   1522.01

Great Britain

Economic Trends   1573
Financial Statistics   2020

United States

Capital Market Developments   858
Consumer Credit Guide   1152
Kiplinger Washington Letter   2917
Lanston Letter   2966
Peter Dag Investment Letter   3753.02

INTERIOR DESIGN.   See also fields

Progressive Architecture   3895

INTERNAL REVENUE SERVICE (IRS) (US)

Association Taxation   342
Bank Tax Report   505
Campaign Practices Reports   742
Code and Regulations   976
Compendium of Internal Revenue
   Service Rulings   1061
Corporation Law & Tax Report   1219
Custom House Guide   1285
Federal Income, Gift and Estate
   Taxation   1927
Federal Revenue Forms—With Official
   Instructions   1959

Federal Taxes Service   1968
Federal Tax Forms   1969
How to Analyze, Design and Install an
   Employee Stock Ownership Plan
   2420
How to Handle Tax Audits, Requests
   for Rulings, Fraud Cases and Other
   Procedures Before IRS   2421
Internal Revenue Bulletin   2645
Internal Revenue Manual-Audit &
   Administration   2646
Internal Revenue Service Annual
   Report of the Commissioner of
   Internal Revenue   2647
Internal Revenue Service Chief Counsel
   Annual Report   2648
International Foundation Legal
   Legislative Reporter News Bulletin
   2681
Journal of Pension Planning and
   Compliance   2872
Monthly Digest of Tax Articles   3290
Real Estate Tax Ideas   4026
Tax Practitioners Forum   4567
Tax Research Techniques   4568

INTERNATIONAL AGENCIES.   See also names

Europa Year Book   1767
Government Publications Review   2250
International Year Book and
   Statesmen's Who's Who   2744
Statesman's Year Book, 1980-81 edition
   4408

INTERNATIONAL BANK FOR RECONSTRUCTION AND DEVELOPMENT (IBRD) (WORLD BANK)

Development Forum: Business Edition
   1375
Finance and Development   1988
World Bank Annual Report, 1980
   5043
World Debt Tables   5054

INTERNATIONAL BANKING.   See
Banking and Finance, International

INTERNATIONAL BONDS.   See
Stocks and Bonds, International Bonds

INTERNATIONAL CENTRE FOR SETTLEMENT OF INVESTMENT DISPUTES (ICSID)

International Centre for Settlement of
   Investment Disputes, Annual Report
   2665

INTERNATIONAL COOPERATIVE EFFORTS.   Note: Covers material in all fields

Achievement   39
Agricultural Co-operative Bulletin   95
Agro Service International   116
American Bulletin of International
   Technology Transfer   163
European Industrial Relations Review
   1778
European Report   1786
Government Regulation of Business
   Ethics: International Payoffs   2251
International Bibliography, Information,
   Documentation   2659
International Commercial Arbitration
   2667
International Labour Organization
   Publications   2699
International Law of Development:
   Basic Documents   2701
International Tax Treaties of All
   Nations   2734
International Telecommunications
   Agreements   2735
Investment Laws of the World:
   Developing Nations   2764
Law and Policy of Intergovernmental
   Primary Commodity Agreements
   2978
Libradoc   3007
Marine Policy   3121
Oil and Gas, the North Sea
   Exploitation   3601
Tax Treaties   4573
Transnational Economic and Monetary
   Law: Transactions and Contracts
   4690
World Economic Service   5060

INTERNATIONAL DEVELOPMENT, AGENCY FOR (AID) (US)

Agency for International Development
   Research & Development Abstracts
   86
Development Digest   1373
Proposed Foreign Aid Program,
   Summary Presentation to Congress
   3903

INTERNATIONAL EXPORT ASSOCIATION (GREAT BRITAIN)

Newsletter   3465.03

INTERNATIONAL FINANCE CORPORATION (IFC)

International Finance Corporation
   (IFC), 1980 Annual Report   2679

INTERNATIONAL FLEETS. *See* Ships and Shipping, International Fleets

INTERNATIONAL MONETARY FUND (IMF)

Finance and Development 1988
International Monetary Fund Survey 2709
International Monetary Fund Annual Report on Exchange Restrictions 2711
Midland Bank Review 3227
Transnational Economic and Monetary Law: Transactions and Contracts 4690

INTERNATIONAL MONETARY SYSTEM. *See* Currency

INTERNATIONAL RELATIONS

AP–Dow Jones Financial Wire 280
Defense Week 1355.02
Holt Executive Advisory 2379
International Perspectives 2718
Keesing's Contemporary Archives 2905
Powell Alert 3814
Time 4619

Africa

Africa 77

Canada

International Perspectives 2718

Korea (South)

Korean Trade News 2922

South Africa

South Africa Yearbook 4337

INTERPRETERS. *See* Translators

INTERSTATE COMMERCE COMMISSION (ICC) (US)

Hawkins Motor Carrier-Freight Forward Service 2351
Hawkins Rail Carrier Service 2352
Interstate Commerce Commission Annual Report 2745
Interstate Commerce Commission Practitioners' Journal 2747
Interstate Commerce Commission Reports Decisions of the ICC of the United States 2748

INVENTIONS. *See also* Patents

Abstract Newsletters, Government Inventions for Licensing 2.16

Invention Intelligence 2749
Invention Management 2750
Inventor 2751
Licensing in Foreign and Domestic Operations 3010
Research Disclosure 4087

INVENTORIES. *See also* subjects, eg, Oil, Inventories

Journal of Purchasing & Materials Management 2876
Manufacturers' Shipments, Inventories, and Orders. M3–1 3110
Production & Inventory Control Handbook 3865
Production & Inventory Management 3866
Purchasing Managers Report on Business 3953
Small Business Bibliographies 4299

Canada

Inventories, Shipments and Orders in Manufacturing Industries 2754
Merchandising Inventories 3192
Wholesale Trade 4971

Great Britain

Business Monitor, Production Series 710

United States

Current Surveys—M:D11 Manufacturers' Shipments, Inventories, and Orders 1283
Economic Week 1575

INVENTORS ASSOCIATIONS, INTERNATIONAL FEDERATION OF

Inventor 2751

INVESTIGATORS AND DETECTIVES

Regency International Directory 4045

INVESTMENT ADVISERS ACT OF 1940

Rules and Regulations 4151.01
Securities & Exchange Commission Docket 4227

INVESTMENT BANKERS

Investment Management 2764.01
Northwestern Banker 3545
Security Dealers Directory 4239

INVESTMENT COMPANIES

Moody's Bank and Finance Manual and News Reports 3308
General Information Bulletin 2212
Spectrum One: Investment Company Stock Holdings Survey 4360
Spectrum Two: Investment Company Portfolios 4360.01
Vickers Guide to Investment Company Portfolios 4853

INVESTMENT COMPANY ACT OF 1940

Rules and Regulations 4151.01

INVESTMENT COMPANY INSTITUTE

Mutual Funds Forum 3348

INVESTMENT TRUSTS, REAL ESTATE. *See* Real Estate Investment Trusts

INVESTMENTS (GENERAL). *See also* Investment Bankers. Investment Companies. Financial Analysis. Foreign Investments. Trust Companies. Types, e.g., Real Estate. Stocks and Bonds

Bank Fact Book 474
Bank of England Quarterly Bulletin 488
Barron's 509
Baxter 515
Boardroom Reports 568
Business Periodicals Index 716
Consumer Information Catalog 1154
Dow Jones International News Wire 1499
Euromoney 1765
Financial Analyst's Handbook 1994
Financial Tactics and Terms for the Sophisticated International Investor, 1974 2022
Forecaster 2107
Income Investor 2484
Institutional Investor 2601
Intelligence Digest Business Trends 2638
International Center for Settlement of Investment Disputes, Annual Report 2665
International Licensing 2702
Investment and Business Opportunity News 2760
Investment Bulletin 2761
Investment Laws of the World 2763
Investment Laws of the World: Developing Nations 2764
Investors Chronicle 2770

Investors Review and Financial World
2775
Money Management Unitholder   3270
SAVVY   4190.01
Sophisticated Investor   4330
Statistical Service   4442
Tax Havens of the World   4554
United Business and Investment Report
4755
Value Line Convertible Strategist   4839
VNR Investor's Dictionary   4862.02
Whaley–Eaton Foreign Letter   4959

Africa

Investment Africa   2758

Alaska

Alaska Business News Letter   137
Alaska Industry   139

Arkansas

Financial Trend   2032

Australia

Australian Investment and Economic
Newsletter   405
Handbook for Industrialists   2313
Midas   3215

California

Kiplinger California Letter   2913

Canada

Financial Post Magazine   2013
Financial Post Newspaper   2014
Financial Times of Canada   2027
General Information Bulletin   2212
Investment Statistics: Service Bulletin
2768
Meetings, Conferences & Conventions:
A Financial Post Guide   3188
Money Reporter, Canadian Edition
3272

Europe

Financial Times of Canada   2027

Great Britain

Bank of England Quarterly Bulletin
488
Investment Analyst   2759
Investors Chronicle   2770
Investors Review and Financial World
2775
Money Management   3269
Money Management and Unitholder
3270
Planned Savings   3777

Louisiana

Financial Trend   2032

New Mexico

Financial Trend   2032

New Zealand

New Zealand Financial Times   3503

Oklahoma

Financial Trend   2032

South Africa

Financial Mail   2005

Switzerland

Swiss–American Chamber of
Commerce. Yearbook   4522

Texas

Financial Trend   2032

Third World

International Law of Development:
Basic Documents   2701

United States

Blue Sky Law Reports   566
Business & Capital Reporter   658
Credit and Capital Markets   1244
Financial Times of Canada   2027
Kiplinger Washington Letter   2917
Money Reporter, US Edition   3273
Peter Dag Investment Letter   3753.02
Select Information Exchange (SIE)
Guide to Business & Investment
Books   4255
United States Banker   4794
Venture Captial   4846
Zweig Forecast   5108

INVESTMENTS, MANAGEMENT OF

Institutional Investor   2601
Journal of Portfolio Management   2874

INVESTMENTS, TAXATION

Federal Tax Course   1966
Financial Times Tax Newsletter   2029
Planned Savings   3777
Tax Haven & Investment Report
4553.03

INVESTMENTS, WOMEN

Executive Woman   1811

INVESTOR RELATIONS. *See*
Corporations, Investor Relations

IOWA

From the State Capitals   2169-2191
Iowa Manufacturers Directory, 1979–80
2776.01
State and Local Taxes   4386
State Legislative Reporting Service
4396
State Tax Reports   4413
Statistical Profile of Iowa   4436

IRAN

Developing Business in the Middle East
and North Africa   1371
Iran Economic News   2779
Iran Service   2779.01
Near East Business   3422

IRAQ

Developing Business in the Middle East
and North Africa   1371

IRELAND, NORTHERN. *See also*
Great Britain

Atlas of Ireland   346
Census of Production for Northern
Ireland   877
District Councils, Summary of
Statements of Accounts, Northern
Ireland   1469
Family Expenditure Survey, Northern
Ireland   1884
Northern Ireland Digest of Statistics
3538
Social and Economic Trends in
Northern Ireland   4311
Statistical Review of Farming in
Northern Ireland   4440

IRELAND, REPUBLIC OF

Atlas of Ireland   346
Confederation of Irish Industry (CII)
Economic Trends   1106
Confederation of Irish Industry
(CII)/ESRI Business Forecast   1107
Food Processing in Ireland   2095
Ireland International Reference Manual
2779.02
Irish Statistical Bulletin   2781
Selling Today   4257
Statistical Abstract of Ireland   4419
Trade Statistics of Ireland   4676

IRISH STOCK EXCHANGE

Analyst's Service   216
British Company Service   610
Registrar's Service   4054

IRON AND STEEL

Achievement   39
Inventories of Steel Mill Shapes M33-3
   2753
Iron and Steel   2784
Iron and Steel International   2786
Statistics of World Trade in Steel
   4456
Steel Service   4461
United Nations Industrial Development
   Organization (UNIDO) Guides to
   Information Sources.
   UNIDO/LIB/SER.D/Rev.1—
   Information Sources on the Iron and
   Steel Industry   4767.09
Worldcasts   5047

Canada

Amer Iron & Steel Institute. Annual
   Statistics Report   193
Primary Iron and Steel   3843

Europe

Annual Bulletin of Steel Statistics for
   Europe   242
Pig-irons and Steel: Basis Prices   3771

European Communities

Euro-Abstracts: Scientific and Technical
   Publications and Patents, Sections I
   and II. Section I: Euratom and EEC
   Research Section II: Coal and Steel
   1759
Iron and Steel: Monthly Statistics
   2787

Great Britain

Achievement   39

Japan

Zosen   5107

United States

Amer Iron & Steel Institute. Annual
   Statistics Report   193
Metals Daily   3196.01
Steel Mill Products   1977

IRRIGATION

Irrigation Age   2789

ISRAEL

British–Israel Trade Journal   615

ISRAEL DISCOUNT BANK

Business Review and Economic News
   from Israel   720

ITALY

Economic News from Italy   1556
Italy: An Economic Profile   2793

JAPAN

Focus Japan   2074
Japanese Breakthroughs   2797.01
Japanese Economic Service   2797.02
Japan External Trade Organization
   (JETRO) Business Information Series
   2801
Japan External Trade Organization
   (JETRO) Marketing Series   2802
Japan International Reference Manual
   2802.02
Japan Letter   2803

JEWELS AND JEWELRY

Accent   6
Department Store Jewelry Buyers
   Directory   1364
Gifts & Tablewares   2227
Jewelers' Circular-Keystone   2807
Jewelry Newsletter International   2808
National Jeweler   3389

JOB MARKET. *See* Labor

JOBS. *See* Labor

JOHANNESBURG STOCK
EXCHANGE (SOUTH AFRICA)

Johannesburg Stock Exchange Monthly
   Bulletin   2815

JOURNALISM. *See also* Periodicals.
Publications. Newspapers

Media Reporter   3178
United Kingdom News Contact
   Directory   4760.01

JUDICIARY. *See also* Court
Reporters. Legal Services. Specific
courts, eg, Supreme Court (US)

Canada

Canada Federal Court Reports   748
Canada Supreme Court Reports   766

Europe

European Commercial Cases   1769

European Economic Community

Common Market Law Reports   1037
Reports of Cases Before the Court
   4075

United States

Federal Taxes Citator   1967
Federal Taxes Service   1968
Hawkins Civil Aeronautics Board
   Service   2349
Hawkins Federal Maritime Commission
   Service   2350
Hawkins Motor Carrier—Freight
   Forwarder Service   2351
Hawkins Rail Carrier Service   2352
Inheritance Taxes   2578
Legal Contents   2995.01
Standard Research Consultants (SRC)
   Quarterly Reports   4378
Who's Who in American Law   4978

KANSAS

From the State Capitals   2169-2191
Kansas Manufacturers & Products
   Directory, 1980–81   2904.01
Kansas State Industrial Directory, 1981
   2904.02
State and Local Taxes   4386
State Legislative Reporting Service
   4396
State Tax Reports   4413

KENTUCKY

From the State Capitals   2169-2191
Kentucky Manufacturers Directory,
   1981   2908.02
Kentucky State Industrial Directory,
   '81   2908.03
State and Local Taxes   4386
State Legislative Reporting Service
   4396
State Tax Reports   4413

KEOGH PLAN

How to Set Up and Run a Qualified
   Pension or Profit Sharing Plan for a
   Small or Medium Size Business
   2424
Money Reporter US Edition   3273
Spencer's Retirement Plan Service
   4362

KITCHENS

Domestic Heating   1492
Housewares Promotions   2407
Kitchen Business   2918
Kitchen Planning   2919

KNITTING AND KNIT GOODS

Drapers Record   1505.02

LABELS AND LABELING

Food Drug Cosmetic Law Reports
2084
Nutrition Action 3558.01
Trade Regulation Reports 4671
Trade Regulation Rules 4672

LABOR (GENERAL). *See also* Blue
Collar Workers. Labor-Management
Relations. Labor Unions. Personnel
Management. Personnel Policies.
Professions. White Collar Workers.
Work Study. Subjects subhead Labor

Ball State Business Review 454
Benefits International 521
Bulletin of Labour Statistics 645
Business & Public Affairs 665
Business International (BI) Data 697
CIS Abstracts Bulletin 948
Dow Jones–Irwin Business Almanac
1501
Enterprise 1714
Handbook of Labor Statistics 2328
Industrial Participation 2535
Institute of Personnel Management
Digest 2599
International Educational Materials
Exchange 2676
International Labour Organization
Publications 2699
International Labour Review 2700
Journal of Human Resources 2860
Labor Market Information Directory
2938
Labor News Memorandum 2941
Labour & Society 2948
Legislative Review 3001
Major Programs 3064
Monthly Labor Review 3291
Omega 3619
Social and Labour Bulletin 4312
Work Related Abstracts 5029
Year Book of Labour Statistics 5095

Africa

Middle East and North Africa 3217

Alaska

Labor Market Information Directory
2938
Statistical Quarterly 4437

Arizona

Arizona Statistical Abstract 317.03

Arkansas

Arkansas. The Great Location in the
Sunbelt 321

Australia

Confederation of Australian Industry
(CAI) News 1098
Guide to Investment 2296

Canada

Canada Manpower and Immigration
Review 758
Canadian Labour 812
Canadian Transport 841
Datafacts 1330
McGill University Industrial Relations
Centre Review 3159
Working Conditions in Canadian
Industry, 1978 and 1979 5023

Europe

Doing Business in Europe 1486

Florida

Florida Employment Statistics 2067
Labor Force Estimates 2931
Labor Market Trends 2940

Georgia

Georgia Statistical Abstract 2220

Great Britain

British Labour Statistics. Year Book
618
Department of Employment Gazette
1361
Industrial Participation 2535
Industrial Relations Review and Report
2547
Institute of Personnel Management
Digest 2599
Labour Research 2955
National Westminster Bank Quarterly
Review 3413

Japan

Japan External Trade Organization
(JETRO) Business Information Series
2801

Middle East

Middle East and North Africa 3217

New York City

New York City Business Fact Book
Part 2: Population & Housing 3475

New York State

Labor Area Summary 2927
Labor News Memorandum 2941

New Zealand

Labour & Employment Gazette 2947
Life and Business in New Zealand
3011
New Zealand Prices, Wages & Labour
3512

Oklahoma

Oklahoma Labor Market 3617

South Carolina

Directory of Labor Market Information
1439

Third World

International Educational Materials
Exchange 2676
Labour, Capital and Society 2949.01

United States

AFL-CIO News 76.02
Census of Manufacturers, 1977 876
Census of Population 876.01
Employee Relations Law Journal 1648
Labor Unity 2945
McGill University Industrial Relations
Centre Review 3159
Solidarity 4327
Worklife Magazine 5026

Virginia

Labor Market Information Directory
2939

Washington (State)

Washington State Labor Market
Information Directory 4895

LABOR, CHILD LABOR

Education and Work 1593
From the State Capitals: Wage-Hour
Regulation 2190
Wage-Hour Guide 4869

LABOR, CONTRACTS

Collective Bargaining Negotiations &
Contracts 977
Industrial Relations Guide 2541
Labour Agreements Data Bank 2946

Canada

Wage Developments Resulting from
Collective Bargaining Settlements
4868.01

LABOR, DEPARTMENT OF (ALASKA)

Labor Market Information Directory 2938

LABOR, DEPARTMENT OF (US)

Employment and Training Administration (ETA) Interchange 1653
Employment and Training Report of the President 1655
Research and Development Projects 4082
Worklife Magazine 5026

LABOR, EMPLOYEE BENEFITS

Benefits International 521
Business Insurance 695
Employee Benefit Costs in Canada 1642
Employee Benefit Plan Review (EBPR) 1643
Employee Benefit Plan Review (EBPR) Research Reports 1644
Forms and Workbook Under ERISA, for Pension and Profit Sharing Plans 2147
Industrial Relations News 2545
International Benefits Information Service 2658
International Foundation of Employee Benefit Plans Digest 2682
Pension Plan Guide Summary 3725
Pensions Directory 3730
Pension World 3732
Personnel Management, Communications 3747
Plan Administrator's Compliance Manual 3776
Risk Management 4134
Small Business Report 4301.01
Social and Labour Bulletin 4312
Textbook for Employee Benefit Plan Trustees, Administrators and Advisors 4598

Canada

Canadian Risk Management and Business Insurance 830
Corporate Insurance in Canada 1209
Employee Benefit Costs in Canada 1642
Employee Benefits Journal 1645
Legislative Review 3001
Working Conditions in Canadian Industry, 1978 and 1979 5023

Far East

Asia/Pacific Compensation Survey 330

Europe

European Compensation Survey 1771

Great Britain

Incomes Data Services (IDS) Studies 2489

New York State

Unemployment Insurance Fund, Evaluation of the New York State 4743

United States

Current Wage Developments 1284
Employee Benefits Journal 1645
International Foundation Legal Legislative Reporter News Bulletin 2681
Labor Unity 2945
Pension Plan Guide 3724
Railroad Retirement Board Annual Report 3991
Railroad Retirement Board Quarterly Review 3992
Tax Management Compensation Planning Journal 4559

LABOR, EMPLOYMENT RATE

Consumer Attitudes and Buying Plans 1150
Dow Jones—Irwin Business Almanac 1501
Economic Inquiry 1553
Employment Review 1664
International Labour Documentation 2698
Labour Force Statistics 2952
Monthly Labor Review 3291
Sound of the Economy 4332
Statistical Yearbook 4444
Year Book of Labour Statistics 5095

Alabama

Alabama Economic Abstract 135

Alaska

Alaska Economic Trends 138
Statistical Quarterly 4437
Trade and Regulated Industries Occupational Employment Statistics 4650

Arizona

Annual Planning Information 253
Arizona Labor Market Newsletter 312
Arizona Review 317

Arkansas

Basics of Plant Location in Arkansas 514

Australia

Bankers' Magazine of Australasia 470

California

Economic Outlook: California Report 1558
Orange County Business 3634
Union-Tribune Annual Review of San Diego Business Activity 4753
Union-Tribune Index 4754

Canada

Canada Manpower and Immigration Review 758
Employment, Earnings and Hours 1660
Historical Labour Force Statistics, Actual Data, Seasonal Factors, Seasonally Adjusted Data 2374
Labour Force 2951
Saskatchewan Monthly Statistical Review 4182

Europe

Unemployment: Monthly Bulletin 4745.01

Far East

Quarterly Bulletin of Statistics for Asia and the Pacific 3959

Florida

Dimensions 1398
Florida Economic Indicators 2066
Florida Employment Statistics 2067
Florida Statistical Abstract 2069
Labor Force Estimates 2931
Labor Market Trends 2940

Great Britain

Department of Employment Gazette 1361
Department of Employment Research 1362
Economic Trends 1573
Labour Research Department Fact Service 2956

Management Information Manual
3081
Monthly Digest Annual Supplement
3288
Social Trends   4321

Hawaii

All about Business in Hawaii   145
First Hawaiian Bank Economic
Indicators   2047

Illinois

Illinois Economic Data Sheets   2438

Ireland, Republic of

Confederation of Irish Industry
(CII)/ESRI Business Forecast   1107
Trade Union Information   4679

Kansas

Kansas Economic Indicators   2904

Louisiana

Louisiana Business Review   3047
Louisiana Economic Indicators
3047.01
Louisiana Economy   3048

New Mexico

Economy   1577

New York City

New York City Business Fact Book
Part 2: Population & Housing   3475

New York State

Labor Area Summary   2927
New York State Business Fact Book
Part 2: Population & Housing   3482
New York State Dept of Labor Annual
Planning Report   3483
Unemployment Insurance Fund,
Evaluation of the New York State
4743

New Zealand

Bankers' Magazine of Australasia   470
Handbook for Investors—New Zealand
2314

North Carolina

North Carolina Industrial Data File
3534

Oklahoma

Oklahoma Annual Planning Report
3611

Oregon

County Economic Indicators   1238

United States

Area Trends in Employment &
Unemployment   308
Citibank Monthly Economic Letter
949
Consumer Information Catalog   1154
Current Population Survey, P:D6   1281
Employment & Earnings   1652
Employment by Type and Broad
Industrial Source   1657
Federal Reserve Bank of San Francisco
Western Economic Indicators   1954
From the State Capitals:
Unemployment Compensation   2188
Kiplinger Washington Letter   2917
Predicasts Basebook   3828
Regional Employment by Industry,
1940–1970   4046
Research and Development Projects
4082
State and Area Forecasting Service
4383.01
Statistical Indicator Reports   4428
Survey of Current Business   4514
United States Regional Forecasts   4815
Update   4827

Utah

Statistical Review of Government in
Utah   4441
Utah Economic and Business Review
4835

Washington

Washington State Labor Market
Information Directory   4895

West Virginia

Labor Market Trends   2940.01
West Virginia Economic Profile   4955

LABOR, EQUAL OPPORTUNITY EMPLOYMENT

Employee Relations Bulletin   1646
Industrial Relations News   2545
Personnel Journal   3744
Woman Executive's Bulletin   5011

Canada

Business & Professional Woman   663
Canadian Labour Law Reports   813

United States

Bureau of National Affairs (BNA)
Policy & Practice Series   650

Employee Relations Law Journal   1648
Employment Discrimination: Sex   1659
Employment Practices   1661.01
Employment Practices Decisions   1662
Equal Employment Opportunity
Commission (EEOC)—Affirmative
Action Manuals   1732
Equal Employment Opportunity
Commission (EEOC) Compliance
Manual   1733
Equal Employment Opportunity Review
1734
Equal Employment Opportunity Today
1735
Fair Employment Practice Service
1877
Fair Employment Practices (FEP)
Guidelines   1878
Fair Employment Report   1879
From the State Capitals: Wage-Hour
Regulation   2190
Labor Relations Reporter   2943
Race Relations & Industry   3983
Union Labor Report   4752
Wage-Hour Guide   4869

LABOR, GOVERNMENT REGULATIONS, LAWS AND PROGRAMS

Employee Benefit Plan Review (EBPR)
Research Reports   1644
Employee Relations Bulletin   1646
Employment Safety and Health Guide
1665
Health & Safety Information Bulletin
2356
Industrial Health Foundation Legal
Series   2526
International Occupational Safety and
Health Information Centre   2715
Investing, Licensing and Trading
Conditions Abroad   2755
Job Safety and Health   2811.01
Monthly Labor Review   3291
Occupational Safety and Health Act
(OSHA) Compliance Letter   3564
Rules and Regulations and Statements
of Procedure of the National Labor
Relations Board, Series 8, 1973
4152
Social and Labour Bulletin   4312
What's Ahead in Personnel   4960
White Collar Management   4967

Canada

Canada Labour Service   757
Canada Manpower and Immigration
Review   758
Canadian Labour Law Reports   813
Labour Standards in Canada   2957
Legislative Review   3001

LABOR, HEALTH HAZARDS AND SAFETY

United States

Best's Safety Directory   541
From the State Capitals: Workmen's
  Compensation   2191
Job Safety and Health   2811.01
Job Safety & Health Report   2812
Labor Relations Guide   2942
Law of Workmen's Compensation
  2986
Mine Safety and Health Reporter
  3234
Occupational Safety and Health Act
  (OSHA) Compliance Letter   3564
Occupational Safety and Health
  Decisions   3566
Occupational Safety and Health
  Reporter   3567
Statistical Bulletin   4426
Union Labor Report   4752
Workmen's Compensation for
  Occupational Injuries and Death
  (Desk Edition)   5027
Workmen's Compensation Law Reports
  5028

LABOR, JOB MARKET

Indicators of Industrial Activity
  2505.01
Job Corps Happenings   2809
Journal of Human Resources   2860
Labour Force Statistics   2952
Occupational Outlook Handbook,
  1980–81 edition   3562
Occupational Outlook Quarterly   3563
Statistical Bulletin   4425

Alaska

Alaska Economic Trends   138
Alaska-Occupational Employment
  Forecast   141
Labor Market Information Directory
  2938
Unfilled Job Openings Report   4746

Arizona

Annual Planning Information   253
Job Openings: Indicator of
  Occupational Demand   2811

Canada

Canada Manpower and Immigration
  Review   758

Florida

Florida Statistical Abstract   2069
Labor Market Trends   2940

Great Britain

Department of Employment Gazette
  1361

Ireland, Republic of

Confederation of Irish Industry
  (CII)/ESRI Business Forecast   1107
Trade Union Information   4679

New York City

New York City Business Fact Book
  Part 2: Population & Housing   3475
Review of Business   4120

New Zealand

Handbook for Investors—New Zealand
  2314

South Carolina

Directory of Labor Market Information
  1439

Texas

Texas Facts   4596.01

United States

Consumer Information Catalog   1154
Employment and Training Report of
  the President   1655
Predicasts Basebook   3828
Research and Development Projects
  4082

Utah

Utah Economic and Business Review
  4835

Virginia

Labor Market Information Directory
  2939

West Virginia

Labor Market Trends   2940.01

LABOR, OLDER WORKERS

Aging and Work   88.01

LABOR, PRODUCTIVITY.   *See also*
Methods-Time Measurement

Aggregate Productivity Measures   88
Ergonomics   1740
Ergonomics Abstracts   1741
International Journal of Production
  Research   2695
Journal of Human Resources   2860

Journal of Industrial Economics   2861
Manage   3067
Public Productivity Review   3930
Supervisor's Production Planner   4500
TIPS—Technical Infomation Periodicals
  Service   4624
World of Work Report   5073
Year Book of Labour Statistics   5095

LABOR, RESEARCH ON

Abstract Newsletters, Administration
  and Management   2.03
Auber Bibliography   346.01
International Labour Organization
  Publications   2699
International Labour Review   2700
Department of Employment Research
  1362
Fair Employment Practice Service
  1877
Key to Economic Science and
  Managerial Sciences   2912.01
Occupational Safety and Health
  Reporter   3567
Research and Development Projects
  4082

LABOR, SPANISH-SPEAKING AMERICANS

SER Network News   4264
SER Newsletter   4266
SER Women's Update   4270.01

LABOR, STRIKES

Strike Preparation Manual   4479

Canada

Strikes and Lockouts in Canada 1979
  4480

New York State

Statistics on Work Stoppages   4458
Work Stoppages in New York State
  5032

United States

Union Labor Report   4752

LABOR, SUPERVISORY PERSONNEL

Impact   2441
Manage   3067
Supervision   4499
Supervisor's Production Planner   4500

LABOR, TRAINING

Abstract Newsletters, Behavior &
  Society   4908

American Society for Personnel
  Administrative Handbook of
  Personnel and Industrial Relations
  205
Anbar Management Publications
  Personnel & Training Abstracts 220
Confederation of British Industry (CBI)
  Education and Training Bulletin
  1100
Development Directory Human
  Resource Management 1373.02
Education and Work 1593
Employment and Training
  Administration (ETA) Interchange
  1653
Employment and Training Reporter
  1654
Employment and Training Report of
  the President 1655
Industrial Relations News 2545
International Labour Documentation
  2698
Manpower and Vocational Education
  Weekly 3098
Personnel Journal 3744
Research and Development Projects
  4082
Texas Facts 4596.01
Training 4684
Training and Development Journal
  4685
United Nations Industrial Development
  Organization (UNIDO) Guides to
  Information Sources.
  UNIDO/LIB/SER.D/Rev.1—
  Information Sources on Industrial
  Training 4767.03
World of Work Report 5073

LABOR, UNEMPLOYMENT. *See*
Labor, Employment Rate

LABOR, UNEMPLOYMENT
INSURANCE

Alaska

Statistical Quarterly 4437

Canada

Digest of Benefit Entitlement and
  Principles/Unemployment Insurance
  1385

New York State

Unemployment Insurance Fund,
  Evaluation of the New York State
  4743

United States

Comparison of State Unemployment
  Insurance Laws 1059
From the State Capitals:
  Unemployment Compensation 2188
Payroll Guide 3710
Significant Provisions of State
  Unemployment Insurance Laws
  4285
Unemployment Insurance Reports
  4744
Unemployment Insurance Statistics
  4745

LABOR, UNIONS. *See* Labor
Unions

LABOR, WAGES AND HOURS

Employee Relations Bulletin 1646
Handbook of Wage and Salary
  Administration, 1972 2339
Monthly Labor Review 3291
Retail Wages 4117
Voice of Small Business 4865
Year Book of Labour Statistics 5095

Alaska

Wage Rates for Selected Occupations
  4871

Argentina

Latin American Services 2976.01

Australia

Workforce 5022

Bolivia

Latin American Services 2976.01

Brazil

Latin American Services 2976.01

Canada

Canadian Labour Law Reports 813
Employment, Earnings and Hours
  1660
Estimates of Labour Income 1757
Wage Developments Resulting from
  Major Collective Bargaining
  Settlements 4868.01
Wage Rates, Salaries & Hours of
  Labour 4872
Working Conditions in Canadian
  Industry, 1978–79 5023

Chile

Latin American Services 2976.01

Colombia

Latin American Services 2976.01

Ecuador

Latin American Services 2976.01

Europe

European Compensation Survey 1771
European Economic Service 1774.01
West European Living Costs 1977
  4952

Far East

Asia/Pacific Compensation Survey 330
Quarterly Bulletin of Statistics for Asia
  and the Pacific 3959

Florida

Florida Employment Statistics 2067

Great Britain

Annual Abstract of Statistics 234
Bargaining Report 508.01
Changes in Rates of Wages & Hours of
  Work 906
CSO Macro-Economic Databank
  1265.01
Incomes Data Reports 2485
Incomes Data Services (IDS) Focus
  2487
Incomes Data Services (IDS) Studies
  2489
Labour Research Department Fact
  Service 2956
New Earnings Survey 3437
Time Rates of Wages and Hours of
  Work 4620

Japan

Japan Economic Yearbook 2797

Maine

Census of Maine Manufactures 875

Mexico

Latin American Services 2976.01

New York State

Employment Review 1664

New Zealand

Employer 1650

Handbook for Investors—New Zealand 2314

New Zealand Prices, Wages & Labour 3512

Peru

Latin American Services   2976.01

South Carolina

Directory of Labor Market Information 1439

United States

Bureau of National Affairs (BNA) Policy & Practice Series   650

Collective Bargaining Negotiations & Contracts   977

Current Wage Developments   1284

Employment & Earnings   1652

Federal Wage-Hour Handbook for Banks   1976

Labor Cases   2930

Labor Law Guide   2934

Labor Relations Reporter   2943

Labor Unity   2945

Payroll Guide   3710

Payroll Management Guide   3711

Wage-Hour Guide   4869

Uruguay

Latin American Services   2976.01

Venezuela

Latin American Services   2976.01

Washington (State)

Washington State Labor Market Information Directory   4895

West Virginia

West Virginia Industrial Wage Survey 4956

LABOR, WOMEN.   *See also* Labor— Equal Employment Opportunity

Business & Professional Women   664

Industrial Health Foundation Medical Series   2528

1975 Handbook on Women Workers 3522

Women's Work   5016

Working Woman   5025

Canada

Business & Professional Woman   663

Women in the Labour Force: Facts & Figures   5014

Great Britain

Business & Professional Women   664

United States

Employment Discrimination: Sex   1659

From the State Capitals: Wage-Hour Regulation   2190

SER Women's Update   4270.01

LABOR, WORKMEN'S COMPENSATION

Benefits Review Board Black Lung Reporter   522

Benefits Review Board Longshore Reporter   522.01

Best's Casualty Loss Reserve Development   525

Canadian Employment Safety and Health Guide   789.01

Canadian Labour Law Reports   813

Law of Workmen's Compensation 2986

Legislative Review   3001

Personnel Journal   3744

Workmen's Compensation for Occupational Injuries and Death (Desk Edition)   5027

Workmen's Compensation Law Reports 5028

LABORATORIES.   *See also* Computer-Aided Laboratory Functions

Dental Laboratory Review   1359

Laboratory Equipment Digest   2928

Laboratory Product News   2929

Lab World   2959

LABOR-MANAGEMENT RELATIONS

American Society for Personnel Administration Handbook of Personnel and Industrial Relations 205

ASPA Handbook of Personnel and Industrial Relations   332.02

British Journal of Industrial Relations 616

Current Wage Developments   1284

Development Directory Human Resource Management   1373.02

Employee Relations in Action   1647

Executive Action Report   1796

Impact   2441

Incomes Data Services (IDS) International Reports   2488

Industrial and Labor Relations Review 2509

Industrial Participation   2535

Industrial Relations Guide   2541

Industrial Relations Journal   2542

Industrial Relations News   2545

Industrial Relations Research in Canada   2546

Industrial Society   2552

International Labour Documentation 2698

Journal of Collective Negotiations in the Public Sector   2832

Journal of European Industrial Training 2853

Labor Law Developments   2933

Management Decision   3077

Monthly Labor Review   3291

New York University Annual Conference on Labor   3489

Panel   3690

Personnel Administrator   3739

Personnel Guide   3742

Personnel Journal   3744

Personnel Psychology   3750

Roberts' Dictionary of Industrial Relations, 1971 Edition   4138

Short Courses and Seminars   4284

Social and Labour Bulletin   4312

Special Report   4356

Strike Preparation Manual   4479

Summary of Labor Arbitration Awards 4493

Work and People   5021

Works Management   5030

World of Work Report   5073

Australia

Employers' Review   1651

Impact   2441

Work and People   5021

Workforce   5022

California

Labour Arbitration Cases   2949

Canada

Canadian Industrial Relations & Personnel Developments   802

Collective Bargaining Review   978

Labour Agreements Data Bank   2946

McGill University Industrial Relations Centre Review   3159

Europe

The Brussels Report   632

European Industrial Relations Review 1778

Great Britain

European Industrial Relations Review 1778

Incomes Data Reports   2485

Incomes Data Services (IDS) Focus 2487
Incomes Data Services (IDS) International Reports 2488
Industrial Cases Reports 2511
Industrial Participation 2535
Industrial Relations Law Reports 2544
Industrial Relations Review and Report 2547
Industrial Relations Week 2548
Industrial Society 2552
Industrial Tribunal Reports 2555
Legal Information Bulletin 2996

New York State

Collective Bargaining Settlements in New York State 979

New Zealand

Employer 1650

United States

Bureau of National Affairs (BNA) Policy & Practice Series 650
Collective Bargaining Negotiations & Contracts 977
Construction Labor Report 1132
Daily Labor Report 1301
Employee Relations Law Journal 1648
Federal Mediation & Conciliation Service Annual Report 1931
Guidebook to Labor Relations 2274
Health Labor Relations Reports 2362
Job Safety and Health 2811.01
Labor Arbitration Awards 2924
Labor Arbitration Reports 2926
Labor Cases 2930
Labor Law Guide 2934
Labor Law Journal 2935
Labor Law Reports 2936
Labor Relations Guide 2942
Labor Relations Reporter 2943
McGill University Industrial Relations Centre Review 3159
National Labor Relations Board (NLRB) Case Handling Manual 3390
National Labor Relations Board (NLRB) Decisions 3392
National Mediation Board Annual Report 3393
National Mediation Board Reports of Emergency Boards 3394
Public Personnel Administration— Labor-Management Relations 3927
Register of Reporting Labor Organizations 4052
Research and Development Projects 4082

Retail Services Labor Report 4112
Rules and Regulations and Statements of Procedure of the National Labor Relations Board, Series 8, 1973 4152
Union Labor Report 4752
White Collar Report 4968

LABOR-MANAGEMENT RELATIONS, GOVERNMENT REGULATIONS

Australia

Workforce 5022

Canada

Canadian Labour Law Reports 813
Legislative Review 3001

United States

Daily Labor Report 1301
From the State Capitals: General Bulletin 2172
From the State Capitals: Labor Relations 2178
Labor Law 2932
Labor Law Developments 2933
Labor Relations Reporter 2943
Retail Service Labor Report 4112
White Collar Report 4968

LABOR-MANAGEMENT RELATIONS, RESEARCH ON

Abstract Newsletters, Administration and Management 2.03
British Journal of Industrial Relations 616

LABOR-MANAGEMENT REPORTING AND DISCLOSURE ACT (US)

Guidebook to Labor Relations 2274
Register of Reporting Labor Organizations 4052

LABOR RELATIONS ACT, NATIONAL (US)

Guidebook to Labor Relations 2274

LABOR RELATIONS BOARD, NATIONAL (NLRB) (US)

Classified Index of Dispositions of ULP Charges by the General Counsel of the National Labor Relations Board 955
Classified Index of National Labor Relations Board Decisions & Related Court Decisions 956

Guidebook to Labor Relations 2274
International Foundation Legal Legislative Reporter News Bulletin 2681
Labor Law Developments 2933
National Labor Relations Board (NLRB) Case Handling Manual 3390
National Labor Relations Board (NLRB) Case Handling Manual 3391
National Labor Relations Board (NLRB) Decisions 3392
Rules and Regulations and Statements of Procedure of the National Labor Relations Board, Series 8, 1973 4152
Weekly Summary of NLRB Cases 4940

LABOR STATISTICS, BUREAU OF (US)

Major Programs 3064

LABOR STUDIES, INTERNATIONAL INSTITUTE FOR

International Educational Materials Exchange 2676
Labour & Society 2948

LABOR UNIONS

Directory of National Unions and Employee Associations 1449
Employee Relations Bulletin 1646
Industrial Relations News 2545
Labor Law 2932
Retail Service Labor Report 4112
World Guide to Trade Associations 5067

Africa

AALC Reporter 79

Australia

Employers' Review 1651

Canada

Canadian Labour 812
Directory of Labour Organizations in Canada, 1980 1439.01
Labour Organizations in Canada 2954

European Economic Community

Trade Union Information 4678

Great Britain

Bargaining Report 508.01
Employment Digest 1658

Historical Directory of Trade Unions
2373.01
Labour Research   2955
Trade Union Handbook, 2nd edition
4677

Ireland, Republic of

Trade Union Information   4679

Maine

Census of Maine Manufacturers   875
Directory of Maine Labor
Organizations   1441

United States

Daily Labor Report   1301
Labor Law Journal   2935
Labor Law Reports   2936
Register of Reporting Labor
Organizations   4052
Union Labor Report   4752
White Collar Report   4968

LABOUR CONGRESS, CANADIAN

Canadian Labour   812

LABOUR ORGANIZATION, INTERNATIONAL (ILO)

International Labour Documentation
2698

LAMB

Livestock Market News Reports   3030
Restaurant Buyers Guide   4098

LAMPS AND LIGHTING

Electric Lamps. MQ-36B   1611
Electric Lamps. M36D   1612
Fluorescent Lamp Ballasts. MQ-36C
2071
IES Lighting Review   2434
Lighting Equipment News   3018

LAND SALES REGISTRATION, OFFICE OF INTERSTATE (US)

Land Development Law Reporter
2960

LANDFILL. *See* Waste Materials

LAND TAX ACT (NEW ZEALAND)

New Zealand Income Tax Law &
Practice   3506

LAND USE PLANNING. *See also* Zoning

Environmental Comment   1721
Journal of Regional Science   2879
Land Development Law Reporter
2960
Land Economics   2961
Land Use Digest   2962
Land Use Law and Zoning Digest
2963
Land Use Planning Abstracts   2964
Land Use Planning Report   2965
Lawyers Title News   2991
Oxford Agrarian Studies   3672
Transportation Planning and
Technology   4693

Canada

Northern Perspectives   3540

Florida

Dimensions   1398

United States

Washington Report   4890

LASERS. *See also* Research and Development, Lasers and Optics

Abstract Newsletter, Physics   2.26
Directory of Defense Electronic
Products and Services: US Suppliers
1426
DMS Military Laser & EO   1475.21
DMS Military Laser & EO Europe
1475.22
Laser Focus   2967
Laser Focus Buyers' Guide   2968
Laser Report   2969
Optics and Laser Technology   3632
Science Research Abstracts Journal,
Parts A&B   4197

LATIN AMERICA. *See* American Nations and Western Hemisphere Possessions

LAW AND LEGISLATION. *See also* Judiciary. Legal Services. Subjects

Antitrust Bulletin   272
Business Index   690.01
Connecticut Business and Industry
Assn (ABIA) News   1116
Current Law Index   1277.01
Digest of Commercial Laws of the
World   1386
Economic and Social Committee of the
Euorpean Communities. Bulletin
1537

European Directory of Business
Information Sources & Services
1773
Forex Service   2145
Government Regulation of Business
Ethics: International Payoffs   2251
Holt Executive Advisory   2379
Industrial Property Reports from
Socialist Countries   2537.01
International Law of Development:
Basic Documents   2701
Investment Laws of the World   2763
Investment Laws of the World:
Developing Nations   2764
Journal of International Law &
Economics   2864
Journal of World Trade Law   2901
Latin America and the Development of
the Law of the Sea   2970
Legal Contents   2995.01
Syracuse Journal of International Law
& Commerce   4524
Transnational Economic and Monetary
Law: Transactions and Contracts
4690
Transport Laws of the World   4696

American Nations

Informational and Technical
Publication of the General Secretariat
of the Organization of American
States (OAS)   2569

Australia

Australian Business Law Review   388
Australian National Economic &
Legislative Report   413
Handbook for Industrialists   2313

Belgium

Oil and Gas, the North Sea
Exploitation   3601

Brazil

Brazilian–American Business
Review/Directory   585

Canada

Bills/Public and Private   553
British Columbia Statute Citator   608
Canada Corporation Act Bulletin   745
Canada Gazette/Part II   750
Canada Gazette/Part III   751
Canada Statute Citator   765
Committees of Parliament/Minutes of
Proceedings and Evidence   1020
Corpus Almanac of Canada   1224

Debates of the House of Commons
1346
Debates of the Senate   1347
Dominion Report Service   1494
Ontario Statute Citator   3626
Ottawa Letter   3650

Denmark

Oil and Gas, the North Sea
Exploitation   3601

Europe

Commercial Laws of Europe   1004.01
Compnay Law in Europe, 3rd edition
1053.01
European Directory of Business
Information Sources & Services
1773
European Law Digest   1782
European Law Letter   1783

European Economic Community

Common Market Law Reports   1037
European Law Digest   1782
European Law Letter   1783
Trade Secrets and Know-How
throughout the World   4675

European Economic Community

Commercial Laws of Europe   1004.01

Great Britain

Black's Law Dictionary, 4th Edition
561
Company Secretary's Review   1055
Management Information Manual
3081
Oil and Gas, the North Sea
Exploitation   3601

Illinois

Daily Legislative Report   1302

Middle East

Commercial Laws of the Middle East
1004.02

Netherlands

Oil and Gas, the North Sea
Exploitation   3601

New York State

Capital Journal   857.01

New Zealand

Capital Letter   857.02

North Carolina

North Carolina Industrial Data File
3534

Norway

Oil and Gas, the North Sea
Exploitation   3601

Spain

Spain–US   4353

Sweden

Oil and Gas, the North Sea
Exploitation   3601

United States

Babson's Washington Forecast Letter
445
Black's Law Dictionary, 5th edition
561
Congressional Action   1111
Congressional Index   1114
Congressional Legislative Reporting
1115
CQ Almanac, 1980   1241
Legal Resource Index   2996.01
Local Government Law   3039
State Government News   4392
State Government Research Checklist
4392.01
State Legislative Leadership, Committee
and Staff   4395
State Legislative Reporting Service
4396
State Slate: A Guide to Legislative
Procedures and Lawmakers   4407
Suggested State Legislation 1980   4490
Washington Report   4889

LAW ENFORCEMENT.   *See* Police
(General)

LAWYERS.   *See* Legal Services

LEAD

Lead and Zinc Statistics   2993
Nonferrous Metal Data   3532

Canada

Lead Data   2994

France

Lead Data   2994

Germany (West)

Lead Data   2994

Great Britain

Lead Data   2994

United States

Lead Data   2994

LEADERS AND LEADERSHIP.
Note: Covers material about prominent
people throughout the world

International Who's Who   2742
International Yearbook and Statesmen's
Who's Who   2744

Africa

Africa   77
Africa South of the Sahara   82
Middle East and North Africa   3217

Australia

Far East and Australasia   1892

Far East

Far East and Australasia   1892

Indonesia

Indonesia Letter   2506

Middle East

Middle East and North Africa   3217

Saudi Arabia

Who's Who in Saudi Arabia   4991

LEASING COMPANIES

Polk's World Bank Directory North
American Edition   3801

LEATHER AND LEATHER GOODS.
See also products, eg, Footwear

Canadian Footwear Journal   793
United Nations Industrial Development
Organization Guides to Information
Sources. UNIDO/LIB/SER D/3 and
Corr—Information Sources on the
Leather and Leather Goods Industry
4770

LEGAL SERVICES.   *See also*
Judiciary. Law and Legislation

Arbitration Journal   299
Best's Recommended Insurance
Adjusters   117
Business Lawyer   704
Law of Advertising   2979

Lawyer's Register by Specialties and
Fields of Law   2990
Taxation for Lawyers   4539

Canada

Almanac and Directory 1981   148.01
Hines Insurance Counsel   2373

United States

Hines Insurance Counsel   2373
Who's Who in American Law   4978

LEISURE ACTIVITIES.   *See*
Entertainment. Recreation. Sports and
Sporting Goods. Travel and Resorts

LETTERHEADS

Letterheads, Volumes I to III   3006.01

LIABILITY INSURANCE.   *See*
Insurance, Liability

LIABILITY INSURANCE
CONTRACT, GENERAL

Law of Liability Insurance   2983

LIABILITY LAWS

Product Liability Legislation for Client
and Counsel   3874.01

LIBRARIES.   *See also* Archives and
Records. Information Retrieval.
Microfilm and Microfiche

Bowker Annual of Library and Book
Trade Information   580
Directory of Special Libraries and
Information Centers   1457
Information Hotline   2572
International Guide to Library,
Archival and Information Science
Associations   2684
Journal of Documentation   2844.02
Journal of the American Society for the
Information Science   2888.01
Libradoc   3007
London Classification of Business
Studies   3040.01
Magazines for Libraries   3058
World of Learning   5072

American Nations

Statistics—America   4449

Canada

Subject Directory of Special Libraries
and Information Centers. Vol 1:
Business and Law Libraries,

Including Military and
Transportation Libraries   4484

Europe

Statistics—Europe   4452

Texas

Business Information for Dallas   691

United States

Abstract Newsletters, Library and
Information Sciences   2.20
Current Periodical Publications in
Baker Library   1279
Recent Additions to Baker Library
4033.01
Subject Directory of Special Libraries
and Information Centers. Vol 1:
Business and Law Libraries,
Including Military and
Transportation Libraries   4484

LIBRARIES, COLLECTIONS

Subject Directory of Special Libraries
and Information Centers. Vol. 1:
Business and Law Libraries,
Including Military and
Transportation Libraries   4484

LIBRARIES, PERSONNEL

Directory of Special Libraries and
Information Centers   1457

LICENSES AND LICENSING.   *See
also* Franchises. Subjects, eg,
Automobiles, Licenses

Abstract Newsletters, Government
Inventions for Licensing   2.16
American Bulletin of International
Technology Transfer   163
Drug License Opportunities   1508.01
East/West Technology Digest   1527
International Intertrade Index   2686
International Licensing   2702
Investing, Licensing and Trading
Conditions Abroad   2755
Law and Business of Licensing   2977
Licensing in Foreign and Domestic
Operations   3010
New Product—New Business Digest
3458
Petrochemical News   3754
Selected Business Ventures   4252
Unit   4754.01

Bulgaria

Business Eastern Europe   677

Canada

British Columbia Export/Import
Opportunities   601.02
Building Permits   640

Czechoslovakia

Business Eastern Europe   677

Europe (West)

New From Europe   3445.01

Germany (East)

Business Eastern Europe   677

Hungary

Business Eastern Europe   677

Poland

Business Eastern Europe   677

Rumania

Business Eastern Europe   677

Union of Soviet Socialist Republics
(USSR)

Business Eastern Europe   677

United States

Abstract Newsletters, Government
Inventions for Licensing   2.16
American Bulletin of International
Technology Transfer   163
Brief Guide to Business Regulations
and Services in Texas   592.01

Yugoslavia

Business Eastern Europe   677

LIFE COMPANY TAX ACT (US)

Federal Taxation of Life Insurance
Companies   1963

LIFE INSURANCE.   *See* Insurance,
Life

LIFE-SUPPORT SYSTEMS

Abstract Newsletters, Biomedical
Technology & Human Factors
Engineering   2.06

LIGHT BULBS.   *See* Lamps and
Lighting

LIPSTICK. *See* Beauty and Grooming Aids. Cosmetics and Toiletries

LIQUEFIED NATURAL GAS

Analysis of LNG Marine Transportation 213
Pipeline & Gas Journal 3772

LIQUEFIED PETROLEUM GAS

LP/Gas 3049
Platt's LP Gaswire 3783.02
Practical Guide to LP/Gas Utilization 3822

LIQUOR. *See also* Alcoholism

Annual Statistical Review of the Distilled Spirits Industry 262
Bottom Line 579
Food and Drink 2079
From the State Capitals: Liquor Control 2179
Hospitality 2393
Impact 2441.01
Liquor Control Law Reports 3023
Liquor Handbook 3024
Rocky Mountain Journal 4139
Spirits Bulletin 4363
Supplier Price Index 4505
Thomson's Liquor Guide 4613

LITERARY AND ARTISTIC WORKS, INTERNATIONAL UNION FOR PROTECTION OF (BERNE, SWITZERLAND)

Copyright 1201

LIVESTOCK. *See also* types, e.g., Cattle

Agricultural Price Report 103
British Journal of Nutrition 617
Chicago Mercantile Exchange Yearbook 937
Doane's Agricultural Report 1476
Feed Industry Red Book 1978
Feed Industry Review 1979
Financial Facts About the Meat Packing Industry 2000
Foreign Agriculture Circulars 2111
In Brief 2476.02
Livestock and Products Reports 3027
Outlook and Situation Reports 3653.01
Statistical Review of Livestock and Meat Industries 4441.01
Tropical Agriculture 4722
World Animal Review 5041
World Farming 5064

Australia

Australian Meat & Livestock Corp Annual Report 410
In Brief 2476.02
Meat Producer and Exporter 3163
Meat Statistics 3164
Statistical Review of Livestock and Meat Industries 4441.01

Canada

Handbook of Agricultural Statistics, Part VI: Livestock and Animal Products, 1871–1973 2320

European Economic Community

Agricultural Markets: Prices (Two Series) 101
Agricultural Production (Two Series) 104

Great Britain

Livestock Farming 3028

Illinois

Illinois Agricultural Statistics 2436

Iowa

Wallaces' Farmer 4875

North Dakota

North Dakota Crop and Livestock Statistics 3536

South Dakota

South Dakota Crop and Livestock Reporter 4344

United States

Census of Agriculture Preliminary Reports for Counties, States, and the United States, 1978 874
Feedstuffs 1980
Livestock Market News Reports 3030

LOANS. *See* Credit

LOBBYISTS AND LOBBYING

Campaign Contributions and Lobbying Laws 740.01
Congressional Insight 1114.01
CQ Almanac, 1980 1241
Lobbying Reports 3035

LOGOTYPES

Trademarks/7 4663.01

World of Logotypes, Volumes I & II 5072.01

LONDON CHAMBER OF COMMERCE AND INDUSTRY

Economic Report 1566

LONGEVITY. *See also* Vital Statistics

Statistical Bulletin 4426

LOUISIANA

Financial Trend 2032
From the State Capitals 2169–2191
Louisiana Business Review 3047
Louisiana Economic Indicators 3047.01
Louisiana State Industrial Directory, 1981 3048.02
State and Local Taxes 4386
State Legislative Reporting Service 4396
State Tax Reports 4413

LUMBER AND LUMBER PRODUCTS. *See also* specific types, eg, Paper

Canadian Forest Industries 794
Chicago Mercantile Exchange Yearbook 937
Commercial Bulletin 999
Fingertip Facts and Figures 2038
Forest Products Service 2144
Random Lengths 4002
Random Lengths Export 4002.01
Random Lengths Yearbook 4003
Timber Tax Journal 4618
Unasylva: An International Journal of Forestry and Forest Products 4739
Yearbooks of Forest Products Statistics 5099

Alaska

Alaska Industry 139

Australia

Construction Equipment News 1129

Canada

British Columbia Lumberman 603
Canadian Forestry Statistics 795
Production, Shipments and Stocks on Hand of Sawmills East of the Rockies 3871
Production, Shipments and Stocks on Hand of Sawmills in British Columbia 3872

MANAGERS AND MANAGEMENT, EDUCATION

MANAGERS AND MANAGEMENT, EMPLOYEE BENEFITS

MANAGERS AND MANAGEMENT, EXECUTIVE RECRUITING

MANAGERS AND MANAGEMENT, FRINGE BENEFITS. *See* Managers and Management, Employee Benefits

MANAGERS AND MANAGEMENT, INDUSTRIAL

MANAGERS AND MANAGEMENT, INSTITUTIONAL AND PUBLIC

Public Productivity Review   3930

MANAGERS AND MANAGEMENT RESEARCH ON. *See* Research and Development, Managers and Management

MANAGERS AND MANAGEMENT, SALARIES

Compensation Review   1062
Current Compensation References   1272
Executive Compensation Service Top Management Report   1802.01
Handbook of Wage and Salary Administration, 1972   2339
Management Compensation in Canada, 1977; and the Remuneration of Chief Executive Officers in Canada, 1977   3075
New Earnings Survey   3437
Rewarding Executive Talent: Salary and Benefit Practices by Industry and Position   4130
Salary Survey   4163
Top Executive Compensation   4637

Brazil

Executive Compensation Service. Reports on International Compensation. Brazil   1801

Canada

Administrative Mgt Society Guide to Mgt Compensation   58

United States

Administrative Mgt Society Guide to Mgt Compensation   58
Executive Compensation Service. Techniciaries Report   1802

MANAGERS AND MANAGEMENT, WOMEN

Executive Woman   1811
SAVVY   4190.01
Woman Executive's Bulletin   5011
Women's Work   5016
Working Woman   5025

MANPOWER. *See* Labor. Personnel Management

MANUFACTURERS AND MANUFACTURING. *See also* subjects

Announcements of Mergers and Acquisitions   233
Annual Survey of Manufacturers   266
Handbook for Manufacturing Enterpreneurs   2315
Handbook of Modern Manufacturing Management, 1970   2332
Import/Export File   2442.02
Industrial Planning and Programming Series   2536
International Licensing   2702
Management Aids   3072
Manufacturers' Export Sales and Orders of Durable Goods M4-A   3109
Mississippi Manufacturers Directory   3245
New Trade Names, 1976 and 1977 Supplements   3473
Official Industrial Directory for Puerto Rico   3585
Organization for Economic Co-operation and Development (OECD) Economic Outlook   3641
Plant Engineering Directory and Specifications Catalog   3779
Production   3864
Production Engineering   3867
Production Handbook, 3rd edition, 1972   3868
Smaller Manufacturer   4303
Reference Book of Manufacturers   4040
Statistical Yearbook   4444
Survey of Industrial Purchasing Power   4516
TIPS—Technical Information Periodicals Service   4624
Trade Names Dictionary   4665

Alabama

Alabama Directory of Mining and Manufacturing, 1980–81 edition   134.07
Alabama Mining & Manufacturing Directory, 1980–81   136

Alaska

Alaska Economic Trends   138

Argentina

Argentina Reference Bk   309

Arizona

Arizona Business   311
Arizona: Manufacturers' Directory, 1980   313
Arizona Statistical Abstract   317.03

Arkansas

Arkansas: Manufacturers' Directory, 1980   320
Arkansas USA   321.01
Basics of Plant Location in Arkansas   514
Directory of Arkansas Manufacturers   1409

Australia

Australian Market Guide   408
Western Australia Manufacturers Directory   4950

California

California: Manufacturers' Register, 1981   738.01
California Manufacturers' Register, 1981   738.02

Canada

British Columbia Manufacturers' Directory   604
Canada: Scott's Trade Directory, Metro Toronto, 1st edition, 1980–81   762.04
Canada: Scott's Trade Directory, Toronto Vicinity, 1st edition, 1980–81   762.05
Consumption of Containers and Other Packaging Supplies by the Manufacturing Industries   1179
Canadian Trade Index, 1981   840
Edmonton and Area Manufacturers' Directory   1586
Inventories, Shipments and Orders in Manufacturing Industries   2754
Manufacturing Industries of Canada: National and Provincial Areas   3116.01
Manufacturing Industries of Canada, Sub-Provincial Areas   3117
Saskatchewan's Financial & Economic Position   4183
Scott's Industrial Directory. Atlantic Manufacturers   4208
Scott's Industrial Directory. Ontario Manufacturers   4209
Scott's Industrial Directory. Quebec Manufacturers   4210
Scott's Industrial Directory. Western Manufacturers   4211

China, People's Republic of

Soviet-Eastern Europe-China Business & Trade   4351

Colorado

Business Economic Outlook Forum
678
Colorado: Manufacturers' Directory,
1980–81   987
Directory of Colorado Manufacturers
1418

Connecticut

Connecticut: Directory of Connecticut
Manufacturers, 1981   1117.01
Connecticut–Rhode Island: Directory of
Manufacturers, 1981   1117.02

Dominican Republic

Caribbean Business   862

Europe (East)

Soviet-Eastern Europe-China Business
& Trade   4351

Far East

Asian Business   326.02
Asia/Pacific Compensation Survey   330
Asia Research Bulletin   331

Florida

Florida Statistical Abstract   2069
Labor Market Trends   2940

Georgia

Georgia Manufacturers' Directory,
1980–81   2218.01
Georgia Manufacturing Directory
2219

Great Britain

Confederation of British Industry (CBI)
Industrial Trends Survey   1101
Kelly's Manufacturers & Merchants
Directory   2907
Manufacturers' Agent   3107
United Kingdom Kompass Register
4759

Guam

Economic Censuses of Outlying Areas,
1977, OAC 77   1547.01

Hawaii

Directory of Manufacturers, State of
Hawaii, 1981–82   1443
Hawaii Annual Economic Review
2347
Hawaii: Manufacturers' Directory,
1981–82   2348.01

Idaho

Idaho: Manufacturing Directory,
1978–79   2431.06
Manufacturing Directory of Idaho
3114

Illinois

Chicago: Geographic Edition, 1981
935.01
Illinois Manufacturers' Directory, 1981
2438.01

Iowa

Iowa Manufacturers' Directory,
1979–80   2776.01

Ireland, Republic of

Guide to Irish Manufacturers   2297
Irish Export Directory   2780
Thom's Commercial Directory   4612

Kansas

Directory of Manufacturers and
Products   1442.01
Kansas Manufacturers & Products
Directory, 1980–81   2904.01

Kentucky

Kentucky Manufacturers' Directory,
1981   2908.02

Louisiana

Louisiana Manufacturers' Directory,
1981   3048.01

Maine

Census of Maine Manufactures   875
Maine, Vermont, New Hampshire:
Directory of Manufacturers, 1979
3061.02

Maryland

Directory of Maryland Manufacturers,
1979–80   1445

Massachusetts

Massachusetts: Directory of
Manufacturers, 1981–82   3149.01
Massachusetts: Manufacturers'
Directory, 1980   3149.02

Michigan

Directory of Michigan Manufacturers
1447

Michigan: Harris Michigan Industrial
Directory, 1980–81   3208.01
Michigan: Manufacturers' Directory,
1980   3209.01

Minnesota

Minnesota: Manufacturers' Directory,
1979–80   3240.01

Mississippi

Mississippi: Manufacturers' Directory,
1980   3245.01

Missouri

Missouri Directory of Manufacturing
and Mining   3249
Missouri: Manufacturing & Mining
Directories, 1980   3249.01
Missouri's New and Expanding
Manufacturers   3250

Montana

Montana: Manufacturers' Directory,
1976–77   3276.01

Nebraska

Directory of Nebraska Manufacturers
1450
Nebraska: Manufacturers' Directory,
1980–81   3423.01

Nevada

Nevada: Industrial Directory, 1981
3430.01

New Hampshire

Maine, Vermont, New Hampshire:
Directory of Manufacturers, 1979
3061.02

New Mexico

Economy   1577
New Mexico: Manufacturing & Mining
Directory, 1981–82   3455

New York City

New York City Business Fact Book
Part 1: Business & Manufacturing
3474

New York State

New York: Manufacturers' Directory,
1980–81   3476.01
New York State Business Fact Book
Part 1: Business & Manufacturing
3481

New Zealand

General Statistics   2217

North Carolina

North Carolina Manufacturers'
   Directory, 1981–82   3534.01

North Dakota

North Dakota Manufacturers'
   Directory, 1980–81   3536.01

Ohio

Ohio: Manufacturers' Guide, 1981
   3593.03

Oklahoma

Oklahoma Directory of Manufacturers
   and Products   3615
Oklahoma: Manufacturers & Products
   Directory, 1980   3617.01

Oregon

Directory of Oregon Manufacturers
   1452
Oregon: Manufacturers' Directory,
   1980–81   3637

Pennsylvania

Pennsylvania: Directory of
   Manufacturers, 1980   3716.01

Puerto Rico

Caribbean Business   862
Economic Censuses of Outlying Areas,
   1977, OAC 77   1547.01

Rhode Island

Connecticut–Rhode Island: Directory of
   Manufacturers, 1981   1117.02

South Africa

South Africa Yearbook   4337

South Dakota

South Dakota: Manufacturers &
   Processors Directory, 1980   4345
South Dakota Manufacturers Directory,
   1981 edition   4345.01

Tennessee

Tennessee: Directory of Manufacturers,
   1981   4593

Texas

Texas: Manufacturers' Directory, 1980
   4597.02

*Union of Soviet Socialist Republics
(USSR)*

Soviet Eastern Europe-China Business
   and Trade   4351

United States

American Industry   185
Census of Manufactures, 1977   876
Central Atlantic States: Manufacturers'
   Directory, 1981   886
Co-op News   1198
Co-op Source Directory   1198.01
Corporate Report Fact Book   1213
Current Surveys—M:D11
   Manufacturers' Shipments,
   Inventories, and Orders   1283
New England: Manufacturers'
   Directory, 1980   3443.01
Sources of State Information and State
   Industrial Directories   4336
Thomas Register of American
   Manufacturers   4611
Trade Lists   4658

Utah

Utah: Manufacturers' Directory,
   1979–80   4835.01

Vermont

Maine, Vermont, New Hampshire:
   Directory of Manufacturers, 1979
   3061.02

Virgin Islands

Caribbean Business   862
Economic Censuses of Outlying Areas,
   1977, OAC 77   1547.01

Washington (State)

Washington Manufacturers' Register,
   1980–81   4888.01
Washington Manufacturers' Register,
   1980–81   4888.02

West Virginia

West Virginia Manufacturing Directory
   4957

Wisconsin

Wisconsin Manufacturers' Directory,
   1981   5008.01

Wyoming

Wyoming: Directory of Manufacturing
   and Mining, 1980   5089.02

MANUFACTURERS AND MANUFACTURING, AGENTS

Verified Directory of Manufacturers'
   Representatives, 1977 Edition   4847

Great Britain

British Commercial Agents Review
   609
Manufacturers' Agent   3107

United States

Trade Lists   4658

MANUFACTURERS AND MANUFACTURING, DISTRIBUTION

Anbar Management Publications
   Marketing Distribution Abstracts
   219
Distribution   1468
Sales & Marketing Management   4165
Trade Lists   4658
Trade Names Dictionary   4665
Traffic Management   4681

MANUFACTURERS AND MANUFACTURING, FINANCES

Confederation of British Industry (CBI)
   Industrial Trends Survey   1101
Management Aids   3072
Manufacturers' Export Sales and Orders
   of Durable Goods. M4-A   3109
Manufacturers' Shipments, Inventories,
   and Orders. M3-1   3110
Reference Book of Manufacturers
   4040

Argentina

Argentina Reference Bk   309

Australia

Australian Market Guide   408

Canada

Financial Post Survey of Industrials
   2017
Industry Price Indexes   2563

Maine

Census of Maine Manufacturers   875

Marketing Science Institute Newsletter 3135
Market Research Abstracts 3137
Market Research Society (MRS) Newsletter 3139
Mintel 3242
Sales Manager's Building 4174

Africa

Statistics Africa 4448

American Nations

Statistics—America 4449

Australia

B & T Advertising Marketing & Media Weekly 455
B & T Yearbook 456
Statistics—Asia & Australasia 4450

Canada

Directory of US and Canadian Marketing Surveys and Services, 1979–80, 3rd edition 1462
Market Research Handbook 3138

Europe

American & European Market Research Reports 155
European Journal of Marketing 1781
Statistics—Europe 4452

Far East

Statistics—Asia & Australasia 4450

Great Britain

Brad Advertiser & Agency List 581
European Journal of Marketing 1781
Market Research Society, Yearbook 3140
Retail Business 4102.01

United States

American & European Market Research Reports 155
Directory of US and Canadian Marketing Surveys and Services, 1979–80, 3rd edition 1462

MARKET RESEARCH SOCIETY (MRS)

Market Research Society (MRS) Newsletter 3139

MARKETING. *See also* Consumer Market. Computer-Aided Marketing. Drop Shipping. Market Research. Marketing Services

ABI/INFORM 2.01
Ad Day/USA 50
Advanced Retail Marketing 62.01
Advertising and Marketing Intelligence (AMI) 66.01
Agri Marketing 115
Anbar Management Services Publications Marketing & Distribution Abstracts 219
Chain Merchandiser Magazine 899
Concise Guide to International Markets 1093
Coopers & Lybrand Banker 1196
Coop Marketing & Management 1197
Counselor 1234
Croner's Reference Book for World Traders 1257
Dartnell Marketing Manager's Handbook, 1973 Edition 1319
Dartnell Sales and Marketing Executive Service 1322
Direct Marketing 1402
Equifax News 1737
European Directory of Business Information Sources & Services 1773
Executive Action Report 1796
Gallagher Report 2206
Handbook of Modern Marketing, 1970 2333
Incentive Marketing and Sales Promotion 2478
Incentive Travel Manager 2479
Industrial Distribution 2517
Industrial Marketing 2533
Industrial Marketing Management 2534
Journal of Advertising Research 2820
Journal of Management Studies 2866
Journal of Marketing 2867
Journal of Marketing Research 2868
Key to Economic Science and Managerial Sciences 2912.01
Long Range Planning 3044
Management Decision 3077
Marketing 3127
Marketing & Media Decisions 3127.01
Marketing Communications 3127.03
Marketing for Sales Executives 3130
Marketing Ideas 3130.01
Marketing Information Guide 3131
Marketing Letter, The 3132
Marketing News 3133
Marketing Science Institute Newsletter 3135
Marketing Times 3136

Media Industry Newsletter 3173
Mintel 3242
Modern Business Reports 3255
Pittsburgh Business Review 3774
Potentials in Marketing 3812
Predi-Briefs 3826
Principal International Business 3844
Sales & Marketing Management 4165
SCAN 4191
Small Business Bibliographies 4299
Small Business Report 4301.01
Survey of Selling Costs 4518
Telephone Marketing Report 4586.01
Topicator 4638
Trade Names Dictionary 4665
World Directory of Marketing Communications Periodicals 5057
World Marketing 5069
World Markets Intelligence Report 5070

Alaska

Pacific Banker and Business 3676

Arizona

Pacific Banker and Business 3676

California

Pacific Banker and Business 3676

Europe

Business Europe 681
European Directory of Business Information Sources & Services 1773
European Journal of Marketing 1781

Great Britain

Advertiser's Annual 65
European Journal of Marketing 1781
Marketing 3127
Quarterly Review of Marketing 3971

Hawaii

Pacific Banker and Business 3673

Idaho

Pacific Banker and Business 3676

Japan

Japan External Trade Organization (JETRO) Marketing Series 2802

Montana

Pacific Banker and Business 3676

Nevada

Pacific Banker and Business   3676

New Zealand

New Zealand Business Who's Who
3495

Oregon

Pacific Banker and Business   3676

United States

Abstract Newsletters, Business &
Economics   2.08
Survey of Buying Power Data Service
4511

Utah

Pacific Banker and Business   3676

Washington (State)

Pacific Banker and Business   3676

MARKETING, INSTITUTE OF (GREAT BRITAIN)

Marketing   3127

MARKETING, MINORITIES

Black Enterprise   560
Gibson Report   2225

MARKETING, OVERSEAS

Export Times   1854
Iowa Exporting Companies Directory
2776
Iowa World Trade Guide   2777
Media International   3174

MARKETING, PERSONNEL

Digest of Executive Opportunities
1389
Principal International Businesses
3844

MARKETING ASSOCIATION, AMERICAN

Marketing News   3133

MARKETING SCIENCE INSTITUTE (US)

Marketing Science Institute Newsletter
3135

MARYLAND

Central Atlantic States: Manufacturers'
Directory, 1981   886

Directory of Maryland Manufacturers,
1979–80   1445
District of Columbia   1469.01
From The State Capitals   2169–2191
Maryland Magazine   3146
Maryland Manufacturers' Directory,
1979–80   3146.01
Maryland: State Industrial Directory,
1980   3146.02
Maryland Statistical Abstract, 1980
edition   3147
State and Local Taxes   4386
State Legislative Reporting Service
4396
State Tax Reports   4413

MASSACHUSETTS

Massachusetts Business & Economic
Report   3148
From the State Capitals   2169–2191
Massachusetts: Directory of
Manufacturers, 1981–82   3149.01
Massachusetts: Manufacturers'
Directory, 1980   3149.02
Massachusetts: Service Directory,
1979–80   3149.03
Massachusetts: State Industrial
Directory, 1981   3149.04
New England: Manufacturers'
Directory, 1980   3443.01
State and Local Taxes   4386
Stae Legislative Reporting Service
4396
State Tax Reports   4413

MASS TRANSPORTATION. *See*
Transit Systems. Types eg, Buses

MATERIALS. *See* Composite
Materials. Materials Handling and
Engineering. Raw Materials. Subjects
and types, eg, Ceramics

MATERIALS HANDLING AND ENGINEERING

Abstract Newsletters, Materials Science
2.21
Bulk   643
Handling & Shipping   2340
International Journal of Physical
Distribution, Land Materials
Management   2694
Journal of Purchasing & Materials
Management   2876
Material Handling Engineering   3152
Materials Engineering   3153
Modern Materials Handling   3256
New Equipment Digest   3444
Storage Handling Distribution   4475

MATHEMATICAL STUDIES, INSTITUTE OF

Statisticians and Others in Allied
Professions   4447

MATHEMATICS. *See also*
Accounting and Auditing. Actuarial
Methods. Operations Research.
Statistical Methods

ACM Transactions on Mathematical
Software   40.02
Annals of Probability   228
Applied Mathematics Modelling   287
Decision Line   1348
Decision Sciences   1352
Econometrica   1534
Journal of Mathematical Economics
2868.01
Mathematical
Programming/Mathematical
Programming Studies   3154.01
Mathematical Social Sciences   3154.02
Statisticians and Others in Allied
Professions   4447

MATTRESSES. *See* Beds, Bedding
and Mattresses

MEASUREMENT. *See* Measuring
and Testing

MEASURING AND TESTING

Selected Business Ventures   4252
Solid State Abstracts Journal   4328

MEAT

Chicago Mercantile Exchange Yearbook
937
Financial Facts about the Meat Packing
Industry   2000
Foreign Agriculture Circulars   2111
In Brief   2476.02
Outlook and Situation Reports
3653.01
Statistical Review of Livestock and
Meat Industries   4441.01
United Nations Industrial Development
Organization Guides to Information
Sources.
UNIDO/LIB/SER.D/1/Rev. 1—
Information Sources on the Meat
Processing Industry   4768
Urner Barry's Price Current   4833.01

Australia

Australian Meat & Livestock Corp
Annual Report   410
In Brief   2476.02

Meat Producer and Exporter 3163
Meat 3164
Statistical Review of Livestock and
  Meat Industries 4441.01

United States

Livestock Market News Reports 3030
Meat, Poultry and Seafood Digest
  3164.01
Restaurant Buyers Guide 4098

MECHANICAL DEVICES

Mechanical & Electrical Cost Data
  3164.02

MEDIA. *See* Communications
Systems. Types, eg, Television and
Radio

MEDIATION AND CONCILIATION SERVICE, FEDERAL (US)

Federal Mediation & Conciliation
  Service Annual Report 1931

MEDICAID

Health Insurance Underwriter 2361
Medicare–Medicaid Guide 3184
Schechter Report/Labs 4191.01

MEDICAL ASSOCIATIONS

World Guide to Scientific Associations
  and Learned Societies 5066

MEDICARE

Health Insurance Underwriter 2361
Medicare–Medicaid Guide 3184
Medicare Report 3185
Payroll Management Guide 3711
Schechter Report/Labs 4191.01
Social Security and Medicare Explained
  4316
Unemployment Insurance Reports
  4744

MEDICINE AND HEALTH. *See*
also Accidents and Safety. Biomedicine.
Hospitals. Insurance. Health. Life
Support Systems. Nurses and Nursing.
Nursing and Rest Homes. Physicians
and Surgeons

Aslib Directory, Volume 2 333.01
Abstracts on Health Effects of
  Environmental Pollutants (HEEP) 4
Clinica 966
Consumer Sourcebook, 1st Edition
  1175
Co-op Consumers 1191.02

Dialog 1375.03
Emergency Preparedness News
  1640.01
Health Care Letter 2357
Health Care Management Review
  2358
Health Media Buyer's Guide 2363
Health Services Research 2365
Hospitals: Journal of the American
  Hospital Association 2396
Hospital Week 2398
IMS Monitor Report 2476.01
International Journal of Health Services
  2693
Law of Advertising 2979
Medical Economics 3180
Medical Meetings 3181.01
Medical School Rounds 3182
Medical World News 3183
Medicare Report 3185
Time 4619
World Health Environmental Surveys
  5067.01

Africa

Africa Research Bulletin 81

Australia

Hospital Journal of Australia 2394

Canada

Perspective Canada 3752
Perspectives Canada III 3753.01

Great Britain

Health and Personal Social Services
  Statistics for England 2354
Social Trends 4321

United States

Biomedical Communications 554.02
Consumer Information Catalog 1154
Health Services Research 2365
Long Term Care 3045
Statistical Bulletin 4426
Washington Health Record 4887.01

Wales

Health and Personal Social Services
  Statistics for Wales 2355

MEDICINE AND HEALTH, EDUCATION

American Hospital Association Guide
  to the Health Care Field 178

Biomedical Communications 554.02
Hospital Medical Staff 2395

MEDICINE AND HEALTH, EQUIPMENT

Abstract Newsletters, Biomedical
  Technology & Human Factors
  Engineering 2.06
Bio-Medical Insight 555
Bio-Medical Scoreboard 556
Clinica 966
Health Care Product News 2359
Health Grants and Contracts Weekly
  2360
Health Service Buyers Guide 2364
Hospital Equipment & Supplies 2391
Hospital Journal of Australia 2394
IMS Monitor Report 2476.01
Medical & Healthcare Marketplace
  Guide, 3rd edition, 1981 3179
Medical Marketing & Media 3181
Worldwide Guide to Medical
  Electronics Marketing
  Representation, 1977 5088

MEDICINE AND HEALTH, FINANCES

Abstract Newsletters, Health Planning
  and Health Services Research 2.17
Clinica 966
Health Services Research 2365
Topics in Health Care Financing 4639

MEDICINE AND HEALTH, GOVERNMENT REGULATIONS AND PROGRAMS

Abstract Newsletters, Health Planning
  and Health Services Research 2.17
Clinica 966
Long Term Care 3045
Medical Marketing & Media 3181
National Health Insurance Reports
  3378
Schechter Report/Labs 4191.01
Washington Health Record 4887.01
Washington Report on Health
  Legislation 4891
Washington Report on Medicine &
  Health 4892

MEDICINE AND HEALTH, MALPRACTICE

Best's Casualty Loss Reserve
  Development 525
Hospital Week 2398
National Association of Insurance
  Commissioners (NAIC) Malpractice
  Claims 3358

MEDICINE AND HEALTH, PERSONNEL

Clinica 966
Executive Compensation Service Top
  Management Report 1802.01
Health Care Management Review
  2358
Health Labor Relations Reports 2362
Medical Economics 3180

MEDICINE AND HEALTH, RESEARCH ON

Abstract Newsletters, Biomedical
  Technology & Human Factors
  Engineering 2.06
Abstract Newsletters, Government
  Inventions for Licensing 2.16
Abstract Newsletters, Health Planning
  and Health Services Research 2.17
Abstract Newsletters, Medicine &
  Biology 2.22
Biological Abstracts/RRM 554.01
Health Services Research 2365
Medical World News 3183
Research Programs in the Medical
  Sciences 4091.01

MEETINGS, CONFERENCES AND SEMINARS. *See also* Conventions.
Subjects subhead Conferences on

Keesing's Contemporary Archives
  2905
Manage 3067
Medical Meetings 3181.01
Meeting News 3186
Meetings & Incentive Travel 3187
Potentials in Marketing 3812
Successful Meetings 4487

MEN'S AND BOYS' WEAR. *See* Apparel

MENTAL HEALTH

Abstract Newsletters, Medicine &
  Biology 2.22
Industrial Health Foundation Nursing
  Series 2529
Journal of Non-White Concerns in
  Personnel and Guidance 2870

Australia

Australian Hospitals and Health
  Services Yearbook 403

MERCHANT FLEET. *See* Ships and Shipping, Merchant Fleet

MERCHANT MARINE (US)

Merchant Marine Data Sheet 3194

MERCHANT MARINE ACT OF 1970

Standard Specifications for Tanker
  Construction 4380

METAL COLLAPSIBLE TUBES

Tube Topics 4732

METAL INDUSTRY. *See* Metal Products

METAL PRODUCTS *See also* Metal Collapsible Tubes

American Machinist 199
American Machinist (Magazine) 200
American Metal Market 201
Australia's International Engineering
  Exhibitions (AIEE) 422
Commodities Survey 1023
Foundry Management & Technology
  2158
Industry Mart 2562
Iron Age 2782
Iron Age Metalworking International
  2783
Metalworking Machinery. MQ-35W
  3201
Metalworking Production 3202
Nonferrous Metal Data 3532
33 Metal Producing 4607
United Nations Industrial Development
  Organization Guides to Information
  Sources. UNIDO/LIB/SER D/5—
  Information Sources on the Foundry
  Industry 4772
Welding and Metal Fabrication 4944

Australia

Metal and Engineering Industry
  Yearbook 3196

United States

Dun & Bradstreet Metalworking
  Marketing Directory 1513
Metalworking Directory 3200
Mississippi Metalworking Services
  Directory 3246

METALS AND METALLURGY. *See also* Metal Products. Specific metals

American Metal Market 201
Coal Week International 973
Commodities Weekly Technical Report
  and Currency Exchange Rates 1024
Engineering and Mining Journal 1706
Engineering and Mining Journal—
  Annual Buyers' Guide 1707
Engineering and Mining Journal (E &
  MJ) International Directory of

Mining and Mineral Processing
  Operations 1708
Foundry Management & Technology
  2158
Green's Commodity Market Comments
  2266
Iron and Steel International 2786
Lynch International Investment Survey
  3051
Mineral Facts and Problems 3231
Precision Metal 3825
Solid State Abstracts Journal 4328
Trade and Economic Development
  4647
World Commodity Report 5048

Australia

Australian Mining 411

India

Engineering & Metal's Review 1704

United States

Abstract Newsletters, Government
  Inventions for Licensing 2.16
Metals Week Insider Report 3198
Metals Daily 3196.01

METALS AND METALLURGY, NONFERROUS METALS

Metals Week 3197
Metals Week Price Handbook 3199

METALS AND METALLURGY, PRICES

American Metal Market 201
Engineering and Mining Journal 1706
Green's Commodity Market Comments
  2266
Metals Week 3197
Metals Week Price Handbook 3199

Canada

Northern Miner 3539

United States

Metals Week Insider Report 3198

METEOROLOGY. *See* Weather

METHODS-TIME MEASUREMENT

Methods-Time Measurement (MTM)
  Journal 3204

METHODS-TIME MEASUREMENT ASSOCIATION FOR STANDARDS AND RESEARCH

Methods-Time Measurement (MTM)
  Journal 3204

Jobson's Mining Year Book   2813
Who's Pegging Where   4975.01

Canada

Canadian Mining Journal   819
Canadian Weekly Stock Charts: Mines
& Oils   848
General Review of the Mineral
Industries   2216
Northern Miner   3539
Quebec Corporation Manual   3979

Colorado

Business Economic Outlook Forum
678

Great Britain

United Kingdom Mineral Statistics
4760

New Mexico

Economy   1577
New Mexico: Manufacturing & Mining
Directory, 1981–82   3455

Missouri

Missouri: Manufacturing & Mining
Directories, 1980   3249.01

South Africa

South Africa Yearbook   4337

United States

Federal Trade Commission. Quarterly
Financial Report for Mfg, Mining &
Trade Corporations   1975
Mine Safety and Health Reporter
3234

Wyoming

Wyoming: Directory of Manufacturing
and Mining, 1980   5089.02

MINING APPEALS BOARD (US)

Occupational Safety and Health
Decisions   3566

MINNESOTA

From the State Capitals   2169–2191
Minnesota 3240
Minnesota: Manufacturers Directory,
1979–80   3240.01
Minnesota: State Industrial Directory,
1980   3240.02
State and Local Taxes   4386

State Legislative Reporting Service
4396
State Tax Reports   4413

MINORITIES. *See also* Commerce
and Industry, Blacks. Commerce and
Industry, Minorities. Fields of activities,
eg, Labor, Minorities. Types, eg, Blacks

Data on Selected Racial Groups
Available from Bureau of the Census,
No 40, Revised May, 1977   1338
Directory of Data Sources on Racial
and Ethnic Minorities   1425
Gibson Report   2225
Journal of Non-White Concerns in
Personnel and Guidance   2870
Minority Business Information Institute
(MBII) Newsletter   3241
Race Relations & Industry   3983

MINORITY BUSINESS
DEVELOPMENT AGENCY

Commerce: Journal of Minority
Business   996.01

MINORITY BUSINESS
ENTERPRISE, OFFICE OF (US)

Access   7

MINORITY BUSINESSES. *See*
Commerce and Industry, Blacks.
Commerce and Industry, Minorities.
Subjects, eg, Accounting and Auditing,
Minority Businesses

MISSILES

Backlog of Orders for Aerospace
Companies MQ-37D   446
DMS Missiles & Satellites (Europe)
1475.24
DMS Missiles/Spacecraft   1475.25
Missile/Ordnance Letter   3244

MISSISSIPPI

From the State Capitals   2169–2191
Mississippi Manufacturers Directory
3245
Mississippi: Manufacturers' Directory,
1980   3245.01
Mississippi Metalworking Services
Directory   3246
Mississippi: State Industrial Directory,
1981   3246.01
State and Local Taxes   4386
State Legislative Reporting Service
4396
State Tax Reports   4413

MISSOURI

From the State Capitals   2169–2191
Missouri Corporate Planner   3248
Missouri: Manufacturing and Mining
Directories, 1980   3249.01
Missouri: State Industrial Directory,
1981   3250.01
More Facts   3319.01
State and Local Taxes   4386
State Legislative Reporting Service
4396
State Tax Reports   4413

MOBILE HOMES. *See* Housing,
Mobile Homes

MODELS (SIMULATIONS)

Applied Mathematics Modelling   287
International Journal of Systems
Science   2697
Journal of Policy Modelling   2872.02
Transportation Planning and
Technology   4693

MONETARY INDICATORS. *See*
Currency

MONEY. *See* Currency

MONEY MARKET FUNDS. *See*
Currency, Markets

MONEY MARKETS. *See* Currency

MONEY SUPPLY. *See* Currency,
Money Supply

MONTANA

From the State Capitals   2169–2191
Montana Business Quarterly   3276
Montana: Manufacturers Directory,
1976–77   3276.01
Montana: State Industrial Directory,
1981   3276.02
State and Local Taxes   4386
State Legislative Reporting Service
4396
State Tax Reports   4413

MONTREAL STOCK EXCHANGE

Montreal Stock Exchange Daily Official
News Sheet   3306
Montreal Stock Exchange Monthly
Review   3307

MORTALITY. *See* Death

United States

Bank Pooled Funds   498
Consensus of Insiders   1119
Graphoscope   2261
Moody's Dividend Record   3312
Mutual Fund Fact Book   3345
Mutual Fund Performance Review
   3346
Mutual Funds Guide   3349
Vickers Guide to Investment Company
   Portfolios   4853
Wiesenberger Financial Services   5001

MUTUAL INSURANCE COMPANIES, NATIONAL ASSOCIATION OF

Mutual Insurance Bulletin   3351

MUTUAL SAVINGS BANKS.   See
Banking and Finance, Mutual Savings
Banks

NASA.   See Aeronautics and Space
Administration, National (NASA) (US)

NATIONAL BANK OF AUSTRALIA

National Bank of Australasia. National
   Bank Monthly Summary   3364

NATIONAL BANKS.   See Banking
and Finance, National Banks

NATIONALIZATION OF
INDUSTRY.   See Commerce and
Industry, Nationalization of Industry

NATIONAL SECURITIES AND
RESEARCH CORP.

National Forecast   3377

NATURAL GAS.   See Gas
(Illuminating and Fuel)

NATURAL RESOURCES.   See also
Raw Materials. Research and
Development, Resource Management

Farmline   1901.01
Land Economics   2961
Lynch International Investment Survey
   3051
Resources and Energy   4096.02
Resources Policy   4097
United Nations Institute for Training
   and Research (UNITAR) Important
   for the Future   4790
Valuation   4838

Africa

African Trade/Commerce Africain   80

Arctic and Antarctic

Arctic Alternative   301
Northern Perspectives   3540

Arkansas

Basics of Plant Location in Arkansas
   514

Australia

Guide to Investment   2296

Canada

Arctic Alternatives   301
Canada–United Kingdom Year Book
   771
Northern Perspectives   3540
Saskatchewan Monthly Statistical
   Review   4182

Maryland

Maryland Statistical Abstract, 1980
   edition   3147

Mexico

Natural Resources (Mexican)   3419

United States

Abstract Newsletters, Natural
   Resources & Earth Sciences   2.24

West Virginia

West Virginia Economic Profile   4955

NATURE AND WILDLIFE

Leisure, Recreation and Tourism
   Abstracts   3004.01
Unasylva: An International Journal of
   Forestry and Forest Products   4739

NAVY.   See Armament and Defense

NEBRASKA

Business in Nebraska   694
Directory of Nebraska Manufacturers
   1450
From the State Capitals   2169–2191
Nebraska: Manufacturers' Directory,
   1980–81   3423.01
Nebraska Now   3424
Nebraska: State Industrial Directory,
   1981   3425
Nebraska Statistical Handbook   3426
State and Local Taxes   4386
State Legislative Reporting Service
   4396
State Tax Reports   4413

NEGROES.   See Blacks

NEVADA

From the State Capitals   2169–2191
Nevada Review of Business &
   Economics   3431
State and Local Taxes   4386
State Legislative Reporting Service
   4396
State Tax Reports   4413

NEW ENGLAND (US)

New England: Manufacturers
   Directory, 1980   3443.01

NEW HAMPSHIRE

From the State Capitals   2169–2191
Maine, Vermont, New Hampshire:
   Directory of Manufacturers, 1979
   3061.02
New England: Manufacturers'
   Directory, 1980   3443.01
New Hampshire: State Industrial
   Directory, 1980–81   3448
State and Local Taxes   4386
State Legislative Reporting Service
   4396
State Tax Reports   4413

NEW JERSEY

From the State Capitals   2169–2191
New Jersey: Directory of
   Manufacturers, 1981–82   3450.01
New Jersey Economic Outlook   3451
New Jersey Policy Council Annual
   Report   3452
New Jersey: State Industrial Directory,
   1980   3453.01
State and Local Taxes   4413
State Legislative Reporting Service
   4396
State Tax Reports   4413

NEW JERSEY BUSINESS AND
INDUSTRY ASSOCIATION

New Jersey Business   3450

NEW MEXICO

Financial Trend   2032
From State Capitals   2169–2191
New Mexico Business   3454
New Mexico: Manufacturing & Mining
   Directory, 1981–82   3455
New Mexico: State Industrial Directory,
   1981   3455.01
State and Local Taxes   4386
State Legislative Reporting Service
   4396
State Tax Reports   4413

NEW PRODUCTS. *Note:* Material covers all fields. *See also* Research and Development, New Products

Advertising Age   66
Agri Marketing   115
American Industry   185
Chemical/Energy New Product
  Directory, 1980   922.01
Drug and Cosmetic Industry   1508
Electrical Construction and
  Maintenance (Annual)   1601
Electronic Component News   1620
Electronic New Product Directory,
  1978–79   1630.01
Gibson Report   2225
Health & Safety in Industry   2356.01
Health Care Product News   2359
Heating & Air Conditioning Journal
  2366
Incentive Marketing   2477
Industrial Maintenance and Plant
  Operation   2532
Industrial Product Bulletin   2536.01
Industrial Purchasing Agent   2538
Information and Records Management
  2570
International Intertrade Index   2686
International New Product Newsletter
  2714
Invention Intelligence   2749
Japan Chemical Directory   2795.02
LabData   2923
Marketing Times   3136
Mintel   3242
National Office Machine Dealers Assn
  (NOMDA) Spokesman   3397
Petrochemical News   3754
Photographic Trade News   3766
Potentials in Marketing   3812
Rountree Report   4143
Salesman's Opportunity Magazine
  4175
Selected Business Ventures   4252
Technology Forecasts and Technology
  Surveys   4581
Unit   4754.01
What's New in Building   4961
What's New in Electronics   4961.01
What's New in Industry   4963.01
World Products   5075

Canada

Engineering Digest   1709
New Equipment News   3445
Ontario Business News   3620
Volume Retail Merchandising   4867

Europe (West)

New From Europe   3445.01
New Products & Processes From
  Western Europe   3458.01

Great Britain

Sales Management and Sales
  Engineering   4172

Japan

New From Japan   3446

United States

Product Liability Legislation for Client
  and Counsel   3874.01

NEVADA

Nevada: Industrial Directory, 1981
  3430.01
Nevada: State Industrial Directory,
  1980   3431.01

NEWS

Business Index   690.01
National Newspaper Index   3396.01

NEWSLETTERS.   *See also* subjects

How to Buy, Sell and Price Newsletter
  Properties   2420.01
Hudson's Washington News Media
  Contacts Directory   2427
Inside Look at the Newsletter Field
  2589
Newsletter on Newsletters   3466
Newsletter Yearbook/Directory   3467

NEW SOUTH WALES.   *See*
Australia

NEWSPAPERS.   *See also*
Advertising, Newspapers. News subjects

Bacon's Publicity Checker   448
Editor & Publisher   1584.01
Gallagher Report   2206
Information Bank I and II   2570.02
Key Issues Tracking (KIT)   2910.01
Media Industry Newsletter   3173

California

Metro CALIFORNIA media   3204.02

Canada

Ayer Directory of Publications   443
Canadian News Index   820
Matthews' List   3155

Europe

Bacon's International Publicity Checker
  447
Willings Press Guide   5002

Great Britain

Advertiser's Annual   65
British Rate & Data   622
Hollis Press and Public Relations
  Annual   2377
Willings Press Guide   5002

New York City Metropolitan Area

New York City Business Fact Book
  Part 1: Business & Manufacturing
  3474
New York Publicity Outlets   3479

United States

Ayer Directory of Publications   443
Family Page Directory   1885
Index to Black Newspapers   2500
Newsbank Library   3462.01
New York Times Index, The   3488

Washington (DC)

Hudson's Washington News Media
  Contacts Directory   2427

**NEWSPAPERS, CIRCULATION
AND MARKETS**

Audit Bureau of Circulations Factbook
  348
Audit Bureau of Circulations (ABC)
  News Bulletin   349
Media Guide International:
  Business/Professional Publications
  Edition   3171
Media Guide International:
  Newspapers/Newsmagazines Edition
  3172
Newspaper Circulation Analysis   3468
Newspaper Rates & Data   3470
Print Media Production Data   3850

Canada

Ayer Directory of Publications   443
Editor & Publisher Market Guide
  1585

Great Britain

British Rate & Data   622

United States

Ayer Directory of Publications   443
Editor & Publisher Market Guide
  1585

NEWSPAPERS, LAWS ON

Media Law Reporter   3175

NEWSPAPERS, PERSONNEL

Editor & Publisher   1584.01
Family Page Directory   1885
Linage Booster   3019

NEWSPAPERS, PRINTING AND PRODUCTION

Editor & Publisher   1584.01
Printing Impressions   3849

NEWSPAPERS, PROMOTION

Idea Newsletter   2433

NEWSPAPERS, RATES

Media Guide International:
   Business/Professional Publications
   Edition   3171
Media Guide International:
   Newspapers/Newsmagazines Edition
   3172
Newspaper Circulation Analysis   3468
Newspaper Rates & Data   3470
Print Media Production Data   3850

Canada

Ayer Directory of Publications   443
Canadian Advertising Rates & Data
   774

Great Britain

British Rate & Data   622

United States

Ayer Directory of Publications   443

NEW VENTURES. *See* Commerce
and Industry, New Ventures

NEW YORK CITY

Annual Summary of Business Statistics,
   New York State   265
New York City Business Fact Book
   Part 1: Business & Manufacturing
   3474
New York City Business Fact Book
   Part 2: Population & Housing   3475

NEW YORK MERCANTILE EXCHANGE

New York Mercantile Exchange
   Statistical Yearbook   3477

NEW YORK STATE

Annual Summary of Business Statistics,
   New York State   265

Business Trends in New York State
   726
Capital Journal   857.01
From the State Capitals   2169–2191
New York: Manufacturers Directory,
   1980–81   3476.01
New York State Business Fact Book
   Part 1: Business & Manufacturing
   3481
New York State Business Fact Book
   Part 2: Population & Housing   3482
New York: State Industrial Directory,
   1980   3483.01
Omnibus   3619.01
Quarterly Summary of Business
   Statistics, New York State   3975
State and Local Taxes   4386
State Legislative Reporting Service
   4396
State Tax Reports   4413

NEW YORK STOCK EXCHANGE

Barron's   509
Chartcraft Weekly Service   912
Daily Graphs New York Stock
   Exchange/OTC   1298
Daily Stock Price Records   1306
Dow Jones Investor's Handbook   1500
Moody's Industrial Manual and News
   Reports   3314
New York Stock Exchange (NYSE)
   Fact Book   3484
New York Stock Exchange (NYSE)
   Guide   3485
New York Stock Exchange (NYSE),
   Statistical Highlights   3486
Standard New York Stock Exchange
   (NYSE) Stock Reports   4375
Stock Guide   4466
Trade Levels Option Report   4656
Trade Levels Report   4657

NEW YORK TIMES, THE (PUBLICATION)

Information Bank I and II   2570.02
Key Issue Tracking (KIT)   2910.01
National Newspaper Index   3396.01
New York Times Index, The   3488

NEW YORK UNIVERSITY

New York University Annual
   Conference on Labor   3489
New York University Annual Institute
   on Federal Taxation   3490

NEW ZEALAND

Australia and New Zealand (ANZ)
   Bank Business Indicators   380
Business Indicators   690.02
Capital Letter   857.02

Catalogue of New Zealand Statistics 4th
   edition, 1978 & 80   870
Economic News Bulletin   1555
Handbook for Investors—New Zealand
   2314
Information Releases   2573.03
Life and Business in New Zealand
   3011
Monthly Abstract of Statistics   3277
National Business Review   3365
New Zealand Official Yearbook   3511
New Zealand Trade Report   3513.01
Pocket Digest of New Zealand Statistics
   3790
Quarterly Predictions of National
   Income & Expenditure   3967
Trans-Tasman   4699

NEW ZEALAND EMPLOYERS FEDERATION

Employer   1650

NIGERIA

Economic & Financial Review   1536
Economic Indicators   1552
Federal Ministry of Industries Annual
   Report   1932
Handbook of Commerce and Industry
   in Nigeria   2325
Nigeria Newsletter   3517.01
Trade Report   4673

NLRB. *See* Labor Relations Board,
National (US)

NO-FAULT PLANS. *See* Insurance,
No-Fault

NOISE

Noise Control Report   3528
Transportation Planning and
   Technology   4693

Canada

Canadian Environmental Control
   Newsletter   791
Guidelines for the Administration of
   the Canada Noise Control
   Regulations, 1975   2283

United States

Abstract Newsletters, Environmental
   Pollution & Control   2.15
Noise Regulation Reports   3529

NOISE POLLUTION. *See* Noise

NON-PAYING STOCK ISSUES. *See* Stocks and Bonds, Non-Paying Stock Issues

NONPROFIT ORGANIZATIONS. *See* Institutions and Agencies, Non-Profit. Foundations

NORTH ATLANTIC TREATY ORGANIZATION (NATO)

DMS NATO/Europe   1475.26
DMS NATO Weapons   1475.27

NORTH CAROLINA

Apparel South   282.02
Central Atlantic States: Manufacturers Directory, 1981   886
From the State Capitals   2169–2191
North Carolina Industrial Data File 3534
North Carolina: Manufacturers Directory, 1981–82   3534.01
North Carolina: State Industrial Directory, 1980   3535.01
North Carolina Review of Business & Economics   3535
State and Local Taxes   4386
State Legislative Reporting Service 4396
State Tax Reports   4413

NORTH DAKOTA

From the State Capitals   2169–2191
North Dakota: Manufacturers Directory, 1980–81   3536.01
North Dakota: State Industrial Directory, 1981   3536.02
State and Local Taxes   4413

NORTH SEA

North Sea Letter   3543
Walter Skinner's North Sea and Europe Offshore Year Book and Buyer's Guide   4293

NUCLEAR ENERGY AND POWER. *See* Atomic Power and Weapons

NUCLEAR FUEL. *See* Atomic Power and Weapons, Nuclear Fuel

NUCLEAR WEAPONS. *See* Atomic Power and Weapons

NUMISMATICS

Forecaster   2107

NURSES AND NURSING

Industrial Health Foundation Nursing Series   2529
Nursing Administration Quarterly 3557
Nursing Management   3558

NURSING AND REST HOMES

Australian Hospitals and Health Services Yearbook   403
Current Literature on Aging   1278
Fitch Hospital and Other Non-profit Institutional Ratings   2053
Long Term Care   3045

NUTRITION. *See* Food, Nutrition

OAS. *See* American States, Organization of (OAS)

OCCUPATIONAL AND PHYSICAL THERAPY

Abstract Newsletters, Medicine & Biology   2.22

OCCUPATIONAL SAFETY. *See* Labor, Health Hazards and Safety

OCCUPATIONAL SAFETY AND HEALTH ACT (US) AND ADMINISTRATION

Best's Safety Directory   541
Employment Safety and Health Guide 1665
Job Safety & Health Report   2812
Occupational Safety and Health Act (OSHA) Compliance Letter   3564
Occupational Safety and Health Act (OSHA) Report   3565
Occupational Safety and Health Decisions   3566

OCCUPATIONS AND PROFESSIONS. *See* Professions

OCEAN RESOURCES. *See also* Marine Biology. Research and Development, Water Resources

Marine Policy   3121
Maritime and Construction Aspects of Ocean Thermal Energy Conversion (OTEC) Plant Ships   3122
Ocean Development and International Law   3570
Oceanic Abstracts   3570.01
Ocean Resources Engineering   3572
Underwater Information Bulletin   4740

OCEANS AND OCEANOGRAPHY. *See also* Coastal Areas. Hydrology. Marine Biology. Ocean Resources

Abstract Newsletters, Ocean Technology & Engineering   2.25
Latin America and the Development of the Law of the Sea   2970
Marine Policy   3121
Ocean Construction & Engineering Report   3568
Oceanic Abstracts   3570.01
Underwater Letter   4741

OECD. *See* Economic Cooperation and Development, Organization for (OECD)

Financial Market Trends   2008
Guide to Legislation on Restrictive Business Practices   2299
Indicators of Industrial Activity 2505.01
Labour Force Statistics   2952
Main Economics Indicators   3061
OECD Import-Export Microtables 3575.01
Statistics of Foreign Trade, Series B: Annual Tables by Reporting Country 4453.01
Statistics of Foreign Trade, Series C: Annual Tables by Country   4453.02

OFFICE BUILDINGS. *See* Buildings

OFFICE EQUIPMENT. *See also* specific types, eg, Office Furniture

Office Equipment and Products 3578.01
Office Equipment News   3579
Office Equipment News   3579.01
Office Products News   3580
Office World News   3582

OFFICE FURNITURE

Contract   1185
Geyer's Dealer Topics   2223
National Office Products Assn (NOPA) Industry Report   3398
Office Equipment News   3579

OFFICE MACHINE DEALERS ASSOCIATION, CANADA

Canadian Office Machine Dealers Assn (COMDA) Key   823

OFFICE MACHINES. *See also* Copying Machines

Administrative Mgt   57
Canadian Office Machine Dealers Assn (COMDA) Key   823

Canadian Office Products and
Stationery 824
Geyer's Dealer Topics 2223
National Office Machine Dealers Assn
(NOMDA) Spokesman 3397
National Office Products Assn (NOPA)
Industry Report 3398
Office Equipment News 3579
Office World News 3582
Special Report 4356

OFFICE PRODUCTS ASSOCIATION, NATIONAL

National Office Products Assn (NOPA)
Industry Report 3398

OFFICE SERVICES

West European Living Costs 1977
4952

OFFICE SUPPLIES. *See also*
Business Forms

Canadian Office Products and
Stationery 824
Geyer's Dealer Topics 2223
National Office Products Assn (NOPA)
Industry Report 3398
Office Equipment News 3579
Office World News 3582
Special Report 4356
Stationery & Office Supplies 4417

OFFICE SYSTEMS. *See also*
Automation. Computer-Aided
Management Techniques. Word
Processing

Administrative Mgt 57
Automated Business Communications
Program 423
Electric Data Processing, EDP Industry
Report 1590
Electronic Office Management and
Technology 1631.01
Handbook of Modern Office
Management and Administrative
Services 2334
Modern Office Procedures 3257
Office Administration Handbook 3577
Office Automation Reporting Service
3578
Officemation Management 3579.02
Officemation Product Reports 3579.03
Office Products News 3580
Office Systems Reports 3581.01
Practice Administration Manual 3823
Special Report 4356

OFFICE WORKERS. *See* White
Collar Workers

OFFSHORE OIL AND GAS. *See*
Gas (Illuminating and Fuel), Offshore.
Oil (Petroleum and Gasoline), Offshore

OHIO

Development News Notes 1375.01
From the State Capitals 2169–2191
Ohio Developer 3593.01
Ohio: Industrial Directory, 1981
3593.02
Ohio: Manufacturers Guide, 1981
3593.03
State and Local Taxes 4386
State Legislative Reporting Service
4396
State Tax Reports 4413

OIL (PETROLEUM) AND GASOLINE. *See also* Creosote Oil.
Gasoline and Service Stations. Oil
Shale. Pipelines. Tar Sands-Based
Petroleum

Achievement 39
Annual Survey of Oil and Gas.
MA-13K 269
AP–Dow Jones Petroleum News
Service 281
Chemical Horizons North American
Report 925
Chemical Horizons Overseas Report
925.01
Chilton's Oil and Gas Energy 940
Company Acreage and Activity
Statistics 1051
Dow Jones International Energy Wire
1498
Energy Developments 1679
Foreign Scouting Service 2136
International Oil and Gas Field
Records 2716
International Oil News 2717
International Petroleum Encyclopedia
2720
Japanese Newsletter 2800
Law and Policy of the
Intergovernmental Primary
Commodity Agreements 2978
Law of Pooling and Unitization—
Voluntary, Compulsory 2985
Manual of Oil and Gas Terms,
Annotated 3103
Oil & Gas Journal 3595
Oil and Gas Law 3596
Oil Daily 3603
Organization for Economic
Co-operation and Development
(OECD) Economic Outlook 3641

Pipeline & Gas Journal 3772
Platt's Oilgram Marketscan 3784.01
Platt's Oilgram News 3785
Platt's Oilgram News/Wire 3785.01
Platt's Oil Marketing Bulletin 3786.01
Quarterly Oil Statistics 3966
Rocky Mountain Mineral Law Institute
4140
Walter Skinner's Oil and Gas
International Year Book 4294
Walter Skinner's Who's Who in World
Oil and Gas 4295
Tax Sheltered Investments 4570
Twentieth Century Petroleum Statistics
4736
World Production and Reserve
Statistics 5074

Alaska

Alaska Business News Letter 137
Alaska Industry 139
Alaska: Petroleum & Industrial
Directory, 1980 141.01

Australia

Annual Mining Review 251
Lipscombe Report 251

California

Oil in California 3605

Canada

Canadian Petroleum 827
Crude Petroleum and Natural Gas
Production 1262
Daily Oil Bulletin 1303
Miscellaneous Petroleum and Coal
Products Industries 3243
Oil Pipe Line Transport 3607

Great Britain

Achievement 39
Oilman 3606

Iran

Iran Economic News 2779

Nevada

Oil in California 3605

Nigeria

Nigeria Newsletter 3517.01

Middle East

Middle East 3216

North Sea

North Sea Letter   3543

Texas

Oil in Texas   3605.01

United States

Current Wholesale Trade   1284.01
IPAA Statistical and Economic Reports
  2777.01
Oil in the Mid-Continent   3605.02
Oil in the Rockies   3605.03
Petroleum Independent   3760
PI Reports   3773
United States Oil and Gas Production
  News   4813.01

OIL (PETROLEUM) AND GASOLINE, CRUDE

Drilling Service   1505.03
Energy Service   1694
Platt's Oil Price Handbook   3787

Canada

Refined Petroleum Products   4043

United States

Crude Petroleum and Natural Gas.
  M:T58   1263

OIL (PETROLEUM) AND GASOLINE, DRILLING STARTS

AP–Dow Jones Petroleum News
  Service   281
Chilton's Oil and Gas Energy   940
Dow Jones International Energy Wire
  1498
Oil & Gas Journal   3595
Oil, Gas & Petrochem Equipment
  3604
Petroleum Engineer International   3759
Profile—A Continuing Study of Oil and
  Gas Programs   3891

Australia

Jobson's Mining Year Book   2813
Trans-Tasman   4699

Canada

Daily Oil Bulletin   1303

Colorado

Rocky Mountain Journal   4139

New Zealand

Trans-Tasman   4699

United States

IPAA Statistical and Economic Reports
  2777.01
National Wildcat Monthly   3413.01
PI Reports   3773

OIL (PETROLEUM) AND GASOLINE, EQUIPMENT AND FACILITIES

Cost Forecasting Service   1227
Oil, Gas & Petrochem Equipment
  3604

OIL (PETROLEUM) AND GASOLINE, EXPLORATION

Annual Survey of Oil and Gas.
  MA-13K   269
Company Acreage and Activity
  Statistics   1051
Energy Developments   1679
Exploration and Economics of the
  Petroleum Industry   1815
Foreign Scouting Service   2136
Johnson Survey   2816.01
Licences and Exploration Information
  System (LEXIS)   3009

Australia

Annual Mining Review   251
Oil and Gas Bulletin   3594

Belgium

Oil and Gas, the North Sea
  Exploitation   3601

Canada

Canadian Oil Register   825
National Exploration Daily   3373.01

Denmark

Oil and Gas, the North Sea
  Exploitation   3601

Great Britain

Achievement   39
North Sea Letter   3543
Oil and Gas, the North Sea
  Exploitation   3601

Netherlands

Oil and Gas, the North Sea
  Exploitation   3601

Norway

Oil and Gas, the North Sea
  Exploitation   3601

Sweden

Oil and Gas, the North Sea
  Exploitation   3601

United States

National Exploration Daily   3373.01

OIL (PETROLEUM) AND GASOLINE, FINANCES

Energy Development   1679
Energy Service   1694
Oil & Gas Journal   3595
Petroleum Economist   3758
Petroleum Outlook   3761
Quarterly Oil Statistics   3966

Australia

Oil and Gas Bulletin   3594

Canada

Canadian Weekly Stock Charts: Mines
  & Oils   848

Great Britain

Dun & Bradstreet Composite Register
  1511

OIL (PETROLEUM) AND GASOLINE, GOVERNMENT REGULATIONS AND PROGRAMS

Annual Institute on Oil and Gas Law
  and Taxation   250
AP–Dow Jones Petroleum News
  Service   281
Oil and Gas Law: Abridged Edition
  3597

American Nations

Mining and Petroleum Legislation of
  Latin America and the Caribbean
  3239

Belgium

Oil and Gas, the North Sea
  Exploitation   3601

Canada

Oil and Gas Reporter   3599

Denmark

Oil and Gas, the North Sea
  Exploitation   3601

Great Britain

Oil and Gas, the North Sea Exploitation 3601

Netherlands

Oil and Gas, the North Sea Exploitation 3601

Norway

Oil and Gas, the North Sea Exploitation 3601

Sweden

Oil and Gas, the North Sea Exploitation 3601

United States

Law of Federal Oil and Gas Leases 2982
Law of Oil and Gas Leases 2984
Oil & Gas Price Regulation Analyst 3598.01
Oil and Gas Reporter 3599
United States Oil and Gas Production News 4813.01
United States Oil Week 4813.02

OIL (PETROLEUM) AND GASOLINE, IMPORTS AND EXPORTS

Quarterly Oil Statistics 3966

Canada

Refined Petroleum Products 4043

United States

Summary of US Export and Import Merchandise Trade 4495

OIL (PETROLEUM) AND GASOLINE, LEASING

Law of Federal Oil and Gas Leases 2982
Law of Oil and Gas Leases 2984
Oil and Gas Law: Abridged Edition 3597

United States

Oil and Gas Lease Reports 3598
Oil in California 3605
Oil in the Mid-Continent 3605.02
Oil in the Rockies 3605.03

OIL (PETROLEUM) AND GASOLINE, OFFSHORE

Business News 713
Construction News 1137
Construction News Magazine 1138
International Petroleum Encyclopedia 2720
Ocean Construction Locator 3569
Ocean Oil Weekly Report 3571
Offshore 3590
Offshore Rig Newsletter 3592
Oil, Gas & Petrochem Equipment 3604
Petroleum Engineer International 3759

Belgium

Oil and Gas, the North Sea Exploitation 3601

Denmark

Oil and Gas, the North Sea Exploitation 3601

Europe

Walter Skinner's North Sea and Europe Offshore Year Book and Buyer's Guide 4293

Great Britain

Construction News 1137
Oil and Gas, the North Sea Exploitation 3601

Netherlands

Oil and Gas, the North Sea Exploitation 3601

North Sea

North Sea Letter 3543
North Sea Petroleum: An Investment & Marketing Opportunity . . . How Big . . . How Soon . . . How to Participate 3544
Offshore 3590
Walter Skinner's North Sea and Europe Offshore Year Book and Buyer's Guide 4293

Norway

Norwegian American Commerce 3548
Oil and Gas, the North Sea Exploitation 3601

Sweden

Oil and Gas, the North Sea Exploitation 3601

Texas

Oil in Texas 3605.01

United States

Offshore Rig Location Report 3591

OIL (PETROLEUM) AND GASOLINE, PRICES

AP–Dow Jones Petroleum News Service 281
Dow Jones International Energy Wire 1498
Energy Developments 1679
International Petroleum Encyclopedia 2720
IPAA Statistical and Economic Reports 2777.01
Oil Daily 3603
Oil & Gas Price Regulation Analyst 3598.01
Petroleum Economist 3758
Platt's Bunkerwire 3783.01
Platt's Oilgram Marketscan 3784.01
Platt's Oilgram Price Report 3786
Platt's Oil Price Handbook 3787
Platt's Oil Regulation Report 3787.01
United States Oil Week 4813.02

OIL (PETROLEUM) AND GASOLINE, REFINING

Energy Service 1694
International Petroleum Encyclopedia 2720
Oil & Gas Journal 3595
Oil, Gas & Petrochem Equipment 3604
Petroleum Refineries 3762
Quarterly Oil Statistics 3966
Refined Petroleum Products 4043
Twentieth Century Petroleum Statistics 4736

OIL (PETROLEUM) AND GASOLINE, SHIPPING

AP–Dow Jones Petroleum News Service 281
Bunker Fuels FT810 648
Lloyd's Monthly List of Laid Up Vessels 3033.03
Platt's Bunkerwire 3783.01
Refined Petroleum Products 4043

OIL (PETROLEUM) AND GASOLINE, TAXATION

Annual Institute on Oil and Gas Law and Taxation 250
Oil & Gas Tax Quarterly 3600

United States

Federal Taxation of Oil and Gas Transactions 1964
Oil & Gas Taxes Natural Resources 3600.01

OIL PRODUCING AND EXPORTING COUNTRIES (OPEC)

International Petroleum Encyclopedia 2720
MidEast Markets Business Information 3226
Trade and Economic Development 4647

OILS AND FATS

Fats and Oils—Oilseed Crushings. M20J 1908
Fats and Oils—Production, Consumption, and Stocks. M20K 1909
Monthly Price Review 3294
Oils and Fats 3609
Outlook and Situation Reports 3653.01
United Nations Industrial Development Organization Guides to Information Sources. UNIDO/LIB/SER D/7—Information Sources on the Vegetable Oil Processing Industry 4774

OIL SHALE

Fuel 2195

OKLAHOMA

Financial Trend 2032
From the State Capitals 2169–2191
Oklahoma Business Bulletin 3614
Oklahoma Directory of Manufacturers and Products 3615
Oklahoma: Manufacturers & Products Directory, 1980 3617.01
Oklahoma Now! 3618
Oklahoma: State Industrial Directory, 1981 3618.01
Statistical Abstract of Oklahoma 4420
State and Local Taxes 4386
State Legislative Reporting Service 4396
State Tax Report 4413

OLDER WORKERS. See Labor, Older Workers

ONTARIO (CANADA). See Canada

OPEC. See Oil Producing and Exporting Countries (OPEC)

OPEN-END FUNDS. See Mutual Funds

OPERATIONS RESEARCH. See also Computer-Aided Management Techniques

Computers & Operations Research 1086
Decision Line 1348
Decision Sciences 1352
European Journal of Operational Research 1781.01
International Abstracts in Operations Research 2652
Journal of Accounting Research 2818
Journal of Bank Research 2824
Journal of the American Society for the Information Science 2888.01
Journal of the Operational Research Society 2896
Operations Research 3629
Operations Research Letters 3629.01
Operations Research/Management Science 3630
Organization Dynamics 3640

OPTHAMOLOGY. See Eyes and Eyesight

OPTICS. See also Research and Development, Lasers and Optics

Laser Focus 2967
Laser Report 2969
Optics and Laser Technology 3632
Refractories MQ-32C 4044
Science Research Abstracts Journal, Parts A&B 4197

ORAL PROSTHETIC DEVICES

Dental Laboratory Review 1359

ORANGE COUNTY (CALIFORNIA)

Orange County Business 3634
Orange County Illustrated 3635

OREGON

From State the Capitals 2169–2191
Oregon: Manufacturers Directory, 1980–81 3637
Oregon: State Industrial Directory, 1980 3638
State and Local Taxes 4386
State Legislative Directory, 1980 4396
State Tax Reports 4413

ORGANIZATIONAL COMMUNICATION

Automated Business Communications Program 423
Corporate Communications Report 1204
Information Industry & Technology Service 2573
International Association of Business Communicators News 2656
Journal of Business Communication 2828
Journal of Organizational Communication 2871
Manage 3067
Office Automation Reporting Service 3578
Ragan Report 3989
Reporter's Report 4062.02

ORNAMENTAL CROPS

Fresh Fruit and Vegetable and Ornamental Crops Market News Reports 2166

OSHA. See Occupational Safety and Health Law and Administration

OUTDOOR ADVERTISING. See Advertising, Outdoor

OUTDOOR LIGHTING. See Lamps and Lighting

OVER-THE-COUNTER TRADING. See Stocks and Bonds, Over-the-Counter

PACIFIC COAST STOCK EXCHANGE

Pacific Coast Stock Exchange Guide 3678
Trade Levels Option Report 4656

PACKAGING. See Containers and Packaging

PAILS AND DRUMS

Steel Shipping Drums and Pails. M34K 4462

PAINTS AND ALLIED PRODUCTS

Finishing Industries 2039
Modern Paint & Coatings 3258
Paint Manufacture 3687
Paint, Varnish, and Lacquer M28F 3688

United Nations Industrial Development Organization Guides to Information Sources. UNIDO/LIB/SER D/18—Information Sources on the Paint and Varnish Industry 4785

PAPER AND PAPER PRODUCTS.
See also Commercial Paper

Chemical Horizons North American Report 925
Chemical Horizons Overseas Report 925.01
Forest Products Service 2144
Paper and Packaging Bulletin 3690
Paper Merchant Performance 3692
Paper Sales 3693
Paper Trade Journal 3694
Paper Year Book 3695
Pulp and Paper 3945
Pulp & Paper Canada 3946
Pulp and Paper Quarterly Statistics 3947
Pulp, Paper, and Board M26A 3948
United Nations Industrial Development Organization (UNIDO) Guides to Information Sources. UNIDO/LIB/SER.D/Rev.1—Information Sources on the Utilization of Agricultural Residues for the Production of Panels, Pulp and Paper 4767.15
United Nations Industrial Development Organization Guides to Information Sources. UNIDO/LIB/SER D/11—Information Sources on the Pulp and Paper Industry 4778
Yearbooks of Forest Products Statistics 5099

PAPERBACK BOOKS. *See* Books, Paperbacks

PARLIAMENT. *See* Government, Parliament

PARTICLEBOARD

Forest Products Service 2144
Pulp, Paper, and Board M26A 3948

PARTNERSHIPS

Business Organizations with Tax Planning 715
Canada Tax Service 769
Partnerships and Taxes: A Practical Guide 3697
United States Master Tax Guide 4811

PASSENGER SHIPS. *See* Ships and Shipping, Passenger Ships

PASSPORTS AND VISAS

Australia

Visa Information Guide 4859

Great Britain

Visa Information Guide 4859

New Zealand

Visa Information Guide 4859

United States

Visa Information Guide 4859

PATENT AND TRADEMARK OFFICE (US)

Patent Attorneys & Agents Registered to Practice Before the US Patent Office 3699
Trademark Official Gazette 4659
Trademark Reporter 4662
Trademark Research Service 4662.01

PATENTING EXAMINING CORPORATION (US)

Manual of Patent Examining Procedure 3104

PATENT OFFICE (CANADA)

Patent Office Record/Canada 3703

PATENTS. *See also* Inventions

Abstracts from Technical and Patent Publications 3
Bureau of National Affairs (BNA) Patent, Trademark & Copyright Journal 649
Business & Acquisition Newsletter 657
Central Patents Index, 1981 890.01
Electrical Patents Index, 1981 1604.01
Forms and Agreements for Architects, Engineers and Contractors 2146
International Intertrade Index 2686
International Invention Register 2687
Invention Management 2750
Inventor 2751
Licensing in Foreign and Domestic Operations 3010
National Aeronautics and Space Administration (NASA) Activities 3356
On-line Search Service, 1981 3619.05
Research Disclosure 4087
United States Patents Quarterly 4814
World Patents Abstract, 1981 5073.01
World Patents Index, 1981 5073.02

Canada

Patent Office Record/Canada 3703

Europe (East)

East/West Technology Digest 1527

European Communities

Euro-Abstracts: Scientific and Technical Publications and Patents, Section I and Section II. Section I: Euratom and EEC Research. Section II: Coal and Steel 1759

Union of Soviet Socialist Republics (USSR)

East/West Technology Digest 1527

United States

Annual Indexes of Patents 248
Manual of Classification 3102
Patent Fraud and Inequitable Conduct 3700
Patent Invalidity: A Statistical and Substantive Analysis 3701
Patent Official Gazette 3704
Trademark Official Gazette 4659

PATENTS, GOVERNMENT REGULATION, LAWS AND PROGRAMS

Intellectual Property Law Review 2636.02
Patent and Trademark Review 3698
Patents and Trademarks 3705
Patents Throughout the World 3706

Australia

Annual of Industrial Property Law 252

Canada

Annual of Industrial Property Law 252
Canadian Patent Reporter 826

France

Annual of Industrial Property Law 252

Germany (West)

Annual of Industrial Property Law 252

Great Britain

Annual of Industrial Property Law 252
Fleet Street Patent Law Reports 2062

Japan

Annual of Industrial Property Law
252

New Zealand

Annual of Industrial Property Law
252

South Africa

Annual of Industrial Property Law
252

United States

Annual of Industrial Property Law
252
Bureau of National Affairs (BNA)
Patent, Trademark & Copyright
Journal 649
Manual of Patent Examining Procedure
3104
Patent Attorneys & Agents Registered
to Practice Before the US Patent
Office 3699
Patent Fraud and Inequitable Conduct
3700
Patent Invalidity: A Statistical and
Substantive Analysis 3701
United States Patents Quarterly 4814

PAYROLL TAXES. *See* Taxation,
Payroll Taxes

PAY TELEVISION. *See* Television,
Pay TV

PENNSYLVANIA

From the State Capitals 2169–2191
Pennsylvania: Directory of
Manufacturers, 1980 3716.01
Pennsylvania: State Industrial
Directory, 1980 3717.02
State and Local Taxes 4386
State Legislative Reporting Service
4396
State Tax Reports 4311

PENSION PLANS. *See also*
Employee Retirement Security Act
(ERISA). Keogh Plan

Benefits International 521
Employee Benefit Plan Review (EBPR)
Research Reports 1644
How to Set Up and Run a Qualified
Pension or Profit Sharing Plan for a
Small or Medium-Size Business
2424
Industrial Relations News 2545
Institutional Investor 2601

Journal of Accounting, Auditing and
Finance 2817.02
Journal of Pension Planning and
Compliance 2872
Journal of the Institute of Actuaries
2892
Money Management Unitholder 3270
Pension Actuary 3719
Pension and Profit Sharing Forms
3721
Pension and Profit Sharing Guide
3722
Pension and Profit Sharing Plans 3723
Pension Plan Guide Summary 3725
Pension Plans Service 3726
Pension Pulse Beats 3726.01
Pensions Directory 3730
Pension Tables for Actuaries 3731
Pension World 3732
Personnel Journal 3744
Plan Administrator's Compliance
Manual 3776
Professional Corporations and
Associations 3885
Profit Sharing Design Manual 3893
Spencer's Retirement Plan Service
4362
Viewpoint 4857

Canada

Canada Corporation Manual 746
Canada Tax Manual 768
Canadian Risk Management and
Business Insurance 830
Money Reporter, Canadian Edition
3272

Great Britain

Employment Digest 1658
Incomes Data Services (IDS) Studies
2489
Insurance Companies and Private
Pension Funds 2615
Money Management and Unitholder
3270
Savings Market 4190

United States

Consensus of Insiders 1119
Current Government Reports 1276
Employee Relations Law Journal 1648
Money Reporter, US Edition 3273
Pension and Profit Sharing 3720
Pension Reporter 3727
Pension & Investment Age 3729
Successful Personal Money
Management 1977 4488

**PENSION PLANS, GOVERNMENT
REGULATIONS**

Pension Plans Service 3726

Canada

Canadian Employment Benefits and
Pension Guide 789

United States

Pension Reporter 3727

PENSION PLANS, TAXATION

Journal of Pension Planning and
Compliance 2872
Pension Reporter 3727

PERFUMES. *See* Cosmetics and
Toiletries

PERIODICALS. *See also*
Newsletters. News. Newspapers

Bacon's International Publicity Checker
447
Information Bank I and II 2570.02
Key Issues Tracking (KIT) 2910.01
Magazine Industry Market Place: The
Directory of American Periodical
Publishing 3056.02
Magazines for Libraries 3058
Media Guide International:
Business/Professional Publications
Edition 3171
Media Guide International:
Newspapers/Newsmagazines Edition
3172
Printing Impressions 3849
Reporter's Report 4062.02
Ulrich's International Periodicals
Directory 4737

Canada

Ayer Directory of Publications 443
Canadian Advertising Rates & Data
774
Canadian Business Index 778.01
Canadian News Index 820.01
Standard Periodical Directory 4377

United States

Ayer Directory of Publications 443
metro CALIFORNIA media 3204.02
Readers' Guide to Periodical Literature
4009
Standard Periodical Directory 4377

**PERIODICALS, AIRLINE AND
IN-FLIGHT MAGAZINES**

Media Guide International: Airline/
Inflight Magazines Edition 3170

PERIODICALS, CONSUMER

PERIODICALS, PROFESSIONAL

Africa

American Nations

Australia

Europe

Far East

Great Britain

Union of Soviet Socialist Republics (USSR)

United States

PERIODICALS, TRADE AND BUSINESS. *See also* subjects

American Nations

Canada

Africa

Australia

Europe

Far East

Union of Soviet Socialist Republics (USSR)

United States

PERMITS. *See* Licenses and
Licensing. Subjects

PERSIAN GULF

PERSONAL EXPENDITURES. *See*
Consumer Market, Spending. Families,
Finances

PERSONAL COMPUTERS. *See*
Computers, Personal

PERSONNEL. *See* Personnel
Management. Personnel Policies.
Subjects

PERSONNEL MANAGEMENT

PETROLEUM ASSOCIATION OF AMERICA, INDEPENDENT (IPAA)

Petroleum Independent　3760

PETS.　*See also* Pet Food. Pet Shops. Veterinary Medicine

Pets/Supplies/Marketing　3764

PHARMACEUTICALS.　*See* Drugs and Drug Trade

PHARMACOLOGY.　*See* Drugs and Drug Trade

PHILADELPHIA-BALTIMORE-WASHINGTON STOCK EXCHANGE

Philadelphia Stock Exchange Guide　3765

PHILANTHROPY.　*See also* Foundations. Fund Raising

Fund Raising Management　2200

PHILIPPINES

Journal of Philippine Development　2872.01
Philippine Development　3765.01
Philippine Economic Indicators　3765.02
Philippine Letter　3765.03
Philippine Statistical Yearbook　3765.04

PHONOGRAPHS.　*See* Recording and Playback Equipment

PHOTOGRAPHY AND PHOTOGRAPHIC FILM

Art Direction　322
Creativity/9　1241.02
Dataguide　1334
Industrial Photography　2535.01
Photographic Trade News　3766
Professional Photographic Equipment Directory & Buying Guide, 1976 Edition　3889
Ragan Report　3989
Reporter's Report　4062.02

PHYSICAL THERAPY.　*See* Occupational and Physical Therapy

PHYSICIANS AND SURGEONS

Hospital Medical Staff　2395
Physician's Management　3768

PHYSICS.　*See also* Magnetohydrodynamics

Abstract Newsletters, Physics　2.26
Science Research Abstracts Journal　4197

PHYSICS, SOLID STATE

Solid State Abstracts Journal　4328

PIGS.　*See also* Meat. Pork and Ham

National Hog Farmer　3379

United States

Livestock Market News Reports　3030

PILLOWCASES.　*See* Beds, Bedding and Mattresses

PILOTS.　*See* Airplanes, Personnel

PIPELINES

Abstract Newsletters, Transportation　2.28
Chilton's Oil and Gas Energy　940
Daily Oil Bulletin　1303
Hydrologic Aspects of Northern Pipeline Development, 1974　2431
International Petroleum Encyclopedia　2720
Oil Pipe Line Transport　3607
Pipeline & Gas Journal　3772
Reference Book of Transportation　4041

PIPES AND PIPING

Heating/Piping/Air Conditioning　2368

PLANTS (HORTICULTURE).　*See* Ornamental Crops. Horticulture. Plants and Trees

PLANTS AND SITES.　*See* Commerce and Industry, Plants and Sites. Industrial Parks. Manufacturers and Manufacturing, Plants and Equipment

PLANTS AND TREES

Food and Agriculture Organization (FAO) Plant Protection Bulletin　2076

PLASTICS

Advances in Plastics Technology　64.01
American Machinist (Magazine)　200
Chemical Horizons North American Report　925

Chemical Horizons Overseas Report　925.01
Modern Plastics　3260
Modern Plastics Encyclopedia　3261
Modern Plastics International Report　3262
Plastic Bottles　3781
Plastics World　3783
Polymer　3807

Australia

Metal and Engineering Industry Yearbook　3196
Process and Chemical Engineering　3859

Canada

Canadian Plastics　828

Europe

Plastics Industry Europe　3782

Great Britain

British Plastics and Rubber　619

Japan

Plastics Industry News　3782.01

Third World

Petrochemical Series　3756

PLATINUM

American Board of Trade Spot and Forward Markets　160

PLUMBERS AND PLUMBING

Contractor　1187
Domestic Heating　1492
Heating-Plumbing Air Conditioning　2369

PLUMBERS AND PLUMBING, FIXTURES.
See also Bathrooms. Kitchens, Equipment

Domestic Heating　1492
Plumbing Fixtures MQ-34E　3789

PLYWOOD

American Board of Trade Spot and Forward Markets　160
Construction Type Plywood　1142
Forest Products Service　2144
Random Lengths　4002
Yearbooks of Forest Products Statistics　5099

PNEUMATICS

Hydraulics & Pneumatics   2430

POISONS. *See* Accidents and Safety. Health Hazards and Safety. Pesticide and Pests. Toxicology

POLICE (GENERAL)

Public Productivity Review   3930

POLISHES. *See* Waxes

POLITICAL AND ECONOMIC INTEGRATION. *See* Economics, Political. European Economic Community (EEC) (Common Market)

Journal of Common Market Studies   2839

POLITICAL SCIENCE. *See* Government

POLITICS. *See* Elections. Government

POLLS. *See* Surveys and Polls

POLLUTION. *See* types, eg, Air Pollution. Environmental Protection

POLYMERS

Petrochemical Series   3756
Plastics Industry News   3782.01
Platt's Polymerscan   3787.03
Polymer   3807

POPULATION. *See also* Vital Statistics

Business International (BI) Data   697
Demographic Yearbook   1357
Development Forum   1374
Economic Development & Cultural Change   1548
Food & Agriculture Organization of the United Nations (FAO) Production Yearbook   2077
Futures   2204
Grindlays Bank Economic Reports   2267
International Journal of Social Economics   2696
International Year Book and Statesmen's Who's Who   2744
Journal of Regional Science   2879
Land Use Planning Abstracts   2964
Monthly Bulletin of Statistics   3283
Sales and Marketing Management Survey of Buying Power (Part I)   4166

Sales and Marketing Management Survey of Buying Power (Part II)   4167
Statistical Yearbook   4444
Worldcasts   5047
World Tables 1980   5080

Africa

Middle East and North Africa   3217

Alabama

Alabama Economic Abstract   135

American Nations

Caribbean Year Book, 1977–78   864

Arizona

Annual Planning Information   253
Arizona Statistical Abstract   317.03
Statistical Abstract of Arizona   4418

California

Union-Tribune Annual Review of San Diego Business Activity   4753

Canada

British Columbia Facts and Statistics   602
Canada   743
Canada Manpower and Immigration Review   758
Canada–United Kingdom Year Book   771
Income After Tax, Distribution by Size in Canada   2480
Income Distributions by Size in Canada   2481
Income Distributions by Size in Canada, Preliminary Estimates   2482
Market Research Handbook   3138
Quarterly Estimates of Population for Canada and the Provinces   3963.01
Survey of Buying Power   4510

Far East

Basic Facts, Developing Member Countries (DMCs) of Asian Development Bank (ADB)   512
Quarterly Bulletin of Statistics for Asia and the Pacific   3959

Florida

Florida Outlook   2068
Florida Statistical Abstract   2069
Kiplinger Florida Letter   2915

Georgia

Georgia Statistical Abstract   2220

Great Britain

Annual Estimates of the Population of England and Wales and Local Authority Areas   245
General Household Survey   2210
Monthly Digest Annual Supplement   3288
Population Projections   3810
Population Trends   3811
Social Trends   4321

Hawaii

Hawaii Annual Economic Review   2347
State of Hawaii Data Book   4403

Illinois

Illinois Economic Data Sheets   2438

Iowa

Statistical Profile of Iowa   4436

Louisiana

Louisiana Economy   3048

Maryland

Maryland Statistical Abstract, 1980 Edition   3147

Middle East

Middle East and North Africa   3217

New Jersey

New Jersey Economic Policy Council Annual Report   3452

New Mexico

Economy   1577

New York City

New York City Business Fact Book Part 2: Population & Housing   3475

New York State

New York State Business Fact Book Part 2: Population & Housing   3482

New Zealand

New Zealand Vital Statistics   3515

Oklahoma

Oklahoma Annual Planning Report   3611

Oregon

County Economic Indicators   1238

Scotland

Annual Estimates of the Population of
   Scotland   246

South Africa

South Africa Yearbook   4337

United States

Census of Population   876.01
Census Retrieval System   880
Current Population Survey   1281
Personal Income, Population, Per
   Capita Personal Income   3737
Predicasts   3828
Reference Manual on Population and
   Housing Statistics from the Census
   Bureau, 1977   4042
Review of Regional Economics &
   Business   4127
SRI Microfiche Library   4368.02
State and Area Forecasting Service
   4383.01
Statistical Bulletin   4426
Statistical Reference Index   4438
Survey of Buying Power   4510
Survey of Buying Power Data Service
   4511
Survey of Buying Power Forecasting
   Service   4511.01
Survey of Buying Power Part II   4512
United States Census Report   4794.03

Utah

Utah Economic and Business Review
   4835

Wales

Annual Estimates of the Population of
   England and Wales and Local
   Authority Areas   245

West Indies

Caribbean Year Book, 1977–78   864

PORK AND HAM

Restaurant Buyers Guide   4098

PORTS.   *See* Ships and Shipping,
Ports

POSTAL SERVICE

Almanac and Directory 1981   148.01
West European Living Costs 1977
   4952

POSTAL SYSTEM.   *See* Postal
Service

POTATOES

Belgium

Agra Europe Potato Markets   91

Canada

Agra Europe Potato Markets   91
Fraser's Potato Newsletter   2163

France

Agra Europe Potato Markets   91

Germany (West)

Agra Europe Potato Markets   91

Great Britain

Agra Europe Potato Markets   91

Netherlands

Agra Europe Potato Markets   91

United States

Agra Europe Potato Markets   91
Fraser's Potato Newsletter   2163

POTTERY.   *See* Ceramics and Pottery

POULTRY.   *See also* Eggs

Chicago Mercantile Exchange Yearbook
   937
Feed Industry Red Book   1978
Feed Industry Review   1979
Outlook and Situation Reports
   3653.01
Urner Barry's Price Current   4833.01

Canada

Production and tocks of Eggs and
   Poultry   3866.01

Illinois

Illinois Agricultural Statistics   2436

United States

Feedstuffs   1980
Meat, Poultry, and Seafood Digest
   3164.01
Monthly Price Review   3294
Poultry Market News Reports   3813
Restaurant Buyers Guide   4098
Weekly Insiders Poultry Report   4934
Weekly Insiders Turkey Letter   4935

POWER.   *See* Energy

**POWER COMMISSION, FEDERAL
(FPC) (US)**

Federal Power Service   1934

PREFABRICATED HOUSING.   *See*
Housing, Prefabricated

PREFERRED STOCKS.   *See* Stocks
and Bonds, Preferred Stocks

PREMIUMS

From the State Capitals: Merchandising
   2180
Incentive Marketing and Sales
   Promotion   2478
Nielsen Reporter   3516.01
Potentials in Marketing   3812
Premium, Incentive and Travel Buyers
   3833
Premium/Incentive Business   3834

PRESIDENTS (POLITICAL).   *See*
Government, Chief Executive. Leaders
and Leadership

PRICE-EARNINGS RATIO.   *See*
Stocks and Bonds, Price-Earnings Ratio

PRICE-FIXING

Trade Regulation Reports   4671

PRICES.   *See also* Cost of Living.
Economies. Price-Fixing. Names of
commodities, e.g., Gold

Consumer Price Index (CPI) Detailed
   Report   1163
Indicators of Industrial Activity
   2505.01
Monthly Commodity Price Bulletin
   3286
National Income & Expenditure
   Accounts   3381
Price Index Numbers for Current Cost
   Accounting   3838
State and Area Forecasting Service
   4383.01

PRICES, WHOLESALE

Economic Inquiry   1553
Producer Prices and Price Indexes
   3862.01

Alabama

Alabama Economic Abstract   135

Arizona

Arizona Review   317

European Economic Community

Purchase Prices of the Means of
Production   3948.01

Far East

Quarterly Bulletin of Statistics for Asia
and the Pacific   3959

Ireland, Republic of

Confederation of Irish Industry
(CII)/ESRI Business Forecast   1107

Nebraska

Business in Nebraska   694

Switzerland

Swiss-American Chamber of Commerce.
Yearbook   4522

United States

Monthly Price Review   3294
Weekly Insiders Poultry Report   4934
Weekly Insiders Turkey Letter   4935

PRIME MINISTERS.   *See*
Government, Chief Executive

PRINTS AND PRINTING.   *See also*
Books, Printing and Production.
Lithography Screen Printing Industry.
Other products

Catalog of Copyright Entries   868
Dataguide   1334
In-Plant Printguide   2583
In-Plant Reproductions   2583.01
Package Printing   3682
Printing Impressions   3849
United Nations Industrial Development
Organization Guides to Information
Sources. UNIDO/LIB/SER D/14—
Information Sources on the Printing
and Graphics Industry   4781

Great Britain

British Printer   620
Graphix   2260

United States

Printing and Publishing   3848

PRINTS AND PRINTING OFFSET

In-Plant Printguide   2583
Offset Printer   3589

PRISONS

From the State Capitals: Institutional
Building   2176

PRIVACY

Access Reference Service   8
Access Reports   9
Access Reports Privacy   9.02

PRIVATE BONDS.   *See* Stocks and
Bonds, Private Bonds

PRIVATE UTILITIES.   *See also*
types

Compustat   1070
Power   3817
Moody's Public Utility Manual and
News Reports   3318
Valuation   4838

PROBABILITY THEORY.   *See*
Actuarial Methods. Mathematics.
Statistical Methods

PRODUCE.   *See* Fruits and
Vegetables

PRODUCT RATINGS.   *See* Product
Testing and Ratings

PRODUCT SAFETY.   *See also*
specific products and fields of use

Consumer Newsweek   1160
LabData   2923
National Electronic Injury Surveillance
System (NEISS) Data Highlights
3373
Product Liability   3873
Product Safety News   3877
Products Liability Reports   3879
Product Standards Index   3881

Canada

Canadian Product Safety Guide   829
Hazardous Products Act and
Regulations/Office Consolidation
2353

United States

Food Drug Cosmetic Law Reports
2084
Product Safety & Liability Reporter
3876

PRODUCTION.   *See* Commerce and
Industry, Production. Other subjects

PRODUCTION ENGINEERING.
See also Quality Control

International Journal of Production
Research   2695
ISMEC   2790
Production & Inventory Control
Handbook   3865
Production & Inventory Management
3866
Production Engineering   3867

PRODUCTIVITY.   *See* Labor,
Productivity. Work Study, Organization
and Methods

PRODUCTS.   *See* Commerce and
Industry, Products. Computer-Aided
Product Development. New Products.
Product Safety. Product Testing and
Ratings

**PRODUCT TESTING AND
RATINGS.**   *See also* Product Safety

Canadian Consumer   786
Consumer Reports   1171
Consumers Index to Product
Evaluations and Information Sources
1174
Consumers' Research   1177
Marketing Times   3136

PROFESSIONAL ASSOCIATIONS.
See Associations (Professional,
Scientific, Technical and Trade)

PROFESSIONAL CORPORATIONS

How to Save Taxes and Increase Your
Wealth with a Professional
Corporation   2423
Professional Corporations and
Associations   3885
Professional Corporations Handbook
3886

Canada

British Columbia Corporation Manual
600

United States

Professional Corporation Guide   3884
Professional Corporations Handbook
3886

**PROFESSIONAL CORPORATIONS,
EMPLOYEE BENEFITS**

Professional Corporation Guide   3884
Professional Corporations and
Associations   3885

RADAR

Directory of Defense Electronic
Products and Services: U.S. Suppliers
1426
DMS Radar & Sonar 1475.29

RADIATION

Abstract Newsletters, Environmental
Pollution & Control 2.15
Radiation Report 3988

RADIO. *See* Television and Radio

RADIOSOTOPES. *See* Radiation

RADIO STATIONS. *See* Television
and Radio Stations

RAILROAD ADJUSTMENT
BOARD, NATIONAL (US)

National Mediation Board Annual
Report 3393
National Mediation Board Reports of
Emergency Boards 3394

RAILROAD RETIREMENT BOARD
(US)

Railroad Retirement Board Annual
Report 3991
Railroad Retirement Board Quarterly
Review 3992

RAILROADS

International Railway Journal 2724
On-line Database 3619.04
Pocket List of Railroad Officials
3790.01
Railroad Research Bulletin 3990.01
Railroad Revenues, Expenses and
Income 3993
Railway Age 3995
Reference Book of Transportation
4041
Yearbook of Railroad Facts 5097

Canada

Decisions of the Railway Transport
Committee 1354
Railway Operating Statistics 3998
Railway Transport Service Bulletin
3999

New England

Boston Marine Guide 577

United States

Interstate Commerce Commission
Annual Report 2745

Modern Railroads 3265
National Mediation Board Annual
Report 3393
Rail News Update 3989.01
Railroad Mileage by States 3990
United States Rail News 4815

Washington (DC)

Railroad Mileage by States 3990

RAILROADS, ACCIDENTS AND
SAFETY

Railway Accidents 3994
Regulations for Transportation of
Dangerous Commodities by Rail
4057

RAILROADS, ASSOCIATION OF
AMERICA

Indexes of Railroad Material Prices and
Wage Rates 2498
Yearbook of Railroad Facts 5097

RAILROADS, EMPLOYEE
BENEFITS

Railroad Retirement Board Annual
Report 3991
Railroad Retirement Board Quarterly
Review 3992

RAILROADS, EQUIPMENT

Indexes of Railroad Material Prices and
Wage Rates 2498
On-line Database 3619.04
Operating and Traffic Statistics 3627
Property Investment and Condensed
Income Account 3900
Railroad Research Bulletin 3990.01
Statistics of Railroads of Class I in the
United States 4454
Transportation Service 4694

RAILROADS, FREIGHT

Hawkins Rail Carrier Service 2352
International Freighting Weekly 2683
Operating and Traffic Statistics 3627
Transportation Service 4694

Canada

Official Railway Guide, Freight Service
Edition 3585.02
Railway Carloadings 3996
Railway Freight Traffic 3997
Regulations for Transportation of
Dangerous Commodities by Rail
4057

Mexico

Official Railway Guide, Freight Service
Edition 3585.02

United States

Official Railway Guide, Freight Service
Edition 3585.02

RAILROADS, GOVERNMENT
REGULATIONS

Decisions of the Railway Transport
Committee 1354
On-line Database 3619.04
Railroad Research Bulletin 3990.01
Regulations for Transportation of
Dangerous Commodities by Rail
4057

RAILROADS, LABOR

Determinations of the National
Mediation Board, Volume 1 through
6 1369.02
Indexes of Railroad Material Prices and
Wage Rates 2498
National Mediation Board Annual
Report 3393
National Mediation Board Reports of
Emergency Boards 3394
Railroad Retirement Board Quarterly
Review 3992
Statistics of Railroads of Class I in the
United States 4454

RAILROADS, PASSENGER

Metropolitan 3205
Official Railway Guide, Passenger
Travel Edition 3585.03
Operating and Traffic Statistics 3627
Travel Weekly 4706

RAILROADS, RATES

Boston Marine Guide 577
Indexes of Railroad Material Prices and
Wage Rates 2498
Routes Yearbook 4144

RAILWAY LABOR ACT (US)

Determinations of the National
Mediation Board, Volumes 1 through
6 1369.02
National Mediation Board Annual
Report 3393
National Mediation Board Reports of
Emergency Boards 3394

RAILWAY TRANSPORT
COMMITTEE (CANADA)

Decisions of the Railway Transport
Committee 1354

RAW MATERIALS

World Markets Intelligence Report
5070

Australia

Kompass Register, Australia   2920

Belgium

Kompass Register, Belgium &
Luxembourg   2920.01

Brazil

Kompass Register, Brazil   2920.02

Denmark

Kompass Register, Denmark   2920.03

France

Kompass Register, France   2920.04

Germany (West)

Kompass Register, West Germany
2920.13

Great Britain

Commodities Survey   1023
United Kingdom Kompass Register
4759

Indonesia

Kompass Register, Indonesia   2920.06

Italy

Kompass Register, Italy   2920.07

Luxembourg

Kompass Register, Belgium &
Luxembourg   2920.01

Morocco

Kompass Register, Morocco   2920.08

Netherlands

Kompass Register, Holland   2920.05

Norway

Kompass Register, Norway   2920.09

Spain

Kompass Register, Spain   2920.01

Sweden

Kompass Register, Sweden   2920.11

Switzerland

Kompass Register. Switzerland
2920.12

REAL ESTATE.   See also Agriculture, Land

Appraisal Journal   291
Appraiser   292
Bibliography of Appraisal Literature
548
Journal of Property Management   2875
Lawyers Title News   2991
Licensing in Foreign and Domestic
Operations   3010
Real Estate Appraisal Terminology
4010
Real Estate Forum   4013
Real Estate "Insider"   4014
Real Estate Investing Letter   4015
Real Estate News   4023
Real Estate Perspectives   4023.02
Real Estate Review   4024
real estate today   4028
Realty Bluebook   4031
Realty Roundup   4032
Site Selection Handbook   4290
Tax Sheltered Investments   4570
Valuation   4838

American Nations

Caribbean Business News   863

Australia

Real Estate Journal   4020

California

California Services Register, 1981
738.04
Journal of Commerce Review   2837
Orange County Business   3634

Canada

Appraisal Institute Magazine (AIM)
290
Canadian Real Estate   829.01
Canadian Real Estate Journal   829.02
Corpus Almanac of Canada   1224

Colorado

Rocky Mountain Journal   4139

Connecticut

Commercial Record   1009

Delaware

Building and Realty Record   634

New Jersey

Building and Realty Record   634

Florida

Kiplinger Florida Letter   2915

Great Britain

Cumbria Weekly Digest   1266
Daltons Weekly   1315
Estates Gazette   1754
Estates Times   1755
Management Information Manual
3081

Massachusetts

Banker & Tradesman   465
Western Massachusetts Commercial
News   4951

New York City Metropolitan Area

Realty   4030

New Zealand

Property   3898

Pennsylvania

Building and Realty Record   634

United States

Business & Capital Reporter   658
Mortgage and Real Estate Executives
Report   3319.02
News & Views   3461.01
Real Estate Appraiser and Analyst
4011
Real Estate Newsletter   4023.01
Realty   4030

Washington (DC) Metropolitan Area

Realtor   4029

REAL ESTATE, ADVERTISING

Real Estate News   4023
Real Estate Sales Handbook, 8th
edition   4025

REAL ESTATE, AGENTS

National Assn of Realtors' Who's Who
3360
National Roster of Realtors   3403
Real Estate Sales Handbook, 8th
edition   4025

REAL ESTATE, FINANCES.   See also Foreclosures. Mortgages

How to Plan for Tax Savings in Real
Estate Transactions   2422

RECORDINGS (DISC AND TAPE) AND PLAYBACK EQUIPMENT

Billboard 551
Catalog of Copyright Entries 868
Graphis Annual 2258
Photographis 3767

RECORDKEEPING. *See* Archives and Records. Information Retrieval. Office Systems

RECORDS MANAGEMENT. *See* Archives and Records. Information Retrieval. Office Systems

RECORDS (PHONOGRAPHS). *See* Recordings (Disc and Tape)

RECREATION. *See also* Recreational Goods. Recreational Vehicles. Types, e.g., Travel and Resorts

Directory Information Service 1406
Executive Lifestyle Newsletter 1804
Managing the Leisure Facility 3095.03

California

Orange County Illustrated 3635

Great Britain

Management Information Manual 3081

RECREATION, HEALTH HAZARDS AND SAFETY

Family Safety 1886

RECREATION, PRICES

West European Living Costs 1977 4952

RECREATIONAL VEHICLES

Jenkins Mobile Industry News Letter 2805
National Electronic Injury Surveillance System NEISS Data Highlights 3373
National Injury Information Clearinghouse, Statistical Data from National Electronic Injury Surveillance System 3386

RECYCLING

Commercial Bulletin 999
Conservation and Recycling 1120
Solid Wastes Management 4329.01

REFINERIES. *See* Oil (Petroleum) and Gasoline, Refining

REFRACTORIES. *See* Optics

REFRIGERATION

Airconditioning & Refrigeration Business 120
Australian Refrigeration, Air-Conditioning and Heating 413.01
Quick Frozen Foods Directory of Frozen Food Processors 3982

REGULATED INDUSTRIES. *See also* types, eg, Electric Light and Power

Trade and Regulated Industries Occupational Employment Statistics 4650

REHABILITATION EFFORTS. *See also* subjects, eg, Alcoholism

Rehabilitation Counseling Bulletin 4059

REINSURANCE. *See* Insurance, Reinsurance

REITS. *See* Real Estate Investment Trusts (REITS)

RELIGION

Africa Research Bulletin 81
Middle East and North Africa 3217

RELIGIOUS EDIFICES

Kelly's Post Office London Directory 2908

RENT CONTROL. *See* Housing, Rent Control

RENTAL EQUIPMENT. *See* Equipment Leasing

RENTS AND RENTING. *See also* Equipment Leasing. Housing, Rent Controls. Housing, Rentals. Subjects

RESALES. *See* Sales and Salespeople, Resales

RESEARCH AND DEVELOPMENT. *See also* Research Associations. Research (Basic). Subject headings

Akron Business & Economic Review 132
Bulletin 643.01
Conference Papers Index 1110

Journal of the Society of Research Administrators 2897
R&D Abstracts 3999.01
Research Management 4090
Technology Forecasts and Technology Surveys 4581

Europe (East)

East/West Technology Digest 1527

Great Britain

Business Monitors Miscellaneous Series 712
Development Digest 1373.01
R&D Abstracts 3999.01

Third World

Bulletin 643.01

Union of Soviet Socialist Republics (USSR)

East/West Technology Digest 1527

RESEARCH AND DEVELOPMENT, AIR CONDITIONING AND HEATING

Heating & Air Conditioning Journal 2366

RESEARCH AND DEVELOPMENT, COMPOSITE MATERIALS

Abstract Newsletters, Materials Sciences 2.21
Composites 1068

RESEARCH AND DEVELOPMENT, DRUGS AND DRUG TRADE

Pharma Prospects 3764.03

RESEARCH AND DEVELOPMENT, ENERGY

Abstract Newsletters, Energy 2.14
Energy Daily 1678
Energy Info 1682
Energy-Related Research and Development Funds MNT59 1689
Energy Research Bureau 1691
Energy Research Programs, 1980 1692
Energy Today 1699
Federal Contract Opportunities: Energy/Environment 1917.01
Financial Post Survey of Energy & Resources 2015
Fuel 2195
Fuel Abstracts and Current Titles 2196
Fusion Power Report 2203.01

International Journal of Ambient
Energy 2689.01
International Journal of Energy
Research 2692

RESEARCH AND DEVELOPMENT, ENVIRONMENT

Ecology USA 1533.01
Federal Contract Opportunites:
Energy/Environment 1917.01
Pollution Abstracts 3803
Washington Environmental Protection
Report 4886

RESEARCH AND DEVELOPMENT, FUEL

Alternative Energy: Trends & Forecasts
149.01
Fuel 2195
Fuel Abstracts and Current Titles
2196
International Journal of Energy
Research 2692

RESEARCH AND DEVELOPMENT, GOVERNMENTAL

Canada

Ottawa R&D Report 3651

Great Britain

Developing Digest 1373.01

United States

Abstract Newsletters, Administration
and Management 2.03
Abstract Newsletters, Agriculture and
Food 2.04
Abstract Newsletters, Behavior and
Society 2.05
Abstract Newsletters, Biomedical
Technology & Human Factors
Engineering 2.06
Abstract Newsletters, Building Industry
Technology 2.07
Abstract Newsletters, Business &
Economics 2.08
Abstract Newsletters, Chemistry 2.09
Abstract Newsletters, Civil Engineering
2.10
Abstract Newsletters, Communication
2.11
Abstract Newsletters, Computers,
Control & Information Theory 2.12
Abstract Newsletters, Electrotechnolgy
2.13
Abstract Newsletters, Energy 2.14
Abstract Newsletters, Environmental
Pollution & Control 2.15

Abstract Newsletters, Government
Inventions for Licensing 2.16
Abstract Newsletters, Health Planning
and Health Services Research 2.17
Abstract Newsletters, Industrial and
Mechanical Engineering 2.18
Abstract Newsletters, Information for
Innovators 2.19
Abstract Newsletters, Library and
Information Sciences 2.20
Abstract Newsletters, Materials Sciences
2.21
Abstract Newsletters, Medicine &
Biology 2.22
Abstract Newsletters, NASA Earth
Resources Survey Program 2.23
Abstract Newsletters, Natural
Resources & Earth Sciences 2.24
Abstract Newsletters, Ocean
Technology & Engineering 2.25
Abstract Newsletters, Physics 2.26
Abstract Newsletters, Problem Solving
Information for State & Local
Governments 2.27
Abstract Newsletters, Transportation
2.28
Abstract Newsletters, Urban and
Regional Technology &
Development, Urban Technology
2.29
Federal Research Report 1934.02
Space Setter 4352

RESEARCH AND DEVELOPMENT, INDUSTRIAL

Akron Business & Economic Review
132
Industrial Research & Development
2549
Industrial Research Laboratories of the
United States 2550
New Product—New Business Digest
3458
Production & Inventory Management
3866
Technical Survey 4578

RESEARCH AND DEVELOPMENT, INTERNATIONAL

Agency for International Development
Research and Development Abstracts
86

RESEARCH AND DEVELOPMENT, LASERS AND OPTICS

DMS Military Laser & EO 1475.21
DMS Military Laser & EO Europe
1475.22
Laser Focus 2967

RESEARCH AND DEVELOPMENT, MANAGERS AND MANAGEMENT

Abstract Newsletters, Administration
and Management 2.03
California Management Review 738
Effective Manager 1598.01
Executive Bulletin 1798
Human Resources Management 2429
Key to Economic Science and
Managerial Sciences 2912.01
Management Review and Digest 3087
Operations Research Letters 3629.01
Organizational Dynamics 3640
R&D Management Digest 3999.02
R&D Research and Development
3999.03
Research Management 4090
Survey Reports 4520

RESEARCH AND DEVELOPMENT, MILITARY

DMS Aerospace Intelligence 1475.02
DMS Contract Quarterly (Agency CQ,
Company CQ, County CQ,
Production CQ, RDT&E & Service
CQ) 1475.09
DMS Defense Market 1475.11
DMS Defense RDT&E Budget
Handbook 1475.13
DMS NATO Weapons 1475.27
Military Research Letter 3229

RESEARCH AND DEVELOPMENT, NEW PRODUCTS

New Product—New Business Digest
3458

RESEARCH AND DEVELOPMENT, SHIPS AND SHIPPING

Annual Report of the Maritime
Administration 256

RESEARCH AND DEVELOPMENT, WATER RESOURCES

Abstract Newsletters, NASA Earth
Resources Survey Program 2.23
Research Reports Supported by Office
of Water Research and Technology
4094
Water Resources Thesaurus 4900

RESEARCH ASSOCIATIONS

World Guide to Scientific Associations
and Learned Societies 5066
World of Learning 5072

Major Mass Market Merchandisers
3063
Nationwide Directory of Sporting
Goods Buyers 3415
Nationwide Men's & Boys' Wear 3416
Nationwide Women's & Children's
Wear 3417

RETAILING, CHAIN STORES

Chain Merchandiser Magazine 899
Chain Store Age, General Merchandise
Edition 900.01
Fairchild's Financial Manual of Retail
Stores 1876

Canada

Retail Trade 4114

RETAILING, COLLEGE STORES

College Store Journal 983

RETAILING CONVENIENCE STORES

C-Store Business 1265.01

RETAILING, CREDIT

Creditalk 1243
Stores 4476

RETAILING, DELIVERY SERVICES

Drop Shipping Source Directory of
Major Consumer Product Lines
1506
Retail Operations News Bulletin 4108

RETAILING, DEPARTMENT STORES

Chain Store Age, Executive Edition
900
Chain Store Age, General Merchandise
Edition 900.01
Current Retail Trade 1282
Department Store Jewelry Buyers
Directory 1364
Department Store Sales 1365
Fairchild's Financial Manual of Retail
Stores 1876
Nationwide Women's & Children's
Wear 3417
Retail Control 4103

California

Union-Tribune Index 4754

Canada

Department Store Sales and Stocks
1366

Florida

Apparel South 282.02

Georgia

Apparel South 282.02

North Carolina

Apparel South 282.02

United States

Apparel South 282.02

RETAILING, DISCOUNT HOUSES

Catalog Showroom Business 869
Chain Store Age, Executive Edition
900
Discount Store News 1465
Fairchild's Financial Manual of Retail
Stores 1876

RETAILING, EQUAL OPPORTUNITY EMPLOYMENT

Personnel News & Views 3748

RETAILING, FREIGHT FORWARDING

Traffic Topics 4683

RETAILING GOVERNMENT REGULATIONS. *See also* Sunday Sales

Consumer Credit Guide 1152

RETAILING, HOME CENTER STORES

ABS 2.02
Chain Store Age, Executive Edition
900
Do It Yourself and Home Improvement
Marketing 1490
National Home Center News 3379.01

RETAILING, INDEPENDENT STORES

Nationwide Women's & Children's
Wear 3417

Canada

Retail Trade 4114

Great Britain

Daltons Weekly 1315

RETAILING, INSTALLMENT SALES

Consumer Credit Guide 1152
NAIC Reporter 3355

RETAILING, PERSONNEL

Employee Relations Bulletin 1646
Personnel News & Views 3748

Alaska

Trade and Regulated Industries
Occupational Employment Statistics
4650

Australia

Australian Market Guide 408

United States

Census of Retail Trade, 1977 878
Retail Service Labor Report 4112

RETAILING, PRICES. *See also* Cost of Living

Australia

Consumer Price Index 1161

Canada

Consumer Price Index 1162

RETAILING, RESEARCH ON

Journal of Retailing 2881
Retailing Today 4105

RETAILING, SECURITY SYSTEMS

Retail Operations News Bulletin 4108

RETIRED PEOPLE. *See also* Pension Plans. Housing, Vacation and Retirement Homes

Best's Retirement Income Guide
538.01
Current Literature on Aging 1278
Institute for Social Research Newsletter
2594
Spencer's Retirement Plan Service
4362
Successful Personal Money
Management 1977 4488

RETIREMENT. *See* Retired People

RHODE ISLAND

Connecticut–Rhode Island: Directory of
Manufacturers, 1981 1117.02

From the State Capitals   2169–2191
Rhode Island: State Industrial
   Directory, 1981–82   4133
State and Local Taxes   4386
State Legislative Reporting   4396
State Tax Reports   4413

RICE

Grain Market News Reports   2254
Outlook and Situation Reports
   3653.01

RIOTS

Security Management   4243

RISK MANAGEMENT. *See*

Actuarial Methods. Insurance, Risk
Management

ROAD ACCIDENTS. *See* Traffic

Safety, Accidents

ROADS. *See* Highways. Streets

ROBBERIES AND THEFTS. *See*

subjects, eg, Banking and Finance,
Bank Robberies

ROBINSON-PATMAN ACT (US)

Antitrust Laws and Trade Regulation
   273

ROBOTS. *See* Automation

ROCHESTER, UNIVERSITY OF

Carnegie–Rochester Conference Series
   on Public Policy   864.01

ROCKETS

National Aeronautics and Space
   Administration (NASA) Activities
   3356

ROCKS. *See* Boulders and Rocks

ROOFING

Roofing Siding Insulation.
   Incorporating Solar Contractor   4141

ROYAL MINT (GREAT BRITAIN)

Royal Mint Annual Report   4147

ROYALTIES

Intellectual Property Management:
   Law/Business/Strategy   2637

ROYALTY. *See* Leaders and

Leadership. Government, Chief
Executive

RUBBER

Chemical Horizons North American
   Report   925
Chemical Horizons Overseas Report
   925.01
Rubber: Supply and Distribution for the
   United States MA-30A   4149
Rubber Trends   4149.01
Rubber World   4150
United Nations Industrial Development
   Organization (UNIDO) Guides to
   Information Soruces.
   UNIDO/LIB/SER.D/Rev.1—
   Information Sources on the Natural
   and Synthetic Rubber Industry
   4767.11

Great Britain

British Plastics and Rubber   619

RUGS. *See* Carpets and Rugs

RURAL AREAS

Agricultural Finance Review   100
Farmline   1901.01
World Agricultural Economics & Rural
   Sociology Abstracts   5036

Australia

Primary Industry Survey   3842

Great Britain

Development Digest   1373.01

United States

Urban Affairs Reports   4829

SAFE DEPOSIT

Safe Deposit Handbook   4156

SAFETY. *See* Accidents and Safety.

Safety Engineering. Subjects

SAFETY ENGINEERING

Best's Loss Control Engineering
   Manual   534
Health & Safety in Industry   2356.01
Industrial Safety Product News
   2551.01

SALARIES. *See also* Labor, Wages

and Hours. Managers and Management,
Salaries. Professions, Salaries

Bank Officer Cash Compensation
   Survey, 1979   489.01
Compensation Review   1062
Current Compensation References
   1272
Executive Compensation Service Top
   Management Report   1802.01
Salary Survey   4164

SALES AND SALESPEOPLE. *See*

also Market Research. Sales Promotion.
Fields of sales

Boardroom Reports   568
Business Monitor, Production Series
   710
Chain Merchandiser Magazine   899
Creative Selling   1241.01
Dartnell Sales and Marketing Executive
   Service   1322
Dartnell Sales Manager's Handbook,
   13th edition   1323
Digest of Executive Opportunities
   1389
Encyclopedia of Advertising, 1969
   Edition   1669
Executive Action Report   1796
Executive Compensation Service Top
   Management Report   1802.01
Gallagher Report   2206
Incentive Marketing and Sales
   Promotion   2478
Incentive Travel Manager   2479
Linage Booster   3019
Marketing for Sales Executives   3130
Marketing Letter, the   3132
Premium/Incentive Business   3834
Sales & Marketing Management   4165
Sales Manager's Building   4174
Salesman's Opportunity Magazine
   4175
SCAN   4191
Specialty Salesman & Business
   Opportunities   4359
Success Unlimited   4489
Telephone Marketing Report   4586.01

Bulgaria

Business Eastern Europe   677

Canada

Canadian Commercial Law Guide
   784.01
Financial Post Survey of Industrials
   2017
Sales Prospector   4176
Survey of Buying Power   4510

Czechoslovakia

Business Eastern Europe 677

Europe

Economic & Social Committee of the
European Communities. Bulletin
1537
European Compensation Survey 1771

Germany (East)

Business Eastern Europe 677

Great Britain

Sales Management and Sales
Engineering 4172
Selling Today 4257

Hungary

Business Eastern Europe 677

Ireland, Republic of

Confederation of Irish Industry
(CII)/ESRI Business Forecast 1107

Poland

Business Eastern Europe 677

Rumania

Business Eastern Europe 677

*Union of Soviet Socialist Republics
(USSR)*

Business Eastern Europe 677

United States

American Salesman 203
Sales Prospector 4176
State Sales Guides 4406
Survey of Buying Power 4510
Survey of Buying Power Data Service
4511
Survey of Buying Power Forecasting
Service 4511.01
Survey of Buying Power Part II 4512
Survey of Selling Costs 4518
White Collar Report 4968

Yugoslavia

Business Eastern Europe 677

SALES AND SALESPEOPLE,
RESALES

From the State Capitals: Merchandising
2180

SALES AND SALESPEOPLE, SELF
EMPLOYED

Specialty Salesman 4358

SALES AND SALESPEOPLE,
TRAINING

Survey of Selling Costs 4518

SALES ENGINEERS, INSTITUTE
OF (GREAT BRITAIN)

Sales Management and Sales
Engineering 4172

SALES PROMOTION. *See also*
Advertising. Promotion and Publicity.
Public Relations

Dartnell Sales Promotion Handbook,
7th edition 1324
Doing Business with Eastern Europe
1489

SALES TAX. *See* Taxation, Sales and
Use Tax

SALT. *See* Sodium

SASKATCHEWAN (CANADA)

Saskatchewan Monthly Statistical
Review 4182

SATELLITES

Abstract Newsletters, Communication
2.11
DMS Missiles & Satellites (Europe)
1475.24
National Aeronautics and Space
Administration (NASA) Activities
3356
Satellite News 4183.01
Weekly Government Abstracts.
Communications 4914

SAUDI ARABIA

Developing Business in the Middle East
and North Africa 1371
Saudi Arabia Newsletter 4183.02
Who's Who in Saudi Arabia 4991

SAVINGS. *See* Banking and Finance.
Credit Unions. Savings and Loan
Associations. Types, eg, Pension Plans

SAVINGS AND LOAN
ASSOCIATIONS

Directory of American Savings and
Loan Associations 1408
Economic Briefs 1541

Federal Aids to Financing 1911
Liquidity Portfolio Manager 3021.01
Payment Systems Newsletter 3708
Savings Association News 4188
Savings and Loan Fact Book 4185
Savings and Loan Investor 4186
Savings and Loan Letter 4186.01
Savings and Loan News 4187
Savings & Loan Reporter 4187.01
United States Banker 4794
Washington Banktrends 4884
Washington Financial Reports 4887

SAVINGS AND LOAN
ASSOCIATIONS, GOVERNMENT
REGULATIONS, LAWS AND
PROGRAMS

Savings and Loan Fact Book 4185
Savings Association News 4188
Washington Notes 4888.03

SAVINGS BANKS. *See* Banking and
Finance

SBA. *See* Small Business
Administration (SBA) (US)

SCHOLARSHIPS AND GRANTS

Comsearch Printouts 1092
Foundation Directory 2154
Foundation Grants Index 2156

SCHOOL BUSES. *See* Education,
School Buses

SCHOOLS. *See* Colleges and
Universities. Education. Fields of study.
Names

SCIENCE. *See also* Scientists. Specific
disciplines, eg, Physics

Applied Science & Technology Index
(ASTI) 288
College Recruiting Report 982
Conference Papers Index 1110
Dialog 1375.03
Directory Information Service 1406
Executive Compensation Service Top
Management Report 1802.01
International Journal of Systems
Science 2697
Medical World News 3183
R&D Abstracts 3999.01
R&D Management Digest 3999.02
Scientific, Engineering Technical
Manpower Comments 4201
Scientific Information Notes 4202

SEEDS (CROP)

Doane's Agricultural Report   1476

SELF-EMPLOYMENT. *See*
Entrepreneurs and Small Businesses.
Partnerships. Professional Corporations

SERVICE INDUSTRIES.   *See also*
types

Announcements of Mergers and
   Acquisitions   233
Financial Post Survey of Industrials
   2017

California

California: Services Register, 1981
   738.03
California: Services Register, 1981
   738.04

Great Britain

Business Monitor, Service and
   Distributive Series   711
United Kingdom Kompass Register
   4759

Illinois

Illinois Services Directory, 1980–81
   2438.02

Massachusetts

Massachusetts: Service Directory,
   1979–80   3149.03

United States

Census of Service Industries, 1977   879
Monthly Selected Services Receipts
   3299
Retail Services Labor Report   4112

SEWERS.   *See* Waste Materials and
Disposal

SEX DISCRIMINATION.   *See*
subjects. Women

SHEEP.   *See also* Lamb. Wool

Report on Livestock Surveys: Cattle,
   Sheep   4070

SHEETS.   *See* Beds, Bedding and
Mattresses

SHELLFISH.   *See* Fish and Fish
Products

SHERMAN ANTITRUST ACT (US)

Acts   46
Antitrust Laws & Trade Regulation
   273

SHIPBUILDING.   *See also* Marine
Engineering. Research and
Development, Ships and Shipping

Annual Report of the Maritime
   Administration   256
Commerce Yearbook of Ports, Shipping
   & Shipbuilding   996.03
DMS Ships/Vehicles/Ordnance
   1475.31

SHIPBUILDING, DIESEL MERCHANT SHIPS

Standard Specifications for Diesel
   Merchant Ship Construction   4379

SHIPBUILDING, GOVERNMENT REGULATIONS

AN, AND, & MS Standards   216.01
Standard Specifications for Tanker
   Construction   4380

SHIPBUILDING, MILITARY SHIPS

DMS Ships/Vehicles/Ordnance
   1475.31

SHIPBUILDING, SPECIALIZED SHIPS

Maritime and Construction Aspects of
   Ocean Thermal Energy Conversion
   (OTEC) Plant Ships   3122

SHIPBUILDING, TANKERS

Final Environmental Impact Statement
   of Maritime Administration Tanker
   Construction Program   1986
Standard Specifications for Tanker
   Construction   4380

SHIPPING AGENTS AND DEPOTS

International Freighting Weekly   2683
Routes Yearbook   4144

SHIPPING AND MERCHANT MARINE ACT

Hawkins Federal Maritime Commission
   Service   2350

SHIPS AND SHIPPING.   *See also*
Marine Engineering. Insurance, Marine.
Navigation; Research and Development,
Ships and Shipping. Shipbuilding.
Shipping Agents and Depots

Export Shipping Manual   1851
Fairplay International Shipping Weekly
   1880
Fairplay International World Ships on
   Order   1881
Fairplay World Shipping Yearbook
   1882
Hawkins Federal Maritime Commission
   Service   2350
Lloyd's List   3032.03
Lloyd's Monthly List of Laid Up
   Vessels   3033.03
Lloyd's Ship Manager   3033.04
Lloyd's Shipping Economist   3330.05
Lloyd's Shipping Index   3033.06
Lloyd's Voyage Record   3033.07
Maritime and Construction Aspects of
   Ocean Thermal Energy Conversion
   (OTEC) Plant Ships   3122
Oceanic Abstracts   3570.01
Reference Book of Transportation
   4041
Seatrade   4217
Shipping and Trade News   4275
Statistical Analysis of the World's
   Merchant Fleets   4423

Africa

Trade and Credit: Problems and
   Resolutions in the Middle East and
   North Africa, in Asia and the Pacific
   and in Latin America   4646.01

American Nations

Caribbean Business News   863
Caribbean Year Book, 1977–78   864
Trade and Credit: Problems and
   Resolutions in the Middle East and
   North Africa, in Asia and the Pacific
   and in Latin America   4646.01

California

Commercial News (WCN)   1007

Canada

Decisions and Orders of the Water
   Transport Committee   1351
Water Transport Service Bulletin   4901

Europe

Lloyd's European Loading List
   3032.01

Great Britain

Lloyd's Loading List, UK edition
3033

India

Commerce Yearbook of Ports, Shipping
& Shipbuilding   996.03

Iran

Iran Economic News   2779

Japan

Shipping and Trade News   4275
Zosen   5107

Korea (South)

Korean Trade Directory   2921

Middle East

Businessman's Guide to the Arab
World   709
Trade and Credit: Problems and
Resolutions in the Middle East and
North Africa, in Asia and the Pacific
and in Latin America   4646.01

New England

Boston Marine Guide   577

United States

Annual Report of the Maritime
Administration   256
Daily Commercial News   1293
United States Ocean Shipping
Technology Forecast and Assessment,
Final Report   4813
United States Waterborne Exports and
General Imports FT985   4822
Vessel Entrances and Clearances.
FT975   4848

West Indies

Caribbean Year Book, 1977–78   864

SHIPS AND SHIPPING, ACCIDENTS AND SAFETY

Lloyd's Ship Manager   3033.04
Lloyd's Shipping Economist   3033.05
Lloyd's Weekly Casualty Reports
3034

SHIPS AND SHIPPING, BULK CARRIERS

Statistical Analysis of the World's
Merchant Fleets   4423

SHIPS AND SHIPPING, CONTAINERSHIPS

Routes Yearbook   4144

SHIPS AND SHIPPING, CRUISES

Cruises & Sea Voyages   1264

SHIPS AND SHIPPING, DIESEL MERCHANT SHIPS

Standard Specifications for Diesel
Merchant Ship Construction   4379

SHIPS AND SHIPPING, FREIGHTERS

Export Shipping Manual   1851
International Freighting Weekly   2683
Statistical Analysis of the World's
Merchant Fleets   4423

Great Britain

Registry of Ships   4056

United States

Merchant Marine Data Sheet   3194

SHIPS AND SHIPPING, GOVERNMENT REGULATIONS

Fairplay International Shipping Weekly
1880
Lloyd's Law Reports   3032.02
Lloyd's Maritime & Commercial Law
Quarterly   3033.01
Lloyd's Maritime Law Newsletter
3033.02
World Shipping Laws   5078.01

Canada

Decisions and Orders of the Water
Transport Committee   1351

United States

Federal Carriers Reports   1916

SHIPS AND SHIPPING, MARITIME CHARTER FIXTURES

Chartering Annual   917
Maritime Research Center Newsletter
3124

SHIPS AND SHIPPING, PASSENGER SHIPS

Cruises & Sea Voyages   1264
Statistical Analysis of the World's
Merchant Fleets   4423

SHIPS AND SHIPPING, PORTS

Abstract Newsletters, Ocean
Technology & Engineering   2.25
Commerce Yearbook of Ports, Shipping
& Shipbuilding   996.03

Canada

Water Transport Service Bulletin   4901

Great Britain

Annual Digest of Port Statistics, Vols I
and II   244
Quarterly Bulletin of Port Statistics
3958
Statistics of Trade through United
Kingdom Ports   4455

United States

Vessel Entrances and Clearances.
FT975   4848

SHIPS AND SHIPPING, TANKERS

AP–Dow Jones Petroleum News
Service   281
Dow Jones International Energy Wire
1498
Energy Service   1694
Statistical Analysis of the World's
Merchant Fleets   4423
Zosen   5107

SHOES. *See* Footwear

SHOPPING CENTERS

Chain Store Age, Executive Edition
900
Directory of Shipping Centers in
Hawaii   1456
Downtown Idea Exchange   1505
Realty Roundup   4032
Shopping Center Newsletter   4283
Shopping Center World   4283.01

SHOPS. *See* Retailing

SIDING

Roofing Siding Insulation.
Incorporating Solar Contractor   4141

SIGNS AND SYMBOLS. *See also*
Trademarks

Abbreviations Dictionary, 6th Edition,
1981   1
Signs of the Times   4286

SILVER

Annual Review of the Silver Market 259
International Monetary Market Yearbook 2713
International Reports 2727
Silver Data 4287
World's Monetary Stocks of Gold, Silver and Coins—On a Calendar Year Basis 5079

United States

Silver Data 4287

SIMULATORS

DMS Military Simulators 1475.23

SKYLAB. *See* Aeronautics and Space

SLATE. *See* Brick and Tile

SLUM CLEARANCE. *See* Area Development and Renewal. Urban Areas

SMALL BUSINESS ADMINISTRATION (SBA) (US)

Amer Journal of Small Business 196
National Association of Small Business Investment Companies (NASBIC) News 3362
Small Business Administration Annual Report 4298

SMALL BUSINESSES. *See* Entrepreneurs and Small Businesses. Partnerships. Fields

SMALL BUSINESS INSTITUTE

Journal of Small Business Management 2884

SMOKING. *See* Tobacco

SNACK FOODS. *See* Food, Snack Foods

SOAPS AND DETERGENTS

Advertising Substantiation Program 72
Happi 2341.01
United Nations Industrial Development Organization (UNIDO) Guides to Information Sources. UNIDO/LIB/SER.D/1/Rev.1—Information Sources on the Soap and Detergent Industry 4767.14

SOCIAL AND WELFARE WORK.
See also Social Security

Consumer Sourcebook, 1st Edition 1175
Current Literature on Aging 1278
International Journal of Social Economics 2696
Journal of Urban Analysis 2900

Great Britain

Health and Personal Social Services Statistics for England 2354
Monthly Digest Annual Supplement 3288

United States

Economic Opportunity Report 1556.02
Health Grants and Contracts Weekly 2360

Utah

Statistical Review of Government in Utah 4441

Wales

Health and Personal Social Services Statistics for Wales 2355

SOCIAL CONDITIONS. *See also*
specific areas, eg, Rural Areas. Geographic regions

Business & Society Review 667
Development Forum: Business Edition 1375
Economic Development & Cultural Change 1548
Institute for Social Research Newsletter 2594
Labour & Society 2948
Monthly Letter 3292
New York Times 3487
Progress in Planning 3894
Socio-Economic Planning Sciences 4324
Stateman's Year-Book, 1980–81 edition 4408
Statistical Yearbook 4444
Technological Forecasting and Social Change 4580
Transdex 4687.01
World Economic and Social Indicators 5059
World Tables, 1980 5080

Africa

Africa Guide 1981 78
Africa South of the Sahara 82

Alaska

Alaska Review of Social & Economic Conditions 142

American Nations

Hanson's Latin American Letter 2341
Informational and Technical Publications of the General Secretariat of the Organization of American States (OAS) 2569
Inter-American Economic Affairs 2641
Latin America & Caribbean 1981 2969.01
Latin American Index 2975
Noticias 3549

Canada

British Columbia Facts and Statistics 602
Edmonton Report 1588
North 3533
Perspective Canada 3752

China, People's Republic of

China Letter 942
Information Peking (Beijing) 2573.02

Egypt

Developing Business in the Middle East and North Africa 1371

Europe

Breve 587
Statistics—Europe 4452

European Economic Community

Bulletin of the European Communities 646
Common Market News 1038
Economic & Social Committee of the European Communities. Bulletin 1537

Far East

Asia & Pacific 1981 324.02
Asia Letter 325
Economic and Social Commission for Asia and the Pacific 1536.01
Quarterly Reviews 3972

Florida

Dimensions 1398

Georgia

Georgia Statistical Abstract 2220

Great Britain

Britain in Context 596.01
Leisure, Recreation and Tourism
Abstracts 3004.01
Monthly Digest Annual Supplement
3288
Social Trends 4321

Hawaii

All about Business in Hawaii 145

Inida

India News 2504

Iraq

Developing Business in the Middle East
and North Africa 1371

Ireland, Northern

Atlas of Ireland 346
Social and Economic Trends in
Northern Ireland 4311

Ireland, Republic of

Atlas of Ireland 346
Statistical Abstract of Ireland 4419

Massachusetts

Industry 2558

Middle East

Middle East Review 1981 3219.01

New Zealand

Life and Business in New Zealand
3011

Oklahoma

Statistical Abstract of Oklahoma 4420

Philippines

Philippine Letter 3765.03

Saudi Arabia

Developing Business in the Middle East
and North Africa 1371

South Africa

South Africa Yearbook 4337

Third World

Ceres: Food and Agriculture
Organization (FAO) Review on
Development 894

Overseas Development Institute (ODI)
Review 3657
South The Third World Magazine
4349.01
Third World Quarterly 4606.01

United States

Abstract Newsletters, Behavior &
Society 2.05
Babson's Washington Forecast Letter
445
Bicentennial Statistics 550
Newsbank Library 3462.01
SRI Microfiche Library 4368.02
Statistical Abstract of the United States
4421
Statistical Reference Index 4438

SOCIAL CREDIT

Abundance 5

SOCIAL ECONOMICS

Review of Social Economy 4129

SOCIAL SCIENCES. *See also*
specific disciplines

Amer Journal of Economics &
Sociology 195
Aslib Directory, Volume 2 333.01
Contents Pages in Management 1184
Current Contents: Social and
Behavioral Sciences 1273
Dialog 1375.03
Evaluation Studies Review Annual
1793
International Encyclopedia of the Social
Sciences, 1977 Condensed Version
2677
International Journal of Social
Economics 2696
Journal of Economic Issues 2846
Mathematical Social Sciences 3154.02
National Institute of Economic Social
Research Annual Report 3387
Public Relations Quarterly 3933
Social Sciences Citation Index 4314
Social Sciences Index 4315

SOCIAL SECURITY

Actuary 48
Benefits International 521
International Benefits Information
Service 2658
Pension Actuary 3719
Social Security and Medicare Explained
4316

Great Britain

Social Security Statistics 4319

United States

Annual Statistical Supplement, Social
Security Bulletin 263
Legislative Series 3002
Payroll Management Guide 3711
Pension and Profit Sharing 3720
Social Security Beneficiaries in
Metropolitan Areas 4317
Unemployment Insurance Reports
4744

SOCKS. *See* Hosiery

SODIUM

Mining Lease Reports 3239.01

SOFTWARE. *See* Computers

SOIL

Abstract Newsletters, NASA Earth
Resources Survey Program 2.23
Abstract Newsletters, Natural
Resources & Earth Sciences 2.24
Earth Surface Processes and Landforms
1522
Tropical Agriculture 4722

SOLAR ENERGY. *See* Energy, Solar

SONAR

DMS Radar & Sonar 1475.29

SOUTH AFRICA, REPUBLIC OF

International Gold Digest 2683.01
South Africa Yearbook 4337

SOUTH AMERICA. *See* American
Nations and Western Hemisphere
Possessions

SOUTH CAROLINA

Central Atlantic States: Manufacturers
Directory, 1981 886
From the State Capitals 2169–2191
South Carolina: Industrial Directory,
1981 4342.01
South Carolina: State Industrial
Directory, 1980 4342.02
State and Local Taxes 4386
State Legislative Reporting Service
4396
State Tax Reports 4413

SOUTH DAKOTA

From the State Capitals   2169–2191
South Dakota: Manufacturers &
  Processors Directory, 1980   4345
South Dakota: State Industrial
  Directory, 1981   4345.02
State and Local Taxes   4386
State Legislative Reporting Service
  4396
State Tax Reports   4413

SOUTHWESTERN LEGAL FOUNDATION

Exploration and Economics of the
  Petroleum Industry   1815

SPACE. *See* Aeronautics and Space

SPECIALTY ADVERTISING. *See*
Advertising, Specialty

SPEECHWRITING

Speechwriter's Newsletter   4361.05

SPICES

United Nations Industrial Development
  Organization (UNIDO) Guides to
  Information Sources.
  UNIDO/LIB/SER.D/Rev.1—
  Information Sources on the Coffee,
  Cocoa, Tea and Spices Industry
  4767.06

SPORTS AND SPORTING GOODS.
See also Skiing Industry

Africa   77
Buying Offices and Accounts   729
Hardware, Tools, and Do-It-Yourself
  2406
Managing the Leisure Facility   3095.03
Nationwide Directory of Sporting
  Goods Buyers   3415
Orange County Illustrated   3635
Sporting Goods Business   4364
Sporting Goods Market   4364.01

SPOT AND FORWARD CONTRACT
MARKETS. *See* Commodities.
Currency

STANDARDS AND
STANDARDIZATION. *See also*
Uniform Commercial Code

AN, AND & MS Standards   216.01
Annual Book of ASTM Standards, 1981
  236.01
Dimensions   1397
Identified Sources of Supply   2433.01

Metric Standards   3204.01
Mill-Hdbk-5C Handbook   3228.01
Military and Federal Standards and
  Specifications   3228.02
National Aerospace Standards   3356.01
National Electrical Manufacturers
  Association Standards Publications
  3372
Standards and Specifications
  Information Bulletin   4378.01
Underwriters Laboratories Standards
  for Safety   4741.01

STARVATION. *See* Hunger

STATE AND LOCAL
GOVERNMENT. *See* Government,
State and Local. Names of states and
localities

STATE-CHARTERED BANKS. *See*
Banking and Finance, State-Chartered
Banks

STATES (US). *See also* state names

Banker's Letter of the Law   468
Directory of Federal Statistics for Local
  Areas: A Guide to Sources, 1976
  1430
Sources of State Information and State
  Industrial Directories   4336

STATIONERY

Canadian Office Products and
  Stationery   824
Geyer's Dealer Topics   2223
Stationery & Office Supplies   4417

STATISTICAL ASSOCIATION,
AMERICAN

Statisticians and Others in Allied
  Professions   4447

STATISTICAL METHODS. *See also*
Statistical Studies

American Statistician   206
Annals of Statistics   229
Best's Underwriting Newsletter   544
Current Index to Statistics—
  Applications, Methods, Theory   1277
Economic Education Bulletin   1550
Estadistica   1744
Financial Statistics: Explanatory
  Handbook   2021
Guide to Official Statistics   2300
Handbook of Sampling for Auditing
  and Accounting   2337
International Statistical Review   2728

Journal of the American Statistical
  Assn   2889
Statistician   4446
Statistics—Asia & Australasia   4450
Statistics—Europe   4452

STATISTICAL STUDIES. *See also*
Surveys and Polls. Vital Statistics.
Subjects

Econometrica   1534
Quality Control and Applied Statistics
  3956
Statisticians and Others in Allied
  Professions   4447
Statistics—Europe   4452
Thorndike Encyclopedia of Banking
  and Financial Tables   4615

Africa

Statistics—Africa   4448

American Nations

Statistics—America   4449

Canada

Infomat   2567
Statistics Canada Daily   4451

Great Britain

Statistical News   4430

STEAM. *See* Energy, Steam

STEEL. *See* Iron and Steel

STEREOS. *See* Recordings

STEVEDORING

Benefits Review Board Longshore
  Reporter   522.01
Commerce Yearbook of Ports, Shipping
  & Shipbuilding   996.03

STOCKBROKERS

Nelson's Directory of Securities
  Research Information   3428
Wall Street Letter   4880

Canada

Security Dealers Directory   4239

Great Britain

Extel Issuing House Year Book   1861

United States

Security Dealers Directory   4239

STOCKHOLDERS RESOLUTIONS.
See Stocks and Bonds, Stockholders Resolutions

STOCKINGS. *See* Hosiery

STOCK OPTIONS. *See* Stocks and Bonds, Stock Options

STOCKS AND BONDS. *See also* Corporations, Investors Relations. Currency, Monetary Stocks. Financial Analysis. Mutual Funds. Securities Exchanges. Names of specific exchanges. Stockbrokers

Analystics   214
AP–Dow Jones Econ Report   278
AP–Dow Jones Financial Wire   280
Barron's   509
Barron's Market Laboratory, 1977 Edition   510
Baylor Business Studies   516
Best's Market Guide   535
Bondholder's Register   571
Capital International Perspective   856
Dow Jones International News Wire 1499
Dow Jones Investor's Handbook   1500
EVM Market Week   1794
Federal Reserve Bank of New York Quarterly Review   1937
Financial Analysts Journal   1995
Financial Digest   1997
Financial Executive's Handbook, 1970 1999
Financial Times Actuaries Share Indices   2024
Fleet Street Letter   2061
Forbes   2103
Goldsmith–Nagan, Bond & Money Market Letter   2235
Income Investor   2484
Indicator Digest   2505
Investment Bulletin   2761
Investors Intelligence   2773
Investors Research Service   2774
Journal of Portfolio Management   2874
Media/General (M/G) Financial Weekly Market Digest   3169
Money   3267
Mortgage Backed Securities Reports 3320
National Monthly Bond Summary 3395
New York Times   3487
NOW Machine   3551
Secondary Market Reporter   4220
Securities Week   4237
Security Industry & Product News 4241

Share-Owners   4272
Smart Money   4307
Stock Market Research Library   4467
Stock Trader's Almanac   4470
Technical Trends   4579
United Business and Investment Report 4755
Value Line Convertible Strategist   4839
Value Line OTC Special Situations Service   4841
Wall Street Advisor   4876
Wall Street Journal   4878
Wall Street Journal Index   4879
Wall Street Letter   4880
Wall Street Review of Books   4881
Who's Who in the Securities Industry 4994

American Nations

Caribbean Business News   863

Australia

Australian Stock Exchange Journal 416
Company Review Service   1054
Jobson's Mining Year Book   2813

California

California Eligible Securities List   736

Canada

Bank of Canada Review   485
Blue Book of CBS Stock Reports   563
Canadian Business Service Investment Reporter   782
Financial Post Corporation Service 2011
Investor's Digest of Canada   2772
Montreal Stock Exchange Daily Official News Sheet   3306
Montreal Stock Exchange Monthly Review   3307
Record of New Issues   4034
Record of Valuation Day Prices   4036
Record of Warrants   4037
Toronto Stock Exchange Company Manual   4640
Toronto Stock Exchange Daily Record 4640.01
Toronto Stock Exchange Management of Change in the Canadian Securities Industry   4640.02
Toronto Stock Exchange Members' Manual   4640.03
Toronto Stock Exchange Review   4641
Toronto Stock Exchange "300" Stock Price Indexes Manual   4641.01

Toronto Stock Exchange "300" Total Return Indexes Manual   4641.02
Vancouver Stock Exchange Annual Report   4842
Vancouver Stock Exchange Review 4843

Dominican Republic

Caribbean Business   862

Europe

Euromarket Letter   1763
Euromarket News   1764

Great Britain

Analyst's Service   216
British Company Service   610
Capital Gains Tax Service   855.01
Extel Handbook of Market Leaders 1860
Investors Chronicle News Letter   2771
Money Management and Unitholder 3270
Planned Savings   3777
Savings Market   4190
United Kingdom & International Point & Figure Library   4755.01

Illinois

Chicago Board Options Exchange Guide   935

Ireland, Republic of

Analyst's Service   216
British Company Service   610

Israel

Business Review and Economic News from Israel   720
Stock Exchange Information Service 4464

Japan

Japan Stock Journal   2803.01

Massachusetts

Boston Stock Exchange Guide   578

Mexico

Rubio's Mexican Financial Journal 4151

New Zealand

National Business Review   3365

STOCKS AND BONDS, BOND INTEREST

STOCKS AND BONDS, CHARTS

STOCKS AND BONDS, COMMERCIAL PAPER BONDS

STOCKS AND BONDS, COMMON STOCKS

South Africa

Johannesburg Stock Exchange Monthly
Bulletin 2815

United States

Chartcraft Weekly Service 912
Commercial and Financial Chronicle
997
Daily Graphs American Stock
Exchange/OTC 1297
Daily Graphs New York Stock
Exchange/OTC 1298
Holt 500 Trading Portfolio 2380
Holt Investment Advisory 2381
Investment Quality Trends 2766
Johnson's Investment Company Service
2816
Moody's Dividend Record 3312
Moody's Handbook of Common Stocks
3313
Moody's Industrial Manual and News
Reports 3314
New York Stock Exchange (NYSE)
Fact Book 3484
Northwest Investment Review 3546
Northwest Stock Guide 3547
Spectrum One: Investment Company
Stock Holdings Survey 4360
Stock Guide 4466
Trendline Service: Daily Action Stock
Charts 4711
Vickers Guide to College Endowment
Portfolios 4850
Vickers Guide to Insurance Company
Portfolios—Common Stocks 4851
Vickers Guide to Investment Company
Portfolios 4853

Canada

Toronto Stock Exchange Daily Record
4640.01
Toronto Stock Exchange "300" Stock
Price Indexes Manual 4641.01
Toronto Stock Exchange "300" Total
Return Indexes Manual 4641.02

STOCKS AND BONDS, CONVERTIBLE BONDS

Bond Guide 570
Fixed Income Investor 2057
Moody's Bond Record 3309
Spectrum Convertibles Holdings Survey
of Convertible Bonds and Convertible
Preferred Stocks 4359.02
Spectrum Six-Insider Ownership Based
on Forms 3 and 4 4361.04
Vickers Guide to Investment Company
Portfolios 4853

STOCKS AND BONDS, CONVERTIBLE DEBT

Vickers Guide to Bank Trust Guide
4849

STOCKS AND BONDS, CORPORATE BONDS

Blue List of Current Municipal
Offerings 564
Bond Guide 570
Committee on Uniform Security
Identification Procedures (CUSIP)
Corporate Directory 1016
Directory of Bond Agents 1411
Fitch Corporate Bond Ratings Book
2051
Fitch Rating Register 2051
Johnson's Investment Company Service
2816
Money Manager 3271
Moody's Bond Record 3309
Spectrum Three Institutional Stock
Holdings Survey 4361.01
Spectrum Five Five Percent Ownership
Based on 13D, 13G and 14D-1
Filings 4361.03
Spectrum Six Insider Ownership Based
on Forms 3 and 4 4361.04
Vickers Guide to Insurance Company
Portfolios—Corporate Bonds 4852

STOCKS AND BONDS, CUSIP

Committee on Uniform Security
Identification Procedures (CUSIP)
Corporate Directory 1016
Committee on Uniform Security
Identification Procedures (CUSIP):
Digest of Changes in CUSIP 1017
Committee on Uniform Security
Identification Procedures (CUSIP)
Directory of User Numbers 1018
Committee on Uniform Security
Identification Procedures (CUSIP)
Master Directory 1019

STOCKS AND BONDS, DIVIDENDS

Capital Adjustments 852
Client Directed Screen 962
Cycli-Graphs 1290
National Investor Relations Institute IR
Update 3388
Security Charts 4238
Stock Market Research Library 4467

Australia

Extel Australian Company Service
1856
Extel Overseas Companies Service
1863

Canada

Canadian Daily Stock Charts 788
Canadian Weekly Stock Charts:
Industrials 847
Financial Post Corporation Service
2011
Toronto Stock Exchange "300" Total
Return Indexes Manual 4641.02
Toronto Stock Exchange Weekly
Summary 4642
Vancouver Stock Exchange Review
4843

Europe

Extel European Company Service
1859
Extel Overseas Companies Services
1863

Great Britain

Analyst's Service 216
British Company Service 610
Extel Dividend Record 1858.01

Ireland, Republic of

Analyst's Service 216
British Company Service 610

North America

Extel North American Company
Service 1862
Extel Overseas Companies Services
1863

United States

American Exchange Stock Reports
173
Canadian Daily Stock Charts 788
Daily Stock Price Records 1306
Dividend Record (Daily) 1470
Dividend Record (Weekly) 1471
Moody's Dividend Record 3312
Stock Summary 4469
Stock Values & Dividends for Tax
Purposes 4472

STOCKS AND BONDS, EARNINGS

Client Directed Screen 962
Cycli-Graphs 1290
Security Charts 4238
Value Line Investment Survey 4840

Canada

Canadian Daily Stock Charts 788
Canadian Weekly Stock Charts:
Industrials 847

Great Britain

British Company Service 610

Ireland, Republic of

British Company Service 610

United States

American Exchange Stock Reports
173
Canadian Daily Stock Charts 788
Earnings Forecaster 1521
Standard New York Stock Exchange
(NYSE) Stock Reports 4375
Stock Summary 4469

STOCKS AND BONDS, EMPLOYEE OWNERSHIP PLANS

How to Analyze, Design and Install an
Employee Stock Ownership Plan
2420

STOCKS AND BONDS, EUROBONDS

AP–Dow Jones Bankers Report 277
Borrowing in International Capital
Markets 576
Euromarket Letter 1763
Financial Market Trends 2008
International Reports 2727

STOCKS AND BONDS, FOREIGN SECURITIES

Moody's Dividend Record 3312

STOCKS AND BONDS, FRAUDS, SWINDLING, AND EMBEZZELMENT

Business Crime: Criminal Liability of
the Business Community 676.01

STOCKS AND BONDS, GOVERNMENT BONDS

Blue List of Current Municipal
Offerings 564
Bond Buyer's Municipal Finance
Statistics Book 569.01
Daily Bond Buyer 1291
Fitch Rating Register 2051
Fitch Investors Municipal Bond
Reports 2055
Investment Dealers' Digest 2762
Money Manager 3271
Moody's Municipal Credit Reports on
Line 3316.01
NOW Machine 3551
Weekly Bond Buyer 4903

Canada

Bank of Canada Weekly Financial
Statistics 486
Ontario Corporation Manual 3621

Florida

This Week 4608

United States

Best's Market Guide 535
Bond Guide 570
Directory of Bond Agents 1411
Johnson's Investment Company Service
2816
Moody's Bond Record 3309
Moody's Municipal and Government
Manual and News Reports 3315
Municipal Bond Selector 3338
Municipal Finance Journal 3338.01
This Week 4608

STOCKS AND BONDS, GOVERNMENT REGULATIONS

News for Investors 3463
Securities and Federal Corporate Law
4232
Securities Law Review 4233
Securities Week 4237
Wall Street Letter 4880

Arkansas

Financial Trend 2032

Australia

Australian Securities Law Reports 415

Canada

Business Law Reports, Vol 1 702
Canadian Securities Law Reports 834
Ontario Securities Commission Weekly
Summary 3625

Louisiana

Financial Trend 2032

New Mexico

Financial Trend 2032

Oklahoma

Financial Trend 2032

Texas

Financial Trend 2032

United States

Blue Sky Law Reports 566
Directory of Companies Filing Annual
Reports with the US Securities &
Exchange Commission 1419
Executive Disclosure Guide 1803
Federal Securities Law Reports 1960
National Assn of Securities Dealers
(NASD) Manual 3361
New York Stock Exchange (NYSE)
Guide 3485
Private Placements and Restricted
Securities 3855
Review of Securities Regulation 4128
SEC Compliance Financial Reporting
and Forms 4219
Secured Transactions Guide 4221
Securities & Exchange Commission
Annual Report to Congress 4224
Securities & Exchange Commission
Decisions & Reports 4225
Securities & Exchange Commission
Docket 4227
Securities & Exchange Commission
News Digest 4228
Securities & Exchange Commission
Official Summary 4229
Securities Regulation 4234
Securities Regulation & Law Report
4235
Securities Regulation Law Journal
4236
Securities Week 4237

STOCKS AND BONDS, HOLDING COMPANIES

Securities & Exchange Commission
News Digest 4228

STOCKS AND BONDS, INCOME BONDS

Moody's Dividend Record 3312
Savings Market 4190

STOCKS AND BONDS, INDEXES

Barron's Market Laboratory, 1977
Edition 510
Daily Stock Price Records 1306
Graphoscope 2261
Point & Figure Summary 3792
Ratio Index Services 4007
Selected Interest and Exchange Rates
4253
Toronto Stock Enchange "300" Stock
Price Indexes Manual 4641.01
Toronto Stock Exchange "300" Total
Return Indexes Manual 4641.02

STOCKS AND BONDS, INDUSTRIAL DEVELOPMENT BONDS

Moody's Bond Record 3309
Savings Market 4190

STOCKS AND BONDS, INSIDER TRADING

Consensus of Insiders 1119
Investors Intelligence 2773
Spectrum Six Insider Ownership Based on Forms 3 and 4 4361.04
Weekly Insider Report 4932

STOCKS AND BONDS, INSTITUTIONAL INVESTORS

Institutional Investor 2601
Vickers Traders Guide 4853.01

Canada

Vickers Guide to Insurance Company Portfolios—Common Stocks 4851

United States

Best's Market Guide 535
Corporate Examiner 1206
Spectrum Three Institutional Stock Holdings Survey 4361.01
Spectrum Four Institutional Portfolios 4361.02
Stock Summary 4469
Vickers Guide to Bank Trust Guide 4849
Vickers Guide to College Endowment Portfolios 4850
Vickers Guide to Insurance Company Portfolios—Common Stocks 4851
Wright Investors Services 5089.01

STOCKS AND BONDS, INTERNATIONAL BONDS

Euromoney 1765
Euromoney Syndication Guide 1766.01
International Bond Service 2661

STOCKS AND BONDS, LIQUIDITY

Liquidity Report 3022

STOCKS AND BONDS, MUNICIPAL BONDS. See Stocks and Bonds, Government Bonds

STOCKS AND BONDS, NEW ISSUES

Securities & Exchange Commission Statistical Bulletin 4231

Canada

Financial Post Corporation Service 2011
Record of New Issues 4034
Toronto Stock Exchange Review 4641

Great Britain

Extel Book of Prospectuses and New Issues 1858
Extel Issuing House Year Book 1861
Monthly New Issues and Placings Service 3293

Ireland, Republic of

Monthly New Issues and Placings Service 3293

STOCKS AND BONDS, NON-PAYING ISSUES

Moody's Dividend Record 3312

STOCKS AND BONDS, OVER-THE-COUNTER TRADING

Bank and Quotation Record 458
Daily Graphs American Stock Exchange/OTC 1297
Daily Graphs-New York Stock Exchange/OTC 1298
Daily Stock Price Records 1306
Dow Jones Investor's Handbook 1500
Market Chronicle 3126
Over-the-Counter Stock Reports 3669
Rocky Mountain Journal 4139
Securities & Exchange Commission Statistical Bulletin 4231
Stock Guide 4466
Stock Summary 4469

STOCKS AND BONDS, PLACINGS

Monthly New Issues and Placings Service 3293
Private Placements and Restricted Securities 3855

STOCKS AND BONDS, PREFERRED STOCKS

Called Bond Record 739
Dow Jones Investor's Handbook 1500
Fitch Rating Register 2051
Fitch Institutional Reports 2054
Fixed Income Investor 2057
Moody's Dividend Record 3312
RHM Convertible Survey 4131
Spectrum Convertibles Holdings Survey of Convertible Bonds and Convertible Preferred Stocks 4359.02
Stock Guide 4466

Vickers Guide to Bank Trust Guide 4849
Vickers Guide to Investment Company Portfolios 4853

STOCKS AND BONDS, PRICE-EARNINGS RATIO

Barron's Market Laboratory 1977 Edition 510
Moody's Investors Fact Sheets 3314.01
Stock Summary 4469

STOCKS AND BONDS, PRICES

Asian Wall Street Journal 329
Bank and Quotation Record 458
Blue List of Current Municipal Offerings 564
Client Directed Screen 962
Dow Jones Investor's Handbook 1500
Growth Stock Outlook 2269
Liquidity Report 3022
National Monthly Bond Summary 3395
National Monthly Stock Summary 3396
New York Times 3487
NOW Machine 3551
Security Charts 4238
Stock Market Research Library 4467

Canada

Canadian Daily Stock Charts 788
Canadian Weekly Stock Charts: Industrials 847
Canadian Weekly Stock Charts: Mines & Oils 848
Commercial and Financial Chronicle 997
Graphoscope 2261
Industry Price Indexes 2563
Point and Figure Digest 3791
Point & Figure Summary 3792
Record of Valuation Day Prices 4036
Toronto Stock Exchange Review 4641

Great Britain

Analyst's Service 216
Extel Handbook of Market Leaders 1860

Ireland, Republic of

Analyst's Service 216

Japan

Japan Stock Journal 2803.01

United States

Canadian Daily Stock Charts 788
Capital Market Developments 858
Commercial and Financial Chronicle
  997
Daily Graphs American Stock
  Exchange/OTC 1297
Daily Graphs-New York Stock
  Exchange/OTC 1298
Daily Stock Price Records 1306
Financial Trend's Corporate Directory
  Service 2033
Graphoscope 2261
Market Chronicle 3126
Northwest Stock Guide 3547
Point and Figure Digest 3791
Point & Figure Summary 3792
Standard New York Stock Exchange
  (NYSE) Stock Reports 4375
Statistical Indicator Reports 4428
Statistical Service 4442

STOCKS AND BONDS, PRIVATE BONDS

Fitch Hospital and Other Nonprofit
  Institutional Ratings 2053

STOCKS AND BONDS, PUBLIC BONDS

Directory of Bond Agents 1411
Fitch Institutional Reports 2054

STOCKS AND BONDS, PUT AND CALL OPTIONS

RHM Survey of Warrants. Options &
  Low-Price Stocks 4132
Trade Levels Option Report 4656

STOCKS AND BONDS, STOCKHOLDERS RESOLUTIONS

News for Investors 3463

STOCKS AND BONDS, STOCK OPTIONS

Daily Graphs Stock Option Guide
  1300
Dow Jones Stock Options Handbook
  1504
Profit Sharing Design Manual 3893
Value Line Convertible Strategist 4839

Canada

Toronto Stock Exchange Daily Record
  4640.01
Vancouver Stock Exchange Review
  4843

United States

Dunn & Hargitt Market Guide 1517

Tax Desk Book for the Closely Held
  Corporation 4546

STOCK AND BONDS, TAXATION

Great Britain

Extel Fixed Interest Record 1859.01

United States

Dividend Record (Daily) 1470
Dividend Record (Weekly) 1471

STOCKS AND BONDS, TENDER OFFERS

Tenders 4590

STOCKS AND BONDS, TRANSFERS

Stock Transfer Guide 4471

Great Britain

Registrar's Service 4054

Ireland, Republic of

Registrar's Service 4054

United States

Inheritance Taxes 2578

STOCKS AND BONDS, VALUATION

Dow Jones Securities Valuation
  Handbook 1503
Unquoted Companies Service 4825

STOCKS AND BONDS, VOLUME TRADING

Cycli-Graphs 1290
NOW Machine 3551
Security Charts 4238
Stock Market Research Library 4467
Trade Levels Report 4657

Canada

Canadian Weekly Stock Charts:
  Industrials 847
Canadian Weekly Stock Charts: Mines
  & Oils 848
Security Transactions with Nonresidents
  4249
Toronto Stock Exchange Daily Record
  4640.01
Vancouver Stock Exchange Annual
  Report 4842
Vancouver Stock Exchange Review
  4843

United States

Capital Market Developments 858
Daily Graphs American Stock
  Exchange/OTC 1297
Daily Graphs-New York Stock
  Exchange/OTC 1298
Daily Stock Price Records 1306
Securities & Exchange Commission
  Statistical Bulletin 4231
Standard New York Stock Exchange
  (NYSE) Stock Reports 4375

STOCKS AND BONDS, WARRANTS

Record of Warrants 4037
RHM Survey of Warrants. Options &
  Low-Price Stocks 4132

STOCK TRANSFERS. *See* Stocks
and Bonds, Transfers

STORES. *See* Retailing. Shopping
Guides

STREETS. *See also* Highways and
Expressways

From the State Capitals: Highway
  Financing and Construction 2173
Kelly's Post Office London Directory
  2908

STRIKES. *See* Labor, Strikes

SUBCHAPTER S. *See* Corporations,
Subchapter S

SUB-SAHARA. *See* Africa,
Sub-Sahara

SUBSIDIARIES. *See* Corporations,
Subsidiaries .

SUGAR AND OTHER SWEETENERS

Foreign Agriculture Circulars 2111
Outlook and Situation Reports
  3653.01

SUNDAY SALES

From the State Capitals: Merchandising
  2180

SUPERMARKETS

Chain Store Age, Executive Edition
  900
Fairchild's Financial Manual of Retail
  Stores 1876
Food Promotions 2096
Progressive Grocer 3896
Supermarket Business 4497
Supermarket News 4498

SUPERVISORY MANAGEMENT.

See Personnel Management. Personnel Policies. Labor, Supervisory Personnel

SUPREME COURT (CANADA)

Canada Supreme Court Reports 766

SUPREME COURT (US)

Guidebook to Labor Relations 2274
Hawkins Civil Aeronautics Board
Service 2349
Hawkins Federal Maritime Commission
Service 2350
Hawkins Motor Carrier-Freight
Forwarder Service 2351
Hawkins Rail Carrier Service 2352
Roberts' Dictionary of Industrial
Relations, 1971 Edition 4138
United States Supreme Court Bulletin
4817

SURTAX. *See* Taxation, Surtax

SURVEYING AND SURVEYORS

Royal Institution of Chartered
Surveyors Year Book 4146

SURVEYS AND POLLS. *See also*

Measuring and Testing. Statistical
Studies

Fraser Opinion Letter 2161
Gallup Survey 2207
Infomat 2567
New Surveys 3472
Statistics Canada Daily 4451

SURVEYS AND POLLS, CENSUS

Data on Selected Racial Groups
Available from Bureau of the Census,
No 40, Revised May 1977 1338
Directory of Federal Statistics for Local
Areas: A Guide to Sources, 1976
1430

United States

Bureau of the Census Catalog 651
Bureau of the Census Catalog of
Publications, 1790–1972 652
Data User News 1345
Reference Manual on Population and
Housing Statistics from the Census
Bureau, 1977 4042
Statistical Abstract of the United States
4421

SWITZERLAND

Economic Survey of Switzerland 1572
Swiss-American Chamber of Commerce.
Yearbook 4522

SWLF LABOR LAW INSTITUTE

Labor Law Developments 2933

SYNAGOGUES. *See* Religious

Edifices

SYNFUEL. *See* Fuel, Synfuels

SYNTHETICS. *See* types, eg, Plastics

SYSTEMS DEVELOPMENT AND

DESIGN. *See* Computers

SYSTEMS ENGINEERING. *See*

Computers

TABLEWARE

Gifts & Tablewares 2227

TAFT-HARTLEY LAW (US)

Guidebook to Labor Relations 2274
Labor Law 2932

TANKERS. *See* Ships and Shipping,

Tankers

TANKS

DMS Tanks Market Study and Forecast
1475.33

TAPE DECKS. *See* Recordings

TAPE RECORDERS. *See*

Recordings

TARIFFS AND TRADE, GENERAL

AGREEMENT ON (GATT)

Basic Instruments and Selected
Documents (BISD) 513
GATT Activities 2209
Trade Negotiation Information Service
4666
Transnational Economic and Monetary
Law: Transactions and Contracts
4690

TARIFFS AND QUOTAS

Airtrade 127
Custom House Guide 1285
Tax-Free Trade Zones of the World
4553.02
Transnational Economic and Monetary
Law: Transactions and Contracts
4690

American Nations

CECON Trade News 873

Australia

Australian Tax Review 418
Imports 2443
Imports Cleared for Home
Consumption: Part 1 Chapter 1–67 of
Customs Tariff 2445
Tariff Brief 4530
Tariff Insight 4531

Canada

Customs Tariff Complete Service 1289

Europe

Inventory of Taxes, 1979 edition
2754.01

Great Britain

Anglo Amer Trade News 225
Bill of Entry Service 552
Report of the Commissioners of Her
Majesty's (HM) Customs and Excise
4064

United States

Anglo American Trade News 225
Customs Bulletin 1287
Customs Regulations of the United
States 1288
Tariff Schedules of the United States
Annotated 4532
United States Customs and
International Trade Guide 4794.04

TAR SANDS-BASED PETROLEUM

Fuel 2195

TAXATION. *See also* Keogh Plan.

Other Taxation Headings

Accountants' Index 23
Accountants' Index Quarterly Service
24
Atlantic Economic Journal 344
Ball State Business Review 454
Business Studies 723
Compendium of Commercial Finance
Law 1060
Coopers & Lybrand Banker 1196
Coopers & Lybrand Newsletter
1196.01
Dow Jones–Irwin Business Almanac
1501
Economic Inquiry 1553
Federal Tax Articles 1961
Financial Times Tax Newsletter 2029
Foreign Tax and Trade Briefs 2137
Income Taxes Worldwide 2492
International Tax Report 2733
Investment and Taxation Monograph
2760.01

Journal of Taxation 2887
Massachusetts Certified Public
    Accountants Review 3149
Money 3267
Monthly Tax Report 3304
People and Taxes 3733
Retail Roundup 4109
Review of Income and Wealth 4123
Taxation for Accountants 4538
Taxation for Lawyers 4539

Arkansas

Basics of Plant Location in Arkansas
514

Australia

Australian Business Law Review 388
Australian Federal Tax Reports 401
Australian Sales Tax Guide 414
Australian Tax Review 418
Guide to Investment 2296

Canada

C A Magazine 739.01
Canada Tax Service 769
Canadian Current Tax 787
Canadian Master Tax Guide, 36th
    edition, 1981 816
Canadian Tax Journal 836
Corpus Almanac of Canada 1224
Provincial Taxation Services 3909
Provincial Tax Reports 3910

Europe

Business Europe 681
European and Middle East Tax Report
    1768
European Taxation 1787
Inventory of Taxes, 1979 edition
    2754.01
Tax Systems of Western Europe
    4572.01
West European Living Costs 1977
    4952

Florida

Guidebook to Florida Taxes 2272

Germany (West)

World Tax Series—Germany 5081

Great Britain

British Tax Guide 623
British Tax Report 623.01
British Tax Review 624
Management Information Manual
    3081
Money Management 3269

Rates and Rateable Values in England
    and Wales 4004
Report of the Commissioners of Her
    Majesty's (HM) Inland Revenue
    4065
Taxation 4537
Tax Digests 4546.01
Tolley's Taxation in the Channel
    Islands and Isle of Man 1977 4635

Hawaii

Taxes of Hawaii 4548

Massachusetts

Massachusetts Certified Public
    Accountants Review 3149

Mexico

Taxes of the State of Mexico 4549

Michigan

Guidebook to Michigan Taxes 2276

Middle East

European and Middle East Tax Report
    1768

New Jersey

Guidebook to New Jersey Taxes 2277
New Jersey Economic Policy Annual
    Report 3452

New Mexico

New Mexico Business 3454

New York City

Guidebook to New York Taxes 2278

New York State

Guidebook to New York Taxes 2278

New Zealand

Australian Business Law Review 388
Life and Business in New Zealand
    3011

North Carolina

Guidebook to North Carolina Taxes
2279

Ohio

Guidebook to Ohio Taxes 2280

Pennsylvania

Guidebook to Pennsylvania Taxes
2281

Puerto Rico

Puerto Rico Tax Reports 3944

Scotland

Rates and Rateable Values in Scotland
4005

Texas

Texas Facts 4596.01
Texas Means Business 4597.03

United States

Certified Public Accountants (CPA)
    Client Bulletin 897
Comparative State Income Tax Guide
    with Forms 1058
Current Government Reports 1276
Daily Report for Executives 1305
Daily Tax Report 1307
Facts and Figures on Government
    Finance 1872
Federal Tax Coordinator 2nd 1965
Federal Taxes Service 1968
Federal Tax Guide Reports 1971
From the State Capitals: Taxes Local
    Nonproperty 2186
Internal Revenue Service Annual
    Report of the Commissioner of
    Internal Revenue 2647
Internal Revenue Service Publications
    2649
Kess Tax Practice Report 2909
Major Tax Planning—University of
    Southern California Law Center
    Annual Institute on Federal Taxation
    3065
Monthly Digest of Tax Articles 3290
Monthly Tax Features 3303
News Summary 3471
New York University Annual Institute
    on Federal Taxation 3490
Research Institute of American (RIA)
    Tax Guide 4089
Standard Research Consultants (SRC)
    Quarterly Reports 4378
State Tax Cases Reports 4409
State Tax Guide 4410
State Tax Handbook 4412
State Tax Reports 4413
State Tax Review 4414
Tax Action Coordinator 4533
Tax Adviser 4534
Taxes 4547
Taxes on Parade 4550
Tax Management Program 4561
Tax Newsletter 4562
Tax Practice Management 4566
Tax Review 4569
Texas Facts 4596.01
Texas Means Business 4597.03

Viewpoint 4857
Views 4857.01
Wisconsin CPA 5007

Utah

Statistical Review of Government in Utah 4441
Utah Economic and Business Review 4835

Virginia (West)

West Virginia Economic Profile 4955

Wales

Rates and Rateable Values in England and Wales 4004

Washington (DC)

Comparative State Income Tax Guide with Forms 1058

Wisconsin

Wisconsin CPA 5007

TAXATION, AUDITS

How to Handle Tax Audits, Requests for Rulings, Fraud Cases and Other Procedures Before IRS 2421
Practical Accountant 3821
Tax Practice Management 4566

TAXATION, CAPITAL GAINS

Capital Adjustments 852
Timber Tax Journal 4618

Great Britain

British Tax Guide 623
Tolley's Income Tax 1977/78 4634

Ireland, Republic of

Tolley's Taxation in the Republic of Ireland 1977/78 4636

United States

Internal Revenue Service Publications 2649

TAXATION, CORPORATE AND BUSINESS

European and Middle East Tax Report 1768
Executive Action Report 1796
Financial Times Tax Newsletter 2029
How to Take Money Out of a Closely Held Corporation 2425

Information Guide for Doing Business in Countries Abroad 2571
International Tax Haven Directory 2731
International Tax Report 2733
Journal of Futures Markets 2858
Kiplinger Tax Letter 2916
Subchapter S: Planning & Operation 4482
Tax and Trade Guide Series 4535
Taxation Publications 4541
Tax Executive 4551
Tax Laws of the World 4557
Tax Planning International 4564
Tax Planning Tips From the Tax Advisor, 1981 4565.01

California

Guidebook to California Taxes 2271

Canada

Canada Tax Manual 768
Canadian Tax Reports 838
Corporation Taxation Statistics 1222
Provincial Taxation Services 3909

Europe

The Brussels Report 632
Doing Business in Europe 1486

Great Britain

British Tax Guide 623
British Tax Report 623.01
Tolley's Corporation Tax 1977/78 4632

Ireland, Rep of

Tolley's Taxation in the Republic of Ireland 1977/78 4636

Massachusetts

Guidebook to Massachusetts Taxes 2275

New Jersey

Guidebook to New Jersey Taxes 2277

New York City

Guidebook to New York Taxes 2278

New York State

Guidebook to New York Taxes 2278

North Carolina

Guidebook to North Carolina Taxes 2279

Ohio

Guidebook to Ohio Taxes 2280

Pennsylvania

Guidebook to Pennsylvania Taxes 2281

United States

Accounting Desk Book, 6th edition 33
Automatic Tax Planner 425
Business International Washington (BIW) 699.01
Business Organizations with Tax Planning 715
Capital Changes Reports 853
Certified Public Accountants (CPA) Client Bulletin 897
Corporate Controllers and Treasurers Report 1204.01
Corporation Law & Tax Report 1219
Daily Report for Executives 1305
Doing Business in the United States 1488
Executives Tax Report & What's Happening in Taxation 1809
Federal Tax Course 1966
Federal Tax Return Manual 1972
Internal Revenue Service Publications 2649
Internal Revenue Service Statistics of Income: Corporation Income Tax Returns 2650
Internal Revenue Service Tax Guide for Small Business (344) 2651
Journal of Corporate Taxation 2843
Kess Tax Practice Report 2909
Research Institute of American (RIA) Tax Guide 4089
State Corporate Income Tax Forms 4388
State Income Taxes 4394
Tax Action Coordinator 4533
Tax, Financial and Estate Planning for the Owner of a Closely Held Corporation 4553.01
Tax Ideas 4555
Tax Planning Review 4565
United States Master Tax Guide 4811

Wisconsin

Guidebook to Wisconsin Taxes 2282

TAXATION, EMPLOYMENT TAXES

Working with the Revenue Code—1977 5025

TAXATION, ESTATE AND GIFT TAXES

Estate Planning Desk Book, 5th edition
1750
Federal Estate and Gift Taxes
Explained, Including Estate Planning
1922
Federal Tax Forms   1969
Monthly Tax Report   3304
Tax Facts on Life Insurance   4553
Tax Treaties   4573

Australia

Australian Estate and Gift Duty
Reports   398

California

Guidebook to California Taxes   2271

Canada

Canada Tax Service   769
Canadian Estate Planning and
Administration Reports   791.01
Provincial Inheritance and Gift Tax
Reports   3907

Florida

Guidebook to Florida Taxes   2272

Illinois

Guidebook to Illinois Taxes   2273

Massachusetts

Guidebook to Massachusetts Taxes
2275

Michigan

Guidebook to Michigan Taxes   2276

New Jersey

Guidebook to New Jersey Taxes   2277

North Carolina

Guidebook to North Carolina Taxes
2279

Ohio

Guidebook to Ohio Taxes   2280

United States

Code and Regulations   976
Federal Estate and Gift Tax Reports
1923
Federal Income, Gift and Estate
Taxation   1927

Federal Revenue Forms—With Official
Instructions   1959
Federal Tax Forms   1969
Federal Tax Guide   1970
Income, Employment, Estate & Gift
Tax Provisions: Internal Revenue
Code   2483
Inheritance Taxes   2578
Insurance Guide   2623
Internal Revenue Service Publications
2649
Tax Treaties   4574
United States Master Tax Guide   4811
United States Tax Cases   4819

Wisconsin

Guidebook to Wisconsin Taxes   2282

TAXATION, EXCISE TAXES

Canada

Canada Tax Service   769
Canadian Sales Tax Reports   833
Customs Tariff Complete Service   1289

Great Britain

Report of the Commissioners of Her
Majesty's (HM) Customs and Excise
4064

United States

Federal Tax Forms   1969
Federal Tax Guide   1970
United States Excise Tax Guide   4797
United States Tax Cases   4819

TAXATION, FOREIGN INVESTMENTS

Financial Times Tax Newsletter   2029
International Tax Treaties of All
Nations   2734
Tax Management International Journal
4560
United States Taxation of International
Operations   4818

Mexico

Doing Business in Mexico   1487

United States

Doing Business in Canada   1484
Doing Business in Mexico   1487
Income Taxation of Foreign Related
Transactions   2490
International Tax   2732

TAXATION, FORMS

Annotated Tax Forms   230
Federal Revenue Forms—with Official
Instructions   1959
Federal Tax Forms   1969
State Corporate Income Tax Forms
4388
State Personal Income Tax Forms
4405
1040 Preparation   4591

TAXATION, FRAUDS

Business Crime: Criminal Liability of
the Business Community   676.01
How to Handle Tax Audits, Requests
for Rulings, Fraud Cases and Other
Procedures Before IRS   2421

TAXATION, GIFT TAXES.   See
Taxation, Estate and Gift Taxes

TAXATION, GOVERNMENT REGULATIONS, LAWS AND PROGRAMS

Cumulative Changes   1268
Estate Planners' Complete Guide and
Workbook   1746
Foreign Tax Law Bi-Weekly Bulletin
2138
From the State Capitals: General
Bulletin   2172
How to Handle Tax Audits, Requests
for Rulings, Fraud Cases and Other
Procedures Before IRS   2421
How to Plan for Tax Savings in Real
Estate Transactions   2422
How to Use Tax Shelters Today   2426
Internal Revenue Service Tax Guide for
Small Business (344)   2651
International Accounting and Financial
Report   2653
International Tax Haven Directory
2731
Investing, Licensing and Trading
Conditions Abroad   2755
Mutual Savings Bank Guide to Federal
Income Tax Law   3352
National Public Accountant   3401
People and Taxes   3733
Subchapter S: Planning & Operation
4482
Taxation Publications   4541
Tax Legislation Update   4557.01
Tax Planning International   4564

Australia

Australian Federal Tax Reports   401
Australian Tax Cases   417

Canada

Canada Tax Cases   767
Canada Tax Manual   768
Canadian Current Tax   787
Canadian Income Tax Act, Regulations
  & Rulings   798
Canadian Sales Tax Reports   833
Canadian Tax News   837
Dominion Tax Cases   1495

Europe

European Law Digest   1782

Great Britain

British Tax Review   624
Income Tax Digest and Accountants'
  Review   2491

New Zealand

Australian Tax Cases   417

Scotland

Accountants Magazine   26

United States

Advance Session Laws   64
All-State Sales Tax Reports   147
All States Tax Guide   148
Annotated Tax Forms   230
Association Taxation   342
Certified Public Accountants (CPA)
  Client Bulletin   897
Code and Regulations   976
Farmer's Tax Report   1898
Federal Estate and Gift Taxes
  Explained, Including Estate Planning
  1922
Federal Excise Tax Reports   1924
Federal Income, Gift and Estate
  Taxation   1927
Federal Revenue Forms—With Official
  Instructions   1959
Federal Taxation of Oil and Gas
  Transactions   1964
Federal Taxes Citator   1967
Federal Taxes Service   1968
Federal Tax Guide   1970
From the State Capitals: General
  Bulletin   2172
Internal Revenue Bulletin   2645
Internal Revenue Service Annual
  Report of the Commissioner of
  Internal Revenue   2647
Internal Revenue Service Chief Counsel
  Annual Report   2648
Kess Tax Practice Report   2909
Major Tax Planning—University of
  Southern California Law Center

Annual Institute on Federal Taxation
  3065
Monthly Digest of Tax Articles   3290
News Summary   3471
Prentice-Hall Federal Tax Handbook
  3835
Property Taxes   3902
Real Estate Law Journal   4021
Real Estate Tax Ideas   4026
Standard Federal Tax Reports   4373
State Income Taxes   4394
State and Local Taxes   4386
State Tax Cases Reports   4409
State Tax Review   4414
Tax Adviser   4534
Tax Court Memorandum Decisions
  4544
Tax Court Reports   4545
Taxes   4547
Tax Exempt News   4551.01
Tax Law Review   4556
Tax Newsletter   4562
Tax Research Techniques   4568
United States Taxation of International
  Operations   4818
United States Tax Cases   4819
United States Tax Week   4820
Virginia Accountant   4858

Virginia

Virginia Accountant Quarterly   4858

TAXATION, INCOME TAX

Better Investing   545
Forecaster   2107
Income Taxes Worldwide   2492
International Tax Haven Directory
  2731
Monthly Tax Report   3304
Mutual Savings Bank Guide to Federal
  Income Tax Law   3352
Tax-Exempt Organizations   4552
Tax Laws of the World   4557
Tax Planning International   4564
Tax Treaties   4573

California

Guidebook to California Taxes   2271

Canada

Canada Income Tax Guide   753
Canada Income Tax Regulations
  Service   754
Canada Tax Manual   768
Canada Tax Service   769
Canadian Income Tax Act, Regulations
  & Rulings   798
Canadian Income Tax (Revised)   799

Canadian Institute of Chartered
  Accounts/Canadian Bar Association
  (CICA/CBA) Recommendations on
  the Income Tax Act   804
Canadian Tax Reports   838
Provincial Taxation Services   3909

Florida

Guidebook to Florida Taxes   2272

Great Britain

British Tax Guide   623
Money Management   3269
Tolley's Income Tax 1977/78   4634

Illinois

Guidebook to Illinois Taxes   2273

Massachusetts

Guidebook to Massachusetts Taxes
  2275

New Jersey

Guidebook to New Jersey Taxes   2277

New York City

Guidebook to New York Taxes   2278

New York State

Guidebook to New York Taxes   2278

New Zealand

Australian Master Tax Guide   409
New Zealand Incomes & Income Tax
  3505
New Zealand Income Tax Law &
  Practice   3506
New Zealand Master Tax Guide   3509

North Carolina

Guidebook to North Carolina Taxes
  2279

Ohio

Guidebook to Ohio Taxes   2280

Pennsylvania

Guidebook to Pennsylvania Taxes
  2281

United States

Client's Monthly Alert   964
Code and Regulations   976
Estate Planner's Complete Guide and
  Workbook   1746
Executives Tax Report & What's
  Happening in Taxation   1809

TAXATION, PARTNERSHIPS.   *See*
Partnerships, Taxation

TAXATION, PAYROLL TAXES

TAXATION, PERSONAL

TAXATION, PLANNING

TAXATION, PROPERTY TAXES.
See also Real Estate, Taxation

TAXATION, RESEARCH ON

**TAXATION, SALES AND USE
TAXES**

TAXATION, SMALL BUSINESSES

Federal Tax Return Manual   1972
Internal Revenue Service Tax Guide for
    Small Business 344   2651
Small Business Report   4301.01
Small Business Tax Control   4302.01

TAXATION, SURTAX

British Tax Guide   623

TAXATION, TAX-EXEMPT STATUS

Association Taxation   342
Tax Exempt News   4551.01

TAXATION, TAX SHELTERS AND HAVENS

Client's Monthly Alert   964
How to Use Tax Shelters Today   2426
Tax-Free Trade Zone of the World
    4553.02
Tax Haven & Investment Report
    4553.03
Tax Shelter Opportunities in Real
    Estate   4571
Tax Shelters in Executive Compensation
    4572
International Tax Haven Directory
    2731
Money   3267
Real Estate Tax Shelter Desk Book
    4027
Spencer's Retirement Plan Service
    4362
Tax Havens of the World   4554
Tax Sheltered Investments   4570

TAXATION, TREATIES AND AGREEMENTS

Financial Times Tax Newsletter   2029
International Tax Treaties of All
    Nations   2734
Tax Treaties   4573

TAXATION, UNINCORPORATED BUSINESS

Guidebook to Michigan Taxes   2276
Guidebook to New York Taxes   2278

TAXATION, VALUE ADDED TAX

Standard Research Consultants (SRC)
    Quarterly Reports   4378
Tolley's Taxation in the Republic of
    Ireland 1977/78   4636

TAXATION, WITHHOLDING RATES

International Withholding Tax Treaty
    Guide   2743

TAXATION, WOMEN

Woman CPA   5010
Women in Business   5013

TAX CODE AND REGULATIONS (1954) (US)

Cumulative Changes   1268
Federal Tax Coordinator 2nd   1965

TAX-EXEMPT STATUS. See Taxation, Tax-Exempt Status

Private Foundations Reports   3852

TAX HAVENS. See Taxation, Tax Shelters and Havens

TAXICABS

Automotive Fleet   429

TAX REDUCTION AND SIMPLIFICATION ACT OF 1977 (US)

Kess Tax Practice Report   2909

TAX REFORM ACT OF 1976 (US)

Dow Jones Securities Valuation
    Handbook   1503
Estate Planners' Complete Guide and
    Workbook   1746
Federal Tax Coordinator 2nd   1965
How to Handle Tax Audits, Request
    for Rulings, Fraud Cases and Other
    Procedures Before IRS   2421
How to Plan for Tax Savings in Real
    Estate Transactions   2422
How to Use Tax Shelters Today   2426
Journal of Real Estate Taxation   2878
Kess Tax Practice Report   2909
Real Estate Tax Shelter Desk Book
    4027
Subchapter S: Planning & Operation
    4482
Tax Facts on Life Insurance   4553
Tax Sheltered Investments   4570

TAX SHELTERS. See Taxation, Tax Shelters and Havens

TEA

United Nations Industrial Development
    Organization (UNIDO) Guides to
    Information Sources.
    UNIDO/LIB/SER.D/Rev.1—
    Information Sources on the Coffee,
    Cocoa, Tea and Spices Industry
    4767.06

TECHNICAL WORKERS

Europe

European Compensation Survey   1771

Far East

Asia/Pacific Compensation Survey   330

United States

White Collar Report   4968

TECHNICAL WRITING

Journal of Technical Writing and
    Communication   2888

TECHNOLOGY. See also Science.
Other subjects

American Bulletin of International
    Technology Transfer   163
Applied Science & Technology Index
    (ASTI)   288
Appropriate Technology   293
Conference Papers Index   1110
Dialog   1375.03
Futures   2204
R&D Abstracts   3999.01
R&D Management Digest   3999.02
Science and Public Policy   4196
Scientific, Engineering, Technical
    Manpower Comments   4201
Scientific Information Notes   4202
Service to Business & Industry   4268
Technological Forecasting and Social
    Change   4580
Technology Forecasts and Technology
    Surveys   4581
Technology Growth Markets and
    Opportunities   4581.01
Technology Transfer Action   4582
Unit   4754.01

Europe

Eruo-Abstracts: Scientific and Technical
    Publications and Patents, Section I
    and II. Section I: Euratom and EEC
    Research. Section II: Coal and Steel
    1759

Europe (East)

East/West Technology Digest   1527

Europe (West)

New Products & Processes From
    Western Europe   3458.01

Far East

Far Eastern Technical Review   1892.01

TELEVISION AND RADIO, PROGRAMS

Hall Radio Report 2310.02
Home Video Report 4856
National Radio Publicity Directory 3402
TV Publicity Outlets—Nationwide 4735
TV World 4735.01

Canada

Broadcasting/Cable Yearbook 627

United States

Broadcasting/Cable Yearbook 627
TV Facts 4734.01

TELEVISION AND RADIO STATIONS AND NETWORKS

Broadcast Investor 628
Hollis Press and Public Relations Annual 2377
Media Industry Newsletter 3173
National Radio Publicity Directory 3402
Network Rates & Data 3430
Spot Radio Rates & Data 4366
Spot Radio Small Markets Edition 4367
Spot Television Rates & Data 4368
Statistical Trends in Broadcasting 4443
Television Factbook, 1980 4589
TV Publicity Outlets—Nationwide 4735

Australia

Trans-Tasman 4699

Canada

Broadcasting/Cable Yearbook 627
Matthews' List 3155

Great Britain

Advertiser's Annual 65
British Rate & Data 622

New York City Metropolitan Area

New York Publicity Outlets 3479

New Zealand

Trans-Tasman 4699

United States

Broadcasting/Cable Yearbook 627
Cable & Station Coverage Atlas, 1980–81 730

Washington (DC)

Hudson's Washington News Media Contacts Directory 2427

TELEVISION AND RADIO STATIONS AND NETWORKS, MARKET DATA

British Rate & Data 622
metro CALIFORNIA media 3204.02
Network Rates & Data 3430
Nielsen Newscast 3516
Spot Radio Rates & Data 4366
Spot Radio Small Markets Edition 4367
Spot Television Rates & Data 4368

TELEVISION AND RADIO STATIONS AND NETWORKS, PERSONNEL

metro CALIFORNIA media 3204.02
Spot Radio Rates & Data 4366
TV Publicity Outlets—Nationwide 4735

TELEVISION AND RADIO STATIONS AND NETWORKS, RATES

Cable TV Regulation 732
Network Rates & Data 3430
Spot Radio Rates & Data 4366
Spot Radio Small Markets Edition 4367
Spot Television Rates & Data 4368

Canada

Canadian Advertising Rates & Data 774

Great Britain

British Rate & Data 622

New York Metropolitan Area

New York Publicity Outlets 3479

TEMPLES. See Religious Edifices

TENNESSEE

From the State Capitals 2169–2191
State and Local Taxes 4386
State Legislative Reporting Service 4396
State Tax Reports 4413
Survey of Business 4508
Tennessee Business and Industrial Review 4592
Tennessee: Directory of Manufacturers, 1981 4593

Tennessee: State Industrial Directory, 1981 4593.01
Tennessee Statistical Abstract, 1980 edition 4594

TESTS AND MEASUREMENTS.
See also Surveys and Polls

Guide to Graduate Management Education, 1980–81 2294
Nondestructive Testing (NDT) International 3530

TEXAS

Brief Guide to Business Regulations and Services in Texas 592.01
Dallas/Fort Worth Business 1314.01
From the State Capitals 2169–2191
Financial Trend 2032
Kiplinger Texas Letter 2916.01
State and Local Taxes 4386
State Legislative Reporting Service 4396
State Tax Reports 4413
Texas Facts 4596.01
Texas Industrial Update 4597.01
Texs: Manufacturers Directory, 1980 4597.02
Texas Means Business 4597.03

TEXAS INDUSTRIAL COMMISSION

Texas Ideas Newsletter 4597
Texas Industrial Update 4597.01

TEXTBOOKS

Book Publishers (BP Report) 573
Educational Marketer 1592

TEXTILES

Broadwoven Fabrics Finished MA-22S 629
Clemson University Textile Marketing Letter 961
Cotton Manmade Fiber Staple, and Linters (Consumption and Stocks, and Spindle Activity) M22P 1230
Fiber Producer 1983
Journal of the Textile Institute 2897
Nonwovens Industry 3532.01
Review of Industrial Management and Textile Science 4123.01
Textile Institute and Industry 4599
Textile Organon 4602
Textile World 4603
Textile World Fact File Buyers' Guide 4604
Woven Fabrics: Production, Inventories, and Unfilled Orders. M22A 5089

Africa

African Textiles   79.03

Australia

Textile Journal Annual Buying Guide
   4600
Textile Journal/Australia   4601

Great Britain

British Clothing Manufacturer   599.01
Drapers Record   1505.02

India

Directory of Wool, Hosiery, & Fabrics
   1462.01

TEXTILES, EQUIPMENT

Textile Journal/Australia   4601
Textile World   4603

TEXTILES, IMPORTS AND EXPORTS

Cotton Manmade Fiber Staple, and
   Linters (Consumption and Stocks,
   and Spindle Activity) M22P   1230

TEXTILES, MARKETING

Clemson University Textile Marketing
   Letter   961
Textile World Fact File Buyers' Guide
   4604

TEXTILES, RESEARCH ON

Journal of the Textile Institute   2897

THEATER

Catalog of Copyright Entries   868
Time   4619

THERMAL ENERGY.   *See* Energy, Thermal

THIRD WORLD

Bulletin   643.01
Ceres: Food and Agriculture
   Organization (FAO) Review on
   Development   894
International Licensing   2702
Labour, Capital and Society   2949.01
Oxford Economic Papers   3674
Public Administration and
   Development   3920.01
South-The Third World Magazine
   4349.01
Third World Quarterly   4606.01

TILE.   *See* Brick and Tile

TIME-SHARING.   *See* Computers, Time-Sharing

TIN

Tin News   4623

TITANIUM

Titanium Ingot, Mill Products and
   Castings DIB-991   4625

TOBACCO

Bi-weekly Index of the Tobacco Scene
   (BITS)   559
Foreign Agriculture Circulars   2111
Outlook and Situation Report   3653.01
Tobacco Barometer   4627
Tobacco Market News Reports   4628
Tobacco Merchants Association Guide
   to Tobacco Taxes   4629
Tobacco Reporter   4630

TORONTO STOCK EXCHANGE

Toronto Stock Exchange Company
   Manual   4640
Toronto Stock Exchange Daily Record
   4640.01
Toronto Stock Exchange Management
   of Change in the Canadian Securities
   Industry   4640.02
Toronto Stock Exchange Members'
   Manual   4640.03
Toronto Stock Exchange Review   4641
Toronto Stock Exchange "300" Stock
   Price Indexes Manual   4641.01
Toronto Stock Exchange "300" Total
   Return Indexes Manual   4641.02
Toronto Stock Exchange Weekly
   Summary   4642

TOURISM.   *See* Travel and Resorts

TOWELS

Sheets, Pillowcases, and Towels.
   MQ-23X   4273

TOXICOLOGY

Canadian Employment Safety and
   Health Guide   789.01
Dangerous Properties of Industrial
   Materials Report   1316.01
Industrial Health Foundation
   Chemical-Toxicological Series   2524
State Regulation Report: Toxic
   Substances & Hazardous Waste
   4405.01
Toxic Materials News   4643.01

Toxic Materials Reference Service
   4643.02
Toxic Substances Journal   4643.04
Toxic Substances Sourcebook   4644

TOYS

National Electronic Injury Surveillance
   System (NEISS) Data Highlights
   3373
Playthings   3788
Toys Hobbies and Crafts   4645
Toys Magazine   4645.01

TRACTORS

Implement & Tractor   2442
Owner Operator   3671
Tractors, Except Garden Tractors
   M35S   4646
Truck & Off-Highway Industries
   4722.01

TRADE.   *Note:* Covers only very general material. *See also* Foreign Trade. Imports and Exports. Trade Fairs. World Trade Centers. Commodity names

Monthly Bulletin of Statistics   3283
Statistical Yearbook   4444
United Nations Conference on Trade
   and Development Guide to
   Publications   4765
World Trade Centers Association
   (WTCA) News   5083

Africa

African Business & Trade   79.02
African Trade/Commerce Africain   80
Africa Research Bulletin   81
Middle East and North Africa   3217
Statistical and Economic Information
   Bulletin for Africa   4424

Alaska

Alaska Economic Trends   138

Belgium

United States Belgium Trade Directory,
   1980–81 edition   4794.01

Canada

Canada Commerce   744

Far East

Quarterly Bulletin of Statistics for Asia
   and the Pacific   3959

Great Britain

Quarterly Trade Statistics of the United
Kingdom   3978

Middle East

Middle East and North Africa   3217

Nigeria

Trade Report   4673

United States

Business & Capital Reporter   658

**TRADE, GOVERNMENT
REGULATIONS**

Antitrust & Trade Regulation Report
271

**TRADE, INDUSTRY AND PRICES,
DEPARTMENT OF GREAT
BRITAIN**

Trade Promotions Guide   4669

**TRADE AGREEMENTS PROGRAM
(US)**

Operation of the Trade Agreements
Program   3628

TRADE ASSOCIATIONS. *See*
Associations (Professional, Scientific,
Technical and Trade)

**TRADE COMMISSION, FEDERAL
(FTC) (US)**

Antitrust Laws and Trade Regulation
273
Federal Trade Commission Annual
Report   1973
Federal Trade Commission Decisions
1974
Land Development Law Reporter
2960
Trade Practice Rules   4668
Trade Regulation Rules   4672
Warranty Watch   4883

**TRADE COMMISSION,
INTERNATIONAL (US)**

International Trade Commission
Annual Report   2737

**TRADE DEVELOPMENT COUNCIL
NEWS, HONG KONG**

Hong Kong Trader   2388

TRADE FAIRS

Export Times   1854
International Intertrade Index   2686
Investment and Business Opportunity
News   2760
Lighting Equipment News   3018
Meeting News   3186
Successful Meetings   4487
Trade Promotions Guide   4669
World's Fair   5078
World Trade Centers Association
(WTCA News)   5083

TRADEMARKS

Bureau of National Affairs (BNA)
Patent, Trademark & Copyright
Journal   649
Executive Newsletter   1807
Franchising   2160
Intellectual Property Management:
Law/Business/Strategy   2637
Licensing in Foreign and Domestic
Operations   3010
Trademark Reporter   ·4662
Trademarks/7   4663.01
United States Patents Quarterly   4814

Canada

Canadian Trade Index, 1981   840
Trade Marks Journal   4663

Europe (East)

Doing Business with Eastern Europe
1489

Switzerland

Swiss Export Directory, 1978–80, 13th
edition   4523

United States

Trademark Alert   4658.01
Trademark Official Gazette   4659
Trademark Research Service   4662.01

**TRADEMARKS, GOVERNMENT
REGULATIONS, LAWS AND
PROGRAMS**

Intellectual Property Management:
Law/Business/Strategy   2637
Patent and Trademark Review   3698
Patents and Trademarks   3705

Canada

Canadian Patent Reporter   826

Great Britain

Fleet Street Patent Law Reports   2062

United States

Bureau of National Affairs (BNA)
Patent, Trademark & Copyright
Journal   649
State Trademark Statutes   4415
United States Patents Quarterly   4814

TRADE NAMES. *See* Brand and
Trade Names

TRADE SECRETS

Trade Secrets   4674
Trade Secrets and Know-How
Throughout the World   4675

TRADE UNIONS. *See* Labor Unions

TRADING

Daily Stock Price Records   1306

TRAFFIC

Abstract Newsletter, Urban Technology
2.29
Louisiana Economic Indicators
3047.01

**TRAFFIC, ACCIDENTS AND
SAFETY**

Family Safety   1886
Highway & Vehicle/Safety Report
2371
Safe Driver   4157
Traffic Safety   4682

Canada

Road Transport Service Bulletin   4137

Great Britain

Road Accidents   4135

United States

From the State Capitals: Motor Vehicle
Regulation   2182

TRAILERS. *See* Housing, Mobile
Homes

TRAINFERRIES. *See* Ships and
Shipping, Trainferry

TRAINING. *See* Labor, Training

TRANSFER TAXES. *See* Taxation, Transfer Taxes

TRANSIT SYSTEMS

Downtown Idea Exchange   1505
Metropolitan   3205
Progress in Planning   3894
Public Transit Report   3937

Canada

Canadian Advertising Rates & Data
764
Road Transport Service Bulletin   4137

New York City

Registry of Manhattan Office Spaces
4055

United States

From the State Capitals: Urban Transit
& Bus Transportation   2189

TRANSLATORS

Business Travel Costs Worldwide
724.01
Transdex   4687.01
Translation & Translators: An
International Directory and Guide
4689

TRANSPORTATION.   *See also*
Hazardous Cargoes. Transit Systems.
Types, eg, Automobiles

Business Periodicals Index   716
Dangerous Goods Shipping Regulations
1316
International Journal of Systems
Science   2697
Journal of Regional Science   2879
Journal of Transport Economics and
Policy   2898
Lloyd's List   3032.03
Metropolitan   3205
Multinational Executive Travel
Companion   3335
Progress in Planning   3894
Reference Book of Transportation
4041
Research on Transport Economies
4091
Transportation Planning and
Technology   4693
Transportation Service   4694
Transport Laws of the World   4696

Africa

Economic Bulletin for Africa   1543

Alaska

Alaska Industry   139

Arkansas

Basics of Plant Location in Arkansas
514
Transportation Arkansas   4691.01

Australia

Handbook for Industrialists   2313

California

Orange County Business   3634

Canada

Canadian Transport   841
Consolidation of General Orders of the
Board of Transport Commissioners
for Canada   1122
Official Directory of Industrial &
Commercial Traffic Executives   3584
Road Transport Service Bulletin   4137

Colorado

Colorado Regional Profiles   988

Europe

Europe's 5000 Largest Companies
1792

European Economic Community

Europa Transport: Observation of the
Transport Markets (Three Series)
1766.02

Far East

Quarterly Bulletin of Statistics for Asia
and the Pacific   3959
Transport and Communication Bulletin
for Asia and the Far East   4691

Georgia

Georgia Statistical Abstract   2220

Great Britain

Regional Trends   4049.01
Transport Statistics, Great Britain
1964–74   4698

Illinois

Commerce   993

Massachusetts

Industry   2558

New Zealand

New Zealand Transport   3514

North Carolina

North Carolina Industrial Data File
3534

Texas

Texas Facts   4596.01

United States

Daily Traffic World   1309
Interstate Commerce Commission
Annual Report   2745
Moody's Transportation Manual &
News Reports   3319
Official Directory of Industrial &
Commercial Traffic Executives   3584
Property Investment and Condensed
Income Account   3900
Texas Facts   4596.01
Transportation Business Report   4692

West Virginia

West Virginia Economic Profile   4955

TRANSPORTATION,
GOVERNMENT REGULATIONS
AND PROGRAMS

Interstate Commerce Commission
Practitioners' Journal   2747

Canada

Consolidation of General Orders of the
Board of Transport Commissioners
for Canada   1122

Mexico

Communication and Transportation
Laws (Mexican)   1041

United States

Abstract Newsletters, Transportation
2.28
Daily Traffic World   1309
Interstate Commerce Commission
Annual Report   2745
Interstate Commerce Commission
Reports Decisions of the ICC of the
United States   2748
Transportation Business Report   4692
Transport Laws of the World   4696
Urban Affairs Reports   4829

TRANSPORTATION, RATES

Interstate Commerce Commission
Reports Decisions of the ICC of the
United States   2748

Transportation Service   4694
West European Living Costs 1977
4952

**TRANSPORTATION SAFETY
BOARD, NATIONAL (US)**

National Transportation Safety Board
Service   3409

TRAVEL AND RESORTS. *See also*
Hotels and Motels. Ships and Shipping,
Cruises. Travel Agents. Travel
(Business)

Consumer Attitudes and Buying Plans
1150
Cruises & Sea Voyages   1264
Executive Lifestyle Newsletter   1804
Incentive Marketing and Sales
Promotion   2478
Information Peking (Beijing)   2573.02
International Tourism Quarterly
2735.01
Journal of Travel Research   2899
Lodging Hospitality   3040
Motel/Hotel "Insider"   3323
Service World International   4270
Travel Agency   4700
Travelweek   4705
Travel Weekly   4706
Visa Information Guide   4859
World Travel Directory   5084

Africa

Owen's Commerce & Travel and
International Register   3670

Alaska

Alaska Business News Letter   137
Alaska Industry   139

American Nations

Homes Overseas   2384

Canada

Canadian Travel News   844
Edmonton Report on Business and
Travel Development   1588
Ontario Business News   3620
Spectrum   4359.01
Travel Between Canada and Other
Countries   4701

Cyprus

Owen's Commerce & Travel and
International Register   3670

Europe

Travel Trade Gazette Europa   4703

Far East

Homes Overseas   2384
Owen's Commerce & Travel and
International Register   3670

Florida

Florida Outlook   2068
Kiplinger Florida Letter   2915

Georgia

Georgia Business   2218

Gibraltar

Owen's Commerce & Travel and
International Register   3670

Great Britain

Business Monitors Miscellaneous Series
712
Leisure, Recreation and Tourism
Abstracts   3004.01
Management Information Manual
3081
National Travel Survey   3410
Travel Trade Directory   4702
Travel Trade Gazette United Kingdom
and Ireland   4704

Hawaii

Hawaii Annual Economic Review
2347

Ireland, Republic of

Travel Trade Gazette United Kingdom
and Ireland   4704

Louisiana

Louisiana Business Review   3047
Louisiana Economic Indicators
3047.01

Malta

Owen's Commerce & Travel and
International Register   3670

Mexico

Mexican American Review   3206.01

Middle East

Middle East Travel   3221
Mideast Business Exchange   3225
Owen's Commerce & Travel and
International Register   3670

Nebraska

Nebraska Now   3424

New Zealand

Life and Business in New Zealand
3011

Scandinavia

Travel Trade Gazette Europa   4703

Spain

Spain–US   4353

Switzerland

Swiss-American Chamber of Commerce.
Yearbook   4522

United States

Travel Between Canada and Other
Countries   4701

TRAVEL AGENTS

Travel Trade Directory   4702
Travel Trade Gazette Europa   4703
Travel Trade Gazette United Kingdom
and Ireland   4704
Travelweek   4705
Travel Weekly   4706
World Travel Directory   5084

TRAVEL (BUSINESS)

Business Travel Costs Worldwide
724.01
Business Traveller   725
Export Times   1854
Information Peking (Beijing)   2573.02
Multinational Executive Travel
Companion   3335
Overseas Assignment Directory Service
3655
Travel Weekly   4706

**TRAVEL AND RESORTS,
INCENTIVE PROGRAMS**

Incentive Travel Manager   2479
Premium, Incentive and Travel Buyers
3833

**TRAVEL AND RESORTS. RESORT
TIMESHARING**

Digest of State Land Sales Regulation
1392
Resort Timesharing Law Reporter
4096.01

TREATIES AND AGREEMENTS.
See also International Cooperative
Efforts. Subjects

Keesing's Contemporary Archives
2905

TRUSTS, GOVERNMENT REGULATIONS

Modern Trust Forms and Checklists 3266
Trust Audit Manual 4727
Trust Letter 4729
Wills, Estates and Trusts 5003

TRUSTS, TAXATION

Estate Planner's Complete Guide and Workbook 1746
Successful Estate Planning Ideas & Methods 4486
United States Master Tax Guide 4811

TRUTH-IN-LENDING ACT (US)

Consumer Credit and Truth-in-Lending Compliance Report 1151

TUNGSTEN

Tungsten Statistics 4733

TUNNELS AND TUNNELLING

Tunnels and Tunnelling 4734

TURKEYS. *See* Poultry

TURPENTINE

Naval Stores Market News Reports 3420

ULTRASONICS

Non-Destructive Testing (NDT) International 3530
Ultrasonics 4738

UMW. *See* Mine Workers of America, United (UMW)

UNDERDEVELOPED COUNTRIES. *See* Third World

UNDERWRITERS LABORATORIES

Underwriters Laboratories Standards for Safety 4741.01

UNDERWRITING. *See* Insurance, Underwriting. Investments, Underwriting

UNEMPLOYMENT INSURANCE. *See* Labor, Unemployment Insurance

UNIFORM CLASSIFICATION. *See* Standards and Standardization

UNIFORM COMMERCIAL CODE

Uniform Commercial Code Law Journal 4750
Uniform Commercial Code Law Letter 4751

UNIFORM SECURITY IDENTIFICATION PROCEDURES, COMMITTEE ON (CUSIP)

Committee on Uniform Security Identification Procedures (CUSIP): Digest of Changes in CUSIP 1017

UNINCORPORQTED BUSINESS TAXES. *See* Taxation, Unincorporated Business Taxes

UNIONS. *See* Labor Unions

UNITED KINGDOM. *See* Great Britain

UNITED NATIONS (UN)

Development Forum 1374
Government Publications Review 2250
International Bibliography, Information, Documentation 2659
International Tax Treaties of All Nations 2734
International Year Book and Statesmen's Who's Who 2744
Soviet-Eastern Europe-China Business & Trade 4351
Trade and Economic Development 4647
UNDOC: Current Index 4742.01
United Nations Chronicle 4764.01

UNITED NATIONS CONFERENCE ON TRADE AND DEVELOPMENT

Transnational Economic and Monetary Law: Transactions and Contracts 4690
United Nations Conference on Trade and Development Guide to Publications 4765

UNITED NATIONS DEVELOPMENT PROGRAM

Development Forum: Business Edition 1375

UNITED NATIONS ECONOMIC COMMISSION FOR AFRICA

African Trade/Commerce Africain 80

UNITED STATES

Statesman's Year Book, 1974–75 Edition 4408
Statistical Abstract of the United States 4421

URANIUM

Mining Lease Reports 3239.01
Nuclearfuel 3552
Uranium Information 4828
Uranium Information Western 4828.01

URBAN AREAS

Downtown Idea Exchange 1505
Downtown Implementation Guide 1505.01
Federal Reserve Bank of Philadelphia Business Review 1938
From the State Capitals: Housing and Redevelopment 2174
Journal of Regional Science 2879
Journal of Urban Analysis 2900
Urban Affairs Reports 4829
Urban Land 4832
Urban Studies 4833

Great Britain

Development Digest 1373.01

URBAN AREAS, PLANNING AND DEVELOPMENT

Committee for Economic Development Newsletter 1012
Journal of Urban Analysis 2900
Neighborhood & Rehab Report 3427
Regional Science and Urban Economics 4047

URBAN AREAS, RESEARCH ON

Abstract Newsletters, Urban and Regional Technology & Development, Urban Technology 2.29

URUGUAY

Latin American Services 2976.01

USE TAX. *See* Taxation, Sales and Use Taxes

UTAH

From the State Capitals 2169–2191
State and Local Taxes 4386
State Legislative Reporting Service 4396
State Tax Reports 4413

Statistical Abstract of Utah   4422
Utah Economic and Business Review
4835
Utah: Manufacturers' Directory,
1979–80   4835.01
Utah: State Industrial Directory,
1980–81   4835.02

UTILITIES.   *See* Private Utilities.
Public Utilities. Types, eg, Electric
Light and Power

VACATION HOMES.   *See* Housing,
Vacation and Retirement Homes

VACATIONS.   *See* Housing, Vacation
Homes. Ships and Shipping, Cruises.
Skiing Industry. Travel and Resorts,
Geographic areas

VALUE ADDED TAX.   *See* Taxation,
Value Added Tax

VANCOUVER STOCK EXCHANGE

Vancouver Stock Exchange Review
4843

VANDALISM

Security Management   4243

VEGETABLES.   *See* Fruits and
Vegetables

VEHICLES.   *See* types

VENDING MACHINES

International Vending Buyer's Guide
and Directory   2741
Vending Times   4844

VENDORS (STREET)

Vending Times   4844

VENEZUELA

Andean Group Regional Report
222.01
Latin American Services   2976.01

VENTURE CAPITAL.   *See* Capital
Markets. Investments (General).
Venture Capital Companies

VENTURE CAPITAL COMPANIES

Business & Acquisition Newsletter   657
National Association of Small Business
Investment Companies (NASBIC)
News   3362

VERMONT

From the State Capitals   2169–2191
Maine, Vermont, New Hampshire:
Directory of Manufacturers, 1979
3061.02
New England: Manufacturers
Directory, 1980   3443.01
State and Local Taxes   4386
State Legislative Reporting Service
4396
State Tax Reports   4413
Vermont: State Industrial Directory,
1981   4847.01

VETERINARY MEDICINE

Abstract Newsletters, Agriculture &
Food   2.04
Animal Health International   225

VIBRATION ANALYSIS

Non-Destructive Testing (NDT)
International   3530

VIDEO EQUIPMENT.   *See*
Television and Radio, Equipment

VIRGINIA

Central Atlantic States: Manufacturers
Directory, 1981   886
From the State Capitals   2169–2191
State and Local Taxes   4386
State Legislative Reporting Service
4396
State Tax Reports   4413
Virginia: Industrial Directory, 1980–81
4858.01
Virginia: State Industrial Directory,
1981   4858.02

VISAS.   *See* Passports and Visas

VITAL STATISTICS.   *See also*
Births. Death. Population. Surveys and
Polls, Census

Data User News   1344.01
Demographic Yearbook   1357
Directory of Data Files, Bureau of the
Census   1424
Monthly Bulletin of Statistics   3283
Population and Vital Statistics Report
3809
SRI Microfiche Library   4368.02
Stateman's Year-Book, 1980–81 edition
4408
Statistical Reference Index   4438

Africa

Middle East and North Africa   3217

American Nations

Informational and Technical
Publications of the General
Secretariat of the Organization of
American States (OAS)   2569

Australia

Statistics Asia & Australasia   4450
World Tables, 1980   5080

Canada

Market Research Handbook   3138

Far East

Statistics Asia & Australasia   4450

Great Britain

Facts in Focus   1873
Guide to Official Statistics   2300
Monthly Digest of Statistics   3289

Hawaii

State of Hawaii Data Book   4403

Ireland, Northern

Atlas of Ireland   346
Northern Ireland Digest of Statistics
3538

Ireland, Republic of

Atlas of Ireland   346

Michigan

Michigan Statistical Abstract, 1980
3211

Middle East

Middle East and North Africa   3217

Nebraska

Nebraska Statistical Handbook   3426

Scotland

Scottish Abstract of Statistics   4203

United States

Census Retrieval System   880
Data User News   1345
Statistical Abstract of the United States
4421

Venezuela

Venezuela Up-to-Date   4845

Wales

Digest of Welsh Statistics 1396

VOCATIONAL GUIDANCE. *See also* Employment Agencies and Counseling Services

Counselor Education and Supervision 1236
Guidepost 2285
Inform 2568
Journal of Employment Counseling 2851
Measurement and Evaluation in Guidance 3161
Personnel and Guidance Journal 3741
Vocational Guidance Quarterly 4863

VOCATIONAL GUIDANCE, MINORITIES

Journal of Non-White Concerns in Personnel and Guidance 2870

VOCATIONAL TRAINING. *See* Colleges and Universities, Vocational Training. Education, Vocational. Labor, Training. Subjects

VOLUME TRADING. *See* Stocks and Bonds, Volume Trading

WAGES. *See* Labor, Wages and Hours

WALES

Agricultural Statistics: England & Wales 107
Annual Estimates of the Population of England and Wales and Local Authority Areas 245
Criminal Statistics, England and Wales 1255
Digest of Welsh Statistics 1396
Health and Personal Social Services Statistics for Wales 2355
Local Government Financial Statistics, England and Wales 3038
Welsh Economic Trends 4948

WALLS AND INTERIOR SURFACES

Flooring 2064

WALL STREET JOURNAL (PUBLICATION)

National Newspaper Index 3396.01
Wall Street Journal Index 4879

WAREHOUSES. *See also* commodities stored

Handling & Shipping 2340
Industrial Distribution 2517
Nevada: Industrial Directory, 1981 3430.01

WARRANTIES

Acts 46
Canadian Product Safety Guide 829
Warranty Watch 4883

WASHINGTON (STATE)

From the State Capitals 2169–2191
Seattle Business Journal 4218
State and Local Taxes 4386
State Legislative Reporting Service 4396
State Tax Reports 4413
Washington: Manufacturers Register, 1980–81 4888.01
Washington Manufacturers Register, 1980–81 4888.02
Washington State Economy: Review and Outlook 4893

WASHINGTON (DC)

District of Columbia 1469.01
From the State Capitals 2169–2191
Maryland: State Industrial Directory, 1980 3146.02
State and Local Taxes 3486
State Legislative Reporting Service 3496
State Tax Reports 4413
Washington Information Directory, 1980–81 4887.02

WASTE MATERIALS AND DISPOSAL. *See also* Hazardous Cargoes

Communicators Directory, 1980 edition 1046
Construction Methods & Hazardous Waste News 2353.01
Journal of Urban Analysis 2900
Management Aids 3072
Pollution Abstracts 3803
Solid Waste Reference Service 4328.01
Solid Waste Report 4329
Solid Wastes Management 4329.01
United Nations Industrial Development Organization (UNIDO) Guides to Information Sources. UNIDO/LIB/SER.D/Rev.1— Information Sources on Bioconversion of Agricultural Wastes 4767.01

Australia

Modern Cleaning & Maintenance 3255.01

Canada

Eco/Log Week 1533

United States

Abstract Newsletters, Environmental Pollution & Control 2.15
Pollution Control Guide 3804
Sewage Treatment Construction Grants Manual 4271
State Regulation Report: Toxic Substances & Hazardous Waste 4405.01

WATER. *See also* Energy, Hydro. Hydrology. Ocean Resources. Oceans and Oceanography. Research and Development, Water Resources. Water Pollution

Rocky Mountain Mineral Law Institute 4140
Underwater Information Bulletin 4740
Water Resources Thesaurus 4900

New York City

New York City Business Fact Book Part I: Business & Manufacturing 3474

United States

Abstract Newsletters, NASA Earth Resources Survey Program 2.23
Selected Water Resources Abstracts (SWRA) 4254

WATER, RESEARCH. *See* Research and Development, Water Resources

WATER POLLUTION

Clean Water Report 959
Oceanic Abstracts 3570.01
Pollution Abstracts 3803
Underwater Information Bulletin 4740

Canada

Canadian Environmental Control Newsletter 791
Eco/Log Week 1533

United States

Abstract Newsletters, Environmental Pollution & Control 2.15
Pollution Control Guide 3804

Sewage Treatment Construction Grants
Manual 4271
Water Pollution Control 4899

WATER POLLUTION CONTROL ACT, FEDERAL (US)

Sewage Treatment Construction Grants
Manual 4271

WATER TRANSPORT COMMITTEE (CANADA)

Decisions and Orders of the Water
Transport Committee 1351

WAXES AND POLISHES

Happi 2341.01

WEALTH (PERSONAL)

Inland Revenue Statistics 2579

WEATHER

Geo Abstracts 2217.01
Weekly Weather and Crop Bulletin
4943

New York City

New York City Business Fact Book
Part I: Business & Manufacturing
3474

WEIGHTS AND MEASURES

Canadian Product Safety Guide 829

WELDING

Welding and Metal Fabrication 4944
Welding Design & Fabrication 4945
Welding Distributor 4946

WELFARE. *See* Social and Welfare
Work

WEST INDIES (BRITISH WEST INDIES)

Caribbean Year Book, 1977–78 864
West Indies Chronicle 4953

WEST VIRGINIA

Central Atlantic States: Manufacturers
Directory, 1981 886
From the State Capitals 2169–2191
Labor Market Trends 2940.01
Outlook and Situation Reports
3653.01
State and Local Taxes 4386
State Legislative Reporting Service
4396

State Tax Reports 4413
West Virginia: State Industrial
Directory, 1980–81 4957.01

WHITE COLLAR WORKERS

Modern Office Procedures 3257
Office Administration Handbook 3577

Europe

European Compensation Survey 1771

United States

White Collar Report 4968

WHITE COLLAR WORKERS, WAGES AND HOURS

Canada

Office Salary Surveys 3581

Great Britain

Incomes Data Reports 2485

United States

Office Salary Surveys 3581

WHOLESALE TRADE. *See also*
Product and commodity names

Trade and Regulated Industries
Occupational Employment Statistics
4650

Alabama

Alabama Economic Abstract 135

Argentina

Argentina Reference Bk 309

Australia

Australian Market Guide 408

New York City

New York City Business Fact Book
Part 1: Business & Manufacturing
3474

New York State

New York State Business Fact Book
Part 1: Business & Manufacturing
3481

Puerto Rico

Commercial Directory for Puerto Rico
and the Virgin Islands 1001

United States

Co-op News 1198
Current Wholesale Trade 1284.01

Virgin Islands

Commercial Directory for Puerto Rico
and the Virgin Islands 1001

WILLS AND ESTATES. *See also*
Taxation, Estate and Gift Taxes

DLB Advanced Sales Reference Service
1473
Estate Planner's Letter 1747
Estate Planning 1748
Estate Planning Review 1752
Money 3267
Practical Accountant 3821
Successful Estate Planning Ideas &
Methods 4486
Tax Facts on Life Insurance 4553
Tax Letter Service 4558
Trusts and Estates 4730.01
Wills, Estates and Trusts 5003
Wills Trusts Forms 5004

Canada

Canadian Estate Planning and
Administration Reports 791.01

New York State

New York Estates, Will, Trusts 3476

United States

Federal Estate and Gift Tax Reports
1923
Successful Personal Money
Management 4488
Wills, Estates and Trusts 5003

WILLS AND ESTATES, TAXATION

Estate Planners' Complete Guide and
Workbook 1746
Estate Planner's Letter 1747
Federal Revenue Forms—With Official
Instructions 1959
Federal Tax Course 1966
Inheritance, Estate and Gift Tax
Reports 2577
Inheritance Taxes 2578
Insurance Guide 2623
Subchapter S: Planning & Operation
4482
Successful Estate Planning Ideas &
Methods 4486
Successful Personal Money
Management 1977 4488

Tax, Financial and Estate Planning for the Owner of a Closely Held Corporation 4553.01
Tax Letter Service 4558
Tax Practice Management 4566
Tax Treaties 4573
Tax Treaties 4574

WIND POWER. *See* Energy, Wind Power

WINE AND BRANDY

Thomson's Liquor Guide 4613
United Nations Industrial Development Organization (UNIDO) Guides to Information Sources. UNIDO/LIB/SER.D/Rev.1— Information Sources on the Beer and Wine Industry 4767.05
Wine Bulletin 5005
Wine Marketing Handbook 5006

WIRES

Copper-Base Mill and Foundry Products. DIB-917 1199
Inventories of Brass and Copper Wire Mill Shapes M33K 2752

WIRETAPPING AND OTHER FORMS OF SURVEILLANCE

Law of Electronic Surveillance 2981

WISCONSIN

From the State Capitals 2169–2191
State and Local Taxes 4386
State Legislative Reporting Service 4396
State Tax Reports 4413
Wisconsin Manufacturers Directory, 1981 5008.01
Wisconsin State Industrial Directory, 1981 5008.02

WITHHOLDING RATES. *See* Taxation, Withholding Rates

WOMEN. *See also* Labor, Equal Employment Opportunity fields of activity

Business & Professional Woman 663
Business & Professional Women 664
Executive Woman 1811
From Nine to Five 2168
1975 Handbook on Women Workers 3522
SAVVY 4190.01
Woman Executive's Bulletin 5011
Women in Business 5013

Women's Work 5016
Working Woman 5025

Africa

Africa Woman 83

Canada

Women in the Labour Force: Facts & Figures 5014

United States

Who's Who of American Women 4998

WOMEN'S AND GIRLS' WEAR. *See* Apparel

WOOD PULP AND RELATED PRODUCTS. *See also* Paper and Paper Products

United Nations Industrial Development Organization (UNIDO) Guides to Information Sources. UNIDO/LIB/SER.D/Rev.1— Information Sources on the Utilization of Agricultural Residues for the Production of Panels, Pulp and Paper 4767.15
United Nations Industrial Development Organization (UNIDO) Guides to Information Sources. UNIDO/LIB/SER.D/Rev.1— Information Sources on Woodworking Machinery 4767.16
United Nations Industrial Development Organization Guides to Information Sources. UNIDO/LIB/SER D/9— Information Sources on the Building Board Industry Based on Wood and Other Fibrous Materials 4776
United Nations Industrial Development Organization Guides to Information Sources. UNIDO/LIB/SER D/11— Information Sources on the Pulp and Paper Industry 4778
Yearbooks of Forest Products Statistics 5099

Canada

Pulp and Paper 3945

North America

Forest Products Service 2144

United States

Abstract Newsletters, Materials Science 2.21

Forest Industries Newsletter 2142
Pulp and Paper 3945
Washington Report 4890

WOOL

Commercial Bulletin 999
Consumption on the Woolen and Worsted Systems. M22D 1180
Directory of Wool, Hosiery & Fabrics 1462.01
General Imports of Cotton, Wool, and Manmade Fiber Manufacturers 2211
Livestock and Products Reports 3027
Outlook and Situation Reports 3653.01
Wool 5018

WORD PROCESSING

Information & Word Processing Report 2570.01
Officemation Product Reports 3579.03
Word Processing Information Systems 5020

WORKMEN'S COMPENSATION. *See* Labor, Workmen's Compensation

WORK STUDY, ORGANIZATION AND METHODS. *See also* Methods-Time Measurement

Methods-Time Measurement (MTM) Journal 3204
Work Study 5033
World of Work Report 5073

WORLD BANK. *See* International Bank for Reconstruction and Development (IBRD)

WORLD TRADE CENTERS

World Trade Centers Association (WTCA News) 5083
World Trade Information Center 5083.01

WYOMING

From the State Capitals 2169–2191
State and Local Taxes 4386
State Legislative Reporting Service 4396
State Tax Reports 4413
Wyoming: Directory of Manufacturing and Mining, 1980 5089.02

YUGOSLAVIA

Business News 714

ZERO-BASE BUDGETING

Zero-Base Digest 5105

ZINC

Lead and Zinc Statistics 2993
Non-ferrous Metal Data 3532
Zinc Data 5106

United States

Zinc Data 5106

ZONING

Dimensions 1398
Land Development Law Reporter
  2960
Land Use Law and Zoning Digest
  2963
Land Use Planning Abstracts 2964
Law of Zoning and Planning 2987

PUBLISHERS' INDEX

ABBOTT, LANGER & ASSOC
Box 275
Park Forest, IL 60466

College Recruiting Report   982

ABWA CO, INC. *See* **American Business Women's Association**

ACADEMIC PUBLISHING CO
PO Box 42
Snowden Station
Montreal, Quebec, Canada H3X 2H7

Economic Planning   1563

ADEAST ENTERPRISES, INC
907 Park Square Bldg
Boston, MA 02116

AdEast   51

ADMINISTRATIVE MANAGEMENT SOCIETY
Maryland Ave
Willow Grove, PA 19090

Administrative Management Society
(AMS) Guide to Management
Compensation   58
Management World   3092
Office Salary Survey   3581

ADVANCED PERSONNEL SYSTEMS
756 Lois Ave
Sunnyvale, CA 94087

Development Directory—Human
Resource Management   1373.02
Manpower Planning   3100

Personnel Alert   3740.01
Training and Development Alert
4684.01

ADVANCED TECHNOLOGY PUBLICATIONS, INC
1001 Watertown St
West Newton, MA 02165

Laser Focus   2967
Laser Focus Buyers' Guide   2968
Laser Report   2969

ADVANCE MORTGAGE CORP
Publication Dept
406 City National Bank Bldg
Detroit, MI 48232

US Housing Markets   4804

ADVERTISING ASSN
Abford House
15 Wilton Rd
London, England SW1V 1NJ

Advertising Magazine   68.01

ADVERTISING CHECKING BUREAU, INC
165 N Canal St
Chicago, IL 60606

SCAN   4191

ADVERTISING/ COMMUNICATIONS TIMES
121 Chestnut St
Philadelphia, PA 19106

Advertising Communications Times
(ACT)   67
Building & Realty Record   634

ADVERTISING RESEARCH FOUNDATION
3 E 54th St
New York, NY 10022

Journal of Advertising Research   2820

ADVERTISING SPECIALTY INST
1120 Wheeler Way
Langhorne, PA 19047

Counselor   1234
imprint   2476

ADVERTISING TRADE PUBLICATIONS, INC
10 E 39th St
New York, NY 10016

Advertising Techniques   73
Art Direction   322
Best Financial Advertising   522.02
Corporate Design Systems   1205.01
Creativity/9   1241.02
Italian Illustrators/2   2791.01
Letterheads, Volumes I to III   3006.01
Pubblicita in Italia (Advertising in
Italy)   3920
Trademarks/7   4663.01
World of Logotypes, Volumes I & II
5072.01

AED. *See* **Associated Equipment Distributors**

AFL–CIO. *See* **American Federation of Labor—Congress of Industrial Organizations**

AFRICA JOURNAL LTD
Kirkman House
54a Tottenham Court Rd
London, England W1P OBT

Africa 77
Africa Woman 83

AFRICAN AMERICAN LABOR CENTER
(AFL-CIO)
1125 15th St NW
Suite 404
Washington, DC 20005

AALC Reporter 79

AFRICA RESEARCH LTD
18 Lower North St
Exeter, Devon, England EX4 3EN

Africa Research Bulletin 81

AGRA EUROPE (LONDON) LTD
Agroup House
16 Lonsdale Gardens
Tunbridge Wells, Kent, England TN1 1PD

Agra Europe 89
Agra Europe Eurofish Report 90
Agra Europe Potato Markets 91
Agra Europe Preserved Milk 92
Green Europe 2264

AGRI BUSINESS PUBLICATIONS, INC
5520 Touhy Ave, Suite G
Skokie, IL 60077

Agri Finance 114
Agri Marketing 115

AIR TRANSPORT ASSOCIATION OF AMERICA
1709 New York Ave NW
Washington, DC 20006

Air Transport 128

ALABAMA (STATE)

ALABAMA DEVELOPMENT OFFICE
State Capitol
Montgomery, AL 36130

Alabama Development News 134
Alabama Directory of Mining and Manufacturing, 1980–81 edition 134.01

(ALABAMA END)

ALASKA (STATE)

DEPT OF LABOR
Employment Security Div
Research & Analysis Section
Box 3-7000
Juneau, AK 99801

Alaska Economic Trends 138
Alaska—Occupational Employment Forecast 141
Government 1975—Occupational Employment Statistics 2246
Labor Market Information Directory 2938
Statistical Quarterly 4437
Trade and Regulated Industries— Occupational Employment Statistics 4650
Unfilled Job Openings Report 4746
Wage Rates for Selected Occupations 4871

(ALASKA END)

ALDEN PRESS LTD
Osney Mead, Oxford, England

Institute of Actuaries Journal 2595
Institute of Actuaries Students' Society Journal 2596
Institute of Actuaries Year Book 2596.01

G R ALLEN
PO Box 1367
Wellington, New Zealand

New Zealand Financial Times 3503

ALLIANCE OF AMERICAN INSURERS
20 N Wacker Dr
Chicago, IL 60606

Journal of American Insurance 2822

ALUMINUM ASSOC, INC
818 Connecticut Ave NW
Washington, DC 20006

Aluminum Statistical Review 152
World Aluminum Abstracts 5040

AMALGAMATED CLOTHING AND TEXTILE WORKERS UNION
15 Union Sq
New York, NY 10003

Labor Unity 2945

AMERICAN ACCOUNTING ASSN
Paul L Gerhardt, Admin Secy
5517 Bessie Dr
Sarasota, FL 33583

Accounting Review 36

AMERICAN AGRICULTURAL ECONOMICS ASSN
Dept of Agricultural Economics
University of Kentucky
Lexington, KY 40506

American Journal of Agricultural Economics 194

AMERICAN ARBITRATION ASSN
140 W 51 St
New York, NY 10020

Arbitration in the Schools 298
Arbitration Journal 299
Commercial Arbitration Yearbook 998
Labor Arbitration in Government 2925
Lawyers' Arbitration Letter and Digest of Court Decisions 2989
News and Views from the American Arbitration Association 3462
New York No-Fault Arbitration Reports 3478
Summary of Labor Arbitration Awards 4493

AMERICAN ASSEMBLY OF COLLEGIATE SCHOOLS OF BUSINESS
11500 Olive Street Rd, Suite 142
St Louis, MO 63141

American Assembly of Collegiate Schools of Business (AACSB) Newsline 156

AMERICAN ASSN OF COMMODITY TRADERS
10 Park St
Concord, NH 03301

Commodity Journal 1030
Journal of Investment Finance/National Spot Market Weekly Price Bulletin 2865

AMERICAN ASSOCIATION OF ENGINEERING SOCIETIES, INC
345 E 47th St
New York, NY 10017

Who's Who in Engineering, 4th edition —1980 4983

**AMERICAN ASSN OF
UNIVERSITY WOMEN**
Sales Office
2401 Virginia Ave NW
Washington, DC 20037

Educational Financial Aids (JJ4), 1981
  1591

AMERICAN BANKER
1 State Street Plaza
New York, NY 10004

American Banker   157

AMERICAN BANKERS ASSN
1120 Connecticut Ave NW
Washington, DC 20036

Agricultural Banker   94
American Bankers Association (ABA)
  Bank Card Letter   158
American Bankers Association (ABA)
  Bank Installment Lender's Report
  159
Bankers Schools Directory, 1977–78
  edition   472
Bank Fact Book   474
Bank Insurance & Protection Bulletin
  480
Bank Marketing Newsletter   483
Bank Personnel News   496
Bank Protection Manual, 1974 edition
  499
Capital   851
Construction Lending Handbook   1133
Delinquency Rates on Bank Installment
  Loans   1356
Digest of Bank Insurance   1384
Federal Wage–Hour Handbook for
  Banks   1976
Gallup Survey   2207
Installment Lending Directory   2592
Leaders Letter   2995
Nacha Quarterly Update   3354
Proceedings of the 1972 National
  Operations and Automation
  Conference—"The Common
  Denominator—Management"   3858
Results of the 1972 National
  Automation Survey   4101
Safe Deposit Handbook   4156
State Banking Law Service   4387
Thruput   4617
Trust Letter   4729
Trust Management Update   4730
Urban and Community Economic
  Development   4830

AMERICAN BAR ASSN
Sect of Labor Relations Law
1155 E 60 St
Chicago, IL 60637

Business Lawyer   704

**AMERICAN BOARD OF TRADE
SPOT AND FORWARD MARKETS**
9 South William St
New York, NY 10004

American Board of Trade (ABT) Spot
  and Forward Options Market   160

AMERICAN BUILDING SUPPLIES
1760 Peachtree Rd NW
Atlanta, GA 30357

ABS   2.02
Fiber Producer   1983

**AMERICAN BUREAU OF METAL
STATISTICS, INC**
420 Lexington Ave
New York, NY 10017

Aluminum Data   150
Copper Data   1200
Gold Data   2233
Lead Data   2994
Non-Ferrous Metal Data   3532
Silver Data   4287
Zinc Data   5106

**AMERICAN BUSINESS
COMMUNICATION ASSN**
911 South 6th St
Univ of Illinois
Champaign, IL 61820

Journal of Business Communications
  2828

AMER BUSINESS LAW ASSN
c/o Wharton School, Univ of
Pennsylvania
Philadelphia, PA 19104

American Business Law Journal   165

**AMERICAN BUSINESS MEN'S
RESEARCH FOUNDATION**
1208 Michigan National Tower
Lansing, MI 48933

Bottom Line   579
Monday Morning Report   3266.01

**AMERICAN BUSINESS WOMEN'S
ASSN**
9100 Ward Parkway
PO Box 8728
Kansas City, MO 64114

Woman in Business   5013

**AMERICAN CHAMBER OF
COMMERCE OF MEXICO**
AC Lucerna 78
Mexico 6, DF, Mexico

Mexican-American Review   3206.01

**AMERICAN CHAMBER OF
COMMERCE**
(United Kingdom)
75 Brook St
London, England W1Y 2EB

Anglo American Trade Directory   224
Atlantic Anglo American Trade News
  343.01

AMERICAN CHEMICAL SOCIETY
1155 16th St NW
Washington, DC 20036

Chemical & Engineering News   920

**AMERICAN COUNCIL OF LIFE
INSURANCE**
1850 K St NW
Washington, DC 20006

Life Insurance Fact Book   3014

**AMERICAN COUNCIL ON
CONSUMER INTERESTS**
162 Stanley Hall
University of Missouri
Columbia, MO 65211

American Council on Consumer
  Interests. Journal of Consumer
  Affairs Newsletter, Consumer
  Education Forum   168

**AMERICAN DATA PROCESSING,
INC**
22929 Industrial Dr E
St Clair Shores, MI 48080

Computer Yearbook   1090

AMERICAN ECONOMIC ASSN
1313 21st Ave S
Nashville, TN 37212

American Economic Review   170
Index of Economic Articles 1969–1976
  2496
Job Openings for Economists   2810
Journal of Economic Literature   2847

AMERICAN ELSEVIER
52 Vanderbilt Ave
New York, NY 10017

Abbreviations Dictionary   1

AMERICAN FEDERATION OF INFORMATION PROCESSING SOCIETIES PRESS
1815 North Lynn St
Arlington, VA 22209

American Federation of Information
Processing Societies Conference
Proceedings   175
American Federation of Information
Processing Societies Office
Automation Conference   175.01
American Federation of Information
Processing Societies Personal
Computing Festival   175.02

AMERICAN FEDERATION OF LABOR–CONGRESS OF INDUSTRIAL ORGANIZATIONS
815 16th St NW Room 402
Washington, DC 20006

AFLabor-CIO News   76.02

AMERICAN FINANCE ASSOCIATION
Graduate School of Business
Administration
New York University
100 Trinity Place
New York, NY 10006

Journal of Finance   2854

AMERICAN FOOTWEAR INDUSTRIES ASSOCIATION
Suite 900, 1611 N Kent St
Arlington, VA 22209

Footwear Manual   2101

AMERICAN FROZEN FOOD INSTITUTE
1700 Old Meadow Rd
McLean, VA 22102

Frozen Food Pack Statistics   2192

AMERICAN GAS ASSOCIATION
Bureau of Statistics
1515 Wilson Blvd
Arlington, VA 22209

Gas Facts: A Statistical Record of the
Gas Utility Industry   2208

AMERICAN HOSPITAL ASSN
840 North Lake Shore Dr
Chicago, IL 60611

American Hospital Association Guide
to the Health Code Field   178
Cross-Reference   1261
Health Services Research   2365

Hospital Statistics: Data from the
American Hospital Association
Annual Survey   2397
Hospital Week   2398
National Hospital Economic Activity
3380

AMERICAN HOSPITAL PUBLISHING, INC
211 E Chicago Ave
Chicago, IL 60611

Hospital Medical Staff   2395
Hospitals   2396
Trustee   4728
Volunteer Leader   4868

AMERICAN INDUSTRIAL DEVELOPMENT COUNCIL
215 W Pershing Rd, Suite 707
Kansas City, MO 64108

American Industrial Development
Council Journal   181

AMERICAN INSTITUTE COUNSELORS, INC
PO Box 567
Great Barrington, MA 01230

Investment Bulletin   2761

AMERICAN INSTITUTE FOR DECISION SCIENCES
Univ Plaza
140 Decatur St SE
Atlanta, GA 30303

Decision Line   1348
Decision Sciences   1352

AMERICAN INSTITUTE FOR ECONOMIC RESEARCH
Great Barrington, MA 01230

Economic Education Bulletin   1550
Research Reports   4091.02

AMERICAN INSTITUTE OF BANKING
1120 Connecticut Ave
Washington, DC 20036

American Institute of Banking Leaders
Letter   186

AMERICAN INSTITUTE OF CERTIFIED PUBLIC ACCOUNTANTS
1211 Ave of the Americas
New York, NY 10036

Accountants' Index   23
Accountants' Index Quarterly Service
24
Accountants International Studies   25

Accounting Trends & Techniques   38
American Institute of Certified Public
Accountants (AICPA) Professional
Standards   187
American Institute of Certified Public
Accountants (AICPA) Washington
Report   191
CPA Client Bulletin   897
CPA Letter   898
Industry Audit Guides   2560
Journal of Accountancy   2817
Management Advisory Services
Guidelines Series   3070
Management of an Accounting Practice
Handbook   3082
Professional Accounting in 30 Countries
3882
Securities Exchange Commission
Quarterly   4230
Statements on International Accounting
Standards   4400
Tax Adviser   4534
Tax Planning Tips From the Tax
Adviser   4565.01
Tax Practice Management   4566
Tax Research Techniques   4568
Technical Practice Aids   4576

AMERICAN INSTITUTE OF COOPERATION
1800 Massachusetts Ave NW, Suite 504
Washington, DC 20036

American Cooperation   167

AMERICAN INSTITUTE OF FOOD DISTRIBUTION, INC
28-06 Broadway
Fair Lawn, NJ 07410

Food Institute Reports   2089

AMERICAN INSTITUTE OF INDUSTRIAL ENGINEERS, INC
Industrial & Labor Relations Div
25 Technology Park
Norcross, GA 30092

Industrial Engineering   2519

AMERICAN INST OF REAL ESTATE APPRAISERS
430 N Michigan Ave
Chicago, IL 60611

Appraisal Journal   291
Appraiser   292

AMERICAN INTERNATIONAL INVESTMENT CORP
351 California St
San Francisco, CA 94104

World Currency Charts   5053

AMERICAN IRON AND STEEL INSTITUTE
1000 16th St NW
Washington, DC 20036

American Iron and Steel Institute.
  Annual Statistical Report   193

AMERICAN JOURNAL OF ECONOMICS & SOCIOLOGY, INC
5 E 44th St
New York, NY 10017

American Journal of Economics and
  Sociology   195

AMERICAN LAND TITLE ASSN
1828 L St NW
Washington, DC 20036

Title News   4626

AMERICAN MANAGEMENT ASSNS, INC
135 W 50 St
New York, NY 10020

AMACOM-Catalog of Resources for
  Professional AMA Management   153
AMA Management Handbook   153.01
Compensation Review   1062
Course Catalog-Management
  Development Guide   1239.01
Current Compensation References
  1272
Executive Compensation Service.
  Reports on International
  Compensation. Brazil   1801
Executive Compensation Service.
  Technician Report   1802
Executive Compensation Service. Top
  Management Report   1802.01
Management Briefings   3073
Management Review   3086
Organizational Dynamics   3640
Personnel   3738
Supervisory Management   4501
Survey Reports   4520

AMERICAN MARKETING ASSN
222 S Riverside Plaza
Chicago, IL 60606

Journal of Marketing   2867
Journal of Marketing Research   2868
Marketing News   3133

AMERICAN MEAT INSTITUTE
PO Box 3556
Washington, DC 20007

Financial Facts About the Meat
  Packing Industry   2000

AMERICAN NUCLEAR SOC
555 N Kensington Ave
La Grange Park, IL 60525

Communicators Directory, 1980 edition
  1046

AMERICAN PAPER INSTITUTE
260 Madison Ave
New York, NY 10016

Wood Pulp and Fiber Statistics   5017

AMERICAN PERSONNEL AND GUIDANCE ASSN
2 Skyline Place, Suite 400
Falls Church, VA 22041

Counseling and Values   1233
Counselor Education and Supervision
  1236
Directory of Counseling Services   1423
Guidepost   2285
Humanist Educator   2428
Inform   2568
Journal of Employment Counseling
  2851
Journal of Non-White Concerns in
  Personnel and Guidance   2870
Measurement and Evaluation in
  Guidance   3161
Personnel and Guidance Journal   3741
Rehabilitation Counseling Bulletin
  4059
School Counselor   4193

AMERICAN PLANNING ASSOCIATION
1313 E 60th St
Chicago, IL 60637

Land Use Law and Zoning Digest
  2963

AMERICAN PRODUCTION & INVENTORY CONTROL SOCIETY, INC
Watergate Bldg, Suite 504
2600 Virginia Ave NW
Washington, DC 20037

Production & Inventory Control
  Handbook   3865
Production & Inventory Management
  3866

AMERICAN RISK & INSURANCE ASSN
c/o Dr. R E Johnson
297 Brooks Hall
University of Georgia
Athens, GA 30602

Journal of Risk and Insurance   2882

AMERICAN SOCIETY FOR INFORMATION SCIENCE
1010 16th St NW
Washington, DC 20036

Annual Review of Information Science
  and Technology/Volume 15   258
Bulletin of the American Society for
  Information Science   645.01
Computer-Readable Data Bases
  1081.02
Information Science Abstracts   2574

AMERICAN SOCIETY FOR PERSONNEL ADMINISTRATION
30 Park Dr
Berea, OH 44017

American Society for Personnel
  Administration (ASPA) Handbook of
  Personnel and Industrial Relations
  205
Personnel Administrator   3739
Salary Survey   4163
Strike Preparation Manual   4479

AMERICAN SOCIETY FOR QUALITY CONTROL
161 W Wisconsin Ave
Milwaukee, WI 53203

Journal of Quality Technology   2877

AMERICAN SOCIETY FOR TESTING AND MATERIALS
1916 Race St
Philadelphia, PA 19103

Annual Book of ASTM Standards
  236.01

AMERICAN SOC FOR TRAINING & DEVELOPMENT, INC
Box 5307
Madison, WI 53705

Training and Development Journal
  4685

AMERICAN SOCIETY OF APPRAISERS
Dulles International Airport
Box 17265
Washington, DC 20041

Bibliography of Appraisal Literature
  548
Valuation   4838

AMERICAN SOCIETY OF ASSOCIATION EXECUTIVES
1575 Eye St NW
Washington, DC 20005

Association Management 339
Who's Who in Association Management
4979

**AMERICAN SOC OF CHARTERED
LIFE UNDERWRITERS**
270 Bryn Mawr Ave
Box 59
Bryn Mawr, PA 19010

Chartered Life Underwriters (CLU)
Journal 915

**AMERICAN SOC OF PENSION
ACTUARIES**
1700 K St NW, Suite 404
Washington, DC 20006

Pension Actuary 3719
Pension Tables for Actuaries 3731

AMERICAN STATISTICAL ASSN
806 15th St NW, Suite 640
Washington, DC 20005

American Statistician 206
Current Index to Statistics—
Applications, Methods, Theory 1277
Journal of the American Statistical
Assn 2889
Statisticians and Others in Allied
Professions 4447

AMERICAN TRUCKING ASSN
1616 P St NW
Washington, DC 20036

American Trucking Trends 210
Executive and Ownership Report
1796.01
Financial Analysis of The Motor
Carrier Industry 1992
Financial and Operating Statistics,
Motor Carrier Quarterly Report
1996
Monthly Truck Tonnage Report 3305
Motor Carrier Annual Report 3326
Motor Carrier Statistical Summary
3327
Research Review 4095
Weekly Truck Tonnage Report 4941

**AMERICAN UNIVERSITY PRESS
SERVICES, INC**
1 Park Ave
New York, NY 10016

Ad Guide: An Advertiser's Guide to
Periodicals 52

**AMERICAN WOMAN'S SOCIETY
OF CPAs**
Circulation Dept
The Woman CPA
PO Box 944
Cincinnati, OH 45201

Woman CPA 5010

AMERITRUST CO
900 Euclid Ave
Cleveland, OH 44101

American Business Activity from 1790
to Today 164

AMES PUBLISHING Div, Chilton
1 W Olney Ave
Philadelphia, PA 19120

Industrial Distributor News 2518
Industrial Maintenance and Plant
Operation 2532
Industrial Safety Product News
2551.01

AMIVEST CORP
505 Park Ave
New York, NY 10022

Liquidity Report 3022

ANBAR PUBLICATIONS LTD
PO Box 23
Wembley, England HA9 8DJ

Anbar Management Publications.
Accounting and Data Processing
Abstracts 217
Anbar Management Publications.
Bibliography 218
Anbar Management Publications.
Marketing and Distribution Abstracts
219
Anbar Managements Publications.
Personnel & Training Abstracts 220
Anbar Management Publications.
Smaller Business Management
Abstracts 220.01
Anbar Management Publications. Top
Management Abstracts 221
Anbar Management Publications. Work
Study and O & M Abstracts 222

ARTHUR ANDERSEN & CO
69 W Washington
Chicago, IL 60602

Tax and Trade Guide Series 4535

RONALD ANDERSON & ASSOC
90-92 Langridge St
Collingwood, Vic 3066, Australia

Primary Industry Newsletter 3841
Primary Industry Survey 3842
World Agricultural Report 5037

ANNY PUBLICATIONS. *See*
**Advertising News of New York
Publications**

**APARTMENT OWNERS &
MANAGERS ASSN OF AMERICA**
65 Cherry Ave
Watertown, CT 06795

Apartment Management Report 274
Apartment Owners & Managers Assn
of America (AOMA) Newsletter
275

APPRAISAL INST OF CANADA
309-93 Lombard Ave
Winnipeg 2, Man, Canada R3B 3B1

Appraisal Institute Magazine (AIM)
290
Directory of Designated Members
1426.01

ARAMTEK CORP
122 E 42nd St
New York, NY 10017

Aramtek Mideast Monthly 297

**AREA DEVELOPMENT
MAGAZINE**
432 Park Ave South
New York, NY 10016

Area Development 303

ARIZONA (STATE)

DEPT OF ECONOMIC SECURITY
Labor Market Information, Research
and Analysis
PO Box 6123
Phoenix, AZ 85005

Annual Planning Information 253
Arizona Labor Market Newsletter 312
Job Openings: Indicator of
Occupational Demand 2811

**OFFICE OF ECONOMIC
PLANNING & DEVELOPMENT**
Executive Tower, RM 505
1700 West Washington
Phoenix, AZ 85007

Arizona: an Economic Profile 310

(ARIZONA END)

ARIZONA STATE UNIVERSITY
College of Business Administration
Bureau of Business and Economic
Research
Tempe, AZ 85281

Arizona Business   311

ARKANSAS (STATE)

**DEPT OF ECONOMIC
DEVELOPMENT**
One Capitol Mall
Little Rock, AR 72201

Arkansas Economic Report   319
Arkansas. The Great Location in the
  Sunbelt   321
Arkansas USA   321.01
Basics of Plant Location in Arkansas
  514
Directory of Arkansas Manufacturers
  1409
Inside Arkansas   2588
Transportation Arkansas   4691.01

(ARKANSAS END)

ASIA LETTER LTD
PO Box 54149
Los Angeles, CA 90054

Asean Briefing   324
Asia Letter   325
China Letter   942
Indonesia Letter   2506
Japan Letter   2803
Philippine Letter   3765.03

ASIAN DEVELOPMENT BANK
PO Box 789
Manila, Philippines 2800

Annual Report   254
Asian Agricultural Survey   326
Basic Facts, Developing Member
  Countries (DMCs) of Asian
  Development Bank (ADB)   512
Key Indicators of Developing Member
  Countries of Asian Development
  Bank (ADB)   2910
Southeast Asia's Economy in the 1970s
  4346

ASIA RESEARCH PTE LTD
International Plaza
10 Anson Rd
Singapore 2

Asean Business Quarterly   324.01
Asia Research Bulletin   331

ASLIB
3 Belgrave Sq
London, England SW1X 8PL

Aslib Directory, Vol 1   333
Aslib Directory, Vol 2   333.01
Journal of Documentation   2844.02
London Classification of Business
  Studies   3040.01
Online Bibliographic Databases
  3619.03

A/S/M COMMUNICATIONS, INC
230 Park Ave
New York, NY 10169

Adweek   74.01

A/S/M PUBLICATIONS INC
514 Shatto Pl
Los Angeles, CA 90020

ADWEEK/West   74.01

ASPEN SYSTEMS CORP
1600 Research Blvd
Rockville, MD 20850

Health Care Management Review
  2358
Nursing Administration Quarterly
  3557
Nursing Management   3558
Topics in Health Care Financing   4639

**ASSOCIATED EQUIPMENT
DISTRIBUTORS**
615 W 22nd St
Oak Brook, IL 60521

Associated Equipment Distributors
  (AED) Edition of Construction
  Equipment Buyers Guide   334
Construction Equipment Distribution
  (CED)   1128
Cost-of-Doing-Business Survey   1228
Rental Compilation   4061
Serial Number Field Guide   4262
Serial Number Location Guide For
  Construction Equipment   4263

ASSOCIATED INDUSTRIES OF MA
4005 Prudential Tower
Boston, MA 02199

Industry   2558

**ASSN FOR COMPARATIVE
ECONOMIC STUDIES**
c/o Roger Skurski
Dept of Economics
Univ of Notre Dame
Notre Dame, IN 46556

Assn for Comparative Economic
  Studies (ACES) Bulletin   338

**ASSOCIATION FOR COMPUTING
MACHINERY**
Special Interest Group on Business
Data Processing
1133 Ave of the Americas
New York, NY 10036

ACM Guide to Computing Literature
  Annual   40
ACM Transactions on Database
  Systems   40.01
ACM Transactions on Mathematical
  Software   40.02
ACM Transactions on Programming
  Languages and Systems   40.03
Communications of the ACM   1043
Computing Reviews   1091
Computing Surveys   1091.01
Journal of the Association for
  Computing Machinery   2889.02

**ASSN FOR EVOLUTIONARY
ECONOMICS**
Dept of Economics
343 College of Bus Adm
University of Nebraska-Lincoln
Lincoln, NE 68588

Journal of Economic Issues (JEI)   2846

ASSN FOR SOCIAL ECONOMICS
c/o William R Waters
De Paul University
25 E Jackson Blvd
Chicago, IL 60604

Review of Social Economy   4129

**ASSN FOR SYSTEMS
MANAGEMENT**
24587 Bagley Rd
Cleveland, OH 44138

Journal of Systems Management   2886

ASSN OF AMERICAN RAILROADS
Economics & Finance Dept
American Railroads Bldg
Washington, DC 20036

Indexes of Railroad Material Prices and
  Wage Rates   2498
Operating and Traffic Statistics   3627
Property Investment and Condensed
  Income Account   3900
Rail News Update   3989.01
Railroad Mileage by States   3990
Railroad Revenues, Expenses, and
  Income   3993

Revenues, Expenses, and Freight Traffic 4118

Statistics of Railroads of Class I in the United States 4454

Weekly Carloading Statement 4904

Yearbook of Railroad Facts 5097

ASSOCIATION OF CERTIFIED ACCOUNTANTS
29 Lincoln's Inn Fields
London, England WC2A 3EE

Certified Accountant 895

ASSOCIATION OF CONSULTING MANAGEMENT ENGINEERS
230 Park Ave
New York, NY 10169

Directory of Members 1446

ASSN OF FOREMEN & SUPERVISORS
20 Hunter St
Parramotta, NSW Australia 895

Impact 2441

ASSOCIATION OF INDIAN ENGINEERING INDUSTRY
172 Jor Bagh
New Delhi, India 110003

Engineering & Metals Review 1704
Handbook of Statistics, 1980 2337.01

ASSN OF INTERSTATE COMMERCE COMMISSION PRACTITIONERS
1112 ICC Bldg
Washington, DC 20423

Interstate Commerce Commission (ICC) Practitioners' Journal 2747

ASSN OF SCIENTIFIC TECHNICAL AND MANAGERIAL STAFFS
10/26A Jamestown Rd
London, England NW1 7DT

Association of Scientific Technical and Managerial Staffs Journal 341

ATCOM, INC
2315 Broadway
New York, NY 10024

Car Dealer "Insider" 859
Car Rental and Leasing "Insider" 866
Funeral Service "Insider" 2201
Leisure Beverage "Insider" 3004
Motel/Hotel "Insider" 3323
Real Estate "Insider" 4014
Truck "Insider" 4723

ATLANTIC ECONOMIC SOCIETY
Box 258
Worden, IL 62097

Atlantic Economic Journal 344

ATLANTIC PROVINCES ECONOMIC COUNCIL
One Sackville Place
Halifax, NS, Canada B3J 1K1

Atlantic Report 345

AUDIT BUREAU OF CIRCULATIONS
123 N Wacker Dr
Chicago, IL 60606

Audit Bureau of Circulations (ABC) Factbook 348
Audit Bureau of Circulations (ABC) News Bulletin 349

AUDIT INVESTMENT RESEARCH
230 Park Ave, Suite 555
New York, NY 10017

Realty Stock Review 4033

AUERBACH PUBLISHERS
6560 N Park Dr
Pennsauken, NJ 08109

Auerbach Applications Software Reports 350
Auerbach Business Minicomputer Systems Reports 351
Auerbach Buyers' Guide to Word Processing 355
Auerbach Computer Programming Management 356
Auerbach Data Base Management 357
Auerbach Data Center Operations Management 358
Auerbach Data Communications Management 359
Auerbach Data Communications, Minicomputers and Data Handling Reports 360
Auerbach Data Communications Notebook 361
Auerbach Data Communications Report 362
Auerbach Data Processing Management 363
Auerbach EDP Notebook/International 364
Auerbach General-Purpose Minicomputer Reports 369
Auerbach/Infotech International's Computer State of the Art Reports 370
Auerbach Input/Output Reports 371
Auerbach Microform Reports 372

Auerbach Minicomputer Notebook/International 373
Auerbach Peripherals and Data Handling Reports 374
Auerbach Software Reports 375
Auerbach Standard EDP Reports 376
Auerbach Systems Development Management 377
Auerbach Systems Software Reports 378
Auerbach Time Sharing Reports 379
Distributed Processing Management 1467
EDP (Electronic Data Processing) Auditing 1589
Electronic Office Management and Technology 1631.01
Financial/Retail Systems Reports 2018.01
Office Systems Reports 3581.01
Plug-Compatible Peripherals Reports 3788.01

AUSTRALIA

BUREAU OF STATISTICS
PO Box 10
Belconnen ACT 2616, Australia

Australia at a Glance 382
Australian Capital Territory Statistical Summary 389
Australian Exports, Country by Commodity 400
Australian Imports, Country by Commodity 404
Balance of Payments 451
Banking 475.01
Consumer Price Index 1161
Crops 1260
Digest of Current Economic Statistics 1387
Exports, Australia 1828
Exports of Major Commodities by Country 1853
Foreign Investment 2117.01
Foreign Investment in Enterprise in Australia 2119
Fruit Statistics 2194
Imports 2443
Imports Cleared for Home Consumption 2445
Labour Force 2950
Labour Statistics 2958
Livestock Statistics 3026.01
Manufacturing Establishments, Details of Operations by Industry Class 3116
Meat 3164
Monthly Review of Business Statistics, Ref No 1.4 3297

Northern Territory Statistical Summary 3542
Official Year Book of Australia   3587
Overseas Trade, Part I: Exports and Imports   3661
Overseas Trade, Part 2: Comparative and Summary Tables   3662
Overseas Trade (Preliminary), Part 1—Exports   3663
Production Statistics   3873
Retail Sales of Goods   4111
Seasonally Adjusted Indicators   4216
Social Indicators   4313
Wheat Statistics   4966
Wool Statistics   5018

COMMONWEALTH DEPARTMENT OF SCIENCE AND TECHNOLOGY
GPO Box 2288U
Melbourne, Vic 3001, Australia

International Occupational Safety and Health Information Centre (CIS)   2715

DEPT OF INDUSTRIAL DEVELOPMENT AND DECENTRALISATION
32 St George's Terrace
Perth, WA 6000, Australia

Enterprise   1713
Western Australian Manufacturers Directory   4950

DEPT OF SCIENCE & TECHNOLOGY
Human Relations Branch
PO Box 449
Woden, ACT 2606 Australia

Work and People   5021

DEPT OF TRADE & RESOURCES
PO Box 69
Commerce Court Postal Sta
Toronto, Ont, Canada M5L 1B9

Australian Trading News   420

GOVERNMENT PUBLISHING SERVICE
Publishing Branch
PO Box 84
Canberra, ACT 2600, Australia

Australia Dept of the Treasury. Round-Up of Economic Statistics   392
Quarterly Review of the Rural Economy   3971.01

(AUSTRALIA END)

AUSTRALIA & NEW ZEALAND BANKING GROUP LTD
551 Collins St
Melbourne, Vic 3000, Australia

Australia and New Zealand (ANZ) Bank Business Indicators   380

AUSTRALIAN AGRICULTURAL ECONOMIC SOCIETY
Suite 302, Clunies Ross House
191 Royal Parade
Parkville, Vic 3052, Australia

Australian Journal of Agricultural Economics   406

AUSTRALIAN CHAMBER OF COMMERCE
PO Box E139
Canberra, ACT 2600, Australia

Canberra Comments   849

AUSTRALIAN CONSUMERS' ASSN
28-30 Queen St
Chippendale, NSW 2008, Australia

Choice   945

AUSTRALIAN COUNCIL OF TRADE UNIONS
254 La Trobe St
Melbourne, Vic 3000, Australia

Australian Congress of Trade Unions Bulletin   390

AUSTRALIAN INSTITUTE OF CREDIT MANAGEMENT
c/o Ley Pulford & Co
37 Swanston St
Melbourne, Vic 3000, Australia

Credit Review   1248
Credo   1254

AUSTRALIAN MEAT AND LIVESTOCK CORP
GPO Box 4129
Sydney, NSW 2001, Australia

Australian & Live-stock Corp Annual Report   410
In Brief   2476.02
Meat Producer and Exporter   3163
Statistical Review of Live-stock and Meat Industries   4441.01

AUSTRALIAN SOCIETY OF ACCOUNTANTS
170 Queen St
Melbourne, Vic 3000, Australia

Australian Accountant   383

AUTOMATIC DATA PROCESSING
Network Services Division
175 Jackson Plaza
Ann Arbor, MI 48106

ADP Network Services   60

AVCO FINANCIAL SERVICES
620 Newport Center Dr
PO Box 2210
Newport Beach, CA 92660

Money Tree   3274

AYER PRESS
1 Bala Ave
Bala Cynwyd, PA 19004

Ayer Directory of Publications   443

BABSON'S REPORTS, INC
Wellesley Hills, MA 02181

Babson's Investment & Barometer Letter   444
Babson's Washington Forecast Letter   445

BACON'S PUBLISHING CO
14 E Jackson Blvd
Chicago, IL 60604

Bacon's International Publicity Checker   447
Bacon's Publicity Checker   448

BALLINGER PUBLISHING CO
17 Dunster St
Harvard Square
Cambridge, MA 02138

Real Estate Appraisal Terminology   4010

BALL STATE UNIVERSITY
College of Business
Muncie, IN 47306

Ball State Business Review   454
Ball State Journal for Business Educators   454.01

BANK ADMINISTRATION INSTITUTE
303 South NW Highway
Box 500
Park Ridge, IL 60068

Bank Officer Cash Compensation Survey, 1979   489.01
Community Bank Series on Operations and Automation   1048
Issues in Bank Regulation   2791
Journal of Bank Research   2824

Magazine of Bank Administration
3057
Survey of Bank Personnel Policies and
Practices   4507
Trust Audit Manual   4727

BANKERS DIGEST, INC
1208 Mercantile Securities Bldg
Dallas, TX 75201

Bankers Digest   467
Texas Banking Red Book   4595

**BANKERS' INSTITUTE OF
AUSTRALASIA**
51 Queen St
Melbourne, Vic 3000, Australia

Bankers' Magazine of Australasia   470

BANKERS MONTHLY, INC
601 Skokie Blvd
Northbrook, IL 60062

Bankers Monthly, National Magazine
of Banking and Investments   471

BANKERS PUBLISHING CO
210 South St
Boston, MA 02111

Munn's Encyclopedia of Banking and
Finance   3342

BANKERS TRUST CO
PO Box 318, Church St Station
New York, NY 10015

Credit and Capital Markets   1244
Current Business Picture   1271

BANK MARKETING ASSN
309 W Washington St
Chicago, IL 60606

Bank Marketing   482

BANK OF AMERICA
Dept 3124
Box 37000
San Francisco, CA 94137

Economic Outlook: California Report
1558
Economic Outlook: Global Report
1559
Economic Outlook: US Report   1560
Small Business Reporter   4302

BANK OF CANADA
Distribution Section
Secretary's Dept
Ottawa, Canada K1A 0G9

Bank of Canada Review   485
Bank of Canada Weekly Financial
Statistics   486

BANK OF ENGLAND
Economics Division
Threadneedle St
London, England EC2R 8AH

Bank of England Annual Report and
Accounts   487
Bank of England Quarterly Bulletin
488

BANK OF HAWAII
Economics Division
PO Box 2900
Honolulu, HI 96846

Bank of Hawaii Monthly Review   491
Construction in Hawaii   1131
Hawaii Annual Economic Review
2347

BANK OF MONTREAL
Economics Dept
PO Box 6002
Montreal, Quebec, Canada H3C 3B1

Bank of Montreal Business Review
492

BANK OF NEW SOUTH WALES
GPO Box 1
Sydney, NSW 2001, Australia

Bank of New South Wales Review
493
Etruscan   1758

BANK OF NEW ZEALAND
PO Box 2392
Wellington, New Zealand

Business Indicators   690.02
Handbook for Investors—New Zealand
2314
Life and Business in New Zealand
3011
Overseas Investment and Business in
New Zealand   3659

BANK OF NOVA SCOTIA
44 King St W
Toronto, Ont, Canada M5H 1H1

Bank of Nova Scotia Monthly Review
494

**BANKRUPTCY TRUSTEES' &
LIQUIDATORS' ASSN OF
AUSTRALIA**
Box 129, GPO
Sydney, NSW 2001, Australia

Australian Bankruptcy Bulletin   386

**BANQUE CANADIENNE
NATIONALE**
500 Place d'Armes
Montreal, Quebec, Canada H2Y 2W3

Monthly Letter   3292

BARCLAYS BANK
Group Economics Dept
54 Lombard St
London, England EC3P 3AH

Abecor Country Reports   2
Barclays Review   508
Commodities Survey   1023
Financial Market Surveys   2007

BARNES & NOBLE, INC
Div of Harper & Row Publishers, Inc
10 E 53 St
New York, NY 10022

Dictionary of Economics   1378

**BARNETT BANKS OF FLORIDA,
INC**
100 Laura St, PO Box 40789
Jacksonville, FL 32231

This Week   4608

BASIL BLACKWELL PUBLISHER
108 Cowley Rd
Oxford, England OX4 1JF

Journal of Business Finance and
Accounting   2830
Journal of Common Market Studies
2839
Journal of Economic Affairs   2845.01
Journal of Industrial Economics   2861
Journal of Management Studies   2866
Oxford Bulletin of Economics &
Statistics   3673
R & D (Research and Development)
Management   3999.03
Social Policy and Administration
4313.01
World Economy   5062

BAXTER
1030 E Putnam Ave
Greenwich, CT 06830

Baxter   515

BAYARD PUBLICATIONS, INC
1234 Summer St
Stamford, CT 06905

Insurance Marketing   2632

BAYLOR UNIVERSITY
Hankamer School of Business
Box 6278
Waco, TX 76798

Baylor Business Studies   516

BAYWOOD PUBLISHING CO, INC
120 Marine St
Farmingdale, NY 11735

International Journal of Health Services
2693
Journal of Collective Negotiations in
the Public Sector   2832
Journal of Educational Technology
Systems   2850
Journal of Environmental Systems
2852
Journal of Technical Writing and
Communication   2888

BELENOS PUBLICATIONS LTD
50 Fitzwilliam Sq W
Dublin 2, Ireland

Business and Finance   661

**BELGIAN AMERICAN CHAMBER
OF COMMERCE IN THE UNITED
STATES, INC**
50 Rockefeller Plaza
New York, NY 10020

Belgian American Trade Review   520
US–Belgium Trade Directory   4794.01

BELL & HOWELL
Micro Photo Division
Old Mansfield Rd
Wooster, OH 44691

Federal Telephone Directories   1972.01
Index to Black Newspapers   2500
Transdex   4687.01

MATTHEW BENDER & CO, INC
235 E 45th St
New York, NY 10017

American Law of Mining   197
Annual Inst on Oil and Gas Law and
Taxation   250
Antitrust Laws and Trade Regulation
273
Benefits Review Board–Black Lung
Reporter   522
Benefits Review Board–Longshore
Reporter   522.01
Business Crime: Criminal Liability of
the Business Community   676.01
Business Organizations with Tax
Planning   715
Computer Law: Evidence and
Procedure   1079.01

Corporate Acquisitions and Mergers
1203
Corporate Counsel's Annual   1205
Doing Business in Brazil   1483.01
Doing Business in Canada   1484
Doing Business in Japan   1486.01
Doing Business in Mexico   1487
Doing Business in the US   1488
Drug Product Liability   1509
EEC Competition Law Reporter
1597.02
Employment Discrimination   1659
Exploration and Economics of the
Petroleum Industry   1815
Federal Income, Gift, and Estate
Taxation   1927
Federal Power Service   1934
Federal Taxation of Life Insurance
Companies   1963
Federal Taxation of Oil and Gas
Transactions   1964
Foreign Tax and Trade Briefs   2137
Franchising   2160
Income Taxation of Foreign Related
Transactions   2490
International Withholding Tax Treaty
Guide   2743
Labor Law   2932
Labor Law Developments   2933
Law of Advertising   2979
Law of Associations: An Operating
Legal Manual for Executives and
Counsel   2980
Law of Federal Oil and Gas Leases
2982
Law of Liability Insurance   2983
Law of Oil and Gas Leases   2984
Law of Pooling and Unitization—
Voluntary, Compulsory   2985
Law of Workmen's Compensation
2986
Local Government Law   3039
Major Tax Planning—University of
Southern California Law Center
Annual Institute on Federal Taxation
3065
Manual of Oil and Gas Terms,
Annotated   3103
New York University Annual
Conference on Labor   3489
New York University Annual Institute
on Federal Taxation   3490
Oil and Gas Law   3596
Oil and Gas Law: Desk Edition   3597
Oil and Gas Reporter   3599
Oil & Gas Tax Quarterly   3600
Pension and Profit Sharing Plans   3723
Private Investors Abroad   3854
Products Liability   3878
Professonal Corporations and
Associations   3885
Rocky Mountain Mineral Law Institute
4140

Tax-Free Trade Zones of the World
4553.02
Tax Havens of the World   4554
Trademark Protection and Practice
4660
Trade Secrets   4674
US Customs and International Trade
Guide   4794.01
US Tax Week   4820
Workmen's Compensation for
Occupational Injuries and Death
(Desk Edition)   5027
World Law of Competition   5068.01

BERKELEY ENTERPRISES, INC
815 Washington St
Newtonville, MA 02160

Computers and People   1087

BERL PUBLICATIONS LTD
PO Box 10-010
Wellington, New Zealand

New Zealand Economist   3500

ARNOLD BERNHARD & CO, INC
711 3rd Ave
New York, NY 10017

Value Line Convertible Strategist   4839
Value Line Investment Survey   4840
Value Line OTC Special Situations
Service   4841

A M BEST & CO
Ambest Rd
Oldwick, NJ 08858

Best's Agents Guide to Life Insurance
Companies   523
Best's Aggregates & Averages   524
Best's Casualty Loss Reserve
Development   525
Best's Directory of Recommended
Insurance Adjustors   526
Best's Directory of Recommended
Insurance Attorneys   526.01
Best's Flitcraft Compend   527
Best's Insurance Management Reports:
Life–Health Edition   528
Best's Insurance Management Reports:
Property–Casualty Edition   529
Best's Insurance Report: Life–Health
530
Best's Insurance Report:
Property–Casualty   531
Best's Insurance Securities Research
532
Best's Key Rating Guide   533
Best's Loss Control Engineering
Manual   534
Best's Market Guide   535
Best's Reproductions of Convention
Statements   538

Best's Retirement Income Guide
538.01
Best's Review. Life/Health Insurance
Edition 539
Best's Review. Property–Casualty
Insurance Edition 540
Best's Safety Directory 541
Best's Settlement Options Manual 542
Best's Underwriting Guide 543
Best's Underwriting Newsletter 544

BILLBOARD PUBLICATIONS INC
PO Box 24970
Nashville, TN 37202

Amusement Business 212
Billboard 551
Managing the Leisure Facility 3095.03

BILL COMMUNICATIONS, INC
633 3rd Ave
New York, NY 10017

Incentive Marketing 2477
Successful Meetings 4487

**BIOSCIENCES INFORMATION
SERVICE OF BIOLOGICAL
ABSTRACTS**
2100 Arch St
Philadelphia, PA 19103

Abstracts on Health Effects of
Environmental Pollutants (HEEP) 4
Biological Abstracts (BA) 554
Biological Abstracts/RPM 554.01

BLACK'S GUIDE
PO Box 2090, 332 Broad St
Red Bank, NJ 07701

Black's Guides for New York,
Philadelphia, and Washington
560.01

**WILLIAM BLACKWOOD & SONS
LTD**
32 Thistle St
Edinburgh, Scotland EH2 1HA

Scottish Bankers Magazine 4204

JOHN BLAIR & CO
717 5th Ave
New York, NY 10022

Statistical Trends in Broadcasting
4443

WILLIAM F BLAND CO
Box 1421
Stamford, CT 06904

International Oil News 2717
Petrochemical News 3754

BLUE LIST PUBLISHING CO
25 Broadway
New York, NY 10004

Blue List of Current Municipal
Offerings 564

BLUE REPORTS, INC
5205 Leesburg Pike
Falls Church, VA 22041

Blue Reports 565

CLARK BOARDMAN CO LTD
435 Hudson St
New York, NY 10014

Forms and Agreements for Architects,
Engineers, and Contractors 2146
Going Public 2232
Intellectual Property Law Review
2636.02
Intellectual Property Management:
Law/Business/Strategy 2637
Land Use and Environment Law
Review 2961.01
Law and Business of Licensing 2977
Law of Electronic Surveillance 2981
Law of Zoning and Planning 2987
Licensing in Foreign and Domestic
Operations 3010
Lindey on Entertainment, Publishing
and the Arts 3019.01
Patent and Trademark Review 3968
Patent Fraud and Inequitable Conduct
3700
Patent Invalidity: A Statistical and
Substantive Analysis 3701
Patents Throughout the World 3706
Private Placements and Restricted
Securities 3855
Securities and Federal Corporate Law
4232
Securities Law Review 4233
Tax Sheltered Investments 4570
Trademarks Throughout the World
4664
Trade Secrets and Know-How
Throughout the World 4675

BOARDROOM REPORTS, INC
500 5th Ave
New York, NY 10036

Boardroom Reports 568

BOBIT PUBLISHING CO
2500 Artesia Blvd
Redondo Beach, CA 90278

Automotive Fleet 429
Metropolitan 3205
School Bus Fleet 4192

BOND BUYER
1 State St Plaza
New York, NY 10004

Bond Buyer's Municipal Finance
Statistics Book 569.01
Daily Bond Buyer 1291
Money Manager 3271
Weekly Bond Buyer 4903

BONDHOLDER'S REGISTER
5 The White House, Beacon Rd
Crowborough, Sussex, England TN6
1AB

Bondholder's Register 571

BORDER PRESS AGENCY LTD
12 Lonsdale St
Carlisle, England CA1 1DD

Cumbria Weekly Digest 1266

R R BOWKER CO
1180 Ave of the Americas
New York, NY 10036

American Art Directory 155.01
American Book Publishing Record
161
American Book Trade Directory 162
American Library Directory 198
Association of Executive Recruiting
Consultants 340.01
Audiovisual Market Place 347
Book Marketing Handbook 571.01
Book Marketing Handbook: Tips and
Techniques for the Sale and
Promotion of Scientific, Technical,
Professional, and Scholarly Books
and Journals 571.02
Books in Print 575
Bowker Annual of Library and Book
Trade Information 580
Economic Regulation of Business and
Industry 1565
Energy Research Programs, 1980 1692
Forthcoming Books 2149
Industrial Research Laboratories of the
United States, 1979 2550
Information Industry Market Place: An
International Directory of
Information Products and Services
2573.01
International Book Trade Directory
2661.01
International Guide to Library,
Archival, and Information Science
Associations 2684

International Literary Market Place
2703
Literary Market Place (LMP) 3026
Magazine Industry Market Place: The
Directory of American Periodical
Publishing 3056.02
Magazines for Libraries 3058
Publishers and Distributors of the
United States 3938
Publishers' Trade List Annual 3940
Publishers Weekly 3941
Publishing and Bookselling 3942
Research Programs in the Medical
Sciences 4091.01
Scientific, Engineering, and Medical
Societies Publications in Print 4200
Scientific and Technical Books and
Serials in Print 1977 4199
Subject Guide to Books in Print 4485
Translation and Translators: An
International Directory and Guide
4689
Ulrich's International Periodicals
Directory 4737
Who Distributes What and Where: An
International Directory of Publishers,
Imprints, Agents and Distributors
4970
World Guide to Scientific Associations
and Learned Societies 5066
World Guide to Trade Associations
5067

BOYNTON & ASSOCIATES
Clifton House
Clifton, VA 22024

Model Retailer 3251

BRADFORD'S DIRECTORY
PO Box 276
Fairfax, VA 22030

Bradford's Directory of Marketing
Research Agencies & Management
Consultants in the US & the World
584

BRAMSON PUBLISHING CO
Box 101
Bloomfield Hills, MI 48013

Production 3864

**BRAZILIAN–AMERICAN
CHAMBER OF COMMERCE, INC**
22 W 48 St, Rm 603
New York, NY 10036

Brazilian–American Business
Review/Directory 585
US–Brazil Business Listing 4794.02

BRENNAN PUBLICATIONS
148 Birchover Way
Allestree, Derby, England

Media Reporter 3178

BRENTWOOD PUBLISHING CORP
825 S Barrington Ave
Los Angeles, CA 90049

Association and Society Manager
Magazine 335
Incentive Travel Manager 2479

C BREWER & CO LTD
Box 1826
Honolulu, HI 96801

C Brewer Today 588

**BRICKER'S INTERNATIONAL
DIRECTORY**
425 Family Farm Rd
Woodside, CA 94062

Bricker's International Directory of
University Executive Development
Programs 592

BRIGHAM YOUNG UNIVERSITY
c/o H Keith Hunt, 395 JKB
Provo, Utah 84602

Journal of Advertising 2819

BRITISH AGENTS REGISTER
23 Victoria Ave
Harrogate, Yorkshire, England HG1
5RE

British Commercial Agents Review
609

BRITISH COLUMBIA (CANADA)

**MINISTRY OF INDUSTRY AND
SMALL BUSINESS
DEVELOPMENT**
Parliament Buildings
Victoria BC, Canada V8V 1X4

British Columbia Business Bulletin
599.02
British Columbia Economic Activity,
1980 Review and Outlook 601.01
British Columbia Export/Import
Opportunities 601.02
British Columbia Facts and Statistics
602
British Columbia Industry and Small
Business News 602.01
British Columbia Manufacturers'
Directory 604

British Columbia Review and Outlook
607
Directory of Importers and
Manufacturers' Agents in British
Columbia 1980 1435
Directory of Public Buying Agencies in
British Columbia 1455
Establishing a Business 1742
External Trade Report 1864

*(BRITISH COLUMBIA, CANADA
END)*

BRITISH INST OF MANAGEMENT
Parker St
London, England WC2B 5PT

Management Review and Digest 3087

**BRITISH INTERNAL
COMBUSTION ENGINE
RESEARCH INST LTD**
111/112 Buckingham Ave
Slough, Berks, England

Abstracts from Technical and Patent
Publications 3

**BRITISH–ISRAEL CHAMBER OF
COMMERCE**
Information & Trade Center
126-134 Baker St
London, England W1M 1FH

British-Israel Trade Journal 615

**BRITISH PROPERTY
FEDERATION**
35 Catherine Place
London, England SW1E 6DY

Property Journal 3901

**BROADCASTING PUBLICATIONS
INC**
1735 De Sales St NW
Washington, DC 20036

Broadcasting 625
Broadcasting/Cable Yearbook 627

BROOKINGS INSTITUTION
1775 Massachusetts Ave NW
Washington, DC 20036

Brookings Papers on Economic Activity
629.01

BROOKLYN PUBLIC LIBRARY
Grand Army Plaza
Brooklyn, NY 11238

Service to Business & Industry 4268

BUILDING MAINTENANCE COST INFORMATION SERVICE
85–87 Clarence St
Kingston Upon Thames
Surrey, England KT1 1RB

BMCIS   566.01

BULGARIAN CHAMBER OF COMMERCE AND INDUSTRY
11a Stamboliiski Blvd
Sofia, Bulgaria   104

Economic News of Bulgaria   1556.01
List of Bulgarian Foreign Trade
　　Organizations   3025

BUREAU OF BUSINESS PRACTICE
24 Rope Ferry Rd
Waterford, CT 06386

Fair Employment Practices (FEP)
　　Guidelines   1878
Occupational Safety and Health Act
　　(OSHA) Compliance Letter   3564
Personnel Advisory Bulletin   3740
Purchasing Executive's Bulletin   3951
Safety Management   4158
Sales Manager's Bulletin   4174
Security Management   4243
Woman Executive's Bulletin   5011

BUREAU OF NATIONAL AFFAIRS, INC
1231 25th St NW
Washington, DC 20037

Affirmative Action Compliance Manual
　　for Federal Contractors   76.01
Air Pollution Control   125
Antitrust & Trade Regulation Report
　　271
ASPA Handbook of Personnel and
　　Industrial Relations   333.02
Bureau of National Affairs (BNA)
　　Policy & Practice Series   650
Bureau of National Affairs (BNA)
　　Patent, Trademark, & Copyright
　　Journal   649
Chemical Regulation Reporter   928
Collective Bargaining Negotiations &
　　Contracts   977
Construction Labor Report   1132
Corporate Practice Series   1211
Daily Labor Report   1301
Daily Report for Executives   1305
Daily Tax Report   1307
Employment and Training Reporter
　　1654
Energy Users Report   1701
Environment Reporter   1730

Equal Employment Opportunity
　　Commission (EEOC)—Affirmative
　　Action Manuals   1732
Export Shipping Manual   1851
Fair Employment Practice Service
　　1877
Federal Contracts Report   1918
Government Employee Relations
　　Report   2240
Government Manager   2245
Housing & Development Reporter
　　2410
International Environment Reporter
　　2677.01
International Trade Reporter's US
　　Import Weekly   2740.01
Job Safety and Health   2811.01
Labor Arbitration Reports   2926
Labor Relations Reporter   2943
Law Reprints Trade Regulation Series
　　2988
Media Law Reporter   3175
Mine Safety and Health Reporter
　　3234
Noise Regulation Reporter   3529
Occupational Safety and Health
　　Reporter   3567
Pension Reporter   3727
Product Safety & Liability Reporter
　　3876
Retail Services Labor Report   4112
Roberts' Dictionary of Industrial
　　Relations, 1971 edition   4138
Securities Regulation & Law Report
　　4235
Sewage Treatment Construction Grants
　　Manual   4271
Tax Management Compensation
　　Planning Journal   4559
Tax Management International Journal
　　4560
Tax Management Program   4561
Union Labor Report   4752
US Export Weekly   4800
US Patents Quarterly   4814
Washington Financial Reports   4887
Water Pollution Control   4899
White Collar Report   4968

BUSINESS COMMUNICATIONS INC
PO Box 4-AA
Anchorage, AK 99509

Alaska Business Newsletter   137
Alaska Industry   139

BUSINESS COUNCIL OF NEW YORK STATE, INC
10 State St
Albany, NY 12207

Capital Journal   857.01
Omnibus   3619.01

BUSINESS GRADUATES ASSN
87 Jermyn St
London, England SW1Y 69JD

Business Graduate   685

BUSINESS INTERNATIONAL CORP
1 Dag Hammarskjold Plaza
New York, NY 10017

Asia/Pacific Compensation Survey   330
BI/Metrics   553.01
Business Asia   668
Business China   674
Business Eastern Europe   677
Business Europe   681
Business International   696
Business International (BI)/Data   697
Business International (BI) Forecasts
　　for World Markets   698
Business International Money Report
　　699
Business International Washington
　　(BIW)   699.01
Business Latin America   700
Doing Business with Eastern Europe
　　1489
European Compensation Survey   1771
Executive Living Costs in Major Cities
　　Worldwide   1806
FFO/Latin America (FFO/LA)   1982
Financing Foreign Operations   2035
Investing, Licensing, and Trading
　　Conditions Abroad   2755
Iran Service   2779.01
Research Reports   4092

BUSINESS PUBLISHERS, INC
PO Box 1067
Silver Spring, MD 20910

Air/Water Pollution Report   131
Clean Water Report   959
Coal Daily   970
Ecology USA   1533.01
Emergency Preparedness News
　　1640.01
Energy Resources Report   1693
Fair Employment Report   1879
Federal Contract Opportunities:
　　Energy/Environment   1917.01
Federal Research Report   1934.02
Fusion Power Report   2203.01
Hazardous Waste News   2353.01
Job Safety & Health Report   2812
Land Use Planning Report   2965
Latin American Energy Report
　　2974.01

Minerals Week   3233
Noise Control Report   3528
Nuclear Waste News   3554.01
Practical Solar   3822.01
Public Transit Report   3937
Sludge Newsletter   4297
Solar Energy Intelligence Report
  4326.02
Solid Waste Reference Service   4328.01
Solid Waste Report   4329
State Regulation Report: Toxic
  Substances & Hazardous Waste
  4405.01
Toxic Materials News   4643.01
Toxic Materials Reference Service
  4643.02
Toxic Materials Transport   4643.03
US Census Report   4794.03
US Rail News   4815
World Environmental Directory
  5063.01

BUSINESS SCIENCE CORP
1700 Ygnacio Valley Rd, Suite 222
Walnut Creek, CA 94598

Journal of Applied Management   2823

BUSINESS SURVEYS LTD
PO Box 21
Dorking, Surrey, England RH5 4EE

Reports Index   4074.01
Research Index   4088

BUTTERWORTH & CO LTD
2265 Midland Ave
Scarborough, Ont, Canada M1P 4S1

Canadian Current Tax   787
Canadian Income Tax   799

CAHNERS PUBLISHING CO, INC
221 Columbus Ave
Boston, MA 02116

Appliance Manufacturer   285
Brick & Clay Record   591
Building Design & Construction   637
Building Supply News   642
Ceramic Data Book   891
Ceramic Industry   893
Construction Equipment   1127
Electronic Business   1619
Foodservice Equipment Dealer   2098
Institutions/VFM   2603
Modern Materials Handling   3256
Modern Railroads   3265
Package Engineering   3681
Plastics World   3783
Professional Builder   3883
Purchasing   3949

Security Distributing & Marketing
  (SDM)   4240
Security World   4250
Service World International   4270
Traffic Management   4681
US Industrial Directory   4806

**CALIFORNIA CREDIT UNION
LEAGUE**
2322 S Garey Ave
Pomona, CA 91766

California Credit Union League
  (CCUL) Digest   735

**CALIFORNIA SOCIETY OF
CERTIFIED PUBLIC
ACCOUNTANTS**
1000 Welch Rd
Palo Alto, CA 94304

Outlook   3651.01

CALLAHAN PUBLICATIONS
PO Box 3751
Washington, DC 20007

Military Research Letter   3229
Missile/Ordnance Letter   3244
Renegotiation/Management Letter
  4060
Space Letter   4352
Underwater Letter   4741
Washington Environmental Protection
  Report   4886

**CAMBRIDGE SCIENTIFIC
ABSTRACTS**
6611 Kenilworth Ave, Suite 437
Riverdale, MD 20840

Computer & Information Systems
  Abstracts Journal   1072
Electronics & Communications
  Abstracts Journal   1634
Safety Science Abstracts Journal   4161
Science Research Abstracts Journal,
  Parts A&B   4197
Solid State Abstracts Journal   4328

CAMBRIDGE UNIVERSITY PRESS
32 E 57th St
New York, NY 10022

British Journal of Nutrition   617
Economic Journal   1554
Experimental Agriculture   1814
Journal of Agricultural Science   2821
Journal of Dairy Research   2844
Journal of the Marine Biological
  Association of the UK   2894

QUENTIN CAMERON
PO Box 376
Hamilton Central, Qld 4007, Australia

Oil and Gas Bulletin   3594

CANADA

**CANADIAN INTERNATIONAL
DEVELOPMENT AGENCY**
200 Promenade Du Portage
Hull, PQ, Canada K1A OG4

Annual Aid Review   236

DEPT OF AGRICULTURE
Regional Development & International
Affairs Branch
Ottawa, Ont, Canada K1A 0C5

Agriculture Abroad   112
Canadian Farm Economics   792

**DEPARTMENT OF
COMMUNICATIONS**
300 Slater St
Ottawa, Ont, Canada K1A 0C8

In Search/En Quete   2586

**DEPT OF INDUSTRY, TRADE,
AND COMMERCE**
235 Queen St
Ottawa, Canada K1A 0H5

Canada Commerce   744

DEPT OF LABOUR
Ottawa, Ont, Canada K1A 0J2

Collective Bargaining Review   978
Industrial Relations Research in
  Canada   2546
Labour Organizations in Canada   2954
Labour Standards in Canada   2957
Wage Rates, Salaries, & Hours of
  Labour   4872
Women in the Labour Force: Facts &
  Figures   5014

**LABOUR CANADA,
COMMUNICATIONS SERVICES
DIRECTORATE**
Ottawa, Ont, Canada K1A 0J2

Directory of Labour Organizations in
  Canada, 1980   1439.01
Guidelines for the Administration of
  the Canada Noise Control
  Regulations, 1975   2283
Legislative Review   3001
Strikes and Lockouts in Canada 1979
  4480

Debates of the House of Commons 1346

Debates of the Senate 1347

Decisions and Orders of the Motor Vehicle Committee 1349

Decisions and Orders of the Water Transport Committee 1351

Decisions of the Air Transport Committee 1353

Decisions of the Railway Transport Committee 1354

Digest of Benefit Entitlement and Principles/Unemployment Insurance 1385

Export and Import Permits Act Handbook 1820

Food and Drug Act and Regulations (Departmental Consolidation)/ Complete Service 2080

Government of Canada Telephone Directory/National Capital Region 2247

Handbook of Air Carrier Legislation 2321.01

Hazardous Products Act and Regulations/Office Consolidation 2353

International Perspectives 2718

Journal of the Fisheries Research Board of Canada 2890

Market Research Handbook 3138

North 3533

Optimum/A Forum for Management 3633

Patent Office Record/Canada 3703

Perspectives Canada III 3753.01

Regulations for Transportation of Dangerous Commodities by Rail 4057

Trade Marks Journal 4663

(CANADA END)

CANADA REPORT
Box 5040
Toronto, Ont, Canada M5W 1N4

Canada Report 761

CANADA JAPAN TRADE COUNCIL
Suite 903, 75 Albert St
Ottawa, Ont, Canada K1P 5E7

Canada–Japan Trade Council Newsletter 756

CANADA LAW BOOK LTD
240 Edward St
Aurora, Ont, Canada L4G 3S9

British Columbia Statute Citator 608
Canada Statute Citator 765

Canadian Business Law Journal 779
Canadian Patent Reporter 826
Labour Arbitration Cases 2949
Ontario Statute Citator 3626

CANADA–UK CHAMBER OF COMMERCE
British Columbia House
3 Lower Regent St
London, England SW1Y 4NZ

Canada–UK Trade News 770
Canada–UK Year Book 771

CANADIAN ANALYST LTD
32 Front St W
Toronto, Ont, Canada M5J 1C5

Canadian Daily Stock Charts 788
Graphoscope 2261
Point and Figure Digest 3791
Point & Figure Summary 3792

CANADIAN ARCTIC RESOURCES COMMITTEE
46 Elgin St, Room 11
Ottawa, Ont, Canada K1P 5K6

Arctic Alternatives 301
Northern Perspectives 3540

CANADIAN BROTHERHOOD OF RAILWAY, TRANSPORT, & GENERAL WORKERS
2300 Carling Ave
Ottawa, Ont, Canada K2B 7G1

Canadian Transport 841

CANADIAN CERTIFIED GENERAL ACCOUNTANTS' ASSN
740-1176 W Georgia St
Vancouver, BC, Canada V6E 4A2

CGA Magazine 896

CANADIAN ENGINEERING PUBLICATIONS LTD
32 Front St W, Suite 501
Toronto, Ont, Canada M5J 2H9

Engineering Digest 1709
New Equipment News 3445
Volume Retail Merchandising 4867

CANADIAN FEDERATION OF BUSINESS & PROFESSIONAL WOMEN'S CLUBS
No 115, 56 Sparks St
Ottawa, Ont, Canada K1P 5A9

Business & Professional Woman 663

CANADIAN IMPERIAL BANK OF COMMERCE
Commerce Court West
Toronto, Ont, Canada M5L 1A2

Spectrum 4359.01

CANADIAN IMPORTERS ASSN, INC
60 Harbour St, 5th Floor
Toronto, Ont, Canada M5J 1B7

Import Canada: A Guide to Canadian Importing 2442.01
Import/Export File 2442.02
Importweek 2475

CANADIAN INDEPENDENT ADJUSTERS' CONFERENCE
55 Queen St E, Suite 1404
Toronto, Ont, Canada M5C 1R6

Canadian Independent Adjuster 800

CANADIAN INST OF CHARTERED ACCOUNTANTS
250 Bloor St E
Toronto, Ont, Canada M4W 1G5

CA Magazine 739.01
Canadian Institute of Chartered Accountants/Canadian Bar Association (CICA/CBA) Recommendations on the Income Tax Act 804
CICA Handbook 945.02
International Accounting Standards 2654
Management Advisory Services Manual, 1977 3071
Practice Administration Manual 3823
Professional Engagement Manual 3887

CANADIAN INSTITUTE OF MANAGEMENT
2175 Sheppard Ave E, Suite 110
Willowdale, Ont, Canada M2J 1W8

Canadian Manager 815

CANADIAN LABOUR CONGRESS
2841 Riverside Dr
Ottawa, Ont, Canada K1V 8X7

Canadian Labour 812

CANADIAN MANUFACTURERS ASSN
1 Yonge St
Toronto, Ont, Canada M5E 1J9

Canadian Trade Index 1981 840

**CANADIAN NEWSPAPER
SERVICES INTERNATIONAL, LTD**
55 Eglinton Ave E, Suite 604
Toronto, Ont, Canada M4P 1G8

Blue Book of Canadian Business   562

**CANADIAN OFFICE MACHINE
DEALERS ASSN**
15 Dyas Rd
Don Mills, Ont, Canada M3B 1V7

Canadian Office Machine Dealers Assn
   Key   823

CANADIAN REAL ESTATE ASSN
99 Duncan Mill Rd
Don Mills, Ont, Canada M3B 1Z2

Canadian Real Estate   829.01
Canadian Real Estate Journal   829.02

CANADIAN TAX FOUNDATION
130 Adelaide St W, Box 6
Toronto, Ont, Canada M5H 3P5

Canadian Tax Journal   836

**CAPITAL COMMUNICATIONS
LTD**
Suite 306, 77 Metcalfe St
Ottawa, Ont, Canada K1P 5L6

Ottawa R&D Report   3651

CAPITAL INTERNATIONAL SA
15 rue de Cendrier, 1201
Geneva, Switzerland

Capital International Perspective   856

CAPITAL PUBLISHING CORP
Box 348
Wellesley Hills, MA 02181

Guide to Selling a Business   2302
Guide to Venture Capital Sources
   2309
Source Guide for Borrowing Capital
   4334
Venture Capital   4846

CAPITOL PUBLICATIONS, INC
Suite G-12, 2430 Pennsylvania Ave NW
Washington, DC 20037

Blue Chip Economic Indicators   563.01
Economic Opportunity Report
   1556.02
Education and Work   1593
Health Grants and Contracts Weekly
   2360
Manpower and Vocational Education
   Weekly   3098
Schechter Report/Labs   4191.01

Small Business Tax Control   4302.01
Tax Exempt News   4551.01
United States Oil Week   4813.02

CARIBOOK LTD
1255 Yonge St
Toronto, Ont, Canada M4W 1Z3

Caribbean Business News   863
Caribbean Year Book   864

CARROLL PUBLISHING CO
1058 Thomas Jefferson St NW
Washington, DC 20007

Defense Industry Organization Service
   1355.01
Energy Executive Directory   1680.01
Federal Executive Directory   1925
Federal Organization Service
   Military/Civil Charts   1933
State Executive Directory   4389.01

CARSWELL CO, LTD
2330 Midland Ave
Agincourt, Ont, Canada M1S 1P7

Business Law Reports Volume 1   702
Canadian Tax News   837

MANUEL CASIANO, INC
Box 6253, Loiza St Station
Santurce, Puerto Rico 00914

Caribbean Business   862

CASSELL AND CO LTD
35 Red Lion Square
London, England WC1 4SG

Modern Publicity   3263

CATALYST
PO Box 547
Fallbrook, CA 92028

International Invention Register   2687

CBD RESEARCH LTD
154 High St
Beckenham, Kent, England BR3 1EA

Current African Directories   1269
Current British Directories   1270
Current European Directories   1275
Statistics—Asia & Australasia   4450

CBIA SERVICE CORP. *See* Conn
Business and Industry Service Corp

CB MEDIA LTD
56 The Esplanade, Suite 214
Toronto, Ont, Canada M5E 1R5

Canadian Business   778

CCH AUSTRALIA LTD. *See*
Commerce Clearing House, Inc

CCH CANADIAN LTD
6 Garamond Ct
Don Mills, Ont, Canada M3C 1Z5

British Columbia Corporations Law
   Guide   601
British Columbia Real Estate Law
   Guide   607
Canada Corporations Law Reports
   747
Canada Income Tax Guide   753
Canadian Business Management
   Development   780
Canadian Commercial Law Guide
   784.01
Canadian Corporate Secretary's Guide
   786.01
Canadian Employment Benefits and
   Pension Guide   789
Canadian Employment Safety and
   Health Guide   789.01
Canadian Energy News   790
Canadian Environmental Control
   Newsletter   791
Canadian Estate Planning and
   Administration Reports   791.01
Canadian Government Programs and
   Services   796
Canadian Income Tax Act, Regulations,
   & Rulings   798
Canadian Industrial Relations &
   Personnel Developments   802
Canadian Insurance Law Reports   807
Canadian Labour Law Reports   813
Canadian Master Tax Guide   816
Canadian Product Safety Guide   829
Canadian Sales Tax Reports   833
Canadian Securities Law Reports   834
Canadian Tax Reports   838
Dominion Report Service   1494
Dominion Tax Cases   1495
Ontario Corporations Law Guide
   3622
Ontario Real Estate Law Guide   3623
Ottawa Letter   3650
Provincial Tax Reports   3910
Sales Tax Guide—Canada   4178

**CENTER FOR BUSINESS
INFORMATION**
7, Rue Buffon 75005
Paris, France

European Directory of Business
   Information Sources & Services
   1773

CENTER FOR SCIENCE IN THE PUBLIC INTEREST
1755 S St NW
Washington, DC 20009

Nutrition Action   3558.01

CENTRAL BANK OF IRELAND
PO Box No 559, Dame St
Dublin 2, Ireland

Central Bank of Ireland Quarterly
   Bulletin and Annual Report   889

CHAIN MERCHANDISER
65 Crocker Ave
Piedmont, CA 94611

Chain Merchandiser Magazine   899

CHAMBER OF COMMERCE OF HAWAII
Dillingham Transportation Bldg
735 Bishop St
Honolulu, HI 96813

Directory of Manufacturers, State of
   Hawaii 1981–82   1443
Directory of Shopping Centers in
   Hawaii   1456
Hawaii Facts and Figures   2348
Legislative Action Bulletin   2997
Voice of Business   4864
Who's Who in Government   4986

CHAMBER OF COMMERCE OF THE UNITED STATES
1615 H St NW
Washington, DC 20062

Association Taxation   342
Congressional Action   1111
Financial Management Handbook for
   Associations   2006
International Report   2726
Nation's Business   3414
Public Affairs Report   3922
Washington Report   4889

CHAMBRE DE COMMERCE FRANCAISE AU CANADA
1080 Beaver Hall Hill, Suite 826
Montreal, Que, Canada H2Z 1S8

Action Canada France   45

H V CHAPMAN & ASSOC LTD
Suite 700, 2 Bloor St W
Toronto, Ont, Canada M4W 1A1

Management Compensation in Canada,
   1980; The Remuneration of Chief
   Executive Officers in Canada, 1980;
   and Sales Representatives
   Compensation in Canada, 1980
   3075

CHARLESON PUBLICATIONS CO
124 E 40th St
New York, NY 10016

Product Marketing   3875

ALAIN CHARLES PUBLISHING LTD
27 Wilfred St
London, England SW1E 6PR

African Textiles   79.03
Far Eastern Technical Review   1892.01
Media International   3174
TV World   4735.01
West African Farming & Food
   Processing   4948.01
West African Technical Review   4949

CHART ANALYSIS LTD
37-39 St Andrew's Hill
London, England EC4V 5DD

Commodities Weekly Technical Report
   and Currency Exchange Rates   1024
Commodity Trading Recommendations
   1032.01
Currency   1268.01
United Kingdom International Point &
   Figure Library   4755.01

CHARTCRAFT, INC
1 West Ave
Larchmont, NY 10538

Chartcraft Commodity Service   910
Chartcraft Weekly Service   912

CHARTER PUBLISHING
641 Lexington Ave
New York, NY 10022

Discount Merchandiser   1464

CHARTERED INSURANCE INST
20 Aldermanbury
London, England EC2V 7HY

Chartered Insurance Institute (CII)
   Journal   914

CHASE TRADE INFORMATION CORP
1 World Trade Center
78th Floor
New York, NY 10048

Arab Aid: Who Gets It, For What, and
   How   295
Arab Investors: Who They Are, What
   They Buy, and Where   296
Chase World Guide for Exporters and
   Export Credit Reports   918
Developing Business in the Middle East
   and North Africa   1371
International Trade Financing:
   Conventional and Nonconventional
   Practices   2739.01
Trade and Credit: Problems and
   Resolutions in the Middle East and
   North Africa, in Asia and the Pacific
   and in Latin America   4646.01

CHAUNTER PUBLICATIONS LTD
PO Box 17-159
Wellington, New Zealand

New Zealand Trade Report   3513.01
Property   3898

CHEMICAL ABSTRACTS SERVICE
2540 Olentangy River Rd
PO Box 3012
Columbus, OH 43210

Chemical Abstracts   918.01
Chemical Industry Notes   925.02

CHEMICAL DAILY CO LTD
19016 Shibaura 3-Chome
Minato-Ku
Tokyo 108, Japan

Japan Chemical Annual   2795.01
Japan Chemical Directory   2795.02
Japan Chemical Week   2795.03

CHICAGO ASSN OF COMMERCE & INDUSTRY
130 S Michigan Ave
Chicago, IL 60603

Chicagoland Development   936
Commerce   993

CHICAGO MERCANTILE EXCHANGE
444 W Jackson Blvd
Chicago, IL 60606

Chicago Mercantile Exchange Yearbook
   937
International Monetary Market
   Yearbook   2713

CHILTON CO
Chilton Way
Radnor, PA 19089

Accent   6
Automotive Industries   430

Automotive Industries/International 431
Automotive Marketing 433
Chilton's Market/Plant Data Bank 939
Chilton's Oil & Gas Energy 940
Commercial Car Journal 1000
Control Equipment Master 1188
Distribution 1468
Electronic Component News 1620
Food Engineering 2085
Food Engineering International 2086
Hardware Age 2343
Instrument & Apparatus News 2604
Instruments & Control Systems 2606
Iron Age 2782
Iron Age Metalworking International (IAMI) 2783
Jewelers' Circular-Keystone 2807
Motor/Age 3325
Outlook 3652
Owner Operator 3671
Product Design & Development 3863
Review of Optometry 4126
Specialist 4353.01
Target Twenty 4529
Truck & Off-Highway Industries 4722.01
Update 4826

CITIBANK
399 Park Ave
New York, NY 10043

Citabank Monthly Economic Letter 949
Economic Week 1575
Sound of the Economy 4332

CITICORP
399 Park Ave
New York, NY 10043

Citicorp Reports 950

CLEMSON UNIV
College of Industrial Management & Textile Science, Sirrine Hall
Clemson, SC 29631

Clemson University Textile Marketing Letter 961
Review of Industrial Management and Textile Science 4123.01

CLEMSON UNIVERSITY
Cooperative Extension Service
Dept of Agricultural Economics and Rural Sociology
Clemson, SC 29631

Palmetto Economics 3689

CLEWORTH PUBLISHING CO, INC
1 River Rd
Cos Cob, CT 06807

United States Banker 4794

COLLEGE PLACEMENT COUNCIL, INC
Box 2263
Bethlehem, PA 18001

College Placement Annual 981
Directory of Career Planning and Placement Offices 1416
Directory of College Recruiting Personnel 1417.01
Journal of College Placement 2833
Salary Survey 4164

COLUMBIA PUBLISHING & DESIGN
Box 1467
127 W Yakima Ave
Yakima, WA 98907

Ag Marketer 88.02

COLUMBIA UNIVERSITY
Graduate School of Business
8th Floor, Uris Hall
New York, NY 10027

Columbia Journal of World Business 992

COLUMBIA UNIVERSITY PRESS
562 W 113th St
New York, NY 10025

Foundation Directory 2154

COMMERCE CLEARING HOUSE, INC
4025 W Peterson Ave
Chicago IL 60646

Accountancy Law Reports 17
Accountants Securities and Exchange Commission (SEC) Practice Manual 27
Accounting Articles 30
Advance Session Laws 64
All-State Sales Tax Reports 147
Americn Institute of Certified Public Accountants (AICPA) Professional Standards—Accounting 188
American Institute of Certified Public Accountants (AICPA) Professional Standards—Auditing, Management Advisory Services, Tax Practice 189
American Institute of Certified Public Accountants (AICPA) Professional Standards—Ethics & Bylaws 190

American Stock Exchange Guide 208
Australian Corporate Affairs Reports 391
Australian Estate and Gift Duty Reports 398
Australian Federal Tax Reports 401
Australian Master Tax Guide 409
Australian National Economic & Legislative Report 413
Australian Sales Tax Guide 414
Australian Securities Law Reports 415
Australian Tax Cases 417
Australian Trade Practices Reports 419
Automobile Insurance 428
Aviation Cases 436
Aviation Law Reports 438
Balance of Payments Reports 452
Bankruptcy Law Reports 500
Blue Sky Law Reports 566
Board of Contract Appeals Decisions 567
Boston Stock Exchange Guide 578
British Tax Guide 623
Business Law Cases for Australians 701
California Eligible Securities List 736
Capital Changes Reports 853
Chicago Board Options Exchange Guide 935
Code and Regulations 976
College and University Reports 980
Commercial Laws (Mexican) 1004
Commodity Futures Law Reports 1027
Common Market Reports 1039
Communication & Transportation Laws (Mexican) 1041
Compliance Guide for Plan Administrators 1066
Congressional Index 1114
Congressional Legislative Reporting 1115
Consumer Credit Guide 1152
Consumer Product Safety Guide 1168
Contract Appeals Decisions 1186
Copyright Revision Act of 1976 1202
Corporation Law Guide 1220
Cost Accounting Standards Guide 1225
Daily Legislative Report 1302
Doing Business in Europe 1486
Employment Practices 1661.01
Employment Practices Decisions 1662
Employment Safety and Health Guide 1665
Energy Management 1686
Equal Employment Opportunity Commission (EEOC) Compliance Manual 1733
Estate Planning Review 1752

**COMMERCE CLEARING HOUSE
CANADIAN LTD See CCH Canadian
Ltd**

COMMERCE PUBLICATIONS LTD
Manek Makal
6th Floor
90 Veer Nariman Rd
PO Box 11017
Bombay 400 020, India

**COMMERCIAL BANK OF
AUSTRALIA LTD**
114 Collins St
Melbourne, Vic 3000, Australia

COMMERCIAL WEST
5100 Edina Industrial Blvd
Edina, MN 55435

**COMMISSION OF THE
EUROPEAN COMMUNITIES**
Office for Official Publications of the
European Communities
CP 1003,
Luxembourg 1, Luxembourg

Economic Situation in the Community
1571
Energy Statistics Yearbook 1978   1697
Euro-Abstracts: Scientific and Technical
Publications and Patents   1759
Euro-Abstracts. Section II. Coal and
Steel   1760
Eurostatistics   1792.02
Graphs and Notes on the Economic
Situation in the Community   2262
Industrial Statistics plus Yearbook
2553
Inventory of Taxes, 1979 edition
2754.01
Iron and Steel   2784
Pig-iron and Steel: Basis Prices   3771
Reports of Cases Before the Court
4075
Managements in the Community
4100.01
Statistical Office of the European
Communities Balances of Payments
Geographical Breakdown   4433
Statistical Office of the European
Communities. Basis Statistics of the
Community   4433.01
Statistical Office of the European
Communities. Monthly External
Trade Bulletin   4434
Statistical Office of the European
Communities. National Accounts
ESA   4435
Trade Union Information   4678
Yearbook of Agricultural Statistics
5090.01

**COMMITTEE FOR ECONOMIC
DEVELOPMENT**
477 Madison Ave
New York, NY 10022

Committee for Economic Development
Newsletter   1012

**COMMITTEE FOR MONETARY
RESEARCH & EDUCATION, INC**
Box 1630
Greenwich, CT 06830

Committee for Monetary Research &
Education (CMRE) Money Tracts
1013

COMMODITIES MAGAZINE, INC
219 Parkade
Cedar Falls, IA 50613

Commodities   1022

**COMMODITY INFORMATION
SERVICE CO**
33 W Ridge Pike
Limerick, PA 19468

Daily Trader's Guide   1308

**COMMODITY RESEARCH
BUREAU**
1 Liberty Plaza
New York, NY 10006

Commodity Chart Service   1026
Commodity Year Book   1033
Commodity Yearbook Statistical
Abstract Service   1034
Futures Market Service   2205

**COMMUNICATION CHANNELS,
INC**
6285 Barfield Rd
Atlanta, GA 30328

Adhesives Age   52.01
Apparel South   282.02
Container News   1181
Elastomerics   1599
Fence Industry   1980.01
Modern Paint & Coatings   3258
National Real Estate Investor   3402.01
Pension World   3732
Shopping Center World   4283.01
Solid Wastes Management   4329.01
Specialty Salesman   4358
Trusts and Estates   4730.01

**COMMUNICATIONS MARKETING,
INC**
5100 Edina Industrial Blvd
Edina, MN 55435

Feed Industry Red Book   1978
Feed Industry Review   1979
Grain Age   2253

**COMMUNITY DEVELOPMENT
SERVICES, INC**
399 National Press Bldg
Washington, DC 20045

Community Development Digest   1049
Housing Affairs Letter   2408
Housing Market Report   2413
Managing Housing Letter   3095.01
Neighborhood & Rehab Report   3427

**COMPUTER DIRECTIONS
ADVISORS, INC**
8750 Georgia Ave
Silver Spring, MD 20910

Bank Pooled Funds   498
Insurance Company Funds   2616

Mutual Fund Performance Review
3346
Spectrum Convertibles—Holding Survey
of Convertible Bonds and
Convertable Preferred Stocks
4359.02
Spectrum One—Investment Company
Stock Holdings Survey   4360
Spectrum Two—Investment Company
Portfolios   4360.01
Spectrum Three—Institutional Stock
Holdings Survey   4361.01
Spectrum Four—Institutional Portfolios
4361.02
Spectrum Five—Five Percent
Ownership   4361.03
Spectrum Six—Insider Ownership
4361.04

**CONFEDERATION OF
AUSTRALIAN INDUSTRY**
PO Box 14
Canberra City, ACT 2600 Australia

Confederation of Australian Industry
(CAI) News   1098

**CONFEDERATION OF BRITISH
INDUSTRY**
Centre Point, 103 New Oxford St
London, England WC1A 1DU

Confederation of British Industry (CBI)
Economic Situation Report   1099
Confederation of British Industry (CBI)
Education and Training Bulletin
1100
Confederation of British Industry (CBI)
Industrial Trends Survey   1101
Confederation of British Industry (CBI)
Members Bulletin   1102
Confederation of British Industry (CBI)
Overseas Reports   1103
West European Living Costs 1977
4952

**CONFEDERATION OF IRISH
INDUSTRY**
Confederation House, Kildare St
Dublin 2, Ireland

Confederation of Irish Industry (CII)
Economic Trends   1106
Confederation of Irish Industry
(CII/ESRI) Business Forecast   1107
Confederation of Irish Industry (CII)
Newsletter   1108
Food Processing in Ireland   2095

CONFERENCE BOARD, INC
845 3rd Ave
New York, NY 10022

COOPERATIVE PRESS LTD
Progress House, 418 Chester Rd
Manchester, England M16 9HP

Co-Operative News 1195
Coop Marketing & Management 1197

COOPERS & LYBRAND
1251 Ave of the Americas
New York, NY 10020

Coopers & Lybrand Banker 1196
Coopers & Lybrand Newsletter
  1196.01
Federal Petroleum Regulatory
  Newsletter 1933.01
Insurance Update 2636.01
Ireland International Reference Manual
  2779.02
Japan International Reference Manual
  2802.02
Real Estate Newsletter 4023.01
Retail Roundup 4109
Savings and Loan Letter 4186.01
Securities Update 4236.01

COPLEY NEWSPAPERS
7776 Ivanhoe Ave
PO Box 1530
La Jolla, CA 92038

South Bay Economic Review 4342
Union-Tribune Annual Review of San
  Diego Business Activity 4753
Union-Tribune Index 4754

CORDOVAN CORP
5314 Bingle Rd
Houston, TX 77092

Atlanta Business Chronicle 343
Dallas/Fort Worth Business 1314.01
Houston Business Journal 2417
Houston Public Companies Directory
  2418
Los Angeles Business Journal 3046.01
Miami Business Journal 3208
Phoenix Business Journal 3765.05
San Diego Business Journal 4179
San Francisco Business Journal 4180
Seattle Business Journal 4218

**CORNELL UNIVERSITY,
GRADUATE SCHOOL OF
BUSINESS AND PUBLIC
ADMINISTRATION**
Ithaca, NY 14853

Administrative Science Quarterly 59

**CORNELL UNIVERSITY, NY
STATE SCHOOL OF INDUSTRY &
LABOR RELATIONS**
Ithaca, NY 14853

Industrial & Labor Relations Review
  2509

CORPCOM SERVICES, INC
112 E 31st St
New York, NY 10016

Corporate Communications Report
  1204

**CORPUS INFORMATION
SERVICES LTD**
151 Bloor St W
Toronto, Ont, Canada M5S 1S4

Canadian Occupational Health & Safety
  News 820.02
Canadian Occupational Safety and
  Health Legislation 821
Corpus Administrative Index 1223
Corpus Almanac of Canada 1224
Corpus Chemical Report 1224.01
Eco/Log Canadian Pollution
  Legislation 1532
Eco/Log Week 1533
Energy Analects 1676
Polyfacts 3806
Public Sector 3935

COTTON GIN & OIL MILL PRESS
PO Box 18092
Dallas, TX 75218

Cotton Gin and Oil Mill Press 1229

**COUNCIL OF BETTER BUSINESS
BUREAUS, INC**
1150 17 St NW
Washington, DC 20036

News & Views 3461

**COUNCIL OF STATE
GOVERNMENTS**
Iron Works Pike, PO Box 11910
Lexington, KY 40578

Book of the States 572
State Administration officials (Classified
  by Functions) 4383
State Elective Officials and the
  Legislatures 4389
State Government 4391
State Government News 4392
State Government Research Checklist
  4392.01
State Headlines 4393

State Legislative Leadership,
  Committees and Staff (RM-664)
  4395
Suggested State Legislation 4490

**COWAN INVESTMENT SURVEY
PTY LTD**
405 Bourke St
Melbourne, Vic 3000 Australia

Midas 3215

**CRAIN AUTOMOTIVE GROUP,
INC**
965 E Jefferson Ave
Detroit, MI 48207

Automotive News 434

CRAIN COMMUNICATIONS, INC
740 Rush St
Chicago, IL 60611

Advertising Age 66
Business Insurance 695
Industrial Marketing 2533
Pensions & Investments Age 3729

**CRAMB TARIFF SERVICES ACT
PTY LTD**
PO Box 179
Civic Sq, ACT 2608, Australia

Tariff Brief 4530
Tariff Insight 4531

CRANE, RUSSAK & CO, INC
3 E 44th St
New York, NY 10017

Coastal Zone Management Journal
  974
Digital Systems for Industrial
  Automation 1396.01
Energy Sources 1695
Energy Systems and Policy 1698
Information Society 2575
Ocean Development and International
  Law 3570

**CREATIVE RESEARCH GROUP,
INC**
82 W Main St
Ramsey, NJ 07446

Jersey Business Review 2806

**CREATIVE STRATEGIES
INTERNATIONAL**
4340 Stevens Creek Blvd
Suite 275
San Jose, CA 95129

Technology Growth Markets and
  Opportunities 4581.01

CREDIT UNION NATIONAL ASSN, INC
Communications Division, PO Box 431B
Madison, WI 53701

Credit Union Executive   1249
Credit Union Magazine   1250
Credit Union Manager Newsletter
   1251

A C CROFT INC
PO Box 2440
Costa Mesa, CA 92627

Personnel Journal   3744

CRONER PUBLICATIONS, INC
211-03 Jamaica Ave
Queens Village, NY 11428

Croner's Reference Book for Exporters
   1256
Croner's Reference Book for World
   Traders   1257
Croner's Road Transport Operation
   1258
Employment Digest   1658
Trade Directories of the World   4654

CROSSROADS PRESS, INC
PO Box 833 Honolulu, HI 96808

All About Business in Hawaii   145
Pacific Business News   3677
Taxes of Hawaii   4548

CURTIS GUILD & CO PUBLISHERS, INC
88 Broad St
Boston, MA 02110

Commercial Bulletin   999

CURTIS INTERNATIONAL LTD
1100 Waterway Blvd
Indianapolis, IN 46202

Indiana Business Magazine   2503

CW COMMUNICATIONS, INC
375 Cochituate Rd, PO Box 880
Framingham, MA 01701

Computer Business News   1073
Computer Management—United
   Kingdom   1080
Computerworld   1089
Info World   2576.01

PETER DAG INVESTMENT LETTER
65 Lakefront Dr
Akron, OH 44319

Peter Dag Investment Letter   3753.02

DAILY JOURNAL PUBLICATIONS
210 S Spring St
Los Angeles, CA 90012

Journal of Commerce Review   2837

DALLAS PUBLIC LIBRARY
Business and Technology Division
1954 Commerce St
Dallas, TX 75201

Business Information for Dallas   691

DANA CHASE PUBLICATIONS, INC
York St at Park Ave
Elmhurst, IL 60126

Appliance Magazine   284

DARTNELL CORP
4660 Ravenswood Ave
Chicago, IL 60640

Dartnell Advertising Managers'
   Handbook, 2nd edition 1977   1317
Dartnell Direct Mail and Mail Order
   Handbook, 3rd edition 1980   1318
Dartnell Marketing Manager's
   Handbook, 1973 edition   1319
Dartnell Public Relations Handbook,
   2nd edition 1979   1321
Dartnell Sales and Marketing Executive
   Service   1322
Dartnell Sales Manager's Handbook,
   13th edition 1980   1323
Dartnell Sales Promotion Handbook,
   7th edition 1979   1324
From Nine to Five   2168
Office Administration Handbook   3577
Supervisor's Production Planner   4500

DATA COURIER, INC
620 S 5th St
Louisville, KY 40202

ABI/INFORM   2.01
Conference Papers Index   1110
ISMEC   2790
Oceanic Abstracts   3570.01
Pharmaceutical News Index   3764.02
Pollution Abstracts   3803

DATA PROCESSING MANAGEMENT ASSN
505 Busse Highway
Park Ridge, IL 60068

Data Management   1335

DATA RESOURCES, INC
29 Hartwell Ave
Lexington, MA 02173

Agriculture and Commodities Service
   111
Canadian Economic Service   788.01
Chemicals Services   928.01
Coal Service   971.02
Consumer Products Service   1169
Consumer Research Service   1171.01
Cost Forecasting Service   1227
Drilling Service   1505.03
East Asian Economic Service   1522.01
Energy Service   1694
European Economic Service   1774.01
Forest Products Service   2144
Insurance Service   2636
Japanese Economic Service   2797.02
Latin American Service   2976.01
Steel Service   4461
State and Area Forecasting Service
   4383.01
Transportation Service   4694
United States Economic Service
   4796.01

ALAN DAVIS PUBLISHING PTY, LTD
GPO Box 4560
Sydney, NSW, 2001, Australia

Australian Stock Exchange Journal
   416

RICHARD DE BOO LTD
70 Richmond St
Toronto, Ont, Canada M5C 2M8

Alberta Corporation Manual   143
Almanac and Directory 1981   148.01
British Columbia Corporation Manual
   600
Canada Corporation Manual   746
Canada Income Tax Regulations
   Service   754
Canada Labour Service   757
Canada Tax Cases   767
Canada Tax Manual   768
Canada Tax Service   769
Ontario Corporation Manual   3621
Provincial Taxation Service   3909
Quebec Corporation Manual   3979

DECISIONS PUBLICATIONS, INC
342 Madison Ave
New York, NY 10017

Encyclomedia   1667
Marketing & Media Decisions   3127.01

DEGOLYER AND MACNAUGHTON
One Energy Square
4925 Greenville Ave
Dallas, TX 75206

Twentieth Century Petroleum Statistics
4736

DEMPA PUBLICATIONS, INC
380 Madison Ave
New York, NY 10017

Asia Electronics Union   324.03
Electronics Buyers' Guide   1634.01
Japan Fact Book   2802.01
Journal of Electronic Engineering
2850.01
Journal of the Electronics Industry
2889.03
Office Equipment and Products
3578.01

DERWENT PUBLICATIONS LTD
Rochdale House
128 Theobalds Rd
London, England WC1X 8RP

Central Patents Index, 1981   890.01
Electrical Patents Index, 1981   1604.01
On-Line Search Service, 1981   3619.05
World Patents Abstracts, 1981
5073.01
World Patents Index, 1981   5073.02

**DEVELOPMENT CORP FOR
WALES**
Pearl Assurance House
Greyfriars Rd
Cardiff, CF1 3AG, Wales

Progress Wales   3897

**DEVELOPMENT PUBLICATIONS
LTD**
Box 84, Sta A
Willowdale, Ont, Canada M2N 5S7

Short Courses and Seminars   4284

**DIALOG INFORMATION
RETRIEVAL SERVICE**
3460 Hillview Ave
Palo Alto, CA 94304

Dialog   1375.03

**DIGEST REPORTING SERVICE
LTD**
869 Portage Ave
Winnipeg, Man, Canada R3G ON8

Digest: Business & Law Journal   1383

DIRECTORIES INTERNATIONAL
1718 Sherman Ave
Evanston, IL 60201

Advertising World   74

Media Guide International:
Airline/Inflight Magazines Edition
3170
Media Guide International:
Business/Professional Publications
Edition   3171
Media Guide International:
Newspapers/Newsmagazines Edition
3172

DIRECTOR PUBLICATIONS INC
408 Olive St
St Louis, MO 63102

Bank Board Letter   461

DISCLOSURE INC
4827 Rugby Ave
Bethesda, MD 20014

Securities Exchange Commission (SEC)
Disclosure Reports   4226

**DISTILLED SPIRITS COUNCIL OF
THE US, INC**
1300 Penn Bldg
Washington, DC 20004

Annual Statistical Review of the
Distilled Spirits Industry   262
Supplier Price Index   4505

DMS, INC
DMS Bldg, 100 Northfield St
Greenwich, CT 06830

DMS Aerospace Agencies   1475
DMS Aerospace Companies   1475.01
DMS Aerospace Intelligence   1475.02
DMS Agency Profile   1475.03
DMS "AN" Equipment   1475.04
DMS Civil Aircraft   1475.05
DMS Code Name Handbook   1475.06
DMS Company Profile   1475.07
DMS Contracting Intelligence   1475.08
DMS Contract Quarterly   1475.09
DMS Defense Budget Intelligence
1475.10
DMS Defense Market   1475.11
DMS Defense Procurement Budget
Handbook   1475.12
DMS Defense RDT & E Budget
Handbook   1475.13
DMS Electronic Systems   1475.14
DMS Electronic Warfare   1475.15
DMS Foreign Military Sales CQ
1475.16
DMS Gas Turbine Engines/Gas
Turbine Markets   1475.17
DMS International Defense Intelligence
1475.18
DMS Middle East/Africa   1475.19
DMS Military Aircraft   1475.20

DMS Military Laser & EO   1475.21
DMS Military Laser & EO Europe
1475.22
DMS Military Simulators   1475.23
DMS Missiles & Satellites (Europe)
1475.24
DMS Missiles/Spacecraft   1475.25
DMS NATO/Europe   1475.26
DMS NATO Weapons   1475.27
DMS Operation & Maintenance
1475.28
DMS Radar & Sonar   1475.29
DMS Rapid Deployment Force
1475.30
DMS Ships/Vehicles/Ordnance
1475.31
DMS South America/Australasia
1475.32
DMS Tanks-Market Study and Forecast
1475.33
DMS Turbine Intelligence   1475.34
DMS World Aircraft Forecast   1475.35
DMS World Helicopter Forecast
1475.36

DOANE AGRICULTURAL SERVICE
8900 Manchester Rd
St Louis, MO 63144

Doane's Agricultural Report   1476

DOCUMENTS INDEX
Box 195
McLean, VA 22101

Guide to US Government Publications
2307

DORN COMMUNICATIONS, INC
7101 York Ave S,
Minneapolis MN 55435

Corporate Report, Kansas City   1212
Corporate Report Fact Book   1213

DOW JONES & CO, INC
22 Cortlandt St
New York, NY 10007

AP–Dow Jones Bankers Report   277
AP–Dow Jones Economic Report   278
AP–Dow Jones Eurofinancial Report
279
AP–Dow Jones Financial Wire   280
AP–Dow Jones Petroleum News
Service   281
Asian Wall Street Journal   329
Barron's   509
Barron's Market Laboratory   510
Dow Jones Commodities Handbook
1496
Dow Jones International Banking Wire
1497

Marketing in Europe   3130.02
Motor Business   3325.01
Multinational Business   3333
Paper and Packaging Bulletin   3690
Quarterly Economic Reviews Service
  3962.01
Quarterly Energy Reviews   3962.02
Retail Business   4102.01
Rubber Trends   4149.01

**ECONOMIC SOCIETY OF
AUSTRALIA AND NEW ZEALAND**
Queensland Branch, Dept of Economics
Univ of Queensland St Lucia
Brisbane, Qld 4067, Australia

Economic Analysis & Policy   1535

**ECONOMIC STATISTICS BUREAU
OF WASHINGTON, DC**
PO Box 10163
Washington, DC 20018

Handbook of Basic Economic Statistics
  2323

ECONOMIST NEWSPAPER LTD
25 St James's St
London, England SW1A 1HG

Economist   1576

ECONOMIST PUBLISHING CO
12 E Grand Ave
Chicago, IL 60611

Who's Who in the Securities Industry
  4994

EDISON ELECTRIC INSTITUTE
1111 19th St NW
Washington, DC 20036

Edison Electric Institute (EEI)
  Pocketbook of Electric Utility
  Industry Statistics   1583
Edison Electric Institute (EEI)
  Statistical Year Book   1584
Electric Perspectives   1614
Year-End Summary of the Electric
  Power Situation   5100

EDITOR & PUBLISHER CO, INC
575 Lexington Ave
New York, NY 10022

Editor & Publisher   1584.01
Editor & Publisher Market Guide
  1585

EDMONTON, CANADA

**EDMONTON BUSINESS
DEVELOPMENT DEPT**
2410 Oxford Tower
10235 101 St
Edmonton, Alberta, Canada T5J 3G1

Edmonton and Area Manufacturers
  Directory   1586
Edmonton Economic Report   1587
Edmonton Report on Business and
  Travel Development   1588

(EDMONTON, CANADA, END)

EIC. *See* **Environmental Information
Center**

ELECTRONICS INDUSTRIES ASSN
2001 I St NW
Washington, DC 20006

Electronic Industries Association.
  Monthly Statistical Report. US
  Imports (by Country) of Electronic
  Products Within Scope of the EIA
  Consumer Electronics Group   1623
Electronic Industries Association.
  Quarterly Statistical Report. US
  Exports (by Country) of Electronic
  Products Within Scope of the EIA
  Consumer Electronic Group
  1623.01
Electronic Industries Association.
  Quarterly Statistical Report. US
  Imports and Exports (by Country) of
  Electronic Products Within Scope of
  the EIA Communications Division
  1624
Electronic Industries Association.
  Quarterly Statistical Report. US
  Imports and Exports (by Country) of
  Electronic Products Within Scope of
  the EIA Industrial Electronics
  Division   1625
Electronic Industries Association.
  Quarterly Statistical Report. US
  Imports and Exports (by Country) of
  Electronic Products Within Scope of
  the EIA Parts Division   1626
Electronic Industries Association.
  Quarterly Statistical Report. US
  Imports and Exports (by Country) of
  Electronic Products Within Scope of
  the EIA Solid State Products
  Division   1627
Electronic Industries Association.
  Quarterly Statistical Report. US
  Imports and Exports (by Country) of
  Electronic Products Within Scope of
  the EIA Tube Division   1628
Electronic Market Data Book   1629
Electronic Market Trends   1630
Electronics Foreign Trade   1636

ELECTRONIC PERIODICALS, INC
33393 Aurora Rd
Cleveland, OH 44139

Electronic Distributing   1621

ELITE PUBLISHING CORP
11-03 46th Ave
Long Island City, NY 11101

Economic News from Italy   1556

**EMPLOYERS' FEDERATION OF
NEW SOUTH WALES**
PO Box A233
Sydney South, NSW 2000, Australia

Employers' Review   1651

**ENCYCLOPEDIA BRITANNICA
CORP**
425 N Michigan Ave
Chicago, IL 60611

New Encyclopedia Britannica   3438

ENGINEERING INDEX, INC
345 E 47th St
New York, NY 10017

Engineering Index   1710

ENTERPRISE PUBLICATIONS
20 N Wacker Dr
Chicago, IL 60606

Industrial Relations News   2545
Investor Relations Newsletter   2769
Recruiting Trends   4038
What's Ahead in Personnel   4960

ENVIRONEWS, INC
1097 National Press Bldg
Washington, DC 20045

Environmental Health Letter   1722
Occupational Health & Safety Letter
  3560

**ENVIRONMENT INFORMATION
CENTER (EIC), INC**
Catalog Order Dept
292 Madison Ave
New York, NY 10017

Energy Directory Update   1680
Energy Index   1681
Energy Information Abstracts   1683
Energy Information Locator   1684
Energyline   1685
Envirofiche   1718
Enviroline   1719
Environment Abstracts   1720
Environment Index   1726
Environment Regulation Handbook
  1728

Land Use Planning Abstracts   2964
State Environmental Laws &
    Regulations   4390
Toxic Substances Sourcebook   4644

EQUIFAX, INC
Box 4081
Atlanta, GA 30302

Equifax News   1737

EQUITY MEDIA, INC
7616 LBJ Freeway
Dallas, TX 75251

Financial Trend   2032
Financial Trend's Corporate Directory
    Service   2033

ERNST & WHINNEY
200 National City Center
Cleveland, OH 44114

International Series   2727.01

ESTATES GAZETTE LTD
151 Wardour St
London, England W1V 4BN

Estates Gazette   1754

**EUROMONEY PUBLICATIONS
LTD**
Nester House
Playhouse Yard
London, England EC4V 5EX

Currency Risk and the Corporation
    1268.03
Directory of Euromarket Borrowers
    1427.01
Euromoney   1765
Euromoney Currency Report   1766
Euromoney Syndication Guide
    1766.01
Hambro Euromoney Directory   2311
Management of Foreign Exchange Risk
    3083
Trade Financing   4654.01

**EUROMONITOR PUBLICATIONS
LTD**
18 Doughty St
London, England WC1N 2PM

Consumer Europe   1153
European Marketing Data & Statistics
    1785
Retail Trade International   4116

EUROPA PUBLICATIONS LTD
18 Bedford Square
London, England WC1B 3JN

Africa South of the Sahara   82
Europa Year Book   1767
Far East and Australasia   1892
International Who's Who   2742
Middle East and North Africa   3217
Who's Who in Saudi Arabia   4991
The World of Learning   5072

**EUROPEAN COMMUNITY
INFORMATION SERVICE**
2100 M St NW, Suite 707
Washington, DC 20037

Agricultural Markets: Prices (Two
    Series)   101
Agricultural Production (Two Series)
    104
Balance of Payments: Global Data
    451.01
Basic Statistics   514.01
Coal: Monthly Bulletin   971.01
Electrical Energy: Monthly Bulletin
    1601.01
Energy Statistics (Three Series)   1696
Euro-Abstracts: Scientific and Technical
    Publications and Patents, Sections I
    and II   1759
Europe Transport: Observation of the
    Transport Markets (Three Series)
    1766.02
European Economy   1774.02
European Investment Bank Annual
    Report   1780
Eurostatistics (Bulletin of General
    Statistics)   1792.03
Fisheries: Quantity and Value of
    Landings   2048
Green Europe: Newsletter on the
    Common Agricultural Policy
    2264.01
Hydrocarbons: Monthly Bulletin
    2431
Industrial Short Term Trends
    2551.02
Iron and Steel: Monthly Statistics
    2787
Monthly External Trade Bulletin
    3290.01
Official Journal of the European
    Communities   3585.01
Purchase Prices of the Means of
    Production   3948.01
Unemployment: Monthly Bulletin
    4745.01

**EUROPEAN ECONOMIC
COMMUNITY SAVINGS BANK
GROUP**
92-94 Square E Plasky
Brussels, Belgium 1040

E E/Epargne Europe   1598

**EUROPEAN ECONOMIC DATA
PUBLISHING CO LTD**
4 Cleveland Square
London, England W2 6DH

Common Market News   1038

EUROPEAN LAW CENTRE LTD
4 Bloomsburg Sq
London, England WC1A 2RL

Annual of Industrial Property Law
    252
Commercial Laws of Europe   1004.01
Common Market Law Reports   1037
Eurolaw Commercial Intelligence   1762
European Commercial Cases   1769
European Human Rights Reports
    1776
European Law Digest   1782
Fleet Street Patent Law Reports   2062
Industrial Property Reports from
    Socialist Countries   2537.01

EUROPE INFORMATION SERVICE
46 Ave Albert Elisabeth
Brussels, Belgium 1040

Agro Service International   116
EEC/Asia Report   1597.01
European Report   1786
Europe Energy   1788
Europe Environment   1789
Multinational Service   3337
World Economic Service   5060

EURO PUBLICATIONS LTD
31 Churchill Way, Cardiff
Glamorgan, Wales CF1 4HE

Business News   713

EVM ANALYSTS, INC
10921 Wilshire Blvd
Suite 1007
Westwood Village
Los Angeles, CA 90024

EVM Market Week   1794

**EXECUTIVE COMMUNICATIONS,
INC**
400 E 54th St
New York, NY 10022

Ad Day/USA   50
New Business Report   3434

**EXECUTIVE ENTERPRISES
PUBLISHING CO, INC**
33 W 60 St
New York, NY 10023

Corporate Accounting Reporter
    1202.01

Employee Relations Law Journal   1648
Equal Employment Opportunity Review
   1734
Equal Employment Opportunity Today
   1735
Enviromental Regulation Analyst
   1724
Oil & Gas Price Regulation Analyst
   3598.01
Toxic Substances Journal   4643.04

EXECUTIVE REPORTS CORP
Englwood Cliffs, NJ 07632

Executives Credit and Collections
   Letter   1807.02
Tax Shelter Opportunities in Real
   Estate   4571
Tax Shelters in Executive Compensation
   4572

EXECUTIVE SCIENCES INST, INC
PO Drawer M
Whippany, NJ 07981

Operations Research/Management
   Science   3630
Quality Control and Applied Statistics
   3956

EXECUTIVE WOMAN
Box 3101, Grand Central Station
New York, NY 10017

Executive Woman   1811

**EXPORT–IMPORT BANK OF THE
UNITED STATES**
811 Vermont Ave NW
Washington, DC 20571

Eximbank Record   1812
Export–Import Bank of the United
   States. Annual Report   1826

**EXPORT TIMES PUBLISHING
LTD**
60 Fleet St
London, England EC4Y 1LA

Business Traveller   725
Export Times   1854

**EXTEL STATISTICAL SERVICES
LTD**
37-45 Paul St
London, England EC2A 4PB

Analyst's Service   216
British CI Sector   599
British Company Service   610
Capital Gains Tax Service   855.01
Extel Australian Company Service
   1856

Extel Book of Prospectuses and New
   Issues   1858
Extel Dividend Record   1858.01
Extel European Company Service
   1859
Extel Fixed Interest Record   1859.01
Extel Handbook of Market Leaders
   1860
Extel Issuing House Year Book   1861
Extel North American Company
   Service   1862
Extel Overseas Companies Services
   1863
International Bond Service   2661
Monthly New Issues and Placings
   Service   3293
Registrar's Service   4054
Unquoted Companies Service   4825
Wardleycards   4881.01

FACTS ON FILE, INC
460 Park Ave S
New York, NY 10016

Direct Marketing Marketplace/1981
   1402.01
Exchange Rate Outlook (ERO)
   1794.01
Facts on File Weekly News Digest
   1874
TV Facts   4734.01
World Directory of Multinational
   Exterprises   5058

FAIRCHILD PUBLICATIONS, INC
Book Div
7 E 12 St
New York, NY 10003

American Metal Market   201
Directory of Defense Electronic
   Products & Services: US Suppliers
   1426
Electronic News Financial Fact Book &
   Directory   1631
Encyclopedia of Advertising, 1969
   edition   1669
Fairchild's Financial Manual of Retail
   Stores   1876
Nelson's Directory of Securities
   Research Information   3428
Supermarket News   4498

FAIRPLAY PUBLICATIONS LTD
301 E 64th St
New York, NY 10021

Fairplay International Shipping Weekly
   1880
Fairplay International World Ships on
   Order   1881
Fairplay World Shipping Yearbook
   1882

FAR EAST TRADE PRESS LTD
Rm 1913, Hanglung Centre
2-20 Paterson St Causeway Bay
Hong Kong, China

Asian Building & Construction   326.01
Asian Business   326.02

FARM CREDIT CORP
PO Box 2314, Postal Station D
Ottawa, Ont, Canada K1P 6J9

Farm Credit Corporation Statistics
   1894.01

FCIB. *See* **Foreign Credit Interchange
Bureau**

**FEDERAL LEGAL PUBLICATIONS,
INC**
157 Chambers St
New York, NY 10007

Antitrust Bulletin   272
Journal of Reprints for Antitrust Law
   and Economics   2880

FEDERAL PUBLICATIONS
1120 20th St NW
Washington, DC 20036

Briefing Papers   593
Briefing Papers Collection   594
Communiqué   1047
Comptroller General's Procurement
   Decisions   1069
Construction Briefings   1125.01
Construction Contractor   1126
Extraordinary Contractual Relief
   Reporter   1867
Government Contractor   2238
Government Contracts Citator
   2238.01
Yearbook of Procurement Articles
   5096.01

**FEDERAL RESERVE BANK OF
ATLANTA**
Research Dept
PO Box 1731
Atlanta, GA 30301

Caribbean Basin Economic Survey   861
Economic Review   1570
Update   4827

**FEDERAL RESERVE BANK OF
BOSTON**
Boston, MA 02106

Mutual Savings Bank Report   3353
New England Economic Indicators
   3440
New England Economic Review   3441

FEDERAL RESERVE BANK OF CHICAGO
Research Dept
Box 834
Chicago, IL 60690

Economic Perspectives   1562

FEDERAL RESERVE BANK OF DALLAS
Station K
Dallas, TX 75222

Condition Report of Weekly Reporting Commercial Banks—Eleventh Federal Reserve District   1096
Federal Reserve Bank of Dallas Annual Report   1935
Voice of the Federal Reserve Bank of Dallas   4866

FEDERAL RESERVE BANK OF KANSAS CITY
925 Grand Ave
Kansas City, MO 64198

Economic Review   1571
Financial Letter   2004.01

FEDERAL RESERVE BANK OF MINNEAPOLIS
Research Dept
250 Marquette Ave
Minneapolis, MN 55480

Federal Reserve Bank of Minneapolis Quarterly Review   1935.01
Statistical Releases (Agricultural Credit Conditions Survey)   4439

FEDERAL RESERVE BANK OF NEW YORK
Publications Section
33 Liberty St
New York, NY 10045

Federal Reserve Bank of New York Annual Report   1936
Federal Reserve Bank of New York Quarterly Review   1937

FEDERAL RESERVE BANK OF PHILADELPHIA
Philadelphia, PA 19105

Federal Reserve Bank of Philadelphia Business Review   1938
Fed in Print   1977

FEDERAL RESERVE BANK OF RICHMOND
PO Box 27622
Richmond, VA 23261

Federal Reserve Bank of Richmond Annual Report   1939
Federal Reserve Bank of Richmond Economic Review   1940

FEDERAL RESERVE BANK OF SAN FRANCISCO
PO Box 7702
San Francisco, CA 94120

Federal Reserve Bank of San Francisco Business & Financial Letter   1951
Federal Reserve Bank of San Francisco Economic Review   1952
Federal Reserve Bank of San Francisco Pacific Basin Economic Indicators   1953
Federal Reserve Bank of San Francisco Western Economic Indicators   1954

FEDERAL STATE REPORTS INC
5203 Leesburg Pike #1201
Falls Church, VA 22041

Campaign Contributions and Lobbying Laws   740.01
Dairy Industry Newsletter   1310
Of Consuming Interest   3576
Product Liability Legislation for Client and Counsel   3874.01
State Slate: A Guide to Legislative Procedures and Lawmakers   4407
Warranty Watch   4883

FIELDMARK MEDIA
25 W 43rd St
New York, NY 10036

Supermarket Business   4497

FINANCIAL ANALYSTS FEDERATION
1633 Broadway
New York, NY 10019

Financial Analysts Federation Membership Directory   1993
Financial Analysts Journal   1995

FINANCIAL EXECUTIVES INSTITUTE
633 3rd Ave
New York, NY 10017

Financial Executive   1998

FINANCIAL MAIL
PO Box 10493
Johannesburg 2000, South Africa

Financial Mail   2004.02

FINANCIAL POST
481 University Ave
Toronto, Ont, Canada M5W 1A7

Financial Post Canadian Markets, 1981   2010
Financial Post Corporation Service   2011
Financial Post Directory of Directors   2012
Financial Post Investment Databank   2012.01
Financial Post Magazine   2013
Financial Post Newspaper   2014
Financial Post Survey of Mines & Energy Resources   2015
Financial Post Survey of Industrials   2017
Investor's Digest of Canada   2772
Meetings, Conferences, & Conventions: A Financial Post Guide   3188

FINANCIAL TIMES BUSINESS INFORMATION LTD
Bracken House, 10 Cannon St
London, England EC4P 4BY

Banker   464
BRU Export Finance Service   631
Business Information Service-Financial Times   692.01
Community Markets   1050
Euromarket Letter   1763
European Energy Report   1775.01
European Law Letter   1783
Financial Mail   2005
Financial Times Actuaries Index Monthly Sheets   2023
Financial Times Actuaries Share Indices   2024
Financial Times International Business Yearbook   2025
Financial Times Newspaper   2026
Financial Times Quarterly Actuaries Indices   2028
Financial Times Tax Newsletter   2029
Financial Times World Hotel Directory   2030
Financial Times World Insurance Year Book   2031
Guide to Financial Times Statistics   2293
International Banking Report   2657
International Coal Report   2666
Investors Chronicle   2770
Investors Chronicle (IC) News Letter   2771
McCarthy Information Services   3158.01
Mid East Markets   3226
Money Management   3269
North Sea Letter   3543
Share-Owners   4272
Trends in International Banking and Capital Markets   4717

Walter Skinner's Mining International
Year Book   4292
Walter Skinner's North Sea and Europe
Offshore Year Book and Buyer's
Guide   4293
Walter Skinner's Oil and Gas
International Year Book   4294
Walter Skinner's Who's Who in World
Oil and Gas   4295
World Accounting Report   5034
World Banking Survey   5045
World Business Weekly   5046.01
World Commodity Report   5048
World Insurance Report   5068
World Solar Markets   5079.01

FINANCIAL TIMES BUSINESS PUBLISHING LTD
Greystoke Place, Fetter Lane
London, England EC4A 1ND

Money Management and Unitholder
3270

FINANCIAL TIMES OF CANADA
920 Yonge St
Suite 5000
Toronto, Ont, Canada M4W 3L5

Financial Times of Canada   2027

FINANCIAL WEEKLY
Westgate House, 9 Holborn
London, England EC1N 2NE

Financial Weekly   2033.01
Westgate Commodities Letter   4953
Westgate Tax Planners Letter   4953.01

FINAX PUBLICATIONS LTD
31 Curzon St
London, England W1Y 7AE

International Tax Haven Directory
2731
Tax Planning International   4564

FINDERHOOD, INC
15 W 38th St
New York, NY 10018

Finderhood Report   2036

FINDLAY PUBLICATIONS LTD
10 Letchworth Dr
Bromley, Kent, England BR2 9BE

Eureka   1758.01
Machinery & Production Engineering
3053
Works Management   5030

FINNISH–AMERICAN CHAMBER OF COMMERCE
Finland House
540 Madison Ave
New York, NY 10022

Finnish–American Chamber of
Commerce Newsletter   2040

FIRST HAWAIIAN BANK
Research Division
PO Box 3200
Honolulu, HI 96801

First Hawaiian Bank Business Outlook
Forum   2046
First Hawaiian Bank Economic
Indicators   2047

FIRST NATIONAL BANK OF CHICAGO
Business & Economic Research
Division
One First National Plaza
Chicago, IL 60670

First Chicago World Report   2044

FISCAL PRESS LTD
Fiscal House
36 Lattimore Rd
St. Albans, Herts, England AL1 3XW

Income Tax Digest and Accountants'
Review   2491

FITCH INVESTORS SERVICE
12 Barclay St
New York, NY 10007

Fitch Commercial Paper Reports   2050
Fitch Corporate Bond Ratings Book
2051
Fitch Rating Register   2051.01
Fitch Hospital and Other Nonprofit
Institutional Ratings   2053
Fitch Institutional Reports   2054
Fitch Investors Municipal Bond
Reports   2055

FLEET STREET LETTER, LTD
80 Fleet St
London, England EC4Y 1JH

Fleet Street Letter   2061

FLORIDA BANKERS ASSN
505 N Mills Ave
Box 6847
Orlando, FL 32803

Florida Banker   2065

FLORIDA (STATE)

DEPT OF LABOR AND EMPLOYMENT SECURITY
Div of Employment Security
Bureau of Research and Analysis
Caldwell Bldg
Tallahassee, FL 32301

Florida Economic Indicators   2066
Florida Employment Statistics   2067
In-Season Farm Labor Report ES-223
2587
Labor Force Estimates   2931
Labor Market Trends   2940

(FLORIDA END)

FORBES, INC
60 5th Ave
New York, NY 10011

Forbes   2103
Forbes Special Situation Survey   2104

FORD INVESTOR SERVICES
11722 Sorrento Valley Rd
Suite I
San Diego, CA 92121

Client-Directed Screen   962
Data Base Service   1325
Ford Value Report   2105
Investment Management Report   2765
Specialized Monthly Reports   4354

FORECASTER PUBLISHING CO
19623 Ventura Blvd
Tarzana, CA 91356

Forecaster   2107

FOREIGN CREDIT INSURANCE ASSN
1 World Trade Center, 9th Floor
New York, NY 10048

Foreign Credit Insurance Assn (FCIA)
News   2112

FOREIGN CREDIT INTERCHANGE BUREAU, NATIONAL ASSN OF CREDIT MGMT
475 Park Ave S
New York, NY 10016

Foreign Credit Interchange Bureau
(FCIB) International Bulletin   2113

FOREIGN TAX LAW ASSN
PO Box 340
Alachua, FL 32616

Commercial Laws of the World   1005
Foreign Tax Law Bi-Weekly Bulletin
2138
Tax Laws of the World   4557

**FOREST INDUSTRIES
COMMITTEE ON TIMBER
VALUATION AND TAXATION**
1250 Connecticut Ave
Washington, DC 20036

Timber Tax Journal 4618

**FORTYEIGHT GROUP OF
BRITISH TRADERS WITH CHINA**
84–86 Rosebery Ave
London, England EC1K 5RR

China Trade and Economic Newsletter
943

FOUNDATION CENTER
888 7th Ave
New York, NY 10106

Comsearch Printouts 1092
Corporate Foundation Profiles 1208.01
Directory of Evaluation Consultants
1428.01
Foundation Center National Data Book
2152
Foundation Center Source Book Profiles
2153
Foundation Directory 2155
Foundation Grants Index 2156

**FOUNDATION FOR THE
ADVANCEMENT OF
INTERNATIONAL BUSINESS
ADMINISTRATION INC**
64 Ferndale Dr
Hastings-on-Hudson, NY 10706

International Executive 2678

FOURTH ESTATE GROUP
PO Box 9344
Wellington, New Zealand

Capital Letter 857.02
National Business Review 3365
New Zealand Business Who's Who
3495
New Zealand Data Processing 3499

HARRY FRASER
Charlottetown RR #1
Hazelbrook, PE1, Canada C1A 7J6

Fraser's Potato Newsletter 2163

FRASER MANAGEMENT ASSOC
309 South Willard St
PO Box 494
Burlington, VT 05402

Energy Research Bureau 1691
Fraser Opinion Letter 2161

**FRENCH CHAMBER OF
COMMERCE IN THE US, INC**
1350 Ave of the Americas
New York, NY 10019

French–American Commerce 2165
French American News 2165.01

FROST & SULLIVAN, INC
106 Fulton St
New York, NY 10038

American and European Market
Research Reports 155

FULL CIRCLE MARKETING CORP
6500 Midnight Pass Road
Penthouse Suite #504, PO Box 2527
Sarasota, FL 33578

Barter Communique 511

FUND RAISING INSTITUTE
Box 365
Ambler, PA 19002

Fund Raising Institute (FRI) Monthly
Portfolio 2199

GALE RESEARCH CO
Book Tower
Detroit, MI 48226

Acronyms and Initialisms Dictionary
42
Consultants and Consulting
Organizations Directory 1144
Consumer Sourcebook 1175
Directory Information Service 1406
Directory of British Associations 1412
Directory of European Associations
1428
Directory of Special Libraries and
Information Centers 1457
Encyclopedia of Associations 1670
Encyclopedia of Business Information
Sources 1671
Encyclopedia of Governmental
Advisory Organizations 1673
Encyclopedia of Information Systems
and Services 1674
New Consultants 3435
New Governmental Advisory
Organizations 3447
New Research Centers 3459
New Trade Names 3473
Research Centers Directory 4085
Statistics—Africa 4448
Statistics—America 4449
Statistics—Europe 4452
Statistics Sources 4459
Subject Directory of Special Libraries
and Information Centers. 4484

Trade Names Dictionary 4665
Who's Who in Consulting 4982
World Guide to Abbreviations of
Organizations 5065

GALLAGHER REPORT, INC
230 Park Ave
New York, NY 10017

Gallagher Report 2206

GATEWAY PUBLICATIONS
Foley Trading Estate
Foley St
Hereford, England HR1 2SN

Export 1816

GAVIN-JOBSON ASSOCIATES
488 Madison Ave
New York, NY 10022

Liquor Handbook 3024
Wine Marketing Handbook 5006

GEE & CO (PUBLISHERS) LTD
151 Strand
London, England WC2R 1JJ

Accountant 18

**GENERAL AGREEMENT ON
TARIFF & TRADE**
Centre William Rappard
154 rue de Lausanne
1211 Geneva 21, Switzerzerland

Basic Instruments and Selected
Documents (BISD) 513
GATT Activities 2209
International Trade 2736

GENERAL ELECTRIC CO
Business Growth Services
120 Erie Blvd, Room 591
Schenectady, NY 12305

New Product–New Business Digest
3458
Selected Business Ventures 4252
TIPS—Technical Information
Periodicals Service 4624

**GENERAL EXECUTIVE SERVICES,
INC**
Park St Bldg
New Canaan, CT 06840

Digest of Executive Opportunities
1389

GEO ABSTRACTS LTD
University of East Anglia
Norwich, England NR4 7TJ

Geo Abstracts 2217.01

GEORGE WASHINGTON UNIV
National Law Center
2000 H ST NW, Rm B-01
Washington, DC 20052

Journal of International Law &
  Economics   2864

GEORGIA (STATE)

**GEORGIA DEPT OF INDUSTRY
AND TRADE**
1400 North Omni International
PO Box 1776
Atlanta, GA 30301

Georgia Manufacturing Directory
  2219

GEORGIA END)

GEORGIA STATE UNIVERSITY
College of Business Administration
Business Publishing Division
University Plaza
Atlanta, GA 30303

Business   653
Directory of Foreign Manufacturers in
  the United States   1432

**GERMAN–AMERICAN CHAMBER
OF COMMERCE, INC**
666 5th Ave
New York, NY 10103

American Subsidiaries of German
  Firms   209
German–American Trade News   2221

**GEYER–MCALLISTER
PUBLICATIONS, INC**
51 Madison Ave
New York, NY 10010

Administrative Management   57
Geyer's Dealer Topics   2223
Geyer's Who Makes it Directory   2224
Information & Word Processing Report
  2570.01
Playthings   3788
Word Processing Information Systems
  5020

**D PARKE GIBSON
INTERNATIONAL, INC**
475 5th Ave
New York, NY 10017

Gibson Report   2225
Race Relations and Industry   3983

**GLASGOW CHAMBER OF
COMMERCE**
30 George Square
Glasgow, Scotland G2 1EQ

Industrial Index to Glasgow & West of
  Scotland   2531
Journal of the Glasgow Chamber of
  Commerce   2891

**GLASS CONTAINER
MANUFACTURERS INSTITUTE**
1800 K St NW
Washington, DC 20006

Glass Containers   2229

GLOBE AND MAIL LTD
444 Front St W
Toronto, Ont, Canada M5V 2S9

Globe and Mail Report on Business
  2231

GEORGE GODWIN LTD
1–3 Pemberton Row
London, England EC4P 4HL

Directory of Official Architecture and
  Planning   1451
Directory of Technical and Further
  Education   1459

GOLDSMITH–NAGAN, INC
1120 19th St NW
Washington, DC 20036

Goldsmith–Nagan Bond and Money
  Market Letter   2235

**GOODYEAR GIBBS (CARIBBEAN)
LTD**
27–29 Beak St
London, England W1R 3LB

Caribbean and West Indies Chronicle
  860

**GORDON AND BREACH SCIENCE
PUBLISHERS LTD**
One Park Ave
New York, NY 10016

Journal of Urban Analysis   2900
Transportation Planning and
  Technology   4693

**GOVERNMENT BUSINESS
WORLDWIDE REPORTS**
PO Box 5651
Washington, DC 20016

Defense & Economy World Report
  1354.02

**GOVERNMENT DATA
PUBLICATIONS**
422 Washington Bldg
Washington, DC 20005

Directory of Government Production
  Prime Contractors   1434
Government Prime Contracts Monthly
  2248
Research and Development (R&D)
  Contracts Monthly   4079
Research & Development Directory
  4080
US Research and Development (R&D)
  4816

**GOVERNMENT DEVELOPMENT
BANK FOR PUERTO RICO**
Box 42001
San Juan, PR 00940

Puerto Rico Business Review   3943

GOWER PUBLISHING CO LTD
1 Westmead, Farnborough
Hampshire, England GU14 7RU

Accounting Law and Practice Manual
  15
Company Administration Handbook
  1052
Company Law in Europe   1053.01
Direct Mail Databook   1399.01
Economic Outlook   1557
Employment Law Manual   1661
Historicl Directory of Trade Unions
  2373.01
Multinational Corporations   3334
Retail Trade Developments in Great
  Britain   4115
Sources of Asian/Pacific Economic
  Information   4334.01
Sources of European Economic
  Information   4335
Sources of World Financial and
  Banking Information   4336.01
Tax Systems of Western Europe
  4572.01
Trade Union Handbook   4677
Who's WHo in Finance   4984
World Index of Economic Forecasts
  5067.02
World's Largest Industrial Enterprises
  5078.02

**GRADUATE MANAGEMENT
ADMISSIONS COUNCIL**
PO Box 966
Princeton, NJ 08541

Guide to Graduate Management
  Education 1980–81   2294

GRALLA PUBLICATIONS
1515 Broadway
New York, NY 10036

Bank Systems and Equipment   503
Catalog Showroom Business   869
Contract   1185
Health Care Product News   2359
Kitchen Business   2918
Meeting News   3186
Multi-Housing News   3332
National Jeweler   3389
Premium/Incentive Business   3834
Professional Furniture Merchant   3888
Sporting Goods Business   4364

GRANVILLE MARKET LETTER, INC
Drawer O
Holly Hill, FL 32017

Granville Market Letter   2257

EARL GRAVES PUBLISHING CO, INC
295 Madison Ave
New York, NY 10017

Black Enterprise   560

GREAT BRITAIN

COMMONWEALTH AGRICULTURAL BUREAUX
Central Sales Branch
Farnham House, Farnham Royal
Slough, England SL2 3BN

GB Agricultural Engineering Abstracts   98
Leisure, Recreation and Tourism Abstracts   3004.01
World Agricultural Economics and Rural Sociology Abstracts   5036

HER MAJESTY'S STATIONERY OFFICE (HMSO)
PO Box 569
London, England SE1 9NH

Acquisitions and Mergers of Companies   41
Agricultural Statistics: England and Wales   107
Agricultural Statistics: Scotland   109
Agricultural Statistics: United Kingdom   110
Annual Abstract of Statistics 1975   234
Annual Digest of Port Statistics, Volumes I and II   244
Annual Estimates of the Population of England and Wales and Local Authority Areas   245

Annual Estimates of the Population of Scotland   246
Bank of England Report   489
Betting and Gaming Bulletin   546
Betting Licensing Statistics   547
Bill of Entry Service   552
British Business   598
British Labour Statistics Year Book   618
Business Monitor, Production Series   710
Business Monitor, Service, and Distributive Series   711
Business Monitors   712
Casualties to Vessels and Accidents to Men   867
Catering Trades   871
Census of Production for Northern Ireland   877
Changes in Rates of Wages and Hours of Work   906
Cinemas   946
Civil Aviation Authority Monthly Statistics   952
Civil Service Statistics   954
Company Finance   1053
Contents of Recent Economic Journals   1183
Control of Immigration Statistics   1190
Criminal Statistics, England and Wales   1255
CSO Macro-Economic Databook   1265.01
Defense Statistics   1354.01
Department of Employment Gazette   1361
Dept of Employment Research   1362
Digest of UK Energy Statistics   1394
Digest of Welsh Statistics   1396
District Councils, Summary of Statements of Accounts, Northern Ireland   1469
Economic Trends   1573
Economic Trends Annual Supplement   1574
Education Statistics for the UK   1596
Energy Trends   1700
Facts in Focus   1873
Family Expenditure Survey   1883
Family Expenditure Survey, Northern Ireland   1884
Financial Statement and Budget Report   2019
Financial Statistics   2020
Financial Statistics: Explanatory Handbook   2021
Fire and Loss Statistics for the United Kingdom   2041
First Destination of University Graduates   2045
General Household Survey   2210

Government Publications (Great Britain)   2249
Guide to Official Statistics   2300
Health and Personal Social Services Statistics for England   2354
Health and Personal Social Services Statistics for Wales   2355
Household Food Consumption and Expenditure (National Food Survey)   2403
Housing and Construction Statistics   2409
Industrial Tribunal Reports   2555
Inland Revenue Statistics   2579
Input–Output Tables   2584
Input–Output Tables for the UK   2585
Insurance Business Statistics   2613
Insurance Companies and Private Pension Funds   2615
Local Financial Returns, Scotland   3037
Local Government Financial Statistics, England and Wales   3038
Memorandum by the Chief Secretary to the Treasury Appropriation Accounts   3188.01
Monthly Bulletin of Construction Indices   3281
Monthly Digest Annual Supplement   3288
Monthly Digest of Statistics   3289
National Income and Expenditure "Blue Book"   3382
National Travel Survey   3410
New Earnings Survey   3437
Northern Ireland Digest of Statistics   3538
Number of Road Vehicles, New Registrations   3556
Overseas Trade Analysed in Terms of Industries   3660
Overseas Trade Statistics of the UK   3665
Population Projections   3810
Population Trends   3811
Price Index Numbers for Current Cost Accounting   3838
Public Expenditure White Papers   3923.01
Quarterly Bulletin of Port Statistics   3958
Quarterly Trade Statistics of the United Kingdom   3978
Railway Accidents   3994
R&D Abstracts   3999.01
Rates and Rateable Value in England and Wales   4004
Rates and Rateable Values in Scotland   4005
Regional Trends   4049.01
Registry of Ships   4056

Report of the Commissioners of HM
    Customs and Excise   4064
Report of the Commissioners of HM
    Inland Revenue   4065
Report on the Census of Production
    4074
Retail Trade   4113
Road Accidents   4135
Scottish Abstract of Statistics   4203
Scottish Economic Bulletin   4205
Scottish Sea Fisheries Statistical Tables
    4207
Sea Fisheries Statistical Tables   4214
Social and Economic Trends in
    Northern Ireland   4311
Social Security Statistics   4319
Social Trends   4321
Spirits Bulletin   4363
Statistical News   4430
Statistical Review of Farming in
    Northern Ireland   4440
Statistics of Trade through United
    Kingdom Ports   4455
Survey of Personal Incomes   4517
Time Rates of Wages & Hours of Work
    4620
Trade Promotions Guide   4669
Transport Statistics, Great Britain
    1964–74   4698
UK Balance of Payments "Pink Book"
    4756
United Kingdom Mineral Statistics
    1975   4760
Welsh Economic Trends   4948
Wine Bulletin   5005

ROYAL MINT
Tower Hill
London, England EC3N 4DR

Royal Mint Annual Report   4147

(GREAT BRITAIN END)

**GREATER PUBLICATIONS PTY,
LTD**
Box 2608, GPO
Sydney, NSW 2001, Australia

B & T Advertising Marketing & Media
    Weekly   445
B & T Yearbook   456

GREENTREE PUBLISHING CORP
PO Box 9
New City, NY 10956

Central New York Business Review
    890
Orange–Rockland–Westchester Business
    Review   3636

GRINDLAYS BANK LTD
Economics Dept
23 Fenchurch St
London, England EC3P 3ED

Grindlays Bank Economic Reports
    2267

DENNY GRISWOLD
127 E 80th St
New York, NY 10021

Public Relations News   3932

GROLIER INC
Sherman Turnpike
Danbury, CT 06816

Encyclopedia Americana, International
    edition   1668

GROWTH STOCK OUTLOOK, INC
4405 East–West Highway
Bethseda, MD 20014

Growth Stock Outlook   2269
Junior Growth Stocks   2902

**GUIDES TO MULTINATIONAL
BUSINESS, INC**
Harvard Sq, Box 92
Cambridge, MA 02138

Ambassadors' Directory   153.02
Businessman's Guide to the Arab
    World   709
Business Travel Cost Worldwide
    724.01
Europe's 5000 Largest Companies
    1792
Information Peking (Beijing)   2573.02
Multinational Executive Travel
    Companion   3335

HALEVI & CO
54 Haneviim St
Jerusalem, Israel 95141

Stock Exchange Information Service
    4464

HAL PUBLICATIONS, INC
1180 Avenue of the Americas
New York, NY 10036

Working Woman   5025

**ALEXANDER HAMILTON
INSTITUTE**
1633 Broadway
New York, NY 10019

Executive's Personal Development
    Letter   1808
Financial Management Letter   2006.01

Marketing Letter   3132
Modern Business Reports   3255

HANDY & HARMAN
850 3rd Ave
New York, NY 10022

Annual Review of the Silver Market
    259

HAROLD D HANSEN
Box 327
Washington Depot, CT 06794

Family Page Directory   1885
metro CALIFORNIA media   3204.02
New York Publicity Outlets   3479
TV Publicity Outlets Nationwide
    4735

**HARCOURT BRACE
JOVANOVICH, INC**
757 3rd Ave
New York, NY 10017

Body Fashions/Intimate Apparel
    Incorporating Hosiery and
    Underwear   569
Brown's Directory   630
Communications News   1042
Dental Industry News   1358
Dental Laboratory Review   1359
Dental Management   1360
Drug & Cosmetic Catalog   1507
Drug & Cosmetic Industry   1508
Electronic Technician Dealer   1638
Fast Service   1907
Flooring   2064
Food Management   2090
Home & Auto   2383
Housewares   2404
Kitchen Planning   2919
LP/Gas   3049
Ocean Resources Engineering   3572
Paper Sales   3693
Paper Year Book   3695
Petroleum Engineer International   3759
Pets/Supplies/Marketing   3764
Physician's Management   3768
Pipeline & Gas Journal   3772
PSM Retail Manual   3914
Practical Guide to LP/Gas Utilization
    3822
PSM Retail Manual   3914
Quick Frozen Foods   3981
Quick Frozen Foods Directory of
    Frozen Food Processors   3982
Rent All   4062
Roofing Siding Insulation   4141
Snack Food   4308
Snack Food Blue Book   4309

Telephone Engineer & Management
 4585
Telephone Engineer & Management
 Directory 4586
Tobacco Reporter 4630
Toys, Hobbies, & Crafts 4645

**HARTMAN COMMUNICATIONS,
INC**
77 N Miller Rd, PO Box 5417
Akron, OH 44313

Rubber World 4150

HARVARD UNIVERSITY
Graduate School of Business
Administration
Baker Library
Soldiers Field
Boston, MA 02163

Baker Library Core Collection, An
 Author and Subject Guide 449
Business History Review 686
Current Periodical Publications in
 Baker Library 1279
Harvard Business Review 2345
Publications by the Faculty of the
 Harvard Business School 3923
Recent Additions to Baker Library
 4033.01
Working Papers in Baker Library: A
 Quarterly Checklist 5024

HAWAII (STATE)

**DEPT OF PLANNING AND
ECONOMIC DEVELOPMENT**
PO Box 2359
Honolulu, HI 96804

Economy of Hawaii 1579
Starting a Business in Hawaii 4381
State of Hawaii Data Book 4403

(HAWAII END)

HAWKINS PUBLISHING CO, INC
Suite 220, 933 N Kenmore St
Arlington, VA 22201

Hawkins Civil Aeronautics Board
 Service 2349
Hawkins Federal Maritime Commission
 Service 2350
Hawkins Motor Carrier–Freight
 Forwarder Service 2351
Hawkins Rail Carrier Service 2352
National Transportation Safety Board
 3409

HAYDEN PUBLISHING CO, INC
50 Essex St
Rochelle Park, NJ 07662

Computer Decisions 1075
Computer Times 1088
Electronic Design's Gold Book
 1620.01

HAYMARKET PUBLISHING LTD
76 Dean St
London, England W1

Management Today 3091

HBJ NEWSLETTERS, INC
757 Third Ave
New York, NY 10017

Aviation Monthly 439
Managing: People & Organizations
 3095.02
Real Estate Investing Letter 4015
Rental House & Condo Investor
 4061.01

HEALTH INSURANCE INSTITUTE
1850 K St NW
Washington, DC 20006

Source Book of Health Insurance Data
 4333

HEARST CORP
224 W 57th St
New York, NY 10019

American Druggist 169

**HEAVY & CHEMICAL
INDUSTRIES NEWS AGENCY**
Daiichifuji Bldg, 2-15
Kandajinbo-Cho
Chiyoda-Ku, Tokyo, Japan

Japan Trade and Industry News 2804

HELDREF PUBLICATIONS
4000 Albemarle St NW
Washington, DC 20016

Journal of Business Education 2829

JOHN S HEROLD, INC
35 Mason St
Greenwich, CT 06830

Johnson Survey 2816.01
Petroleum Outlook 3761

HINE'S LEGAL DIRECTORY INC
Professional Center Bldg, PO Box 71
Glen Ellyn, IL 60137

Hines Insurance Adjusters 2372
Hines Insurance Counsel 2373

HIRSCH ORGANIZATION, INC
6 Deer Trail
Old Tappan, NJ 07675

Mutual Funds Almanac 3347
Smart Money 4307
Stock Trader's Almanac 4470

HITCHCOCK PUBLISHING CO
Hitchcock Bldg
Wheaton, IL 60187

Infosystems 2576

BETSY HOGAN ASSOCIATES
PO Box 360
Brookline, MA 02146

Equal Employment News 1731

HOKE COMMUNICATIONS, INC
224 7th St
Garden City, NY 11535

Direct Marketing 1402
Friday Report 2167
Fund Raising Management 2200
Fundraising Weekly 2200.01
Marketing Information Guide 3131

HOLLIS DIRECTORIES
Contact House
Lower Hampton Rd
Sunbury-On-Thames
Middlesex, England TW16 5HG

Hollis Press and Public Relations
 Annual 2377

T J HOLT & CO
290 Port Rd West
Westport, CT 06880

Holt Executive Advisory 2379
Holt 500 Trading Portfolio 2380
Holt Investment Advisory 2381

HOMEFINDERS LTD
10 East Rd
London, England N1

Homes Overseas 2384

**HONG KONG TRADE
DEVELOPMENT COUNCIL**
548 5th Ave
New York, NY 10036

Apparel Magazine 282.01
Hong Kong Cable 2386
Hong Kong Enterprise 2387

Hong Kong Trader   2388
Toys Magazine   4645.01

HOUSEHOLD & PERSONAL PRODUCTS INDUSTRY
Box 555, 26 Lake St
Ramsey NJ 07446

Carpet & Rug Industry   864.02
Happi   2341.01
Nonwovens Industry   3532.01

ICA CONSUMER COMMITTEE FDB
Rockildevej 65, 2620 Albertslund
Denmark

Co-op Consumers   1191.02

ICC PUBLISHING CORP, INC
801 2nd Ave, Suite 1204
New York, NY 10017

ICC World Economic Yearbook
2431.01

IC PUBLICATIONS LTD
122 E 42nd St, Suite 1121
New York, NY 10017

African Business   79.01
Egypt/North Africa   1598.02
Gulf States   2310.01
Middle East   3216
Middle East Industry & Transport
3218
Middle East Travel   3221
New African   3432
Nigeria Newsletter   3517.01
Saudi Arabia Newsletter   4183.02

IDC EUROPA LTD
2 Bath Rd
London, England W4 1LN

European Computer Market
Forecast-Eurocast 1981   1772

ILLINOIS BANKERS ASSN
188 W Randolph St
Chicago, IL 60601

Illinois Banker   2437

ILLINOIS (STATE)

DEPT OF BUSINESS AND ECONOMIC DEVELOPMENT
222 S College St
Springfield, IL 62706

Illinois Economic Data Sheets   2438

(ILLINOIS END)

ILLINOIS STATE UNIVERSITY
Dept of Finance
Williams Hall
Normal, IL 61761

Journal of Financial Education   2856

IMSWORLD PUBLICATIONS LTD
York House, 37 Queen Square
London, England WC1N 3BE

Animal Health International   225
Drug License Opportunities   1508.01
IMS Monitor Report   2476.01
New Product Card Index   3457.02
Pharmaceutical Marketletter   3764.01
World Directory of Pharmaceutical
Manufacturers   5058.01
World Health Environmental Surveys
5067.01
World License Review   5068.02
World Pharmaceutical Introductions
5073.03

INCOMES DATA SERVICES LTD
140 Great Portland St
London, England W1N 5TA

Incomes Data Report   2485
Incomes Data Services (IDS) Briefs
2486
Incomes Data Services (IDS) Focus
2487
Incomes Data Services (IDS)
International Reports   2488
Incomes Data Services (IDS) Studies
2489

INCORPORATED COUNCIL OF LAW REPORTING FOR ENGLAND & WALES
3 Stone Bldgs, Lincoln's Inn
London, England, WC2A 3XN

Industrial Cases Reports   2511

INDEPENDENT BANKERS ASSN OF AMERICA
Sauk Centre, MN 56378

Independent Banker   2494
Washington Weekly Report   4897

INDEPENDENT PETROLEUM ASSN OF AMERICA
1101 16th St NW
Washington, DC 20036

IPAA Statistical and Economic Reports
2777.01
Petroleum Independent   3760

INDEPENDENT SURVEY CO, LTD
PO Box 6000
Vancouver, BC, Canada V6B 4B9

Canadian Weekly Stock Charts:
Industrials   847
Canadian Weekly Stock Charts: Mines
& Oils   848

(INDIA)

EMBASSY OF INDIA
Commerce Wing
2107 Massachusetts Ave NW
Washington, DC 20008

Embassy of India Commercial Bulletin
1640
India News   2504

(INDIA END)

INDIANA UNIVERSITY
Graduate School of Business
Bloomington, IN 47401

Business Horizons   687

INDICATOR RESEARCH GROUP, INC
Indictor Bldg
Palisades Park, NJ 07650

Income Investor   2484
Indicator Digest   2505
International Gold Digest   2683.01

INDPROP PUBLISHING CO, INC
PO Box 2060
Red Bank, NJ 07701

American Industrial Properties Report
183
American Industrial Properties Report
(AIPR) Worldwide Guide for
Foreign Investment   184

INDUSTRIAL ACCIDENT PREVENTION ASSN
c/o Jack Oldham
2 Bloor St E, 23rd Floor
Toronto, Ont, Canada M4W 3C2

Accident Prevention   11

INDUSTRIAL FOUNDATION FOR ACCIDENT PREVENTION
Box 28
Mosman Park, Western Australia 6012

Industrial Foundation for Accident
Prevention (IFAP) News   2521

INDUSTRIAL HEALTH FOUNDATION, INC
5231 Centre Ave
Pittsburgh, PA 15232

Industrial Health Foundation
Chemical–Toxicological Series   2524
Industrial Health Foundation
Engineering Series   2525
Industrial Health Foundation Legal
Series   2526
Industrial Health Foundation
Management Series   2527
Industrial Health Foundation Medical
Series   2528
Industrial Health Foundation. Nursing
Series   2529
Industrial Hygiene Digest   2530

INDUSTRIAL OPPORTUNITIES LTD
13-14 Homewell
Havant, Hamp, England PO9 1EE

Research Disclosure   4087

INDUSTRIAL PARTICIPATION ASSN
78 Buckingham Gate
London, England SW1E 6PQ

Industrial Participation   2535

INDUSTRIAL RELATIONS SERVICE
170 Finchley Rd
London, England NW3 6BP

European Industrial Relations Review
1778
Health & Safety Information Bulletin
2356
Industrial Relations Law Reports
2544
Industrial Relations Review & Report
2547
Legal Information Bulletin   2996

INDUSTRIAL RESEARCH INST
265 Post Rd W
Westport, CT 06880

Research Management   4090

INDUSTRIAL SOCIETY
Peter Runge House
3 Carlton House Terrace
London, England SW1Y 5DG

Industrial Society   2552

INFORMATION ACCESS CORP
404 Sixth Ave
Menlo Park, CA 94025

American Buys   154.01
Business Index   690.01
Current Law Index   1277.01
Legal Resource Index   2996.01
Magazine Index   3056.01
National Newspaper Index   3396.01

INFORMATION COORDINATORS, INC
1435-37 Randolph St
Detroit, MI 48226

Work-Related Abstracts   5029

INFORMATION FOR INDUSTRY
Hay Group
229 S 18th St
Philadelphia, PA 19103

Directors & Boards   1404
Mergers & Acquisitions   3195

INFORMATION RESOURCES PRESS
1700 Moore St, Suite 700A
Arlington, VA 22209

EIS   1598.03

INFORMATION SCIENCE ABSTRACTS
PO Box 8510
Philadelphia, PA 19101

Information Science Abstracts   2574

INSTITUTE FOR BUSINESS PLANNING, INC
IBP Plaza
Englewood Cliffs, NJ 07632

Accounting Desk Book   33
Business Acquisitions Desk Book with
Checklists and Forms   655
Estate Planning Desk Book   1750
Real Estate Financing Desk Book
4012
Real Estate Tax Shelter Desk Book
4027
Tax Desk Book for the Closely-Held
Corporation   4546

INSTITUTE FOR INTERNATIONAL RESEARCH LTD
70 Warren St
London, England W1P 5PA

British Tax Report   623.01
China Business Report   940.01
Currency Forecasting Service   1268.02
European and Middle East Tax Report
1768
International Accounting & Financial
Report   2653

International Tax Report   2733
Re Report   4078.01
Tax Haven & Investment Report
4553.03

INST FOR INVENTION & INNOVATION, INC
85 Irving St
Arlington, MA 02174

Copyright Management   1201.01
Invention Management   2750

INSTITUTE FOR PRODUCT SAFETY
1410 Duke University Rd
Durham, NC 27701

Product Safety News   3877
Product Standards Index   3881

INSTITUTE FOR SCIENTIFIC INFORMATION
325 Chestnut St
Philadelphia, PA 19106

Current Contents: Social and
Behavioral Sciences   1273
Social Sciences Citation Index   4314

INSTITUTE OF ACTUARIES
Staple Inn Hall, High Holborn
London, England WC1V 7QJ

Journal of the Institute of Actuaries
2892

INST OF ADMINISTRATIVE ACCOUNTING
Walter House
418-422 Strand
London, England WC2R 0PW

Administrative Accounting   55

INSTITUTE OF BANKERS
10 Lombard St
London, England EC3V 9AS

Journal of the Institute of Bankers
2893

INST OF CHARTERED ACCOUNTANTS IN ENGLAND AND WALES
PO Box 433, Chartered Acc's Hall
Moorgate Place
London, England EC2P 2BJ

Accountancy   13
Accountants Digests   20
Accounting & Business Research   29
Tax Digests   4546.01

**INST OF CHARTERED
ACCOUNTANTS IN IRELAND**
7 Fitzwilliam Place
Dublin 2, Ireland

Accountancy Ireland   14

**INST OF CHARTERED
ACCOUNTANTS IN SCOTLAND**
Accountants' Publishing Co Ltd
27 Queen St
Edinburgh, EH2 1LA, Scotland

Accountants Magazine   26
Institute of Chartered Accountants of
   Scotland Official Directory   2597

INST OF CREDIT MANAGEMENT
12 Queens Sq
Brighton, England BN1 3FD

Credit Management   1247

INSTITUTE OF DIRECTORS
116 Pall Mall
London, England SW1Y 5ED

Director   1403

**INSTITUTE OF DIRECTORS IN
AUSTRALIA**
16 O'Connell St
Sydney, NSW 2000, Australia

Australian Director   393

**INST OF INTERNAL AUDITORS,
INC**
249 Maitland Ave
Altamonte Springs, FL 32701

Internal Auditor   2644
Internos   2744.01

**INSTITUTE OF MANAGEMENT
SCIENCES**
146 Westminster St
Providence, RI 02903

Interfaces   2643
Management Science   3088

**INSTITUTE OF MANAGEMENT
SERVICES**
1 Cecil Ct, London Rd, Enfield
Middlesex, England EN2 6DD

Management Services   3090

INST OF MARKETING
Moor Hall
Cookham Maidenhead
Berks, England SL6 9QH

Marketing   3127
Quarterly Review of Marketing   3971

**INSTITUTE OF MATHEMATICAL
STATISTICS**
c/o Heebok Park
3401 Investment Blvd, No 6
Hayward, CA 94545

Annals of Probability   228
Annals of Statistics   229

**INST OF PATENTEES &
INVENTORS**
Staple Inn Bldgs South
335 High Holborn
London, England WC1V 7PX

Inventor   2751

**INST OF PERSONNEL
MANAGEMENT**
Central House, Upper Woburn Pl
London, England WC1H 0HX

Institute of Personnel Management
   (IPM) Digest   2599
Personnel Management   3745

**INSTITUTE OF POLYMER
INDUSTRY, INC**
Central PO Box 1176
Tokyo 100-91, Japan

Plastics Industry News   3782.01

INST OF PUBLIC AFFAIRS
401 Collins St
Melbourne, Vic 3000, Australia

Institute of Public Affairs (IPA) Review
   2600

INST OF PUBLIC RELATIONS
1 Great James St
London, England WC1N 3DA

Register of Members   4051.01

**INSTITUTE OF PURCHASING &
SUPPLY**
York House, Westminster Bridge Rd
London, England SE1 7UT

Procurement Weekly   3861
Purchasing & Supply   3950

**INSTITUTE OF REAL ESTATE
MANAGEMENT**
430 N Michigan Ave
Chicago, IL 60611

Journal of Property Management   2875

**INSTITUTE OF SALES
MANAGEMENT**
Concorde House, 24 Warwick New Rd
Royal Leamington Spa
Warwickshire, England CV32 5JH

Sales Management and Sales
   Engineering   4172

**INSTITUTE OF SUPERVISORY
MANAGEMENT**
22 Bore St
Lichfield, Staffs, England WS13 6LP

Supervisory Management   4502

INSTITUTIONAL INVESTOR, INC
488 Madison Ave
New York, NY 10022

Corporate Financing Week   1208
Institutional Investor   2601
Institutional Investor International
   Edition   2602
Journal of Portfolio Management   2874
Pensions Directory   3730
Wall Street Letter   4880

INSURANCE FIELD CO, INC
4325 Old Shepherdsville Rd, Box 18441
Louisville, KY 40218

Adjusters' Reference Guide   53
Insurance Agency Computer Power
   2609
Insurance Field Magazine   2621
Insurance Industry Newsletter   2624
Pension Pulse Beats   3726.01
Producer News   3862

INSURANCE FORUM, INC
PO Box 245
Ellettsville, IN 47429

Insurance Forum   2622

**INSURANCE INFORMATION
INSTITUTE**
110 William St
New York, NY 10038

Insurance Facts   2620
Journal of Insurance   2862

**INSURANCE INSTITUTE OF
CANADA**
55 University Ave
Toronto, Ont, Canada M5J 2H7

Insurance Institute of Canada Annual
   Report   2626

**INSURANCE PUBLISHING &
PRINTING CO**
34 Lower High St Stourbridge
West Midlands, England DY8 1TA

Fur Review   2203
Insurance Brokers' Monthly   2612

**INTELLIGENCE INTERNATIONAL
LTD**
17 Rodney Rd
Cheltenham, Glos, England GL50 1HX

Intelligence Digest BUSINESS
   TRENDS   2638

INTERACTIVE DATA CORP
486 Totten Pond Rd
Waltham, MA 02154

Analytics   214

**INTER-AMERICAN AFFAIRS
PRESS**
Box 181
Washington, DC 20044

Hanson's Latin America Letter   2341
Inter-American Economic Affairs
   2641

**INTER-AMERICAN
DEVELOPMENT BANK**
808 17th St NW
Washington, DC 20577

Ec onomic & Social Progress in Latin
   America Annual Report   1538
Inter-American Development Bank
   Annual Report   2639
Inter-American Development Bank
   (IDB) News   2640

**INTERFAITH CENTER ON
CORPORATE RESPONSIBILITY**
475 Riverside Dr, Rm 566
New York, NY 10027

Corporate Examiner   1206

**INTERMEDIATE TECHNOLOGY
PUBLICATIONS LTD**
9 King St
London, England WC2E 8HN

Appropriate Technology   293

INTERNATIONAL ADVANCEMENT
Box 75537
Los Angeles, CA 90075

American Bulletin of International
   Technology Transfer   163

**INTERNATIONAL ADVERTISING
ASSN**
475 5th Ave
New York, NY 10017

Concise Guide to International Markets
   1093
World Advertising Expenditures, 1976
   5035
World Directory of Marketing
   Communications Periodicals   5057

**INTERNATIONAL AIR
TRANSPORT ASSOCIATION**
IBM Bldg, Five Place Ville Marie
Montreal 2, Que, Canada

World Air Transport Statistics   5039

**INTERNATIONAL ASSN FOR
RESEARCH IN INCOME &
WEALTH**
Box 1962, Yale Station
New Haven, CT 06520

Review of Income & Wealth   4123

**INTERNATIONAL ASSOCIATION
OF BUSINESS COMMUNICATORS**
870 Market St, Suite 940
San Francisco, CA 94102

International Assn of Business
   Communicators (IABC) News   2656
Journal of Organizational
   Communication   2871

**INTERNATIONAL ASSOCIATION
OF INSURANCE COUNSEL**
20 N Wacker Dr, Suite 3705
Chicago, IL 60606

Insurance Counsel Journal   2617

**INTERNATIONAL BANKTRENDS,
INC**
910 16th St NW
Washington, DC 20006

Access Reports-Privacy   902
Bank Director   461.01
International Banktrends   2657.01
Investment Management   2764.01
Washington Banktrends   4884

**INTERNATIONAL BIO-MEDICAL
INFORMATION SERVICE, INC**
PO Box 756
Miami, FL 33156

Bio-Medical Insight   555
Bio-Medical Scoreboard   556
Medical & Healthcare Marketplace
   Guide   3179

Medical School Rounds   3182
Worldwide Guide to Medical
   Electronics Marketing Representation
   5088

**INTERNATIONAL BUREAU OF
FISCAL DOCUMENTATION**
Muiderpoort
PO Box 20237
1000HE Amsterdam, Netherlands

European Taxation   1787

**INTERNATIONAL
BUSINESS–GOVERNMENT
COUNSELLORS, INC**
1625 I St NW
Washington, DC 20006

Brussels Report   632
Washington International Business
   Report   4888

**INTERNATIONAL CENTRE FOR
SETTLEMENT OF INVESTMENT
DISPUTES**
Washington, DC 20433

Investment Laws of the World   2763

**INTERNATIONAL CITY
MANAGEMENT ASSOCIATION**
1140 Connecticut Ave NW
Washington, DC 20036

Municipal Yearbook   3341

**INTERNATIONAL CONSUMER
CREDIT ASSOCIATION**
243 N Lindbergh Blvd
St Louis, MO 63141

Consumer Trends   1178.01
Credit World   1253

**INTERNATIONAL CO-OPERATIVE
ALLIANCE**
11 Upper Grosvenor St
London, England W1X 9PA

Agricultural Co-operative Bulletin   95
Libradoc   3007
Review of International Co-operation
   4124

**INTERNATIONAL COTTON
ADVISORY COMMITTEE**
1225 19th St NW
Washington, DC 20036

Cotton: Monthly Review of the World
   Situation   1232

INTERNATIONAL DATA CORP
214 Third Ave
Waltham, MA 02254

Automated Business Communications
  Program 423
Autotransaction Industry Report
  435.01
Computer Output Program 1081.01
Corporate Plannng Service 1210
Datacomm Advisor 1326
Data Files 1331
Distributed Processing Report Service
  1467.01
EDP (Electronic Data Processing)
  Industry Report 1590
EDP (Electronic Data Processing)
  Japan Report 1590.01
Information Industry and Technology
  Service 2573
Office Automation Reporting Service
  3578
Services and Software Information
  Program 4267
Telecom Insider 4582.01

INTERNATIONAL EXPORT ASSN
PO Box 1
Bourne, Lincolnshire, England

Newsletter 3645.03

INTERNATIONAL FOUNDATION OF EMPLOYEE BENEFIT PLANS
18700 W Bluemound Rd, Box 69
Brookfield, WI 53005

Employee Benefits Journal 1645
International Foundation (IF) Legal
  Legislative Reporter. News Bulletin
  2681
International Foundation of Employee
  Benefit Plans. Digest 2682
Textbook for Employee Benefit Plan
  Trustees, Administrators, & Advisors
  4598

INTERNATIONAL INSTITUTE FOR LABOUR STUDIES
CP 6, CH-1211
Geneva 22, Switzerland

International Educational Materials
  Exchange 2676
Labour and Society 2948

INTERNATIONAL INTERTRADE INDEX
Box 636, Federal Square
Newark, NJ 07101

International Intertrade Index 2686

INTERNATIONAL LABOUR ORGANIZATION
1750 New York Ave NW
Washington, DC 20006

Bulletin of Labour Statistics 645
CIS 947
CIS Abstracts Bulletin 948
International Labour Documentation
  2698
International Labour Organization
  (ILO) Publications 2699
International Labour Review 2700
Legislative Series 3002
Social & Labour Bulletin 4312
Year Book of Labour Statistics 5095

INTERNATIONAL LEAD & ZINC STUDY GROUP
Metro House, 58 St James's St
London, England SW1A 1LH

Lead and Zinc Statistics 2993

INTERNATIONAL LICENSING LTD
92 Cannon Lane
Pinner, Middlesex, England HA5 1HT

International Licensing 2702

INTERNATIONAL MONETARY FUND
19th and H Sts NW
Washington, DC 20431

Central Banking Legislation: A
  Collection of Central Bank,
  Monetary, and Banking Laws 888
Direction of Trade 1400
Finance and Development 1988
Government Finance Statistics
  Yearbook 2244
International Financial Statistics 2680
International Monetary Fund (IMF)
  Survey 2709
International Monetary Fund Annual
  Report of the Executive Directors
  2710
International Monetary Fund Annual
  Report on Exchange Restrictions
  2711
International Monetary Fund Balance
  of Payments Yearbook 2712
Staff Papers 4369
Surveys of African Economies 4521
Tape Subscriptions to IFS, DOT, BOP,
  and GFS 4528

INTERNATIONAL NEWSPAPER PROMOTION ASSN
PO Box 17422
Dulles International Airport
Washington, DC 20041

Idea Newsletter 2433

INTERNATIONAL PUBLICATIONS SERVICE
114 E 32nd St
New York, NY 10016

International Directory of Computer
  and Information System Services
  2672

INTERNATIONAL REPORTS, INC
200 Park Avenue South
New York, NY 10003

Foreign Letter 2120
Forex Service 2145
International Business Intelligence
  2662
International Commercial Financing
  Intelligence 2668
International Country Risk Guide
  2670
International Reports 2727
Special Telex Service (STS) 4357

INTERNATIONAL REVIEW SERVICE
15 Washington Place
New York, NY 10003

Energy Developments 1679
State-Owned Energy Enterprises 4404
Trade and Economic Development
  4647

INTERTEC PUBLISHING CORP
9221 Quivera Rd, PO Box 12901
Overland Park, KS 66212

Implement & Tractor 2442
Lawn & Garden Marketing 2978.01
Meat, Poultry and Seafood Digest
  3164.01
Video Systems 4856
World Farming 5064

INVESTMENT COMPANY INST
1775 K St NW
Washington, DC 20006

Monthly Statistics 3301
Mutual Fund Fact Book 3345
Mutual Funds Forum 3348

INVESTMENT DEALERS' DIGEST
150 Broadway
New York, NY 10038

Investment Dealers' Digest   2762
Mutual Fund Directory   3344

INVESTOR RESPONSIBILITY RESEARCH CENTER
1522 K St NW, Suite 806
Washington, DC 20005

News for Investors   3463

INVESTORS INTELLIGENCE, INC
2 East Ave
Larchmont, NY 10538

Investors Intelligence   2773

INVESTORS RESEARCH CO
PO Box 30, 1900 State St
Santa Barbara, CA 93102

Investors Research Service   2774

IOWA DEVELOPMENT COMMISSION
250 Jewett Bldg
Des Moines, IA 50309

Iowa Exporting Companies Directory
  2776
Iowa World Trade Guide   2777
Statistical Profile of Iowa   4436

IPC BUSINESS PRESS LTD
205 E 42nd St
New York, NY 10017

Applied Ergonomics   286
Applied Mathematics Modelling   287
Composites   1068
Computer-Aided Design   1071
Cryogenics   1265
Energy Policy   1687
Food Policy   2094
Fuel   2195
Fuel Abstracts and Current Titles
  2196
Futures   2204
Iron and Steel International   2786
Marine Policy   3121
Microprocessors   3214
Non-Destructive Testing (NDT)
  International   3530
Optics and Laser Technology   3632
Policy Publications Review   3795
Polymer   3807
Resources Policy   4097
Science and Public Policy   4196
Telecommunications Policy   4583
Tropical Agriculture   4722
Ultrasonics   4738
Underwater Information Bulletin   4740
Welding and Metal Fabrication   4944

IRELAND

CENTRAL STATISTICS OFFICE
Earlsfort Terrace
Dublin 2, Ireland

Irish Statistical Bulletin   2781
Statistical Abstract of Ireland   4419
Trade Statistics of Ireland   4676

(IRELAND END)

IRISH CONGRESS OF TRADE
Unions Research Service
19 Ragland Rd
Ballsbridge
Dublin 4, Ireland

Trade Union Information   4679

IRISH EXPORT BOARD
Strand Rd
Sandymount
Dublin 4, Ireland

Export   1817
Irish Export Directory   2780

PETER ISAACSON PUBLICATIONS
46-49 Porter Street
Prahran, Vic 3181, Australia

Australian Directory of Exports   394
Australian Hospital   402
Australian Hospitals and Health
  Services Yearbook   403
Aviation News/Airmarket   440
Datascope   1344
Graphix   2260
Hospitality   2393
Hotel, Motel, and Travel Directory
  2400
Metal and Engineering Industry
  Yearbook   3196
New DP Index   3436
Pacific Computer Weekly   3679
Travelweek   4705
Visa Information Guide   4859

ISRAEL DISCOUNT BANK OF NEW YORK
511 5th Ave
New York, NY 10017

Business Review and Economic News
  from Israel   720

ITALY

ITALIAN EMBASSY
Commercial Office
1601 Fuller St NW
Washington, DC 20009

Italian Trade Topics   2792
Italy: An Economic Profile   2793

(ITALY END)

ITALY–AMERICA CHAMBER OF COMMERCE, INC
350 5th Ave, Suite 3015
New York, NY 10001

United States–Italy Trade Directory
  4808

JOHN JACKSON & ASSOC PTY LTD
Box A 771
Sydney South, NSW 2000, Australia

Australian Building and Construction
  News   387

JANUZ MARKETING COMMUNICATIONS, INC
PO Box 1000
Lake Forest, IL 60045

Creative Selling   1241.01
Execu-Time   1794.02
Januz Direct Marketing Letter   2795
Telephone Marketing Report   4586.01

JAPAN JOURNAL, INC
CPO Box 702
Tokyo, Japan   100–91

Japan Stock Journal   2803.01

JAPAN TRADE CENTRE
1221 Avenue of the Americas
New York, NY 10020

Focus Japan   2074
Japan External Trade Organization
  (JETRO) Business Information Series
  2801
Japan External Trade Organization
  (JETRO) Marketing Series   2802

JENKINS PUBLISHING CO
306 W Main St
Mascoutah, IL 62258

Jenkins Mobile Industry News Letter
  2805

JOHANNESBURG STOCK EXCHANGE
PO Box 1174
Johannesburg, South Africa 2000

Johannesburg Stock Exchange Monthly
  Bulletin   2815

JOHNSON'S CHARTS, INC
545 Elmwood Ave
Buffalo, NY 14222

Johnson's Investment Co Service   2816

**JOHNSTON INTERNATIONAL
PUBLISHING CORP**
386 Park Ave, South
New York, NY 10016

Automobile International   427
Export/El Exportador   1821
Industrial World/Industrial World en
   Español   2556
Modern Africa   3252
Modern Asia   3253
Near East Business   3422
World Automotive Market   5041.01

BETHUNE JONES
321 Sunset Ave
Asbury Park, NJ 07712

From the State Capitals: Agriculture
   and Food Products   2169
From the State Capitals: Airport
   Construction and Financing   2170
From the State Capitals: Federal Action
   Affecting the States   2171
From the State Capitals: General
   Bulletin   2172
From the State Capitals: Highway
   Financing and Construction   2173
From the State Capitals: Housing and
   Redevelopment   2174
From the State Capitals: Industrial
   Development   2175
From the State Capitals: Institutional
   Building   2176
From the State Capitals: Insurance
   Regulation   2177
From the State Capitals: Labor
   Relations   2178
From the State Capitals: Liquor
   Control   2179
From the State Capitals: Merchandising
   2180
From the State Capitals: Milk Control
   2181
From the State Capitals: Motor Vehicle
   Regulation   2182
From the State Capitals: Personnel
   Management   2183
From the State Capitals: Public Utilities
   2184
From the State Capitals: Small Loans,
   Sales Finance, Banking   2185
From the State Capitals: Taxes—Local
   Nonproperty   2186
From the State Capitals: Taxes—
   Property   2187

From the State Capitals:
   Unemployment Compensation   2188
From the State Capitals: Urban Transit
   & Bus Transportation   2189
From the State Capitals: Wage–Hour
   Regulation   2190
From the State Capitals: Workmen's
   Compensation   2191

JOURNAL OF COMMERCE LTD
2000 W 12th Ave
Vancouver, BC, Canada V6J 2G2

Journal of Commerce   2834

JSB PRODUCTIONS LTD
PO Box 46475, Station G
Vancouver, BC, Canada V6R 4G7

British Columbia Municipal Yearbook
   606

E E JUDGE & SONS, INC
PO Box 866
Westminster, MD 21157

Almanac of the Canning, Freezing,
   Preserving Industries   149

PAUL KAGAN ASSOCIATES, INC
100 Merrick Rd
Rockville Center, NY 11570

Broadcast Investor   628
Cablecast   731
Cable TV Regulation   732
Multicast   3331
Pay TV Newsletter   3712

ROBERT KAHN AND ASSOCIATES
PO Box 249
Lafayette, CA 94549

Retailing Today   4105

**KANSAS DEPT OF ECONOMIC
DEVELOPMENT**
503 Kansas Ave, Room 626
Topeka, KS 66003

Directory of Manufacturers and
   Products   1442.01

KELLY'S DIRECTORIES LTD
Windsor Court, East Grinstead House
East Grinstead, West Susses, England
RH19 1XB

Advertiser's Annual   65
British Industry and Services in the
   Common Market   614
International Businessman's Who's
   Who   2663

International Year Book and
   Statesmen's Who's Who   2744
Kelly's Manufacturers and Merchants
   Directory   2907
Kelly's Post Office London Directory
   2908
Kelly's Regional Directory of British
   Industry and Services   2908.01
Laxton's Building Price Book   2992
United Kingdom News Contact
   Directory   4760.01

KENNEDY & KENNEDY, INC
Templeton Rd
Fitzwilliam, NH 03447

Consultants News   1145
Directory of Executive Recruiters
   1429
Directory of Management Consultants
   1442
Directory of Outplacement Firms
   1453
Executive Recruiter News   1807.01
International Directory of Executive
   Recruiters   2673

KENNEDY SINCLAIRE, INC
524 Hamburg Turnpike, PO Box 34
Wayne, NJ 07470

Down to Business   1504.01

JAMES C KILLINGSWORTH
PO Box 1816
Newport Beach, CA 92663

Orange County Business   3634
Orange County Illustrated   3635

LLEWELLYN KING
300 National Press Bldg
Washington, DC 20045

Defense Week   1355.02
Energy Daily   1678
Metals Daily   3196.01

**KIPLINGER WASHINGTON
EDITORS, INC**
1729 H St NW
Washington, DC 20006

Changing Times   907
Kiplinger Agricultural Letter   2912.02
Kiplinger California Letter   2913
Kiplinger Florida Letter   2915
Kiplinger Tax Letter   2916
Kiplinger Texas Letter   2916.01
Kiplinger Washington Letter   2917

B KLEIN PUBLICATIONS, INC
Box 8503
Coral Springs, FL 33065

Directory of Mailing List Houses   1440
Guide to American Directories   2286
Mail Order Business Directory   3059

CHARLES H KLINE & CO, INC
330 Passaic Ave
Fairfield, NJ 07006

Directory of US and Canadian
   Marketing Surveys & Services   1462

**KNOWLEDGE INDUSTRY
PUBLICATIONS, INC**
701 Westchester Ave
White Plains, NY 10604

Book Publisher's (BP) Report   573
Educational Marketer   1592
Home Video Report   2384.01
IDP Report   2433.02
Overseas Assignment Directory Service
   3655

KOMPASS PUBLISHERS LTD
Windosr Court, East Grinstead House
East Grinstead, West Sussex, England
RH19 1XD

British Exports   613
Export Services   1832
Kompass Register, Australia   2920
Kompass Register, Belgium &
   Luxembourg   2920.01
Kompass Register, Brazil   2920.02
Kompass Register, Denmark   2920.03
Kompass Register, France   2920.04
Kompass Register, Holland   2920.05
Kompass Register, Indonesia   2920.06
Kompass Register, Italy   2920.07
Kompass Register, Morocco   2920.08
Kompass Register, Norway   2920.09
Kompass Register, Spain   2920.10
Kompass Register, Sweden   2920.11
Kompass Register, Switzerland
   2920.12
Kompass Register, West Germany
   2920.13
UK Kompass Register   4759
UK Trade Names   4762

KOREAN TRADERS ASSN, INC
460 Park Ave, Room 555
New York, NY 10022

Korean Trade Directory   2921
Korean Trade News   2922

LABOUR RESEARCH DEPT
78 Blackfriars Rd
London, England SE1 8HF

Bargaining Report   508.01
Labour Research   2955
Labour Research Dept Fact Service
   2956

LAKEWOOD PUBLICATIONS INC
731 Hennepin Ave
Minneapolis, MN 55403

Airport Services Management   126
Food Plant Ideas   2093
Potentials in Marketing   3812
Training   4684

**LAND DEVELOPMENT INSTITUTE
LTD**
1401 16th St NW
Washington, DC 20036

Digest of State Land Sales Regulation
   1392
Land Development Law Reporter
   2960
Resort Timesharing Law Reporter
   4096.01

AUBREY G LANSTON & CO
20 Broad St
New York, NY 10005

Lanston Letter   2966

**LATIN AMERICAN NEWSLETTERS
LTD**
Greenhill House
90-93 Cowcross St
London, England EC1M 6BL

Andean Group Regional Report
   222.01
Brazil Regional Report   586
Caribbean Regional Report   863.01
Latin America Commodities Report
   2972
Latin America Weekly Report   2976.02
Mexico and Central America Regional
   Report   3206.02
Southern Cone Regional Report
   4347.01

LAVENTHOL AND HORWATH
1845 Walnut St
Philadelphia, PA 19103

Health Care Letter   2357
Monthly Tax Report   3304
Trend of Business in Hotels (Canada)
   4714
Trend of Business in the Lodging
   Industry   4715

LAW BOOK CO LTD
31 Market St
Sydney, NSW 2000, Australia

Australian Business Law Review   388
Australian Tax Review   418

LAWRENCE-LETTER & CO
427 W 12 St
Kansas City, MO 64105

Association Management Scope   340
Management/Scope   3089

**LAWYERS TITLE INSURANCE
CORP**
Box 27567
Richmond, VA 23261

Lawyers Title News   2991

**LAWYER TO LAWYER
CONSULTATION PANEL**
5325 Naiman Pkwy
Solon, OH 44139

Lawyer's Register by Specialties and
   Fields of Law   2990

**LEBHAR-FRIEDMAN
PUBLICATIONS, INC**
425 Park Ave
New York, NY 10022

Chain Store Age, Executive Edition
   900
Chain Store Age, General Merchandise
   Edition   900.01
Chain Store Age, Supermarkets Edition
   901
Discount Store News   1465
Drug Store News   1509.01
National Home Center News   3379.01
Nation's Restaurant News   3414.01

LEGAL CONTENTS
PO Box 3014
Northbrook, IL 60062

Legal Contents   2995.01

**LEGISLATIVE RESEARCH
INTERNATIONAL**
PO Box 1511
Washington, DC 20013

News from the Hill   3464

LENDING LAW FORUM, INC
Box 85, Rockville Centre
New York, NY 11571

Lending Law Forum   3005

LEVIATHAN HOUSE
11 John Princes St
Cavendish Sq
London, England W1M 9HB

Business Who's Who   728

S JAY LEVY
Box 26
Chappaqua, NY 10514

Industry Forecast   2561

LINK HOUSE PUBLICATIONS LTD
Link House
Dingwall Ave
Croydon, England CR9 2TA

Do It Yourself Retailing and Home
   Improvement Marketing   1490

LIPSCOMBE & ASSOCIATES
PO Box 158
Claremont, WA 6010, Australia

Executive Briefing   1797
Lipscombe Report   3021
Who's Pegging Where   4975.01

LITTLEFIELD, ADAMS & CO
81 Adams Dr
Totawa, NJ 07512

Dictionary of Economics and Business
   1379
Dictionary of Insurance   1380

LLOYDS BANK LTD
PO Box 215, Lombard St
London, England EC3P 3BS

Lloyd's Bank Economic Bulletin   3031
Lloyds Bank Review   3032

LLOYD'S OF LONDON PRESS LTD
Sheepen Place
Colchester, Essex, England CO3 3LP

Lloyd's European Loading List
   3032.01
Lloyd's Law Reports   3032.02
Lloyd's List   3032.03
Lloyd's Loading List   3033
Lloyd's Maritime & Commercial Law
   Quarterly   3033.01
Lloyd's Maritime Law Newsletter
   3033.02
Lloyd's Monthly List of Laid Up
   Vessels   3033.03
Lloyd's Ship Manager   3033.04
Lloyd's Shipping Economist   3033.05
Lloyd's Shipping Index   3033.06
Lloyd's Voyage Record   3033.07

Lloyd's Weekly Casualty Reports
   3034
Product Liability International   3874

LOMOND PUBLICATIONS, INC
PO Box 56
Mt Airy, MD 21771

R & D Management Digest   3999.02

**LONDON CHAMBER OF
COMMERCE & INDUSTRY**
69-75 Cannon St
London, England EC4N 5AB

Commerce International   996
Eastern Europe   1523
Economic Report   1566

**LONDON SCHOOL OF
ECONOMICS AND POLITICAL
SCIENCE**
Houghton St
London, England WC2A 2AE

British Journal of Industrial Relations
   616
Journal of Transport Economics and
   Policy   2898

**LONG ISLAND COMMERCIAL
REVIEW, INC**
303 Sunnyside Blvd
Plainview, NY 11803

Long Island Business Newsweekly and
   Reference Series   3042

LONGMAN GROUP LTD
Longman House
Burnt Mill
Harlow, Essex, England CM20 2JE

Education   1590.02
Education Year Book   1597
International Statistical Review   2728
International Journal of Ambient
   Energy   2689.01
Keesing's Contemporary Archives
   2905
Review of Economic Studies   4121
Statistician   4446
Urban Studies   4833

LORNE, CALDOUGH LTD
Tower Suite, 1 White Hall Place
London, England SW1

Business Ideas Letter   688

JACK LOTTO
265 Jericho Turnpike, PO Box 639
Floral Park, NY 11001

Disclosure Record   1463

LOUISIANA STATE UNIVERSITY
College of Business Administration
Division of Research, 3139 CEBA
Baton Rouge, LA 70803

Louisiana Business Review   3047
Louisiana Economic Indicators
   3047.01

LOUISIANA TECH UNIVERSITY
Division of Administration and
Business Research
PO Box 5796 Tech Station
Ruston, LA 71270

Louisiana Economy   3048

LYNCH-BOWES, INC
120 Broadway, Suite 1749
New York, NY 10271

Lynch International Investment Survey
   3051

MACLAREN PUBLISHERS LTD
Box 109, Davis House
69-77 High St
Croydon, Surrey, England CR9 1QH

Incentive Marketing and Sales
   Promotion   2478

MACLEAN-HUNTER LTD
30 Old Burlington St
London, England W1X 2AE

Airtrade   127
Brad Advertiser & Agency List   581
Brad Directories & Annuals   583
British Plastics & Rubber   619
British Printer   620
British Rate & Data   621
Business Systems & Equipment   724
Cruises & Sea Voyages   1264
Dataguide   1334
Domestic Heating   1492
Fraser's Canadian Trade Directory
   2162
Heating & Air Conditioning Journal
   2366
International Freighting Management
   2682.01
International Freighting Weekly   2683
Lighting Equipment News   3018
Modern Purchasing   3264
Oilman   3606
Packaging News   3684
Printer   3589
Record of New Issues   4034
Record of Valuation Day Prices   4036
Record of Warrants   4037
Routes Yearbook   4144

Survey of Predecessor and Defunct
  Companies 4517.01
Travel Agency 4700

MACMILLAN PUBLISHING CO
866 3rd Ave
New York, NY 10022

International Encyclopedia of the Social
  Sciences 2677

MACRO COMMUNICATIONS, INC
150 E 58th St
New York, NY 10159

Financial World 2034

**MADISON AVENUE MAGAZINE,
INC**
369 Lexington Ave
New York, NY 10017

Madison Avenue 3056

MAINE NATIONAL BANK
400 Congress St, PO Box 919
Portland, ME 04104

Maine Business Indicators 3060

MAINE (STATE)

DEPT OF MANPOWER AFFAIRS
Bureau of Labor
State House Station #45
Augusta, ME 04333

Census of Maine Manufacturers 875
Directory of Maine Labor
  Organizations 1441

(MAINE END)

MAIN LAFRENTZ & CO
380 Park Ave
New York, NY 10017

News Summary 3471
Tax Newsletter 4562
Viewpoint 4857

MALAYSIAN TIN BUREAU
2000 K St NW
Washington, DC 20006

Tin News 4623

MANAGEMENT CONTENTS
PO Box 3014
Northbrook, IL 60062

Management Contents 3076

**MANAGEMENT INFORMATION
CORP**
140 Barclay Center
Cherry Hill, NJ 08034

Datacom & Distributed Processing
  Report 1326.01
Data Entry Awareness Report 1328
Officemation Management 3579.02
Officemation Product Reports 3579.03
Packaged Software Reports 3680
Small Business Computer News 4300

**MANAGEMENT SERVICES ASSOC,
INC**
Box 3750
Austin, TX 78764

Tax Correspondent 4543

MAN AND MANAGER, INC
799 Broadway
New York, NY 10003

Businessman & The Law 707
Corporate Security 1214
Employee Relations in Action 1647
Occupational Safety and Health Act
  (OSHA) Report 3565
White Collar Management 4967

**MANCHESTER BUSINESS
SCHOOL**
Booth St West
Manchester, England M15 6PB

Contents Pages in Management 1184
Manchester Business School Review
  3096

ANDREW R MANDALA
PO Box 30240
Washington, DC 20014

Condominium Lenders Guide 1096.01
Credit Union Commentary 1248.01
Liquidity Portfolio Manager 3021.01
Mortgage Backed Securities Reports
  3320
Mortgage Commentary 3322
Mortgage Securities Manual & Pricing
  Guide 3322.01
Oliver Jones Report 3618.02
Savings & Loan Reporter 4187.01
Secondary Market Reporter 4220

MANITOBA, CANADA

(MANITOBA, CANADA, END)

**MANUFACTURER PUBLISHING
CO**
8543 Puritan Ave
Detroit, MI 48238

Directory of Michigan Publishers 1447
Michigan Manufacturer & Financial
  Record 3209

**MANUFACTURERS' AGENT
PUBLISHING CO INC**
663 5th Ave
New York, NY 10022

Verified Directory of Manufacturers'
  Representative 4847

MANUFACTURERS AGENTS ASSN
13A West St
Reigate
Surrey, England RH2 9BL

Manufacturers Agent 3107

**MANUFACTURERS HANOVER
TRUST CO**
Corporate Communications Dept
350 Park Ave
New York, NY 10022

Business Report 719
Economic Report 1567
Financial Digest 1997

MANUFACTURERS' NEWS, INC
3 E Huron St
Chicago, IL 60611

Alabama: Mining & Manufacturing
  Directory 136
Alabama: State Industrial Directory
  136.01
Alaska: Petroleum & Industrial
  Directory 141.01
Arizona: Manufacturers Directory 313
Arizona: State Industrial Directory
  317.02
Arkansas: Manufacturers' Directory
  320
Arkansas: State Industrial Directory
  320.01
California: Manufacturers Register
  738.01
California: Services Register 738.03
California: State Industrial Directory
  738.05
Canada: Scott's Atlantic Industrial
  Directory 762.01
Canada: Scott's Ontario Industrial
  Directory 762.02
Canada: Scott's Quebec Industrial
  Directory 762.03
Canada: Scott's Trade Directory, Metro
  Toronto 762.04
Canada: Scott's Trade Directory,
  Toronto Vicinity 762.05
Canada: Scott's Western Canada
  Industrial Directory 762.06

Central Atlantic States: Manufacturers
Directory 886
Chicago: Geographic Edition 935.01
Colorado: Manufacturers Directory
987
Connecticut: Directory of Connecticut
Manufacturers 1117.01
Connecticut-Rhode Island: Directory of
Manufacturers 1117.02
Connecticut: State Industrial Directory
1117.03
Delaware: State Industrial Directory
1355.03
District of Columbia 1469.01
Europe's 5000 Largest Companies
Directory 1792.01
Florida: Industries Directory 2067.01
Florida: State Industrial Directory
2068.01
Georgia: Manufacturers Directory
2218.01
Georgia: State Industrial Directory
2219.01
Hawaii: Manufacturers Directory
2348.01
Idaho: Manufacturing Directory
2431.06
Illinois: Manufacturers Directory
2438.01
Illinois: Services Directory 2438.02
Indiana: Industrial Directory 2503.01
Indiana: State Industrial Directory
2503.02
Iowa: Manufacturers Directory
2776.01
Kansas: Manufacturers & Products
Dirctory 2904.01
Kansas: State Industrial Directory
2904.02
Kentucky: Manufacturers Directory
2908.02
Kentucky: State Industrial Directory
2908.03
Louisiana: Manufacturers Directory
3408.01
Louisiana: State Industrial Directory
3048.02
Maine: State Industrial Directory
3061.01
Maine, Vermont, New Hampshire:
Directory of Manufacturers 3061.02
Maryland: Manufacturers Directory
3146.01
Maryland: State Industrial Directory
3146.02
Massachusetts: Directory of
Manufacturers 3149.01
Massachusetts: Manufacturers Directory
3149.02
Massachusetts: Service Directory
3149.03

Massachusetts: State Industrial
Directory 3149.04
Michigan: Harris Michigan Industrial
Directory 3208.01
Michigan: Manufacturers Directory
3209.01
Michigan: State Industrial Directory
3210
Minnesota: Manufacturers Directory
3240.01
Minnesota: State Industrial Directory
3240.02
Mississippi: Manufacturers Directory
3245.01
Mississippi: State Industrial Directory
3246.01
Missouri: Manufacturing & Mining
Directories 3249.01
Missouri: State Industrial Directory
3250.01
Montana: Manufacturers Directory
3276.01
Montana: State Industrial Directory
3276.02
Nebraska: Manufacturers Directory
3423.01
Nebraska: State Industrial Directory
3425
Nevada: Industrial Directory 3430.01
Nevada: State Industrial Directory
3431.01
New England: Manufacturers Directory
3443.01
New Hampshire: State Industrial
Directory 3448
New Jersey: Directory of Manufacturers
3450.01
New Jersey: State Industrial Directory
3453.01
New Mexico: Manufacturing & Mining
Directory 3455
New Mexico: State Industrial Directory
3455.01
New York: Manufacturers Directory
3476.01
New York: State Industrial Directory
3483.01
North Carolina: Manufacturers
Directory 3534.01
North Carolina: State Industrial
Directory 3535.01
North Dakota: Manufacturing
Directory 3536.01
North Dakota: State Industrial
Directory 3536.02
Ohio: Industrial Directory 3593.02
Ohio Manufacturers Guide 3593.03
Oklahoma: Manufacturers & Products
Directory 3617.01
Oklahoma: State Industrial Directory
3618.01

Oregon: Manufacturers Directory
3637
Oregon: State Industrial Directory
3638
Pennsylvania: Directory of
Manufacturers 3716.01
Pennsylvania: State Industrial Directory
3717.02
Puerto Rico: Official Industrial & Trade
Directory 3943.01
Rhode Island: State Industrial
Directory 4133
South Carolina: Industrial Directory
4342.01
South Carolina: State Industrial
Directory 4342.02
South Dakota: Manufacturers &
Processors Directory 4345
South Dakota: State Industrial
Directory 4345.02
Tennessee: Directory of Manufacturers
4593
Tennessee: State Industrial Directory
4593.01
Texas: Manufacturers Directory
4597.02
Utah: Manufacturers Directory
4835.01
Utah: State Industrial Directory
4835.02
Vermont: State Industrial Directory
4847.01
Virginia: Industrial Directory 4858.01
Virginia: State Industrial Directory
4858.02
Washington: Manufacturers Register
4888.01
Washington: State Industrial Directory
4894.01
West Virginia: State Industrial
Directory 4957.01
Wisconsin: Manufacturers Directory
5008.01
Wisconsin: State Industrial Directory
5008.02
Wyoming: Directory of Manufacturing
and Mining 5089.02

MARINE GUIDE PUBLISHING CO
88 Broad St
Boston, MA 02110

Boston Marine Guide 577

MARITIME RESEARCH, INC
11 Broadway
New York, NY 10004

Chartering Annual 917
Maritime Research Center Newsletter
3124

MARKET CHRONICLE
45 John St, Suite 911
New York, NY 10038

Market Chronicle 3126

MARKETING DEVELOPMENT
402 Border Rd
Concord, MA 01742

Chemical/Energy New Product
Directory 922.01
Electronic New Product Directory
1630.01
Security/Fire Equipment
Manufacturers' Directory 4240.01

MARKETING ECONOMICS INSTITUTE LTD
441 Lexington Ave
New York, NY 10017

Marketing Economics Institute (MEI)
Marketing Economics Guide 3128
Marketing Economics Key Plants
3129

MARKETING SCIENCE INSTITUTE
14 Story St
Cambridge, MA 02138

Marketing Science Institute Newsletter
3135

MARKET RESEARCH SOCIETY
15 Belgrave Square
London, England SW1X 8PF

International Directory of Market
Research Organizations 2674
Journal of the Market Research Society
2895
Market Research Abstracts 3137
Market Research Society (MRS)
Newsletter 3139
Market Research Society. Yearbook
3140

MARPEP PUBLISHING LTD
Suite 700, 133 Richmond St
Toronto, Ont, Canada M5H 3M8

Blue Book of CBS Stock Reports 563
Canadian Business Service Investment
Reporter 782
Canadian News Facts 820
Commodity & Currency Reporter
1024.01
Energy Update 1700.01
Money Reporter, Canadian Edition
3272
Money Reporter, US Edition 3273

MARPLE'S BUSINESS NEWSLETTER
444 Colman Bldg
Seattle, WA 98104

Marple's Business Newsletter 3144

MARQUIS PUBLICATIONS
200 E Ohio St, Rm 5604
Chicago, IL 60611

Who's Who in America 4977
Who's Who in American Law 4978
Who's Who in Finance and Industry
4985
Who's Who in the East 4992
Who's Who in the Midwest 4993
Who's Who in the South and Southwest
4995
Who's Who in the West 4996
Who's Who in the World 4997
Who's Who of American Women
4998
World Who's Who in Science 5085

MARYLAND (STATE)

DEPT OF ECONOMIC & COMMUNITY DEVELOPMENT
2525 Riva Rd
Anapolis, MD 21401

Directory of Maryland Manufacturers
1445
Maryland Magazine 3146
Maryland Statistical Abstract 3147

(MARYLAND END)

MASSACHUSETTS INSTITUTE OF TECHNOLOGY
Alfred P Sloan School of Management
Cambridge, MA 02139

Sloan Management Review 4296

MASSACHUSETTS SOCIETY OF CERTIFIED PUBLIC ACCOUNTANTS, INC
Three Center Plaza
Boston, MA 02108

Massachusetts CPA Review 3149

MBH COMMODITY ADVISORS, INC
Box 353
Winnetka, IL 60093

MBH Weekly Commodity Futures
Trading Letter 3158

MCB PUBLICATIONS
International Inst of Social Economics
200 Keighley Rd, Bradford
W Yorkshire, England BD9 4JQ

European Journal of Marketing 1781
International Journal of Physical
Distribution and Materials
Management 2694
International Journal of Social
Economics 2696
Journal of European Industrial Training
2853
Journal of Operations & Production
Management 2870.01
Leadership & Organization
Development 2994.01
Management Decision 3077
Managerial Finance 3093
Managerial Law 3094

MCCARRON BIRD
594 Lonsdale St
Melbourne, Vic 3000, Australia

Insurance Record of Australia and New
Zealand 2635

MCGILL UNIVERSITY
Centre for Developing Studies
815 Sherbrooke St W
Montreal, Que, Canada H3A 2R6

Labour, Capital and Society 2949.01

MCGILL UNIVERSITY
Industrial Relations Centre
Samuel Bronfman Bldg
1001 Sherbrooke St W
Montreal, Que, Canada H3A 1G5

Labour Agreements Data Bank 2946
McGill University Industrial Relations
Centre Review 3159

MCGRAW-HILL BOOK CO
Hightstown-Princeton Rd
Hightstown, NJ 08520
(For McGraw-Hill Periodicals
See McGraw-Hill Publications)

Aerospace Facts and Figures 76
American Machinist 199
Aviation Week & Space Technology,
Marketing Directory Issue 442
Chemical Engineering—Equipment
Buyers' Guide Issue 924
Chemical Week—Buyers' Guide Issue
930
Coal Age—Annual Buyers' Guide 969
Coal Mine Directory 971
Condensed Computer Encyclopedia
1094

Consumer Market Research Handbook
    1158
Director's Handbook   1405
Dodge Construction Systems Costs
    1480
Dodge Digest of Building Costs and
    Specifications   1481
Dodge Guide for Estimating Public
    Works Construction Costs   1482
Electrical Construction and
    Maintenance (Annual)   1601
Electrical Wholesaling   1606
Electrical World   1608
Electronics—Buyers' Guide   1635
Engineering and Mining Journal—
    Annual Buyers' Guide   1707
Engineering and Mining Journal (E &
    M J) International Directory of
    Mining and Mineral Processing
    Operations   1708
Engineering News Record—Directory
    of Design Firms   1712
Handbook for Auditors   2312
Handbook of Advertising Management,
    1970 edition   2316
Handbook of Business Administration
    2324
Handbook of Marketing Research
    2329
Handbook of Modern Accounting
    2331
Handbook of Modern Manufacturing
    Management   2332
Handbook of Modern Marketing, 1970
    Edition   2333
Handbook of Modern Office
    Managment and Administrative
    Services   2334
Handbook of Modern Personnel
    Administration   2335
Handbook of Public Relations: The
    Standard Guide to Public Affairs and
    Communications   2336
Handbook of Sampling for Auditing
    and Accounting   2337
Handbook of Wage and Salary
    Administration   2339
Keystone Coal Industry Manual   2911
Materials Handbook: An Encyclopedia
    for Purchasing Managers, Engineers,
    Executives, and Foremen, 1971
    Edition   3154
McGraw-Hill Dictionary of Modern
    Economics: A Handbook of Terms
    and Organizations   3160
Metals Week Price Handbook   3199
Modern Plastics Encyclopedia   3261
North Sea Petroleum: An Investment &
    Marketing Opportunity . . . How Big
    . . . How Soon . . . How to
    Participate   3544

Platt's Oilgram Legislative Service
    3784
Platt's Oil Price Handbook   3787
Power—Electric Utility Generation
    Planbook   3818
Purchasing Handbook   3952
Registry of Manhattan Office Spaces
    4055
Rewarding Executive Talent: Salary and
    Benefit Practices by Industry and
    Position   4130
Successful Personal Money
    Management 1977   4488

MCGRAW-HILL PUBLICATIONS CO
1221 Ave of Americas
New York, NY 10020

American Machinist (Magazine)   200
Architectural Record   300
Aviation Week & Space Technology
    441
Business Week   727
Chemical Engineering   923
Chemical Week   929
Chemical Week Newswire Service   931
Chemical Week Pesticides Register
    932
Coal Age   968
Coal Week   972
Coal Week International   973
Data Communications   1327
Dodge Building Cost Calculator and
    Valuation Guide   1477
Dodge Bulletins   1478
Dodge Construction Potentials Bulletin
    1479
Dodge/Scan Microfilm System   1483
Electrical Construction and
    Maintenance   1600
Electrical Marketing Newsletter   1604
Electrical Week   1605
Electrical Wholesaling (Magazine)
    1607
Electrical World (Magazine)   1609
Electronics   1632
Engineering & Mining Journal (E/MJ)
    Mining Activity Digest   1641
Engineering and Mining Journal   1706
Engineering News-Record   1711
Fleet Owner   2059
Fuel Price Analysis   2197
Green Markets   2265
Housing   2407.01
ICW's Africa Construction Business
    Report   2431.02
ICW's Asia Construction Business
    Report   2431.03
ICW's Latin America Construction
    Business Report   2431.04

ICW's Mideast Construction Business
    Report   2431.05
Industry Mart   2562
International Construction Week   2669
International Management   2704
Keystone News-Bulletin   2912
Long Term Care   3045
Medical World News   3183
Metals Week   3197
Metals Week Insider Report   3198
Modern Plastics   3260
Modern Plastics International Report
    3262
Nuclearfuel   3552
Nucleonics Week   3555
Petrochemical Scan   3755
Platt's Bunkerwire   3783.01
Platt's LP Gaswire   3783.02
Platt's OHA Digest   3783.03
Platt's Oilgram Marketscan   3784.01
Platt's Oilgram News   3785
Platt's Oilgram News/Wire   3785.01
Platt's Oilgram Price Report   3786
Platt's Oil Marketing Bulletin   3786.01
Platt's Oil Regulation Report   3787.01
Platt's Petrochemical Scan   3787.02
Platt's Polymerscan   3787.03
Power   3817
Professional Standards Review
    Organizations (PSRO) Letter   3890
Securities Week   4237
Textile World   4603
Textile World—Fact File Buyers' Guide
    4604
33 Metal Producing   4607
Washington Health Record   4887.01
Washington Report on Health
    Legislation   4891
Washington Report on Medicine &
    Health   4892

MEAL. *See* **Media Expenditure
Analysis Ltd**

R S MEANS CO, INC
100 Construction Plaza
Kingston, MA 02364

Appraisal Manual   291.01
Building Construction Cost Data   635
Building Systems Cost Guide   642.01
Mechanical & Electrical Cost Data
    3164.02
Repair and Remodeling Cost Data
    4062.01

MEDIA EXPENDITURE ANALYSIS LTD
110 St Martin's Lane
London, England WC2N 4BH

Media Expenditure Analysis Ltd
(MEAL) Reports 3167

**MEDIA GENERAL FINANCIAL
SERVICES, INC**
PO Box C-32333
Richmond, VA 23293

Industriscope 2557
Media/General (M/G) Financial
Weekly Market Digest 3169

MEDIA INDUSTRY NEWSLETTER
75 E 55th St
New York, NY 10022

Media Industry Newsletter 3173

MEDIA INFORMATION LTD
Hale House
Green Lanes
London, England N13 5TP

PR Planner—Europe 3911
PR Planner—UK 3912

MEDIA RECORDS, INC
370 7th Ave
New York, NY 10001

Business Publication Advertising Report
716.01
Financial Advertising Report 1991
Media Records Blue Book 3176
Media Records Green Book 3177

MEDICAL ECONOMICS CO
550 Kinderkamack Rd
Oradell, NJ 07649

Drug Topics 1510
Medical Economics 3180

**MERCANTILE GAZETTE OF NEW
ZEALAND LTD**
Box 20-034
Christchurch 5, New Zealand

Insurance Directory of New Zealand
2619
Mercantile Gazette of New Zealand
3190
New Zealand Company Directory &
Executive 3498

**MERCURY HOUSE BUSINESS
PUBLICATIONS LTD**
Waterloo Rd
London, England SE1 8UL

Industrial Relations Journal 2542
Journal of General Management 2859
Office Equipment News 3579

MERRILL ANALYSIS, INC
Box 228
Chappaqua, NY 10514

Technical Trends 4579

**METAL TUBE PACKAGING
COUNCIL OF NORTH AMERICA**
118 E 61 St
New York, NY 10021

Tube Topics 4732

**METHODS–TIME MEASUREMENT
ASSN FOR STANDARDS &
RESEARCH**
16-01 Broadway
Fair Lawn, NJ 07410

Methods–Time Measurement (MTM)
Journal 3204

**METROPOLITAN LIFE
INSURANCE CO**
1 Madison Ave
New York, NY 10010

Statistical Bulletin 4426

MEXLETTER SA
Apartado Postal 1335
Mexico 1 DF, Mexico

Mexletter 3207

MICHIGAN (STATE)

MICHIGAN DEPT OF COMMERCE
PO Box 30225
Lansing, MI 48909

Michigan Plant Location Directory
3209.02
Michigan Statistical Abstract 3211

(MICHIGAN END)

MICHIGAN STATE UNIVERSITY
Bureau of Business and Economic
Research
5J Berkey Hall
East Lansing, MI 48824

(MSU) Business Topics 3330

MICHIGAN STATE UNIVERSITY
Dept of Agricultural Economics
E Lansing, MI 48824

Michigan Farm Economics 3108

**MICROFILMING CORP OF
AMERICA**
1620 Hawkins Ave, PO Box 10
Sanford, NC 27330

New York Times Index 3488

MICROFILM PUBLISHING INC
PO Box 313, Wykagyl Station
New Rochelle, NY 10804

International Micrographic Source
Book 2708
Micrographics Newsletter 3212

MICROINFO LTD
PO Box 3
Newman Lane
Alton, Hampshire, England GU34 2PG

Energy Report 1690
Health & Safety in Industry 2356.01
Microinfo 3213
Pollution 3802
World Markets Intelligence Report
5070
World Video Report 5084.01

MICROMEDIA LTD
144 Front St W
Toronto, Ont, Canada M57 2L7

Canadian Business Index 778.01
Canadian News Index 820.01

MIDLAND BANK LTD
Griffin House, PO Box 2
Silver Street Head
Sheffield, England S1 3GG

Midland Bank Review 3227

**MILLER FREEMAN
PUBLICATIONS**
500 Howard St
San Francisco, CA 94105

Pulp & Paper 3945

MILLER PUBLISHING CO
2501 Wayzata Blvd, PO Box 67
Minneapolis, MN 55405

Feedstuffs 1980

MINNESOTA (STATE)

**DEPT OF ECONOMIC
DEVELOPMENT**
480 Cedar St
St Paul, MN 55101

Minnesota 3240

(MINNESOTA END)

MINORITY BUSINESS INFORMATION INSTITUTE
295 Madison Ave
New York, NY 10017

Minority Business Information Institute (MBII) Newsletter   3241

MIN PUBLISHING. *See* **Media Industry Newsletter**

MINTEL PUBLICATIONS
20 Bockingham St
London, England WC2N 6EE

Mintel   3242
Retail Intelligence   4106

MISSISSIPPI RESEARCH AND DEVELOPMENT CENTER
PO Drawer 2470
Jackson, MS 39205

Mississippi Manufacturers Directory   3245
Mississippi Metalworking Services Directory   3246

MISSOURI (STATE)

MISSOURI DIVISION OF COMMERCE & INDUSTRIAL DEVELOPMENT
PO Box 118
Jefferson City, MO 65102

Missouri Corporate Planner   3248
Missouri Directory of Manufacturing and Mining   3249
Missouri's New and Expanding Manufacturers   3250
MOre Facts   3319.01

(MISSOURI END)

MODERN PRODUCTIONS LTD
First Floor, Midland House, Box 3159
73 Great North Rd
Auckland 1, New Zealand

Forest Industries Review   2143
Management   3068
Office Equipment News   3579.01
White's Air Directory and Who's Who in New Zealand Aviation   4969.01

MONITOR TRADE PUBLICATIONS, INC
150 W 28 St
New York, NY 10001

International Insurance Monitor   2685

MONTREAL STOCK EXCHANGE
800 Victoria Square, PO Box 61
Montreal, Que, Canada H4Z 1A9

Montreal Stock Exchange Daily Official News Sheet   3306
Montreal Stock Exchange Monthly Review   3307

MOODY'S INVESTOR'S SERVICE INC
99 Church St
New York, NY 10007

Moody's Bank and Finance Manual and News Reports   3308
Moody's Bond Record   3309
Moody's Bond Survey   3310
Moody's Commercial Paper Reports   3311
Moody's Dividend Record   3312
Moody's Handbook of Common Stocks   3313
Moody's Industrial Manual and News Reports   3314
Moody's Investors Fact Sheets   3314.01
Moody's Municipals and Governments Manual and News Reports   3315
Moody's Municipal Credit Reports   3316
Moody's Municipal Credit Reports On Line   3316.01
Moody's Over-the-Counter (OTC) Industrial Manual and News Reports   3317
Moody's Public Utility Manual and News Reports   3318
Moody's Transportation Manual and News Reports   3319

MORECROSS LTD
100 Fleet St
London, England EC4Y 1DE

Investors Review and Financial World   2775

ROBERT MOREY ASSOCIATES
PO Box 98
Dana Point, CA 92629

Advanced Battery Technology   61
Energy Info   1682

MORGAN–GRAMPIAN PUBLISHERS LTD
30 Calderwood St
London, England SE18 6QH

Accountants Weekly   28
American City & County   166
Autotrade   435
Building Design   636

Building Refurbishment   641.01
Chemical Age   919
Chief Executive   937.01
Civil Engineering   953
Construction Plant & Equipment   1139
Contractor   1187
Control & Instrumentation   1187.01
Daltons Weekly   1315
Design Engineering/UK   1369
Design Engineering/USA   1369.01
Directory of Industrial Distributors   1436
Electronic Engineering   1622
Electronics Times   1637
Engineer   1702
Estates Times   1755
Food Manufacture   2091
Industrial Distribution   2517
Industrial Products Bulletin   2536.01
Industrial Purchasing News   2539
Laboratory Equipment Digest   2928
Livestock Farming   3028
Manufacturing Chemist Aerosol Review   3112
Manufacturing Chemist & Aerosol News   3113
Mart   3144.01
Metalworking Production   3202
Metalworking Production Machine Tools Survey   3203
Municipal Index   3339
Process Engineering   3860
Travel Trade Directory   4702
Travel Trade Gazette Europa   4703
Travel Trade Gazette UK & Ireland   4704
Tunnels & Tunnelling   4734
What's New in Building   4961
What's New in Electronics   4961.01
What's New in Farming   4962
What's New in Industry   4963.01

SYDNEY MORREL & CO, INC
152 E 78th St
New York, NY 10021

Australia Newsletter   399
Guide to Investment   2296

ROBERT MORRIS ASSOCIATES
1616 PNB Bldg
Philadelphia, PA 19107

Annual Statement Studies   261
Journal of Commercial Bank Lending   2858

MORTGAGE BANKERS ASSN OF AMERICA
1125 15th St NW
Washington, DC 20005

Mortgage Banker   3321

MOTOR
224 W 57th St
New York, NY 10019

Motor   3324

**MOTOR VEHICLE
MANUFACTURERS' ASSOCIATION
OF THE UNITED STATES**
320 New Center Bldg
Detroit, MI 48202

Automobile Facts and Figures   426
Facts and Figures of the Automotive
    Industry   1871

MUNROE PUBLICATIONS INC
PO Drawer 7
Indian Rocks Beach, FL 33535

Food Promotions   2096
Housewares Promotions   2407

MURRAY STATE UNIVERSITY
College of Business and Public Affairs
School of Business
Murray, KY 42071

Business & Public Affairs   665

**NATIONAL ASSN OF
ACCOUNTANTS**
919 3rd Ave
New York, NY 10022

Management Accounting   3069

**NATIONAL ASSN OF BANK
WOMEN**
500 N Michigan Ave
Suite 1400
Chicago, IL 60611

National Association of Bank Women
    (NABW) Journal   3357

**NATIONAL ASSOCIATION OF
BUSINESS ECONOMISTS**
28349 Chagrin Blvd
Cleveland, OH 44122

Business Economics   679

**NATIONAL ASSN OF COLLEGE
STORES, INC**
528 E Lorain St
Oberlin, OH 44074

College Store Journal   983

**NATIONAL ASSN OF CREDIT
MANAGEMENT**
475 Park Ave South
New York, NY 10016

Credit and Financial Management
    1245

**NATIONAL ASSN OF HEALTH
UNDERWRITERS**
145 N Ave
Box 278
Hartland, WI 53029

Health Insurance Underwriter   2361

**NATIONAL ASSN OF HOSIERY
MANUFACTURERS**
PO Box 4098, 516 Charlottetown Mall
Charlotte, NC 28204

Hosiery Statistics   2389

**NATIONAL ASSN OF
INSTALLMENT COMPANIES**
38 W 32 St
New York, NY 10001

NAIC Reporter   3355

**NATIONAL ASSN OF INSURANCE
COMMISSIONERS**
350 Bishops Way
Brookfield, WI 53005

Financial Review of Alien Insurers
    2018.02
Proceedings of the NAIC   3857.01

**NATIONAL ASSN OF
INVESTMENT CLUBS**
1515 E Eleven Mile Rd
Royal Oak, MI 48067

Better Investing   545

**NATIONAL ASSN OF
MANUFACTURERS**
1776 F St NW
Washington, DC 20006

Enterprise   1714

**NATIONAL ASSN OF MUTUAL
INSURANCE COMPANIES**
3707 Woodview Trace
PO Box 68700
Indianapolis, IN 46268

Mutual Insurance Bulletin   3351

**NATIONAL ASSN OF MUTUAL
SAVINGS BANKS**
200 Park Ave
New York, NY 10017

Directory of the Mutual Savings Banks
    of the United States   1460
Mutual Savings Bank Guide to Federal
    Income Tax Law   3352

National Assn of Mutual Savings
    Banks' Annual Report   3359
National Fact Book of the Mutual
    Savings Bank Industry   3374
Savings Bank Journal   4189

**NATIONAL ASSN OF PERSONNEL
CONSULTANTS**
1012 14th St NW
Washington, DC 20005

Directory of the National Association
    of Personnel Consultants   1461
Personnel Consultant   3741.01

**NATIONAL ASSN OF
PURCHASING MANAGEMENT**
Publication Sales Office
49 Sheridan Ave
Albany, NY 12210

Journal of Purchasing & Materials
    Management   2876
Purchasing Managers Report on
    Business   3953

**NATIONAL ASSN OF REAL
ESTATE INVESTMENT TRUSTS,
INC**
1101 17th St NW
Washington, DC 20036

Compendium of Internal Revenue
    Service Rulings   1061
Directory of National Assn of Real
    Estate Investment Trusts (NAREIT)
    Members   1448
Real Estate Investment Trusts (REIT)
    Fact Book   4018
Real Estate Investment Trusts (REIT)
    Industry Statistics   4019

NATIONAL ASSN OF REALTORS
430 N Michigan Ave
Chicago, IL 60611

Existing Home Sales Series   1813
National Assn of Realtors Who's Who
    3360
National Roster of Realtors   3403
Real Estate Sales Handbook   4025

**NATIONAL ASSOCIATION OF
SMALL BUSINESS INVESTMENT
COMPANIES**
618 Washington Bldg
Washington, DC 20005

National Association of Small Business
    Investment Companies (NASBIC)
    News   3362

**NATIONAL AUTOMOBILE
DEALERS ASSOCIATION**
8400 Westpark Dr
McLean, VA 22102

Franchised New Car & Truck Dealer
Facts   2159

**NATIONAL BANK OF
AUSTRALASIA LTD**
500 Bourke St
Melbourne, Vic 3000, Australia

Australian Investment and Economic
Newsletter   405
National Bank of Australasia National
Bank Monthly Summary   3364

NATIONAL BANK OF CANADA
500 Place d'Armes
Montreal, Que, Canada H2Y 2W3

National Bank of Canada, Economic
Review   3364.01

**NATIONAL BUSINESS AIRCRAFT
ASSOCIATION**
One Farragut Sq S
Washington, DC 20006

Business Flying   683

**NATIONAL BUSINESS
EDUCATION ASSN**
1914 Association Dr
Reston, VA 22091

Business Education Forum   680

**NATIONAL CENTER FOR PUBLIC
PRODUCTIVITY**
John Jay College of Criminal Justice
445 W 59th St
New York, NY 10019

Public Productivity Review   3930

NATIONAL COAL ASSOCIATION
Coal Bldg, 1130 17th St NW
Washington, DC 20036

Coal Data   970.01

**NATIONAL COMMERCIAL
FINANCE CONFERENCE INC**
One Penn Plaza
New York, NY 10001

Compendium of Commercial Finance
Law   1060
Journal of the Asset-Based Financial
Services   2889.01

**NATIONAL CONSUMER FINANCE
ASSN**
1000 16th St NW
Washington, DC 20036

Credit   1242
Finance Facts   1989
Finance Facts Yearbook   1990

**NATIONAL CONTRACT
MANAGEMENT ASSN**
6728 Old McLean Village Dr
McLean, VA 22101

National Contract Management Assn
(NCMA) Journal   3367
National Contract Management Assn
(NCMA) Magazine   3368

**NATIONAL COUNCIL FOR
US–CHINA TRADE**
Suite 350, 1050 17th St NW
Washington, DC 20036

CBR Index and Microfiche   872.01
China Business Review   941

**NATIONAL COUNCIL ON THE
AGING**
1828 L St NW, Suite 504
Washington, DC 20036

Aging and Work   88.01
Current Literature on Aging   1278
Perspective on Aging   3753

**NATIONAL COUNSELOR
REPORTS**
Task Bldg
Kerrville, TX 78028

Business & Capital Reporter   658
How and Where to Get Capital:
Dollars in Your Future   2419

**NATIONAL CREDIT UNION
ADMINISTRATION**
1776 G St NW
Washington, DC 20456

Credit Union Statistics   1252
Items of Current Interest   2793.01
National Credit Union Administration
(NCUA) Annual Report   3369
NCUA Review   3421

**NATIONAL FEATURES
SYNDICATE**
#1 National Press Bldg
Washington, DC 20045

Medicare Report   3185

**NATIONAL FEDERATION OF
INDEPENDENT BUSINESS**
150 W 20th Ave
San Mateo, CA 94403

National Federation of Independent
Business (NFIB) Quarterly Economic
Report for Small Business   3375

**NATIONAL FOREIGN TRADE
COUNCIL**
10 Rockefeller Plaza
New York, NY 10020

Breve   587
Noticias   3549

**NATIONAL FOREST PRODUCTS
ASSN**
1619 Massachusetts Ave NW
Washington, DC 20036

API/NFPA Environmental Report
282
Fingertip Facts and Figures   2038
Forest Industries Newsletter   2142
Washington Report   4890

**NATIONAL INFORMATION
CENTER FOR EDUCATIONAL
MEDIA**
University Park
Univ of Southern California
Los Angeles, CA 90007

National Information Center for
Educational Media (NICEM)
Newsletter   3385
Total Information Package for
1980–1982   4643

**NATIONAL INSTITUTE OF
ECONOMIC AND SOCIAL
RESEARCH**
2 Dean Trench St
Smith Square
London, England SW1P 3HE

National Institute of Economic & Social
Research Annual Report   3387

**NATIONAL INVESTOR
RELATIONS INSTITUTE**
1730 K St NW
Suite 307
Washington, DC 20006

National Investor Relations Institute IR
Update   3388

NATIONAL LP-GAS ASSOCIATION
1301 W 22nd St
Oak Brook, IL 60521

LP-Gas Industry Market Facts   3050

NATIONAL MACHINE TOOL BUILDERS' ASSOCIATION
7901 Westpark Dr
McLean, VA 22102

Economic Handbook of the Machine
Tool Industry   1551

NATIONAL MANAGEMENT ASSN
2210 Arbor Blvd
Dayton, OH 45439

Manage   3067

NATIONAL MINORITY BUSINESS CAMPAIGN
1201 12th Ave N
Minneapolis, MN 55411

Guide to Obtaining Minority Business
Directories   2299.01
Purchasing People in Major
Corporations   3954
Try Us National Minority Business
Directory   4731

NATIONAL NEWS SERVICE
4 Water St
Arlington, MA 02174

Bank and Quotation Record   458
Commercial and Financial Chronicle
997

NATIONAL OFFICE MACHINE DEALERS ASSN
1510 Jarvis Ave
Elk Grove Village, IL 60007

National Office Machine Dealers Assn
(NOMDA) Spokesman   3397

NATIONAL OFFICE PRODUCTS ASSN
301 N Fairfax St
Alexandria, VA 22314

National Office Products Assn (NOPA)
Industry Report   3398
Special Report   4356

NATIONAL PAPER TRADE ASSOCIATION
420 Lexington Ave
New York, NY 10170

Paper Merchant Performance   3692

NATIONAL PLANNING ASSN
1606 New Hampshire Ave NW
Washington, DC 20009

Looking Ahead and Projection
Highlights   3046
New International Realities   3449

NATIONAL QUOTATION BUREAU
116 Nassau St
New York, NY 10038

National Monthly Bond Summary
3395
National Monthly Stock Summary
3396

NATIONAL RAILWAY PUBLICATION CO
424 W 33rd St
New York, NY 10001

Official Railway Guide, Freight Service
Edition   3585.02
Official Railway Guide, Passenger
Travel Edition   3585.03
Pocket List of Railroad Officials
3790.01

NATIONAL REGISTER PUBLISHING CO
5201 Old Orchard Rd
Skokie, IL 60077

Directory of Corporate Affiliations
1422
Standard Directory of Advertisers
4371
Standard Directory of Advertising
Agencies   4372

NATIONAL RESEARCH BUREAU, INC
424 N 3rd St
Burlington, IA 52601

American Salesman   203
Shopping Center Newsletter   4283
Supervision   4499

NATIONAL RESEARCH DEVELOPMENT CORP OF INDIA
20 Ring Rd, Lajpat Nagar-IV
New Delhi—110024, India

Invention Intelligence   2749

NATIONAL RETAIL MERCHANTS ASSN
100 W 31st St
New York, NY 10001

Creditalk   1243
Employee Relations Bulletin   1646
Personnel News & Views   3748
Retail Accounting Manual—Revised
4102
Retail Control   4103
Retail Operations News Bulletin   4108
Stores   4476
Traffic Topics   4683

NATIONAL SAFETY COUNCIL
444 N Michigan Ave
Chicago, IL 60611

Family Safety   1886
Industrial Supervisor   2554
National Safety News   3404
Safe Driver   4157
Safe Worker   4162
Traffic Safety   4682

NATIONAL SECURITIES & RESEARCH CORP
605 3rd Ave
New York, NY 10016

National Forecast   3377

NATIONAL SMALL BUSINESS ASSN
1604 K St
Washington, DC 20006

Voice of Small Business   4865

NATIONAL SOCIETY OF ACCOUNTANTS FOR COOPERATIVES
Virginia Commonwealth University
1015 Floyd Ave
Richmond, VA 23284

Cooperative Accountant   1192

NATIONAL SOCIETY OF PUBLIC ACCOUNTANTS
1010 North Fairfax St
Alexandria, VA 22314

National Public Accountant   3401

NATIONAL SPORTING GOODS ASSN
717 N Michigan Ave
Chicago, IL 60611

Sporting Goods Market   4364.01

NATIONAL STANDARDS ASSN, INC
5161 River Rd
Washington, DC 20016

AN, AND & MS Standards   216.01
Identified Sources of Supply   2433.01
Metric Standards   3204.01
Mil-Hdbk-5C Handbook   3228.01
Military and Federal Standards and
Specifications   3228.02
National Aerospace Standards   3356.01
National Electrical Manufacturers
Association Standards Publications
3372

Standards and Specifications
  Information Bulletin   4378.01
Underwriters Laboratories Standards
  for Safety   4741.01

NATIONAL TAX ASSN–TAX INSTITUTE OF AMERICA
21 E State St
Columbus, OH 43215

National Tax Journal   3407

NATIONAL UNDERWRITER CO
420 E 4th St
Cincinnati, OH 45202

Agent's and Buyer's Guide   87
DLB Advanced Sales Reference Service
  1473
DLB Agent's Service   1474
Fire, Casualty, & Surety Bulletins
  2042
Life Financial Reports   3013
Life Rates & Data   3017
National Underwriter   3411
National Underwriter: Life & Health
  Insurance Edition   3412
Policy Statistics Service   3796
Tax Facts on Life Insurance   4553
Who Writes What   5000

NATIONAL VOCATIONAL GUIDANCE ASSN
Suite 400
5203 Leesburg Pike
Falls Church, VA 22041

Vocational Guidance Quarterly   4863

NATIONAL WESTMINSTER BANK LTD
41 Lothbury
London, England EC2P 2BP

National Westminster Bank Quarterly
  Review   3413

NEBRASKA (STATE)

DEPT OF ECONOMIC DEVELOPMENT
Box 94666, 301 Centennial Mall South
Lincoln, NE 68509

Directory of Nebraska Manufacturers
  1450
Nebraska Now   3424
Nebraska Statistical Handbook   3426

(NEBRASKA END)

NETHERLANDS CHAMBER OF COMMERCE IN US, INC
1 Rockefeller Plaza
New York, NY 10020

Netherlands–American Trade   3429

NEW ENGLAND BUSINESS MAGAZINE
31 Milk St
Boston, MA 02109

New England Business Magazine   3439

NJ MANUFACTURERS ASSN
50 Park Place
Newark, NJ 07101

New Jersey Business   3450

NEW JERSEY (STATE)

OFFICE OF ECONOMIC POLICY
142 W State St
Trenton, NJ 08625

New Jersey Economic Outlook   3451
New Jersey Economic Policy Council
  Annual Report   3452

OFFICE OF INTERNATIONAL TRADE
744 Broad St, Rm 1709
Newark, NJ 07102

New Jersey International Report   3453

(NEW JERSEY END)

NEWKIRK PRODUCTS INC
55 Grant Ave
Albany, NY 12206

Monthly Digest of Tax Articles   3290

DAN NEWMAN CO
57 Lakeview Ave
Clifton, NJ 07011

Business Ideas Newsletters   689

NEWS CIRCLE
2007 Wilshire Blvd, Suite 900
Los Angeles, CA 90057

Mideast Business Exchange   3225

NEWSBANK, INC
58 Pine St
New Canaan, CT 06840

Newsbank Library   3462.01

NEWSLETTER CLEARINGHOUSE
44 Market St
Rhinebick, NY 12572

How to Buy, Sell and Price Newsletter
  Properties   2420.01
Hudson's Washington News Media
  Contacts Directory   2427
Inside Look at the Newsletter Field
  2589
Newsletter on Newsletters   3466
Newsletter Yearbook/Directory   3467
Public Relations Quarterly   3933

NEWSLETTERS INTERNATIONAL
2600 S Gessner Rd
Houston, TX 77063

Business & Acquisition Newsletter   657
Department Store Jewelry Buyers
  Directory   1364
Jewelery Newsletter International
  2808

NEW SOUTH WALES, AUSTRALIA

DEPT OF AGRICULTURE
Division of Marketing and Economics
PO Box K220 Haymarket
Sydney, NSW 2000, Australia

Commodity Bulletin   1025
Review of Marketing and Agricultural
  Economics   4125
Weekly Marketing Notes   4935.01

DEPT OF INDUSTRIAL DEVELOPMENT & DECENTRALISATION
Box 2626, GPO
Sydney, 2001, Australia

Handbook for Industrialists   2313

(NEW SOUTH WALES END)

NEW YORK BUSINESS PUBLICATION, INC
105 Wolf Rd
Albany, NY 12205

Capital District Business Review   854

NEW YORK CREDIT & FINANCIAL MANAGEMENT ASSN
71 W 23 St
New York, NY 10010

Credit Executive   1246

NEW YORK MERCANTILE EXCHANGE
4 World Trade Center
New York, NY 10048

New York Mercantile Exchange
Statistical Yearbook   3477

NEW YORK (STATE)

DEPT OF COMMERCE
99 Washington Ave
Albany, NY 12245

Annual Summary of Business Statistics,
New York State   265
Business Trends in New York State
726
New York City Business Fact Book.
Part 1: Business & Manufacturing
3474
New York City Business Fact Book.
Part 2: Population & Housing   3475
New York State Business Fact Book.
Part 1: Business & Manufacturing
3481
New York State Business Fact Book.
Part 2: Population and Housing
3482
Quarterly Summary of Business
Statistics, New York State   3975

DEPT OF LABOR
Div of Research and Statistics
State Office Bldg Campus
Albany, NY 12240

Collective Bargaining Settlements in
New York State   979
Employment Review   1664
Labor Area Summary   2927
Labor News Memorandum   2941
New York State Dept of Labor Annual
Planning Report   3483
Statistics on Work Stoppages   4458
Unemployment Insurance Fund,
Evaluation of the New York State
4743
Work Stoppages in New York State
5032

(NEW YORK END)

**NEW YORK STATE BANKERS
ASSN**
485 Lexington Ave
New York, NY 10017

New York State Banker   3480

NEW YORK STOCK EXCHANGE
11 Wall St
New York, NY 10005

New York Stock Exchange (NYSE)
Fact Book   3484
New York Stock Exchange (NYSE)
Statistical Highlights   3486

NEW YORK TIMES
229 W 43 St
New York, NY 10036

New York Times   3487

**NEW YORK TIMES
INFORMATION SERVICE INC**
Mt. Pleasant Office Pk 1719A Route 10
Parsippany, NJ 07054

Advertising and Marketing Intelligence
(AMI)   66.01
Information Bank I and II   2570.02
Key Issues Tracking (KIT)   2910.01

NEW YORK UNIV
Inst of Retail Management, 202 Tisch
Hall
Washington Sq
New York, NY 10003

Journal of Retailing   2881

NEW ZEALAND

DEPT OF LABOUR
Private Bag
Wellington 1, New Zealand

Labour & Employment Gazette   2947

**DEPT OF STATISTICS (PRIVATE
BAG)**
Mulgrave St
Wellington, New Zealand

Catalogue of New Zealand Statistics
870
Dept of Statistics. Annual Report of the
Government Statistician   1363
General Statistics   2217
Information Releases   2573.03
Monthly Abstract of Statistics   3277
New Zealand Agricultural Statistics
3491
New Zealand Balance of Payments
3493
New Zealand Building and
Construction Statistics   3494
New Zealand Census of Building and
Construction   3496
New Zealand Exports   3501
New Zealand External Trade, Country
Analyses   3502
New Zealand Imports   3504
New Zealand Incomes and Income Tax
3505
New Zealand Industrial Production
3507
New Zealand Insurance Statistics   3508
New Zealand National Income &
Expenditure   3510

New Zealand Official Yearbook   3511
New Zealand Prices, Wages, & Labor
3512
New Zealand Report & Analysis of
External Trade   3513
New Zealand Transport   3514
New Zealand Vital Statistics   3515
Pocket Digest of New Zealand Statistics
3790

GOVERNMENT PRINTING OFFICE
Private Bag
Wellington 1, New Zealand

New Zealand Report of the Dept of
Trade and Industry   4066

(NEW ZEALAND END)

**NEW ZEALAND CHAMBERS OF
COMMERCE**
Box 1071
Wellington, New Zealand

New Zealand Commerce   3497

**NEW ZEALAND ECONOMIC
NEWS LTD**
PO Box 1026
Wellington, New Zealand

Economic News Bulletin   1555

NEW ZEALAND EMPLOYERS FED
Research & Information Service Div
PO Box 1786, Federation House
95-99 Molesworth St
Wellington, New Zealand

Employer   1650

**NEW ZEALAND INSTITUTE OF
ECONOMIC RESEARCH**
Box 3479
Wellington, New Zealand

Quarterly Predictions of National
Income & Expenditure   3967
Quarterly Survey of Business Opinion
3977

A C NIELSEN CO
Media Research Groups
Nielsen Plaza
Northbrook, IL 60062

Nielsen Newscast   3516
Nielsen Researcher   3517
Nielsen Reporter   3516.01

NIHON KEIZAI SHIMBUN, INC
1-9-5 Otemachi, Chiyoda-Ku
Tokyo 100, Japan

Japan Economic Journal   2796.01

MARTINUS NIJHOFF
9-11 Lange Voorhout
The Hague, The Netherlands

Economic Titles/Abstracts 1572.01
Key to Economic Science and
Managerial Sciences 2912.01

NIGERIA

CONSULATE GENERAL OF NIGERIA
575 Lexington Ave
New York, NY 10022

Economic & Financial Review 1536
Federal Ministry of Industries Annual
Report 1932
Handbook of Commerce and Industry
in Nigeria 2325
Trade Report 4673

(NIGERIA END)

NORTH AMERICAN PUBLISHING CO
401 N Broad St
Philadelphia, PA 19108

American Inport/Export Bulletin 179
American School and University 204
Business Forms Reporter 684
Custom House Guide 1285
In Plant Reproductions 2583
Lab World 2959
Marketing Bestsellers 3127.02
Media and Methods 3165
Package Printing 3682
Printing Impressions 3849
What's New In Home Economics
4963

NORTH AMERICAN STUDENTS OF COOPERATION
Box 7293
Ann Arbor, MI 48107

CO-OP 1191.01
New Harbinger: A Journal of the
Cooperative Movement 3448

NORTH CAROLINA (STATE)

DEPT OF COMMERCE
430 N Salisbury St
Raleigh, NC 27611

North Carolina Industrial Data File
3534

(NORTH CAROLINA END)

NORTHERN MINER PRESS LTD
77 River St
Toronto, Ont, Canada M5A 3P2

Northern Miner 3539

NORTH HOLLAND PUBLISHING CO
Box 211
1000 AE Amsterdam, The Netherlands

Carnegie-Rochester Conference Series
on Public Policy 864.01
Economics Letters 1571.02
European Economic Review 1774
European Journal of Operational
Research 1781.01
Industrial Marketing Management
2534
Information & Management 2568.01
International Abstracts in Operations
Research 2652
Journal of Accounting and Economics
2817.01
Journal of Banking & Finance 2823.02
Journal of Business Research 2831.01
Journal of Development Economics
2844.01
Journal of Econometrics 2845
Journal of Economic Behavior and
Organization 2845.02
Journal of Economic Dynamics and
Control 2845.03
Journal of Financial Economics
2855.01
Journal of International Economics
2863.01
Journal of Mathematical Economics
2868.01
Journal of Monetary Economics
2868.02
Journal of Policy Modeling 2872.02
Journal of Public Economics 2875.01
Mathematical
Programming/Mathematical
Programming Studies 3154.01
Mathematical Social Sciences 3154.02
Operations Research Letters 3629.01
Regional Science and Urban Economics
4047
Resources and Energy 4096.02
Review of Economics and Statistics
4120.01
Technological Forecasting and Social
Change 4580
World Economy 5062.01

NORTHWESTERN BANKER CO
306 15th St
Des Moines, IA 50309

Northwestern Banker 3545

NORTHWOOD PUBLISHING LTD
Elm House, 10-16 Elm St
London, England WC1X 0BP

Brewery Manual and Who's Who in
British Brewing 589
British Clothing Manufacturer 599.01
Building Conservation 634.01
Building Trades Journal 642.02
Construction News 1137
Construction News Magazine 1138
Consulting Engineers' Who's Who and
Year Book 1147
Drapers Record 1505.02
Men's Wear 3189.01

NORWEGIAN–AMERICAN CHAMBER OF COMMERCE, INC
800 3rd Ave
New York, NY 10022

Norwegian–American Commerce 3548

OCEANA PUBLICATIONS
75 Main St
Dobbs Ferry, NY 10522

Commercial Laws of the Middle East
1004.02
Comparative State Income Tax Guide
with Forms 1058
Constitutions of the Countries of the
World 1123
Copyright Protection in the Americas
1201.02
Digest of Commercial Laws of the
World 1386
Federal Consumer Protection: Law,
Rules & Regulations 1917
Government Regulation of Business
Ethics: International Payoffs 2251
International Commercial Arbitration
2667
International Law of Development:
Basic Documents 2701
International Tax Treaties of All
Nations 2734
International Telecommunications
Agreements 2735
Investment Laws of the World:
Developing Nations 2764
Latin America and the Development of
the Law of the Sea 2970
Law and Policy of Intergovernmental
Primary Commodity Agreements
2978
Mining and Petroleum Legislation of
Latin America and the Caribbean
3239
Oil and Gas, the North Sea
Exploitation 3601
Patents and Trademarks 3705
Product Liability 3873

Transnational Economic & Monetary
   Law: Transactions and Contracts
   4690
Transport Laws of the World   4696
World Shipping Laws   5078.01

J R O'DWYER CO, INC
271 Madison Ave
New York, NY 10016

O'Dwyer's Directory of Corporate
   Communications   3573
O'Dwyer's Directory of Public
   Relations Executives   3573.01
O'Dwyers Directory of Public Relations
   Firms   3574
Jack O'Dwyer's Newsletter   3575

OHIO (STATE)

DEPT OF ECONOMIC &
COMMUNITY DEVELOPMENT
PO Box 1001
Columbus, OH 43216

Development News Notes   1375.01
Ohio Developer   3593.01

(OHIO END)

OHIO SOCIETY OF CERTIFIED
PUBLIC ACCOUNTANTS
PO Box 306
Dublin, OH 43017

Ohio CPA Journal   3593

OHIO STATE UNIVERSITY PRESS
2070 Neil Ave
Columbus, OH 43210

Journal of Money, Credit, & Banking
   2869

OIL DAILY
850 3rd Ave
New York, NY 10022

Oil Daily   3603

OKLAHOMA (STATE)

DEPT OF INDUSTRIAL
DEVELOPMENT
PO Box 53424
Oklahoma City, OK 73152

Oklahoma Directory of Manufacturers
   and Products   3615
Oklahoma NOW!   3618

EMPLOYMENT SECURITY
COMMISSION
Research & Planning Division
Will Rogers Bldg
Oklahoma City, OK 73105

Oklahoma Annual Planning Report
   3611
Oklahoma Economic Indicators   3616
Oklahoma Labor Market   3617

(OKLAHOMA END)

OMICRON DELTA EPSILON
FRATERNITY
Long Island University
Dept of Economics
Brooklyn, NY 11201

American Economist   171

WM O'NEIL & CO, INC
PO Box 24933
Los Angeles, CA 90024

Daily Graphs—American Stock
   Exchange Over the Counter   1297
Daily Graphs—NY Stock
   Exchange/Over the Counter   1298
Daily Graphs—Stock Option Guide
   1300

ONLINE, INC
11 Tannery Lane
Weston, CT 06883

DATABASE   1324.01
ONLINE   3619.02
Online Terminal Guide and Directory
   3619.06

ONTARIO, CANADA

MINISTRY OF INDUSTRY &
TOURISM
Queen's Park
Toronto, Ont, Canada M7A 2E1

Ontario Business News   3620

ONTARIO SECURITIES
COMMISSION
10 Wellesley St E
Toronto, Ont, Canada M7A 2H7

Ontario Securities Commission Weekly
   Summary   3625

(ONTARIO, CANADA END)

OPERATIONS RESEARCH
SOCIETY OF AMERICA
428 E Preston St
Baltimore, MD 21202

Operations Research   3629

OPPORTUNITY PRESS, INC
6 North Michigan Ave, Suite 1405
Chicago, IL 60602

Salesman's Opportunity Magazine
   4175

OREGON (STATE)

ECONOMIC DEVELOPMENT
DEPT
155 Cottage St
Salem, OR 97310

County Economic Indicators   1238
Directory of Oregon Manufacturers
   1452
Directory of Oregon State Services to
   Business   1453
International Trade Directory   2739

(OREGON END)

ORGANIZATION FOR ECONOMIC
COOPERATION & DEVELOPMENT
Publications Center
1750 Pennsylvania Ave NW
Washington, DC 20006

Financial Market Trends   2008
Guide to Legislation on Restrictive
   Business Practices   2299
Indicators of Industrial Activity
   2505.01
Labour Force Statistics   2952
Main Economics Indicators   3061
Nuclear Law Bulletin   3553
OECD Import-Export Microtables
   3575.01
Organization for Economic Cooperation
   and Development (OECD) Economic
   Outlook   3641
Organization for Economic Cooperation
   and Development (OECD) Economic
   Surveys   3642
Organization for Economic Cooperation
   and Development (OECD) Financial
   Statistics   3643
Organization for Economic Cooperation
   and Development (OECD) Observer
   3644
Pulp and Paper Quarterly Statistics
   3947
Quarterly National Accounts   3965
Quarterly Oil Statistics   3966
Research on Transport Economics
   4091
Statistics of Foreign Trade, Monthly
   Bulletin   4453
Statistics of Foreign Trade, Series B
   4453.01
Statistics of Foreign Trade, Series C
   4453.02

ORGANIZATION OF AMERICAN STATES
17th & Constitution Ave NW
Washington, DC 20006

CECON Trade News   873
Informational and Technical
   Publications of the General
   Secretariat of the Organization of
   American States (OAS)   2569
Estadistica   1744
Official Records of the Organization of
   American States   3586

ORIENTAL ECONOMIST
1-4 Hongokucho 1-chrome
Nihonbashi, Chuo-ku, Tokyo, 103
Japan

Japan Company Handbook   2796
Japan Economic Yearbook   2797
Oriental Economist   3648

ALAN OSBORNE & ASSOC LTD
Unit 5, Seager Buildings
Brookmill Rd
London, England SE8

Protection   3904

OVERSEAS DEVELOPMENT INST
10-11 Percy St
London, England W1P OJB

Overseas Development Institute (ODI)
   Review   3657

**OVERSEAS TRADE RESEARCH
FUND OF THE ECONOMIC
RESEARCH COUNCIL**
55 Park Lane
London, England W1Y 3DH

Britain and Overseas   596

**OWEN'S COMMERCE & TRAVEL
LTD**
106 Belsize Lane
London, England NW3 5BB

Owen's Commerce & Travel &
   International Register   3670

**OXBRIDGE COMMUNICATIONS,
INC**
40 E 34th St
New York, NY 10016

Standard Periodical Directory   4377

OXFORD UNIVERSITY PRESS
Subscription Dept
Press Rd, Neasden
London, England NW10 0DD

Oxford Economic Papers   3674

PACIFIC BANKER AND BUSINESS
109 W Mercer St, C#19081
Seattle, WA 98119

Pacific Banker and Business   3676

C A PAGE PUBLISHING CO
3181 Fernwood Ave
Lynwood, CA 90262

Commercial News (WCN)   1007
Daily Commercial News   1293

PANEL PUBLISHERS
14 Plaza Rd
Greenvale, NY 11548

Automatic Tac Planner   425
Estate Planner's Complete Guide and
   Workbook   1746
Forms and Workbook under ERISA for
   Pension and Profit Sharing Plans
   2147
How to Analyze, Design, and Install an
   Employee Stock Ownership Plan
   2420
How to Handle Tax Audits, Requests
   for Rulings, Fraud Cases, and Other
   Procedures Before IRS   2421
How to Plan for Tax Savings in Real
   Estate Transactions   2422
How to Save Taxes and Increase Your
   Wealth with a Professional
   Corporation   2423
How to Set Up and Run a Qualified
   Pension or Profit-Sharing Plan for a
   Small or Medium-Size Business
   2424
How to Take Money Out of a Closely
   Held Corporation   2425
How to Use Tax Shelters Today   2426
International Tax Journal   2732
Journal of Pension Planning and
   Compliance   2872
Municipal Finance Journal   3338.01
Partnerships and Taxes: A Practical
   Guide   3697
Subchapter S: Planning & Operation
   4482
Tax, Financial and Estate Planning for
   the Owner of a Closely Held
   Corporation   4553.01

PANNELL KERR FORSTER
420 Lexington Ave
New York, NY 10170

Trends in the Hotel Industry   4718

**PAPER MAKERS ADVERTISING
ASSN**
PO Box 2
90 Elm St
Westfield, MA 01086

Direct Advertising (D/A)   1399

W PARR & CO
Rex Bldg, Alderley Rd
Cheshire, England SK9 1HZ

European Industrial & Commercial
   Review   1777

PAYMENT SYSTEMS, INC
100 Peachtree St
Atlanta, GA 30303

Payment Systems Action Report   3707
Payment Systems Newsletter   3708

**PEAT, MARWICK, MITCHELL &
CO, CERTIFIED PUBLIC
ACCOUNTANTS**
345 Park Ave
New York, NY 10022

Management Focus   3079

**PENNSYLVANIA INST OF
CERTIFIED PUBLIC
ACCOUNTANTS**
1100 Lewis Tower Bldg
225 S 15th St
Philadelphia, PA 19102

Pennsylvania CPA Spokesman   3716

PENNSYLVANIA (STATE)

DEPT OF COMMERCE
415 South Office Bldg
Harrisburg, PA 17120

Pennsylvania Industrial Directory
   3717
Pennsylvania Statistical Abstract   3718

(PENNSYLVANIA END)

**PENNSYLVANIA STATE
UNIVERSITY**
Cooperative Extension Service
2 Weaver Bldg
University Park, PA 16802

Farm Economics   1895
Pennsylvania Business Survey   3715

PENSION PUBLICATIONS
30 Queen Anne's Gate
London, England SW1H 9AW

Benefits International   521

PENTON-IPC
614 Superior Ave W
Cleveland, OH 44113

Air Conditioning & Refrigeration
   Business   120
Air Transport World   129
Energy Management   1686.01

Foundry Management & Technology
2158
Government Product News   2248.01
Handling & Shipping   2340
Heating/Piping/Air Conditioning
2368
Hydraulics & Pneumatics   2430
Industry Week   2566
Lodging Hospitality   3040
Machine Design   3052
Material Handling Engineering   3152
Materials Engineering   3153
Modern Office Procedures   3257
New Equipment Digest   3444
Occupational Hazards   3559
Power Transmission Design   3820
Precision Metal   3825
Production Engineering   3867
Progressive Architecture   3895
Restaurant Hospitality   4099
School Product News   4195
Welding Design & Fabrication   4945
Welding Distributor   4946

**PERFORMANCE GUIDE
PUBLICATIONS INC**
PO Box 2604
Palos Verdes Peninsula, CA 90274

Performance Guide Publications.
Mutual Funds and Timing, Managed
Accounts   3735

PERGAMON PRESS, INC
Maxwell House
Fairview Park
Elmsford, NY 10523

Accident Analysis and Prevention   10
Accounting, Organizations, & Society
35
Annals of Occupational Hygiene   227
Automatica   424
Building and Environment   633
Computers & Industrial Engineering
1084
Computers & Operations Research
1086
Conservation and Recycling   1120
Government Publications Review   2250
Journal of the Operational Research
Society   2896
Long Range Planning   3044
Omega   3619
Progress in Planning   3894
Regional Studies   4049
Socio-Economic Planning Sciences
4324
World Development   5055

PERSONNEL PSYCHOLOGY, INC
Box 6965, College Sta
Durham, NC 27708

Personnel Psychology   3750

**PETER/GLENN PUBLICATIONS,
INC**
17 E 48th St
New York, NY 10017

National Radio Publicity Directory
3402

PETROCONSULTANTS SA
8-10 Rue Muzy
PO Box 228, 1211
Geneva 6, Switzerland

Company Acreage and Activity
Statistics   1051
Foreign Scouting Service   2136
International Oil and Gas Field
Records   2716
Licenses and Exploration Information
System (LEXIS)   3009
World Production and Reserve
Statistics   5074

**PETROLEUM INFORMATION
CORP**
PO Box 2612, 1375 Delaware
Denver, CO 80201

Coal Information   970.02
Energy Information   1682.01
Mining Lease Reports   3239.01
National Exploration Daily   3373.01
National Geothermal Service   3377.01
National Wildcat Monthly   3413.01
Oil and Gas Lease Reports   3598
Oil in California   3605
Oil in Texas   3605.01
Oil in the Mid-Continent   3605.02
Oil in the Rockies   3605.03
PI Reports   3773
United States Oil and Gas Production
News   4813.01
Uranium Information   4828
Uranium Information Western
4828.01

**PETROLEUM PRESS BUREAU,
LTD**
107 Charterhouse ST
London, England EC1M 6AA

Petroleum Economist   3758

PETROLEUM PUBLISHING CO
PO Box 1941
Houston, TX 77001

Japanese Newsletter   2800
International Petroleum Encyclopedia
2720
Ocean Oil Weekly Report   3571
Offshore   3590
Oil & Gas Journal   3595
Oil, Gas, & Petrochemical Equipment
3604

**PHARMACEUTICAL
MANUFACTURERS ASSN**
1155 15 St NW
Washington, DC 20005

Annual Survey Report—Ethical
Pharmaceutical Industry Operations
270
Prescription Drug Industry Factbook
3836

REPUBLIC OF THE PHILIPPINES
National Economic and Development
Authority
PO Box 1116
Manila, Philippines

Journal of Philippine Development
2872.01
Philippine Development   3765.01
Philippine Economic Indicators
3765.02
Philippine Statistical Yearbook
3765.04

PHILLIPS PUBLISHING, INC
7315 Wisconsin Ave
Bethesda, MD 20014

Data Channels   1325.01
Hall Radio Report   2310.02
Satellite News   4183.01
Telephone News   4586.02
VideoNews   4855

P H PRESS LTD
Waterloo Rd
Stockport, Cheshire, England SK1 3BN

Policy Holder Insurance Journal   3794

PICK PUBLICATIONS, INC
8543 Puritan Ave
Detroit, MI 48238

Directory of Michigan Manufacturers
1447
Michigan Manufacturer & Financial
Record   3209

PICK PUBLISHING CORP
21 West St
New York, NY 10006

Pick's Currency Yearbook   3769
Pick World Currency Report   3770

PIERIAN PRESS
5000 Washtenaw Ave, Box 1808
Ann Arbor, MI 48104

Consumers Index to Product
Evaluations and Information Sources
1174
Guide to Trade and Securities Statistics
2305

PILOT BOOKS
347 5th Ave
New York, NY 10016

Directory of Franchising Organizations
1433

PJB PUBLICATIONS LTD
18a Hill St
Richmond, Surrey, England TW9 1TN

Chinica   966
Pharma Prospects   3764.03
Scrip World Pharmaceutical News
4212

PLANNING EXECUTIVES INSTITUTE
Box 70
Oxford, OH 45056

Managerial Planning   3095

PLASTICS INDUSTRY EUROPE
31 Alington Grove
Wallington, Surrey, England SM6 9NH

Plastics Industry Europe   3782

PLUS PUBLICATIONS, INC
2626 Pennsulvania Ave NW
Washington, DC 20037

Access Reference Service   8
Access Reports   9
Campaign Practices Reference Service
741
Campaign Practices Reports   742
Health Labor Relations Reports   2362
Lobbying Reports   3035
National Health Insurance Reports
3378

POLITICS & MONEY PUBLISHING CO
14 South Hill Park Gardens
London, England NW3

Politics and Money   3797

R L POLK & CO
2001 Elm Hill Pike, PO Box 1340
Nashville, TN 37202

Polk's Daily Bank Information Service
3798
Polk's World Bank Directory   3799
Polk's World Bank Directory,
International Edition   3800
Polk's World Bank Directory, North
American Edition   3801

PORTER CORP
PO Box 350
Westport, CT 06881

Electric Vehicle News   1617.01

PRACTICAL ACCOUNTANT
964 3rd Ave
New York, NY 10155

Client's Monthly Alert   964
Practical Accountant   3821

PREDICASTS, INC
200 University Circle, Research Center
11001 Cedar Ave
Cleveland, OH 44106

Chemical Horizons North American
Report   925
Chemical Horizons Overseas Report
925.01
Custom Market Extract Reports   1286
Marketing Ideas   3130.01
Planning Ideas   3777.01
Predi-Briefs   3826
Predicasts Basebook   3828
Predicasts F & S Index Europe
3828.01
Predicasts F & S Index Europe Annual
3828.02
Predicasts F & S Index International
3828.03
Predicasts F & S Index International
Annual   3828.04
Predicasts F & S Index of Corporate
Change   3828.05
Predicasts F & S Index United States
3828.06
Predicasts F & S Index United States
Annual   3828.07
Predicasts Forecasts   3828.08
Predicasts Overview of Markets &
Technology (PROMT)   3828.09
Predicasts Source Directory   3829
Predicasts Terminal System   3830
PTS Index Services   3916
PTS Federal Index—File 48   3917
PTS Abstract Services   3915
PTS Statistical Services   3919
Technical Survey   4578
World Casts   5047

PRENTICE-HALL INC
Englewood Cliffs, NJ 07632

Accountant's Handbook of Formulas
and Tables   22
All States Tax Guide   148
Annotated Tax Forms   230
Capital Adjustments   852
Consumer and Commercial Credit
1149

Control of Banking   1189
Corporate Treasurer's and Controller's
Encyclopedia   1215
Corporation Forms   1217
Corporation Service   1221
Corporation Service Management
Edition   1221.01
Cumulative Changes   1268
Dictionary for Accountants   1376
Energy Controls   1677
Equal Opportunity in Housing   1736
Executive Action Report   1796
Executives Tax Report & What's
Happening in Taxation   1809
Farmer's Tax Report   1898
Federal Aids to Financing   1911
Federal revenue Forms—with Official
Instructions   1959
Federal Tax Course   1966
Federal Tax Guide   1970
Federal Taxes Citator   1967
Federal Taxes Service   1968
Foreign Investment in Canada   2118
Industrial Relations Guide   2541
Inheritance Taxes   2578
Insurance Guide   2623
Labor Relations Guide   2942
Lesly's Public Relations Handbook
3006
Oil & Gas Taxes Natural Resources
3600.01
Payroll Guide   3710
Pension and Profit Sharing   3720
Pension and Profit Sharing Forms
3721
Pension and Profit Sharing Guide
3722
Personnel Management—
Communications   3747
Personnel Management—Policies and
Practices   3747.01
Plan Administrator's Compliance
Manual   3776
Prentice-Hall Federal Tax Handbook
3835
Professional Corporation Guide   3884
Profit Sharing Design Manual   3893
Property Taxes   3902
Public Personnel Administration—
Labor-Management Relations   3927
Public Personnel Administration—
Policies and Practices for Personnel
3928
Sales Taxes   4177
Securities Exchange Commission
Compliance—Financial Reporting
and Forms   4219
Securities Regulation   4234
State & Local Taxes   4386
State Income Taxes   4394

Successful Estate Planning Ideas &
    Methods 4486
Tax-Exempt Organizations 4552
Tax Ideas 4555
Tax Treaties 4574
US Taxation of International
    Operations 4818
Wage-Hour Guide 4869
Wills, Estates, and Trusts 5003
Wills Trusts Forms 5004

J G PRESS, INC
Box 323
Emmaus, PA 18049

In Business 2476.03

PRESTEL HEADQUARTERS
Post-Office Telecommunications
Telephone House, Temple Ave
London, England EC4Y 0HL

Prestel 3837

**PRESTWICK INTERNATIONAL,
INC**
PO Box 205
Burnt Hills, NY 12027

Japanese Breakthroughs 2797.01
New From Europe 3445.01
New From Japan 3446
New Products & Processes From
    Western Europe 3458.01

PRICE WATERHOUSE & CO
60 Broad St
New York, NY 10004

Information Guide for Doing Business
    in Countries Abroad 2571

PRINT
6400 Goldsboro Rd NW
Washington, DC 20034

Print 3847

PROBE, INC
78 Randall Ave
Rockville Centre, NY 11570

Probe 3856

**PROFESSIONAL PUBLISHING
CORP**
122 Paul Dr
San Rafael, CA 94903

Realty Bluebook 4031

PROFIT PRESS, INC
400 E 89 St
New York, NY 10028

Food Industry Newsletter 2087

**PROGRESSIVE GROCER
PUBLISHING CO**
708 3rd Ave
New York, NY 10017

C-Store Business 1265.02
Progressive Grocer 3896
Progressive Grocer Marketing
    Guidebook 3896.01
Progressive Grocer Market Scope
    3896.02

**PROSPECTOR RESEARCH
SERVICES, INC**
751 Main St, PO Box 518
Waltham, MA 02154

Sales Prospector 4176

P R PUBLISHING CO, INC
PO Box 600
Exeter, NH 03833

PR Blue Book International 3824
PR Reporter 3913
Who's Who in Public Relations
    (International) 4989

PTN PUBLISHING CORP
250 Fulton Ave
Hempstead, NY 11550

Information and Records Management
    2570
Photographic Trade News 3766
Professional Photographic Equipment
    Directory & Buying Guide 3889
Security Industry & Product News
    4241

**PUBLIC AFFAIRS INFORMATION
SERVICE, INC**
11 W 40th St
New York, NY 10018

Public Affairs Information Service
    Bulletin 3921

PUBLICATIONS FOR INDUSTRY
21 Russell Woods Rd
Great Neck, NY 11021

American Industry 185
Industrial Purchasing Agent 2538

**PUBLIC CITIZEN'S TAX REFORM
GROUP**
Box 14198
Washington, DC 20044

People and Taxes 3733

**PUBLICORP COMMUNICATIONS
INC**
Box CP 1029
Pointe Claire, Que, Canada H9S 4H9

Matthews' CATV 3154.03
Matthews' List 3155

PUBLIC RELATIONS AIDS, INC
221 Park Ave South
New York, NY 10003

Publicist 3925

**PUBLIC RELATIONS SOCIETY OF
AMERICA**
845 3rd Ave
New York, NY 10022

Public Relations Journal 3931
Public Relations Register 3934

**PUBLISHING & DISTRIBUTING
CO LTD**
Mitre House
177 Regent St
London, England W1R 7FB

Thapar's First International Import &
    Export Directory of the World 4605

**PURCHASING MANAGEMENT
ASSN OF ARIZONA**
49 E Thomas Rd, Suite 108
Phoenix, AZ 85012

Arizona Purchaser 316

QUEENSLAND, AUSTRALIA

DEPT OF PRIMARY INDUSTRIES
Marketing Services Branch
William St
Brisbane, Qld 4000, Australia

Report on Production Trends 4072
Weekly Market Review 4936

(QUEENSLAND, AUSTRALIA END)

QUESTOR ASSOCIATES
Real Estate Syndication Reporter
115 Sansome St
San Francisco, CA 94104

Real Estate Syndication Reporter
    4025.01
Real Estate Syndication Reporter
    Newsletter 4025.02

**LAWRENCE RAGAN
COMMUNICATIONS, INC**
407 S Dearborn St
Chicago, IL 60605

Ragan Report   3989
Reporter's Report   4062.02
Speechwriter's Newsletter   4361.05

**RAILROAD RESEARCH
INFORMATION SERVICE**
Transportation Research Board
National Academy of Sciences
2101 Constitution Ave NW
Washington, DC 20418

On-line Database   3619.04
Railroad Research Bulletin   3990.01

RAND MCNALLY & CO
8255 N Central Park
Skokie, IL 60076

Rand McNally Commercial Atlas and
   Marketing Guide   4000
Rand McNally International Bankers
   Directory   4001

**RANDOM LENGTHS
PUBLICATIONS INC**
Box 867
Eugene, OR 97440

Random Lengths   4002
Random Lengths Export   4002.01
Random Lengths Yearbook   4003

REAL ESTATE FORUM, INC
30 E 42 St
New York, NY 10017

Real Estate Forum   4013
Realty Roundup   4032

**REAL ESTATE INSTITUTE OF
NEW SOUTH WALES**
Box A624
Sydney, NSW 2000, Australia

Real Estate Journal   4020

REAL ESTATE NEWS
720 S Dearborn St
Chicago, IL 60605

Real Estate News   4023

**REALTORS NATIONAL
MARKETING INSTITUTE**
National Assn of Realtors
430 N Michigan Ave
Chicago, IL 60611

Real Estate Perspectives   4023.02
real estate today   4028

REALTY
80-34 Jamaica Ave
Woodhaven, NY 11421

Realty   4030

RECORD PUBLISHING CO
750 Old Main St
Rocky Hill, CT 06067

Commercial Record   1009

REDGRAVE PUBLISHING CO
430 Manville Rd
Pleasantville, NY 10570

Wall Street Review of Books   4881

**REGENCY INTERNATIONAL
PUBLICATIONS LTD**
Newstone House
127 Sandgate Rd
Folkestone, Kent, England CT20 2BL

Regency International Directory   4045

**REGIONAL SCIENCE RESEARCH
INST**
Wentworth Bldg, 256 N Pleasant St
Amherst, MA 01002

Journal of Regional Science   2879

KEN REISS
633 3rd ave
New York, NY 10017

Sales and Marketing Management
   Survey of Buying Power (Part I)
   4166
Sales and Marketing Management
   Survey of Buying Power (Part II)
   4167
Sales and Marketing Management
   Survey of Industrial Purchasing
   Power   4168
Sales and Marketing Managment
   Survey of Selling Costs   4169

**REPORTING ON GOVERNMENTS,
INC**
80 Park Ave
New York, NY 10016

Reporting on Governments   4063

REPORTS, INC
700 Orange St
Wilmington, DE 19801

Regulatory News Release   4058
Report on Credit Unions   4069

**RESEARCH AND REVIEW
SERVICE OF AMERICA**
PO Box 1727
Indianapolis, IN 46206

Advanced Underwriting Service   63
Estate Planner's Letter   1747
Fraternal Monitor   2164
In Focus   2566.01

Market Builder Magazine   3125.01
Pension Plans Service   3726
Tax Letter Service   4558

**RESEARCH INSTITUTE OF
AMERICA, INC**
589 5th Ave
New York, NY 10017

Federal Tax Coordinator   1965
Marketing for Sales Executives   3130
Research Institute of America (RIA)
   Tax Guide   4089
Tax Action Coordinator   4533
You and the Law   5101

RESERVE RESEARCH, LTD
50 Broad St
New York, NY 10004

Powell Alert   3814
Powell Gold Industry Guide &
   International Mining Analyst   3815
Powell Monetary Analyst   3816

RESOURCE PROGRAMS, INC
521 5th Ave
New York, NY 10175

Profile—A Continuing Study of Oil and
   Gas Programs   3891

RETAIL COUNCIL OF CANADA
Suite 212, 214 King St
Toronto, Ont, Canada M5H 1K4

Department Store Sales   1365
Retail Sales   4110
Retail Wages   4117

RHM ASSOC, INC
417 Northern Blvd
Great Neck, NY 11021

RHM Convertible Survey   4131
RHM Survey of Warrants, Options, &
   Low-Price Stocks   4132

**RISK & INSURANCE
MANAGEMENT SOCIETY, INC**
205 E 42 St
New York, NY 10017

Risk Management   4134

MARTIN ROBERTS & ASSOC
PO Box 5254
Beverly Hills, CA 90210

Videocassette & CATV Newsletter
   4854

ROBERTS PUBLISHING CORP
45 John St
New York, NY 10038

Insurance Advocate   2608

SHEPARD D ROBINSON
410 Grove Ave
Barrington, IL 60010

Manufactured Housing Newsletter
3106

ROCKY MOUNTAIN JOURNAL
1590 S Federal
Denver, CO 80219

Rocky Mountain Journal   4139

RONALD PRESS CO
Div of John Wiley & Sons Inc
605 Third Ave
New York, NY 10016

Production Handbook   3868

ROOSEVELT UNIVERSITY
Heller College of Business
Administration
430 S Michigan Ave
Chicago, IL 60605

Business & Society   666

ROUGH NOTES CO, INC
1200 N Meridian St
Indianapolis, IN 46204

Insurance Sales   2635.01
Policy, Form, & Manual Analysis
Service   3793
Rough Notes   4142

ROUNTREE PUBLISHING CO, INC
117 Brixton Rd
Garden City, NY 11530

Rountree Report   4143

VICTOR M RUBIO Y CIA, SA
Paseo de la Reforma 292-601
Mexico, DF Mexico

Rubio's Mexican Financial Journal
4151

S J RUNDT ASSOCIATES
130 E 63 St
New York, NY 10021

Rundt's Weekly Intelligence   4153

**RURAL BANK OF NEW SOUTH
WALES**
GPO Box 41
Sydney, NSW 2001, Australia

Trends   4716

RUTGERS UNIVERSITY
Graduate School Management
92 New St
Newark, NJ 07102

Journal of International Business
Studies   2863
Maritime Policy and Management
3123

SAGE PUBLICATIONS INC
275 S Beverly Dr
Beverly Hills, CA 90212

Evaluation Studies Review Annual
1793
Public Finance Quarterly   3924

ST JOHN'S UNIVERSITY
Business Research Inst
Rm 203, St John Hall
Jamaica, NY 11439

Review of Business   4120

ST MARTIN'S PRESS, INC
175 5th Ave
New York, NY 10010

Atlas of Ireland   346
Britain in Context   596.01
Statesman's Year-Book   4408
Who's Who 1980–81   4975.02

**SALES AND MARKETING
EXECUTIVES INTERNATIONAL,
INC**
380 Lexington Ave
New York, NY 10168

Marketing Times   3136

**SALES AND MARKETING
MANAGEMENT**
Sales Builders Div
633 3rd Ave
New York, NY 10017

Sales & Marketing Management   4165
Survey of Buying Power—Part I   4510
Survey of Buying Power Data Service
4511
Survey of Buying Power Forecasting
Service   4511.01
Survey of Buying Power—Part II
4512
Survey of Industrial Purchasing Power
4516
Survey of Selling Costs   4518

SALESMAN'S GUIDE, INC
1140 Broadway
New York, NY 10001

Buying Offices and Accounts   729
Gift & Housewares Buyers   2226
Major Mass Market Merchandisers
3063
Nationwide Directory Sporting Goods
Buyers   3415
Nationwide Men's & Boys' Wear   3416
Nationwide Women's & Children's
Wear   3417
Premium, Incentive, and Travel Buyers
3833

HOWARD W SAMS CO, INC
4300 W 62 St
Indianapolis, IN 46268

Computer Dictionary and Handbook
1076

SAMSON PUBLICATIONS LTD
12-14 Hill Rise
Richmond, Surrey, England TW10
6UA

Computer Report   1082
Industrial Relations Week   2548
Management Information Manual
3081
Middle East Week   3222
Motor Report International   3328

T K SANDERSON ORGANIZATION
200 E 25 St
Baltimore, MD 21218

Directory of American Savings & Loan
Associations   1408

SASKATCHEWAN, CANADA

BUREAU OF STATISTICS
TC Douglas Bldg, 3475 Albert St
Regina, Sask, Canada S4S 6X6

Saskatchewan Economic Review   4181
Saskatchewan Monthly Statistical
Review   4182

DEPT OF FINANCE
Legislative Bldg, Room 117
Regina, Sask, Canada S4S 0B3

Saskatchewan's Financial & Economic
Position   4183

(SASKATCHEWAN, CANADA END)

SAVINGS & LOAN INVESTOR
PO Box 7163
Long Beach, CA 90807

Savings and Loan Investor   4186

SAVINGS ASSN LEAGUE OF NY STATE
700 White Plains Rd
Scarsdale, NY 10583

Savings Association News   4188

SAVVY
PO Box 2495
Boulder, CO 80321

Savvy   4190.01

SAWELL PUBLICATIONS LTD
127 Stanstead Rd
London, England SE23 1JE

Work Study   5033

SCHNELL PUBLISHING CO
100 Church St
New York, NY 10007

Chemical Marketing Reporter   926

SCHOONMAKER ASSOCIATES
Drawer M
Coram, NY 11727

Mainly Marketing   3062

SCIENCE ASSOCIATES/INTERNATIONAL, INC
1841 Broadway
New York, NY 10023

Information Hotline   2572

SCIENTIFIC MANPOWER COMMISSION
1776 Massachusetts Ave NW
Washington, DC 20036

Scientific, Engineering, Technical
Manpower Comments   4201

W D SCOTT & CO
100 Pacific Highway
North Sydney, NSW 2060, Australia

Australian Economy: Economic
Advisory Service   396

SCOTT'S INDUSTRIAL DIRECTORIES
PO Box 365
Oakville, Ont, Canada L6J 5M5

Scott's Industrial Directory. Atlantic
Manufacturers   4208
Scott's Industrial Directory. Ontario
Manufacturers   4209
Scott's Industrial Directory. Quebec
Manufacturers   4210

Scott's Industrial Directory. Western
Manufacturers   4211

SEATRADE PUBLICATIONS LTD
Fairfax House
Colchester, England CO1 1RJ

Seatrade   4217

SEATTLE–FIRST NATIONAL BANK
1001 4th Ave, Box 3586
Seattle, WA 98124

Quarterly Summary of Pacific
Northwest Industries   3976
Seafirst Magazine   4213

SECURITIES RESEARCH CO
Division of United Business Service Co
208 Newbury St
Boston, MA 02116

Stock Market Research Library   4467

SECURITY LETTER, INC
475 5th Ave
New York, NY 10017

Security Letter   4242

SECURITY PACIFIC NATIONAL BANK
PO Box 2097
Terminal Annex
Los Angeles, CA 90051

California Construction Trends   733
California International Trade   737
Census Retrieval System   880
Northern Coastal California—Economic
Trends in the Seventies   3537
Economic Report   3962
Security Pacific National Bank
International Trade Data Bank
4244
Security Pacific National Bank Monthly
Summary of Business Conditions,
Central Valley Counties of California
4245
Security Pacific National Bank Monthly
Summary of Business Conditions in
Southern California   4246
Security Pacific National Bank Monthly
Summary of Business Conditions,
Northern Coastal Counties of
California   4247
Security Pacific National Bank (SPNB)
California Databank   4248
Southern California—Economic Trends
in the Seventies   4347

SELECT INFORMATION EXCHANGE
2095 Broadway
New York, NY 10023

Select Information Exchange (SIE)
Guide to Business & Investment
Books   4255
Sophisticated Investor   4330

SELL'S PUBLICATIONS LTD
Sells House, 39 East St
Epsom, Surrey, England KT17 1BQ

Aviation Europe   437.01
British Exporters   612
Government & Municipal Contractors
2236
Health Service Buyers Guide   2364
Hotel, Restaurant, & Catering Supplies
2401
Scottish National Register of Classified
Trades   4206
Sell's British Exporters   4258
Sell's Building Index   4259
Sell's Directory   4260

SER–JOBS FOR PROGRESS INC
8585 N Stennons Freeway, Suite 401
Dallas, TX 75247

SER Network News   4264
SER Newsletter   4266
SER Women's Update   4270.01

SETON HALL UNIVERSITY
Division of Research, Graduate School
of Business
South Orange, NJ 07079

Mid-Atlantic Journal of Business
3215.01

IP SHARP ASSOCIATES
145 King St
Toronto, Canada M5H 1J8

Computer Network of Databases   1081

M E SHARPE, INC
80 Business Park Dr
Armonk, NY 10504

Challenge   902
Chinese Economic Studies   944
Eastern European Economics   1524
International Studies of Management &
Organization   2730
Japanese Economic Studies   2798
Matekon   3151
Problems of Economics   3857
Soviet and Eastern European Foreign
Trade   4350

SHEFFER CO
PO Box 19909
Houston, TX 77024

Ocean Construction & Engineering
    Report   3568
Ocean Construction Locator   3569
Offshore Rig Location Report   3591
Offshore Rig Newsletter   3592

SHELBY PUBLISHING CORP
555 Washington St
Wellesley Hills, MA 02181

John Liner Letter   3020

SIC PUBLISHING CORP
8705 N Port Washington Rd
Milwaukee, WI 53217

Wisconsin Industrial Product News
    5008

**SIGNS OF THE TIMES
PUBLISHING CO**
407 Gilbert Ave
Cincinnati, OH 45202

Screen Printing   4211.01
Signs of the Times   4286
Sportswear Graphics   4365
Visual Merchandising   4862

**SIMMONS–BOARDMAN
PUBLISHING CORP**
350 Broadway
New York, NY 10013

Banking   475
International Railway Journal (IRJ)
    2724
Marine Engineering/Log   3120
Plant Location   3780
Railway Age   3995

SINO–BRITISH TRADE COUNCIL
25 Queen Anne's Gate
London, England SW1H 9BU

Sino–British Trade   4289

THOMAS SKINNER DIRECTORIES
Windsor House
East Grimstead House
West Sussex, England RH19 1XE

Bankers Almanac and Year Book   466
Bank Sorting Code Numbers   502
Directory of Directors   1427
Royal Institution of Chartered
    Surveyors Year Book   4146
Willings Press Guide   5002

SMALL BUSINESS REPORT
497 Lighthouse Ave
Monterey, CA 93940

Small Business Report   4301.01

**SMALLER MANUFACTURERS
COUNCIL**
339 Blvd of the Allies
Pittsburgh, PA 15222

Smaller Manufacturer   4303

**SOCIAL CREDIT CO-ORDINATING
CENTRE**
Montagu Chambers
Mexborough, S Yorkshire, England S64
9AJ

Abundance   5

**SOCIETY FOR ADVANCEMENT
OF MANAGEMENT**
135 W 50th St
New York, NY 10020

Advanced Management Journal   62

**SOCIETY FOR INTERNATIONAL
DEVELOPMENT**
Palazzo della Civilta del Lavoro
00144 Rome, Italy

International Development Review
    2671

SOCIETY OF ACTUARIES
208 S La Salle St
Chicago, IL 60604

Actuary   48
Society of Actuaries Year Book   4323

**SOCIETY OF CHARTERED
PROPERTY & CASUALTY
UNDERWRITERS**
Kahler Hall
Providence Rd, (CB #9)
Malvern, PA 19355

Chartered Property & Casualty
    Underwriters (CPCU) Annals   916

**SOCIETY OF INVESTMENT
ANALYSTS**
211-213 High St
Bromley, Kent, England BR1 1NY

Investment Analyst   2759

**SOCIETY OF MANAGEMENT
ACCOUNTANTS OF CANADA**
154 Main St E
Hamilton, Ont, Canada L8N 3C3

Cost and Management   1226

**SOCIETY OF MANUFACTURING
ENGINEERS**
One SME Dr, PO Box 930
Dearborn, MI 48128

Manufacturing Engineering   3115

**SOCIETY OF REAL ESTATE
APPRAISERS**
645 N Michigan Ave
Chicago, IL 60611

Real Estate Appraiser and Analyst
    4011
SREA Briefs   4368.01

**SOCIETY OF RESEARCH
ADMINISTRATORS**
2855 E Coast Hwy, Suite 225
Corona del Mar, CA 92625

Journal of the Society of Research
    Administrators   2897

SOLAR ENERGY DIGEST
PO Box 17776
San Diego, CA 92117

Solar Energy Digest   4326.01
Solar Engineering Magazine   4326.03
Solar Heating and Cooling Magazine
    4326.04

SOLAR VISION, INC
Church Hill
Harrisville, NH 03450

Solar Age   4326

**SOUTH AFRICAN CONSULATE
GENERAL**
Consul (Commercial)
425 Park Ave, Suite 1200
New York, NY 10022

South Africa Yearbook   4337

**SOUTHAM COMMUNICATIONS
LTD**
1450 Don Mills Rd
Don Mills, Ont, Canada M3B 2X7

Administrative Digest   56
British Columbia Lumberman   603
Canadian Architect   775
Canadian Chemical Processing   784
Canadian Consulting Engineer   785
Canadian Footwear Journal   793
Canadian Forest Industries   794
Canadian Industrial Equipment News
    801
Canadian Mining Journal   819
Canadian Office Products and
    Stationery   824

Canadian Oil Register   825
Canadian Petroleum   827
Canadian Plastics   828
Canadian Transportation & Distribution
    Management   842
Canadian Travel News   844
Construction West   1143
Daily Commercial News and
    Construction Record   1294
Daily Commercial News Progress
    Report   1295
Daily Oil Bulletin   1303
Electrical Equipment News   1603
Electronics & Communications   1633
Engineering & Contract Record   1703
Executive   1795
Gifts & Tablewares   2227
Health Care   2356.02
Heating–Plumbing Air Conditioning
    2369
Journal of Commerce   2835
Laboratory Product News   2929
Meetings & Incentive Travel   3187
Pulp & Paper Canada   3946
Shop   4282
Southam Building Guide   4340
Southam Building Reports   4341
Water & Pollution Control   4898

SOUTH CAROLINA (STATE)

**EMPLOYMENT SECURITY
COMMISSION**
1550 Gadsden St, Box 995
Columbia, SC 29202

Directory of Labor Market Information
    1439

(SOUTH CAROLINA END)

SOUTH DAKOTA (STATE)

**DEPT OF ECONOMIC AND
TOURISM DEVELOPMENT**
South Dakota Idea, 221 S Central
Pierre, SD 57501

South Dakota Manufacturers Directory
    4345.01

(SOUTH DAKOTA END)

**SOUTHERN AGRICULTURAL
ECONOMICS ASSN**
c/o H. Evan Drummond, Sec-Treas
FRE, McCarty Hall, Univ of Florida
Gainesville, FL 32611

Southern Journal of Agricultural
    Economics   4349

SOUTHERN ECONOMIC ASSN
University of North Carolina at Chapel
Hill
Hanes Hall
Chapel Hill, NC 27514

Southern Economic Journal   4348

SOUTHERN HARDWARE
1760 Peachtree Rd NW
Atlanta, GA 30357

National Hardware Wholesalers Guide
    3377.02
Southern Hardware   4348.01

**SPAIN–US CHAMBER OF
COMMERCE**
500 5th Ave
New York, NY 10110

Span–US   4353

**SPECIALIST NEWSLETTERS PTY
LTD**
PO Box 430, Milsons Point
Sydney, NSW 2061, Australia

Adbrief   49
Cover Note   1240
Workforce   5022

SPECIAL LIBRARIES ASSN
235 Park Ave South
New York, NY 10003

Directory of Business and Financial
    Services   1414
Insurance Literature   2630
Insurance Periodicals Index   2633
Special Libraries Directory of Greater
    New York   4355

**SPECIALTY SALESMAN
MAGAZINE, INC**
Div of Communication Channels, Inc
6285 Barfield Rd
Atlanta, GA 30328

Specialty Salesman & Business
    Opportunities   4359

**CHARLES D SPENCER & ASSOC,
INC**
222 W Abrams St
Chicago, IL 60606

Employee Benefit Plan Review   1643
Employee Benefit Plan Review (EBPR)
    Research Reports   1644
International Benefit Information
    Service (IBIS)   2658

Spencer's Retirement Plan Service
    4362

L STAMBOVSKY
333 Bridge St
Springfield, MA 01103

Western Massachusetts Commercial
    News   4951

STAMLER PUBLISHING CO
297 Main St, PO Box 3367, SC Station
Branford, CT 06405

Highway & Vehicle/Safety Report
    2371

STANDARD & POOR'S CORP
25 Broadway
New York, NY 10004

American Exchange Stock Reports
    173
Analysts Handbook   215
Bond Guide   570
Called Bond Record   739
Commercial Paper Ratings Guide
    1008
Committee on Uniform Security
    Identification Procedures (CUSIP)
    Corporate Directory   1016
Committee on Uniform Security
    Identification Procedures (CUSIP):
    Digest of Changes in CUSIP   1017
Committee on Uniform Security
    Identification Procedures (CUSIP)
    Directory of User Numbers   1018
Committee on Uniform Security
    Identification Procedures (CUSIP)
    Master Directory   1019
Compmark Data Services   1067
Compustat   1070
Daily Stock Price Record   1306
Directory of Bond Agents   1411
Dividend Record (Daily)   1470
Dividend Record (Weekly)   1471
Earnings Forecaster   1521
Fixed Income Investor   2057
Industry Surveys   2565
Municipal Bond Selector   3338
Outlook   3653
Over-the-Counter Stock Reports   3669
Ratio Index Services   4007
Registered Bond Interest Record   4050
Register of Corporations, Directors, and
    Executives   4051
Review of Securities Regulation   4128
Security Dealers Directory   4239
Standard Corporation Records   4370
Standard NYSE Stock Reports   4375
Statistical Service   4442
Stock Guide   4466

Stock Summary 4469
Trendline Services Current Market
Perspectives 4710
Trendline Service Daily Action Stock
Charts 4711
Trendline Service: OTC Chart Manual
4713

STANDARD PUBLISHING
1073 Hancock St
Quincy, MA 02169

Standard—Northeast's Insurance
Weekly 4376

**STANDARD RATE AND DATA
SERVICE, INC**
5201 Old Orchard Rd
Skokie, IL 60077

British Rate & Data 622
Business Publication Rates & Data
717
Canadian Advertising Rates & Data
774
Community Publication Rates and Data
1050.01
Consumer Magazine & Farm
Publication Rates & Data 1156
Co-op News 1198
Co-op Source Directory 1198.01
Direct Mail List Rates & Data 1401
Network Rates & Data 3430
Newspaper Circulation Analysis 3468
Newspaper Rates & Data 3470
Print Media Production Data 3850
Spot Radio Rates & Data 4366
Spot Radio Small Markets Edition
4367
Spot Television Rates & Data 4368

**STANDARD RESEARCH
CONSULTANTS**
26 Broadway
New York, NY 10004

Standard Research Consultants (SRC)
Quarterly Reports 4378

**STANFORD RESEARCH
INSTITUTE INTERNATIONAL**
Menlo Park, CA 94025

Chemical Economics Handbook 921
Chemical Economics Newsletter 922
Directory of Chemical Producers USA
1417

STANFORD UNIV,
Food Research Institute
Stanford, CA 94305

Food Research Institute Studies 2097

STATISTICAL INDICATOR ASSOC
North Egremont, MA 01252

Statistical Indicator Reports 4428

STIMULUS PUBLISHING CO, LTD
Suite 906, 67 Yonge St
Toronto, Ont, Canada M5E 1J8

Stimulus 4463

**STOCK EXCHANGE RESEARCH
PTY LTD**
20 Bond St
Sydney, 2000, Australia

Annual Industrial Review 249.01
Annual Mining Review 251
Company Review Service 1054
Statex Service 4416

STOCK RESEARCH CORP
50 Broadway
New York, NY 10004

Weekly Insider Report 4932

STOKES & LINDLEY–JONES LTD
Alverstoke House
21 Montpelier Row
Blackheath
London, England SE3 0SR

Automotive, Spares & Accessories
434.01
Building Materials 639
Chemists' & Druggists' Supplies &
Toiletries 933
Food & Drink 2079
Hospital Equipment & Supplies 2391
Hotel & Catering Equipment &
Supplies 2399
Housewares Incorporating Gifts &
Fancy Goods 2405
Housewares Incorporating Hardware,
Tools and Do-It-Yourself 2406
Stationery & Office Supplies 4417

STONE & COX LTD
100 Simcoe St, 2nd Floor
Toronto, Ont, Canada M5H 3G2

Canadian Insurance 806
Canadian Insurance Law Service 808
Corporate Insurance in Canada 1209
Provincial Results (Underwriting)
3908
Stone and Cox General Insurance
Register 4473
Stone and Cox Life Insurance Tables
4474
Underwriting Results in Canada 4742

SUCCESS UNLIMITED, INC
401 N Wabash
Chicago, IL 60611

Success Unlimited 4489

SUNSHINE ENTERPRISES LTD
PO Box 2873
St Thomas, USUI 00801

Spotlite 4365.01

**SWEET & MAXWELL STEVENS
PERIODICALS**
11 New Fetter Lane
London, England EC4P 4EE

British Tax Review 624
Journal of Business Law 2831

SWITZERLAND

**CONSULATE GENERAL OF
SWITZERLAND**
444 Madison Ave
New York, NY 10022

Economic Survey of Switzerland 1572
Swiss–American Chamber of Commerce
Yearbook 4522
Swiss Export Directory 4523

(SWITZERLAND END)

SYRACUSE UNIVERSITY
College of Law
Syracuse, NY 13210

Syracuse Journal of International Law
& Commerce 4524

SYSTEM DEVELOPMENT CORP
2500 Colorado Ave
Santa Monica, CA 90406

SDC Search Service 4212.01

SYSTEMS RESEARCH INST
Publications Div
PO Box 74524
Los Angeles, CA 90004

Dictionary of Administration and
Management 1377

**TASCO PUBLISHING
CORPORATION**
305 E 53rd St
New York, NY 10022

Impact 2441.01

TAXATION PUBLISHING CO LTD
98 Park St
London, England W1Y 4BR

Taxation 4537

TAX EXECUTIVES INST
425 13th St NW
Washington, DC 20004

Tax Executive   4551

TAX FOUNDATION, INC
1875 Connecticut Ave NW
Washington, DC 20009

Facts & Figures on Government
    Finance   1872
Monthly Tax Features   3303
Tax Review   4569

TAYLOR & FRANCIS LTD
4 John St
London, England WC1N 2ET

Ergonomics   1740
Ergonomics Abstracts   1741
International Journal of Control   2690
International Journal of Electronics
    2691
International Journal of Production
    Research   2695
International Journal of Systems
    Science   2697

TCR SERVICE INC
140 Sylvan Ave
Englewood Cliffs, NJ 07632

Trademark Alert   4658.01
Trademark Research Service   4662.01

**TECHNICAL PRESS
PUBLICATIONS**
Eucharistic Congress Bldg No 1
5/1 Convent St, Colaba
Bombay 400 039, India

Chemical Age of India   919.01
Indian Chemical Directory   2503.03

TECHNICAL PUBLISHING CO
1301 South Grove Ave
Barrington, IL 60010

Consulting Engineer   1146
Datamation   1336
Industrial Research & Development
    2549
Plant Engineering   3778
Plant Engineering Directory and
    Specifications Catalog   3779
Pollution Engineering   3805
Power Engineering   3819
Purchasing World   3955

**TECHNOLOGY FORECASTS AND
TECHNOLOGY SURVEYS**
Suite 208, 205 S Beverly Dr
Beverly Hills, CA 90212

Alternative Energy: Trends & Forecasts
    149.01
Technology Forecasts and Technology
    Surveys   4581

**TECHNOLOGY NEWS CENTER,
INC**
PO Box 2549
Rando Palos Verdes, CA 90274

Technology Transfer Action   4582

**TECHNOMIC PUBLISHING CO
INC**
265 Post Rd W
Westport, CT 06880

Health Media Buyer's Guide   2363
Medical Marketing & Media   3181

**TELECOMMUNICATIONS
PUBLISHING**
1293 National Press Bldg
Washington, DC 20045

Telecommunications Reports   4584

TELEVISION DIGEST, INC
1836 Jefferson Pl NW
Washington, DC 20036

Cable & Station Coverage Atlas   730
Television Factbook   4589
Weekly Television Digest with
    Consumer Electronics   4940.01

TEMPLE UNIVERSITY
School of Business Administration
Philadelphia, PA 19122

Journal of Economics & Business
    2848

TENNESSEE (STATE)

**DEPT OF ECONOMIC &
COMMUNITY DEVELOPMENT**
1007 Andrew Jackson Bldg
Nashville, TN 37219

Tennessee Business and Industrial
    Review   4592

(TENNESSEE END)

TERMINUS MEDIA, INC
1819 Peachtree Rd, NE
Atlanta, GA 30309

Media Fax   3168

TEXAS (STATE)

**TEXAS INDUSTRIAL
COMMISSION**
Capitol Station
Box 12728
Austin, TX 78711

Brief Guide to Business Regulations
    and Services in Texas   592.01
Texas Facts   4596.01
Texas Ideas Newsletter   4597
Texas Industrial Update   4597.01
Texas Means Business   4597.03

(TEXAS END)

**TEXTILE ECONOMICS BUREAU,
INC**
489 5th Ave
New York, NY 10017

Textile Organon   4602

TEXTILE INSTITUTE
10 Blackfriars St
Manchester, England M3 5DR

Journal of the Textile Institute   2897
Textile Institute and Industry   4599

THIRD WORLD FOUNDATION
New Zealand House
80 Haymarket
London, England SW1Y 4TS

South—The Third World Magazine
    4349.01
Third World Quarterly   4606.01

THOMAS PUBLISHING CO
1 Penn Plaza, 250 West 34th
New York, NY 10001

American Export Register   174
Industrial Equipment News   2520
Thomas Grocery Register   4610
Thomas Register of American
    Manufacturers   4611

THOMPSON BUREAU
5395 S Miller St
Littleton, CO 80123

Topicator   4638

THOM'S DIRECTORIES LTD
38 Merrion Sq
Dublin 2, Ireland

Thom's Commercial Directory   4612

**THOMSON PUBLICATIONS PTY
LTD**
47 Chippen St, PO Box 65
Chippendale, NSW 2008, Australia

Australian Advertising Rate and Data Service   384
Australian Electronics Engineering   397
Australian Mining   411
Australian Mining Yearbook   412
Australia's International Engineering Exhibitions (AIEE)   422
Building Products News   641
Construction Equipment News   1129
Construction and Road Transport   1125
Electrical Engineer   1602
Factory Equipment News   1868
IES Lighting Review   2434
MEDIA '81   3166
Mingay's Electrical Supplies Guide   3235
Mingay's Price Service—Appliance Edition   3236
Mingay's Price Service—Radio/TV Edition   3237
Mingay's Retailer & Merchandiser   3238
Process and Chemical Engineering   3859
Tenders   4590
Thomson's Liquor Guide   4613

THORNE STEVENSON & KELLOGG
2300 Yonge St, Suite 1800
Toronto, Ont, Canada M4P 1G2

Employee Benefit Costs in Canada   1642

TIME, INC
Time & Life Bldg
New York, NY 10020

Fortune   2150
Fortune Double 500 Directory   2151
Money   3267
Time   4619

TIMES BOOKS
3 Park Ave
New York, NY 10016

Times Atlas of the World: Revised Comprehensive Edition   4621

TIMES BOOKS
16 Golden Sq
London, England WC1X 8EZ
W1R4BN

Times 1000   4622

TIMES MIRROR PRESS
1115 S Boyle Ave
Los Angeles, CA 90023

California International Trade Register   737.01
California Manufacturers Register   738.02
California Services Register   738.04
Washington Manufacturers Register   4888.02

TOBACCO MERCHANTS ASSN
Statler Hilton
7th Ave & 33rd St
New York, NY 10001

Bi-weekly Index of the Tobacco Scene (BITS)   559
Tobacco Barometers   4627
Tobacco Merchants Assn (TMA) Guide to Tobacco Taxes   4629

TOKYO NEWS SERVICE, LTD
Tsukiji Hamarikyu Bldg
3-3 Ipukyi 5-chome
Chuoku, Tokyo (104), Japan

Shipping and Trade News   4275
Zosen   5107

TOLLEY PUBLISHING CO, LTD
44a High St
Croydon, Surrey, England CR9 1UU

Company Secretary's Review   1055
Tolley's Corporation Tax   4632
Tolley's Employment Handbook   4633
Tolley's Income Tax   4634
Tolley's Taxation in the Channel Islands and Isle of Man   4635
Tolley's Taxation in the Republic of Ireland   4636

TORONTO BOARD OF TRADE
PO Box 60
3 First Canadian Place
Toronto, Ont, Canada M5X 1C1

Metropolitan Toronto Board of Trade. Journal   3206

TORONTO DOMINION BANK
PO Box 1
Toronto-Dominion Centre
Toronto, Ont, Canada M5K 1A2

Canada's Business Climate   762

TORONTO STOCK EXCHANGE
234 Bay St
Toronto, Ont, Canada M5J 1R1

Toronto Stock Exchange—Company Manual   4640
Toronto Stock Exchange—Daily Record   4640.01

Toronto Stock Exchange—Management of Change in the Canadian Securities Industry   4640.02
Toronto Stock Exchange—Members' Manual   4640.03
Toronto Stock Exchange Review   4641
Toronto Stock Exchange—"300" Stock Price Indexes   4641.01
Toronto Stock Exchange—"300" Total Return Indexes   4641.02
Toronto Stock Exchange Weekly Summary   4642

TOUCHE ROSS & CO
1633 Broadway
New York, NY 10019

Business Studies   723
Investment and Taxation Monograph   2760.01

TRADE LEVELS, INC
301 E Colorado Blvd, Suite 400
Pasadena, CA 91101

Trade Levels Option Report   4656
Trade Levels Report   4657

TRAFFIC SERVICE CORP
1435 G St NW, Suite 815
Washington, DC 20005

Daily Traffic World   1309
Official Directory of Industrial & Commercial Traffic Executives   3584

TRANSCOMMUNICATIONS INTERNATIONAL, INC
426 Statler Office Bldg
Boston, MA 02116

International New Product Newsletter   2714

TRANS-TASMAN NEWS SERVICE LTD
PO Box 377
Wellington, New Zealand

Trans-Tasman   4699

TRENDS PUBLISHING, INC
233 National Press Bldg
Washington, DC 20045

Energy Today   1699
Environment Report   1729
Radiation Report   3984
Scientific Information Notes   4202

TRINC TRANSPORTATION CONSULTANTS, DIVISION OF DUN & BRADSTREET
475 L'Enfant Plaza SW, Suite 4200
PO Box 23091
Washington, DC 20024

Trinc's Blue Book of the Trucking
  Industry   4719
Trinc's Red Book of the Trucking
  Industry   4721

TRUST COMPANIES ASSN OF CANADA
Suite 400, Board of Trade Bldg
11 Adelaide St W
Toronto, Ont, Canada M5H 1L9

General Information Bulletin   2212

TUDOR PRESS LTD
Tudor House, 3 Delfield Close
Watford, Herts, England WD1 3LB

Insurance Record   2634

TUFTY COMMUNICATIONS
986 National Press Bldg
Washington, DC 20045

Zero-Base Digest   5105

JOHN TURREL
Rt 2
Mt Vernon, IL 62864

Electric Letter   1613

TURRET PRESS LTD
4 Local Board Rd
Watford, Herts, England WD1 2JS

Bulk   643
Ceramic Industries Journals   892
Cleaning, Maintenance & Big Building
  Management   958
Finishing Industries   2039
Heating & Ventilating Engineer   2367
Insulation   2607
Milling, Feed & Fertiliser   3229.01
Music Trades International   3343
Paint Manufacture   3687
Radio & Electric Retailing   3986
Storage Handling Distribution   4475

TWIN COAST NEWSPAPERS, INC
110 Wall St
New York, NY 10005

Exporters Directory   1821.01
Journal of Commerce and Commercial
  2836

UNDERWRITER PRINTING & PUBLISHING CO
50 East Palisade Ave, PO Box 9806
Englewood, NJ 07631

Insurance Almanac   2610
Insurance Casebook   2614
Insurance Department Service   2618
Telephone Tickler   4587
Weekly Underwriter   4942
Who's Who Among Professional
  Insurance Agents   4976
Who's Who in Insurance   4988
Who's Who in Risk Management
  4990

UNDERWRITERS LABORATORIES, INC
333 Pfingsten Rd
Northbrook, IL 60062

Lab Data   2923

UNION OF INTERNATIONAL ASSOCIATIONS
1 rue aux Laines
Brussels, Belgium 1000

Yearbook of International
  Organizations   5093

UNIPUB
345 Park Ave S
New York, NY 10010

International Bibliography, Information,
  Documentation   2659

UNITED AUTOMOBILE, AEROSPACE AND AGRICULTURAL IMPLEMENT WORKERS OF AMERICA
8000 E Jefferson Ave
Detroit, MI 48214

Solidarity   4327

UNITED BUSINESS PUBLICATIONS, INC
475 Park Ave S
New York, NY 10016

Audiovisual Communications   346.02
Biomedical Communications   554.02
Government Data Systems   2239.01
Industrial Photography   2535.01
Marketing Communications   3127.03
Medical Meetings   3181.01
Videography   4854.01

UNITED BUSINESS SERVICE CO
210 Newbury St
Boston, MA 02116

Cycli-Graphs   1290
Security Charts   4238
United Business & Investment Report
  4755
United Mutual Fund Selector   4764

UNITED CALIFORNIA BANK
Research and Planning Division
707 Wilshire Blvd (W14-2)
Los Angeles, CA 90017

Forecast   2106

UNITED COMMERCIAL TRAVELLERS' ASSN, ASTMS
Bexton Lane, Knutsford
Cheshire, England WA16 9DA

Selling Today   4257

UK FEDERATION OF BUSINESS & PROFESSIONAL WOMEN CLUBS
54 Bloomsbury St
London, England WC1B 3QU

Business & Professional Women   664

UNITED NATIONS

UN CONFERENCE ON TRADE & DEVELOPMENT (UNCTAD)
Palais des Nations
Geneva 10, CH-1211 Switzerland

Handbook of International Trade and
  Development Statistics, 1979   2327
Monthly Commodity Price Bulletin
  3286
Tungsten Statistics   4733
United Nations Conference on Trade
  and Development (UNCTAD) Guide
  to Publications   4765
United Nations Conference on Trade
  and Development (UNCTAD)
  Monthly Bulletin   4766

DEPT OF ECONOMIC AND SOCIAL AFFAIRS
United Nations
Rm A-3315
New York, NY 10017

World Economic Survey   5061

UN DIVISION FOR ECONOMIC & SOCIAL INFORMATION
Palais des Nations
Geneva 10, CH-1211 Switzerland

Development Forum   1374
Development Forum: Business Edition
  1375

UNITED NATIONS ECONOMIC COMMISSION FOR AFRICA
PO Box 3001
Addis Ababa, Ethiopia

African Trade/Commerce Africain   80
Investment Africa   2758
Statistical and Economic Information
   Bulletin for Africa   4424

ECONOMIC AND SOCIAL COMMISSION FOR ASIA AND THE PACIFIC
United Nations Bldg, Rajadamnern Ave
Bangkok 2, Thailand

Economic & Social Commission for
   Asia and the Pacific   1536.01

FOOD AND AGRICULTURE ORGANIZATION OF THE UNITED NATIONS
Via delle Terme di Caracalla
Rome 00100, Italy

Food and Agriculture Organization
   Ceres (FAO) Review on
   Development   894
Food and Agriculture Organization
   (FAO) Commodity Review and
   Outlook   2075
Food and Agriculture Organization
   (FAO) Plant Protection Bulletin
   2076
Food and Agriculture Organization
   Production Yearbook   2077
Food and Agriculture Organization
   Trade Yearbook   2078
Food and Nutrition   2082
Monthly Bulletin of Agricultural
   Economics and Statistics   3278
State of Food and Agriculture   4402
Unasylva: An International Journal of
   Forestry and Forest Products   4739
World Animal Review   5041
Yearbooks of Fishery Statistics   5098
Yearbooks of Forest Products Statistics
   5099

UNITED NATIONS INDUSTRIAL DEVELOPMENT ORGANIZATION
Vienna International Centre
PO Box 300, A-1400
Vienna, Austria

Fertilizer Industry Series   1981
Food Industry Studies   2088
Industrial Development Abstracts
   2514
Industrial Planning and Programming
   Series   2536
Petrochemical Series   3756

Thesaurus of Industrial Development
   Terms   4606
Training for Industry Series   4686
United Nations Industrial Development
   Organization (UNIDO) Guides to
   Information Sources.
   UNIDO/LIB/SER.D/Rev. 1—
   Information Sources on
   Bioconversion of Agricultural Wastes
   4767.01
United Nations Industrial Development
   Organization (UNIDO) Guides to
   Information Sources.
   UNIDO/LIB/SER.D/Rev. 1—
   Information Sources on Industrial
   Maintenance and Repair   4767.02
United Nations Indusrial Development
   Organization (UNIDO) Guides to
   Information Sources.
   UNIDO/LIB/SER.D/Rev. 1—
   Information Sources on Industrial
   Training   4767.03
United Nations Industrial Development
   Organization (UNIDO) Guides to
   Information Sources.
   UNIDO/LIB/SER.D/Rev. 1—
   Information Sources on
   Non-conventional Sources of Energy
   4767.04
United Nations Industrial Development
   Organization (UNIDO) Guides to
   Information Sources.
   UNIDO/LIB/SER.D/1/Rev. 1—
   Information Sources on the Beer and
   Wine Industry   4767.05
United Nations Industrial Development
   Organization (UNIDO) Guides to
   Information Sources.
   UNIDO/LIB/SER.D/Rev. 1—
   Information Sources on the Coffee,
   Cocoa, Tea and Spices Industry
   4767.06
United Nations Industrial Development
   Organization (UNIDO) Guides to
   Information Sources.
   UNIDO/LIB/SER.D/Rev. 1—
   Information Sources on the Dairy
   Product Manufacturing Industry
   4767.07
United Nations Industrial Development
   Organization (UNIDO) Guides to
   Information Sources.
   UNIDO/LIB/SER.D/Rev. 1—
   Information Sources on the
   Electronics Industry   4767.08
United Nations Industrial Development
   Organization (UNIDO) Guides to
   Information Sources.
   UNIDO/LIB/SER.D/Rev. 1—
   Information Sources on the Iron and
   Steel Industry   4767.09

United Nations Industrial Development
   Organization (UNIDO) Guides to
   Information Sources.
   UNIDO/LIB/SER.D/1/Rev. 1—
   Information Sources on the Machine
   Tool Industry   4767.10
United Nations Industrial Development
   Organization (UNIDO) Guides to
   Information Sources.
   UNIDO/LIB/SER.D/Rev. 1—
   Information Sources on the Natural
   and Synthetic Rubber Industry
   4767.11
United Nations Industrial Development
   Organization (UNIDO) Guides to
   Information Sources.
   UNIDO/LIB/SER.D/Rev. 1—
   Information Sources on the
   Packaging Industry   4767.12
United Nations Industrial Development
   Organization (UNIDO) Guides to
   Information Sources.
   UNIDO/LIB/SER.D/Rev. 1—
   Information Sources on the
   Petrochemical Industry   4767.13
United Nations Industrial Development
   Organization (UNIDO) Guides to
   Information Sources.
   UNIDO/LIB/SER.D/1/Rev. 1—
   Information Sources on the Soap and
   Detergent Industry   4767.14
United Nations Industrial Development
   Organization (UNIDO) Guides to
   Information Sources.
   UNIDO/LIB/SER.D/Rev. 1—
   Information Sources on the
   Utilization of Agricultural Residues
   for the Production of Panels, Pulp
   and Paper   4767.15
United Nations Industrial Development
   Organization (UNIDO) Guides to
   Information Sources.
   UNIDO/LIB/SER.D/Rev. 1—
   Information Sources on
   Woodworking Machinery   4767.16
United Nations Industrial Development
   Organization Guides to Information
   Sources. UNIDO/LIB/SER D/1 Rev
   1—Information Sources on the Meat
   Processing Industry   4768
United Nations Industrial Development
   Organization Guides to Information
   Sources. UNIDO/LIB/SER D/2—
   Information Sources on the Cement
   and Concrete Industry   4769
United Nations Industrial Development
   Organization Guides to Information
   Sources. UNIDO/LIB/SER D/3 and
   Corr—Information Sources on the
   Leather and Leather Goods Industry
   4770

UN INSTITUTE FOR TRAINING & RESEARCH

801 UN Plaza
New York, NY 10017

UNITED NATIONS PUBLICATIONS

United Nations, Rm A-3315
New York, NY 10017

UNITED NATIONS STATISTICAL OFFICE

United Nations
New York, NY 10017

Yearbook of National Accounts
   Statistics 5096

US BUREAU OF THE CENSUS. *See*
**US Department of Commerce, Bureau
of the Census**

**US AGENCY FOR
INTERNATIONAL DEVELOPMENT**
Washington, DC 20523

Agency for International Development
   (AID) Research and Development
   Abstracts 86
Development Digest 1373
Proposed Foreign Aid Program 3903

US BUREAU OF MINES
Publications Distribution Branch
4800 Forbes Ave
Pittsburgh, PA 15213

Foreign Mineral Reports 2135
Mineral Facts and Problems 3231
Mineral Industry Surveys 3232
Preliminary Annual Area Reports
   3831
Preliminary Annual Data on
   Commodities 3832

US CIVIL AERONAUTICS BOARD
Bureau of Accounts and Statistics
Washington, DC 20428

Handbook of Airline Statistics 2322

US COPYRIGHT OFFICE. *See* **US
Library of Congress, Copyright Office**

US CUSTOMS SERVICE
Washington, DC 20229

Customs Bulletin 1287
Customs Regulations of the United
   States 1288
Exporting to the United States 1827

**US DEPARTMENT OF
AGRICULTURE**
Agricultural Marketing Service
306 Annex Bldg
Washington, DC 20250

Cotton Market News Reports 1231
Dairy Market News Reports 1312
Fresh Fruit and Vegetable and
   Ornamental Crops Market News
   Reports 2166
Grain Market News Reports 2254

Livestock Market News Reports 3030
Naval Stores Market News Reports
   3420
Poultry Market News Reports 3813
Tobacco Market News Reports 4628

US DEPT OF AGRICULTURE
Crop Reporting Board
Economics & Statistics Service (ESS)
Washington, DC 20250

Agricultural Price Report 103
Dairy Products Reports 1313
Illinois Agricultural Statistics 2436
Livestock and Products Reports 3027
North Dakota Crop and Livestock
   Statistics 3536
South Dakota Crop and Livestock
   Reporter 4344

US DEPT OF AGRICULTURE
ESS Publications, Room 0054-S
Washington, DC 20250

Agricultural Economics Research 97
Agricultural Finance Outlook 99
Agricultural Finance Review 100
Agricultural Outlook 102
Agricultural Statistics 106
Developments in Price Spreads for
   Farm Foods 1375.02
Economic Indicators of the Farm
   Sector: Income and Balance Sheet
   Statistics 1552.01
Economic Indicators of the Farm
   Sector: Production and Efficiency
   Statistics 1552.02
Evaluation of Pesticide Supplies and
   Demand 1792.04
Farmline 1901.01
Farm Real Estate Market
   Developments 1903
Foreign Agricultural Trade of the
   United States 2108
Handbook of Agricultural Charts
   2317
National Food Review 3376
Outlook and Situation Report 3653.01
Outlook for US Agricultural Exports
   3654
World Agricultural Situation 5038
World Agricultural Supply and
   Demand Estimate 5038.01

US DEPT OF AGRICULTURE
Agricultural Cooperative Service
GHI Bldg, Rm 550
Washington, DC 20250

Farmer Cooperatives 1897

US DEPT OF AGRICULTURE
Foreign Agricultural Service
Information Service Staff, Rm 5918
Washington, DC 20250

Foreign Agriculture 2110
Foreign Agriculture Circulars 2111
Weekly Roundup of World Production
   and Trade 4939

US DEPT OF AGRICULTURE
NOAA/USDA Joint Agricultural
Weather Facility
USDA S Bldg, Room 3526
Washington, DC 20250

Weekly Weather and Crop Bulletin
   4943

US DEPT OF COMMERCE
14th St between Constitution Ave and
E St NW
Washington, DC 20203

Business America 656
Commerce Business Daily 995
Commerce Publications Update 996.02
Construction Reports—Housing Starts
   1141
Data User News 1345
Dimensions 1397
Foreign Economic Trends 2116
Survey of Current Business 4514

US DEPT OF COMMERCE
Bureau of Economic Analysis
Washington, DC 20230

Business Conditions Digest Data File
   676
Employment by Type and Broad
   Industrial Source 1657
Foreign Direct Investment in the
   United States 2115
Local Area Personal Income 1973–1978
   3036
National Income and Product Accounts
   3383
Personal Income, Population, Per
   Capita Personal Income 3737
Regional Employment by Industry,
   1940–1970 4046
Transfer Payments by Major Source
   4688
US Direct Investment Abroad, 1966
   4796

**US DEPARTMENT OF
COMMERCE**
Bureau of the Census
Washington, DC 20233

US DEPT OF COMMERCE

Industry and Trade Admin
Bureau of Export Development
Washington, DC 20230

US DEPT OF COMMERCE
International Trade Administration
Washington, DC 20230

Commercial News USA   1006
Export Administration Regulations
   1818
Export Administration Report   1819
Foreign Economic Trends and Their
   Implications for the US   2117
International Economic Indicators &
   Competitive Trends   2675
Overseas Business Reports   3656
Summary of US Export Administration
   Regulations   4494
United States Industrial Outlook   4807

US DEPT OF COMMERCE
Minority Business Development Agency
Main Commerce Bldg
Washington, DC 20230

Access   7
Commerce: Journal of Minority
   Business   996.01

US DEPT OF COMMERCE
National Technical Information Service
5285 Port Royal Rd
Springfield, VA 22161

Abstract Newsletters, and Management
   Administration   2.03
Abstract Newsletters, Agriculture &
   Food   2.04
Abstract Newsletters, Behavior &
   Society   2.05
Abstract Newsletters, Biomedical
   Technology & Human Factors
   Engineering   2.06
Abstract Newsletters, Building Industry
   Technology   2.07
Abstract Newsletters, Business &
   Economics   2.08
Abstract Newsletters, Chemistry   2.09
Abstract Newsletters, Civil Engineering
   2.10
Abstract Newsletters, Communication
   2.11
Abstract Newsletters, Computers,
   Control & Information Theory   2.12
Abstract Newsletters, Electrotechnology
   2.13
Abstract Newsletters, Energy   2.14
Abstract Newsletters, Environmental
   Pollution & Control   2.15
Abstract Newsletters, Government
   Inventions for Licensing   2.16
Abstract Newsletters, Health Planning
   and Health Services Research   2.17
Abstract Newsletters, Industrial &
   Mechanical Engineering   2.18

Abstract Newsletters, Information for
   Innovations   2.19
Abstract Newsletters, Library &
   Information Sciences   2.20
Abstract Newsletters, Materials Sciences
   2.21
Abstract Newsletters, Medicine &
   Biology   2.22
Abstract Newsletters, NASA Earth
   Resources Survey Program   2.23
Abstract Newsletters, Natural
   Resources & Earth Sciences   2.24
Abstract Newsletters, Ocean
   Technology & Engineering   2.25
Abstract Newsletters, Physics   2.26
Abstract Newsletters, Problem-Solving
   Information for State & Local
   Governments   2.27
Abstract Newsletters, Transportation
   2.28
Abstract Newsletters, Urban
   Technology   2.29
Directory of Computerized Data Files
   & Related Technical Reports   1420
Directory of Computer Software and
   Related Technical Reports   1421

US DEPT OF LABOR
Bureau of Labor Statistics
441 G St NW
Washington, DC 20212

Consumer Price Index (CPI) Detailed
   Report   1163
Current Wage Developments   1284
Directory of National Unions &
   Employee Associations   1449
Employment & Earnings   1652
Handbook of Labor Statistics   2328
Major Programs   3064
Monthly Labor Review   3291
Occupational Outlook Handbook   3562
Occupational Outlook Quarterly   3563
Producer Prices and Price Indexes
   3862.01

US DEPT OF LABOR
Employment & Training Administration
Washington, DC 20210

Area Trends in Employment &
   Unemployment   308
Comparison of State Unemployment
   Insurance Laws   1059
Employment and Training
   Administration (ETA) Interchange
   1653
Employment and Training Report to
   the President   1655
Job Corps Happenings   2809
Research and Development Projects
   4082

Significant Provisions of State
   Unemployment Insurance Laws
   4285
Unemployment Insurance Statistics
   4745
Worklife Magazine   5026

US DEPT OF LABOR
Employment Standards Adm
200 Constitution Ave NW
Washington, DC 20210

Employment Standards Digest   1666

US DEPT OF LABOR
Labor Management Services
Administration
Washington, DC 20216

Register of Reporting Labor
   Organizations   4052

US DEPT OF LABOR
Women's Bureau
200 Constitution Ave NW
Washington, DC 20210

1975 Handbook on Women Workers
   3522

US DEPT OF THE INTERIOR
Washington, DC 20240

Annual Indexes to SWRA   249
Research Reports Supported by Office
   of Water Research and Technology
   4094
Selected Water Resources Abstracts
   (SWRA)   4254
Water Resources Thesaurus   4900

US DEPT OF THE TREASURY
Washington, DC 20226

Annual Report of the Secretary of the
   Treasury on the State of the Finances
   257
Monthly Treasury Statement of
   Receipts and Outlays of the US Govt
   3304.01
Monthly Statement of United States
   Currency and Coin   3298
Treasury Bulletin   4708
Treasury Combined Statement of
   Receipts, Expenditures, and Balances
   of the US Govt   4709

US DEPT OF THE TREASURY
Bureau of the Mint
15th & Pennsylvania Ave NW
Washington, DC 20220

World's Monetary Stocks of Gold,
   Silver, and Coins—on a Calendar
   Year Basis   5079

US DEPT OF TRANSPORTATION
Federal Aviation Administration
800 Independence Ave
Washington, DC 20591

Federal Aviation Administration (FAA)
  General Aviation News   1912
Federal Aviation Administration (FAA)
  Statistical Handbook of Aviation
  1913

US FARM CREDIT ADMINISTRATION
Public Affairs Div
Washington, DC 20578

Annual Report of the Farm Credit
  Administration   255

US FEDERAL DEPOSIT INSURANCE CORP
Washington, DC 20429

Changes Among Operating Banks &
  Branches   904
Federal Deposit Insurance Corp Annual
  Report   1919
Federal Deposit Insurance Corporation
  —Law, Regulations and Related Acts
  1920
Trust Assets of Insured Commercial
  Banks   4726
US Federal Deposit Insurance Corp.
  Bank Operating Statistics   4801

US FEDERAL HOME LOAN BANK BOARD
1700 G St NW
Washington, DC 20552

Economic Briefs   1541
Federal Home Loan Bank Board
  Journal   1926
Savings and Home Financing Source
  Book   4184

US FEDERAL MEDIATION & CONCILIATION SERVICE
2100 K St NW
Washington, DC 20427

Federal Mediation & Conciliation
  Service Annual Report   1931

US FEDERAL RESERVE SYSTEM
Board of Governors
Washington, DC 20551

Capital Market Developments   858
Federal Reserve Bulletin   1956
Federal Reserve Chart Book on
  Financial and Business Statistics
  1957

Federal Reserve System Annual Report
  1958
Public Periodic Releases   3926
Selected Interest and Exchange Rates
  4253

US FEDERAL TRADE COMMISSION
Washington, DC 20580

Acts   46
Advertising Substantiation Program   72
Federal Trade Commission Annual
  Report   1973
Federal Trade Commission Decisions
  1974
Federal Trade Commission. Quarterly
  Financial Report for Manufacturing,
  Mining, & Trade Corporations   1975
Trade Practice Rules   4668
Trade Regulation Rules   4672

US GENERAL SERVICES ADMINISTRATION
18th and F Sts NW
Washington, DC 20405

Business Service Centers   721
Consumer Information Catalog   1154

US GOVT PRINTING OFFICE
Superintendent of Documents
Washington, DC 20402

Monthly Catalog of US Government
  Publications   3285
Official Congressional Directory   3583
Printing and Publishing   3848
Superintendent of Documents Price
  Lists   4496
US Government Manual   4803

INTERNAL REVENUE SERVICE
12th & Constitution Ave
Washington, DC 20224

Internal Revenue Bulletin   2645
Internal Revenue Service Annual
  Report of the Commissioner of
  Internal Revenue   2647
Internal Revenue Service Chief Counsel
  Annual Report   2648
Internal Revenue Service Publications
  2649
Internal Revenue Service Statistics of
  Income: Corporation Income Tax
  Returns   2650
Internal Revenue Service Tax Guide for
  Small Business 344   2651

US INTERNATIONAL TRADE COMMISSION
Washington, DC 20436

Imports of Benzenoid Chemicals &
  Products   2474
International Trade Commission
  Annual Report   2737
International Trade Commission
  Quarterly Report to the Congress &
  the East–West Foreign Trade Board
  on Trade between the US & the
  Nonmarket Economy Countries
  2738
Operation of the Trade Agreements
  Program   3628
Tariff Schedules of the US Annotated
  4532

US INTERSTATE COMMERCE COMMISSION
12th St & Constitution Ave NW
Washington, DC 20423

Interstate Commerce Commission
  Annual Report   2745
Interstate Commerce Commission
  Reports, Decisions of the ICC of the
  US   2748

US LIBRARY OF CONGRESS
Copyright Office
Washington, DC 20559

Catalog of Copyright Entries   868

US MARITIME ADMINISTRATION
Commerce Bldg, 14th & E Sts NW
Washington, DC 20230

Analysis of LNG Marine
  Transportation   213
Annual Report of the Maritime
  Administration   256
Arctic Marine Commerce Study   302
Final Environmental Impact Statement
  of Maritime Administration Tanker
  Construction Program   1986
Maritime and Construction Aspects of
  Ocean Thermal Energy Conversion
  (OTEC) Plant Ships   3122
Merchant Marine Data Sheet   3194
Standard Specifications for Diesel
  Merchant Ship Construction   4379
Standard Specifications for Tanker
  Construction   4380
Statistical Analysis of the World's
  Merchant Fleets   4423
US Ocean Shipping Technology
  Forecast and Assessment, Final
  Report   4813

NATIONAL AERONAUTICS AND SPACE ADMINISTRATION
Washington, DC 20546

National Aeronautics and Space Administration (NASA) Activities 3356

US NATIONAL INJURY INFORMATION CLEARINGHOUSE
US Consumer Product Safety Commission
5401 Westbord Ave, Room 625
Washington, DC 20207

NEISS Data Highlights   3373
National Injury Information Clearinghouse. Tabulation of Data from National Electronic Injury Surveillance System   3386

US NATIONAL LABOR RELATIONS BOARD
1717 Pennsylvania Ave NW
Washington, DC 20570

Classified Index of Dispositions of ULP Charges by the General Counsel of the National Labor Relations Board 955
Classified Index of National Labor Relations Board Decisions & Related Court Decisions   956
National Labor Relations Board Case Handling Manual   3391
Rules and Regulations and Statements of Procedure of the National Labor Relations Board   4152
Weekly Summary of NLRB Cases 4940

US NATIONAL MEDIATION BOARD
1425 K St NW
Washington, DC 20572

Determinations of the National Mediation Board   1369.02
National Mediation Board Annual Report   3393
National Mediation Board Reports of Emergency Boards   3394

US OFFICE OF CONSUMER AFFAIRS
Health and Human Services Dept
621 Reporters Bldg
Washington, DC 20201

Consumer Action Update   1147.01

US PATENT AND TRADEMARK OFFICE
Washington, DC 20231

Annual Indexes of Patents   248
Manual of Classification   3102

Manual of Patent Examining Procedure 3104
Patent Attorneys & Agents Registered to Practice Before the US Patent Office   3699
Patent Official Gazette   3704
Trademark Official Gazette   4659

US RAILROAD RETIREMENT BOARD
844 Rush St
Chicago, IL 60611

Railroad Retirement Board Annual Report   3991
Railroad Retirement Board Quarterly Review   3992

US SECURITIES & EXCHANGE COMMISSION
Washington, DC 20549

Accounting Series Releases   37
Directory of Companies Filing Annual Reports with the US Securities & Exchange Commission   1419
Rules and Regulations   4151.01
Securities & Exchange Commission Annual Report to Congress   4224
Securities & Exchange Commission Decisions & Reports   4225
Securities & Exchange Commission Docket   4227
Securities & Exchange Commission News Digest   4228
Securities & Exchange Commission Official Summary   4229
Securities & Exchange Commission Statistical Bulletin   4231

US SMALL BUSINESS ADMINISTRATION
1030 15 St NW, Suite 250
Washington, DC 20417

Management Aids   3072
Small Business Administration Annual Report   4298
Small Business Bibliographies   4299
Small Business Management Series 4301
Starting and Managing Series   4382

US SOCIAL SECURITY ADMINISTRATION
Office of Research & Statistics
Washington, DC 20201

Annual Statistical Supplement, Social Security Bulletin   263
Current Medicare Survey Reports 1279

Social Security Beneficiaries in Metropolitan Areas   4317
Social Security Bulletin   4318

(UNITED STATES END)

US BREWERS ASSOCIATION
1750 K St NW
Washington, DC 20006

Brewing Industry in the US: Brewers Almanac   590

US INDEPENDENT TELEPHONE ASSOCIATION
1801 K St NW, Suite 1201
Washington, DC 20006

Independent Telephone Statistics   2495

US LEAGUE OF SAVINGS ASSN
111 E Wacker Dr
Chicago, IL 60601

Savings and Loan Fact Book   4185
Savings & Loan News   4187
Washington Notes   4888.03

US NEWS AND WORLD REPORT
PO Box 2629
Boulder, CO 80322

US News and World Report   4812

US TRADEMARK ASSN
6 E 45th St
New York, NY 10017

Executive Newsletter   1807
State Trademark Statutes   4415
Trademark Reporter   4662

US-YUGOSLAV ECONOMIC COUNCIL, INC
51 E 42nd St
New York, NY 10017

Business News   714

UNITED TECHNICAL PUBLICATIONS INC
645 Stewart Ave
Garden City, NY 11530

Office Products News   3580
Office World News   3582

UNITED TRADE PRESS LTD
33-35 Bowling Green Lane
London, England EC1R 0DA

Industrial Safety   2551

UNIVERSTIY OF AKRON
College of Business Administration
302 E Buchtel Ave
Akron, OH 44325

Akron Business and Economic Review
132

UNIVERSITY OF ALABAMA
College of Commerce & Business
Administration
Center for Business and Economic
Research
PO Box AK
University, AL 35486

Alabama Business   133
Alabama Economic Abstract   135

UNIVERSITY OF ALASKA
Institute of Social and Economic
Research, 707 A St, Suite 206
Anchorage, AK 99501

Alaska Review of Social & Economic
Conditions   142

UNIVERSITY OF ARIZONA
College of Business and Public
Administration
Div of Economic and Business
Research
Tucson, AZ 85721

Arizona Review   317
Arizona's Economy   317.01
Arizona Statistical Abstract   317.03

UNIVERSITY OF ARKANSAS
College of Business Administration
Bureau of Business and Economic
Research
Fayetteville, AR 72701

Arkansas Business and Economic
Review   318

UNIVERSITY OF BALTIMORE
1420 N Charles St
Baltimore, MD 21201

American Journal of Small Business
196
University of Baltimore Business
Review   4823

**UNIVERSITY OF CALIFORNIA AT
BERKELEY**
Graduate School of Business
Administration
Berkeley, CA 94720

California Management Review   738

**UNIVERSITY OF CALIFORNIA
PRESS**
2223 Fulton St
Berkeley, CA 94720

Business Information Sources   693

UNIVERSITY OF CHICAGO
Graduate School of Business
1101 E 58th St
Chicago, IL 60637

Journal of Accounting Research   2818

UNIVERSITY OF CHICAGO PRESS
5801 S Ellis Ave
Chicago, IL 60637

Economic Development & Cultural
Change   1548
Journal of Business   2827
Journal of Political Economy   2873

UNIVERSITY OF COLORADO
Graduate School of Business
Administration
Business Research Division
Boulder, CO 80309

Business Economic Outlook Forum
678
Colorado Business Review   984
Colorado City Retail Sales by Standard
Industrial Classification   985
Colorado County and State Retail Sales
by Standard Industrial Classification
986
Colorado Ski and Winter Recreation
Statistics   989
Directory of Colorado Manufacturers
1418
Journal of Travel Research   2899
National Ski Area Association (NSAA)
Economic Analysis of North
American Ski Areas   3406

UNIVERSITY OF FLORIDA
College of Business Administration
Bureau of Economic and Business
Research
221 Matherly Hall
Gainesville, FL 32611

Dimensions   1398
Florida Outlook   2068
Florida Statistical Abstract   2069

UNIVERSITY OF GEORGIA
College of Business Administration
Division of Research
Athens, GA 30602

Georgia Business   2218
Georgia Statistical Abstract   2220

UNIVERSITY OF IDAHO
Center for Business Development and
Research
Moscow, ID 83843

Idaho Statistical Abstract   2432
Manufacturing Directory of Idaho
3114

**UNIVERSITY OF ILLINOIS AT
URBANA-CHAMPAIGN**
Agricultural Experiment Station
Urbana, IL 61801

Illinois Agricultural Economics   2435
Illinois Research   2439

UNIVERSITY OF LANCASTER
Dept of Systems, Bailrigg
Lancaster, England LA1 4YR

Journal of Applied Systems Analysis
2823.01

UNIVERSITY OF LEEDS
School of Economic Studies
Leeds, England LS2 9JT

Bulletin of Economic Research   644

**UNIVERSITY OF
MASSACHUSETTS**
School of Business Administration
Amherst, MA 01002

Massachusetts Business & Economic
Report   3148

UNIVERSITY OF MELBOURNE
Institute of Applied Economic and
Social Research
Parkville, Vic 3052, Australia

Australian Economic Review   395

UNIVERSITY OF MICHIGAN
Graduate School of Business
Administration
Ann Arbor, MI 48109

Human Resource Management   2429
Personnel Management Abstracts   3746

UNIVERSITY OF MICHIGAN
Institute for Social Research
PO Box 1248
Ann Arbor, MI 48106

Institute for Social Research (ISR)
Newsletter   2594

UNIVERSITY OF MONTANA
Bureau of Business and Economic
Research
Missoula, MT 59812

Montana Business Quarterly   3276

UNIVERSITY OF NEBRASKA—LINCOLN
Bureau of Business Research
200 CBA
Lincoln, NE 68588

Business in Nebraska   694
Nebraska Journal of Economics &
  Business   3423

UNIVERSITY OF NEVADA, RENO
Bureau of Business and Economic
Research
Reno, NV 89557

Nevada Review of Business &
  Economics   3431

UNIVERSITY OF NEW MEXICO
Bureau of Business and Economic
Research
Institute for Applied Research Services
Albuquerque, NM 87131

Economy   1577
New Mexico Business   3454

UNIVERSITY OF NORTH CAROLINA AT GREENSBORO
School of Business and Economics
Center for Applied Research
Greensboro, NC 27412

North Carolina Review of Business &
  Economics   3535

UNIVERSITY OF OKLAHOMA
Center for Economic and Management
Research
College of Business Administration
307 W Brooks St, Rm 4
Norman, OK 73019

Oklahoma Business Bulletin   3614
Review of Regional Economics &
  Business   4127
Statistical Abstract of Oklahoma   4420

UNIVERSITY OF OKLAHOMA
School of Journalism
860 Vanvleet Oval, Rm 101
Norman, OK 73019

Cecil H Brite Lecture Series in
  Advertising and Publications
  Management   597

UNIVERSITY OF OXFORD
Institute of Agricultural Economics
Dartington House
Little Clarendon St
Oxford, England

Oxford Agrarian Studies   3672

UNIVERSITY OF PITTSBURGH
Graduate School of Business
Bureau of Business Research
Pittsburgh, PA 15213

Pittsburgh Business Review   3774

UNIVERSITY OF RHODE ISLAND
Research Center in Business and
Economics
Kingston, RI 02881

New England Journal of Business &
  Economics   3443

UNIVERSITY OF SOUTH CAROLINA
Division of Research
College of Business Administration
Columbia, SC 29208

Business and Economic Review   660

UNIVERSITY OF SOUTH DAKOTA
School of Business
Business Research Bureau
Vermillion, SD 57069

South Dakota Business Review   4343

UNIVERSITY OF SUSSEX
Institute of Development Studies
Brighton, England BN1 9RE

Bulletin   643.01
Development Digest   1373.01

UNIVERSITY OF TENNESSEE
Center for Business and Economic
Research
College of Business Administration
100 Glocker Bus Admin Bldg
Knoxville, TN 37916

Survey of Business   4508
Tennessee Statistical Abstract   4594

UNIVERSITY OF TEXAS AT AUSTIN
Bureau of Business Research
PO Box 7459
Austin, TX 78712

Texas Business Review   4596

UNIVERSITY OF UTAH
Dept of Economics
Salt Lake City, UT 84112

Statistical Abstract of Utah   4422
Utah Construction Report   4834
Utah Economic & Business Review
  4835

UNIVERSITY OF WASHINGTON
Graduate School of Business
Mackenzie Hall
Seattle, WA 98195

Journal of Contemporary Business
  2842
Journal of Financial & Quantitative
  Analysis   2855

UNIVERSITY OF WESTERN ONTARIO
School of Business Administration
London, Ont, Canada N6A 3K7

Business Quarterly   718

UNIVERSITY OF WISCONSIN PRESS
Journals Div, 114 N Murray St
Madison, WI 53715

Journal of Consumer Affairs   2840
Journal of Human Resources   2860
Land Economics   2961

URBAN LAND INSTITUTE
1090 Vermont Ave NW
Washington, DC 20005

Environmental Comment   1721
Environmental Impact Handbook
  1723
Industrial Development Handbook
  2515
Land Use Digest   2962
Urban Land   4832

URNER BARRY PUBLICATIONS
PO Box 389
Toms River, NJ 08753

Monthly Price Review   3294
Restaurant Buyers Guide   4098
Seafood Price—Current   4215
Urner Barry's Price-Current   4833.01
Weekly Insiders Dairy and Egg Letter
  4933
Weekly Insiders Poultry Report   4934
Weekly Insiders Turkey Letter   4935

UTAH FOUNDATION
308 Continental Bank Bldg
Salt Lake City, UT 84101

Statistical Review of Government in
  Utah   4441

VALLEY NATIONAL BANK OF ARIZONA
Box 71
Phoenix, AZ 85001

Arizona Progress   315

VALUE TREND ANALYSIS
7440 Girard Ave, #4
La Jolla, CA 92037

Investment Quality Trends   2766

VANCE PUBLISHING CORP
133 E 58th St
New York, NY 10022

Paper Trade Journal   3694

VANCOUVER BOARD OF TRADE
1177 W Hastings St
Vancouver, BC, Canada V6E 2K3

Sounding Board   4331
Trade Letter and Business Barometer
   4655

VANCOUVER STOCK EXCHANGE
536 Howe St
Vancouver, BC, Canada V6C 2E1

Vancouver Stock Exchange Annual
   Report   4842
Vancouver Stock Exchange Review
   4843

VAN NOSTRAND REINHOLD
135 W 50 St
New York, NY 10001

Advances in Plastics Technology   64.01
Advertising Cost Control Handbook
   68
Dangerous Properties of Industrial
   Materials   1316.01
Encyclopedia of Management   1675
VNR Dictionary of Business and
   Finance   4862.01
VNR Investor's Dictionary   4862.02

VENDING TIMES, INC
211 E 43rd St
New York, NY 10036

International Vending Buyer's Guide &
   Directory   2741
Vending Times   4844

VENEZUELA

EMBASSY OF VENEZUELA
2437 California St NW
Washington, DC 20008

Venezuela Up-to-Date   4845

(VENEZUELA END)

VICKERS ASSOCIATES, INC
226 New York Ave
Huntington, NY 11743

Vickers Guide to Bank Trust Guide
   4849
Vickers Guide to College Endowment
   Portfolios   4850
Vickers Guide to Insurance Company
   Portfolios—Common Stocks   4851
Vickers Guide to Insurance Company
   Portfolios—Corporate Bonds   4852
Vickers Guide to Investment Company
   Portfolios   4853
Vickers Traders Guide   4853.01

VINCENT PRESS
10 Hill View Rd
Twickenham Middx, England TW1
1EB

Journal of World Trade Law   2901

VIRGINIA SOCIETY OF CPA'S
700 E Main St Bldg, Suite 1010
Richmond, VA 23219

Virginia Accountant Quarterly   4858

VIRGINIA (STATE)

VA EMPLOYMENT COMMISSION
703 E Main St
Richmond, VA 23211

Labor Market Information Directory
   2939

(VIRGINIA END)

VISION, INC
13 E 75th
New York, NY 10021

Vision—The Inter-American Magazine
   4860

WADHAM PUBLICATIONS LTD
109 Vanderhoof Ave, Suite 101
Toronto, Ont, Canada M4G 2J2

Automotive Marketer   432
Canadian Risk Management & Business
   Insurance   830
Canadian Underwriter   845
Motor Truck   3329

WALKER & CO
720 5th Ave
New York, NY 10019

World Trade Annual   5082

WALKER'S MANUAL, INC
5855 Naples Plaza, Suite 101
Long Beach, CA 90803

Walker's Manual of Western
   Corporations   4872

WALLACE–HOMESTEAD CO
1912 Grand Ave
Des Moines, IA 50305

Wallaces Farmer   4875

WALL STREET ADVISOR
PO Box 2591
Ormond Beach, FL 32074

Wall Street Advisor   4876

ROY W WALTERS & ASSOC
Whitney Rd
Mahwah, NJ 07430

Behavioral Sciences Newsletter   519
Executive Lifestyle Newsletter   1804

WARD PUBLICATIONS
Box 380
Petaluma, CA 94952

News Front/Business Trends   3465
News Front/Business Trends Databank
   3465.01
News Front/Business Trends Directory
   3465.02

WARD'S COMMUNICATIONS, INC
28 W Admas St
Detroit, MI 48226

Ward's Automotive Yearbook   4882

**WARREN, GORHAM, AND
LAMONT, INC**
210 South St
Boston, MA 02111

Bank Auditing & Accounting Report
   459
Bank Automation Newsletter   460
Bank Director's Report   462
Banker's Letter of the Law   468
Bankers Magazine   469
Bank Executive's Report   473
Banking Law Journal   477
Bank Installment Lending Newsletter
   479
Bank Loan Officers Report   481
Bank Marketing Report   484
Bank Officer's Handbook of
   Commercial Banking Law   490
Bank Operations Report   495
Bank Personnel Report   497
Bank Security Report   501
Bank Tax Report   505
Bank Teller's Report   506
Business & Society Review   667
Computer Law and Tax Report   1079

Consumer Credit and Truth-in-Lending Compliance Report 1151
Corporate Controllers and Treasurers Report 1204.01
Corporation Law & Tax Report 1219
Effective Manager 1598.01
Estate Planning 1748
Executive Compensation and Employee Benefits Report 1798.01
Journal of Accounting, Auditing and Finance 2817.02
Journal of Business Strategy 2831.02
Journal of Corporate Taxation 2843
Journal of Real Estate Taxation 2878
Journal of Taxation 2887
Kess Tax Practice Report 2909
Modern Banking Forms 3254
Modern Trust Forms and Checklists 3266
Mortgage and Real Estate Executives Report 3319.02
Real Estate Law Journal 4021
Real Estate Law Report 4022
Real Estate Review 4024
Real Estate Tax Ideas 4026
Securities and Exchange Commission (SEC) Accountig Report 4222
Securities Regulation Law Journal 4236
Taxation for Accountants 4538
Taxation for Lawyers 4539
Tax Law Review 4556
Thorndike Encyclopedia of Banking and Financial Tables 4615
Uniform Commercial Code Law Journal 4750
Uniform Commercail Code Law Letter 4751
Wiesenberger Financial Services 5001

WARREN PUBLISHING CORP
210 South St
Boston, MA 02111

Banker & Tradesman 465

WASHINGTON BOARD OF REALTORS, INC
1511 K St NW
Washington, DC 20005

Realtor 4029

WASHINGTON (STATE)

DEPT OF COMMERCE & ECONOMIC DEVELOPMENT
Research Div
General Administration Bldg
Olympia, WA 98504

Announced New Plants and Expansions in the State of Washington 231
Washington State Economy: Review and Outlook 4893
Washington State Foreign Trade Trends 4894

EMPLOYMENT SECURITY DEPT
Research and Statistics Branch
Olympia, WA 98504

Washington State Labor Market Information Directory 4895

(WASHINGTON END)

WASHINGTON MONITOR
499 National Press Bldg
Washington, DC 20045

Access Reports/Freedom of Information 9.01
Congress Daily 1110.01
Congress in Print 1110.02
Congressional Monitor 1115.01
Congressional Record Scanner 1115.02
Congressional Yellow Book 1115.03
Federal Yellow Book 1976.01
Weekly Regulatory Monitor 4938

WEBB CO
1999 Shepard Rd
St Paul, MN 55116

Beef 517
Beef Buying Guide 518
Farmer 1896
Farm Industry News 1900
Irrigation Age 2789
National Hog Farmer 3379

WELLENS PUBLISHING
Guilsborough, Northampton, England NN6 8PY

Industrial & Commercial Training, The Management of Human Resources 2507

WELLS FARGO BANK
Public Relations Dept
PO Box 44000
San Francisco, CA 94144

Wells Fargo Bank Business Review 4947

WELT PUBLISHING CO
1151 K St NW
Washington, DC 20005

African Business & Trade 79.02
East/West Technology Digest 1527
Latin American Index 2975

Soviet-Eastern Europe-China Business & Trade 4351

WERBEL PUBLISHING CO
595 Old Willets Path
Smithtown, NY 11787

General Insurance Guide 2213

WESTERN ECONOMIC ASSN
Dept of Economics
California State University
Long Beach, Ca 90840

Economic Inquiry 1553

WESTERN ILLINOIS UNIVERSITY
Center for Business and Economic Research
Macomb, IL 61455

Journal of Behavioral Economics 2825

WESTERN RESERVE PRESS
PO Box 675
Ashtabula, OH 44004

Handbook for Manufacturing Entrepreneurs, 1973 2315

WEST PUBLISHING CO
50 W Kellogg Bldg, PO Box 3526
St Paul, MN 55165

Black's Law Dictionary 561

WEST VIRGINIA SOCIETY OF CPAS
Box 1142
Charleston, WV 25324

West Virginia CPA 4954

WEST VIRGINIA (STATE)

DEPT OF EMPLOYMENT SECURITY
Labor and Economic Research
112 California Ave
Charleston, WV 25305

Labor Market Trends 2940.01

GOVERNOR'S OFFICE OF ECONOMIC AND COMMUNITY DEVELOPMENT
1900 Washington St E
Charleston, WV 25305

West Virginia Economic Profile 4955
West Virginia Industrial Wage Survey 4956
West Virginia Manufacturing Directory 4957

(WEST VIRGINIA END)

WEST VIRGINIA UNIVERSITY
Bureau of Business Research
Morgantown, WV 26506

Auber Bibliography   346.01
Business Law Review   703
Journal of Small Business Management
2884

WHALEY–EATON CORP
1141 National Press Bldg
Washington, DC 20004

Transportation Business Report   4692
Whaley–Eaton American Letter   4958
Whaley–Eaton Foreign Letter   4959

WHEATLAND JOURNALS LTD
177 Hagden Lane
Watford, England WD1 8LW

Packaging   3683

WHITE MERCANTILE AGENCY
240 Queen St
Brisbane, Qld 4000, Australia

White Mercantile Gazette   4969

WHITSED PUBLISHING LTD
55 Bloor St W, Suite 1201
Toronto, Ont, Canada M4W 3K2

Canadian Office   822
Computer Data   1074

WHO OWNS WHOM LTD
6–8 Bowhill St
London, England EC2A 4BU

Who Owns Whom: Australia & Far
East   4972
Who Owns Whom: Continental Europe
4973
Who Owns Whom: North America
4974
Who Owns Whom: United Kingdom &
Republic of Ireland   4975

WICHITA STATE UNIVERSITY
College of Business Administration
Center for Business and Economic
Research
023 Clinton Hall, Box 48
Wichita, KS 67208

Kansas Economic Indicators   2904

JOHN WILEY AND SONS, INC
605 3rd Ave
New York, NY 10158

Accountants' Cost Handbook   19
Accountants' Handbook   21
Biotechnology and Bioengineering   557
Color Research and Application   991
Earth Surface Processes and Landforms
1522
Financial Handbook   2002
International Journal for Energy
Research   2692
International Journal for Numerical
Methods in Engineering   2689
Journal of Earthquake Engineering and
Structural Dynamics   2845
Journal of Futures Markets   2858
Journal of the American Society for
Information Science   2888.01
Public Administration and
Development   3920.01
Quarterly Journal of Economics   3964
Software: Practice & Experience   4325
Strategic Management Journal   4478.01

**WILLAMETTE MANAGEMENT
ASSOC**
534 SW 3rd Ave, Suite 400
Portland, OR 97204

Northwest Investment Review   3546
Northwest Stock Guide   3547

WILLIAMS & GLYNS BANK LTD
Economics Office
7 Capthall Ave
London, England EC2R 7HB

Monthly Summary of Business
Conditions in the United Kingdom
3302
Three Banks Review   4616

H W WILSON CO
950 University Ave
Bronx, NY 10452

Applied Science and Technology Index
(ASTI)   288
Business Periodicals Index   716
Cumulative Book Index   1267
Readers' Guide to Periodical Literature
4009
Social Sciences Index   4315

WISCONSIN INSTITUTE OF CPAS
600 E Mason St
Milwaukee, WI 53202

Wisconsin CPA   5007

WOMEN'S WORK
1302 18th St NW, Suite 203
Washington, DC 20036

Women's Work   5016

WOOTTEN PUBLICATIONS LTD
150/152 Caledonian Rd
London, England N1 9RD

Planned Savings   3777
Savings Market   4190

WORK IN AMERICA INST, INC
700 White Plains Rd
Scarsdale, NY 10583

World of Work Report   5073

WORLD BANK
1818 H St NW
Washington, DC 20433

Borrowing in International Capital
Markets   576
Commodity Trade and Price Trends
1031
International Centre for Settlement of
Investment Disputes (ICSID)   2665
International Finance Corporation
(IFC), 1980 Annual Report   2679
World Bank Annual Report, 1980
5043
World Bank Atlas   5044
World Debt Tables   5054
World Economic and Social Indicators
5059
World Tables 1980   5080

**WORLD COUNCIL OF CREDIT
UNIONS**
PO Box 391
Madison, WI 53701

World Council of Credit Unions
Annual Report   5049
World Council of Credit Unions
Newsletter   5050
World Reporter   5077

**WORLD INTELLECTUAL
PROPERTY ORGANIZATION**
34 Chemin des Colombettes
1211 Geneva 20, Switzerland

Copyright   1201
Industrial Property   2537

WORLD OF INFORMATION
21 Gold St, Saffron Walden
Essex, England CB10 1EJ

Africa Guide 1981   78
Asia & Pacific 1981   324.02
Gulf Guide & Diary 1981   2310
Latin America & Caribbean 1981
2969.01
Middle East Review 1981   3219.01

WORLD'S FAIR LTD
PO Box 57
Union St
Oldham, Lanc, England 0L1 1DY

World's Fair   5078

**WORLD TRADE ACADEMY
PRESS, INC**
50 E 42nd St
New York, NY 10017

Directory of American Firms Operating
   in Foreign Countries   1407
Directory of Foreign Firms Operating
   in the US   1431
Multinational Marketing and
   Employment Directory   3336

WORLD TRADE CENTERS ASSN
One World Trade Center, Suite 55W
New York, NY 10048

World Trade Centers Association
   (WTCA News)   5083

**WORLD TRADE INFORMATION
CENTER**
1 World Trade Center
Suite 86001
New York, NY 10048

World Trade Information Center
   5083.01

WORLD TRADE MAGAZINES LTD
World Trade House, 145 High St
Riverhead, Sevenoaks, Kent, England
TN13 1XJ

Achievement   39

**WRIGHT INVESTMENT
PUBLICATIONS**
Park City Plz
10 Middle St
Bridgeport, CT 06604

Wright Investors Service   5089.01

YAFFA PUBLISHING GROUP
432-436 Elizabeth St
Surry Hills, NSW 2001, Australia

Advertising News   69
Australian Refrigeration,
   Air-Conditioning and Heating
   413.01
Clothing Industry News   967.01
Food Manufacturing News   2092
Hospital Journal of Australia   2394
Men's Wear   3189.02
Modern Cleaning & Maintenance
   3255.01
Packaging News   3685
Textile Journal Annual Buying Guide
   4600
Textile Journal/Australia   4601

ARTHUR YOUNG & CO
277 Park Ave
New York, NY 10017

Executive Compensation Letter   1799
News & Views   3461.01
Taxation Publications   4541
Tax Legislation Update   4457.01
Views   4857.01

ZIFF–DAVIS PUBLISHING CO
1156 15th St NW
Washington, DC 20005

Aerospace Daily   75
Aviation Daily   437
Business & Commercial Aviation   659
Flying   2072
Flying Annual & Buyers' Guide   2073
Travel Weekly   4706
World Aviation Directory   5042
World Travel Directory   5084

GARY ZIMMERMAN
GPO Box 114
Brooklyn, NY 11202

MONEY BEGETS MONEY: A Guide
   to Personal Finance   3268

**ZWEIG SECURITIES ADVISORY
SERVICE, INC**
747 3rd Ave
New York, NY 10017

Traders Hotline   4673.01
Zweig Forecast   5108

SOURCES OF BUSINESS INFORMATION

1
Abbreviations Dictionary, 6th edition, 1981
American Elsevier, 52 Vanderbilt Ave, New York, NY 10017. Telephone (212) 867-9040.

Dictionary of shortened and abbreviated usage, including contractions, nicknames, signs, symbols, and abbreviations used in business and industry. Price $35.00.

2
Abecor Country Reports
Barclays Bank, Group Economics Dept, 54 Lombard St, London, England, EC3P 3AH. Telephone (44) (01) 283-8989.

Pamphlet. Covers the economies of over 100 countries throughout the world. Price free of charge.

2.01
ABI/INFORM
Data Courier, Inc, 620 S 5th St, Louisville, KY 40202. Telephone (502) 582- Telex 204235.

.e service. Provides access to business information. Contains abstracts of cles on accounting, economics, information science, marketing, and other lated subjects. Price available on request.

2.02
ABS
American Building Supplies, 1760 Peachtree Rd, NW, Atlanta, GA 30357. Telephone (404) 874-4462.

Monthly magazine. Reports on home improvement and building materials market. Focuses on merchandising trends. Price $35.00 per year.

2.03
Abstract Newsletters, Administration and Management
US Dept of Commerce, National Technical Information Service, 5285 Port Royal Rd, Springfield, VA 22161. Telephone (703) 487-4630.

Weekly newsletter. Provides information on government conducted or sponsored research projects on administration, management informaion systems, personnel management, and labor relations. Price $70.00 per year.

2.04
Abstract Newsletters, Agriculture & Food
US Dept of Commerce, National Technical Information Service, 5285 Port Royal Rd, Springfield, VA 22161. Telephone (703) 487-4630.

Weekly newsletter. Reviews government conducted or sponsored research projects on agricultural engineering, agricultural economics, food technology, veterinary medicine, and related topics. Price $60.00 per year.

2.05
Abstract Newsletters, Behavior & Society
US Dept of Commerce, National Technical Information Service, 5285 Port Royal Rd, Springfield, VA 22161. Telephone (703) 487-4630.

Weekly newsletter. Supplies material on government conducted or sponsored research on pyschology and society, Includes information on job training, education, law, and the humanities. Price $60.00 per year.

2.06
Abstract Newsletters, Biomedical Technology & Human Factors Engineering
US Dept of Commerce, National Technical Information Service, 5285 Port Royal Rd, Springfield, VA 22161. Telephone (703) 487-4630.

Weekly newsletter. Contains information on government sponsored or conducted biomedical technology and engineering research. Covers instruments, prosthetics, life-support systems, and space biology. Price $50.00 per year.

2.07
Abstract Newsletters, Building Industry Technology
US Dept of Commerce, National Technical Information Service, 5285 Port Royal Rd, Springfield, VA 22161. Telephone (703) 487-4630.

Weekly newsletter. Provides data on government conducted or sponsored building technology research projects. Includes information on design, management, materials, and equipment. Price $65.00 per year.

2.08
Abstract Newsletters, Business & Economics

US Dept of Commerce, National Technical Information Service, 5285 Port Royal Rd, Springfield, VA 22161. Telephone (703) 487-4630.

Weekly newsletter. Covers business and economics research conducted or sponsored by the government. Includes such topics as manufacturing and production, marketing, consumer affairs, banking and finance, and minority business. Price $65.00 per year.

2.09
Abstract Newsletters, Chemistry

US Dept of Commerce, National Technical Information Service, 5285 Port Royal Rd, Springfield, VA 22161. Telephone (703) 487-4630.

Weekly newsletter. Carries material on government conducted or sponsored chemical research activities. Includes such subjects as chemical process engineering, industrial polymer, photo and radiation, and theoretical chemistry. Price $70.00 per year.

2.10
Abstract Newsletters, Civil Engineering

US Dept of Commerce, National Technical Information Service, 5285 Port Royal Rd, Springfield, VA 22161. Telephone (703) 487-4630.

Weekly newsletter. Reports on civil and structural engineering research sponsored or conducted by the government. Covers highway engineering, flood control, construction equipment and materials, and soil and rock mechanics. Price $70.00 per year.

2.11
Abstract Newsletters, Communication

US Dept of Commerce, National Technical Information Service, 5285 Port Royal Rd, Springfield, VA 22161. Telephone (703) 487-4630.

Weekly newsletter. Provides information on communications research conducted or sponsored by the government. Includes data on common carriers and satellites, policies and regulations, and radio and television equipment. Price $55.00 per year.

2.12
Abstract Newsletters, Computers, Control & Information

US Dept of Commerce, National Technical Information Service, 5285 Port Royal Rd, Springfield, VA 22161. Telephone (703) 487-4630.

Weekly newsletter. Carries material on computers, control systems, and information theory research conducted or sponsored by the government. Discusses hardware, software, and pattern recognition. Price $80.00 per year.

2.13
Abstract Newsletters, Electrotechnology

US Dept of Commerce, National Technical Information Service, 5285 Port Royal Rd, Springfield, VA 22161. Telephone (703) 487-4630.

Weekly newsletter. Reports on government conducted or sponsored electrotechnology research programs. Includes information on antennas, circuits, electronic tubes, components, and semi-conductors. Price $55.00 per year.

2.14
Abstract Newsletters, Energy

US Dept of Commerce, National Technical Information Service, 5285 Port Royal Rd, Springfield, VA 22161. Telephone (703) 487-4630.

Weekly newsletter. Reports on government conducted or sponsored energy research projects. Includes such topics as energy use, supply and demand, sources, fuel conversion processes, power and heat generation, engines, and fuels. Price $80.00 per year.

2.15
Abstract Newsletters, Environmental Pollution & Control

US Dept of Commerce, National Technical Information Service, 5285 Port Royal Rd, Springfield, VA 22161. Telephone (703) 487-4630.

Weekly newsletter. Discusses environmental pollution and control research conducted or sponsored by the government. Covers air, noise, solid waste, water pollution, radiation, environmental health and safety. Price $80.00 per year.

2.16
Abstract Newsletters, Government Inventions for Licensing

US Dept of Commerce, National Technical Information Service, 5285 Port Royal Rd, Springfield, VA 22161. Telephone (703) 487-4630.

Weekly newsletter. Reports on government inventions available for licensing. Covers mechanical devices and fields of nuclear technology, biology and medicine, metallurgy, and electrotechnology. Price $180.00 per year.

2.17
Abstract Newsletters, Health Planning and Health Services Research

US Dept of Commerce, National Technical Information Service, 5285 Port Royal Rd, Springfield, VA 22161. Telephone (703) 487-4630.

Weekly newsletter. Reports on government conducted or sponsored health planning research. Covers health services and facilities, costs, manpower requirements and training, and government and private agency activities. Price $60.00 per year.

2.18
Abstract Newsletters, Industrial & Mechanical Engineering

US Dept of Commerce, National Technical Information Service, 5285 Port Royal Rd, Springfield, VA 22161. Telephone (703) 487-4630.

Weekly newsletter. Covers industrial and mechanical engineering research conducted or sponsored by the government. Includes information on quality control, plant design and maintenance, environmental engineering, and machinery and tools. Price $65.00 per year.

2.19
Abstract Newsletters, Information for Innovators

US Dept of Commerce, National Technical Information Service, 5285 Port Royal Rd, Springfield, VA 22161. Telephone (703) 487-4630.

Biweekly newsletter. Provides abstracts in nontechnical language on federally sponsored research and development, selected and interpreted for innovative potential. Includes foreign technology and extensive collateral references. Price $85.00 per year.

2.20
Abstract Newsletters, Library and Information Sciences
US Dept of Commerce, National Technical Information Service, 5285 Port Royal Rd, Springfield, VA 22161. Telephone (703) 487-4630.

Weekly newsletter. Carries material on government conducted or sponsored library and information science research. Reports on systems, marketing, and personnel. Price $50.00 per year.

2.21
Abstract Newsletters, Materials Sciences
US Dept of Commerce, National Technical Information Service, 5285 Port Royal Rd, Springfield, VA 22161. Telephone (703) 487-4630.

Weekly newsletter. Reports on materials science research programs conducted or sponsored by the government. Includes such topics as ablation, adhesives, ceramics, elastomers, plastics, alloys, wood, and paper products. Price $70.00 per year.

2.22
Abstract Newsletters, Medicine & Biology
US Dept of Commerce, National Technical Information Service, 5285 Port Royal Rd, Springfield, VA 22161. Telephone (703) 487-4630.

Weekly newsletter. Supplies information on government conducted or sponsored medical and biological research. Covers dentistry, nutrition, occupational and physical therapy, pharmacology, and psychiatry. Price $60.00 per year.

2.23
Abstract Newsletters, NASA Earth Resources Survey
US Dept of Commerce, National Technical Information Service, 5285 Port Royal Rd, Springfield, VA 22161. Telephone (703) 487-4630.

Bimonthly newsletter. Contains information on NASA's Earth Resources Survey Program research. Pertains to Skylab's and earth resources satellites' feedback on the earth's soil, water, and vegetation. Price $50.00 per year.

2.24
Abstract Newsletters, Natural Resources & Earth
US Dept of Commerce, National Technical Information Service, 5285 Port Royal Rd, Springfield, VA 22161. Telephone (703) 487-4630.

Weekly newsletter. Supplies data on natural resources research projects conducted or sponsored by the government. Covers mineral industries, soil conservation, forestry, and geology. Price $60.00 per year.

2.25
Abstract Newsletters, Ocean Technology & Engineering
US Dept of Commerce, National Technical Information Service, 5285 Port Royal Rd, Springfield, VA 22161. Telephone (703) 487-4630.

Weekly newsletter. Covers government conducted or sponsored ocean technology and engineering research. Includes information on oceanography, hydrography, underwater construction, and port engineering. Price $55.00 per year.

2.26
Abstract Newsletters, Physics
US Dept of Commerce, National Technical Information Service, 5285 Port Royal Rd, Springfield, VA 22161. Telephone (703) 487-4630.

Weekly newsletter. Reports on physics research projects sponsored or conducted by the government. Includes such topics as optics and lasers, solid-state physics, nuclear physics, thermodynamics, and quantum mechanics. Price $60.00 per year.

2.27
Abstract Newsletters, Problem Solving Information for State & Local Governments
US Dept of Commerce, National Technical Information Service, 5285 Port Royal Rd, Springfield, VA 22161. Telephone (703) 487-4630.

Weekly newsletter. Carries government conducted or sponsored research reports on problem solving for state and local governments. Includes such topics as finance, human resources, transportation, energy, and community development. Price $50.00 per year.

2.28
Abstract Newsletters, Transportation
US Dept of Commerce, National Technical Information Service, 5285 Port Royal Rd, Springfield, VA 22161. Telephone (703) 487-4630.

Weekly newsletter. Reports on transportation research conducted or sponsored by the government. Covers air, pipeline, surface and subsurface transportation. Price $70.00 per year.

2.29
Abstract Newsletters, Urban and Regional Technology & Development, Urban Technology
US Dept of Commerce, National Technical Information Service, 5285 Port Royal Rd, Springfield, VA 22161. Telephone (703) 487-4630.

Weekly newsletter. Carries material on urban technology research conducted or sponsored by the government. Includes such subjects as urban administration, housing, sanitation, health services, pollution control and traffic. Price $50.00 per year.

3
Abstracts from Technical and Patent Publications
British Internal Combustion Engine Research Institute Ltd, 111/112 Buckingham Ave, Slough, Berkshire, England. Telephone Slough 27371.

Weekly report. Presents abstracts from papers on technical research and patents on internal combustion engine parts and processes. Notes pertinent conferences. Price £50.00 per year.

4
Abstracts on Health Effects of Environmental Pollutants (HEEP)
Biosciences Information Service of Biological Abstracts, 2100 Arch St, Philadelphia, PA 19103. Telephone (215) 568-4016.

Monthly journal. Contains abstracts of research reports on the effect of environmental pollutants on health. Includes topics on industrial medicine, occupational health, and animal research. Price $130.00 per year. Annual cumulative index $55.00.

5
Abundance
Social Credit Co-Ordinating Centre, Montaqu Chambers, Mexborough, South Yorkshire, England S64 9AJ.

Quarterly magazine. Discusses social credit in Great Britain and other parts of world. Notes related international economic issues. Price 20p per issue.

6
Accent
Chilton Co, Chilton Way, Radnor, PA 19089. Telephone (215) 687-8200.
Monthly magazine. Reports on developments in fashion jewelry business. Price $12.00.

7
Access
US Dept of Commerce, Minority Business Development Agency, Main Commerce Bldg, Washington, DC 20230. Telephone (202) 377-2000.
Magazine. Reports on the activities of the Office of Minority Business Enterprise. Discusses minority business problems and trends. Price available on request.

8
Access Reference Service
Plus Publications, Inc, 2626 Pennsylvania Ave NW, Washington, DC 20037. Telephone (202) 333-5444.
Information service, with updates as needed. Contains laws, regulations, and court decisions covering application of the Freedom of Information Act, Privacy Act, Federal Advisory Committee Act, and related federal statutes. Price $182.00 per year.

9
Access Reports
Plus Publications, Inc, 2626 Pennsylvania Ave NW, Washington, DC 20037. Telephone (202) 333-5444.
Fortnightly report. Covers federal and state news and legislation, regulations, and judicial actions that affect freedom of information and privacy. Price $147.00 per year.

9.01
Access Reports/Freedom of Information
Washington Monitor, 499 National Press Bldg, Washington, DC 20045. Telephone (202) 347-7757.
Fortnightly newsletter. Reports on freedom of information developments. Price $189.00 per year.

9.02
Access Reports-Privacy
International Banktrends, Inc, 910 16th St, NW, Washington, DC 20006. Order from Access Reports, Inc, 910 16th St, NW, Washington, DC 20006. Telephone (202) 466-7490.

Biweekly newsletter and reference file. Combines general and technical news on information handling, including protection and availability of information. Price $389.00 per year.

10
Accident Analysis and Prevention
Pergamon Press, Inc, Maxwell House, Fairview Park, Elmsford, NY 10523. Telephone (914) 592-7700. Telex 13-7328.
Quarterly journal. Publishes papers on accidental injury and damage, including medical, legal, and educational aspects. Has tables, charts, and graphs. Price $95.00 per year.

11
Accident Prevention "Store Safety"
Industrial Accident Prevention Assn, 2 Bloor St East, 23rd Floor, Toronto, Ont, Canada M4W 3C2. Telephone (416) 965-8888.
Monthly report. Discusses occupational safety and health issues. Focuses on Canadian industry. Notes Industrial Accident Prevention Association activities. Price free of charge.

13
Accountancy
Institute of Chartered Accountants in England and Wales, PO Box 433, Chartered Accountants' Hall, Moorgate Place, London, England EC2P 2BJ. Order from Accountancy, 56–66 Goswell Rd, London, England EC1M 7AB. Telephone (44) (01) 628 7060.
Monthly journal. Covers British accounting field, including new legislation and techniques. Notes international accounting developments. Price £18.80 per year.

14
Accountancy Ireland
Institute of Chartered Accountants in Ireland, 7 Fitzwilliam Pl, Dublin 2, Ireland. Telephone (353) (1) 760 401.
Bimonthly magazine of interest to Irish accountants. Includes section on accountants' education. Price £7.00 per year. ISBN 0 903854.

15
Accountancy Law and Practice Manual
Gower Publishing Co Ltd, 1 Westmead, Farnborough, Hampshire, England GU14 7RU. Telephone Farnborough (0252) 519221. Telex 858623.

Manual, with loose-leaf binder periodically updated. Provides guide to developments in accountancy laws, standards, practices, and taxation. Includes British and international standards. Price $90.00. ISBN 0 566 02090 4.

17
Accountancy Law Reports
Commerce Clearing House, Inc, 4025 W Peterson Ave, Chicago, IL 60646. Telephone (312) 583-8500.
Two loose-leaf books, plus monthly reports. Provide information on state laws regulating practice of accounting. Price $180.00 per year.

18
Accountant
Gee & Co (Publishers) Ltd, 151 Strand, London, England WC2R 1JJ. Telephone (44) (01) 836 0832.
Weekly magazine. Reports on accounting, industry, and commerce. Price $60.00 per year.

19
Accountants' Cost Handbook **1960**
John Wiley & Sons, Inc, 605 Third Ave, New York, NY 10158. Telephone (212) 850-6418.
Book. Covers manufacturing cost accounting theory and practice. Price $39.-00. ISBN 0-8260-2705-9.

20
Accountants Digests
Institute of Chartered Accountants in England & Wales, PO Box 433, Chartered Accountants' Hall, Moorgate Place, London, England EC2P 2BJ. Telephone (44) (01) 628 7060.
Periodic digests. Deal with accounting, legislative, and management topics which affect accountants. Price £35.00.

21
Accountants' Handbook, 6th edition
John Wiley & Sons, Inc, 605 Third Ave, New York, NY 10158. Telephone (212) 850-6418.
Book. Covers commercial and financial accounting theory, rules, and procedures. Price $75.00. ISBN 0-471-05505-0.

22
Accountant's Handbook of Formulas and Tables
Prentice-Hall, Inc, Englewood Cliffs, NJ 07632. Telephone (201) 592-2000. Telex 13-5423.

Book. Contains tables and formulas frequently used in accountancy. Price $32.-95. ISBN 0-13-001255-6.

23
Accountants' Index
American Institute of Certified Public Accountants, 1211 Ave of the Americas, New York, NY 10036. Telephone (212) 575-6200.

Annual book. Provides bibliographic information on books, pamphlets, articles; and speeches on accounting, auditing, taxation, finance, and management. Price $47.50 per copy.

24
Accountants' Index Quarterly Service
American Institute of Certified Public Accountants, 1211 Ave of the Americas, New York, NY 10036. Telephone (212) 575-6200.

Annual book, with three quarterly supplements. Provides a bibliography of books, pamphlets, articles; and speeches on accounting, auditing, taxation, finance, management, and related business subjects. Price $135.00 per year.

25
Accountants International Studies
American Institute of Certified Public Accountants, 1211 Ave of the Americas, New York, NY 10036. Telephone (212) 575-6200.

Series of studies. Covers accounting and auditing practices in the US, the United Kingdom, and Canada. Price $3.75 for each study.

26
Accountants Magazine
Institute of Chartered Accountants in Scotland, 27 Queen St, Edinburgh, Scotland EH2 1LA. Telephone (44) (031) 225 5673. Telex 727530.

Monthly magazine. Focuses on general and Scottish accounting subjects, including tax and legislative developments. Price £12.00 per year.

27
Accountants Securities and Exchange Commission (SEC) Practice Manual
Commerce Clearing House, Inc, 4025 W Peterson Ave, Chicago, IL 60646. Telephone (312) 583-8500.

Loose-leaf book, plus monthly reports. Provides help in preparing and filing financial statements with the Securities and Exchange Commission. Price $200.00 per year.

28
Accountants Weekly
Morgan–Grampian Ltd, Morgan–Grampian House, Calderwood St, London, England SE18 6QH. Order from Morgan–Grampian Publishing Co, 2 Park Ave, New York, NY 10016. Telephone England 855 7777. Telex 896238 MORGAN G. New York (212) 340-9700. Telex 425592 MGI UI.

Weekly magazine. Evaluates accounting standards and methods in Great Britain. Price $65.00 per year.

29
Accounting and Business Research
Institute of Chartered Accountants in England & Wales, PO Box 433, Chartered Accountants' Hall, Moorgate Pl, London, England EC2P 2BJ. Telephone (44) (01) 628 7060.

Quarterly magazine. Examines new ideas, research, and advanced theoretical studies in accounting and business fields. Price £24.00.

30
Accounting Articles
Commerce Clearing House, Inc, 4025 W Peterson Ave, Chicago, IL 60646. Telephone (312) 583-8500.

Two loose-leaf books, plus monthly reports. Carry articles on accounting and management services published in accounting, business, and other periodicals. Price $230.00 per year.

33
Accounting Desk Book, 6th edition
Institute for Business Planning, Inc, IBP Plz, Dept. 7102-81, Englewood Cliffs, NJ 07632. Telephone (201) 592-2040.

Book. Covers major accounting subjects, including tax treatment of business transactions and recent tax law changes. Price $34.95. ISBN 0-87624-009-0.

35
Accounting, Organizations & Society
Pergamon Press, Inc, Maxwell House, Fairview Park, Elmsford, NY 10523. Telephone (914) 592-7700. Telex 13-7328.

Quarterly magazine. Publishes research on behavioral, organizational, and social aspects of accounting. Price $85.00 per year.

36
Accounting Review
American Accounting Assn, Paul L Gerhardt, Adm Secy, 5517 Bessie Dr, Sarasota, FL 33583. Telephone (813) 921-7747.

Quarterly report. Contains articles on accounting theory, research, and educational methods. Price $7.50 per issue.

37
Accounting Series Releases
US Securities & Exchange Commission, Washington, DC 20549. Telephone (202) 775-4833.

Publication. Compiles Securities and Exchange Commission Accounting Series Releases 1 to 195. Price $7.25.

38
Accounting Trends & Techniques
American Institute of Certified Public Accountants, 1211 Ave of the Americas, New York, NY 10036. Telephone (212) 575-6200.

Annual book. Surveys accounting practices followed in annual reports of corporations of all sizes in a wide variety of industries. Price $35.00 per copy.

39
Achievement
World Trade Magazines Ltd, World Trade House, 145 High St, Riverhead, Sevenoaks, Kent, England TN13 1XJ. Telephone 0732-58144.

Monthly magazine. Discusses international project management. Emphasizes power generation, iron and steel, chemicals and petrochemicals, and oil exploration and production. Price $18.00 per year.

40
ACM Guide to Computing Literature Annual
Association for Computing Machinery, 1133 Ave of the Americas, New York, NY 10036. Telephone (212) 265-6300

Annual book. Lists more than 10,000 books, papers, and reports on computer science. Covers 200 computer categories. Price $50.00.

40.01

ACM Transactions on Database Systems
Association for Computing Machinery, 1133 Ave of the Americas, New York, NY 10036. Telephone (212) 265-6300.

Quarterly journal. Covers new developments in database design and implementation. Reports research results in hardware architecture, system software, applications, and other areas. Price $50.00 per year.

40.02

ACM Transactions on Mathematical Software
Association for Computing Machinery, 1133 Ave of the Americas, New York, NY 10036. Telephone (212) 265-6300.

Quarterly journal. Discusses mathematical and associated software research. Offers machine-readable algorithms with test examples. Price $50.00 per year.

40.03

ACM Transactions on Programming Languages and Systems
Association for Computing Machinery, 1133 Ave of the Americas, New York, NY 10036. Telephone (212) 265-6300.

Quarterly journal. Offers research on programming languages and systems. Compares language features, and analyzes design and implementation of particular languages. Price $50.00 per year.

41

Acquisitions and Mergers of Companies
Her Majesty's Stationery Office, PO Box 569, London, England SE1 9NH. Telephone (44) (01) 928 1321.

Quarterly report on company acquisitions and mergers in Great Britain. Price $4.00 per year.

42

Acronyms and Initialisms Dictionary
Gale Research Co, Book Tower, Detroit, MI 48226. Telephone (313) 961-2242.

Book. Covers shortened and abbreviated usage, including equipment, processes, and names of organizations. Price $82.00.

43

Across the Board
Conference Board, Inc, 845 3rd Ave, New York, NY 10022. Telephone (212) 759-0900.

Monthly magazine. Contains information and projections relevant to business and industry. Is aimed at managerial personnel. Price available on request.

45

Action Canada France
Chambre de Commerce Francaise au Canada, 1080 Beaver Hall Hill, Suite 826, Montreal, Que, Canada H2Z 1S8. Telephone (514) 866-2797.

Monthly magazine. Concerns commercial, industrial, and financial exchanges between France and Canada. English and French. Price $15.00 per year. ISSN 03187306.

46

Acts
US Federal Trade Commission, Washington, DC 20580. Order from Distribution and Duplication Branch, Federal Trade Commission, Washington, DC 20580. Telephone (202) 523-3598.

Series of publications. Contains texts of 30 trade acts, including the Consumer Credit Protection Act, Magnuson-Moss Warranty Act, and Sherman Antitrust Act. Price free of charge.

48

Actuary
Society of Actuaries, 208 S LaSalle St, Chicago, IL 60604. Telephone (312) 236-3833.

Monthly newsletter. Reports on actuarial field. Discusses ERISA and Social Security regulations. Notes Society of Actuaries' activities. Price $4.50 per year.

49

Adbrief
Specialist Newsletters Pty Ltd, PO Box 430, Milsons Point, Sydney, NSW 2061, Australia. Telephone (61) (02) 922 3255.

Weekly newsletter. Covers advertising and media in Australia. Price $107.00 per year.

50

Ad Day/USA
Executive Communications, Inc, 400 E 54th St, New York, NY 10022. Telephone (212) 421-3713.

Weekly newsletter. Gives terse rundown of advertising and marketing news. Price $55.00 per year.

51

AdEast
AdEast Enterprises, Inc, 907 Park Sq Bldg, Boston, MA 02116. Telephone (617) 423-1122.

Monthly newspaper. Comments on advertising in New England and other parts of the US. Price $18.00 per year.

52

Ad Guide: An Advertister's Guide to Periodicals 1979-1980
American University Press Services, Inc, 1 Park Ave, New York, NY 10016. Telephone (212) 889-3510.

Biannual book. Guides advertisers to over 2500 scholarly periodicals. Includes rates and an index to periodicals. Price $50.00 per copy.

52.01

Adhesives Age
Communication Channels, Inc, 6285 Barfield Rd, Atlanta, GA 30328. Telephone (404) 256-9800.

Monthly magazine. Covers the application, technology, and sale of industrial adhesives. Emphasizes industrial consumer problems and solutions. Price $21.00 per year.

53

Adjusters' Reference Guide
Insurance Field Co, Inc, PO Box 18441, 4325 Old Shepherdsville Rd, Louisville, KY 40218. Telephone (502) 459-7910.

Loose-leaf report, with quarterly updating. Contains technical insurance articles and a full set of specimen policies and forms in general US use. Price $160.00 per year, $70.00 per year, quarterly updates.

54

Admap
Admap Publications Ltd, 28 Great Queen St, London, England WC2B 5BB. Telephone (44) (01) 405 5328. Telex 265906.

Monthly magazine for advertising trade. Includes articles on advertising and marketing, as well as trade news items. Price £25.00 per year.

55

Administrative Accounting
Institute of Adm Accounting, Walter House, 418-422 Strand, London, England WC2R 0PW. Telephone (44) (01) 240-3106.

Quarterly magazine. Covers current developments in the accounting profession and British matters affecting the Institute of Administrative Accounting. Price £2.00 per year.

56
Administrative Digest
Southam Communications Ltd, 1450 Don Mills Rd, Don Mills, Ont, Canada M38 2X7. Telephone (416) 445-6641. Telex 06 966612.

Monthly magazine. Provides information on business products and equipment. Price $35.00 per year.

57
Administrative Management
Geyer-McAllister Publications Inc, 51 Madison Ave, New York, NY 10010. Telephone (212) 689-4411.

Monthly magazine. Emphasizes information of interest to business systems/office products executives and administrators. Price $16.00 per year.

58
Administrative Management Society Guide to Management Compensation
Adm Management Society, Maryland Ave, Willow Grove, PA 19090. Telephone (215) 659-4300.

Annual report. Surveys middle-management salaries and fringe benefits in US and Canadian companies. Price $75.00 per year.

59
Administrative Science Quarterly
Cornell University, Graduate School of Business and Public Adm, Ithaca, NY 14853. Telephone (607) 256-5117.

Quarterly report. Contains articles on management theory and practice. Price $16.00 individuals, $32.00 institutions, $15.00 students per year. ISSN 0001-8392.

60
ADP Network Services
Automatic Data Processing, Network Services Div, 175 Jackson Plaza, Ann Arbor, MI 48106. Telephone (313) 769-6800.

Service. Offers information on data bases. Provides description, uses, access, and features. Price available on request.

61
Advanced Battery Technology
Robert Morey Assoc, PO Box 98, Dana Point, CA 92629. Telephone (714) 496-2574.

Monthly newsletter. Follows aspects of the battery industry. Price $60.00 per year.

62
Advanced Management Journal
Society for Advancement of Management, 135 W 50th St, New York, NY 10020. Telephone (212) 586-8100.

Quarterly journal. Offers articles on management topics for middle managers, presidents of small companies, educators, consultants, and business students. Price $16.50 per year. ISSN 0036-0805.

62.01
Advanced Retail Marketing
Downtown Research and Development Center, 270 Madison Ave, Suite 1505, New York, NY 10016. Telephone (212) 889-5666.

Semimonthly newsletter. Discusses marketing strategies, consumer promotion techniques, consumer behavior trends, and advertising techniques for the retailing industry. Price $185.00 per year.

63
Advanced Underwriting Service
Research and Review Service of America, Inc, PO Box 1727, Indianapolis, IN 46206. Telephone (317) 297-4360.

Six-volume book and monthly report. Cover subjects related to advanced insurance markets, including estate planning, taxes, community property, and government benefits. Price $95.00 for books, $90.00 for updates.

64
Advance Session Laws
Commerce Clearing House, Inc, 4025 W Peterson Ave, Chicago, IL 60646. Telephone (312) 583-8500.

Periodic reports. Pertain to new business and tax laws passed by state legislatures. Price available on request.

64.01
Advances in Plastics Technology
Van Nostrand Reinhold, 135 W 50th St, New York, NY 10020. Telephone (212) 265-8700.

Quarterly journal. Covers new processes and techniques in the plastics field. Available on microfiche. Price $100.00 per year domestic, $124.00 per year international, $31.00 per back copy.

65
Advertiser's Annual
Kelly's Directories Ltd, Windsor Court, E Grinstead House, E Grinstead, W Sussex, England RH19 1XB. Telephone (44) (01) 0342 26972.

Annual book. Contains material on British advertising agencies and clients, marketing, and direct mail. Also covers newspapers, television and radio stations, and public relations companies. Price £30.00 per copy.

66
Advertising Age
Crain Communications, Inc, 740 Rush St, Chicago, IL 60611. Telephone (312) 649-5219.

Weekly newspaper. Contains news of advertising campaigns, account changes, personnel shifts, and new products. Discusses pertinent legislation and regulation and includes market research information. Price $40.00 per year.

66.01
Advertising and Marketing Intelligence (AMI)
New York Times Information Service, Inc, Mt Pleasant Office Pk, 1719A 10, Parsippany, NJ 07054. Telephone (201) 530-5850. Telex 136390.

Database. Provides information on advertising and marketing fields. Identifies new products, consumer trends, and research. Price $165.00 per hour.

67
Advertising Communications Times (ACT)
Advertising/Communications Times, 121 Chestnut St, Philadelphia, PA 19106. Telephone (215) 629-1666.

Monthly newspaper. Covers news and issues affecting the advertising and broadcasting industry in eastern Pennsylvania, northern New Jersey, and Delaware. Price $18.00 per year.

68
Advertising Cost Control Handbook
Van Nostrand Reinhold, 135 W 50th St, New York, NY 10001. Telephone (212) 265-8700.

Book. Provides a guide to controlling advertising costs. Price $18.95. ISBN 0-442-26954-4.

68.01
Advertising Magazine
Advertising Assn, Abford House, 15 Wilton Rd, London, England SW1V 1NJ. Telephone (44) (01) 828 2771.

Quarterly magazine. Covers general topics, such as marketing and consumerism, of interest to the advertising industry in Great Britain. Price $25.00 per year.

69
Advertising News
Yaffa Publishing Group, GPO Box 606, Yaffa Publishing Group, 432-436 Elizabeth St, Surry Hills, NSW 2001, Australia. Order from Sydney, NSW 2001, Australia. Telephone (61) (02) 699-7861. Telex 21887.

Semimonthly magazine. Reports on Australian advertising, media, and communications industries. Includes a semiannual guide to clients and their agencies and semiannual list of Australian and New Zealand agencies and consultants. Price $30.00 (Australia) per year.

72
Advertising Substantiation Program
US Federal Trade Commission, Washington, DC 20580. Order from National Technical Information Service, 5285 Port Royal Rd, Springfield, VA 22161. Telephone (703) 487-4650.

Series of reports. Presents information supplied by manufacturers of consumer products to substantiate advertising. Includes such products as air conditioners, automobiles, cold remedies, soaps and detergents, and hearing aids. Price free of charge.

73
Advertising Techniques
Advertising Trade Publications, Inc, 10 E 39th St, New York, NY 10016. Telephone (212) 889-6500.

Monthly magazine. Reports on professionals' handling of specific advertising campaigns. Focuses on success stories in visual advertising. Price $7.50 per year.

74
Advertising World
Directories International, 1718 Sherman Ave, Evanston, IL 60201. Telephone (312) 491-0019.

Bimonthly magazine. Devoted to international advertising. Emphazies media planning and buying. Price $24.00 per year.

74.01
ADWEEK
A/S/M Communications, Inc, 230 Park Ave, New York, NY 10017. Telephone (212) 661-8080.

Weekly magazine. Publishes brief articles and announcements of events in advertising field, especially of the New York City region. Price $30.00 per year.

74.02
ADWEEK/West
A/S/M Publications Inc, 514 Shatto Pl, Los Angeles, CA 90020. Telephone (213) 384-7100.

Weekly publication. Features news of advertising industry in US West. Notes media, agencies, and clients. Price $1.00 per year.

75
Aerospace Daily
Ziff-Davis Publishing Co, 1156 15th St NW, Washington, DC 20005. Telephone (202) 293-3400.

Daily newsletter. Covers trade news and trends in the aerospace industry. Price $610.00 per year.

76
Aerospace Facts and Figures
McGraw-Hill Book Co, Hightstown-Princeton Rd, Hightstown, NJ 08520. Telephone (609) 448-1700. Telex 843449.

Annual book. Provides statistics on the US aerospace industry. Price $6.95.

76.01
Affirmative Action Compliance Manual for Federal Contractors
Bureau of National Affairs, Inc, 1231 25th St, NW, Washington, DC 20037. Telephone (202) 452-4200.

Loose-leaf books, with monthly updates. Provide guide to Office of Federal Contract Compliance Program procedures, regulations, and policies. Price $135.00 per year.

76.02
AFL-CIO News
American Federation of Labor and Congress of Industrial Organizations, Room 402, 815 16th St NW, Washington, DC 20006. Telephone (202) 637-5032.

Weekly newspaper. Covers labor issues and trends, including legislation. Price $2.00 per year.

77
Africa
Africa Journal Ltd, Kirkman House, 54a Tottenham Court Rd, London, England W1P 0BT. Telephone (44) (01) 637 9341. Order from (212) 552-2222.

Monthly magazine. Contains articles on African politics, personalities, and economic conditions. Includes features on sports, the arts, and relations with non-African governments. Price £15.00 per year.

78
Africa Guide 1981
World of Information, 21 Gold St, Saffron Walden, Essex, England, CB10 1EJ. Telephone Saffron Walden 21150 (STD 0799 21150). Telex England 817197 a/b Jaxpress G.

Annual book. Provides analysis of commercial, economic, political, and social developments in Africa, with separate chapters about each country. Price $43.00. ISBN 0-904439-19-4.

79
African-American Labor Center (AALC) Reporter
African-American Labor Center AFL-CIO, 1125 15th St, NW, Suite 404, Washington, DC 20005. Telephone (202) 293-3603.

Bimonthly newsletter. Carries news about the programs and issues in which the organization is involved in Africa.

79.01
African Business
IC Publications Ltd, 122 E 42nd St, Suite 1121, New York, NY 10017. Telephone (212) 867-5159. Telex 425442.

Monthly journal. Covers African business developments. Examines economic trends. Price $50.00 per year.

79.02
African Business & Trade
Welt Publishing Co, 1511 K St, NW, Washington, DC 20005. Telephone (202) 737-8080.

Bimonthly report. Covers trade and economic developments in the sub-Sahara market. Price $195.00 per year.

79.03
African Textiles
Alain Charles Publishing Ltd, 27 Wilfred St, London England SW1E 6PR. Telephone (44) (01) 828-6107. Telex 28905.

Magazine. Covers entire field of African textiles from machinery to garment manufacturing for international audience. Price $25.00 per year.

80
African Trade/Commerce Africain
United Nations Economic Commission for Africa, Africa Hall, PO Box 3001, Addis Ababa, Ethiopia. Telephone 47200.

Quarterly magazine. Concerns intra-African trade developments. Notes natural resources of specific countries and includes information on the activities of the United Nations Economic Commission for Africa, African Chambers of Commerce, and Africa Trade Centre. Articles in English and French. Price free of charge.

81
Africa Research Bulletin
Africa Research Ltd, 18 Lower North St, Exeter, Devon, England EX4 3EN.

Monthly bulletin. Follows current events in Africa, including material on politics, education, health, religion, trade, and economics. Price $260.00 per year.

82
Africa South of the Sahara
Europa Publications Ltd, 18 Bedford Sq, London, WC1B 3JN, England. Telephone (44) (01) 580 8236.

Annual book on Africa south of the Sahara. Encompasses history, politics, social problems, agriculture, industry, regional organizations, and major personalities. Price $90.00.

83
Africa Woman
Africa Journal Ltd, Kirkman House, 54a Tottenham Court Rd, London, England W1P 0BT. Telephone (44) (01) 637-9341.

Monthly magazine. Reports on the activities of African women and on fashion, beauty, and family topics. Price £15.00 per year.

86
Agency for International Development (AID) Research and Development Abstracts
US Dept of State, Agency for International Development, Washington, DC 20523. Telephone (202) 655-4000.

Publication. Abstracts papers on international research and development. Price available on request.

87
Agent's and Buyer's Guide
National Underwriter Co, 420 E 4th St, Cincinnati, OH 45202. Telephone (513) 721-2140.

Annual book on property-liability insurance. Provides information on which companies write policies for unusual and hard-to-place risks. Price $11.50.

88
Aggregate Productivity Measures
Statistics Canada, User Services, Publications Distribution, Ottawa, Ont, Canada K1A 0V7. Telephone (613) 992-3151.

Annual report. Provides data on Canadian output per person employed and per man-hour. Shows unit labor costs for all industries—including manufacturing, agriculture, and service industries—and notes comparisons with corresponding US official statistics. Price $7.20. ISSN 0317-7882.

88.01
Aging and Work
National Council on the Aging, Inc, 1828 L St, NW, Suite 504, Washington, DC 20036. Telephone (202) 223-6250.

Quarterly magazine. Focuses on problems of middle-aged and older workers. Includes abstracts of material from other journals. Price $30.00 per year, $8.00 per copy.

88.02
Ag-Marketer
Columbia Publishing & Design, PO Box 1467, Yakima, WA 98907. Telephone (509) 248-2452.

Monthly magazine offering marketing information for diversified farm operators in the Northwest. Price $8.00 per year.

89
Agra Europe
Agra Europe (London) Ltd, Agroup House, 16 Lonsdale Gardens, Tunbridge Wells, Kent, England TN1 1PD. Telephone Tunbridge Wells (0892) 33813. Telex 95114.

Weekly bulletin. Contains information on European agricultural markets. Puts emphasis on common market policy. Price $235.00 per year.

90
Agra Europe Eurofish Report
Agra Europe (London) Ltd, Agroup House, 16 Lonsdale Gardens, Tunbridge Wells, Kent, England TN1 1PD. Telephone Tunbridge Wells (0892) 33813. Telex 95114.

Semimonthly report. Covers developments in the fishing and fish processing industries in EEC countries. Notes legislation, regulations, and grants. Tables. Price £221.00 per year.

91
Agra Europe Potato Markets
Agra Europe (London) Ltd, Agroup House, 16 Lonsdale Gardens, Tunbridge Wells, Kent, England TN1 1PD. Telephone Tunbridge Wells (0892) 33813. Telex 95114.

Weekly report. Contains potato production, market, and price information from the Netherlands, Belgium, West Germany, France, Great Britain, Canada, and the US. Tables. Price £310.00 per year.

92
Agra Europe Preserved Milk
Agra Europe (London) Ltd, Agroup House, 16 Lonsdale Gardens, Tunbridge Wells, Kent, England TN1 1PD. Telephone Tunbridge Wells (0892) 33813. Telex 95114.

Monthly report. Provides information on prices, production, stocks, imports, and exports of whole and skim milk powder, condensed milk, casein, and whey powder. Covers common market countries, Scandinavia, Austria, Switzerland, the US, Canada, New Zealand, and Australia. Tables and charts. Price £81.00 per year.

93
Agribusiness in the Middle East and North Africa
Chase World Information Corp, 1 World Trade Center, Suite 4627, New York, NY 10048. Telephone (212) 552-3378. Telex RCA 235444, WU: 141489.

Series of six reports, one each for Saudi Arabia, Iran, Egypt, Syria, Sudan, and Iraq. Each covers the resources and development plans for all aspects of agribusiness. Price $4800.00 per year for full series of six reports.

94
Agricultural Banker
American Bankers Assn, 1120 Connecticut Ave NW, Washington, DC 20036. Telephone (202) 467-4123.

Monthly newsletter. Pertains to federal legislation and regulation affecting agricultural banking, particularly lending trends. Price $24.00 per year.

95
Agricultural Co-operative Bulletin
International Co-Operative Alliance, 11 Upper Grosvenor St, London, England W1X 9PA. Telephone (44) (01) 449 5991.

Monthly newsletter on agricultural activities of International Co-Operative Alliance. Covers also national and international agricultural cooperative developments. French summaries. Price £2.00. ISSN 0002-1415.

96
Agricultural Economics Bulletin for Africa
United Nations Publications, Rm A-3315, New York, NY 10017. Telephone (212) 754-8302.

Report. Provides statistics and other information dealing with agricultural economics in Africa. Price available on request.

97
Agricultural Economics Research
US Dept of Agriculture, ESS Publications, Room 0054-S, Information Div, Washington, DC 20250. Order from Superintendent of Documents, US Government Printing Office, Washington, DC 20402. Telephone (202) 783-3238.

Quarterly report. Presents technical agricultural economics research. Includes interim reports on Economic Research Service work in progress. Price $8.00 per year domestic, $10.00 per year foreign.

98
Agricultural Engineering Abstracts
Commonwealth Agricultural Bureaux, Central Sales Branch, Farnham House, Farnham Royal, Slough, England SL2 3BN. Telephone Farnham Common 2281. Telex 847964.

Monthly magazine. Provides abstracts of articles on agricultural and horticultural engineering. Covers plant and animal sciences. Price $180.00 per year.

99
Agricultural Finance Outlook
US Dept of Agriculture, ESS Publications, Room 0054-S, Washington, DC 20250. Telephone (202) 447-7255.

Annual report. Reviews finances of farm operators by region. Provides forecasts on financial matters. Price free of charge.

100
Agricultural Finance Review
US Dept of Agriculture, ESS Publications, Room 0054-S, Washington, DC 20250. Telephone (202) 447-7255.

Annual report. Discusses agricultural finance. Includes topics on farm and rural credit, insurance, taxation, and rural development. Price free of charge.

101
Agricultural Markets: Prices (Two Series)
European Community Information Service, 2100 M St, NW, Suite 707, Washington DC 20037. Telephone (202) 862-9500, Telex 248455.

Monthly publications. Give prices for European Economic Community (Common Market) agricultural markets, vegetable, and livestock products. Price $101.00 per year, $63.00 each for separate series on vegetable or livestock products.

102
Agricultural Outlook
US Dept of Agriculture. ESS Publications, Room 0054-S, Washington, DC 20250. Order from Superintendent of Documents, US Government Printing Office, Washington, DC 20402. Telephone (202) 783-3238.

Report issued 11 times per year. Discusses food and agriculture outlook. Covers commodities, marketing, world agriculture and trade, farm income, and transportation. Tables. Price $19.00 per year domestic, $23.50 per year foreign.

103
Agricultural Price Report
US Dept of Agriculture, Crop Reporting Board, Economics and Statistics Service (ESS), Room 0005 S Bldg, Washington, DC 20250. Telephone (202) 447-4021.

Monthly report. Indicates prices received by farmers for principal crops and livestock products. Price free of charge.

104
Agricultural Production (Two Series)
European Community Information Service, 2100 M St, NW, Suite 707, Washington, DC 20037. Telephone (202) 862-9500, Telex 247455.

Quarterly publications. Reports on crop production and livestock production in European communities' member countries. Price $52.50 per year, $31.50 each for series on crop or animal production.

105
Agricultural Situation
US Dept of Agriculture. Order from ESCS Information Staff, Room 5855-S, USDA, Washington, DC 20250. Telephone (202) 655-4000.

Monthly report. Features articles on trends and research in agricultural field. Includes statistical summaries and economic and marketing developments affecting farmers. Price $5.00 per year.

106
Agricultural Statistics
US Dept of Agriculture. ESS Publications, Room 0054-S, Washington, DC 20250. Order from Superintendent of Documents, US Government Printing Office, Washington, DC 20402. Telephone (202) 783-3238.

Annual report. supplies statistical agricultural data. Price $7.00. ISSN 001-000-04129-1.

107
Agricultural Statistics: England and Wales
Her Majesty's Stationery Office, PO Box 569, London, England SE1 9NH. Telephone (44) (01) 928 1321.

Annual publication. Contains agricultural statistics for Great Britain and Wales. Price £4.25 per year.

109
Agricultural Statistics, Scotland
Her Majesty's Stationery Office, PO Box 569, London, England SE1 9NH. Telephone (44) (01) 928 1321.

Annual report. Gives statistics on agriculture in Scotland. Price £6.00 per year.

110
Agricultural Statistics: United Kingdom
Her Majesty's Stationery Office, PO Box 569, London, England SE1 9NH. Telephone (44) (01) 928 1321.

Annual report. Publishes British agricultural statistics. Price £4.00 per year.

111
Agriculture and Commodities Service
Data Resources, Inc, 29 Hartwell Ave, Lexington, MA 02173. Telephone (617) 861-0165.

Monthly report. Gives forecasts concerning US agriculture. Includes acres planted, yield, production, inventories, and commodity prices. Price available on request.

112
Agriculture Abroad
Canadian Dept of Agriculture, Regional Development and International Affairs Branch,RD & IA Branch, Ottawa, Canada K1A 0C5.

Bimonthly magazine. Offers a digest of agricultural policies in various countries, including Ireland, Mexico, the Union of Soviet Socialist Republics, US, and Great Britain. English and French. Price free of charge. ISSN 0002-1717.

113
Agriculture the Third Century
US Dept of Agriculture. Order from Superintendent of Documents, US Government Printing Office, Washington, DC 20402. Telephone (202) 655-4000.

Irregular report. Summarizes results of Economic Research Service economic projections program. Includes national and regional projections of US food and fiber production and use and trade through 1985 for major commodities. Price available on request.

114
Agri Finance
Agri Business Publications, Inc, 5520 Touhy Ave, Suite G, Skokie, IL 60077. Telephone (312) 676-4060.

Magazine issued nine times per year. Discusses agricultural financial management, tax, and legislation. Price $19 per year.

115
Agri Marketing
Agri Business Publications, Inc, 5520 Touhy Ave, Suite G, Skokie, IL 60076. Telephone (312) 676-4060.

Monthly magazine and annual directory. Discusses agricultural market techniques, new products for farmers, and farm market research. Is aimed at sellers to farm markets. Directory lists top 150 agricultural companies, farm publications accepting advertising, radio stations with farm programming, and agricultural associations. Price $20.00 per year.

116
Agro Service International
Europe Information Service, 46 Ave Albert Elisabeth, Brussels, Belgium 1040. Telephone (32) (02) 736.11.93. Telex 26005b Eurinf.

Semimonthly report. Covers world agricultural economy, international agricultural agreements, agricultural commodities for foodstuffs, and 'green' Europe in the world framework. Price $330.00 per year.

118
Air Carrier Operations in Canada
Statistics Canada, User Services, Publications Distribution, Ottawa, Ont, Canada K1A 0V7. Telephone (613) 992-3151.

Quarterly report. Discusses operations of 750 domestic and foreign air carriers operating in Canada. Covers passengers, miles and hours flown, goods and mail carried, and finances. Price $28.80 per year. ISSN 0008-2570.

119
Air Carriers Regulations/Office Consolidation
Supply and Services Canada, Publishing Centre, Printing and Publishing, Ottawa,Ont, Canada K1A 0S9. Telephone (613) 238-1601.

Loose-leaf volume, plus update service. Covers Canadian air carrier regulations. Bilingual. Price $9.00.

120
Airconditioning & Refrigeration Business
Penton/IPC, 614 Superior Ave W, Cleveland, OH 44113. Telephone (216) 696-0300.

Monthly magazine. Reports on air conditioning and refrigeration industry. Discusses manufacturing, marketing, installation, and service. Price $24.00.

122
Air Navigation Radio Aids
Supply and Services Canada, Publishing Centre, Printing and Publishing, Ottawa, Ont, Canada K1A 0S9. Telephone (613) 238-1601.

Quarterly report. Discusses radio aids for air navigation. Price $2.00 per year.

123
Air Passenger Origin and Destination, Canada-United States Report
Statistics Canada, User Services, Publications Distribution, Ottawa, Ont, Canada K1A 0V7. Telephone (613) 992-3151.

Annual report. Presents data on Canadia-US passenger origins and destinations. Price $30.00. ISSN 0705-4343.

124
Air Passenger Origin and Destination, Domestic Report
Statistics Canada, User Services, Publications Distribution, Ottawa, Ont, Canada K1A 0V7. Telephone (613) 992-3151.

Annual report. Provides statistics on Canadian domestic air-passenger traffic. Price $18.00. ISSN 0703-2692.

125
Air Pollution Control
Bureau of National Affairs, Inc, 1231 25th St, NW, Washington, DC 20037. Telephone (202) 452-4200.

Loose-leaf books, with biweekly updates. Covers air pollution control standards and programs, including permits and licenses, research documents, monitoring and enforcement, and control technology. Includes reference file. Price $215.00 per year.

126
Airport Services Management
Lakewood Publications, Inc, 731 Hennepin Ave, Minneapolis, MN 55403. Telephone (612) 333-0471.

Monthly magazine. Presents business information for the ground support market for commercial, government, and military aviation. Price $18.00 per year.

127
Airtrade
Maclean-Hunter Ltd, 30 Old Burlington St, London, England W1X 2AE. Telephone (44) (01) 434 2233.

Monthly journal. Offers in-depth articles concerning the movement of cargo by air. Includes news on tariffs. Price available on request.

128
Air Transport
Air Transport Assn of America, 1709 New York Ave NW, Washington, DC 20006. Telephone (202) 872-4000.

Annual report. Provides statistics on airline operations, including costs, income, and performance. Price available on request.

129
Air Transport World
Penton/IPC, 614 Superior Ave W, Cleveland, OH 44113. Order from Reinhold Publishing Div, Penton/IPC, 600 Summer St, Stamford, CT 06904. Telephone (203) 348-7531.

Monthly magazine. Focuses on commercial airlines. Price $24.00 per year.

130
Air Transport World
Reinhold Publishing Co, 600 Summer St, Stamford CT 06904. Telephone (203) 348-7531.

Monthly report. Covers developments and gives statistics for air freight and passenger services. Price $5.00 per year.

131
Air/Water Pollution Report
Business Publishers, Inc, Box 1067, Silver Spring, MD 20910. Telephone (301) 587-6300.

Weekly newsletter. Reports on environmental pollution. Price $237.00 per year.

132
Akron Business and Economic Review
University of Akron, College of Business Adm, 302 E Buchtel Ave, Akron, OH 44325. Telephone (216) 375-7045.

Quarterly report. Discusses economic, accounting, business, and finance subjects. Emphasizes research. Price $6.00 per year.

133
Alabama Business
University of Alabama, College of Commerce and Business Administration, Center for Business and Economic Research, PO Box AK, University, AL 35486. Telephone (205) 348-6191.

Monthly report. Alabama economic and business topics. Provides statistics for general Alabama business indicators. Tables and charts. Includes occasional scholarly articles. Price free of charge. ISSN 0002-4163.

134
Alabama Development News
Alabama Development Office, State Capitol, Montgomery, AL 36130. Telephone (205) 832-6980.

Monthly newsletter. Deals with new and expanding industry announcements and economic growth in Alabama. Price free of charge.

134.01
Alabama Directory of Mining and Manufacturing, **1980–1981 edition**
Alabama Development Office, State Capitol, Montgomery, AL 36130. Telephone (205) 832-6980.

Annual directory. Contains listings of 5000 mining and manufacturing firms in Alabama, including addresses, contact name and title, telephone number, employment, and product. Includes parent company, geographic location, resource, and international sections. Price $25.00.

135
Alabama Economic Abstract
University of Alabama, College of Commerce and Business Administration, Graduate School of Business, Center for Business and Economic Research, PO Box AK, Univeristy, AL 35486. Telephone (205) 348-6191.

Book. Provides economic and demographic statistics for Alabama, such as population, housing, employment, income, prices, and wholesale and retail trade. Price available on request.

136
Alabama Mining & Manufacturing Directory, **1980-81**
Manufacturers' News, Inc, 3 E Huron St, Chicago, IL 60611. Telephone (312) 337-1084

Biennial book. Lists Alabama mining and manufacturing firms by name and locations. Price $40.00.

136.01
Alabama: State Industrial Directory **1980**
Manufacturers' News, Inc, 3 E Huron St, Chicago, IL 60611. Telephone (312) 337-1084.

Annual book. Identifies 5000 Alabama industrial companies. Price $55.00.

137
Alaska Business News Letter
Business Communications, Inc, PO Box 4-AA, Anchorage, AK 99509. Telephone (907) 279-7407.

Weekly newsletter. Contains information about business and industry in Alaska. Includes fields of building, tourism, fisheries, investments, and petroleum. Price $65.00 per year.

138
Alaska Economic Trends
Alaska Dept. of Labor, Employment Security Div, Research & Analysis Section, Box 3-7000, Juneau, AK 99801. Telephone (907) 465-2700.

Monthly report on Alaska's economy. Includes employment trends, trade statistics, banking activity, and construction and manufacturing data. Highlights one aspect of the state's economy each month. Charts and graphs. Price free of charge.

139
Alaska Industry
Business Communications, Inc, PO Box 4-AA, Anchorage, AK 99509. Telephone (907) 279-7407.

Monthly magazine for executives in Alaskan industries, including oil and gas, construction, mining, fisheries, transportation, timber, communication, trade, investments, and tourism. Price $12.50 per year.

141
Alaska—Occupational Employment Forecast
Alaska Dept of Labor, Employment Security Div, Research & Analysis Section, Box 3-7000, Juneau, AK 99801. Telephone (907) 465-2700.

Annual report. Provides statistical forecast of the number of jobs expected to be open in Alaska from 1977 to 1982. Estimates the type of jobs. Price available on request.

141.01
Alaska: Petroleum & Industrial Directory, **1980**
Manufacturers' News, Inc, 3 E Huron St, Chicago, IL 60611. Telephone (312) 337-1084.

Annual book. Names 2800 Alaskan petroleum and industrial firms. Identifies key personnel. Price $40.00.

142
Alaska Review of Social & Economic Conditions
University of Alaska, Institute of Social and Economic Research, 707 A St, Suite 206, Anchorage, AK 99506. Telephone (907) 278-9621.

Irregularly issued report. Provides information on social and economic conditions in Alaska. Price free of charge.

143
Alberta Corporation Manual
Richard De Boo, Ltd, 70 Richmond St, Toronto, Ont, Canada M5C 2M8. Telephone (416) 367-0714.

Three loose-leaf books. Contain corporate statutes and regulations in Alberta, Canada. Include such subjects as incorporation, dissolution, and credit unions. Price $125.00 per year.

145
All about Business in Hawaii

Crossroads Press, Inc, PO Box 833, Honolulu, HI 96808. Telephone (808) 521-0021.

Annual magazine. Reports on major Hawaiian industries. Includes information about economy, government, labor, and social conditions. Price $3.95 per copy.

146
Allen Report

Richard C Allen, 1631 Kingston Rd, Placentia, CA 92670. Telephone (714) 541-3371.

Weekly newsletter. Offers advice on trading in the commodity futures market. Price $295.00 per year.

147
All-State Sales Tax Reports

Commerce Clearing House, Inc, 4025 W Peterson Ave, Chicago, IL 60646. Telephone (312) 583-8500.

Four loose-leaf books, plus biweekly reports. Discuss sales and use tax laws. Digest court decisions. Price $455.00 per year.

148
All States Tax Guide

Prentice-Hall, Inc, Englewood Cliffs, NJ 07632. Telephone (201) 592-2000. Telex 13-5423.

Weekly loose-leaf service. Explains the tax laws of each state. Suggests ways to choose the best tax state. Price $330.00 per year.

148.01
1981 Almanac and Directory

Richard De Boo Ltd, 70 Richmond St, Toronto, Ont, Canada M5C 2M8. Telephone (416) 367-0714.

Directory. Lists all levels of Canadian government, post offices, lawyers, publishers, courts, banks, and insurance companies. Price $35.95.

149
Almanac of the Canning, Freezing, Preserving Industries

E E Judge & Sons, Inc, PO Box 866, Westminster, MD 21157. Telephone (301) 876-2052.

Annual. Gives statistics, law & regulations, on US and world food process. Price $24.50.

149.01
Alternative Energy: Trends & Forecasts

Technology Forecasts and Technology Surveys, Suite 208, 205 S Beverly Dr, Beverly Hills, CA 90212. Telephone (213) 273-3486.

Monthly newsletter. Reports on news, advances and major trend forecasts in all areas of alternative energy. Includes solar, synfuels, electric, hydrogen, and nuclear fusion. Price $75.00 per year.

150
Aluminum Data

American Bureau of Metal Statistics, Inc, 420 Lexington Ave, New York, NY 10170. Telephone (212) 867-9450. Telex 14-7130.

Monthly report. Gives US aluminum statistics, including data on imports and exports and supply in the US. Price $75.00 per year.

151
Aluminum Ingot and Mill Products

US Dept of Commerce, Bureau of the Census, Washington, DC 20233. Telephone (202) 449-1600.

Monthly report with annual summary. Presents data on aluminum ingot and mill products. Covers quantity of shipments, receipts and month-end inventories by type of aluminum shape and type of producer. Notes defense shipments. Price $3.75 per year.

152
Aluminum Statistical Review

Aluminum Assn, Inc, 818 Connecticut Ave, NW, Washington, DC 20006. Telephone (202) 862-5100.

Annual report. Focuses on statistical data on aluminum industry. Tables and charts. Price $10.00.

153
AMACOM Catalog of Resources for Professional Management

American Management Assns, 135 W 50th St, New York, NY 10020. Telephone (212) 586-8100.

Semiannual catalog. Describes AMA publications and educational programs. Price available on request.

153.01
AMA Management Handbook

American Management Assns, 135 W 50th St, New York, NY 10020. Telephone (212) 586-8100.

Book. Management theory and practice. Price $43.50.

153.02
Ambassadors' Directory

Guides to Multinational Business, Inc, Harvard Sq, Box 92, Cambridge, MA 02138. Telephone (617) 868-2288.

Book. Lists names and addresses of over 7000 embassies relative to 185 countries. Gives names and addresses of resident and accredited ambassadors throughout the world. Price $150.00.

154.01
America Buys

Information Access Corporation, 404 Sixth Ave, Menlo Park, CA 94025. Telephone (800) 227-8431.

Annual book. Indexes information on over 40,000 products, including evaluations, brand name references, consumer buying information, and brand comparisons. Price $94.00.

155
American and European Market Research Reports

Frost & Sullivan, Inc, 106 Fulton St, New York, NY 10038. Telephone (212) 233-1080. Telex 235986.

Reports. Analyze market research trends. Offer forecasts for American and European markets for a segment of one industry. Price $600.00 to $1000.00 each.

155.01
American Art Directory

RR Bowker Co, 1180 Ave of the Americas, New York, NY 10036. Order from RR Bowker Co, PO Box 1807, Ann Arbor, MI 48106. Telephone (212) 764-5100.

Biennial directory. Gives information on 2500 museums and art associations in the US and Canada, plus art schools, art library statistics, scholarships, reference works, directors, and supervisors of art education in schools, and corporations supporting the visual arts. Price $49.50. ISBN 0-8352-1250-5. ISSN 0065-6968.

156

*American Assembly of Collegiate
Schools of Business Newsline*
American Assembly of Collegiate Schools
of Business, 11500 Olive St. Rd., Suite
142, St Louis, MO 63141. Telephone
(314) 872-8481.

Newsletter published six times per year.
Presents articles relevant to the adminis-
tration of college-level business schools.
Covers AACSB internal activities. Price
$8.00 per year.

157

American Banker
American Banker, One State St Plaza,
New York, NY 10004. Telephone (212)
943-8200. Telex 12-5818.

Daily newspaper (except Saturday and
Sunday). Covers news related to banking,
including legislation, mergers, money
markets, and international developments.
Price $295.00 per year.

158

*American Bankers Assn (ABA) Bank
Card Newsletter*
American Bankers Assn, 1120 Connecti-
cut Ave NW, Washington, DC 20036.
Telephone (202) 467-4123.

Monthly newsletter. Covers bank credit
card field. Sends subscribers mailings on
the American Bankers Association, Bank
Card Division, conferences, workshops,
schools, and statistical surveys. Price
$22.00 per year members, $28.00 per year
nonmembers.

159

*American Bankers Assn (ABA) Bank
Installment Lender's Report*
American Bankers Assn, 1120 Connecti-
cut Ave NW, Washington, DC 20036.
Telephone (202) 467-4123.

Monthly newsletter. Reports on legislative developments, court decision, and innovations in the installment lending field.
Price $12.00 per year.

160

*American Board of Trade Spot and
Forward Market*
American Board of Trade Spot and For-
ward Markets, 9 S. William St., New
York, NY, 10004. Telephone (212) 943-
0100.

Booklets. Offers spot and forward contract markets. Cobers, gold, silver,
platium, copper, plywood, British pound,
Swiss franc, German mark, Canadian dollar, and Japanese yen. Price free of
charge.

161

American Book Publishing Record
RR Bowker Co, 1180 Ave of the Americas, New York, NY 10036. Order from
RR Bowker Co, PO Box 13746, Philadelphia, PA 19101. Telephone (212) 764-
5100.

Monthly magazine. Lists newly published
American books by subject (Dewey Deci-
mal arrangement). Gives each entry's
price, classification number, and publisher. Price $25.00 per year. ISSN 0002-
7707.

162

American Book Trade Directory
R R Bowker Co, 1180 Ave of the Ameri-
cas, New York, NY 10036. Order from R
R Bowker Co, PO Box 1807, Ann Arbor,
MI 48106. Telephone (212) 764-5100.

Annual directory. Gives information
about book outlets in the US and Canada.
Provides statistics and lists. Price $54.95.
ISBN 0-8352-0928-8. ISSN 0065-795X.
1252-1.

163

*American Bulletin of International
Technology Transfer*
International Advancement, PO Box
75537, Los Angeles, CA 90075. Telephone (213) 931-7481.

Bimonthly pamphlet. Lists product and
service opportunities offered and wanted
for direct foreign investments, licensing,
and joint venture agreements in the US
and abroad. Is vehicle for international
exchange of technology, capital, and management resources. Price $360.00 per
year.

164

*American Business Activity from 1790
to Today*
Ameri Trust Co, 900 Euclid Ave, Cleveland, OH 44101. Telephone (216) 687-
5046.

Annual pamphlet. Graphs chronologi-
cally—and briefly discusses—business activity since 1790. Price free of charge.

165

American Business Law Journal
American Business Law Assn, c/o Wharton School, University of Pennsylvania,
Philadelphia, PA 19104. Nonmembers
order from Frank P Land, School of Business, University of North Carolina
Greensboro, Greensboro, NC 27412.

Magazine published four times per year.
Presents articles on business law. Price
$12.00 per year, $14.00 foreign. ISSN
0002-7766.

166

American City & Country
Morgan-Grampian Ltd, Morgan-Gram-
pian House, Calderwood St, London,
England SE18 6QH. Telephone (44) (01)
855-7777. Telex 896238. Order from
Morgan-Grampian Publishing Co, 2
Park Ave, New York, NY 10016. Tele-
phone (212) 340-9700. Telex 425592
MGI UI.

Monthly magazine. Covers local government, engineering, and management.
Price $30.00 per year.

167

American Cooperation
American Institute of Cooperation, 1800
Massachusetts Ave, NW, Suite 504,
Washington, DC 20036. Telephone (202)
296-6825.

Annual book. Covers issues pertinent to
cooperatives. Contains current statistics
and forecasts. Price $9.50 per copy.

168

*American Council on Consumer
Interests.*
American Council on Consumer Interests, Journal of Consumer Affairs, Newsletter, Consumer Education Forum.
American Council on Consumer Interests, 162 Stanley Hall, Columbia, MO
65211. Telephone (314) 882-3817.

Annual service: two journals, two forums,
nine newsletters and annual conference
report per year. Provides information on
consumer research, legislation, and resource materials. Price $25.00 per year
individual; and $40.00 per year institu-
tional.

169

American Druggist
Hearst Corp, 224 W 57th St, New York,
NY 10019. Telephone (212) 262-4167.

Monthly magazine. Covers trade news
and trends in the drug industry. Price
$12.00 per year. ISSN 0002-824X.

170

American Economic Review
American Economic Assn, 1313 21st Ave S, Nashville, TN 37212. Telephone (615) 322-2595.

Quarterly journal. Contains articles on economic subjects. Reports proceedings and papers of American Economic Association annual meeting. Price $100.00 per year (with Journal of Economic Literature), $15.00 per back copy.

171

American Economist
Omicron Delta Epsilon Fraternity, Long Island University, Brooklyn Center, Brooklyn, NY 11201. Order from Omicron Delta Epsilon, Department of Economics, PO Drawer AS, University of Alabama, University, AL 35486. Telephone (205) 348-7842.

Semiannual magazine. Discusses economic research and theories. Reviews recent books. Price $6.00 per year.

172

American Exchange (AMEX) Databook
American Stock Exchange, Inc, 86 Trinity Pl, New York, NY 10006. Telephone (212) 938-6000.

Annual report. Gives volume, price, and other AMEX statistics for an eight-year period. Price available on request.

173

American Exchange Stock Reports
Standard & Poor's Corp, 25 Broadway, New York, NY 10004. Telephone (212) 248-2525.

Quarterly reports revised twice a week. Cover stocks listed on American Stock Exchange. Analyze company activities and financial results and provide statistics on earnings and dividends. Price $610.00 per year daily edition; $495.00 per year weekly edition.

174

American Export Register
Thomas Publishing Co, One Penn Plz, New York, NY 10001. Telephone (212) 695-0500.

Annual directory. Lists over 37,000 manufacturers who export products worldwide. Provides 3033 product classifications and alphabetical listings in English, French, German, Spanish, and Japanese. Price $60.00.

175

American Federation of Information Processing Societies Conference Proceedings
American Federation of Information Processing Societies Press, 1815 N Lynn St, Arlington, VA. 22209. Telephone (703) 558-3600.

Annual report. Covers new developments in computer theory and practice. Price $60.00.

175.01

American Federation of Information Processing Societies Office Automation Conference
American Federation of Information Processing Societies Press, 1815 N Lynn St, Arlington, VA 22209. Telephone (703) 558-3600.

Annual digest. Covers developments in office automation. Price available on request.

175.02

American Federation of Information Processing Societies Personal Computing Festival
American Federation of Information Processing Societies Press, 1815 N Lynn St, Arlington VA 22209. Telephone (703) 558-3600.

Annual digest. Covers developments in personal computers. Price available on request.

177

American Freedom from Hunger Foundation. Bulletin
American Freedom from Hunger Foundation, 1625 Eye St, NW, Suite 719, Washington, DC 20006. Telephone (202) 254-3487.

Monthly newsletter. Articles pertain to antihunger movement and legislation, and hunger in the US and abroad. Price $5.00 per year.

178

American Hospital Association Guide to the Health Care Field
American Hospital Assn, 840 N Lake Shore Dr, Chicago, IL 60611. Telephone (312) 280-6000.

Annual book. Acts as a guide to registered US hospitals; international, national, state, and regional hospital associations; and hospital educational programs. Price $55.00. ISBN 0-87258-203-5.

179

American Import/Export Bulletin
North American Publishing Co, 401 N Broad St, Philadelphia, PA 19108. Telephone (215) 574-9600.

Monthly report. Discusses US import-export news. Includes information on product sales, marketing, finance, and distribution. Price $15.00 per year.

181

American Industrial Development Council Journal
American Industrial Development Council, Inc, 215 W Pershing Rd, Suite 707, Kansas City, MO 64108. Telephone (816) 474-4558.

Quarterly journal. Publishes papers on economic, social, and political developments bearing on industrial development. Price $36.00 per year.

182

American Industrial Development Council Newsletter
American Industrial Development Council, Inc, 215 W Pershing Rd, Suite 707, Kansas City, MO 64108. Telephone (816) 474-4558.

Bimonthly newsletter. Gives news of the American Industrial Development Council, including information on membership, conferences, and seminars. Offers brief articles about industrial development. Price available free to members only.

183

American Industrial Properties Report
Indprop Publishing Co, Inc, PO Box 2060, Red Bank, NJ 07701. Telephone (201) 842-7433.

Magazine issued nine times per year. Covers site selection and economic development. Price $15.00 per year.

184

American Industrial Properties Report (AIPR) Worldwide Guide for Foreign Investment
Indprop Publishing Co, Inc, PO Box 2060, Red Bank, NJ 07701. Telephone (201) 842-7433.

Annual magazine. Offers guidance for US companies seeking to locate outside the country. Provides information on manufacturing facilities, partnerships, licensee agreements, and branch offices. Price $5.00 per copy.

185

American Industry
Publications For Industry, 21 Russell Woods Rd, Great Neck, NY 11021. Telephone (516) 487-0990.

Monthly newspaper. Reports on manufacturing industries. Includes information on new equipment, products, and systems. Price $11.00 per year.

186

American Institute of Banking. Leaders Letter
American Institute of Banking, 1120 Connecticut Ave, Washington, DC 20036. Telephone (202) 467-4151.

Newsletter issued eight times per year. Contains articles on American Institute of Banking's chapters, activites. Price free of charge.

187

American Institute of Certified Public Accountants (AICPA) Professional Standards
American Institute of Certified Public Accountants, 1211 Ave of the Americas, New York, NY 10036. Nonmembers may order from Commerce Clearing House, Inc, 4025 W Peterson Ave, Chicago, IL 60646. Telephone (212) 575-6200.

Three loose-leaf books. Cover professional standards in auditing, Management Advisory Services, tax practice, accounting, ethics and quality control. Price $140.00 per year.

188

American Institute of Certified Public Accountants (AICPA) Professional Standards—Accounting
Commerce Clearing House, Inc, 4025 W Peterson Ave, Chicago, IL 60646. Telephone (312) 583-8500.

Book. Covers statements and interpretations of the Accounting Principles Board and its successor, the Financial Accounting Standards Board. Price $10.00.

189

American Institute of Certified Public Accountants (AICPA) Professional Standards—Auditing, Management Advisory Services, Tax Practice
Commerce Clearing House, Inc, 4025 W Peterson Ave, Chicago, IL 60646. Telephone (312) 583-8500.

Book. Includes statements of the American Institute of Certified Public Accountants on auditing standards, management advisory services, and responsibilities in tax practice. Price $10.00.

190

American Institute of Certified Public Accountants (AICPA) Professional Standards—Ethics & Bylaws
Commerce Clearing House, Inc, 4025 W Peterson Ave, Chicago, IL 60646. Telephone (312) 583-8500.

Book. Covers the ethics and conduct of the American Institute of Certified Public Accountants. Includes the bylaws. Price $8.75.

191

American Institute of Certified Public Accountants (AICPA) Washington Report
American Institute of Certified Public Accountants, 1211 Ave of the Americas, New York, NY 10036. Telephone (212) 575-6200.

Weekly newsletter on federal and congressional legislative activities relating to the accounting profession. Price $38.00 per year.

192

American Investors Service
Chestnutt Corp, 88 Field Point Rd, Greenwich, CT 06830. Telephone (203) 622-1600.

Weekly service. Analyzes current stock market activity and shows changes over a two-week period for selected stocks. Ranks stocks by percentage strength and provides charts indicating industrial group stock trends. Price available on request.

193

American Iron and Steel Institute Annual Statistical Report
American Iron and Steel Institute, 1000 16th St, NW, Washington, DC 20036. Telephone (202) 452-7021.

Annual report. Contains US and Canadian statistics on production, economics, and finance of the iron and steel industry. Price $15.00.

194

American Journal of Agricultural Economics
American Agricultural Economics Assn, Dept of Agricultural Economics, University of Kentucky, KY 40506. Telephone (606) 258-5688.

Quarterly journal. Concentrates on agriculture and its contribution to the general economy. Price free to members of AAEA, $35.00 per year nonmembers.

195

American Journal of Economics and Sociology
American Journal of Economics and Sociology, Inc, 5 E 44th St, New York, NY 10017. Telephone (212) 986-8684.

Quarterly magazine. Presents research on economics and other social sciences. Price $10.00 per year.

196

American Journal of Small Business
University of Baltimore, 1420 North Charles St, Baltimore, MD 21201. Telephone (301) 659-3262.

Quarterly magazine. Discusses small business management and finance. Notes the activities of the Small Business Administration and includes book reviews and special features. Price $18.00 per year. ISSN 0363-9428.

197

American Law of Mining
Matthew Bender & Co, 235 W 45th St, New York, NY 10017. Telephone (212) 661-5050.

Loose-leaf volumes, with annual supplements. Provide coverage of US mining laws. Index. Price $350.00 for five volumes.

198

American Library Directory **1976–1977**
R R Bowker Co, 1180 Ave of the Americas, New York, NY 10036. Order from R R Bowker Co, PO Box 1807, Ann Arbor, MI 48106. Telephone (212) 764-5100.

Annual directory. Arranges over 32,000 US and over 3000 Canadian libraries by state/province and city. Notes personal and special collections. Gives statistical data on print and nonprint holdings, finances, and state and federal funding. Price $54.95. ISBN 0-8352-1251-3. ISSN 0065-910X.

199

American Machinist
McGraw-Hill Book Co, Hightstown-Princeton Rd, Hightstown, NJ 08520. Telephone (609) 448-1700. Telex 843449.

Directory with periodic updates. Provides inventory of metalworking manufacturing equipment. Price $30.00.

200
American Machinist (Magazine)
McGraw-Hill Publications Co, 1221 Ave of the Americas, New York, NY 10020. Telephone (212) 997-1221. Telex TWX 7105814879 WUI 62555.

Monthly magazine. Focuses on metal-working manufacturing industries and engineering. Includes material on plastics technology. Price $30.00 per year US, $35.00 Canada, $60.00 elsewhere.

201
American Metal Market
Fairchild Publications, Inc, 7 E 12th St, New York, NY 10003. Telephone (212) 741-4130.

Daily newspaper. Covers news of the metals industry, including the latest prices for metals and scrap. Price $215.00 per year.

202
American Register of Exporters & Importers
American Register, 90 W Broadway, New York, NY 10007. Telephone (212) 227-4030.

Annual directory. Supplies information on US exporters and importers, chambers of commerce, foreign embassies, and foreign trade associations in the US. Contains product indexes in English, Spanish, French, and German. Price $40.00 per copy.

203
American Salesman
National Research Bureau, Inc, 424 N 3rd St, Burlington, IA 52601. Telephone (319) 752-5415.

Monthly magazine. Supplies information about and of interest to American salespersons. Price $19.00 per year. ISSN 0003-0902.

204
American School and University
North American Publishing Co, 401 N Broad St, Philadelphia, PA 19108. Telephone (215) 574-9600.

Monthly magazine. Discusses educational facilities, purchasing, and business management. Emphasizes construction and maintenance of school and university plants. Price $25.00 per year.

205
American Society for Personnel Administration (ASPA) Handbook of Personnel and Industrial Relations
American Society for Personnel Administration, 30 Park Dr, Berea, OH 44017. Order from ASPA Book Service, 30 Park Dr, Berea, OH 44017. Telephone (216) 826-4790.

Book. Contains personnel and industrial relations information. Includes such subjects as manpower management systems, staffing policies, and manpower training and development. Price $5.00.

206
American Statistician
American Statistical Assn, 806 15th St NW, Washington, DC 20005. Telephone (202) 393-3253.

Quarterly publication. Discusses issues related to statistics, especially statistical education and statistical computing. Price $12.00 per year.

207
American Statistics Index
Congressional Information Service, Inc, 4520 EW Highway, Suite 800, Washington, DC 20014. Telephone (301) 654-1550.

Service composed of monthly, quarterly, and annual indexes and abstracts. Covers statistical data published by US government departments, agencies, and offices. Price $1165.00 per year.

208
American Stock Exchange Guide
Commerce Clearing House, Inc, 4025 W Peterson Ave, Chicago, IL 60646. Telephone (312) 583-8500.

Two loose-leaf books plus monthly reports. Carry the directory, constitution, and rules for the American Stock Exchange. Price $140.00 per year.

209
American Subsidiaries of German Firms
German–American Chamber of Commerce, Inc, 666 5th Ave, New York, NY 10103. Telephone (212) 974-8830.

Yearly book. Lists American subsidiaries of German firms alphabetically by German parent, and US subsidiary and by product. Price $50.00.

210
American Trucking Trends
American Trucking Assn, Inc, 1616 P St NW, Washington, DC 20036. Telephone (202) 797-5351.

Annual report. Covers trucking industry developments. Notes truck registrations, tonnage and mileage, freight products, and financial data. Tables and charts. Price free of charge.

212
Amusement Business
Billboard Publications, Inc, PO Box 24970, Nashville, TN 37202. Telephone (615) 748-8120.

Weekly newspaper. Reports on mass entertainment business, including facility operations and management, events, spending, promotions, and routes of touring attractions, carnivals, and circuses. Price $2.00 per copy; $35.00 per year. ISSN 08668.

213
Analysis of LNG Marine Transportation
US Maritime Adm, Commerce Bldg, 14th & E Sts NW, Washington, DC 20230. Order from National Technical Information Service, 5285 Port Royal Rd, Springfield, VA 22161. Telephone (703) 487-4650.

Publication. Analyzes marine transportation of liquefied natural gas. Price $18.50.

214
Analystics
Interactive Data Corp, 486 Totten Pond Rd, Waltham, MA 02154. Telephone (617) 890-1234.

Data retrieval service. Provides security and corporate financial information. Offers processing facilities to analyze data-bases. Price available on request.

215
Analysts Handbook
Standard & Poor's Corp, 25 Broadway, New York, NY 10004. Telephone (212) 248-2525.

Annual book with monthly updating. Gives composite corporate per share data on a true comparison basis for 95 industries. Price $365.00 per year.

216
Analyst's Service
Extel Statistical Services Ltd, 37-45 Paul St, London, England EC2A 4PB. Telephone 01-253 3400. Telex. 262687.

Card service with weekly updates. Provides a 10-year record of capital changes, balance sheets, profit and loss accounts, stock prices, and dividends for 1500 companies listed on the British and Irish stock exchanges. Is designed as a reference source for stock analysts. Price £670.00 per year.

216.01
AN, AND & MS Standards
National Standards Assn, Inc, 5161 River Rd, Washington, DC 20016. Telephone (301) 951-1310. Telex 89-8452.

Twenty-volume set. Provides standards for automotive, marine, and aircraft components. Price $590.00 per year.

217
Anbar Management Publications
Accounting and Data Processing
Abstracts
Anbar Publications Ltd, PO Box 23, Wembley, England HA9 8DJ. Telephone (44) (01) 902 4489. Telex 935779.

Publication issued eight times per year and separate annual index. Contains abstracts of articles from accounting and data processing periodicals, mostly British and American. Supplies copies of articles. Price £67.00 per year. ISSN 0001-4796.

218
Anbar Management Publications
Bibliography
Anbar Publications Ltd, PO Box 23, Wembley, England HA9 8DJ. Telephone (44) (01) 902 4489. Telex 935779.

Annual bibliography. Lists books, pamphlets, and films and audio-visual material covered by Anbar Management Services abstracts. Price £5.00 per copy. ISSN 0003-2808.

219
Anbar Management Publications
Marketing & Distribution Abstracts
Anbar Publications Ltd, PO Box 23, Wembley, England HA9 8DJ. Telephone (44) (01) 902 4489. Telex 935779.

Publication issued eight times per year and separate annual index. Contains abstracts of articles from marketing and distribution periodicals, mostly British and American. Supplies copies of articles. Price £67.00 per year. ISSN 0305-0661.

220
Anbar Management Publications
Personnel Training Abstracts
Anbar Publications Ltd, PO Box 23, Wembley, England HA9 8DJ. Telephone (44) (01) 902 4489. Telex 935779.

Publication issued eight times per year and separate annual index. Contains abstracts of articles from personnel and training periodicals, mostly British and American. Supplies copies of articles. Price £67.00 per year. ISSN 0305-067X.

220.01
Anbar Management Publications
Smaller Business Management Abstracts
Anbar Publications Ltd, PO Box 23, Wembley, England HA9 8DJ. Telephone (44) (01) 902 4489. Telex 935779.

Publication issued eight times per year, with separate annual index. Contains abstracts of articles from management periodicals, mostly British and American. Supplies copies of articles. Price £38.00 per year. ISSN 01434780.

221
Anbar Management Publications Top
Management Abstracts
Anbar Publications Ltd, PO Box 23, Wembley, England HA9 8DJ. Telephone (44) (01) 902 4489. Telex 935779.

Publication issued eight times per year and separate annual index. Contains abstracts of articles from management periodicals, mostly British and American. Supplies copies of articles. Price £67.00 per year. ISSN 0049-4100.

222
Anbar Management Publications Work
Study & O and M Abstracts
Anbar Publications Ltd, PO Box 23, Wembley, England HA9 8DJ. Telephone (44) (01) 902 4489. Telex 935779.

Publication issued eight times per year and separate annual index. Contains abstracts of articles from work study, organization, and methods periodicals, mostly British and American. Supplies copies of articles. Price £67.00 per year. ISSN 0305-0653.

222.01
Andean Group Regional Report
Latin American Newsletters Ltd, Greenhill House, 90–93 Cowcross St, London, England EC1M 6BL. Telephone (44)(01) 251-0012. Telex 261117.

Monthly newsletter. Examines economic and political developments in Bolivia, Colombia, Ecuador, Peru, and Venezuela. Price £40, $90.00 (US) per year.

223
Andrews Newsletter
R E Andrews and Assocs, 25743 N Hogan Dr, Valencia, CA 91355. Telephone (805) 259-3742.

Monthly newsletter. Covers stock market cycles, interest rate trends, and economic and industrial developments. Price $100.00 per year.

224
Anglo American Trade Directory
American Chamber of Commerce (United Kingdom), 75 Brook St, London, England W1Y 2EB. Telephone (44) (01) 493-0381.

Biennial book. Offers directory to British and American companies having trade and/or investment relations. Price $50.00.

225
Animal Health International
IMS World Publications Ltd, York House, 37 Queen Sq, London, England WCIN 3BE. Telephone (44) (01) 242-0112. Telex 263298.

Quarterly report. Discusses new drugs for animals. Covers research developments. Price $1000.00 per year.

226
Anglo-Israel Trade Journal
Anglo-Israel Chamber of Commerce, 8/12 Brook St, London, England W1Y 1AB. Telephone (44) (01) 493 0140.

Monthly magazine. Refers to trade between Israel and other countries, especially the United Kingdom.

227
Annals of Occupational Hygiene
Pergamon Press, Inc, Maxwell House, Fairview Park, Elmsford, NY 10523. Telephone (914) 592-7700. Telex 13-7328.

Quarterly magazine. Publishes articles on occupational health and safety. Price $80.00 per year.

228
Annals of Probability
Institute of Mathematical Statistics, c/o Heebok Park, Treasurer, 3401 Investment Blvd, No 6, Hayward, CA 94545. Telephone (415) 783-8141.

Bimonthly reports. Contains articles on probability theory. Price $44.00. ISSN 0091-1798.

229
Annals of Statistics
Institute of Mathematical Statistics, c/o Heebok Park, Treasurer, 3401 Investment Blvd, No 6, Hayward, CA 94545. Telephone (415) 783-8141.

Bimonthly report. Contains articles on statistical theory. Price $50.00 per year. ISSN 0090-5364.

230
Annotated Tax Forms
Prentice-Hall, Inc, Englewood Cliffs, NJ 07632. Telephone (201) 592-2000. Telex 13-5423.

Loose-leaf service issued six times per year. Contains model tax procedural forms, including an explanation of their function with references to statutes and rulings. Price $228.00 per year.

231
Announced New Plants & Expansions in the State of Washington
Washington Dept of Commerce & Economic Development, Research Div, Genl Adm Bldg, Olympia, WA 98504. Telephone (206) 753-5600.

Quarterly reports. Cover new industrial plants and expansions of existing ones in Washington State. Price free of charge.

232
Announcement of Foreign Investment in US Manufacturing Industries
Conference Board, Inc, 845 3rd Ave, New York, NY 10022. Telephone (212) 759-0900.

Quarterly listing. Provides data on foreign direct investment, classified by state and industry. Offers anticipated spending and employment figures. Price available on request.

233
Announcements of Mergers and Acquisitions
Conference Board, Inc, 845 3rd Ave, New York, NY 10022. Telephone (212) 759-0900.

Monthly listing. Announces mergers and acquisitions in manufacturing, mining, wholesale and retail trade, and service industries. Includes names, locations, industries, and product classes. Price available on request.

234
Annual Abstract of Statistics
Her Majesty's Stationery Office, PO Box 569, London, England SE1 9NH. Telephone (44) (01) 928 1321.

Annual service. Provides statistics on British economic subjects, such as wages, consumer expenditure, industrial production, energy consumption, and imports and exports over a ten-year period. Price $11.90 per year.

235
Annual Abstract of Statistics
Nigerian Consulate General, 575 Lexington Ave, New York, NY 10022. Telephone (212) 752-1670.

Annual publication. Offers abstracts of statistics on Nigeria. Price $1.25.

236
Annual Aid Review
Canadian International Development Agency, 200 Promenade Du Portage, Hull, PQ Canada K1A 0G4. Telephone (613) 997-6100. Telex 053-4140.

Annual report. Summarizes Canada's development assistance program as reported to the Development Assistance Committee of Organization for Economic Cooperation and Development. Covers volume, terms, and aid distribution. Tables. Price free of charge.

236.01
Annual Book of ASTM Standards, **1981**
American Society for Testing and Materials, 1916 Race St, Philadelphia, PA 19103. Telephone (215) 299-5400.

Annual book in 48 volumes. Contains 6400 standards for materials, products, systems, and services. Price $1750.00 for complete set, prices for individual volumes available on request.

237
Annual Bulletin of Coal Statistics for Europe
United Nations Publications, Room A-3315, New York, NY 10017. Telephone (212) 754-8302.

Annual report. Provides statistics on European coal industry. Price available on request.

238
Annual Bulletin of Electric Energy Statistics for Europe
United Nations Publications, Rm A-3315, New York, NY 10017. Telephone (212) 754-8302.

Annual report. Provides cumulative statistics on electricity in Europe. Price available on request.

239
Annual Bulletin of Gas Statistics for Europe
United Nations Publications, Rm A-3315, New York, NY 10017. Telephone (212) 754-8302.

Annual report. Provides cumulative statistics on European gas industry. Price available on request.

240
Annual Bulletin of General Energy Statistics for Europe
United Nations Publications, Rm A-3315, New York, NY 10017. Telephone (212) 754-8302.

Annual report. Cumulative statistics on energy in Europe. Price available on request.

241
Annual Bulletin of Housing and Building Statistics for Europe
United Nations Publications, A-3315, New York, NY 10017. Telephone (212) 754-8302.

Annual report. Contains cumulative statistics on housing and building in Europe. Price available on request.

242
Annual Bulletin of Steel Statistics for Europe
United Nations Publications, Rm A-3315, New York, NY 10017. Telephone (212) 754-8302.

Annual report. Cumulative statistics on European steel. Price available on request.

243
Annual Demographic File **March Supplement. P:D38**
US Dept of Commerce, Bureau of the Census, Washington, DC 20233. Order information from Chief, Population Division, Bureau of the Census, Washington, DC 20233. Telephone (202) 655-4000.

Annual service. Contains modified basic family and person records. Includes information on family and household characteristics, age, race, sex, income, and work experience. Price $80.00 per reel.

244
Annual Digest of Port Statistics **Vols I and II**
Her Majesty's Stationery Office, PO Box 569, London, England SE1 9NH. Telephone: (44) (01) 928 1321.

Annual books. Provide statistics on British port activity. Price £10.00 per volume.

245
Annual Estimates of the Population of England and Wales and Local Authority Areas
Her Majesty's Stationery Office, PO Box 569, London, England SE1 9NH. Telephone (44) (01) 928 1321.

Annual report. Estimates population of Great Britain, Wales, and local areas. Price £3.00 per year.

246
Annual Estimates of the Population of Scotland
Her Majesty's Stationery Office, PO Box 569, London, England SE1 9NH. Telephone (44) (01) 928 1321.

Annual report. Estimates population of Scotland. Price £1.25 per year.

247
Annual Housing Survey **1975 (Final). H–150–75**
US Dept of Commerce, Bureau of the Census, Washington, DC 20233. Telephone (202) 655-4000.

Series of six reports. Surveys housing characteristics, including neighborhood quality, finances, and urban and rural housing. Maps. Price varies.

248
Annual Indexes of Patents
Patent and Trademark Office, Washington, DC 20231. Order from Superintendent of Documents, Government Printing Office, Washington, DC 20402. Telephone (202) 783-3238.

Two-volume annual index. Provides an alphabetical list of patentees for US patents issued during year, and an index of patents by subject of invention. Price varies.

249
Annual Indexes to Selected Water Resources Abstracts (SWRA)
US Dept of the Interior, Washington, DC 20240. Order from National Technical Information Service, US Dept of Commerce, 5825 Port Royal Rd, Springfield, VA 22161. Telephone (202) 343-8435.

Annual report. Contains indexes to Selected Water Resources Abstracts. Price $50.00.

249.01
Annual Industrial Review
Stock Exchange Research Pty Ltd, 20 Bond St, Sydney, 2000, Australia. Order from Financial Analysis & Publications, PO Box 256, Australia Sq, Sydney, 2000 Australia. Telephone (61)(02) 231-0066.

Book. Discusses all industrial companies in Australia. Includes financial and operational details. Price $60.00 (Australian).

250
Annual Institute on Oil and Gas Law and Taxation
Matthew Bender & Co, 235 W 45th St, New York, NY 10017. Telephone (212) 661-5050.

Annual book. Covers legal and tax problems confronted by the oil and gas industries. Price $65.00 per year.

251
Annual Mining Reveiw
Stock Exchange Research Pty Ltd, 20 Bond St, Sydney, 2000, Australia. Order from Financial Analysis & Publications, PO Box 256, Australia Sq, Sydney, 2000 Australia. Telephone (61) (02) 231-0066

Book. Discusses all mining and oil companies in Australia. Includes financial and exploration details. Price $50.00 (Australia).

252
Annual of Industrial Property Law
European Law Centre Ltd, 4 Bloomsbury Sq, London, WC1A 2RL, England. Telephone (44) (01) 404 4300. Telex 21746.

Annual book. Provides information on patent and other industrial property legislative developments in Australia, New Zealand, Canada, France, West Germany, Japan, South Africa, the United Kingdom, and the US. Price $102.00.

253
Annual Planning Information
Arizona Dept of Economic Security, Manpower Information and Analysis Section, PO Box 6123, Phoenix, AZ 85005. Telephone (602) 255-3871.

Annual report. Covers the economic developments, employment, population, and labor force in Arizona. Price free of charge.

254
Annual Report
Asian Development Bank, PO Box 789, Manila, Phillippines 2800. Telephone 8317251, 8317211. Telex 23103 PH RCA, 40571 PM ITT.

Annual report. Provides the financial statement for the Asian Development Bank. Discusses loans granted and technical assistance offered. Tables and charts. Price free of charge.

255
Annual Report of the Farm Credit Administration
Farm Credit Administration Public Affairs Div, Washington, DC 20578. Telephone (202) 755-2170.

Annual report. Gives statistical and narrative account to Congress on work of the cooperative Farm Credit System. Price free of charge.

256
Annual Report of the Maritime Administration
US Maritime Adm Commerce Bldg, 14th & E Sts NW, Washington, DC 20230. Order from Superintendent of Documents, US Government Printing Office, Washington, DC 20402. Telephone (202) 783-3238.

Annual report. Describes the activities of the Maritime Administration. Covers US shipbuilding, ship operations, and research and development. Tables. Price $2.75 per copy.

257
Annual Report of the Secretary of the Treasury on the State of the Finances
US Dept of the Treasury, Bureau of Government Financial Operations, Pennsylvania Ave and Madison Pl NW, Washington, DC 20226. Order from Superintendent of Documents, Government Printing Office, Washington, DC 20402. Telephone (202) 566-2000.

Two-volume report. Carries data on the state of US finances. Covers policy, administration, fiscal operations, organizational units, and supporting exhibits. Statistical index containing historical tables. Price available on request.

258

Annual Review of Information Science and Technology /Volume 15, 1980
American Society for Information Science, 1010 16th St, NW, Washington, DC 20036. Order from Knowledge Industry Publications, Inc, 2 Corporate Park Dr, White Plains, NY 10604. Telephone (914) 328-9157.

Annual book. Discusses developments and trends in various specialty areas of information science. Price available on request.

259

Annual Review of the Silver Market
Handy & Harman, 850 3rd Ave, New York, NY 10022. Telephone (212) 752-3400.

Annual booklet. Reports on the silver market for previous year. Includes information on the future of silver, industrial consumption, imports and exports, related international legislation. Tables. Price free of charge.

260

Annual Rural Planning Report
Arizona Dept of Economic Security, Manpower Information and Analysis Section, PO Box 6123, Phoenix, AZ 85005. Telephone (602) 271-3871.

Annual report. Discusses Arizona's rural employment trends, services offered to rural people, and community development activities. Price free of charge.

261

Annual Statement Studies
Robert Morris Assoc, 1616 PNB Bldg, Philadelphia, PA 19107. Telephone (215) 665-2850.

Annual book. Contains balance sheets, income statements, and 16 widely used ratios for 313 industries in 5 categories: manufacturing, wholesaling, retailing, servicing, and contracting. Price $22.20.

262

Annual Statistical Review of the Distilled Spirits Industry
Distilled Spirits Council of the US, Inc, 1300 Penn Bldg, Washington, DC 20004. Telephone (202) 628-3544.

Annual report. Presents statistics on operations of the US distilled spirits beverage distilling industry. Includes information on production, taxes, consumption, retail outlets, foreign trade. Tables, charts, and graphs. Price free of charge.

263

Annual Statistical Supplement, Social Security Bulletin
US Social Security Adm, Office of Research and Statistics, Washington, DC 20201. Order from Superintendent of Documents, US Government Printing Office, Washington, DC 20402. Telephone (202) 953-3600.

Annual report. Presents general time-series statistical data on Social Security and the economy and on interprogram Social Security. Summarizes related legislation. Tables. Price $4.50.

264

Annual Statistics Transport and Communications, Tourism
Commission of the European Communities, Office for Official Publications of the European Communities, CP 1003, Luxembourg 1, Luxembourg. Telephone (352) 490081. Telex PUBLOF 1325.

Annual publication. Contains statistical data on transportation, communications, and tourism within the European community. Price 100 Belgian francs.

265

Annual Summary of Business Statistics, New York State
New York Dept of Commerce, 99 Washington Ave, Albany, NY 12245. Telephone (518) 474-8670.

Annual publication. Gives statistical tables on New York State's economic performance and on various regions within the state. Price free of charge.

266

Annual Survey of Manufacturers
US Dept of Commerce, Bureau of the Census, Washington, DC 20233. Telephone (202) 499-1600.

Annual report for intercensal years. Provides statistics on manufacturing activity and employment for industry groups, individual industries, and geographic regions. Price available on request.

267

Annual Survey of Manufacturers, 1974. M74(AS)
US Dept of Commerce, Bureau of the Census, Washington, DC 20233. Telephone (202) 655-4000.

Series of reports. Presents statistics on 1974 manufacturers' expenditures for new plants and equipment, book value of fixed assets, rental payments for buildings and equipment, and fuels and electric energy consumed. Price $2.40.

268

Annual Survey of Manufactures, 1975. M75(AS)
US Dept of Commerce, Bureau of the Census, Washington, DC 20233. Telephone (202) 655-4000.

Series of reports. Provides 1975 data on value of product shipments for 1500 classes of manufactured products. Offer preliminary statistics on quantity and cost of purchased fuels and electric energy for major energy-consuming industry groups. Price varies.

269

Annual Survey of Oil and Gas
US Dept of Commerce, Bureau of the Census, Washington, DC 20233. Telephone (202) 449-1600.

Annual report. Presents year-end statistics on oil and gas field exploration, development, and production. Includes comparative figures for previous years. Price $1.10.

270

Annual Survey Report—Ethical Pharmaceutical Industry Operations
Pharmaceutical Manufacturers Assoc, 1155 15th St NW, Washington, DC 20005. Telephone (202) 463-2060.

Statistical survey. Covers operations and expenditures of the pharmaceutical industry. Price free of charge.

271

Antitrust & Trade Regulation Report
Bureau of National Affairs, Inc, 1231 25th St NW, Washington, DC 20037. Telephone (202) 452-4200.

Loose-leaf books, with updates. Cover developments in antitrust and trade regulation and note federal and state activity. Provide bibliographies of books and articles. Price $364.00 per year.

272

Antitrust Bulletin
Federal Legal Publications, Inc, 157 Chambers St, New York, NY 10007. Telephone (212) 243-5775.

Quarterly bulletin. Discusses American antitrust issues, international restrictive trade practices, and proposed legislation. Reviews legal and economics books. Price $60.00 per year.

273
Antitrust Laws and Trade Regulation
Matthew Bender & Co, 235 E 45th St, New York, NY 10017. Telephone (212) 661-5050.

Loose-leaf books, with supplements four times per year and covering newsletter. Analyze provisions and applications of the Sherman, Clayton, Robinson-Patman, and Federal Trade Commission Acts. Price $650.00 (16 volumes); $350.00 per year.

274
Apartment Management Report
Apartment Owners & Managers Assn of America, 65 Cherry Ave, Watertown, CT 06795. Telephone (203) 274-2589.

Monthly newsletter. Deals with the property management of multifamily housing, including condominiums. Price $22.00 per year.

275
Apartment Owners and Managers Assn of America Newsletter
Apartment Owners & Managers Assn of America, 65 Cherry Ave, Watertown, CT 06795. Telephone (203) 274-2589.

Monthly newsletter. Covers such issues as zoning, construction, technology, legislation, renting strategies, and new products in the multifamily housing field. Price $35.00.

276
APC Tablet
Alltech Publishing Co, 212 Cooper Ctr, N Park Dr & Browning Rd, Pennsauken, NJ 08109. Telephone (609) 662-2122.

Monthly newsletter. Reports on data processing industry developments. Includes profiles of companies and information on new products and applications. Price $30.00 per year.

277
AP-Dow Jones Bankers Report
Dow Jones & Co, Inc, 22 Cortlandt St, New York, NY 10007. Telephone (212) 285-5000.

Continuous service. Provides data on international money and capital markets. Gives Eurocurrency and Eurobond market prices and notes interest rates, exchange rates, and new banking legislation. Price available on request.

278
AP-Dow Jones Economic Report
Dow Jones & Co, Inc, 22 Cortlandt St, New York, NY 10007. Telephone (212) 285-5000.

Daily service. Reports on economic news, including financial, industrial, and political information affecting corporate investments and stock markets. Price available on request.

279
AP-Dow Jones Eurofinancial Report
Dow Jones & Co, Inc, 22 Cortlandt St, New York, NY 10007. Telephone (212) 285-5000.

Daily service. Reports on European financial and business news and money market activities. Price available on request.

280
AP-Dow Jones Financial Wire
Dow Jones & Co, Inc, 22 Cortlandt St, New York, NY 10007. Telephone (212) 285-5000.

Daily service. Provides information on international stock exchanges, commodity and money markets. Reports on corporate, political, and economic news. Price available on request.

281
AP-Dow Jones Petroleum News Service
Dow Jones & Co, Inc, 22 Cortlandt St, New York, NY 10007. Telephone (212) 285-5000.

Daily service. Provides data on petroleum and petrochemicals, including government regulations, drilling news, oil shipping developments, and price changes. Price available on request.

282
API/NFPA Environmental Report
American Paper Institute, 1619 Massachusetts Ave NW, Washington, DC 20036. Telephone (202) 332-1050.

Monthly report. Discusses legislation, regulation, and judicial developments in environmental areas affecting the forest industries. Price free to association members.

282.01
Apparel Magazine
Hong Kong Trade Development Council, 548 5th Ave, New York, NY 10036. Telephone (212) 582-6610.

Semiannual magazine. Reports on fashion industry in Hong Kong. Price available on request.

282.02
Apparel South
Communication Channels, Inc, 6285 Barfield Rd, Atlanta, GA 30328. Telephone (404) 256-9800.

Monthly magazine. Reports on retail apparel news from major cities throughout the South and from the three major apparel marts in Miami, Atlanta, and Charlotte. Includes Southern fashion trends, merchandising displays, and New York fashions. Price $16.00 per year.

283
Apparel Trades Book
Dun & Bradstreet, Box 3224, Church St Station, New York, NY 10008. Telephone (212) 285-7346.

Book. Provides credit information on 110,000 retail and wholesale clothing outlets. Price on request. Available to Dun & Bradstreet subscribers only.

284
Appliance Magazine
Dana Chase Publications, Inc, York St at Park Ave, Elmhurst, IL 60126. Telephone (312) 834-5280.

Monthly magazine. Contains current statistics and other information on the appliance industry. Price $24.00 per year, $37.00 per year foreign.

285
Appliance Manufacturer
Cahners Publishing Company, Inc, 221 Columbus Ave, Boston, MA 02116. Telephone (617) 536-7780.

Monthly magazine. Covers trends and technology affecting the appliance industry. Price $20.00 per year.

286
Applied Ergonomics
IPC Business Press Ltd, 205 E 42nd St., New York, NY 10017. Telephone (212) 889-0700. Telex 421710.

Quarterly magazine on ergonomics. Provides information on equipment, systems, and buildings, including industrial and domestic applications. Price $104.00. ISSN 0003-6870.

287
Applied Mathematics Modelling
IPC Business Press Ltd, 205 E 42nd St, New York, NY 10017. Telephone (212) 889-0700. Telex 421710.

Quarterly magazine. Offers brief, up-to-date papers on advances in mathematical modelling. Includes a discussion of the applicability of a particular model to specific problem. Price $169.00. ISSN 0307-904X.

288
Applied Science and Technology Index (ASTI)
H W Wilson Co, 950 University Ave, Bronx, NY 10452. Telephone (212) 588-8400.

Monthly publication (except July) with quarterly cumulations and a bound annual. Covers articles published in a wide range of scientific and technological journals, including those on the hard sciences, engineering, and industrial and communications technology. Price available on request.

289
Appraisal Briefs
Society of Real Estate Appraisers, 7 S Dearborn, Chicago, IL 60603. Telephone (312) 346-7422.

Weekly newsletter. Reports on the activities affecting appraisers in Federal agencies, state governments, counties and cities. Price $10.00 per year.

290
Appraisal/Institute Magazine (AIM)
Appraisal Institute of Canada, 309-93 Lombard Ave, Winnipeg, Manitoba, Canada R3B 3B1. Telephone (204) 942-0751.

Quarterly magazine. Furnishes information on real estate appraisals in Canada. Price $10.00 per year.

291
Appraisal Journal
American Institute of Real Estate Appraisers, 430 N Michigan Ave, Chicago, IL 60611. Telephone (312) 440-8141.

Quarterly journal. Covers theory and the practice of appraising, including legal aspects. Price $25.00 per year.

291.01
Appraisal Manual
R S Means Co, Inc, 100 Construction Plz, Kingston, MA 02364. Telephone (617) 747-1270.

Annual valuation resource. Provides building illustrations, descriptions, and costs to aid in estimates for residential, commercial, industrial, and institutional structures. Price $33.00.

292
Appraiser
American Institute of Real Estate Appraisers, 430 N Michigan Ave, Chicago, IL 60611. Telephone (312) 440-8141.

Monthly bulletin. Covers current trends in appraisal practice. Price $7.50 per year.

293
Appropriate Technology
Intermediate Technology Publications Ltd, 9 King St, London, England WC2E 8HN. Telephone (44) (01) 836 9434.

Quarterly magazine. Discusses developmental technology. Includes technical articles, book reviews, and readers' contributions. Price £6.00 individuals and non-profit organizations, £8.00 all other subscribers.

294
Approved Wright Investment List (AWIL)
Wright Investors' Service, Wright Bldg, 500 State St, Bridgeport, CT 06604. Telephone (203) 377-9444.

Quarterly service, with monthly updating. Contains investment analyses and projections for selected stocks. Includes 10-year records and five-year projections. Price $500.00 per quarter.

295
Arab Aid: Who Gets It, For What, and How
Chase Trade Information Corp, 1 World Trade Center, 78th Floor, New York, NY 10048. Telephone (212) 432-8072. Telex RCA 235444.

Report, with upcoming second edition. Covers Arab concessionary leading and foreign aid. Price $290.00 for first edition.

296
Arab Investors: Who They Are, What They Buy, and Where
Chase Trade Information Corp, 1 World Trade Center, 78th Floor, New York, NY 10048. Telephone (212) 432-8072. Telex RCA 235444.

Two-volume report. Describes public and private investment institutions, commercial firms, consortiums, and private family holdings in the Middle East. Volume I covers investment outside the Arab world, Volume II focuses within the Arab world. Price $345.00 per volume.

297
Aramtek Mideast Review
Aramtek Corp, 122 E 42nd St, New York, NY 10017. Telephone (212) 490-2990.

Quarterly report for executives doing business in the Middle East. Offers concise coverage of business activities, plus feature articles. Price $125.00 per year.

298
Arbitration in the Schools
American Arbitration Assn, 140 W 51st St, New York, NY 10020. Telephone (212) 977-2000.

Monthly magazine. Summarizes awards and recommendations involving employees of public and private educational institutions. Price $75.00 per month.

299
Arbitration Journal
American Arbitration Assn, 140 W 51st St, New York, NY 10020. Telephone (212) 977-2000.

Quarterly journal. Pertains to arbitration law and practice in various fields. Price $20.00 per year.

300
Architectural Record
McGraw-Hill Publications Co, 1221 Ave of the Americas, New York, NY 10020. Telephone (212) 997-1221. Telex TWX 7105814879 WUI 62555.

Monthly magazine, plus four spotlight issues. Discusses architectural and related engineering issues, and residential and nonresidential construction. Price $35.00 per year US, $37.00 Canada, $59.00 elsewhere.

301
Arctic Alternatives
Canadian Arctic Resources Committee, 46 Elgin St, Room 11, Ottawa, Ont, Canada K1P 5K6. Telephone (613) 236-7379.

Report. Gives proceedings of Canadian Arctic Resources Committee's First National Workshop on People, Resources, and the Environment North of 60. Price $5.95. ISBN 0-9690998-5-1.

302

Arctic Marine Commerce Study

US Maritime Adm, GAO Bldg, 5 & G Sts NW, Washington, DC 20235. Order from National Technical Information Service, 5285 Port Royal Rd, Springfield, VA 22161. Telephone (703) 487-4650.

Report. Covers the Arctic marine commerce field. Price $15.00.

303

Area Development

Area Development Magazine, 432 Park Ave S, New York, NY 10016. Telephone (212) 532-4360.

Monthly magazine. Discusses corporate plant and office building sites and planning. Cites case histories. Price $30.00 per year.

304

Area Economic Projections

US Dept of Commerce, Bureau of Economic Analysis, Washington, DC 20230. Order from Information Services Div, Bureau of Economic Analysis, Washington, DC 20230. Telephone (202) 523-0777.

Information service. Provides data and projections for total personal income, population, per capita income, total employment, and 37 industry earnings. Includes state areas, economic areas, water planning areas, and Standard Metropolitan Statistical Areas. Price $250.00.

305

Area Manpower Summary

West Virginia Dept of Employment Security, Research & Statistics Div, 112 California Ave, Charleston, WV 25305. Telephone (304) 348-2660.

Monthly report. Covers employment and wage data for various West Virginia regions and the nearby areas by Ohio and Kentucky. Tables. Price free of charge.

306

Area Statistics **Vol II, 1976 (Construction)**

US Dept of Commerce, Bureau of the Census, Washington, DC 20233. Telephone (202) 655-4000.

Report. Provides statistics on the number of construction firms and proprietors, the average number of employees, and the total receipts with and without payroll. Price $12.00.

307

Area Statistics **Vol II, 1976 (Wholesale Trade)**

US Dept of Commerce, Bureau of the Census, Washington, DC 20233. Telephone (202) 655-4000.

Series of reports. Summarizes wholesale trade data for the US, regions, states, and other geographic areas. Indicates the kind of business, number of establishments, sales, inventories, operating expenses, payroll, and number of employees. Price $20.00.

308

Area Trends in Employment & Unemployment

US Dept of Labor, Employment & Training Adm, Washington, DC 20213. Telephone (202) 376-6730.

Monthly report. Indicates areas of substantial or persistent unemployment. Tables. Price free of charge.

309

Argentina-Reference Book

Dun & Bradstreet, Box 3224, Church St Station, New York, NY 10008. Telephone (212) 285-7346.

Biannual book. Lists over 110,000 Argentine manufacturers, wholesalers, retailers, and agents. Estimates financial strength and credit standing. Price available on request. Available to Dun & Bradstreet subscribers only.

310

Arizona: An Economic Profile

Office of Economic Planning & Development, Executive Tower, Rm 505, 1700 W Washington, Phoenix, AZ 85007. Telephone (602) 271-5374.

Annual report. Covers Arizona's economic development. Tables and maps. Price free of charge.

311

Arizona Business

Arizona State University, College of Business Adm, Bureau of Business and Economic Research, Tempe, AZ 85281. Telephone (602) 965-3961.

Monthly journal. Carries articles on all phases of business and the economy for those interested in business administration. Tables. Price free of charge.

312

Arizona Business & Industry

Trailbeau Publications, Inc, 2823 N 48th St, Phoenix, AZ 85008. Telephone (602) 955-3411.

Monthly magazine. Covers Arizona business and industrial news. Includes company profiles. Price $12.00 per year.

313

Arizona Manufacturers Directory, **1980**

Manufacturers' News, Inc, 3 E Huron St, Chicago, IL 60611. Telephone (312) 337-1084.

Annual book. Lists Arizona manufacturing companies by name and location. Price $30.00.

314

Arizona Mining and Manufacturing

Arizona Dept of Economic Security, Manpower Information and Analysis Section, PO Box 6123, Phoenix, AZ 85005. Telephone (602) 271-3871.

Annual report. Provides data on most of the mining and manufacturing companies in Arizona. Price free of charge.

315

Arizona Progress

Valley National Bank of Arizona, Box 71, Phoenix, AZ 85001.

Pamphlet issued nine times per year. Provides statistics on Arizona's economic progress. Price free of charge.

316

Arizona Purchaser

Purchasing Management Assn of Arizona, 49 E Thomas Rd, Suite 108, Phoenix, AZ 85021. Telephone (602) 277-8432

Monthly publication. Discusses activities of the Purchasing Management Association of Arizona and Arizona's economic conditions. Provides professional development oriented articles for purchasing professionals, as well as articles on general management techniques and philosophies. Price $15.00 per year.

317

Arizona Review

University of Arizona, College of Business & Public Administration, Div of Economic and Business Research, Tucson, AZ 85721. Telephone (602) 626-2155.

Quarterly magazine. Covers business and economic issues in Arizona. Includes tables and graphs. Price free of charge.

317.01
Arizona's Economy
University of Arizona, College of Business & Public Adm, Div of Economic and Business Research, Tucson, AZ 85721. Telephone (602) 626-2155.

Monthly newsletter. Provides indicators of economic activity for Arizona. Includes an analysis of economic conditions. Price free of charge.

317.02
Arizona: State Industrial Directory, 1981
Manufacturers' News, Inc, 3 E Huron St, Chicago, IL 60611. Telephone (312) 337-1084.

Annual book. Provides information on industrial firms in Arizona. Price $35.00.

317.03
Arizona Statistical Abstract
University of Arizona, College of Business & Public Adm, Div of Economic and Business Research, Tucson, AZ 85721. Telephone (602) 626-2155.

Book. Provides economic and socioeconomic data for Arizona. Topics include population, labor force, income, and industries. Price $9.95.

318
Arkansas Business and Economic Review
University of Arkansas, College of Business Adm, Bureau of Business and Economic Research, Fayetteville, AR 72701. Telephone (501) 575-4151.

Quarterly report. Provides a statistical review of Arkansas and national economic trends, as well as supplies economic indicators, including employment, manufacturing production, construction and agricultural cash receipts. Table and charts. Price free of charge.

319
Arkansas Economic Report
Arkansas Dept of Economic Development, One Capital Mall, Little Rock, AR 72201. Telephone (501) 371-2431.

Quarterly newsletter. Contains economic news items, including new and expanded industry listings, state economic trends, and department programs. Price free of charge.

320
Arkansas: Manufacturers' Directory, 1980
Manufacturers' News, Inc, 3 E Huron St, Chicago, IL 60611. Telephone (312) 337-1084.

Annual book. Identifies 2500 Arkansas manufacturing firms by name, location, and product. Price $38.00.

320.01
Arkansas: State Industrial Directory, 1981
Manufacturers' News, Inc, 3 E Huron St, Chicago, IL 60611. Telephone (312) 337-1084.

Annual book. Lists industrial companies in Arkansas and identifies executives. Price $40.00.

321
Arkansas. The Great Location in the Sunbelt
Arkansas Dept of Economic Development, One Capital Mall, Little Rock, AR 72201. Telephone (501) 371-2431.

Booklet. Offers information about Arkansas's geography, economy, natural resources, government, and work force. Price free of charge.

321.01
Arkansas USA
Arkansas Dept of Economic Development, One Capitol Mall, Little Rock, AR 72201. Telephone (501) 371-2431.

Brochure. Promotes Arkansas's industries and products to European markets. Available in English, French, and German. Price free of charge.

322
Art Direction
Advertising Trade Publications, Inc, 10 E 39th St, New York, NY 10016. Telephone (212) 889-6500.

Monthly magazine. Includes features on developments in advertising art, photography, graphic design, packaging, and supplies. Price $16.00 per year.

324
ASEAN Briefing
Asia Letter Ltd, PO Box 54149, Los Angeles, CA 90054. Telephone (213) 322-4222.

Monthly newsletter. Provides commentary and analysis of economic, political, and trade trends in the five ASEAN countries and within the ASEAN organization. Price $36.00 per year.

324.01
Asean Business Quarterly
Asia Research Pte Ltd, 2815, International Plaza, 10 Anson Rd, Singapore 2. Order from Asia Research Pte Ltd, PO Box 91, Alexandra Post Office, Singapore 3. Telephone 2221545/6. Telex RS21374 PRINTIM.

Quarterly journal. Covers economic and business developments in Southeast Asian nations. Includes economic indicators and forecasts. Price $34.00 per year.

324.02
Asia & Pacific 1981
World of Information, 21 Gold St, Saffron Walden, Essex, England CB10 1EJ. Telephone Saffron Walden 21150 (Std. 0799 21150). Telex England 817197 a/b Jaxpress G.

Annual book. Contains analysis of commercial economic, political, and social developments in Asia and the Pacific including Australasia. Includes chapters on every country. Price $43.00. ISBN 0-904439-22-4.

324.03
Asia Electronics Union
Dempa Publications, Inc, 380 Madison Ave, New York, NY 10017. Telephone (212) 867-0900.

Monthly journal. Covers Asian electronics industry. Reports on exports. Price $60.00 per year air mail.

325
Asia Letter
Asia Letter Ltd, PO Box 54149, Los Angeles, CA 90054. Telephone (213) 322-4222.

Weekly newsletter. Covers economic, social, and political developments in Asian countries pertinent to companies doing business in the region. Price $100.00 per year.

326
Asian Agricultural Survey
Asian Development Bank, PO Box 789, Manila, Phillippines 2800. Order from University of Washington Press, Seattle, WA 98105; or University of Tokyo Press, 7-3-1 Hongo, Bunkyo-ku. Telephone (206) 543-8870.

Book. Surveys agricultural activity in Asian countries. Price $10.00 for hardbound; $5.00 for paperbound.

326.01
Asian Building & Construction
Far East Trade Press Ltd, Room 1913, Hanglung Centre, 2–20 Paterson St, Causeway Bay, Hong Kong, China. Telephone 5-760775. Telex 83434.

Monthly magazine. Reports on building and construction in Asia. Price £24.00 per year.

326.02
Asian Business
Far East Trade Press Ltd, Room 1913, Hanglung Centre, 2-20 Paterson St, Causeway Bay, Hong Kong, China. Telephone 5-760775. Telex 83434.

Monthly magazine. Reports on Asian business developments. Includes information on manufacturing and trade. Price $25.00 per year.

327
Asian Economy—Economic and Social Survey of Asia and the Pacific
United Nations Publications, United Nations Plz, Room A-3315, New York, NY 10017. Telephone (212) 754-8302.

Report. Provides statistics and other economic information for Asia and the Far East. Price available on request.

328
Asian Industrial Development News
United Nations Economic & Social Commission for Asia & the Pacific, United Nations Bldg, Bangkok 2, Thailand. Telephone 813544.

Publication. Covers industrial development in Asia. Price $1.50.

329
Asian Wall Street Journal
Dow Jones & Co, Inc, 22 Cortlandt St, New York, NY 10007. Order from Dow Jones & Co, Inc, PO Box 300, Princeton, NJ 08540. Telephone (212) 285-5000.

Daily newspaper. Discusses business and financial news affecting Asian business and trade. Includes US and foreign stock prices and a review of international money and commodities markets. Price $206.00 per year.

330
Asia/Pacific Compensation Survey
Business International Corp, 1 Dag Hammarskjold Plz, New York, NY 10017. Telephone (212) 750-6300.

Annual computerized comparisons of wages, fringe benefits, and allowances in ten Asian countries, broken down by managerial, technical, sales, clerical, and blue collar job classifications. Price $980.00 per series; $165.00 per country.

331
Asia Research Bulletin
Asia Research Pte Ltd, 2815, International Plaza, 10 Anson Rd, Singapore 2. Order from Asia Research Pte Ltd, PO Box 91, Alexandra Post Office, Singapore 3. Telephone 2221545/6. Telex RS21374 PRINTIM.

Five separate monthly reports. Covers Asian economic developments. Includes information on economic policies, manufacturing, trade, commodities, and energy. Notes political trends. Price $193.20 per year.

332
ASI Microfiche Library
Congressional Information Service, Inc, 4520 E-W Highway, Suite 800, Washington, DC 20014. Telephone (301) 654-1550.

Microfiche file, with monthly updates. Collects federal statistical publications. Price $10,295.00 per year.

333
Aslib Directory, Volume 1
Aslib, 3 Belgrave Sq, London, England SWIX 8PL. Telephone (44) (01) 235-5050. Telex 23667.

Book. Lists sources of information in science, technology, and commerce in Great Britain. Price £33.00. ISBN 0-85142-104-0.

333.01
Aslib Directory, Volume 2
Aslib, 3 Belgrave Sq, London, England SWIX 8PL. Telephone (44)(01) 235-5050. Telex 23667.

Book. Lists information sources in the social sciences, medicine, and the humanities. Price £48.00. ISBN 0-85142-130-X.

333.02
ASPA Handbook of Personnel and Industrial Relations
Bureau of National Affairs, Inc, 1231 25th St, NW, Washington, DC 20037. Telephone (202) 452-4276.

Book. Covers theory and practice of personnel and industrial relations. Exhibits, figures, tables, topical, and name index. Price $45.00. ISBN 0-87179-307-5.

334
Associated Equipment Distributors (AED) Edition of Construction Equipment Buyers Guide
Associated Equipment Distributors, 615 W 22nd St, Oak Brook, IL 60521. Telephone (312) 654-0650.

Annual book. Offers a guide to US and Canadian distributors of construction equipment and the manufacturers they represent. Gives manufacturer and product listings. Price $20.00 per copy.

335
Association & Society Manager Magazine
Brentwood Publishing Corp, 825 S Barrington Ave, Los Angeles, CA 90049. Telephone (213) 826-8388.

Bimonthly magazine. Edited for the managers of trade and professional societies and associations. Price $30.00 per year.

336
Associated Industries (AI) Bulletin
Associated Industries of New York State, Inc, 150 State St, Albany, NY 12207. Telephone (518) 465-3547.

Irregular reports. Provides news on labor issues and benefits and taxation in New York State. Price free of charge.

337
Associated Industries (AI) Update
Associated Industries of New York State, Inc, 150 State St, Albany, NY 12207. Telephone (518) 465-3547.

Irregularly issued newsletter. Covers the activities of the Associated Industries of New York State. Notes New York State labor, business, and tax news. Price free of charge.

338
Association for Comparative Economic Studies (ACES) Bulletin
Assn for Comparative Economic Studies, c/o Roger Skurski, Dept of Economics, University of Notre Dame, Notre Dame, IN 46556. Telephone (219) 283-7340.

Journal. Publishes studies of economic systems, planning, development, and research. Price $25.00.

339
Association Management
American Society of Assn Executives, 1575 Eye St NW, Washington, DC 20005. Telephone (202) 626-ASAE.

Monthly magazine. Contains information on trends in the management of associations. Price $15.00 per year.

340
Association Management Scope
Lawrence-Leiter and Co, 427 W 12th St, Kansas City, MO 64105. Telephone (816) 474-8340.

Semiannual newsletter. Provides information on management methods for trade, professional, service, and volunteer associations. Price free of charge.

340.01
Association of Executive Recruiting Consultants: **1980 Directory**
R R Bowker Co, 1180 Ave of the Americas, New York, NY 10036. Order from R R Bowker Co, PO Box 1807, Ann Arbor, MI 48106. Telephone (212) 764-5100.

Directory. Lists 58 member firms of Association of Executive Recruiting Consultants. Gives key information and specialization areas, and brief profiles of senior management and professional recruiting personnel of each firm. Price $38.50. ISBN 0-8352-1256-4. ISSN 0195-6981.

341
Association of Scientific, Technical and Managerial Staffs (ASTMS) Journal
Assn of Scientific Technical and Managerial Staffs, 10/26A Jamestown Rd, London, England NW1 7DT. Telephone (44) (01) 267 4422.

Bimonthly report. Provides news of ASTMS activities and policies. Price free of charge to members.

342
Association Taxation
Chamber of Commerce of the US, 1615 H St, NW, Washington, DC 20062. Telephone (202) 659-6231.

Monthly newsletter. Reports developments at the Internal Revenue Service, in the courts, and in Congress that affect the tax-exempt status of associations and chambers of commerce. Price $25.00 per year.

343
Atlanta Business Chronicle
Cordovan Corp, 5314 Bingle Rd, Houston, TX 77092. Order from Atlanta Business Chronicle, 1750 Century Circle, Atlanta, GA 30345. Telephone (404) 325-2442.

Weekly newspaper. Contains feature articles on various segments of Atlanta business. Price $24.00 per year.

343.01
Atlantic Anglo American Trade News
American Chamber of Commerce (United Kingdom), 75 Brook St, London, England W1Y 2EB. Telephone (44) (01) 493-0381.

Monthly magazine. Discusses British-American trade subjects, including new products, airline routes, company news, and tax legislation. Notes the activities of the American Chamber of Commerce (United Kingdom). Price $30.00.

344
Atlantic Economic Journal
Atlantic Economic Society, Box 258, Worden, IL 62097.

Journal. Discusses general economic trends and research. Includes such topics as taxation, inflation and world trade. Provides book reviews. Price $50.00 per year, $60.00 overseas..

345
Atlantic Report
Atlantic Provinces Economic Council, One Sackville Pl, Halifax, NS, Canada B3J 1K1. Telephone (902) 422-6516.

Quarterly report. Analyzes economic conditions and trends in the Atlantic provinces of Canada. Price $12.00 per year. (Subscriptions available only to libraries.) ISSN 0004-6841.

346
Atlas of Ireland
St Martin's Press, Inc, 175 5th Ave, New York, NY 10010. Telephone (212) 674-5151.

Book. Contains 250 color maps detailing economic, physical, social, and demographic data on Ireland. Price $99.50.

346.01
Auber Bibliography
West Virginia University, Bureau of Business Research, Morgantown, WV 26506. Telephone (304) 293-5837.

Annual bibliography. Lists more than 2300 papers, reports, journals, and books on economics, business, agriculture, and labor. Price $12.50. ISSN 0066-8767.

346.02
Audio Visual Communications
United Business Publications, Inc, 475 Park Ave S, New York, NY 10016. Telephone (212) 725-2300.

Monthly magazine. Reports on audiovisual media news. Includes annual Buyer's Guide and Who's Who. Price $13.50 per year.

347
Audiovisual Market Place
R R Bowker Co, 1180 Ave of the Americas, New York, NY 10036. Order from R R Bowker Co, PO Box 1807, Ann Arbor, MI 48106. Telephone (212) 764-5100.

Annual directory. Lists producers, suppliers, and services for audiovisual materials. Covers in a reference section such topics as literature, associations, funding sources, and government agencies. Price $29.95 paperbound. ISBN 0-8352-1201-7. ISSN 0067-0553.

348
Audit Bureau of Circulations (ABC) Factbook
Audit Bureau of Circulations, 123 N Wacker Dr, Chicago, IL 60606. Telephone (312) 236-7994.

Annual book. Provides facts about the Audit Bureau of Circulations and related industry activities. Price $15.00. ISSN 0098-2520.

349
Audit Bureau of Circulations (ABC) News Bulletin
Audit Bureau of Circulations, 123 N Wacker Dr, Chicago, IL 60606. Telephone (312) 236-7994.

Quarterly magazine. Presents news about the Audit Bureau of Circulations and related industry activities. Price free to members.

350
Auerbach Applications Software Reports
Auerbach Publishers, Inc, 6560 N Park Dr, Pennsauken, NJ 08109. Telephone (609) 662-2070. Telex 831 464.

Book, plus monthly reports. Evaluates applications software products. Provides pricing, operational characteristics, and hardware requirements. Price $325.00.

351
*Auerbach Business Minicomputer
Systems Reports*
Auerbach Publishers, Inc, 6560 N Park
Dr, Pennsauken, NJ 08109. Telephone
(609) 662-2070. Telex: 831 464.
Two-volume set, plus monthly reports.
Discusses business minicomputer sys-
tems. Compares specifications, mainte-
nance and support policies, and prices.
Price $410.00.

352
*Auerbach Buyers' Guide to Business
Minicomputer Systems*
Auerbach Publishers, Inc, 6560 N Park
Dr, Pennsauken, NJ 08109. Telephone
(609) 662-2070. Telex 831 464.
Semiannual book. Analyzes performance
capabilities and specifications of major US
business minicomputer systems. Describes several classes of systems, and includes directory of suppliers. Price
$59.00.

353
*Auerbach Buyers' Guide to Data
Base/Data Communications Software*
Auerbach Publishers, Inc, 6560 N Park
Dr, Pennsauken, NJ 08109. Telephone
(609) 662-2070. Telex 831 464.
Annual book. Provides information on
data base systems and data communica-
tions control. Notes computer's use in in-
formation storage and retrieval. Price
$59.00.

355
*Auerbach Buyers' Guide to Word
Processing*
Auerbach Publishers, Inc, 6560 N Park
Dr, Pennsauken, NJ 08109. Telephone
(609) 662-2070. Telex 831 464.
Semiannual book. Reports on the word
processing industry. Analyzes different
systems and applications. Specification
charts. Price $59.00.

356
*Auerbach Computer Programming
Management*
Auerbach Publishers, Inc, 6560 N Park
Dr, Pennsauken, NJ 08109. Telephone
(609) 662-2070. Telex: 831 464.
Book, plus bimonthly reports. Focuses on
computer programming management,
standards, and techniques. Price $175.00.

357
Auerbach Data Base Management
Auerbach Publishers, Inc, 6560 N Park
Dr, Pennsauken, NJ 08109. Telephone
(609) 662-2070. Telex 831 464.
Book, plus bimonthly reports. Focuses on
management of data base systems. Discusses components, design, and current
trends. Price $225.00.

358
*Auerbach Data Center Operations
Management*
Auerbach Publishers, Inc, 6560 N Park
Dr, Pennsauken, NJ 08109. Telephone
(609) 662-2070. Telex 831 464.
Books, plus bimonthly reports. Discusses
data center operations management, emphasizing problems. Includes such topics
as computer performance measurement
and operations control. Price $210.00.

359
*Auerbach Data Communications
Management*
Auerbach Publishers, Inc, 6560 N Park
Dr, Pennsauken, NJ 08109. Telephone
(609) 662-2070. Telex 831 464.
Book, plus bimonthly reports. Analyzes
data communications methods and pro-
ducts, with emphasis on systems manage-
ment. Price $175.00.

360
*Auerbach Data Communications,
Minicomputers and Data Handling
Reports*
Auerbach Publishers, Inc, 6560 N Park
Dr, Pennsauken, NJ 08109. Telephone
(609) 662-2070. Telex 831 464.
Five-volume set, plus monthly reports.
Evaluates data communications systems
and products, minicomputers, and data
handling equipment. Includes informa-
tion on peripherals, terminals, and mi-
crocomputers. Price $850.00.

361
*Auerbach Data Communications
Notebook*
Auerbach Publishers, Inc, 6560 N Park
Dr, Pennsauken, NJ 08109. Telephone
(609) 662-2070. Telex 831 464.
Two-volume set, plus monthly reports.
Covers 1200 data communications sys-
tems and devices, including modems,
multiplexors, and data entry equipment.
Explains data communications functions,
identifies components, evaluates products
and services. Price $350.00.

362
Auerbach Data Communications Reports
Auerbach Publishers, Inc, 6560 N Park
Dr, Pennsauken, NJ 08109. Telephone
(609) 662-2070. Telex 831 464.
Three-volume set, plus monthly reports.
Covers data communications equipment,
including facsimile equipment, audio-
response systems, modems, and multi-
plexors. Price $745.00.

363
Auerbach Data Processing Management
Auerbach Publishers, Inc, 6560 N Park
Dr, Pennsauken, NJ 08109. Telephone
(609) 662-2070. Telex 831 464.
Three-volume set, plus monthly reports.
Deals with data processing installation.
Discusses operations, technology, man-
agement. Tables, charts, and graphs.
Price $285.00.

364
Auerbach EDP Notebook/International
Auerbach Publishers, Inc, 6560 N Park
Dr, Pennsauken, NJ 08109. Telephone
(609) 662-2070. Telex 831 464.
Four-volume set, plus monthly reports.
Describes electronic data processing products in the US, Europe, and Japan. Includes product analysis, user reactions,
specification charts, and prices; and such
devices as minicomputers, data communications equipment and software. Price
$425.00.

365
*Auerbach Executive Checklist for
Finance and Administration*
Auerbach Publishers, Inc, 6560 N Park
Dr, Pennsauken, NJ 08109. Telephone
(609) 662-2070. Telex 831 464.
Book. Provides information for corporate
financial administrators. Includes such
topics as inventory control, management
information, credit control, and accounting systems. Price $145.00.

366
*Auerbach Executive Checklist for
Production*
Auerbach Publishers, Inc, 6560 N Park
Dr, Pennsauken, NJ 08109. Telephone
(609) 662-2070. Telex 831 464.
Book. Discusses production topics, in-
cluding production assets, control, and
planning. Price $89.00.

367

Auerbach Executive Checklist for Sales and Marketing

Auerbach Publishers, Inc, 6560 N Park Dr, Pennsauken, NJ 08109. Telephone (609) 662-2070. Telex 831 464.

Book. Contains sales and marketing information. Includes such topics as communications and planning and managing sales people. Price $89.00.

368

Auerbach Executive Checklist for the Chief Executive Officer

Auerbach Publishers, Inc, 6560 N Park Dr, Pennsauken, NJ 08109. Telephone (609) 662-2070. Telex 831 464.

Book. Deals with corporate management, assets, profits, costs, and labor relations. Price $145.00.

369

Auerbach General-Purpose Minicomputer Reports

Auerbach Publishers, Inc, 6560 N Park Dr, Pennsauken, NJ 08109. Telephone (609) 662-2070. Telex 831 464.

Two-volume set, plus monthly reports. Contains reports on general purpose minicomputers. Compares purchase prices and maintenance rates. Price $410.00.

370

Auerbach/Infotech International's Computer State of the Art Reports

Auerbach Publishers, Inc, 6560 N Park Dr, Pennsauken, NJ 08109. Telephone (609) 662-2070. Telex 831 464.

Series of reports. Covers numerous aspects of computing, including minicomputer systems, software engineering, microprocessors, and future systems. Price $1295.00.

371

Auerbach Input/Output Reports

Auerbach Publishers, Inc, 6560 N Park Dr, Pennsauken, NJ 08109. Telephone (609) 662-2070. Telex 831 464.

Three-volume set, plus monthly reports. Provides information on computer peripheral and data handling equipment and on microform equipment and processes. Price $625.00.

372

Auerbach Microfilm Reports

Auerbach Publishers, Inc, 6560 N Park Dr, Pennsauken, NJ 08109. Telephone (609) 662-2070. Telex 831 464.

Book, plus monthly reports. Contains information on new microfilm equipment and processes, including retrieval systems, duplicators, cameras, and computer output microfilm. Price $225.00.

373

Auerbach Minicomputer Notebook/International

Auerbach Publishers, Inc, 6560 N Park Dr, Pennsauken, NJ 08109. Telephone (609) 662-2070. Telex 831 464.

Two-volume set, plus monthly reports. Reports on major minicomputer systems of the US, Europe, and Japan, including business minicomputers, office computers, and intelligent terminals. Price $245.00.

374

Auerbach Peripherals and Data Handling Reports

Auerbach Publishers, Inc, 6560 N Park Dr, Pennsauken, NJ 08109. Telephone (609) 662-2070. Telex 831 464.

Two-volume set, plus monthly reports. Covers over 2000 pieces of data processing equipment, including key-to-storage systems, financial terminals, and tape drives. Tables and charts. Price $460.00.

375

Auerbach Software Reports

Auerbach Publishers, Inc, 6560 N Park Dr, Pennsauken, NJ 08109. Telephone (609) 662-2070. Telex 831 464.

Two-volume set, plus monthly reports. Evaluates applications and systems software packages. Price $475.00.

376

Auerbach Standard EDP Reports

Auerbach Publishers, Inc, 6560 N Park Dr, Pennsauken, NJ 08109. Telephone (609) 662-2070. Telex 831 464.

Nine-volume set, plus monthly reports. Analyzes and compares large, medium, and small general purpose computers, business minicomputer systems, system software, and standard peripherals. Includes prices. Price $2195.00.

377

Auerbach Systems Development Management

Auerbach Publishers, Inc, 6560 N Park Dr, Pennsauken, NJ 08109. Telephone (609) 662-2070. Telex 831 464.

Book, plus bimonthly reports. Covers all aspects of computer systems development and design, including systems specifications and implementation and information systems analysis. Price $210.00.

378

Auerbach Systems Software Reports

Auerbach Publishers, Inc, 6560 N Park Dr, Pennsauken, NJ 08109. Telephone (609) 662-2070. Telex 831 464.

Book, plus monthly reports. Evaluates systems software packages, input-output capabilities, and maintenance support. Price $325.00.

379

Auerbach Time Sharing Reports

Auerbach Publishers, Inc, 6560 N Park Dr, Pennsauken, NJ 08109. Telephone (609) 662-2070. Telex 831 464.

Book, plus bimonthly reports. Gives time-sharing service rates, equipment, and applications. Includes specification charts and company records. Price $295.00.

380

Australia and New Zealand (ANZ) Bank Business Indicators

Australia & New Zealand Banking Group Ltd, 55 Collins St, Melbourne, Vic 3000, Australia.

Monthly magazine. Contains data on New Zealand's and Australia's bank business indicators. Price free of charge.

382

Australia at a Glance Cat No 1309.0, latest edition

Australian Bureau of Statistics, Box 10, Belconnen, ACT 2616, Australia. Order from Australian Government Publishing Service, PO Box 84, Canberra, ACT 2600, Australia.

Annual booklet. Covers Australia's population, domestic products, government finance, mining, building, labor and trade. Price free of charge.

383

Australian Accountant

Australian Society of Accountants, 170 Queen St, Melbourne, Vic 3000, Australia. Telephone (61) (03) 6024466.

Monthly magazine (except January). Gives Australian accounting and business news. Offers a supplement of professional notices. Price $25.00 per year.

384

Australian Advertising Rate and Data Service

Thomson Publications Pty Ltd, 47 Chippen St, PO Box 65, Chippendale, NSW 2008, Australia. Telephone 699-6731. Telex TPAS AA22226.

Five periodically updated books, with loose-leaf supplements. Provide data on advertising in Australian newspapers; consumer, business, rural, and international press; and on radio and television. Include data on rates, mechanicals, personnel, and deadlines. Price $1248.00 (Australian) per year.

386

Australian Bankruptcy Bulletin

Bankruptcy Trustees' & Liquidators' Assn of Australia, Box 129, GPO Sydney NSW, 2001 Australia. Telephone (61) (02) 233-6922.

Quarterly report. Covers matters connected with the Australian Bankruptcy Act and acts of various companies. Price $30.00 per year.

387

Australian Building and Construction News

John Jackson & Associates Pty Ltd, Box A, 771 Sydney S, NSW 2000, Australia.

Monthly newspaper. Pertains to the Australian building and construction industry. Provides statistical analysis of flow of funds and notes previous month's developments in all projects. Price $176 (Australian) per year.

388

Australian Business Law Review

Law Book Co, Ltd, 31 Market St, Sydney, NSW Australia 2000. Telephone (61) (02) 290 1299.

Bimonthly report. Contains commentaries on legislation affecting banking, investment, industrial relations, insurance, and taxation in Australia and New Zealand. Price $48.50. ISSN 0310-1053.

389

Australian Capital Territory Statistical Summary Cat No 1307.0

Australian Bureau of Statistics, Box 10, Belconnen, ACT 2616, Australia. Order from Australian Government Publishing Service, PO Box 84, Canberra, ACT 2600, Australia. Telephone (61) (062) 52 7911.

Annual report. Presents statistical data on ACT's population, employment, housing, economy, climate, and social conditions. Chronological table of events and ordinances promulgated since 1974. Price free of charge.

390

Australian Council of Trade Unions Bulletin

Australian Council of Trade Unions, 254 La Trobe St, Melbourne, Vic 3000, Australia. Telephone (61) (03) 347-3925.

Bimonthly newspaper. Carries news affecting trade unions in Australia. Contains articles on government action, legislation, wages, arbitration, and the economy. Price available on request. ISSN 0314-2868.

391

Australian Corporate Affairs Reports

Commerce Clearing House, Inc, 4025 W Peterson Ave, Chicago, IL 60646. Telephone (312) 583-8500.

Two loose-leaf books, plus monthly reports. Interprets regulations applying to the operation of companies doing business in Australian states. Price $500.00 per year.

392

Australian Dept of the Treasury. Round-Up of Economic Statistics

Australian Government Publishing Service, Publishing Branch, PO Box 84, Canberra, ACT 2600, Australia. Telephone (61) (62) 95 4411. Telex AA62013.

Publication. Presents economic statistics on Australia. Price $8.50 per 12 issues.

393

The Australian Director

Institute of Directors in Australia, 16 O'Connell St, Sydney, NSW 2000, Australia. Telephone (61) (02) 231-6355.

Bimonthly journal. Discusses topics of interest to Australian business directors, including economic trends and business legislation and notes news of the Australian Institute of Directors. Price $2.50 (Australian) per copy.

394

Australian Directory of Exports

Peter Isaacson Publications, 46-49 Porter St, Prahran, Vic 3181, Australia. Telephone (61) (03) 51 8431. Telex 30880.

Annual book. Surveys Australia's major industries. Lists products for export, exporters, and services available to overseas companies. Price $28.50.

395

Australian Economic Review

University of Melbourne, Institute of Applied Economic & Social Research, Parkville, Vic 3052, Australia. Telephone (61) (603) 341-5295.

Quarterly. Discusses recent Australian economic developments, international economic trends, and foreign trade. Includes economic forecasts. Price $74.00 (Australian) per year. ISSN 004-9018.

396

Australian Economy: Economic Advisory Service

W D Scott & Company, 100 Pacific Hwy, North Sydney, NSW 2060, Australia. Telephone (61) (02) 929-0033.

Biweekly bulletins, plus special reports. Deal with the impact of major economic events on business in Australia. Price $200.00 (Australian) per year.

397

Australian Electronics Engineering

Thomson Publications (Australia) Pty Ltd, 47 Chippen St, PO Box 65, Chippendale, NSW 2008, Australia. Telephone 699-6731. Telex TPAS AA22226.

Monthly magazine. Reports on new electronics engineering products, systems, techniques, and research. Includes information on telecommunication engineering; also covers Australian news. Price $43.00 (Australian) per year.

398

Australian Estate and Gift Duty Reports

Commerce Clearing House, Inc, 4025 W Peterson Ave, Chicago, IL 60646. Telephone (312) 583-8500.

Two loose-leaf volumes, plus monthly reports. Cover Australian federal and state gift duties and estate taxes. Price $310.00 per year.

399

Australia Newsletter

Sydney Morrell & Co., Inc, 152 E 78th St, New York, NY 10021. Telephone (212) 249-7255. Telex 62396.

Monthly newsletter. Reports on Australian business and economics news, foreign trade activity, and new plant construction. Price free of charge.

400

Australian Exports, Country by Commodity **Cat No 5411.0**

Australian Bureau of Statistics, Box 10, Belconnen, ACT 2616, Australia. Order from Australian Government Publishing Service, PO Box 84, Canberra, ACT 2600, Australia. Telephone (61) (062) 52 7911.

Annual report. Gives the quantity and value of Australian exports to approximately 190 countries. Provides a detailed description of each export item. Price $8.65 (Australian).

401

Australian Federal Tax Reports

Commerce Clearing House, Inc, 4025 W Peterson Ave, Chicago, IL 60646. Telephone (312) 583-8500.

Seven loose-leaf books, plus biweekly reports. Explore Australian federal tax system and basic tax statute. Price $750.00 per year.

402

Australian Hospital

Peter Isaacson Publications, 46-49 Porter St, Prahran, Vic 3181, Australia. Telephone (61) (03) 51 8431. Telex 30880.

Monthly newspaper (January-February issue combined) geared to hospital administrators in Australia. Price $15.00 per year.

403

Australian Hospitals and Health Services Yearbook

Peter Isaacson Publications, 46-49 Porter St, Prahran, Vic 3181, Australia. Telephone (61) (03) 51 8431. Telex 30880.

Annual book. Lists Australian public and private hospitals, institutions for mentally ill and handicapped, and nursing homes. Price $28.50.

404

Australian Imports, Country by Commodity **Cat No 5414.0**

Australian Bureau of Statistics, Box 10, Belconnen, ACT 2616, Australia. Order from Australian Government Publishing Service, PO Box 84, Canberra, ACT 2600, Australia. Telephone (61) (062) 52 7911.

Annual report. Shows Australia's imports by country of origin. Notes quantity, value, and description for each. Five-year tables. Price $12.75 (Australian).

405

Australian Investment and Economic Newsletter

National Bank of Australasia Ltd, 500 Bourke St, Melbourne, Vic 3000, Australia. Telephone (61) (03) 63 0471. Telex 30241.

Weekly newsletter. Furnishes material on Australian economic, financial, and investment developments. Price free of charge.

406

Australian Journal of Agricultural Economics

Australian Agricultural Economic Society, Suite 302, Clunies Ross House, 191 Royal Parade, Parkville, Vic 3052, Australia. Telephone 347-1277.

Magazine issued three times per year. Provides information on agricultural economics, with emphasis on Australia. Includes agricultural prices and interest rates. Price free to members of the society.

407

Australian Key Business Directory

Dun & Bradstreet, Box 3224, Church St Station, New York, NY 10008. Telephone (212) 285-7346.

Annual book. Provides a directory to several thousand of the largest public and private businesses in Australia whose net worth is Australian $100,000. Price on request. Available to Dun & Bradstreet subscribers only.

408

Australian Market Guide

Dun & Bradstreet, Box 3224, Church St Station, New York, NY 10008. Telephone (212) 285-7346.

Biannual book. Contains over 130,000 listings of Australian manufacturers, wholesalers, retailers, and agents. Includes credit appraisal. Price on request. Available to Dun & Bradstreet subscribers only.

409

Australian Master Tax Guide

Commerce Clearing House, Inc, 4025 W Peterson Ave, Chicago, IL 60646. Telephone (312) 583-8500.

Book. Explains Australian income tax. Price $18.00.

410

Australian Meat & Live-stock Corp Annual Report

Australian Meat and Live-stock Corp, GPO Box 4129, Sydney, NSW 2001, Australia. Telephone (02) 267-9488. Telex AA 22887.

Annual report. Provides statistics on Australian domestic and export meat markets. Covers Australian Meat and Live-stock Corp activities. Price free of charge.

411

Australian Mining

Thomson Publications (Australia) Pty Ltd, 47 Chippen St, PO Box 65, Chippendale, NSW 2008, Australia. Telephone 699-6731. Telex TPAS AA22226.

Monthly magazine. Reports on Australian mining industries, including coal and metal mining. Notes mining technology developments. Price $68.00 (Australian) per year.

412

Australian Mining Year Book

Thomson Publications (Australia) Pty Ltd, 47 Chippen St, PO Box 65, Chippendale, NSW 2008, Australia. Telephone 699-6731. Telex TPAS AA22226.

Annual book. Provides information on the Australian mining industry. Includes an equipment buyers' guide, statistics, mine location maps, and a directory of companies operating in Australia. Price $25.00 (Australian).

413

Australian National Economic & Legislative Report

Commerce Clearing House, Inc, 4025 W Peterson Ave, Chicago, IL 60646. Telephone (312) 583-8500.

Loose-leaf book, plus weekly reports. Provides coverage of Australian economic and legislative developments. Includes economic statistics. Price $355.00 per year.

413.01

Australian Refrigeration, Air-Conditioning and Heating

Yaffa Publishing Group, 432-436 Elizabeth St, Surry Hills, NSW 2010, Australia. Order from Yaffa Publishing Group, GPO Box 606, Sydney, NSW 2001, Australia. Telephone (61) (02) 699-7861. Telex 21887.

Monthly magazine. Covers Australian refrigeration, air-conditioning, and heating industries. Pric available on request.

414

Australian Sales Tax Guide

CCH Australia Ltd, PO Box 230, North Ryde, NSW 2113, Australia. Telephone 583-8500.

Bimonthly loose-leaf volume. Provides a guide to Australian sales tax legislation, cases and rulings. Includes an index. Price $100.00 (Australian). ISBN 0909720 37 1.

415

Australian Securities Law Reports

Commerce Clearing House, Inc, 4025 W Peterson Ave, Chicago, IL 60646. Telephone (312) 583-8500.

Loose-leaf volume plus monthly reports. Reproduces full text of pertinent laws, regulations, court decisions, and related material pertaining to the securities industry in Australia. Price $360.00 per year.

416

Australian Stock Exchange Journal

Alan Davis Publishing Pty, Ltd, GPO Box 4560, Sydney NSW, 2001, Australia. Telephone (61) (02) 233-8433.

Monthly journal. Provides statistics for Australian stocks and other equity securities. Contains articles on Australian and international economic and financial issues. Price $18.00 (Australian) per year.

417

Australian Tax Cases

Commerce Clearing House, Inc, 4025 W Peterson Ave, Chicago, IL 60646. Telephone (312) 583-8500.

Loose-leaf volume, plus biweekly reports. Covers tax decisions of the High Court of Australia Administrative Boards and key decisions of the Supreme Court of New Zealand. Price $255.00 per year.

418

Australian Tax Review

Law Book Co, Ltd, 31 Market St, Sydney, NSW Australia 2000. Telephone (61) (02) 290 1299.

Quarterly report. Analyzes Australian taxes and customs duties. Price $42.50. ISSN 0311-094X

419

Australian Trade Practices Reports

Commerce Clearing House, Inc, 4025 W Peterson Ave, Chicago, IL 60646. Telephone (312) 583-8500.

Two loose-leaf books, plus monthly reports. Cover the rules, regulations, and standards governing trade practices and consumer protection under the Australian Trade Practices Act. Price $490.00 per year.

420

Australian Trading News

Australian Dept of Trade & Resources, PO Box 69, Commerce Court Postal Station, Toronto, Ont, Canada M5L 1B9. Telephone (416) 367-0783. Telex 06-219762.

Quarterly magazine. Reports on Australian industrial developments and products available for export. Price free of charge.

421

Australian Women's Wear and Clothing Industry News

Yaffa Publishing Group, GPO Box 606, Sydney, NSW 2001, Australia. Telephone (61) (02) 69 7861. Telex 21887.

Semimonthly newsletter. Reports on Australian women's clothing industry. Price $40.00 (Australian) per year.

422

Australia's International Engineering Exhibitions AIEE

Thomson Publications (Australia) Pty Ltd, 47 Chippen St, PO Box 65, Chippendale, NSW 2008, Australia. Telephone 699-6731. Telex TPAS AA22226.

Annual publication. Covers Australia's International Engineering Exhibition. Shows over 100 companies that participate in the industrial exhibition sponsored by the metal trades industry.

423

Automated Business Communications Program

International Data Corp, 214 3rd Ave, Waltham, MA 02254. Telephone (617) 890-3700. Telex 92-3401.

Continuous information service. Examines and reports on latest developments in automated office processing and communications equipment. Includes communication services. Price available on request.

424

Automatica

Pergamon Press, Inc, Maxwell House, Fairview Park, Elmsford, NY 10523. Telephone (914) 592-7700. Telex 13-7328.

Bimonthly magazine. Publishes research papers on design and control on systems, particularly automatic control. Stresses applications. Charts, tables, and graphs. Price $145.00 per year.

425

Automatic Tax Planner

Panel Publishers, 14 Plaza Rd, Greenvale, NY 11548. Telephone (516) 484-0006.

Two volume loose-leaf service, with quarterly supplements. Provides worksheets for tax planning. Covers corporate stock redemptions, tax-free exchanges, and corporate reorganizations. Price $110.00 per year. ISBN 0-916592-01-4.

426

Automobile Facts and Figures

Motor Vehicle Manufacturers' Assn of the US, 320 New Ctr Bldg, Detroit, MI 48202. Telephone (313) 872-4311.

Annual report. Provides statistical analysis of auto production and use. Price free of charge.

427

Automobile International

Johnston International Publishing Corp, 386 Park Ave S, New York, NY 10016. Telephone (212) 689-0120. Telex 66811 Jonst.

Report carries information on production, export, and registration of motor vehicles throughout the world. Price $50.00 per year.

428

Automobile Insurance

Commerce Clearing House, Inc, 4025 W Peterson Ave, Chicago, IL 60646. Telephone (312) 583-8500.

Loose-leaf book, plus biweekly report. Covers motor vehicle insurance decisions, including financial responsibility and compulsory and no-fault insurance. Price $425.00 per year.

429

Automotive Fleet

Bobit Publishing Co, 2500 Artesia Blvd, Redondo Beach, CA 90278. Telephone (213) 376-8788.

Monthly magazine. Discusses issues affecting passenger car fleets and the light truck industry. Price $15.00 per year.

430

Automotive Industries

Chilton Co, Chilton Way, Radnor, PA 19089. Telephone (215) 687-8200.

Monthly publication. Carries information on new automotive manufactured products, design, developments and production techniques. Price $25.00 per year.

431

Automotive Industries/International

Chilton Co, Chilton Way, Radnor, PA 19089. Telephone (215) 687-8200.

Monthly magazine. Provides information about international automotive manufacturing, design, engineering, production and marketing. Price $25.00 per year.

432
Automotive Marketer
Wadham Publications Ltd, 109 Vanderhoof Ave, Suite 101, Toronto, Ont, Canada M4G 2J2. Telephone (416) 425-9021.

Quarterly magazine. Discusses automotive aftermarket, including oil and gasoline, tires, repairs, maintenance, and equipment. Emphasizes Canadian news. Price $5.00 per copy.

433
Automotive Marketing
Chilton Co, Chilton Way, Radnor PA 19089. Telephone (215) 687-8200.

Monthly magazine. Covers buying and retailing of automotive parts. Price $24.00 per year.

434
Automotive News
Crain Automotive Group Inc, 965 E Jefferson Ave, Detroit, MI 48207. Telephone (313) 567-9520.

Weekly report. Covers new developments and statistics on production and sales of cars and trucks in the US and Canada. Price $35.00 per year.

434.01
Automotive, Spares & Accessories
Stokes & Lindley-Jones Ltd, Alverstock House, 21 Montpelier Row, Blackheath, London, England SE3 0SR. Telephone (01) 852-9865.

Biannual report. Provides information on British transport, spares, and accessories available for export. Price £25.00 for three years to qualified subscribers.

435
Autotrade
Morgan–Grampian Ltd, Morgan–Grampian House, Calderwood St, London, England SE18 6QH. Order from Morgan–Grampian Publishing Co, 2 Park Ave, New York, NY 10016. Telephone (44) (01) 855 7777. Telex 896238 MORGAN G. New York (212) 340-9700. Telex 425592 MGI UI.

Monthly magazine. Provides industry news for the auto supplies industry in Great Britain. Price $75.00 per year.

435.01
Autotransaction Industry Report
International Data Corp, 214 3rd Ave, Waltham, MA 02254. Telephone (617) 890-3700. Telex 92-3401.

Semimonthly newsletter. Covers key issues and events in computer automation products, services, and regulations. Price available on request.

436
Aviation Cases
Commerce Clearing House, Inc, 4025 W Peterson Ave, Chicago, IL 60646. Telephone (312) 583-8500.

Fourteen books. Cover court decisions on federal aviation regulations. Include a discussion of insurance and liability problems. Price $47.50 per volume.

437
Aviation Daily
Ziff-Davis Publishing Co, 1156 15th St NW, Washington, DC 20005. Telephone (202) 293-3400.

Daily newsletter. Covers trade news and trends in the aviation industry. Price $610.00 per year.

437.01
Aviation Europe
Sell's Publications Ltd, Sell's House, 39 E St, Epsom Surrey, England KT17 1BQ. Telephone Epsom 26376. Telex 21792 A/B Mono K LDN.

Book. Covers major European aerospace groups and component manufacturers and suppliers of all products and services for aircraft constructors, designers of defense systems, and end users in commercial and service aviation. Price £20.00.

438
Aviation Law Reports
Commerce Clearing House, Inc, 4025 W Peterson Ave, Chicago, IL 60646. Telephone (312) 583-8500

Four loose-leaf volumes, plus monthly reports. Carry full coverage of federal aviation controls, with statutes, regulations, decisions, and air liabilities. Price $655.00 per year.

439
Aviation Monthly
HBJ Newsletter, Inc. 757 Thrid Ave, New York, NY 10017. Telephone (212) 888-3335.

Monthly newsletter. Discusses aviation safety. Reports on commercial and private accidents. Price $27.00 per year.

440
Aviation News/Airmarket
Peter Isaacson Publications, 46-49 Porter St, Prahran, Vic 3181, Australia. Telephone (61)(03) 51 8431. Telex 30880.

Monthly newspaper directed at Australian aviation and aerospace industries. Includes news of commercial airlines and military aircraft. Price $15.00 per year.

441
Aviation Week & Space Technology
McGraw-Hill Publications Co, 1221 Ave of the Americas, New York, NY 10020. Telephone (212) 997-1221. Telex TWX 7105814879 WUI 62555.

Weekly magazine. Reports on aerospace industry's technical and market developments. Includes material on air transport, commercial and military aircraft, avionics, and space industries. Price $47.00 per year.

442
Aviation Week & Space Technology Marketing Directory Issue
McGraw-Hill Book Co, Hightstown-Princeton Rd, Hightstown, NJ 08520. Telephone (609) 448-1700. Telex 843449.

Annual directory. Provides a guide to aerospace products. Includes products for air transport, commercial aviation, avionics, military aircraft, and space industries. Price $4.00.

443
Ayer Directory of Publications
Ayer Press, 1 Bala Ave, Bala Cynwyd, PA 19004. Telephone (215) 664-6205.

Annual book. Lists US, US territory, and Canadian newspapers, magazines, and trade publications. Includes names of editor, publisher and national advertising manager, address, periodicity, circulation, and advertising rates. Price $66.00.

444
Babson's Investment & Barometer Letter
Babson's Reports, Inc, Wellesley, MA 02181. Telephone (617) 235-0900.

Weekly newsletter lists buy, hold, and sell options on promising stocks. Reports on current market activity and reviews companies in the news. Subscription includes an annual forecast issue. Price $96.00 per year.

445
Babson's Washington Forecast Letter
Babson's Reports, Inc, Wellesley Hills, MA 02181. Telephone (617) 235-0900.

Weekly newsletter. Interprets and forecasts the impact of federal legislation in economic, environmental, social, and other areas. Price $36.00 per year.

446

Backlog of Orders for Aerospace Companies

US Dept of Commerce, Bureau of the Census, Washington, DC 20233. Telephone (202) 449-1600.

Quarterly report, with annual summary. Presents data on the backlog of orders, net new orders, and net sales reported by manufacturers of complete aircraft, space vehicles, missiles, and selected parts. Price $4.75 per year.

447

Bacon's International Publicity Checker

Bacon's Publishing Co, 14 E Jackson Blvd, Chicago, IL 60604. Telephone (312) 922-8419.

Annual loose-leaf book. Provides publicity guide to western European markets. Enables subscriber to reach over 7500 business, trade, and industrial publications, plus over 600 newspapers in 15 countries. Price $120.00.

448

Bacon's Publicity Checker

Bacon's Publishing Co, 14 E Jackson Blvd, Chicago, IL 60604. Telephone (312) 922-8419.

Two annual loose-leaf books, with quarterly revisions. List over 4000 business, trade, industrial, professional, farm, and consumer magazines that use publicity material. Include list 1815 daily and 7429 weekly newspapers. Price $110.00.

449

Baker Library. Core Collection, an Author & Subject Guide

Harvard University, Graduate School of Business Adm, Baker Library, Soldiers Field, Boston, MA 02163. Telephone (617) 495-6405.

Annual index. Covers 4000 books in Baker Library's reading room collection, with emphasis on recent titles. Price $15.00.

451

Balance of Payments Cat No 5301-0

Australian Bureau of Statistics, Box 10 Belconnen, ACT 2616, Australia. Order from Australian Government Publishing Service, PO Box 84, Canberra, ACT 2600, Australia. Telephone (61) (062) 52 7911.

Annual report. Shows Australia's and international balance of payments. Includes the value of principal imports and exports. Price $1.50 (Australian).

451.01

Balance of Payments: Global Data

European Community Information Service, 2100 M St NW, Suite 707, Washington, DC 20037. Telephone (202) 862-9500. Telex 248455.

Quarterly publication. Gives global balance of payments data. Price $10.50.

452

Balance of Payments Reports

Commerce Clearing House, Inc, 4025 W Peterson Ave, Chicago, IL 60646. Telephone (312) 583-8500.

One loose-leaf volume, plus monthly reports. Discusses proposals designed to produce favorable balance of payment situations. Price $225.00 per year.

454

Ball State Business Review

Ball State University, College of Business, Muncie, IN 47306. Telephone (317) 285-5926.

Biannual journal. Presents articles on economics, management, higher education, taxation, employment, accounting finance, marketing, data processing, and other business-related topics. Price free of charge.

454.01

Ball State Journal for Business Educators

Ball State University, College of Business, Muncie, IN 47306. Telephone (317) 285-5926.

Biannual journal. Contains articles on business and business education topics. Price free of charge.

455

B & T Advertising Marketing & Media Weekly

Greater Publications Pty Ltd, GPO Box 2608, Sydney, 2001, Australia. Telephone (61) (02) 61 8143.

Weekly magazine. Reports on the Australian radio, television, advertising, market research, newspapers, and magazines. Price $55.00 per year.

456

B & T Yearbook

Greater Publications Pty Ltd, GPO Box 2608, Sydney, 2001, Australia. Telephone (61) (02) 61 8143.

Annual book. Provides information on the Australian radio and television industry, newspapers and magazines, advertising and market research. Price available on request.

458

Bank and Quotation Record

National News Service, Inc, 4 Water St, Arlington, MA 02174. Telephone (617) 643-7900.

Monthly report designed for the professional investor. Lists quotations and ranges of all listed stocks, including over-the-counter securities. Price $110.00 per year.

459

Bank Auditing & Accounting Report

Warren, Gorham & Lamont, Inc, 210 S St, Boston, MA 02111. Telephone (617) 423-2020.

Monthly report. Contains information on bank financial management, including auditing, accounting, controls, budgeting, and systems. Price $64.00 per year.

460

Bank Automation Newsletter

Warren, Gorham & Lamont, Inc, 210 S St, Boston, MA 02111. Telephone (617) 423-2020.

Monthly newsletter. Reports on bank electronic data processing services and products, including electronic funds transfer systems. Price $72.00 per year.

461

Bank Board Letter

Director Publications, Inc, 408 Olive St, St Louis, MO 63102. Telephone (314) 421-5445.

Monthly newsletter. Stresses topics of concern to bank directors and bank management such as bank stock trading, loans to political candidates, and federal bank regulation. Price $37.00 per year.

461.01

Bank Director

International Banktrends, Inc, 910 16th St, NW, Washington, DC 20006. Order from Bank Director, Inc, 910 16th St, NW, Washington, DC 20006. Telephone (202) 466-7490.

Biweekly report. Gives directors and members of financial institution boards news on trends, as well as technical information grounded in the fiduciary relationship and general corporate operations. Price $100.00 per year.

462

Bank Director's Report

Warren, Gorham & Lamont, Inc, 210 S St, Boston, MA 02111. Telephone (617) 423-2020.

Monthly newsletter. Contains information on banking developments and trends, with emphasis on the role of the bank director. Price $56.00 per year.

463

Bank Directory of the Ninth Federal Reserve District

Commercial West, 5100 Edina Industrial Blvd, Edina, MN 55435. Telephone (612) 835-5853.

Annual directory. Provides a guide to the banks of the Ninth Federal Reserve District. Price $26.00 per year.

464

Banker

Financial Times Business Information Ltd, Bracken House, 10 Cannon St, London, England EC4P 4BY. Order from Financial Times Ltd, 75 Rockefeller Plz, New York, NY 10019. Telephone (44) (01) 248-8000. Telex 886341-2.

Monthly journal. Contains articles on monetary and financial issues, international economic relations, credit, and fiscal policies. Reviews major policy documents. Surveys new financial services of banks. Price $64.00 per year.

465

Banker & Tradesman

Warren Publishing Corp, 210 S St, Boston, MA 02111. Telephone (617) 426-4495.

Weekly newspaper. Reports on Massachusetts' banking and real estate industry developments. Lists every real estate transfer, along with the name of the mortgagee and the amount of loan. Price $75.00 per year.

466

Bankers Almanac and Year Book

Thomas Skinner Directories, Windsor Court, E Grinstead House, W Sussex, England RH16 1XE. Order from IPC Business Press Ltd New York, 205 E 42nd St, New York, NY 10017. Telephone (212) 867-2080.

Annual directory. Lists and supplies essential information on banks throughout the world. Includes a special section on British banks. Price $120.00 per year. ISBN 611 00647 2.

467

Bankers Digest

Bankers Digest, Inc, 1208 Mercantile Securities Bldg, Dallas, TX 75201. Telephone (214) 747-4522.

Weekly magazine. Reports on Texas bank news. Notes officer and director changes, new bank applications and charters, and bank association meetings. Includes as a special feature a section on the legal aspects of banking. Price $12.00 per year.

468

Banker's Letter of the Law

Warren, Gorham & Lamont, Inc, 210 S St, Boston, MA 02111. Telephone (617) 423-2020.

Monthly newsletter. Covers current court decisions and changes in state and federal laws and regulations that affect banking. Price $54.00 per year.

469

Bankers Magazine

Warren, Gorham & Lamont, Inc, 210 S St, Boston, MA 02111. Telephone (617) 423-2020.

Bimonthly magazine. Discusses bank planning, operations, controls and management. Price $48.00 per year.

470

Bankers' Magazine of Australasia

Bankers' Institute of Australasia, 51 Queen St, Melbourne, Vic 3000, Australia. Telephone (61) (03) 61 2985.

Bimonthly magazine. Covers interest rates, law, employment—and other topics of interest to bankers—in Australia and New Zealand. Price $16.00 (Australian). ISSN 0005-5468.

471

Bankers Monthly, National Magazine of Banking and Investments

Bankers Monthly, Inc, 601 Skokie Blvd, Northbrook, IL 60062. Telephone (312) 498-2580.

Monthly magazine. Covers developments and issues in the banking and finance industries. Price $15.00 per year.

472

Bankers Schools Directory **1977–78 edition**

American Bankers Assn, 1120 Connecticut Ave NW, Washington, DC 20036. Telephone (202) 467-4123.

Booklet. Features information on schools run by the American Bankers Association. Includes fees and admission requirements. Price $8.00.

473

Bank Executive's Report

Warren, Gorham & Lamont, Inc, 210 S St, Boston, MA 02111. Telephone (617) 432-2020.

Semimonthly report. Supplies information on bank policy and management. Covers federal regulations, operations, and loan portfolios. Price $110.00 per year.

474

Bank Fact Book

American Bankers Assn, 1120 Connecticut Ave NW, Washington, DC 20036. Telephone (202) 467-4123.

Book. Presents basic banking information. Includes such subjects as controlling the money supply, bank regulations, loans, investments, and trusts. Price $3.00.

475

Banking

Simmons-Boardman Publishing Corp, 350 Broadway, New York, NY 10013. Telephone (212) 966-7700.

Monthly journal of the American Bankers Association. Offers articles about bank management and long-range planning for commercial banks and trust companies. Price $10.00 per year.

475.01

Banking, **Cat No 5605.0**

Australian Bureau of Statistics, Box 10, Belconnen, ACT 2616, Australia. Order from Australian Government Publishing Service, PO Box 84, Canberra, ACT 2600, Australia.

Quarterly magazine. Covers Australian banking and related statistics. Price free of charge.

476

Banking and Currency **Ref No 5.1, 1972–73 latest edition**

Australian Bureau of Statistics, Box 17 GPO, Canberra, ACT 2600, Australia. Order from Australian Government Publishing Service, PO Box 84, Canberra, ACT 2600, Australia. Telephone (062) 52 7911.

Annual report. Covers the operations of the Reserve Bank of Australia, the Commonwealth Development Bank of Australia, Australian trading and savings banks, coinage, and overseas exchange. Price $1.90 (Australian).

477
Banking Law Journal
Warren, Gorham & Lamont, Inc, 210 S
St, Boston, MA 02111. Telephone (617)
423-2020.

Monthly magazine. Covers banking law
developments. Includes digests of cases
and book reviews. Price $58.00 per year.

479
Bank Installment Lending Newsletter
Warren, Gorham & Lamont, Inc, 210 S
St, Boston, MA 02111. Telephone (617)
423-2020.

Monthly report. Discusses regulations
and trends affecting bank installment
loans. Evaluates proposed legislation and
includes case histories. Price $58.00 per
year.

480
Bank Insurance & Protection Bulletin
American Bankers Assn, 1120 Connecti-
cut Ave NW, Washington, DC 20036.
Telephone (202) 467-4123.

Monthly newsletter. Contains articles on
insurance and other means of protection
against bank swindling. Price $6.50 per
year.

481
Bank Loan Officers Report
Warren, Gorham & Lamont, Inc, 210 S
St, Boston, MA 02111. Telephone (617)
423-2020.

Monthly report. Covers commercial
bank lending, including term loans, commercial and industrial loans, construction financing, and real estate loans.
Notes legal requirements. Price $56.00
per year.

482
Bank Marketing
Bank Marketing Assn, 309 W Washington St, Chicago, IL 60606. Telephone
(312) 782-1442.

Monthly magazine for bank executives.
Covers the marketing of banking services.
Includes sales promotion, bank planning,
and public relations. Price free to members, $48.00 to nonmembers in US, $60.00
foreign.

483
Bank Marketing Newsletter
American Bankers Assn, 1120 Connecti-
cut Ave NW, Washington, DC 20036.
Telephone (202) 467-4123.

Monthly newsletter. Acquaints user with
regulatory and legislative issues relevant
to the banking field. Includes coverage of
development in competing industries.
Price $22.50 per year.

484
Bank Marketing Report
Warren, Gorham & Lamont, Inc, 210 S
St, Boston, MA 02111. Telephone (617)
423-2020.

Monthly report. Focuses on bank marketing techniques. Includes information on
advertising, promotions, and innovative
banking services. Price $56.00 per year.

485
Bank of Canada Review
Bank of Canada, Distribution Section, Ot-
tawa, Ont, Canada K1A OG9.

Monthly review. Features graphs and tables on Canadian banking, economic,
labor force, foreign trade, and monetary
topics. English and French texts. Price
$10.00 per year. CN ISSN 0045-1460.

486
*Bank of Canada Weekly Financial
Statistics*
Bank of Canada, Distribution Section,
Secy's Dept, Ottawa, Ont, Canada K1A
OG9.

Weekly report in table form. Gives financial statistics for the Bank of Canada, Canadian government finances and securities, chartered banks' finances, and
interest and exchange rates. Includes
graphs. Price free of charge.

487
*Bank of England Annual Report and
Accounts*
Bank of England, Economics Div,
Threadneedle St, London, England EC2R
8AH. Telephone (44) (01) 601 4030.

Pamphlet. Annual report on the Bank of
England's policies, activities, and accounts. Price free of charge. ISSN 0308-
5279.

488
Bank of England Quarterly Bulletin
Bank of England, Economics Div,
Threadneedle St, London, England EC2R
8AH. Telephone (44) (01) 601 4030.

Quarterly bulletin. Offers commentary on
fiscal trends in Great Britain. Contains
extensive statistical tables on banking,
financial, economic, and monetary activity in Great Britain and elsewhere. Price
£21.00. ISSN 0005-5166.

489
Bank of England. Report
Her Majesty's Stationery Office, PO Box
569, London, England SE1 9NH. Telephone (44) (01) 928-1321.

Annual report on the Bank of England
from the Select Committee on Nationalized Industries, with minutes of evidence
and appendexes. Includes observations by
the chancellor of Exchequer. Price £3.60
per year.

489.01
*Bank Officer Cash Compensation
Survey, 1979*
Bank Adm Inst, PO Box 500, 303 S, NW
Hwy, Park Ridge, IL 60068. Telephone
(312) 693-7300.

Nine annual books. Survey bank officers'
salaries, annual bonuses, ages, education,
reporting level, number of subordinate
employees, and years in position. Each
volume covers separate US geographic region, with combined regional data. Price
$30.00 per volume, $200 for complete series, $100 BMI member discount.

490
*Bank Officer's Handbook of Commercial
Banking Law*
Frederick K Beutel, Warren, Gorham &
Lamont, Inc, 210 S St, Boston, MA
02111. Telephone (617) 423-2020.

Book. Covers typical banking business
legal problems. Price available on request.

491
Bank of Hawaii Monthly Review
Bank of Hawaii, Economics Div, PO Box
2900, Honolulu, HI 96846. Telephone
(808) 537-8269.

Monthly newsletter. Pertains to business
activity in Hawaii. Price free of charge.

492
Bank of Montreal Business Review
Economics Dept, Bank of Montreal, PO
Box 6002, Montreal, Que, Canada H3C
3B1. Telephone (514) 877-6961.

Monthly newsletter. Covers current
trends in Canadian business and finance.
Price free of charge.

493
Bank of New South Wales Review
Bank of New South Wales, GPO Box 1,
Sydney, NSW 2001, Australia.

Irregular reports. Surveys current economic conditions in Australia and New
Zealand. Price free of charge.

494

Bank of Nova Scotia. Monthly Review

Bank of Nova Scotia, 44 King St, W, Toronto, Ont, Canada MSH 1H1.

Monthly newsletter. Covers economic and business trends mainly in Canada. English and French editions. Price free of charge. ISSN 0005-5328.

495

Bank Operations Report

Warren, Gorham & Lamont, Inc, 210 S St, Boston, MA 02111. Telephone (617) 423-2020.

Monthly report. Discusses bank operations management techniques. Includes such topics as electronic data processing control, check handling, credit and debit cards, and electronic funds transfer systems. Price $56.00 per year.

496

Bank Personnel News

American Bankers Assn, 1120 Connecticut Ave NW, Washington, DC 20036. Telephone (202) 467-4123.

Monthly newsletter. Offers bank personnel and employee relations news and analyses of federal regulations affecting employment practices. Price $18.00 per year.

497

Bank Personnel Report

Warren, Gorham & Lamont, Inc, 210 S St, Boston, MA 02111. Telephone (617) 423-2020.

Monthly report. Discusses bank personnel management subjects, including compensation, employee communications, retirement plans, and unionization. Price $58.00 per year.

498

Bank Pooled Funds

Computer Directions Advisors, Inc, 8750 Georgia Ave, Silver Spring, MD 20910. Telephone (301) 565-9544.

Monthly report. Provides information on bank pooled funds. Includes list of participating banks, individual fund results, and performance charts. Price $400.00 per year.

499

Bank Protection Manual, **1974 edition**

American Bankers Assn, 1120 Connecticut Ave NW, Washington, DC 20036. Telephone (202) 467-4123.

Loose-leaf manual. Reviews procedures for handling external criminal attacks against financial institutions. Aids in complying with Bank Protection Act Periodic revisions. Price $35.00.

500

Bankruptcy Law Reports

Commerce Clearing House, Inc, 4025 W Peterson Ave, Chicago, IL 60646. Telephone (312) 583-8500.

Three loose-leaf books, plus biweekly reports. Cover various phases of bankruptcy and debt readjustment law and practice. Price $325.00 per year.

501

Bank Security Report

Warren, Gorham & Lamont, Inc, 210 S St, Boston, MA 02111. Telephone (617) 423-2020.

Monthly report. Contains information on bank security programs. Covers surveillance systems, computer fraud, burglary, forgery, and embezzlement. Price $56.00 per year.

502

Bank Sorting Code Numbers

Thomas Skinner Directories, Windsor Court, E Grinstead House, W Sussex, England RH19 1XE. Order from IPC Business Press Ltd New York, 205 E 42nd St, New York, NY 10017. Telephone (212) 867-2080.

Yearbook. Offers a directory to sorting code numbers for British banks. Price £ 1.80 per year. ISBN 611 00650 2.

503

Bank Systems & Equipment

Gralla Publications, 1515 Broadway, New York, NY 10036. Telephone (212) 869-1300.

Monthly magazine. Covers operations and systems management in the banking field. Focuses on computer systems. Price available on request.

505

Bank Tax Report

Warren, Gorham & Lamont, Inc, 210 S St, Boston, MA 02111. Telephone (617) 423-2020.

Semimonthly report. Discusses bank tax issues. Covers court decisions and Internal Revenue Service regulations and rulings and includes information on tax planning. Price $72.00 per year.

506

Bank Teller's Report

Warren, Gorham & Lamont, Inc, 210 S St, Boston, MA 02111. Telephone (617) 423-2020.

Monthly report. Offers suggestions for bank tellers on customer relations, cross-selling bank services, and improving efficiency. Price $38.00 per year.

508

Barclays Review

Barclays Bank, Group Economics Depart., 54 Lombard St, London, England EC3P 3AH. Telephone (44)(01) 283 8989.

Quarterly magazine. Expresses the Barclays Bank's views on economic and financial developments in the United Kingdom and other parts of the world. Price free of charge.

508.01

Bargaining Report

Labour Research Dept, 78 Blackfriars Rd, London, England SE1 8HF. Telephone (44)(01) 928-3649.

Bimonthly journal. Covers trade union negotiations and survey results on occupational pay and conditions. Price £10.00 per year.

509

Barron's

Dow Jones & Co, Inc, 22 Cortlandt St, New York, NY 10007. Telephone (212) 285-5000, 5243.

Weekly newspaper. Provides financial and investment news. Includes information on commodities and international trading. Contains tables on New York Stock Exchange transactions. Price $32.00 per year.

510

Barron's Market Laboratory, **1977 edition**

Dow Jones & Co, Inc, 22 Cortlandt St, New York, NY 10007. Order from Dow Jones & Co, Inc, PO Box 300, Princeton, NJ 08540. Telephone (212) 285-5000.

Book. Contains US and foreign stock indexes, bond data, price-earnings ratios, and other stock market statistics. Price $4.95. ISBN 0-87128-529-0.

511

Barter Communique

Full Circle Marketing Corp, PO Box 2527, Sarasota, FL 33578. Telephone (813) 349-3300.

Quarterly newspaper. Discusses advertising barter news and other advertising and barter techniques. Price $20.00 per year.

512
Basic Facts, Developing Member Countries (DMCs) of Asian Development Bank (ADB)
Asian Development Bank, PO Box 789, Manila, Phillippines 2800. Telephone 80-26-31. Telex 7425071.

Annual pamphlet. Supplies basic information on Asian countries, including gross domestic product, population, public debt, exchange rates, and foreign trade. Price free of charge.

513
Basic Instruments and Selected Documents (BISD)
General Agreement on Tariffs and Trade, Centre William Rappard, 154 rue de Lausanne, 1211 Geneva 21, Switzerland. Telephone 022-31 02 31.

Annual series. Contains important decisions, resolutions, recommendations, and reports adopted by GATT's member states during the period covered by each yearly supplement. Price $25.00 per year.

514
Basics of Plant Location in Arkansas
Arkansas Dept of Economic Development, One Capitol Mall, Little Rock, AR 72201. Telephone (501) 371-2431.

Booklet. Discusses manufacturing opportunities in Arkansas. Covers transportation, natural resources, labor force, industrial financing, education, and taxes. Price free of charge.

514.01
Basic Statistics
European Community Information Service, 2100 M St, NW, Suite 707, Washington, DC 20037. Telephone (202) 862-9500. Telex 248455.

Annual publication. Gives European Communities member countries' statistical information on agriculture, industry, trade, and relations with nonmember countries. Price available on request.

515
Baxter
Baxter, 1030 E Putnam Ave, Greenwich, CT 06830. Telephone (203) 637-4559.

Weekly bulletin. Offers advice concerning investments. Covers such areas as inflation and currency markets. Price $125.00 per year.

516
Baylor Business Studies
Baylor University, Hankamer School of Business, Box 6278, Waco, TX 76798. Telephone (817) 755-1011.

Quarterly journal. Provides articles on business, industry, and stocks. Tables. Price $1.50 per year. ISSN 0005-724X.

517
Beef
The Webb Co, 1999 Shepard Rd, St Paul, MN 55116. Telephone (612) 690-7200.

Monthly magazine. Reports on beef cattle. Subjects include feed and diseases. Price available on request.

518
Beef Buying Guide
The Webb Co, 1999 Shepard Rd, St Paul, MN 55116. Telephone (612) 690-7200.

Annual book. Provides a list of beef manufacturers, auction and terminal markets, commission firms, products, and supplies. Price available on request.

519
Behavioral Sciences Newsletter
Roy W Walters & Assoc, Whitney Rd, Mahwah, NJ 07430. Telephone (201) 891-5757.

Semimonthly newsletter. Deals with latest developments in behavioral sciences as they apply to business and industry. Price $66.00 per year.

520
Belgian American Trade Review
Belgian-American Chamber of Commerce in the United States, Inc., 50 Rockefeller Plz, New York, NY 10020. Telephone (212) 247-7613. Telex 232872 BACC UR.

Monthly magazine. Reports on Belgium's international trade and economic developments. Price $15.00 per year (third class); $22.00 per year (airmail).

521
Benefits International
Pension Publications Ltd, 30 Queen Anne's Gate, London, England SW1H 9AW. Telephone (44) (01) 222-8033. Telex 916283.

Monthly magazine. Assesses issues relating to international employee benefits, including social insurance and security plans, pension funds, and benefits for foreign workers. Price $150.00 per year.

522
Benefits Review Board–Black Lung Reporter
Matthew Bender & Co, 235 E 45th St, New York, NY 10017. Telephone (212) 661-5050.

Annual service. Covers decisions of the Benefits Review Board in black lung workmen's compenstion cases. Price $450.00 per year.

522.01
Benefits Review Board–Longshore Reporter
Matthew Bender & Co, 235 E 45th St, New York, NY 10017. Telephone (212) 661-5050.

Annual service. Contains coverage of longshore workmen's compensation decisions of the Benefits Review Board. Price $450.00 per year.

522.02
Best Financial Advertising
Advertising Trade Publications, Inc, 10 E 39th St, New York, NY 10016. Order from Art Direction Book Co, 10 E 39th St, New York, NY 10016. Telephone (212) 889-6500.

Annual book. Contains ads for financial institutions, arranged by subject matter. Includes illustrations. Price $30.00.

523
Best's Agents Guide to Life Insurance Companies
A M Best Co, Ambest Rd, Oldwick, NJ 08858. Telephone (201) 439-2200.

Book. Profiles over 1300 life insurance companies including policyholder ratings. Contains operating and financial facts and lists states and territories where each company is licensed. Price $20.00.

524
Best's Aggregates & Averages
A M Best Co, Ambest Rd, Oldwick, NJ 08858. Telephone (201) 439-2200.

Annual book. Presents statistical survey of fire-marine and casualty-surety business. Gives cumulative past histories and figures on underwriting expenses by company and groups. Price $110.00.

525
Best's Casualty Loss Reserve Development
A M Best Co, Ambest Rd, Oldwick, NJ 08858. Telephone (201) 439-2200.

Annual five-volume series. Provides analysis of property-casualty insurance company loss reserves. Covers auto liability, general liability, multi-peril, worker's compensation, and medical malpractice. Price $280.00 per volume, $1230 for complete set.

526

Best's Directory of Recommended Insurance Adjusters

A M Best Co, Ambest Rd, Oldwick, NJ 08858. Telephone (201) 439-2200.

Annual book. Contains the names of 2400 American, Canadian, and foreign adjusting offices recommended by insurance companies. Includes reference tables and charts on key insurance laws by state and province. Price $15.00

526.01

Best's Directory of Recommended Insurance Attorneys

A M Best Co, Ambest Rd, Oldwick, NJ 08858. Telephone (201) 439-2200.

Annual book. Supplies names of over 3000 law firms recommended by insurance companies listed by state and city. Tables and charts show key elements of insurance laws. Maps. Price $25.00.

527

Best's Flitcraft Compend

A M Best Co, Ambest Rd, Oldwick, NJ 08858. Telephone (201) 439-2200.

Annual Book. Shows comparative policy premium rates of all major life insurance companies. Summarizes 10- and 20-year policy provisions. Contains cash value tables and statistics. Price $13.50.

528

Best's Insurance Management Reports: Life-Health Edition

A M Best Co, Ambest Rd, Oldwick, NJ 08858. Telephone (201) 439-2200.

Weekly four-part newsletter. Provides concise accounts of the latest news in the life and health insurance fields, plus stock index, prices, and statistical data. Price $150.00 per year.

529

Best's Insurance Management Report: Property-Casualty Edition

A M Best Co, Ambest Rd, Oldwick, NJ 08858. Telephone (201) 439-2200.

Weekly four-part newsletter. Digests major events in property and casualty insurance arena. Includes stock index, and prices. Washington Review, Statistical Studies and Perspectives. Price $150.00 per year.

530

Best's Insurance Report: Life Health

A M Best Co, Ambest Rd, Oldwick, NJ 08858. Telephone (201) 439-2200.

Service. Provides detailed analysis of financial and operating results for 1300 life-health insurance companies, plus summary data on 600 smaller carriers. Includes policyholders' ratings and financial size categories. Price $150.00 per year.

531

Best's Insurance Report: Property-Casualty

A M Best Co, Ambest Rd, Oldwick, NJ 08858. Telephone (201) 439-2200.

Service. Gives detailed analysis of financial and operating results for 1300 major property-casualty insurance companies, plus summary data on 2000 smaller mutual companies. Includes policyholders' ratings and financial size categories. Price $270.00 per year.

532

Best's Insurance Securities Research Series

A M Best Co, Ambest Rd, Oldwick, NJ 08858. Telephone (201) 439-2200.

Annual service. Consists of comprehensive financial reports on over 135 major stock, captive, mutual, and reciprocal insurance companies. Covers six year period for each company. Price $1400.00 per year (including monthly summaries and reports).

533

Best's Key Rating Guide

A M Best Co, Ambest Rd, Oldwick, NJ 08858. Telephone (201) 439-2200.

Annual book. Tenders five-year operating and financial figures on over 1300 major property-casualty carriers policyholder ratings. Includes figures on over 2000 smaller mutual insurance companies. Price $35.00.

534

Best's Loss Control Engineering Manual

A M Best Co, Ambest Rd, Oldwick, NJ 08858. Telephone (201) 439-2200.

Book, with update service. Provides standards for safety engineers and field underwriters in evaluating loss exposure in over 700 key industrial and commercial classifications. Price $110.00 per year, plus $30.00 per year for supplements.

535

Best's Market Guide

A M Best Co, Ambest Rd, Oldwick, NJ 08858. Telephone (201) 439-2200.

Annual three-volume set of books. Analyzes the investment portfolios of over 1200 insurance companies. Provides volumes as arranged by corporate stock holdings, corporate bond holdings, and municipal bonds. Price $1040.00 for complete set.

536

Best's Directory of Recommended Insurance Adjusters

A M Best Co, Ambest Rd, Oldwick, NJ 08858. Telephone (201) 439-2200.

Annual book. Contains the names of 2400 American, Canadian, and foreign adjusting offices recommended by insurance companies. Includes reference tables and charts on key insurance laws by state and province. Price $15.00

538

Best's Reproductions of Convention Statements

A M Best Co, Ambest Rd, Oldwick, NJ 08858. Telephone (201) 439-2200.

Book. Provides principal schedules from the annual Convention Statements of property-casualty insurance companies. Reproduces pages on assets, liabilities, premiums and losses from over 100 major companies. Price $460.00.

538.01

Best's Retirement Income Guide

A M Best Co, Ambest Rd, Oldwick, NJ 08858. Telephone (201) 439-2200.

Biannual report. Provides analysis of annuity policies offered by insurance companies, including costs, loading fee, interest rates, and options. Price $21.00 per year.

539

Best's Review: Life/Health Insurance Edition

A M Best Co, Ambest Rd, Oldwick, NJ 08858. Telephone (201) 439-2200.

Monthly magazine. Contains analyses of trends in life and health insurance fields. Statistics. Price $14.00 per year.

540

Best's Review: **Property-Casualty Insurance Edition**

A M Best Co, Ambest Rd, Oldwick, NJ 08858. Telephone (201) 439-2200.

Monthly magazine. Interprets developments in the property and casualty insurance industry. Price $14.00 per year.

541

Best's Safety Directory

A M Best Co, Ambest Rd, Oldwick, NJ 08858. Telephone (201) 439-2200.

Annual two-volume book. Reports on industrial safety, hygiene, and security. Contains OSHA analysis and product buyers guides. Price $35.00.

542

Best's Settlement Options Manual

A M Best Co, Ambest Rd, Oldwick, NJ 08858. Telephone (201) 439-2200.

Book. Gives precalculated income and cash value figures on policies written since 1900 by companies that write 95% of US life insurance. Is designed for professionals using programming to sell insurance. Price $55.00 per year.

543

Best's Underwriting Guide

A M Best Co, Ambest Rd, Oldwick, NJ 08858. Telephone (201) 439-2200.

Loose-leaf volumes, with continuous updates. Describes industrial and commercial underwriting risk classifications. Includes hazard indexes. Price $110.00 per year, plus $25.00 per year for supplements.

544

Best's Underwriting Newsletter

A M Best Co, Ambest Rd, Oldwick, NJ 08858. Telephone (201) 439-2200.

Monthly newsletter. Covers developments in the property-casualty insurance underwriting field. Offers advice and interprets actuarial and statistical studies. Price $30.00 per year.

545

Better Investing

National Assn of Investment Clubs, 1515 E Eleven Mile Rd, Royal Oaks, MI 48067. Telephone (313) 543-0612.

Monthly magazine. Offers investment advice. Recommends specific stocks and groups of stocks and comments on tax issues. Price $8.00 per year. ISSN 0006-016X.

546

Betting and Gaming Bulletin

Her Majesty's Stationery Office, PO Box 569, London, England SE1 9NH. Order-from Bill of Entry Service, HM Customs and Excise, King's Beam House, Mark Lane, London, England EC3 7HE. Telephone (44) (01) 928 1321.

Monthly report. Covers betting and gaming in Great Britain. Price £4.83 per year.

547

Betting Licensing Statistics

Her Majesty's Stationery Office, PO Box 569, London, England SE1 9NH. Telephone (44) (01) 928 1321.

Annual report. Supplies statistical material on betting licensing in Great Britain. Price £1.25per year.

548

Bibliography of Appraisal Literature

American Society of Appraisers, Dulles International Airport, PO Box 17265, Washington, DC 20041. Telephone (703) 620-3838.

Lists approximately 17,000 entries for use in numerous appraisal disciplines, including real estate, machinery and equipment, and personal property. Price $30.00 per copy.

550

Bicentennial Statistics

US Dept of Commerce, Bureau of the Census, Washington, DC 20233. Telephone (202) 449-1600.

Report. Contains historical, statistical time series on social, political, and economic characteristics of the US from colonial times to 1976. Price $.90.

551

Billboard

Billboard Publications, Inc, PO Box 24970, Nashville, TN 37202. Telephone (615) 748-8140.

Weekly news magazine. Reports on the music industry. Lists bestselling records and albums and notes new stereo and tape products. Charts. Price $110.00 per year.

552

Bill of Entry Service

Her Majesty's Stationery Office, PO Box 569, London, England SE1 9NH. Telephone (44) (01) 928 1321.

Publication. Provides information on the British bill of entry service. Price available on request.

553

Bills/Public and Private

Supply and Services Canada, Canadian Govt Publishing Centre, Hull, Que, Canada K1A 0S9. Telephone (819) 994-3475, 2085.

Report. Provides information on bills in Canadian House of Commons and Senate. Bilingual. Price $286.80 per year.

553.01

BI/Metrics

Business International Corp, 1 Dag Hammarskjold Plaza, New York, NY 10017. Telephone (212) 750-6300.

Monthly report. Covers the medium and long-term outlook for all major currencies. Contains detailed forecasts based on econometric models designed for currency forecasting. Price $960.00 per year.

554

Biological Abstracts (BA)

Biosciences Information Service of Biological Abstracts, 2100 Arch St, Philadelphia, PA 19103. Telephone (215) 568-4016.

Semimonthly reference journal. Provides abstracts from literature on biological and biomedical research from over 100 countries. Price $1675.00, $1500.00 per year educational.

554.01

Biological Abstracts/RRM

Biosciences Information Service of Biological Abstracts, 2100 Arch St, Philadelphia, PA 19103. Telephone (215) 568-4016.

Monthly report. Summarizes books, reports, reviews, and meetings on biological and medical research. Price $840.00, $760.00 educationai per year.

554.02

Biomedical Communications

United Business Publications, Inc, 475 Park Ave S, New York, NY 10016. Telephone (212) 725-2300.

Bimonthly journal. Discusses media coverage of medical education and health care. Price $8.75 per year.

555

Bio-Medical Insight

International Bio-Medical Information Service, Inc, PO Box 756, Miami, FL 33156. Telephone (305) 665-4856.

Bimonthly newsletter. Covers over 20 annual biomedical trade shows in the US and overseas. Reports on business environment, markets, and technology. Price $320.00 per year. ISSN 0090-161X.

556
Bio-Medical Scoreboard
International Bio-Medical Information Service, Inc, PO Box 756, Miami, FL 33156. Telephone (305) 665-4856.

Monthly newsletter, plus annual index. Provides financial data on over 450 US-based medical and biomedical firms. Price $160.00 per year. ISSN 0095-0971.

557
Biotechnology and Bioengineering
John Wiley and Sons, Inc, 605 3rd Ave, New York, NY 10158. Telephone (212) 850-6515. Telex 12-7063.

Monthly magazine. Presents original research on all aspects of biochemical and microbial technology. Includes articles on products, process development and design, and equipment. Price $170.00.

558
Bituminous Coal Data
National Coal Association, Coal Bldg, 1130 17th St NW, Washington, DC 20036.

Annual report. Covers bituminous coal productions, sales, and other industry data. Price $10.00. ISSN 00067-897X.

559
Bi-weekly Index of the Tobacco Scene (BITS)
Tobacco Merchants Assn of the US, Statler Hilton, 7th Ave & 33rd St, New York, NY 10001. Telephone (212) 239-4435.

Biweekly report. Provides index to newspaper and periodical articles on tobacco, organized by subject. Areas include advertising, health, and corporations. Price $25.00 per year.

560
Black Enterprise
Earl Graves Publishing Co, Inc, 295 Madison Ave, New York, NY 10017. Telephone (212) 889-8220.

Monthly magazine geared to black people in business and professionals. Provides information on money, management, and marketing. Price $10.00 per year.

560.01
Black's Guides for New York, Philadelphia and Washington
Black's Guide, PO Box 2090, 332 Broad St, Red Bank, NJ 07701. Telephone (201) 842-6060.

Annual directories. Separate editions list office space availability for the New York metropolitan area, Philadelphia-South Jersey area, and Baltimore-Washington area. Include maps. Price $25.00 per edition.

561
Black's Law Dictionary, 5th edition.
West Publishing Co, 50 W Kellog Blvd, PO Box 3526, St Paul, MN 55165. Telephone (612) 228-2500.

Book. Provides a dictionary of terminology for US and British law. Price available on request.

562
Blue Book of Canadian Business
Canadian Newspaper Services International Ltd, 55 Eglinton Ave E, Suite 604, Dept A, Toronto, Ont, Canada M4P 1G8. Telephone (416) 487-4725.

Annual hardcover book. Contains basic information on over 2000 major companies doing business in Canada, including company profiles, rankings, and business index. Price $59.50 per issue.

563
Blue Book of CBS Stock Reports
Marpep Publishing Ltd, Suite 700, 133 Richmond St W, Toronto, Ont, Canada M5H 3M8. Telephone (416) 869-1177.

Biweekly loose-leaf report. Assesses over 230 key Canadian stocks. Contains detailed report on each company, including a five-year statistical analysis for each company. Price $150 per year. ISSN 0384-7802.

563.01
Blue Chip Economic Indicators
Capitol Publications, Inc, Suite G-12, 2430 Pennsylvania Ave, NW, Washington, DC 20037. Telephone (202) 452-1600.

Monthly newsletter. Provides economic information based on poll of 40 economists on 11 key indicators. Includes forecasts. Price $222.00 per year.

564
Blue List of Current Municipal Offerings
Blue List Publishing Co, 25 Broadway, New York, NY 10004. Telephone (212) 248-3111.

Daily publication of computer printouts listing municipal and corporate bond offering prices. Price $360.00 per year.

565
Blue Reports
Blue Reports, Inc, 5252 Leesburg Pike, Falls Church, VA. 22041 Telephone (703) 820-4200.

Daily mimeographed report. Provides news of private and government municipal construction projects in Washington, DC, Virginia, and Maryland. Includes federal projects nationally. Price $560.00 per year.

566
Blue Sky Law Reports
Commerce Clearing House, Inc, 4025 W Peterson Ave, Chicago, IL 60646. Telephone (312) 583-8500.

Four loose-leaf books, plus monthly reports. Interpret state blue sky statutes and regulations. Note selected legal investment laws. Price $385.00 per year.

566.01
BMCIS
Building Maintenance Cost Information Service, 85–87 Clarence St, Kingston upon Thames, Surrey, England KT1 1RB. Telephone (44)(01) 546-7554.

Annual service. Provides information on building maintenance costs in Great Britain. Notes legislation. Price available on request.

567
Board of Contract Appeals Decisions
Commerce Clearing House, Inc, 4025 W Peterson Ave, Chicago, IL 60646. Telephone (312) 583-8500.

Two books per year. Report on decisions of the Armed Services Board of Contract Appeals and other appeals boards. Price $47.50 per volume. ISSN 8450.

568
Boardroom Reports
Boardroom Reports, Inc, 500 5th Ave, New York, NY 10110. Telephone (212) 354-0005.

Semimonthly magazine for executives. Discusses new ideas about such subjects as advertising, investments, law, management, personnel, selling and taxes. Price $44.00 per year.

569
Body Fashions/Intimate Apparel incorporating Hosiery and Underwear
Harcourt Brace Jovanovich Publications, 757 3rd Ave, New York, NY 10017. Order from Harcourt Brace and Jovanovich Publications, 1 East 1st St, Duluth, MN 55802. Telephone (218) 727-8511.

Monthly magazine. Covers manufacturing and marketing news for foundation garments, sleepwear, robes, swimwear, hosiery, and underwear industries. Price $16.00 per year.

569.01
Bond Buyer's Municipal Finance Statistics Book
Bond Buyer, 1 State St Plz, New York, NY 10004. Telephone (212) 943-8200.

Annual book. Provides data on state and local government bonds and related financing. Tables. Price $20.00.

570
Bond Guide
Standard & Poor's Corp, 25 Broadway, New York, NY 10004. Telephone (212) 248-2525.

Monthly report. Gives data on 3900 corporate bonds, including current yield, registered and coupon bonds, bond quality ratings, municipal bonds, and convertible bonds. Price $89.00.

571
Bondholder's Register
Bondholder's Register, 5 The White House, Beacon Rd, Crowborough, Sussex, England TN6 1AB. Telephone 08926 62439.

Semimonthly newsletter. Reports on bearer securities' redemptions, rights, and dividends. Includes biannual indexes of bond redemptions and equities. Price £ 46.50 per year.

571.01
Book Marketing Handbook
RR Bowker Co, 1180 Ave of the Americas, New York, NY 10036. Telephone (212) 764-5100.

Book. Covers all aspects of book marketing, advertising, promotion, and exploitation. Contains over 500 numbered subject entries in 44 chapters. Provides four appendixes, including glossary of book marketing and promotion terms. Price $45.00. ISBN 0-8352-1286-6.

571.02
Book Marketing Handbook: Tips and Techniques for the Sale and Promotion of Scientific, Technical, Professional, and Scholarly Books and Journals
R R Bowker Co, 1180 Ave of the Americas, New York, NY 10036. Order from R R Bowker Co, PO Box 1807, Ann Arbor, MI 48106. Telephone (212) 764-5100.

Book. Discusses book marketing techniques, including direct mail, space advertising, telephone marketing, publicity, outlets, and specialized marketing. Includes professional journals. Appendixes, glossary, index. Price $45.00. ISBN 0-8352-1286-6.

572
Book of the States, **1980-81 edition**
Council of State Governments, Iron Works Pike, PO Box 11910, Lexington, KY 40578. Telephone (606) 252-2291.

Book. Serves as reference for information on state government. Tables and statistics. Price $28.00 per copy.

573
Book Publishers (BP Report)
Knowledge Industry Publications, 701 Westchester Ave, White Plains, NY 10604. Telephone (914) 694-8686.

Weekly newsletter. Covers the book publishing industry in the US and internationally. Includes educational publishing. Price $19.50 per year. ISSN 0145-9457.

575
Books in Print
R R Bowker Co, 1180 Ave of the Americas, New York, NY 10036. Order from R R Bowker Co, PO Box 1807, Ann Arbor, MI 48106. Telephone (212) 764-5100.

Annual four-volume book. Indexes about 550,000 books by author and title. Includes price, publisher, and other information. Price $110.00. ISBN 0-8352-1300-5. ISSN 0068-0214.

576
Borrowing in International Capital Markets
World Bank, 1818 H St NW, Washington, DC 20433. Telephone (202) 393-6360.

Quarterly pamphlet. Presents data on foreign and international bonds issues and Publicized Eurocurrency Credits. Includes individual transactions and statistics on borrowing countries. Tables. Price free of charge.

577
Boston Marine Guide
Marine Guide Pub Co, 88 Broad St, Boston, MA 02110. Telephone (617) 357-9452.

Weekly newspaper. Reports on New England shipping, trucking, airfreight, and railroad industries, including information on schedules and rates. Price $10.00 per year.

578
Boston Stock Exchange Guide
Commerce Clearing House, Inc, 4025 W Peterson Ave, Chicago, IL 60646. Telephone (312) 583-8500.

Loose-leaf book, plus monthly reports. Includes a directory and constitution and the rules of the Boston Stock Exchange. Price $130.00 per year.

579
Bottom Line
American Business Men's Research Foundation, 1208 Michigan National Tower, Lansing, MI 48933. Telephone (517) 487-9276.

Quarterly magazine. Provides articles about alcoholic products: their manufacture and sale and use for beverage, industrial and other purposes. Notes alcohol's relation to health and problem drinking. Price $8.00 per year, $12.00 foreign.

580
Bowker Annual of Library and Book Trade Information
R R Bowker Co, 1180 Ave of the Americas, New York, NY 10036. Order from R R Bowker Co, PO Box 1807, Ann Arbor, MI 48106. Telephone (212) 764-5100.

Annual book. Provides news and analyses of interest to library and book trades, including federal agency reports, grant information, copyright law, statistics, salaries, and reference and directory information. Price $29.95. ISBN 0-8352-1273-4. ISSN 0068-0540.

581

Brad Advertiser & Agency List

Maclean-Hunter Ltd, 30 Old Burlington St, London, England W1X 2AE. Telephone (44) (01) 434 2233.

Report issued quarterly. Supplies information on British advertisers, agencies, brand names, market research, and direct mail companies. Price available on request.

583

Brad Directories & Annuals

Maclean-Hunter Ltd, 30 Old Burlington St, London, England W1X 2AE. Telephone (44) (01) 434 2233.

Annual publication. Covers all reference books and directories published annually in Great Britain for all consumer, trade, and technical publications. Price available on request.

584

Bradford's Directory of Marketing Research Agencies & Management Consultants in the US & the World, **13th edition**

Bradford's Directory, PO Box 276, Dept E, Fairfax, VA 22030. Telephone (703) 560-7484.

Irregularly revised book. Gives alphabetical listings by state and city of over 750 marketing research and management firms, with information about services available. Provides international listings by countries. Contains an index of agencies, key personnel, and classified service-guide. Price $25.50 per copy.

585

Brazilian-American Business Review/Directory

Brazilian-American Chamber of Commerce, Inc, 22 W 48th St, New York, NY 10036. Telephone (212) 575-9030.

Annual directory. Reports on Brazil's business, economic, trade, and legal developments. Lists Brazilian-American Chamber of Commerce members and their activities. Price $10.00.

586

Brazil Regional Report

Latin American Newsletters Ltd, Greenhill House, 90-93 Cowcross St, London, England EC1M 6BL. Telephone (44) (01) 251-0012. Telex 261117.

Monthly newsletter. Focuses on Brazil's economy and politics. Price £40, $90.00 US per year.

587

Breve

National Foreign Trade Council, 10 Rockefeller Plz, New York, NY 10020. Telephone (212) 58 1-6420.

Weekly newsletter. Summarizes European news dealing with political, economic, and social developments affecting US trade and foreign investment. Price $60.00 per year members only.

588

C Brewer Today

James D Sylvester, C. Brewer & Co Ltd, Box 1826, Honolulu, HI 96801. Telephone (808) 536-4461.

Monthly tabloid. Intended for salaried employees of C Brewer and Co Ltd, a diversified agribusiness company engaged in the production, processing, and marketing of sugar, molasses, coffee, spices, macadamia nuts, rice, chemicals, and fertilizers. Price free of charge.

589

Brewery Manual and Who's Who in British Brewing, **1980 edition**

Northwood Publications Ltd, Elm House, 10-16 Elm St, London, England. WC1X 0BP. Order from Northwood Publications Ltd, Northwood House, 93–99 Goswell Rd, London, England EC1 V7QA. Telephone (44) (01) 253 9355. Telex 894461.

Book. Surveys British brewing companies. Discusses subsidiaries, directors, and personnel. Includes a guide to suppliers of brewing machinery and equipment. Price £7.95.

590

Brewing Industry in the US **Brewers Almanac**

US Brewers Association, 1750 K St NW, Washington, DC 20006. Telephone (202) 466-2400.

Annual report. Gives production, sales, foreign trade, and other related statistics. Price available on request.

591

Brick & Clay Record

Cahners Publishing Company, Inc, 221 Columbus Ave, Boston, MA 02116. Telephone (617) 536-7780.

Monthly magazine. Contains articles on the production of brick and other heavy clay products. Price $12.00 per year.

592

Bricker's International Directory of University Sponsored Executive Development Programs

Bricker's International Directory, 425 Family Farm Rd, Woodside, CA 94062. Telephone (415) 851-3090.

Annual directory. Lists over 200 university executive development programs in the US, Canada, Europe, and Australia. Price $85.00. ISBN 0-9604804-0-4. ISSN 0361-1108.

592.01

Brief Guide to Business Regulations and Services in Texas

Texas Industrial Commission, Capitol Station, Box 12728, Austin, TX 78711. Telephone (512) 472-5059.

Directory. Lists agencies which issue permits or licenses for new businesses in Texas. Price free of charge.

593

Briefing Papers

Federal Publications, Inc, 1120 20th St, NW, Washington, DC 20036. Telephone (202) 337-7000.

Bimonthly loose-leaf report. Discusses basic principles and guidelines of federal government contracts. Price $112.00 per year.

594

Briefing Papers Collection

Federal Publications, Inc, 1120 20th St, NW, Washington, DC 20036. Telephone (202) 337-7000.

Four books with updates. Contain information on federal government contracts that originally appeared in Briefing Papers. Include a bibliography and indexes. Price $395.00.

595

Briefs

Council of State Governments, Iron Works Pike, PO Box 11910, Lexington, KY 40511. Telephone (606) 252-2291.

Biweekly publication. Analyzes federal government developments affecting states. Includes intermittent in-depth reports. Price $20.00 per year.

596

Britain and Overseas

Overseas Trade Research Fund of the Economic research Council, 55 Park Ln, London, England W1Y 3DH. Telephone (44) (01) 499 3000.

Quarterly journal. Digests news about the British economy. Carries articles on trade, inflation, the common market, and the purchasing power of the pound. Price £2.00, $6.00 per year foreign.

596.01
Britain in Context
St Martin's Press, Inc, 175 5th Ave, New York, NY 10010. Telephone (212) 674-5151.

Book. Provides economic and social data of Great Britain in diagrams, charts, and text. Draws comparisons with other countries and time periods. Price $22.50.

597
Cecil H Brite Lecture Series in Advertising and Publications Management
University of Oklahoma, School of Journalism, 860 Van Vleet Oval, Rm 101, Norman, OK 73019. Telephone (405) 325-2721.

Annual pamphlet. Presents article on advertising or communications industry topic. Price free of charge.

598
British Business
Her Majesty's Stationery Office, PO Box 569, London, England SE1 9NH. Telephone (44) (01) 928-1321.

Weekly magazine. Contains statistics on British wholesale prices, retail sales, industrial production, and other economic indicators. Includes commentary from the Departments of Industry, Trade and Prices, and Consumer Protection. Price £18.72 per year.

599
British CI Sector
Extel Statistical Services Ltd, 37-45 Paul St, London, England EC2A 4PB. Telephone (44) (01) 253 3400. Telex 262687.

Annual card service, with daily updates. Covers British capital investments. Price £1,200.00 per year.

599.01
British Clothing Manufacturer
Northwood Publications Ltd, Elm House, 10–16 Elm St, London, England WC1X OBP. Order from Subscription Manager, 23–29 Emerald St, London, England WC1N 3QJ. Telephone (44)(01) 404-5531. Telex 21746.

Monthly magazine. Aimed at top executives, technologists, and cloth buyers in Britain's ready-to-wear sector. Provides coverage of new equipment, products, services, and new fabric trends and availability. Price £15.00 United Kingdom, £25.00 overseas.

599.02
British Columbia Business Bulletin
Ministry of Industry and Small Business Development, Parliament Buildings, Victoria, BC, Canada V8V 1X4. Telephone (604) 387-6701.

Monthly report. Summarizes current British Columbia economic and business indicators. Price free of charge.

600
British Columbia Corporation Manual
Richard De Boo Ltd, 70 Richmond St, Toronto, Ont, Canada M5C 2M8. Telephone (416) 367-0714.

Three loose-leaf books. Contain statutes and regulations affecting corporations in British Columbia, Canada. Include material on cooperative associations, credit unions, and professional corporations. Price $125.00 per year.

601
British Columbia Corporations Law Guide
CCH Canadian Ltd, 6 Garamond Ct, Don Mills, Ont, Canada M3C 1Z5. Telephone (416) 429-2992.

Loose-leaf book, plus monthly updates. Covers British Columbia Companies Act and related regulations. Price $160.00 per year.

601.01
British Columbia Economic Activity, 1980 Review and Outlook
Ministry of Industry and Small Business Development, Parliament Buildings, Victoria, BC, Canada V8V 1X4. Telephone (604) 387-6701.

Annual book. Summarizes British Columbia's economic activity during the previous year. Offers economic forecast. Contains statistical supplement with 10-year historical perspective. Price free of charge.

601.02
British Columbia Export/Import Opportunities
Ministry of Industry and Small Business Development, Parliament Buildings, Victoria, BC, Canada V8V 1X4. Telephone (604) 387-6701.

Bimonthly report. Lists foreign inquiries on import, export, and licensing opportunities. Price free of charge.

602
British Columbia Facts and Statistics
Ministry of Industry and Small Business Development, Vic, BC, Canada V8V 1X4. Telephone (604) 387-6701.

Booklet. Furnishes statistics on the resources, people, and economy of British Columbia. Price free of charge.

602.01
British Columbia Industry and Small Business News
Ministry of Industry and Small Business Development, Parliament Buildings, Victoria, BC, Canada V8V 1X4. Telephone (604) 387-6701.

Newsletter. Reports on business activity and government programs in British Columbia. Price free of charge.

603
British Columbia Lumberman
Southam Communications Ltd, 1450 Don Mills Rd, Don Mills, Ont, Canada M3B 2X7. Order from Southam Communications Ltd, 2000 W 12th Ave, Vancouver, BC V6J 2G2, Canada. Telephone (604) 731-1171. Telex 04-51158.

Monthly magazine. Contains information on British Columbia's forest industry. Price available on request.

604
British Columbia Manufacturers' Directory
Ministry of Industry and Small Business Development, Vic, BC, Canada V8V 1X4. Telephone (604) 387-6701.

Annual directory. Lists manufacturers in British Columbia. Indicates products both alphabetically and by product classification. Price free of charge.

605
British Columbia Market News
Ministry of Economic Development, Vic, BC, Canada V8V 4R9. Order from Box 10111, 700 W Georgia St, Vancouver, BC, Canada V7Y 1C6. Telephone Victoria (604) 387-6701; Vancouver (604) 668-2878.

Monthly newsletter. Covers economic development in British Columbia, including manufacturing, government programs, and exports and imports. Price available on request.

606

British Columbia Municipal Yearbook
JSB Production Ltd, PO Box 46475, Station G, Vancouver, BC V6R 4G7 Canada. Telephone (604) 228-9213.

Annual book. Provides data on British Columbia's municipalities, school districts, and regional districts. Price $7.00.

607

British Columbia Review and Outlook
Ministry of Industry and Small Business Development, Vic, BC, Canada V8V 1X4. Telephone (604) 387-6701.

Annual book. Reviews British Columbia's economy. Includes material on foreign trade, capital investment, and major industries. Price free of charge.

608

British Columbia Statute Citator
Canada Law Book Ltd, 240 Edward St, Aurora, Ont, L4G 3S9, Canada. Telephone (416) 859-3880.

Loose-leaf book, plus quarterly updates. Provides citation and chapter number of all acts in Revised Statutes of British Columbia, 1960. Includes information on regulations, and relevant court cases. Price $57.00 per year, $25.00 additional for binder and contents.

609

British Commercial Agents Review
British Agents Register, 23 Victoria Ave, Harrogate N Yorkshire, England HG1 5RE. Telephone STD 0423 60608.

Monthly report. Discusses role of manufacturer's agent, with emphasis on Great Britain. Advertises opportunities for agents. Price $25.00.

610

British Company Service
Extel Statistical Services Ltd, 37-45 Paul St, London, England EC2A 4PB. Telephone (44) (01) 253 3400. Telex 262687.

Annual card service, with daily updating. Provides financial and other information on most companies listed on the British and Irish stock exchanges. Includes balance sheets, dividend records, yields, and earnings. Price £1,700.00 per year.

611

British Economy in Figures
Lloyds Bank Ltd, PO Box 215, Lomard St, London, England EC3P 3BS. Telephone 01-626 1500.

Annual pamphlet. Gives figures on British national income, production, manpower, prices, trade, government finance, and quality of life. Price free of charge.

613

British Exports
Kompass Publishers Ltd, Windsor Court, East Grinstead House, Grinstead, West Sussex, England RH19 1XD. Telephone 0342 26972.

Annual book. Furnishes a registry to 18,000 British products available for export. Notes British exporter and corresponding overseas agency. Price £25.00 per copy.

614

British Industry and Services in the Common Market
Kelly's Directories Ltd, Windsor Court, E Grinstead House, W Sussex, England RH19 1XB. Telephone(44) (01) 0342 26972.

Annual book. Gives a roster of British companies providing goods and services needed by EEC buyers. Notes British company agents in common market countries and British companies involved in import and export services. Price £25.00 per copy.

615

British-Israel Trade Journal
British-Israel Chamber of Commerce, Information & Trade Centre, 126-134 Baker St, London, England WIM 1FH. Telephone (44) 01-486-4143.

Bimonthly journal. Provides news and features about bilateral British-Israeli trade, investments, and joint ventures. Price available on request.

616

British Journal of Industrial Relations
London School of Economics & Political Science, Houghton St, London, England WC2A 2AE. Telephone (44) (01) 242 2288, Ext. 247.

Magazine issued three times per year. Contains articles by experts on industrial relations. Encompasses the results of current research. Price $40.00 per year.

617

British Journal of Nutrition
Cambridge University Press, 32 E 57th St, New York, NY 10022. Telephone (212) 688-8885.

Bimonthly journal. Provides papers on clinical, human, experimental, and farm animal nutrition. Price $230.00 per year.

618

British Labour Statistics Year Book
Her Majesty's Stationery Office, PO Box 569, London, England SE1 9NH. Telephone (44) (01) 214 6159. Telex 915564.

Annual book. Contains detailed British labor statistics for previous year with some data on earlier years. Price £20.00 per year. ISBN 011 361097 1.

619

British Plastics and Rubber
Maclean-Hunter Ltd, 30 Old Burlington St, London, England W1X 2AE. Telephone (44) (01) 434 2233.

Monthly journal. Provides news and technical articles on all aspects of the plastics and rubber industries. Focuses on British developments. Price available on request.

620

British Printer
Maclean-Hunter Ltd, 30 Old Burlington St, London, England W1X 2AE. Telephone (44) (01) 434 2233.

Monthly journal. Presents articles by specialists on Great Britain's printing and graphic arts. Covers technological development and exhibitions. Price available on request.

621

British Rate & Data
Maclean-Hunter Ltd, 30 Old Burlington St, London, England W1X 2AE. Telephone (44) (01) 434 2233.

Publication. Gives details on the British advertising media, including newspapers, television, and numerous other forms. Price available on request.

622

British Rate & Data
Standard Rate & Data Service, Inc, 5201 Old Orchard Rd, Skokie, IL 60077. Telephone (312) 470-3100.

Monthly book. Lists advertising rates and information for British television and radio stations, newspapers, and periodicals. Price $310.00 per year.

623

British Tax Guide
Commerce Clearing House, Inc, 4025 W Peterson Ave, Chicago, IL 60646. Telephone (312) 583-8500.

Four loose-leaf books, plus monthly reports. Cover Great Britain's surtax, and income, corporate, and capital gains taxes. Price $450.00 per year.

623.01
British Tax Report

Inst for International Research Ltd, 70 Warren St, London, England W1P 5PA. Telephone (44) (01) 388-2663. Telex 263504.

Monthly report. Analyzes British tax news. Discusses tax planning for individuals and companies. Price $185.00 per year.

624
British Tax Review

Sweet and Maxwell/Stevens Periodicals, 11 New Fetter Ln, London, England EC4P 4EE. Order from Carswell Co Ltd, 2330 Midland Ave, Agincourt, Ont, Canada MIS 1P7. Telephone England (44) (01) 583 9855. Telex 263398. Canada (416) 291-8421.

Bimonthly periodical. Contains articles and notes on British tax topics and recent cases. Includes book reviews. Price $71.00 per year.

625
Broadcasting

Broadcasting Publications, Inc, 1735 De Sales St NW, Washington, DC 20036. Telephone (202) 638-1022.

Weekly magazine. Reports on radio, television and cable TV news. Notes new equipment, FCC rule changes, and people in the business. Price $50.00 per year.

627
Broadcasting/Cable Yearbook

Broadcasting Publications, Inc, 1735 De Sales St NW, Washington, DC 20036. Telephone (202) 638-1022.

Yearbook. Lists information on all US and Canadian radio and television stations and cable TV systems. Includes a guide to equipment manufacturers and program services producers. Price $60.00.

628
Broadcast Investor

Paul Kagan Assocs, Inc, 100 Merrick Rd, Rockville Centre, NY 11570. Telephone (516) 764-5516.

Semimonthly newsletter. Contains reports on investments in radio-television stations. Digests FCC files on station sales. Price $215.00 per year.

629
Broadwoven Fabrics Finished

US Dept of Commerce, Bureau of the Census, Washington, DC 20233. Telephone (202) 449-1600.

Quarterly report. Contains data on the production of woolen, worsted, and other fabrics. Price $.25.

629.01
Brookings Papers on Economic Activity

Brookings Institution, 1775 Massachusetts Ave, NW, Washington, DC 20036. Telephone (202) 797-6000.

Journal issued three times per year. Provides analyses of economic developments. Offers research studies on the American economy. Price available on request.

630
Brown's Directory

Harcourt Brace Jovanovich Publications, 757 3rd Ave, New York, NY 10017. Order from Harcourt Brace and Jovanovich Publications, 1 E 1st St, Duluth, MN 55802. Telephone (218) 727-8511.

Annual directory. Contains data on US and Canadian natural gas utilities and personnel. Price $95.00 per copy.

631
BRU Export Finance Service

Financial Times Business Information Ltd, Bracken House, 10 Cannon St, London, England EC4P 4BY. Order from Financial Times Ltd, 75 Rockefeller Plz, New York, NY 10019. Telephone (44) (01) 248-8000. Telex 886341-2.

Quarterly loose-leaf service with annual supplement. Details terms at which exports are financed and insured in the US, Great Britain, Germany, France, Belgium, Italy, Japan, South Africa, and the Netherlands. Price $210.00 per year.

632
Brussels Report

International Business-Government Counsellors, Inc, 1625 Eye St NW, Washington, DC 20006. Telephone (202) 872-8181. Telex 440511.

Biweekly report on EEC. Includes material on company law, consumer affairs, government procurement, industrial policy, corporate tax, and industrial democracy. Emanates from Brussels. Price $252.00 per year.

633
Building and Environment

Pergamon Press, Inc, Maxwell House, Fairview Park, Elmsford, NY 10523. Telephone (914) 592-7700. Telex 13-7328.

Quarterly journal. Publishes original papers and review articles on building and architectural topics. Includes book reviews. Price $85.00 per year.

634
Building and Realty Record

Advertising Communications Times, 121 Chestnut St, Philadelphia, PA 19106. Telephone (215) 629-1611.

Monthly newspaper. Covers news and issues affecting the development and real estate of eastern Pennsylvania, Southern New Jersey, and Delaware. Price $8.50 per year.

634.01
Building Conservation

Northwood Publications Ltd, Elm House, 10–16 Elm St, London, England WC1X OBP. Order from Subscription Manager, 23–29 Emerald St, London, England WC1N 3QJ. Telephone (44)(01) 404-5531. Telex 21746.

Monthly magazine. Geared to persons holding senior positions within the professional or industrial areas of repair, restoration, reconstruction, and rehabilitation of building structures and infrastructures. Price £24.00 per year.

635
Building Construction Cost Data

R S Means Co, Inc, 100 Construction Plaza, Kingston, MA 02364. Telephone (617) 747-1270.

Annual book. Presents updated cost data for building materials, installation, crews, and equipment. Price $24.50.

636
Building Design

Morgan–Grampian Ltd, Morgan–Grampian House, Calderwood St, London, England SE18 6QH. Order from Morgan–Grampian Publishing Co, 2 Park Ave, New York, NY 10016. Telephone England 855 7777. Telex 896238 MORGAN G. Telephone New York (212) 340-9700. Telex 425592 MGI UI.

Weekly newspaper. Contains articles about architecture published for those concerned with improving natural and man-made environment. Price $65.00 per year.

637

Building Design & Construction
Cahners Publishing Co, Inc, 221 Columbus Ave, Boston, MA 02116. Telephone (617) 536-7780.

Monthly magazine. Contains articles on news and trends in building construction. Includes coverage of architecture, engineering, contracting, and building ownership. Price $25.00 per year.

639

Building Materials
Stokes & Lindley-Jones Ltd, Alverstoke House, 21 Montpelier Row, Blackheath, London, England SE3 0SR. Telephone (44) (01) 852 9865.

Biannual report. Tells of building materials ready for export from Great Britain. Price £25.00 for three years to qualified subscribers.

640

Building Permits
Statistics Canada, User Services, Publications Distribution, Ottawa, Ont, Canada K1A 0V7. Telephone (613) 992-3151.

Monthly report. Provides information on building permits issued by Canadian municipalities. Covers the number of new dwelling units by type and value of residential, commercial, governmental, and institutional building construction. Price $42.00 per year. ISSN 0318-8809.

641

Building Products News
Thomson Publications (Australia) Pty Ltd, 47 Chippen St, PO Box 65, Chippendale, NSW 2008, Australia. Telephone 699-6731. Telex TPAS AA22226.

Monthly magazine. Reports on building products and construction topics. Stresses Australian experience. Price $52.00 (Australian) per year.

641.01

Building Refurbishment
Morgan-Grampian Ltd, Morgan-Grampian House, Calderwood St, London England SE18 6QH. Telephone (44) (01) 855-7777. Telex 896238. Order from Morgan-Grampian Publishing Co, 2 Park Ave, New York, NY 10016. Telephone (212) 340-9700. Telex 425592 MGI UI.

Bimonthly magazine. Covers building refurbishment and maintenance, including technology, design, products, and equipment. Price $20.00 per year.

642

Building Supply News
Cahners Publishing Co, Inc, 221 Columbus Ave, Boston, MA 02116. Telephone (617) 536-7780.

Monthly magazine. Provides marketing and management information for retail and wholesale building supply establishments. Price $35.00 per year.

642.01

Building Systems Cost Guide
R S Means Co, Inc, 100 Construction Plz, Kingston, MA 02364. Telephone (617) 747-1270.

Annual book. Provides illustrations, descriptions, specifications, and updated costs for building systems ranging from excavation through specialties and equipment. Price $32.00.

642.02

Building Trades Journal
Northwood Publications Ltd, Elm House, 10–16 Elm St, London, England WC1X OBP. Order from Subscription Manager, 23–29 Emerald St, London, England WC1N 3QJ. Telephone (44)(01)404-5531. Telex 21746.

Weekly publication. Reports on Great Britain's building industry for the small to medium sized builder. Price £20.00 per year.

643

Bulk
Turret Press Ltd, 4 Local Board Rd, Watford, Herts, England WD1 2JS. Order from UK Publishers, Inc, PO Box 36420 Fort Logan, Denver, CO 80236. Telephone Watford (0923) 46199.

Bimonthly magazine. Covers handling of bulk materials. Includes buyers' guide. Price £51.00 per year.

643.01

Bulletin
University of Sussex, Institute of Development Studies at the Brighton, England BN1 9RE. Telephone Brighton (0273) 606261. Telex 877159. RR Hove IDS. Cable: Development Brighton.

Quarterly bulletin. Contains brief articles on international and Third World development problems and research results. Price $27.00 per year.

644

Bulletin of Economic Research
University of Leeds, School of Economic Studies, Leeds, England LS2 9JT. Telephone 31751.

Biannual magazine. Presents articles on theoretical and applied economic research. Subjects include modern macroeconomics, international economics, and applied econometric work. Price $18.00 per copy.

645

Bulletin of Labour Statistics
International Labour Organization, 1750 New York Ave NW, Suite 330, Washington, DC 20006. Telephone (202) 396-2315.

Quarterly report with eight supplements. Complements annual data presented in Yearbook of Labour Statistics. Price $28.50 per year.

645.01

Bulletin of the American Society for Information Science
American Society for Information Science, 1010 16th St, NW, Washington, DC 20036. Telephone (202) 659-3644.

Bimonthly journal. Reports on information science developments. Price available on request.

646

Bulletin of the European Communities
Commission of the European Communities, Office for Official Publications of the European Communities, CP 1003, Luxembourg 1, Luxembourg. Telephone (352) 490081. Telex PUBLOF 1325.

Contains features and news items on activity within the European community. Covers economic, agricultural, environmental, social, and political topics. Price $38.50 per year.

647

Bulletin on Documentation
Commission of the European Communities, Office for Official Publications of the European Communities, CP 1003, Luxembourg 1, Luxembourg. Telephone Luxembourg 490081. Telex PUBLOF 1325.

Weekly report. Provides information on the European community publications in six languages. Price $42.00 per year.

648
Bunker Fuels
US Dept of Commerce, Bureau of the Census, Washington, DC 20233. Telephone (202) 449-1600.

Monthly and annual report. Contains data on the value and quantity of oil and coal of domestic and foreign origin laden on US and foreign flag vessels. Shows quantity for each customs district. Price $3.25 per year.

649
Bureau of National Affairs (BNA)
Patent, Trademark & Copyright Journal
Bureau of National Affairs, Inc, 1231 25th St NW, Washington, DC 20037. Telephone (202) 452-4200.

Loose-leaf books, with weekly updates. Analyze developments in patent, trademark, and copyright fields. Give text of major legislation, opinions, and speeches. Include a calendar and an index. Price $364.00 per year.

650
Bureau of National Affairs (BNA)
Policy & Practice Series
Bureau of National Affairs, Inc, 1231 25th St NW, Washington, DC 20037. Telephone (202) 452-4200.

Loose-leaf books, with updates. Cover employer-employee relations, labor laws, collective bargaining, wages and hours, and equal employment opportunity. Include special survey reports. Price $564.00 per year.

651
Bureau of the Census Catalog
US Dept of Commerce, Bureau of the Census, Washington, DC 20233. Telephone (202) 449-1600.

Quarterly book, with monthly supplements. Lists publications, data files, and special tabulations of the Bureau of Census. Price $19.00 per year.

652
Bureau of the Census Catalog of
Publications, 1790–1972
US Dept of Commerce, Bureau of the Census, Washington, DC 20233. Order from Superintendent of Documents, Government Printing Office, Washington, DC 20402. Telephone (202) 783-3238.

Catalog. Contains bibliography of sources for Census Bureau statistics from 1790 to 1972. Price $7.10.

653
Business
Georgia State University, College of Business Adm, Business Publishing Div, Univ Plz, Atlanta, GA 30303. Telephone (404) 658-4253.

Bimonthly magazine. Provides management technique ideas for managers in all types and sizes of business organizations. Price $15.00 per year. ISSN 0163-531X.

654
A G Bush Library Abstracts
University of Chicago, Industrial Relations Center, A G Bush Library, 1225 E 60th St, Chicago, IL 60637. Telephone (312) 753-2024.

Monthly report. Provides abstracts of books and articles on organizations, management, personnel, human behavior, work force, and industrial relations. Price $15.00 per year. ISSN 0001-1304.

655
Business Acquisitions Desk Book
with Checklists and Forms, 2nd
edition
Institute for Business Planning, Inc, IPB Plz, Dept 7102-81, Englewood Cliffs, NJ 07632. Telephone (201) 592-2040.

Book. Advises businessmen on the acquisitions of other companies. Discusses how to evaluate a company's assets and liabilities. Checklists and forms. Price $39.50. ISBN 0-87624-050-3.

656
Business America
US Dept of Commerce, 14th St between Constitution Ave and E St NW, Washington, DC 20230. Order from Superintendent of Documents, US Government Printing Office, Washington, DC 20402. Telephone (202) 783-3238.

Report. Covers US and international business developments. Evaluates economic conditions and various US industries. Price $41.00 per year.

657
Business & Acquisition Newsletter
Newsletters International, 2600 S Gessner Rd, Houston, TX 77063. Telephone (713) 783-0100.

Monthly newsletter. Reports on companies that want to buy or sell companies, product lines, and patents. Notes firms seeking or possessing venture capital. Price $100.00 per year.

658
Business & Capital Reporter
National Counselor Reports, Inc, Task Bldg, Kerrville, TX 78028. Telephone (512) 257-5050.

Monthly newsletter. Lists nationwide lending and investment opportunities ranging from $10,000 to $10,000,000. Includes such ventures as those involving agriculture, trade, and land development. Price $100.00 for 12 issues.

659
Business & Commercial Aviation
Ziff-Davis Publishing Co, 1156 15th St NW, Washington, DC 20005. Order from Ziff-Davis Publishing Co, Hangar C-1, White Plains, NY 10604. Telephone (914) 548-1912.

Monthly magazine. Covers trade news and trends in the business and commercial aviation industry. Price available on request.

660
Business and Economic Review
University of South Carolina, Div of Research, College of Business Adm, Columbia, SC 29208. Telephone (803) 777-2510.

Bimonthly report. Contains articles on business and economic topics of interest to managers in the private or public sectors. Includes current South Carolina statistical indicators. Price free of charge.

661
Business and Finance
Belenos Publications Ltd, 50 Fitzwilliam Sq W, Dublin 2, Ireland. Telephone (353) (01) 764587 and 760869.

Weekly magazine. Reports on business conditions in the Republic of Ireland. Price available on request.

663
Business & Professional Woman
Canadian Federation of Business and Professional Women's Clubs, 56 Sparks St, Ottawa, Canada K1P 5A9. Telephone (613) 234-7619.

Magazine published five times per year. Concerned with the economic status of women. Publishes news and information about economic, employment, and social conditions. Price $3.00 per year.

664

Business & Professional Women
United Kingdom Federation of Business & Professional, Women, 54 Bloomsbury St, London, England WC1B 3QU. Telephone (44) (01) 580 9686.

Quarterly magazine. Discusses British business opportunities for women and legislation affecting women workers. Notes international women's employment trends. Price £1.00 per year.

665

Business & Public Affairs
Murray State University, College of Business & Public Affairs, Murray, KY 42071. Telephone (502) 762-4181.

Semiannual magazine. Covers business, labor, accounting, economics and management issues. Price free of charge.

666

Business & Society
Roosevelt University, Heller College of Business Adm, 430 S Michigan Ave, Chicago, IL 60605. Telephone (312) 341-3822.

Semiannual magazine. Discusses issues of corporate social responsibility, such as advertising and environmental protection. Price $3.00 for two years.

667

Business & Society Review
Warren, Gorham & Lamont, Inc, 210 S St, Boston, MA 02111. Telephone (617) 423-2020.

Quarterly report. Discusses social responsibilities of business. Price $38.00 per year.

668

Business Asia
Business International Corp, 1 Dag Hammarskjold Plz, New York, NY 10017. Telephone (212) 750-6300.

Weekly newsletter. Covers trade opportunities and business developments in Asia and the Pacific. Price $450.00 per year.

669

Business Automation Reference Service. Computer Equipment
Alltech Publishing Co, 212 Cooper Ctr, N Park Dr & Browning Rd, Pennsauken, NJ 08109. Telephone (609) 662-2122.

Two-volume loose-leaf set with monthly updates. Supplies charts and abstracts on computer and peripheral systems, including printers, tape drives, and disk drive. Price $100.00 per year.

670

Business Automation Reference Service. Computer Software
Alltech Publishing Co, 212 Cooper Ctr, N Park Dr & Browning Rd, Pennsauken, NJ 08109. Telephone (609) 662-2122.

Two-volume loose-leaf set, with monthly updates. Provides charts and abstracts on computer software. Price $100.00 per year.

671

Business Automation Reference Service. Office Equipment
Alltech Publishing Co, 212 Cooper Ctr, N Park Dr & Browning Rd, Pennsauken, NJ 08109. Telephone (609) 662-2122.

Two-volume loose-leaf set, with monthly updates. Contains charts and abstracts related to the automated office equipment field. Includes devices for microfilming, word processing, and copying. Price $100.00 per year.

672

Business Automation Reference Service. Peripheral Equipment
Alltech Publishing Co, 212 Cooper Ctr, N Park Dr & Browning Rd, Pennsauken, NJ 08109. Telephone (609) 662-2122.

Two-volume loose-leaf set with monthly updates. Provides charts and abstracts on data communications, data collections, OCR devices, and key-to-storage. Price $100.00 per year.

673

Business Books and Serials in Print, **3rd edition, 1977**
R R Bowker Co, 1180 Ave of the Americas, New York, NY 10036. Order from R R Bowker Co, PO Box 1807, Ann Arbor, MI 48106. Telephone (212) 764-5100.

Book. Gives finding, ordering, and bibliographic data for more than 31,500 titles, which are indexed by author, title, and business subjects. Includes a directory of publishers. Price $37.50. ISBN 0-8352-0965-2. ISSN 0000-0396.

674

Business China
Business International Corp, 1 Dag Hammarskjold Plz, New York, NY 10017. Telephone (212) 750-6300.

Biweekly report. Discusses opportunities for establishing or expanding markets in the People's Republic of China, Vietnam, North Korea, Cambodia, Laos, Mongolia, and the Soviet Far East. Price $265.00 per year.

675

Business Conditions Bulletin
Arthur Young & Co, 277 Park Ave, New York, NY 10017. Telephone (212) 922-4724.

Quarterly report. Presents analyses of current and forecasted economic and business conditions in Canada. Price free of charge.

676

Business Conditions Digest
US Dept of Commerce, Bureau of Economic Analysis, Washington, DC 20230. Order from Budget Office, Bureau of Economic Analysis, Washington, DC 20230. Telephone (202) 523-0961.

Information service. Furnishes data on national income and product accounts, employment, production, trade, fixed capital investment, prices, profits, money credit, and foreign trade. Price $100.00

676.01

Business Crime: Criminal Liability of the Business Community
Matthew Bender & Co, 235 E 45th St, New York, NY 10017. Telephone (212) 661-5050.

Six-volume book with semiannual updates. Covers business crime law and practice. Includes information on securities fraud, bank fraud, and corporate tax fraud. Price $360.00.

677

Business Eastern Europe
Business International Corp, 1 Dag Hammarskjold Plz, New York, NY 10017. Telephone (212) 750-6300.

Weekly report. Discusses new developments on and sales and licensing opportunities in the Union of Soviet Socialist Republics, Bulgaria, East Germany, Czechoslovakia, Hungary, Poland, Rumania, and Yugoslavia. Price $560.00 per year.

678

Business Economic Outlook Forum
University of Colorado, Business Research Div, Graduate School of Business Adm, Boulder, CO 80309. Telephone (303) 492-8227.

Annual report. Analyzes and forecasts Colorado's economy. Includes data on population, agriculture, mining, manufacturing, construction, and retail trade. Tables and charts. Price free of charge.

679
Business Economics
National Assn of Business Economists, 28349 Chagrin Blvd, Cleveland, OH 44122. Telephone (216) 464-7986.

Quarterly publications. Contains articles of interest to the professional business economist. Price $15.00 per year, $23.00 overseas.

680
Business Education Forum
National Business Education Assn, 1914 Association Dr, Reston, VA 22091. Telephone (703) 860-0213.

Magazine published eight times per year. Discusses business education, including teacher education, curriculum, and specific subjects. Price available only to members.

681
Business Europe
Business International Corp, 1 Dag Hammarskjold Plz, New York, NY 10017. Telephone (212) 750-6300.

Weekly eight-page report. Discusses the opportunities and dangers of doing business with, within, and from Europe, emphasizing marketing, finance, taxation and management, and the European Economic Community. Price $690.00 per year.

681.01
Business Executives' Expectations
Conference Board, Inc, 845 3rd Ave, New York, NY 10022. Telephone (212) 759-0900.

Quarterly report. Surveys executives' views on current and prospective economic conditions, and the outlook for their industries. Contains monthly topical question. Price available on request.

682
Business Failure Record
Dun & Bradstreet, Inc, c/o Dun Donnelly Publishing Corp, 666 5th Ave, New York, NY 10019. Telephone (212) 489-2200.

Annual report. Gives statistics on business failures. Price available on request.

683
Business Flying
National Business Aircraft Assn, One Farragut Sq, Washington, DC 20006. Telephone (415) 642-6682.

Quarterly report. Provides statistics on usage, safety marketing, and other aspects of business and corporate flying. Price $16.95.

684
Business Forms Reporter
North American Publishing Co, 401 N Broad St, Philadelphia, PA 19108. Telephone (215) 574-9600.

Monthly magazine. Covers the business forms industry, including printing plates, ink technology, and other equipment developments. Includes a directory of forms manufacturers and forms equipment suppliers. Price $18.00 per year.

685
Business Graduate
Business Graduates Assn, 87 Jermyn St, London, England SW1Y 69JD. Telephone 01-930 9368.

Journal published about three times a year to advance business and management practices and education in Great Britain. Price £15.00 per year. ISSN: 0306-3895.

686
Business History Review
Harvard University, Graduate School of Business Adm, Baker 217, Soldiers Field, Boston, MA 02163. Telephone (617) 495-6364.

Quarterly journal. Contains articles on business in a historical context, the evolution of business practices, and the interaction of businesspeople with their economic, political, and social environments. Price $15.00 individuals, $20.00 institutions and abroad.

687
Business Horizons
Indiana University, Graduate School of Business, Bloomington, IN 47405. Telephone (812) 337-5507.

Bimonthly report. Covers management theory and practice. Price $15.00 per year. ISSN 0007-6813.

688
Business Ideas Letter
Lorne, Caldough Ltd, Tower Suite, 1 White Hall Pl, London, England SW1. Telephone (44) (01) 930-5577.

Monthly newsletter. Offers advice on part-time businesses and for people interested in becoming self-employed. Price £29.50 per year.

689
Business Ideas Newsletter
Dan Newman Co, 57 Lakeview Ave, Clifton, NJ 07011. Telephone (201) 340-1166.

Monthly newsletter. Offers brief business, advertising, and promotional suggestions. Price $25.00 per year.

690
Business in Brief
Chase Manhattan Bank, Economics Group, 1 Chase Manhattan Plz, New York, NY 10015. Telephone (212) 552-3704.

Bimonthly newsletter. Reports on business and economic developments in the US and abroad. Price free of charge.

690.01
Business Index
Information Access Corp, 404 6th Ave, Menlo Park, CA 94025. Telephone (800) 227-8431.

Monthly microfilm service. Includes abstracts and index of all articles, reviews, news, and related business material from 325 business periodicals, and over 1100 general and legal periodicals. Catalogs business books and reports from the Library of Congress MARC (Machine Readable Cataloguing) database. Price $1860.00 per year.

690.02
Business Indicators
Bank of New Zealand, PO Box 2392, Wellington, New Zealand. Telex 3344 MONARCH.

Monthly pamphlet. Reports economic statistics and trends in New Zealand. Price free of charge.

691
Business Information for Dallas
Dallas Public Library, Business and Technology Div, 1954 Commerce St, Dallas, TX 75201. Telephone (214) 748-9071, ext. 226.

Bimonthly newsletter. Reports on Dallas Public Library newspapers, periodicals, books, on-line data bases, and information services covering business, finance, economic, and stock market developments. Price free of charge.

692
Business Information Reports
Dun & Bradstreet, Box 3224, Church St Station, New York, NY 10008. Telephone (212) 285-7346.

Information service. Reports on businesses' credit ratings. Gives immediate access to rating changes. Price on request. Available to Dun & Bradstreet subscribers only.

692.01
Business Information Service-Financial Times
Financial Times Business Information Ltd, Bracken House, 10 Cannon St, London, England EC4P 4BY. Order from Business Information Service, Financial Times, Bracken House, 10 Cannon St, London, England EC4P 4BY. Telephone (44)(01) 248-8000.

On-line service. Offers access to Financial Times files on companies, industries, and markets. Price available on request.

693
Business Information Sources
Lorna M Daniells, University of California Press, 2223 Fulton St, Berkeley, CA 94720. Telephone (415) 642-4247.

Book. Provides listing of business indexes, directories, publications, and statistical sources. Makes recommendations for a basic bookshelf. Price $14.95. ISBN 0-520-024946-1.

694
Business in Nebraska
University of Nebraska-Lincoln, Bureau of Business Research, 200 CBA, Lincoln, NE 68588. Telephone (402) 472-2334.

Monthly newsletter. Surveys Nebraska's economic conditions and business developments. Tables indicate prices, retail sales, banking activity, and other economic indicators. Price free of charge.

695
Business Insurance
Crain Communications, Inc, 740 Rush St, Chicago, IL 60611. Telephone (312) 649-5221.

Weekly newspaper. Discusses property and liability insurance, employee benefits, plant security and safety, and related business insurance topics. Price $30.00 per year.

696
Business International
Business International Corp, 1 Dag Hammarskjold Plz, New York, NY 10017. Telephone (212) 750-6300.

Weekly eight-page report. Discusses worldwide business problems and opportunities, emphasizing international management problems, laws and regulations, and business forecasts. Price $435.00 per year.

697
Business International (BI) Data
Business International Corp, 1 Dag Hammarskjold Plz, New York, NY 10017. Telephone (212) 750-6300.

On-line computer information service. Provides demographic, economic, and labor data for 131 countries, plus projections of population growth, industrial production and COL indexes, labor costs and conditions, exports and imports, and exchange and interest rates. Price $480.00 per year.

698
Business International (BI) Forecast for World Markets
Business International Corp, 1 Dag Hammarskjold Plz, New York, NY 10017. Telephone (212) 750-6300.

Regularly updated reports. Includes short-term forecasts of political, social, and economic conditions in major countries. Covers business conditions, historical data, government measures, and trade patterns. Graphs of key indicators from 1960 through forecast period. Price $60.00 per forecast.

699
Business International Money Report
Business International Corp, 1 Dag Hammarskjold Plz, New York, NY 10017. Telephone (212) 750-6300.

Weekly eight-page report. Analyzes the world financial and currency markets. Provides updates on interest and exchange rates. Price $598.00 per year.

699.01
Business International Washington (BIW)
Business International Corp, 1 Dag Hammarskjold Plaza, New York, NY 10017. Telephone (212) 750-6300.

Fortnightly report. Provides information for executives concerned about the impact of US Government on international corporate operations. Covers trends in taxation, trade restrictions, export financing, restrictive business practices, and incoming-outgoing investment. Price $195.00 per year.

700
Business Latin America
Business International Corp, 1 Dag Hammarskjold Plz, New York, NY 10017. Telephone (212) 750-6300.

Weekly analysis of regional developments throughout Latin America. Price $435.00 per year.

701
Business Law Cases for Australians
Commerce Clearing House, Inc, 4025 W Peterson Ave, Chicago, IL 60646. Telephone (312) 583-8500.

Monthly newsletter. Covers legislative and legal decisions affecting Australian business. Offers digests of actual case. Price $85.00 per year.

702
Business Law Reports. Volume 11
Carswell Co, Ltd, 2330 Midland Ave, Agincourt, Ont, Canada M1S 1P7. Telephone (416) 291-8421.

Monthly reports. Provides Canadian business law decisions and pertinent rulings of government agencies. Includes information on incorporations, consumer protection laws, and security regulations. Price $44.50.

703
Business Law Review
West Virginia University, Bureau of Business Research, Morgantown, WV 26506. Telephone (304) 293-5837.

Semiannual journal. Considers business law issues, such as teacher training and legislative changes. Contains comments, case digests and book reviews. Price $4.00 per year individuals. ISSN 0145-9074.

704
Business Lawyer
American Bar Assn, 1155 E 60th St, Chicago, IL 60637. Telephone (312) 947-3860.

Journal issued five times per year. Contains reports and commentary on developments in business-oriented law. Price $25.00 per year.

706

Business/Management Book Review
Industrial Bookshelf, Inc, 777 Mountain Ave, Murray Hill, NJ 07974. Telephone (201) 464-9062.

Fortnightly newsletter. Reviews new business and management books, noting qualifications of author, format, and audience to whom book is addressed. Price $15.00 per year.

707

Businessman & The Law
Man and Manager, Inc, 799 Broadway, New York, NY 10003. Telephone (212) 677-0640.

Semimonthly report. Presents legal cases and their effect on day-to-day business decisions. Annual index. Price $48.00 per year.

708

Businessman's Guide to Brazil
Guides to Multinational Business, Inc, Harvard Sq, Box 92, Cambridge, MA 02138. Telephone (617) 868-2288.

Annual book. Provides information about Brazil. Notes government, finance, transportation, and shipping data. Is designed to aid the foreign businessperson. Price $20.00.

709

Businessman's Guide to the Arab World
Guides to Multinational Business, Inc, Harvard Sq, Box 92, Cambridge, MA 02138. Telephone (617) 868-2288.

Annual book. Provides information about Arab countries for foreign businesspersons. Includes government, shipping, finance, and insurance data. Price $40.00.

710

Business Monitor, Production Series
Her Majesty's Stationery Office, PO Box 569, London, England SE1 9NH. Telephone (44) (01) 928 1321.

Series of monthly, annual, and quarterly reports. Monthly magazine. Provides summary figures on sales, production, orders, and inventories for selected British industries. Price available on request.

711

Business Monitor, Service and Distribution Series
Her Majesty's Stationery Office, PO Box 569, London, England SE1 9NH. Telephone (44) (01) 928 1321.

Series of monthly, annual, and quarterly reports. Provides summary on business activity in British retail distribution and service fields. Prices available on request.

712

Business Monitors Miscellaneous Series
Her Majesty's Stationery Office, PO Box 569, London, England SE1 9NH. Telephone (44) (01) 928-1321.

Series of statistics. Provides information on overseas transactions, travel, industrial research, motor vehicle registrations, and other subjects. Price available on request.

713

Business News
Euro Publications Ltd, 31 Churchill Way, Cardiff, Wales CF1 4HE. Order from 205 E 42 St, New York, NY 10017. Telephone Cardiff 0222 387508. New York (212) 867-2080.

Magazine issued six times per year. Covers business and industrial developments in Wales and South West England. Notes general British economic conditions and offshore oil drilling activity. Price £3.00 per year.

714

Business News
US-Yugoslav Economic Council, Inc, 51 E 42nd St, New York, NY 10017. Telephone (212) MU7-7797.

Monthly newsletter. Discusses Yugoslav business news and export trends. Indicates business opportunities for US firms. Price $75.00 per year.

715

Business Organizations with Tax Planning
Matthew Bender & Co, 235 E 45th St, New York, NY 10017. Telephone (212) 661-5050.

15-volume set of books. Provides information on the establishment, operation, dissolution, liquidation, and reorganization of all business organizations, including corporations, partnerships, and associations. Cites state and federal tax statutes. Price $650.00.

716

Business Periodicals Index
H W Wilson Co, 950 University Ave, Bronx, NY 10452. Telephone (212) 588-8400.

Monthly publication (except August) with quarterly cumulations and a bound annual. Provides an index to 272 business publications. Covers economics, finance, investments, management and personnel administration, transportation, and related subjects. Price available on request.

716.01

Business Publication Advertising Report
Media Records, Inc, 370 7th Ave, New York, NY 10001. Telephone (212) 736-7490.

Annual report. Lists advertising space and investments in trade publications by advertiser. Price available on request.

717

Business Publications Rates & Data
Standard Rate & Data Service, Inc, 5201 Old Orchard Rd, Skokie, IL 60077. Telephone (312) 470-3100.

Monthly book. Indicates advertising rates and information for 3600 business, trade, and technical publications. Price $125.00 per year.

718

Business Quarterly
University of Western Ontario, School of Business Adm, London, Ont, Canada N6A 3K7.

Quarterly magazine. Discusses business management topics. Includes results of business research. Price $16.00 for one year, $25.00 for two years.

719

Business Report
Manufacturers Hanover Trust Co, Corporate Communications Dept, 350 Park Ave, New York, NY 10022. Telephone (212) 350-3300. Telex 232337, 420966, 62814, 82615.

Quarterly report. Analyzes US business conditions. Statistics. Price free of charge.

720

Business Review and Economic News from Israel
Israel Discount Bank of New York, 511 5th Ave, New York, NY 10017. Telephone (212) 551-8500. Telex 420250.

Quarterly booklet. Reviews Israeli economic, industrial, and stock market developments. Notes Israel Discount Bank news. Price free of charge.

721
Business Service Centers
US General Services Adm, 18th and F Sts NW, Room 6034, Washington, DC 20405. Telephone (202) 566-1240.

Information service. Concerns General Services Administration business service centers, located throughout the US, that offer counseling to business people, provide publications on doing business with the federal government, and information on current bidding opportunities. Price free of charge.

723
Business Studies
Touche Ross International, 1633 Broadway, New York, NY 10019. Telephone (212) 489-1600.

Series of 20 books. Each describes investment factors, business practices, accounting and auditing, taxation, and other factors affecting business in a country. Also included in this series is *Tax & Trade Profiles*, similar in content but each book covers 10–15 countries. Price available on request.

724
Business Systems & Equipment
Maclean-Hunter Ltd, 30 Old Burlington St, London, England W1X 2AE. Telephone (44) (01) 434 2233.

Publication. Presents detailed, concise news about new business equipments, applications, and installations. Price available on request.

724.01
Business Travel Costs Worldwide
Guides to Multinational Business, Inc, Harvard Sq, Box 92, Cambridge, MA 02138. Telephone (617) 868-2288.

Book. Offers guide to business travel and entertainment expenses for over 70 countries. Includes data on hotel accommodations, restaurants, transportation, entertainment, secretarial, and translation services. Price $125.00.

725
Business Traveller
Export Times Publishing Ltd, 60 Fleet St, London, England EC4Y 1LA. Telephone (44) (01) 583-0968. Telex 27808.

Quarterly magazine. Suggests ways business travelers can save money, especially on air flights. Spotlighted in articles are cities frequented by businesspeople. Price $15.00 per year (Airmail).

726
Business Trends in New York State
New York Dept of Commerce, 99 Washington Ave, Albany, NY 12245. Telephone (518) 474-8670.

Monthly report. Reviews business activity in New York State. Gives statistical summary of significant economic indicators. Tables and graphs. Price free of charge.

727
Business Week
McGraw-Hill Publications Co, 1221 Ave of the Americas, New York, NY 10020. Telephone (212) 997-1221. Telex TWX 7105814879 WUI 62555.

Weekly magazine. Reports on US and international business and economic topics. Is aimed at business management personnel. Includes industrial, European, international, and five US regional editions. Price $34.95 per year.

728
Business Who's Who, 1974
Leviathan House, 11 John Princes St, Cavendish Sq, London, England W1M 9HB. Order from Hippocrene Books, Inc, 171 Madison Ave, New York, NY 10016. Telephone (212) 685-4371.

Book. Gives biographical data on top executives of major British companies. Includes boards of directors of the largest British companies. Price $30.00. ISBN 0-900537-21-3, H-316.

729
Buying Offices and Accounts
Salesman's Guide, Inc, 1140 Broadway, New York, NY 10001. Telephone (212) 684-2985.

Book. Lists paid and commission resident buying offices serving 11,000 accounts connected with sporting goods and men's, women's, and children's wear. Price $35.00.

730
Cable & Station Coverage Atlas
Television Digest, Inc, 1836 Jefferson Pl, NW, Washington, DC 20036. Telephone (202) 872-9200.

Annaul book. Contains maps indicating communities with cable systems and television station coverage. Includes cable television regulations. Price $96.50.

731
Cablecast
Paul Kagan Assoc, Inc, 100 Merrick Rd, Rockville Centre, NY 11570. Telephone (516) 764-5516.

Semimonthly newsletter. Provides financial analysis of cable television industry and CATV systems. Price $250.00 per year.

732
Cable TV Regulation
Paul Kagan Assoc, Inc, 100 Merrick Rd, Rockville Centre, NY 11570. Telephone (516) 764-5516.

Semimonthly newsletter. Deals with the federal, state, and local regulation of cable television. Includes listing of all rate increases. Price $150.00 per year.

733
California Construction Trends
Security Pacific National Bank, PO Box 2097, Terminal Annex, Los Angeles, CA 90015. Telephone (213) 613-5382.

Monthly magazine. Covers residential and nonresidential building permit activity in California. Price available on request.

735
California Credit Union League (CCUL) Digest
California Credit Union League, 2322 S Graey Ave, Pomona, CA 91766. Telephone (714) 628-6044.

Weekly newsletter. Contains news of credit union operations, technical information, legislative/regulatory advocacy, and training/educational programs. Price $100.00 per year.

736
California Eligible Securities List
Commerce Clearing House, Inc, 4025 W Peterson Ave, Chicago, IL 60646. Telephone (312) 583-8500.

Monthly newsletter. Lists eligible securities in California. Price $90.00 per year. ISSN 9995.

737
California International Trade
Security Pacific National Bank, PO Box 2097, Terminal Annex, Los Angeles, CA 90051. Telephone (213) 613-5414.

Magazine. Covers California's trade, particularly major trading partners and import and export trends. Price available on request.

737.01
California International Trade Register, 1980–81
Times Mirror Press, 1115 S Boyle Ave, Los Angeles, CA 90023. Telephone (213) 265-6767.

Biennial book. Lists California businesses involved in foreign trade. Includes import and export sections. Price $59.95.

738
California Management Review
University of California at Berkeley, Graduate School of Business Adm, Berkeley, CA 94720. Telephone (415) 642-7129.

Quarterly report. Covers a wide range of management concerns. Includes articles on management research. Price $15.00 US, Canada, South America, $20.00 foreign.

738.01
California: Manufacturers Register, 1981
Manufacturers' News, Inc, 3 E Huron St, Chicago, IL 60611. Telephone (312) 337-1084.

Annual directory. Lists 19,500 California manufacturing firms and notes products. Price $85.00.

738.02
California Manufacturers Register, 1981
Times Mirror Press, 1115 S Boyle Ave, Los Angeles, CA 90023. Telephone (213) 265-6767.

Annual book. Lists 19,000 manufacturers in California. Notes branch plants, products, and number of employees. Price $85.00.

738.03
California: Services Register, 1981
Manufacturers' News, Inc, 3 Huron St, Chicago, IL 60611. Telephone (312) 337-1084.

Annual directory. Provides information on service companies in California. Price $60.00.

738.04
California Services Register, 1981
Times Mirror Press, 1115 S Boyle Ave, Los Angeles, CA 90023. Telephone (213) 265-6767.

Annual book. Lists 12,000 service companies in California. Covers construction, insurance, real estate, finance, and other industries. Price $60.00.

738.05
California: State Industrial Directory, 1981
Manufacturers' News, Inc, 3 E Huron St, Chicago, IL 60611. Telephone (312) 337-1084.

Annual book. Identifies 14,000 industrial firms in California. Notes executives and number of employees. Price $70.00.

739
Called Bond Record
Standard & Poor's Corp, 25 Broadway, New York, NY 10004. Telephone (212) 248-2525.

Semiweekly loose-leaf service. Reports on bond and preferred stock calls, sinking fund proposals, definitive securities, defaulted bond data, and income bond interest payments. Supplies a calendar. Price $371.00 per year.

739.01
CA Magazine
Canadian Inst of Chartered Accountants, 250 Bloor St E, Toronto, Ont, Canada M4W 1G5. Telephone (416) 962-1242.

Monthly magazine. Contains news and information dealing with accounting, auditing, management, and taxation. Price $20.00 per year Canada $30.00 other countries.

740
Cambridge Studies in Applied Econometrics
John Wiley and Sons, Inc. 605 3rd Ave, New York, NY 10016. Telephone (212) 867-9800. Telex 12-7063.

Book series, three volumes. Cover theory and practice in field of ergonomics (volume 1). Focus on economic analysis and include models and projections (volumes 2 and 3). Price available on request.

740.01
Campaign Contributions and Lobbying Laws
Federal-State Reports, Inc, 5203 Leesburg Pike, #1201, Falls Church, VA 22041. Telephone (703) 379-0222.

Handbook, with periodic updates. Condenses over 100 laws which regulate campaign contributions and lobbying in 50 states and at the US federal level. Price $150.00 per year.

741
Campaign Practices Reference Service
Plus Publications, Inc, 2626 Pennsylvania Ave NW, Washington, DC 20037. Telephone (202) 333-5444.

Information service, with monthly updates. Analyzes laws, regulations, and judicial decisions covering federal campaign practices and financing. Price $131.00 per year.

742
Campaign Practices Reports
Plus Publications, Inc, 2626 Pennsylvania Ave NW, Washington, DC 20037. Telephone (202) 333-5444.

Fortnightly report. Contains news related to federal and state campaign practices and financing, including legislation, court cases, and Internal Revenue Service rulings. Price $97.00 per year.

743
Canada
Statistics Canada, User Services, Publications Distribution, Ottawa, Ont, Canada K1A OV7. Telephone (613) 992-3151.

Yearbook. Discusses Canadian environment, population, economy, and governmental services. Price $18.00 per year. ISSN 0068-8142.

744
Canada Commerce
Dept of Industry, Trade and Commerce, 235 Queen St., Ottawa, Ont, Canada K1A 0H5. Telephone (613) 995-7489.

Monthly magazine. Reports on Canadian trade. Price free of charge.

745
Canada Corporation Act Bulletin
Supply and Services Canada, Canadian Govt Publishing Centre, Hull, Que, Canada K1A 0S9. Telephone (819) 994-3475, 2085.

Monthly report. Provides information on Canada's Corporation Act. Bilingual. Price $27.60 per year.

746
Canada Corporation Manual
Richard De Boo Ltd, 70 Richmond St, Toronto, Ont, Canada M5C 2M8. Telephone (416) 367-0714.

Three loose-leaf books. Contain Canadian statutes and regulations affecting corporations, pension funds, and investment companies. Price $145.00 per year.

747
Canada Corporations Law Reports
CCH Canadian Ltd, 6 Garamond Ct, Don Mills, Ont, Canada M3C 1Z5. Telephone (416) 429-2992.

Two loose-leaf books, plus monthly updates. Covers federal legislation governing companies under Canadian charter. Include commentary based on Canada Business Corporations Act. Price $185.00 per year.

748
Canada Federal Court Reports
Supply and Services Canada, Canadian Govt Publishing Centre, Hull, Que, Canada K1A 0S9. Telephone (819) 994-3475, 2085.

Monthly report. Contains news of Canadian federal courts. Bilingual. Price $50.40 per year.

749
Canada Gazette/Part I
Supply and Services Canada, Canadian Govt Publishing Centre, Hull, Que, Canada K1A 0S9. Telephone (819) 994-3475, 2085.

Weekly magazine. Contains government notices, proclamations, and divorce notices. Bilingual. Price $25.00 per year.

750
Canada Gazette/Part II
Supply and Services Canada, Canadian Govt Publishing Centre, Hull, Que, Canada K1A 0S9. Telephone (819) 994-3475, 2085.

Semimonthly magazine. Covers Canadian statutory orders and regulations. Bilingual. Price $25.00 per year.

751
Canada Gazette/Part III
Supply and Services Canada, Canadian Govt Publishing Centre, Hull, Que, Canada K1A 0S9. Telephone (819) 994-3475, 2085.

Irregularly published magazine. Contains public acts of Canada. Bilingual. Price $25.00 per year.

752
Canada Handbook
Supply and Services Canada, Publishing Centre, Printing and Publishing, Ottawa, Ont, Canada K1A 0S9. Telephone (613) 238-1601.

Annual book. Summarizes recent social, economic, and cultural developments in Canada. Price $2.95.

753
Canada Income Tax Guide
CCH Canadian Ltd, 6 Garamond Ct, Don Mills, Ont, Canada M3C 1Z5. Telephone (416) 429-2992.

Loose-leaf book plus 18 reports per year. Explains Canadian federal income tax law. Illustrates with court decisions. Price $130.00 per year.

754
Canada Income Tax Regulations Service
Richard De Boo Ltd, 70 Richmond St, Toronto, Ont, Canada M5C 2M8. Telephone (416) 367-0714.

Two loose-leaf volumes. Notes continuing changes in Canadian income tax regulations, bulletins, and tax rulings. Provides historical notes, pertinent court cases, and index. Revised and supplemental pages issued frequently. Price $110.00 per year.

756
Canada–Japan Trade Council Newsletter
Canada–Japan Trade Council, Suite 903, 75 Albert St, Ottawa, Ont, Canada K1P 5E7. Telephone (613) 233-4047.

Monthly newsletter with information on business, trade, and investment between Canada and Japan. Price free of charge. ISSN 0045-4214.

757
Canada Labour Service
Richard De Boo Ltd, 70 Richmond St, Toronto, Ont, Canada M5C 2M8. Telephone (416) 367-0714.

Three loose-leaf volumes plus monthly updates. Consolidates all Canadian federal and provincial labor legislation. Summarizes recent developments. Price $149.00 per year.

758
Canada Manpower and Immigration Review
Canadian Dept of Manpower & Immigration (CN), Room U-802, Canada Manpower and Immigration Review, Ottawa, Ont, Canada K1A 0J9.

Quarterly report. Reviews Canadian manpower and immigration developments. Notes legislation and job creation programs. Tables provide unemployment, population, and other labor statistics. English and French. Price free of charge.

759
Canada Postal Guide/Part I
Supply and Services Canada, Publishing Centre, Printing and Publishing, Ottawa, Ont, Canada K1A 0S9. Telephone (613) 238-1601.

Loose-leaf book plus update service. Presents Canadian postal laws and general regulations. Price $13.50.

760
Canada Postal Guide/Part II
Supply and Services Canada, Publishing Centre, Printing and Publishing, Ottawa, Ont, Canada K1A 0S9. Telephone (613) 238-1601.

Loose-leaf book plus update series. Covers international mail, including rates. Price $20.00.

761
Canada Report
Canada Report, Box 5040, Toronto, Ont, Canada M5W 1N4.

Weekly newsletter on Canadian business and economic trends. Includes financial, industrial, political, and governmental information. Price $69.00 per year. ISSN 0384-9252.

762
Canada's Business Climate
Toronto-Dominion Bank, PO Box 1, Toronto Dominion Centre, Toronto, Ont, Canada M5K 1A2.

Quarterly report. Analyzes current Canadian business and economic trends. Offers forecasts for economic indicators, gross national product, personal income, employment, business investment, and exports and imports. Tables and charts. Price free of charge. ISSN 0045-4303.

762.01
Canada: Scott's Atlantic Industrial Directory 2nd edition, 1979–80
Manufacturers' News, Inc, 3 Huron St, Chicago, IL 60611. Telephone (312) 337-1084.

Biennial book. Identifies industrial firms in Canada's Atlantic provinces (New Brunswick, Nova Scotia, Prince Edward Island, Newfoundland). Price $57.75.

762.02
Canada: Scott's Ontario Industrial Directory 12th edition, 1981–82
Manufacturers' News, Inc, 3 Huron St, Chicago, IL 60611. Telephone (312) 337-1084.

Biennial book. Contains information on 14,500 industrial companies in Ontario. Price $98.50.

762.03
Canada: Scott's Quebec Industrial Directory, 10th edition, 1980–81
Manufacturers' News, Inc, 3 Huron St, Chicago, IL 60611. Telephone (312) 337-1084.

Biennial book. Lists 11,000 industrial firms in Quebec. Includes information about executives. Price $98.50.

762.04
Canada: Scott's Trade Directory, Metro Toronto, 1st edition, 1980–81
Manufacturers' News, Inc, 3 Huron St, Chicago, IL 60611. Telephone (312) 337-1084.

Book published every 18 months. Lists manufacturing and non-manufacturing companies in the metropolitan Toronto area. Price $90.00.

762.05
Canada: Scott's Trade Directory, Toronto Vicinity, 1st edition, 1980–81
Manufacturers' News, Inc, 3 Huron St, Chicago, IL 60611. Telephone (312) 337-1084.

Book published every 18 months. Lists businesses and manufacturing companies in 11 cities in the vicinity of Toronto. Price $60.00.

762.06
Canada: Scott's Western Canada Industrial Directory 5th edition, 1980–81
Manufacturers' News, Inc, 3 Huron St, Chicago, IL 60611. Telephone (312) 337-1084.

Biennial book. Lists industrial firms in western Canada (Manitoba, Saskatchewan, Alberta, and British Columbia). Price $98.50.

763
Canada's International Investment Position
Statistics Canada, User Services, Publications Distribution, Ottawa, Ont, Canada K1A OV7. Telephone (613) 992-3151.

Annual report. Supplies detailed analysis of foreign investments in Canada and Canadian investments abroad. Notes relative position of foreign capital in ownership and control of Canadian industry, investment financing, and income distribution. Price $9.60. ISSN 0318-8868.

764
Canada's Mental Health
Supply and Services Canada, Publishing Centre, Printing and Publishing, Ottawa, Ont, Canada K1A 0S9. Telephone (613) 238-1601.

Quarterly magazine. Covers mental health in Canada. Price $3.00 per year.

765
Canada Statute Citator
Canada Law Book Ltd, 240 Edward St, Aurora, Ont, L4G 3S9, Canada. Telephone (416) 859-3880.

Two loose-leaf books plus quarterly updates. Lists citation and chapter number of every act in Revised Statutes of Canada. Notes year enacted and in-force date. Price $52.00 per year, $38.00 additional for binder and contents (including relevant court cases).

766
Canada Supreme Court Reports
Supply and Services Canada, Canadian Govt Publishing Centre, Hull, Que, Canada, KIA 0S9. Telephone (819) 9994-3475.

Monthly report. Covers news of Canada's Supreme Court. Bilingual. Price $50.40 per year.

767
Canada Tax Cases
Richard De Boo Ltd, 70 Richmond St, Toronto, Ont, Canada M5C 2M8. Telephone (416) 367-0714.

Loose-leaf issued twice monthly plus bound volume at end of year. Contains complete text of judgments on Canadian federal cases. Price $145.00.

768
Canada Tax Manual
Richard De Boo Ltd, 70 Richmond St, Toronoto, Ont, Canada M5C 2M8. Telephone (416) 367-0714.

Loose-leaf service with monthly updates. Provides data on Canadian Income Tax Act. Covers such subjects as personal, corporate, property, income, and pension funds. Price $109.00 per year (includes annual copy of Act and Regulations).

769
Canada Tax Service
Richard De Boo Ltd, 70 Richmond St, Toronto, Ont, Canada M5C 2M8. Telephone (416) 367-0714.

Six loose-leaf binders with four updates each month. Provides commentary on Canadian federal income taxes and excise taxes. Contains full texts of acts, regulations and tax rulings. Price $319.00 per year.

770
Canada–United Kingdom Trade News
Canada–United Kingdom Chamber of Commerce, British Columbia House, 3 Regent St, London, England SW1 4NZ. Telephone 01-930 2794.

Monthly magazine. Discusses Canadian–British trade. Subjects include freight transportation, nationalized industries, and specific industry trends. Price £7.50, $20.00 Canada, $20.00 US per year.

771
Canada–United Kingdom Year Book
Canada–United Kingdom Chamber of Commerce, British Columbia House, 3 Regent St, London, England SW1 4NZ. Telephone 01-930 2794.

Yearbook. Supplies information on Canadian provinces, including population, industries, and natural resources. Lists Canadian–United Kingdom Chamber of Commerce members. Price £7.50, $20.00 Canada, $20.00 US per copy.

772
Canada Year Book
Supply and Services Canada, Publishing Centre, Printing and Publishing, Ottawa, Ont, Canada K1A OS9. Telephone (613) 238-1601.

Annual book. Covers economic, social, and political developments in Canada. Includes material on United Nations, education, arts, scientific research, and government programs. Price $10.00 per year.

773
Canadiana
Supply and Services Canada, Publishing Centre, Printing and Publishing, Ottawa, Ont, Canada K1A 0S9. Telephone (613) 238-1601.

Monthly report. Lists publications of interest to Canada received at National Library of Canada. Bilingual. Price $9.00 per year.

774
Canadian Advertising Rates & Data
Standard Rate & Data Service, Inc, 5201 Old Orchard Rd, Skokie, IL 60077. Telephone (312) 470-3100.

Monthly book. Contains advertising rates and related information for Canadian radio and television stations and networks, newspapers and periodicals, and transportation industry. Price $114.00 per year.

775
Canadian Architect
Southam Communications Ltd, 1450 Don Mills Rd, Don Mills, Ont, Canada M3B 2X7. Telephone (416) 445-6641. Telex 06 966612.

Monthly magazine. Deals with architectural field in Canada, including business and creative aspects. Price $47.00 per year.

776
Canadian Balance of International Payments. System of National Accounts
Statistics Canada, User Services, Publications Distribution, Ottawa, Ont, Canada K1A OV7. Telephone (613) 992-3151.

Annual report. Discusses and provides statistical analysis of current and capital account transactions between Canada and other countries. Price $12.00. ISSN 0318-8817.

777
Canadian Book of Corporate Management
Dun & Bradstreet, Box 3224, Church St Station, New York, NY 10008. Telephone (212) 285-7346.

Directory. Lists names, titles, and functions of key officers and managers in Canada's 6000 leading companies. Price available on request.

778
Canadian Business
CB Media Limited, 56 The Esplanade, Suite 214, Toronto, Ont, Canada M5E 1R5. Telephone (416) 364-4266.

Monthly magazine. Covering all aspects of Canadian business and current events affecting it. Price $18.00 per year. ISSN 0008-3100.

778.01
Canadian Business Index
Micromedia Ltd, 144 Front St W, Toronto, Ont, Canada M57 2L7. Telephone (416) 593-5211.

Monthly publication, with annual cumulation. Provides subject and personal name index for articles in over 176 Canadian business periodicals. Price $425.00 per year.

779
Canadian Business Law Journal
Canada Law Book Ltd, 240 Edward St, Aurora, Ont, L4G 3S9, Canada. Telephone (416) 859-3880.

Quarterly report plus annual book. Covers Canadian business and commercial law subjects, with emphasis on new legislation and court cases. Price $46.00 per volume.

780
Canadian Business Management Developments
CCH Canadian Ltd, 6 Garamond Ct, Don Mills, Ont, Canada M3C 1Z5. Telephone (416) 441-2992.

Loose-leaf book, plus semimonthly newsletter. Reports business world news. Cumulative topical index. Price $175.00 per year.

781
Canadian Business Review
Conference Board in Canada, Suite 100, 25 McArthur Rd, Ottawa, Ont, Canada K1L 6R3. Telephone (613) 746-1261.

Quarterly magazine. Reports on research and conference activities of Conference Board in Canada. Includes articles by authorities in business, government, and education. Price $2.00 per copy. ISSN 0317-4026.

782
Canadian Business Service Investment Reporter
Marpep Publishing Ltd, Suite 700, 133 Richmond St W, Toronto, Ont, Canada M5H 3M8. Telephone (416) 869-1177.

Weekly newsletter. Analyzes Canadian stocks. Recommends portfolios. Considers market outlook and individual companies. Price $145.00 per year. ISSN 0700-5539.

783
Canadian Business Trends
Conference Board in Canada, Suite 100, 25 McArthur Rd, Ottawa, Ont, Canada K1L 6R3. Telephone (613) 746-1261.

Three chart folders. Focuses on Canadian economy. Price available on request.

784
Canadian Chemical Processing
Southam Communications Ltd, 1450 Don Mills Rd, Don Mills, Ont, Canada M3B 2X7. Telephone (416) 445-6641. Telex 06-966612.

9 issues per year magazine. Offers technical information on chemical processing in Canada. Price $33.00 per year.

784.01
Canadian Commercial Law Guide
CCH Canadian Ltd, 6 Garamond Ct, Don Mills, Ont, Canada M3C 1Z5. Telephone (416) 429-2992.

Two-loose leaf books plus monthly updates. Give full text and commentary on Canadian federal and provincial laws relating to consumer protection and sales contracts. Price $195.00 per year.

785
Canadian Consulting Engineer
Southam Communications Ltd, 1450 Don Mills Rd, Don Mills, Ont, Canada M3B 2X7. Telephone (416) 445-6641. Telex 06 966612.

Monthly magazine. Discusses engineering field in Canada. Price $33.00 per year.

786
Canadian Consumer
Consumers' Assn of Canada, 200 First Ave, Ottawa, Ont, Canada K1S 5J3. Telephone (613) 238-4840.

Bimonthly magazine. Contains Canadian consumer information, including results of product testing, buying guides, and legislation. English and French editions. Price $10.00 per year. ISSN 0008-3275 (English).

786.01
Canadian Corporate Secretary's Guide
CCH Canadian Ltd, 6 Garamond Ct, Don Mills, Ont, Canada M3C 1Z5. Telephone (416) 441-2992.

Loose-leaf book, plus monthly updates. Reference manual for corporate secretaries and administrators. Includes duties and responsibilities, information on incorporation, and administration. Tables and finding lists. Price available on request.

787
Canadian Current Tax
Butterworth & Co (Canada) Ltd, 2265 Midland Ave, Scarborough, Ont, Canada M1P 4S1. Telephone (416) 292-1421.

Weekly loose-leaf service provides commentary on the tax field, including legislation and regulation. Price $30.00 per year. ISSN 409915491-01.

788
Canadian Daily Stock Charts
Canadian Analyst Ltd, 32 Front St W, Toronto, Ont, Canada M5J 1C5. Telephone (416) 363-4431.

Weekly service. Contains daily bar charts for 350 Canadian stocks. Provides price, earnings, and dividend data. Price $284.00 per year.

788.01
Canadian Economic Service
Data Resources, Inc, 29 Hartwell Ave, Lexington, MA 02173. Telephone (617) 861-0165.

Quarterly and annual report. Provides Canadian economic forecasts. Data cover consumption, investment, trade, public spending, fianance, prices, and industrial output. Price available on request.

789
Canadian Employment Benefits and Pension Guide
CCH Canadian Ltd, 6 Garamond Ct, Don Mills, Ont, Canada M3C 1Z5. Telephone (416) 429-2992.

Two loose-leaf books plus monthly updates. Presents Canadian and Quebec pension plans and provincial private pension plan legislation. Price $195.00 per year.

789.01
Canadian Employment Safety and Health Guide
CCH Canadian Ltd, 6 Garamond Ct, Don Mills, Ont, Canada M3C 1Z5. Telephone (416) 441-2992.

Two loose-leaf books, plus monthly reports. Discuss Canadian federal and provincial law and regulations pertaining to employment safety and health. Include inspection enforcement, workmen's compensation, and toxic substances. Price $225.00 per year.

790
Canadian Energy News
CCH Canadian Ltd, 6 Garamond Ct, Don Mills, Ont, Canada M3C 1Z5. Telephone (416) 429-2992. Telex 053-3601.

Semimonthly newsletter. Covers Canadian legislative and administrative activities, economic and technological developments related to energy problems. Price $150.00 per year.

791
Canadian Environmental Control Newsletter
CCH Canadian Ltd, 6 Garamond Ct, Don Mills, Ont, Canada M3C 1Z5. Telephone (416) 429-2992.

Semimonthly loose-leaf report on Canadian pollution and environmental control. Price $130.00 per year.

791.01
Canadian Estate Planning and Administration Reports
CCH Canadian Ltd, 6 Garamond Ct, Don Mills, Ont, Canada M3C 9Z9. Telephone (416) 429-2992.

Two loose-leaf books, plus monthly updates. Cover estate planning and administration in Canada. Include pertinent forms, precedents, examples, and corporation directory. Price $170.00 per year.

792
Canadian Farm Economics
Canada Dept of Agriculture Regional Development and International Affairs Branch (RD & IA Branch), Ottawa, Canada K1A OC5. Order from Publications Manager, Room E-132, Economics Branch, Canada Dept of Agriculture, Sir John Carling Bldg, Ottawa, Canada K1A OC5.

Bimonthly magazine. Provides articles on agricultural economics and agribusiness. Covers such topics as dairy policy, grain farming, beef marketing, and aid to developing countries. English and French. Price free of charge.

793
Canadian Footwear Journal
Southam Communications Ltd, 1450 Don Mills Rd, Don Mills, Ont, Canada M3B 2X7. Telephone (416) 445-6641. Telex 06-966612.

Journal issued nine times per year. Covers the footwear and leather industries in Canada. Price $22.00 per year.

794
Canadian Forest Industries
Southam Communications Ltd, 1450 Don Mills Rd, Don Mills, Ont, Canada M3B 2X7. Telephone (416) 445-6641. Telex 06-966612.

Monthly magazine. Covers production, equipment, and management of wood products industries. Price $33.00 per year.

795
Canadian Forestry Statistics
Statistics Canada, User Services, Publications Distribution, Ottawa, Ont, Canada K1A OV7. Telephone (613) 992-3151.

Annual report. Provides data on Canadian forestry industry. Includes classification of forest land and inventory estimates of timber by species. Price $7.20. ISSN 0575-805X.

796
Canadian Government Programs and Services
CCH Canadian Ltd, 6 Garamond Ct, Don Mills, Ont, Canada M3C 1Z5. Telephone (416) 429-2992.

Loose-leaf book plus monthly updates. Offers guide to Canadian federal government organization. Includes information on all departments. Lists members of Senate and House of Commons. Price $130.00 per year.

797
Canadian Government Publications Monthly Catalogue
Supply and Services Canada, Publishing Centre, Printing and Publishing, Ottawa, Ont, Canada K1A OS9. Telephone (613) 238-1601.

Monthly book. Provides catalog of Canadian government publications. Bilingual. Price $6.00 per year.

798
Canadian Income Tax Act, Regulations, and Rulings
CCH Canadian Ltd, 6 Garamond Ct, Don Mills, Ont, Canada M3C 1Z5. Telephone (416) 429-2992.

Two loose-leaf volumes. Contains consolidated texts of Income Tax Act and Income Tax Regulations for Canada, with historical notes and interpretations. Price $130.00 per year.

799
Canadian Income Tax (Revised)
Butterworth & Co (Canada) Ltd, 2265 Midland Ave, Searborough, Ont, Canada M1P 4S1. Telephone (416) 292-1421.

Twelve looseleaf volumes covering the application of Canadian income tax law. Includes also Canadian Current Tax. Price $240.00 per year. ISBN 0-409-81950-6.

800
Canadian Independent Adjuster
Canadian Independent Adjusters' Conference, 55 Queen St E, Suite 1404, Toronto, Ont, Canada M5C 1R6. Telephone (416) 362-7466.

Quarterly magazine covering national and international information about the adjusting aspect of insurance. Price $8.00 per year, $10.00 outside Canada. ISSN 0083828.

801
Canadian Industrial Equipment News
Southam Communications Ltd, 1450 Don Mills Rd, Don Mills, Ont, Canada M3B 2X7. Telephone (416) 445-6641. Telex 06-966612.

Monthly publication. Supplies information on Canadian industrial equipment. Price $47.00 per year.

802
Canadian Industrial Relations and Personnel Developments
CCH Canadian Ltd, 6 Garamond Ct, Don Mills, Ont, Canada M3C 1Z5. Telephone (416) 429-2992.

Loose-leaf book plus weekly updates. Reviews and analyzes developments in Canadian industrial relations and personnel. Monthly digest gives Canadian economic indicators. Price $175.00 per year.

803
Canadian Industrial Stock Charts
Independent Survey Co Ltd, PO Box 6000, 1775 Pine St, Vancouver, BC, Canada V6B 4B9. Telephone (604) 736-6757.

Monthly service. Provides charts showing weekly price ranges, trading volumes, and relative strengths for Canadian industrials. Price $120.00 per year.

804
Canadian Institute of Chartered Accountants/Canadian Bar Association (CICA/CBA) Recommendations on the Income Tax Act
Canadian Institute of Chartered Accountants, 250 Bloor St E, Toronto, Ont, Canada M4W 1G5. Telephone (416) 962-1242.

Book. Contains recommendations on Canadian Income Tax Act by Joint Taxation Committee of Canadian Bar Association and Canadian Institute of Chartered Accountants. Price $11.00.

806
Canadian Insurance
Stone and Cox Ltd, 100 Simcoe St, 2nd Floor, Toronto, Ont, M5H 3G2, Canada. Telephone (416) 593-1310.

Monthly magazine. Covers general insurance issues with emphasis on Canada. Topics include reinsurance, life insurance, and taxation. Price $10.00 per year. ISSN 0008-3879.

807
Canadian Insurance Law Reports
CCH Canadian Ltd, 6 Garamond Ct, Don Mills, Ont, Canada M3C 1Z5. Telephone (416) 429-2992.

Loose-leaf book plus monthly updates. Contains full text of decisions from Canadian provincial and federal courts on all types of insurance matters. Price $165.00 per year.

808
Canadian Insurance Law Service
Stone and Cox Ltd, 100 Simcoe St, 2nd Floor, Toronto, Ont, M5H 3G2, Canada. Telephone (416) 593-1310.

Series of loose-leaf books with regular updates. Provides information on Canadian and provincial insurance laws and regulations. Notes legislative changes and court rulings. Price $525.00 for complete service. ISBN 919468-01-2.

810
Canadian International Trade Classification
Statistics Canada, User Services, Publications Distribution, Ottawa, Ont, K1A OV7, Canada. Telephone (613) 992-3151.

Irregular report. Lists Canadian International Trade Classification commodity code headings and Import Commodity Classification headings. Price $9.75.

811
Canadian Key Business Directory
Dun & Bradstreet, Box 3224, Church St Station, New York, NY 10008. Order from Dun & Bradstreet of Canada, Marketing Services Div, Suite 1107, 415 Yonge St, Toronto, Ont, Canada M5B 2E7. Telephone (212) 285-7346.

Directory. Provides marketing guide to Canada's major companies. Gives name and title of each company's key executives, annual sales volume, and primary and secondary lines of business. Price $125.00.

812
Canadian Labour
Canadian Labour Congress, 2841 Riverside Dr, Ottawa, Ont, Canada K1V 8X7. Telephone (613) 521-3400.

The official journal of the Canadian Labour Congress. Deals with news of union activity, as well as ideas and events affecting working people in Canada. Bilingual. Price free of charge. ISSN 0008-4336.

813
Canadian Labour Law Reports
CCH Canadian Ltd, 6 Garamond Ct, Don Mills, Ont, Canada M3C 1Z5. Telephone (416) 429-2992.

Three loose-leaf books plus semi-monthly updates. Give Canadian federal and provincial laws on labor elations, fair wages, fair employment practices, and workmen's compensation. Price $275.00 per year.

815
Canadian Manager
Canadian Inst of Management, 2175 Sheppard Ave E, Suite 110, Willowdale, Ont, Canada, M2J 1W8. Telephone (416) 493-0155.

Bimonthly magazine. Discusses business management techniques and Canadian economic and business developments. Price $8.00 per year.

816
Canadian Master Tax Guide, 36th edition, 1981
CCH Canadian Ltd, 6 Garamond Ct, Don Mills, Ont, Canada M3C 1Z5. Telephone (416) 429-2992.

Book. Offers tax guide for Canada. Price $14.75 paperbound; $20.00 hardbound.

817
Canadian Mineral Reviews
Supply and Services Canada, Publishing Centre, Printing and Publishing, Ottawa, Ont, Canada K1A 0S9. Telephone (613) 238-1601.

Loose-leaf book. Covers Canadian mineral industry and resources. Price $18.00 per year.

818
Canadian Minerals Yearbook
Supply and Services Canada, Publishing Centre, Printing and Publishing, Ottawa, Ont, Canada K1A 0S9. Telephone (613) 238-1601.

Annual book. Reports on developments in Canadian mining industry. Deals with specific commodities. Statistical summaries, tables, and maps. Price $9.00.

819
Canadian Mining Journal
Southam Communications Ltd, 1450 Don Mills Rd, Don Mills, Ont, Canada M3B 2X7. Telephone (416) 455-6641. Telex 06 966612.

Monthly magazine. Reports on Canadian mining industry. Price $55.00 per year.

820
Canadian News Facts
Marpep Publishing Ltd, Suite 700, 133 Richmond St W, Toronto, Canada M5H 3M8. Telephone (416) 869-1177.

Biweekly newsletter. Covers Canadian political and economic news. Price available on request.

820.01
Canadian News Index
Micromedia Ltd, 144 Front St W, Toronto, Ont, Canada M57 2L7. Telephone (416) 593-5211.

Monthly publication, with annual cumulation. Provides subject and personal name index for 34 major Canadian newspapers and magazines. Price $425.00 per year.

820.02
Canadian Occupational Health & Safety News
Corpus Information Service Ltd, 1450 Don Mills Rd, Don Mills, Ont, Canada M3B 2X7. Telephone (416) 445-7101.

Biweekly newsletter. Covers occupational safety and health in Canada. Price $127.00 (Canadian) per year. ISSN 06-966612.

821
Canadian Occupational Safety and Health Legislation
Corpus Information Services Ltd, 1450 Don Mills Rd. Don Mills, Ont, Canada, M3B 2X7. Telephone (416) 445-7101. Telex. 06-966612.

Twelve-volume loose-leaf compilation plus monthly update service. Covers occupational health and safety in Canada. Price available on request.

822
Canadian Office
Whitsed Publishing Ltd, 55 Bloor St W, Suite 1201, Toronto, Ont, Canada M4W 3K2. Telephone (416) 967-6200.

Monthly magazine. Reports on office management topics. Covers technology, records management, business computing, and communications. Price $20.00 per year. ISSN 0319-2148.

823
Canadian Office Machine Dealers Assn (COMDA) Key
Canadian Office Machine Dealers Assn, 15 Dyas Rd, Don Mills, Ont, Canada M3B 1V7. Telephone (416) 441-1717.

Bimonthly magazine. Discusses office machine news, including new products. Reports on activities of Canadian Office Machine Dealers Association. Price free to qualified subscribers.

824
Canadian Office Products and Stationery
Southam Communications Ltd, 1450 Don Mills Rd, Don Mills, Ont, Canada M3B 2X7. Telephone (416) 445-6641. Telex 06 966612.

Bimonthly magazine. Covers office equipment and stationery business in Canada. Price $22.00 per year.

825
Canadian Oil Register
Southam Communications Ltd, 1450 Don Mills Rd, Don Mills, Ont, Canada M3B 2X7. Order from Southam Communications Ltd, Suite 200-1201 5th St, SW, Calgary, AB Canada.

Annual reference manual. Supplies material on companies and personnel active in oil, natural gas, and synthetic energy exploration fields. Price $75.00.

826
Canadian Patent Reporter
Canada Law Book Ltd, 240 Edward St, Aurora, Ont, L4G 3S9 Canada. Telephone (416) 859-3880.

Monthly report plus six to eight books per year. Discusses Canadian court cases on patents, industrial designs, copyrights, and trademarks. Includes decisions of Commissioner of Patents and Registrar of Trademark. Price $60.00 per volume.

827
Canadian Petroleum
Southam Communications Ltd, 1450 Don Mills Rd, Don Mills, Ont, Canada M3B 2X7. Order from Southam Communications Ltd, Suite 200-1201 5th St, SW, Calgary, AB, Canada.

Monthly magazine. Covers various phases of Canadian oil and gas industry. Price $33.00 per year.

828
Canadian Plastics
Southam Communications Ltd, 1450 Don Mills Rd, Don Mills, Ont, Canada M3B 2X7. Telephone (416) 445-6641. Telex 06-966612.

Monthly magazine. Deals with Canadian plastics industry. Is aimed at personnel of companies supplying materials. Price $33.00 per year.

829
Canadian Product Safety Guide
CCH Canadian Ltd, 6 Garamond Ct, Don Mills, Ont, Canada, M3C 1Z5. Telephone (416) 441-2992.

Two loose-leaf books, plus monthly reports. Provide text and commentary on 150 Canadian federal and provincial consolidated statutes and regulations related to safety and standards of consumer products. Include packaging and labeling, hazardous products, peticides, warranties, weights, and measures. Price $170.00 per year.

829.01
Canadian Real Estate
Canadian Real Estate Assn, 99 Duncan Mill Rd, Don Mills, Ont, Canada M3B 1Z2. Telephone (416) 445-9910.

Monthly newspaper containing information about Canadian real estate. Includes reports on government legislation. Price $7.00 per year. ISSN 0315-3843.

829.02
Canadian Real Estate Journal
Canadian Real Estate Assn, 99 Duncan Mill Rd, Don Mills, Ont, Canada M3B 1Z2. Telephone (416) 445-9910.

Quarterly magazine. Contains technical articles on real estate and trends in the industry. Price $5.00 per year members, $15.00 per year nonmembers.

830
Canadian Risk Management and Business Insurance
Wadham Publications Ltd, 109 Vanderhoof Ave, Suite 101, Toronto, Ont, Canada M4G 2J2. Telephone (416) 425-9021.
Bimonthly magazine. Discusses corporate property and liability insurance, employee pension and welfare programs, plant security and fire protection services, and related topics, with emphasis on Canada. Price $7.00 per year.

833
Canadian Sales Tax Reports
CCH Canadian Ltd, 6 Garamond Ct, Don Mills, Ont, Canada M3C 1Z5. Telephone (416) 429-2992.
Loose-leaf book plus monthly updates. Reviews Canadian federal sales and excise taxes, regulations, and court decisions. Price $175.00 per year.

834
Canadian Securities Law Reports
CCH Canadian Ltd, 6 Garamond Ct, Don Mills, Ont, Canada M3C 1Z5. Telephone (416) 429-2992.
Three loose-leaf books plus monthly updates. Provides full texts of Canadian provincial securities Acts, regulations, and applicable provisions of related federal statutes. Includes bylaws and rules of Canada's stock exchanges. Price $230.00 per year.

835
Canadian Statistical Review
Statistics Canada, User Services, Publications Distribution, Ottawa, Ont, K1A 0V7, Canada. Telephone (613) 992-3151.
Monthly review. Offers statistical summary of current Canadian economic indicators. Includes articles on economy. Tables and charts. Price $42.00 per year. ISSN 0380-0563.

836
Canadian Tax Journal
Canadian Tax Foundation, 130 Adelaide St, W, Box 6, Toronto, Ont, Canada M5H 3P5. Telephone (416) 863-9784.
Bimonthly magazine. Covers Canadian tax issues for professionals. Notes cross-border concerns. Yearly subscription with membership only. Price $6.00 per individual copy (discounts for bulk orders).

837
Canadian Tax News
Carswell Company Ltd, 2330 Midland Ave, Agincourt, Ont, Canada M1S 1P7. Telephone (416) 291-8421.
Monthly report. Reviews Canadian tax law developments and explains provisions. Tables. Price $75.00 per year.

838
Canadian Tax Reports
CCH Canadian Ltd, 6 Garamond Ct, Don Mills Ont, Canada M3C 1Z5. Telephone (416) 429-2992.
Six loose-leaf books plus weekly updates. Covers Canadian federal, corporate, and personal income tax laws. Price $400.00 per year.

840
Canadian Trade Index, 1981
Canadian Manufacturers' Association, 1 Yonge St, Toronto, Ont, Canada M5E 1J9. Telephone (416) 363-7261.
Annual book. Index lists more than 13,000 Canadian manufacturing companies alphabetically, geographically, by products manufactured, and by trademarks and/or brand names. Services section. Price $63.00 per year.

841
Canadian Transport
Canadian Brotherhood of Railway, Transport, and General Workers, 2300 Carling Ave, Ottawa, Int, Canada K2B-7G1.
Monthly newspaper. Discusses Canadian labor and transportation news. Price $6.00 (Canadian) per year. ISSN 0045-5466.

842
Canadian Transportation and Distribution Management
Southam Communications Ltd, 1450 Don Mills Rd, Don Mills, Ont, Canada M3B 2X7. Telephone (416) 445-6641. Telex 06 966612.
Monthly magazine. Deals with traffic and distribution connected with freight carriers and shipping in Canada. Price $33.00 per year.

843
Canadian Transport Commission General and Other Orders
Supply and Services Canada, Publishing Centre, Printing and Publishing, Ottawa, Ont, Canada K1A 0S9. Telephone (613) 238-1601.

Irregular report. Covers general and other orders of Canadian Transport Commission. Bilingual. Price $3.00 per year.

844
Canadian Travel News
Southam Cumminications Ltd, 1450 Don Mills Rd, Don Mills, Ont, Canada M3B 2X7. Telephone (416) 445-6641. Telex 06-966612.
Fortnightly newspaper. Covers Canadian travel industry. Is aimed at agents, carriers and tour operators. Price $33.00 per year.

845
Canadian Underwriter
Wadham Publications Ltd, 109 Vanderhoof Ave, Suite 101, Toronto, Ont, Canada M4G 2J2. Telephone (416) 425-9021.
Monthly magazine. Discusses general insurance topics with emphasis on Canadian firms. Price $10.00 per year.

846
Canadian Weather Review
Supply and Services Canada, Publishing Centre, Printing and Publishing, Ottawa, Ont, Canada K1A 0S9. Telephone (613) 238-1601.
Monthly report on Canada's weather. Bilingual. Price $4.25 per year.

847
Canadian Weekly Stock Charts: Industrials
Independent Survey Co, Ltd, PO Box 6000, Vancouver, BC, Canada V6B 4B9. Telephone (604) 736-6757.
Monthly publication. Provides charts showing three years of weekly price ranges, trading volumes, relative strength, and moving average for Canadian industrial stocks. Price $158.00 per year.

848
Canadian Weekly Stock Charts: Mines and Oils
Independent Survey Co, Ltd, PO Box 6000, Vancouver, BC, Canada V6B 4B9. Telephone (604) 736-6757.
Monthly publication. Provides charts showing three years of weekly price ranges, trading volumes, relative strength, and moving average for Canadian mining and oil stocks. Price $160.00 per year.

849
Canberra Comments
Australian Chamber of Commerce, PO Box E139 Canberra, ACT 2600, Australia. Telephone 73 2381. Telex 62507.
Monthly newsletter on Australia's business and economic conditions. Price $7.50 (Australian) per year.

850
Canned Food: Stocks, Pack, Shipments
US Dept of Commerce, Bureau of the Census, Washington, DC 20233. Telephone (202) 449-1600.
Series of five reports. Presents estimates of wholesale distributions' and canners' stocks of selected canned food items (vegetables, fruits, juices, and fish). Includes data on shipments, carryover, and pack. Price $1.25 per season.

851
Capital
American Bankers Assn, 1120 Connecticut Ave NW, Washington, DC 20036. Telephone (202) 467-4123
Weekly newsletter. Provides information on bank legislation in Congress, decisions of federal regulatory agencies, and conditions in bond and money markets. Price $30.00.

852
Capital Adjustmets
Prentice-Hall, Inc, Englewood Cliffs, NJ 07632. Telephone (201) 592-2000. Telex 13-5423.
Weekly loose-leaf service. Provides information on tax effects of stock sales and dividends. Tables. Price $381.00 per year.

853
Capital Changes Reports
Commerce Clearing House, Inc, 4025 W Peterson Ave, Chicago, IL 60646. Telephone (312) 583-8500.
Six loose-leaf books plus weekly reports. Provides news and discussion of income tax results of changes in corporate structure. Price $395.00 per year.

854
Capital District Business Review
New York Business Publications Inc, 105 Wolf Rd, Albany, NY 12205. Telephone (518) 458-7000.
Monthly magazine analyzes local business and development news in the New York capital district. Price $9.95 per year.

855
Capital Energy Letter
Capital Energy Letter, Inc, National Press Bldg, Washington, DC 20045. Telephone (202) 347-8737.
Weekly newsletter reporting on the energy field. Focuses on Congress, the administration, and federal agencies. Price $325.00 per year.

855.01
Capital Gains Tax Service
Extel Statistical Services Ltd, 37-45 Paul St, London, England EC2A 4PB. Telephone (44) (01) 253-3400. Telex 262687.
Annual book with monthly supplements. Contains base date prices for all British securities listed on or after April 5, 1965, plus every capital event since that date. Aids capital gains tax calculations. Price £64.00 per year.

856
Capital International Perspective
Capital International SA, 15 rue du cendrier, 1201 Geneva, Switzerland. Telephone (022) 32 01 30. Telex 23 341.
Monthly and quarterly magazines (16 isues per year). Monthlies focus on stock performances and comparisons of market valuation factors within countries and international industry groups. Quarterlies include graphs on 1600 of the world's largest companies. English, French, and German. Price $830.00 per year.

857
Capital Investment and Supply Conditions in Manufacturing
Conference Board, Inc, 845 3rd Ave, New York, NY 10022. Telephone (212) 759-0900.
Quarterly supplement. Estimates current use of facilities, availability of funds for capital investment, shortages, and production bottlenecks. Price available on request.

857.01
Capital Journal
Business Council of New York State, Inc, 150 State St, Albany, NY 12207. Telephone (518) 465-3547.
Weekly report during legislative session. Covers New York State government and legislative news which affect business. Lists introduction of pertinent bills. Price free of charge to members.

857.02
Capital Letter
Fourth Estate Group, PO Box 9344, Wellington, New Zealand. Telephone (64) (4) 859-019.
Weekly newsletter. Reviews New Zealand government, administration, legislation, and law. Price $65.00 per year.

858
Capital Market Developmets
US Federal Reserve System, Board of Governors, Washington, DC 20551. Order from Publication Services, Division of Administrative Services, Board of Governors of the Federal Reserve System, Washington, DC 20551. Telephone (202) 452-3245.
Weekly report. Summarizes selected interest rates and yields, security offerings, stock market prices and volume, and mortgage market information. Price $15.00 per year.

859
Car Dealer "Insider"
Atcom, Inc, Atcom Bldg, 2315 Broadway, New York, NY 10024. Telephone (212) 873-3760.
Weekly newsletter. Provides news pertaining to industry. Price $57.00 per year.

860
Caribbean and West Indies Chronicle
Goodyear Gibbs (Caribbean) Ltd, 27-29 Beak St, London, England W1R 3LB. Telephone (44) (01) 439-8820.
Bimonthly magazine. Discusses West Indies economic and political news. Includes information on the development of individual islands and territories. Price $36.00.

861
Caribbean Basin Economic Survey
Federal Reserve Bank of Atlanta, Research Dept, PO Box 1731, Atlanta, GA 30301. Telephone (404) 586-8788.
Quarterly magazine. Examines economic issues in Mexico, Colombia, Venezuela, Central America, Caribbean Islands, Guyana, Surinam, and French Guyana. Price free of charge.

862
Caribbean Business
Manuel Casiano, Inc, PO Box 6253, Loiza St Station, Santurce, Puerto Rico 00914. Telephone (809) 728-3000.

Weekly newspaper of Puerto Rican manufacturing, commecial and financial news. Also covers the Dominican Republic and Virgin Islands. Price $19.00 per year.

863
Caribbean Business News
Caribook Ltd, 1255 Yonge St, Toronto, Ont, Canada M4W 1Z3. Telephone (416) 925-1086.

Monthly newspaper covers business news of 30 Caribbean countries. Includes government activity, real estate news, analysis of economic trends and reports on industry, finance, trade, shipping, and others. Price $17.50 per year. ISSN 0045-5792.

863.01
Caribbean Regional Report
Latin American Newsletters Ltd, Greenhill House, 90-93 Cowcross St, London, England EC1M 6BL. Telephone (44) (01) 251-0012. Telex 261117.

Newsletter issued irregularly. Covers political developments. Discusses role of foreign investment. Price £40, $90.00 US per year.

864
Caribbean Year Book 1977-78
Caribook Ltd, 1255 Yonge St, Toronto, Ont, Canada M4W 1Z3. Telephone (416) 925-1086.

Annual book covering all Caribbean and West Indies countries. Includes business directories, history, geography, government, population, trade and industry statistics, directory of exporters, and shipping. Price $30.00. ISSN 0083-8233.

864.01
Carnegie-Rochester Conference Series on Public Policy
North-Holland Publishing Co, PO Box 211, 1000 AE Amsterdam, The Netherlands. Order from Elsevier/North-Holland, Inc, 52 Vanderbilt Ave, New York, NY 10017. Telephone (212) 867-9040.

Semiannual book. Covers conferences on public economic policy organized by the University of Rochester and Carnegie-Mellon University. Price $104.00 per year. ISSN 0167-2231.

864.02
Carpet & Rug Industry
Household & Personal Products Industry, Box 555, 26 Lake St, Ramsey, NJ 07446. Telephone (201) 825-2552.

Monthly magazine. Reports on carpet and rug industry developments. Notes design and color trends, new equipment, and industry meetings. Price $18.00 per year.

865
Carpet and Rugs
US Dept of Commerce, Bureau of the Census, Washington, DC 20233. Telephone (202) 449-1600.

Quarterly report with annual summary. Presents statistics on quantity and value of shipments of rugs and carpeting. Indicates yarns and fabrics consumed in manufacture. Price $1.25 per year.

866
Car Rental and Leasing "Insider"
Atcom, Inc, Atcom Bldg, 2315 Broadway, New York, NY 10024. Telephone (212) 873-3760.

Weekly newsletter. Provides information of interest to car rental and leasing industry. Price $57.00.

867
Casualties to Vessels and Accidents to Men
Her Majesty's Stationery Office, PO Box 569, London, England SE1 9NH. Telephone (44) (01) 928 1321.

Annual publication. Covers casualties to British vessels and men for 1973 and 1974. Price availablee £1.50.

868
Catalog of Copyright Entries
US Libary of Congress, Copyright Office, Washington, DC 20559. Order from Superintendent of Documents, Government Printing Office, Washington, DC 20402. Telephone (202) 783-3238.

Semiannual and quarterly publication. Lists nondramatic literary works, serials and periodicals, performing arts, motion pictures and filmstrips, visual arts, maps, sound recordings, and renewal copyright registrations, for which copyrights have been registered. Price $215.00.

869
Catalog Showroom Business
Gralla Publications, 1515 Broadway, New York, NY 10036. Telephone (212) 869-1300.

Publication. Provides news of developments in catalog showroom field. Price available on request.

870
Catalogue of New Zealand Statistics, 4th edition 1978
New Zealand Dept of Statistics, Private Bag, Wellington, New Zealand. Telephone Wellington 729119.

Catalogue. Supplies statistics on New Zealand. Price $6.00 (New Zealand).

871
Catering Trades
Her Majesty's Stationery Office, PO Box 569, London, England SE1 9NH. Telephone (44) (01) 928-1321.

Monthly report on British catering trades. Price £4.00 per year.

872
Caveat Emptor/Consumers Bulletin
Consumer Education Research Center, 17 Freeman St, West Orange, NJ 07052. Telephone (201) 675-8474.

Monthly magazine. Discusses consumer issues, with emphasis on frauds, dishonest medical behavior, deceptive advertising, and government conflict-of-interest cases. Price $10.00 per year.

872.01
CBR Index and Microfiche
National Council for US-China Trade, Suite 350, 1050 17th St, NW, Washington, DC 20036. Telephone (202) 828-8300.

Six volumes. Provide subject, company, name, and country index to China Business Review, plus six years of China Business Review and supplements on microfiche. Price $160.00.

873
CECON Trade News
Organization of American States, 17th St and Constitution Ave NW, Washington, DC 20006. Order from OAS General Secretariat, Dept of Publications, 6840 Industrial Rd, Springfield, VA 22151. Telephone (703) 941-1617.

Monthly newsletter. Reports on American nations' tariff and duty news. Includes information on trade bills pending in US Congress. Price $35.00 per year.

874
Census of Agriculture Preliminary Reports for Counties, States, and the United States, 1978
US Dept of Commerce, Bureau of Census, Washington, DC 20233. Telephone (202) 449-1600.

Series of reports. Provides agricultural statistics for the US, regions, states, and counties. Includes information on number of farms, income and sales, machinery and equipment, crops, and livestock. Price available on request.

874.01
Census of Governments, 1977
US Dept of Commerce, Bureau of Census, Washington, DC 20233. Telephone (202) 449-1600.

Series of reports. Supplies data on numbers and characteristics of governments in US. Notes revenues, expenditures, debt, and public employees. Price available on request.

875
Census of Maine Manufactures
Maine Dept of Manpower Affairs, Bureau of Labor, State House Station #45, Augusta, ME 04333. Telephone (207) 289-3331.

Annual booklet. Provides statistics on Maine's manufacturing. Reports on investment in plant modernization, organized workers, wages, and product valuation. Tables, charts, and graphs. Price free of charge.

876
Census of Manufactures, 1977
US Dept of Commerce, Bureau of Census, Washington, DC 20233. Telephone (202) 449-1600.

Report. Provides statistics on wide range of US industries and manufacturing firms, based on 1977 census. Covers employment, payroll, expenditures, and quantity and value of materials consumed and products shipped. Price available on request.

876.01
Census of Population
US Dept of Commerce, Bureau of Census, Washington, DC 20233. Telephone (202) 449-1600.

Two-volume book. Contains population data from the 1970 census. Includes information on labor force, personal and family characteristics of the population, and income. Price available on request.

877
Census of Production for Northern Ireland
Her Majesty's Stationery Office, PO Box 569, London, England SE1 9NH. Telephone (44) (01) 928 1321.

Annual census of production for Northern Ireland. Price £2.50 per year.

878
Census of Retail Trade
US Dept of Commerce, Bureau of Census, Washington, DC 20233. Telephone (202) 449-1600.

Series of reports. Covers retail trade in US. Provides statistics on number of establishments, finances, and employment. Price available on request.

879
Census of Service Industries, 1977
US Dept of Commerce, Bureau of Census, Washimgton, DC 20233. Telephone (202) 449-1600.

Series of reports. Provides statistics on service industries in US. Indicates receipts, payroll, and employment. Price available on request.

880
Census Retrieval System
Security Pacific National Bamk, PO Box 2097, Terminal Annex, Los Angeles, CA 90051. Telephone (213) 613-5414.

Computer service. Provides population and demographic information from the 1980 Census. Price available on request.

881
Census Publications. **Volume IV**
Statistics Canada, Publications Distribution, Ottawa, Ont, K1A 0T6, Canada. Telephone (613) 992-2959.

Annual report. Provides Canadian agricultural statistics. Shows number of farms, crops, livestock, machinery, and socioeconomic characteristics of farm operators and their households. Includes provincial data. Price $46.00.

882
Census Publications. **Volume V**
Statistics Canada, Publications Distribution, Ottawa, Ont, K1A 0T6, Canada. Telephone (613) 992-2959.

Annual report. Supplies data on major Canadian demographic, economic, family, housing, and agricultural trends. Price $34.00.

883
Census Publications. **Volume VI**
Statistics Canada, Publications Distribution, Ottawa, Ont, K1A 0T6, Canada. Telephone (613) 992-2959.

Annual report. Presents detailed account of organization, planning, and procedures involved in 1971 Canadian Census. Price $8.00.

884
Census Publications. **Volume VII**
Statistics Canada, Publications Distribution, Ottawa, Ont, K1A 0T6, Canada. Telephone (613) 992-2959.

Annual report. Contains information on Canadian retail trade. Covers location, size, and type of business. Summarizes annual sales and operative revenue and expenditures. Price $9.00.

885
Census Publications. **Volume VIII**
Statistics Canada, Publications Distribution, Ottawa, Ont, K1A 0T6, Canada. Telephone (613) 992-2959.

Annual report. Covers Canadian wholesale trade. Describes business locations and size and kind of businesses. Includes financial data. Price $6.00.

886
Central Atlantic States: Manufacturers Directory, 1981
Manufacturers' News, Inc, 3 Huron St, Chicago, IL 60611. Telephone (312) 337-1084.

Biennial book. Covers manufaturers in Maryland, Delaware, Virginia, West Virginia, North Carolina, and South Carolina. Price $50.00.

887
Centerpoint
University of Idaho, Center of Business Development and Research, Moscow, ID 83843. Telephone (208) 885-6611, 6612.

Quarterly newsletter. Discusses national and Idaho economic and business subjects. Includes information on taxes and employment. Price free of charge.

888
Central Banking Legislation: **A Collection of Central Bank, Monetary, and Banking Laws**
International Monetary Fund, 19th & H Sts NW, Washington, DC 20431. Telephone (202) 393-6362.

Two-volume book. Contains central bank, monetary, and banking laws for 38 countries. Price $10.00.

889

Central Bank of Ireland **Quarterly Bulletin and Annual Report**

Central Bank of Ireland, PO Box No 559, Dame St, Dublin 2, Ireland. Telephone 716666.

Annual report, with quarterly bulletins. Covers monetary and general economic developments in Ireland and abroad. Price free of charge.

890

Central New York Business Review

Greentree Publishing Co, PO Box 9, New City, NY 10956. Order from: Greentree Publishing Co, 499 S Warren St, Syracuse, NY 13202. Telephone (315) 471-2433.

Monthly newspaper. Discusses business, agriculture, development and industry in central New York State. Price $5.00 per year.

890.01

Central Patents Index, 1981

Derwent Publications Ltd, Rochdale House, 128 Theobalds Rd, London, England WC1X 8RP. Telephone (44) (01) 242-5823. Telex 267487.

Retrieval service. Provides abstracts for chemical technology patents. Price available on request.

891

Ceramic Data Book

Cahners Publishing Company, Inc, 221 Columbus Ave, Boston, MA 02116. Telephone (617) 536-7780.

Annual catalog, data file, and purchasing directory for fine ceramics and heavy clay products. Price available on request.

892

Ceramic Industries Journals

Turret Press Ltd, 4 Local Board Rd, Watford, Herts, England WD1 2JS. Order from UK Publishers Inc, PO Box 36420 Fort Logan, Denver, CO 80236. Telephone Watford (0923) 46199.

Bimonthly magazine plus yearly directory. Brings together three journals: British Clayworker; Ceramics; and Clayworker. Price £52.00 per year.

893

Ceramic Industry

Cahners Publishing Company, Inc, 221 Columbus Ave, Boston, MA 02116. Telephone (617) 536-7780.

Monthly magazine. Covers manufacture of fine ceramics, including porcelain, enamel, whiteware, glass, and electronic ceramics. Price $12.00 per year.

894

Ceres: Food and Agriculture Organization (FAO) Review on Development

Food and Agriculture Organization of the United Nations, Via delle Terme di Caracalla, Rome 00100, Italy. Order from UNIPUB, 345 Park Ave, S, New York, NY 10010. Telephone (212) 636-4707.

Bimonthly report. Covers Third World development, including agricultural, economic, and social progress. Price $12.00 per year.

895

Certified Accountant

The Assn of Certified Accountants', 29 Lincoln's Inn Fields, London, England, WC2A 3EE.

Bimonthly magazine provides information on and news of the accounting field in Great Britain. Price 75p per copy.

896

Certified General Accountants' (CGA) Magazine

Canadian Certified General Accountants' Association, 740-1176 W Georgia St, Vancouver, BC, Canada, V6E 4A2. Telephone (604) 669-3555.

Magazine issued nine times per year. Discusses accounting methods and trends and Canadian economic and financial issues. Price $9.00 per year. ISSN 0318-742X.

897

Certified Public Accountants (CPA) Client Bulletin

American Inst of Certified Public Accountants, 1211 Ave of the Americas, New York, NY 10036. Telephone (212) 575-6200.

Monthly report. Discusses tax, business management, and accounting subjects for accounting clients. Notes new tax legislation. Price $100.00 per year (available to AICPA members only).

898

Certified Public Accountants (CPA) Letter

American Inst of Certified Public Accountants, 1211 Avenue of the Americas, New York, NY 10036. Telephone (212) 575-6200.

Semimonthly newsletter. Offers concise reports on accounting and auditing. Price $35.00 per year.

899

Chain Merchandise Magazine

Chain Merchandizer, 65 Crocker Ave, Piedmont, CA 94611. Telephone (415) 547-4545.

Bimonthly periodical. Covers merchandising and sales for chain retail and direct sales markets and their suppliers. Price $3.00 per year.

900

Chain Store Age, Executive Edition

Lebhar-Friedman Publications, Inc, 425 Park Ave, New York, NY 10022. Telephone (212) 371-9400.

Monthly report. Reports on retail operations and capital expenditures for specialty, drug, discount, department, home center, shopping center, and supermarket stores. Price available on request.

900.01

Chain Store Age, General Merchandise Edition

Lebhar-Friedman Publications, Inc, 425 Park Ave, New York, NY 10022. Telephone (212) 371-9400.

Monthly report. Discusses merchandising and operations of department stores and chain stores. Price $7.00 per year.

901

Chain Store Age. Supermarkets Edition

Lebhar-Friedman Publications, Inc, 425 Park Ave, New York, NY 10022. Telephone (212) 371-9400.

Monthly report. Provides coverage of trade news and trends in the supermarket industry. Price available on request.

902

Challenge

M E Sharpe, Inc, 80 Business Park Dr, Armonk, NY 10504. Telephone (914) 273-1800.

Bimonthly magazine. Offers nontechnical articles on major economic issues by well-known economists. Price $30.00 per year institutions, $25.00 per year individuals.

904

Changes Among Operating Banks & Branches

United States Federal Deposit Insurance Corp, Washington, DC 20429. Telephone (202) 389-4221.

Annual report. Supplies information on changes in number and classification of operating banks and branches. Price free of charge.

906

Changes in Rates of Wages and Hours of Work

Her Majesty's Stationery Office, PO Box 569, London, England SE1 9NH. Telephone (44) (01) 928-1321. Telex 266455.

Monthly report. Furnishes data on changes of rates of wages and hours for workers in Great Britain. Price £7.66 per year.

907

Changing Times

Kiplinger Washington Editors, Inc, 1729 H St NW, Washington, DC 20006. Telephone (202) 887-6400.

Monthly magazine. Offers advice on personal finances, including saving, investing, shopping, taxation, housing, and other topics. Price $12.00 per year.

908

Chart Book of the Melbourne Share Price Index

Stock Exchange of Melbourne Ltd, GPO Box 1784Q, Melbourne, Vic 3001, Australia.

Annual report. Provides stock price indices for groups of Australian stocks. Charts and tables. Price $5.50 (Australian). ISSN 0311-3655.

910

Chartcraft Commodity Service

Chartcraft, Inc, 1 West Ave, Larchmont, NY 10538. Telephone (914) 834-5181.

Weekly service. Supplies point and figure charts on commodity futures. Includes charts for actively traded over-the-counter gold stocks and futures. Price $180.00 per year.

912

Chartcraft Weekly Service

Chartcraft, Inc, 1 West Ave, Larchmont, NY 10538. Telephone (914) 834-5181.

Weekly loose-leaf report provides point and figure technique for analyzing stocks listed on New York and American stock exchanges. Graphs and charts. Price $180.00 per year.

914

Chartered Insurance Inst (CII) Journal

Chartered Insurance Inst, 20 Aldermanbury, London, England EC2V 7HY. Telephone (44) (01) 606-3835.

Annual volume in three parts, issued in December, April, and August, covering general insurance topics. Price £1.00 each part. ISSN 0309-4928.

915

Chartered Life Underwriters (CLU) Journal

American Society of Chartered Life Underwriters, 270 Bryn Mawr Ave, Box 59, Bryn Mawr, PA 19010. Telephone (215) 896-4300.

Quarterly magazine. Covers opinion and research in health insurance and life insurance fields. Price $9.00 per year.

916

Chartered Property and Casualty Underwriters (CPCU) Annals

Society of Chartered Property and Casualty Underwriters, Kahler Hall, Providence Rd (CB #9), Malvern, PA 19355. Telephone (215) 648-0440.

Quarterly magazine. Publishes articles on insurance-related subjects. Price $8.00 per year.

917

Chartering Annual

Maritime Research, Inc, 11 Broadway, New York, NY 10004. Telephone (212) 269-3061.

Annual publication. Lists maritime charter fixtures reported throughout year by commodity and week of fixture. Price $40.00

918

Chase World Guide for Exporters and Export Credit Reports

Chase Trade Information Corp, 1 World Trade Center, 78th Floor, New York, NY 10048. Telephone (212) 432-8072. Telex RCA 235444.

Annual loose-leaf, plus updates. Contains information on financing export shipments. Updates cover credit terms for shipments to principal world markets. Price $390.00 (for both publications).

918.01

Chemical Abstracts

Chemical Abstracts Service, 2540 Olentangy River Rd, PO Box 3012, Columbus, OH 43210. Telephone (614) 421-6940.

Weekly journal. Contains abstracts of articles on chemical research and chemical engineering. Includes indexes. Price $5500.00 per year. ISSN 0009-2258.

919

Chemical Age

Morgan–Grampian Ltd, Morgan–Grampian House, Calderwood St, London, England SE18 6QH. Order from Morgan–Grampian Publishing Co, 2 Park Ave, New York, NY 10016. Telephone (44) (01) 855-7777. Telex 896238 MORGAN G. New York (212) 340-9700. Telex 425592 MGI UI.

Weekly newspaper. Reports on investment, construction, and financial performance in international chemical and contracting industries. Price $76.00 per year.

919.01

Chemical Age of India

Technical Press Publications, Eucharistic Congress Bldg No 1, 5/1 Convent St, Colaba, Bombay 400 039, India. Telephone 231446, 231156. Telex 11 3479 CHEMIN.

Monthly journal. Covers Indian chemical and allied process industry. Emphasizes technology transfer, consultancy, and management topics. Price $40.00 per year.

920

Chemical and Engineering News

American Chemical Society, 1155 16th St NW, Washington, DC 20036. Telephone (800) 424-6747.

Weekly magazine. Covers developments in the chemical process industries, includes reports on federal legislation. Price $24.00 per year, $39.00 per year foreign.

921

Chemical Economics Handbook

Stanford Research Institute International, Menlo Park, CA 94025. Telephone (415) 859-3346.

Loose-leaf service with monthly supplements. Provides market research for international chemical industry. Supplies data on production, sales, consumption, exports, and imports. Includes Chemical Economics Newsletter and direct consultation service. Price $15,500.00 per year.

922

Chemical Economics Newsletter
Stanford Research Institute International, Menlo Park, CA 94025. Telephone (415) 859-3346.

Bimonthly newsletter. Analyzes worldwide chemical industry developments. Discusses production and consumption rates for specific chemicals. Price free of charge.

922.01

Chemical/Energy New Product Directory, 1980
Marketing Development, 402 Border Rd, Concord, MA 01742. Telephone (617) 369-5382.

Book. Surveys 3171 significant new chemical and energy products introduced in 1979. Lists by company and seven digit Standard Industrial Classification (SIC). Price $385.00.

923

Chemical Engineering
McGraw-Hill Publications Co, 1221 Avenue of the Americas, New York, NY 10020. Telephone (212) 997-1221. Telex TWX 7105814879 WUI 62555.

Biweekly magazine. Covers chemical engineering field, including equipment and plant construction. Price available on request.

924

Chemical Engineering—Equipment Buyers' Guide Issue
McGraw-Hill Book Co, Hightstown-Princeton Rd, Hightstown, NJ 08520. Telephone (609) 448-1700. Telex 843449.

Annual publication. Lists suppliers and equipment for the chemical process industry. Price $35.00.

925

Chemical Horizon North American Report
Predicasts, Inc, 11001 Cedar Ave, Cleveland, OH 44106. Telephone (216) 795-3000.

Weekly newsletter. Summarizes developments in the chemical, paper, rubber, plastics, fibers, and petroleum industries in the US, Canada, and Mexico. Price $132.00 per year.

925.01

Chemical Horizons Overseas Report
Predicasts, Inc, 11001 Cedar Ave, Cleveland, OH 44106. Telephone (216) 795-3000.

Weekly newsletter. Summarizes developments in the chemical, paper, rubber, plastics, fibers, and petroleum industries (excluding US, Mexico, and Canada). Price $132.00 per year.

925.02

Chemical Industry Notes
Chemical Abstracts Service, 2540 Olentangy River Rd, PO Box 3012, Columbus, OH 43210. Telephone (614) 421-6940.

Weekly journal. Summarizes articles in chemical industry publications. Indexes material by keyword, corporate name, or personal name. Price $700.00 per year. ISSN 0045-639X.

926

Chemical Marketing Reporter
Schnell Publishing Co, 100 Church St, New York, NY 10007. Telephone (212) 732-9820.

Weekly newspaper. Contains industry news and lists 3,000 current prices of chemicals and associated materials. Price $45.00 per year.

927

Chemical Purchasing
Myers Publishing Co, Inc, 381 Park Ave S, New York, NY 10016. Telephone (212) 684-1063.

Monthly magazine. Presents information on chemical purchasing and related topics. Price $15.00 per year.

928

Chemical Regulation Reporter
Bureau of National Affairs, Inc, 1231 25th St NW, Washington, DC 20037. Telephone (202) 452-4200.

Loose-leaf books with weekly updates. Covers chemical laws and regulations. Includes current material and reference file. Price $407.00 per year.

928.01

Chemicals Services
Data Resources, Inc, 29 Hartwell Ave, Lexington, MA 02173. Telephone (617) 861-0165.

Quarterly report. Provides forecasts of US petrochemical production by process, price, consumption, capacity, and manufacturing costs. Price available on request.

929

Chemical Week
McGraw-Hill Publications Co, 1221 Avenue of the Americas, New York, NY 10020. Telephone (212) 997-1221. Telex TWX 7105814879 WUI 62555.

Weekly magazine. Pertains to chemical process management. Includes data on technical and nontechnical developments, environmental issues, and financing trends. Price $26.00 per year.

930

Chemical Week—Buyers' Guide Issue
McGraw-Hill Book Co, Hightstown-Princeton Rd, Hightstown, NJ 08520. Telephone (609) 448-1700. Telex 843449.

Annual guide. Contains inventory of chemicals, their raw materials, and packaging products. Price $30.00.

931

Chemical Week Newswire Service
McGraw-Hill Publications Co, 1221 Ave of the Americas, New York, NY 10020. Telephone (212) 997-6375. Telex TWX 7105814879 WUI 62555.

Daily service. Provides chemical process industry news. Price $2500.00 per year.

932

Chemical Week Pesticides Register
McGraw-Hill Publications Co, 1221 Ave of the Americas, New York, NY 10020. Telephone (212) 997-1221. Telex TWX 7105814879 WUI 62555.

Data-based report. Provides technical, safety, and marketing information needed for registering pesticides with Environmental Protection Administration. Price $95.00 per year. ISBN 0-07-047948-8.

933

Chemists' and Druggists' Supplies and Toiletries
Stokes & Lindley-Jones Ltd, Alverstoke House, 21 Montpelier Row, Blackheath, London, England SE3 OSR. Telephone (44) (01) 852 9865.

Biannual report. Informs importers of British chemists' and druggists' supplies and toiletries available for export sale. Price £25.00 for 3 years to qualified subscribers.

934

Cheques Cashed
Statistics Canada, User Services, Publications Distribution, Ottawa, Ont, Canada K1A 0V7. Telephone (613) 992-3151.

Monthly magazine. Reports on value of checks cashed against individual accounts by type of deposit account for 50 Canadian cities. Notes turnover ratios by type of account. Price $18.00 per year. ISSN 0705-5404.

935
Chicago Board Options Exchange Guide
Commerce Clearing House, Inc, 4025 W Peterson Ave, Chicago, IL 60646. Telephone (312) 583-8500.

Loose-leaf book plus monthly report. Includes directory, constitution, rules, and listed securities of Chicago Board Options Exchange. Price $160.00 per year.

935.01
Chicago: Geographic Edition, 1981
Manufacturers' News, Inc, 3 Huron St, Chicago, IL 60611. Telephone (312) 337-1084.

Biennial directory. Contains information on 12,000 Chicago firms and 50,000 executives. Includes maps. Price $49.95.

936
Chicagoland Development
Chicago Assn of Commerce & Industry, 130 S Michigan Ave, Chicago, IL 60603. Telephone (312) 786-0111.

Monthly magazine. Covers Chicago industrial, commercial, community planning, and development trends. Includes housing news. Price $25.00 per year.

937
Chicago Mercantile Exchange Yearbook
Chicago Mercantile Exchange, 444 W Jackson Blvd, Chicago, IL 60606. Telephone (312) 648-1000.

Yearbook. Contains price ranges for futures traded on Chicago Mercantile Exchange. Provides statistical information on eggs, random-length and stud lumber, live beef cattle, feeder cattle, frozen pork bellies, live hogs and fresh broiler chickens, potatoes, and other commodities. Price $6.00.

937.01
Chief Executive
Morgan-Grampian Ltd, Morgan-Grampian House, Calderwood St, London, England SE18 6QH. Telephone (44) (01) 855-7777. Telex 896238 MORGAN G. Order from Morgan-Grampian Publishing Co, 2 Park Ave, New York, NY 10016. Telephone (212) 340-9700. Telex 425592 MGI UI.

Monthly magazine. Carries articles on policies of successful companies for chief executives of enterprises employing at least 100 people. Price $55.00 per year.

938
Chief Executive's Handbook
Dow Jones-Irwin, Inc, 1818 Ridge Rd, Homewood, IL 60430. Telephone (312) 798-3100.

Book. Discusses the many facets of corporation management. Price $37.50.

939
Chilton's Market/Plant Data Bank
Chilton Co, Chilton Way, Radnor, PA 19089. Telephone (215) 687-8200.

Information service. Provides data on industrial locations for major industries. Price available on request.

940
Chilton's Oil and Gas Energy
Chilton Co, Chilton Way, Radnor, PA 19089. Telephone (215) 687-8200.

Monthly newsletter. Covers oil and gas exploration, drilling, production, processing, pipelines, and legislation. Price $80.00.

940.01
China Business Report
Inst for International Research Ltd, 70 Warren St, London, England W1P 5PA. Telephone (44) (01) 388-2663. Telex 263504.

Monthly report. Analyzes developments in China's trade. Advises on negotiating techniques. Price $205.00 per year.

941
China Business Review
National Council for US–China Trade, Suite 350, 1050 17th St NW, Washington, DC 20036. Telephone (202) 828-8300.

Bimonthly magazine. Assesses issues affecting US–People's Republic of China trade and Chinese economic and industrial developments. Price $60.00 per year.

942
China Letter
Asia Letter Ltd, PO Box 54149, Los Angeles, CA 90054. Telephone (213) 322-4222.

Monthly newsletter. Covers economic, political, trade, and social developments and trends in the People's Republic of China. Provides background, commentary, and current major business deals. Price $175.00 per year.

943
China Trade and Economic Newsletter
The Fortyeight Group of British Traders with China, 84-86 Rosebery Avenue, London EC1R 5RR, England. Telephone (44) (01) 837 2223/4.

Monthly newsletter. Covers China's trade and economic news. Offers statistics on China's trade with United Kingdom and other countries. Price $50.00 surface mail, $70.00 airmail.

944
Chinese Economic Studies
M E Sharpe, Inc, 80 Business Park Dr, Armonk, NY 10504. Telephone (914) 273-1800.

Quarterly journal. Supplies translations from books and periodicals published in China and Japan on economics. Price $127.00.

945
Choice
Australian Consumers' Assn, 28-30 Queen St, Chippendale, NSW 2008, Australia. Telephone (612) 698-9200.

Monthly magazine. Evaluates Australian consumer products. Reports are based on Australian Consumers' Association tests. Includes prices. Price $20.00 (Australian) per year.

945.01
Choosing Life
Stone and Cox Ltd, 100 Simcoe St, 2nd Floor, Toronto, Ont, Canada M5H 3G2. Telephone (416) 593-1310.

Annual book. Provides comparative prices for life insurance products in Canada, as well as explanation of titles and terms used in common policies. Compares net costs and net payments at selected ages for some 60 companies. Price $5.00. ISBN 0-919468-05-5.

945.02
CICA Handbook
Canadian Institute of Chartered Accountants, 250 Bloor St E, Toronto, Ont, Canada M4W IG5. Telephone (416) 962-1242.

Loose-leaf book, with regular revisions. Contains recommendations on accepted accounting, auditing, and financial reporting standards. Topical index. Price $15.00, one year of revisions $10.00; three years $27.00.

946
Cinemas
Her Majesty's Stationery Office, PO Box 569, London, England SE1 9NH. Telephone (44) (01) 928 1321.
Annual publication on motion pictures in Great Britain. Price £1.25 peryear.

947
CIS
International Labour Organization, 1750 New York Ave, Suite 330, Washington, DC 20006. Telephone (202) 376-2315.
Computerized service. Provides data on occupational safety and health. Offers abstracts, cumulative indexes, thesaurus, bibliographies, and information sheets. Price $165.00.

948
CIS Abstracts Bulletin
International Labour Organization, 1750 New York Ave, Suite 330, Washington, DC 20006. Order from International Occupational Safety and Health Information Centre, International Labour Office, 1211, Geneva 22, Switzerland. Telephone (202) 376-2315.
Bulletin. Provides abstracts of articles, reports, books, and films on occupational safety and health. Price $165.00.

948.01
CIS/Index
Congressional Information Service, Inc, 4520 E-W Highway, Suite 800, Washington, DC 20014. Telephone (301) 654-1550.
Two-volume set of indexes and abstracts, with monthly updates and quarterly cumulations. Provides information on Congressional publications, hearings, and documents. Price $985.00 per year.

948.02
CIS/Microfiche Library
Congressional Information Service, Inc, 4520 E-W Highway, Suite 800, Washington, DC 20014. Telephone (301) 654-1550.
Microfiche file, with monthly updates. Covers reports issued by Congressional committees and subcommittees. Includes all hearings. Price $5775.00 per year.

949
Citibank Monthly Economic Letter
Citibank, Economic Dept, 399 Park Ave, New York, NY 10022. Telephone (212) 559-4022.

Monthly report. Considers US and international economic developments, including domestic monetary policy, unemployment, and inflation. Price free of charge.

950
Citicorp Reports
Citicorp, 399 Park Ave, New York, NY 10043. Telephone (212) 559-0233.
Annual report. Presents Citicorp's financial statement and stand on public issues. Tables. Price free of charge.

952
Civil Aviation Authority Monthly Statistics
Her Majesty's Stationery Office, PO Box 569, London, England SE1 9NH. Order from Library, Civil Aviation Authority, Aviation House, 129 Kingsway, London, England WC2B 6NN. Telephone (44) (01) 928-1321.
Monthly publication. Supplies statistics on aviation in Great Britain. Price £36.00 per year.

953
Civil Engineering
Morgan–Grampian Ltd, Morgan–Grampian House, Calderwood St, London, England SE18 6QH. Order from Morgan–Grampian Publishing Co, 2 Park Ave, New York, NY 10016. Telephone (44) (01) 855-7777. Telex 896238 MORGAN G. New York (212) 340-9700. Telex 425592 MGI UI.
Monthly magazine. Contains information relevant to contractors involved in major projects in Great Britain and throughout world. Price $45.00 per year.

954
Civil Service Statistics
Her Majesty's Stationery Office, PO Box 569, London, England SE1 9NH. Telephone (44) (01) 928-1321.
Annual report. Presents British civil service statistics. Price £7.50 per year.

955
Classified Index of Dispositions of ULP Charges by the General Counsel of the National Labor Relations Board
US National Labor Relations Board, 1717 Pennsylvania Ave NW, Washington, DC 20570. Order from Superintendent of Documents, US Government Printing Office, Washington, DC 20402. Telephone (202) 655-4000.

Book, paperback. Provides index to advice and appeals memoranda and dispositions issued by National Labor Relations Board General Counsel, 1976–79. Price $10.00.

956
Classified Index of National Labor Relations Board Decisions & Related Court Decisions
US National Labor Relations Board, 1717 Pennsylvania Ave NW, Washington, DC 20570. Telephone (202) 655-4000.
Book issued irregularly with supplements. Provides index to National Labor Relations Board and related court decisions. Price $21.00

957
Clay Construction Products
US Dept. of Commerce, Bureau of the Census, Washington, DC 20233. Telephone (202) 449-1600.
Monthly report with annual summary. Supplies information on production and value of shipments of brick and clay construction products. Price $3.25 per year.

958
Cleaning Maintenance & Big Building Management
Turret Press Ltd, 4 Local Board Rd, Watford, Herts, England WD1 2JS. Telephone Watford (0923) 46199.
Monthly magazine. Presents material on maintaining and servicing buildings. Price £23.86 per year, $55.00 US per year.

959
Clean Water Report
Business Publishers, Inc, P.O. Box 1067, Silver Spring, MD 20910. Telephone (301) 587-6300
Biweekly newsletter. Contains information on water pollution. Price $97.00 per year.

961
Clemson University Textile Marketing Letter
Clemson University College of Industrial Management and Textile Science, Sirrine Hall, Clemson, SC 29631. Telephone (803) 656-3177.
Monthly (except July and August). Reports on textile industry, including various fibers. Features marketing and sales trends. Price $10.00 per year.

962

Client-Directed Screen

Ford Investor Services, 11722 Sorrento Valley Rd, Suite I, San Diego, CA 92121. Telephone (714) 755-1327.

Information service. Provides data on 1400 common stocks selected according to investor's particular needs. Includes earnings, dividends, stock prices. Offers monitoring of specific stock portfolio. Price $108.00 per year.

964

Client's Monthly Alert

The Practical Accountant, 964 3rd Ave, New York, NY 10155. Telephone (212) 935-9210.

Monthly bulletin designed to be sent by accountants to clients. Deals with topics such as tax planning, tax shelters, and stock profits. Price $36.00 for three months for 50 copies.

965

Client Tax Digest

Arthur Young & Co, 277 Park Ave, New York, NY 10017. Telephone (212) 922-4724.

Irregular report. Deals with Australian federal budget and taxation. Price free of charge.

966

Clinica

PJB Publications Ltd, 18a Hill St, Richmond, Surrey, England, TW9 ITN. Telephone (44) (01) 940 8849.

Fortnightly newsletter. Covers world medical equipment news, including government regulations concerning product manufacturing and marketing, product development, and new medical/surgical techniques and technologies. Also notes non-regulatory factors affecting the health care industry, financial data, and people in the field. Price £169.00 European countries, £179.00 other countries.

967

Closures for Containers

US Dept of Commerce, Bureau of the Census, Washington, DC 20233. Telephone (202) 449-1600.

Monthly report with annual summary. Contains data on shipments of closures for glass, metal, and plastics containers, by type of closure. Price $3.25 per year.

967.01

Clothing Industry News

Yaffa Publishing Group, 432-436 Elizabeth St, Surry Hills NSW 2010, Australia. Order from Yaffa Publishing Group, GPO Box 606, Sydney, NSW 2001, Australia. Telephone (61) (02) 699-7861. Telex 21887.

Newsletter irregularly issued. Contains news of Australia's clothing industry. Includes government regulations and labor developments. Price available on request.

967.02

Coal

Commission of the European Communities, Office for Official Publications of the European Communities, CP 1003, Luxembourg 1, Luxembourg. Telephone (352) 490081. Telex PUBLOF 1325.

Monthly bulletin. Provides statistics indicating short-term movements in the coal industry. Price $10.50 per year.

968

Coal Age

McGraw-Hill Publications Co, 1221 Ave of the Americas, New York, NY 10020. Telephone (212) 997-1221. Telex TWX 7105814879 WUI 62555.

Monthly magazine. Reports on coal production subjects, including mine management, engineering, and safety. Price $16.00 per year.

969

Coal Age—Annual Buyers' Guide

McGraw-Hill Book Co, Hightstown-Princeton Rd, Hightstown, NJ 08520. Telephone (609) 448-1700. Telex 843449.

Annual guide. Contains information on equipment and supplies needed in coal mining. Included free with Coal Age magazine subscription. Price $16.00 per year.

970

Coal Daily

Business Publishers, Inc, PO Box 1067, Silver Spring, MD 20910. Telephone (301) 587-6300.

Daily newsletter. Reports on coal industry developments. Price $397.00 per year.

970.01

Coal Data

National Coal Assn, 1130 17th St, NW, Washington, DC 20036, Attn: Publications Section. Telephone (202) 463-2635.

Annual report. Is statistical compilation of national energy production, consumption and reserves over past five years. Includes coal production, preparation, consumption, stocks, distribution, machinery, safety, and other topics. Reports on anthracite and the latest National Bituminous Coal Industry wage agreement. Price $50.00, $35.00 for nonprofit organizations.

970.02

Coal Information

Petroleum Information Corp, PO Box 2612, 1375 Delaware, Denver, CO 80201. Telephone (303) 825-2181.

Monthly report. Supplies information on fee coal leases in Wyoming, North Dakota, South Dakota, New Mexico, Utah, Colorado, Montana, and Nebraska. Price $300.00 per year.

971

Coal Mine Directory

McGraw-Hill Book Co, Hightstown-Princeton Rd, Hightstown, NJ 08520. Telephone (609) 448-1700. Telex 843449.

Directory. Provides data on coal mines and production companies. Price $35.00.

971.01

Coal: Monthly Bulletin

European Community Information Service, 2100 M St, NW, Suite 707, Washington, DC 20037. Telephone (202) 862-9500 Telex 248455.

Monthly bulletin. Gives information on coal industry in European Communities member countries. Price $10.50.

971.02

Coal Service

Data Resources, Inc, 29 Hartwell Ave, Lexington, MA 02173. Telephone (617) 861-0165.

Quarterly report. Forecasts coal demand production, prices, and distribution for 18 producing states, 13 consuming regions, eight demand sectors, two mine types, and six sulfur types. Price available on request.

972

Coal Week

McGraw-Hill Publications Co, 1221 Ave of the Americas, New York, NY 10020. Telephone (212) 997-1221. Telex TWX 7105814879 WUI 62555.

Weekly report. Analyzes domestic coal industry developments. Covers prices, markets, and related operations. Price $327.00 per year US, $367.00 foreign.

973
Coal Week International
McGraw-Hill Publications Co, 1221 Ave of the Americas, New York, NY 10020. Telephone (212) 997-6375, telex TWX 7105814879 WU1 62555.

Weekly report. Covers world coal industry news and metallurgical industry developments. Price $467.00 US, $507.00 foreign.

974
Coastal Zone Management Journal
Crane, Russak & Company, Inc, 3 East 44th St, New York, NY 10017. Telephone (212) 867-1490. Telex 423921.

Quarterly magazine. Discusses coastal zone resources. Reports on development, conservation, and management techniques. Price $48.00 per year.

975
Coband: Continental Bank Annotated Digest
Continental Illinois Bank and Trust Co of Chicago, 231 S LaSalle, Chicago, IL. Telephone (312) 828-2345.

Weekly report. Contains abstracts of articles on banking, finance, and business from journals in these fields. Service includes quarterly and annual indexes. Price available on request.

976
Code and Regulations
Commerce Clearing House, Inc, 4025 W Peterson Ave, Chicago, IL 60646. Telephone (312) 583-8500.

Four loose-leaf books plus monthly report. Gives full texts of Internal Revenue Code and income, estate, and gift tax regulations. Price $195.00 per year.

977
Collective Bargaining Negotiations & Contracts
Bureau of National Affairs, Inc, 1231 25th St NW, Washington, DC 20037. Telephone (202) 452-4200.

Loose-leaf books with biweekly updates. Discusses current labor contract settlements, selected texts, wage patterns, and current bargaining issues. Includes contract clause finder. Price $365.00 per year.

978
Collective Bargaining Review
Canadian Dept of Labour, Ottawa, Ont, K1A 0J2, Canada. Order from Publishing Centre, Supply and Services, Ottawa, K1A 0S9, Canada. Telephone (819) 997-2582.

Monthly book. Summarizes major provisions of Canadian collective agreements covering 500 employees or more. Lists bargaining units in current negotiation. Price free of charge.

979
Collective Bargaining Settlements in New York State
New York State Dept of Labor, Div of Research and Statistics, State Office Bldg Campus, Albany, NY 12240. Order from Division of Research and Statistics, Room 6804, New York State Dept of Labor, 2 World Trade Center, New York, NY 10047. Telephone (212) 488-5030.

Monthly report. Summarizes collective bargaining settlements affecting 50 or more workers in New York State. Price free of charge.

980
College and University Reports
Commerce Clearing House, Inc, 4025 W Peterson Ave, Chicago, IL 60646. Telephone (312) 583-8500.

Two loose-leaf books plus weekly reports. Discusses federal programs assisting institutions of higher education. Price $680.00 per year.

981
College Placement Annual
College Placement Council, Inc, PO Box 2263, Bethlehem, PA 18001. Telephone (215) 868-1421.

Annual occupational directory containing career information about approximately 1300 employers. 512 pp. Price $5.00 per copy.

982
College Recruiting Report
Abbott, Langer & Assoc, PO Box 275, Park Forest, IL 60466. Telephone (312) 756-3990.

Annual report. Provides information on starting salaries of college graduates in engineering, scientific and technical, and nontechnical fields. Price $75.00 per copy.

983
College Store Journal
National Assn of College Stores, Inc, 528 E Loraine St, Oberlin, OH 44074. Telephone (216) 775-1561.

Bimonthly magazine. Reports on college stores' management, merchandising, and design. Notes activities of National Association of College Stores. Price $20.00 per year.

984
Colorado Business Review
University of Colorado, Graduate School of Business Administration, Business Research Div, Boulder, CO 80309. Telephone (303) 492-8227.

Monthly report. Covers Colorado regional business dates. Price $10.00 per year.

985
Colorado City Retail Sales by Standard Industrial Classification
University of Colorado, Graduate School of Business Administration, Business Research Div, Boulder, CO 80309. Telephone (303) 492-8227.

Quarterly and annual report. Provides information on Colorado city retail sales by standard industrial classification. Includes county reports. Price $35.00 per year.

987
Colorado: Manufacturers Directory, 1980–81
Manufacturers' News, Inc, 3 Huron St, Chicago, IL 60611. Telephone (312) 337-1084.

Biennial book. Lists 3500 Colorado manufacturers. Notes executives and number of employees. Price $38.00.

989
Colorado Ski and Winter Recreation Statistics, **1980 edition**
University of Colorado, Graduate School of Business Administration, Business Research Div, Boulder, CO 80309. Telephone (303) 492-8227.

Report. Provides statistical analysis of Colorado's ski and winter recreation industry. Includes data on finances and characteristics of skiers. Price $25.00.

991
Color Research and Application
John Wiley and Sons, Inc, 605 3rd Ave, New York, NY 10158. Telephone (212) 850-6515. Telex 12-7063.

Quarterly journal. Reports on the science, technology, and application of color in business, art, design, education, and industry. Price $40.00 per year.

992

Columbia Journal of World Business

Columbia University, Graduate School of Business, 8th Fl Uris Hall, New York, NY 10027. Telephone (212) 280-3431.

Quarterly magazine. Presents articles on business topics of global or comparative interest that deal with practical experience or applied theory. Price $16.00 individuals, $32.00 per year businesses.

993

Commerce

Chicago Assn of Commerce & Industry, 130 S Michigan Ave, Chicago, IL 60603. Telephone (312) 786-0111.

Monthly magazine. Focuses on Chicago business developments. Notes leading enterprises, economic conditions, transportation issues, and industrial development. Price $15.00 per year.

994

Commerce

Commerce Publications Ltd, Manek Mahal, 6th Floor, 90 Veer Nariman Rd, PO Box No 11017, Bombay 400 020, India. Telephone, 253505, 253562. Telex CORE-011-6915.

Weekly magazine. Covers Indian economic and financial news. Includes surveys of selected industries. Price $63.00.

995

Commerce Business Daily

US Dept of Commerce, 14th St between Constitution Ave and E St NW, Washington, DC 20230. Order from Superintendent of Documents, US Government Printing Office, Washington, DC 20402. Telephone (202) 783-3238.

Daily newspaper. Lists US government procurement invitations, contract awards, subcontracting leads, sales of surplus property, and foreign business opportunities. Price $105.00 per year.

996

Commerce International

London Chamber of Commerce & Industry, 69-75 Cannon St, London, England EC4N 5AB. Order from Queensway House, 2 Queensway, Redhill, Surrey RH1 1QS, England. Telephone (44) (0737) 68611. Telex 948669.

Monthly magazine. Provides information about London Chamber of Commerce activities, as well as news and analysis of industrial and commercial affairs in Great Britain and world. Price £15.00 Foreign. £12.00 per year.

996.01

Commerce Journal of Minority Business

US Department of Commerce, Minority Business Development Agency, Main Commerce Bldg, Washington, DC 20230. Telephone (202) 377-1936.

Quarterly magazine. Reports on the activities of the Minority Business Development Agency. Discusses minority business development problems and trends. Price free of charge.

996.02

Commerce Publications Update

US Dept of Commerce, 14th St between Constitution Ave and E St NW, Washington, DC 20230. Order from Superintendent of Documents, US Government Printing Office, Washington, DC 20402. Telephone (202) 783-3238.

Biweekly newsletter. Contains a list of the Department of Commerce publications. Includes key business indicators, such as personal income, gross national product, civilian labor force, and imports. Price $17.00 per year domestic, $21.25 per year foreign.

996.03

Commerce Yearbook of Ports, Shipping & Shipbuilding

Commerce Publications Ltd, Manek Mahal, 6th Floor, 90 Veer Nariman Rd, PO Box No 11017, Bombay 400 020, India. Telephone 253505, 253392, 253562. Telex CORE-011-6915.

Annual book. Provides information on major Indian ports. Lists shipping agents, stevedores, and marine insurers. Price Rs 30.

996.04

Commerce Yearbook of Road Transport

Commerce Publications Ltd, Manek Mahal, 6th Floor, 90 Veer Nariman Rd, PO Box No 11017, Bombay 400 020, India. Telephone 253505, 253392, 253562. Telex CORE-011-6915.

Annual book. Covers road transportation in India. Reports on automobile manufacturers, transport companies, and trade organizations. Price Rs 35.

997

Commercial and Financial Chronicle

National News Service, Inc, 4 Water St, Arlinton, MA 02174. Telephone (617) 643-7900.

Weekly publication. Lists more than 4000 stocks, including daily high, low, and closing prices; yearly range; and weekly volume of trading for US and Canadian stock exchanges. Price available on request.

998

Commercial Arbitration Yearbook

American Arbitration Assn, 140 W 51st St, New York, NY 10020. Telephone (212) 977-2000.

Book. Reviews arbitration law and practice in Comecon countries and Rules of International Chamber of Commerce. Price Volume II $19.75, Volume III $23.-70, Volume IV $32.50, Volume V $32.50.

999

Commercial Bulletin

Curtis Guild & Co Publishers, Inc, 88 Broad St, Boston, MA 02110. Telephone (617) 357-9450.

Weekly newspaper. Covers wool, lumber, building materials, energy, and recycling trades. Price $16.00 per year.

1000

Commercial Car Journal

Chilton Co, Chilton Way, Radnor, PA 19089. Telephone (215) 687-8200.

Monthly journal. Offers material about commercial truck, truck tractors, trailers, buses and offroad vehicles in fleets.Price $28.00 per year.

1001

Commercial Directory for Puerto Rico and the Virgin Islands

Dun & Bradstreet, Box 3224, Church St Station, New York, NY 10008. Telephone (212) 285-7346.

Directory. Publishes information on 10,000 retailers and 2000 wholesalers in Puerto Rico and Virgin Islands. Prices on request. Available to Dun & Bradstreet subscribers only.

1004

Commercial Laws (Mexican)

Commerce Clearing House, Inc, 4025 W Peterson Ave, Chicago, IL 60646. Telephone (312) 583-8500.

Monthly loose-leaf report. Deals with Mexico's commercial laws. Price $58.50 per year. (Prices subject to change with Mexican currency fluctuations.)

1004.01
Commercial Laws of Europe
European Law Centre Ltd, 4 Bloomsbury Sq, London, England WC1A 2RL. Telephone (44) (01) 404-4300. Telex 21746.

Monthly report. Provides full texts and explanatory notes on commercial laws in Western European countries. Includes information on European Economic Community. Price $276.00 ISSN 0141-7258.

1004.02
Commercial Laws of the Middle East
Oceana Publications, Inc, 75 Main St, Dobbs Ferry, NY 10522. Telephone (914) 693-1320.

Loose-leaf service in five binders. Provides information on commercial laws of the Middle East on a country-by-country basis. Price $85.00 per binder. ISBN 0-379-2467-3.

1005
Commercial Laws of the World
Foreign Tax Law Assn, Inc, PO Box 340, Alachua, FL 32616

Twenty-nine loose-leaf binders, supplemented monthly. Contain full text of commerical codes, company acts, and other business laws for 100 countries. Price $625.00, annual renewal $175.00.

1006
Commercial News USA
US Dept of Commerce, International Trade Administration, Washington, DC 20230. Telephone (202) 377-3355.

Monthly magazine. Provides commerical news for the US Foreign Service. Limited courtesy copies available on request.

1007
Commercial News (WCN)
C A Page Publishing Co, 3181 Fernwood Ave, Lynwood, CA 90262. Telephone (213) 774-2480.

Weekly newspaper. Reports on shipping, with emphasis on southern California. Price $5.00 per year.

1008
Commercial Paper Ratings Guide
Standard & Poor's Corp, 25 Broadway, New York, NY 10004. Telephone (212) 924-6400.

Loose-leaf reports, with quarterly updates. Provide monthly credit information on over 600 commercial paper issues and issuers. Price $400.00 per year.

1009
Commercial Record
Record Publishing Co, 750 Old Main St, Rocky Hill, CT 06067. Telephone (203) 563-3796.

Weekly newspaper. Contains information on Connecticut real estate and business. Price $138.00 per year. Subscriptions not accepted outside the US.

1010
Commercial Transactions Desk Book
Institute for Business Planning, Inc, IPB Plaza, Englewood Cliffs, NJ 07632. Telephone (201) 592-2040.

Book. Explains how UCC covers commercial transactions. Outlines points to include in legal document. Price $34.95. ISBN 0-87624-095-3.

1011
Commercial West
Commercial West, 5100 Edina Industrial Blvd, Edina, MN 55435. Telephone (612) 835-5853.

Weekly magazine. Covers banking and finance in Midwest. Price $29.00 per year.

1012
Committee for Economic Development Newsletter
Committee for Economic Development, 477 Madison Ave, New York, NY 10022. Telephone (212) 688-2063.

Annual newsletter. Reports on Committee for Economic Development's policies on US and international economic issues, government management, education, and urban development. Price free of charge.

1013
Committee for Monetary Research & Education (CMRE) Money Tracts
Committee for Monetary Research & Education, Inc, Box 1630, Greenwich, CT 06830. Telephone (203) 661-2533.

Bimonthly booklet. Presents papers on monetary and economic issues, particularly role of sound money in a free society. Price varies.

1015
Committee on Uniform Security Identification Procedures (CUSIP) Conversion Service
Standard & Poor's Corp, 25 Broadway, New York, NY 10004. Telephone (212) 248-2525.

Information service. Offers assistance in converting securities files to CUSIP. (Committee on Uniform Security Identification Procedures.) Price available on request.

1016
Committee on Uniform Security Identification Procedures (CUSIP) Corporate Directory
Standard & Poor's Corp, 25 Broadway, New York, NY 10004. Telephone (212) 248-2525.

One-volume book plus supplements. Gives CUSIP (Committee on Uniform Security Identification Procedures) numbers and descriptions for 45,000 corporate issue stocks and bonds. Price $470.00 per year.

1017
Committee on Uniform Security Identification Procedures (CUSIP): Digest of Changes in CUSIP
Standard & Poor's Corp, 25 Broadway, New York, NY 10004. Telephone (212) 248-2525.

Fortnightly report. Covers changes in CUSIP (Committee on Uniform Security Identification Procedures), including material on acquisitions and mergers. Price $92.00 per year.

1018
Committee on Uniform Security Identification Procedures (CUSIP) Directory of User Numbers
Standard & Poor's Corp, 25 Broadway, New York, NY 10004. Telephone (212) 248-2525.

Directory. Lists all available CUSIP (Committee on Uniform Security Identification Procedures) user numbers. Is reserved for users to assign to securities not qualifying for CUSIP official identification. Price available on request.

1019
Committee on Uniform Security Identification Procedures (CUSIP) Directory
Standard & Poor's Corp, 25 Broadway, New York, NY 10004. Telephone (212) 248-2525.

Annual directory. Lists CUSIP (Committee on Uniform Security Identification Procedures) numbers and descriptions for more than 1,000,000 stocks, bonds, and warrants. Price $680.00 per year.

1020
Committees of Parliament/Minutes of Proceedings and Evidence
Supply and Services Canada, Canadian Govt Publishing Centre, Hull, Que, Canada, KIA 0S9. Telephone (819) 994-3475; 2085.

Report. Contains minutes of proceedings and evidence of Canada's Senate, House of Commons, and Joint Committees. Usually bilingual. Price available on request.

1022
Commodities
Commodities Magazine, Inc, 219 Parkade, Cedar Falls, Iowa 50613. Telephone (319) 277-6341.

Monthly magazine provides information on commodity futures and trading. Price $34.00 per year.

1023
Commodities Survey
Barclays Bank, Group Economics Dept, 54 Lombard St, London, England EC3P 3AH.Telephone (44) (01) 283-8989.

Quarterly reports. Analyze price trends and medium—term prospects for the major metal, raw material and soft commodity markets. Price free of charge.

1024
Commodities Weekly Technical Report and Currency Exchange Rates
Chart Analysis Ltd, 37-39 St Andrew's Hill, London, England EC4V 5DD. Telephone (44) (01) 236-5211. Telex 883356.

Weekly report. Provides charts on 24 commodities and metals, plus currency exchange rates. Includes price predictions and overbought–oversold indicators. Price £250.00 per year.

1024.01
Commodity & Currency Reporter
Marpep Publishing Ltd, Suite 700, 133 Richmond St W, Toronto, Ont, Canada M5H 3M8. Telephone (416) 869-1177.

Weekly report. Offers news and advice for commodity futures traders. Price available on request.

1025
Commodity Bulletin
New South Wales, Dept of Agriculture, Div of Marketing and Economics, PO Box K220, Haymarket, Sydney, NSW 2000, Australia. Telephone (61) (02) 2176666.

Monthly bulletin. Provides information relating to agricultural commodities in New South Wales, Australia. Price free of charge.

1026
Commodity Chart Service
Commodity Research Bureau, Inc, One Liberty Plz—47th floor, New York, NY 10006. Telephone (212) 267-3600.

Weekly loose-leaf service. Charts cover all actively traded commodites. Price $265.00 per year.

1027
Commodity Futures Law Reports
Commerce Clearing House, Inc, 4025 W Peterson Ave, Chicago, IL 60646. Telephone (312) 583-8500.

Two Loose-leaf books plus semimonthly reports. Covers Commodity Exchange Act and regulations of Commodity Exchange Authority and Commodity Futures Trading Commission. Full text. Price $290.00 per year.

1028
Commodity Imports
United Nations Publications, Room LX 2300, New York, NY 10017. Telephone (212) 754-1234.

Report. Contains data on commodity trade. Price $6.00.

1030
Commodity Journal
American Assn of Commodity Traders, 10 Park St, Concord, NH 03301. Order from Commodity Journal, Subscription Dept, 10 Park St, Concord, NH 03301. Telephone (603) 224-2376.

Monthly journal. Examines regional, national, and global commodity markets. Focuses on spot, forward, and option contracts. Price $20.00 per year.

1031
Commodity Trade and Price Trends, 1980 edition
World Bank, 1818 H St, NW, Washington, DC 20433. Telephone (202) 393-6360.

Paperback book. Presents factual, historical information on the trend of developing countries. Provides 80 market price quotations for 51 commodities which figure importantly in international trade. Available in English, French and Spanish. Price $15.00 per year. Mimeographed publication contains data on export trade of developing nations. Offers 68 market price quotations for 42 commodities. Tables and charts. English, French, and Spanish. Price free of charge.

1032
Commodity Trade Statistics
United Nations Publications, Room A-3315, New York, NY 10017. Telephone (212) 754-8302.

Publication issued 28 times per year. Provides data on trade of major trading nations by commodity groups. Price $50.00 per year.

1032.01
Commodity Trading Recommendations
Chart Analysis Ltd, 37-39 St Andrew's Hill, London, England EC4V 5DD. Telephone (44) (01) 236-5211.

Service. Provides specific buy and sell recommendations when markets produce suitable opportunities. Price £150.00 per year.

1033
Commodity Year Book
Commodity Research Bureau, Inc, One Liberty Plz—47th Floor, New York, NY 10006. Telephone (212) 267-3600.

Annual book. Statistical tables and charts are used to appraise commodity market trends. Price $22.95 each.

1034
Commodity Yearbook Statistical Abstract Service
Commodity Research Bureau, Inc, One Liberty Plz—47th floor, New York, NY 10006. Telephone (212) 267-3600.

Three times yearly. Statistical data for commodity market are presented with charts and tables. Intended to update the Commodity Year Book. Price $45.00 per year.

1037
Common Market Law Reports
European Law Centre Ltd, 4 Bloomsbury Sq, London, WC1A 2RL, England. Telephone (44) (01) 404-4300. Telex 21746.

Weekly report. Discusses European Community legal developments. Includes European Court of Justice and selected national court decisions. Price $390.00 per year.

1038
Common Market News
European Economic Data Publishing Co Ltd, 4 Cleveland Sq, London, England W2 6DH. Telephone (44) (01) 723-9681.

Monthly journal. Provides information on European Economic Community, including coverage of social, political, economic, commercial, and agricultural affairs. European Court of Justice. Price $56.00 per year. ISSN 0305-8670.

1039
Common Market Reports
Commerce Clearing House, Inc, 4025 W Peterson Ave, Chicago, IL 60646. Telephone (312) 583-8500.

Four loose-leaf books plus biweekly reports. Explains laws, regulations, and court decisions governing business operations in European Economic Community. Price $745.00 per year.

1041
Communication and Transportation Laws (Mexican)
Commerce Clearing House, Inc, 4025 W Peterson Ave, Chicago, IL 60646. Telephone (312) 583-8500.

Monthly loose-leaf binder. Reports on Mexico's transportation and communication laws. Price $58.50 per year. (Prices subject to change with Mexican currency fluctuations.)

1042
Communications News
Harcourt Brace Jovanovich Publications, 757 3rd Ave, New York, NY 10017. Order from Harcourt Brace and Jovanovich Publications, 1 E 1st St, Duluth, MN 55802. Telephone (218) 727-8511.

Monthly report. Provides information on communications systems' design, engineering, construction, and maintenance. Notes telephone and broadcasting industry news. Price $7.00 per year.

1043
Communications of the ACM
Assn for Computing Machinery, 1133 Ave of the Americas, New York, NY 10036. Telephone (212) 265-6300.

Monthly journal. Presents technical articles on computers. Includes information on systems performance evaluation, programming, and applications. Price $55.00 per year.

1044
Communications Service Bulletin
Statistics Canada, User Services, Publications Distribution, Ottawa, Ont, K1A 0V7, Canada. Telephone (613) 992-3151.

Irregular report. Provides statistical summary of information on Canadian telecommunications. Contains data on telephones, radio, television, and cable television. Price $18.00 per year. ISSN 0380-0334.

1045
Communicator
Institute of Public Relations, 1 Great James St, London, England WC1N 3DA. Telephone (44) (01) 405-5505.

Monthly newsletter. Contains international and British public relations news items. Reports or Institute of Public Relations' activities. Price free to members of the Institute. ISSN 0307 9252.

1046
Communicators Directory, 1980 edition
American Nuclear Society, 555 Kensington Ave, La Grange Park, IL 60525. Telephone (312) 352-6611.

Directory. Lists names of 500 energy experts in fields of nuclear power, waste management, safety, solar power, and other forms of energy. Includes addresses. Price $12.00 per copy.

1047
Communique
Federal Publications, Inc, 1120 20th St, NW, Washington, DC 20036. Telephone (202) 337-7000.

Fortnightly newsletter. Reports news about federal government's contracts. Price $228.00 per year.

1048
Community Bank Series on Operations and Automation
Bank Administration Inst, PO Box 500, 303 S Northwest Hwy, Park Ridge, IL 60068. Telephone (312) 693-7300.

Series of reports. Covers community banks' operations and automation. Contains information on demand deposit accounting, savings and time deposit accounting, general ledger and automated financial reporting, customer information files, and automation alternatives. Price $50.00.

1049
Community Development Digest
Community Development Services Inc, National Press Bldg, Washington, DC 20045. Telephone (202) 638-6113.

Twice-monthly report on rules and changes in the Community Development Block Grant program. Includes housing news and all aspects of community development. Price $147.00 per year.

1050
Community Markets
Financial Times Business Information Ltd, Bracken House, 10 Cannon St, London, England EC4P 4BY. Order from Financial Times Ltd, 75 Rockefeller Plz, New York, NY 10019. Telephone (44) (01) 248-8000. Telex 886341-2.

Monthly publication. Covers the activities of the European Commission, Council of Ministers, European Parliament, Court of Justice, and European Investment Bank. Price $215.00 per year.

1050.01
Community Publication Rates and Data
Standard Rate & Data Service, Inc, 5201 Old Orchard Rd, Skokie, IL 60077. Telephone (312) 470-3100.

Semiannual book. Reports on advertising rates and related information for weekly newspapers and shopping guides in metropolitan and other areas. Price $18.00 per year.

1051
Company Acreage and Activity Statistics
Petroconsultants SA, 8-10 Rue Muzy, PO Box 1211, Geneva 6, Switzerland. Telephone 36 88 11. Telex 27 763 PETRO CH.

Annual report. Offers statistics on oil exploration and production of every oil company outside North America and Communist block. Price 1500 Swiss francs.

1052

Company Administration Handbook, **4th edition**

Gower Publishing Co, Ltd, 1 Westmead, Farnborough, Hampshire, England GU14 7RU. Telephone Farnborough (0252) 519221. Telex 858623.

Book. Provides advice for office personnel responsible for administration. Includes information on accounting and management of employees and physical assets. Price $58.00. ISBN 0 566 02154 4.

1053

Company Finance

Her Majesty's Stationery Office, PO Box 569, London, England SE1 9NH. Telephone (44) (01) 928-1321.

Annual publication. Addresses itself to company finance in Great Britain. Price £3.50 per year.

1053.01

Company Law in Europe, 3rd Edition

Gower Publishing Co, Ltd, 1 Westmead, Farnborough, Hampshire, England GU14 7RU. Telephone Farnborough (0252) 519221. Telex 858623.

Manual. Provides survey of law relating to companies within individual European countries. Contains bibliography listing further information sources. Price $97.50. ISBN 0566 02245 1.

1054

Company Review Service

Stock Exchange Research Pty Ltd, 20 Bond St, Sydney, 2000, Australia. Telephone (61) (02) 231-0066.

Annual report with weekly updates. Reviews company balance sheets and activities. Covers 1000 Australian Stock Exchange companies. Price $2500.00 (Australian) per year.

1055

Company Secretary's Review

Tolley Publishing Co Ltd, 44a High St, Croydon, Surrey, England CR9 1UU. Telephone (44) (01) 686-9144.

Fortnightly journal. Covers legislation, regulations, and announcements issued by British Government, EEC, and professional organizations. Price available on request.

1056

Comparative Analysis

Investors Management Sciences, Inc, 7400 S Alton Ct, Englewood, CO 80110. Telephone (303) 771-6510; (800) 525-8640 (toll free).

Computerized information service provides financial data on 4000 US companies, including income statements, balance sheets, reconciliations, and retained earnings statements. Price available on request.

1057

Comparative Investment Analyses (CIA)

Wright Investors' Service, Wright Bldg, 500 State St, Bridgeport, CT 06604. Telephone (203) 377-9444.

Weekly service. Provides data on all New York Stock Exchange stocks by industry group. Offers comparative investment evaluations. Includes updated earnings and dividends. Price $500.00 per quarter.

1058

Comparative State Income Tax Guide with Forms

Oceana Publications, Inc, 75 Main St., Dobbs Ferry, NY 10522. Telephone (914) 693-5944.

Three loose-leaf books with annual supplement. Provides data on tax structures of 50 states and District of Columbia. Includes copies of state income tax forms. Price $225.00. ISBN 0-379-10120-3.

1059

Comparison of State Unemployment Insurance Laws

US Dept of Labor, Employment & Training Administration, Washington, DC 20213. Telephone (202) 376-6730.

Loose-leaf report with biannual updates. Compares state unemployment insurance coverage, employer taxation, and benefits. Tables. Price $12.45.

1060

Compendium of Commercial Finance Law

National Commercial Finance Conference, Inc, One Penn Plz, New York, NY 10001. Telephone (212) 594-3490.

Five loose-leaf books with periodic updates. Offers material on commercial finance law, including federal tax lien filing statutes, uniform commercial code, interest statutes, corporate guaranties, and secret liens. Price $250.00 per year.

1061

Compendium Internal Revenue Service

National Assn of Real Estate Investment Trusts, Inc, 1101 17th St NW, Washington, DC 20036. Telephone (202) 785-8717.

Loose-leaf book with periodic updating. Reports on all Internal Revenue Service rulings and legislative changes that affect taxes on real estate investment trust income. Price available to members only.

1062

Compensation Review

American Management Assns, 135 W 50th St, New York, NY 10020. Telephone (212) 586-8100.

Quarterly report. Provides information on developments in compensation. Price $24.75 per year.

1064

Complete Aircraft and Aircraft Engines

US Dept of Commerce, Bureau of the Census, Washington, DC 20233. Telephone (202) 449-1600.

Monthly report and annual summary. Contains information on shipments and unfilled orders to complete civilian aircraft and aircraft parts. Includes data on engines and engine parts and on exports. Price $4.75 per year.

1065

Complete Guide to Organizing and Managing the Responsibilities of the Plan Administrator

Panel Publishers, 14 Plaza Rd, Greenvale, NY 11548. Telephone (516) 484-0006.

Book. Offers guide to responsibilities of pension, profit-sharing, and employee-benefit plans administrator. Provides information on records maintenance and compliance requirements. Price $75.00.

1066

Compliance Guide for Plan Administrators

Commerce Clearing House, Inc, 4025 W Peterson Ave, Chicago, IL 60646. Telephone (312) 583-8500.

Two loose-leaf book, monthly reports, and fortnightly newsletter. Covers reporting and disclosure rules of Employee Retirement Income Security Act as they affect plan administrators. Includes forms. Price $275.00 per year.

1067
Compmark Data Services
Standard & Poor's Corp, 25 Broadway, New York, NY 10004. Telephone (212) 248-2525.

Information service in variety of formats. Provides facts on more than 37,000 US and international corporations. Also covers 405,000 corporate executives, with 72,000 biographies. Price available on request.

1068
Composites
IPC Business Press Ltd, 205 E 42nd St, New York, NY 10017. Telephone (212) 889-0700. Telex 421710.

Quarterly magazine presents articles on composite materials, with emphasis on applied research. Price $124.80 per year. Price $135.80 air mail. ISSN 0010-4361.

1069
Comptroller General's Procurement Decisions
Federal Publications, Inc, 1120 20th St, NW, Washington, DC 20036. Telephone (202) 337-7000.

Monthly report. Reproduces all published and unpublished contract decisions of General Accounting Office's comptroller general. Price $380.00 per year.

1070
Compustat
Standard & Poor's Compustat Services, Inc, 7400 S Alton Ct, Englewood, CO 80112. Telephone (303) 771-6510; (800) 525-8640.

Annual service provides computerized library of financial information on approximately 6500 companies. Includes industrial, bank, utility, and special files. Price available on request.

1071
Computer-Aided Design
IPC Business Press Ltd, 205 E 42nd St, New York, NY 10017. Telephone (212) 889-0700. Telex 421710.

Quarterly magazine provides enlightment on computer-aided design in all aspects of engineering and building design. Notes conferences and pertinent literature. Price $124.80. ISSN 0010-4485.

1072
Computer and Information Systems Abstracts Journal
Cambridge Scientific Abstracts, 6611 Kenilworth Ave, Suite 437, Riverdale, MD 20840. Telephone (301) 951-1327.

Twenty issues per year. Provides indexed abstracts from more than 8500 periodicals on scientific and technical aspects of computer industry. Price $470.00 per year.

1073
Computer Business News
CW Communications Inc, 375 Cochituate Rd, Box 880, Framingham, MA 01701. Telephone (617) 879-0700.

Weekly newspaper. Covers computer sales and distribution developments. Price $25.00 per year.

1074
ComputerData
Whitsed Publishing Ltd, 55 Bloor St W, Suite 1201, Toronto, Ont, Canada M4W 3K2. Telephone (416) 967-6200.

Monthly magazine. Reports on developments in the field of business computing for computer industry and users. Emphasizes Canada. Price $25.00 per year. ISSN 0383-7319.

1075
Computer Decisions
Hayden Publishing Co, Inc, 50 Essex St, Rochelle Park, NJ 07662. Telephone (201) 843-0550.

Monthly magazine on computer trade. Addresses itself to managers. Price free of charge.

1076
Computer Dictionary and Handbook
Howard W Sams, Co, Inc, 4300 W 62nd St, Indianapolis, IN 46268. Telephone (317) 298-5400.

Book. Contains definitions of computer terminology and discussion of systems and techniques. Price $29.95. ISBN 0-672-21632-9.

1078
Computerized Data Sheet
Financial Post, 481 University Ave, Toronto, Ont, Canada M5W 1A7. Telephone (416) 595-1811.

Annual computerized data sheets. Give financial information about 250 Canadian companies. Analyzes profits and growth rates. Supply regular updates. Price $125.00 per month.

1079
Computer Law and Tax Report
Warren, Gorham & Lamont, Inc, 210 South St, Boston, MA 02111. Telephone (617) 423-2020.

Monthly report. Discusses laws relating to computer use. Notes conferences and new publications. Price $64.00 per year.

1079.01
Computer Law: Evidence and Procedure
Matthew Bender & Co, 235 E 45th St, New York, NY 10017. Telephone (212) 661-5050.

Loose-leaf book with supplements as needed. Discusses evidence and discovery procedures which apply to computers. Price $60.00, plus additional charge for revisions.

1080
Computer Management—United Kingdom
CW Communications, Inc, 375 Cochituate Rd, Box 880, Framingham, MA 01701. Telephone (617) 879-0700.

Monthly magazine. Covers British computer industry hardware, software, terminals, and supply products. Price $40.00.

1081
Computer Network of Databases
IP Sharp Assc, 145 King St, Toronto, Canada M5H 1J8. Telephone (416) 364-5361.

Computer network. Provides databases in fields such as energy, aviation, finance, and insurance. Prices available on request.

1081.01
Computer Output Program
International Data Corporation, 214 3rd Ave, Waltham, MA 02254. Telephone (617) 890-3700. Telex 92-3401.

Continuous information service. Offers analysis of all aspects of computer output, including printers, microfiche, microfilm, and paper forms. Price available on request.

1081.02
Computer-Readable Data Bases: A Directory and Data Sourcebook, **1979 edition**
American Society for Information Science, 1010 16th St, NW, Washington, DC 20036. Order from Knowledge Industry Publications, Inc, 2 Corporate Park Dr, White Plains, NY 10604. Telephone (914) 328-9157.

Directory. Supplies information on computer-readable databases. Notes producer, coverage, year of origin, availability, and other information. Price $95.00.

1082
Computer Report
Samsom Publications Ltd, 12-14 Hill Rise, Richmond, Surrey, England TW10 6UA. Telephone (44) (01) 948-4251.

Weekly newsletter. Offers news and comment on computer companies, products, and services. Price $125.00 per year. ISSN 0306-6886.

1084
Computers and Industrial Engineering
Pergamon Press, Inc, Maxwell House, Fairview Park, Elmsford, NY 10523. Telephone (914) 592-7700. Telex 13-7328.

Quarterly journal. Covers computerized industrial engineering applications, and implementation of different industrial engineering techniques on computers. Graphs, charts, tables. Price $100.00 per year.

1086
Computers & Operations Research
Pergamon Press, Inc, Maxwell House, Fairview Park, Elmsford, NY 10523. Telephone (914) 592-7700. Telex 13-7328.

Quarterly magazine. Reports on computers and operations research and their application to problems of world concern. Price $165.00 per year.

1087
Computers and People
Berkeley Enterprises, Inc, 815 Washington St, Newtonville, MA 02160. Telephone (617) 332-5453.

Monthly report. Covers developments in the information processing field. Price $9.50 per year. ISSN 0361-1442.

1088
Computer Times
Hayden Publishing Co, Inc, 50 Essex St, Rochelle Park, NJ 07662. Telephone (201) 843-0550. Telex TWX 710 990-5071.

Monthly newspaper. Focuses on minicomputer and microcomputer. Price free to qualified persons.

1089
Computerworld
CW Communications, Inc, 375 Cochituate Rd, Box 880, Framingham, MA 01701. Telephone (617) 879-0700.

Weekly newspaper. Covers EDP/MIS business industry, including hardware products, software systems, data communications, and industrial trends. Price $36.00.

1090
Computer Yearbook
American Data Processing Inc, 22929 Industrial Dr E, St Clair Shores, MI 48080. Telephone (313) 773-4252.

Book, revised triennially. Provides information on new developments and on applications and manufacturers. Price $39.-00. ISSN 0069-8180.

1091
Computing Reviews
Assn for Computing Machinery, Special Interest Group on Business Data Processing, 1133 Ave of the Americas, New York, NY 10036. Telephone (212) 265-6300.

Monthly report. Reviews both books and articles on computers and related topics. Price $40.00 per year. ISSN 0010-4884.

1091.01
Computing Surveys
Assn for Computing Machinery, 1133 Ave of the Americas, New York, NY 10036. Telephone (212) 265-6300.

Quarterly journal. Presents surveys on computer topics. Covers database techniques, architecture, security, and ethics. Price $40.00 per year.

1092
Comsearch Printouts
Foundation Center, 888 7th Ave, New York, NY 10106. Telephone (212) 975-1120.

Annual computer printout series. Lists grants by over 300 foundations in 68 subject areas, 12 geographic areas, and four special topical concentrations. Includes fields within the arts, sciences, and humanities. Price $4.00 (microfiche), $12.00 (paper printout).

1093
Concise Guide to International Markets
International Advertising Assn, 475 5th Ave, New York, NY 10017. Order from Leslie Stinton & Partners, 39A London Road, Kingston-upon-Thames, Surrey, England KT2 6ND. Telephone (212) 684-1583.

Book. Carries concise data and statistics on advertising and marketing in 100 world markets. Contains more than 100 maps. Price $38.00.

1094
Condensed Computer Encyclopedia
McGraw-Hill Book Co, Hightstown-Princeton Rd, Hightstown, NJ 08520. Telephone (609) 448-1700. Telex 843449

Book. Contains definitions of computer terms and systems. Price $19.95.

1096
Condition Report of Weekly Reporting Commercial Banks—Eleventh Federal Reserve District
Federal Reserve Bank of Dallas, Station K, Dallas, TX 75222. Telephone (214) 651-6111.

Weekly report on balances of assets and liabilities of major commercial banks in 11th Federal Reserve District. Price free of charge.

1096.01
Condominium Lenders Guide
Andrew R Mandala, PO Box 30240, Washington, DC 20014. Telephone (301) 654-5580.

Binder, with monthly supplements. Provides information on condominium law. Price $150.00 per year.

1097
Confectionery Including Chocolate Products. **M20C**
US Dept of Commerce, Bureau of the Census, Washington, DC 20233. Telephone (202) 449-1600.

Monthly report with annual summary. Presents estimated dollar sales of manufacturers-wholesalers for confectionery and competitive chocolate products by geographic areas and by specified states. Includes poundage and export figures. Price $3.25 per year.

1098
Confederation of Australian Industry (CAI) News
Confederation of Australian Industry, PO Box 14, Canberra City, Act 2600, Australia. Telephone (61) (062) 732311. Telex AA62733.

Monthly newsletter. Reports on Australian business news, labor issues, economic developments, and Confederation of Australian Industry activities. Price free of charge. ISSN: 0155-2090.

1099

Confederation of British Industry (CBI) Economic Situation Report

Confederation of British Industry, Centre Point, 103 New Oxford St, London, England WC1A 1DU. Telephone (44) (01) 379-7400. Telex 21332.

Monthly report discusses the Confederation's view of economic trends. Price £ 50.00 per year.

1100

Confederation of British Industry (CBI) Education and Training Bulletin

Confederation of British Industry, Centre Point, 103 New Oxford St, London, England WC1A 1DU. Telephone (44) (01) 379-7400.

Quarterly bulletin discusses education and training developments of interest to industry. Price members £10.00 per year, nonmembers £12.00 per year.

1101

Confederation of British Industry (CBI) Industrial Trends Survey

Confederation of British Industry, Centre Point, 103 New Oxford St., London, England WC1A 1DU. Telephone (01) 379-7400. Telex 21332.

Quarterly reviews latest trends in output, employment and investment plans for 33 manufacturing industries. Price members £60.00 per year, £17.00 per copy. Nonmembers £1100.00 per year, £30.00 per copy.

1102

Confederation of British Industry (CBI) Members Bulletin

Confederation of British Industry, Centre Point, 103 New Oxford St, London, England WC14 1DU.. Telephone (44) (01) 3790-7400. Telex 21332.

Semimonthly report. Covers British industrial developments. Notes occupational safety topics and international news. Free of charge.

1103

Confederation of British Industry (CBI) Overseas Reports

Confederation of British Industry, Centre Point, 103 New Oxford St, London, England WC1A 1DU. Telephone 01-379-7400.

Monthly report. Reviews international business conditions and markets. Price £ 40.00 per year (members only).

1106

Confederation of Irish Industry (CII) Economic Trends

Confederation of Irish Industry, Confederation House, Kildare St, Dublin 2, Ireland. Telephone 77 98 01. Telex 4711.

Monthly summary of current Irish economic situation. Subscription includes CII newsletter. Price available on request.

1107

Confederation of Irish Industry (CII)/ESRI Business Forecast

Confederation of Irish Industry, Confederation House, Kildare St, Dublin 2, Ireland. Telephone 77 98 01. Telex 24711.

Monthly report. Surveys Irish businessmen's views on current industrial climate. Includes export, sales, price, and employment data. Price free to survey participants.

1108

Confederation of Irish Industry (CII) Newsletter

Confederation of Irish Industry, Confederation House, Kildare St, Dublin 2, Ireland. Telephone 77 98 01. Telex 24711.

Weekly newsletter covering full range of industrial subjects in Ireland. Subscription includes CII Economic Trends. Price available on request.

1109

Conference Board Cumulative Index

Conference Board, Inc, 845 3rd Ave, New York, NY 10022. Telephone (212) 759-0900.

Annual book. Subject index to Conference Board publications. Price free of charge.

1110

Conference Papers Index

Data Courier, Inc, 620 S 5th St, Louisville, KY 40202. Telephone (502) 582-4111. Telex 204235.

Monthly journal. Cites and indexes research findings and papers presented at scientific and technical conferences, and meetings throughout the world. Price $435.00 per year.

1110.01

Congress Daily

Washington Monitor, 499 National Press Bldg, Washington, DC 20045. Telephone (202) 347-7757.

Daily report. Covers news of Congress. Price $200.00 per year.

1110.02

Congress in Print

Washington Monitor, 499 National Press Bldg, Washington, DC 20045. Telephone (202) 347-7757.

Weekly report. Provides information on congressional hearings, committee reports, prints, and staff studies. Price $70.00 per year.

1111

Congressional Action

Chamber of Commerce of the US, 1615 H St, NW, Washington, DC 20062. Telephone (202) 659-6231.

Weekly report. Discusses congressional issues of interest to US Chamber of Commerce members. Price available to members only.

1114

Congressional Index

Commerce Clearing House, Inc, 4025 W Peterson Ave, Chicago, IL 60646. Telephone (312) 583-8500.

Two loose-leaf books plus weekly reports. Traces action on all public bills and resolutions from introduction to final disposition. Price $405.00 per year.

1114.01

Congressional Insight

Congressional Quarterly, Inc, 1414 22nd St, NW, Washington, DC 20037. Telephone (202) 296-6800.

Weekly newsletter. Analyzes Congressional politics. Discusses lobbying practices. Price $138.00 per year.

1115

Congressional Legislative Reporting

Commerce Clearing House, Inc, 4025 W Peterson Ave, Chicago, IL 60646. Telephone (312) 583-8500.

Periodic reports. Covers congressional subjects of subscriber's choice, with texts on bills and laws. Price $975.00 per year plus annual charge for each subject.

1115.01

Congressional Monitor

Washington Monitor, 499 National Press Bldg, Washington, DC 20045. Telephone (202) 347-7757.

Daily advisory service. Lists scheduled congressional committee and subcommittee hearings up to two months in advance. Includes witness lists and floor action summaries. Price $600.00 per year.

1115.02
Congressional Record Scanner
Washington Monitor, 499 National Press Bldg, Washington, DC 20045. Telephone (202) 347-7757.

Report published almost daily. Reviews the Congressional Record. Price $330.00 per year.

1115.03
Congressional Yellow Book
Washington Monitor, 499 National Press Bldg, Washington, DC 20045. Telephone (202) 347-7757.

Loose-leaf directory with quarterly updates. Lists members of Congress, their committees, and key staff aides. Notes district offices. Price $85.00 per year.

1116
Connecticut Business and Industry Assn (CBIA) News
Connecticut Business and Industry Assn (CBIA) Service Corp, 60 Washington St, Hartford, CT 06106. Telephone (203) 549-6060.

Monthly magazine. Reports on political, legislative, economic, and other developments that affect business and industry in Connecticut. Price $8.00 per year.

1117
Connecticut CPA
Connecticut Society of Certified Public Accountants, 179 Allyn St, Suite 501, Hartford, CT 06103. Telephone (203) 525-1153.

Quarterly magazine. Addresses itself to tax and accounting procedures in Connecticut. Limited courtesy copies available on request.

1117.01
Connecticut Directory of Connecticut Manufacturers, 1981
Manufacturers' News, Inc, 3 Huron St, Chicago, IL 60611. Telephone (312) 337-1084.

Annual book. Lists Connecticut manufacturing companies by name, location, and product. Price $27.50.

1117.02
Connecticut-Rhode Island: Directory of Manufacturers, 1981
Manufacturers' News, Inc, 3 Huron St, Chicago, IL 60611. Telephone (312) 337-1084.

Annual book. Identifies manufacturing firms in Connecticut and Rhode Island. Price $59.50.

1117.03
Connecticut: State Industrial Directory, 1981
Manufacturers' News, Inc, 3 Huron St, Chicago, IL 60611. Telephone (312) 337-1084.

Annual book. Names 6132 Connecticut businesses. Identifies executives and products. Price $50.00.

1118
Consensus
Consensus, Inc, 30 W Pershing Rd, Kansas City, MO 64108. Telephone (816) 471-3862.

Weekly newspaper. Reports on national commodity futures with recommendations from over 50 sources. Includes charts, price quotes, brokerage reports and sentiment index. Price $291.00 per year.

1119
Consensus of Insiders
Consensus of Insiders, PO Box 10247, Fort Lauderdale, FL 33305. Telephone (305) 563-6827.

Weekly newsletter. Provides information on insiders' stock trading. Indicates transactions of stock exchange members, specialist, and traders. Includes data on pension and mutual funds, foreign funds, and banks and insurance companies. Price $180.00 per year.

1120
Conservation and Recycling
Pergamon Press, Inc, Maxwell House, Fairview Park, Elmsford, NY 10523. Telephone (914) 592-7700. Telex 13-7328.

Journal. Provides information on conservation and reclamation of energy and materials, excluding air and water. Price $70.00 per year.

1121
Consolidated Ledger Abstract
Dun & Bradstreet, Box 3224, Church St Station, New York, NY 10008. Telephone (212) 285-7346.

Monthly report. Provides information on past due accounts in building and construction lines. Price available on request. (Available to Dun & Bradstreet subscribers only.)

1122
Consolidation of General Orders of the Board of Transport Commissioners for Canada
Supply and Services Canada, Canadian Govt Publishing Centre, Hull, Que, Canada, K1A 0S9. Telephone (819) 994-3475.

Book, with supplements. Consolidates general orders of Canada's Board of Transport Commision. Price available on request.

1123
Constitutions of the Countries of the World
Oceana Publications, Inc, 75 Main St, Dobbs Ferry, NY 10522. Telephone (914) 693-5944.

Loose-leaf service, 15 binders. Contains constitutions of independent countries. Reflects changes as they occur. Price $1200.00 for all material published to date and still in print. $75.00 per supplement. ISBN 0-379-00467-4.

1125
Construction and Road Transport
Thomson Publications (Australia) Pty Ltd, 47 Chippen St, PO Box 65, Chippendale, NSW 2008, Australia. Telephone 699-6731. Telex TPAS AA22226.

Monthly magazine. Discusses trucking subjects, with emphasis on Australia. Presents road tests and user reports. Price $60.00 (Australian) per year.

1125.01
Construction Briefings
Federal Publications, Inc, 1120 20th St, NW, Washington, DC 20036. Telephone (202) 337-7000.

Bimonthly report. Discusses construction contract topics. Price $112.00 per year.

1126
Construction Contractor
Federal Publications, Inc, 1120 20th St, NW, Washington, DC 20036. Telephone (202) 337-7000.

Biweekly loose-leaf report. Focuses on legal aspects of construction contract operations. Price $236.00 per year.

1127
Construction Equipment
Cahners Publishing Company, Inc, 221 Columbus Ave, Boston, MA 02116. Telephone (617) 536-7780.

Monthly magazine reports on purchase, maintenance use, and management of heavy construction equipment. Price $25.00 per year.

1128
Construction Equipment Distribution (CED)

Associated Equipment Distributors, 615 W 22nd St, Oak Brook, IL 60521. Telephone (312) 654-0650.

Magazine. Covers business aspects of construction equipment industry. Price $15.00 per year.

1129
Construction Equipment News

Thomson Publications (Australia) Pty Ltd, 47 Chippen St, PO Box 65, Chippendale, NSW 2008, Australia. Telephone 699-6731. Telex TPAS AA22226.

Monthly magazine. Carries material on new construction equipment. Covers mining and logging industries. Focuses on Australian situation. Price $60.00 (Australia) per year.

1130
Construction in Canada

Statistics Canada, User Services, Publications Distribution, Ottawa, Ont, K1A 0V7, Canada. Telephone (613) 992-3151.

Annual report. Supplies data on Canadian construction for two preceeding years and estimates for current year. Covers value of new and repair work, types on structures, and labor and material costs. Price $8.40. ISSN 0527-4974.

1131
Construction in Hawaii

Bank of Hawaii, Economics Div, PO Box 2900, Honolulu, HI 96846. Telephone (808) 537-8269.

Annual report. Reviews Hawaiian construction trends. Discusses residential, commercial, and industrial construction, and mortgage activity. Tables, charts, and maps. Price free of charge.

1132
Construction Labor Report

Bureau of National Affairs, Inc, 1231 25th St NW, Washington, DC 20037, Telephone (202) 452-4200.

Loose-leaf books with weekly updates. Concerns labor-management relations in construction industry. Includes facts on collective bargaining, equal employment opportunity, job safety, and union activity. Index. Price $350.00 per year.

1133
Construction Lending Handbook

American Bankers Assn, 1120 Connecticut Ave NW, Washington, DC 20036. Telephone (202) 467-4123.

Book. Reviews construction lending by commercial banks. Covers permanent financing, construction loan participation and servicing, and bonding. Price $6.00.

1134
Construction Machinery

US Dept of Commerce, Bureau of the Census, Washington, DC 20233. Telephone (202) 449-1600.

Annual report. Presents final data on construction machinery shipments for each year. Includes export information. Price $.50.

1135
Construction Machinery

US Dept of Commerce, Bureau of the Census, Washington, DC 20233. Telephone (202) 449-1600.

Quarterly report. Supplies data on quantity and value of total construction machinery shipments and exports. Includes information on specific pieces of equipment. Price $1.70 per year.

1137
Construction News

Northwood Publications, Ltd, Elm House, 10-16 Elm St, London, England WC1X 0BP. Order from Subscription Manager, 23-29 Emerald St, London, England WC1N 3QJ. Telephone (44) (01) 404-5531. Telex 21746.

Weekly newspaper. Reports on British and international construction industry. Includes information on public and private contracts, offshore oil and gas developments, and jobs. Price £26.00 per year. ISSN 0010-6860.

1138
Construction News Magazine

Northwood Publications Ltd, Elm House, 10-16 Elm St, London, England WC1X 0BP. Order from Subscription Manager, 23-29 Emerald St, London, England WC1N 3QJ. Telephone (44) (01) 404-5531.

Monthly magazine. Reports on international construction market and new technology. Notes offshore oil and gas developments. Free supplement once a month within the weekly issue of Construction News. ISSN 0306-3232.

1139
Construction Plant & Equipment

Morgan–Grampian Ltd, Morgan–Grampian House, Calderwood St, London, England SE18 6QH. Order from Morgan–Grampian Publishing Co, 2 Park Ave, New York, NY 10016. Telephone (44) (01) 855-7777. Telex 896238 MORGAN G. New York (212) 340-9700. Telex 425592 MGI UI.

Monthly magazine. Pertains to use of construction plants and equipment. Is geared to specifiers and buyers. Price $45.00 per year.

1140
Construction Price Statistics

Statistics Canada, User Services, Publications Division, Ottawa, Ont, K1A 0V7, Canada. Telephone (613) 992-3151.

Monthly report. Contains statistics on Canadian construction prices. Gives residential and nonresidential input price indexes. Price $36.00 per year. ISSN 0319-8243.

1141
Construction Reports—Housing Starts, May 1977

US Dept of Commerce, 14th St between Constitution Ave and E St NW, Washington, DC 20203. Order from Customer Services Section (DUSD), Bureau of the Census, Washinton, DC 20233. Telephone (301) 449-1600.

Report. Provides information on US housing starts. Price $14.00 per year.

1142
Construction Type Plywood

Statistics Canada, User Services, Publications Distribution, Ottawa, Ont, Canada K1A 0V7. Telephone (613) 992-3151.

Monthly report. Supplies data on production, domestic and export shipments, and stocks of construction type plywood. Price $18.00 per year. ISSN 0708-6229.

1143
Construction West

Southam Communications Ltd, 1450 Don Mills Rd, Don Mills, Ont, Canada M3B 2X7. Order from Southam Communications Ltd, 2000 W 12th Ave, Vancouver, BC, Canada V6J 2G2. Telephone (604) 731-1171. Telex 04-51158.

Monthly magazine. Contains information on construction activity in western Canada. Price available on request.

1144
Consultants and Consulting Organizations Directory, **5th edition**
Gale Research Co, Book Tower, Detroit, Michigan, 48226. Telephone (313) 961-2242.

Directory providing information on firms and individuals offering business, industrial, and governmental consultation services. Price $190.00. ISBN 0352-3.

1145
Consultant News
Kennedy & Kennedy, Inc, Templeton Rd, Fitzwilliam, NH 03447. Telephone (603) 585-2299.

Monthly newsletter. Discusses management and consultant issues. Notes trends in fees and services and personnel changes. Price $56.00 per year.

1146
Consulting Engineer
Technical Publishing Co, 1301 S Grove Ave, Barrington, IL 60010. Telephone (312) 381-1840.

Monthly magazine. Provides information on consulting engineer topics. Discusses commercial, public, industrial, and institutional project designs. Includes quarterly product directory. Price $25.00 per year.

1147
Consulting Engineers' Who's Who and Year Book 1980
Northwood Publications Ltd, Elm House, 10-16 Elm St, London WC1X 0BP, England. Telephone (44) (01) 278-2345. Telex 21746.

Annual book. Lists members of British Association of Consulting Engineers. Includes directory to firms, special services, and overseas offices. Price £10.00.

1147.01
Consumer Action Update
US Office of Consumer Affairs, Health, and Human Services Dept, 621 Reporters Bldg, Washington, DC 20201. Telephone (202) 755-8810.

Semimonthly newsletter. Reports on consumer protection issues, laws, applications, and government agency rulings. Price free of charge, limited distribution.

1148
Consumer Affairs Bulletin
International Cooperative Alliance, 11 Upper Grosvenor St, London, England W1X 9PA. Telephone (44) (01) 499-5991.

Monthly newsletter covers international consumer activities. Emphasizes energy, food, and health areas. English and French editions. Price £2.00 per year. ISSN 0010-7115.

1149
Consumer and Commercial Credit
Prentice-Hall, Inc, Englewood Cliffs, NY 07632. Telephone (201) 592-2000. Telex 13-5423.

Biweekly loose-leaf service. Covers consumer and commercial credit regulations, including Uniform Commerical Code, Uniform Consumer Credit Code, Truth-in-Lending law. Price $276.00 per year for 1 state; $360.00 for each additional state.

1150
Consumer Attitudes and Buying Plans
3rd Conference Board, Inc, 845 3rd Ave, New York, NY 10022. Telephone (212) 759-0900.

Monthly survey. Reports consumer confidence, employment, and buying plans, including durable goods and vacations. Price available on request.

1151
Consumer Credit and Truth-in-Lending Compliance Report
Warren, Gorham & Lamont, Inc, 210 S St, Boston, Ma 02111. Telephone (800) 225-2263.

Monthly report. Provides information on changes in consumer credit field. Includes coverage of Equal Credit Opportunity Act and Truth-in-Lending Act. Price $68.00 per year.

1152
Consumer Credit Guide
Commerce Clearing House, Inc, 4025 W Peterson Ave, Chicago, IL 60646. Telephone (312) 853-8500.

Five loose-leaf books plus fortnightly reports. Carries texts of consumer protection laws, including retail installment sales acts, truth-in-lending laws, credit card, and interest-usuary laws. Price $375.00 per year.

1153
Consumer Europe 1981/82
Euromonitor Publications Ltd, 18 Doughty St, London, England, WCIN 2 PN. Telephone (44) (01) 242-0042

Biennial handbook. Statistics cover Europe's major household markets. Includes data on consumer research, sales, market trends, and imports and exports in 12 product groups. Price $204.00 US.

1153.01
Consumer Income
US Dept of Commerce, Bureau of Census, Washington, DC 20233. Telephone (202) 449-1600.

Series of reports. Contains information on US consumer income. Covers families and individuals. Notes characteristics of the population below the poverty level. Price available on request.

1154
Consumer Information Catalog
US General Services Administration, 18th and F Sts NW, Room G142, Washington, DC 20405. Order from Consumer Information Catalog, Pueblo, CO 81009. Telephone (202) 566-1794.

Quarterly pamphlet. Lists more than 200 federal consumer publications. Subjects include automobiles, food and nutrition, health, gardening, housing, energy conservation, employment and money management. Price free of charge.

1156
Consumer Magazine & Farm Publication Rates & Data
Standard Rate & Data Service, Inc, 5201 Old Orchard Rd, Skokie, IL 60077. Telephone (312) 470-3100.

Monthly magazine. Provides profiles and advertising rates for consumer and farm magazines. Includes analysis of markets. Price $106.00 per year.

1158
Consumer Market Research Handbook, **1972 edition**
McGraw-Hill Book Co, Highstown-Princeton Rd, Hightstown, NJ 08520. Telephone (609) 448-1700. Telex 843449.

Book. Provides information on the practice of market research. Price $28.50. ISBN 0-07-094234-X.

1160
Consumer Newsweekly
Consumer News, Inc, 813 National Press Bldg, Washington, DC 20045. Telephone (202) 737-1190.

Weekly newsletter. Reports on consumer issues, including advertising, product safety, and consumer legislation. Includes product ratings. Price $15.00 per year.

1161
Consumer Price Index Cat No 6401.0
Australian Bureau of Statistics, PO Box 10, Belconnen, ACT 2616, Australia. Order from Australian Government Publishing Service, PO Box 84, Canberra, ACT 2600, Australia. Telephone (61) (062) 52 7911.

Quarterly report. Reviews movement of retail prices in six Australian state capitals and Canberra for selected goods and services. Price free of charge.

1162
Consumer Price Index
Statistics Canada, User Services, Publications Distribution, Ottawa, Ont, K1A 0V7, Canada. Telephone (613) 992-3151.

Monthly index. Summarizes Canadian retail price movements and contributory factors in 15 regional cities. Includes historical data and seasonally adjusted price movements. Price $30.00 per year. ISSN 0703-9352.

1163
Consumer Price Index (CPI) Detailed Report
US Dept of Labor, Bureau of Labor Statistics, Dept of Labor, 441 G St NW, Washington, DC 20212. Telephone (202) 523-1221.

Monthly report. Contains detailed Consumer Price Index data. Measures retail price changes, consumer purchasing power, and inflation or deflation. Price $15.00 per year.

1165
Consumer Prices & Price Indexes
Statistics Canada, User Services, Publications Distribution, Ottawa, Ont, K1A 0V7, Canada. Telephone (613) 992-3151.

Quarterly report. Supplies Canadian consumer prices and price index data. Includes historical, comparative, and regional information. Price $28.80 per year. ISSN 0380-691X.

1167
Consumer Product Safety Commission—Consumer Product Hazard Index, 1978
US National Injury Information Clearinghouse, US Consumer Product Safety Commission, 1750 K St NW, Washington, DC 20207. Telephone (301) 492-6424.

Annual index. Ranks products and related activities in terms of associated injuries. Includes sports and sporting goods, electric appliances, and lamps, paints, and cosmetics. Price free.

1168
Consumer Product Safety Guide
Commerce Clearing House, Inc, 4025 W Peterson Ave, Chicago, IL 60646. Telephone (312) 583-8500.

Three loose-leaf books plus weekly reports. Provides text of Consumer Product Safety Act, and rules, regulations, and court decisions implementing and interpreting act. Price $350.00 per year.

1171
Consumer Reports
Consumers Union of US, Inc, Blaisedell Rd, Orangeburg, NY 10962. Telephone (914) 359-8200.

Monthly magazine. Gives comparative shopping information, product testing results, advice on goods and services. Price $11.00 per year.

1171.01
Consumer Research Service
Data Resources, Inc, 29 Hartwell Ave, Lexington, MA 02173. Telephone (617) 861-0165.

Quarterly report. Provides projections of consumer market by age and income. Surveys consumer spending patterns by age and income for specific products. Price available on request.

1172
Consumers Digest
Consumers Digest Inc, 4401 W Devon Ave, Chicago, IL 60646. Telephone (312) 286-7606.

Bimonthly magazine. Offers test reports, ratings, and recommendations on variety of consumer goods. Extra issue in January. Price $10.00 per year.

1173
Consumers Digest Guide to Discount Buying
Consumer's Digest, Inc, 4401 W Devon Ave, Chicago, IL 60646. Telephone (312) 286-7606.

Annual book. Gives digest of test reports, ratings, and recommendations for variety of consumer goods. Price $2.95.

1174
Consumers Index to Product Evaluations and Information Sources
Pierian Press, 5000 Washtenaw, Ann Arbor, MI 48104. Telephone (313) 434-5530.

Quarterly and annual cumulative service. Provides index to evaluations of products in standard consumer magazines and specialty publications. Price $59.50 per year.

1175
Consumer Sourcebook, 3rd edition
Gale Research Co, Book Tower, Detroit, Michigan 48226. Telephone (313) 961-2242.

Book containing consumer information sources, including government organizations, centers, and institutes. Topics include health, social welfare, and consumer fraud. Price $78.00. ISBN 0381-7.

1177
Consumers' Research
Consumers' Research, Inc, Washington, NJ 07882. Telephone (201) 689-3300.

Monthly magazine. Provides consumers with information, including test results, on many products and advice about purchase of services. Price $15.00 per year.

1178
Consumers Union News Digest
Consumers Union of US, Inc, Blaisedell Rd, Orangeburg, NY 10962. Telephone (914) 359-8200.

Semimonthly newsletter. Abstracts consumer-oriented articles from other magazines and newspapers. Price $36.00 per year.

1178.01
Consumer Trends
International Consumer Credit Assn, 243 N Lindbergh Blvd, St. Louis, MO 63141. Telephone (314) 991-3030.

Semimonthly newsletter. Reports on developments in consumer credit and financial fields. Price $30.00 per year.

1179
Consumption of Containers and Other Packaging Supplies by the Manufacturing Industries
Statistics Canada, User Services, Publications Distribution, Ottawa, Ont, Canada K1A 0V7. Telephone (613) 992-3151.

Annual report. Provides detailed breakdown of Canadian manufacturing industries' consumption of containers and related supplies. Price $5.40. ISSN 0576-0186.

1179.01
Consumption on the Cotton System
M22P
US Dept of Commerce, Bureau of Census, Washington, DC 20233. Telephone (202) 449-1600.

Monthly report with annual summary. Provides data for cotton-growing states. Indicates consumption and stocks of cotton and manmade fiber staple. Price $3.90 per year.

1180
Consumption on the Woolen and Worsted Systems
US Dept of Commerce, Bureau of the Census, Washington, DC 20233. Telephone (202) 449-1600.

Monthly report and annual summary. Presents data on quantity of fibers consumed in woolen spinning and worsted combing mills by class of fiber. Price $3.60 per year.

1181
Container News
Communication Channels, Inc, 6285 Barfield Rd, Atlanta, GA 30328. Telephone (404) 256-9800.

Monthly magazine.Covers the movement of containerized cargo and other cargo via more than one mode of transportation. Price $19.00 per year.

1183
Contents of Recent Economic Journals
Her Majesty's Stationery Office, PO Box 569, London, England SE1 9NH. Telephone (44) (01) 928-1321.

Weekly magazine. Reproduces contents pages of journals in economics and related subjects received by British Department of Industry Library. Price £24.50 per year.

1184
Contents Pages in Management
Manchester Business School, Booth St W, Manchester, England M15 6PB. Telephone (44) (061) 273-8228. Telex 668354.

Fortnightly magazine. Consists of tables of contents from about 200 publications relating to management, accounting, economics, and social sciences. Price £48.00 per year.

1185
Contract
Gralla Publications, 1515 Broadway, New York, NY 10036. Telephone (212) 869-1300.

Report. Covers furnishing and interior architecture for commercial interiors. Is aimed at specifiers, buyers, and users of contract furnishings. Price available on request.

1186
Contract Appeals Decisions
Commerce Clearing House, Inc, 4025 W Peterson Ave, Chicago, IL 60646. Telephone (312) 583-8500.

Loose-leaf book plus biweekly reports. Carries decisions of Armed Services Board of Contract Appeals and other appeals boards rulings on contract problems. Price $375.00 per year.

1187
Contractor
Morgan–Grampian Ltd, Morgan–Grampian House, Calderwood St, London, England SE18 6QH. Order from Morgan–Grampian Publishing Co, Circulation Dept, Berkshire Common, Pittsfield, MA 01201. Telephone (413) 499-2550. Telex 425592 MGI UI.

Semimonthly magazine. Covers US air conditioning, heating, and plumbing industries. Price $36.00 per year.

1187.01
Control & Instrumentation
Morgan-Grampian Ltd, Morgan-Grampian House, Calderwood St, London, England SE18 6QH. Telephone (44) (01) 855-7777. Telex 896238. Order from Morgan-Grampian Publishing Co, 2 Park Ave, New York, NY 10016. Telephone (212) 340-9700. Telex 425592 MGI UI.

Monthly magazine. Reports on control and instrumentation development for industry. Price $100.00 per year.

1187.02
Control Data Computerized Data Base Service
Control Data Corp, 8100 34 Ave S, Minneapolis, MN 55440. Order from Literature and Distribution Control Data Corp, 308 N Dale St, St. Paul, MN 55103. Telephone (612) 292-2100. Telex 290-435.

Database service. Provides information on computer hardware and software. Price available on request.

1188
Control Equipment Master
Chilton Co, Chilton Way, Radnor, PA 19089. Telephone (215) 687-8200.

Annual book. Catalogs equipment for instrumentation and controls market. Price $55.00.

1189
Control of Banking
Prentice-Hall, Inc, Englewood Cliffs, NJ 07632. Telephone (201) 592-2000. Telex 13-5423.

Semimonthly loose-leaf service. Presents rules and interpretations relative to national banks and state-chartered banks that are members of Federal Reserve System or are insured by Federal Deposit Insurance Corporation. Price $273.00 per year.

1190
Control of Immigration Statistics
Her Majesty's Stationery Office, PO Box 569, London, England SE1 9NH. Telephone (44) (01) 928 1321.

Annual report. Carries statistics on Great Britain's immigration. Price £9.50 per year.

1191
Converted Flexible Packaging Products
US Dept of Commerce, Bureau of the Census, Washington, DC 20233. Telephone (202) 449-1600.

Quarterly report with annual summary. Presents information on value of shipments of converted flexible packaging products. Price $1.25 per year.

1191.01
CO-OP
North American Students of Cooperation, Box 7293, Ann Arbor, MI 48107. Telephone (313) 663-0889.

Bimonthly magazine. Reports on consumer cooperatives. Price $10.50 per year.

1191.02
Co-Op Consumers
ICA Consumer Committee, FDB, Roskildevej 65, 2620 Albertslund, Denmark.

Quarterly newsletter. Covers international consumer activities. Emphasizes energy, food, and health areas. English, French, German, Spanish, and Danish editions. Price £4.00 per year.

1192
Cooperative Accountant
National Society of Accountants for Cooperatives, 1015 Floyd Ave, Richmond, VA 23284. Telephone (804) 770-8823.

Quarterly report. Deals with accounting, tax, and related subjects concerned with cooperatives. Price $10.00 per year.

1193
Co-Operative Consumer
Consumer Press Ltd, PO Box 1050, Saskatoon, Sask, Canada S7K 3M9. Telephone (306) 244-3118.

Semimonthly newspaper. Reports on cooperatives, with emphasis on Canadian farm and consumer cooperatives. Includes discussion of consumer issues. Price $9.60 per year.

1195
Co-Operative News
Co-Operative Press Ltd, Progress House, 418 Chester Rd, Manchester, England M16 9HP. Telephone (44) (061) 872 2991. Telex 668867.

Weekly newspaper. Discusses news of British cooperative movement. Includes consumer and economic issues. Price £ 14.00 per year.

1196
Coopers & Lybrand Banker
Coopers & Lybrand, 1251 Ave of the Americas, New York, NY 10020. Order from Manager of Publications, PO Box 682, Times Sq Station, New York, NY 10108. Telephone (212) 489-1100.

Periodic newsletter. Covers major developments in accounting and reporting, marketing, and taxation. Price free of charge.

1196.01
Coopers & Lybrand Newsletter
Coopers & Lybrand, 1251 Ave of the Americas, New York, NY 10020. Order from Manager of Publications, PO Box 682, Times Sq Station, New York, NY 10108. Telephone (212) 489-1100.

Monthly newsletter. Covers international accounting, auditing, and tax developments. Includes 24-month index of aticles. Price free of charge.

1197
Coop Marketing & Management
Co-Operative Press Ltd, Progress House, 48 Chester Rd, Manchester, England M16 9HP. Telephone (44) (061) 872-2991. Telex 668867.

Monthly magazine discusses cooperative marketing and management techniques. Includes food and nonfood cooperatives. Highlights various products. Price £14.50 per year. ISSN 0307-8604.

1198
Co-op News
Standard Rate and Data Service, Inc, 5201 Old Orchard Rd, Skokie, IL 60077. Telephone (312) 470-3450.

Semimonthly newspaper. Reports news on cooperative advertising. Covers manufacturers, media, retailers, wholesalers, and government agencies. Price $48.00 per year.

1198.01
Co-op Source Directory
Standard Rate and Data Service, Inc, 5201 Old Orchard Rd, Skokie, IL 60077. Telephone (312) 470-3450.

Semiannual book. Provides detailed summaries of manufacturer co-op advertising programs for all media. Price $120.00 per year.

1199
Copper-Base Mill and Foundry Products
US Dept of Commerce, Bureau of the Census, Washington, DC 20233. Telephone (202) 449-1600.

Quarterly report and annual summary. Contains data on shipments of brass mill products, copper wire mill products, brass and bronze foundry products, and copperbase powder mill products. Tables. Price $1.25 per year.

1199.01
Copper Controlled Materials, ITA-9008
US Dept of Commerce, Bureau of Census, Washington, DC 20233. Telephone (202) 449-1600.

Quarterly report with annual summary. Provides data on shipments of copperbase mill products in the US. Price $1.25 per year.

1200
Copper Data
American Bureau of Metal Statistics, Inc, 420 Lexington Ave, New York, NY 10170. Telephone (212) 867-9450. Telex 14-7130.

Monthly report. Covers copper industry in US and abroad. Features statistics on production, imports and exports, and shipments of refined stocks. Price $200.00 per year.

1201
Copyright
World Intellectual Property Organization, 34 Chemin des Colombettes, 1211 Geneva 20, Switzerland. Telephone (41) (022) 99 91 11. Telex Geneve 2 23 76.

Monthly report. Covers activities of International (Berne) Union for Protection of Literary and Artistic Works. Contains texts of laws, court decisions, and copyright news items. Price 105 Swiss francs.

1201.01
Copyright Management
Inst for Invention & Innovation, Inc, 85 Irving St, Arlington, MA 02174. Telephone (617) 646-0093.

Monthly journal. Presents articles on the administration of literary/artistic property rights, plus brief reviews of selected organizations, publications, and coming events. Price $84.00 per year. ISSN 0161-4010.

1201.02
Copyright Protection in the Americas
Oceana Publications, Inc, 75 Main St, Dobbs Ferry, NY 10522. Telephone (914) 693-1320.

Two binders. Cover copyright laws and regulations in North and South America. Note treaties and conventions as of May 1978. Price $75.00 per binder. ISBN 0-379-20675-7.

1202
Copyright Revision Act of 1976
Commerce Clearing House, Inc, 4025 W Peterson Ave, Chicago, IL 60646. Telephone (312) 583-8500.

Book. Explains 1976 comprehensive revision of US Copyright Law. Includes selected committee reports. Price $12.50.

1202.01
Corporate Accounting Reporter
Executive Enterprises Publications Co Inc, 33 W 60th St, New York, NY 10023. Telephone (212) 489-2670.

Semimonthly newsletter. Provides information for corporate accounting managers on latest developments in corporate accounting field. Price $72.00 per year.

1203

Corporate Acquisitions and Mergers

Matthew Bender & Co, 235 E 45th St, New York, NY 10017. Telephone (212) 661-5050.

Three-volume set of books. Covers procedures involved in purchase, sale, or reorganization of corporation. Discusses state and federal laws, Justice Department policies and industry guidelines. Price $180.00.

1204

Corporate Communications Report

Corpcomst Services, Inc, 112 E 31 St, New York, NY 10016. Telephone (212) 889-2450.

Bimonthly newsletter. Highlights trends in corporate communications and investor relations. Price $65.00 per year.

1204.01

Corporate Controllers and Treasurers Report

Warren, Gorham & Lamont, Inc, 210 S St, Boston, MA 02111. Telephone (800) 225-2263.

Monthly report. Covers corporate financial topics. Includes information on taxation and legal developments. Price $56.00 per year.

1205

Corporate Counsel's Annual

Matthew Bender & Co, 235 E 45th St, New York, NY 10017. Telephone (212) 661-5050.

Two volumes. Reviews corporate law practices. Includes bibliography of law review articles, comments, and notes. Price $120.00.

1205.01

Corporate Design Systems

Advertising Trade Publications, Inc, 10 E 39th St, New York, NY 10016. Order from Art Direction Book Co, 10 E 39th St, New York, NY 10016. Telephone (212) 889-6500.

Annual book. Presents corporate design programs of 9 international conglomerates. Price $30.00.

1206

Corporate Examiner

Interfaith Center on Corporate Responsibility, Corporate Information Center, 475 Riverside Dr, Rm. 566, New York, NY 10115. Telephone (212) 870-2293.

Monthly newsletter. Examines policies of major US corporations in developing nations, energy, military production, OSHA, community reinvestment, agribusiness, and other areas. Includes news of church and other institutional investors. Price $25.00 per year. ISSN 0361-2309.

1208

Corporate Financing Week

Institutional Investor, Inc, 488 Madison Ave, New York, NY 10022. Telephone (212) 832-8888.

Weekly newsletter. Covers new developments and trends in corporate finance. Price $195.00 per year.

1208.01

Corporate Foundation Profiles

Foundation Center, 888 7th Ave, New York, NY 10106. Telephone (212) 975-1120.

Book. Contains comprehensive descriptions of 215 corporate foundations. Provides brief information on over 300 smaller corporate foundations. Price $50.00.

1209

Corporate Insurance in Canada

Stone and Cox Ltd, 100 Simcoe St, 2nd Floor, Toronto, Ont, M5H 3G2, Canada. Telephone (416) 593-1310.

Annual magazine. Reports on Canadian and general corporate insurance subjects. Lists corporate insurance and employee benefits and business insurance companies. Price $2.00 per year.

1210

Corporate Planning Service

International Data Corporation, 214 3rd Ave, Waltham, MA 02254. Telephone (617) 890-3700. Telex 92-3401.

Continuous information service. Provides to suppliers of EDP (Electronic Data Processing) hardware and services analyses of vendor strategies, user profiles, examination of new technological trends, and projections for future growth of specific markets. Price available on request.

1211

Corporate Practice Series

Bureau of National Affairs, Inc, 1231 25th St, NW, Washington, DC 20037. Telephone (202) 452-4200.

Monthly portfolio series, with weekly updates. Covers principal legal areas of corporate operations. Includes weekly Washington Memorandum newsletter, index, and portfolio file. Price $366.00 per year.

1212

Corporate Report, Kansas City

Dorn Communications, Inc, 7101 York Ave S, Minneapolis, MN 55435. Order from Dorn Communications, Inc, 4149 Pennsylvania, Kansas City, MO 64111. Telephone (612) 835-6855.

Monthly magazine. Covers business and finance news in the Kansas City area. Price $18.00 per year.

1213

Corporate Report Fact Book

Dorn Communications, Inc, 7101 York Ave S, Minneapolis, MN 55435. Telephone (612) 835-6855.

Annual books with midyear supplements. Lists publicity owned corporations in the 9th and 10th Federal Reserve Districts. Include data on balance sheets, operations, and officers. Price $54.00 per volume.

1214

Corporate Security

Man & Manager, Inc, 799 Broadway, New York, NY 1003. Telephone (212) 677-0640.

Semimonthly report. Presents case histories to help administrators secure plants, offices, personnel, and facilities. Annual index. Price $66.00 per year.

1215

Corporate Treasurer's and Controller's Encyclopedia **1974**

Prentice-Hall, Inc, Englewood Cliffs, NJ 07632. Telephone (201) 592-2000. Telex 13-5423.

Book. Covers theory and practice of corporate financial management. Price $54.50. ISBN 0-13-176156-0.

1216

Corporation Financial Statistics

Statistics Canada, User Services, Publications Distribution, Ottawa, Ont, K1A 0V7, Canada. Telephone (613) 992-3151.

Annual review. Contains, aggregate balance sheet, and income and expense, profit, and retained earnings information for Canadian corporations, classified by industry. Includes data analysis. Price $12.00. ISSN 0575-8262.

1217
Corporation Forms
Prentice-Hall, Inc, Englewood Cliffs, NJ 07632. Telephone (201) 592-2000. Telex 13-5423.

Monthly loose-leaf service. Provides forms for corporate transactions with explanations. Offers continuous new forms and ideas. Price $204.00 per year.

1219
Corporation Law & Tax Report
Warren, Gorham, & Lamont, Inc, 210 South St, Boston, MA 02111. Telephone (617) 423-2020.

Semimonthly report. Considers corporate law and tax topics. Evaluates court decisions, legislative changes, and Internal Revenue Service rulings. Price $72.00 per year.

1220
Corporation Law Guide
Commerce Clearing House, Inc, 4025 W Peterson Ave, Chicago, IL 60646. Telephone (312) 583-8500.

Two loose-leaf books plus fortnightly reports. Deals with state corporate law and practice and federal and state controls affecting business management. Price $175.00 per year.

1221
Corporation Service
Prentice-Hall, Inc, Englewood Cliffs, NJ 07632. Telephone (201) 592-2000. Telex 13-5423.

Biweekly loose-leaf service. Covers corporate topics such as financing, dividends, closed corporations, and small businesses. Price $303.00 per year for one state, $39.00 per year for each additional state.

1221.01
Corporation Management Edition
Prentice-Hall, Inc, Englewood Cliffs, NJ 07632. Telephone (201) 592-2000. Telex 13-5423.

Biweekly loose-leaf service. Explains corporate law and statutes. Covers all states. Forms and text of laws. Price $228.00 per year.

1222
Corporation Taxation Statistics
Statistics Canada, User Services, Publications Distribution, Ottawa, Ont, Canada K1A 0V7. Telephone (613) 992-3151.

Annual report. Supplies statistical data on Canadian corporate taxation by industry and province. Includes reconciliation of corporate profit with taxable income and with taxes. Price $9.60. ISSN 0576-0119.

1223
Corpus Administrative Index
Corpus Information Services, Ltd, 1450 Don Mills Rd, Don Mills, Ont, Canada M3B 2X7. Telephone (416) 455-7101. Telex 06-966612.

Bimonthly directory. Prints names, titles, addresses, telephone, and telex numbers for more than 12,000 of Canada's top government executives. Price $177.00 (Canadian) per year.

1224
Corpus Almanac of Canada
Corpus Information Services, Ltd, 1450 Don Mills Rd, Don Mills, Ont, Canada M3B 2X7. Telephone (416) 445-7101. Telex 06-966612

Annual two-volume set offers reference material on Canada. Has sections on government, education, taxation, law, and real estate. Price $67.00 (Canadian) per year. ISBN 0-919217-03-6.

1224.01
Corpus Chemical Report
Corpus Information Services, Ltd, 1450 Don Mills Rd, Don Mills, Ont, Canada M3B 2X7. Telephone (416) 445-7101. Telex 06-966612.

Weekly newsletter analyzes developments in Canadian chemical process industries. Price $367.00 (Canadian) per year. ISSN 0315-257X.

1225
Cost Accounting Standards Guide
Commerce Clearing House, Inc, 4025 W Peterson Ave, Chicago, IL 60646. Telephone (312) 583-8500.

One loose-leaf book plus monthly reports. Covers cost accounting standards required of defense contractors for federal government. Price $175.00 per year.

1226
Cost and Management
Society of Management Accountants of Canada, 154 Main St E, Hamilton, Ont, Canada L8N 3C3. Telephone (416) 525-4100.

Bimonthly journal. Publishes articles on accounting and management sciences. Analyzes subjects leading to development of the accountant in management. Price $7.50 per year. ISSN 0010-9592.

1227
Cost Forecasting Service
Data Resources, Inc, 29 Hartwell Ave, Lexington, MA 02173. Telephone (617) 861-0165.

Quarterly report. Forecasts prices of components and machinery and wage rates for construction projects. Offers specific cost indexes for chemical plant, refinery, and oil rig construction. Price available on request.

1228
Cost-Of-Doing-Business Survey
Associated Equipment Distribution, 615 W 22nd St, Oak Brook, IL 60521. Telephone (312) 654-0650.

Annual survey. Reports on heavy, general, and light equipment distributors. Offers balance and work sheets. Price $50.00 per copy.

1229
Cotton Gin and Oil Mill Press
Cotton Gin and Oil Mill Press, PO Box 18092, Dallas, TX 75218. Telephone (214) 288-7511.

Fortnightly magazine. Reports on cotton ginning, cotton seed crushing, and oilseed processing industries. Price $5.00 per year.

1230
Cotton Man-made Fiber Staple, and Linters (Consumption and Stocks, and Spindle Activity)
US Dept of Commerce, Bureau of the Census, Washington, DC 20233. Telephone (202) 449-1600.

Monthly report with annual summary. Supplies data for cotton growing states on consumption and stocks of cotton and man-made fiber staples. Includes data on cotton system spindles in place and spindle hours and on exports and imports of cotton, man-made fiber staples, and linters. Price $3.90 per year.

1231
Cotton Market News Reports
US Department of Agriculture, 306 Annex Bldg, Agricultural Marketing Service, Washington, DC 20250. Telephone (202) 447-7857.

Intermittent reports. Covers cotton market information, including prices, varieties planted, and cottonseed. Price free of charge.

1232
Cotton: Monthly Review of the World Situation
International Cotton Advisory Committee, 1225 19th St, NW, Suite 320, Washington, DC 20036. Telephone (202) 463-6660.

Monthly report with quarterly bulletins. Covers issues and developments and gives statistics for cotton products worldwide. Price available on request.

1233
Counseling and Values
American Personnel and Guidance Assn, 2 Skyline Place, Suite 400, 5203 Leesburg Pike, Falls Church, VA 22041. Telephone (703) 820-4700.

Quarterly magazine. Discusses counseling and guidance issues. Includes information on student personnel administration and psychological services in educational institutions. Price $10.00 per year.

1234
Counselor
Advertising Specialty Inst, 1120 Wheeler Way, Langhorne, PA 19047. Telephone (215) 752-4200.

Monthly magazine. Covers specialty advertising. Notes use of media and marketing, plus other trends. Price $25.00 per year.

1235
Counselor
National Employment Assn, 1835 K St NW, Suite 910, Washington, DC 20006. Telephone (202) 331-8040.

Bimonthly newsletter. Reports on issues affecting private employment agencies and on National Employment Association activities. Price $3.00 per year.

1236
Counselor Education and Supervision
American Personnel and Guidance Assn, 2 Skyline Place, Suite 400, 5203 Leesburg Pike, Falls Church, VA 22k041. Telephone (703) 820-4700.

Quarterly magazine. Reports on guidance counselor preservice and in-service preparation and supervision. Covers theory, research, and practice. Price $10.00 per year.

1237
County Business Patterns, 1974
US Dept of Commerce, Bureau of the Census, Washington, DC 20233. Telephone (202) 449-1600.

Series of reports for each state, District of Columbia, and US. Presents data for 1974 on employment, size of firms, and payrolls by type of business and by state and county. Prices available on request.

1238
County Economic Indicators
Oregon Economic Development Dept. 155 Cottage St NW, Salem, OR 97310. Telephone (503) 373-1200.

Annual publication. Provides statistics on economic trends in Oregon counties. Covers personal income, population, employment, and retail sales. Price $2.50.

1239
Courier—European Communities—Africa, the Caribbean and the Pacific
Commission of the European Communities, Office for Official Publications of the European Communities, CP 1003, Luxembourg 1, Luxembourg. Telephone 352 490081. Telex PUBLOF 1325.

Bimonthly magazine. Contains articles on European Community, Africa, the Caribbean, and the Pacific. Price free of charge.

1239.01
Course Catalog—Management Development Guide
American Management Associations, 135 W 50th St, New York, NY 10020. Telephone (212) 586-8100.

Catalog. Lists management development courses, home-study programs, on-site training program, and special American Management. Associations services. Groups career opportunities by subject and region. Indexed. Price $4.25.

1240
Cover Note
Specialist Newsletters Pty Ltd, PO Box 430, Milsons Point, Sydney, NSW 2061, Australia. Telephone (61) (02) 922 3255.

Weekly newsletter. Reports on Australian insurance industry, including bank encroachment into field. Price $120.00 per year.

1241
CQ Almanac, 1980
Congressional Quarterly, Inc, 1414 22nd St, NW, Washington, DC 20037 Telephone (202) 887-8500.

Annual book. Covers events in Congress. Provides summaries of legislation and charts of roll-call votes. Includes lobby registrations. Price $96.00.

1241.01
Creative Selling
Januz Marketing Communications, Inc, PO Box 1000, Lake Forest, IL 60045. Telephone (312) 295-6550.

Semimonthly newsletter. Provides tested sales techniques for professional salespersons and other self-help ideas. Price $48.00 per year, $96.00 per two years, $120.00 per three years. ISSN 0163-1748.

1241.02
Creativity/9
Advertising Trade Publications, Inc, 10 E 39th St, New York, NY 10016. Order from Art Direction Book Co, 10 E 39th St, New York, NY 10016. Telephone (212) 889-6500.

Annual book. Provides review of selected advertising art, photography, and design. Includes illustrations. Price $26.50.

1242
Credit
National Consumer Finance Assn, 1000 16th St NW, Washington, DC 20036. Telephone (202) 638-1340.

Bimonthly magazine for consumer finance management personnel. Reports on consumer finance issues and trends. Price available on request.

1243
Creditalk
National Retail Merchants Assn, 100 W 31st St, New York, NY 10001. Telephone (212) 244-6780.

Monthly newsletter. Provides synopsis of credit developments, including state and federal legislation, credit technology, and ideas for retail credit executives. Price $9.00 per year.

1244
Credit and Capital Markets
Bankers Trust Co, PO Box 318, Church St Station, New York, NY 10015. Telephone (212) 692-7122.

Annual pamphlet. Analyzes credit and capital markets in US. Forecasts performance for coming year. Contains statistical tables on fund sources and use. Price free of charge.

1245

Credit and Financial Management

National Assn of Credit Management, 475 Park Ave S, New York, NY 10016. Telephone (212) 725-1700.

Monthly magazine. Reports on credit and financial management topics such as company asset management, including accounts receivable investment, inventory control, EDP, cash flow projections, and debt-equity financing. Price $15.00 per year.

1246

Credit Executive

New York Credit & Financial Management Assn, 71 W 23rd St, New York, NY 10010. Telephone (212) 741-4710.

Bimonthly newsletter. Contains current news on credit and financial management. Is geared to executives in field. Price free to members.

1247

Credit Management

Inst of Credit Management, 12 Queen Sq, Brighton, England BN1 3FD. Telephone Brighton (0273) 26644.

Quarterly magazine. Contains articles on British credit. Reviews pertinent legislation and court cases. Notes news of Institute of Credit Management. Price £2.00 per issue; free to members of the Institute.

1248

Credit Review

Australian Inst of Credit Management, c/o Ley Pulford & Co, 37 Swanston St, Melbourne, Vic 3000, Australia. Telephone (61) (03) 63-77-48.

Bimonthly magazine. Deals with credit management for Australian credit managers. Price $15.00 (Australian) per year.

1248.01

Credit Union Commentary

Andrew R Mandala, PO Box 30240, Washington, DC 20014. Telephone (301) 654-5580.

Weekly newsletter. Discusses developments affecting credit unions. Price $110.00 per year.

1249

Credit Union Executive

Credit Union National Assn, Inc, PO Box 431B, Madison, WI 53701. Telephone (608) 231-4000.

Quarterly magazine. Discusses credit union issues. Notes new regulations and technology. Price $12.00 per year.

1250

Credit Union Magazine

Credit Union National Assn, Inc, PO Box 431B, Madison, WI 53701. Telephone (608) 231-4000.

Monthly magazine. Provides reports relevant to credit unions management and finance. Price $11.00 per year.

1251

Credit Union Manager Newsletter

Credit Union National Assn, Inc, PO Box 431B, Madison, WI 53701. Telephone (608) 231-4000.

Biweekly newsletter. Contains news and advice for credit union managers. Price $52.00 per year.

1252

Credit Union Statistics

National Credit Union Administration, 1776 G St, NW, Washington, DC 20456. Telephone (202) 357-1050.

Monthly statistical report. Supplies data on credit union assets, loans, savings, and loan-to-share ratios. Price free of charge.

1253

Credit World

International Consumer Credit Assn, 243 N Lindbergh Blvd, St Louis, MO 63141.

Bimonthly magazine. Presents articles on consumer credit. Reviews new laws and reports on activities of International Consumer Credit Association. Price $15.00 per year.

1254

Credo

Australian Inst of Credit Management, Victorian Division, c/o Ley Pulford & Co, 37 Swanston St, Melbourne, Vic 3000, Australia. Telephone (61) (03) 63-77-48.

Bimonthly magazine. Covers credit management topics. Price $10.00 (Australian) per year.

1255

Criminal Statistics, England and Wales

Her Majesty's Stationery Office, PO Box 569, London, England SE1 9NH. Telephone (44) (01) 928-1321.

Annual report. Furnishes statistical information on crime in Great Britain and Wales. Price £5.50.

1256

Croner's Reference Book for Exporters

Croner Publications Ltd, 211-03 Jamaica Ave, Queens Village, NY 11428. Order from Croner Publications Ltd, Croner House, 173 Kingston Rd, New Malden, Surrey, England KT3 3SS. Telephone (212) 942-8966.

Loose-leaf book with monthly supplements. Provides information on British export regulations and import regulations of 200 countries with which United Kingdom trades. Price £26.90.

1257

Croner's Reference Book for World Traders

Croner Publications, Inc, 211-03 Jamaica Ave, Queens Village, NY 11428. Telephone (212) 464-0866.

Loose-leaf books with monthly updates. Contains sources of information on trade and marketing in countries throughout the world. Price $85.00 per year.

1258

Croner's Road Transport Operation

Croner Publications Ltd, 211-03 Jamaica Ave, Queens Village, NY 11428. Order from Croner Publications Ltd, Croner House, 173 Kingston Rd, New Malden, Surrey, KT3 3SS, England, Telephone (212) 942-8966.

Loose-leaf book with monthly updates. Contains information on laws governing freight operations in Great Britain and Europe. Includes directory of freight services. Price £23.50 per year.

1260

Crops Cat No 7302.0

Australian Bureau of Statistics, PO Box 10, Belconnen, ACT 2616, Australia. Order from Australian Government Publishing Service, PO Box 84, Canberra, ACT 2600, Australia. Telephone (062) 52 7911.

Annual report. Statistics show Australian rural land use for crops, vegetables, and grasses. Notes value of exports and imports. Price free of charge.

1261

Cross-Reference

American Hospital Assn, 840 N Lake Shore Dr, Chicago, IL 60611. Telephone (312) 280-6000.

Bimonthly magazine. Carries articles, reviews, and reports on patient and staff education in hospitals. Price $10.00 per year. ISSN 0190-0447.

1262
Crude Petroleum and Natural Gas Production
Statistics Canada, User Services, Publications Distribution, Ottawa, Ont, Canada K1A 0V7. Telephone (613) 992-3151.

Monthly report. Provides information on Canadian production and disposition of crude petroleum and natural gas, by provinces. Monthly and cumulative tables. Price $30.00 per year. ISSN 0702-6846.

1263
Crude Petroleum and Natural Gas
US Dept of Commerce, Bureau of the Census, Washington, DC 20233. Order information from Chief, Manufacturing and Mineral Industries Division, Bureau of the Census, Washington, DC 20233. Telephone (202) 449-1600.

Information service. Provides data on value of shipments of crude petroleum and natural gas for groups of companies ranked by size of operation. Indicates whether or not producing company drills. Prices available on request.

1264
Cruises & Sea Voyages
Maclean–Hunter Ltd, 30 Old Burlington St, London, England W1X 2AE. Telephone (44) (01) 434-2233.

Annual directory. Provides guide to various types of vacations at sea. Lists sailing individually. Maps and charts. Price available on request.

1265
Cryogenics
IPC Business Press Ltd, 205 E 42nd St, New York, NY 10017. Telephone (212) 889-0700. Telex 421710.

Monthly magazine presents review articles and original research on cryogenics. Price $286.00 per year. ISSN 0011-2275.

1265.01
CSO Macro-Economic Databank
Her Majesty's Stationery Office, PO Box 569, London, England SE1 9NH. Telephone (44) (01) 928-1321

Data service. Contains economic statistics, including industrial production, national income and expenditure, balance of payments, and wages and earnings. Price available on request.

1265.02
C-Store Business
Progressive Grocer Pub Co, 708 3rd Ave, New York, NY 10017. Telephone (212) 490-1000.

Bimonthly publication. Covers news and trends in the convenience store industry. Price $18.00 per year. ISSN 0193-919x.

1266
Cumbria Weekly Digest
Border Press Agency Ltd, 12 Lonsdale St, Carlisle, England CA1 1DD. Telephone 0228-24321.

Weekly newspaper. Covers business news in Northwest England. Includes information on property sales. Price £25.66 per year.

1267
Cumulative Book Index
H W Wilson, Co, 950 University Ave, Bronx, NY 10452. Telephone (212) 588-8400.

Index of all English-language books published in the world. Updated monthly (except August) with quarterly and annual cumulative editions. Price available on request.

1268
Cumulative Changes
Prentice-Hall, Inc, Englewood Cliffs, NJ 07632. Telephone (201) 592-2000. Telex 13-5423.

Quarterly loose-leaf service. Gives exact wording of every amended section of 1954 tax code. Charts. Price $207.00 per year.

1268.01
Currency
Chart Analysis Ltd, 37–39 St Andrew's Hill, London, England EC4V 5DD. Telephone (44) (01) 236-5211.

Weekly chart service. Provides information on six currency exchange rates. Price £500.00 per year.

1268.02
Currency Forecasting Service
Inst for International Research Ltd, 70 Warren St, London, England W1P 5PA. Telephone (44) (01) 388-2663. Telex 263504.

Weekly report. Issues forecasts on currency trends based on analyses of international political and economic factors. Price $495.00 per year.

1268.03
Currency Risk and the Corporation
Euromoney Publications Ltd, Nestor House, Playhouse Yard, London, England, EC4V 5EX. Telephone (44) (01) 236-7111. Telex 8812246 Eurmon G.

Book. Covers policies, objectives, strategies, and techniques in defining, measuring, and managing foreign exchange exposures. Includes discussion of taxation, disclosure, profitability analysis, and evaluation. Price $90.00. ISBN 0-90312-14X.

1269
Current African Directories
CBD Research, Ltd, 154 High St, Beckenham, Kent, England BR3 1EA. Telephone (44) (01) 650-7745.

Book. Offers guide to directories concerned with Africa and sources of information on business enterprises in Africa. Price $38.00. ISBN 900246-11-1.

1270
Current British Directories, 9th edition, 1979
CBD Research, Ltd, 154 High St, Beckenham, Kent, England BR3 1EA. Telephone (01) 650-7745.

Book published every three years. Supplies guide to directories of all kinds published in Great Britain, Ireland, British Commonwealth, and South Africa. Price $105.00. ISBN 900246-31-6.

1271
Current Business Picture
Bankers Trust Co, PO Box 318, Church St Station, New York, NY 10015. Telephone (212) 692-7122.

Biannual pamphlet. Offers analysis of current economic and business trends. Forecasts business climate for upcoming months. Price free of charge.

1272
Current Compensation References
American Management Assns, 135 W 50th St, New York, NY 10020. Telephone (212) 586-8100.

Monthly newsletter. Contains brief summaries of current articles on compensation appearing in industry, trade, and government publications. Price $25.00.

1273
Current Contents: Social and Behavioral Sciences
Inst for Scientific Information, 3501 Market St, University City Science Center, Philadelphia, Pa 19104. Telephone (215) 386-0100.

Weekly index of articles published in social and behavioral science journals. Includes tables of contents. Price $190.00 per year.

1274

Current Cotton Statistics

US Dept of Commerce, Bureau of Census, Washington, DC 20233. Telephone (202) 449-1600.

Series of reports. Provides US cotton statistics. Includes information on ginnings by counties and states. Price available on request.

1275

Current European Directories

CBD Research, Ltd, 154 High St, Beckenham, Kent, England BR3 1EA. Telephone (44) (01) 650-7745.

Book. Provides guide to international, national, city, and specialized directories and reference works for all countries of continental Europe. Price available on request. ISBN 900246-02-2.

1276

Current Government Reports

US Dept of Commerce, Bureau of the Census, Washington, DC 20233. Order from Subscriber Services Section (Publications) Bureau of the Census, Washington, DC 20233. Telephone (202) 449-1600.

Series of reports. Contain information on state and local government employment, tax revenues, and finances of employee retirement systems. Price $20.50 per year.

1277

Current Index to Statistics—
Applications, Methods, Theory

American Statistical Assn, 806 15th St NW, Suite 640, Washington, DC 20005. Telephone (202) 393-3253.

Annual index. Directs user to more than 6000 articles from statistical journals and related publications. Price $22.00 per year.

1277.01

Current Law Index

Information Access Corp, 404 6th Ave, Menlo Park, CA 94025. Telephone (800) 227-8431.

Monthly and quarterly book, with annual cumulations. Provides subject access, listing of article and book review authors, tables of cases and statutes, and titles of all books on legal subjects and other materials reviewed. Price $300.00 per year American Association of Law Libraries members, $340.00 per year non-members.

1278

Current Literature on Aging

National Council on the Aging, Inc, 1828 L St NW, Suite 504, Washington, DC 20036. Telephone (202) 223-6250.

Quarterly publications. Annotates recent books and articles on aging and related subjects, including nursing homes, retirement and social services. Price $10.00 per year, non members.

1279

Current Periodical Publications in
Baker Library

Harvard University, Graduate School of Business Adm, Baker Library, Soldiers Field, Boston, MA 02163. Telephone (617) 495-6405.

Annual Book. Includes 6500 active serial titles: magazines, journals, bulletins, statistical annuals, yearbooks, proceedings of conferences, directories, government annual reports, and loose-leaf services. Divided into three parts by title, subject, and geographic region. Library of Congress numbers. Price $26.00.

1280

Current Population Reports

US Dept of Commerce, Bureau of the Census, Washington, DC 20233. Telephone (202) 449-1600.

Annual and biennial reports. Covers population characteristics, estimates and projections, farm population, and consumer income per household. Price $110.00 per year.

1281

Current Population Survey

US Dept of Commerce, Bureau of the Census, Washington, DC 20233. Order information from Chief, Population Division, Bureau of the Census, Washington, DC 20233. Telephone (202) 449-1600.

Information service. Covers labor force, population characteristics, and consumer income. Topics include mobility, marital and family status, black and Spanish-origin population. Price available on request.

1282

Current Retail Trade

US Dept of Commerce, Bureau of the Census, Washington, DC 20233. Telephone (202) 449-1600.

Weekly, advance monthly, monthly, and annual reports. Presents data on retail, including department store, sales. Indicates sales by business group and by geographic area. Price $25.00 per year.

1283

Current Surveys—MND11
Manufacturers' Shipments, Inventories,
and Orders

US Dept of Commerce, Bureau of the Census, Washington, DC 20233. Order information from Chief, Manufacturing and Mineral Industries Division, Bureau of the Census, Washington, DC 20233. Telephone (202) 449-1600.

Information service. Supplies statistics on manufacturers' shipments, inventories, and orders for industry groups. Price $80.00 per reel.

1284

Current Wage Developments

US Dept of Labor, Bureau of Labor Statistics, 441 G St NW, Washington, DC 20212. Telephone (202) 523-1221.

Monthly report. Indicates wage and benefit changes resulting from collective bargaining settlements and unilateral management decisions. Includes special reports on wage trends and tables. Price $12.00 per year.

1284.01

Current Wholesale Trade

US Dept of Commerce, Bureau of Census, Washington, DC 20233. Telephone (202) 449-1600.

Series of reports. Covers wholesale trade sales and inventories in US. Includes fuel oil statistics. Price available on request.

1285

Custom House Guide

North American Publishing Co, 401 N Broad St, Philadelphia, PA 19108. Telephone (215) 574-9600.

Annual book. Provides information on US tariff schedules, duty rates, shipping, commerce, customs regulations, and Internal Revenue Code. Price $119.00 per copy.

1286

Custom Market Extract Reports

Predicasts, Inc, 200 University Circle Research Cntr, 11001 Cedar Ave, Cleveland, OH 44106. Telephone (216) 795-3000.

Computerized sets of abstracts. Provides digests of articles covering specific industrial or business topic requested by client. Price $325.00.

1287

Customs Bulletin

US Customs Service, Washington, DC 20229. Order from Superintendent of Documents, Washington, DC 20402. Telephone (202) 783-3238.

Weekly newsletter. Contains current amendments to Customs Regulations and decisions of US Court of International Trade and US Court of Customs and Patent Appeals. Price $85.00 per year.

1288

Customs Regulations of the United States

US Customs Service, Washington, DC 20229. Order from Superintendent of Documents, Washington, DC 20402. Telephone (202) 783-3238.

Loose-leaf book. Discusses regulations for carrying out customs, navigation, and other laws administered by US Customs Service. Price $37.00.

1289

Customs Tariff Partial Service

Supply and Services Canada, Canadian Govt Publishing Centre, Hull, Que, Canada K1A 0S9. Telephone (819) 994-3475, 2085.

Annual service. Consolidates Canadian Customs Tariff Act. Includes supplements. Price available on request.

1290

Cycli-Graphs

United Business Service Co, 210 Newbury St, Boston, MA 02116. Telephone (617) 267-8855.

Quarterly set of charts. Provides monthly price ranges, relative market performance, volumes, earnings, and dividends for 1105 stocks. Includes industry group and selected business charts. Price $54.00 per year.

1291

Daily Bond Buyer

Bond Buyer, One State St Plz, New York, NY 10004. Telephone (212) 943-8200. Telex 12-9233.

Daily newspaper (except Saturday and Sunday). Reports on municipal bond news. Tables and charts. Price $825.00 per year.

1292

Daily Checklist of Canadian Government Publications

Supply and Services Canada, Publishing Centre, Printing and Publishing, Ottawa, Ont, Canada K1A 0S9. Telephone (613) 238-1601.

Daily report. Provides checklist of Canadian government publications. Bilingual. Price $35.00 per year.

1293

Daily Commercial News

C A Page Publishing Co, 3181 Fernwood Ave, Lynwood, CA 90262. Telephone (213) 744-2480.

Daily newspaper. Covers shipping industry, with emphasis on West Coast ports. Includes inbound and outbound tables, calendar of arrivals and sailings. Price $42.00 per year.

1294

Daily Commercial News (and Construction Record)

Southam Communications Ltd, 1450 Don Mills Rd, Don Mills, Ont, Canada, M3B 2X7. Order from Southam Communication Ltd, 34 St Patrick St, Toronto, Ont, Canada M5T 1V2. Telephone (416) 598-2222. Telex 06 22740.

Daily report. Focuses on construction and industrial growth in eastern Canada. Price available on request.

1295

(Daily Commercial News) Progress Report

Southam Communications Ltd, 1450 Don Mills Rd, Don Mills, Ont, Canada M3B 2X7. Order from Southam Communication Ltd, 34 St Patrick St, Toronto, Ont, Canada M5T 1V2. Telephone (416) 598-2222. Telex 06 22740.

Monthly newspaper. Views building and engineering markets in eastern Canada. Price available on request.

1297

Daily Graphs. American Stock Exchange/OTC

William O'Neil & Co, Inc, PO Box 24933, Los Angeles, CA 90024. Telephone (213) 820-2583.

Weekly information service. Provides daily charting of 874 common stocks on American Stock Exchange and 150 selected over-the-counter stocks. Lists 67 facts per stock, including daily price and volume activity. Price $290.00 per year.

1298

Daily Graphs—NY Stock Exchange/OTC

William O'Neil & Co, Inc, PO Box 24933, Los Angeles, CA 90024. Telephone (213) 820-2583.

Weekly information service. Charts provide 67 facts, including daily price and volume activity, for nearly all New York Stock Exchange common stocks plus 50 selected over-the-counter stocks. Price $325.00 per year.

1300

Daily Graphs Stock Option Guide

William O'Neil & Co, Inc, PO Box 24933, Los Angeles, CA 90024. Telephone (213) 820-2583.

Weekly information service. Presents statistical data on all listed call and put options, plus daily chart on each underlying stock. Price $120.00 per year.

1301

Daily Labor Report

Bureau of National Affairs, Inc, 1231 25th St NW, Washington, DC 20037. Telephone (202) 452-4200.

Daily newsletter. Reports on major labor activity in US, including legislation, court and agency rulings, union events, an arbitration awards. Price $2189.00 per year.

1302

Daily Legislative Report

Commerce Clearing House, Inc, 4025 W Peterson Ave, Chicago, IL 60646. Telephone (312) 583-8500.

Daily loose-leaf report. Provides coverage of Illinois legislature when in session. Price $400.00 per year. ISSN 9998.

1303

Daily Oil Bulletin

Southam Communications Ltd, 1450 Don Mills Rd, Don Mills, Ont, Canada M3B 2X7. Order from Southam Communication Ltd, Suite 200-1201 5th St, SW, Calgary, AB, Canada.

Daily report. Covers Canadian oil and gas field. Includes data on drilling, field operations, governmental transactions, production, and pipeline and plant projects. Price available on request.

1305

Daily Report for Executives

Bureau of National Affairs, Inc, 1231 25th St NW, Washington, DC 20037. Telephone (202) 452-4200.

Daily newsletter on Washington developments affecting US business and industries. Includes reports on legislation, taxation, and national economy. Price $2983.00 per year.

1306
Daily Stock Price Records
Standard & Poor's Corp, 25 Broadway, New York, NY 10004. Telephone (212) 248-2525.

Quarterly books. Give data on over 6400 issues on the New York, American and Over-the-Counter Exchanges. Price $189.00, $178.50, and $206.00 per year respectively.

1307
Daily Tax Report
Bureau of National Affairs, Inc, 1231 25th St NW, Washington, DC 20037. Telephone (202) 452-4200.

Daily newsletter. Provides tax information through summaries and analyses of developments in Washington. Biweekly and bimonthly indexes. Price $801.00 per year.

1308
Daily Trader's Guide
Commodity Information Service Co, 33 W Ridge Pike, Limerick, PA 19468. Telephone (215) 489-4188.

Weekly report and daily hot line. Trading recommendations on "standard unit" of ten futures for trading in commodities futures. Price $750.00 per year.

1309
Daily Traffic World
Traffic Service Corp, 1435 G St NW, Suite 815, Washington, DC 20005. Telephone (202) 783-7325.

Daily newspaper. Reports on transportation industry news. Covers legislative and regulatory developments. Price $340.00 per year.

1310
Dairy Industry Newsletter
Federal State Reports, Inc, 5203 Leesburg Pike, #1201, Falls Church, VA 22041. Telephone (703) 379-0222.

Biwekly report. Covers Washington developments affecting producers, processors, and retailers, as well as dairy industry representatives. Price $95.00 per year.

1311
Dairying and Dairy Products
Australian Bureau of Statistics, Box 17 GPO, Canberra, ACT 2600, Australia. Order from Australian Government Publishing Service, PO Box 84, Canberra, ACT 2600, Australia. Telephone (61) (062) 52 7911.

Annual report. Offers data on Australian dairy cattle used for milk or cream, butter production, cheeses, and other dairy-related topics. Appendix presents rural holdings classified by area and size of milk cattle herd. Price available on request.

1312
Dairy Market News Reports
US Department of Agriculture, Room 2764-S, Agricultural Marketing Service, Washington, DC 20250. Telephone (202) 447-7461.

Irregular reports. Discuss dairy market news, including minimum class and producer prices, and receipts and sales in federal order markets. Give cold storage holdings. Price free of charge.

1313
Dairy Products Report
US Dept of Agriculture, Crop Reporting Board, Economics and Statistics Service (ESS), Room 0005 S Bldg, Washington, DC 20250. Telephone (202) 447-4021.

Monthly report. Indicates production of butter, cheese, frozen products, evaporated, condensed and dry milk, whey products, and prices. Includes annual summary of production. Price free of charge.

1314
Dairy Review
Statistics Canada, User Services, Publications Distribution, Ottawa, Ont, Canada, K1A 0V7. Telephone (613) 992-3151.

Monthly report. Supplies statistical summary of Canadian dairy industry. Includes data on milk production, farm value, and cash income from dairying. Price $30.00 per year. ISSN 0300-0753.

1314.01
Dallas/Fort Worth Business
Cordovan Corp, 5314 Bingle Rd, Houston, TX 77092. Order from Dallas/Fort Worth Business, 11300 N Central Expressway, Dallas, TX, 75243. Telephone (214) 692-5846.

Weekly newspaper. Contains feature articles on various segments of Dallas/Fort Worth business. Price $24.00 per year.

1315
Daltons Weekly
Morgan–Grampian Ltd, Morgan–Grampian House, Calderwood St, London, England SE18 6QH. Order from Morgan–Grampian Publishing Co, 2 Park Ave, New York, NY 10016. Telephone (44) (01) 855-7777. Telex 896238 MORGAN G. New York (212) 340-9700. Telex 425592 MGI UI.

Weekly newspaper contains advertisements for accommodations, property, shops, and small businesses for sale in Great Britain. Price $34.00 per year.

1316
Dangerous Goods Shipping Regulations
Supply & Services Canada, Canadian Govt Publishing Centre, Hull, Que, Canada K1A 0S9. Telephone (819) 994-3475, 2085.

Book plus supplements. Contains regulations governing shipment of dangerous materials in Canada. Price $24.00.

1316.01
Dangerous Properties of Industrial Materials Report
Van Nostrand Reinhold, 135 West 50th St, New York, NY 10020. Telephone (212) 265-8700.

Bimonthly journal. Analyzes common industrial substances for toxicity, flammability, and explosiveness. Gives countermeasures, reactions, and disposal methods. Price $120.00 per year, $20.00 per back issue.

1317
Dartnell Advertising Managers' Handbook, 2nd edition 1977
Dartnell Corp, 4660 Ravenswood Ave, Chicago, IL 60640. Telephone (312) 561-4000.

Book. Theory and practice of advertising management. Price available on request.

1318
Dartnell Direct Mail and Mail Order Handbook, 1980 3rd edition
Dartnell Corp, 4660 Ravenswood Ave, Chicago, IL 60640. Telephone (312) 561-4000.

Book. Practical guide to direct mail and mail order operations. Price available on request.

1319
Dartnell Marketing Manager's
Handbook, **1973 edition**
Dartnell Corp, 4660 Ravenswood Ave, Chicago, IL 60640. Telephone (312) 561-4000.

Book. Covers theory and practice of marketing management. Price available on request.

1321
Dartnell Public Relations Handbook
2nd edition
Dartnell Corp, 4660 Ravenswood Ave, Chicago, IL 60640. Telephone (312) 561-4000.

Book. Theory and practice in the public relations field. Price available on request.

1322
Dartnell Sales and Marketing Executive
Service
Dartnell Corp, 4660 Ravenswood Ave, Chicago, IL 60640. Telephone (312) 561-4000.

Monthly service. Gives information on management, marketing, and sales. Includes sales checking chart and advice on use of direct mail and running of successful sales meetings. Price $13.00 per month.

1323
Dartnell Sales Manager's Handbook,
13th edition 1980
Dartnell Corp, 4660 Ravenswood Ave, Chicago, IL 60640. Telephone (312) 561-4000.

Book. Theory and practice of sales management. Price available on request.

1324
Dartnell Sales Promotion Handbook,
7th edition 1979
Dartnell Corp, 4660 Ravenswood Ave, Chicago, IL 60640. Telephone (312) 561-4000.

Book. Theory and practice of organizing a sales promotion campaign. Price available on request.

1324.01
DATABASE
Online, Inc, 11 Tannery Lane, Weston, Ct 06883. Telephone (203) 227-8466.

Quarterly magazine. Focuses on databases. Discusses commercial uses and creation of in-house databases. Price $52.00 per year.

1325
Data Base Service
11722 Sorrento Valley Rd, Suite I, San Diego, CA 92121. Telephone (714) 755-13270.

Monthly service. Provides computerized data base for 1400 common stocks, or any portion of it, on magnetic tape. Price $900.00 per year.

1325.01
Data Channels
Phillips Publishing, Inc, 7315 Wisconsin Ave, Bethesda, Md 20014. Telephone (301) 986-0666.

Monthly newsletter. Covers the data communication industry, including regulations, technology, and trade shows. Price $97.00 per year.

1326
Datacom Advisor
International Data Corporation, 214 3rd Ave, Waltham, MA 02254. Telephone (617) 890-3700. Telex 92-3401.

Monthly periodical. Covers data communications industry, from network management to regulatory policies. Price available on request.

1326.01
Datacomm & Distributed Processing
Report
Managment Information Corp, 140 Barclay Ctr, Cherry Hill, NJ 08034. Telephone (609) 428-1020.

Monthly report. Evaluates distributed processing systems and communications networks. Price $245.00 per year, $135.00 renewal.

1327
Data Communications
McGraw-Hill Publications Co, 1221 Ave of the Americas, New York, NY 10020. Telephone (212) 997-1221. Telex TWX 7105814879 WUI 62555.

Monthly magazine. Discusses data communications topics, including terminals, multiplexers, processors, and other equipment. Price $18.00 per year.

1328
Data Entry Awareness Report
Management Information Corp, 140 Barclay Ctr, Cherry Hill, NJ 08034. Telephone (609) 428-1020.

Monthly report. Evaluates data entry products such as key-to-disc, voice entry, portable data recorders, and intelligent terminals. Suggests management techniques. Price $245.00 per year, $135.00 renewal.

1329
Data Entry Today
Management Information Corp, 140 Barclay Ctr, Cherry Hill, NJ 08034. Telephone (609) 428-1020.

Book. Provides data entry management information. Covers keypunch, point-of-sale, and voice recognition systems. Includes equipment selection guide. Price $50.00.

1330
Datafacts
Conference Board in Canada, Suite 100, 25 McArthur Rd, Ottawa, Ont, Canada K1L 6R3. Telephone (613) 746-1261.

Quarterly loose-leaf report. Offers tables and charts on Canadian quarterly labor market statistics by region and industry for 3-year period. Price available on request.

1331
Data Files
International Data Corporation, 214 3rd Ave, Waltham, MA 02254. Telephone (617) 890-3700. Telex 92-3401.

Magnetic tapes or printouts, with summary. Provide descriptions of computer installations throughout the world, multiple-unit buyers of mini- and micro-computers, and software vendors and buyers. Price available on request.

1334
Dataguide
Maclean–Hunter Ltd, 30 Old Burlington St, London, England W1X 2AE. Telephone (44) (01) 434-2233.

Annual publication. Presents tabulated printing equipment specifications under various categories, including typesetting, composition and makeup, and camera and darkroom. Price available on request.

1335
Data Management
Data Processing Management Association, 505 Busse Hwy, Park Ridge, IL 60068. Telephone (312) 825-8124.

Monthly magazine. Discusses issues in the field of information processing. Price $16.00. ISSN 0022-0329.

1336

Datamation

Technical Publishing Co, 1301 S Grove Ave, Barrington, IL 60010. Order from Technical Publishing Co, 666 5th Ave, New York, NY 10019. Telephone (212) 489-2200.

Monthly magazine. Covers international electronic data processing industry. Reports on new equipment and techniques. Price available on request.

1337

Data News—Brazil

CW Communications, Inc, 797 Washington St, Newton, MA 02160. Telephone (617) 965-5800.

Biweekly newspaper in Portuguese with English summary. Reports on Brazil's computer hardware, software, terminals, and services. Price $50.00.

1338

Data on Selected Racial Groups Available from Bureau of the Census, **No 40, Revised May 1977**

US Dept of Commerce, Bureau of the Census, Washington, DC 20233. Telephone (202) 449-1600.

Report. Provides information on sources of data for selected minority races available from Bureau of Census. Describes racial categories used. Price $1.00.

1344

Datascope

Peter Isaacson Publications, 46-49 Porter St, Prahran, Vic 3181, Australia. Telephone (03) 51 8431. Telex 30880.

Fortnightly newspaper concerning data processing equipment and services. Emphasizes small business systems. Includes material on work processing and micrographic systems. Price $15.00 (Australian) per year.

1344.01

Data User News

US Dept of Commerce, Bureau of Census, Washington, DC 20233. Telephone (202) 449-1600.

Monthly report. Discusses new Census Bureau products, services, and programs. Highlights developments in statistical areas. Price $14.00 per year.

1345

Data User News

US Dept of Commerce, 14th St between Constitution Ave and E St NW, Washington, DC 20230. Order from Superintendent of Documents, US Government Printing Office, Washington, DC 20402. Telephone (202) 783-3238.

Magazine. Presents new Census Bureau statistical information. Notes Census Bureau activities and personnel changes. Price $14.00 per year.

1346

Debates of the House of Commons

Supply and Services Canada, Canadian Govt Publishing Centre, Hull, Que, Canada K1A 0S9. Telephone (819) 994-3475, 2085.

Daily report. Covers proceedings of Canada's House of Commons. Price $30.00 per year.

1347

Debates of the Senate

Supply and Services Canada, Canadian Govt Publishing Centre, Hull, Que, Canada K1A 0S9. Telephone (819) 994-3475, 2085.

Reports. Covers proceedings of Canada's Senate. Price $30.00 per year.

1348

Decision Line

American Inst for Decision Sciences, University Plz, 140 Decatur St, SE, Atlanta, GA 30303. Telephone (404) 658-4000.

Discusses internal affairs of AIDS. Includes material on computer systems. Price $4.00 per year.

1349

Decisions and Orders of the Motor Vehicle Committee

Supply and Services Canada, Canadian Govt Publishing Centre, Hull, Que, Canada K1A 0S9. Telephone (819) 994-3475, 2085.

Irregular published reports. Contains decisions of Canada's Motor Vehicle Committee. Bilingual. Price $3.00.

1350

Decisions and Orders of the Telecommunications Committee

Supply and Services Canada, Publishing Centre, Printing and Publishing, Ottawa, Ont, Canada K1A 0S9. Telephone (613) 238-1601.

Irregular report on decisions and orders of Canada's Telecommunications Committee. Bilingual. Price $5.00.

1351

Decisions and Orders of the Water Transport Committee

Supply and Services Canada, Canadian Govt Publishing Centre, Hull, Que, Canada K1A 0S9. Telephone (819) 994-3475, 2085.

Irregular report. Covers decisions and orders of the Canadian Water Transport Committee. Bilingual. Price $7.50 per year.

1352

Decision Sciences

American Inst for Decision Sciences, University Plz, 140 Decatur St, SE, Atlanta, Ga 30303. Telephone (404) 658-4000.

Quarterly journal. Publishes articles concerned with the application of computer systems and mathematics to the solution of problems of organized groups. Is the official publication of the AIDS. Models, tables, and graphs. Price $27.00 per year.

1353

Decisions of the Air Transport Committee

Supply and Services Canada, Canadian Govt, Publishing Centre, Hull, Que, Canada K1A 0S9. Telephone (819) 994-3475, 2085.

Irregular report. Contains decisions of the Canadian Air Transport Committee. Bilingual. Price $65.00 per year.

1354

Decisions of the Railway Transport Committee

Supply and Services Canada, Canadian Govt Publishing Centre, Hull, Que, Canada, K1A 0S9. Telephone (819) 994-3475, 2085.

Irregular report. Provides decisions of the Canadian Railway Transport Committee. Bilingual. Price $5.00.

1354.01

Defense Statistics

Her Majesty's Stationary Office, PO Box 569, London, England SE1 9NH. Telephone (44) (01) 928-1321.

Annual book. Contains statistics on British armed forces. Covers equipment, finances, and personnel. Price £4.00.

1354.02
Defense & Economy World Report
Government Business Worldwide Reports, PO Box 5651, Washington, DC 20016. Telephone (202) 966-6379.

Weekly report. Contains information on armament and military procurement in the US and abroad. Surveys defense policy, equipment, and requirements and votes international cooperative projects and arms exports and controls. Price $265.00 per year. ISSN 0364-9008.

1355.01
Defense Industry Organization Service
Carroll Publishing Co, 1058 Thomas Jefferson St, NW, Washington, DC 20007. Telephone (202) 333-8620.

Semiannual service with two supplemental mailings. Provides charts of the organization structure and personnel of 120 largest defense contractors. Includes major aerospace and electronics companies. Price $435.00 per year.

1355.02
Defense Week
Llewllyn King, 300 National Press Bldg, Washinton, DC 20045. Telephone (202) 638-7430.

Weekly publication. Covers weapons development and acquisition, corporate profiles, Congress, Defense Department, and White House. Includes information on the defense budget, defense policy, and domestic and international strategic affairs. Price $500.00 per year, $550.00 oversees.

1355.03
Delaware: State Industrial Directory
1980
Manufacturers' News, Inc, 3 Huron St, Chicago, Il 60611. Telephone (312) 337-1084.

Annual book. Identifies 584 Delaware industrial firms by name, location, and product. Price $15.00.

1356
Delinquency Rates on Bank Installment Loans
American Bankers Assn, 1120 Connecticut Ave NW, Washington, DC 20036. Telephone (202) 467-4123.

Quarterly newsletter. Contains material on bank installment loans. Features graphs and tables on personal, home, property improvements, and check credit loans. Price $10.00 per year.

1357
Demographic Yearbook
United Nations Publications, Rm A-3315, New York, NY 10017. Telephone (212) 754-8302.

Annual book. Provides a compilation of UN demographic information. Price $48.-00.

1358
Dental Industry News
Harcourt Brace Jovanovich Publications, 757 3rd Ave, New York, NY 10017. Order from Harcourt Brace and Jovanovich Publications, 1 E 1st St, Duluth, MN 55802. Telephone (218) 727-8511.

Monthly magazine. Reports on dental products and practice. Price $10.00 per year.

1359
Dental Laboratory Review
Harcourt Brace Jovanovich Publications, 757 3rd Ave, New York, NY 10017. Order from Harcourt Brace and Jovanovich Publications, 1 E 1st St, Duluth, MN 55802. Telephone (218) 727-8511.

Monthly report plus annual directory. Covers the processing of oral prosthetic devices and other dental laboratory developments. Price $10.00 per year.

1360
Dental Management
Harcourt Brace Jovanovich Publications, 757 3rd Ave, New York, NY 10017. Order from Harcourt Brace and Jovanovich Publications, 1 E 1st St, Duluth, MN 55802. Telephone (218) 727-8511.

Monthly magazine. Focuses on dental practice and financial management. Notes the political and social problems affecting the profession. Price $15.00 per year.

1361
Department of Employment Gazette
Her Majesty's Stationery Office, PO Box 569, London, England SE1 9NH. Telephone (44) (01) 928-1321.

Monthly service. Contains information on employment in Great Britain. Price £ 27.72 per year.

1362
Department of Employment Research
Her Majesty's Stationery Office, PO Box 569, London, England SE1 9NH. Telephone (44) (01) 928 1321. Telex 266455.

Annual report. Covers employment research in Great Britain. Price £1.75. ISBN 0 11 3611005.

1363
Dept of Statistics. Annual Report of the Government Statistician
New Zealand Dept of Statistics, Mulgrave St, (Private Bag), Wellington, New Zealand. Telephone (64) (04) 729119.

Annual report. Covers New Zealand's Government Statistician. Price $.30 (New Zealand).

1364
Department Store Jewelry Buyers Directory
Newsletters International, 2600 S Gessner Rd, Houston, TX 77063. Telephone (713) 783-0100.

Annual book. Contains a directory of department stores selling fine and costume jewelry. Notes buyers' names and stores' addresses and telephone numbers. Price $150.00 per copy.

1365
Department Store Sales
Retail Council of Canada, Suite 212, 214 King St, Toronto, Ont, Canada M5H 1K4. Telephone (416) 598-4684.

Monthly report. Contains statistics on department store sales in Canada and provinces. Price $11.00 per year members, $22.00 per year nonmembers.

1366
Department Store Sales and Stocks
Statistics Canada, User Services, Publications Distribution, Ottawa, Ont, Canada K1A 0V7. Telephone (613) 992-3151.

Monthly report. Supplies data on Canadian department store sales and inventories by the number of outlets, provinces, and selected metropolitan areas. Monthly and cumulative tables. Price $30.00 per year. ISSN 0380-7045.

1367
Descriptive Bulletin on Radiological Protection
Commission of the European Communities, Office for Official Publications of the European Communities, CP 1003, Luxembourg 1, Luxembourg. Telephone (352) 490081. Telex PUBLOF 1325.

Monthly report. Covers radiological protection. Price free of charge.

1369
Design Engineering /UK
Morgan-Grampian Ltd, Morgan-Grampian House, Calderwood St, London, England SE18 6QH. Telephone (44) (01) 855-7777. Telex 896238 MORGAN G.

Monthly journal. Provides ideas for industrial designers. Price $50.00 per year.

1369.01
Design Engineering/USA
Morgan-Grampian Ltd, Morgan-Grampian House, Calderwood St, London, England, SE18 6QH. Telephone (44) (01) 855-7777. Telex 896238. Order from Morgan-Grampian Publishing Co, 2 Park Ave, New York, NY 10016. Telephone (212) 340-9700. Telex 425592 MGI UI.

Monthly magazine. Provides ideas for industrial designers. Price $25.00.

1369.02
Determinations of the National Mediation Board, Volumes 1 through 6
National Mediation Board, 1425 K St, NW, Washington, DC 20402. Telephone (202) 523-5995.

Irregularly issued booklet. Contains determinations of the National Mediation Board, Volumes I through VI. Includes significant determinations relating to Railway Labor Act. Price available on request.

1371
Developing Business in the Middle East and North Africa
Chase Trade Information Corp, 1 World Trade Center, 78th Floor, New York, NY 10048. Telephone (212) 432-8072.

Five books covering the Persian Gulf states, Algeria, Iraq, Egypt, and Saudi Arabia. Each study covers critical issues, including economic and social conditions, government development plans, and official policy on foreign investment. Price $375.00 for Gulf states, $185.00 for four other books.

1372
Developing Country Foodgrain Projections for 1985
Sandra C Hadler and Maw-Chengh Yang, World Bank, 1818 H St NW, Washington, DC 20433. Telephone (202) 393-6360.

Publication gauging long-run grain problems of developing countries. Provides projections to 1985 for individual grains for 6 regions and 21 countries. Price free of charge.

1373
Development Digest
US Agency for International Development, Washington, DC 20523. Order from Superintendent of Documents, Government Printing Office, Washington, DC 20402. Telephone (202) 783-3238.

Publication. Summarizes international development work of the US Agency for International Development. Price available on request.

1373.01
Development Digest
University of Sussex, Institute of Development Studies, Brighton, England BN1 9RE. Telephone Brighton (0273) 606261. Telex 877159 RR Hove IDS. Cable Development Brighton.

Semiannual publication. Summarizes current research in the United Kingdom on development problems, emphasizing policy implications. Subjects include urban and rural problems, technology, and education. Price $18.00 per year.

1373.02
Development Directory-Human Resource Management
Advanced Personnel Systems, 756 Lois Ave, Sunnyvale, CA 94087. Telephone (408) 736-2433.

Semiannual directory with bimonthly supplement. Lists public seminars and conferences on topics in personnel management, management development, and employee relations. Covers over 300 public and private organizations. Price $75.00 per year. ISSN 0197-3436.

1374
Development Forum
UN Dir for Economic & Social Information, Palais des Nations, CH-1211, Geneva 10, Switzerland. Order from UN Dep of Public Information and the United Nations University, Palais des Nations, CH 1211, Geneva 10, Switzerland.

Newspaper issued nine times per year. Reports on international development, environment, population, and economic subjects. Stresses the activities of the United Nations. English, French, German, Spanish, and Serbo-Croatian editions. Price free of charge.

1375
Development Forum: Business Edition
UN Div for Economic & Social Information, Palais des Nations, CH-1211, Geneva 10, Switzerland.

Semimonthly newspaper. Pertains to international economic and social developments. Lists contracts funded by the World Bank and United Nations Development Program. Price $250.00 per year.

1375.01
Development News Notes
State of Ohio, Department of Economic and Community Development, PO Box 1001, Columbus, OH 43216. Telephone (614) 466-7772

Biweekly newsletter. Contains information on Ohio economic and business trends. Price available on request.

1375.02
Developments in Price Spreads for Farm Foods
US Dept of Agriculture, ESS Publications, Room 0054-S, Washington, DC 20250. Telephone (202) 447-7255.

Annual report. Contains statistics on farm to retail price spreads for market basket of farm foods. Includes data on selected food, such as beef and pork. Free of charge.

1375.03
Dialog
Dialog Information Retrieval Service, 3460 Hillview Ave, Palo Alto, CA 94304. Telephone (415) 858-2700. Telex 334499.

Information service with more than 100 databases. Provides access to references to articles and reports on science, technology, business, medicine, social science, current affairs, and humanities. Price available on request.

1376
Dictionary for Accountants
Eric L Kohler, Prentice-Hall, Inc, Englewood Cliffs, NJ 07632. Telephone (201) 592-2000.

Book. Defines accounting and related terms. Price $26.00. ISBN 013-209783-4.

1377
Dictionary of Administration and Management 1981 Edition
Systems Research Institute, Publications Div, PO Box 74524, Los Angeles, CA 90004.

Book. Covers terms and concepts related to administration and management. Includes annotated directory of leadership resources. Price $24.95. ISBN 0-912352-04-3.

1378
Dictionary of Economics, **5th edition**
Barnes & Noble, Inc, Div of Harper &
Row Publishers, Inc, 10 E 53rd St, New
York, NY 10022. Telephone (212) 593-
7000.

Book. Defines terms in economics and includes descriptions of organizations. Price
$4.95 paperback.

1379
Dictionary of Economics and Business
1974
Littlefield, Adams & Co, 81 Adams Dr,
Totawa, NJ 07512. Telephone (201) 256-
8600.

Paperback book. Defines over 5000 terms
encountered in college business and economics courses. Price $7.95.

1380
Dictionary of Insurance
Littlefield, Adams & Co, 81 Adams Dr,
Totawa, NJ 07512. Telephone (201) 256-
8600.

Paperback book. Contains over 4000 entries explaining words and phrases in all
fields of insurance. Price $5.95.

1383
Digest: Business & Law Journal
Digest Reporting Service Ltd, 869 Por-
tage Ave, Winnipeg, Man, Canada R3G
ON8. Telephone 772-9710.

Weekly report. Contains real estate and
credit information for Manitoba, Canada.
Includes data on bankruptcies, mortgages, and real estate sales. Price $120.00
per year.

1384
Digest of Bank Insurance **1973 edition**
American Bankers Assn, 1120 Connecti-
cut Ave NW, Washington, DC 20036.
Telephone (202) 467-4123.

Loose-leaf book. Analyzes insurance requirements for banking. Periodic revisions. Price $20.00.

1385
*Digest of Benefit Entitlement and
Principles/Unemployment Insurance*
Supply and Services Canada, Canadian
Govt Publishing Centre, Hull, Que, Can-
ada K1A 0S9. Telephone (819) 994-3475,
2085.

Book, with update service. Discusses Canadian benefit entitlement principles and
unemployment insurance. Price $12.00.

1386
*Digest of Commercial Laws of the
World*
Oceana Publications, Inc, 75 Main St,
Dobbs Ferry, NY 10522. Telephone (914)
693-5944.

Six loose-leaf binders. Summarize international commercial laws for over 60
countries. Price $500.00, $150.00 subscription service.

1387
*Digest of Current Economic Statistics
(Cat No 1305.0)*
Australian Bureau of Statistics, PO Box
10, Belconnen, ACT 2616, Australia.
Order from Australian Government Pub-
lishing Service, PO Box 84, Canberra,
ACT 2600, Australia. Telephone (062) 52
7911.

Monthly report. Summarizes Australia's
current economic statistics. Covers production, overseas trade, taxation, unemployment, and other topics. Price free of
charge.

1388
*Digest of Environmental Protection
Legislation in Canada—to January
1977* **6th edition**
Canadian Industries Ltd, CIL House,
Box 10, Montreal, Que, Canada H3C
2R3. Telephone (514) 874-3000.

Two softcover volumes. Contain digests
of provincial and federal Canadian legislation and regulations relevant to environmental protection. Price $20.00 per set.

1389
Digest of Executive Opportunities
General Executive Services, Inc, Park St
Bldg, New Canaan, CT 06840. Telephone
(203) 966-1673.

Weekly report. Describes executive job
opportunities in general management,
sales and marketing, manufacturing,
finance, and other fields. Price $95.00 for
20 weeks.

1391
Digest of Investment Advices
N H Mager, Editor, Digest of Advices,
Inc, 233 Broadway, New York, NY
10007. Telephone (212) 233-6018.

Monthly newsletter. Offers a digest of investment advisory services and financial
and economic publications. Price $25.00
per year.

1392
Digest of State Land Sales Regulation
Land Development Institute, Ltd, 1401
16th St, NW, Washington, DC 20036.
Telephone (202) 232-2144.

Loose-leaf volume, plus quarterly updates. Covers state regulations on sale of
subdivided land, condominiums, and resort timesharing in 50 states, District of
Columbia, and six major Canadian provinces. Price $125.00 per year, $95.00 libraries.

1393
Digest of Statistics
Consulate General of Nigeria, 575 Lexington Ave, New York, NY 10022. Telephone (212) PL2-1670.

Quarterly digest of statistics pertaining to
Nigeria. Price 50 kobo.

1394
*Digest of United Kingdom Energy
Statistics*
Her Majesty's Stationery Office, PO Box
569, London, England SE1 9NH. Tele-
phone (44) (01) 928 1321.

Annual report. Digests energy statistics.
Price £8.50 per year.

1396
Digest of Welsh Statistics
Her Majesty's Stationery Office, PO Box
569, London, England SE1 9NH. Telephone (44) (01) 928 1321.

Annual service. Provides vital statistics
from all government departments for
Wales. Price £6.75 per year.

1396.01
*Digital Systems for Industrial
Automation*
Crane, Russak & Co Inc, 3 East 44th St,
New York, NY 10017. Telephone (212)
867-1490.

Quarterly magazine. Examines theoretical and computational subjects in relation
to the needs of industrial organizations.
Covers micro-electronic equipment, intelligent machines, and robot application.
Price $70.00 per volume.

1397
Dimensions
US Dept of Commerce, 14th St between
Constitutional Ave and E St NW, Wash-
ington, DC 20230. Order from Superin-
tendent of Documents, US Government
Printing Office, Washington, DC
20402230. Telephone (202) 783-3238.

Magazine. Contains information on standards and standardization. Includes such topics as metrication and building safety. Price $11.00 per year, $13.75 foreign.

1398
Dimensions
University of Florida, College of Business Adm, Bureau of Economic & Business Research, 221 Matherly Hall, Gainesville, FL 32611. Telephone (904) 392-0171.

Quarterly magazine. Reports on Florida's economic growth, government, land management, social conditions, and other topics. Includes tabular data on the labor force and commercial bank activities. Price $15.00 per year.

1399
Direct Advertising (D/A)
Paper Makers Advertising Assn, PO Box 2, 90 Elm St, Westfield, MA 01086. Telephone (413) 568-1986.

Quarterly magazine. Deals with the graphic arts. Highlights a different theme in each issue. Price free of charge.

1399.01
Direct Mail Databook, 3rd Edition
Gower Publishing Co Ltd, 1 Westmead, Farnborough, Hampshire, England GU14 7RU. Telephone Farnborough (0252) 519221. Telex 858623.

Book. Supplies data on direct mail organizations and lists for the European continent. Contains articles that cover aspects of the direct mail industry in Europe. Price $54.00. ISBN 0 566 02177 3.

1400
Direction of Trade
International Monetary Fund, 19th & H Sts NW, Washington, DC 20431. Telephone (202) 393-6362.

Monthly book on the trade of 36 countries. Contains comparative data for the preceding year. Tables. Price $16.00 per year.

1401
Direct Mail List Rates & Data
Standard Rate & Data Service, Inc, 5201 Old Orchard Rd, Skokie, IL 60077. Telephone (312) 470-3100.

Quarterly book. Indicates the source of 50,000 business, consumer, farm, and co-operative mailing lists and rental rates. Price $92.00 per year.

1402
Direct Marketing
Hoke Communications, Inc, 224 7th St, Garden City, NY 11535. Telephone (516) 746-6700.

Monthly magazine. Emphasizes direct mail advertising and other direct marketing techniques for any kind of business. Price $30.00 per year.

1402.01
Direct Marketing Marketplace/1981
Facts on File, Inc, 460 Park Ave S, New York, NY 10016. Telephone (212) 265-2011.

Directory. Lists alphabetically by category company name, address, phone number, key executives, product, and other specific direct marketing data. Price $40.00.

1403
Director
Institute of Directors, 116 Poll Mall, London, SW1Y 5ED, England. Telephone (44) (01) 839-1233.

Monthly magazine geared to British business directors. Covers business trends and methods and boardroom control. Includes reports on the Institute of Directors. Price £24.00, $57.00 per year.

1404
Directors & Boards
Information for Industry, The Hay Group, 229 S 18th St, Philadelphia, PA 19103. Telephone (215) 875-2330.

Quarterly journal. Offers articles on corporate directors, boards, and activities. Price $48.00 per year.

1405
Director's Handbook
McGraw-Hill Book Co, Hightstown-Princeton Rd, Hightstown, NJ 08520. Telephone (609) 448-1700. Telex 843449.

Book. Covers management practices in Great Britain. Price available on request.

1406
Directory Information Service
Gale Research Co, Book Tower, Detroit, MI 48226. Telephone (313) 961-2242.

Reference guide published three times a year. Lists directories in 15 subject areas, including government, science, business, education, and leisure. Price $58.00 per year.

1407
Directory of American Firms Operating in Foreign Countries
World Trade Academy Press, Inc, 50 E 42nd St, New York, NY 10017. Telephone (212) 697-4999.

Annual book. Provides a guide to 4200 US corporations operating overseas. Includes information on subsidiaries, branches, products, and services. Price $125.00.

1408
Directory of American Savings and Loan Associations
T K Sanderson Organization, 200 E 25th St, Baltimore, MD 21218. Telephone (301) 235-3383.

Annual directory. Lists main and branch offices of savings and loan associations for the 50 states, the District of Columbia, Puerto Rico, and Guam, with addresses, officials, telephone numbers and assets. Price $40.00.

1409
Directory of Arkansas Manufacturers
Arkansas Dept of Economic Development, One Capitol Mall, Little Rock, AR 72201. Order from Arkansas Industrial Development foundation, PO Box 1784, Little Rock, AR 72203. Telephone (501) 371-1121.

Annual book. Lists manufacturing operations in Arkansas by city, product, and alphabetically by company. Price $25.00.

1410
Directory of Associations in Canada
University of Toronto Press, Front Campus, Toronto, Ont, Canada M5S 1A6.

Directory. Lists Canadian associations alphabetically and by subject. Includes company, name, address, and top executive. Price $37.50.

1411
Directory of Bond Agents
Standard & Poor's Corp, 25 Broadway, New York, NY 10004. Telephone (212) 248-2525.

Loose-leaf book, plus bimonthly updates. Identifies the paying agent, registrar, co-registrar, trustee, and conversion agent for over 20,000 publicly held corporate and municipal bonds. Includes title of issue, state, form, and exchange fee. Price $371.00 per year.

1412

Directory of British Associations, **6th edition**

Gale Research Co, Book Tower, Detroit, MI 48226. Telephone (313) 961-2242.

Directory. Lists the interests and activities of Great Britain and Ireland. Provides a listing of the publications for associations in these countries—including trade, scientific, technical, and professional. Price $125.00.

1413

Directory of British Importers

Dun & Bradstreet, Box 3224, Church St Station, New York, NY 10008. Telephone (212) 285-7346.

Directory. Lists 470 importers in Great Britain. Price available on request, to Dun & Bradstreet subscribers only.

1414

Directory of Business and Financial Services, **1976 edition**

Special Libraries Assn, 235 Park Ave S, New York, NY 10003. Telephone (212) 477-9250.

Directory. Presents a guide to more than 1000 business and financial services in the US and Canada. Subject index and publishers index. Price $18.80. ISBN 0-87111-212-4.

1415

Directory of Canadian Commercial Air Services

Supply and Services Canada, Publishing Centre, Printing and Publishing, Ottawa, Ont, Canada K1A 0S9. Telephone (613) 238-1601.

Loose-leaf directory, plus update service. Covers Canadian commerical air services. Bilingual. Price $7.50.

1416

Directory of Career Planning and Placement Offices

College Placement Council, Inc, PO Box 2263, Bethlehem, PA 18001. Telephone (215) 868-1421.

Annual directory. Contains information on placement personnel and interview dates at 1900 two- and four-year college campuses. Price $10.00 per copy.

1417

Directory of Chemical Producers USA

Stanford Research Inst, Stanford Research Inst International, Menlo Park, CA 94025. Telephone (415) 859-3627.

Annual directory, with two supplements. Lists major US chemical producers and their products. Price $595.00.

1417.01

Directory of College Recruiting Personnel

College Placement Council, Inc, PO Box 2263, Bethlehem, PA 18001. Telephone (215) 868-1421.

Annual directory. Contains information on college recruiting personnel at 1700 companies and government agencies. Price $10.00.

1418

Directory of Colorado Manufacturers

University of Colorado, Graduate School of Business Adm, Business Research Div, Boulder, CO 80309. Telephone (303) 492-8227.

Book revised approximately every 18 months. Lists Colorado manufacturing firms alphabetically and by city and product. Price $30.00. ISBN 0-89478-031-X.

1419

Directory of Companies Filing Annual Reports with the US Securities & Exchange Commission

US Securities & Exchange Commission, Washington, DC 20549. Order from Superintendent of Documents, Government Printing Office, Washington, DC 20402. Telephone (202) 755-4833.

Book series. Lists companies required to file annual reports with the Securities and Exchange Commission under the Securities Exchange Act of 1934. Includes alphabetical and industry group listings. Price available on request.

1420

Directory of Computerized Data Files & Related Technical Reports

US Dept of Commerce, National Technical Information Service, 5285 Port Royal Rd, Springfield, VA 22161. Telephone (703) 487-4808.

Directory. Lists by subject, computerized data files available from US government agencies. Contains a description of the contents of files. Price $40.00. Order number, PB 80–217003.

1421

Directory of Computer Software and Related Technical Reports, **1980**

US Dept of Commerce, National Technical Information Service, 5285 Port Royal Rd, Springfield, VA 22161. Telephone (703) 487-4808.

Directory. Provides single information source on computer programs—machine readable software—and directly re;ated selected technical reports from over 100 federal agencies covering 27 subject categories. Price $40.00. Order Number, PB80–110232.

1422

Directory of Corporate Affliations

National Register Publishing Co, Inc, 5201 Old Orchard Rd, Skokie, IL 60077. Telephone (312) 470-3100.

Book, with five bimonthly updating reports. Offers a directory to 4500 US parent corporations. Gives their domestic and foreign divisions, subsidiaries and affiliates, with subsidiaries and affiliates cross-indexed. Price $109.00. ISBN 0-87217-002-0.

1423

Directory of Counseling Services

American Personnel and Guidance Assn, 2 Skyline Place, Suite 400, 5203 Leesburg Pike, Falls Church, VA 22041. Telephone (717) 820-4700.

Book. Lists over 300 accredited counseling services and agencies in the US and Canada. Price $6.00.

1424

Directory of Data Files, Bureau of the Census

US Dept of Commerce, Bureau of Census, Washington, DC 20233. Telephone (202) 449-1600.

Book. Describes the Census Bureau's holdings of machine-readable data and provides information on how they may be obtained. Price available on request.

1425

Directory of Data Sources on Racial and Ethnic Minorities

US Dept of Commerce, Bureau of the Census, Washington, DC 20233. Order from Superintendent of Documents, Government Printing Office, Washington, DC 20402. Telephone (202) 783-3238.

Directory. Provides information on minority-group data published by various federal agencies. Price $1.50.

1426

Directory of Defense Electronic Products & Services: US Suppliers

Fairchild Publications, Inc, 7 E 12th St, New York, NY 10003. Telephone (212) 741-4280.

Directory. Supplies technical descriptions and specifications for US electronic products and services for defense. Includes telecommunications equipment, radar, and lasers. Price $40.00.

1426.01
Directory of Designated Members
Appraisal Institute of Canada, 309-93 Lombard Ave, Winnipeg, Manitoba, Canada R3B 3B1. Telephone (204) 942-0751.

Annual publication. Furnishes names and addresses of all designated members of Appraisal Institute of Canada. Price free of charge.

1427
Directory of Directors
Thomas Skinner Directories, Windsor Court, E Grinstead House, E Grinstead, W Sussex, England RH19 1XE. Order from IPC Business Press Ltd New York, 205 E 42nd St, New York, NY 10017. Telephone (212) 867-2080.

Annual book. Offers a directory to company directors. Price £75.00 per year. ISBN 611 00649 9.

1427.01
Directory of Euromarket Borrowers
Euromoney Publications Ltd, Nestor House, Playhouse Yard, London, England EC4V 5EX. Telephone (44) (01) 236-7111. Telex 8812246 Eurmon G.

Directory. Provides bankers with listings of corporate, sovereign, state, government agency, and bank borrowers in the market. Price $50.00. ISBN 0-903121-16-6.

1428
Directory of European Associations, **3rd edition**
Gale Research Co, Book Tower, Detroit, MI 48226. Telephone (313) 961-2242.

Directory. Contains information on over 9000 European industrial, trade, and professional associations (excluding Great Britain and Ireland). Price $175.00.

1428.01
Directory of Evaluation Consultants
Foundation Center, 888 7th Ave, New York, NY 10106. Telephone (212) 975-1120.

Book. Describes over 550 individuals and organizations experienced in the design and conduct of evaluation. Price $8.95.

1429
Directory of Executive Recruiters
Kennedy & Kennedy, Inc, Templeton Rd, Fitzwilliam, NH 03447. Telephone (603) 585-2200.

Annual book. Lists members of the Association of Executive Recruiting Consultants and other firms and individuals doing executive recruiting. Price $12.00 per paid.

1430
Directory of Federal Statistics for Local Areas: A Guide to Sources
US Dept of Commerce, Bureau of the Census, Washington, DC 20233. Order from Subscriber Services Section (Publications), Bureau of the Census, Washington, DC 20233. Telephone (202) 449-1600.

Book. Cites tables from reports on states and local areas issued by the Census Bureau and other federal agencies. Price available on request.

1431
Directory of Foreign Firms Operating in the US
World Trade Academy Press, Inc, 50 E 42nd St, New York, NY 10017. Telephone (212) 697-4999.

Annual book. Provides information on foreign businesses operating in the US. Price $85.00.

1432
Directory of Foreign Manufacturers in the United States,
Georgia State University, College of Business Adm, Business Publishing Div, Univ Plz, Atlanta, GA 30303. Telephone (404) 658-4253.

Book. Surveys foreign investment in US manufacturing. Indicates which industries and states have the highest concentration of investment. Index by parent company, parent company's country of origin, and by major products produced. Price $34.95. ISBN 0-88406-128-0.

1433
Directory of Franchising Organizations
Pilot Books, 347 5th Ave, New York, NY 10016. Telephone (212) 685-0736.

Annual book. Lists nation's top money-making franchises. Offers concise descriptions and facts about franchising. Price $3.50.

1434
Directory of Government Production Prime Contractors
Government Data Publications, 422 Washington Bldg, Washington, DC 20005. Telephone (202) 966-6379.

Annual book. Lists names and addresses of organizations that received government production prime contracts during the past fiscal year. Price $15.00.

1435
Directory of Importers and Manufacturers' Agents in British Columbia 1980
Ministry of Industry and Small Business Development, Parliment Buildings, Victoria, BC, Canada V8V 1X4. Telephone (604) 387-6701.

Directory. Provides a roster of importers and manufacturers' agents in British Columbia. Includes product lines. Price free of charge.

1436
Directory of Industrial Distributors
Morgan-Grampian Ltd, Morgan-Grampin House, Calderwood St, London, England SE18 6QH. Order from Morgan-Grampian Publishing Co, 2 Park Ave, New York, NY 10016. Telephone (212) 340-9700. Telex 425592 MGI UI.

Book published every three years. Provides marketing guide for industrial distributors in the US. Price $300.00.

1439
Directory of Labor Market Information
South Carolina Employment Security Commission, 1550 Gadsden St, PO Box 995, Columbia, SC 29202. Telephone (803) 758-8983.

Directory. Lists reports that provide information on South Carolina's labor market, economic conditions, wages, and types of employment. Price available on request.

1439.01
Directory of Labour Organizations in Canada, 1980
Labour Canada, Communications Services Directorate, Ottawa, Ont, Canada K1A OJ2. Order from Canadian Government, Publishing Centre, Supply and Services Canada, 45 Sacre-Coeur Blvd, Hull, Que, K1A OS9. Telephone (819) 997-2617.

Annual publication. Includes statistics on union membership and information on national and international unions, independent labor organizations, and labor congresses. Bilingual. Price $4.00.

1440
Directory of Mailing List Houses
B Klein Publications, Inc, PO Box 8503, Coral Spring, FL 33065. Telephone (305) 752-1708.

Annual directory. Lists 2000 mailing list specialists geographically and indicates the nature of the lists. Price $30.00.

1441

Directory of Maine Labor Organizations
Maine Dept of Manpower Affairs, Bureau of Labor, State House Station #45, Augusta, ME 04333. Telephone (207) 289-3331.

Annual book. Lists Maine labor organizations and councils and identifies officials. Price available on request.

1442

Directory of Management Consultants
Kennedy & Kennedy, Inc, Templeton Rd, Fitzwilliam, NH 03447. Telephone (603) 585-2200.

Directory. Lists 583 US management consultant firms, indexed by services offered, industries served, and geographic area. Price $37.50.

1442.01

Directory of Manufacturers and Products
Kansas Dept of Economic Development, 503 Kansas Ave, Room 626, Topeka, KS 66603. Telephone (913) 296-3481.

Annual directory. Lists Kansas manufacturers and products. Price $20.00.

1443

Directory of Manufacturers, State of Hawaii, **1981–82**
Chamber of Commerce of Hawaii, Dillingham Transportation Bldg, 735 Bishop St, Honolulu, HI 96813. Telephone (808) 531-4111.

Biennial publication. Lists all Hawaiian manufacturers. Includes brand, trade, and manufacturers' names. Price $15.00.

1445

Directory of Maryland Manufacturers, **1979–1980**
Maryland Dept of Economic & Community Development, 2525 Riva Rd, Annapolis, MD 21401. Telephone (301) 269-2041.

Book. Contains data on more than 3096 Maryland manufacturers, including addresses, personnel, and products. Price $18.00.

1446

Directory of Members
Assn of Consulting Management Engineers, 230 Park Ave, New York, NY 10169. Telephone (212) 697-9693.

Annual book. Describes services offered by major management consulting firms. Price free of charge.

1447

Directory of Michigan Manufacturers
Pick Publications, Inc, 8543 Puritan Ave, Detroit, MI 48238. Telephone (313) 864-9388.

Annual directory. Lists about 15,000 Michigan manufacturers alphabetically, geographically, and by product. Mailing labels and lists available. Price $95.00.

1448

Directory of National Association of Real Estate Investment Trusts (NAREIT) Members
National Assn of Real Estate Investment Trusts, Inc, 1101 17th St NW, Washington, DC 20036. Telephone (202) 785-8717.

Annual directory. Lists National Association of Real Estate Investment Trusts members. Notes each trust's investment policies and officers and includes an abbreviated balance sheet. Price $5.00.

1449

Directory of National Unions & Employee Associations
US Dept. of Labor, Bureau of Labor Statistics, 441 G St NW, Washington, DC 20212. Telephone (202) 523-1221.

Biennial book, with irregular supplements. Lists names of officers and professional employees, the number of members and locals of each US labor union. Includes information on union membership, structure, and function, and on state labor organizations. Price $5.00.

1450

Directory of Nebraska Manufacturers
Nebraska Dept of Economic Development, Box 94666, 301 Centennial Mall S, Lincoln, NE 68509. Telephone (402) 471-3111.

Directory. Lists manufacturing firms in Nebraska. Price $10.00.

1451

Directory of Official Architecture and Planning, **23rd Edition, 1980**
George Godwin Ltd, The Builder House, 1–3 Pemberton Row, London, England EC4P 5HL. Telex 25212 Builda G. Order from International Ideas, Inc, 1627 Spruce St, Philadelphia, PA 19103. Telephone (215) 546-0932.

Directory. Lists name and addresses of British local and central government officials concerned with architecture, planning, and related services. Maps of new regions in England, Wales, and Scotland and indexes. Price $40.00. ISBN 07114 5503 1.

1452

Directory of Oregon Manufacturers
Oregon Economic Development Depart. 155 Cottage St NE, Salem, OR 97310. Telephone (503) 373-1200.

Biennial book. Lists all manufacturers in Oregon alphabetically, geographically, and by product. Supplies employment data. Price $25.00.

1453

Directory of Outplacement Firms
Kennedy & Kennedy, Inc, Templeton Rd, Fitzwilliam, NH 03447. Telephone (603) 585-6544.

Annual book. Lists 43 firms offering outplacement services, primarily at the executive level. Price available on request.

1455

Directory of Public Buying Agencies in British Columbia
Ministry of Industry and Small Business Development, Parliament Buildings, Victoria, BC, Canada V8V1X4. Telephone (604) 387-6701.

Directory. Acts as a guide to British Columbian businesses and manufacturers wanting to sell goods or services to provincial and municipal governments or other public agencies. Price free of charge.

1456

Directory of Shopping Centers in Hawaii
Chamber of Commerce of Hawaii, Dillingham Transportation Bldg, 735 Bishop St, Honolulu, HI 96813. Telephone (808) 531-4111.

Book, with periodic updating. Lists Hawaiian shopping centers. Indicates the number of stores and developer. Tables. Price available on request.

1457

Directory of Special Libraries and Information Centers, **6th edition**
Gale Research Co, Book Tower, Detroit, MI 48226. Telephone (313) 961-2242.

Book. Lists 14,000 research libraries and specialized information centers. Provides supplemental volumes containing a geographic-personnel index and an updating of the fourth edition. Price $160.00. ISBN 0289-6.

1459
Directory of Technical & Further Education 18th edition, 1980
George Godwin Ltd, 1-3 Pemberton Row, London, England EC4P 4HL. Order from International Ideas Inc, 1627 Spruce St, Philadelphia, PA 19103. Telephone (215) 546-0932.

Biennial book. Serves as a directory to British colleges below the University level, particularly those that concentrate on vocational education. Names department heads and identifies the range of courses offered. Price $60.00 per year. ISBN 07114 5515 5.

1460
Directory of the Mutual Savings Banks of the United States
National Assn of Mutual Savings Banks, 200 Park Ave, New York, NY 10017. Telephone (212) 973-5432.

Annual book. Lists all US mutual savings banks. Contains information on banks' assets, deposits, mortgage investments, and financial services. Price $30.00 per copy.

1461
Directory of the National Association of Personnel Consultants
National Assn of Personnel Consultants, 1012 14th St NW, Washington, DC 20005. Telephone (202) 638-1721.

Annual directory to private personnel placement services. Lists over 2500 services, noting employment specialties. Price $8.50.

1462
Directory of US and Canadian Marketing Surveys and Services, 3rd edition, 1979–80
Charles H Kline & Co, Inc, 330 Passaic Ave, Fairfield, NJ 07006. Telephone (201) 227-6262. Telex 13-9170 KLINECO.

Loose-leaf book. Provides a directory to 2500 marketing services and published studies covering US, Canadian, and international industrial and consumer markets. Two updated supplements. Price $125.00.

1462.01
Directory of Wool, Hosiery & Fabrics
Commerce Publications Ltd, Manek Mahal, 6th Floor, 90 Veer Nariman Rd, PO Box No 11017, Bombay 400 020, India. Telephone 253505, 253392, 253562. Telex CORE-011-6915.

Annual directory. Supplies information on India's wool, hoisery, and fabric industries. Price Rs 100.

1463
Disclosure Record
Jack Lotto, 265 Jericho Tpke, PO Box 639, Floral Park, NY 11001. Telephone (212) 347-1100 or (516) 328-8811. Telex 510-223-0408.

Weekly newspaper. Publishes corporate transcripts of business and economic reports and financial announcements. Price $50.00 per year.

1464
Discount Merchandiser
Charter Publishing, Inc, 641 Lexington Ave, New York, NY 10022. Telephone (212) 872-8430.

Monthly report. Covers industry news and gives statistics on some companies. Price $20.00 per year. ISSN 0012-3579.

1465
Discount Store News
Lebhar-Friedman Publications, Inc, 425 Park Ave, New York, NY 10022. Telephone (212) 371-9400.

Fortnightly report. Covers news and trends in discount store industry. Price $7.50 per year. ISSN 0012-3587.

1467
Distributed Processing Management
Auerbach Publishers, Inc, 6560 N Park Dr, Pennsauken, NJ 08109. Telephone (609) 662-2070. Telex 831 464.

Book, updated bimonthly. Provides information on planning, designing, implementing, and administering an effective Distributed Data Processing (DDP) system. Includes case studies. Price $200.00.

1467.01
Distributed Processing Reporting Service
International Data Corp, 214 3rd Ave, Waltham, MA 02254. Telephone (617) 890-3700. Telex 92-3401.

Monthly newsletters, special reports, and spot news analyses. Covers intersection of computers and communications. Price available on request.

1468
Distribution
Chilton Co, Chilton Way, Radnor, PA 19089. Telephone (215) 687-8200.

Monthly magazine. Covers facets of physical distribution, including transportation, storage, handling, packaging, and containerization. Price $20.00.

1469
District Councils, Summary of Statements of Accounts, Northern Ireland
Her Majesty's Stationery Office, PO Box 569, London, England SE1 9NH. Telephone (44) (01) 928 1321.

Annual publication. Summarizes the district councils' statements of accounts in Northern Ireland. Price £1.50 per year.

1469.01
District of Columbia
Manufacturers' News, Inc, 3 Huron St, Chicago, IL 60611. Telephone (312) 337-1084.

Annual directory. Lists 4000 Maryland industrial firms by name, location, and product. Includes information on District of Columbia. Price $35.00.

1470
Dividend Record (Daily)
Standard & Poor's Corp, 25 Broadway, New York, NY 10004. Telephone (212) 248-2525.

Daily loose-leaf report. Contains dividend information on over 9800 listed and unlisted issues. Includes a notice of dividend meetings and the tax status of dividend supplements. Price $200.00 per year.

1471
Dividend Record (Weekly)
Standard & Poor's Corp, 345 Hudson St, New York, NY 10014. Telephone (212) 924-6400.

Weekly loose-leaf report. Contains details on stock dividends for over 9800 listed and unlisted issues. Includes a notice of dividend meetings and the tax status of dividend supplements. Price $100.00 per year.

1472
Dixie Business
Dixie Business, PO Box 119, Atlanta, GA 30301. Telephone (404) 289-7878.

Quarterly journal. Covers business news in the South. Price $5.00 per year.

1473

DLB Advanced Sales Reference Service

National Underwriter Co, 420 E 4th St, Cincinnati, OH 45202. Telephone (513) 721-2140.

Eight loose-leaf books and monthly updates. Cover all aspects of life insurance, including taxation, estate planning, and business insurance. Report on recent revenue rulings. Price $184.00 per year.

1474

DLB Agent's Service

National Underwriter Co, 420 E 4th St, Cincinnati, OH 45202. Telephone (513) 721-2140.

Three loose-leaf books and monthly updates. Discuss selling ideas for life insurance agents. Price $61.00 per year.

1475

DMS Aerospace Agencies

DMS, Inc, DMS Bldg, 100 Northfield St, Greenwich, CT 06830. Telephone (203) 661-7800. Telex 131526.

Monthly report. Discusses organization, budget, and current activities of US agencies involved in high technology aerospace systems. Includes data on specific projects and budgets. Price $585.00 per year.

1475.01

DMS Aerospace Companies

DMS, Inc, DMS Bldg, 100 Northfield St, Greenwich, CT 06830. Telephone (203) 661-7800. Telex 131526.

Monthly report. Covers sales, organization, and activities of 80 major US defense and aerospace contractors. Discusses programs and sales trends. Price $585.00 per year.

1475.02

DMS Aerospace Intelligence

DMS, Inc, DMS Bldg, 100 Northfield St, Greenwich, CT 06830. Telephone (203) 661-7800. Telex 131526.

Weekly newsletter. Presents information on US defense and aerospace policies. Notes research and development programs. Price $125.00 per year.

1475.03

DMS Agency Profile

DMS, Inc, DMS Bldg, 100 Northfield St, Greenwich, CT 06830. Telephone (203) 661-7800. Telex 131526.

Annual book. Lists 145 US defense agencies and indicates dollars each spent under relevant Federal Supply Classification code, Program Element number, or service code during the past three years. Price $430.00.

1475.04

DMS "AN" Equipment

DMS, Inc, DMS Bldg, 100 Northfield St, Greenwich, CT 06830. Telephone (203) 661-7800. Telex 131526.

Monthly report. Provides contracting data on 5000 US military electronic systems. Identifies all major components by agency, company, and contract. Price $585.00 per year.

1475.05

DMS Civil Aircraft

DMS, Inc, DMS Bldg, 100 Northfield St, Greenwich, CT 06830. Telephone (203) 661-7800. Telex 131526.

Monthly report. Monitors more than 125 commercial and general aviation aircraft and helicopters in development or production around the world. Includes data on current users, inventories, and performance. Price $585.00 per year.

1475.06

DMS Code Name Handbook

DMS, Inc, DMS Bldg, 100 Northfield St, Greenwich, CT 06830. Telephone (203) 661-7800. Telex 131526.

Annual book. Provides definitions for 12,-000 terms, acronyms, and codes used in defense and aerospace industries. Price $95.00.

1475.07

DMS Company Profile

DMS, Inc, DMS Bldg, 100 Northfield St, Greenwich, CT 06830. Telephone (203) 661-7800. Telex 131526.

Two-volume book. Lists 20,000 companies which were awarded defense contracts during the past three years. Indicates type of contract. Price $430.00.

1475.08

DMS Contracting Intelligence

DMS, Inc, DMS Bldg, 100 Northfield St, Greenwich, CT 06830. Telephone (203) 661-7800. Telex 131526.

Biweekly newsletter. Covers latest US military contracting information. Notes recent awards, supplemental contracts, and foreign military sales contracts. Price $200.00 per year.

1475.09

DMS Contract Quarterly (Agency CQ, Company CQ, County CQ, Production CQ, RDT&E & Service CQ)

DMS, Inc, DMS Bldg, 100 Northfield St, Greenwich, CT 06830. Telephone (203) 661-7800. Telex 131526.

Five-volume quarterly series. Provides information on defense contracts valued at more than $10,000 awarded during the previous three months. Notes company name and location, awarding agency, dollar amount, code and contract numbers. Price available on request.

1475.10

DMS Defense Budget Intelligence

DMS, Inc, DMS Bldg, 100 Northfield St, Greenwich, CT 06830. Telephone (203) 661-7800. Telex 131526.

Weekly newsletter. Covers US defense budgeting process from initial request through authorizations and appropriations. Price $125.00 per year.

1475.11

DMS Defense Market

DMS, Inc, DMS Bldg, 100 Northfield St, Greenwich, CT 06830. Telephone (203) 661-7800. Telex 131526.

Monthly report. Provides information on US defense programs and projects for each armed service. Includes detailed funding figures. Price $585.00 per year.

1475.12

DMS Defense Procurement Budget Handbook

DMS, Inc, DMS Bldg, 100 Northfield St, Greenwich, CT 06830. Telephone (203) 661-7800. Telex 131526.

Annual book. Lists every program element, project, or line item in the Defense Department's procurement budget request. Price $31.00.

1475.13

DMS Defense RDT & E Budget Handbook

DMS, Inc, DMS Bldg, 100 Northfield St, Greenwich, CT 06830. Telephone (203) 661-7800. Telex 131526.

Annual book. Lists every program element, project, or line item in the Defense Department's annual research and development budget request. Price $31.00.

1475.14
DMS Electronic Systems
DMS, Inc, DMS Bldg, 100 Northfield St, Greenwich, CT 06830. Telephone (203) 661-7800. Telex 131526.

Monthly report. Covers US electronic programs for military and civil applications. Notes budgets, contractors, and systems makeup. Price $585.00 per year.

1475.15
DMS Electronic Warfare
DMS, Inc, DMS Bldg, 100 Northfield St, Greenwich, CT 06830. Telephone (203) 661-7800. Telex 131526.

Monthly report. Provides information on electronic warfare systems. Notes airborne, sea-based, and land-based models for each program. Price $685.00 per year.

1475.16
DMS Foreign Military Sales CQ
DMS, Inc, DMS Bldg, 100 Northfield St, Greenwich, CT 06830. Telephone (203) 661-7800. Telex 131526.

Annual book. Details over 2,500 contracts in excess of $10,000 involving sales of US military equipment and services to foreign countries. Indicates company, awarding agency, and type. Price $452.00.

1475.17
DMS Gas Turbine Engines/Gas Turbine Markets
DMS, Inc, DMS Bldg, 100 Northfield St, Greenwich, CT 06830. Telephone (203) 661-7800. Telex 131526.

Monthly report. Discusses world use of gas turbine engines. Notes engines in development or production, Compares competing models within market areas. Price $1015.00 per year.

1475.18
DMS International Defense Intelligence
DMS, Inc, DMS Bldg, 100 Northfield St, Greenwich, CT 06830. Telephone (203) 661-7800. Telex 131526.

Weekly newsletter. Reports on developments in the international weapons market. Notes country requirements, pending negotiations, recent acquisitions, and deliveries. Price $125.00 per year.

1475.19
DMS Middle East/Africa
DMS, Inc, DMS Bldg, 100 Northfield St, Greenwich, CT 06830. Telephone (203) 661-7800. Telex 131526.

Monthly report. Covers arms purchases and requirements of 29 countries in the Middle East and Africa. Notes military organizations. Price $585.00 per year.

1475.20
DMS Military Aircraft
DMS, Inc, DMS Bldg, 100 Northfield St, Greenwich, CT 06830. Telephone (203) 661-7800. Telex 131526.

Monthly report. Discusses combat and support aircraft and helicopters in development or production worldwide. Notes aircraft variants, armament, contractors, and production status. Price $585.00 per year.

1475.21
DMS Military Laser & EO
DMS, Inc, DMS Bldg, 100 Northfield St, Greenwich, CT 06830. Telephone (203) 661-7800. Telex 131526.

Monthly report. Covers US military development and procurement programs involving lasers and electro–optical equipment. Notes contractors and funding. Price $685.00 per year.

1475.22
DMS Military Laser & EO Europe
DMS, Inc, DMS Bldg, 100 Northfield St, Greenwich, CT 06830. Telephone (203) 661-7800. Telex 131526.

Annual study. Covers all military applications of laser and electro-optical technology in Europe. Price $380.00.

1475.23
DMS Military Simulators
DMS, Inc, DMS Bldg, 100 Northfield St, Greenwich, CT 06830. Telephone (203) 661-7800. Telex 131526.

Monthly report. Discusses all military simulator and trainer programs funded by US. Includes current inventory and 5-year forecast. Price $685.00 per year.

1475.24
DMS Missiles & Satellites (Europe)
DMS, Inc, DMS Bldg, 100 Northfield St, Greenwich, CT 06830. Telephone (203) 661-7800. Telex 131526.

Monthly report. Provides information on major European missiles and spacecraft. Notes designation, originating authority, status, cost, quantity, users, and timetables. Price $685.00 per year.

1475.25
DMS Missiles/Spacecraft
DMS, Inc, DMS Bldg, 100 Northfield St, Greenwich, CT 06830. Telephone (203) 661-7800. Telex 131526.

Monthly report. Contains information on US missile and space programs in development or production. Notes sponsoring agencies, contractors, and applications. Price $585.00 per year.

1475.26
DMS NATO/Europe
DMS, Inc, DMS Bldg, 100 Northfield St, Greenwich, CT 06830. Telephone (203) 661-7800. Telex 131526.

Monthly report. Covers military purchases and requirements of NATO and 21 European countries. Discusses arms buying patterns and recent acquisitions. Price $585.00 per year.

1475.27
DMS NATO Weapons
DMS, Inc, DMS Bldg, 100 Northfield St, Greenwich, CT 06830. Telephone (203) 661-7800. Telex 131526.

Monthly report. Covers more than 80 NATO research and development, and procurement programs being jointly produced by two or more NATO countries. Price $685.00 per year.

1475.28
DMS Operation & Maintenance
DMS, Inc, Dms Bldg, 100 Northfield St, Greenwich, CT 06830. Telephone (203) 661-7800. Telex 131526.

Annual book. Identifies business opportunities at various facilities of the Department of Defense, Energy, NASA, and other government agencies. Analyzes the future level of activity at key installations. Price $755.00.

1475.29
DMS Radar & Sonar
DMS, Inc, DMS Bldg, 100 Northfield St, Greenwich, CT 06830. Telephone (203) 661-7800. Telex 131526.

Monthly report. Provides information on US radar and sonar systems. Notes designation, executive agency, contractors, status, mission, and funding. Price $685.00 per year.

1475.30
DMS Rapid Deployment Force
DMS, Inc, DMS Bldg, 100 Northfield St, Greenwich, CT 06830. Telephone (203) 661-7800. Telex 131526.

Annual study. Discusses Rapid Deployment Force concept. Includes equipment reports and forecasts. Price $755.00.

1475.31
DMS Ships/Vehicles/Ordnance
DMS, Inc, DMS Bldg, 100 Northfield St, Greenwich, CT 06830. Telephone (203) 661-7800. Telex 131526.

Monthly report. Covers US Navy, Coast Guard, and Marine Administration ships in development or construction. Price $585.00 per year.

1475.32
DMS South America/Australasia
DMS, Inc, DMS Bldg, 100 Northfield St, Greenwich, CT 06830. Telephone (203) 661-7800. Telex 131526.

Monthly report. Discusses military requirements and purchases by 32 countries in South America and Australasia. Notes arms buying patterns and recent acquisitions. Price $585.00 per year.

1475.33
DMS Tanks-Market Study and Forecast
DMS, Inc, DMS Bldg, 100 Northfield St, Greenwich, CT 06830. Telephone (203) 661-7800. Telex 131526.

Annual report. Discusses 40 tanks in development or production worldwide. Discusses marketing opportunities for each. Price $755.00.

1475.34
DMS Turbine Intelligence
DMS, Inc, DMS Bldg, 100 Northfield St, Greenwich, CT 06830. Telephone (203) 661-7800. Telex 131526.

Weekly newsletter. Reports on the international gas turbine engine market. Notes contracts, companies, product innovations, and personnel. Price $125.00 per year.

1475.35
DMS World Aircraft Forecast
DMS, Inc, DMS Bldg, 100 Northfield St, Greenwich, CT 06830. Telephone (203) 661-7800. Telex 131526.

Three-volume annual report. Provides 10-year forecast of all military and commercial aircraft production and inventories. Price $3265.00.

1475.36
DMS World Helicopter Forecast
DMS, Inc, DMS Bldg, 100 Northfield St, Greenwich, CT 06830. Telephone (203) 661-7800. Telex 131526.

Annual book. Contains inventories and 10-year forecasts for all military services and major commercial helicopter operators. Notes powerplant, number of engines, and weight of each helicopter. Price $1760.00.

1476
Doane's Agricultural Report
Doane Agricultural Service, Inc, 8900 Manchester Rd, St Louis, MO 63144. Telephone (314) 968-1000.

Weekly report. Advises farmers when to buy livestock, seed, and fertilizer and when to sell crops and livestock. Suggests new farm production and tax saving procedures. Price $34.50.

1477
Dodge Building Cost Calculator and Valuation Guide
McGraw-Hill Publications Co, 1221 Ave of the Americas, New York, NY 10020. Telephone (212) 997-1221. Telex TWX 7105814879 WUI 62555. Order from McGraw-Hill Information Systems Co, 1221 Ave of the Americas, New York, NY 10020.

Annual guide. Updates average construction costs per square foot for replacing or duplicating new and old buildings. Includes city and historical indexes. Updated three times a year. Price $89.00 per year.

1478
Dodge Bulletins
McGraw-Hill Publications Co, 1221 Ave of the Americas, New York, NY 10020. Telephone (212) 997-1221. Telex TWX 7105814879 WUI 62555.Order from McGraw-Hill Information Systems Co, 1221 Ave of the Americas, New York, NY 10020.

Information service. Compiles reports on planned construction projects in the US. Includes information on when projects will be ready for bidding and who will award contracts. Price available on request.

1479
Dodge Construction Potentials Bulletin
McGraw-Hill Publications Co, 1221 Ave of the Americas, New York, NY 10020. Telephone (212) 997-1221. Telex TWX 7105814879 WUI 62555. Order from McGraw-Hill Information Systems Co, 1221 Ave of the Americans, New York, NY 10020.

Monthly bulletin. Offers a statistical summary of new construction activity for the US and nine regional areas. Price available on request.

1480
Dodge Construction Systems Costs
McGraw-Hill Book Co, Hightstown-Princeton Rd, Hightstown, NJ 08520. Telephone (609) 448-1700. Telex 843449.

Annual publication. Provides cost data on building systems and assemblies. Enables architects to analyze the cost of design alternatives. Price $43.80.

1481
Dodge Digest of Building Costs and Specifications
McGraw-Hill Book Co, Hightstown-Princeton Rd, Hightstown, NJ 08520. Telephone (609) 448-1700. Telex 843449.

Semiannual digest. Provides specifications and successful bid data on recent building projects. Includes adjustment indexes for 184 metropolitan areas. Price $132.00.

1482
Dodge Guide for Estimating Public Works Construction Costs
McGraw-Hill Book Co, Hightstown-Princeton Rd, Hightstown, NJ 08520. Telephone (609) 448-1700. Telex 843449.

Annual book. Provides a guide to the costs for public works heavy construction projects. Offers data on materials, labor, equipment. Price $31.80.

1483
Dodge/Scan Microfilm System
McGraw-Hill Publications Co, 1221 Ave of the Americas, New York, NY 10020. Telephone (212) 997-1221. Telex TWX 7105814879 WUI 62555.

Daily service. Supplies construction bidding documents on 35 mm film to subconstractors and building product manufacturers and suppliers. Price available on request.

1483.01
Doing Business in Brazil
Matthew Bender & Co, 235 E 45th St, New York, NY 10017. Telephone (212) 661-5050.

Loose-leaf book. Examines business practices in Brazil. Includes information on changes in pertinent laws. Price $135.00.

1484
Doing Business in Canada
Matthew Bender & Co, 235 E 45th St, New York, NY 10017. Telephone (212) 661-5050.

Two volumes, book with periodic updates. Discusses how to establish a business in Canada. Notes federal and provincial legislation affecting business transactions. Price $215.00.

1486
Doing Business in Europe
Commerce Clearing House, Inc, 4025 W Peterson Ave, Chicago, IL 60646. Telephone (312) 583-8500.

Loose-leaf book, plus monthly reports. Provides an overview of company, tax, labor, and financial requirements for business operations in Europe. Price $325.00 per year.

1486.01
Doing Business in Japan
Matthew Bender & Co, 235 E 45th St, New York, NY 10017. Telephone (212) 661-5050.

Five-volume loose-leaf book. Provides information on Japan's business world. Includes information on statutes, laws, and court cases. Price $625.00.

1487
Doing Business In Mexico
Matthew Bender & Co, 235 E 45th St, New York, NY 10017. Telephone (212) 661-5050.

Two volumes. Discusses opportunities for US investment in Mexico. Covers taxation and legal aspects. Price $200.00.

1488
Doing Business in United States
Matthew Bender & Co, 235 E 45th St, New York, NY 10017. Telephone (212) 661-5050.

Six volume loose-leaf book with annual supplements. Offers information on doing business in US. Covers legal practices and tax laws. Price $360.00 plus additional charge for revisions.

1489
Doing Business with Eastern Europe
Business International Corp, 1 Dag Hammarskjold Plz, New York, NY 10017. Telephone (212) 750-6300.

Ten-volume, continuously updated reference service. Analyzes, in separate volumes for each East European country, the national market, political context, economy, foreign trade, sales promotion, financing, and trademarks. Price $1700.00 per year.

1490
Do It Yourself Retailing
Link House Publications Ltd, Link House, Dingwall Ave, Croydon, England CR9 2TA. Telephone (44) (01) 686-2599. Telex 947709.

Monthly magazine. Provides information to do-it-yourself and home inprovement shops and stores. Price £7.50 per year.

1491
Domestic and International Transportation of US Foreign Trade 1976
US Dept of Commerce, Bureau of Census, Washington, DC 20233. Telephone (202) 449-1600.

Two-volume report. Contains results of 1976 survey of domestic and international transportation of US foreign trade. Includes origin/destination study of the movement of foreign trade within the US. Price $10.75.

1492
Domestic Heating
Maclean-Hunter Ltd, 30 Old Burlington St, London, England W1X 2AE. Telephone (44) (01) 434-2233.

Monthly journal. Contains material on heating, plumbing, bathrooms, and kitchens for installers, contractors, and replacers in the domestic market. Price available on request.

1494
Dominion Report Service
CCH Canadian, Ltd, 6 Garamond Ct, Don Mills, Ont, Canada M3C 1Z5. Telephone (416) 429-2992.

Loose-leaf book, plus monthly updates. Summarizes and indexes all decisions appearing in Canadian law reports. Price $235.00 per year.

1495
Dominion Tax Cases
CCH Canadian, Ltd, 6 Garamond Ct, Don Mills, Ont, Canada M3C 1Z5. Telephone (416) 429-2992.

Loose-leaf book, plus three reports per month. Gives full texts and digests of all court and Tax Review Board decisions on Canadian federal tax questions. Price $195.00 per year.

1496
Dow Jones Commodities Handbook, 1977 edition
Dow Jones & Co, Inc, 22 Cortlandt St, New York, NY 10007. Order from Dow Jones & Co, Inc, PO Box 300, Princeton, NJ 08540. Telephone (212) 285-5000.

Book. Reviews commodities futures trading in 1976. Anticipates key factors in 1977 markets. Charts. Price $5.95. ISBN 0-87128-528-2.

1497
Dow Jones International Banking Wire
Dow Jones & Co, Inc, 22 Cortlandt St, New York, NY 10007. Telephone (212) 285-5000.

Continuous service. Covers international money markets. Gives interest and exchange rates, capital markets data, and major corporate developments. Price available on request.

1498
Dow Jones International Energy Wire
Dow Jones & Co, Inc, 22 Cortlandt St, New York, NY 10007. Telephone (212) 285-5000.

Continuous service. Reports on international petroleum, petrochemical, and other energy news. Includes price changes, drilling developments, and tanker activities. Price available on request.

1499
Dow Jones International News Wire
Dow Jones & Co, Inc, 22 Cortlandt St, New York, NY 10007. Telephone (212) 285-5000.

Continuous service. Covers international political, corporate, and investment news. Quotes exchange rates and stock and commodity prices. Price available on request.

1500
Dow Jones Investor's Handbook **1977 edition**
Dow Jones & Co, Inc, 22 Cortlandt St, New York, NY 10007. Order from Dow Jones & Co, Inc, PO Box 300, Princeton, NJ 08540. Telephone (212) 285-5000.

Book. Contains complete Dow Jones Averages through 1976. Covers common and preferred stocks and bonds on the New York Stock Exchange and American Stock Exchange and over 2000 over-the-counter securities quotations. Price $4.95. ISBN 0-87128-527-4.

1501

Dow Jones–Irwin Business Almanac

Dow Jones & Co, Inc, 22 Cortlandt St, New York, NY 10007. Order from Dow Jones–Irwin, 1818 Ridge Rd, Homewood, IL 60430. Telephone (212) 285-5000.

Annual book. Provides data on business, finance, and economics. Includes articles on tax, accounting, and labor developments. Tables and graphs. Price $9.95 (paperbound); $15.00 (hardbound).

1502

Dow Jones News/Retrieval

Dow Jones & Co, Inc, 22 Cortlandt St, New York, NY 10007. Telephone (212) 285-5000.

Continuous service. Covers news of 6000 major US corporations and other business matters. Price available on request.

1503

Dow Jones Securities Valuation Handbook, 1977 edition

Dow Jones & Co, Inc, 22 Cortlandt St, New York, NY 10007. Order from Dow Jones & Co, Inc, PO Box 300, Princeton, NJ 08540. Telephone (212) 285-5000.

Book. Provides the December 31, 1976, market values of all securities as required by the 1976 Tax Reform Act. Price $6.95 (paperbound); $9.95 (hardbound). ISBN 0-87128-540-1. ISBN 0-87128-541-X.

1504

Dow Jones Stock Options Handbook, 1977 edition

Dow Jones & Co, Inc, 22 Cortlandt St, New York, NY 10007. Order from Dow Jones & Co, Inc, PO Box 300, Princeton, NJ 08540. Telephone (212) 285-5000.

Book. Provides information on stock options. Summarizes information about companies whose common stocks underlie options. Price $5.95. ISBN 0-87128-531-2.

1504.01

Down To Business

Kennedy Sinclaire, Inc, 524 Hamburg Turnpike, PO Box 34, Wayne, NJ 07470. Telephone (201) 942-2000.

Monthly newsletter. Reports on business and management topics. Price $36.00 per year.

1505

Downtown Idea Exchange

Downtown Research and Development Center, 270 Madison Ave, Suite 1505, New York, NY 10016. Telephone (212) 889-5666.

A twice-monthly newsletter. Deals with revitalizing core cities. Provides data on malls, parking, transit, beautification, shopping, and housing. Price $67.00 per year.

1505.01

Downtown Implementation Guide

Downtown Research and Development Center, 270 Madison Ave, Suite 1505, New York, NY 10016. Telephone (212) 889-5666.

Monthly newsletter. Details legal powers, financial methods, administrative methods, and other tools for implementing plans, projects, and programs in central business districts. Price $73.00 per year.

1505.02

Drapers Record

Northwood Publications Ltd, Elm House, 10-16 Elm St, London, England WC1X OBP. Order from Subscription Manager, 23-29 Emerald St, London, England WC1N 3QJ. Telephone (44) (01) 404-5531. Telex 21746.

Weekly publication. Covers Britain's women's wear, children's wear, textiles, and accessories sections of retail trade. Includes furnishings, yardgoods, handknit yarns, and shoes. Price £27.50 United Kingdom, £55.00 overseas.

1505.03

Drilling Service

Data Resources, Inc, 29 Hartwell Ave, Lexington, MA 02173. Telephone (617) 861-0165.

Quarterly report. Provides data base of historical behavior of oil and gas drilling industry. Forecasts drilling activity, reserve additions, and production of crude oil and natural gas. Price available on request.

1505.04

Drop Shipping News

Consolidated Marketing Services, Inc, PO Box 3328, New York, NY 10017. Telephone (212) 688-8797.

Newsletter. Covers all facets of drop shipping. Includes product sources. Discusses selling products (without inventory) for future delivery through mail order methods using drop shipping. Price $2.00.

1506

Drop Shipping Source Directory of Major Consumer Product Lines, 1977

Consolidated Marketing Services, Inc, PO Box 3328, New York, NY 10017. Telephone (212) 688-8797.

Directory. Lists firms that will make drop shipments of single units of over 57,000 products direct to consumer for retailers, mail order firms, and other establishments. Lists products that are divided into 25 classifications. Price $7.00. ISBN 0-917626-01-X.

1507

Drug & Cosmetic Catalog

Harcourt Brace Jovanovich Publications, 757 3rd Ave, New York, NY 10017. Order from Harcourt Brace and Jovanovich Publications, 1 E 1st St, Duluth, MN 55802. Telephone (218) 727-8511.

Annual catalog. Lists the sources of raw materials, equipment, packaging components, and services for drug and cosmetic manufacturers and distributers. Price $10.00 per copy.

1508

Drug & Cosmetic Industry

Harcourt Brace Jovanovich Publications, 757 3rd Ave, New York, NY 10017. Order from Harcourt Brace and Jovanovich Publications, 1 E 1st St, Duluth, MN 55802. Telephone (218) 727-8511.

Monthly magazine. Covers developments in the drug and cosmetic industries. Notes regulatory action and new products. Price $10.00 per year.

1508.01

Drug License Opportunities

IMS World Publications Ltd, York House, 37 Queen Sq, London, England WCIN 3BE. Telephone (44) (01) 242-0112. Telex 263298.

Semiannual publication, with annual index. Reports on potential drug license opportunities throughout the world. Discusses research developments. Price available on request.

1509
Drug Product Liability
Matthew Bender & Co, 235 W 45th St, New York, NY 10017. Telephone (212) 661-5050.

Loose-leaf book, with annual supplements. Reports on the drug trade, including quality control and marketing, Price $70.00 per volume; $25.00 for update.

1509.01
Drug Store News
Lebhar-Friedman Publications, Inc, 425 Park Ave, New York, NY 10022. Telephone (212) 371-9400.

Fortnightly report. Covers trade news and trends in the chain drug store industry. Price $10.00 per year.

1510
Drug Topics
Medical Economics Co, 680 Kinderkamack Rd, Oradell, NJ 07649. Telephone (201) 262-3030.

Report issued 23 times per year. Provides information on issues affecting drugstores. Price $26.00 per year. ISSN 0012-6616.

1511
Dun & Bradstreet Composite Register
Dun & Bradstreet, Box 3224, Church St Station, New York, NY 10008. Telephone (212) 285-7346.

Annual book. Lists over 200,000 British businesses representing all industries and trades. Provides bank of account and credit recommendation. Price available on request, to Dun & Bradstreet subscribers only.

1512
Dun & Bradstreet Handbook of Credits and Collections
Dun & Bradstreet, Inc, Box 3224, Church St, Station, New York, NY 10008. Telephone (212) 285-7000.

Book. Addresses the theory and practice of credit management. Price $20.00. ISBN 0-690-00590-3.

1513
Dun & Bradstreet Metalworking Marketing Directory
Dun & Bradstreet, Inc, Box 3224, Church St Station, New York, NY 10008. Telephone (212) 285-7346.

Annual book. Offers a list of US metalworking, producing, and distributing operations, with descriptive details on each. Price available on request.

1514
Dun & Bradstreet Reference Book
Dun & Bradstreet, Box 3224, Church St Station, New York, NY 10008. Telephone (212) 285-7346.

Bimonthly book. Lists and rates the financial strength of companies. Notes new business and credit ratings. Price available on request, to Dun & Bradstreet subscribers only.

1515
Dun & Bradstreet Standard Register
Dun & Bradstreet, Box 3224, Church St Station, New York, NY 10008. Telephone (212) 285-7346.

Annual book. Lists over 200,000 businesses. Includes the date of formation, ownership, bank of account, and credit information. Price available on request, to Dun & Bradstreet subscribers only.

1516
Dunn & Hargitt Commodity Service
Dunn & Hargitt, Inc, 22 N 2nd St, Lafayette, IN 47902. Telephone (317) 423-2624.

Weekly newsletter. Advises on the commodity futures market. Analyzes the price outlook for major commodities. Charts of most active contracts. Price $125.00 per year.

1517
Dunn & Hargitt Market Guide
Dunn & Hargitt, Inc, 22 N 2nd St, Lafayette, IN 47902. Telephone (317) 423-2624.

Weekly newsletter. Provides investment advice on stocks and options based on analyses for 1000 leading stocks. Price $95.00 per year.

1519
Dunhill Marketing Guide to Mailing Lists
Dunhill International List Co, Inc, 419 Park Ave S, New York, NY 10016. Telephone (212) 686-3700.

Book. Provides a subject directory to mailing lists. Indicates the cost of the lists and other pertinent data. Price free of charge.

1520
Duns World Letter
Dun & Bradstreet, Box 3224, Church St Station, New York, NY 10008. Telephone (212) 285-7346.

Quarterly newsletter. Contains articles of general international business interest. Assesses current economic trends. Price available on request, to Dun & Bradstreet subscribers only.

1521
Earnings Forecaster
Standard & Poor's Corp, 25 Broadway, New York, NY 10004. Telephone (212) 248-2525.

Weekly newsletter. Provides new and revised earnings estimates for over 1600 companies. Price $231.00 per year.

1522
Earth Surface Processes and Landforms
John Wiley and Sons, Inc, 605 3rd Ave, New York, NY 10158. Telephone (212) 867-9800.

Bimonthly journal. Presents research papers on all aspects of process geomorphology. Covers sediment transfer on hillslopes and rivers, hydrology, weathering and surface geochemistry, soil dynamics and mechanics, and solute and nutrient cycling. Price $170.00 per year.

1522.01
East Asian Economic Service
Data Resources, Inc, 29 Hartwell Ave, Lexington, MA 02173. Telephone (617) 861-0165.

Quarterly report. Forecasts foreign debt positions, inflation rates, domestic demand, production, wages, interest rates, money supply, and balance of payments for South Korea, Taiwan, Australia, Hong Kong, China, India, the Philippines, and other East Asian countries. Price available on request.

1523
Eastern Europe
London Chamber of Commerce & Industry, 69-75 Cannon St, London, England EC4N 5AB. Telephone (44) (01) 248-4444 Ext. 176. Telex 888941.

Biweekly report. Analyzes commercial and economic developments in Eastern Europe. Price £108.00 per year, £126.00 foreign.

1524
Eastern European Economics
M E Sharpe, Inc, 80 Business Park Dr, Armonk, NY 10504. Telephone (914) 273-1800.

Quarterly journal. Contains translations of current writings in economics from East Europe. Price $127.00 per year.

1525
Eastwest Business Cooperation and Joint Ventures
Chase World Information Corp, 1 World Trade Center, Suite 4627, New York, NY 10048. Telephone (212) 552-3378. RCA 235444. WU: 141489.

Series of nine reports, one each for Yugoslavia, Hungary, Poland, Rumania, Czechoslovakia, Bulgaria, German Democratic Republic, the Union of Soviet Socialist Republics, and a ninth covering all of East Europe. Provides guidelines for establishing and conducting successful business relations in the particular country or region. Price $1000.00 for full series.

1526
East-West Markets
Chase World Information Corp, 1 World Trade Center, Suite 4627, New York, NY 10048. Telephone (212) 552-3378. Telex RCA 235444. WU: 141489.

Biweekly newsletter. Analyzes business developments, economic plans, and legislation of Eastern Europe and the Union of Soviet Socialist Republics, with emphasis on East-West trade. Price $375.00 per year.

1527
East/West Technology Digest
Welt Publishing Co, 1511 K St NW, Washington, DC 20005. Telephone (202) 737-8080.

Monthly report. Reviews new Soviet and Eastern European technology. Lists patented inventions, research discoveries, and case studies of East-West licensing agreements. Price $175.00 per year.

1528
East-West Trade Council Newsletter
East-West Trade Council, 1700 Pennsylvania Ave NW, Suite 670, Washington, DC 20006. Telephone (202) 393-6240.

Biweekly newsletter. Covers US trade opportunities with socialist countries, including the Union of Soviet Socialist Republics, Eastern Europe, and Cuba. Price $500.00 (membership included).

1529
Ebasco Cost Newsletter
Ebasco Services, Inc, 2 Rector St, New York, NY 10006. Telephone (212) 785-2200.

Quarterly newsletter. Gives information on the impact of inflation and cost trends on construction materials and labor. Price free of charge.

1530
Ebasco News
Ebasco Services, Inc, 2 Rector St, New York, NY 10006. Telephone (212) 785-2200.

Bimonthly magazine. Features articles and graphics relevant to Ebasco Services's engineering, construction, and consulting activities in the energy and utility fields. Price free of charge.

1531
Ebasco's Analysis of Public Utility Financing
Ebasco Services, Inc, 2 Rector St, New York, NY 10006. Telephone (212) 785-2200.

Annual book. Analyzes investor-owned utility financing and private issues. Quarterly supplements and weekly reports. Price $160.00 per year.

1532
Eco/Log Canadian Pollution Legislation
Corpus Information Services, Ltd, 1450 Don Mills Rd., Don Mills, Ont, Canada M3B 2X7. Telephone (416) 445-7101. Telex 06-966612.

Three-volume loose-leaf compilation, plus bimonthly updating. Covers all Canadian pollution-control laws, regulations, and guidelines. Price $245.00 (Canadian) for binders; $195.00 (Canadian) per year for updating service.

1533
Eco/Log Week
Corpus Information Services Ltd, 1450 Don Mills Rd, Don Mills, Ont, Canada M5S 2X7. Telephone (416) 445-7101. Telex 06-966612.

Weekly newsletter. Gives information about Canadian industrial pollution control, including waste management and the transportation of hazardous goods. Price $247.00 (Canadian) per year.

1533.01
Ecology USA
Business Publishers, Inc, PO Box 1067, Silver Spring, MD 20910. Telephone (301) 587-6300.

Biweekly newsletter. Covers ecological research and news. Price $62.00 per year.

1534
Econometrica
Econometric Society, Dept of Economics, Northwestern University, 2003 Sheridan Rd, Evanston, IL 60201. Order from Econometrica, Econometric Society, Department of Economics, Northwestern University, 2003 Sheridan Road, Evanston, IL 60201. Telephone Evanston (312) 492-3615.

Bimonthly journal. Features articles on economic theory in relation to statistics and mathematics. Tables. Price $36.00 individuals, $63.00 libraries and institutions.

1535
Economic Analysis & Policy
Economic Society of Australia & New Zealand, Queensland Branch, Dept of Economics, University of Queensland, St Lucia, Brisbane, Australia 4067.

Biannual journal. Discusses economic issues, with emphasis on the Australian economy and industry. Includes research topics. Price $9.00 (Australian) per year.

1536
Economic & Financial Review
Consulate General of Nigeria, 575 Lexington Ave, New York, NY 10022. Telephone (212) PL2-1670.

Periodic report. Reviews economic conditions in Nigeria. Price free of charge.

1536.01
Economic and Social Commission for Asia and the Pacific
United National Economic and Social Commission for Asia and the Pacific, The United Nations Bldg, Rajadamnern Ave, Bangkok 2, Thailand. Telephone 2829161-200, 2829381-389. Telex 82392 ESCAP TH, 82315 ESCAP TH.

Annual report. Reviews economic and social developments in Asia and the Pacific. English and French editions. Price $14.00.

1537
Economic & Social Committee of the European Communities. Bulletin
Economic & Social Committee of the European Communities, 2 rue Ravenstein, Brussels, Belgium. Telephone 512 39 20. Telex 25983.

Monthly report. Contains summaries on opinions by the Economic & Social Committee of European Communities on the European community's draft legislation. Price free of charge.

1538
Economic & Social Progress in Latin America Annual Report
Inter-American Development Bank, 808 17th St, NW, Washington, DC 20577. Telephone (202) 634-8000.

Annual book. Presents a detailed review of the economic and social developments in Latin America, with regional descriptions and country-by-country analyses. Statistics. Available on request.

1539
Economic and Social Science Research Assn (ESSRA) Magazine
Economic and Social Science Research Assn, 177 Vauxhall Bridge Rd, London, England SW 1.

Magazine issued three times per year. Publishes articles and news dealing with the fundamentals of economics. Price £1.00 per year. ISSN 0307-1901.

1540
Economic & Social Survey of Asia & the Pacific
United Nations Economic & Social Commission for Asia & the Pacific, United Nations Bldg, Bangkok 2, Thailand. Telephone 813544.

Annual publication. Covers Asian and Pacific economic developments. Subjects include agriculture, industry, transport, trade and payments, monetary and fiscal problems, and development planning. Price $10.00.

1541
Economic Briefs
United States Federal Home Loan Bank Board, 1700 G St NW, Washington, DC 20552. Telephone (202) 377-6687.

Monthly report. Discusses housing and mortgage trends. Indicates housing starts, vacancy rates, housing sales, and the financial situation of savings and loan associations. Price free of charge.

1543
Economic Bulletin for Africa
United Nations Publications, Rm A-3315, New York, NY 10017. Telephone (212) 754-8302.

Irregular report. Provides information on African economic development in agriculture, industry, transport, and public finance. Price available on request.

1544
Economic Bulletin for Asia and the Far Pacific
United Nations Publications, United Nations Plz, Rm A-3315, New York, NY 10017. Telephone (212) 754-8302.

Report. Provides statistics and other information on Asian and Far Eastern economies. Price available on request.

1545
Economic Bulletin for Asia & the Pacific
United Nations Economic & Social Commission for Asia & the Pacific, United Nations Bldg, Bangkok 2, Thailand. Telephone 813544.

Report published three times per year. Provides information on Asian and Pacific economic trends. Covers agriculture, trade, industry, finance, and development. Price $5.00.

1546
Economic Bulletin for Europe
United Nations Publications, Rm A-3315, New York, NY 10017. Telephone (212) 754-8302.

Report. Gives statistics and other economic information for Europe. Price available on request.

1547
Economic Bulletin for Latin America
United Nations Publications, Rm A-3315, New York, NY 10017. Telephone (212) 754-8302.

Report. Provides statistics and other information dealing with economics in Latin America. Price available on request.

1547.01
Economic Census of Outlying Areas, 1977, OAC77
US Dept of Commerce, Bureau of Census, Washington, DC 20233. Telephone (202) 449-1600.

Six reports. Cover 1977 census information on construction, manufacturing, and other industries in Puerto Rico, Virgin Islands, and Guam. Price available on request.

1548
Economic Development & Cultural Change
University of Chicago Press, 5801 S Ellis Ave, Chicago, IL 60637. Telephone (312) 753-3347.

Quarterly journal. Discusses the economic growth and change factors from social, demographic, political, historical, and anthropological viewpoints. Price $35.00 per year. ISSN 0013-0079.

1550
Economic Education Bulletin
American Inst for Economic Research, Great Barrington, MA 01230. Telephone (413) 528-1216.

Monthly report. Discusses general economic and personal finance subjects, including economic theories, the use of statistical indicators to forecast business conditions, annuities, and life insurance. Price $10.00 per year (includes membership in AIER).

1551
Economic Handbook of the Machine Tool Industry
National Machine Tool Builders' Assn, 7901 Westpark Dr, McLean, VA 22102. Telephone (703) 893-2900.

Annual publications. Gives current and historical facts and statistics about the machine tool industry in the US and world trade in machine tools. Price $15.00, plus $2.50 postage and handling.

1552
Economic Indicators
Consulate General of Nigeria, 575 Lexington Ave, New York, NY 10022. Telephone (212) PL2-1670.

Monthly report. Covers Nigeria's economic indicators. Price 35 kobo.

1552.01
Economic Indicators of the Farm Sector: Income and Balance Sheet Statistics
US Dept of Agriculture, ESS Publications, Room 0054-S, Washington, DC 20250. Telephone (202) 447-7255.

Annual report. Covers material relevant to farm assets and debts. Price free of charge.

1552.02
Economic Indicators of the Farm Sector: Production and Efficiency Statistics
US Dept of Agriculture, ESS Publications, Room 0054-S, Washington, DC 20250. Telephone (202) 447-7255.

Annual report. Contains current information on farm production, labor productivity, and farm mechanization; 1976 issue provides historical data. Price free of charge.

1553

Economic Inquiry

Western Economic Assn, Dept of Economics, California State University, Long Beach, CA 90840. Telephone (213) 498-5067.

Quarterly journal. Discusses economic topics and research. Includes articles on monetary policy, unemployment, taxation, and prices. Price $65.00 per year.

1554

Economic Journal

Cambridge University Press, 32 E 57th St, New York, NY 10022. Telephone (212) 688-8885.

Quarterly journal. Covers economics theory and applications and related subjects. Price $75.00 per year.

1555

Economic News Bulletin

New Zealand Economic News Ltd, PO Box 1026, Wellington, New Zealand

Weekly report. Covers economic conditions in New Zealand. Price $55.00 (New Zealand).

1556

Economic News from Italy

Elite Publishing Corp, 11-03 46th Ave, Long Island City, NY 11101. Telephone (212) 937-4606.

Weekly newsletter. Reports on Italian political and economic developments. Price $40.00 per year, $50.00 foreign.

1556.01

Economic News of Bulgaria

Bulgarian Chamber of Commerce and Industry, 11a Stamboliiski Blvd, Sofia, Bulgaria 104. Telephone 87-54-75, 87-26-31.

Monthly newspaper. Reports on Bulgarian economic developments. Notes activities of the Bulgarian Chamber of Commerce and Industry. Price available on request.

1556.02

Economic Opportunity Report

Capitol Publications, Inc, Suite G-12, 2430, Pennsylvania Ave, NW, Washington, DC 20037. Telephone (202) 452-1600.

Weekly newsletter. Focuses on federal actions which affect Community Action Agencies and other federally supported poverty programs. Price $149.00 per year.

1557

Economic Outlook

Gower Publishing Co Ltd, 1 Westmead, Farnborough, Hampshire, England GU14 7RU. Telephone Farnborough (0252) 519221. Telex 858623.

Monthly magazine. Gives a four-year business forecast for the British economy. Includes computer-generated tabulations. Price $130.00.

1558

Economic Outlook: California Report

Bank of America, Editorial Services, Dept 3124, Box 37000, San Francisco, CA 94137. Telephone (415) 622-5515.

Annual report. Analyzes California's economic developments and presents forecasts on income and sales, inflation, employment, residential construction, and agriculture. Includes regional analyses. Charts. Price free of charge.

1559

Economic Outlook: Global Report

Bank of America, Editorial Services, Dept 3124, Box 37000, San Francisco, CA 94137. Telephone (415) 622-5515.

Annual report. Discusses international economic trends and forecasts growth for individual regions and countries. Notes current balance of payments and inflation rates. Tables. Price free of charge.

1560

Economic Outlook: US Report

Bank of America, Editorial Services, Dept 3124, Box 37000, San Francisco, CA 94137. Telephone (415) 622-5515.

Annual report. Presents information on US economic growth and evaluates future growth. Discusses inflation, capital investment, and financial market trends. Tables and charts. Price free of charge.

1561

Economic Overview

Capital Communications Ltd, Suite 705, Burnside Bldg, 151 Slater St, Ottawa, Ont, Canada K1P 5H3. Telephone (613) 235-9183. Telex 053-3601.

Quarterly newsletter. Analyzes the economic indicators and fiscal and monetary policies of Canada and its major trading partners. Price $50.00 per year.

1562

Economic Perspective

Federal Reserve Bank of Chicago, Public Information Center, PO Box 834, Chicago, IL 60690. Telephone (312) 322-5112.

Bimonthly magazine. Discusses business, economic, and banking issues and focuses on the Seventh Federal Reserve District. Price free of charge.

1563

Economic Planning

Academic Publishing Co, PO Box 42, Snowden Station, Montreal, 26 Que, H3X 2H7. Canada. Telephone (514) 737-7615.

Bimonthly magazine. Covers agricultural policies at the international level and economic planning. Price $8.00 US and Canada, $10.00 overseas per year.

1564

Economic Profile of Britain

Lloyds Bank Ltd, PO Box 215, 71 Lombard St, London, England EC3P 3BS. Telephone (44) (01) 626-1500.

Annual pamphlet. Gives the economic picture of Great Britain, including information on national production and incomes, employment, industry, agriculture, banking, and finance. Price free of charge.

1565

Economic Regulation of Business and Industry

R R Bowker Co, 1180 Ave of the Americas, New York, NY 10036. Order from R R Bowker Co, PO Box 1807, Ann Arbor, MI 48106. Telephone (212) 764-5100.

Five books. Document origins and growth of nine US federal regulatory agencies. Price $192.50. ISBN 0-8352-0694-7.

1566

Economic Report

London Chamber of Commerce & Industry, 69-75 Cannon St, London, England EC4N 5AB. Telephone (44) (01) 248-4444 Ext.173. Telex 888941.

Monthly report. Summarizes economic trends in Great Britain. Price £24.00 per year.

1567

Economic Report

Manufacturers Hanover Trust Co, Corporate Communications Dept, 350 Park Ave, New York, NY 10022. Telephone (212) 350-3300. Telex 232337, 420966, 62814, 82615.

Monthly report. Covers the world economy, including foreign trade. Price free of charge.

1568
Economic Report of the President
US Council of Economic Advisors, Executive Office Bldg, Washington, DC 20506.

Annual book. Publishes the economic report of the US president transmitted to Congress and the report of the Council of Economic Advisors. Includes information on world economy. Statistical tables on income, employment, and production. Price $2.90.

1569
Economic Review
Commercial Bank of Australia Ltd, 114 William St, Melbourne, Vic 3000, Australia. Telephone (61) (03) 607-7222.

Quarterly report. Covers the economic and financial conditions in Australia and New Zealand. Charts and graphs. Price free of charge.

1570
Economic Review
Federal Reserve Bank of Atlanta, Research Dept, PO Box 1731, Atlanta, GA 30301. Telephone (404) 586-8788.

Bimonthly report. Examines economic issues, focusing on the Federal Reserve Sixth District area. Charts and tables. Price free of charge.

1571
Economic Review
Federal Reserve Bank of Kansas City, 925 Grand Ave, Kansas City, MO 64198. Telephone (816) 881-2000.

Journal published 10 times per year. Contains articles on economics, banking, and business. Price free of charge.

1571.01
Economic Road Maps
Conference Board, Inc, 845 3rd Ave, New York, NY 10022. Telephone (212) 759-0900.

Semimonthly report. Presents graphic summaries on various economic and management facts of general interest. Price available on request.

1571.02
Economics Letters
North-Holland Publishing Co, PO Box 211, 1000 AE Amsterdam, The Netherlands. Order from Elsevier Sequoia SA, PO Box 851, CH-1001 Lausanne 1, Switzerland.

Journal published eight times per year. Contains concise reports of new results, models, and methods in all fields of economic research. Price $130.50 per year. ISSN 0165-1765.

1572
Economic Survey of Switzerland
Consulate General of Switzerland, 444 Madison Ave, New York, NY 10022. Telephone (212) 758-2560.

Annual report. Reviews Switzerland's economic trends. Provides information on selected industries, trades, and professions. Index of reports. Price free of charge.

1572.01
Economic Titles/Abstracts
Martinus Nijhoff, 9-11 Lange Voorhout, The Hague, The Netherlands. Order from Martinus Nijhoff, 9-11 Lange Voorhout, PO Box 269, The Hague, The Netherlands.

Semimonthly review. Contains abstracts of economic articles. Notes books, special studies, and reports. Includes information on business topics. Price available on request.

1573
Economic Trends
Her Majesty's Stationery Office, PO Box 569, London, England SE1 9NH. Telephone (44) (01) 928 1321.

Monthly service. Contains key British economic indicators: personal income and consumption, retail sales, employment, balance of payments, and others. Price £ 6.45 per year.

1574
Economic Trends Annual Supplement
Her Majesty's Stationery Office, PO Box 569, London, England SE1 9NH. Telephone (44) (01) 928 1321.

Annual supplement. Supplies up to 30-year runs of British economic data. Gives notes and definitions for economic trends and includes a calendar of economic events for the previous year. Price £88.74 per year.

1575
Economic Week
Citibank, Economics Dept, 399 Park Ave, New York, NY 10022. Telephone (212) 559-4022.

Weekly newsletter. Reports on US economic trends. Includes such issues as consumer prices, construction activity, exchange rates, and inventories. Price $110.00 per year.

1576
Economist
Economist Newspaper Ltd, 25 St James's St, London, England SW1A 1HG. Telephone 01 839-7000. Telex 24344.

Weekly news magazine. Covers economic and political news and trends in the United Kingdom and world wide. Price: UK £35, Europe £40, Rest of World £50, USA and Canada US $85.00.

1577
Economy
University of New Mexico, Bureau of Business and Economic Research, Institute for Applied Research Services, Albuquerque, NM 87131. Telephone (505) 277-2216.

Annual report. Evaluates New Mexico's economy, providing related data on employment, agriculture, mining, and manufacturing. Tables. Price free of charge.

1578
Economy of Arizona
Arizona Dept of Economic Security, Manpower Information and Analysis Section, PO Box 6123, Phoenix, AZ 85005. Telephone (602) 271-3871.

Biannual report. Covers economic conditions in Arizona and the US generally. Price free of charge.

1579
Economy of Hawaii
Hawaii State Dept of Planning and Economic Development, PO Box 2359, Honolulu, HI 96804. Telephone (808) 548-4620.

Annual report. Provides an immediate, long-range look at economic conditions in Hawaii. Price free while copies last.

1580
Econoscope View
General Electric Co, Business Growth Services, Building 5-311, 1 River Rd, Schenectady, NY 12345. Telephone (518) 385-2128.

Quarterly report and annual issue. Discusses the prevailing economic conditions for US industries. Covers consumer patterns for over 95 industries. Price $120.00 per year.

1583
Edison Electric Institute (EEI)
Pocketbook of Electric Utility Industry
Statistics
Edison Electric Inst, 1111 19th St, NW, Washington, DC 20036. Telephone (202) 828-7400.

Annual report. Summarizes electric utility industry statistics. Includes data on capacity and production, capital and finance, sales and customers. Price $1.25.

1584
Edison Electric Institute (EEI)
Statistical Year Book
Edison Electric Inst, 1111 19th St, WN, Washington, DC 20036. Telephone (202) 828-7400.

Annual book. Supplies electric utility industry statistics. Includes such subjects as generating capacity, operations, ratios, and customers. Price $15.00.

1584.01
Editor & Publisher
Editor & Publisher, 575 Lexington Ave, New York, NY 10022. Telephone (212) 752-7050. Telex 12-5102.

Weekly magazine. Covers the newspaper business. Notes new production and editing methods, personnel changes, and awards. Price $40.00 per year.

1585
Editor & Publisher Market Guide
Editor & Publisher Co, Inc, 575 Lexington Ave, New York, NY 10022. Telephone (212) 752-7050.

Annual report. Contains market statistics for US and Canadian cities with newspapers. Price $35.00.

1586
Edmonton and Area Manufacturers
Directory
Edmonton Business Development Dept, 2410 Oxford Tower, 10235 101 St, Edmonton, Alberta, Canada T5J 3G1. Telephone (403) 425-5464

Annual directory. Offers a guide to manufacturing firms in the Edmonton, Alberta, area. Price available upon request.

1587
Edmonton Economic Report
Edmonton Business Development Dept, 2410 Oxford Tower, 10235 101 St, Edmonton, Alberta, Canada T5J 1S6. Telephone (403) 425-5464.

Annual report. Provides economic indicators for Edmonton, Alberta metropolitan area. Price free of charge.

1588
Edmonton Report on Business and
Travel Development
Edmonton Business Development Dept, 2410 Oxford Tower, 10235 101 St, Edmonton, Alberta, Canada T5J 3G1. Telephone (403) 425-5464.

Monthly newsletter. Highlights business, industrial, and travel development activities in the Edmonton, Alberta region. Price free of charge.

1589
EDP (Electronic Data Processing)
Auditing
Auerbach Publishers, Inc, 6560 N Park Dr, Pennsauken, NJ 08109. Telephone (609) 662-2070. Telex 831 464.

Book, updated bimonthly. Provides information on performing EDP audits in any industry. Includes material on system environment, management controls, audit planning and methodology, and auditing case studies. Price $160.00.

1590
EDP (Electronic Data Processing)
Industry Report
International Data Corp, 214 Third Ave, Waltham, MA 02254. Telephone (617) 890-3700. Telex 92-3401.

Bimonthly newsletter. Provides latest developments in computer-based information processing. Price available on request.

1590.01
EDP Electronic Data Processing Japan
Report
International Data Corp, 214 Third Ave, Waltham, MA 02254. Telephone (617) 890-3700. Telex 92-3401.

Semimonthly newsletter. Covers latest developments in Japanese computer–communications industry. Price available on request.

1590.02
Education
Longman Group Ltd, Longman House, Burnt Mill, Harlow, Essex England CM20 2JE. Telephone Harlow 26721. Telex 81259.

Weekly magazine. Reports on British educational topics including new products, school buildings, and school meals. Price $78.00 per year. ISSN 0013-1164.

1591
Educational Financial Aids (JJ4), **1981**
American Assn of University Women, Sales Office, 2401 Virginia Ave NW, Washington, DC 20037. Telephone (202) 785-7772.

Booklet on fellowships, scholarships, and internships in higher education available to women. Price $1.00.

1592
Educational Marketer
Knowledge Industry Publications, 701 Westchester Ave, White Plains, NY 10604. Telephone (914) 694-8686.

Biweekly newsletter relevant to the educational market. Gives sales of textbooks and audiovisual materials and reports on federal education funding and school enrollment trends. Price $115.00 per year. ISSN 0013-1806.

1593
Education and Work
Capital Publications, Inc, Suite G-12-2430, Pennsylvania Ave, NW, Washington, DC 20037. Telephone (202) 452-1600.

Biweekly newsletter. Reports on national career education news. Covers Comprehensive Employment and Training Act developments and youth employment issues. Price $103.00 per year.

1596
Education Statistics for the UK
Her Majesty's Stationery Office, PO Box 569, London, England SE1 9NH. Telephone (44) (01) 928 1321.

Annual publication. Provides education statistics for Great Britain. Price £6.00 per year.

1597
Education Year Book **1981**
Longman Group Ltd, Longman House, Burnt Mill, Harlow, Essex, England CM20 2JE. Telephone Harlow 26721. Telex 81259.

Annual book. Provides information about British schools, colleges, local education authorities, and teachers' organizations. Includes information on where to buy educational supplies. Price £18.95.

1597.01
EEC/ASIA Report
Europe Information Service, 46 Ave Albert Elisabeth, Brussels, Belgium 1040. Telephone (32) (02) 736.11.93. Telex Eurinf 26005b.

Monthly report. Covers developments in relations between the European Economic Community and the countries of South and Southeast Asia. Discusses trade, foreign aid, and investment news. Price $270.00 per year.

1597.02
EEC Competition Law Reporter
Matthew Bender & Co, 235 E 45th St, New York, NY 10017. Telephone (212) 661-5050.

Seven-volume book. Covers European Economic Community competition law. Includes Commission decisions, court judgments, and settlements. Price $500.00.

1598
E E/Epargne Europe
European Economic Community Savings Bank Group, 92-94 Square E Plasky, 1040 Brussels, Belgium. Telephone 736 80 47.

Newsletter issued three times per month. Covers the activities and observations of the European Economic Community Savings Bank Group and its members. Price 850 Belgian francs.

1598.01
Effective Manager
Warren, Gorham & Lamont, Inc, 210 S St, Boston, MA 02111. Telephone (800) 225-2263.

Monthly report. Discusses practical strategies for managers. Notes new research findings. Price $42.00 per year.

1598.02
Egypt/North Africa
IPC Publications Ltd, 122 E 42nd St, Suite 1121, New York, NY 10017. Telephone (212) 867-5159. Telex 425442.

Biweekly newsletter. Reports on commercial prospects, trade contacts, and government regulations in Egypt. Price $395.00 per year.

1598.03
EIS
Information Resources Press, 1700 N Moore St, Suite 700A, Arlington, VA 22209. Telephone (703) 558-8270.

Monthly report. Abstracts and indexes environmental impact statements issued by federal government. Price $150.00 per year.

1599
Elastomerics
Communication Channels, Inc, 6285 Barfield Rd, Atlanta, GA 30328. Telephone (404) 256-9800.

Monthly magazine. Focuses on compounding, processing, and testing of elastomers. Price $21.00 per year.

1600
Electrical Construction and Maintenance
McGraw-Hill Publications Co, 1221 Ave of the Americas, New York, NY 10020. Telephone (212) 997-1221. Telex TWX 7105814879 WUI 62555.

Monthly magazine. Provides information on electrical design, installation, maintenance, construction modernization, repairs, and equipment. Price $50.00, Canada $60.00 per year.

1601
Electrical Construction and Maintenance (Annual)
McGraw-Hill Book Co, Hightstown-Princeton Rd, Hightstown, NJ 08520. Telephone (609) 448-1700. Telex 843449.

Annual book. Provides a buying guide to electrical equipment. Emphasizes new products. Price $12.00.

1601.01
Electrical Energy: Monthly Bulletin
European Community Information Service, 2100 M St NW, Suite 707, Washington DC 20037. Telephone (202) 862-9500. Telex 248455.

Monthly bulletin. Reports on electrical energy in European Communities member countries. Price $10.50.

1602
Electrical Engineer
Thomson Publications (Australia) Pty Ltd, 47 Chippen St, PO Box 65, Chippendale, NSW 2008, Australia. Telephone 699-6731. Telex TPAS AA22226.

Monthly magazine. Supplies information on electrical engineering and power generation. Covers Australian developments. Price $47.00 (Australian) per year.

1603
Electrical Equipment News
Southam Communications Ltd, 1450 Don Mills Rd, Don Mills, Ont, Canada M3B 2X7. Telephone (416) 445-6641. Telex 06-966612.

Monthly periodical. Offers information on new and improved electrical equipment. Includes technical literature. Price $33.00 per year.

1604
Electrical Marketing Newsletter
McGraw-Hill Publications Co, 1221 Ave of the Americas, New York, NY 10020. Telephone (212) 997-1221. Telex TWX 7105814879 WUI 62555.

Semimonthly newsletter. Contains material on electrical equipment marketing and sales trends. Notes personnel changes. Price $300.00 per year.

1604.01
Electrical Patents Index, 1981
Derwent Publications Ltd, Rochdale House, 128 Theobalds Rd, London, England WC1X 8RP. Telephone (44) (01) 242-5823. Telex 267487.

Retrieval service. Supplies abstracts of electrical and electronics patents. Price available on request.

1605
Electrical Week
McGraw-Hill Publications Co, 1221 Ave of the Americas, New York, NY 10020. Telephone (212) 997-1221. Telex TWX 7105814879 WUI 62555.

Weekly newsletter. Provides electric utility news, including rates, equipment, and environmental regulation. Lists fuel deliveries by price and supplier. Price $625.00 per year.

1606
Electrical Wholesaling
McGraw-Hill Book Co., Hightstown-Princeton Rd, Hightstown, NJ 08520. Telephone (609) 448-1700. Telex 843449.

Directory. Provides a register of electrical wholesale distributors. Includes a market planning guide. Price $7.00.

1607
Electrical Wholesaling (Magazine)
McGraw-Hill Publications Co, 1221 Ave of the Americas, New York, NY 10020. Telephone (212) 997-1221. Telex TWX 7105814879 WUI 62555.

Magazine issued seven times a year. Provides electrical equipment marketing information. Notes specific products, such as minicomputers and pertinent legislation. Price $18.00 per year.

1608
Electrical World
McGraw-Hill Book Co, Hightstown-Princeton Rd, Hightstown, NJ 08520. Telephone (609) 448-1700. Telex 843449.

Book. Lists US electric utilities. Price $150.00.

1609
Electrical World (Magazine)
McGraw-Hill Publications Co, 1221 Ave of the Americas, New York, NY 10020. Telephone (212) 997-1221. Telex TWX 7105814879 WUI 62555.

Monthly magazine. Covers the electric utility engineering field. Emphasizes technical developments. Price $36.00 per year.

1610
Electric Housewares and Fans: 1976
US Dept of Commerce, Bureau of the Census, Washington, DC 20233. Telephone (202) 449-1600.

Annual report. Presents 1976 data on manufacturers' shipments of electric housewares and fans. Indicates quantity and value. Price $.25.

1611
Electric Lamps
US Dept of Commerce, Bureau of the Census, Washington, DC 20233. Telephone (202) 449-1600.

Quarterly report, with annual summary. Presents data on the production, stocks, and quantity, and value of shipments of electric lamps. Price $4.30 per year.

1612
Electric Lamps
US Dept of Commerce, Bureau of the Census, Washington, DC 20233. Telephone (202) 499-1600.

Monthly report. Contains statistics on the value of domestic shipments of electric lamps for large incandescent (except photo), general lighting (vapor), high intensity, and fluorescent hot cathodes. Price $4.30 per year.

1613
Electric Letter
John Turrel, Rt 2, Mt Vernon, IL 62864. Telephone (618) 242-6549.

Biweekly newsletter. Discusses communications, marketing, conservation, load management, education, and consumer relations for electric utilities. Price $49.00 per year.

1614
Electric Perspectives
Edison Electric Inst, 1111 19th St, NW, Washington, DC 20036. Telephone (202) 828-7400.

Quarterly magazine. Covers issues and new developments in the electric power industry. Is aimed at management. Price $15.00 per year.

1616
Electric Power in Asia and the Pacific
United Nations Publications, United Nations Plaza, Room A-3315, New York, NY 10017. Telephone (212) 754-8302.

Report. Statistics and other information on electric power in Asia and the Far East. Price available on request.

1617
Electric Power Statistics
Statistics Canada, User Services, Publications Distribution, Ottawa, Ont, Canada K1A 0V7. Telephone (613) 992-3151.

Monthly report. Supplies statistics on the Canadian electric power industry. Provides cumulative data by province. Price $30.00 per year. ISSN 0380-0229.

1617.01
Electric Vehicle News
Porter Corp, PO Box 350, Westport, CT 06881. Telephone (203) 226-4600.

Quarterly report. Covers electric vehicles industry. Discusses engineering, marketing, and applications. Price $12.00 per year.

1617.02
Electric Vehicle Progress
Downtown Research and Development Center, 270 Madison Ave, Suite 1505, New York, NY 10016. Telephone (212) 889-5666.

Semimonthly newsletter. Provides management news, technical developments, marketing, research, manufacturing, and government actions on electric vehicles. Aimed at management and technical people in industry and government. Price $210.00 per year.

1618
Electrified Industry
B J Martin Company, Inc, 20 N Wacker Dr, Chicago, IL 60606. Telephone (312) 236-7150.

Monthly magazine. Presents information on electric power and lighting for industrial plants and offices. Evaluates products and provides energy-saving suggestions. Price $9.00 per year.

1619
Electronic Business
Cahners Publishing Co, Inc, 221 Columbus Ave, Boston, MA 02116. Telephone (617) 536-7780.

Monthly magazine. Provides reports and commentary on business and marketing aspects of the electronics industry. Price available on request.

1620
Electronic Component News
Chilton Co, Chilton Way, Radnor, PA 19089. Telephone (215) 687-8200.

Monthly magazine. Covers new products and technology in the electronics market. Price available on request.

1620.01
Electronic Design's Gold Book
Hayden Publishing Co, Inc, 50 Essex St, Rochelle Park, NJ 07662. Telephone (201) 843-0550. Telex TWX 710 990-5071.

Annual four-volume directory. Describes products in electronics industry. Price $45.00–$60.00.

1621
Electronic Distributing
Electronic Periodicals, Inc, 33393 Aurora Rd, Cleveland, OH 44139. Telephone (216) 248-4955.

Magazine published 10 times per year. Focuses on marketing and selling electronic components and equipment through electronic distributors. Price free of charge to qualified recipients.

1622
Electronic Engineering
Morgan-Grampian Ltd, Morgan-Grampian House, Calderwood St, London, England SE18 6QH. Order from Morgan-Grampian Publishing Co, 2 Park Ave, New York, NY 10016. Telephone England (44) (01) 855-7777. Telex 896238 MORGAN G. New York (212) 340-9700. Telex 425592 MGI UI.

Monthly journal. Discusses high technology electronics. Price $47.50 per year.

1623
Electronic Industries Association. Monthly Statistical Report. US Imports (by Country) of Electronic Products within Scope of the EIA Consumer Electronics Group
Electronic Industries Assn, 2001 I St NW, Washington, DC 20006. Telephone (202) 457-4955.

Monthly report. Supplies statistics on US imports of electronic consumer products. Price $1000.00 per year.

1623.01
Electronic Industries Association. Quarterly Statistical Report. US Exports (by Country) of Electronic Products within Scope of the EIA Consumer Electronics Group
Electronic Industries Assn, 2001 I St, NW, Washington, DC 20006. Telephone (202) 457-4955.

Quarterly report. Supplies statistics on US exports of consumer electronic products by country of destination. Price $600.00 per year.

1624
Electronic Industries Association. Quarterly Statistical Report. US Imports and Exports (by Country) of Electronic Products within Scope of the EIA Communications Division
Electronic Industries Assn, 2001 I St NW, Washington, DC 20006. Telephone (202) 457-4950.

Quarterly report. Presents data on US imports and exports, by country, of communications electronic products. Price $200.00 per year.

1625
Electronic Industries Association. Quarterly Statistical Report. US Imports and Exports (by Country) of Electronic Products within Scope of the EIA Industrial Electronics Division
Electronic Industries Assn, 2001 I St NW, Washington, DC 20006. Telephone (202) 457-4950.

Quarterly report. Contains statistical information on US imports and exports, by country, of industrial electronic products. Price $200.00 per year.

1626
Electronic Industries Association. Quarterly Statistical Report. US Imports and Exports (by Country) of Electronic Products within Scope of the EIA Parts Division
Electronic Industries Assn, 2001 I St NW, Washington, DC 20006. Telephone (202) 457-4952.

Quarterly report. Presents data on US imports and exports, by country, of electronic parts products. Price $500.00 per year.

1627
Electronic Industries Association. Quarterly Statistical Report. US Imports and Exports (by Country) of Electronic Products within Scope of the EIA Solid State Products Division
Electronic Industries Assn, 2001 I St NW, Washington, DC 20006. Telephone (202) 457-4950.

Quarterly report. Supplies statistical information on US imports and exports, by country, of electronic solid state products. Price $200.00 per year.

1628
Electronic Industries Association. Quarterly Statistical Report. US Imports and Exports (by Country) of Electronic Products within Scope of the EIA Tube Division
Electronic Industries Assn, 2001 I St NW, Washington, DC 20006. Telephone (202) 457-4950.

Quarterly report. Presents data on US electron tube imports and exports by country. Price $200.00 per year.

1629
Electronic Market Data Book
Electronic Industries Assn, 2001 I St NW, Washington, DC 20006. Telephone (202) 457-4950.

Annual book. Contains current and historical sales data on the electronics industry. Covers a full range of products, world trade patterns, employment, industry earnings, and government needs for electronics. Price $50.00.

1630
Electronic Market Trends
Electronic Industries Assn, 2001 I St NW, Washington, DC 20006. Telephone (202) 457-4950.

Monthly journal. Contains articles on the electronics markets, new technologies, international developments, and policy issues. Provides monthly statistics on domestic sales and foreign trade. Price $150.00 per year.

1630.01
Electronic New Product Directory, 1978–79
Marketing Development, 402 Border Rd, Concord, MA 01742. Telephone (617) 369-5382.

Book. Lists 2205 significant new electronic products introduced by company and Standard Industrial Classification (SIC) number. Price $450.00.

1631
Electronic News Financial Fact Book & Directory
Fairchild Publications, Inc, 7 E 12th St, New York, NY 10003. Telephone (212) 741-4280.

Annual book. Provides profiles of more than 790 electronics corporations. Details sales and earnings, assets and liabilities, and divisions. Price $90.00.

1631.01
Electronic Office Management and Technology
Auerbach Publishers, Inc, 6560 N Park Dr, Pennsauken, NJ 08109. Telephone (609) 662-2070. Telex 831 464.

Two-volume service, updated monthly. Provides information on planning, purchasing, implementing, and managing electronic office technologies. Includes equipment vendors, prices, and evaluations. Price $350.00.

1632
Electronics
McGraw-Hill Publications Co, 1221 Ave of the Americas, New York, NY 10020. Telephone (212) 997-1221. Telex TWX 7105814879 WUI 62555.

Biweekly magazine. Reports on technical advances in electronic equipment. English and Russian editions. Price $30.00 per year.

1633
Electronics & Communications
Southam Communications Ltd, 1450 Don Mills Rd, Don Mills, Ont, Canada M3B 2X7. Telephone (416) 445-6641. Telex 06-966612.

Bimonthly magazine. Covers product information for the electronics industry. Price $21.00 per year.

1634
Electronics & Communications Abstracts Journal
Cambridge Scientific Abstracts, 6611 Kenilworth Ave, Suite 437, Riverdale, MD 20840. Telephone (301) 951-1327.

Magazine, ten issues per year. Compiles indexed abstracts from scientific and technical literature on electronics. Emphasizes the research and application of theories and devices. Price $295.00 per year.

1634.01
Electronics Buyers' Guide
Dempa Publications, Inc, 380 Madison Ave, New York, NY 10017. Telephone (212) 867-0900.

Annual directory. Lists electronics products and manufacturers in Japan, Korea, Taiwan, Hong Kong, and Singapore. Price $54.00.

1635
Electronics-Buyers' Guide
McGraw-Hill Book Co, Hightstown-Princeton Rd, Hightstown, NJ 08520. Telephone (609) 448-1700. Telex 843449.

Annual publication. Provides an inventory of electronics production equipment and products. Price $30.00 per year.

1636
Electronics Foreign Trade
Electronic Industries Assn, 2001 I St NW, Washington, DC 20006. Telephone (202) 457-4950.

Monthly statistical report. Provides information on imports and exports, by individual product category, and for groups of electronic products, as well as balance of trade for the electronic industries. Price $150.00 per year.

1637
Electronics Times
Morgan-Grampian Ltd, Morgan-Grampian House, Calderwood St, London, England SE18 6QH. Telephone (44) (01) 855-7777. Telex 896238. Order from Morgan-Grampian Publishing Co, 2 Park Ave, New York, NY 10016. Telephone (212) 340-9700. Telex 425592 MGI UI.

Weekly tabloid. Covers business, technology and products in the electronics industry. Price $75.00.

1638
Electronic Technician Dealer
Harcourt Brace Jovanovich Publications, 757 3rd Ave, New York, NY 10017. Order from Harcourt Brace and Jovanovich Publications, 1 E 1st St, Duluth, MN 55802. Telephone (218) 727-8511.

Monthly magazine. Reports on the sales and service of television, radio (including citizens bands), and other home entertainment electronic equipment. Price $9.00 per year.

1639
El Ra-Ed
El Ra-Ed Publications Corp, 60 Hamilton Ave, #8G, Staten Island, NY 10301. Telephone (212) 442-3128.

Monthly newspaper. Features business, cultural, and economic events in Arab countries. Lists new business opportunities. English and Arabic texts. Price $.25 per copy.

1640
Embassy of India Commercial Bulletin
Commerce Wing, Embassy of India, 2107 Massachusetts Ave, NW, Washington, DC 20008. Telephone (202) 265-5200.

Semimonthly newsletter. Provides information on Indian trade. Emphasizes exports and growth of specific industries. Price free of charge.

1640.01
Emergency Preparedness News
Business Publishers, Inc, PO Box 1067, Silver Spring, MD 20910. Telephone (301) 587-6300.

Biweekly newsletter. Discusses emergency preparedness and assistance programs. Price $127.00 per year.

1641
E/MJ Mining Activity Digest
McGraw-Hill Publications Co, 1221 Ave of the Americas, New York, NY 10020. Telephone (212) 997-1221. Telex TWX 7105814879 WUI 62555.

Monthly newsletter. Digests reports on international mining activity, including such topics as exploring, smelting, and refining. Price $84.00 per year.

1642
Employee Benefit Costs in Canada
Thorne Stevenson & Kellogg, 2300 Yonge St, Suite 1800, Toronto, Ont, Canada M4P 1G2. Telephone (416) 868-8500.

Biennial report based on national survey. Shows cost of benefits for 21 industries in Canada. Gives statistical tables and US comparison. Price $145.00 (Canadian) per copy.

1643
Employee Benefit Plan Review (EBPR)
Charles D Spencer & Assoc, Inc, 222 W Adams St, Chicago, IL 60606. Telephone (312) 236-2615.

Monthly magazine. Reports on employee benefit programs. Price available on request.

1644
Employee Benefit Plan Review (EBPR) Research Reports
Charles D Spencer & Assoc, Inc, 222 W Adams St, Chicago, IL 60606. Telephone (312) 236-2615.

Seven loose-leaf books on all employee benefits, including texts, analyses and weekly news digest. Price for initial subscription $375.00 per year, $345.00 per year renewal.

1645
Employee Benefits Journal
International Foundation of Employee Benefit Plans, 18700 W Bluemound Rd, Box 69, Brookfield, WI 53005. Telephone (414) 786-6700.

Quarterly magazine. Discusses employee benefit plan management. Notes Canadian and US trends. Price $15.00 per year. ISSN 0361-4050.

1646
Employee Relations Bulletin
National Retail Merchants Assn, 100 W 31st St, New York, NY 10001. Telephone (212) 244-6780.

Monthly report. Deals with retail store employment issues, including union contracts, labor legislation, and decisions by the Wage-Hour Division and EEOC. Price $18.00.

1647
Employee Relations in Action
Man & Manager, Inc, 799 Broadway, New York, NY 10003. Telephone (212) 677-0640.

Monthly newsletter. Covers day-to-day employee problems taken from grievances that have gone to arbitration. Annual index. Price $48.00 per year.

1648
Employee Relations Law Journal
Executive Enterprises Publications Co, Inc, 33 W 60th St, New York, NY 10023. Telephone (212) 489-2670.

Quarterly journal. Deals with labor problems, equal employment opportunity, pensions, and collective bargaining. Price $54.00 per year.

1649
Employee Relocation Council (ERC) Directory
Employee Relocation Council, 333 N Michigan Ave, Chicago, IL 60601. Telephone (312) 346-4151.

Annual directory. Lists real estate brokers and appraisers—and relocation-related services that are equipped to handle problems of the transferee. Price $8.00 per copy. ISBN 0-912614-02-1.

1650
Employer
New Zealand Employers Federation, Research and Information Services Div, PO Box 1786 Federation House, 95-99 Molesworth St, Wellington, New Zealand. Telephone 4-722-453. Telex NZ3937.

Monthly newsletter. Reports on New Zealand labor relations issues such as equal employment, wages, and legislation. Notes the activities of the New Zealand Employers Federation. Price free to federation members.

1651

Employers' Review

Employers' Federation of New South Wales, PO Box A 233, Sydney South, NSW 2000, Australia. Telephone (02) 264-2000.

Monthly magazine. Reports on labor relations in New South Wales and other parts of Australia. Reviews new labor contracts. Price $3.00 per copy.

1652

Employment & Earnings

US Dept of Labor, Bureau of Labor Statistics, 441 G St NW, Washington, DC 20212. Telephone (202) 523-1221.

Monthly report. Provides current employment, hours, earnings, and labor turnover data for the US, including individual states and 200 local areas. Price $22.00 per year.

1653

Employment and Training Administration (ETA) Interchange

US Dept of Labor, Employment & Training Adm, Washington, DC 20213. Telephone (202) 376-6730.

Monthly report. Carries material on the Department of Labor Employment and Training Administration program. Discusses general job training subjects. Price free of charge.

1654

Employment and Training Reporter

Bureau of National Affairs, Inc, 1231 25th St NW, Washington, DC 20037. Telephone (202) 452-4200.

Loose-leaf books, with weekly updates. Detail major developments under the Comprehensive Employment and Training Act. Feature current topics and reference file. Price $496.00 per year.

1655

Employment and Training Report of the President

US Dept of Labor, Employment & Training Adm, Washington, DC 20213. Telephone (202) 376-6730.

Annual report. Contains the Department of Labor's report on employment and training requirements, resources, and use of the Department of Health, Education and Welfare's report on the use of facilities and employment and training program coordination. Price $2.75.

1657

Employment by Type and Broad Industrial Source

US Dept of Commerce, Bureau of Economic Analysis, Washington, DC 20230. Order From Regional Economic Measurement Div, Bureau of Economic Analysis, Washington, DC 20230. Telephone (202) 523-0966.

Information service. Provides data on the number of proprietors and full- and part-time wage and salary employees by major industries for states, counties, and Standard Metropolitan Statistical Areas. Covers most recent six years. Price $1000.00.

1658

Employment Digest

Croner Publications, Inc, 211-03 Jamaica Ave, Queens Village, NY 11428. Order from Croner Publications Ltd, Croner House, 173 Kingston Rd, New Malden, Surrey, England KT3 3SS. Telephone (212) 942-8966.

Fortnightly newsletter. Reports on British labor law developments, including health and safety legislation, pensions, and unions. Notes news in the European community. Price £29.00 per year.

1659

Employment Discrimination

Matthew Bender & Co, 235 E 45th St, New York, NY 10017. Telephone (212) 661-5050.

Four-volume loose-leaf report, with biannual cumulative. Discusses federal and state laws governing sex discrimination in employment. Includes information on racial, religious, and other types of employment discrimination. Price $250.00 per volume.

1660

Employment, Earnings and Hours

Statistics Canada, User Services, Publications Distribution, Ottawa, Ont, Canada K1A 0V7. Telephone (613) 992-3151.

Monthly report. Provides data on Canadian industrial employment, average weekly earnings, weekly hours, and hourly earnings by industry and region. Price $48.00 per year. ISSN 0380-6936.

1661

Employment Law Manual

Gower Publishing Co Ltd, 1 Westmead, Farnborough, Hampshire, England GU14 7RU. Telephone Farnborough (0252) 519221. Telex 858623.

Annual loose-leaf book. Deals with existing British labor legislation, new regulations, and judicial decisions. Offers an updating service. Price $97.00. ISBN 0 7161 0220 X.

1661.01

Employment Practices

Commerce Clearing House, Inc, 4025 W Peterson Ave, Chicago, IL 60646. Telephone (312) 583-8500.

Four loose-leaf books, plus semimonthly reports. Give information about federal and state rules prohibiting discrimination in employment. Price $250.00 per year.

1662

Employment Practices Decisions

Commerce Clearing House, Inc, 4025 W Peterson Ave, Chicago, IL 60646. Telephone (312) 583-8500.

Twenty-two volumes. Contain pertinent federal and state court decisions or discrimination in employment controversies. Price $27.50 per volume.

1664

Employment Review

New York State Dept of Labor, Div of Research and Statistics, State Office Bldg Campus, Albany, NY 12240. Telephone (518) 457-1130.

Monthly report. Offers articles and statistics on employment, earnings and hours, labor turnover, and unemployment for New York State and various geographic areas. Price free of charge.

1665

Employment Safety and Health Guide

Commerce Clearing House, Inc, 4025 W Peterson Ave, Chicago, IL 60646. Telephone (312) 583-8500.

Three loose-leaf books, plus weekly reports. Cover standards, compliance rules, decisions, and regulations of the Occupational Safety and Health Act. Price $335.00 per year.

1666

Employment Standards Digest

US Dept of Labor, Employment Standards Adm, 200 Constitution Ave, NW, Rm C4331, Washington, DC 20210. Order from Superintendent of Documents, US Government Printing Office, Washington, DC 20402. Telephone (202) 783-3238.

Monthly report. Summarizes activities involving the Employment Standards Administration. Price available on request.

1667
Encyclomedia, 1978 edition
Decisions Publications, Inc, 342 Madison Ave, New York, NY 10017. Telephone (212) 953-1888.

Six volumes. Cover different areas of the advertising media in each. Include newspapers, magazines, television, radio, business publications, and out-of-home media. Price $120.00 per year set of six volumes.

1668
Encyclopedia Americana, International edition
Grolier, Inc., Sherman Turnpike, Danbury, CT 06816. Telephone (203) 797-3500.

Thirty-volume encyclopedia of general information. Has a one-volume index and an annual update, the Americana Annual. Price available on request.

1669
Encyclopedia of Advertising, 1969 edition
Fairchild Publications, Inc, 7 E 12th St, New York, NY 10003. Telephone (212) 741-4280.

Book. Covers all aspects of advertising and related fields. Price $20.00. ISBN 0-87005-014-1.

1670
Encyclopedia of Associations, 15th edition
Gale Research Co, Book Tower, Detroit, MI 48226. Telephone (313) 961-2242.

Book. Contains information on over 13,-000 associations in the US. Provides an index by subject, key word, and proper name. Price $120.00. ISBN 0133-4.

1671
Encyclopedia of Business Information Sources, 4th edition
Gale Research Co, Book Tower, Detroit, MI 48226. Telephone (313) 961-2242.

Book. Provides an information source for 1280 business-oriented topics. Lists reference books, periodicals, organizations, and other kinds of information sources. Price $98.00. ISBN 0372-8.

1673
Encyclopedia of Governmental Advisory Organizations, 3rd edition
Gale Research Co, Book Tower, Detroit, MI 48226. Telephone (313) 961-2242.

Book. Provides a guide to US federal advisory committees, task forces, conferences, and similar bodies. Price $190.00. ISBN 0251-9.

1674
Encyclopedia of Information Systems and Services, 4th edition
Gale Research Co, Book Tower, Detroit, MI 48226. Telephone (313) 961-2242.

Book. Describes 1750 organizations involved in information products and services, including publishers, computer companies, and data banks. Price $175.-00. ISBN 0939-4.

1675
Encyclopedia of Management
Van Nostrand Reinhold, Co, 135 W 50th St, New York, NY 10001. Telephone (212) 265-8700.

Book. Provides detailed definitions of management terms and techniques. Price $34.50. ISBN 0-442-23405-8.

1676
Energy Analects
Corpus Information Services, Ltd, 1450 Don Mills Rd, Don Mills, Ont, Canada M3B 2X7. Telephone (416) 445-7101. Telex 06-966612.

Weekly newsletter. Covers developments affecting North American energy industries, with emphasis on Canada. Notes various kinds of power, prices, production, conservation, and marketing. Price $347.00 (Canadian) per year. ISSN 0315-1654.

1677
Energy Controls
Prentice-Hall, Inc, Englewood Cliffs, NJ 07632. Telephone (201) 592-2000. Telex 13-5423.

Weekly loose-leaf service. Contains the text of federal and state energy laws. Reports new energy control developments. Price $450.00 per year.

1678
Energy Daily
Llewellyn King, 300 National Press Bldg, Washington, DC 20045. Telephone (202) 638-4260.

Newsletter published every business day. Covers major energy sources, including research and development, legislation, regulation, and supply and demand. Notes nonconventional sources. Price $650.00 per year, $675.00 overseas.

1679
Energy Developments
International Review Service, 15 Washington Pl, New York, NY 10003. Telephone (212) 751-0833.

Monthly report. Covers petroleum and nuclear energy developments, plus nonconventional sources of energy. Notes commercial activities, financial supply, price, agreements, projects, explorations, and discoveries. Price $250.00 per year.

1680
Energy Directory Update
Environment Information Center (EIC), Inc, Catalog Order Dept, 292 Madison Ave, New York, NY 10017. Telephone (212) 949-9494.

Loose-leaf books, with bimonthly updates. Provide information on organizations and officials involved in the energy field. Includes indexes. Price $125.00.

1680.01
Energy Executive Directory
Carroll Publishing Co, 1058 Thomas Jefferson St, NW, Washington, DC 20007. Telephone (202) 333-8620.

Book published three times per year. Lists energy related offices and personnel of the federal, state, and local governments. Identifies trade association personnel and newsletters. Price $60.00 per year.

1681
Energy Index
Environment Information Center (EIC), Inc, Catalog Order Dept, 292 Madison Ave, New York, NY 10017. Telephone (212) 949-9494.

Annual report. Provides a directory to the year's major events in the energy field, literature, legislation, films, and conferences. Statistics. Price $95.00.

1682
Energy Info
Robert Morey Assoc, PO Box 98, Dana Point, CA 92629. Telephone (714) 496-2574.

Monthly newsletter. Contains news about energy research and development. Price $40.00 per year.

1682.01
Energy Information
Petroleum Information Corp, PO Box 2612, 1375 Delaware, Denver, CO 80201. Telephone (303) 825-2181.

Weekly report. Analyzes current energy developments, including government news and exploration activity. Price $240.00 per year.

1683
Energy Information Abstracts

Environment Information Center (EIC), Inc, Catalog Order Dept, 292 Madison Ave, New York, NY 10017. Telephone (212) 949-9494.

Monthly report. Contains informative abstracts from varied publications on energy and related subjects. Includes a listing of upcoming conferences and newly published books. Price $350.00 per year.

1684
Energy Information Locator

Environment Information Center (EIC), Inc, Catalog Order Dept, 292 Madison Ave, New York, NY 10017. Telephone (212) 949-9494.

Loose-leaf report, with annual updating. Provides a directory to information sources on energy, including indexes, directories, computerized service libraries, and research centers. Includes five indexes. Price $35.00.

1685
Energyline

Environment Information Center (EIC), Inc, Catalog Order Dept, 292 Madison Ave, New York, NY 10017. Telephone (212) 949-9494.

Information service. Provides computerized abstracts, with citations, from reports and periodicals on energy and related subjects. Price available on request.

1686
Energy Management

Commerce Clearing House, Inc, 4025 W Peterson Ave, Chicago, IL 60646. Telephone (312) 583-8500.

Seven loose-leaf books, plus weekly reports. Monitor federal programs concerned with energy resource problems, including those of the Federal Energy Administration. Price $750.00 per year.

1686.01
Energy Management

Penton/IPC, 614 Superior Ave W, Cleveland, OH 44113. Telephone (216) 696-0300.

Bimonthly magazine. Reports on products, systems, and services which provide more efficient use of energy of all types in plants, buildings, and residences. Price $24.00 per year.

1687
Energy Policy

IPC Business Press Ltd, 205 E 42nd St, New York, NY 10017. Telephone (212) 889-0700. Telex 421710.

Quarterly magazine. Discusses energy economics, production, conversion, and use. Includes book reviews. Price $124.80 per year. ISSN 0301-4215.

1688
Energy Prospects in OECD Countries and Possible Demand for OPEC Oil Exports to 1980

Merih Celasun and Frank J P Pinto, World Bank, 1818 H St NW, Washington, DC 20433. Telephone (202) 383-6360.

Mimeographed publication. Analyzes the results of three regional energy models for OECD area. Offers projections of demand for OPEC oil exports. Price free of charge.

1689
Energy Related Research and Development Funds

US Dept of Commerce, Bureau of the Census, Washington, DC 20233. Order information from Chief, Manufacturing and Mineral Industries Div, Bureau of the Census, Washington, DC 20233. Telephone (202) 449-1600.

Annual service. Reports on energy-related research and development funds in the 10 largest manufacturing industries by ratio of company funds to federal funds. Price free of charge.

1690
Energy Report

Microinfo Ltd, PO Box 3, Newman Lane, Alton, Hampshire, England GU34 2PG. Telephone Alton 84300. Telex 858431.

Newsletter. Pertains to the technological aspects of the energy field. Price available on request.

1691
Energy Research Bureau

Fraser Management Associates, Inc, 309 Willard St, PO Box 494, Burlington, VT 05402. Telephone (802) 658-0322.

Newsletter issued 20 times per year. Reports on energy development with special focus on investment opportunities. Gives stock statistics. Price $70.00 per year.

1692
Energy Research Programs 1980

RR Bowker Co, 1180 Avenue of the Americas, New York, NY 10036. Order from RR Bowker Co, PO Box 1807, Ann Arbor, MI 48106. Telephone (212) 764-5100.

Directory. Register of energy-related programs, services, and industries by 3675 parent organizations having 5900 research facilities in the US and Canada. Includes locations, administrators and research personnel, professional staff, and scientific disciplines for each. Geographical, name, and subject indexes. Price $75.-00. ISBN 0-8352-1242-4. ISSN 0195-699X.

1693
Energy Resources Report

Business Publishers, Inc, PO Box 1067, Silver Spring, MD 20910. Telephone (301) 587-6300.

Weekly newsletter. Provides worldwide energy news. Price $217.00 per year.

1694
Energy Service

Data Resources, Inc, 29 Hartwell Ave, Lexington, MA 02173. Telephone (617) 861-0165.

Quarterly report. Offers forecasts on the world demand for crude oils, refined products' prices, tanker rates, refiners' margins. Covers also the US's consumption of oil, gas, coal, and electricity. Price available on request.

1695
Energy Sources

Crane, Russak & Company, Inc, 3 East 44th St, New York, NY 10017. Telephone (212) 867-1490. Telex 423921.

Quarterly magazine. Examines new solutions to energy shortage. Discusses environmental, legal, and social implications. Price $60.00 per year.

1696
Energy Statistics (Three Series)

European Community Information Service, 2100 M St, NW, Suite 707, Washington, DC 20037. Telephone (202) 862-9500. Telex 248455.

Monthly report. Gives energy statistics for European Communities member countries. Price $38.50.

1697
Energy Statistics Yearbook 1978.

Commission of the European Communities, Office for Official Publications of the European Communities, CP 1003, Luxembourg 1, Luxembourg. Telephone (352) 490081. Telex PUBLOF 1325.

Annual book. Provides statistical data on energy. Price $28.00.

1699
Energy Today

Trends Publishing, Inc, 233 National Press Bldg, Washington, DC 20045. Telephone (202) 393-0031.

Semimonthly report. Discusses energy trends. Indicates the sources of studies on energy problems and technology and lists pertinent books and journals. Price $200.00 per year.

1700
Energy Trends

Her Majesty's Stationery Office, PO Box 569, London, England SE1 9NH. Telephone (44) (01) 928 1321.

Monthly report. Covers energy trends. Price free of charge.

1700.01
Energy Update

Marpep Publishing Ltd, Suite 700, 133 Richmond St W, Toronto, Ont, Canada M5H 3M8. Telephone (416) 869-1177.

Biweekly report. Discusses Canadian energy developments and government regulation. Price available on request.

1701
Energy Users Report

Bureau of National Affairs, Inc, 1231 25th St NW, Washington, DC 20037. Telephone (202) 452-4200.

Loose-leaf books, with weekly updates. Review energy policy, supply, and technology. Include current reports, with an index, and a reference file, with a statistics section. Price $350.00 per year.

1702
Engineer

Morgan-Grampian Ltd, Morgan-Grampian House, Calderwood St, London, England SE18 6QH. Order from Morgan-Grampian Publishing Co, 2 Park Ave, New York, NY 10016. Telephone (44) (01) 855-7777. Telex 896238 MORGAN G. New York (212) 340-9700. Telex 425592 MGI UI.

Weekly magazine. Presents material on engineering technology and management in Great Britain. Price $100.00 per year.

1703
Engineering & Contract Record

Southam Communications Ltd, 1450 Don Mills Rd, Don Mills, Ont, Canada M3B 2X7. Telephone (416) 445-6641. Telex 06 966612.

Monthly report. Offers reports on the engineering construction industry in Canada. Price $33.00 per year.

1704
Engineering & Metals Review

Assn of Indian Engineering Industry, 172 Jor Bagh, New Delhi 110003, India. Telephone 615115. Telex 031-3855.

Monthly journal. Covers the engineering and metals industries in India. Price Rs 120 per year.

1705
Engineering and Inspection Manual/Part III

Supply and Services Canada, Publishing Centre, Printing and Publishing, Ottawa, Ont, Canada K1A 0S9. Telephone (613) 238-1601.

Loose-leaf report, with update service. Summarizes airworthiness directives. Price $6.00; updates $.60.

1706
Engineering and Mining Journal

McGraw-Hill Publications Co, 1221 Ave of the Americas, New York, NY 10020. Telephone (212) 997-6375. Telex TWX 7105814879 WUI 62555.

Monthly journal. Provides information on metal and nonmetal mining, milling, smelting, and refining. Lists metal prices. Price $18.00 per year.

1707
Engineering and Mining Journal—Annual Buyers' Guide.

McGraw-Hill Book Co, Hightstown-Princeton Rd, Hightstown, NJ 08520. Telephone (609) 448-1700. Telex 843449.

Annual directory. Provides a buyer's guide to metal and nonmetal mining, milling, smelting, and refining equipment. Is free with an Engineering and Mining Journal subscription. Price $18.00 per year.

1708
Engineering and Mining Journal (E&MJ) International Directory of Mining and Mineral Processing Operations

McGraw-Hill Book Co, Hightstown-Princeton Rd, Hightstown, NJ 08520. Telephone (609) 448-1700. Telex 843449.

Directory. Lists companies, mines, and plants engaged in exploring, mining extractive processing, smelting, and refining metal and nonmetal minerals. Price $55.-00.

1709
Engineering Digest

Canadian Engineering Publications Ltd, 32 Front St, W, Suite 501, Toronto, Ont, Canada M5J 2H9. Telephone (416) 869-1735.

Magazine issued ten times a per year. Provides technical and industrial information for Canadian engineers. Presents abstracts of selected papers and a special section on new products. Price $24.00 per year. ISSN 0013-7901.

1710
Engineering Index

Engineering Index, Inc, 345 E 47th St, New York, NY 10017. Telephone (212) 644-7615.

Monthly and annual publications. Provide bibliographic reference service with complete abstracts and subject index to all fields of engineering. Draw on worldwide sources. Annual is also available on microform. Prices available on request.

1711
Engineering News-Record

McGraw-Hill Publications Co, 1221 Ave of the Americas, New York, NY 10020. Telephone (212) 997-6375. Telex TWX 7105814879 WUI 62555.

Weekly magazine. Reports on engineering construction, including site selection, labor, cost of materials, and new technology. Price $26.00 per year.

1712
Engineering News Record—Directory of Design Firms

McGraw-Hill Book Co, Hightstown-Princeton Rd, Hightstown, NJ 08520. Telephone (609) 448-1700. Telex 843449.

Directory. Offers list of engineering design firms. Price $17.50.

1713
Enterprise
Australian Dept of Industrial Development & Decentralisation, Superannuation Bldg, 32 St George's Ter, Perth 6000, Western Australia. Telephone 25 0471.

Quarterly magazine. Concerns western Australian trade and industry. Price free of charge.

1714
Enterprise
National Assn of Manufacturers, 1776 F St NW, Washington, DC 20006. Telephone (202) 626-3700.

Monthly magazine. Reports on American business issues, including economic,labor, energy, and environmental developments. Price $10.00 per year.

1715
Enterprise Standard Industrial Classification Manual, 1974
US Dept of Commerce, Bureau of the Census, Washington, DC 20233. Order from Superintendent of Documents, Government Printing Office, Washington, DC 20402. Telephone (202) 655-4000.

Book. Contains information on the classification of enterprises by the Office of Management and Budget. Price $.65.

1716
Enterprising Women
Artemis Enterprises, Inc, 525 West End Ave, New York, NY 10024. Telephone (212) 787-6780.

Monthly magazine. Addresses itself to women's role in the economy and professions. Discusses taxes, insurance, and personal finances as well as management issues. Price $18.00 per year.

1718
Envirofiche
Environment Information Center (EIC), Inc, Catalog Order Dept, 292 Madison Ave, New York, NY 10017. Telephone (212) 949-9494.

Monthly service. Supplies microfiche keyed to abstracts' citations in Environment Abstracts, Environment Index, and Enviroline. Provides single-document, on-demand service, or full and partial subscriptions. Price $3500.00.

1719
Enviroline
Environment Information Center (EIC), Inc, Catalog Order Dept, 292 Madison Ave, New York, NY 10017. Telephone (212) 949-9494.

Information service. Provides an on-line data base for environmental topics and documents. Includes abstracts in the citations provided. Price available on request.

1720
Environment Abstracts
Environment Information Center (EIC), Inc, Catalog Order Dept, 292 Madison Ave, New York, NY 10017. Telephone (212) 949-9494.

Monthly magazine. Provides abstracts from journals, documents, conferences, and articles on pollution and other environmental abstracts. Includes an index. Price $325.00 per year.

1721
Environmental Comment
Urban Land Inst, 1090 Vermont Ave, NW, Washington, DC 20005. Telephone (202) 289-8500.

Monthly magazine. Contains information on environmental legislation and issues that affect land development. Includes commentary. Available only to members.

1722
Environmental Health Letter
Environews, Inc, 1097 National Press Bldg, Washington, DC 20045. Telephone (202) 347-3868.

Semimonthly newsletter. Covers all aspects of the environment. Price $110.00 per year.

1723
Environmental Impact Handbook
1090 Vermont Ave, NW, Washington, DC 20005. Telephone (202) 289-8500.

Book. Provides a guide to the residential environmental impact statement, including changes in federal and state guidelines through January 1975. Covers the National Environmental Policy Act of 1969 and related state and local laws. Price $8.-95.

1724
Environmental Regulation Analyst
Executive Enterprises Publications Co, Inc, 33 W 60th St, New York, NY 10023. Telephone (212) 489-2670.

Monthly newsletter. Analyzes impact on business of environmental regulations. Provides practical information on EPA compliance requirements. Price $72.00 per year.

1725
Environmental/Socioeconomic Data Sources
US Dept of Commerce, Bureau of the Census, Washington, DC 20233. Order from Subscriber Services Section (Publications), Bureau of the Census, Washington, DC 20233. Telephone (202) 655-4000.

Book. Provides sources of data on environmental and socioeconomic topics, including demography, economy, housing, and government. Price $1.50.

1726
Environment Index.
Environment Information Center (EIC), Inc, Catalog Order Dept, 292 Madison Ave, New York, NY 10017. Telephone (212) 949-9494.

Annual book. Serves as an index to Environment Abstracts and as a directory to environment-related subjects. Notes environmental books published and films released during the year and environmental officials and conferences. Price $95.00.

1728
Environment Regulation Handbook
Environment Information Center (EIC), Inc, Catalog Order Dept, 292 Madison Ave, New York, NY 10017. Telephone (212) 949-9494.

Four-volume loose-leaf book. Provides reference material to aid in complying with federal environmental laws and regulations. Includes key laws and state regulations. Flow charts and an index. Price $215.00.

1729
Environment Report
Trends Publishing, Inc, 233 National Press Bldg, Washington, DC 20045. Telephone (202) 393-0031.

Semimonthly report. Covers environmental issues, including legislation and technology. Provides a bibliography of related studies and books. Price $200.00 per year.

1730
Environment Reporter
Bureau of National Affairs, Inc, 1231 25th St NW, Washington, DC 20037. Telephone (202) 452-4200.

Loose-leaf books updated. Weekly. Deal with legislative, administrative, judicial, and industrial activity in pollution control and environmental protection. Include full text of decisions on specific cases and monographs. Price $607.00 per year.

1731

Equal Employment News

Betsy Hogan Assoc, PO Box 360, Brookline, MA 02146. Telephone (617) 232-0066.

Monthly newsletter. Provides digest of national equal employment opportunity developments. Includes trends in business, academia, and federal and local government. Price $45.00 per year.

1732

Equal Employment Opportunity Commission (EEOC)—Affirmative Action Manuals

Bureau of National Affairs, Inc, 1231 25th St NW, Washington, DC 20037. Telephone (202) 452-4200.

Two loose-leaf books, supplemented as needed. Provide information on Equal Employment Opportunity Commission procedures and standards and on affirmative action programs requiring compliance by federal contractors. Price $81.00 per year.

1733

Equal Employment Opportunity Commission (EEOC) Compliance Manual

Commerce Clearing House, Inc, 4025 W Peterson Ave, Chicago, IL 60646. Telephone (312) 583-8500.

Loose-leaf books, plus periodic reports. Present facsimile reproductions of the official policies, procedures, and standards of the Equal Employment Opportunity Commission. Price $90.00 per year.

1734

Equal Employment Opportunity Review

Executive Enterprises Publications Co, Inc, 33 W 60th St, New York, NY 10023. Telephone (212) 489-2670.

Monthly report. Advises supervisory personnel on the handling of equal employment opportunity problems. Price $36.00 per year.

1735

Equal Employment Opportunity Today

Executive Enterprises Publications Co, Inc, 33 W 60th St, New York, NY 10023. Telephone (212) 489-2670.

Quarterly journal. Features articles designed to assist employers in responding to equal employment opportunity programs. Price $48.00 per year.

1736

Equal Opportunity in Housing

Prentice-Hall, Inc, Englewood Cliffs, NJ 07632. Telephone (201) 592-2000. Telex 135423.

Biweekly loose-leaf service. Explains federal and state laws on equal opportunity in housing. Reviews court decisions. Price $273.00 per year.

1737

Equifax News

Equifax, Inc, Box 4081, Atlanta, GA 30302. Telephone (404) 885-8167.

Quarterly magazine. Presents material on insurance, marketing, and public image of international interest. Price free of charge.

1738

Equipment Market Abstracts

Predicasts, Inc, 200 University Circle Research Center, 11001 Cedar Ave, Cleveland, OH 44106. Telephone (216) 795-3000.

Monthly set of abstracts. Covers developments in the equipment, electronics, and hard goods industries, as reported in journals and government reports. Is indexed by product, company, country, and trade name. Price $500.00 per year.

1740

Ergonomics

Taylor & Francis Ltd, 4 John St, London WC1N 2ET, England. Telephone (44) (01) 405-2237.

Monthly journal. Deals with the human factors affecting performance and efficiency in work. Notes the design of equipment from various standpoints. Price $200.00 per year. ISSN 0014-0139.

1741

Ergonomics Abstracts

Taylor & Francis Ltd, 4 John St, London, WC1N 2ET, England. Telephone (44) (01) 405-2237.

Quarterly journal. Provides summaries of papers in psychology, physiology, biomechanics, and engineering relevant to the work environment. Price $198.00. ISSN 0046-2446.

1742

Establishing a Business

Ministry of Industry and Small Business Development, Victoria, BC, Canada V8V 1X4. Telephone (604) 387-6701.

Booklet. Outlines government regulations and legislation affecting businesses in British Columbia. Price free of charge.

1743

Establishments Classified by Ratio of Payroll to Value added. **MNT69**

US Dept of Commerce, Bureau of the Census, Washington, DC 20233. Order information from Chief, Manufacturing and Mineral Industries Div, Bureau of the Census, Washington, DC 20233. Telephone (202) 655-4000.

Information service. Provides statistics for business establishments by ratio of payroll to value added. Includes data on the number of establishments, employees, payroll, cost of materials, and related subjects. Price $.60 (microfiche).

1744

Estadistica

Organization of American States, 17th St, and Constitution Ave NW, Washington, DC 20006. Order from OAS General Secretariat, Dept of Publications, 6840 Industrial Rd, Springfield, VA 22151. Telephone (703) 941-1617.

Magazine published every three months. Deals with the problems of statistical administration, theory, and practice in OAS countries. Price $6.00 per year.

1746

Estate Planner's Complete Guide and Workbook

Panel Publishers, 14 Plaza Rd, Greenvale, NY 11548. Telephone (516) 484-0006.

Loose-leaf book, plus quarterly updates. Covers estate, gift, and income taxes. Includes worksheets and examples of forms for wills, trusts, and contracts. Price $98.00. ISBN 0-916592-13-8.

1747

Estate Planner's Letter

Research and Review Service of America, Inc, PO Box 1727, Indianapolis, IN 46206. Telephone (317) 297-4360.

Monthly newsletter. Presents information relating to estate planning, particularly regarding taxation and insurance. Price $33.00 per year.

1748

Estate Planning

Warren, Gorham & Lamont, Inc, 210 S St, Boston, MA 02111. Telephone (800) 225-2263.

Bimonthly magazine. Provides practical help on estate planning for attorneys, accountants, and life insurance personnel. Price $36.00 per year.

1749
Estate Planning Course
Inst for Business Planning, Inc, IPB Plz, Englewood Cliffs, NJ 07632. Telephone (201) 592-2040.

Three loose-leaf books, plus semimonthly cassettes and monthly updates. Provide a review of estate planning techniques and procedures, with emphasis on the Tax Reform Act of 1976. Price $510.00 per year.

1750
Estate Planning Desk Book, 5th edition
Inst for Business Planning, Inc, IPB Plz, Dept. 7102-81, Englewood Cliffs, NJ 07632. Telephone (201) 592-2040.

Book. Covers estate planning and estate and gift taxes. Explains provisions of the Tax Reform Act of 1976 and the Revenue Act of 1978. Tables and charts. Price $29.95. ISSN 0-87624-139-9.

1751
Estate Planning Program
Inst for Business Planning, Inc, IPB Plz, Englewood Cliffs, NJ 07632. Telephone (201) 592-2040.

Two loose-leaf books, with monthly supplements and semimonthly letters. Deal with estate valuation and planning under the Tax Reform Act of 1976. Suggests ways to avoid needless taxes. Price available on request.

1752
Estate Planning Review
Commerce Clearing House, Inc, 4025 W Peterson Ave, Chicago, IL 60646. Telephone (312) 583-8500.

Loose-leaf book, plus monthly newsletter. Provides news and commentary on estate planning. Price $65.00 per year.

1753
Estate Practice & Procedure Program
Inst for Business Planning, Inc, IPB Plz, Englewood Cliffs, NJ 07632. Telephone (201) 592-2040.

Loose-leaf book, with monthly supplements and semimonthly letters. Presents a complete system for estate planning for professionals. Tax tables, worksheets, checklist. Price available on request.

1754
Estates Gazette
Estates Gazette Ltd, 151 Wardour St, London, England W1V 4BN. Telephone (44) (01) 437-0141.

Weekly magazine on real estate investment in Great Britain. Covers the management, purchase, sale, valuation and development of land and buildings. Contains an extensive listings of properties for sale. Price £45.24 per year.

1755
Estates Times
Morgan-Grampian Ltd, Morgan-Grampian House, Calderwood St, London, England SE18 6QH. Order from Morgan-Grampian Publishing Co, 2 Park Ave, New York, NY 10016. Telephone England (44)(01) 855-7777. Telex 896238 MORGAN G. New York (212) 340-9700. Telex 425592 MGI UI.

Weekly newspaper. Contains information about industrial and commercial property in the United Kingdom and overseas. Price $70.00 per year.

1757
Estimates of Labour Income
Statistics Canada, User Services, Publications Distribution, Ottawa, Ont, Canada K1A 0V7. Telephone (613) 992-3151.

Quarterly report. Estimates Canadian wages and supplementary income for industries and regions by month. Provides annual totals for the last 5 years. Price $24.00 per year. ISSN 0318-9007.

1758
Etruscan
Bank of New South Wales, GPO Box 1, Sydney, NSW 2001, Australia

Magazine. Contains articles about banking and the activities of the Bank of New South Wales. Presents features of general interest. Price free of charge.

1758.01
Eureka
Findlay Publications Ltd, 10 Letchworth Dr, Bromley, Kent, England BR2 9BE. Order from Machpress Ltd, 1 Copers Cope Rd, Beckenham, Kent, England BR3 2NB. Telephone (44) (01) 650-4877.

Monthly magazine. Contains information on design engineering and on components used in design function in manufacturing. Price £21.00 per year.

1759
Euro-Abstracts: Scientific and Technical Publications and Patents, Sections I and II
European Community Information Service, 2100 M St, NW, Suite 707, Washington, DC 20037. Telephone (202) 862-9500. Telex 248455.

Monthly publications. Contain abstracts from scientific and technical publications and patents on Euratom and European Economic Community (Common Market) research (Section I); coal and steel (Section II). Price $122.50 per year for both sections, $70.00 per year for individual section.

1760
Euro-Abstracts: Section II. Coal and Steel
Commission of the European Communities, Office for Official Publications of the European Communities, CP 1003, Luxembourg 1, Luxembourg. Telephone (352) 490081. Telex PUBLOF 1325.

Monthly publication. Presents abstracts of scientific and technical articles on coal and steel in six languages. Price free of charge.

1761
Euroguide
Publishing and Distributing Company Ltd, Mitre House, 177 Regent St, London, England W1R 7FB. Telepone (44) (01) 734-6534, 6535.

Book. Provides a guide to European economic, political, financial, and other organizations, including EEC, EFTA, and Comecon. Includes European cultural and travel information. Price $200.00 per year.

1762
Eurolaw Commercial Intelligence
European Law Centre Ltd, 4 Bloomsbury Sq, London, WC1A 2RL, England. Telephone (44) (01) 404-4300. Telex 21746.

Semimonthly survey. Covers European commercial law developments, including information on court cases, industry, labor, taxation, and conferences. Price $174.00 per year.

1763
Euromarket Letter
Financial Times Business Information Ltd, Bracken House, 10 Cannon St, London, England EC4P 4BY. Order from Financial Times Ltd, 75 Rockefeller Plz, New York, NY 10019. Telephone (44) (01) 248-8000. Telex 886341-2.

Weekly newsletter. Reviews activities in Euromarkets. Provides information on Eurobonds, loans, interest rates, and domestic bond and money markets. Price $750.00 per year.

1764

Euromarket News

Commerce Clearing House, Inc, 4025 W Peterson Ave, Chicago, IL 60646. Telephone (312) 583-8500.

Weekly newsletter. Covers major European merger, financial, and stock market news. Includes money trends, and government actions. Price $120.00 per year.

1765

Euromoney

Euromoney Publications Ltd, Nestor House, Playhouse Yard, London EC4V 5EX, England. Telephone (01) 236-7111. Telex 8812246 Eurmon G.

Monthly journal. Provides articles on the international banking and money markets, plus details of syndicated loans and bond issues, and Euromarket data. Price $89.00 per year. ISBN 0014-2433. ISBN 0-903 121 00X.

1766

Euromoney Currency Report

Euromoney Publications Ltd, Nestor House, Playhouse Yard, London, England EC4V 5EX. Telephone (44) (01) 236-7111. Telex 8812246 Eurmon G.

Monthly report, plus regular supplements. Surveys the 15 most critical currencies, plus hedging techniques and regulations. Includes one to five year forecasts. Price $480.00 per year. ISSN 0 143 8719.

1766.01

Euromoney Syndication Guide

Euromoney Publications Ltd, Nestor House, Playhouse Yard, London England EC4V 5EX. Telephone (44) (01) 236-7111. Telex 8812246 Eurmon G.

Monthly service, with weekly updates. Provides all information available on syndicated loans, international bonds, and private placements. Tables. Price $1650.00 per year. ISSN 0260-6747.

1766.02

Europa Transport: Observation of the Transport Markets (Three Series)

European Community Information Service, 2100 M St, NW, Suite 707, Washington DC 20037. Telephone (202) 862-9500. Telex 248455.

Quarterly publications and annual report. European Economic Community (Common Market) Covers transport markets, trends and transport survey. Price $12.30 per year $5.30 for each series or annual report.

1767

Europa Year Book

Europa Publications Ltd, 18 Bedford Sq, London, WC1B 3JN, England. Telephone (44) (01) 580-8236.

Yearbook. Offers detailed information on every country in the world and 1650 international organizations. Price $180.00.

1768

European and Middle East Tax Report

Inst for International Research Ltd, 70 Warren St, London, England W1P 5PA. Telephone (44) (01) 388 2663. Telex 263504.

Biweekly report. Reviews and analyzes tax developments in Europe and the Middle East with recommendations for corporations. Price $295.00 per year.

1769

European Commercial Cases

European Law Centre Ltd, 4 Bloombury Sq, London, England WC1A 2RL. Telephone (44) (01) 404-4300. Telex 21746.

Quarterly report. Contains full texts of decisions of Western European courts on commercial law. Price $210.00 per year. ISSN 0141-7266.

1771

European Compensation Survey

Business International Corp, 1 Dag Hammarskjold Plz, New York, NY 10017. Telephone (212) 750-6300.

Annual computerized comparisons of wages, fringe benefits, and allowances in eight European countries, distinguished by industry and by managerial, technical, sales, clerical, and blue-collar job classifications. Price $1190.00 for series; $230.00 per country.

1772

European Computer Market Forecast-Eurocast **1981**

IDC Europa Ltd, 2 Bath Rd, London, England W4 1LN. Telephone (44) (01) 995-9222. Telex 934287.

Series of reports. Analyzes Western Europe market for computer equipment and services. Profiles principal vendors. Notes user attitudes. Price available on request.

1773

European Directory of Business Information Sources & Services

Center for Business Information, 7, Rue Buffon, 75005 Paris, France. Telephone 707-26-14. Telex 204320.

Annual loose-leaf book, with monthly updating service. Monitors international and European sources of information to provide data on such subjects as finance, economics, insurance, banking, law, marketing, and communications. Price $180.00 per year, plus postage.

1774

European Economic Review

North-Holland Publishing Co, PO Box 211, 1000 AE Amsterdam, The Netherlands. Order from Elsevier/North-Holland, Inc, 52 Vanderbilt Ave, New York, NY 10017. Telephone (212) 867-9040.

Bimonthly journal. Covers European economic research. Emphasizes applied economic work. Price $172.50 per year. ISSN 0014-2921.

1774.01

European Economic Service

Data Resources, Inc, 29 Hartwell Ave, Lexington, MA 02173. Telephone (617) 861-0165.

Monthly report. Gives the European Economic Community's and individual countries' economic forecasts. Covers consumption, investment, trade, prices, wages, finance, and production. Price available on request.

1774.02

European Economy

European Community Information Service, 2100 M St, NW, Suite 707, Washington, DC 20037. Telephone (202) 862-9500. Telex 248455.

Report issued three times per year. Covers all aspects of European Communities economy. Price $24.50 per year.

1775

European Economy-Economic Survey of Europe

United Nations Publications, Rm A-3315, New York, NY 10017. Telephone (212) 754-8302.

Report. Covers economic conditions and trends in Europe. Price available on request.

1775.01

European Energy Report

Financial Times Business Information Ltd, Bracken House, 10 Cannon St, London, England EC4P 4BY. Order from Financial Times Ltd, 75 Rockefeller Plz., New York, NY 10019. Telephone (44) (01) 248-8000. Telex 886341-2.

Fortnightly report. Analyzes energy news, trends, and developments throughout Europe. Price $475.00 per year.

1776
European Human Rights Reports
European Law Centre Ltd, 4 Bloombury Sq, London, England WC1A 2RL. Telephone (44) (01) 404-4300. Telex 21746.

Quarterly report. Contains full texts of decisions of the European Court of Human Rights. Includes selected decisions of the European Commission on Human Rights. Price $162.00 per year. ISSN 0260-4868.

1777
European Industrial & Commercial Review
W Parr & Co, Rex Bldgs, Alderley Rd, Cheshire, England SK9 1HZ. Telephone 09964-27431.

Bimonthly magazine. Reviews European industrial and commercial news. Price £ 6.00 per year.

1778
European Industrial Relations Review
Industrial Relations Service, 170 Finchley Rd, London, England NW3 6BP. Telephone (44) (01) 794-4554.

Monthly report on significant developments in British and European industrial relations. Includes coverage of national and international agreements, the European Economic Community, multinational companies, laws governing employment, and collective bargaining. Price $110.00 per year.

1780
European Investment Bank Annual Report
European Community Information Service, 2100 M St NW, Suite 707, Washington, DC 20037. Telephone (202) 862-9500. Telex 248455.

Publication. Presents the annual report of the European Investment Bank. Price available on request.

1781
European Journal of Marketing
MCB Publications, 200 Keighley Rd, Bradford, W Yorkshire, England BD9 4JQ. Telephone 0274 499821.

Three journals and three monographs per year. Present articles on marketing and market research in Great Britain and Western Europe. Price $168.00 per year.

1781.01
European Journal of Operational Research
North-Holland Publishing Co, PO Box 211, 1000 AE Amsterdam, The Netherlands. Telephone 5159222.

Monthly journal. Contains articles on operations research. Includes book reviews. Price $232.25 per year. ISSN 0304-4130.

1782
European Law Digest
European Law Centre Ltd, 4 Bloomsbury Sq, London, WC1A 2RL, England. Telephone (44) (01) 404-4300. Telex 21746.

Monthly report. Summarizes European law developments and includes laws of individual countries, the European community, and other European organizations. Emphasizes business and tax laws. Price $186.00 per year.

1783
European Law Letter
Financial Times Business Information Ltd, Bracken House, 10 Cannon St, London, England EC4P 4BY. Order from Financial Times Ltd, 75 Rockefeller Plz, New York, NY 10019. Telephone (44) (01) 248-8000. Telex 886341-2.

Monthly newsletter. Surveys European legal developments, including EEC issues. Price $260.00 per year.

1785
European Marketing Data & Statistics, 1981
Euromonitor Publications Ltd, 18 Doughty St, London, England WC1N 2PN. Telephone (44) (01) 242-0042. Order from Gale Research Co, Book Tower, Detroit, MI 48226.

Annual. Offers vital statistics on Eastern and Western Europe, including data on population, employment, trade, food and energy consumption, prices, and taxation. Price $150.00.

1786
European Report
Europe Information Service, 46 Ave Albert Elisabeth, Brussels, Belgium 1040. Telephone 736.11.93. Telex Eurinf 26005b.

Semiweekly report, plus supplements. Features the economic and political activities of the European Economic Community and other international organizations. Focuses on Western Europe. Price $750.00.

1787
European Taxation
International Bureau of Fiscal Documentation, Muiderpoort, PO Box 20237, 1000 HE Amsterdam, Netherlands.

Monthly magazine. Contains articles on the tax structure of countries in Europe. Price DFL 550 per year.

1787.01
European Trends
Economist Intelligence Unit Ltd, Spencer House, 27 St James's Pl, London, England SW1A 1NT. Order from Economist Intelligence Unit Ltd, 75 Rockefeller Plz, New York, NY 10019. Telephone (212) 541-5730. Telex 148393.

Quarterly journal. Reports on developments in the European Economic Community (EEC), and relations between member countries. Focuses on agriculture and economic policies. Price $130.00 per year.

1788
Europe Energy
Europe Information Service, 46 Ave Albert Elisabeth, Brussels, Belgium 1040. Telephone 736.11.93. Telex Eurinf 26005b.

Semimonthly report. Covers energy-related topics pertinent to western Europe. Price $360.00.

1789
Europe Environment
Europe Information Service, 46 Ave Albert Elisabeth, Brussels, Belgium 1040. Telephone 736.11.93. Telex Eurinf 26005b.

Semimonthly report. Covers environmental topics of interest to western Europe. Price $600.00 per year.

1790
Europe's 5,000 Largest Companies
R R Bowker Co, 1180 Ave of the Americas, New York, NY 10036. Telephone (212) 764-5100.

Annual book. Ranks major European companies. Includes financial information. Price available on request.

1791
Europe's 5,000 Largest Companies
Dun & Bradstreet, Box 3224, Church St Station, New York, NY 10008. Telephone (212) 285-7346.

Directory. Covers Europe's 5000 largest companies. Prices available on request, to Dun & Bradstreet subscribers only.

1792

Europe's 5,000 Largest Companies

Guides to Multinational Business, Inc, Harvard Sq, Box 92, Cambridge, MA 02138. Telephone (617) 868-2288.

Annual book. Presents a guide to 5000 European industrial companies and 1500 European banks, trading, transport, and insurance companies. Price $150.00.

1792.01

Europe's 5000 Largest Companies Directory, **1980**

Manufacturers' News, Inc, 3 Huron St, Chicago, IL 60611. Telephone (312) 337-1084.

Annual book. Lists 5000 largest industrial companies in Europe. Includes information on trading companies. Price $85.00.

1792.02

Eurostatistics

Commission of the European Communities, Office for Official Publications of the European Communities, CP 1003, Luxembourg 1, Luxembourg. Telephone (352) 490081. Telex PUBLOF 1325.

Report issued 11 times per year. Provides data for short-term European community economic analysis. Price $28.00 per year.

1792.03

Eurostatistics (Bulletin of General Statistics)

European Community Information Service, 2100 M St, NW, Suite 707, Washington, DC 20037. Telephone (202) 862-9500. Telex 248455.

Monthly bulletin. Provides data for short-term economic analysis of European Economic Community (Common Market) developments. Price $28.00 per year.

1792.04

Evaluation of Pesticide Supplies and Demand

US Dept of Agriculture, ESS Publications, Room 0054-S, Washington, DC 20250. Telephone (202) 447-7255.

Report. Covers use and source of pesticides. Price free of charge.

1793

Evaluation Studies Review Annual

Sage Publications, Inc, 275 S Beverly Dr, Beverly Hills, CA 90212. Telephone (213) 274-8003.

Two-volume review. Presents articles on evaluation theory as it relates to various fields. Price $35.00 per volume.

1794

EVM Market Week

EVM Analysts, Inc, 10921 Wilshire Blvd, Suite 1007, Westwood Village, Los Angeles, CA 90024. Telephone (213) 478-3693.

Weekly newsletter. Covers listed stock options, market conditions, and trading methods. Price $130.00 per year.

1794.01

Exchange Rate Outlook (ERO)

Facts on File, Inc, 460 Park Ave S, New York, NY 10016. Telephone (212) 265-2011.

Monthly report. Provides forecasts of exchange rates for six currencies. Notes developments which affected exchange rates in recent months. Price $350.00 per year.

1794.02

Execu-Time

Januz Marketing Communications, Inc, PO Box 1000, Lake Forest, IL 60045. Telephone (312) 295-6550.

Semimonthly newsletter. Notes ways executives can save time by performing daily tasks more efficiently. Price $56.00 per year, $112.00 two years, $140.00 three years. ISSN 0199-2260.

1795

Executive

Southam Communications Ltd, 1450 Don Mills Rd, Don Mills, Ont, Canada M3B 2X7. Telephone (416) 445-6641. Telex 06 966612.

Monthly magazine. Reflects the economic, political, and social concerns of senior management in Canadian corporations. Price $33.00 per year.

1796

Executive Action Report

Prentice-Hall, Inc, Englewood Cliffs, NJ 07632. Telephone (201) 592-2000. Telex 13-5423.

Weekly newsletter service. Covers management, marketing and sales policies, labor relations, corporate taxation, pollution, and consumerism. Price $156.00 per year.

1796.01

Executive and Ownership Report

American Trucking Assn Inc, 1616 P St, NW, Washington, DC 20036. Telephone (202) 797-5351.

Annual report. Lists corporate officers, stockholders, subsidiaries, and affiliated companies for Class I and Class II motor carriers of property. Price $100.00 per year.

1797

Executive Briefing

Lipscombe & Assoc, PO Box 158, Claremont, WA, Australia 6010. Telephone 386-7899. Telex 92-442.

Monthly newsletter. Covers energy, building, mining, and economic topics for Australia. Statistical tables on western Australia's key business indicators. Price $49.00 (Australian) per year.

1798

Executive Bulletin

Conference Board in Canada, Suite 100, 25 McArthur Rd, Ottawa, Ont, Canada K1L 6R3. Telephone (613) 746-1261.

Irregular reports. Cover economic and management research. Price available on request.

1798.01

Executive Compensation and Employee Benefits Report

Warren, Gorham & Lamont, Inc, 210 South St, Boston, MA 02111. Telephone (617) 423-2020.

Monthly report. Discusses executive compensation subjects, including fringe benefits, tax planning, and insider stock trading. Price $56.00 per year.

1799

Executive Compensation Letter

Arthur Young & Co, 277 Park Ave, New York, NY 10017. Telephone (212) 922-2000.

Bimonthly newsletter. Reports on executive compensation programs. Includes information on health insurance coverage and employee benefits practices. Price free of charge.

1801

Executive Compensation Service. Reports on International Compensation. Brazil

American Management Assns, 135 W 50th St, New York, NY 10020. Telephone (212) 586-8100.

Report. Contains data on top and middle managers' compensation in Brazil. Covers 106 companies and a wide range of industries. Price $155.00.

1802

Executive Compensation Service. Technician Report

American Management Assns, 135 W 50th St, New York, NY 10020. Telephone (212) 586-8100.

Report. Provides salary data on US technicians based on a survey of 650 companies. Covers numerous fields. Price $70.00 members $165.00 nonmembers.

1802.01

Executive Compensation Service Top Management Report

American Management Assns, 135 W 50th St, New York, NY 10020. Telephone (212) 586-8100.

Series of reports. Provides salary data on executives, middle managers, engineers, scientists, salesmen, and health care employees. Includes information on benefits and bonuses. Price available on request.

1803

Executive Disclosure Guide

Commerce Clearing House, Inc, 4025 W Peterson Ave, Chicago, IL 60646. Telephone (312) 583-8500.

Loose-leaf books, monthly reports, and biweekly newsletters. Offer assistance to executives in complying with the Securities and Exchange Commission's reporting and disclosure rules. Price $200.00 per year.

1804

Executive Lifestyle Newsletter

Roy W Walters & Assoc, Whitney Rd, Mahwah, NJ 07430. Telephone (201) 891-5757.

Newsletter. Discusses topics of interest to executives. Includes travel, leisure, and management. Price $54.00 per year.

1806

Executive Living Costs in Major Cities Worldwide

Business International Corp, 1 Dag Hammarskjold Plz, New York, NY 10017. Telephone (212) 750-6300.

Annual survey. Compares the living costs for executives and their families in 77 cities throughout the world. Price $160.00 per city; $3715.00 for all cities.

1807

Executive Newsletter

US Trademark Assn, 6 E 45th St, New York, NY 10017. Telephone (212) 986-5880.

Quarterly newsletter. Discusses trademark issues for management personnel. Topics include protecting corporate trademarks and use of international trademarks. Price $.50 per copy.

1807.01

Executive Recruiter News

Kennedy & Kennedy, Inc, Templeton Rd, Fitzwilliam, NH 03447. Telephone (603) 585-6544.

Monthly newsletter. Covers developments in executive recruiting. Notes personnel changes and activities of associations. Price $48.00 per year.

1807.02

Executive's Credit and Collections Letter

Executive Reports Corp, Englewood Cliffs, NJ, 07632. Telephone (201) 592-2000. Telex 13-5423.

Fortnightly newsletter. Includes credit and collections techniques. Price $131.40 per year.

1808

Executive's Personal Development Letter

Alexander Hamilton Inst, 1633 Broadway, New York, NY 10019. Telephone (212) 397-3580.

Monthly letter. Suggests ways business executives can develop personally to improve business performance. Price $68.00 per year.

1809

Executives Tax Report & What's Happening in Taxation

Prentice-Hall, Inc, Englewood Cliffs, NJ 07632. Telephone (201) 592-2000. Telex 13-5423.

Weekly newsletter service. Provides tax information for business executives. Price available on request.

1810

Executive's Tax Review

Commerce Clearing House, Inc, 4025 W Peterson Ave, Chicago, IL 60646. Telephone (312) 583-8500.

Loose-leaf book, plus monthly newsletter. Provides assistance for tax planning of an executive's personal and business financial affairs. Price $65.00 per year.

1811

Executive Woman

Executive Woman, Box 3101, Grand Central Station, New York, NY 10017. Telephone (212) 661-7139 or (914) 528-2256.

Monthly (except June and July) newsletter for business and professional women. Contains information on credit, investments, education, career opportunities, and business trends. Price $28.00 per year.

1812

Eximbank Record

Export-Import Bank of the US, 811 Vermont Ave NW, Washington, DC 20571. Telephone (202) 566-8990. Telex 89-461.

Newsletter published 10 times a year. Discusses topics of interest to exporters. Price free of charge.

1813

Existing Home Sales Series

National Assn of Realtors, 430 N Michigan Ave, Chicago, IL 60611. Telephone (312) 440-8008. Telex 02 53742.

Monthly report, with cumulative annual report. Provides current data on existing home sales and prices by major regions of the country. Price $36.00 per year.

1814

Experimental Agriculture

Cambridge University Press, 32 E 57th St, New York, NY 10022. Telephone (212) 688-8885.

Quarterly journal. Presents information on experimental agricultural projects. Price $97.50 per year.

1815

Exploration and Economics of the Petroleum Industry

Matthew Bender & Co, 235 E 45th St, New York, NY 10017. Telephone (212) 661-5050.

Annual book. Discusses current petroleum exploration projects, techniques, and finances. Contains proceedings of the Institute held at International Oil and Gas Educational Center of Southwestern Legal Foundation. Price $45.00.

1816

Export

Gateway Publications, Foley Trading Estate, Foley St, Hereford, England HR1 2SN. Telephone Hereford (0432) 65700.

Monthly magazine. Reports on news and techniques affecting British exports. Notes changes in regulations. Price £ 15.00 per year.

1817

Export

Irish Export Board, Strand Rd, Sandymount, Dublin 4, Ireland. Order from 10 E 53rd St, New York, NY 10022. Telephone (212) 371-3600. Telex 420012 IREXUI.

Quarterly magazine. Offers items of general interest related to Irish exports. Price free of charge.

1818

Export Administration Regulations

US Dept of Commerce, International Trade Adm, Office of Export Adm, Washington, DC 20230. Order from Superintendent of Documents, US Govt Printing Office, Washington, DC 20402. Telephone (202) 377-4811.

Annual loose-leaf report. Covers regulations for exports, re-exports, boycotting, licensing and special country licensing provision. Lists commerce offices and commodity control numbers. Price $37.-50.

1819

Export Administration Report

US Dept of Commerce, International Trade Administration, Washington, DC 20230. Order from Publications Distribution, Room 1617, Washington, DC 20230. Telephone (202) 377-2000.

Report. Provides data on East-West international export trade. Price available on request.

1820

Export and Import Permits Act Handbook

Supply and Services Canada, Canadian Govt Publishing Centre, Hull, Que, Canada K1A 0S9. Telephone (819) 994-3475, 2085.

Book, with update service. Details regulations of Canada's Export and Import Permits Act. Bilingual. Price $18.00.

1821

Export/Ed Exportador

Johnston International Publishing Corp, 386 Park Ave S, New York, NY 10016. Telephone (212) 689-0120. Telex 666811 Jonst.

Bimonthly magazine. Covers consumer hard goods available for export, including home appliances, electrical equipment, and building—and other allied—products. Spanish and English editions. Price $40.00 per year, $65.00 two years.

1821.01

Exporters Directory

Twin Coast Newspapers, Inc, 110 Wall St, New York, NY 10005. Order from US Buying Guide, 445 Marshall St, Phillipsburg, NJ 08865. Telephone (201) 859-1300.

Directory. Lists 40,000 exporters and identifies products. Price $175.00.

1822

Exporters' Encyclopaedia—World Marketing Guide

Dun & Bradstreet, Box 3224, Church St Station, New York, NY 10008. Telephone (212) 285-7346.

Annual book, with semimonthly bulletins. Contains data on world export regulations. Price available on request, to Dun & Bradstreet subscribers only.

1823

Exporter's Financial and Marketing Handbook, 1975

Claude M Jonnard, Noyes Data Corp, Park Ridge, NJ 07656. Telephone (201) 391-8484.

Book. Serves as a guide to exporting and marketing abroad. Price $18.00.

1826

Export-Import Bank of the United States Annual Report

Export-Import Bank of the US, 811 Vermont Ave NW, Washington, DC 20571. Telephone (202) 566-8990. Telex 89-461.

Annual report. Discusses the financial conditions and operations of the Export-Import Bank of the US. Price free of charge.

1827

Exporting to the United States

US Customs Service, Washington, Dc 20229. Order from Superintendent of Documents, US Government Printing Office, Washington, DC 20420. Telephone (202) 783-3238.

Booklet. Provides pertinent data for foreign exporters and American importers on US import requirements. Price $4.00.

1828

Exports, Australia (Cat No 5404.0)

Australian Bureau of Statistics, PO Box 10, Belconnen, ACT 2616, Australia. Order from Australian Government Publishing Service, PO Box 84, Canberra, ACT 2600, Australia. Telephone (61) (062) 527911.

Monthly report. Presents statistics on value of Australian exports for approximately 800 commodites, produce, gold, manufactured goods, and petroleum. Price free of charge.

1829

Export News Bulletin

Canadian Export Assn, Suite 1020, 1080 Beaver Hall Hill, Montreal, Que, Canada H2Z 1T7. Telephone (514) 866-4481. Telex 055-60687.

Monthly loose-leaf, with information of interest to Canadian exporters. Includes a Review and Digest Bulletin with a subscription. Price $25.00 per year. ISSN 0316-7631.

1830

Exports by Commodities

Statistics Canada, User Services, Publications Distribution, Ottawa, Ont, Canada K1A 0V7. Telephone (613) 992-3151.

Monthly report. Provides data on the quantity and value of Canadian exports. Indicates the country to which a commodity was exported and cumulative totals. Notes re-exports and nontrade special transactions. Price $60.00 per year. ISSN 0318-238X.

1831

Exports by Countries

Statistics Canada, User Services, Publications Distribution, Ottawa, Ont, Canada K1A 0V7. Telephone (613) 992-3151.

Quarterly report. Gives the value of Canadian exports by country and commodity categories. Contains three-year figures and year-to-date totals. Price $48.00 per year. ISSN 0318-2384.

1832

Export Services

Kompass Publishers Ltd, Stuart House, 41-43 Perrymount Rd, Haywards Heath, West Sussex, England RH16 3DA. Telephone 0444 59188.

Annual publication. Provides information on services for British export firms. Includes sections on freight and finance. Price £20.00.

1833

Exports—FTNT-7508

US Dept of Commerce, Bureau of the Census, Washington, DC 20233. Order information from Chief, Foreign Trade Div, Bureau of the Census, Washington, DC 20233. Telephone (202) 655-4000.

Monthly report. Provides information on US exports of greases, animal and vegetable fats and oils, and glycerine of domestic and foreign origin. Tables. Price available on request.

1834
Exports—FTNT-8501
US Dept of Commerce, Bureau of the Census, Washington, DC 20233. Order information from Chief, Foreign Trade Div, Bureau of the Census, Washington, DC 20233. Telephone (202) 655-4000.

Monthly service. Presents statistics on US exports of steel products and selected commodities by the country of destination and customs district of exportation. Price available on request.

1835
Exports—FTNT-8502
US Dept of Commerce, Bureau of the Census, Washington, DC 20233. Order information from Chief, Foreign Trade Div, Bureau of the Census, Washington, DC 20233. Telephone (202) 655-4000.

Monthly service. Covers US shipments of selected agriculture and earth-moving equipment to Puerto Rico and the Virgin Islands. Price available on request.

1836
Exports—FTNT-8503
US Dept of Commerce, Bureau of the Census, Washington, DC 20233. Order information from Chief, Foreign Trade Div, Bureau of the Census, Washington, DC 20233. Telephone (202) 655-4000.

Monthly and cumulative service. Presents data on US exports of domestic merchandise to Japan. Price available on request.

1837
Exports—FTNT-8504
US Dept of Commerce, Bureau of the Census, Washington, DC 20233. Order information from Chief, Foreign Trade Div, Bureau of the Census, Washington, DC 20233. Telephone (202) 655-4000.

Monthly service. Provides information on US shipments of specified glass to Puerto Rico. Price available on request.

1838
Exports—FTNT-8521
US Dept of Commerce, Bureau of the Census, Washington, DC 20233. Order information from Chief, Foreign Trade Div, Bureau of the Census, Washington, DC 20233. Telephone (202) 655-4000.

Monthly service. Supplies statistics on US shipments of brandy, rum, whiskey, and other distilled alcoholic beverages and compounds containing spirits to Puerto Rico and the Virgin Islands. Price available on request.

1839
Exports—FTNT-8532
US Dept of Commerce, Bureau of the Census, Washington, DC 20233. Order information from Chief, Foreign Trade Div, Bureau of the Census, Washington, DC 20233. Telephone (202) 655-4000.

Monthly service. Contains data on US exports of domestic and foreign merchandise from Customs District 17 (Savannah, Georgia). Price available on request.

1840
Exports—FTNT-8549
US Dept of Commerce, Bureau of the Census, Washington, DC 20233. Order information from Chief, Foreign Trade Div, Bureau of the Census, Washington, DC 20233. Telephone (202) 655-4000.

Monthly service. Reports on US exports of tall oil fatty acids, tall oil and tall oil resin, pine oil (except pine needle oil) and terpenic solvents through specified southern ports. Shows the country of destination. Price available on request.

1841
Exports—FTNT-8562
US Dept of Commerce, Bureau of the Census, Washington, DC 20233. Order information from Chief, Foreign Trade Div, Bureau of the Census, Washington, DC 20233. Telephone (202) 655-4000.

Monthly, cumulative-to-date and cumulative quarterly service. Contains information on US exports of iron and steel products of domestic origin. Indicates the country of destination and customs district. Price available on request.

1842
Exports—FTNT-8568
US Dept of Commerce, Bureau of the Census, Washington, DC 20233. Order information from Chief, Foreign Trade Div, Bureau of the Census, Washington, DC 20233. Telephone (202) 655-4000.

Monthly service. Supplies data on US shipments of selected iron and steel products to Puerto Rico. Price available on request.

1843
Exports—FTNT-8575
US Dept of Commerce, Bureau of the Census, Washington, DC 20233. Order information from Chief, Foreign Trade Div, Bureau of the Census, Washington, DC 20233. Telephone (202) 655-4000.

Monthly service. Contains statistics on US exports of hosiery of domestic and foreign origin. Shows the country of destination and customs district of exportation. Price available on request.

1844
Exports—FTNT-8584
US Dept of Commerce, Bureau of the Census, Washington, DC 20233. Order information from Chief, Foreign Trade Div, Bureau of the Census, Washington, DC 20233. Telephone (202) 655-4000.

Monthly and cumulative year-to-date service. Offers data on US exports of selected electrical merchandise and related products. Shows the country of destination. Price available on request.

1845
Exports—FTNT-8594
US Dept of Commerce, Bureau of the Census, Washington, DC 20233. Order information from Chief, Foreign Trade Div, Bureau of the Census, Washington, DC 20233. Telephone (202) 655-4000.

Monthly service. Reports on US shipments of electric lamps (bulbs) and motor vehicle-sealed beam lamps to Puerto Rico and the Virgin Islands. Price available on request.

1846
Exports—FTNT-EA 675
US Dept of Commerce, Bureau of the Census, Washington, DC 20233. Order information from Chief, Foreign Trade Div, Bureau of the Census, Washington, DC 20233. Telephone (202) 655-4000.

Annual service. Provides information on US exports by products. Price available on request.

1847
Exports—FTNT-EA 676
US Dept of Commerce, Bureau of the Census, Washington, DC 20233. Order information from Chief, Foreign Trade Div, Bureau of the Census, Washington, DC 20233. Telephone (202) 655-4000.

Annual service. Supplies data on US exports by the product and country of destination. Price available on request.

1848
Exports—FTNT-EA 694
US Dept of Commerce, Bureau of the Census, Washington, DC 20233. Order information from Chief, Foreign Trade Div, Bureau of the Census, Washington, DC 20233. Telephone (202) 655-4000.

Annual service. Supplies data on shipments of merchandise from the US to Puerto Rico, the Virgin Islands, and American Samoa. Indicates the customs district of exportation and method of transportation. Price available on request.

1849
Exports—FTNT-EM 594
US Dept of Commerce, Bureau of the Census, Washington, DC 20233. Order information from Chief, Foreign Trade Div, Bureau of the Census, Washington, DC 20233. Telephone (202) 655-4000.

Monthly service. Contains data on US shipments of merchandise to Puerto Rico and the Virgin Islands by the customs district of exportation and method of transportation. Price available on request.

1851
Export Shipping Manual
Bureau of National Affairs, Inc, 1231 25th St NW, Washington, DC 20037. Telephone (202) 452-4200.

Loose-leaf book, with weekly updates. Gives a compendium of shipping facts about countries and regions of export interest. Price $220.00 per year.

1852
Exports—Merchandise Trade
Statistics Canada, User Services, Publications Distribution, Ottawa, Ont, Canada K1A OV7. Telephone (613) 992-3151.

Annual reports. Provide data on Canadian exports by countries, trading areas, and commodities. Price $42.00. ISSN 0317-5375.

1853
Exports of Major Commodities by Country (Cat No 5403.0)
Australian Bureau of Statistics, PO Box 10, Belconnen, ACT 2616, Australia. Order from Australian Government Publishing Service, PO Box 84, Canberra, ACT 2600, Australia. Telephone (062) 52 7911.

Monthly report. Reviews the quantity and value of Australian exports by the country to which each of numerous commodities is assigned. Price free of charge.

1854
Export Times
Export Times Publishing Ltd, 60 Fleet St, London, England EC4Y 1LA. Telephone (44) (01) 353-7582. Telex 27808.

Monthly newspaper. Emphasizes business travel, international trade fairs, and export finance. Is aimed at British business people engaged in overseas marketing. Price $32.00 per year (airmail).

1856
Extel Australian Company Service
Extel Statistical Service Ltd, 37-45 Paul St, London, England EC2A 4PB. Telephone (44) (01) 253-3400. Telex 262687.

Annual card service, with weekly updates. Supplies information on major Australian companies. Covers finances, dividends, products, and subsidiaries. Price £500.00 per year.

1858
Extel Book of Prospectuses and New Issues
Extel Statistical Service Ltd, 37-45 Paul St, London, England EC2A 4PB. Telephone (44) (01) 253-3400. Telex 262687.

Semiannual two-book series. Provides information on British Stock Exchange prospectuses and new issues. Covers offers for sale, sales by tender, reconstructions, placings, and acquisitions. Price £250.00 per year.

1858.01
Extel Annual Dividend Record
Extel Statistical Service Ltd, 37-45 Paul St, London, England EC2A 4PB. Telephone (44) (01) 253-3400. Telex 262687.

Annual book, with periodic updates. Provides dividend information necessary for compiling British income tax returns. Includes interest on convertible loan stocks, debenture stocks and bonds, and unit trust distributions. Price £42.00 per year.

1859
Extel European Company Service
Extel Statistical Service Ltd, 37-45 Paul St, London, England EC2A 4PB. Telephone (44) (01) 253-3400. Telex 262687.

Annual card service, with weekly updates. Describes major European companies. Information includes balance sheets, profit and loss accounts, dividends, and activities. Price £850.00 per year.

1859.01
Extel Fixed Interest Record
Extel Statistical Services Ltd, 37-45 Paul St, London, England EC2A 4PB. Telephone (44) (01) 253-3400. Telex 262687.

Annual book with periodic updates. Provides details of fixed interest securities for British income tax returns. Price £33.00 per year.

1860
Extel Handbook of Market Leaders
Extel Statistical Service Ltd, 37-45 Paul St, London, England EC2A 4PB. Telephone (44) (01) 253-3400. Telex 262687.

Semiannual bound volume. Provides financial and stock price activity information for companies in the F T Actuaries Index. Price £50.00 per year (£60.00 for current edition).

1861
Extel Issuing House Year Book
Extel Statistical Service Ltd, 37-45 Paul St, London, England EC2A 4PB. Telephone (44) (01) 253-3400. Telex 262687.

Annual book. Supplies data on British stock issues. Indicates the brokerage house or stockbroker arranging an issue. Price £50.00 per year.

1862
Extel North American Company Service
Extel Statistical Service Ltd, 37-45 Paul St, London, England EC2A 4PB. Telephone (44) (01) 253-3400. Telex 262687.

Annual card service, with weekly updates. Provides financial and other information on major North American companies. Includes balance sheets, profit and loss accounts, and dividends. Price £840.00 per year.

1863
Extel Overseas Companies Service
Extel Statistical Service Ltd, 37-45 Paul St, London, England EC2A 4PB. Telephone (44) (01) 253-3400. Telex 262687.

Annual card services, with regular updating. Provide financial information on major European, Australian, and North American companies. Include balance sheets, profit and loss accounts, dividends, and activities. Australian Service—£500.00 per year. European Service—£850.00 per year. North American Service—£840.00 per year.

1864
External Trade Report
Ministry of Industry and Small Business Development, Parliament Buildings, Victoria, BC, Canada V8V 1X4. Telephone (604) 387-6701.

Annual report. Provides detailed statistics of imports and exports through British Columbia's custom ports. Data arranged by value, commodity, and country of origin and destination. Price free of charge.

1865
External Trade Review
Consulate General of Nigeria, 575 Lexington Ave, New York, NY 10022. Telephone (212) 752-1670.

Annual report. Reviews external Nigerian trade. Price 50 kobo.

1867
Extraordinary Contractual Relief Reporter
Federal Publications, Inc, 1120 20th St, NW, Washington, DC 20036. Telephone (202) 337-7000.

Four-volume set, with periodic supplements. Contains complete copies of PL 85-804 extraordinary contractual relief decisions issued by government boards. Includes indexes, explanations, statutes, and statistics. Price $360.00 per set; annual supplement $90.00.

1868
Factory Equipment News
Thomson Publications (Australia) Pty Ltd, 47 Chippen St, PO Box 65, Chippendale, NSW 2008, Australia. Telephone 699-6731. Telex TPAS AA22226.

Monthly magazine. Discusses factory equipment developments, with emphasis on Australian news. Price $77.00 (Australian) per year.

1871
Facts and Figures of the Automotive Industry
Motor Vehicle Manufacturers' Assn of the US, 320 New Center Bldg, Detroit, MI 48202. Telephone (313) 872-4311.

Annual report. Gives data on Canadian production and sales of motor vehicles. Price available on request.

1872
Facts and Figures on Government Finance
Tax Foundation, Inc, 1875 Connecticut Ave, NW, Washington, DC 20009. Telephone (202) 328-4500.

Biennial book. Provides data on revenue, expenditures, debt, and tax rates of the US Federal, state, and local government. Includes related economic indicators. Tables. Price $15.00 per copy.

1873
Facts in Focus
Her Majesty's Stationery Office, PO Box 569, London, England SE1 9NH. Telephone (44) (01) 928 1321.

Biennial compendium of official British government statistics. Price £1.50.

1874
Facts on File Weekly News Digest
Facts on File, Inc, 460 Park Ave S, New York, NY 10016. Telephone (212) 265-2011.

Weekly newsletter. Covers current events. Includes cumulative index. Price $315.00 per year.

1876
Fairchild's Financial Manual of Retail Stores
Fairchild Publications, Inc, 7 East 12th St, New York, NY 10003. Telephone (212) 741-4280.

Annual book. Provides corporate profiles and financial assessments of over 475 stores, including department stores, discounters, chain stores, mail order houses, and supermarkets. Price $50.00.

1877
Fair Employment Practice Service
Bureau of National Affairs, Inc, 1231 25th St NW, Washington, DC 20037. Telephone (202) 452-4200.

Two loose-leaf books, plus semiweekly updates. Provide reference and research data for background information on fair employment practices. Summarize latest developments. Price $301.00 per year.

1878
Fair Employment Practices (FEP) Guidelines
Bureau of Business Practice, 24 Rope Ferry Rd, Waterford, CT 06386. Telephone (203) 442-4365.

Monthly loose-leaf newsletter. Analyzes histories regarding job discrimination in terms of the Fair Employment Practice Laws to help management avoid lawsuits and arbitration. Price $48.00 per year.

1879
Fair Employment Report
Business Publishers, Inc, PO Box 1067, Silver Spring, MD 20910. Telephone (301) 587-6300.

Biweekly reporting service. Covers Equal Employment Opportunity (EEO) affairs. Price $107.00 per year.

1880
Fairplay International Shipping Weekly
301 E 64th St, New York NY 10021. Telephone (212) 879-4418.

Weekly magazine. Covers the international shipping scene. Contains articles, news briefs, and special sections on sales, marine insurance, and maritime law. Price $100.00. ISBN 0307-0220.

1881
Fairplay International World Ships on Order
Fairplay Publications Ltd, 301 E 64th St, New York, NY 10021. Telephone (212) 879-4418.

Quarterly magazine supplement to Fairplay International Shipping Weekly. Contains statistics on commercial vessels, except fishing vessels, of 1000 tons dead weight and over. Organized by the type of vessel and country. Price available on request.

1882
Fairplay World Shipping Yearbook
Fairplay Publications Ltd, 301 E 64th St, New York, NY 10021. Telephone (212) 879-4418.

Annual book. Provides detailed data on shipping companies, organizations, and associations. Lists ship sale and purchase brokers. Index and statistics. Price $56.-00.

1883
Family Expenditure Survey
Her Majesty's Stationery Office, PO Box 569, London, England SE1 9NH. Telephone (44) (01) 928 1321. Telex 266455.

Annual service. Provides a detailed breakdown of British household expenditure, analyzed by income, household composition, region, occupation, and sources of income. Price £6.50 per year. ISSN 011 3610 89 0.

1884
Family Expenditure Survey, Northern Ireland
Her Majesty's Stationery Office, PO Box 569, London, England SE1 9NH. Telephone (44) (01) 928 1321.

Annual report. Covers family expenditures in Northern Ireland. Price £4.75 per year.

1885
Family Page Directory
Harold D Hansen, Box 327, Washington Depot, CT 06794. Telephone (203) 868-0200.

Quarterly directory. Offers information pertaining to editors of family pages of 526 of the largest US daily newspapers. Price $45.00 per year.

1886
Family Safety
National Safety Council, 444 N Michigan Ave, Chicago, IL 60611. Telephone (312) 527-4800. Telex 25-3141.

Quarterly magazine. Presents home safety and accident prevention information. Includes articles on car and leisure activity safety. Price $5.25 members, $6.60 nonmembers.

1892
Far East and Australasia
Europa Publications Ltd, 18 Bedford Sq, London, WC1B 3JN, England. Telephone (44) (01) 580-8236.

Annual book. Surveys South Asia, Southeast Asia, Australasia, and the Pacific Islands. Covers history, geography, economy, and major personalities. Price $100.00.

1892.01
Far Eastern Technical Review
Alain Charles Publishing Ltd, 27 Wilfred St, London, England SW1E 6PR. Telephone (44) (01) 828-6107. Telex 28905.

Magazine. Discusses Southeast Asian industrial and technology subjects for international management and industry leaders. Price $28.00 per year.

1893
Far East Week by Week
Laurence French Trade Research, 27 Leinster Sq, London, England W2 4NQ. Telephone London (44) (01) 221-6590.

Weekly newsletter. Focuses on Asia, with special emphasis on international trade and relations. Price £40.00 per year.

1894
Farm Cash Receipts
Statistics Canada, User Services, Publications Distribution, Ottawa, Ont, Canada K1A 0V7. Telephone (613) 992-3151.

Monthly magazine. Reports on the cumulative estimates of income received by Canadian farmers from the sale of farm products by province and commodity. Price $18.00 per year. ISSN 0703-7945.

1894.01
Farm Credit Corporation Statistics
Farm Credit Corp, PO Box 2314, Postal Station D, Ottawa, Ont, Canada, K1P 6J9. Telephone (613) 996-6606.

Annual book. Gives statistics on Canadian farm credit, including borrowing under the Farm Credit Act. Provides profiles of borrowers, and agricultural production. Tables. In English and French. Price free of charge.

1895
Farm Economics
Pennsylvania State University, Cooperative Extension Service, 2 Weaver Bldg, University Park, PA 16802. Telephone (814) 865-2561.

Monthly newsletter. Each issue addresses a current topic in the economics of agriculture. Price free of charge for single issues.

1896
Farmer
The Webb Co, 1999 Shepard Rd, St Paul, MN 55116. Telephone (612) 690-7200.

Semimonthly magazine. Discusses agricultural topics, with emphasis on Minnesota, North Dakota, and South Dakota. Price $6.00 per year.

1897
Farmer Cooperatives
US Dept of Agriculture, Agricultural Cooperative Service, Rm 550, GHI Bldg, Washington, DC 20250. Telephone (202) 447-8915.

Monthly magazine. Reports on farm cooperative achievements. Discusses US Agricultural Cooperative Service technical assistance and research. Price free of charge.

1898
Farmer's Tax Report
Prentice-Hall, Inc, Englewood Cliffs, NJ 07632. Telephone (201) 592-2000. Telex 13-5423.

Fortnightly newsletter. Provides tax information for farmers based on laws, regulations, and court decisions. Price $144.00 per year.

1899
Farm Index
US Dept of Agriculture, Order from Superintendent of Documents, US Government Printing Office, Washington, DC 20402. Telephone (202) 655-4000.

Monthly magazine. Presents research on agricultural economics. Provides data on economic indicators for agricultural development. Tables. Price $7.70 per year.

1900
Farm Industry News
The Webb Co, 1999 Shepard Rd, St Paul, MN 55116. Telephone (612) 690-7200.

Magazine issued nine times per year. Reports on agricultural products. Includes information on machinery, fertilizers, and pesticides. Price available on request.

1901
Farm Input Price Indexes 1971-100
Statistics Canada, User Services, Publications Distribution, Ottawa, Ont, Canada K1A 0V7. Telephone (613) 992-3151.

Quarterly index. Provides the prices of commodities and services used in Canadian farming operations. Includes statistics for the preceding three years and data on eastern and western Canada. Tables. Price $19.20 per year. ISSN 0383-4875.

1901.01
Farmline
US Dept of Agriculture, ESS Publications, Room 0054-S, Washington, DC 20250. Order from Superintendent of Documents, US Government Printing Office, Washington, DC 20402. Telephone (202) 783-3238.

Magazine issued 11 times per year. Gives overall picture of trends in agriculture. Covers developments in rural life, natural resources, farm finances and other topics affecting farm families. Price $10.00 per year domestic, $12.50 per year foreign.

1902
Farm Machines and Equipment
US Dept of Commerce, Bureau of the Census, Washington, DC 20233. Telephone (202) 449-1600.

Annual report. Provides data on shipments of farm machinery and equipment in the US. Indicates the number of manufacturers, exports, imports, and apparent consumption. Price $.35.

1903
Farm Real Estate Market Developments
US Dept of Agriculture, ESS Publications, Room 0054-S, Washinton, DC 20250. Telephone (202) 447-7255.

Annual report, with supplement. Covers farmland values, volume of sales, financing of farm purchases, and factors affecting land market. Provides estimated average value per acre by state. Price free of charge.

1906
Farm Wages in Canada
Statistics Canada, User Services, Publications Distribution, Ottawa, Ont, Canada K1A 0V7. Telephone (613) 992-3151.

Quarterly magazine. Provides average Canadian farm wage rates for Canada excluding Newfoundland. Includes rates by hour, day, and month, with and without board and lodging. Price $12.00 per year. ISSN 0703-2528.

1907
Fast Service
Harcourt Brace Jovanovich Publications, 757 3rd Ave, New York, NY 10017. Order from Harcourt Brace and Jovanovich Publications, 1 E 1st St, Duluth, MN 55802. Telephone (218) 727-8511.

Monthly magazine. Pertains to fast-service restaurant management. Price $15.00 per year.

1908
Fats and Oils—Oilseed Crushings
US Dept of Commerce, Bureau of the Census, Washington, DC 20233. Telephone (202) 449-1600.

Monthly report, with annual summary. Provides data on net receipts, crushings, and end-of-month stocks of raw materials at oil mill locations. Contains statistics on primary products at oil mill locations, on crushings and stock of cottonseed and soybeans at oil mills, and on cottonseed products and soybean products. Notes vegetable oil production. Price $2.70 per year.

1909
Fats and Oil—Production, Consumption, and Stocks
US Dept of Commerce, Bureau of the Census, Washington, DC 20233. Telephone (202) 449-1600.

Monthly report and annual summary. Presents figures on production, consumption, and stocks of selected edible and inedible oils, minor oils, and selected fat and oil products. Notes imports and exports. Price $7.20 per year.

1910
Fedacards
Extel Statistical Service Ltd, 37-45 Paul St, London, England EC2A 4PB. Telephone (44) (01) 253-3400. Telex 23721.

Loose-leaf service, with weekly updates. Supplies information on all companies quoted in Hong Kong. Price £20.00 per year.

1911
Federal Aids to Financing
Prentice-Hall, Inc, Englewood Cliffs, NJ 07632. Telephone (201) 592-2000. Telex 13-5423.

Biweekly loose-leaf service. Discusses federal insurance and guaranty programs for national and state banks, savings and loan associations, mutual savings banks, life insurance companies. Price $261.00 per year.

1912
Federal Aviation Administration (FAA) General Aviation News
US Dept of Transportation, Federal Aviation Adm, 800 Independence Ave, Washington, DC 20591. Order from Superintendent of Documents, US Government Printing Office, Washington, DC 20401. Telephone (202) 275-3050.

Bimonthly magazine. Covers aviation safety for pilots, student pilots, and ground personnel. Includes information on safety problems of helicopters, ballons, gliders, antique, sport, and experimental aircraft. Price $6.20.

1913
Federal Aviation Administration (FAA) Statistical Handbook of Aviation
US Dept of Transportation, Federal Aviation Adm. 800 Independence Ave, Washington, DC 20591. Order from National Technical Information Service, US Dept of Commerce, Operations Center, 5825 Port Royal Rd, Springfield, KVA 22161. Also order from Government Printing Office, Public Documents Dept, Washington, Dc 20402. Telephone (703) 557-4651, 4652, 4653.

Book. Provides aviation statistics. Price $5.00.

1914
Federal Banking Law Reports
Commerce Clearing House, Inc, 4025 W Peterson Ave, Chicago, IL 60646. Telephone (312) 583-8500.

Six loose-leaf books, plus weekly reports. Cover the Federal Reserve System, deposit insurance, national bank acts, and related federal banking and loan measures. Price $390.00 per year.

1916
Federal Carriers Reports
Commerce Clearing House, Inc, 4025 W Peterson Ave, Chicago, IL 60646. Telephone (312) 583-8500.

Four loose-leaf books, plus fortnightly reports. Cover federal regulation and control of motor carriers, water carriers, and freight forwarders. Price $385.00 per year.

1917
Federal Consumer Protection: Law Rules & Regulations
Oceana Publications, Inc, 75 Main St, Dobbs Ferry, NY 10522. Telephone (914) 693-1320.

Loose-leaf service in four binders. Covers federal consumer protection laws and regulations. Includes information on administrative rules. Price $300.00 per set. ISBN 0-379-10025-8.

1917.01
Federal Contract Opportunities: Energy/Environment
Business Publishers, PO Box 1067, Silver Spring, MD 20910. Telephone (301) 587-6300.

Weekly newsletter. Discusses federal energy and environmental contract opportunities. Price $97.00 per year.

1918
Federal Contracts Report
Bureau of National Affairs, Inc, 1231 25th St NW, Washington, DC 20037. Telephone (202) 452-4200.

Loose-leaf books, with updates. Keep subscriber apprised of federal contracting and grants-in-aid developments. Contain often the full text of pertinent documents. Indexes and summary tables of cases. Price $364.00 per year.

1919
Federal Deosit Insurance Corp Annual Report
US Federal Deposit Insurance Corp, Washington, DC 20429. Telephone (202) 389-4221.

Annual report. Discusses the action of the Federal Deposit Insurance Corporation and provides a financial statement. Analyzes bank failures and problem banks. Tables and charts. Price free of charge.

1920
Federal Deosit Insurance CorporationLaw, Regulations and Related Acts
US Federal Deposit Insurance Corp, Washington, DC 20429. Telephone (202) 389-4221.

Annual loose-leaf report, with bimonthly bulletins. Contains the Federal Deposit Insurance Act and other regulations affecting operations of insured banks. Notes statutory or regulatory changes. Price $100.00 for each service per calendar year.

1921
Federal Election Campaign Financing Guide
Commerce Clearing House, Inc, 4025 W Peterson Ave, Chicago, IL 60646. Telephone (312) 583-8500.

Periodic report. Carries the full text of the regulations governing federal election campaign financing as administered by the Federal Election Commission. Price $140.00.

1922
Federal Estate and Gift Taxes Explained, Including Estate Planning
Commerce Clearing House, Inc, 4025 W Peterson Ave, Chicago, IL 60646. Telephone (312) 583-8500.

Book. Explains court decisions, rulings, and estate and gift tax regulations. Price $7.00.

1923
Federal Estate and Gift Tax Reports
Commerce Clearing House, Inc, 4025 W Peterson Ave, Chicago, IL 60646. Telephone (312) 583-8500.

Three loose-leaf books, plus weekly reports. Cover new federal estate and gift tax developments, including estate planning. Price $185.00 per year.

1924
Federal Excise Tax Reports
Commerce Clearing House, Inc, 4025 W Peterson Ave, Chicago, IL 60646. Telephone (312) 583-8500.

Loose-leaf book, plus weekly reports. Covers all federal excise taxes, with laws, decisions, regulations, rulings, and explanations. Price $125.00 per year.

1925
Federal Executive Directory
Carroll Publishing Co, 1058 Thomas Jefferson St, NW, Washington, DC 20007. Telephone (202) 333-8620.

Bimonthly directory. Lists federal personnel and offices. Notes titles and phone numbers. Price $96.00 per year.

1926
Federal Home Loan Bank Board Journal
United States Federal Home Loan Bank Board, 1700 G St NW, Washington, DC 20552. Order from Superintendent of Documents, US Government Printing Office, Washington, DC 20502. Telephone (202) 376-3012.

Monthly magazine. Discusses housing and home finance issues. Reports on the activities and policies of the US Federal Home Loan Bank Board. Provides mortgage, housing, and general fiancial data. Tables. Price $24.50 per year.

1927
Federal Income, Gift and Estate Taxation
Matthew Bender & Co. 235 E 45th St, New York, NY 10017. Telephone (212) 661-5050.

Loose-leaf volumes, monthly supplements, and newsletter. Interpret law for federal income, gift, and estate taxation. Include an index, the text of the 1954 Internal Revenue Code, and relevant House and Senate committee reports. Price $450.00 for 13 volumes with a year's monthly service; 550.00 with two year's monthly service: $275.00.

1928
Federal Income Taxation of Employee Benefits
Clark Boardman Co Ltd, 435 Hudson St, New York, NY 10014. Telephone (212) 929-7500.

Loose-leaf book, periodically revised. Describes federal taxation of employee benefit plans. Includes a detailed analysis of ERISA; and covers bonus plans, pension and profit-sharing plans, deferred compensation, and stock options. Price $47.-50. ISBN 0-87632-077-9.

1929
Federal Income Tax Regulations
Commerce Clearing House, Inc, 4025 W Peterson Ave, Chicago, IL 60646. Telephone (312) 583-8500.

Three loose-leaf books, plus weekly reports. Give final texts of proposed federal income and withholding regulations. Price $170.00 per year.

1930
Federal Index
Predicasts, Inc, 200 University Circle Research Center, 11001 Cedar Ave, Cleveland, OH 44106. Telephone (216) 795-3000.

Monthly computerized information service. Reports on federal legislation, executive orders, government contracts, and other federal developments. Includes such sources as the Congressional Record, Federal Register, Presidential Documents, Commerce Business Daily, and the Washington Post. Price $400.00 per year.

1931
Federal Mediation & Conciliation Service Annual Report
US Federal Mediation and Conciliation Service, 2100 K St NW, Washington, DC 20427. Telephone (202) 653-5290.

Annual report. Discusses the activities of the US Federal Mediation & Conciliation Service. Evaluates private and public collective bargaining issues and provides data on the resolution of cases. Tables. Price free of charge, single copy.

1932
Federal Ministry of Industries Annual Report
Consulate General of Nigeria, 575 Lexington Ave, New York, NY 10022. Telephone (212) PL2-1670.

Annual report on the Nigerian industry. Price free of charge.

1933
Federal Organization Service Military/Civil Charts
Carroll Publishing Co, 1058 Thomas Jefferson St, NW, Washington, DC 20007. Telephone (202) 333-8620.

Quarterly service. Provides charts of 200 federal, civil and military departments. Indicates titles and phone numbers of 18,-000 individuals. Notes organizational changes. Price $600.00 per year.

1933.01
Federal Petroleum Regulatory Newsletter
Coopers & Lybrand, 1251 Ave of the Americas, New York, NY 10020. Order from Manager of Publications, PO Box 682, Times Sq Station, New York, NY 10108. Telephone (212) 489-1100.

Periodic newsletter. Describes developments in government energy regulations. Price free of charge.

1934
Federal Power Service
Matthew Bender & Co, 235 E 45th St, New York, NY 10017. Telephone (212) 661-5050.

Loose-leaf volumes, with a biweekly service. Cover opinions, decisions, and orders of the Federal Power Commission. Price $475.00 per year.

1934.01
Federal Regulatory Directory, 1980–81
Congressional Quarterly, Inc, 1414 22nd St, NW, Washington, DC 20037. Telephone (202) 296-6800.

Annual directory. Provides information on federal agencies. Notes officials, organizations, and responsibilities. Price $25.-00.

1934.02
Federal Research Report
Business Publishers, PO Box 1067, Silver Spring, MD 20910. Telephone (301) 587-6300.

Weekly newsletter. Presents information on federal research grant opportunities. Price $87.00 per year.

1935
Federal Reserve Bank of Dallas Annual Report
Federal Reserve Bank of Dallas, Station K, Dallas, TX 75222. Telephone (214) 651-6111.

Annual report. Contains a statement of condition, earnings, and expenses, volume of operations, and other statistics on the Federal Reserve Bank of Dallas. Price free of charge.

1935.01
Federal Reserve Bank of Minneapolis Quarterly Review
Federal Reserve Bank of Minneapolis, 250 Marquette Ave, Minneapolis, MN 55480. Telephone (612) 340-2341.

Quarterly report. Presents economic research aimed at improving policymaking by Federal Reserve System. Includes review of Ninth Federal Reserve District's economy. Price free of charge.

1936
Federal Reserve Bank of New York Annual Report
Federal Reserve Bank of New York Publications Section, 33 Liberty St, New York, NY 10045. Telephone (212) 791-6134.

Annual report. Analyzes the year's domestic and international economic and financial developments, including Federal Reserve policies. Price free of charge.

1937
Federal Reserve Bank of New York Quarterly Review
Federal Reserve Bank of New York Publications Section, 33 Liberty St, New York, NY 10045. Telephone (212) 791-6134.

Quarterly review. Reports on recent business activity, money and bond markets, and banking and finance. Reprints major speeches by New York Federal Reserve Bank officials. Price free of charge.

1938
Federal Reserve Bank of Philadelphia Business Review
Federal Reserve Bank of Philadelphia, Philadelphia, PA 19105. Telephone (215) 574-6115.

Bimonthly magazine. Publishes articles on business, banking, monetary policy, and urban economics. Price free of charge. ISSN 0007-7011.

1939
Federal Reserve Bank of Richmond Annual Report
Federal Reserve Bank of Richmond (VA), Richmond, VA 23261. Telephone (804) 643-1250.

Annual report. Details the Federal Reserve Bank of Richmond's operations during the year. Price free of charge.

1940
Federal Reserve Bank of Richmond Economic Review
Federal Reserve Bank of Richmond (VA), Richmond, VA 23261. Telephone (804) 643-1250.

Bimonthly review. Focuses on financial and business developments in the Fifth Federal Reserve District. Price free of charge.

1942
Federal Reserve Bank of St Louis Annual US Economic Data
Federal Reserve Bank of St Louis, PO Box 442, St Louis, MO 63166. Telephone (314) 444-8444.

Annual publication. Shows the compounded annual rates of change for monetary indicators, such as Federal Reserve credit and money stock. Includes business indicators, such as corporate profits and gross national product. Statistical tables. Price free of charge.

1943
Federal Reserve Bank of St Louis Federal Budget Trends
Federal Reserve Bank of St Louis, PO Box 442, St Louis, MO 63166. Telephone (314) 444-8444.

Quarterly publication. Relates to selected federal budget measures. Covers expenditures and federal government debt and includes comment on how budget affects the national economy. Tables and charts. Price free of charge.

1944
Federal Reserve Bank of St Louis Monetary Trends
Federal Reserve Bank of St Louis, PO Box 442, St Louis, MO 63166. Telephone (314) 444-8444.

Monthly report. Discusses monetary and selected interest rate conditions. Tables and charts. Price free of charge.

1945
Federal Reserve Bank of St Louis National Economic Trends
Federal Reserve Bank of St Louis, PO Box 442, St Louis, MO 63166. Telephone (314) 444-8444.

Monthly report. Covers national business developments. Includes employment figures, wholesale prices, and the gross national product. Tables, charts, and graphs. Price free of charge.

1946
Federal Reserve Bank of St Louis. Rates of Change in Economic Data for Ten Industrial Countries
Federal Reserve Bank of St Louis, PO Box 442, St Louis, MO 63166. Telephone (314) 444-8444.

Quarterly and annual publication. Offers data on money supply, price indexes, employment, measures of output, and international trade for 10 industrial countries: Belgium, Canada, France, Germany, Italy, Japan, the Netherlands, Switzerland, the United Kingdom, and the US. Statistical tables. Price free of charge.

1947
Federal Reserve Bank of St Louis Review
Federal Reserve Bank of St Louis, PO Box 442, St Louis, MO 63166. Telephone (314) 444-8444.

Monthly review. Contains articles on national and international economic developments. Emphasizes monetary aspects and includes an analysis of various sectors of the Eighth Federal Reserve District. Price free of charge.

1948
Federal Reserve Bank of St Louis. Selected Economic Indicators, Central Mississippi Valley
Federal Reserve Bank of St Louis, PO Box 442, St Louis, MO 63166. Telephone (314) 444-8444.

Quarterly publication. Provides economic data for most St Louis Federal Reserve Bank District metropolitan areas and states. Include employment and personal income data. Price free of charge.

1949
Federal Reserve Bank of St Louis. US Financial Data
Federal Reserve Bank of St Louis, PO Box 442, St Louis, MO 63166. Telephone (314) 444-8444.

Weekly publication. Relates to monetary data. Includes selected interest rate data and brief analyses of current conditions. Tables and charts. Price free of charge.

1950
Federal Reserve Bank of St Louis. US International Transactions and Currency Review
Federal Reserve Bank of St Louis, PO Box 442, St Louis, MO 63166. Telephone (314) 444-8444.

Quarterly review. Provides data on US international trade. Notes consumer prices, interest rates, money supply, and other financial data for selected foreign countries. Tables and charts. Price free of charge.

1951
Federal Reserve Bank of San Francisco Business and Financial Letter
Federal Reserve Bank of San Francisco, PO Box 7702, San Francisco, CA 94120. Telephone (415) 544-2184.

Weekly newsletter. Focuses on current economic issues. Provides banking data for the Twelfth Federal Reserve District. Tables. Price free of charge.

1952
Federal Reserve Bank of San Francisco Economic Review
Federal Reserve Bank of San Francisco, PO Box 7702, San Francisco, CA 94120. Telephone (415) 544-2184.

Quarterly review. Covers broad economic issues in depth. Tables, charts, and graphs. Price free of charge.

1953
Federal Reserve Bank of San Francisco. Pacific Basin Economic Indicators
Federal Reserve Bank of San Francisco, PO Box 7702, San Francisco, CA 94120. Telephone (415) 544-2184.

Quarterly publication. Provides information on the gross national product, money supply, trade, and other economic indicators for major Pacific-area nations. Statistical charts. Price free of charge.

1954
Federal Reserve Bank of San Francisco. Western Economic Indicators
Federal Reserve Bank of San Francisco, PO Box 7702, San Francisco, CA 94120. Telephone (415) 544-2184.

Bimonthly report. Provide information on income and trade, employment, production, construction, and commercial banking in the Twelfth Federal Reserve Bank District. Statistical charts. Price free of charge.

1956
Federal Reserve Bulletin
US Federal Reserve System, Board of Governors, Washington, DC 20551. Order from Publication Services, Div of Adm Services, Board of Governors of the Federal Reserve System, Washington, DC 20551. Telephone (202) 452-3245.

Monthly report. Covers the US Federal Reserve System and its activities. Price $20.00 per year.

1957
Federal Reserve Chart Book on Financial and Business Statistics
US Federal Reserve System, Board of Governors, Washington, DC 20551. Order from Publication Services, Div of Adm Services, Board of Governors of the Federal Reserve System, Washington, DC 20551. Telephone (202) 452-3245.

Monthly book. Provides charts containing financial and business statistics. Includes a copy of the annual Historical Chart Book with a subscription. Price $7.00 per year.

1958
Federal Reserve System Annual Report
US Federal Reserve System, Board of Governors, Washington, DC 20551. Order from Publication Services, Div of Adm Services, Board of Governors of the Federal Reserve System, Washington, DC 20551. Telephone (202) 452-3245.

Annual report on the US Federal Reserve System.

1959
Federal Revenue Forms—With Official Instructions
Prentice-Hall, Inc, Englewood Cliffs, NJ 07632. Telephone (201) 592-2000. Telex 13-5423.

Quarterly loose-leaf service. Contains tax returns and related forms required by the IRS for federal income, estate, and gift taxes. Includes IRS rules and procedures. Price $159 per year.

1960
Federal Securities Law Reports
Commerce Clearing House, Inc, 4025 W Peterson Ave, Chicago, IL 60646. Telephone (312) 583-8500.

Seven loose-leaf books, plus weekly reports. Give details of the Securities and Exchange Commission's control of the securities industry. Price $495.00 per year.

1961

Federal Tax Articles

Commerce Clearing House, Inc, 4025 W Peterson Ave, Chicago, IL 60646. Telephone (312) 583-8500.

Loose-leaf book, plus monthly reports. Lists articles published on federal taxes in business, legal, and accounting periodicals. Price $205.00 per year.

1963

Federal Taxation of Life Insurance Companies

Matthew Bender & Co, 235 E 45th St, New York, NY 10017. Telephone (212) 661-5050.

Three-volume loose-leaf report, with annual supplements. Provides a guide to insurance company taxation. Covers the Life Company Tax Act and federal regulations. Price $195.00.

1964

Federal Taxation of Oil and Gas Transactions

Matthew Bender & Co, 235 E 45th St, New York, NY 10017. Telephone (212) 661-5050.

Two-volume loose-leaf report, with annual supplements. Provides a guide to the application of federal tax laws to oil and gas transactions. Price $165.00.

1965

Federal Tax Coordinator, **2d edition**

Research Inst of America, Inc, 589 5th Ave, New York, NY 10017. Telephone (212) 755-8900.

Twenty-eight loose-leaf books, with updating services. Provide text and analyses of federal tax law, including reforms. Contain examples of tax problems and their solutions. Price available on request.

1966

Federal Tax Course

Prentice-Hall, Inc, Englewood Cliffs, NJ 07632. Telephone (201) 592-2000. Telex 13-5423.

Annually revised and updated volume. Gives an overview of federal income tax provisions affecting business and investment decisions. Notes the effects of federal estate and gift taxes. Price available on request.

1967

Federal Taxes Citator

Prentice-Hall, Inc, Englewood Cliffs, NJ 07632. Telephone (201) 592-2000. Telex 13-5423.

Monthly loose-leaf service. Provides a complete judicial history of every federal tax case and ruling, listing also related tax cases and rulings. Price $273.00 per year.

1968

Federal Taxes Service

Prentice-Hall, Inc, Englewood Cliffs, NJ 07632. Telephone (201) 592-2000. Telex 13-5423

Weekly loose-leaf service. Provides complete federal tax information. Includes all laws, court and tax court decisions, and Internal Revenue Service rulings. Price available on request.

1969

Federal Tax Forms

Commerce Clearing House, Inc, 4025 W Peterson Ave, Chicago, IL 60646. Telephone (312) 583-8500.

Two loose-leaf books, plus monthly reports. Include facsimile tax returns, related forms, and instructions for federal income, estate, gift, and major excise taxes. Price $160.00 per year.

1970

Federal Tax Guide

Prentice-Hall, Inc, Englewood Cliffs, NJ 07632. Telephone (201) 592-2000. Telex 13-5423.

Weekly loose-leaf service. Discusses federal tax laws, including income, estate, gift, and excise tax regulations. Notes new rulings. Price available on request.

1971

Federal Tax Guide Reports **Capital Edition**

Commerce Clearing House, Inc, 4025 W Peterson Ave, Chicago, IL 60646. Telephone (312) 583-8500.

Loose-leaf book, plus weekly reports. Offers guidance on business and personal federal tax problems. Includes an income tax code. Price $200.00 per year.

1972

Federal Tax Return Manual

Commerce Clearing House, Inc, 4025 W Peterson Ave, Chicago, IL 60646. Telephone (312) 583-8500.

Loose-leaf book. Provides a tax return guide that tells how to prepare federal income tax returns for individuals, small businesses, and corporations. Includes tax forms. Price $57.00.

1972.01

Federal Telephone Directories

Bell & Howell Micro Photo Division, Old Mansfield Rd, Wooster, OH 44691. Telephone (216) 264-6666. Telex 98-6496.

Series of directories. Provides telephone numbers of federal offices. Price $71.50 per set.

1973

Federal Trade Commission Annual Report

US Federal Trade Commission, Washington, DC 20580. Order from Distribution and Duplication Branch, Federal Trade Commission, Washington, DC 20580. Telephone (202) 523-3598.

Annual report. Covers business transacted by the US Federal Trade Commission and its costs. Price free of charge.

1974

Federal Trade Commission Decisions

Federal Trade Commission, Washington, DC 20580. Order from Distribution and Duplication Branch, Federal Trade Commission, Washington, DC 20580. Telephone (202) 523-3598.

Series of 94 volumes. Contains Federal Trade Commission decisions, 1915–1979. Price available on request.

1975

Federal Trade Commission. Quarterly Financial Report for Mfg, Mining & Trade Corporations

US Federal Trade Commission, Washington, DC 20580. Order from Distribution and Duplication Branch, Federal Trade Commission, Washington, DC 20580. Telephone (202) 523-3598.

Quarterly report. Presents financial information for US manufacturing, mining, and trade corporations. Price free of charge.

1976

Federal Wage-Hour Handbook for Banks

American Bankers Assn, 1120 Connecticut Ave NW, Washington, DC 20036. Telephone (202) 467-4123.

Book. Covers federal wage and hour laws. Contains texts of Fair Labor Standards Act, Equal Pay Act of 1963, and Age Discrimination in Employment Act of 1967. Price $5.00.

1976.01
Federal Yellow Book
Washington Monitor, 499 National Press Bldg, Washington, DC 20045. Telephone (202) 347-7757.

Loose-leaf directory with bimonthly updates. Lists federal department and agency employees. Provides titles, addresses, and phone numbers. Price $120.00 per year.

1977
Fed in Print
Federal Reserve Bank of Philadelphia, Philadelphia, PA 19105. Telephone (215) 574-6115.

Biannual index to selected subjects published in the Federal Reserve Bank Bulletin and in periodic reviews of Federal Reserve banks. Price free of charge.

1978
Feed Industry Red Book
Communications Marketing, Inc, 5100 Edina Industrial Blvd, Edina, MN 55435. Telephone (612) 835-5888.

Quarterly book. Serves as a reference source on the manufacture of livestock and poultry feeds and pet foods. Covers purchasing, production, and distribution. Price $12.50.

1979
Feed Industry Review
Communications Marketing, Inc, 5100 Edina Industrial Blvd, Edina, MN 55435. Telephone (612) 835-5888.

Quarterly magazine. Contains information on the production and distribution of livestock and poultry feeds. Is aimed at executives in the field. Price $12.50 per year.

1980
Feedstuffs
Miller Publishing Co, 2501 Wayzata Blvd, Minneapolis, MN 55405. Telephone (612) 374-5200.

Weekly newspaper. Covers manufacture and distribution of products and services for livestock and poultry. Price $30.00 US.

1980.01
Fence Industry
Communication Channels, Inc, 6285 Barfield Rd, Atlanta, GA 30328. Telephone (404) 256-9800.

Monthly magazine. Covers all types of fencing and new developments in installation and related products. Price $21.00 per year.

1981
Fertilizer Industry Series
United Nations Industrial Development Organization, Vienna International Centre, PO Box 300, A-1400, Vienna, Austria. Telephone 26310. Telex 135612.

Series of reports. Covers chemical and ammonia fertilizers, fertilizer costs, and supply and demand in South America, Mexico, and Central America. Symbols: ID/SER.F/1-9. Price $.75 to $1.50.

1982
FFO/Latin America (FFO/LA)
Business International Corp, 1 Dag Hammarskjold Plaza, New York, NY 10017. Telephone (212) 750-6300.

Reference service annually updated. Covers major Latin American countries. Designed to help regional management locate new sources of capital for financing sales and investments in individual countries or the entire region. Tables. Price $300.00 per year.

1983
Fiber Producer
American Building Supplies, 1760 Peachtree Rd, NW, Atlanta, GA 30357. Telephone (404) 874-4462.

Monthly magazine. Covers developments in fiber production and textile industries in US and abroad. Price $25.00 per year.

1984
Field Crop Reporting Series
Statistics Canada, User Services, Publications Distribution, Ottawa, Ont, Canada K1A 0V7. Telephone (613) 992-3151.

Eight seasonal reports. Cover Canadian field crop acreage, seeding, growth, harvesting, production, and stocks. Price $12.00 per year. ISSN 0575-8548.

1985
Field Crops and Stocks Reports
US Dept of Agriculture, Crop Reporting Board, Statistical Reporting Service, Washington, DC 20250. Telephone (202) 447-4021.

Series of periodic reports. Provides information on field crop production and stocks. Indicates acreage planted, yield, and prices. Price free of charge.

1986
Final Environmental Impact Statement of Maritime Administration Tanker Construction Program
US Maritime Adm, Commerce Bldg, 14th & E Sts NW, Washington, DC 20230. Order from National Technical Information Service, 5285 Port Royal Rd, Springfield, VA 22161. Telephone (703) 487-4650.

Publication. Presents the final environmental impact statement of the Maritime Administration tanker construction program. Price $26.00 per set.

1987
Finance
IFB Communications Ltd, 8 W 40th St, New York, NY 10018. Order from Finance Publishing Corp, Box 947, Farmingdale, NY 11735. Telephone New York (212) 221-7900.

Monthly magazine. Reports on monetary and business issues. Provides an investment banker-broker directory in the annual issue. Price $35.00 per year.

1988
Finance and Development
International Monetary Fund, 19th & H St NW, Washington, DC 20431. Telephone (202) 393-6362.

Quarterly report. Explains the purposes and work of the International Monetary Fund and International Bank for Reconstruction and Development. Discusses international economic conditions, national and international monetary policies, and trade developments. English, French, Spanish, and German editions; special articles in Arabic and Portuguese. Price free of charge.

1989
Finance Facts
National Consumer Finance Assn, 1000 16 St NW, Washington, DC 20036. Telephone (202) 638-1340.

Monthly newsletter. Reports on consumer financial behavior. Price $6.00 per year.

1990
Finance Facts Yearbook
National Consumer Finance Assn, 1000 16th St NW, Washington, DC 20036. Telephone (202) 638-1340.

Yearbook. Presents data on consumer finances and the consumer finance industry. Price available on request.

1991
Financial Advertising Report
Media Records, Inc, 370 7th Ave, New York, NY 10001. Telephone (212) 736-7490.

Annual report. Summarizes the financial advertising linage by category and advertiser. Price $300.00.

1992
Financial Analysis of the Motor Carrier Industry
American Trucking Assn, Inc, 1616 P St NW, Washington, DC 20036. Telephone (202) 797-5351.

Annual report. Discusses the financial situation of the motor carrier industry. Evaluates various carrier groups. Tables and charts. Price free of charge.

1993
Financial Analysts Federation Membership Directory
Financial Analysts Federation, 1633 Broadway, New York, NY 10019. Telephone (212) 957-2860.

Annual directory. Lists federation members. Price available on request.

1994
Financial Analysts' Handbook, Portfolio Management 1975
Dow Jones–Irwin, 1818 Ridge Rd, Homewood, IL 60430. Telephone (312) 798-6000.

Books. Discusses the theory and practice of investment management. Price $37.50.

1995
Financial Analysts Journal
Financial Analysts Federation, 1633 Broadway, New York, NY 10019. Order from Financial Analysts Journal, PO Box 8021, New York, NY 10049. Telephone (212) 957-2860.

Bimonthly magazine. Presents articles on investment and stock issues. Includes book reviews. Price $36.00 per year.

1996
Financial and Operating Statistics, Motor Carrier Quarterly Report
American Trucking Assn, Inc, 1616 P St NW, Washington, DC 20036. Telephone (202) 797-5351.

Three quarterly reports and one annual report. Contain detailed financial and operating statistics on Class I and II motor carriers with annual revenues over $500,-000. Price $175.00 per year.

1997
Financial Digest
Manufacturers Hanover Trust Co, Corporate Communications Dept, 350 Park Ave, New York, NY 10022. Telephone (212) 350-3300. Telex 232337, 420966, 62814, 82615.

Weekly newsletter. Covers the stock market, business and trade, banking, and credit. Price free of charge.

1998
Financial Executive
Financial Executives Inst, 633 3rd Ave, New York, NY 10017. Telephone (212) 953-0497.

Monthly magazine. Covers new developments and offers practical information in the field of corporate finance. Price $15.00 per year.

1999
Financial Executive's Handbook 1970
Dow Jones-Irwin, Inc, 1818 Ridge Rd, Homewood, IL 60430. Telephone (312) 798-3100.

Book. Covers theory and practice for financial executives. Price $37.50. ISBN 0-87094-008-2.

2000
Financial Facts about the Meat Packing Industry
American Meat Inst, PO Box 3556, Washington, DC 20007. Telephone (703) 841-2400.

Annual report. Gives statistics on meat packing, livestock, and feed. Price available on request.

2001
Financial Flow Accounts
Statistics Canada, User Services, Publications Distribution, Ottawa, Ont, Canada K1A 0V7. Telephone (613) 992-3151.

Quarterly magazine. Provides data on the Canadian economic sector and financial category tables and matrices. Includes a review of financial and monetary developments. Price $36.00 per year. ISSN 0380-092X.

2002
Financial Handbook, 5th Edition
Jules Bogen and Samuel Shipman, John Wiley & Sons, Inc, 605 Third Ave, New York, NY 10158. Telephone (212) 850-6515.

Book. Covers corporate finance, money, and banking. Price $22.00. ISBN 0471-07727-5.

2003
Financial Indicators and Corporate Financing Plans
Conference Board, Inc, 845 3rd Ave, New York, NY 10022. Telephone (212) 759-0900.

Semiannual report. Surveys a panel of senior financial executives of leading US nonfinancial corporations on the business and financial outlook. Price available on request.

2004
Financial Institutions, Financial Statistics
Statistics Canada, User Services, Publications Distribution, Ottawa, Ont, Canada K1A 0V7. Telephone (613) 992-3151.

Quarterly magazine. Supplies financial data for Canadian financial institutions. Includes balance sheet, income and expense statements, retained earnings statements, reserve accounts statements, and source and application of funds statements. Price $36.00 per year. ISSN 0380-075X.

2004.01
Financial Letter
Federal Reserve Bank of Kansas City, 925 Grand Ave, Kansas City, MO 64198. Telephone (816) 881-2000.

Monthly newsletter. Provides credit, economic, and banking information. Lists Tenth Federal Reserve District bank statistics. Price free of charge.

2004.02
Financial Mail
Financial Mail, PO Box 10493, Johannesburg 2000, South Africa. Telephone 28-2121.

Weekly magazine. Reports on South African political, economic, and business news. Includes economic indicators. Price available on request.

2005
Financial Mail
Financial Times Business Information Ltd, Bracken House, 10 Cannon St, London, England EC4P 4BY. Order from Financial Times Ltd, 75 Rockefeller Plz, New York, NY 10019. Telephone (44) (01) 248-8000. Telex 886341-2.

Weekly newsletter. Covers the South African investment business. Price $171.00 per year.

2006
Financial Management Handbook for Associations
Chamber of Commerce of the US, 1615 H St, NW, Washington, DC 20062. Telephone (202) 659-6231.

Book. Discusses financial management topics for US Chamber of Commerce associations. Includes information on internal financial control, budgets, financial reports, and cost controls. Price $5.00.

2006.01
Financial Management Letter
Alexander Hamilton Institute, 1633 Broadway, New York, NY 10019. Telephone (212) 397-3580.

Monthly letter. Describes financial techniques used by companies to control and improve performance. Directed at finance executives. Price $75.00 per year.

2007
Financial Market Survey
Barclays Bank, Group Economics Dept, 54 Lombard St, London, England EC3P 3AH. Telephone (44) (01) 283-8989.

Newsletter issued every two to three months. Reviews developments in the British and international financial markets. Price free of charge.

2008
Financial Market Trends
Organization for Economic Cooperation and Development, Publications Center, 1750 Pennsylvania Ave NW, Washington, DC 20006. Telephone (202) 724-1857.

Magazine issued three times per year. Analyzes international financial markets. Provides data on Eurocurrency deposits, Eurobonds, and other international bank lending and reviews the monetary trends in OECD countries. Price $33.28 per year.

2009
Financial Planning
Inst for Business Planning, Inc, IPB Plz, Englewood Cliffs, NJ 07632. Telephone (201) 592-2040.

Loose-leaf book, with monthly supplements and semimonthly letters. Provides information on trust funds, life insurance, real estate, and other investments. Tables, charts, and worksheets. Price available on request.

2010
Financial Post Canadian Markets, 1981
Financial Post, 481 University Ave, Toronto, Ont, Canada M5W 1A7. Telephone (416) 596-5585.

Annual book. Presents market characteristics for over 400 Canadian markets. Offers census figures and estimates on the best retail markets. Maps, a bibliography, and a directory of advertising agencies. Price $29.00.

2011
Financial Post Corporation Service
Financial Post, 481 University Ave, Toronto, Ont, Canada M5W 1A7. Telephone (416) 596-5585.

Daily booklets. Provide Canadian investment information and data on selected corporations. Include dividend records, records of new issues, and special supplements. Price $195.00 per month (complete service).

2012
Financial Post Directory of Directors
Financial Post, 481 University Ave, Toronto, Ont, Canada M5W 1A7. Telephone (416) 596-5585.

Annual book. Provides a directory to Canada's top executive personnel. Covers 13,000 people and 2100 companies. Price $45.00.

2012.01
Financial Post Investment Databank
Financial Post, 481 University Ave, Toronto, Ont, Canada M5W 1A7. Telephone (416) 596-5693.

On-line printout sheets. Present computerized information on the finances of over 300 Canadian public companies. Encompass 175 ratios for 11 years, balance sheets, and growth rates per share. Price $150.00 per month.

2013
Financial Post Magazine
Financial Post, 481 University Ave, Toronto, Ont, Canada M5W 1A7. Telephone (416) 596-5000.

Monthly magazine. Aimed at business leaders in a leisure environment. Price available only with subscription to Financial Post in Canada.

2014
Financial Post Newspaper
Financial Post, 481 University Ave, Toronto, Ont, Canada M5W 1A7. Order from Financial Post Circulation, Box 9100 Postal Station A, Toronto, Ont, Canada M5W 1V5. Telephone (416) 596-5148.

Weekly newspaper. Covers Canadian business, investments, and public affairs. Includes about 52 special reports with an annual subscription. Price $29.95 per year (Canadian).

2015
Financial Post Survey of Energy Resources
Financial Post, 481 University Ave, Toronto, Ont, Canada M5W 1A7. Telephone (416) 595-1811.

Annual book. Details energy exploration and development activities of more than 400 companies. Notes company officers, finances, subsidiaries, and dividend histories. Statistics on oil and gas. Price $19.95.

2017
Financial Post Survey of Industrials
Financial Post, 481 University Ave, Toronto, Ont, Canada M5W 1A7. Telephone (416) 596-5585.

Publication. Gives investment facts on manufacturing, sales, and service companies. Includes data on company's officers, capital structure, dividend record, long-term debt, and five-year earnings. Price $27.00.

2018
Financial Post Survey of Mines & Energy Resources
Financial Post, 481 University Avenue, Toronto, Ont, Canada M5W 1A7. Telephone (416) 596-5585.

Annual book. Details operations, management, and financial status of some 2000 mining companies. Mineral production and reserves by company and industry, milling plants. Statistics on petroleum, natural gas, uranium, coal, hydro-electric power, production and reserves of oil and gas by company and industry. Price $37.00.

2018.01
Financial/Retail Systems Reports
Auerbach Publishers, Inc, 6560 N Park Dr, Pennsauken, NJ 08109. Telephone (609) 662-2070. Telex 831 464.

Book, updated monthly. Covers optical character, code and mark readers, magnetic ink character recognition, credit authorization terminals, financial terminals, multi-purpose data collection, and other developments in the field for banking, retailing, and other businesses. Price $325.00.

2018.02
Financial Review of Alien Insurers
National Ass of Insurance Commissioners, 350 Bishops Way, Brookfield, WI 53005. Telephone (414) 784-9540.

Annual book. Gives financial and corporate data on the alien insurers and reinsurers appearing in the NAIC Quarterly Listing of Alien Insurers. Price $250.00.

2019
Financial Statement and Budget Report
Her Majesty's Stationery Office, PO Box 569, London, England SE1 9NH. Telephone (44) (01) 928 1321.

Annual report on the state of the British budget and finances. Price £3.25 per year.

2020
Financial Statistics
Her Majesty's Stationery Office, PO Box 569, London, England SE1 9NH. Telephone (44) (01) 928 1321.

Monthly publication statistical. Gives information on British financial topics, including government income and expenditure, money stock, interest rates, and financial accounts for sectors of the economy. Price £4.95 per month.

2021
Financial Statistics: Explanatory Handbook
Her Majesty's Stationery Office, PO Box 569, London, England SE1 9NH. Telephone (44) (01) 928 1321.

Annual book. Explains and gives notes on Financial Statistics. Indicates the relationship between tables and methods used to compile figures. Price £1.35. ISBN 0 11 7242926

2022
Financial Tactics and Terms for the Sophisticated International Investor, 1974
Harper & Row, Inc, 10 E 53rd St, New York, NY 10022. Telephone (212) 593-7000.

Book. Dictionary of investment management terms and practices. Price $7.95.

2023
Financial Times Actuaries Index Monthly Sheets
Financial Times Business Information Ltd, Bracken House, 10 Cannon St, London, England EC4P 4BY. Order from Financial Times Ltd, 75 Rockefeller Plz, New York, NY 10019. Telephone (44) (01) 248-8000. Telex 886341-2.

Monthly sheets. Provide actuarial figures. Price $8.00 per year.

2024
Financial Times Actuaries Share Indices
Financial Times Business Information Ltd, Bracken House, 10 Cannon St, London, England EC4P 4BY. Order from Financial Times Ltd, 75 Rockefeller Plz, New York, NY 10019. Telephone (44) (01) 248-8000. Telex 886341-2.

Publications. Give statistical actuarial indexes for shares. Price $8.00.

2025
Financial Times International Business Yearbook
Financial Times Business Information Ltd, Bracken House, 10 Cannon St, London, England EC4P 4BY. Order from Financial Times Ltd, 75 Rockefeller Plz, New York, NY 10019. Telephone (44) (01) 248-8000. Telex 886341-2.

Annual book. Offers information on international business affairs. Price available on request.

2026
Financial Times Newspaper
Financial Times Business Information Ltd, Bracken House, 10 Cannon St, London, England EC4P 4BY. Order from Financial Times Ltd, 75 Rockefeller Plz, New York, NY 10019. Telephone (44) (01) 248-8000. Telex 886341-2.

Daily newspaper. Covers British and world financial and economic news. Price $200.00 per year.

2027
Financial Times of Canada
Financial Times of Canada, 920 Yonge St, Suite 500, Toronto, Ont, Canada M4W 3L5. Telephone (416) 922-1133.

Weekly newspaper. Covers Canadian business, government, industry, and investment. Includes some European and American coverage. Price $15.00 per year, $26.00, foreign outside Canada. ISSN 0015-2056.

2028
Financial Times Quarterly Actuaries Indices
Financial Times Business Information Ltd, Bracken House, 10 Cannon St, London, England EC4P 4BY. Order from Financial Times Ltd, 75 Rockefeller Plz, New York, NY 10019. Telephone (44) (01) 248-8000. Telex 886341-2.

Quarterly publications. Supply statistical actuarial figures. Price available on request.

2029
Financial Times Tax Newsletter
Financial Times Business Information Ltd, Bracken House, 10 Cannon St, London, England EC4P 4BY. Order from Financial Times Ltd, 75 Rockefeller Plz, New York, NY 10019. Telephone (44) (01) 248-8000. Telex 886341-2.

Monthly newsletter. Surveys world developments in taxation. Includes such topics as: government changes in personal, corporate, and indirect taxes; overseas and domestic investment, and tax treaties. Price $260.00 per year.

2030
Financial Times World Hotel Directory
Financial Times Business Information Ltd, Bracken House, 10 Cannon St, London, England EC4P 4BY. Order from Financial Times Ltd, 75 Rockefeller Plz, New York, NY 10019. Telephone (44) (01) 248-8000. Telex 886341-2.

Directory. Provides a guide to hotels throughout the world. Price available on request.

2031
Financial Times World Insurance Year Book
Financial Times Business Information Ltd, Bracken House, 10 Cannon St, London, England EC4P 4BY. Order from Financial Times Ltd, 75 Rockefeller Plz, New York, NY 10019. Telephone (44) (01) 248-8000. Telex 886341-2.

Annual book. Publishes data on insurance throughout the world. Price available on request.

2032
Financial Trend
Equity Media, Inc, 7616 LBJ Fwy, Dallas, TX 75251. Telephone (214) 239-0161.

Weekly newspaper. Covers industry and investments in Texas, Oklahoma, Arkansas, Louisiana, and New Mexico. Includes such topics as corporate finance, business management, equity investment, commercial banking, venture capital, energy companies, and securities regulation. Price $23.00 per year.

2033
Financial Trend's Corporate Directory Service
Equity Media, Inc, 7616 LBJ Fwy, Dallas, TX 75251. Telephone (214) 239-0161.

Semiannual directory, with 10 updates per year. Lists all publicly held companies in Texas, Oklahoma, Arkansas, Louisiana and New Mexico (listed on stock exchanges or actively traded as over-the-counter stocks). Gives mailing addresses, phone numbers, top officers, revenues, and net earnings. Price $36.00 per year, $50.00 per two years.

2033.01
Financial Weekly
Financial Weekly, Westgate House, 9 Holborn, London, England EC1N 2NE. Telephone (44) (01) 404-0733. Telex 881 2431.

Weekly newspaper. Covers business developments. Price £45.00 per year.

2034
Financial World
Macro Communications, Inc., 150 E 58th New York, NY. 10159. Telephone (212) 826-4360.

Biweekly report. Investment analysis and forecasts for specific companies and industries as a whole. Price $36.00 per year.

2035
Financing Foreign Operations
Business International Corp, 1 Dag Hammarskjold Plz, New York, NY 10017. Telephone (212) 750-6300.

Updated reference service. Provides sources of foreign capital, credits, trade, and investment. Includes such services as a two-volume series covering international finance, cross-border finance, and domestic finance in 31 countries. Price $675.00 per year.

2036
Finderhood Report
Finderhood, Inc, 15 W 38th St, New York, NY 10018. Telephone (212) 840-2423.

Bimonthly report. Covers finder's fees opportunities protected by signed contracts. Price $175.00 for one year.

2037
Fingertip Facts about Alabama
Alabama Development Office, State Capitol, Montgomery, AL 36130. Telephone (205) 832-6810.

Book, revised periodically. Depicts Alabama's major soil types, mineral resources, transportation routes, population distribution, forestry, and other general interest facts. Maps. Price free of charge.

2038
Fingertip Facts and Figures
National Forest Products Assn, 1619 Massachusetts Ave NW, Washington, DC 20036. Telephone (202) 797-5853.

Monthly report. Presents data on lumber production, shipments, consumption, imports, exports, and inventories. Price $15.00 per year.

2039
Finishing Industries
Turret Press Ltd, 4 Local Board Rd, Watford, Herts, England WD1 2JS. Order from Wheatland Journals Ltd, 4 Local Board Rd, Watford, Herts WD1, 2JS England. Telephone Watford (0923) 46199.

Monthly magazine. Provides material on finishing industries. Price $74.50 per year.

2040
Finnish–American Chamber of Commerce Newsletter
Finnish–American Chamber of Commerce, 540 Madison Ave, Finland House, New York, NY 10022. Telephone (212) 832-2588.

Monthly newsletter. Discusses Finnish economic and trade news. Reports on selected industries. Price free of charge. ISSN 0015-2439.

2041
Fire and Loss Statistics for the United Kingdom
Her Majesty's Stationery Office, PO Box 569, London, England SE1 9NH. Telephone (44) (01) 928 1321.

Annual report. Proffers statistics on fire and loss for Great Britain. Price £4.55 per year.

2042
Fire, Casualty & Surety Bulletins
National Underwriter Co, 420 E 4th St, Cincinnati, OH 45202. Telephone (513) 721-2140.

Four loose-leaf books and monthly updates. Provide detailed information on fire, casualty, and marine insurance. Report on unusual insurance plans and on agency operations. Price $148.00 per year.

2044
First Chicago World Report
First National Bank of Chicago, Business and Economic Research Div, 1 First National Plz, Chicago, IL 60670. Telephone (312) 732-3779. Telex 253801-3.

Monthly newsletter. Discusses worldwide economic trends, such as unemployment, gas shortages, and international pricing systems. Includes an evaluation of foreign economies. Price free of charge.

2045
First Destination of University Graduates
Her Majesty's Stationery Office, PO Box 569, London, England SE1 9NH. Telephone (44) (01) 928 1321.

Annual report. Pertains to the first destination of British university graduates. Price £1.85 per year.

2046
First Hawaiian Bank Business Outlook Forum
First Hawaiian Bank, PO Box 3200, Honolulu, HI 96847. Telephone (808) 525-6353.

Annual report. Analyzes US and Hawaiian economic trends and prospects. Price free of charge.

2047
First Hawaiian Bank Economic Indicators
First Hawaiian Bank, PO Box 3200, Honolulu, HI 96847. Telephone (808) 525-6353.

Monthly newsletter. Discusses Hawaii's economy. Price free of charge. ISSN 0015-2757.

2048
Fisheries: Quantity and Value of Landings
European Community Information Service, 2100 M St, NW, Suite 707, Washington DC 20037. Telephone (202) 862-9500. Telex 248455.

Quarterly report. Provides information on quantity and value of fish hauls by European Communities member countries. Price $21.00.

2050
Fitch Commercial Paper Report
Fitch Investors Service, 5 Hanover Sq, New York, NY 10004. Telephone (212) 668-8300.
Annual loose-leaf reports. Provide commercial paper ratings and evaluations of selected companies. Price free of charge (not available to the general public).

2051
Fitch Corporate Bond Ratings Book
Fitch Investors Service, 5 Hanover Sq, New York, NY 10004. Telephone (212) 668-8300.
Monthly report. Lists corporate and municipal bonds, preferred stock and commercial paper ratings issued by Fitch Investors Service. Price $75.00 per year.

2051.01
Fitch Rating Register
Fitch Investors Service, 5 Hanover Sq, New York, NY 10004. Telephone (212) 668-8300.
Monthly report. Lists corporate and municipal bonds, preferred stock and commercial paper ratings issued by Fitch Investors Service. Price $75.00 per year.

2052
Fitch Corporate Bond Review
Fitch Investors Service, 12 Barclay St, New York, NY 10007. Telephone (212) 571-1415.
Bimonthly loose-leaf reports. Rate corporate bond offerings. Include municipal bond offerings. Include a daily inquiry privilege with a subscription. Tables. Price $120.00 per year.

2053
Fitch Hospital and Other Non-profit Institutional Ratings
Fitch Investors Service, 5 Hanover Sq, New York, NY 10004. Order from Fitch Investors Service, 8301 E Prentice Ave, Englewood, CO 80111. Telephone (303) 770-7800.
Annual report with monthly supplements. Lists hospital, nursing home and retirement center bond ratings. Price $45.00 per year.

2054
Fitch Institutional Reports
Fitch Investors Service, 5 Hanover Sq, New York, NY 10004. Telephone (212) 668-8300.
Irregularly issued loose-leaf reports. Rate individual bond and preferred stock issues of public utilities. Price free of charge.

2055
Fitch Investors Municipal Bond Reports
Fitch Investors Service, 5 Hanover Sg, New York, NY 10007. Telephone (212) 668-8300.
Loose-leaf reports. Evaluates municipal bonds. Include a daily inquiry privilege with a subscription. Tables. Price free of charge.

2056
Fixed Capital Flows and Stocks
Statistics Canada, User Services, Publications Distribution, Ottawa, Ont, Canada K1A 0V7. Telephone (613) 992-3151.
Annual report. Provides estimates of fixed nonresidential Canadian capital stocks and flows by major industries according to the 1960 Standard Industrial Classification in constant (1961) and current dollar valuation. Price $8.40. ISSN 0317-5154.

2057
Fixed Income Investor
Standard & Poor's Corp, 25 Broadway, New York, NY 10004. Telephone (212) 248-2525.
Weekly loose-leaf report. Covers developments in the debt securities market, including bonds, commercial paper, and preferred stocks. Statistical analysis of convertible bonds. Price $575.00 per year.

2058
Flat Glass
US Dept of Commerce, Bureau of the Census, Washington, DC 20233. Telephone (202) 449-1600.
Quarterly report, with annual summary. Provides data on the production, inventory, and the value of shipments of flat glass. Price $1.25 per year.

2059
Fleet Owner
McGraw-Hill Publications Co, 1221 Ave of the Americas, New York, NY 10020. Telephone (212) 997-6375. Telex TWX 7105814879 WUI 62555.

Monthly magazine. Covers trucking fleet management, operation, maintenance, and technical developments. Price $25.00 per year.

2061
Fleet Street Letter
Fleet St Letter Ltd, 80 Fleet St, London, England EC4Y 1JH. Telephone (44) (01) 353-7571.
Semimonthly investment newsletter. Discusses British economic and political issues. Notes world economic developments. Price £25 per year.

2062
Fleet Street Patent Law Reports
European Law Centre Ltd, 4 Bloomsbury Sq, London, WC1A 2RL, England. Telephone (44) (01) 404-4300. Telex 21746.
Monthly report. Reviews legal and court developments relating to patents, copyrights, trademarks, and other industrial property issues in England and Scotland. Includes cases from other common law countries, such as Australia and Ireland. Price $225.00.

2063
Flight Comment
Supply and Services Canada, Publishing Centre, Printing and Publishing, Ottawa, Ont, Canada K1A 0S9. Telephone (613) 238-1601.
Bimonthly magazine. Discusses aviation safety, developments, and techniques in Canada. Price $5.00 per year.

2064
Flooring
Harcourt Brace Jovanovich Publications, 757 3rd Ave, New York, NY 10017. Order from Harcourt Brace and Jovanovich Publications, 1 E 1st St, Duluth, MN 55802. Telephone (218) 727-8511.
Monthly magazine. Discusses the flooring industry. Includes information on wall and related interior-surfacing products. Price $8.00 per year.

2065
Florida Banker
Florida Bankers Assn, 505 N Mills Ave, PO Box 6847, Orlando, FL 32803. Telephone (305) 896-0441.
Monthly magazine published 11 times a year. Reports on Florida's banking industry. Includes articles on banking education, local, state and national legislation, and personnel changes. Price $15.00 per year. ISSN 0147-1961.

2066
Florida Economic Indicators
Florida Dept of Labor and Employment Security, Bureau of Research and Analysis, Caldwell Bldg, Tallahassee, FL 32301. Telephone (904) 488-1048.

Monthly newsletter. Carries material on Florida's economic indicators, including the unemployment rate, new incorporations, weekly hours for manufacturing production workers, new vehicle registrations, and sales and use tax collections. Mailing list restricted to Florida-based firms. Single copies available to public upon request. Price free of charge.

2067
Florida Employment Statistics
Florida Dept of Labor and Employment Security, Bureau of Research and Analysis, Caldwell Bldg, Tallahassee, FL 32301. Telephone (904) 488-1048.

Monthly report. Contains estimates of Florida labor force, employment, hours and earnings, and labor turnover. Summarizes economic conditions. Mailing list restricted to Florida-based firms. Single copies available upon request. Price free of charge.

2067.01
Florida: Industries Directory 1981
Manufacturers' News, Inc, 3 Huron St, Chicago, IL 60611. Telephone (312) 337-1084.

Annual book. Identifies 10,000 industrial companies in Florida by name, location, and product. Price $45.00.

2068
Florida Outlook
University of Florida, College of Business Adm, Bureau of Economic & Business Research, 221 Matherly Hall, Gainesville, FL 32611. Telephone (904) 392-0171.

Quarterly service. Forecasts Florida's economic conditions. Covers such factors as population, housing, construction, and tourism. Price $125.00 per year.

2068.01
Florida: State Industrial Directory 1981
Manufacturers' News, Inc, 3 Huron St, Chicago, IL 60611. Telephone (312) 337-1084.

Annual book. Provides information on Florida industries by name, county, city, and product. Price $65.00.

2069
Florida Statistical Abstract
University of Florida, College of Business Adm, Bureau of Economic & Business Research, 221 Matherly Hall, Gainesville, FL 32611. Telephone (904) 392-0171.

Annual book. Provides data on Florida's population, housing, labor force, personal income, employment, farm and manufacturing production, and other topics. Price $11.50 paperbound, $20.00 hardbound. Order the hardbound from University Presses of Florida, 15 NW 15th St, Gainesville, FL 32603.

2070
Flour Milling Products
US Dept of Commerce, Bureau of the Census, Washington, DC 20233. Telephone (202) 449-1600.

Monthly report, with annual summary. Provides data on the quantity of wheat flour produced by geographic region and by state, quantity of straight semolina and blended semolina durum flour and rye flour produced, and rye millfeed production for the US as a whole. Shows wheat flour exports. Price $3.30 per year.

2071
Fluorescent Lamp Ballasts
US Dept of Commerce, Bureau of the Census, Washington, DC 20233. Telephone (202) 449-1600.

Quarterly report, with annual summary. Supplies information on the quantity and value of manufacturers' shipments of fluorescent lamp ballasts by product. Price $1.25 per year.

2072
Flying
Ziff-Davis Publishing Co, 1156 15th St NW, Washington, DC 20005. Order from Ziff-Davis Publishing Co, One Park Ave, New York NY 10016 . Telephone (212) 725-3828.

Monthly magazine. Covers general aviation news for consumers, including new products, air safety, and flying techniques. Price $14.00 per year.

2073
Flying Annual & Buyers' Guide
Ziff-Davis Publishing Co, 1156 15th St NW, Washington, DC 20005. Order from Ziff-Davis Publishing Co, One Park Ave, New York, NY 10016. Telephone (212) 725-3680.

Annual book. Provides information on aviation equipment and maintenance. Includes a listing of manufacturers. Price available on request.

2074
Focus Japan
Japan Trade Center, 1221 Ave of the Americas, New York, NY 10020. Telephone (212) 997-0400.

Monthly magazine. Covers Japanese economic and trade issues. Includes government policies and book reviews and gives a glimpse of the Japanese outside the work environment. Price $28.00 per year.

2075
Food and Agriculture Organization (FAO) Commodity Review & Outlook 1979/1980
Food and Agriculture Organization of the United Nations, Via Delle Terme di Caracalla, Rome, Italy 00100. Order from UNIPUB, 345 Park Ave S, New York, NY 10010. Telephone (212) 686-4707.

Annual report. Summarizes international commodity market developments. Analyzes major agricultural commodities, including fishery and forest products. Price $22.50.

2076
Food and Agriculture Organization (FAO) Plant Protection Bulletin
Food and Agriculture Organization of the United Nations, Via delle Terme di Caracalla, Rome, Italy 00100. Order from UNIPUB, 345 Park Ave S, New York, NY 10010. Telephone (212) 686-4707.

Quarterly report. Discusses the incidence and spread of plant diseases and pests, quarantine measures, prevention, and control. Price $10.00 per year.

2077
Food & Agriculture Organization of the United Nations (FAO) Production Yearbook
Food and Agriculture Organization of the United Nations, Via delle Terme di Caracalla, Rome, Italy 00100. Order from UNIPUB, 345 Park Ave S, New York, NY 10016. Telephone 5797. Telex 61181.

Annual book. Presents data on international food and agriculture, including material on population, wages, and freight rates. Price $28.00 per year.

2078

Food and Agriculture Organization of the United Nations (FAO) Trade Yearbook

Food and Agriculture Organization of the United Nations, Via delle Terme di Caracalla, Rome, Italy 00100. Order from UNIPUB, 345 Park Ave S, New York, NY 10016. Telephone 5797. Telex 61181.

Yearbook. Provides statistical information on international trade in major world agricultural products. Freight rate tables and summaries of trade in agricultural supplies. Price $33.50.

2079

Food & Drink

Stokes & Lindley-Jones Ltd, Alverstoke House, 21 Montpelier Row, Blackheath, London, England SE3 OSR. Telephone (44) (01) 852-9865.

Biannual report. Promotes the sale of British food and drink around the world. Price £25.00 for three years to qualified subscribers.

2080

Food and Drug Act and Regulations (Departmental Consolidation)/Complete Service

Supply and Services Canada, Canadian Govt Publishing Centre, Hull, Que, Canada, K1A 0S9. Telephone (819) 994-3475, 2085.

Book and loose-leaf service. Covers Canadian food and drug laws and regulations. Price $36.00.

2081

Food and Drug Act and Regulations/Partial Amendment Service

Supply and Services Canada, Publishing Centre, Printing and Publishing, Ottawa, Ont, Canada K1A OS9. Telephone (613) 238-1601.

Loose-leaf report, with update service. Presents data on Canada's Food and Drug Act and regulations. Includes information on cosmetics and vitamins. Price $10.50.

2082

Food and Nutrition

Food and Agriculture Organization of the United Nations, Via delle Terme di Caracalla, Rome, Italy 00100. Order from UNIPUB, 345 Park Ave S, New York, NY 10016. Telephone 5797. Telex 61181.

Quarterly report. Discusses developments in international food policies and nutrition. Price $7.00 per year.

2084

Food Drug Cosmetic Law Reports

Commerce Clearing House, Inc, 4025 W Peterson Ave, Chicago, IL 60646. Telephone (312) 538-8500.

Five loose-leaf books with weekly reports. Covers regulation of adulteration, packaging, and labeling of foods, drugs, and cosmetics. Price $820.00 per year.

2085

Food Engineering

Chilton Co, Chilton Wa, Radnor, PA 19089. Telephone (215) 687-8200.

Monthly magazine. Notes developments in major food and beverage industries. Price available on request.

2086

Food Engineering International

Chilton Co, Chilton Way, Radnor, PA 19089. Telephone (215) 687-8200.

Monthly magazine. Covers the overseas food manufacturing industry. Price available on request.

2087

Food Industry Newsletter

Profit Press, Inc, 400 E 89 St, New York, NY 10028. Telephone (212) 534-0366.

Semimonthly newsletter. Covers trends and developments among food manufacturers, primarily management, marketing and sales aspects. Price $95.00 per year.

2088

Food Industry Studies

United Nations Industrial Development Organization, Vienna International Centre, PO Box 300, A-1400, Vienna, Austria. Telephone 26310. Telex 135612.

Series of reports. Covers the food, citrus fruit, milk processing, and food packaging industries. Symbols: ID/SER.I/1-5. Price $.75.

2089

Food Institute Reports: Report on Food Markets; Washington Food Report; Weekly Digest

American Inst of Food Distribution, Inc, 28-06 Broadway, Fair Lawn, NJ 07410. Telephone (201) 791-5570.

Three weekly newsletters. Report on all phases of food production, processing, distribution, and marketing. Cover US government actions and judicial rulings affecting the food industry. Price $175.00 per year (includes membership).

2090

Food Management

Harcourt Brace Jovanovich Publications, 757 3rd Ave, New York, NY 10017. Order from Harcourt Brace and Jovanovich Publications, 1 E 1st St, Duluth, MN 55802. Telephone (218) 727-8511.

Monthly magazine. Reports on the institutional food service industry, including educational and health care institutions. Price $15.00 per year.

2091

Food Manufacture

Morgan-Grampian Ltd, Morgan-Grampian House, Calderwood St, London, England SE18 6QH. Order from Morgan-Grampian Publishing Co, 2 Park Ave, New York, NY 10016. Telephone England (44) (01) 855-7777. Telex 896238 MORGAN G. New York (212) 340-9700. Telex 425592 MGI UI.

Monthly magazine. Serves the food production industries with reports on raw materials, manufacturing processes, packaging, and distribution. Price $95.00 per year.

2092

Food Manufacturing News

Yaffa Publishing Group, 432-436 Elizabeth St, Surry Hills, NSW 2010, Australia. Order from Yaffa Publishing Group, GPO Box 606, Sydney, NSW 2001, Australia. Telephone (61) (02) 699-7861. Telex 21887.

Bimonthly newspaper. Provides information on manufacture and marketing of Australian food products. Price $25.00 Australia per year.

2093

Food Plant Ideas

Lakewood Publications, Inc, 731 Hennepin Ave, Minneapolis, MN 55403. Telephone (612) 333-0471.

Bimonthly magazine. Supplies news relevant to the food processing and manufacturing industries. Price $6.00 per year.

2094

Food Policy

IPC Business Press Ltd, 205 E 42nd St, New York, NY 10017. Telephone (212) 889-0700. Telex 421710.

Quarterly magazine. Deals with food production and policy, particularly agricultural technology, food prices, and government programs. Price $124.80 per year. ISSN 0306-9192.

2095

Food Processing in Ireland

Confederation of Irish Industry, Confederation House, Kildare St, Dublin 2, Ireland. Telephone (353) (01) 77 98 01. Telex 4711.

Report. Reviews the Irish food processing industry and forecasts future growth. Price £27.50.

2096

Food Promotions

Munroe Publications, Inc, PO Drawer 7, Indian Rocks Beach, FL 33535. Telephone (813) 595-5579.

Monthly newspaper. Covers food and nonfood topics. Includes information on supermarkets and food advertising. Price $7.50 per year.

2097

Food Research Institute Studies

Stanford University Food Research Inst, Stanford, CA 94305. Telephone (415) 497-4160.

Journal published three times per year. Presents articles on food and agricultural research and related world economic condition. Price $15.00.

2098

Foodservice Equipment Dealer

Cahners Publishing Company, Inc, 221 Columbus Ave, Boston, MA 02116. Telephone (617) 536-7780.

Monthly magazine. Contains information on food service equipment, including distributors and the design of food service operations. Price $10.00 per year.

2100

Food Trades Directory

Newman Books Ltd, 48 Poland St, London, England W1V 4PP. Telephone (44) (01) 439-0335.

Annual book. Offers directory to food markets. Provides information on food production, processing, distribution, and bulk purchasing, especially in Great Britain. Price $45.00.

2101

Footwear Manual

American Footwear Industries Assn, Suite 900, 1611 N Kent St, Arlington, VA 22209. Telephone (703) 522-7275.

Annual report, with monthly updates. Gives essential statistics on the footwear industry. Price $200.00 per year.

2102

Footwear Statistics

Statistics Canada, User Services, Publications Distribution, Ottawa, Ont, Canada K1A 0V7. Telephone (613) 992-3151.

Monthly report. Covers Canadian production of footwear by size and function. Price $18.00 per year. ISSN 0380-707X.

2103

Forbes

Forbes Inc, 60 5th Ave, New York, NY 10011. Telephone (212) 620-2200.

Biweekly magazine. Covers general business, economic and financial news. Reports on various corporations, executives, stocks, and industries. Price $30.00 per year.

2104

Forbes Special Situation Survey

Forbes Investors Advisory Inst Inc, 60 5th Ave, New York, NY 10011. Telephone (212) 620-2210.

Monthly loose-leaf report. Discusses and recommends the purchase of one speculative equity security in each issue. Price $395.00 per year.

2105

Ford Value Report

Ford Investor Services, 11722 Sorrento Valley Rd, Suite I, San Diego, CA 92121. Telephone (714) 755-1327.

Monthly report. Summarizes standard value analysis and earnings trend analysis for 1400 common stocks. Offers brief commentaries and stock selections. Price $72.00 per year.

2106

Forecast

United California Bank, Research and Planning Div, 707 Wilshire Blvd, Los Angeles, CA 90017. Telephone (213) 614-3383.

Annual report. Analyzes the economy in the US and California for the past year. Forecasts future trends and evaluates money markets, inflation, unemployment, industrial profits, and other indicators. Tables and charts. Price available on request.

2107

Forecaster

Forecaster Publishing Co, Inc, 19623 Ventura Blvd, Tarzana, CA 91356. Telephone (213) 345-4421.

Weekly newsletter. Reports speculative ideas outside the stock market. Covers economic, monetary, numismatic markets, and other unusual money-making fields. Price $90.00 per year. ISSN 0095-294X.

2108

Foreign Agricultural Trade of the United States

US Dept of Agriculture, ESS Publications, Room 0054-S, Washington, DC 20250. Telephone (202) 447-7255.

Bimonthly report. Discusses current US agricultural trade and outlook. Covers exports under government-finance programs, commercial exports, and prices. Tables. Price free of charge.

2110

Foreign Agriculture

US Dept of Agriculture, Foreign Agricultural Service, Information Service Staff, Rm 5918, Washington, DC 20250. Order from Superintendent of Documents, Government Printing Office, Washington, DC 20402. Telephone (202) 783-3238.

Monthly magazine. Reports on international agricultural issues. Discusses government policies, food prices, and export trends. Price $14.00 US, $17.50 foreign.

2111

Foreign Agriculture Circulars

Dept of Agriculture, US Foreign Agricultural Service, Information Service Staff, Rm 5918S, Washington, DC 20250. Telephone (202) 447-7937.

Irregular reports. Provide world agricultural information on specific commodities, including grains, dairy products, livestock and meat, sugar, and tobacco. Price free of charge.

2112

Foreign Credit Insurance Assn (FCIA) News

Foreign Credit Insurance Assn, 1 World Trade Center, 9th Floor, New York, NY 10048. Telephone (212) 432-6300. Telex 12-756.

Thrice yearly newsletter. Discusses changes and improvements in current and new programs for exporters wishing to insure their credit sales. Current emphasis on pieces highlighting service to existing customers. Price free of charge.

2113
Foreign Credit Interchange Bureau (FCIB) International Bulletin
Foreign Credit Interchange Bureau, National Assn of Credit Management, 475 Park Ave S, New York, NY 10016. Telephone (212) 578-4419.
Report. Covers news affecting international credit, collection, and exchange conditions. Includes economic forecasts. Price $150.00 per year.

2115
Foreign Direct Investment in the United States, **1974 edition**
US Dept of Commerce, Bureau of Economic Analysis, Washington, DC 20230. Order from Superintendent of Documents, US Government Printing Office, Washington, DC 20402. Telephone (202) 783-3238.
Two-volume publication. Gives data on foreign investment in the US and its economic impact. Includes US affiliates, balance of payments transactions, foreign share of earnings, and reinvestment. Price $6.00.

2116
Foreign Economic Trends
US Dept of Commerce, 14th St between Constitution Ave and E St NW, Washington, DC 20230. Order from Superintendent of Documents, US Government Printing Office, Washington, DC 20402. Telephone (202) 783-3238.
Series of 140-150 reports per year. Presents business and economic information on foreign countries that offer a current or potential market for US goods. Price $50.00 per year US, $62.50 foreign.

2117
Foreign Economic Trends and Their Implications for the US
US Dept of Commerce, International Trade Administration, Washington, DC 20230. Telephone (202) 377-1470.
Approximately 150 reports per year. Covers economic overseas trends by country, and their effect on the US. Price $50.00 per year.

2117.01
Foreign Investment **Cat No 5305.0**
Australian Bureau of Statistics, Box 10, Belcooen, ACT 2616, Australia. Order from Australian Government Publishing Service, PO Box 84, Canberra, ACT 2600, Australia. Telephone (61) (062) 527911.

Annual report. Analyzes foreign investment in Australia and Australian investment abroad. Price $1.25 (Australian).

2118
Foreign Investment in Canada
Prentice-Hall, Inc, Englewood Cliffs, NJ 07632. Telephone (201) 592-2000. Telex 13-5423.
Loose-leaf book, plus updates. Explains Canada's Foreign Investment Review Act and other Canadian federal and provincial laws that restrict foreign investment. Price $195.00 per year.

2119
Foreign Investment in Enterprise in Australia **Cat No 5306.0**
Australian Bureau of Statistics, Box 10 Belconnen, ACT 2616, Australia. Order from Australian Government Publishing Service, PO Box 84, Canberra, ACT 2600, Australia. Telephone (062) 52 7911.
Quarterly report. Covers the inflow of foreign investment into Australia. Classifies investments by country and industry group. Price free of charge.

2120
Foreign Letter
International Reports, 200 Park Ave S, New York, NY 10003. Telephone (212) 477-0003.
Biweekly report. Analyzes international political news. Focuses on events which will affect world currency developments. Price $95.00 per year.

2134
Foreign Market Reports Index
US Dept of Commerce, Industry and Trade Adm, Bureau of Export Development, Washington, DC 20230. Order from National Technical Information Service, 5285 Port Royal Rd, Springfield, VA 22161. Telephone (202) 377-2000.
Monthly pamphlet. Indexes reports dealing with international market surveys, prospects for exports to foreign countries, industry and trade forecasts, and international finance. Price $10.00 per year.

2135
Foreign Mineral Reports
US Bureau of Mines, Publications Distribution Branch, 4800 Forbes Ave, Pittsburgh, PA 15213. Telephone (412) 621-4500.
Monthly and annual reports. Provides information on foreign mineral industries and markets. Price available on request.

2136
Foreign Scouting Service
Petroconsultants SA, 8-10 Rue Muzy, PO Box 228, 1211 Geneva 6, Switzerland. Telephone 36 88 11. Telex 27 763 PETRO CH.
Monthly reports. Cover technical aspects of international oil exploration and production. Maps. Price varies according to country requested.

2137
Foreign Tax and Trade Briefs
Matthew Bender & Co, 235 E 45th St, New York, NY 10017. Telephone (212) 661-5050.
Loose-leaf volumes with monthly updating. Supply tax and trade information for over 100 foreign countries. Give every class of taxation for each country. Price $180.00 for two volumes; $150.00 per year.

2138
Foreign Tax Law Bi-Weekly Bulletin
Foreign Tax Law Assn, Inc, PO Box 340, Alachua, FL 32616.
Biweekly bulletin. Discusses tax laws in various countries and pending legislation. Price free to members.

2140
Foreign Trade Statistics for Africa-Series A-Direction of Trade
United Nations Publications, Rm A-3315, New York, NY 10017. Telephone (212) 754-8302.
Report. Provides statistics on Africa's foreign trade. Price available on request.

2141
Foreign Trade Statistics for Africa—Series B—Trade by Commodity
United Nations Publications, Rm A-3315, New York, NY 10017. Telephone (212) 754-8302.
Report. Gives a breakdown of Africa's foreign trade by commodity. Price available on request.

2142
Forest Industries Newsletter
National Forest Products Assn, 1619 Massachusetts Ave NW, Washington, DC 20036. Telephone (202) 797-5800.
Weekly newsletter. Covers major government actions relating to forest management, products, manufacturing, and sales. Price $30.00 per year.

2143

Forest Industries Review

Modern Productions Ltd, 1st Floor, Midland House, 73 Great North Rd, PO Box 3159, Auckland 1, New Zealand. Telephone (64) (09) 768-808.

Monthly magazine. Covers the New Zealand forest industries. Is devoted to the production side of the industry. Price $20.00 (New Zealand) per year.

2144

Forest Products Service

Data Resources, Inc, 29 Hartwell Ave, Lexington, MA 02173. Telephone (617) 861-0165.

Quarterly and annual report. Provides forecasts for the North American lumber industry, including supply, demand, and price of Douglas fir products, plywood, particle board, paper, and pulp. Price available on request.

2145

Forex Service

International Reports, Inc, 200 Park Ave S, New York, NY 10003. Telephone (212) 477-0003.

Monthly report. Provides information on current and pending legislation which will affect international finance and trade. Price $235.00 per year.

2146

Forms and Agreements for Architects, Engineers, and Contractors

Clark Boardman Co Ltd, 435 Hudson St, New York, NY 10014. Telephone (212) 929-7500.

Loose-leaf book, periodically revised. Discusses construction industry contracts. Contains information on finance, patents, joint ventures, and nondisclosure agreements. Cites court cases and includes forms. Price $125.00 per two looseleaf volumes. ISBN 0-87632-215-1.

2147

Forms and Workbook Under ERISA, for Pension and Profit Sharing Plans

Panel Publishers, 14 Plaza Rd, Greenvale, NY 11548. Telephone (516) 484-0006.

Two loose-leaf books, with bimonthly supplements. Provide forms and checklists for establishing pension, profit-sharing, and employee benefit plans, including employee stock ownership plans. Price $128.00. ISBN 0-916592-05-7.

2148

Forms of Business Agreements. Vols 1 and 2

Inst for Business Planning, Inc, IPB Plz, Englewood Cliffs, NJ 07632. Telephone (201) 592-2040.

Two loose-leaf books, with monthly supplements. Provide sample forms, agreements and resolutions to cover business, and financial and investment transactions. Price available on request.

2149

Forthcoming Books

R R Bowker Co, 1180 Ave of the Americas, New York, NY 10036. Order from R R Bowker Co, PO Box 13746, Philadelphia, PA 19101. Telephone (212) 764-5100.

Bimonthly magazine. Contains author-title indexes to all books to be published in the coming five-month period. Supplements Books in Print. Price $32.50 per year. ISSN 0015-8119.

2150

Fortune

Time, Inc, Time & Life Bldg, New York, NY 10020. Order from Time, Inc, 541 N Fairbanks Ct, Chicago, IL 60611. Telephone (212) 586-1212.

Semimonthly magazine. Covers business and economic developments. Evaluates specific industries and corporations and notes banking and energy news. Price $20.00 per year.

2151

Fortune Double 500 Directory

Time, Inc, Time & Life Bldg, New York, NY 10020. Order from Time, Inc, 541 N Fairbanks Ct, Chicago, IL 60611. Telephone (212) 586-1212.

Annual book. Provides data on sales, finances, and other aspects of 500 large industrial corporations. Includes information on various categories of business, such as banking, retailing, and utilities. Statistical charts. Price $6.00 per copy.

2152

Foundation Center National Data Book

Foundation Center, 888 7th Ave, New York, NY 10106. Telephone (212) 975-1120.

Two-volume annual directory. Includes material on over 22,000 US private foundations. Provides listings of note assets, grants made, and gifts received. Bases its information on IRS returns. Price $45.00.

2153

Foundation Center Source Book Profiles

Foundation Center, 888 7th Ave, New York, NY 10106. Telephone (212) 975-1120.

Annual loose-leaf service. Provides analytical profiles of over 500 of the largest US foundations by subject area, grant type, and recipient type. Price $200.00 per year.

2154

Foundation Directory, **6th edition**

Columbia University Press, 562 W 113th St, New York, NY 10025. Telephone (212) 678-6750.

Periodically revised book. Contains profiles of over 2800 of the largest grant-making foundations in the US. Price $35.00 per copy. ISBN 0-87954-011-7.

2155

Foundation Directory, **7th edition 1979**

Foundation Center, 888 7th Ave, New York, NY 10106. Order from Columbia University Press, 136 S Broadway, Irvington, NY 10533. Telephone (212) 975-1120.

Directory. Describes 3218 of the largest US foundations. Includes subject index, grant application procedures, and statistical profiles of foundations. Price $41.50.

2156

Foundation Grants Index

Foundation Center, 888 7th Ave, New York NY 10106. Telephone (212) 975-1120.

Annual publication. Lists current foundation grants of $5000 or more by over 400 major foundations. Recipients and subjects of awards indexed. Price $27.00 per year.

2158

Foundry Management & Technology

Penton/IPC, 614 Superior Ave W, Cleveland, OH 44113. Order from Penton/IPC, 111 Chester Ave, Cleveland, OH 44114. Telephone (216) 696-7000.

Monthly magazine. Reports on foundries, with emphasis on management and technology. Price $24.00 per year.

2159

Franchised New Car & Truck Dealer Facts

National Automobile Dealers Assn, 3400 Westpark Dr, McLean, VA 22102. Telephone (703) 821-7000

Annual report. Gives statistics on car and truck production, sales, and franchise operations. Price free of charge.

2160
Franchising
Matthew Bender & Co, 235 E 45th St, New York, NY 10017. Telephone (212) 661-5050.

Two-volume set of books. Provides a guide to franchising. Includes such topics as contracts, trademarks, taxation, and equipment provisions. Price $150.00.

2161
Fraser Opinion Letter
Fraser Management Associates, Inc, 309 Willard St, PO Box 494, Burlington, VT 05402. Telephone (802) 658-0322.

Biweekly newsletter. Offers differing views on current economic events, business, finance, and public thinking trends. Price $45.00 per year.

2162
Fraser's Canadian Trade Directory
Maclean-Hunter Ltd, 481 University Ave, Toronto, Ont, Canada. Telephone (416) 595-1811.

Annual book. Lists Canadian companies and products. Price $45.00.

2163
Fraser's Potato Newsletter
Harry Fraser, Charlottetown RR #1, Hazelbrook, Prince Edward Island, Canada C1A 7J6. Telephone (902) 569-2685.

Weekly newsletter. Reports on US and Canadian potato production. Notes acres planted and harvested and yield and prices. Price $28.00 per year.

2164
Fraternal Monitor
Research and Review Service of America, Inc, PO Box 1727, Indianapolis, IN 46206. Telephone (317) 297-4360.

Monthly magazine. Covers news of interest to field and home office personnel of fraternal benefit societies. Includes society and institutional events, sales and management articles, and a review of new books and products. Price $10.20 per year.

2165
French-American Commerce
French Chamber of Commerce of the US, Inc, 1350 Ave of the Americas, New York, NY 10019. Telephone (212) 581-4554. Telex Fren 237757.

Bimonthly magazine. Discusses French industries, French-American commerce, and economic issues of interest to both countries. English and French. Free to members.

2165.01
French-American News
French Chamber of Commerce of the US, Inc, 1350 Ave of the Americas, New York, NY 10019. Telephone (212) 581-4554.

Monthly newsletter. Covers French, US, and international economic and fi nancial news. Reports on French-American business interests and investments. Price free to members.

2166
Fresh Fruit and Vegetable and Ornamental Crops Market News Reports
US Dept of Agriculture, Agricultural Marketing Service, Room 2503, Washington, DC 20250. Telephone (202) 447-2745.

Irregular reports. Contain information on fresh fruit, vegetable, and ornamental crops market. Cover wholesale prices and shipments. Price free of charge.

2167
Friday Report
Hoke Communications, Inc, 224 7th St, Garden City, NY 11535. Telephone (516) 746-6700.

Weekly newsletter. Contains reports on direct response advertisers and market data centers organizing direct marketing. Price $84.00 per year.

2168
From Nine to Five
Dartnell Corp, 4660 Ravenswood Ave, Chicago, IL 60640. Telephone (312) 561-4000.

Semimonthly report. Provides tips for businesswomen. Bibliography. Price $20.00 per year.

2169
From the State Capitals: Agriculture and Food Products
Bethune Jones, 321 Sunset Ave, Asbury Park, NJ 07712. Telephone (201) 775-4853.

Weekly report. Deals with the regulation of the production, processing, and marketing of food products. Price $120.00 per year.

2170
From the State Capitals: Airport Construction and Financing
Bethune Jones, 321 Sunset Ave, Asbury Park, NJ 07712. Telephone (201) 775-4853.

Monthly report. Emphasizes the planning, financing, and regulation of airports. Price $57.00 per year.

2171
From the State Capitals: Federal Action Affecting the States
Bethune Jones, 321 Sunset Ave, Asbury Park, NJ 07712. Telephone (201) 775-4853.

Mimeographed newsletter. Twenty issues per year. Covers federal legislative and administrative developments affecting state and local governments. Price $72.00 per year.

2172
From the State Capitals: General Bulletin
Bethune Jones, 321 Sunset Ave, Asbury Park, NJ 07712. Telephone (201) 775-4853.

Semimonthly newsletter. Reviews state and local action on taxes, public works, and labor relations. Price $72.00 per year.

2173
From the State Capitals: Highway Financing and Construction
Bethune Jones, 321 Sunset Ave, Asbury Park, NJ 07712. Telephone (201) 775-4853.

Weekly report. Discusses how highway and street modernization programs are being planned, financed, and administered. Price $120.00 per year.

2174
From the State Capitals: Housing and Redevelopment
Bethune Jones, 321 Sunset Ave, Asbury Park, NJ 07712. Telephone (201) 775-4853.

Monthly report. Features information on planning, financing, administration of public housing, slum clearance, urban renewal, and action affecting public and private housing. Price $57.00 per year.

2175
From the State Capitals: Industrial Development
Bethune Jones, 321 Sunset Ave, Asbury Park, NJ 07712. Telephone (201) 775-4853.

Monthly mimeographed report. Covers state and local efforts to attract industry and facilitate expansion of existing plants. Price $57.00 per year.

2176

From the State Capitals: Institutional Building

Bethune Jones, 321 Sunset Ave, Asbury Park, NJ 07712. Telephone (201) 775-4853.

Monthly report. Covers financing and construction of state-operated, aided, and regulated hospitals, colleges, prisons, and other structures. Price $57.00 per year.

2177

From the State Capitals: Insurance Regulation

Bethune Jones, 321 Sunset Ave, Asbury Park, NJ 07712. Telephone (201) 775-4853.

Weekly mimeographed reports. Provides information on the regulation of casualty, life, fire, accident, and health insurance. Price $120.00 per year.

2178

From the State Capitals: Labor Relations

Bethune Jones, 321 Sunset Ave, Asbury Park, NJ 07712. Telephone (201) 775-4853.

Monthly report. Features the regulations affecting labor-management relations in industry, commerce, and government. Price $57.00 per year.

2179

From the State Capitals: Liquor Control

Bethune Jones, 321 Sunset Ave, Asbury Park, NJ 07712. Telephone (201) 775-4853.

Weekly newsletter. Covers regulatory developments affecting the production and marketing of alcoholic beverages. Price $120.00 per year.

2180

From the State Capitals: Merchandising

Bethune Jones, 321 Sunset Ave, Asbury Park, NJ 07712. Telephone (201) 775-4853.

Weekly report. Includes information on such topics as consumer protection, resale pricing, consumer credit, trading stamps and premiums, and Sunday sales. Price $120.00 per year.

2181

From the State Capitals: Milk Control

Bethune Jones, 321 Sunset Ave, Asbury Park, NJ 07712. Telephone (201) 775-4853.

Monthly report. Provides data on the production, processing, marketing, and pricing of milk and other dairy products. Price $57.00 per year.

2183

From the State Capitals: Personnel Management

Bethune Jones, 321 Sunset Ave, Asbury Park, NJ 07712. Telephone (201) 775-4853.

Monthly report. Provides information on civil service and merit programs, public employee salary levels, and related matters in state and local governments. Price $57.00 per year.

2184

From the State Capitals: Public Utilities

Bethune Jones, 321 Sunset Ave, Asbury Park, NJ 07712. Telephone (201) 775-4853.

Weekly report. Surveys the rate regulation of public utilities. Price $120.00 per year.

2185

From the State Capitals: Small Loans, Sales Finance, Banking

Bethune Jones, 321 Sunset Ave, Asbury Park, NJ 07712. Telephone (201) 775-4853.

Monthly report. Discusses regulations affecting small loans, sales finance, and banking. Price $57.00 per year.

2186

From the State Capitals: Taxes—Local Non-Property

Bethune Jones, 321 Sunset Ave, Asbury Park, NJ 07712. Telephone (201) 775-4853.

Monthly report. Discusses municipal taxes and revenue. Emphasizes nonproperty tax trends. Price $57.00 per year.

2187

From the State Capitals: Taxes—Property

Bethune Jones, 321 Sunset Ave, Asbury Park, NJ 07712. Telephone (201) 775-4853.

Monthly newsletter. Provides information on equalization affecting real and personal property taxes. Price $57.00 per year.

2188

From the State Capitals: Unemployment Compensation

Bethune Jones, 321 Sunset Ave, Asbury Park, NJ 07712. Telephone (201) 775-4853.

Monthly report. Covers unemployment compensation changes, job opportunity development programs, and efforts to stimulate employment. Price $57.00 per year.

2189

From the State Capitals: Urban Transit & Bus Transportation

Bethune Jones, 321 Sunset Ave, Asbury Park, NJ 07712. Telephone (201) 775-4853.

Monthly newsletter. Covers the financing and development of mass transportation systems. Price $57.00 per year.

2190

From the State Capitals: Wage-Hour Regulation

Bethune Jones, 321 Sunset Ave, Asbury Park, NJ 07712. Telephone (201) 775-4853.

Monthly report. Reviews the regulations affecting wages and hours, sex discrimination, and child labor laws. Price $57.00 per year.

2191

From the State Capitals: Workmen's Compensation

Bethune Jones, 321 Sunset Ave, Asbury Park, NJ 07712. Telephone (201) 775-4853.

Monthly report. Covers the regulations affecting industrial safety and worker's compensation. Price $57.00 per year.

2192

Frozen Food Pack Statistics

American Frozen Food Inst, 1700 Old Meadow Rd, McLean, VA 22102. Telephone (703) 821-0770.

Annual report. Gives statistics by category for frozen food packing. Price $50.-00.

2193

Fruit and Vegetable Production

Statistics Canada, User Services, Publications Distribution, Ottawa, Ont, Canada K1A OV7. Telephone (613) 992-3151.

Seasonal reports. Provide estimates of planted acreage and production of Canadian vegetable and canning crops. Include estimates of production and value of production of fruit crops. Price $12.00 per year.ISSN 0383-008X.

2194
Fruit Statistics Cat No 7303.0
Australian Bureau of Statistics, PO Box 10, Belconnen, ACT 2616, Australia. Order from Australian Government Publishing Service, PO Box 84, Canberra, ACT 2600, Australia. Telephone (062) 52 7911.

Annual report. Covers the number of trees, area, production, and yield per tree for approximately 25 types of Australian orchard fruits. Includes berries and grapes. Price free of charge.

2195
Fuel
IPC Business Press Ltd, 205 E 42nd St, New York, NY 10017. Telephone (212) 889-0700. Telex 421710.

Quarterly magazine. Publishes research reports on fuel and energy technology. Emphasizes coal research and such alternative energy sources as oil shale and tar sands. Price $329.20 airmail. ISSN 0016-2361.

2196
Fuel Abstracts and Current Titles
IPC Business Press Ltd, 205 E 42nd St, New York, NY 10017. Telephone (212) 889-0700. Telex 421710.

Bimonthly magazine. Furnishes abstracts and titles on the technical aspects of fuel and energy from over 800 publications. Price $234.00. ISSN 0016-2388.

2197
Fuel Price Analysis
McGraw-Hill Publications Co, 1221 Ave of the Americas, New York, NY 10020. Telephone (212) 997-1221. Telex TWX 7105814879 WUI 62555.

Monthly service. Reports all fuel purchases by US generating stations for utilities with a capacity greater than 25 megawatts. Lists the type of fuel and its origin, supplier, quality specification, and price. Price $1200.00 per year.

2199
Fund Raising Institute (FRI) Monthly Portfolio
Fund Raising Inst, Box 365, Ambler, PA 19002. Telephone (215) 646-7019.

Monthly newsletter. Reports on fundraising techniques used by nonprofit organizations. Price $43.00 per year.

2200
Fund Raising Management
Hoke Communications, Inc, 224 7th St, Garden City, NY 11535. Telephone (516) 746-6700.

Monthly magazine. Focuses on private philanthropy. Is designed to aid the professional fund raiser and nonprofit institutions. Price $24.00 per year.

2200.01
Fundraising Weekly
Hoke Communications, Inc, 224 7th St, Garden City, NY 11535. Telephone (516) 746-6700.

Newsletter. Gives latest news on government and private sectors in relation to nonprofit field. Price $64.00 per year.

2201
Funeral Service "Insider"
Atcom, Inc, Atcom Bldg, 2315 Broadway, New York, NY 10024. Telephone (212) 873-3760.

Weekly newsletter. Carries articles pertaining to the funeral profession, including grief counseling, and antitrust guidelines. Price $72.00 per year.

2203
Fur Review
Insurance Publishing & Printing Co, 34 Lower High St, Stourbridge, West Midlands, England DY8 1TA. Telephone Stourbridge 77761. Order from Fur Review Publishing Co, 25 Garlick Hill, London EC4V 2AU, England. Telephone (44) (01) 248-3548.

Monthly magazine. Discusses international trends affecting the fur trade. Price £18.00 per year.

2203.01
Fusion Power Report
Business Publishers, PO Box 1067, Silver Spring, MD 20910. Telephone (301) 587-6300.

Monthly newsletter. Reports on fusion energy research and development. Price $97.00 per year.

2204
Futures
IPC Business Press Ltd, 205 E 42nd St, New York, NY 10017. Telephone (212) 889-0700. Telex 421710.

Bimonthly. Covers methods of long-term forecasting in areas such as economics, population, and technology. Price $72.80 (company rate); $124.80 (individual rate). ISSN 0016-3287.

2205
Futures Market Service
Commodity Research Bureau, Inc, 1 Liberty Plz, 47th Floor, New York, NY 10006. Telephone (212) 267-3600.

Weekly newsletter. Covers the fundamental developments influencing price changes in the futures markets. Price $99.00 per year.

2206
Gallagher Report
Gallagher Report, Inc, 230 Park Ave, New York, NY 10017. Telephone (212) 661-5000.

Weekly report. Presents news and trends in the fields of marketing, advertising, media, and sales. Price $84.00 per year.

2207
Gallup Survey
American Bankers Assn, 1120 Connecticut Ave NW, Washington, DC 20036. Telephone (202) 467-4123.

Pamphlet. Contains the results of the public opinion survey of current banking issues. Price $35.00.

2208
Gas Facts: A Statistical Record of the Gas Utility Industry
American Gas Assn, Bureau of Statistics, 1515 Wilson Blvd, Arlington, VA 22209. Telephone (703) 841-8000.

Annual report. Gives production, sales, storage, financial, and other related statistics for the gas utility industry. Price $25.00.

2209
GATT Activities
General Agreement on Tariffs and Trade, Centre William Rappard, 154 rue de Lausannee, 1211 Geneva 21, Switzerland. Telephone 022-31 02 31.

Annual report. Describes the trade policy issues and other works before the GATT member states and secretariat during the period covered. Price $7.00.

2210

General Household Survey

Her Majesty's Stationery Office, PO Box 569, London, England SE1 0NH. Telephone (44) (01) 928 1321.

Report. Provides a general household survey for Great Britain. Price $7.00 per year.

2211

General Imports of Cotton, Wool, and Man-made Fiber Manufactures

US Dept of Commerce, Bureau of the Census, Washington, DC 20233.

Monthly bulletin. Presents data on US imports of cotton, wool, and man-made fiber manufactures. Notes country of origin. Price $3.60 per year.

2212

General Information Bulletin

Trust Companies Assn of Canada, 11 Adelaide St W, Ste 400, Toronto, Ont, Canada M5H 1L9. Telephone (416) 364-1207.

General Information Bulletin. Supplies financial information for Canadian trust and mortgage loan companies. Includes assets, mortgage loans, investment funds, and other data. Tables. Price free of charge.

2213

General Insurance Guide

Werbel Publishing Co, Inc, 595 Old Willets Path, Smithtown, NY 11787. Telephone (516) 234-1114, (212) 261-6222.

Loose-leaf three-volume book, with quarterly updates. Contains information on property, casualty and health insurance. Price $74.00 first year, $36.00 subsequent years.

2216

General Review of the Mineral Industries

Statistics Canada, User Services, Publications Distribution, Ottawa, Ont, Canada K1A 0V7. Telephone (613) 992-3151.

Annual review. Presents Canadian mining industry data. Includes the production and value of minerals by kind and provinces and average prices of leading minerals. Price $5.40. ISSN 0575-8645.

2217

General Statistics

New Zealand Dept of Statistics, Private Bag, Wellington, New Zealand. Telephone (64) (4) 729119.

Bullentin. Provides statistics on New Zealand's manufacturing industries. Price $1.10.

2217.01

Geo Abstracts

Geo Abstracts Ltd, University of East Anglia, Norwich, England NR4 7TJ. Telephone (44) (01) (0603) 26327.

Annual series of abstracts. Provides information on earth science literature. Covers geography, regional planning, and meteorology. Price available on request.

2218

Georgia Business

University of Georgia, College of Business Adm, Div of Research, Athens, GA 30602. Telephone (404) 542-4085.

Bimonthly magazine. Reports on Georgia's economy and business. Notes tourist travel developments. Tables. Price $6.00 per year.

2218.01

Georgia: Manufacturers Directory, **1980–81**

Manufacturers' News, Inc, 3 Huron St, Chicago, IL 60611. Telephone (312) 337-1084.

Biennial book. Lists 5600 Georgia manufacturing companies. Notes executives and products. Price $33.00.

2219

Georgia Manufacturing Directory

Georgia Dept of Industry & Trade, 1400 N Omni International, PO Box 1776, Atlanta, GA 30301. Telephone (404) 656-3619. Telex 54-2586 GA INTL ATL.

Biennial book. Provides a directory to Georgia manuafacturing firms, products, markets, parent companies, employment, and officers. Price $20.00.

2219.01

Georgia: State Industrial Directory, **1980**

Manufacturers' News, Inc, 3 Huron St, Chicago, IL 60611. Telephone (312) 337-1084.

Annual book. Contains information on Georgia industrial companies. Price $50.-00.

2220

Georgia Statistical Abstract

University of Georgia, College of Business Adm, Div of Research, Athens, GA 30602. Telephone (404) 542-4085.

Biennial publication. Supplies data on the economic, social, and political structure of Georgia. Includes such topics as transportation, education, labor, and population. Tables, charts, and maps. Price $8.50 per copy.

2221

German–American Trade News

German–American Chamber of Commerce, Inc, 666 5th Ave, New York, NY 10019. Telephone (212) 974-8830.

Bimonthly magazine. Focuses on West German economic conditions and industrial developments and American-West German commerce. Price $9.00 per year.

2223

Geyer's Dealer Topics

Geyer-McAllister Publications, Inc, 51 Madison Ave, New York, NY 10010. Telephone (212) 689-4411.

Monthly magazine. Provides information of interest to office machines, furniture, and stationery dealers. Price $14.00 per year.

2224

Geyer's Who Makes It Directory

Geyer-McAllister Publications, Inc, 51 Madison Ave, New York, NY 10010. Telephone (212) 689-4411.

Annual directory. Lists brand and trade names, with information about manufacturers, wholesalers, and industry associations. Available with subscription to Geyer's Dealer Topics only.

2225

Gibson Report

D Parke Gibson International, Inc, 475 5th Ave, New York, NY 10017. Telephone (212) 889-5557.

Monthly report. Deals with marketing for and communications with minority groups. Discusses new products and advertising. Price $25.00. ISSN 0016-9784.

2226

Gifts & Housewares Buyers

Salesman's Guide, Inc, 1140 Broadway, New York, NY 10001. Telephone (212) 684-2985.

Directory, with quarterly supplements. Lists top department, chain, and specialty stores carrying giftware and housewares. Notes the names of buyers and merchandise managers of giftware and housewares. Price $95.00.

2227

Gifts & Tablewares

Southam Communications Ltd, 1450 Don Mills Rd, Don Mills, Ont, Canada M3B 2X7. Telephone (416) 445-6641. Telex 06-966612.

Bimonthly magazine. Deals with the retailing of gifts. Focuses on tableware and jewelry. Price $22.00 per year.

2228

Gilmour's Income Tax Handbook

Richard De Boo Ltd, 70 Richmond St, Toronto, Ont, Canada M5C 2M8. Telephone (416) 368-1784.

Book. Covers the Canadian income tax. Includes such topics as estates and trusts, residence, capital gains, and corporate taxation. Price $28.95.

2229

Glass Containers

Glass Container Manufacturers Inst, 1800 K St NW, Washington, DC 20006. Telephone (202) 872-1280.

Annual report. Contains statistics on shipments of glass containers. Price free of charge.

2230

Glass Containers

US Dept of Commerce, Bureau of the Census, Washington, DC 20233. Telephone (202) 449-1600.

Monthly report, with annual summary. Presents statistics on shipments, the production, and stocks of glass containers by type. Price $3.25 per year.

2230.01

Global Investment Flows

Conference Board, Inc, 845 3rd Ave, New York, NY 10022. Telephone (212) 759-0900.

Quarterly report. Lists transnational investment flows, including name and domicile of investing company, country of investment, manufacturing sector of investment, and anticipated spending and employment figures, when available. Price available on request.

2231

Globe and Mail Report on Business

Globe and Mail Ltd, 444 Front St W, Toronto, Canada M5V 2S9. Telephone (416) 361-5434.

Section of daily Toronto, Canada, Globe and Mail. Deals with economic, business, and financial issues, with emphasis on Canada. Price $52.00 per year.

2232

Going Public

Clark Boardman Co Ltd, 435 Hudson St, New York, NY 10014. Telephone (212) 929-7500.

Loose-leaf book, with annual revisions. Discusses underwriting, business, and tax considerations involved in companies going public. Notes the Securities and Exchange Commission's—and other federal and state—regulations. Price $67.50. ISBN 0-87632-010-8.

2233

Gold Data

American Bureau of Metal Statistics, Inc, 420 Lexington Ave, New York, NY 10170. Telephone (212) 867-9450. Telex 14-7130.

Monthly report. Provides data on mine production and imports and exports of US gold. Price $75.00 per year.

2235

Goldsmith-Nagan Bond & Money Market Letter

Goldsmith-Nagan, Inc, 1120 19th St NW, Washington, DC 20036. Telephone (202) 628-1600.

Biweekly newsletter. Covers bond and money markets and federal monetary policy. Price $198.00 per year.

2236

Government & Municipal Contractors

Sell's Publications Ltd, Sell's House, 39 E St, Epsom Surrey, England KT17 1BQ. Telephone Epsom 26376. Telex 21792 A/B Mono K LDN.

Book. Lists British firms by name and trade that contract to the government, municipal authorities, and nationalized industries. Price £12.00.

2238

Government Contractor

Federal Publications, Inc, 1120 20th St, NW, Washington, DC 20036. Telephone (202) 337-7000.

Biweekly report. Discusses significant federal government contract rulings issued by the courts, the comptroller general, Congress, agencies and other sources. Price $288.00 per year.

2238.01

Government Contracts Citations

Federal Publications, Inc, 1120 20th St, NW, Washington, DC 20036. Telephone (202) 337-7000.

Quarterly report. Lists all citations of US government contracts decisions by courts, Comptroller General, and agency boards. Price $240.00 per year.

2239

Government Contracts Reports

Commerce Clearing House, Inc, 4025 W Peterson Ave, Chicago, IL 60646. Telephone (312) 583-8500.

Nine loose-leaf books, plus weekly reports. Present laws and regulations pertaining to government contract work, from bid to final settlement, including defense procurement, performance, and costs. Price $725.00 per year.

2239.01

Government Data Systems

United Business Publications, Inc, 475 Park Ave S, New York, NY 10016. Telephone (212) 725-2300.

Bimonthly magazine. Reports on government computer systems. Notes new equipment. Price $10.00 per year.

2240

Government Employee Relations Report

Bureau of National Affairs, Inc, 1231 25th St NW, Washington, DC 20037. Telephone (202) 452-4200.

Two books, plus weekly updates. Provide both a summary and in-depth coverage of federal, state, and local public sector employee relations. Include statistics and contracts, a glossary, and an index. Price $370.00 per year.

2244

Government Finance Statistics Yearbook

International Monetary Fund, 19th & H Sts NW, Washington, DC 20431. Telephone (202) 393-6362.

Annual book. Provides government finance statistics for 90 countries. Includes data on revenues, grants, expenditures, and debts. French, Spanish, and English headings. Price $10.00 per volume.

2245

Government Manager

Bureau of National Affairs, Inc, 1231 25th St NW, Washington, DC 20037. Telephone (202) 452-4200.

Biweekly bulletin. Provides guidelines for federal supervisors on government employee relations. Price $66.00 per year.

2246
Government 1975—Occupational Employment Statistics
Alaska Dept of Labor, Employment Security Div, Research & Analysis Section, Box 3-7000, Juneau, AK 99801. Telephone (907) 465-2700.

Report. Tenders statistics on federal, state, and local government employment in Alaska. Price available on request.

2247
Government of Canada Telephone Directory/National Capital Region
Supply and Services Canada, Canadian Govt Publishing Centre, Hull, Que, Canada K1A 0S9. Telephone (819) 994-3475, 2085.

Semiannual book. Lists telephone numbers of Canadian government in the capital region. Price $18.00 per year.

2248
Government Prime Contracts Monthly
Government Data Publications, 422 Washington Bldg, Washington, DC 20005. Telephone (202) 966-6379.

Monthly report. Lists government prime contract awards. Identifies awardee, agency, material involved—that is, the quantity, contract number, and amount of money the award brings. Price $60.00 per year.

2248.01
Government Product News
Penton/IPC, 614 Superior Ave W, Cleveland, OH 44113. Telephone (216) 696-0300.

Monthly magazine. Presents information on products and services utilized in government functions at all levels. Price $24.00 per year.

2249
Government Publications (Great Britain)
Her Majesty's Stationery Office (HMSO), PO Box 569, London, England SE1 9NH, London, England EC1P 1BN.

Monthly list of Great Britain's government publications. Contains parliamentary, government department, and periodic publications. Price available on request.

2250
Government Publications Review
Pergamon Press, Inc, Maxwell House, Fairview Park, Elmsford, NY 10523. Telephone (914) 592-7700. Telex 13-7328.

Quarterly journal. Reports on new developments in production, distribution, processing, and use of government documents. Covers federal, state, municipal, the United Nations, and international agencies. Price $110.00 per year.

2251
Government Regulation of Business Ethics: International Payoffs
Oceana Publications, Inc, 75 Main St, Dobbs Ferry, NY 10522. Telephone (914) 693-5944.

Loose-leaf service in three binders. Reviews existing and proposed international legislation regarding payoffs. Includes case studies. Price $75.00 per binder. ISBN 0-379-10258-7.

2252
Graduate Study in Management
Graduate Business Admissions Council, PO Box 966, Princeton, NJ 08540.

Book. Provides information on 886 graduate management school programs, public and educational administration, hospital administration, and urban planning. Includes, also, information on the Graduate Management Admission Test. Price $7.70.

2253
Grain Age
Communications Marketing, Inc, 5100 Edina Industrial Blvd, Edina, MN 55435. Telephone (612) 835-5888.

Monthly magazine. Pertains to all phases of the grain merchandising and milling industries. Aims at top management. Price available on request.

2254
Grain Market News Reports
US Dept of Agriculture, Agricultural Marketing Service, Room 2078-S, Washington, DC 20250. Telephone (202) 447-7316.

Irregular reports. Supply data on grain markets, including the feed market, grain stocks, and rice information. Price free of charge.

2256
Grain Trade of Canada
Statistics Canada, User Services, Publications Distribution, Ottawa, Ont, Canada K1A 0V7. Telephone (613) 992-3151.

Annual report. Offers statistics on Canadian grain acreage, production, marketing, inspections, receipts, shipments, movement within Canada, exports, and flour milling. Price $8.40. ISSN 0072-5358.

2257
Granville Market Letter
Granville Market Letter, Inc, Drawer O, Holly Hill, FL 32017. Telephone (800) 874-0977.

Newsletter, issued 46 times per year. Makes specific suggestions about stock market transactions. Price $250.00 per year.

2258
Graphis Annual
Advertising Trade Publications, Inc, 19 W 44th St, New York, NY 10036. Telephone (212) YU6-4930.

Annual book. Presents a collection of graphics appearing in and on advertisements, annual reports, booklets, book jackets, magazine covers, trademarks, letterheads, packages, record covers, motion pictures, and television. Price $37.50.

2259
Graphis Posters
Advertising Trade Publications, Inc, 19 W 44th St, New York, NY 10036. Telephone (212) YU6-4930.

Annual book. Presents international advertising, cultural, social, and decorative posters. Price $35.00.

2260
Graphix
Peter Isaacson Publications, 46-49 Porter St, Prahran, Vic 3181, Australia. Telephone (03) 51 8431. Telex 30880.

Fortnightly newspaper. Offers information on printing and publishing processes, including electronic-based technology. Price $15.00 per year.

2261
Graphoscope
Canadian Analyst Ltd, 32 Front St W, Toronto, Ont, Canada M5J 1C5. Telephone (416) 363-4431.

Bimonthly service. Provides market and financial data on Canadian and US stocks and mutual funds. Price charts. Price $110.00 per year.

2262

Graphs and Notes on the Economic Situation in the Community

Commission of the European Communities, Office for Official Publications of the European Communities, CP 1003, Luxembourg 1, Luxembourg. Telephone (352) 490081. Telex PUBLOF 1325.

Monthly report. Presents graphs and notes denoting the economic situation within the European community. Price $13.10 per year.

2263

Green Coffee: Inventories, Imports, and Roastings

US Dept of Commerce, Bureau of the Census, Washington, DC 20233. Telephone (202) 449-1600.

Quarterly report. Presents data on US green coffee inventories, roastings, and imports. Price $1.00 per year.

2264

Green Europe

Agra Europe (London) Ltd, Agroup House, 16 Lonsdale Gardens, Tunbridge Wells, Kent, England TN1 1PD. Telephone Tunbridge Wells (0892) 33813. Telex 95114.

Monthly newspaper. Discusses developments that relate to agricultural and horticultural production and marketing in EEC countries. Tables. Price £54.00 per year.

2264.01

Green Europe: Newsletter on the Common Agricultural Policy

European Community Information Service, 2100 M St, NW, Suite 707, Washington DC 20037. Telephone (202) 862-9500. Telex 248455.

Newsletter issued 10 to 12 times per year. Reports of the European Economic Community Common Market agricultural policy. Price $8.80 per year.

2265

Green Markets

McGraw-Hill Publications Co, 1221 Ave of the Americas, New York, NY 10020. Telephone (212) 997-1221. Telex TWX 7105814879 WUI 62555.

Weekly newsletter. Provides world prices for potash, phosphate, ammonia, and other fertilizer commodities. Discusses developments affecting fertilizer prices. Price $427.00 per year.

2266

Green's Commodity Market Comments

Economic News Agency, Inc, PO Box 174, Princeton, NJ 08540. Telephone (609) 921-6594. Telex 84 34 01.

Biweekly newsletter. Reports on the world market for currency and precious metals. Includes exchange rates, government policies, and production capacities. Price $240.00 per year. ISSN 0017-4076.

2267

Grindlays Bank Economic Reports

Grindlays Bank, Ltd, 23 Fenchurch St, London, England EC3P 3ED. Telephone (44) (01) 626-0545. Telex 885043-6.

Annual reports on 30 countries. Assess recent economic trends and prospects. Include information on population, growth rates, and exchange rates. Tables and charts. Price free of charge.

2269

Growth Stock Outlook

Growth Stock Outlook, Inc, 4405 E-W Hwy, Bethesda, MD 20014. Order from PO Box 9911, Chevy Chase, MD 20015. Telephone (301) 654-5205.

Semimonthly newsletter. Reports on selected stocks with vigorous growth. Includes such stock data as earnings per share, prices, year's growth, and revenues. Published since 1965. Price $95.00 per year.

2271

Guidebook to California Taxes

Commerce Clearing House, Inc, 4025 W Peterson Ave, Chicago, IL 60646. Telephone (312) 583-8500.

Book. Discusses California's personal, corporate income, sales, property, inheritance, and gift taxes. Price $9.00.

2272

Guidebook to Florida Taxes

Commerce Clearing House, Inc, 4025 W Peterson Ave, Chicago, IL 60646. Telephone (312) 583-8500

Book. Discusses Florida's corporate income, sales, use, intangibles, and estate taxes. Price $8.00.

2273

Guidebook to Illinois Taxes

Commerce Clearing House, Inc, 4025 W Peterson Ave, Chicago, IL 60646. Telephone (312) 583-8500.

Book. Offers a detailed treatment of income, sales, use, and inheritance taxes in Illinois. Price $9.00.

2274

Guidebook to Labor Relations

Commerce Clearing House, Inc, 4025 W Peterson Ave, Chicago, IL 60646. Telephone (312) 583-8500.

Book. Covers labor relations rules developed under the National Labor Relations Act, Taft-Hartley Law, and Labor-Management Reporting and Disclosure Act that reflect decisions of the US Supreme Court and National Labor Relations Board. Price $8.50.

2275

Guidebook to Massachusetts Taxes

Commerce Clearing House, Inc, 4025 W Peterson Ave, Chicago, IL 60646. Telephone (312) 583-8500.

Book. Offers a guide to Massachusetts's personal, corporate income, sales, use, insurance, and inheritance taxes. Price $9.-00.

2276

Guidebook to Michigan Taxes

Commerce Clearing House, Inc, 4025 W Peterson Ave, Chicago, IL 60646. Telephone (312) 583-8500.

Book. Covers Michigan's income, sales, use, single business, intangibles, and inheritance taxes. Price $9.00.

2277

Guidebook to New Jersey Taxes

Commerce Clearing House, Inc, 4025 W Peterson Ave, Chicago, IL 60646. Telephone (312) 583-8500.

Book. Discusses New Jersey's personal income, corporation, business, personal property, sales, use, inheritance, and estate taxes. Price $9.00.

2278

Guidebook to New York Taxes

Commerce Clearing House, Inc, 4025 W Peterson Ave, Chicago, IL 60646. Telephone (312) 583-8500.

Book. Covers New York State's tax laws, with emphasis on corporate, personal income, and unincorporated business tax. Includes New York City taxes. Price $9.-00.

2279

Guidebook to North Carolina Taxes

Commerce Clearing House, Inc, 4025 W Peterson Ave, Chicago, IL 60646. Telephone (312) 583-8500.

Book. Covers North Carolina's personal, corporate income, sales, use, inheritance, gift, and intangibles taxes. Treats also taxes on banks and financial institutions. Price $9.00.

2280
Guidebook to Ohio Taxes
Commerce Clearing House, Inc, 4025 W Peterson Ave, Chicago, IL 60646. Telephone (312) 583-8500.

Book. Discusses Ohio's personal, corporation income, sales, use, and estate taxes. Withholding tables. Price $9.00.

2281
Guidebook to Pennsylvania Taxes
Commerce Clearing House, Inc, 4025 W Peterson Ave, Chicago, IL 60646. Telephone (312) 583-8500.

Book. Covers Pennsylvania's personal, corporate income, sales, use, intangibles, and real property tax. Includes material on Philadelphia's and Pittsburgh's taxes. Price $9.00.

2282
Guidebook to Wisconsin Taxes
Commerce Clearing House, Inc, 4025 W Peterson Ave, Chicago, IL 60646. Telephone (312) 583-8500.

Book. Summarizes Wisconsin's personal, corporate income, sales, use, inheritance, gift, and local property taxes. Price $9.00.

2283
Guidelines for the Administration of the Canada Noise Control Regulations, **1975.**
Labour Canada, Communications Services Directorate, Ottawa, Ont, Canada K1A OJ2. Order from Communications Services Directorate, Labour Canada, Ottawa, Ont, Canada K1A OJ2. Telephone (819) 997-2617.

Folder. Covers administration of noise control legislation in Canada. Bilinqual. Price free of charge.

2284
Guide on Financial Administration for Departments and Agencies of the Government of Canada
Supply and Services Canada, Publishing Centre, Printing and Publishing, Ottawa, Ont, Canada K1A 0S9. Telephone (613) 238-1601.

Loose-leaf report, with update service. Provides a guide to financial administration for Canadian government departments and agencies. Price $14.00; updates $6.00.

2285
Guidepost
American Personnel and Guidance Assn, 2 Skyline, Suite 400, 5203 Leesburg Pike, Falls Church, VA 22041. Telephone (703) 820-4700.

Newspaper issued 18 times per year. Covers events affecting guidance counselors, students, and educators. Classified ads. Price $15.00 per year.

2286
Guide to American Directories, **11th edition**
B Klein Publications, Inc, PO Box 8503, Coral Springs, FL 33065. Telephone (305) 752-1708.

Book. Offers a listing of 7000 directories organized by subject. Describes contents of the directories, noting the publisher, date of publication, and cost. Price $55.-00.

2287
Guide to Business Statistics
US Dept of Commerce, Bureau of the Census, Washington, DC 20233. Order from Subscriber Services Section (Publications), Bureau of the Census, Washington, DC 20233. Telephone (202) 655-4000.

Report. Reports on current data for retail and wholesale trade and selected service industries. Price available on request.

2288
Guide to Canada's Capital
Supply and Services Canada, Publishing Centre, Printing and Publishing, Ottawa, Ont, Canada K1A 0S9. Telephone (613) 238-1601.

Book. Presents current and historical information on Canada's national capital. Maps. Bilingual. Price $1.80.

2289
Guide to Canadian Ministries since Confederation, July 1, 1867—April 1, 1973
Supply and Services Canada, Publishing Centre, Printing and Publishing, Ottawa, Ont, Canada K1A 0S9. Telephone (613) 238-1601.

Book. Combines earlier publications on Canadian ministries with new information on the eighteenth, nineteenth, and twentieth ministries. Price $3.60.

2290
Guide to Construction Statistics
US Dept of Commerce, Bureau of the Census, Washington, DC 20233. Order from Construction Statistics Div, Bureau of the Census, Washington, DC 20233. Telephone (202) 655-4000.

Report. Provides a guide to the Bureau of Census's statistical series on construction. Price free of charge.

2291
Guide to Consumer Markets, **1977-1978 Edition**
Conference Board, Inc, 845 3rd Ave, New York, NY 10022. Telephone (212) 759-0900.

Report. Provides information on consumer markets. Price $30.00.

2292
Guide to Current British Journals
R R Bowker Co, 1180 Ave of the Americas, New York, NY 10036. Order from R R Bowker Co, PO Box 1807, Ann Arbor, MI 48106. Telephone (212) 764-5100.

Two books. Provide a guide to 4700 British periodicals, with a listing of publishers represented and titles of their journals. Price $39.95. ISBN 0-85365-207-4. ISSN 0017-5277.

2293
Guide to Financial Times Statistics
Financial Times Business Information Ltd, Bracken House, 10 Cannon St, London, England EC4P 4BY. Order from Financial Times Ltd, 75 Rockefeller Plz, New York, NY 10019. Telephone (44) (01) 248-8000. Telex 886341-2.

Directory. Serves as a guide to statistics supplied by the Financial Times. Price available on request.

2294
Guide to Graduate Management Education, **1980–81**
Graduate Management Admission Council, PO Box 966, Princeton, NJ 08541.

Book. Provides descriptions of 437 graduate management schools and sample of Graduate Management Admission Test (GMAT). Lists schools offering special programs such as public and educational administration, health services management, international business, and MBA combined degrees. Price $4.00 fourth-class, $7.95 priority mail, $10.40 overseas airmail.

2295
Guide to Industry Statistics
US Dept of Commerce, Bureau of the Census, Washington, DC 20233. Order from Data User Services Div, Bureau of the Census, Washington, DC 20233. Telephone (202) 655-4000.

Book. Offers a statistical guide to the 1972 Censuses of Manufactures and Mineral Industries and Annual Survey of Manufactures. Price available on request.

2296
Guide to Investment
Sydney Morrell & Co, Inc, 152 E 78th St, New York, NY 10021. Telephone (212) 249-7255. Telex 62396.

Annual book. Provides information about Victoria, Australia, for foreign investors. Notes gross domestic product, natural resources, industry, business laws and taxes, and labor information. Tables. Price free of charge.

2297
Guide to Irish Manufacturers
Dun & Bradstreet, Box 3224, Church St Station, New York, NY 10008. Telephone (212) 285-7346.

Biannual book. Describes 4000 Irish manufacturers. Notes the line of business, number of employees, and names of directors. Price available on request, to Dun & Bradstreet subscribers only.

2298
Guide to Key British Enterprises
Dun & Bradstreet, Box 3224, Church St Station, New York, NY 10008. Telephone (212) 285-7346.

Annual book. Describes large and middle-range companies in the United Kingdom. Contains lists of products, services, and company subsidiaries. Price £40.00. ISSN 0072-856X.

2299
Guide to Legislation on Restrictive Business Practices
Organization for Economic Cooperation and Development, Publications Center, 1750 Pennsylvania Ave NW, Washington, DC 20006. Telephone (202) 724-1857.

Four volumes, plus periodic supplements. Contain OECD countries' laws on restrictive business practices. Include comments, historical background, and court decisions. Price $325.00.

2299.01
Guide to Obtaining Minority Business Directories
National Minority Business Campaign, 1201 12th Ave N, Minneapolis, MN 55411. Telephone (612) 377-2402.

Annual booklet. Lists local agencies that have compiled a minority business directory for their state or city. Price $3.00.

2300
Guide to Official Statistics
Her Majesty's Stationery Office, PO Box 569, London, England SE1 9NH. Telephone (44) (01) 928 1321.

Annual book on British statistics. Covers 800 topics and identifies 2500 sources. Price £7.50. ISBN 011 630 132 5.

2301
Guide to Recurrent and Special Governmental Statistics
US Dept of Commerce, Bureau of the Census, Washington, DC 20233. Order from Superintendent of Documents, Government Printing Office, Washington, DC 20402. Telephone (202) 655-4000.

Book. Summarizes data found in the most recent reports of the Bureau of Census's state and local government statistics program. Covers government finances, tax revenue, public employment, fire service, and criminal justice. Tables. Price $3.20.

2302
Guide to Selling a Business
Capital Publishing Corp, Box 348, Wellesley Hills, MA 02181. Telephone (617) 235-5405.

Book. Provides information on 1500 acquisition corporations. Covers legal, tax, and estate aspects of mergers. Price $49.-50. ISBN 0-914470-10-8.

2305
Guide to Trade and Securities Statistics
Pierian Press, 5000 Washtenaw, Ann Arbor, MI 48104. Telephone (313) 434-5530.

Service. Provides subject index to sources of trade and securities statistics. Price $20.00. ISBN 0-87650-07707.

2306
Guide to Travel and Residence Expenses for the Multinational Executive
Guides to Multinational Business, Inc, Harvard Sq, Box 92, Cambridge, MA 02138. Telephone (617) 868-2288.

Book. Offers a guide to travel and residence expenses for 55 countries. Includes data on hotel accommodations, restaurants, transportation, apartments, and food. Price $50.00.

2307
Guide to US Government Publications
Andriot, John L, Editor, Documents Index, Box 195, McLean, VA 22101. Telephone (703) 356-2434.

Books with quartly update supplements. List publications of US Government agencies. Price available on request.

2309
Guide to Venture Capital Sources **5th Edition**
Capital Publishing Corp, Box 348, Wellesley Hills, MA 02181. Telephone (617) 235-5405.

Book. Lists 500 sources of venture capital for smaller companies. Indicates types of projects and industries preferred and notes legal aspects. Price $62.50. ISBN 0-914470-12-4.

2310
Gulf Guide and Diary 1981
World of Information, 21 Gold St, Saffron Walden, Essex, England CB10 1EJ. Telephone Saffron Walden 21150 (Std 0799 21150). Telex England 817197 a/b Jaxpress G.

Annual book. Gives information about the Persian Gulf countries, including Iraq, Yemen AR and PDR Yemen. Contains Gregorian and Islamic calendars. Color photographs. Price $14.00. ISBN 0-904439-32-2.

2310.01
Gulf States
IC Publications Ltd, 122 E 42nd St, Suite 1121, New York, NY 10017. Telephone (212) 867-5159. Telex 425442.

Biweekly newsletter. Analyzes Middle Eastern business, political, financial, and international developments. Published in New York. Price $395.00 per year.

2310.02
Hall Radio Report
Phillips Publishing, Inc, 7315 Wisconsin Ave, Bethesda, MD 20014. Telephone (301) 986-0666.

Biweekly newsletter. Reports on the radio broadcasting industry, regulations, programming, management, new products, and marketing. Price $127.00 per year.

2311

Hambro Euromoney Directory
Euromoney Publications Ltd, Nestor House, Playhouse Yard, London, EC4V 5EX, England. Telephone (01) 236-7111. Telex 8812246 Eurmon G.

Annual directory. Contains names of over 2100 organizations in the international money markets, with details on their officers. Periodic updates. Price $40.00.

2312

Handbook for Auditors
McGraw-Hill Book Co, Hightstown-Princeton Rd, Hightstown, NJ 08520. Telephone (609) 448-1700. Telex 843449.

Book. Discusses various aspects of auditing, including new auditing systems. Price $42.50. ISBN 0-07-010200-7.

2313

Handbook for Industrialists
Department of Industrial Development and Decentralisation, Government of New South Wales, Box 2626, GPO, Sydney, 2001, Australia. Telephone (02) 27 2741. Telex AA 20972.

Annual book. Covers investment, trade, law, banking, fuel and power, transportation, industrial conditions, environmental protection, consumer protection and education in New South Wales, Australia. Price free of charge.

2314

Handbook for Investors—New Zealand
Bank of New Zealand, PO Box 2392, Wellington 1, New Zealand. Telex 3344 MONARCH.

Pamphlet for foreign investors in New Zealand. Discusses opportunities and restrictions, currency exchange regulations, taxes, company law, employment, and wages. English and Japanese. Price free of charge.

2315

Handbook for Manufacturing Entrepreneurs, **1973**
Western Reserve Press, PO Box 675, Ashtabula, OH 44004. Telephone (216) 951-6336.

Book. Provides an A-to-Z coverage of the ownership and management of manufacturing companies. Price $19.50.

2316

Handbook of Advertising Management, **1970 edition**
McGraw-Hill Book Co, Hightstown-Princeton Rd, Hightstown, NJ 08520. Telephone (609) 448-1700. Telex 843449.

Book. Covers a wide range of advertising management concerns. Price $32.45. ISBN 0-07-003966-6.

2317

Handbook of Agricultural Charts
US Dept of Agriculture, Order from ESS Publications, Room 0054-S, Washington, DC 20250. Telephone (202) 447-7255.

Annual book. Provides data on key factors in the US economic and agricultural situation. Charts. Price free of charge.

2318

Handbook of Agricultural Statistics, Part I: Field Crops
Statistics Canada, User Services, Publications Distribution, Ottawa, Ont, Canada K1A 0V7. Telephone (613) 992-3151.

Irregular report. Provides statistics on Canadian and provincial field crops from 1971 to 1974. Includes such subjects as acreage, yield, production, prices, and value. Price $2.80.

2320

Handbook of Agricultural Statistics, Part VI: Livestock and Animal Products **1871–1973**
Statistics Canada, User Services, Publications Distribution, Ottawa, Ont, Canada K1A 0V7. Telephone (613) 992-3151.

Irregular report. Presents major Canadian and provincial livestock statistical series from 1871 to 1973. Price $2.10.

2321

Handbook of Agricultural Statistics **Part VII: Dairy Statistics, 1920–73**
Statistics Canada, User Services, Publications Distribution, Ottawa, Ont, Canada K1A 0V7. Telephone (613) 992-3151.

Irregular report. Contains Canadian and provincial dairy statistics from 1920 to 1973. Includes farm and manufacturing production levels, distribution, farm cash receipts, and per capita consumption. Price $1.05.

2321.01

Handbook of Air Carrier Legislation
Supply and Services Canada, Canadian Govt Publishing Centre, Hull, Que, Canada K1A OS9. Telephone (819) 994-3475, 2085.

Book, with update service. Contains Canadian air carrier laws. Price $18.00.

2322

Handbook of Airline Statistics
US Civil Aeronautics Board, Bureau of Accounts and Statistics, Washington, DC 20428. Order from National Technical Information Service, US Dept of Commerce, 5285 Port Royal Rd, Springfield, VA 22151. Telephone (202) 673-5432.

Biennial book. Gives air transport companies financial and air traffic statistics since 1964. Price $12.00.

2323

Handbook of Basic Economic Statistics
Economic Statistics Bureau of Washington, DC, PO Box 10163, Washington, DC 20018. Telephone (202) 393-5070.

Monthly book. Provides statistical data on general business indicators; national product and income; retail, wholesale, and farm prices; Social Security operations; and employment. Price $72.00 per year.

2324

Handbook of Business Administration
McGraw-Hill Book Co, Hightstown-Princeton Rd, Hightstown, NJ 08520. Telephone (609) 448-1700. Telex 843449.

Book. Covers management theory and practice. Price $41.00.

2325

Handbook of Commerce and Industry in Nigeria
Consulate General of Nigeria, 575 Lexington Ave, New York, NY 10022. Telephone (212) PL2-1670.

Handbook. Contains data on commerce and industry in Nigeria. Price free of charge.

2326

Handbook of Industrial Taxes, Financing and Statutory Programs in Arkansas and Neighboring States
Arkansas Industrial Development Commission, 205 State Capitol, Little Rock, AR 72201. Telephone (501) 371-2431.

Booklet. Provides information on laws affecting industry in Arkansas and neighboring states. Covers taxation, finance and labor laws. Tables. Price free of charge.

2327
Handbook of International Trade and Development Statistics, **1979**
United Nations Conference on Trade and Development (UNCTAD), Palais des Nations, 1211 Geneva 10, Switzerland. Telephone (22) 34 60 11. Telex 28 96 96.

Book. Supplies statistical data on world trade and development. Covers the value of trade by regions and countries, commodity prices, financial flows, balance of payments, and related subjects. Price $44.00.

2328
Handbook of Labor Statistics
US Dept of Labor, Bureau of Labor Statistics, 441 G St NW, Washington, DC 20212. Telephone (202) 523-1221.

Annual report. Presents data from the major Bureau of Labor Statistics. Includes related series from other government agencies and foreign countries. Tables. Price $9.50 per copy.

2329
Handbook of Marketing Research, **1974 edition**
McGraw-Hill Book Co, Hightstown-Princeton Rd, Hightstown, NJ 08520. Telephone (609) 448-1700. Telex 843449.

Book. Covers the theory and practice of marketing research. Price $38.50. ISBN 0-07-020462-4.

2331
Handbook of Modern Accounting, **1977**
McGraw-Hill Book Co, Hightstown-Princeton Rd, Hightstown, NJ 08520. Telephone (609) 448-1700. Telex 843449.

Book. Covers accounting theory and practice. Price $27.50.

2332
Handbook of Modern Manufacturing Management, **1970**
McGraw-Hill Book Co, Hightstown-Princeton Rd, Hightstown, NJ 08520. Telephone (609) 448-1700. Telex 843449.

Book. Covers the theory and practice of managing manufacturing operations. Price $29.50. ISBN 0-07-041087-9.

2333
Handbook of Modern Marketing, **1970**
McGraw-Hill Book Co, Hightstown-Princeton Rd, Hightstown, NJ 08520. Telephone (609) 448-1700. Telex 843449.

Book. Covers the theory and practice of marketing. Price available on request.

2334
Handbook of Modern Office Management and Administrative Services, **1972**
McGraw-Hill Book Co, Hightstown-Princeton Rd, Hightstown, NJ 08520. Telephone (609) 448-1700. Telex 843449.

Book. Is a practical guide to office management and administration. Price $37.-80. ISBN 0-07-028630-2.

2335
Handbook of Modern Personnel Administration, **1972**
McGraw-Hill Book Co, Hightstown-Princeton Rd, Hightstown, NJ 08520. Telephone (609) 448-1700. Telex 843449.

Book. Covers personnel administration theory and practice. Price $36.65. ISBN 0-07-019912-4.

2336
Handbook of Public Relations: The Standard Guide to Public Affairs and Communications
McGraw-Hill Book Co, Hightstown-Princeton Rd, Hightstown, NJ 08520. Telephone (609) 448-1700. Telex 843449.

Book. Covers public relations theory and practice. Price $34.90.

2337
Handbook of Sampling for Auditing and Accounting, **1974**
Herbert Arkin, McGraw-Hill Book Co, Hightstown-Princeton Rd, Hightstown, NJ 08520. Telephone (609) 448-1700. Telex 843449.

Book. Discusses statistical sampling. Statistical tables. Price $18.40. ISBN 0-07-002212-7.

2337.01
Handbook of Statistics, **1980**
Assn of Indian Engineering Industry, 172 Jor Bagh, New Delhi 110003, India. Telephone 615115. Telex 031-3855.

Book. Contains statistics on India's engineering industry. Price Rs 75.

2339
Handbook of Wage and Salary Administration, **1972**
McGraw-Hill Book Co, Hightstown-Princeton Rd, Hightstown, NJ 08520. Telephone (609) 448-1700. Telex 843449.

Book. Covers wage and salary administration theory and practice. Price $24.50. ISBN 0-07-053348-2.

2340
Handling & Shipping
Penton/IPC, 614 Superior Ave W, Cleveland, OH 44113. Order from Penton-/IPC, 111 Chester Ave, Cleveland, OH 44114. Telephone (216) 696-7000.

Monthly magazine. Reports on shipping and handling. Includes such topics as warehousing, packaging, and containerization. Price $24.00 per year.

2341
Hanson's Latin American Letter
Inter-American Affairs Press, Box 181, Washington, DC 20044.

Weekly newsletter. Analyzes public policy and economic problems in Latin America. Price $100.00 per year.

2341.01
Happi
Household & Personal Products Industry, Box 555, 26 Lake St, Ramsey, NJ 07446. Telephone (201) 825-2552.

Monthly magazine. Contains news of household and personal products industry. Includes information on cosmetics, soaps, detergents, waxes, and polishes. Price $18.00 per year.

2343
Hardware Age
Chilton Co, Chilton Way, Radnor, PA 19089. Telephone (215) 687-8200.

Monthly magazine. Covers consumer buying trends that aid in successful marketing of products in the hardware/hardlines industry. Price $35.00.

2345
Harvard Business Review
Harvard University, Graduate School of Business Adm, Teele 314, Soldiers Field, Boston, MA 02163. Telephone (617) 495-6800.

Bimonthly review. Provides an analysis of conditions and problems in all areas of business. Price $24.00.

2347
Hawaii Annual Economic Review
Bank of Hawaii, Economics Div, PO Box 2900, Honolulu, HI 96846. Telephone (808) 537-8269.

Annual magazine. Reports on Hawaii's economy, energy resources, people, agriculture, manufacturing, and tourism. Price free of charge.

2348
Hawaii Facts and Figures
Chamber of Commerce of Hawaii, Dillingham Transportation Bldg, 735 Bishop St, Honolulu, HI 96813. Telephone (808) 531-4111.

Annual report. Compiles Hawaiian business statistics. Price $2.00.

2348.01
Hawaii: Manufacturers Directory
1981–82
Manufacturers' News, Inc, 3 Huron St, Chicago, IL 60611. Telephone (312) 337-1084.

Biennial book. Identifies 487 Hawaii manufacturing firms by name and product. Price $35.00.

2349
Hawkins Civil Aeronautics Board Service
Hawkins Publishing Co, Inc, Suite 220, 933 N Kenmore St, Arlington, VA 22201. Telephone (703) 525-9090.

Loose-leaf book. Provides an indexed digest that analyzes the Civil Aeronautics Boards reports and decisions of the federal courts and US Supreme Court relating to the Federal Aviation Act. Monthly supplements. Price $170.00.

2350
Hawkins Federal Maritime Commission Service
Hawkins Publishing Co, Inc, Suite 220, 933 N Kenmore St, Arlington, VA 22201. Telephone (703) 525-9090.

Loose-leaf book. Indexes, digests, and analyzes reports of the Federal Maritime Commission and its predecessors and decisions of the federal courts and the US Supreme Court relating to the Shipping and Merchant Marine Act. Supplies periodic supplements. Price $170.00.

2351
Hawkins Motor Carrier-Freight Forwarder Service
Hawkins Publishing Co, Inc, Suite 220, 933 N Kenmore St, Arlington, VA 22201. Telephone (703) 525-9090.

Four-volume loose-leaf service. Indexes, digests, and analyzes the Interstate Commerce Commission's reports and decisions of the federal courts and US Supreme Court relating to Parts II and IV of the Interstate Commerce Act. Offers monthly supplements. Price $180.00.

2352
Hawkins Rail Carrier Service
Hawkins Publishing Co, Inc, Suite 220, 933 N Kenmore St, Arlington, VA 22201. Telephone (703) 525-9090.

Ten-volume loose-leaf publication. Indexes, digests, and analyzes the Interstate Commerce Commission's reports and decisions of the federal courts and US Supreme Court relating to Parts I and III of the Interstate Commerce Act. Includes monthly supplements. Price $195.00.

2353
Hazardous Products Act and Regulations/Office Consolidation
Supply and Services Canada, Canadian Govt Publishing Centre, Hull, Que, Canada K1A 0S9. Telephone (819) 994-3475, 2085.

Loose-leaf book. Covers Canada's Hazardous Products Act and regulations. Bilingual. Price $8.00.

2353.01
Hazardous Waste News
Business Publishers, Inc, PO Box 1067, Silver Spring, MD 20910. Telephone (301) 587-6300.

Weekly newsletter. Covers hazardous waste management news and regulations. Price $195.00 per year.

2354
Health and Personal Social Services Statistics for England
Her Majesty's Stationery Office, PO Box 569, London, England SE1 9NH. Telephone (44) (01) 928 1321.

Annual report. Gives statistical data on Great Britain's health and personal social services. Price £8.50 per year.

2355
Health and Personal Social Services Statistics for Wales
Her Majesty's Stationery Office, PO Box 569, London, England SE1 9NH. Telephone (44) (01) 928 1321.

Annual report. Supplies statistics on health and personal social services in Wales. Price £5.25 per year.

2356
Health & Safety Information Bulletin
Industrial Relations Service, 170 Finchley Rd, London, England NW3 6BP. Telephone (44) (01) 794-4554.

Monthly report on British industrial health and safety legislation and court decisions. Price £20.00 per year.

2356.01
Health & Safety in Industry
Microinfo Ltd, PO Box 3, Newman Lane, Alton, Hampshire, England GU34 2PG. Telephone Alton 84300. Telex 858431.

Newsletter. Covers all aspects of health and safety, including new products and markets. Price available on request.

2356.02
Health Care
Southam Communications Ltd, 1450 Don Mills Rd, Don Mills, Ont, Canada M3B 2X7. Telephone (416) 445-6641. Telex 06 966612.

Monthly magazine. Provides information on Canadian hospital administration. Price $33.00 per year.

2357
Health Care Letter
Laventhol & Horwath, 1845 Walnut St, Philadelphia, PA 19103. Telephone (215) 491-1600.

Monthly newsletter. Offers news and commentary on health care topics. Price free of charge.

2358
Health Care Management Review
Aspen Systems Corp, 1600 Research Blvd, Rockville, MD 20850. Telephone (800) 638-8437.

Quarterly journal. Provides the latest theories on health care management and the marketing of health services. Price $44.50 per year.

2359
Health Care Product News
Gralla Publications, 1515 Broadway, New York, NY 10036. Telephone (212) 869-1300.

Publication. Carries news on new products in the health care field. Price available on request.

2360
Health Grants and Contracts Weekly
Capitol Publications, Inc, Suite G-12, 2430 Pennsylvania Ave, NW, Washington, DC 20037. Telephone (202) 452-1600.

Weekly newsletter. Covers federal funding opportunities in health and human services. Notes grant deadlines and contract awards. Price $138.00 per year.

2361
Health Insurance Underwriter
National Assn of Health Underwriters, 145 N Ave, Box 278, Hartland, WI 53029. Telephone (414) 367-3248.

Monthly magazine. Discusses health care and disability insurance. Includes Medicaid and Medicare news. Price $6.00 per year.

2362
Health Labor Relations Reports
Plus Publications, Inc, 2626 Pennsylvania Ave NW, Washington, DC 20037. Telephone (202) 333-5444.

Fortnightly report. Reviews congressional and federal agency activities affecting labor-management relations in the health care industry. Price $87.00 per year.

2363
Health Media Buyer's Guide
Technomic Publishing Co, Inc, 265 Post Rd W, Westport, CT 06880. Telephone (203) 226-1151.

Book. Lists over 1000 health journals, indexed alphabetically, by specialty and region. Notes publishers and journal representatives. Price available on request.

2364
Health Service Buyers Guide
Sell's Publications Ltd, Sell's House, 39 East St, Epsom Surrey, England KT17 1BQ. Telephone Epsom 26376. Telex 21792 A/B Mono K LDN.

Book. Offers a buying guide to makers and suppliers of items used in the British National Health Service. Price £12.00.

2365
Health Services Research
American Hospital Assn, 840 N Lake Shore Dr, Chicago, IL 60611. Telephone (312) 280-6381. Order from Health Administration Press, University of Michigan, 1420 Washington Heights, Ann Arbor, MI 48109.

Quarterly magazine. Presents original research on organizing, financing, and using health services. Includes book reviews and reports of national meetings. Price $25.00 per year.

2366
Heating & Air Conditioning Journal
Maclean-Hunter Ltd, 30 Old Burlington St, London, England W1X 2AE. Telephone (44) (01) 434-2233.

Magazine. Covers the technical aspects of heating and air conditioning fields, including research and development and new products. Contains company news. Price available on request.

2367
Heating & Ventilating Engineer
Turret Press Ltd, 4 Local Board Rd, Watford, Herts, England WD1 2JS. Order from Technitrade Journal Ltd, 4 Local Board Rd, Watford, Herts, WD1 2JS England. Telephone Watford (0923) 46199.

Monthly magazine. Addresses itself to the fields of heating, ventilation, and air conditioning. Price £26.50 per year, $61.00 US per year.

2368
Heating/Piping/Air Conditioning
Penton/IPC, 614 Superior Ave W, Cleveland, OH 44113. Order from Reinhold Publishing Div, Penton/IPC, 600 Summer St, Stamford, CT 06904. Telephone (203) 343-7531.

Monthly magazine. Carries reports on heating, piping, air conditioning, and energy management. Price $24.00 per year.

2369
Heating-Plumbing Air Conditioning
Southam Communications Ltd, 1450 Don Mills Rd, Don Mills, Ont, Canada M3B 2X7. Telephone (416) 445-6641. Telex 06-966612.

Monthly publication. Covers heating, plumbing, and air conditioning. Price $33.00 per year.

2370
Highlights of US Export and Import Trade
US Dept of Commerce, Bureau of the Census, Washington, DC 20233. Telephone (202) 449-1600.

Monthly report. Provides data on the quantity and value of US exports and imports by commodity groupings. Notes the country of destination, country of origin, and method of transportation. Price $37.75 per year.

2371
Highway & Vehicle/Safety Report
Stamler Publishing Co, 297 Main St, PO Box 3367, SC Station, Branford, CT 06405. Telephone (203) 488-9808.

Fortnightly newsletter. Covers Washington and other developments in the traffic safety field. Price $90.00 per year.

2372
Hines Insurance Adjusters
Hines's Legal Directory, Inc, Professional Center Bldg, PO Box 71, Glen Ellyn, IL 60137. Telephone (312) 469-3983.

Annual directory of selected independent insurance adjusting companies in the US and Canada. Price $10.00.

2373
Hines Insurance Counsel
Hines's Legal Directory, Inc, Professional Center Bldg, PO Box 71, Glen Ellyn, IL 60137. Telephone (312) 469-3983.

Annual directory of selected defense trial attorneys in the US, and Canada. Includes listings of insurance companies and law offices. Price $10.00.

2373.01
Historical Directory of Trade Unions
Gower Publishing Co Ltd, 1 Westmead, Farnborough, Hampshire, England GU14 7RU. Telephone Farnborough (0252) 519221. Telex 858623.

Four-volume book. Details essential information about all British trade unions, past and present. Price $174.00.

2374
Historical Labour Force Statistics, Actual Data, Seasonal Factors, Seasonally Adjusted Data
Statistics Canada, User Services, Publications Distribution, Ottawa, Ont, Canada K1A 0V7. Telephone (613) 992-3151.

Annual report. Presents statistics on Canadian labor force and employment and unemployment by age, sex, industry, and region. Covers the period from January 1953 to the end of the current year. Price $12.00 per year. ISSN 0703-2684.

2375
History of Political Economy
Duke University Press, PO Box 6697, College Station, Durham, NC 27708. Telephone (919) 684-8111.

Quarterly magazine. Discusses the development of economic analysis and exploration of relation of theory to policy, to other disciplines, and to general social history. Price $28.00, individuals $20.00.

2377
Hollis Press and Public Relations Annual
Hollis Directories, Contact House, Lower Hampton Rd, Sunbury-on-Thames, Middlesex, England TW16 5HG. Telephone 84781 (09327).

Annual directory, with updates throughout year. Lists British public relations firms, radio and television broadcasting stations, newspapers, and government information sources. Price £12.75. ISBN 900967 35 8. ISSN 0073 3059.

2379
Holt Executive Advisory
T J Holt & Co, Inc, 290 Port West, Westport, CT 06880. Telephone (203) 226-8911.

Semimonthly newsletter. Interprets economic developments for businessmen. Comments on domestic politics and international affairs and on legislative and regulatory developments. Price $48.00 per year.

2380
Holt 500 Trading Portfolio
T J Holt & Co, Inc, 290 Port Rd West, Westport, CT 06880. Telephone (203) 226-8911.

Portfolio published at irregular intervals. Instructs participants on high-risk stock market moves. Stresses rapid rather than long-term growth. Price $1000.00 per year.

2381
Holt Investment Advisory
T J Holt & Co, Inc, 290 Port Rd West, Westport, CT 06880. Telephone (203) 226-8911.

Semimonthly information service. Discusses the economy and stock market for investors concerned with long-term capital growth. Price $180.00 per year.

2383
Home & Auto
Harcourt Brace Jovanovich Publications, 757 3rd Ave, New York, NY 10017. Order from Harcourt Brace and Jovanovich Publications, 1 E 1st St, Duluth, MN 55802. Telephone (218) 727-8511.

Semimonthly magazine. Reports on automobile parts and accessories and home products. Discusses merchandising trends. Price $15.00 per year.

2384
Homes Overseas
Homefinders Ltd, 10 E Rd, London, England N1. Telephone (44) (01) 253-4628. Telex 28177.

Monthly magazine. Provides information on holiday and retirement homes in southern Europe. Includes tourist information on USA, Caribbean countries and the Far East. Price $25.00 per year.

2384.01
Home Video Report
Knowledge Industry Publications, Inc, 701 Westchester Ave, White Plains, NY 10604. Telephone (914) 694-8686.

Weekly newsletter. Reports on the production and distribution of video programming and video discs, television advertising, pay television, CATV, and video technology. Price $225.00 per year. ISSN 0300-7057.

2385
Honey Production
Statistics Canada, User Services, Publications Distribution, Ottawa, Ont, Canada K1A 0V7. Telephone (613) 992-3151.

Semiannual report. Supplies the number of Canadian and provincial beekeepers and colonies and data on honey production and value. Price $7.20 per year. ISSN 0319-3799.

2386
Hong Kong Cable
Hong Kong Trade Development Council, 548 5th Ave, New York, NY 10036. Telephone (212) 582-6610.

Monthly newsletter. Provides information on new corporate offices in Hong Kong, and recent Hong Kong trade figures. Emphazies US-Hong Kong trade. Price available on request.

2387
Hong Kong Enterprise
Hong Kong Trade Development Council, 548 5th Ave, New York, NY 10036. Telephone (212) 582-6610.

Monthly magazine. Surveys various Hong Kong industries. Includes photographs and descriptions of products available for export. Price available on request.

2388
Hong Kong Trader
Hong Kong Trade Development Council, 548 5th Ave, New York, NY 10036. Telephone (212) 582-6610.

Bimonthly magazine. Covers recent business activity in Hong Kong. Includes fashion and Hong Kong Trade Development Council news. Price available on request.

2389
Hosiery Statistics
National Assn of Hosiery Manufacturers, PO Box 4098, 516 Charlottetown Mall, Charlotte, NC 28204. Telephone (704) 372-4200.

Annual booklet. Presents statistics on hosiery production, consumption, and fiber content. Presents data on men's, women's and children's wear and includes foreign trade statistics. Tables and graphs. Price $35.00 per copy.

2391
Hospital Equipment & Supplies
Stokes & Lindley-Jones Ltd, Alverstoke House, 21 Montpelier Row, Blackheath, London, England SE3 0SR. Telephone (44) (01) 852-9865.

Annual report. Covers hospital equipment and supplies available for export from Great Britain. Price £25.00 for three years to qualified subscribers.

2393
Hospitality
Peter Isaacson Publications, 46-49 Porter St, Prahran, Vic 3181, Australia. Telephone (03) 51 8431. Telex 30880.

Fortnightly newspaper. Aimed at the food, accomodation, and liquor service industries. Price $20.00 (Australian) per year.

2394
Hospital Journal of Australia
Yaffa Publishing Group, 432-436 Elizabeth St, Surry Hills, NSW 2010, Australia. Order from Yaffa Publishing Group, GPO Box 606, Sydney, NSW 2001, Australia. Telephone (02) 699-7861. Telex 21887.

Monthly magazine. Contains news of Australia's hospitals. Includes information on equipment and administration. Price $40.00 (Australian) per year.

2395
Hospital Medical Staff
American Hospital Publishing, Inc, 211 E Chicago Ave, Chicago, IL 60611. Telephone (312) 951-1100.

Monthly magazine. Reports on the responsibilities of hospital physicians. Includes such subjects as medical staff organization, medical education, and legal problems. Price $12.00 per year. ISSN 0090-0710.

2396
Hospitals
American Hospital Publishing Inc, 211 E Chicago Ave, Chicago, IL 60611. Telephone (312) 951-1100.

Semimonthly journal. Provides background and information on health care and hospital operations. Price $30.00 per year. ISSN 0018-5973.

2397
Hospital Statistics: Data from the American Hospital Association Annual Survey
American Hospital Assn, 840 N Lake Shore Dr, Chicago, IL 60611. Telephone (312) 280-6000.
Annual book. Provides detailed data on US hospitals and their use. Covers, also, personnel, finances, and facilities. Price $18.75. ISBN 0-87258-282-5.

2398
Hospital Week
American Hospital Assn, 840 N Lake Shore Dr, Chicago, IL 60611. Telephone (312) 280-6000.
Weekly newsletter. Covers major events concerned with the health care field. Includes news on legislation, hospital associations, and individual hospitals. Price $15.00 per year.

2399
Hotel & Catering Equipment & Supplies
Stokes & Lindley-Jones Ltd, Alverstoke House, 21 Montpelier Row, Blackheath, London, England SE3 0SR. Telephone (44) (01) 852-9865.
Annual report. Informs importers of hotel and catering equipment and supplies available from Great Britain. Price £25.00 for three years to qualified subscribers.

2400
Hotel, Motel and Travel Directory
Peter Isaacson Publications, 46-49 Porter St, Prahran, Vic 3181, Australia. Telephone (03) 51 8431. Telex 30880.
Annual book. Lists hotels and motels in Australia, Southeast Asia, and the South Pacific. Offers special sections on conventions and tour operators. Price $11.00 (Australian).

2401
Hotel, Restaurant & Catering Supplies
Sell's Publications Ltd, Sell's House, 39 East St, Epsom Surrey, England KT17 1BQ. Telephone Epsom 26376. Telex 21792 A/B Mono K LDN.
Guide. Lists makers and suppliers of supplies for hotel and catering trades. Price £10.00.

2403
Household Food Consumption and Expenditure (National Food Survey)
Her Majesty's Stationery Office, PO Box 569, London, England SE1 9NH. Telephone (44) (01) 928 1321.

Annual report. Surveys household food consumption and expenditure in Great Britain. Price £3.50.

2404
Housewares
Harcourt Brace Jovanovich Publications, 757 3rd Ave, New York, NY 10017. Order from Harcourt Brace and Jovanovich Publications, 1 E 1st St, Duluth, MN 55802. Telephone (218) 727-8511.
Magazine issued 18 times per year. Provides information on housewares and small electrical appliances. Notes sales and marketing trends. Price $8.00 per year.

2405
Housewares Incorporating Gifts & Fancy Goods
Stokes & Lindley-Jones Ltd, Alverstoke House, 21 Montpelier Row, Blackheath, London, England SE3 OSR. Telephone (44) (01) 852-9865.
Annual report. Deals with export items available from Great Britain in housewares, gifts, and fancy goods. Price £25.00 for three years to qualified subscribers.

2406
Housewares Incorporating Hardware, Tools and Do-It-Yourself
Stokes & Lindley-Jones Ltd, Alverstoke House, 21 Montpelier Row, Blackheath, London, England SE3 OSR. Telephone (01) 852-9865.
Annual report. Announces sport, garden, and leisure goods available for export from Great Britain. Price £25.00 for three years to qualified subscribers.

2407
Housewares Promotions
Munroe Publications, Inc, PO Drawer 7, Indian Rocks Beach, FL 33535. Telephone (813) 595-5579.
Bimonthly newspaper. Pertains to promotion of housewares, hardware, and gifts. Price $7.50 per year.

2407.01
Housing
McGraw-Hill Publications Co, 1221 Ave of the Americas, New York, NY 10020. Telephone (212) 997-6375. Telex TWX 7105814879 WUI 62555.
Monthly magazine. Reports on housing construction. Includes topics on architecture, engineering, and finance. Price $33.00 per year.

2408
Housing Affairs Letter
Community Development Services, Inc, 399 National Press Building, Washington, DC 20045. Telephone (202) 638-6113.
Weekly newsletter. Includes legislation, regulations and money markets on housing programs. Price $137.00 per year.

2409
Housing and Construction Statistics
Her Majesty's Stationery Office, PO Box 569, London, England SE1 9NH. Telephone (44) (01) 928 1321.
Quarterly service. Contains figures on output, orders, prices, and finance in British housing, construction, and building materials industries. Price £17.43 per year.

2410
Housing & Development Reporter
Bureau of National Affairs, Inc, 1231 25th St NW, Washington, DC 20037. Telephone (202) 452-4200.
Loose-leaf books with weekly updates. Present major laws, trends, and developments affecting housing and community development programs. Include reference and current developments sections. Price $439.00 per year.

2412
Housing Completions
U.S. Dept. of Commerce, Bureau of the Census, Washington, DC 20233. Telephone (202) 449-1600.
Monthly report. Presents unadjusted and seasonally adjusted data on number of completed new privately and publicly owned housing units. Indicates new privately owned housing units under construction. Price $3.60 per year.

2413
Housing Market Report
Community Development Services, Inc, 399 National Press Building, Washington, DC 20045. Telephone (202) 638-6113.
Twice-monthly report. Covers national housing market. Includes statistics and mortgage rates. Price $127.00 per year.

2414
Housing Starts and Completions
Statistics Canada, User Services, Publications Distribution, Ottawa, Ont, Canada K1A OV7. Telephone (613) 992-3151.

Monthly report. Provides information on construction of new permanent dwellings in Canada. Shows starts, completions, and units under construction. Includes provincial and metropolitan figures. Price $36.00 per year. ISSN 0319-8278.

2415
Housing Starts
US Dept of Commerce, Bureau of the Census, Washington, DC 20233. Telephone (202) 449-1600.

Monthly report. Presents estimates of total housing starts and number of new housing units by location. Includes public and privately owned housing. Indicates distribution of apartment houses. Price $14.00 per year.

2415.01
Housing Units Authorized by Building Permits and Public Contracts, C40
U.S. Dept. of Commerce, Bureau of the Census, Washington, DC 20233. Telephone (202) 449-1600.

Monthly report with annual summary. Presents summary of statistics on number of new housing units authorized by building permits and public contracts. Price $31.05 per year.

2416
Housing Vacancies
US Dept of Commerce, Bureau of the Census, Washington, DC 20233. Telephone (202) 449-1600.

Quarterly report. Presents data on rental and homeowner vacancy rates by location and by housing characteristics. Price $6.00 per year.

2417
Houston Business Journal
Cordovan Corp, 5314 Bingle Rd, Houston, TX 77092. Telephone (713) 688-8811.

Weekly newspaper. Contains feature articles on various segments of Houston business. Price $24.00 per year.

2418
Houston Public Companies Directory
Cordovan Corp, 5314 Bingle Rd, Houston, TX 77092. Telephone (713) 688-8811.

Annual directory. Provides data on Houston corporations. Lists officers, earnings, dividends, and other corporate data. Price available on request.

2419
How and Where to Get Capital: Dollars in Your Future
National Counselor Reports, Inc, Task Bldg, Kerrville, TX 78028. Telephone (512) 257-5050.

Annual book. Lists over 2500 sources of capital, loans, and grants. Notes hundreds of government assistance programs. Price $25.00.

2420
How to Analyze, Design and Install an Employee Stock Ownership Plan
Panel Publishers, 14 Plaza Rd, Greenvale, NY 11548. Telephone (516) 484-0006.

Loose-leaf book, issued periodically. Discusses all aspects of employee stock ownership plans, including SEC and IRS regulations. Price $98.00. ISBN 0-916592-14-6.

2420.01
How to Buy, Sell and Price Newsletter Properties
Newsletter Clearinghouse, 44 W Market St, Rhinebeck, NY 12572 Telephone (914) 876-2081.

Spiral-bound publication. Provides information on buying, selling or appraising newsletter properties, including pricing formula, earnings computation, and negotiating the purchase and sale. Price $20.00.

2421
How to Handle Tax Audits, Requests for Rulings, Fraud Cases and Other Procedures Before IRS
Panel Publishers, 14 Plaza Rd, Greenvale, NY 11548. Telephone (516) 484-0006.

Two loose-leaf books with quarterly supplements. Discuss procedures involved in handling tax audits and fraud cases before Internal Revenue Service. Price $110.00. ISBN 0-916592-08-1.

2422
How to Plan for Tax Savings in Real Estate Transactions
Panel Publishers, 14 Plaza Rd, Greenvale, NY 11548. Telephone (516) 484-0006.

Loose-leaf book with quarterly supplements. Clarifies tax factors affecting real estate. Furnishes information on depreciation, financing, installment sales, subsidized housing, and rehabilitated buildings. Price $98.00. ISBN 0-916592-11-1.

2423
How to Save Taxes and Increase Your Wealth with a Professional Corporation
Panel Publishers, 14 Plaza Rd, Greenvale, NY 11548. Telephone (516) 484-0006.

Loose-leaf book with quarterly supplements. Discusses all aspects of professional corporations, including tax advantages, life and health insurance, and medical expenses. Price $98.00. ISBN 0-916592-09-X.

2424
How to Set Up and Run a Qualified Pension or Profit Sharing Plan for a Small or Medium-Size Business
Panel Publishers, 14 Plaza Rd, Greenvale, NY 11548. Telephone (516) 484-0006.

Two volume loose-leaf service, with bimonthly supplements. Provides information needed to establish and administer pension or profit sharing plan for small or medium-size business. Includes Keogh and individual retirement plans. Price $110.00. ISBN 0-916592-10-3.

2425
How to Take Money Out of a Closely-Held Corporation
Panel Publishers, 14 Plaza Rd, Greenvale, NY 11548. Telephone (516) 484-0006.

Two loose-leaf books with quarterly supplements. Discuss methods of transferring closely held corporate money to stockholders under current tax rules. Price $110.00. ISBN 0-916592-02-2.

2426
How to Use Tax Shelters Today
Panel Publishers, 14 Plaza Rd, Greenvale, NY 11548. Telephone (516) 484-0006.

Loose-leaf book, with quarterly updates. Discusses tax shelters. Measures impact of new tax laws on various forms of investment. Price $98.00. ISBN 0-916592-25-1.

2427
Hudson's Washington News Media Contacts Directory
Newsletter Clearinghouse, 44 W Market St, Rhinebeck, NY 12572. Order from Newsletter Clearinghouse, 7615 Wisconsin Ave, 1200N, Washington, DC 20014. Telephone (301) 986-0666.

Annual directory. Lists newspapers, radio, and television stations, magazines, and newsletters based or represented in Washington. Gives names and assignments of editors and correspondents. Updated quarterly. Price $60.00 per year.

2428

Humanist Educator
American Personnel and Guidance Assn, 2 Skyline Place, Suite 400, 5203 Leesburg Pike, Falls Church, VA 22041. Telephone (703) 820-4700.

Quarterly magazine. Discusses humanist aspects of education. Price $9.00 per year.

2429

Human Resource Management
University of Michigan, School of Business Administration, Ann Arbor, MI 48102. Telephone (313) 764-1817.

Quarterly report. Covers research in management techniques. Price available on request.

2430

Hydraulics & Pneumatics
Penton/IPC, 614 Superior Ave W, Cleveland, OH 44113. Order from Penton/IPC, 1111 Chester Ave, Cleveland, OH 44114. Telephone (216) 696-0300.

Monthly magazine. Reports on the design, operation, and maintenance of fluid power systems. Price $24.00 per year.

2431

Hydrocarbons: Monthly Bulletin
European Community Information Service, 2100 M St, NW, Suite 707, Washington, DC 20037. Telephone (202) 862-9500. Telex 248455.

Monthly bulletin. Reports hydrocarbons development by European Communities' member countries. Price $21.00.

2431.01

ICC World Economic Yearbook, **1980**
ICC Publishing Corp, Inc, 801 2nd Ave, Suite 1204, New York, NY 10017. Telephone (212) 354-4480. Telex US COUNCIL 14-8361 NYK.

Annual book. Analyzes world economic developments. Offers forecasts. Price $28.00.

2431.02

ICW's Africa Construction Business Report
McGraw-Hill Publications Co, 1221 Ave of the Americas, New York, NY 10020. Telephone (212) 997-6375. Telex TWX 7105814879 WUI 62555.

Weekly newsletter. Reports on construction in Africa. Topics include contracting, materials, and finance. Price $295.00 per year.

2431.03

ICW's Asia Construction Business Report
McGraw-Hill Publications Co, 1221 Ave of the Americas, New York, NY 10020. Telephone (212) 997-6375. Telex TWX 7105814879 WUI 62555.

Weekly newsletter. Covers construction developments in Asia. Discusses contracting, materials, and finance. Price $295.00 per year.

2431.04

ICW's Latin America Construction Business Report
McGraw-Hill Publications Co, 1221 Ave of the Americas, New York, NY 10020. Telephone (212) 997-6375. Telex TWX 7105814879 WUI 62555.

Weekly newsletter. Reports on construction in Latin America. Includes information on contracting, materials, and finance. Price $255.00 per year.

2431.05

ICW's Mideast Construction Business Report
McGraw-Hill Publications Co, 1221 Ave of the Americas, New York, NY 10020. Telephone (212) 997-6375. Telex TWX 7105814879 WUI 62555.

Weekly newsletter. Covers Mideast construction news. Provides information on contracting, materials, and finance. Price $365.00 per year.

2431.06

Idaho: Manufacturing Directory **1978–79**
Manufacturers' News, Inc, 3 Huron St, Chicago, IL 60611. Telephone (312) 337-1084.

Biennial book. Names 900 Idaho manufacturing firms. Includes information on executives and number of employees. Price $30.00.

2432

Idaho Statistical Abstract, **1980, 3rd edition**
University of Idaho, Center for Business Development and Research, Moscow, ID 83843. Telephone (208) 885-6611.

Book. Provides Idaho's economic and demographic data. Price $30.00 per copy.

2433

Idea Newsletter
International Newspaper Promotion Assn, PO Box 17422, Dulles International Airport, Washington, DC 20041. Telephone (703) 620-9560.

Monthly magazine. Provides newspaper promotion ideas. Covers advertising, circulation, and public relations. Price available to members only.

2433.01

Identified Sources of Supply
National Standards Assn, Inc, 5161 River Rd, Washington, DC 20016. Telephone (301) 951-1310. Telex 89-8452.

Annual two-volume book. Lists manufacturers and distributors of products conforming to 12,000 military, federal, and aerospace standards. Price $130.00.

2433.02

IDP Report
Knowledge Industry Publications, Inc, 701 Westchester Ave, White Plains, NY 10604. Telephone (914) 694-8686.

Biweekly newsletter. Reports on the information and data base publishing industry, including technological developments, acquisitions, and videotex. Price $195.00 per year.

2434

IES Lighting Review
Thomson Publications (Australia) Pty Ltd, 47 Chippen St, PO Box 65, Chippendale, NSW 2008, Australia. Telephone 699-6731. Telex TPAS AA22226.

Bimonthly magazine. Reports on new lighting products and techniques in Australian commercial, industrial, home, and outdoor illumination. Price available on request.

2435

Illinois Agricultural Economics
University of Illinois at Urbana-Champaign, Agricultural Experiment Station, Urbana, IL 61801. Order from University of Illinois, Agricultural Publications Office, 305 Mumford Hall, Urbana, IL 61801. Telephone (217) 333-1000.

Semiannual magazine. Reports agricultural economics research studies carried on by University of Illinois at Urbana-Champaign Dept of Agricultural Economics. Free of charge.

2436

Illinois Agricultural Statistics
US Dept of Agriculture, Crop Reporting Board, Economics and Statistics Service (ESS), Room 0005 S Bldg, Washington, DC 20250. Order from Illinois Cooperative Crop Reporting Service, PO Box 429, Springfield, IL 62705. Telephone (217) 782-4898.

Annual report. Provides Illinois agricultural data, including farm income, crop production, livestock and poultry, prices. Tables. Free of charge.

2437
Illinois Banker
Illinois Bankers Assn, 188 W Randolph St, Chicago, IL 60601. Telephone (312) 984-1500.

Monthly magazine. Reports on Illinois and general banking news. Notes legislative developments that affect banking. Price $25.00 per year.

2438
Illinois Economic Data Sheets
Illinois Department of Commerce and Community Affairs, 222 S College St, Springfield, IL 62706. Telephone (217) 782-1441.

Monthly report. Covers Illinois unemployment, construction starts, population, new business incorporations, business failures, labor force, farm marketings, and coal production. Statistics. Price free of charge.

2438.01
Illinois: Manufacturers Directory, **1981**
Manufacturers' News, Inc, 3 Huron St, Chicago, IL 60611. Telephone (312) 337-1084.

Annual book. Provides information on 27,000 Illinois manufacturing firms. Notes location, product, and executives. Price $99.50.

2438.02
Illinois: Services Directory **1980–81**
Manufacturers' News, Inc, 3 Huron St, Chicago, IL 60611. Telephone (312) 337-1084.

Annual book. Lists 15,270 service companies in Illinois. Price $70.00.

2439
Illinois Research
University of Illinois at Urbana-Champaign, Agricultural Experiment Station, Urbana, IL 61801. Order from University of Illinois, Agricultural Publications Office, 123 Mumford Hall, Urbana, IL 61801. Telephone (217) 333-1000.

Quarterly magazine. Reports on current research of University of Illinois at Urbana-Champaign Agricultural Experiment Station. Free of charge.

2440
Illustrators 18
Advertising Trade Publications, Inc, 19 W 44th St, New York, NY 10036. Telephone (212) 986-4930.

Annual book. Contains illustrations that won awards at Society of Illustrators Annual National Exhibition. Includes 500 juried selections. Price $24.50.

2441
Impact
Assn of Foremen & Supervisors, 20 Hunter St, Parramatta, NSW, Australia 2150. Telephone (61) (2) 635-4444.

Quarterly magazine. Discusses general and Australian industry news, with emphasis on labor relations and industrial supervision.

2441.01
Impact
Tasco Publishing Corp, 305 E 53rd St, New York, NY 10022. Telephone (212) 751-6500.

Semimonthly newsletter. Covers US alcoholic beverage industry developments. Contains marketing, economic, and research news. Price $78.00 per year.

2442
Implement & Tractor
Intertec Publishing Corp, 9221 Quivera Rd, PO Box 12901, Overland Park, KS 66212. Telephone (913) 888-4664. Telex 42-4156.

Semimonthly magazine. Covers farm equipment developments. Notes trends in product design and construction. Price $8.00 per year.

2442.01
Import Canada: A Guide to Canadian Imports
Canadian Imports Assn, Inc, 60 Harbour St, 5th Floor, Toronto, Ont, Canada M5J 1B7. Telephone (416) 862-0002.

Book. Reports basic Canadian importing procedures. Price $20.00 (Canadian).

2442.02
Import/Export File
Canadian Importers Assn, Inc, 60 Harbour St, 5th Floor, Toronto, Ont, Canada M5J 1B7. Telephone (416) 862-0002.

Semiannual directory. Lists over 1200 worldwide manufacturers offering products on the Canadian market. Price $20.00 (Canadian). ISSN 0383-6304.

2443
Imports (Cat No 5406.0)
Australian Bureau of Statistics, PO Box 10, Belconnen, ACT 2616, Australia. Order from Australian Government Publishing Service, PO Box 84, Canberra, ACT 2600, Australia. Telephone (062) 527911.

Monthly report. Contains tables on value of total Australian imports from selected countries. Includes value of customs and excise revenue collected. Price free of charge.

2444
Imports by Commodities
Statistics Canada, User Services, Publications Distribution, Ottawa, Ont, Canada K1A 0V7. Telephone (613) 992-3151.

Monthly report. Gives value of Canadian imports by country and commodity. Shows monthly figures and cumulative totals. Price $60.00 per year. ISSN 0318-2398.

2444.01
Imports by Countries
Statistics Canada, User Services, Publications Distribution, Ottawa, Ont, Canada KIA OV7. Telephone (613) 992-3151.

Quarterly report. Provides values of Canadian imports by countries and commodity categories for three years. Bilingual. Price $30.00 per year.

2445
Imports Cleared for Home Consumption (Cat No 5412.0)
Australian Bureau of Statistics, PO Box 10, Belconnen, ACT 2616, Australia. Order from Australian Government Publishing Service, PO Box 84, Canberra, ACT 2600, Australia. Telephone (61) (062) 527911.

Annual report. Lists approximately 2000 items cleared for Australian import. Gives tariff, country of origin, quantity, and duty paid for each commodity. Tables and statistics. Price $14.00 (Australian) (microfiche only).

2446
Imports—Merchandise Trade
Statistics Canada, User Services, Publications Distribution, Ottawa, Ont, Canada K1A OV7. Telephone (613) 992-3151.

Annual book. Provides summary tables of Canadian imports by countries and by sections. Indicates free and dutiable imports, and duty initially collected. Price $30.00.

2450
Import—FTNT-8007
US Dept of Commerce, Bureau of the Census, Washington, DC 20233. Order information from Chief, Foreign Trade Division, Bureau of the Census, Washington, DC 20233. Telephone (202) 655-4000.

Monthly service. Contains statistics on US imports for consumption and general imports of crude oil into Virgin Islands from foreign countries. Notes country of origin and method of transportation. Price available on request.

2451
Import—FTNT-8008
US Dept of Commerce, Bureau of the Census, Washington, DC 20233. Order information from Chief, Foreign Trade Division, Bureau of the Census, Washington, DC 20233. Telephone (202) 655-4000.

Monthly service. Supplies data on US imports of crude barytes ore for consumption from Mexico, by customs port of entry. Price $325.00 per year.

2452
Import—FTNT-8015
US Dept of Commerce, Bureau of the Census, Washington, DC 20233. Order information from Chief, Foreign Trade Division, Bureau of the Census, Washington, DC 20233. Telephone (202) 655-4000.

Monthly, cumulative-to-date, and cumulative quarterly information service. Reports on US imports of iron and steel products for consumption. Notes country of origin and customs district. Price available on request.

2453
Import—FTNT-8018
US Dept of Commerce, Bureau of the Census, Washington, DC 20233. Order information from Chief, Foreign Trade Division, Bureau of the Census, Washington, DC 20233. Telephone (202) 655-4000.

Monthly service. Reports on US imports for consumption of woven fabrics of vegetable fibers, suitable for covering cotton bales. Notes country of origin and customs district of entry. Price available on request.

2454
Imports—FTNT-8019
US Dept of Commerce, Bureau of the Census, Washington, DC 20233. Order information from Chief, Foreign Trade Division, Bureau of the Census, Washington, DC 20233. Telephone (202) 655-4000.

Monthly service. Contains information on US imports for consumption and general imports of glass and glass products. Indicates country of origin and customs district of entry. Price available on request.

2455
Imports—FTNT-8026
US Dept of Commerce, Bureau of the Census, Washington, DC 20233. Order information from Chief, Foreign Trade Division, Bureau of the Census, Washington, DC 20233. Telephone (202) 655-4000.

Monthly service. Supplies data on US imports of creosote oil for consumption. Notes country of origin and customs port of entry. Price available on request.

2456
Imports—FTNT-8027
US Dept of Commerce, Bureau of the Census, Washington, DC 20233. Order information from Chief, Foreign Trade Division, Bureau of the Census, Washington, DC 20233. Telephone (202) 655-4000.

Monthly service. Covers US imports of hardboard for consumption. Shows country of origin and customs port of entry. Price available on request.

2457
Imports—FTNT-8031
US Dept of Commerce, Bureau of the Census, Washington, DC 20233. Order information from Chief, Foreign Trade Division, Bureau of the Census, Washington, DC 20233. Telephone (202) 655-4000.

Monthly service. Provides data on US imports for consumption of monosodium glutamate and preparations containing over 50 percent by weight of monosodium glutamate. Indicates country of origin and customs port of entry. Price available on request.

2458
Imports—FTNT-8046
US Dept of Commerce, Bureau of the Census, Washington, DC 20233. Order information from Chief, Foreign Trade Division, Bureau of the Census, Washington, DC 20233. Telephone (202) 655-4000.

Monthly service. Provides data on US imports for consumption and general imports of merchandise from France. Indicates customs district of entry and method of transportation. Price available on request.

2459
Imports—FTNT-8056
US Dept of Commerce, Bureau of the Census, Washington, DC 20233. Order information from Chief, Foreign Trade Division, Bureau of the Census, Washington, DC 20233. Telephone (202) 655-4000.

Monthly service. Presents information on US general imports of casein and casein mixtures. Shows country of origin and customs port of entry. Price available on request.

2460
Imports—FTNT-8058
US Dept of Commerce, Bureau of the Census, Washington, DC 20233. Order information from Chief, Foreign Trade Division, Bureau of the Census, Washington, DC 20233. Telephone (202) 655-4000.

Monthly service. Contains data on US imports of hydraulic cement, cement clinker, and cements n.s.p.f. for consumption. Indicates country of origin and customs port of entry. Price available on request.

2461
Imports—FTNT-8077
US Dept of Commerce, Bureau of the Census, Washington, DC 20233. Order information from Chief, Foreign Trade Division, Bureau of the Census, Washington, DC 20233. Telephone (202) 655-4000.

Monthly service. Contains statistics on US imports of copra, coconut oil, palm-kernel oil, palm oil, tallow, animal oils, fats and greases n.s.p.f. (not edible), and glycerine (crude and refined). Price available on request.

2462
Imports—FTNT-8083

US Dept of Commerce, Bureau of the Census, Washington, DC 20233. Order information from Chief, Foreign Trade Division, Bureau of the Census, Washington, DC 20233. Telephone (202) 655-4000.

Monthly service. Presents data on US general imports of gum arabic, tragacanth, and karaya. Indicates commodity by country or origin and by customs port of entry. Price available on request.

2463
Imports—FTNT-9002

US Dept of Commerce, Bureau of the Census, Washington, DC 20233. Order information from Chief, Foreign Trade Division, Bureau of the Census, Washington, DC 20233. Telephone (202) 655-4000.

Monthly service. Supplies information on US imports of atrazine for consumption by country of origin, customs port of entry, and port of unloading. Price available on request.

2464
Imports—FTNT-9073

US Dept of Commerce, Bureau of the Census, Washington, DC 20233. Order information from Chief, Foreign Trade Division, Bureau of the Census, Washington, DC 20233. Telephone (202) 655-4000.

Monthly service. Reports on US imports of ammonium persulfate for consumption by country of origin and port of entry. Price available on request.

2465
Imports—FTNT-9080

US Dept of Commerce, Bureau of the Census, Washington, DC 20233. Order information from Chief, Foreign Trade Division, Bureau of the Census, Washington, DC 20233. Telephone (202) 655-4000.

Monthly service. Contains data on US imports of roll or cartridge color film produced in United Kingdom and France but shipped or transshipped from country other than country or origin. Price available on request.

2466
Imports—FTNT-9083

US Dept of Commerce, Bureau of the Census, Washington, DC 20233. Order information from Chief, Foreign Trade Division, Bureau of the Census, Washington, DC 20233. Telephone (202) 655-4000.

Monthly service. Supplies data on US imports of gear hobbing machines by country of origin. Price available on request.

2467
Imports—FTNT-IA 236-A

US Dept of Commerce, Bureau of the Census, Washington, DC 20233. Order information from Chief, Foreign Trade Division, Bureau of the Census, Washington, DC 20233. Telephone (202) 655-4000.

Annual service. Offers statistics on US imports of articles of metal manufactured in US that were exported for processing abroad and returned to US for further processing. Includes data on articles assembled abroad from components produced in US. Price available on request.

2468
Imports—FTNT-IA 245-A

US Dept of Commerce, Bureau of the Census, Washington, DC 20233. Order information from Chief, Foreign Trade Division, Bureau of the Census, Washington, DC 20233. Telephone (202) 655-4000.

Annual service. Provides data on US imports for consumption and general imports of articles of metal manufactured in US, exported for processing abroad and returned to US for further processing. Covers articles assembled abroad from US produced components. Price available on request.

2469
Imports—FTNT-IA 245-V

US Dept of Commerce, Bureau of the Census, Washington, DC 20233. Order information from Chief, Foreign Trade Division, Bureau of the Census, Washington, DC 20233. Telephone (202) 655-4000.

Annual service. Contains information on imports for consumption and general imports into Virgin Islands from foreign countries. Notes country or origin and method of transportation. Price available on request.

2470
Imports—FTNT-IA 275

US Dept of Commerce, Bureau of the Census, Washington, DC 20233. Order information from Chief, Foreign Trade Division, Bureau of the Census, Washington, DC 20233. Telephone (202) 655-4000.

Annual service. Supplies data on US imports for consumption and general imports. Price available on request.

2471
Imports—FTNT-IA 276

US Dept of Commerce, Bureau of the Census, Washington, DC 20233. Order information from Chief, Foreign Trade Division, Bureau of the Census, Washington, DC 20233. Telephone (202) 655-4000.

Annual service. Contains data on US imports for consumption and general imports. Indicates country of origin. Price available on request.

2472
Imports—FTNT-IM 145-A

US Dept of Commerce, Bureau of the Census, Washington, DC 20233. Order information from Chief, Foreign Trade Division, Bureau of the Census, Washington, DC 20233. Telephone (202) 655-4000.

Monthly service. Provides information on US imports for consumption and general imports of articles of metal manufactured in US that were exported for processing abroad and returned to US for further processing. Covers articles assembled abroad from US-produced components. Price available on request.

2473
Imports—FTNT-IM 145-V

US Dept of Commerce, Bureau of the Census, Washington, DC 20233. Order information from Chief, Foreign Trade Division, Bureau of the Census, Washington, DC 20233. Telephone (202) 655-4000.

Monthly service. Provides information on imports for consumption and general imports into Virgin Islands from foreign countries. Indicates country of origin and method of transportation. Price available on request.

2474

Imports of Benzenoid Chemicals & Products

US International Trade Commission, Washington, DC 20436. Telephone (202) 523-0161.

Publication. Reports on US imports of benzenoid chemicals and products. Price free of charge.

2475

Importweek

Canadian Importers Assn, Inc, 60 Harbour St, 5th Floor, Toronto, Ont, Canada M5J 1B7. Telephone (416) 862-0002.

Weekly bulletin. Contains information on regulations affecting Canadian importers. Price $20.00 (Canadian) per subscription, available to members only (first subscription free). ISSN 0702-8385.

2476

imprint

Advertising Specialty Inst, 1120 Wheeler Way, Langhorne, PA 19047. Telephone (215) 752-4200.

Quarterly magazine. Is for users of specialty advertising products. Focuses on specific products and current trends in the field. Price $5.00 per year.

2476.01

IMS Monitor Report

IMS World Publications Ltd, York House, 37 Queen Sq, London, England WCIN 3BE. Telephone (44) (01) 242-0112. Telex 263298.

Quarterly magazine. Reports on health care developments, with special emphasis on pharmaceutical sector. Discusses new products. Offers Europe, Americas, Asia, Africa and Australasia editions. Price $510.00 per year, for all three editions.

2476.02

In Brief

Australian Meat and Live-stock Corp, GPO Box 4129, Sydney, NSW 2001, Australia. Telephone (61) (02) 267-9488. Telex AA 22887.

Monthly report. Summarizes Australian livestock and meat industry information. Includes data on world markets. Price free of charge.

2476.03

In Business

J G Press, Inc, Box 323, Emmaus, PA 18049. Telephone (215) 967-4135.

Bimonthly magazine. Discusses small business issues, including accounting, marketing, and advertising. Offers profiles of successful entrepreneurs. Price $14.00 per year.

2477

Incentive Marketing

Bill Communications, Inc, 633 3rd Ave, New York, NY 10017. Telephone (212) 986-4800.

Monthly magazine. Covers specialized research, product planning evaluation, and marketing consultation. Price $25.00 per year.

2478

Incentive Marketing and Sales Promotion

Maclaren Publishers Ltd, PO Box 109, Davis House, 69-77 High St, Croydon, England CR9 1QH. Telephone (44) (01) 688-7788. Telex 946665.

Monthly magazine. Is devoted to consumer and trade sales promotion and marketing. Price $31.00 per year. ISSN 0305-2230.

2479

Incentive Travel Manager

Brentwood Publishing Corp, 825 S Barrington Ave, Los Angeles, CA 90049. Telephone (213) 826-8388.

Monthly magazine. Is for sales and marketing executives involved with incentive travel programs. Price $30.00 per year.

2480

Income After Tax, Distribution by Size in Canada

Statistics Canada, User Services, Publications Distribution, Ottawa, Ont, Canada K1A 0V7. Telephone (613) 992-3151.

Annual report. Supplies after tax income distribution data for Canadian families and individuals by region, age, sex, and other characteristics. Price $7.20. ISSN 0319-0374.

2481

Income Distributions by Size in Canada

Statistics Canada, User Services, Publications Distribution, Ottawa, Ont, Canada K1A 0V7. Telephone (613) 992-3151.

Annual report. Provides estimates of Canadian family and individual incomes by size of income, source, region, age, and sex. Shows composition of income quintiles and characteristics of low income families. Tables. Price $9.60. ISSN 0575-8750.

2482

Income Distributions by Size in Canada, Preliminary Estimates

Statistics Canada, User Services, Publications Distribution, Ottawa, Ont, Canada K1A 0V7. Telephone (613) 992-3151.

Annual report. Contains estimates of Canadian family and individual incomes by size of income, region, family size, number of children, and age and sex of household head. Includes data on characteristics of low income families. Tables. Price $5.40. ISSN 0317-5405.

2483

Income, Employment, Estate & Gift Tax Provisions: Internal Revenue Code

Commerce Clearing House, Inc, 4025 W Peterson Ave, Chicago, IL 60646. Telephone (312) 583-8500.

Book. Contains full texts of income, estate, and gift tax provisions of Internal Revenue Code. Price $12.00.

2484

Income Investor

Indicator Research Group Inc, Indicator Bldg, Palisades Park, NJ 07650. Telephone (201) 947-8800.

Monthly report. Covers high-yield, conservative investments and special situations. Provides analysis of economic and monetary trends. Compares variety of fixed-income and other securities. Price $95.00 per year.

2490

Income Taxation of Foreign Related Transactions

Matthew Bender & Co, 235 E 45th St, New York, NY 10017. Telephone (212) 661-5050.

Four-volume loose-leaf report with semiannual supplements. Discusses US taxation of income earned or invested by US citizens or businesses abroad. Includes information on US taxation of aliens and foreign corporations, western hemisphere trade corporations, and DISC. Price $240.00.

2491

Income Tax Digest and Accountants' Review

Fiscal Press Ltd, Fiscal House, 36 Lattimore Rd, St Albans, Herts, England AL1 3XW. Telephone St Albans 55688.

Monthly report on British tax law cases and proposed tax legislation. Includes Commonwealth and international tax and fiscal reports. Price £20.00 per year.

2492

Income Taxes Worldwide

Commerce Clearing House, Inc, 4025 W Peterson Ave, Chicago, IL 60646. Telephone (312) 583-8500.

Five loose-leaf books and monthly reports. Covers income and related taxes of more than 100 countries. Price $275.00 per year.

2493

Income Tax Service/Act and Regulations

Supply and Services Canada, Publishing Centre, Printing and Publishing, Ottawa, Ont, Canada K1A 0S9. Telephone (613) 238-1601.

Loose-leaf book plus update service. Covers Canadian Income Tax Act and regulations. Price $23.00.

2494

Independent Banker

Independent Bankers Assn of America, Sauk Centre, MN 56378. Telephone (612) 352-6546.

Monthly magazine. Pertains to issues affecting independent bankers. Notes new banking techniques. Reports on activities of independent Bankers Association of America. Price $12.00 per year.

2495

Independent Telephone Statistics

US Independent Telephone Association, 1801 K St, NW, Suite 1201, Washington, DC 20006. Telephone (202) 872-1200.

Two annual booklets. Summarizes statistics of independent telephone industry. Includes information on assets, liabilities, operating ratios and employees. Price $25.00 per copy.

2496

Index of Economic Articles, 1969–1976

American Economic Assn, 1313 21st Ave S, Nashville, TN 37212. Order from Richard D Irwin, Inc, 1818 Ridge Rd, Homewood, IL 60430.

Book. Lists articles from 220 major economic journals and collective volumes published from 1969–1976. Includes selected congressional committee testimony and government documents. Is indexed by subject and author. Price $50.00.

2498

Indexes of Railroad Material Prices and Wage Rates

Assn of American Railroads, Economics and Finance Dept, American Railroads Bldg, Washington, DC 20036. Telephone (202) 293-4063.

Quarterly report. Shows annual indexes of charge-out prices and wage rates, and quarterly indexes of spot prices of railroad fuel, material, and supplies. Free of charge.

2499

Indexes of Real Domestic Product by Industry

Statistics Canada, User Services, Publications Distribution,Ottawa, Ont, Canada K1A 0V7. Telephone (613) 992-3151.

Monthly magazine. Contains indexes of real Canadian output by industry. Includes tables of 120 seasonally adjusted and unadjusted components. Price $36.00 per year. ISSN 0317-3453.

2500

Index to Black Newspapers

Bell & Howell Micro Photo Division, Old Mansfield Rd, Wooster, OH 44691. Telephone (216) 264-6666. Telex 98-6496.

Quarterly index. Serves as guide to 10 black newspapers. Contains personal names and subject sections. Price $225.00 per year.

2501

Index to 1970 Census Summary Tapes

US Dept of Commerce, Bureau of the Census, Washington, DC 20233. Order from Subscriber Services Section (Publications), Bureau of the Census, Washington, DC 20233. Telephone 202 655-4000.

Book. Contains index to all tabulations of 1970 census summary data organized alphabetically by subject variable. Price $2.-60.

2503

Indiana Business Magazine

Curtis International Ltd, 1100 Waterway Blvd, Indianapolis, IN 46202. Telephone (317) 634-1100.

Monthly magazine. Covers business and industry in Indiana. Is geared to corporate executives. Concentrates in certain issues on particular topics, such as energy, construction, manufacturing, graphic arts, and finance. Price $12.00 per year.

2503.01

Indiana: Industrial Directory **1981**

Manufacturers' News, Inc, 3 Huron St, Chicago, IL 60611. Telephone (312) 337-1084.

Annual book. Identifies 12,000 industrial companies in Indiana by location and product. Price $38.50.

2503.02

Indiana: State Industrial Directory **1981**

Manufacturers' News, Inc, 3 Huron St, Chicago, IL 60611. Telephone (312) 337-1084.

Annual book. Provides information on 13,750 Indiana industrial firms by name, county, city, and product. Price $75.00.

2503.03

Indian Chemical Directory

Technical Press Publications, Eucharistic Congress Bldg No 1, 5/1 Convent St, Colaba, Bombay 400 039, India. Telephone 231446, 231156. Telex 11 3479 CHEMIN.

Biennial book. Provides information on Indian chemical plants, equipment, processes, and import-export statistics. Price $45.00.

2504

India News

Commerce Wing, Embassy of India, 2107 Massachusetts Ave, NW, Washington, DC. Order from Information Service of India, 2107 Massachusetts Ave, NW, Washington, DC 20008. Telephone (202) 265-5050.

Weekly newspaper. Reports on Indian political, economic, sociocultural and related developments. Price $5.00 per year.

2505

Indicator Digest

Indicator Research Group, Inc, Indicator Bld., Palisades Park, NJ 07650. Telephone (201) 947-8800.

Fortnightly digest. Surveys stock market, business and monetary trends. Focuses on various stock groups. Reviews stock market indicators. Charts and graphs. Price $125.00 per year.

2505.01

Indicators of Industrial Activity

Organization for Economic Cooperation and Development, Publications Center, 1750 Pennsylvania Ave, NW, Washington, DC 20006. Telephone (202) 724-1857.

Quarterly publication. Presents up-to-date production, deliveries, orders, prices, and employment indicators on an annual, quarterly, and monthly basis for total industrial production in most OECD countries. Price $25.00 per year, $30.90 airmail.

2506
Indonesia Letter
Asia Letter Ltd, PO Box 54149, Los Angeles, CA 90054. Telephone (213) 322-4222.

Monthly report. Relates to Indonesia's economy, focusing on personalities, politics, and foreign business. Includes special reports. Price $175.00 per year.

2507
Industrial & Commercial Training, The Management of Human Resources
Wellens Pub, Guilsborough, Northampton, England NN6 8PY. Telephone (0604) 740379.

Monthly magazine. Reports on human resources management subjects including industrial relations training, worker participation, and employee communications. Price £18.00 per year, $50.00 US.

2508
Industrial and Geographic Distribution of Union Membership in Canada
Labour Canada, PR Branch, 340 Laurier Ave W, Ottawa, Ont, Canada K1A 0J2. Order from Publications Division, Labour Canada, Ottawa, Ont, Canada K1A 0J2. Telephone (819) 997-2031.

Annual publication. Tabulates union membership in Canada by industry, province, and metropolitan area. Price free of charge.

2509
Industrial & Labor Relations Review
Cornell University, New York State School of Industrial & Labor Relations, Box 1000, Ithaca, NY 14853. Telephone (607) 256-3295.

Quarterly journal. Provides original research and analyses of industrial labor relations. Price $12.00 for individuals, $14.00 for institutions per year. ISSN 0019-7939.

2510
Industrial Bulletin
Morgan-Grampian Ltd, Morgan-Grampian House, Calderwood St, London, England SE18 6QH. Order from Morgan-Grampian Pub Co, 2 Park Ave, New York, NY 10016. Telephone England (44)(01) (8551-1) 7777. Telex 896238 MORGAN G. New York (212) 573-8100. Telex 425592 MGI UI.

Monthly magazine. Provides reference source for innovations in manufacturing technology. Price $20.00 per year.

2511
Industrial Cases Reports
Incorporated Council of Law Reporting for England and Wales, 3 Stone Bldgs, Lincoln's Inn, London, England WC2A 3XN.

Monthly report with year-end bound volume. Covers cases concerning industrial matters heard before High Court and Employment Appeal Tribunal in England and Wales. Emphasizes cases relating to employment and unfair dismissals. Price £57.50 per year.

2512
Industrial Corporations, Financial Statistics
Statistics Canada, User Services, Publications Distribution, Ottawa, Ont, Canada K1A 0V7. Telephone (613) 992-3151.

Quarterly magazine. Provides financial information on Canadian industrial corporations. Covers estimated assets, liabilities, shareholders' equity, estimated revenue, expenses, profits, and retained earnings by industry. Price $48.00 per year. ISSN 0380-7525.

2513
Industrial Development
Conway Publications, Inc, Peachtree Air Terminal, 1954 Airport Rd, Atlanta, GA 30341. Telephone (404) 458-6026.

Bimonthly journal. Offers articles on industrial expansion and site location decisions. Subscription includes Site Selection Handbook. Price $39.00 per year. ISSN 0019-8137.

2514
Industrial Development Abstract
United Nations Industrial Development Organization, Vienna International Centre, PO Box 300, A-1400, Vienna, Austria. Telephone 26310. Telex 135612.

Book issued four to six times per year. Provides abstracts on industrial development. Symbols: UMDO/LIB/SER.B/1-40. Price $5.00 each.

2515
Industrial Development Handbook
Urban Land Inst, 1090 Vermont Ave., NW, Washington, DC 20005. Telephone (202) 289-8500.

Book. Covers various aspects of industrial development, including site selection, engineering and design, and financing. Provides 10 case studies. Price $29.00.

2516
Industrial Development News Asia and the Pacific
United Nations Publications, Room A-3315, New York, NY 10017. Telephone (212) 754-8302.

Publications. Provide news on industrial development in Asia and Pacific areas. Price available on request.

2517
Industrial Distribution
Morgan-Grampian Ltd, Morgan-Grampian House, Calderwood St, London, England SE18 6QH. Order from Morgan-Grampian Publishing Co, Circulation Dept, Berkshire Common, Pittsfield, MA 01201. Telephone (413) 499-2550, NY (212) 340-9700. Telex 425592 MGI UI.

Monthly journal. Covers industrial distribution, including warehousing and materials handling. Price $20.00 per year.

2518
Industrial Distributor News
Ames Publishing Div, Chilton, 1 W Olney Ave, Philadelphia, PA 19120. Telephone (215) 224-7000.

Monthly magazine. Reports on sales, marketing, and technical developments within commodity areas for firms engaged in distribution of industrial equipment and supplies. Price $24.00 per year.

2519
Industrial Engineering
American Inst of Industrial Engineers, Inc, Indus & Labor Relations Div, 25 Technology Park, Norcross, GA 30092. Telephone (404) 449-0460.

Monthly magazine. Covers industrial engineering. Emphasizes new developments, products, and services. Price $30.00 per year.

2520
Industrial Equipment News
Thomas Publishing Co, 1 Penn Plaza, 250 W 34th St, New York, NY 10001. Telephone (212) 695-0500.

Monthly newsletter. Discusses new and improved industrial equipment and parts. Offers editions for Europe, Japan, Brazil, and Spanish-speaking Latin America. Free of charge.

2521
Industrial Foundation for Accident Prevention (IFAP) News
Industrial Foundation for Accident Prevention, PO Box 28, Mosman Park, WA 6012, Australia. Telephone (61)335-1344.

Bimonthly newsletter. Discusses occupational safety issues with emphasis on Australian industries. Notes activities of Industrial Foundation for Accident Prevention. Price $5.00 per year.

2522
Industrial Gases
US Dept of Commerce, Bureau of the Census, Washington, DC 20233. Telephone (202) 449-1600.

Monthly report with annual summary. Indicates production of specified industrial gases by type. Supplies data for gaseous, liquid, or solid form, where applicable. Price $3.50 per year.

2524
Industrial Health Foundation
Chemical-Toxicological Series
Industrial Health Foundation, Inc, 5231 Centre Ave, Pittsburgh, PA 15232. Telephone (412) 687-2100.

Irregularly issued technical booklets. Deals with chemical and toxicological issues from occupational safety viewpoint. Price $5.00 per copy. ISSN 0073-7488.

2525
Industrial Health Foundation
Engineering Series
Industrial Health Foundation, Inc, 5231 Centre Ave, Pittsburgh, PA 15232. Telephone (412) 687-2100.

Irregularly issued technical booklets. Deals with specific engineering issues from industrial safety viewpoint. Price $5.00 per copy. ISSN 0073-7496.

2526
Industrial Health Foundation Legal
Series
Industrial Health Foundation, Inc, 5231 Centre Ave, Pittsburgh, PA 15232. Telephone (412) 687-2100.

Irregularly issued technical booklets. Covers legal aspects of occupational health and safety, including workmen's compensation and recent legislation. Price $5.00 per copy. ISSN 0073-750X.

2527
Industrial Health Foundation
Management Series
Industrial Health Foundation, Inc, 5231 Centre Ave, Pittsburgh, PA 15232. Telephone (412) 687-2100.

Technical booklets, issued irregularly. Concerns business management topics related to occupational safety, such as corporate health programs. Price $5.00 per copy.

2528
Industrial Health Foundation Medical
Series
Industrial Health Foundation, Inc, 5231 Centre Ave, Pittsburgh, PA 15232. Telephone (412) 687-2100.

Technical booklets issued irregularly. Deals with industrial medical topics such as health problems of women in industry and industry-related diseases. Price $5.00 per copy. ISSN 0073-7518.

2529
Industrial Health Foundation Nursing
Series
Industrial Health Foundation, Inc, 5231 Centre Ave, Pittsburgh, PA 15232. Telephone (412) 687-2100.

Technical booklets issued irregularly. Deals with industrial nursing practices including role of nurse in employee mental health programs. Price $5.00 per copy. ISSN 0073-7526.

2530
Industrial Hygiene Digest
Industrial Health Foundation, Inc, 5231 Centre Ave, Pittsburgh, PA 15232. Telephone (412) 687-2100.

Monthly abstracts from international occupational health literature. Cover industrial medicine, toxicology, safety, and current books. Price $100.00 per year. ISSN 0019-8382.

2531
Industrial Index to Glasgow & West of
Scotland
Glasgow Chamber of Commerce, 30 George Sq, Glasgow, Scotland G2 1EQ. Telephone (44)(041) 2042121.

Annual index. Lists Glasgow and West Scotland Chamber of Commerce members alphabetically and by product. Price free to members, £15.00 nonmembers.

2532
Industrial Maintenance and Plant
Operation
Ames Publishing Div, Chilton, 1 W Olney Ave, Philadelphia, PA 19120. Telephone (215) 224-7000.

Monthly magazine. Provides news of new products and methods relevant to plant engineering, maintenance and operation. Price $30.00 per year.

2533
Industrial Marketing
Crain Communications, Inc, 740 Rush St, Chicago, IL 60611. Telephone (312) 649-5385.

Monthly newspaper. Discusses business marketing plans. Analyzes effective advertising campaigns. Price $20.00 per year.

2534
Industrial Marketing Management
North-Holland Publishing Co, PO Box 211, 1000 AE Amsterdam, The Netherlands. Order from Elsevier/North-Holland, Inc, 52 Vanderbilt Ave, New York, NY 10017. Telephone (212) 867-9040.

Quarterly journal. Covers industrial marketing management topics, including pricing, distribution, and purchasing behavior. Price $54.00 per year. ISSN 0019-8501.

2535
Industrial Participation
Industrial Participation Assn, 78 Buckingham Gate, London, England SW1E 6PQ Telephone (44)(01) 222-0351

Journal published three times per year. Considers British and international labor issues. Includes company case studies, with emphasis on industrial democracy. Price £4.00 per year (UK), £6.00 foreign.

2535.01
Industrial Photography
United Business Publications, Inc, 475 Park Ave S, New York, NY 10016. Telephone (212) 725-2300.

Monthly magazine. Covers industrial photography and photographic equipment topics. Price $15.00 per year.

2536
Industrial Planning and Programming
Series
United Nations Industrial Development Organization, Vienna International Centre, PO Box 300, A-1400, Vienna, Austria. Telephone 26310. Telex 135612

Series of reports. Contain information on manufacturing establishments and industrial feasibility studies. Symbols: ID/-SER.E12-8. Price $3.00 to $3.50.

2536.01
Industrial Product Bulletin
Morgan-Grampian Ltd, Morgan-Grampian House, Calderwood St, London, England SE18 6QH. Order from Morgan-Grampian Publishing Co, Circulation Dept, Berkshire Common, Pittsfield, MA 01201. Telephone (413) 499-2550.

Bimonthly magazine. Presents innovative, new and improved products, processes and services to the manufacturing industries (SICs 20-39). Price $20.00 per year.

2537
Industrial Property
World Intellectual Property Organization, 32 Chemin des Colombettes, 1211 Geneva 20, Switzerland. Telephone (41)-(022) 999111. Telex Geneve 2 23 76.

Monthly report. Contains information on activities of International (Paris) Union for Protection of Industrial Property and Special Unions and Agreements concerning industrial property. Includes news items, court decisions, texts of laws. Price 115 Swiss francs.

2537.01
Industrial Property Reports from Socialist Countries
European Law Centre Ltd, 4 Bloombury Sq, London, England WC1A 2RL. Telephone (44) (01) 404-4300. Telex 21746.

Semiannual report. Covers intellectual and industrial property law developments in Eastern Europe, China, and other non-European Socialist countries. Includes full texts of legislation and court decisions. Price $216.00 per year. ISSN 0260-4876.

2538
Industrial Purchasing Agent
Publications For Industry, 21 Russell Woods Rd, Great Neck, NY 11021. Telephone (516) 487-0990.

Monthly newspaper. Discusses industrial purchasing topics, specializing in new product information. Price $11.00 per year.

2539
Industrial Purchasing News
Morgan-Grampian Ltd, Morgan-Grampian House, Calderwood St, London, England SE18 6QH. Order from Morgan-Grampian Pub Co, 2 Park Ave, New York NY 10016. Telephone England (44)(01) 855-7777. Telex 896238 MORGAN G. New York (212) 340-9700. Telex 425592 MGI UI.

Monthly magazine. Supplies information on major industrial products. Price $65.00 per year.

2540
Industrial Real Estate
William N Kinnard, Jr and Stephen D Messner American Industrial Development Council, Inc, 215 W Pershing Rd, Suite 707, Kansas City, MO 64108. Order from Society of Industrial Realtors, 1300 Connecticut Ave, NW, Washington, DC 20036. Telephone (816) 474-4558.

Book. Pertains to industrial real estate, its selection and use. Price $12.50 per copy.

2541
Industrial Relations Guide
Prentice-Hall, Inc, Englewood Cliffs, NJ 07632. Telephone (201) 592-2000. Telex 13-5423.

Biweekly loose-leaf service. Discusses industrial labor problems, labor arbitration and collective bargaining issues. Contains contract clauses and alternatives. Price $261.00 per year.

2542
Industrial Relations Journal
Mercury House Business Publications Ltd, Mercury House, Waterloo Rd, London, England SE1 8UL. Telephone (44)-(01) 928-3388.

Quarterly magazine. Reports on industrial relations management topics. Price £12.00 per year.

2544
Industrial Relations Law Reports
Industrial Relations Service, 170 Finchley Rd, London, England NW3 6BP Telephone (44)(01) 794-4554.

Monthly magazine. Carries text of all major industrial relations cases in Britain. Contains index to key issues. Price £53.00 per year.

2545
Industrial Relations News
Enterprise Publications, 20 N Wacker Dr, Chicago, IL 60606. Telephone (312) 332-3571.

Weekly newsletter. Focuses on industrial relations. Covers affirmative actions, education, retirement, unions and related topics. Price $135.00 per year.

2546
Industrial Relations Research in Canada.
Canadian Dept of Labour, Ottawa, Ont, Canada K1A 0J2. Order from Publishing Centre, Supply and Services, Ottawa, Ont, Canada K1A 0S9. Telephone (819) 997-2582.

Annual directory. Acts as guide to Canadian industrial relations research projects under way during year. Gives names and addresses of researchers and lists publications resulting from projects. Free of charge.

2547
Industrial Relations Review & Report
Industrial Relations Service, 170 Finchley Rd, London, England NW3 6BP. Telephone (44)(01) 794-4554.

Bimonthly report. Focuses on labor and personnel management issues in Great Britain. Includes case studies and legal decisions. Price £80.00 per year.

2548
Industrial Relations Week
Samson Publications Ltd, 12–14 Hill Rise, Richmond Surrey, England TW10 6UA. Telephone (44)(01) 948-4251.

Weekly newsletter. Reports on industrial relations in Great Britain. Price $115.00 per year. ISSN 0306-6894.

2549
Industrial Research and Development
Technical Pub Co, 1301 S Grove Ave, Barrington, IL 60010. Telephone (312) 381-1840.

Monthly magazine. Covers industrial and government research and development. Price $36.00 per year.

2550
Industrial Research Laboratories of the United States, **1979**
RR Bowker Co, 1180 Ave of the Americas, New York, NY 10036. Order from RR Bowker Co, PO Box 1807, Ann Arbor, MI 48106. Telephone (212) 764-5100.

Directory. Provides information on approximately 10,000 research and development facilities belonging to almost 6500 nongovernment, nonacademic organizations in the US. Covers location, laboratory personnel, researchers and administrators, giving disciplines of each. Price $75.00. ISBN 0-8352-1135-5. ISSN 0073-7623.

2551
Industrial Safety
United Trade Press Ltd, 33-35 Bowling Green Lane, London, EC1R ODA England. Telephone (44) (01) 837-1212.

Monthly magazine. Covers fire protection, health, safety, and security in British industry. Price 100.00 Swiss francs. ISSN 0019-8757.

2551.01
Industrial Safety Product News
Ames Publishing Div, Chilton, 1 W Olney Ave, Philadelphia, PA 19120. Telephone (215) 224-7000.

Monthly magazine. Reports on safety industry news and new products of interest to industrial safety executives. Price $24.00 per year.

2551.02
Industrial Short-Term Trends
European Community Information Service, 2100 M St, NW, Suite 707, Washington, DC 20037. Telephone (202) 862-9500. Telex 248455.

Monthly publication. Reports short-term industrial trends in European Economic Community (Common Market) countries. Price $17.50.

2552
Industrial Society
Industrial Society, Peter Runge House, 3 Carlton House Terr, London, England SW1Y 5DG. Telephone (44) (01) 839-4300.

Quarterly magazine. Covers British and international management and industrial relations. Price £12.50 per year.

2553
Industrial Statistics plus Yearbook
Commission of the European Communities, Office for Official Publications of the European Communities, CP 1003, Luxembourg, 1 Luxembourg. Telephone (352) 490081. Telex PUBLOF 1325.

Quarterly publication plus yearbook. Contains industrial statistics for European Community. Price $14.50 per year.

2554
Industrial Supervisor
National Safety Council, 444 N Michigan Ave, Chicago, IL 60611. Telephone (312) 527-4800. Telex 25-3141.

Monthly magazine. Contains information on occupational safety designed to help foremen recognize work hazards and communicate with workers on safety issues. Price $5.50 members, $6.90 nonmembers.

2555
Industrial Tribunal Reports
Her Majesty's Stationery Office, PO Box 569, London, England SE1 9NH. Telephone (44) (01) 928 1321.

Pamphlets. Cover industrial tribunals in Great Britain. Price available on request.

2556
Industrial World/Industrial World en Espanol
Johnston International Pub Corp, 386 Park Ave S, New York, NY 10016. Telephone (212) 689-0120. Telex 66811 Jonst.

Monthly magazine. Discusses latest developments in industrial equipment, materials and methods. Spanish and English editions. Price $50.00 per year, $80.00 two years.

2557
IndustriScope
Media General Financial Services, Inc, PO Box C-32333, Richmond, VA 23293. Telephone (804) 649-6569.

Monthly report. Lists stocks by industry group. Notes monthly activity. Price $85.00 per year.

2558
Industry
Associated Industries of Massachusetts, 4005 Prudential Tower, Boston, MA 02199. Telephone (617) 262-1180.

Monthly magazine. Concerns itself with management developments, pollution control, socioeconomic problems, transportation trends, and other business issues. Price $12.00 per year.

2560
Industry Audit Guides
American Inst of Certified Public Accountants, 1211 Ave of the Americas, New York, NY 10036. Telephone (212) 575-6200.

Series of reports. Presents general auditing information and guidelines for auditing and reporting on specific industries, types of business, or aspects of business activity. Prices vary from $4.50 to $7.00 per guide.

2561
Industry Forecast
S Jay Levy, Box 26, Chappaqua, NY 10514. Telephone (914) 238-3665.

Monthly newsletter. Offers economic predictions 6 to 18 months into future. Includes forecasts of production, sales, corporate profits, and prices. Price $85.00 per year.

2562
Industry Mart
McGraw-Hill Publications Co, 1221 Ave of the Americas, New York, NY 10020. Telephone (212) 997-1221. Telex TWX 7105814879 WUI 62555.

Magazine issued eight times per year. Publishes reports on new metalworking products and services. Analyzes technical applications. Price $10.00 per year.

2563
Industry Price Indexes
Statistics Canada, User Services, Publications Distribution, Ottawa, Ont, Canada K1A 0V7. Telephone (613) 992-3151.

Monthly and annual index. Provides manufacturing industry selling prices, wholesale prices, farm product prices, common and preferred stock prices, and average dealers' selling prices. Tables, charts, and graphs. Price $42.00 per year. ISSN 0700-2033.

2564
Industry Series, CC77-1 to -28
US Dept of Commerce, Bureau of Census, Washington, DC 20233. Telephone (202) 449-1600.

Series of reports. Presents data on the construction industry. Covers receipts, employment, payments for materials and equipment, and depreciable assets. Price available on request.

2565
Industry Surveys
Standard & Poor's Corp, 25 Broadway, New York, NY 10004. Telephone (212) 248-2525.

Annual loose-leaf service with monthly updates. Provides economic and investment analysis of more than 65 leading industries. Price $595.00 per year.

2566
Industry Week
Penton/IPC, 614 Superior Ave W, Cleveland, OH 44113. Order from Penton/IPC, 1111 Chester Ave, Cleveland, OH 44114. Telephone (216) 696-7000.

Biweekly magazine. Covers industrial management news. Price $36.00 per year.

2566.01
In Focus
Research and Review Service of America, Inc, PO Box 1727, Indianapolis, IN 46206. Telephone (317) 297-4360.

Monthly newsletter. Condenses articles on life insurance from government, business, and trade publications; house organs, newspapers, and magazines. Price $42.00 per year.

2567
Infomat
Statistics Canada, User Services, Publications Distribution, Ottawa, Ont, Canada K1A 0V7. Telephone (613) 992-3151.

Weekly service. Summarizes major Statistics Canada reports. Contains charts, statistics, and list of publications released during week. Price $72.00 per year. ISSN 0380-0547.

2568
Inform
American Personnel Guidance Assn, 2 Skyline Place, Suite 400, 5203 Leesburg Pike, Falls Church, VA 22041. Telephone (703) 820-4700.

Monthly periodical. Provides information on sources of career information, plus Career Resource Bibliography. Price $25.00 per year.

2568.01
Information & Management
North-Holland Publishing Co, PO Box 211, 1000 AE Amsterdam, The Netherlands. Telephone Telephone 5159222.

Bimonthly journal. Discusses new developments in the field of applied information systems. Focuses on information system development for managerial policies. Price $76.00 per year. ISSN 0378-7206.

2569
Informational and Technical Publications of the General Secretariat of the Organization of American States (OAS)
Organization of American States, 17th St and Constitution Ave NW, Washington, DC 20006. Order from OAS General Secretariat, Dept of Publications, 6840 Industrial Rd, Springfield, VA 22151. Telephone (703) 941-1617.

Service. Includes OAS periodicals and technical and informational publications dealing with culture, education, law, economics, statistics, art and folklore of the American nations. Price $80.00 per year.

2570
Information and Records Management
PTN Publishing Corp, 250 Fulton Ave, Hempstead, NY 11550. Telephone (516) 489-1300.

Monthly magazine. Discusses records management developments including new products. Covers COM systems and office copying methods. Price $7.50 per year.

2570.01
Information & Word Processing Report
Geyer-McAllister Publications, Inc, 51 Madison Ave, New York, NY 10010. Telephone (212) 689-4411.

Semimonthly newsletter. Covers word processing news, practical applications, and equipment. Price $106.00 per year.

2570.02
Information Bank I and II.
New York Times Information Service, Inc, Mt. Pleasant Office Pk, 1719A Route 10, Parsippany, NJ 07054. Telephone (201) 539-5850. Telex 136390.

Database. Provides abstracts of articles from The New York Times and 60 other newspapers and magazines. Includes 1.9 million abstracts dating back to January 1969. Price available on request.

2571
Information Guide for Doing Business in Countries Abroad
Price Waterhouse & Co, 60 Broad St, New York, NY 10004. Telephone (212) 489-8900.

Series of reports. Contains information on running a business in a particular country. Price available on request.

2572
Information Hotline
Science Associates/International, Inc, 1841 Broadway, New York, NY 10023. Telephone (212) 265-4995.

Monthly newsletter. Contains information on new data bases, legislation, information services, and special collections. Intended for information managers and computer center directors. Price $95.00 per year.

2573
Information Industry & Technology Service
International Data Corp, 214 Third Ave, Waltham, MA 02254. Telephone (617) 890-3700. Telex 92-3401.

Continuous information service. Monitors merger of data, word, and communications technologies for banking, finance, and government. Price available on request.

2573.01
Information Industry Market Place: An International Directory of Information Products and Services
RR Bowker Co, 1180 Ave of the Americas, New York, NY 10036. Order from RR Bowker Co, PO Box 1807, Ann Arbor, MI 48106. Telephone (212) 764-5100.

Annual directory. Lists 400 database producers, as well as information centers that collect, analyze, evaluate, and process raw data. Also lists other support services and suppliers, organizations, conferences and courses, reference books, periodicals, and newsletters in the field. Price $32.50. ISBN 0-8352-1291-2. ISSN 0000-0450.

2573.02
Information Peking (Beijing)
Guides to Multinational Business, Inc, Harvard Sq, Box 92, Cambridge, MA 02138. Telephone (617) 868-2288.

Reference guide. Provides information for businessmen and tourists visiting China, including visas, courtesies, health requirements, facilities, and social customs. Contains Peking telephone/address section and location map. Price $30.00.

2573.03
Information Releases
New Zealand Dept of Statistics, Private Bag, Wellington, New Zealand. Telephone (64) (4) 729119.

Irregularly issued booklets. Offers information on New Zealand's economic, trade, and building statistics. Price available on request.

2574
Information Science Abstracts
American Society for Information Science, 1010 Sixteenth St, NW, Washington, DC 20036

Bimonthly journal. Contains abstracts about literature of documentation and related areas. Price $95.00 per year.

2575
Information Society
Crane, Russak & Co, Inc, 3 E 44th St, New York, NY 10017. Telephone (212) 867-1490.

Quarterly magazine. Covers information-related topics, including regulatory issues and transborder data flow. Price $48.00 per volume.

2576

Infosystems

Hitchcock Publishing Co, Hitchcock Bldg, Wheaton, IL 60187. Telephone (312) 665-1000.

Monthly report. Contains articles on topics related to information processing management. Price $25.00 per year.

2576.01

InfoWorld

CW Communications Inc, 375 Cochituate Rd, Box 880, Framingham, MA 01701. Telephone (617) 879-0700.

Biweekly newspaper. Provides information on personal or desktop computers. Price $25.00 per year.

2577

Inheritance, Estate & Gift Tax Reports

Commerce Clearing House, Inc, 4025 W Peterson Ave, Chicago, IL 60646. Telephone (312) 583-8500.

Three loose-leaf books and monthly reports. Covers inheritance, estate, and gift taxes in each state. Price $165.00 per year.

2578

Inheritance Taxes

Prentice-Hall, Inc, Englewood Cliffs, NJ 07632. Telephone (201) 592-2000. Telex 13-5423.

Loose-leaf report with biweekly supplements. Contains information on state and federal inheritance and gift taxes. Includes court decisions and stock transfer information. Price available on request.

2579

Inland Revenue Statistics

Her Majesty's Stationery Office, PO Box 569, London, England SE1 9NH. Telephone (44) (01) 928 1321.

Annual service. Supplies statistical results of British surveys on personal income and personal wealth. Price £10.50 per year.

2580

Innovation World

Raymond Lee Organization, Inc, 230 Park Ave, New York, NY 10017. Telephone (212) 661-7000.

Bimonthly magazine. Covers product ideas including marketing, research and development, packaging, and trademark news. Price $24.00 per year.

2581

Inorganic Chemicals

US Dept of Commerce, Bureau of the Census, Washington, DC 20233. Telephone (202) 449-1600.

Monthly report with annual summary. Contains data on primary production and stocks of specified inorganic chemicals. Price $4.00 per year.

2582

Inorganic Fertilizer Materials and Related Acids

US Dept of Commerce, Bureau of the Census, Washington, DC 20233. Telephone (202) 449-1600.

Monthly report with annual summary. Presents data on production and stocks of nitrogen fertilizer materials, phosphoric acid, and sulfuric acid. Shows production, shipments, consumption, and stocks of superphosphate and other phosphatic fertilizer materials. Price $3.25 per year.

2583

In Plant Reproductions

North American Pub Co, 401 N Broad St, Philadelphia, PA 19108. Telephone (215) 574-9600.

Monthly magazine. Reports on in-plant printing and reproductive processes and equipment, including binding and copying equipment, and platemaking techniques. Price $18.00 per year.

2584

Input-Output Tables

Her Majesty's Stationery Office, PO Box 569, London, England SE1 9NH. Telephone (44) (01) 928 1321.

Annual book of tables. Shows flow of British goods and services between industries and from industries to final demand. Price £2.10 per year.

2585

Input-Output Tables for the UK

Her Majesty's Stationary Office, PO Box 569, London, England SE1 9NH. Telephone (44) (01) 928 1321.

Annual tables on British input and output. Price £per year.

2586

In Search/En Quete

Canadian Dept of Communications, 300 Slater St, Ottawa, Ont, Canada K1A 0C8. Telephone (613) 995-8185.

Quarterly magazine. Contains information and opinion on Canadian telecommunication. Bilingual. Free of charge.

2587

In-Season Farm Labor Report. **ES-223**

Florida Dept of Labor and Employment Security, Bureau of Research and Analysis, Caldwell Bldg, Tallahassee, FL 32301. Telephone (904) 488-1048.

Semimonthly report. Provides estimates of number of seasonal Florida agricultural workers and representative wage rates by area and crop. Discusses factors affecting supply and demand of farm labor. Mailing list restricted to Florida-based firms. Single copies available to public upon request. Price free of charge.

2588

Inside Arkansas

Arkansas Dept of Economic Development, One Capitol Mall, Little Rock, AR 72201. Telephone (501) 371-2431.

Quarterly magazine. Contains articles on Arkansas' industrial and business community. Price free of charge.

2589

Inside Look at the Newsletter Field

Newsletter Clearinghouse, 44 W Market St, Rhinebeck, NY 12572. Telephone (914) 876-2081.

Softcover book. Surveys newsletter industry. Provides information on subscriptions, list rentals, circulation, and frequency of publication. Price $25.00.

2592

Installment Lending Directory

American Bankers Assn, 1120 Connecticut Ave NW, Washington, DC 20036. Telephone (202) 467-4123.

Biennial book. Explains rules under which banks assist one another in collection of installment loans and credit card accounts. Lists participating banks and extent of services. Price $20.00.

2593

NAIC Reporter

National Assn of Installment Companies, Inc, 38 W 32 St, New York, NY 10001. Telephone (212) 239-6520.

Magazine published six times per year. Covers all aspects of installment trade including new products and techniques. Discusses case histories. Price $10.00 per year.

2594

Institute For Social Research

University of Michigan, Inst for Social Research, PO Box 1248, Ann Arbor, MI 48106. Telephone (313) 764-7509.

Quarterly newsletter. Discusses research on social issues including housing, education, income, and retirement. Reports ISR news. Free of charge.

2595
Institute of Actuaries Journal
Alden Press Ltd, Osney Mead, Oxford, England.

Magazine issued three times per year. Offers articles on actuarial topics. Price $10.00.

2596
Institute of Actuaries Students' Society Journal
Alden Press Ltd, Osney Mead, Oxford, England.

Annual journal. Presents material on actuarial subjects. Price $10.00.

2596.01
Institute of Actuaries Year Book
Alden Press Ltd, Osney Mead, Oxford, England.

Annual publication. Provides actuarial information. Price $10.00.

2597
Institute of Chartered Accountants of Scotland Official Directory
Inst of Chartered Accountants of Scotland, 27 Queen St, Edinburgh, Scotland EH2 1LA. Telephone (44) (031) 225-5673. Telex 727530.

Annual book. Offers directory to members of Institute of Chartered Accountants of Scotland. Price £10.00.

2599
Institute of Personnel Management (IPM) Digest
Inst of Personnel Management, Central House Upper Woburn Place, London, England WC1H OHX. Telephone (44) (01) 387-2844.

Monthly magazine. Reports on British and international labor developments and on Inst of Personnel Management and its branches. Price £8.00 per year; Airmail £25.00 per year.

2600
Institute of Public Affairs (IPA) Review
Inst of Public Affairs, (IPA Review), 401 Collins St, Melbourne 3000, Australia. Telephone (3) 612029

Quarterly review. Analyzes economic and political developments from a free enterprise viewpoint. Price $10.00 per year for individuals, $100.00 per year for companies.

2601
Institutional Investor
Institutional Investor Systems, Inc, 488 Madison Ave, New York, NY 10022. Telephone (212) 832-8888.

Monthly magazine. Covers professional investing, pension funds, banking and investment banking, and insurance. Price $80.00 per year.

2602
Institutional Investor International Edition
Institutional Investor , Inc, 488 Madison Ave, New York, NY 10022. Telephone (212) 832-8888.

International edition of monthly magazine. Covers news of international finance including government and corporate finance, currency, and economic conditions. Price $80.00 per year.

2603
Institutions/VFM
Cahners Pub Co, Inc, 221 Columbus Ave, Boston, MA 02116. Telephone (617) 536-7780.

Semimonthly magazine. Contains articles on commercial and institutional foodservice operations. Price available on request.

2604
Instrument & Apparatus News
Chilton Co, Chilton Way, Radnor, PA 19089. Telephone (215) 687-8200.

Monthly magazine. Covers controls and instrumentation including raw materials, engineering, manufacture of machinery, research, and development. Price $25.00.

2605
Instrument Flight Rules Supplement (IFR)
Supply and Services Canada, Publishing Centre, Printing and Publishing, Ottawa, Ont, Canada K1A 0S9. Telephone (613) 238-1601.

Monthly report. Provides terminal and en route data for Canada and North Atlantic. Price $15.00 per year.

2606
Instruments & Control Systems
Chilton Co, Chilton Way, Radnor, PA 19089. Telephone (215) 687-8200.

Monthly magazine. Contains information about techniques and equipment in instrumentation and controls with emphasis on practical use. Price $40.00.

2607
Insulation
Turret Press, 4 Local Board Rd, Watford, Herts, WD1 2JS England. Order from Comprint LTD.,4 Local Board Rd, Watford, Herts, England WD1 2JS. Telephone (44) (0923) 46199.

Monthly magazine. Offers information on insulation. Price $56.00 per year.

2608
Insurance Advocate
Roberts Pub Corp, 45 John St, New York, NY 10038. Telephone (212) 233-3768.

Weekly magazine. Reports on matters relevant to fire, casualty, life and health insurance industries including legal and financial aspects. Price $15.00 per year.

2609
Insurance Agency Computer Power
Insurance Field Co, Inc, PO Box 18441, 4325 Old Shepherdsville Rd, Louisville, KY 40218. Telephone (502) 459-7910.

Loose-leaf report with bimonthly updating. Provides information on insurance automation technology and applications. Price $186.00.

2610
Insurance Almanac
Underwriter Printing & Pub Co, 50 East Palisade Ave, PO Box 9806, Englewood, NJ 07631. Telephone (201) 569-8808.

Annual book. Provides data on operations of 2000 insurance companies. Includes material on associations, conventions, and supervisory authorities. Price $40.00 per year.

2611
Insurance and Other Private Finance
Ref. No. 5.15, 1971-72 final edition
Australian Bureau of Statistics, Box 17 GPO, Canberra, ACT 2600, Australia. Order from Australian Government Pub Service, PO Box 84, Canberra, ACT 2600, Australia. Telephone (61) (062) 527911.

Annual bulletin. Covers operations of insurance and finance companies, installment credit. Price $2.00 (Australian).

2612

Insurance Brokers' Monthly and Insurance Adviser

Insurance Pub & Printing Co, 34 Lower High St, Stourbridge, West Midlands, England DY8 1TA. Telephone Stourbridge 77761.

Monthly publication. Reports on issues that affect insurance brokers. Stresses communication between brokers and clients and between brokers and insurance companies. Price £14.00 per year.

2613

Insurance Business Statistics

Her Majesty's Stationery Office, PO Box 569, London, England SE1 9NH. Telephone (44) (01) 928 1321.

Annual service. Furnishes statistics on British insurance business. Price £3.75 per year.

2614

Insurance Casebook

Underwriter Printing & Pub Co, 50 East Palisade Ave, PO Box 9806, Englewood, NJ 07631. Telephone (201) 569-8808.

Annual book. Compiles significant state and federal court decisions that affect insurance industry. Price $40.00 per year.

2615

Insurance Companies and Private Pension Funds

Her Majesty's Stationery Office, PO Box 569, London, England SE1 9NH. Telephone (44) (01) 928 1321.

Quarterly report on British insurance companies and private pension plans. Price £4.00 per year.

2616

Insurance Company Funds

Computer Directions Advisors, Inc, 8750 Georgia Ave, Silver Spring, MD 20910. Telephone (301) 565-9544.

Monthly report. Covers insurance company funds. Lists participating insurance companies, individual fund results, and performance charts. Price $300.00 per year.

2617

Insurance Counsel Journal

International Assn of Insurance Counsel, 20 N Wacker Dr, Suite 3705, Chicago, IL 60606. Telephone (312) 368-1494.

Quarterly journal. Carries reports on International Association of Insurance Counsel. Contains articles on insurance law. Price $20.00 per year.

2618

Insurance Department Service

Underwriter Printing & Pub Co, 50 East Palisade Ave, PO Box 9806, Englewood, NJ 07631. Telephone (201) 569-8808.

Information service. Provides rulings of state insurance departments and related attorney's generals opinions. Available for all or individual states. Price available on request.

2619

Insurance Directory of New Zealand

Mercantile Gazette of New Zealand, Box 20-034, Christchurch 5, New Zealand. Telephone (64) (3) 583219.

Annual directory. Lists insurance houses and brokers in New Zealand. Price $2.50 (New Zealand).

2620

Insurance Facts

Insurance Information Inst, 110 William St, New York, NY 10038. Telephone (212) 233-7650.

Statistical yearbook. Gives data relating to property, liability, marine and surety insurance. Charts and tables. Price single copies free, additional copies $4.50 each.

2621

Insurance Field Magazine

Insurance Field Co, Inc, PO Box 18441, 4325 Old Shepherdsville Rd, Louisville, KY 40218. Telephone (502) 459-7910.

Quarterly magazine. Covers four annual conventions. Free to qualified subscribers.

2622

Insurance Forum

Insurance Forum, Inc, PO Box 245, Ellettsville, IN 47429.

Monthly newsletter. Discusses controversial insurance industry activities including claims and sales practices and company-agent relations. Price $20.00 per year. ISSN 0095-2923.

2623

Insurance Guide

Prentice-Hall, Inc, Englewood Cliffs, NJ 07632. Telephone (201) 592-2000. Telex 13-5423.

Monthly loose-leaf seqvhce. Presents insurance sales ideas, information on income, estate, and gift taxation of insurance, and current insurance business trends. Price $179.40 per year.

2624

Insurance Industry Newsletter

Insurance Field Co, Inc, PO Box 18441, 4325 Old Shepherdsville Rd, Louisville, KY 40218. Telephone (502) 459-7910.

Weekly newsletter. Reports on general insurance news and developments in property/liability and life/health fields. Includes company and personnel news. Price $57.00 per year.

2626

Insurance Institute of Canada Annual Report

Insurance Inst of Canada, 55 University Ave, Toronto, Ont, Canada M5J 2H7. Telephone (416) 366-1601.

Annual report of Insurance Inst of Canada. Includes committee reports, financial statements, lists of education programs, fellows, and associates. Price free of charge.

2628

Insurance Law Reports: Fire & Casualty

Commerce Clearing House, Inc, 4025 W Peterson Ave, Chicago, IL 60646. Telephone (312) 583-8500.

Loose-leaf book plus biweekly reports. Covers current decisions on fire and casualty insurance laws. Price $340.00 per year.

2629

Insurance Law Reports: Life, Health & Accident

Commerce Clearing House, Inc, 4025 W Peterson Ave, Chicago, IL 60646. Telephone (312) 583-8500.

Loose-leaf book plus biweekly reports. Covers current decisions on life, health, and accident insurance laws. Price $340.00 per year.

2630

Insurance Literature

Special Libraries Assn, 235 Park Ave S, New York, NY 10003. Order from Carol Gottliebsen, INA Corp, Rm 223, 1600 Arch St, Philadelphia, PA 19101. Telephone (215) 241-4000.

Bimonthly report. Contains annotated listing of all types of literature in the insurance field. Price $10.00 per year.

2632

Insurance Marketing

Bayard Publications, Inc, 1234 Summer St, Stamford, CT 06905. Telephone (203) 327-0800.

Monthly magazine. Covers all branches of insurance. Price $10.00 per year.

2633
Insurance Periodicals Index
Special Libraries Assn, Insurance Div, c/o Robert L Enequest, Ed, College Insurance, 123 William St, New York, NY 10038. Telephone (212) 477-9250.

Annual index. Lists articles in periodicals dealing with insurance by subject. Price $40.00 per year. ISSN 0074-073X.

2634
Insurance Record
Tudor Press Ltd, Tudor House, 3 Dellfield Close, Watford, Herts, England WD1 3LB. Telephone Warford (44) (01) (0923) 31757.

Monthly magazine. Discusses international insurance subjects with emphasis on British insurance industry. Reports on legislative changes and activities of British Insurance Association. Price £5.00 per year.

2635
Insurance Record of Australia and New Zealand
McCarron Bird, 594 Lonsdale St, Melbourne, Vic 3000, Australia. Telephone (61) (3) 679651.

Monthly magazine. Contains information about insurance industry in Australia and New Zealand. Price $31.70 per year.

2635.01
Insurance Sales
Rough Notes Co, Inc, 1200 N Meridian St, Indianapolis, IN 46204. Telephone (317) 634-1541.

Monthly magazine. Covers life and health insurance, with an emphasis on sales. Price $8.00 per year.

2636
Insurance Service
Data Resources, Inc, 29 Hartwell Ave, Lexington, MA 02173. Telephone (617) 861-0165.

Quarterly report. Provides forecasts on US property and casualty insurance industry. Gives monthly asset holdings by life insurance company. Price available on request.

2636.01
Insurance Update
Coopers & Lybrand, 1251 Ave of the Americas, New York, NY 10020. Order from Manager of Publications, PO Box 682, Times Sq Station, New York, NY 10108. Telephone (212) 489-1100.

Periodic newsletter. Covers insurance industry news. Price free of charge.

2636.02
Intellectual Property Law Review
Clark Boardman Co Ltd, 435 Hudson St, New York, NY 10014. Telephone (212) 929-7500.

Annual volume that reviews patent law. Price $47.50. ISBN 0-87632-143-0.

2637
Intellectual Property Management: Law/Business/Strategy
Clark Boardman Co Ltd, 435 Hudson St, New York, NY 10014. Telephone (212) 929-7500.

Loose-leaf book periodically revised. Provides guide to legal and business aspects of intellectual property management. Subjects include copyrights, trademarks, royalties and pricing strategies. Price $67.50. ISBN 0-87632-150-3.

2638
Intelligence Digest Business Trends
Intelligence International Ltd and Advance News Services Ltd, 17 Rodney Rd, Cheltenham, Glos, England GL50 1HX. Telephone 0242-517774.

Monthly newsletter. Analyzes international economic, financial, and business trends, and also includes selected advice on commodities and other investments. Price $78.00 per year.

2639
Inter-American Development Bank Annual Report
Inter-American Development Bank, 808 17th St NW, Washington, DC 20577. Telephone (202) 634-8000.

Annual journal. Reports on development trends in Latin America. Notes Inter-American Development Bank activities. Available on request.

2640
Inter-American Development Bank (IDB) News
Inter-American Development Bank, 808 17th St NW, Washington, DC 20577. Telephone (202) 634-8000.

Monthly newsletter. Reports on activities of Inter-American Development Bank and economic and financial developments in Latin America. Free of charge.

2641
Inter-American Economic Affairs
Inter-American Affairs Press, Box 181, Washington, DC 20044.

Quarterly report. Devotes itself to inter-American relations, economics, and public policy. Price $20.00 per year.

2642
Interface-1
Capital Communications Ltd, Suite 705, Burnside Building, 151 Slater St, Ottawa, Ont, Canada K1P 5H3. Telephone (613) 235-9183. Telex 053-3601.

Semimonthly newsletter. Focuses on federal and provincial developments in government-business relations in Canada. Price $100.00 per year.

2643
Interfaces
Inst of Management Sciences, 146 Westminster St, Providence, RI 02903. Telephone (401) 274-2525.

Bimonthly magazine. Pertains to management sciences research and problem solving. Offers case studies. Price $22.00 per volume.

2644
Internal Auditor
Inst of Internal Auditors, Inc, 249 Maitland Ave, Altamonte Springs, FL 32701. Telephone (305) 830-7600.

Bimonthly journal. Discusses current developments in internal auditing philosophy and practice. Covers business applications. Price $16.00 per year.

2645
Internal Revenue Bulletin
Internal Revenue Service, 12th & Constitution Ave, Washington, DC 20024. Order from Superintendent of Documents, Government Printing Office, Washington, DC 20402. Telephone (202) 783-3238.

Weekly report. Announces Internal Revenue Service rulings, Treasury decisions, Executive Orders, legislation, and court decisions related to internal revenue matters. Price varies.

2646
Internal Revenue Manual—Audit & Administration
Commerce Clearing House, Inc, 4025 W Peterson Ave, Chicago, IL 60646. Telephone (312) 583-8500.

Periodic reports. Cover operating and administrative procedures and policies of Internal Revenue Service. Released as revisions become official. Price $430.00 per year.

2647
Internal Revenue Service Annual Report of the Commissioner of Internal Revenue
Internal Revenue Service, 12th & Constitution Ave, Washington, DC 20024. Order from Superintendent of Documents, Government Printing Office, Washington, DC 20402. Telephone (202) 783-3238.

Annual report. Summarizes activities of Internal Revenue Service. Price varies.

2648
Internal Revenue Service Chief Counsel Annual Report
Internal Revenue Service, 12th & Constitution Ave, Washington, DC 20024. Order from Superintendent of Documents, Government Printing Office, Washington, DC 20402. Telephone (202) 783-3238.

Annual report. Discusses activities of Chief Counsel of Internal Revenue Service. Price available on request.

2649
Internal Revenue Service Publications
Internal Revenue Service, 12th & Constitution Ave, Washington, DC 20024. Order from Superintendent of Documents, Government Printing Office, Washington, DC 20402. Telephone (202) 783-3238.

Various publications. Covers federal income and corporate taxes, and taxation of small businesses, gifts, estates, capital assets, farm income, and other areas. Statistics. Price available on request.

2650
Internal Revenue Service Statistics of Income: Corporation Income Tax Returns
Internal Revenue Service, 12th & Constitution Ave, Washington, DC 20024. Order from Superintendent of Documents, Government Printing Office, Washington, DC 20420. Telephone (202) 783-3238.

Annual report. Analyzes corporate income using statistics compiled from corporate tax returns. Price available on request.

2651
Internal Revenue Service Tax Guide for Small Business 344
Internal Revenue Service, 12th & Constitution Ave, Washington, DC 20024. Order from Superintendent of Documents, Government Printing Office, Washington, DC 20420. Telephone (202) 783-3238.

Annual book. Discusses federal tax laws that apply to small business operations. Free of charge.

2652
International Abstracts in Operations Research
North Holland Publishing Co, Box 211, 1000 AE Amsterdam, The Netherlands. Order from Elsevier/ North-Holland Inc, 52 Vanderbilt Ave, New York, NY 10017. Telephone (212) 867-9040.

Bimonthly journal. Provides abstracts of papers published in the field of operations research. Price $146.50 per year. ISSN 0020-580X.

2653
International Accounting & Financial Report
Institute for International Research Ltd, 70 Warren Street, London, England WIP 5PA. Telephone 44 (01) 388 2663. Telex 263504.

Biweekly report. Analyzes international accounting and financial problems. Reviews tax legislation and outlines new accounting techniques. Price $295.00 per year.

2654
International Accounting Standards
Canadian Institute of Chartered Accountants, 250 Bloor St E, Toronto, Ont, Canada M4W 1G5. Telephone (416) 962-1242.

Loose-leaf report. Presents international accounting, auditing, and financial reporting standards issued by International Accounting Standards Committee. Price $3.00 for individual standards, subscriptions to new standards as available, $7.00 per year.

2655
International Air Charter Statistics
Statistics Canada, User Services, Publications Distribution, Ottawa, Ont, Canada K1A 0V7. Telephone (613) 992-3151.

Quarterly report. Reviews all air charter operations between Canada and other countries performed by Canadian and foreign airlines. Price $24.00 per year. ISSN 0705-4297.

2656
International Assn of Business Communicators (IABC) News
International Assn of Business Communicators, 870 Market St, Suite 940, San Francisco, CA 94102. Telephone (415) 433-3400.

Monthly newspaper. Reports on ideas, people, issues, and regulations affecting business communications. Notes International Association of Business Communicators news. Price included in membership fees.

2657
International Banking Report
Financial Times Business Information Ltd, Bracken House, 10 Cannon St, London, England EC4P 4BY. Order from Financial Times Ltd, 75 Rockefeller Plaza, New York, NY 10019. Telephone (44) (01) 248-8000. Telex 886341-2.

Monthly loose-leaf report. Covers international banking trends, mergers, appointments, new branches, and consortiums. Cumulative index. Price $200.00 per year.

2657.01
International Banktrends
International Banktrends, Inc, 910 16th St, NW, Washington, DC 20006. Telephone (202) 466-7490.

Biweekly newsletter. Digests general and technical data pertinent to international banking, commerce, and related interests from a fi nancial and trading slant. Price $100.00 per year.

2658
International Benefits Information Service (IBIS)
Charles D Spencer & Associates, Inc, 222 W Adams St, Chicago, IL 60606. Telephone (312) 236-2615.

Monthly loose-leaf reports plus separate reference on manuals for foreign countries. Furnish data on employee benefits including Social Security. Price available on request.

2659
International Bibliography, Information, Documentation
Unipub, 345 Park Ave S, New York, NY 10010. Telephone (212) 686-4707.

Quarterly service. Lists materials published by the United Nations and other intergovernmental organizations. Price $38.00 per year.

2661
International Bond Service
Extel Statistical Service Ltd, 37-45 Paul St, London, England EC2A 4PB. Telephone (44) (01) 253-3400. Telex 262687.

Loose-leaf service with weekly updates. Supplies details on new and existing bonds on international market. Notes pending changes. Price £360.00 per year.

2661.01
International Book Trade Directory
RR Bowker Co, 1180 Ave of the Americas, New York, NY 10036. Order from RR Bowker Co, PO Box 1807, Ann Arbor; MI 48106. Telephone (212) 764-5100.

Book. Gives information on some 30,000 booksellers and distributors in 170 countries outside the US and Canada. Price $47.00. ISBN 0-89935-060-6.

2662
International Business Intelligence
International Reports, 200 Park Ave S, New York, NY 10003. Telephone (212) 477-0003.

Weekly report. Discusses international business trends, including advice on foreign investment possibilities and project financing. Price $270.00 per year.

2663
International Businessman's Who's Who, 1980 edition
Kelly's Directories Ltd, Windsor Court, East Grinstead House, East Grinstead, West Sussex, England RH19 1XB. Telephone (44) (01) 0342-26972. Telex 95127 INFSER G.

Annual directory. Contains biographical data on outstanding business people to 1980. Price £40.00. ISSN 610-00526X.

2665
International Centre for Settlement of Investment Disputes (ICSID) Annual Report
World Bank, 1818 H St, NW, Washington, DC 20433. Telephone (202) 393-6360.

Annual report. Covers activities of International Centre for Settlement of Investment Disputes. Includes review of pending cases. English, French, and Spanish. Free of charge.

2666
International Coal Report
Financial Times Business Information Ltd, Bracken House, 10 Cannon St, London, England EC4P 4BY. Order from Pasha Publications, Suite 713, 1730 K St, NW, Washington, DC 20006. Telephone (202) 783-2660. Telex 248852.

Fortnightly report. Reviews workdivide coal developments and news. Includes information on consumption, production, imports and exports, and prices. Price $395.00 per year.

2667
International Commercial Arbitration
Oceana Publications, Inc, 75 Main St, Dobbs Ferry, NY 20522. Telephone (914) 693-5944.

Loose-leaf service. Contains documents and papers relating to international commercial arbitration. Includes cases and regulations under New York Convention. Price $75.00 per binder. ISBN 0-379-10150-3.

2668
International Commercial Financing Intelligence
International Reports, 200 Park Ave S, New York, NY 10003. Telephone (212) 477-0003.

Service consisting of annual and periodic reports. Covers new opportunities in international commercial financing, insurance in international finance, and switch and barter trade information. Price $435.00 per year.

2669
International Construction Week
McGraw-Hill Publications Co, 1221 Ave of the Americas, New York, NY 10020. Telephone (212) 997-1221. Telex TWX 7105814879 WUI 62555.

Weekly newsletter. Discusses construction contracting, design, materials, machinery, and finance. Notes new business leads and labor issues. Price $585.00 per year.

2670
International Country Risk Guide
International Reports, 200 Park Ave S, New York, NY 10003. Telephone (212) 477-0003.

Monthly report. Evaluates changes in country risk assessment. Covers currency flights and changes in reserve positions. Price $1900.00 per year.

2671
International Development Review
Society for International Development, Palazzo della Civilta del Lavoro, 00144 Rome, Italy. Telephone (06) 595506, 5917897, Cables SOCINTDEV.

Quarterly journal. Offers articles on economic development of world's nations, particularly underdeveloped countries. Summarizes articles in French and Spanish. Price $25.00 per year. ISSN 0020-6555.

2672
International Directory of Computer and Information System Services, 3d edition
International Publications Service, 114 E 32nd St, New York, NY 10016. Telephone (212) 685-9351.

Book. Describes computer services offered by about 3000 organizations throughout the world. Price $25.00.

2673
International Directory of Executive Recruiters
Kennedy & Kennedy, Inc, Templeton Rd, Fitzwilliam, NH 03447. Telephone (603) 585-2200.

Directory. Lists 600 executive recruiting firms in 150 countries. Price $15.00.

2674
International Directory of Market Research Organisations
Market Research Society, 15 Belgrave Sq, London, England SW1X 8PF. Telephone (44) (01) 235-4709.

Annual directory. Gives particulars on 1,100 market research organizations in over 60 countries. Price $60.00.

2675
International Economic Indicators & Competitive Trends
US Dept of Commerce, International Trade Administration, Washington, DC 20230. Order from Supt of Documents, US Govt Printing Office, Washington, DC 20402. Telephone (202) 783-3238.

Report. Offers data on worldwide economic indicators and competitive trends. Price available on request.

2675.01
International Economic Scoreboard
Conference Board, Inc, 845 3rd Ave, New York, NY, 10022. Telephone (212) 759-0900.

Bimonthly report. Gives leading economic indicators in major industrial countries. Price available on request.

2676

International Educational Materials Exchange

International Inst for Labour Studies, PO Box 6, CH-1211, Geneva 22, Switzerland. Telephone (41) (022) 996111.

Listing service of unpublished documents. Concerns international labor and related areas, with special emphasis on developing nations. Sources include International Institute for Labour Studies. Price varies according to length.

2677

International Encyclopedia of the Social Sciences, **1977, Condensed Version**

Macmillan Pub Co, 866 Third Ave, New York, NY 10022. Telephone (212) 935-2000.

Eight-volume encyclopedia of social science, industrial economics, psychology, and statistics, with biographical supplement. Price $250.00, $280.00 supplement.

2677.01

International Environment Reporter

Bureau of National Affairs, Inc, 1231 25th St, NW, Washington, DC 20037. Telephone (202) 452-4200.

Loose-leaf books, with monthly updates. Provide worldwide environmental information for professionals and government officials. Include reports and analyses of pollution, control developments, and an updated compilation of key foreign and international pollution control laws and regulations. Cumulative index and three indexed reference file binders. Price $494.00 per year.

2678

International Executive

Foundation for the Advancement of International Business Administration, Inc, 64 Ferndale Drive, Hastings-on-Hudson, NY 10706. Telephone (914) 478-0193.

Magazine published three times per year. Summarizes books and articles dealing with international business. Provides extensive bibliography and lists of books and articles of interest, organized by subjects such as management, marketing, and law. Price $27.00 per year.

2679

International Finance Corporation (IFC), 1980 Annual Report

World Bank, 1818 H St, NW, Washington, DC 20433. Telephone (202) 393-6360.

Annual report of International Finance Corporation. Summarizes fiscal year's operations. Assesses investment and trade climate. English, French, and Spanish. Free of charge.

2680

International Financial Statistics

International Monetary Fund, 19th & H St NW, Washington, DC 20431. Telephone (202) 393-6362.

Monthly book. Provides statistics on domestic and international finance, including exchange rates, international liquidity, and government finance. English, French, and Spanish editions. Price $35.00 per year.

2681

International Foundation (IF) Legal Legislative Reporter, News Bulletin

International Foundation of Employee Benefit Plans, 18700 W Bluemound Rd, Box 69, Brookfield, WI 53005. Telephone (414) 786-6700.

Monthly magazine. Covers governmental developments that affect employee benefit trust funds. Notes court cases and National Labor Relations Board and Internal Revenue Service decisions. Price included in cost of membership. ISSN 0458-6700.

2682

International Foundation of Employee Benefit Plans, Digest

International Foundation of Employee Benefit Plans, 18700 W Bluemound Rd, Box 69, Brookfield, WI 53005. Telephone (414) 786-6700.

Monthly magazine. Describes activities of International Foundation of Employee Benefit Plans. Covers developments in benefits in field and governmental news. Price included in cost of membership. ISSN 0146-1141.

2682.01

International Freighting Management

Maclean-Hunter Ltd, 30 Old Burlington St, London, England W1X 2AE. Telephone (44) (01) 434-2233.

Monthly magazine. Covers the management of international and British freight distribution and shipments. Price available on request.

2683

International Freighting Weekly

Maclean-Hunter Ltd, 30 Old Burlington St, London, England W1X 2AE. Telephone (44) (01) 434-2233.

Weekly publication. Covers international freight industry. Includes data on shipping agents, depots, equipment, and services by air, rail, road, and sea. Free to qualified subscribers.

2683.01

International Gold Digest

Indicator Research Group, Inc, Indicator Bldg, Palisades Park, NJ 07650. Telephone (201) 947-8800.

Weekly publication. Reports on South African gold stocks. Shows the activity of various gold companies, and includes gold mining news items. Charts. Price $140.00 per year.

2684

International Guide to Library, Archival, and Information Science Associations

R R Bowker Co, 1180 Ave of the Americas, New York, NY 10036. Order from R R Bowker Co, PO Box 1807, Ann Arbor, MI 48106. Telephone(212) 764-5100.

Book. Provides information on 509 national and international library, archival, and information science associations. Bibliography, appendixes, and indexes. Price $32.50. ISBN 0-8352-1285-8.

2685

International Insurance Monitor

Monitor Trade Publications, Inc, 150 W 28th St, New York, NY 10001. Telephone (212) 255-6112.

Published eight times per year. Covers world insurance markets. Devotes whole issues to specialized coverages. Price $18.50 per year.

2686

International Intertrade Index

International Intertrade Index, PO Box 636, Federal Sq, Newark, NJ 07101. Telephone (201) 623-2864.

Monthly newsletter. Lists new products shown at foreign trade fairs. Notes new foreign processes, licenses, and patents. Price $45.00 per year.

2687

International Invention Register
Catalyst, PO Box 547, Fallbrook, CA 92028.

Quarterly newspaper. Contains register of patents offered for sale or license and manufacturers seeking such patents or products. Price $5.75 per year.

2688

Internatonal Investment Trends
International Investment Trends, PO Box 40, 8027 Zurich 2, Switzerland.

Newsletter issued 17 times per year. Reports on international investment and political trends. Emphasizes gold investments and South African politics. Notes stock market activity and world monetary developments. Price $95.00 per year.

2689

International Journal for Numerical Methods in Engineering
John Wiley and Sons, Inc, 605 3rd Ave, New York, NY 10158. Telephone (212) 850-6515. Telex 12-7063.

Monthly magazine. Contains articles on theory and methods of analyzing geomechanical pheonomena. Price $65.00.

2689.01

International Journal of Ambient Energy
Longman Group Ltd, Longman House, Burnt Mill, Harlow, Essex, England CM20 2JE. Telephone Harlow (0279) 26721. Telex 81259.

Quarterly journal. Provides information on self-regenerating sources of energy and potential uses. Includes information on how new construction can utilize energy sources. Price $72.00 per year.

2690

International Journal of Control
Taylor & Francis Ltd, 4 John St, London, WC1N 2ET, England. Telephone (44) (01) 405-2237.

Monthly journal. Addresses theoretical and practical aspects of machine and process control and automation. Price $465.00 per year. ISSN 0020-7179.

2691

International Journal of Electronics
Taylor & Francis Ltd, 4 John St, London, WC1N 2ET, England. Telephone (44) (01) 405-2237.

Monthly journal. Describes research in active electronic components and systems containing them, especially semiconduction devices and devices using conduction in gases and electrons in a vacuum. Price $340.00 per year. ISSN 0020-7217.

2692

International Journal of Energy Research
John Wiley & Sons, Inc, 605 Third Ave, New York, NY 10158. Telephone (212) 867-9800.

Quarterly magazine. Covers the development and exploitation of traditional and new fuels, and other energy sources. Price $150.00.

2693

International Journal of Health Services
Baywood Publishing Co, Inc, 120 Marine St, Farmingdale, NY 11735. Telephone (516) 249-2464.

Quarterly. Presents information on planning, administration, and evaluation of health services. Price $55.00 per year.

2694

International Journal of Physical Distribution and Materials Management
MCB Publications, 200 Keighley Rd, Bradford, W Yorkshire, BD9 4JQ, England. Telephone 0274 499821.

Three journals plus three monographs per year. Concern managerial effectiveness, particularly in logistics, distribution and materials management. Price $150.00 per year.

2695

International Journal of Production Research
Taylor & Francis Ltd, 4 John St, London, WC1N 2ET, England. Telephone (44) (01) 405-2237.

Bimonthly journal. Deals with research into efficient use of productive resources regardless of technology or product involved. Price $177.00 per year. ISSN 0020-7543.

2696

International Journal of Social Economics
MCB Publications, 200 Keighley Rd, Bradford, W Yorkshire, England, BD9 4JQ. Telephone 0274 499821.

Journal issued six times per year. Discusses economic implications of social theories. Covers socioeconomic aspects of the environment, welfare, income distribution, and demographic trends. Price $168.00 per year.

2697

International Journal of Systems Science
Taylor & Francis Ltd, 4 John St, London, WC1N 2ET, England. Telephone (44) (01) 405-2237.

Monthly magazine. Deals with theory and practice of mathematical modeling, simulation, optimization, and control in regard to biological, economic, industrial, and transportation systems. Price $380.00 per year. ISSN 0020-7721.

2698

International Labour Documentation
International Labour Organization, 1750 New York Ave NW, Suite 330, Washington, DC 20006. Telephone (202) 396-2315.

Monthly report. Contains bibliographic record of current acquisitions of International Labour Organization's Central Library concerning industrial relations, management, manpower planning, and vocational training. Gives abstracts of all titles listed. Price $34.00 per year.

2699

International Labour Organization (ILO) Publications
International Labour Organization, 1750 New York Ave NW, Suite 330, Washington, DC 20006. Telephone (202) 376-2315.

Quarterly booklet. Lists new publications of International Labour Organization including research studies. Notes labor conferences. In 4 languages: English, French, Spanish and German. Free of charge.

2700

International Labour Review
International Labour Organization, 1750 New York Ave NW, Suite 330, Washington, DC 20006. Telephone (202) 376-2315.

Report. Contains articles on international economic and social trends that affect labor. Includes research and book reviews. Price $25.50.

2701

International Law of Development: Basic Documents

Oceana Publications, Inc, 75 Main St, Dobbs Ferry, NY 10522. Telephone (914) 693-5944.

Four-volume set. Contains laws that affect trade and investment for benefit of less developed countries. Includes resolutions adopted at international conferences. Price $180.00. ISBN 0-379-10244-7.

2702

International Licensing

International Licensing Ltd, 92 Cannon Ln, Pinner, Middlesex, England HA5 1HT. Telephone (44) (01) 866-2812.

Monthly publication. Covers business propositions and opportunities with emphasis on the transfer of technology and manufacturing licenses, new developments, agencies and distributorships, joint ventures openings overseas, companies available for acquisition or merger, and industrial projects in the emergent countries. Price $60.00 one year, $96.00 two years, $120.00 three years.

2703

International Literary Market Place

R R Bowker Co, 1180 Ave of the Americas, New York, NY 10036. Order from R R Bowker Co., PO Box 1807, Ann Arbor, MI 48106. Telephone (212) 764-5100.

Annual directory. Provides information about publishers and book trade outside US and Canada. Also lists key people in publishing, book selling, and allied fields. Price $39.50. ISBN 0-8352-1294-7.

2704

International Management

McGraw-Hill Publications Co., 1221 Ave of the Americas, New York, NY 10020. Telephone (212) 997-1221. Telex TWX 7105814879 WUI 62555.

Monthly magazine. Covers international business management methods, systems, and theories. Reviews books. English, Spanish, Arabic, and Farsi editions. Price $40.00 per year, $59.00 for air mail to US and Canada.

2705

International Market Guide— Continental Europe

Dun & Bradstreet, Box 3224, Church St Station, New York, NY 10008. Telephone (212) 285-7346.

Annual book with two supplements per year. Lists over 375,000 European firms in 19 countries. Notes their lines of business and provides general appraisal. Price on request. Available to Dun & Bradstreet subscribers only.

2706

International Market Guide—Latin America

Dun & Bradstreet, Box 3224, Church St Station, New York, NY 10008. Telephone (212) 285-7346.

Biannual book. Contains listing of Latin American firms, their lines of business, and general appraisal. Covers 33 countries. Price on request. Available to Dun & Bradstreet subscribers only.

2707

International Marketing Data & Statistics, **1976–1977 edition**

Euromonitor Publications Ltd, PO Box 115, 41 Russell Sq, London, England WC1B 5DL. Telephone (44) (01) 637-9517.

Handbook. Supplies statistical tables and latest data for 45 countries in Americas, Africa, Asia and Australia. Information is geared to marketing use. Price £30.00 per copy.

2708

International Micrographics Source Book

Microfilm Publishing, Inc, PO Box 313, Wykagyl Station, New Rochelle, NY 10804. Telephone (914) 235-5246.

Biennial book. Acts as source for locating worldwide microfilm services and equipment. Price $49.50.

2709

International Monetary Fund (IMF) Survey

International Monetary Fund, 19th & H St NW, Washington, DC 20431. Telephone (202) 393-6362.

Fortnightly report. Covers International Monetary Fund activities in context of national economic developments and international finance. English, French, and Spanish editions. Price $10.00 per year.

2710

International Monetary Fund Annual Report of the Executive Directors

International Monetary Fund, 19th & H St NW, Washington, DC 20431. Telephone (202) 393-6362.

Annual report. Surveys world economy with emphasis on balance of payments, exchange rates, international liquidity, and trade. Free of charge.

2711

International Monetary Fund Annual Report on Exchange Restrictions

International Monetary Fund, 19th & H St NW, Washington, DC 20431. Telephone (202) 393-6362.

Annual report. Reviews developments that may affect International Monetary Fund member countries' balance of payments. Price first one free. Succeeding copies $5.00.

2712

International Monetary Fund Balance of Payments Yearbook

International Monetary Fund, 19th & H St NW, Washington, DC 20431. Telephone (202) 393-6362.

Annual book plus monthly updates and supplements. Contains balance of payments statistics for more than 100 countries. Price $20.00 per year.

2713

International Monetary Market Yearbook

Chicago Mercantile Exchange, 444 West Jackson Blvd, Chicago, IL 60606. Telephone (312) 648-1000.

Yearbook. Contains data on trading futures in international currencies, US treasury bills, US silver coins, and gold bullion. Price $6.00.

2714

International New Product Newsletter

Transcommunications International Inc, 426 Statler Office Bldg, Boston, MA. 02116. Telephone (617) 426-6647.

Monthly newsletter. Provides information on new industrial products and processes, primarily from foreign sources. Notes products immediately available for manufacture under license. Offers Japanese edition. Price $90.00 per year.

2715

International Occupational Safety and Health Information Centre (CIS)

Commonwealth Dept of Science and Technology, GPO Box 2288U, Melbourne, Vic 3001, Australia. Telephone (61) (03) 665 6438. Telex 30252.

Information service. Presents abstracts of international articles on occupational safety and health. Includes laws, regulations, research, and symposia reports. Provides periodical information sheets on occupational safety topics. Price $160.00 (Australian) per year.

2716
International Oil and Gas Field Records
Petroconsultants SA, 8-10 Rue Muzy, PO Box 228, 1211 Geneva 6, Switzerland. Telephone (36) (22) 8811. Telex 27 763.

Presents data on more than 6000 of world's oil and gas fields, except in US and Canada. Price 150,000 Francs (Swiss).

2717
International Oil News
William F Bland Co, PO Box 1421, Stamford, CT 06904. Telephone (203) 359-1125. Telex 965-952.

Weekly newsletter. Focuses on international oil information. Price $230.00 per year.

2718
International Perspectives
Supply and Services Canada, Canadian Govt Publishing Centre, Hull, Que, Canada K1A 0S9. Telephone (819) 994-3475, 2085.

Bimonthly bulletin. Covers foreign affairs from a Canadian perspective. Price $5.00 per year.

2720
International Petroleum Encyclopedia
Petroleum Publishing Co, PO Box 1941, Houston, TX 77001. Telephone (713) 621-0561.

Annual book. Provides guide to petroleum and gas industry. Reviews OPEC actions, offshore activity, pipeline developments, refining, and price trends. Tables and maps. Price $42.50.

2721
International Philanthropy: A Compilation of Grants by United States Foundations
Foundation Center, 888 7th Ave, New York, NY 10019. Telephone (212) 489-8610.

Book. Describes grants awarded by US foundations in 1976 for international purposes to both domestic and foreign recipients. Statistics. Price $35.00.

2722
International Point & Figure Library
Chart Analysis Ltd, 194-200 Bishopsgate, London, England EC2M 4PE. Telephone (44) (01) 283-4476. Telex 883356.

Weekly book. Provides charts for leading stocks on 18 world stock markets plus Eurobonds and currency exchange rates. Price £300.00 per year.

2724
International Railway Journal (IRJ)
Simmons-Boardman Pub Corp, 350 Broadway, New York, NY 10013. Telephone (212) 966-7700.

Monthly magazine. Provides information about various phases of railroading. Price $17.00 per year.

2725
International Reference Manual
Coopers & Lybrand, 1259 Ave of the Americas, New York, NY. Telephone (914) 489-1100.

Loose-leaf book. Contains information on doing business abroad. Arranged by country. Price available on request.

2726
International Report
Chamber of Commerce of the US, 1615 H St, NW, Washington, DC 20062. Telephone (202) 659-6231.

Monthly newsletter. Reviews legislative policy developments in international trade and investment with emphasis on Chamber's contacts with foreign business and government. Price $30.00 per year.

2727
International Reports
International Reports, Inc, 200 Park Ave S, New York, NY 10003. Telephone (212) 477-0003. Telex RCA 223139 ITT 422963 WU 649160.

Weekly report. Covers international finance including liquidity forecasts, exchange rate projections, evaluations of Euro-Bond Market, interest rate trends, and prospects for gold, silver, and other commodities. Tables. Price $730.00 per year.

2727.01
International Series
Ernst & Whinney, 2000 National City Center, Cleveland, OH 44114. Telephone (216) 861-5000.

Series of reports. Contains analysis of climate for investment and trade in a particular country. Price available on request.

2728
International Statistical Review
Longman Group Ltd, Longman House, Burnt Mill, Harlow, Essex, England CM20 2JE. Telephone Harlow 26721. Telex 81259.

Magazine issued three times per year. Covers statistical techniques and methods. Includes information on macrodescriptive statistics and training of statisticians. Price $30.00 per year. ISSN 0306-7734.

2730
International Studies of Management & Organization
ME Sharpe, Inc, 80 Business Park Dr, Armonk, NY 10504. Telephone (914) 273-1800.

Quarterly journal. Carries translations from scholarly publications on business management published throughout world. Price $127.00 per year.

2731
International Tax Haven Directory
Finax Publications Ltd, 31 Curzon St, London, England W1Y 7AE. Telephone (44) (01) 499-8241. Telex 262570.

Annual book. Offers synopsis of conditions, facilities, and legal requirements in leading tax havens. Includes both personal and corporate tax haven planning. Discusses problems of emigration. Price $22.50 per year.

2732
International Tax Journal
Panel Publishers, 14 Plaza Rd, Greenvale, NY 11548. Telephone (516) 484-0006.

Bimonthly magazine. Discusses US taxation of international operations. Covers research, planning, government compliance, and alternative tax strategies. Price $84.00 per year.

2733
International Tax Report
Inst for International Research Ltd, 70 Warren St, London, England W1P 5PA. Telephone (44) (01) 388 2663. Telex 263504.

Biweekly report. Summarizes and digests international tax news. Recommends worldwide tax opportunities for US corporate taxpayers. Price $325.00 per year.

2734
International Tax Treaties of All Nations
Oceana Publications, Inc, 75 Main St, Dobbs Ferry, NY 10522. Telephone (914) 693-5944.

Twenty volume set. Contains tax treaties published by the United Nations and treaties not yet published. Includes cumulative index. Price $50.00 per volume, $25.00 for index. ISBN 0-379-00725-B and 0-379-20225-5.

2735
International Telecommunications Agreements
Oceana Publications, Inc, 75 Main St, Dobbs Ferry, NY 10522. Telephone (914) 693-5944.

Loose-leaf service. Analyzes international telecommunications agreements. Price $175.00. ISBN 0-379-10045-2.

2735.01
International Tourism Quarterly
Economist Intelligence Unit Ltd, Spencer House, 27 St James's Pl, London, England SW1A 1NT. Order from Economist Intelligence Unit Ltd, 75 Rockefeller Plaza, New York, NY 10019. Telephone (212) 541-5730. Telex 148393.

Quarterly journal. Reports on international tourism trends. Includes statistics. Price $155.00 per year.

2736
International Trade
General Agreement on Tariffs and Trade, Centre William Rappard, 154 rue de Lausanne, 1211 Geneva 21, Switzerland. Telephone 022-31 02 31.

Annual book. Describes international trade during previous year. Analyzes major trends and developments, as well as trade in commodities and trade by major areas and countries. Price $18.00.

2737
International Trade Commission Annual Report
US International Trade Commission, Washington, DC 20436. Telephone (202) 523-0161.

Annual report. Covers public investigations, activities, administration, and finances of US International Trade Commission. Price $1.40 per copy.

2738
International Trade Commission Quarterly Report to the Congress & the East-West Foreign Trade Board on Trade between the US & the Nonmarket Economy Countries
US International Trade Commission, Washington, DC 20436. Telephone (202) 523-0161.

Quarterly report. Provides Congress and East-West Foreign Trade Board with information concerning US trade with nonmarket economy countries. Free of charge.

2739
International Trade Directory
Oregon Economic Development Dept, 155 Cottage St NE, Salem, OR 9l7310. Telephone (503) 373-1200.

Directory. Lists Oregon firms involved in international commerce. Includes type of business and country. Price $10.00.

2739.01
International Trade Financing: Conventional and Nonconventional Practices
Chase Trade Information Corp, 1 World Trade Center, 78th Floor, New York, NY 10048. Telephone (212) 432-8072. Telex RCA 235444.

Book. Provides financing formulas for international trade transactions. Price $360.00.

2740
International Trade News Letter
International Trade News Letter, 160 Broadway, New York, NY 10038. Telephone (212) 964-1484.

Monthly newsletter. Reports on international trade developments including export controls, freight rates, exchange rates, and dumping regulation. Price $15.00 per year.

2740.01
International Trade Reporter's US Import Weekly
Bureau of National Affairs, Inc, 1231 25th St, NW, Washington, DC 20037. Telephone (202) 452-4200.

Loose-leaf books, with weekly updates. Provide reference material on legislative, regulatory, judicial, and industry activities affecting US import policy. Decision section. Reference file. Price $487.00 per year.

2741
International Vending Buyer's Guide & Directory
Vending Times, Inc, 211 E 43 St, New York, NY 10036. Telephone (212) 697-3868.

Annual directory. Provides guide to international vending services. Price $10.00.

2742
International Who's Who
Europa Publications Ltd, 18 Bedford Sq,, London, WC1B 3JN, England. Telephone (44) (01) 580-8236.

Annual book. Contains bibliographies of approximately 15,000 of world's most eminent men and women. Price $90.00.

2743
International Withholding Tax Treaty Guide
Matthew Bender & Co, 235 E 45th St, New York, NY 10017. Telephone (212) 661-5050.

Three-volume loose-leaf report with quarterly supplements. Provides data on international withholding tax rates. Price $100.00 for one volume, $250.00 for complete set.

2744
International Year Book and Statesmen's Who's Who
Kelly's Directories Ltd, Windsor Court, E Grindstead House, E Grindstead, W Sussex, England RH19 1XB. Telephone (44) (01) 0342 26972.

Annual book. Provides information on every country including government, education, and population. Offers biographies of 7000 world leaders and data on United Nations and other international agencies. Price 1980 Edition $45.00 per copy.

2744.01
Internos
Institute of Internal Auditors, Inc, 249 Maitland Ave, Altamonte Springs, FL 32701. Telephone (305) 830-7600.

Monthly newsletter. Covers seminars, conferences, and other Institute of Internal Auditors activities for its membership. Price free of charge.

2745
Interstate Commerce Commission (ICC) Annual Report
US Interstate Commerce Commission, 12th St & Constitution Ave NW, Washington, DC 20423. Order from Superintendent of Documents, US Government Printing Office, Washington, DC 20402. Telephone (202) 783-3238.

Annual report. Summarizes activities of Interstate Commerce Commission. Includes information on railroads, passenger and freight motor carriers, legislation, enforcement, and court actions. Price available on request.

2746
Interstate Commerce Commission (ICC) Permanent Series Reports
Commerce Law Services, Inc, 1747 Pennsylvania Ave NW, Washington, DC 20006. Telephone (202) 466-8166.

Monthly publication. Contains Interstate Commerce Commission decision reports. Provides research and finding aids. Price $350.00 per year.

2747
Interstate Commerce Commission (ICC) Practitioners' Journal
Assn of Interstate Commerce Commission Practitioners, 1112 ICC Bldg, Washington, DC 20423. Telephone (202) 783-9432.

Bimonthly journal. Examines transportation law and related subjects. Price $45.00 per year.

2748
Interstate Commerce Commission Reports, Decisions of the ICC of the US
US Interstate Commerce Commission, 12th St & Constitution Ave, NW, Washington, DC 20423. Order from the Publications Division, Room 1349. Telephone (202) 275-7307 or (800) 424-9312.

Series of reports. Present Interstate Commerce Commission finance, rate of traffic, and motor carrier decisions. Price available on request.

2749
Invention Intelligence
National Research Development Corp of India, 20 Ring Rd, Lajpat Nagar-IV, New Delhi-110024, India. Telephone 693865. Telex 031-3214.

Monthly magazine. Reports on new inventions, products, and processes. Price $12.00 per year.

2750
Invention Management
Inst for Invention & Innovation, Inc, 85 Irving St, Arlington, MA 02174. Telephone (617) 646-0093.

Monthly journal. Presents articles on invention-patent-marketing process plus brief reviews of selected organizations, publications, and coming events. Price $84.00 per year. ISSN 0363-6380.

2751
Inventor
Inst of Patentees and Inventors, Staple Buildings South, 335 High Holborn, London, W.C.1. 7PX. England Telephone (44) (01) 242-7812.

Quarterly journal. Reports topics of interest to inventors. Covers international patent legislation and specific inventions. Includes International Federation of Inventors Associations bulletin. Free of charge to members of IPI.

2752
Inventories of Brass and Copper Wire Mill Shapes
US Dept of Commerce, Bureau of the Census, Washington, DC 20233. Telephone (202) 449-1600.

Monthly, quarterly, and annual reports. Present data on receipts, consumption, and inventories of brass and copper wire mill products, by shape. Show shipments and inventories by type of mill. Price $3.30 per year.

2753
Inventories of Steel Mill Shapes
US Dept of Commerce, Bureau of the Census, Washington, DC 20233. Telephone (202) 449-1600.

Monthly report with annual summary. Contains information on receipts, consumption, and inventories of steel mill shapes. Notes inventories of steel in process and finished steel. Price $3.75 per year.

2754
Inventories, Shipments, and Orders in Manufacturing Industries
Statistics Canada, User Services, Publications Distribution, Ottawa, Ont, Canada K1A 0V7. Telephone (613) 992-3151.

Monthly report. Provides information on values of shipments, new and unfilled orders, and inventories in Canadian manufacturing industries. Includes ratios of value of inventories to shipments. Price $42.00 per year. ISSN 0701-7367.

2754.01
Inventory of Taxes, 1979 edition
Commission of the European Communities, Office for Official Publications of the European Communities, CP 1003, Luxembourg 1, Luxembourg. Telephone (352) 490081. Telex PUBLOF 1325.

Book. Lists duties and taxes in European Community states. Price $30.00.

2755
Investing, Licensing, and Trading Conditions Abroad
Business International Corp, 1 Dag Hammarskjold Plaza, New York, NY 10017. Telephone (212) 750-6300.

Monthly, updated reference service. Rules and laws of 56 countries are interpreted with respect to finance, labor, taxes, remittances, licensing, and trade. Price $685.00 per year.

2756
Investment Advice & Analysis (IAA)
Wright Investors' Service, Wright Bldg, 500 State St, Bridgeport, CT 06604. Telephone (203) 377-9444.

Weekly service. Provides investment recommendations, model trust portfolios, stock market analyses, and data on 100 industry groups. Price $500.00 per quarter.

2757
Investment Advisory Service
Stock Market Analysts Ltd, 58 High St, Esher, Surrey, England KT10 9QY. Telephone ESher 66264.

Monthly service. Offers investment advice. Considers British and foreign stocks, bonds, commodities, gold shares, and equities. Charts and tables. Price available on request.

2758
Investment Africa
United Nations Economic Commission for Africa, Africa Hall, PO Box 3001, Addis Ababa, Ethiopia. Telephone 47200.

Irregular report. Discusses investment opportunities and industrial developments in Africa. Free of charge.

2759
Investment Analyst
Society of Investment Analysts, 211-213 High St, Bromley, Kent, England BR1 1NY. Telephone (44) (01) 464-0811.

Quarterly Journal. Discusses investment and economic topics. Price £10.00.

2760
Investment and Business Opportunity News
Sutton Place Publications, Investments Opportunities Around the World, PO Box 610097, North Miami, FL 33161. Telephone (305) 895-2494.

Bimonthly magazine. Describes business and investment opportunities including franchises and distributorships. Notes conventions and shows. Price $10.00 per year.

2760.01
Investment and Taxation Monograph
Touche Ross International, 1633 Broadway, New York, NY 10019. Telephone (212) 489-1600, ext 4578.

Booklets. Each provides information on individual countries fiscal and corporate laws, investment incentives, taxation, currency regulations, and business entities. Price available on request.

2761
Investment Bulletin
American Inst Counselors, Inc, PO Box 567, Great Barrington, MA 01230. Telephone (413) 528-0140.

Semimonthly newsletter. Features reports on investments, securities, and business trends. Price $25.00 per year.

2762
Investment Dealers' Digest
Investment Dealers' Digest (IDD), Inc, 150 Broadway, New York, NY 10038. Telephone (212) 227-1200.

Weekly magazine. Covers investment news including common stocks, municipal bonds, and foreign securities. Notes corporate financing and market developments. Price $84.00 per year.

2763
Investment Laws of the World
International Centre for Settlement of Investment Disputes, Washington, DC 20433. Order from Oceana Publications, 75 Main St, Dobbs Ferry, NY 10522. Telephone (914) 693-1394.

Ten loose-leaf binders. Cover national legislation and international agreements on foreign investments for 60 developing countries. Price $80.00 per volume.

2764
Investment Laws of the World: Developing Nations
Oceana Publications, Inc, 75 Main St, Dobbs Ferry, NY 10522. Telephone (914) 693-5944.

Eleven loose-leaf binders. Contain national legislation and international agreements on investment laws of 52 developing nations that are parties to ICSID. Price $800.00 per set.

2764.01
Investment Management
International Banktrends, Inc, 910 16th St, NW, Washington, DC 20006. Order from Investment Management, Inc, 910 16th St, NW, Washington DC 20006. Telephone (202) 466-7490.

Biweekly report. Gives general and technical news concerning investment banking and trusts, as well as portfolio management primarily for financial institutions grounded in a professional institutional interest. Price $100.00 per year.

2765
Investment Management Report
11722 Sorrento Valley Rd, Suite I, San Diego, CA 92121. Telephone (714) 755-1327.

Monthly report. Tabulates computerized information for 1400 common stocks. Provides standard value and earnings trend analysis. Includes buy/hold/sell evaluations. Price $144.00 per year.

2766
Investment Quality Trends
Value Trend Analysis, 7440 Girard Ave, Suite 4, La Jolla, CA 92037. Telephone (714) 459-3818.

Semimonthly report plus quarterly reviews. Provide investment advice on 350 selected blue chip stocks. Tables and charts. Price $175.00 per year, $100.00 six months, $15.00 trial subscription.

2767
Investment Statistics: Capital Investment Conditions
Conference Board, Inc, 845 3rd Ave, New York, NY 10022. Telephone (212) 759-0900.

Report. Provides information on capital investment. Price available on request.

2768
Investment Statistics: Service Bulletin
Statistics Canada, User Services, Publications Distribution, Ottawa, Ont, Canada K1A 0V7. Telephone (613) 992-3151.

Report. Provides early release information on Canadian investment statistics. Price $18.00 per year. ISSN 0380-7053.

2769
Investor Relations Newsletter
Enterprise Publications, 20 N Wacker Dr, Chicago, IL 60606. Telephone (312) 332-3571.

Monthly newsletter. Covers current investor relations scene including rule changes, new ideas, communication, and financial reports. Price $70.00 per year.

2770
Investors Chronicle
Financial Times, Business Information Ltd, Bracken House, 10 Cannon St, London, England EC4P 4BY. Order from: Financial Times, Ltd, 75 Rockefeller Plaza, New York, NY 10019. Telephone (44) (01) 248-8000. Telex 886341-2.

Weekly magazine. Reports on British and international investing. Includes articles on stocks, finances, business, and specific companies. Price $80.00 per year.

2771
Investors Chronicle (IC) News Letter
Financial Times, Business Information Ltd, Bracken House, 10 Cannon St, London, England EC4P 4BY. Order from: Financial Times, Ltd, 75 Rockefeller Plaza, New York, NY 10019. Telephone (44) (01) 248-8000. Telex 886341-2.

Weekly newsletter. Provides investment advice on holding, buying, and selling shares in Great Britain. Price $64.00 per year.

2772
Investor's Digest of Canada
Financial Post, 481 University Ave, Toronto, Ont, Canada M5W 1A7. Telephone (416) 596-5670.

Fortnightly newspaper. Analyzes Canadian stock market. Provides financial data for selected corporations. Evaluates specific industries and corporations. Tables. Price $85.00 per year (Canada and the US).

2773
Investors Intelligence
Investors Intelligence, Inc, 2 East Ave, Larchmont, NY 10538. Telephone (914) 834-5181.

Semimonthly report. Evaluates stock market trends, recommends specific stocks, summarizes various investment advisory services' recommendations, and notes insider transactions. Price $60.00 per year.

2774
Investors Research Service
Investors Research Co, PO Box 30, 1900 State St, Santa Barbara, CA 93102. Telephone (805) 965-7078.

Weekly report. Provides stock market analyses. Price $155.00 per year.

2775

Investors Review and Financial World

Morecross Ltd, 100 Fleet St, London, England EC4Y 1DE. Telephone (44) (01) 353-2581/4.

Biweekly magazine. Contains articles about investment and finance in Great Britain and other parts of world. Price £25.00 per year.

2776

Iowa Exporting Companies Directory

Iowa Development Commission, 250 Jewett Bldg, Des Moines, IA 50309. Telephone (515) 281-3585.

Biennial directory. Lists Iowa's manufacturers and products available for overseas marketing. Free of charge.

2776.01

Iowa: Manufacturers Directory, **1979–80**

Manufacturers' News, Inc, 3 Huron St, Chicago, IL 60611. Telephone (312) 337-1084.

Biennial book. Identifies 3,900 Iowa manufacturing companies. Indicates executives and number of employees. Price $26.00.

2777

Iowa World Trade Guide

Iowa Development Commission, 250 Jewett Bldg, Des Moines, IA 50309. Telephone (515) 281-3585.

Book. Provides information on marketing of Iowa's products overseas. Free of charge.

2777.01

IPAA Statistical and Economic Reports

Independent Petroleum Assn of America, 1101 16th St, NW, Washington, DC 20036. Telephone (202) 857-4770.

Series of reports. Covers US oil industry. Includes supply, demand, prices, and drilling and completion costs. Price $100.00 per year.

2778

Iran-American Interchange

Iran-American Chamber of Commerce, Inc, 555 5th Ave, Suite 500, New York, NY 10017. Telephone (212) 986-9560.

Bimonthly newsletter. Reports on Iran's economy, government, foreign trade, and relations with US. Price $42.00 per year.

2779

Iran Economic News

Imperial Embassy of Iran, Economic Section, 5530 Wisconsin Ave NW, Washington, DC 20015. Telephone (301) 654-7930.

Monthly newsletter. Reports on economic developments in Iran. Includes oil, agricultural, trade, and shipping items. Free of charge.

2779.01

Iran Service

Business International Corp, 1 Dag Hammarskjold Plaza, New York, NY 10017. Telephone (212) 750-6300.

Monthly bulletin. Covers the current political and economic outlook in Iran. Price $655.00 per year.

2779.02

Ireland International Reference Manual

Coopers & Lybrand, 1251 Ave of the Americas, New York, NY 10020. Telephone (212) 536-2000.

Booklet. Covers Ireland's business practices and government regulations. Price free of charge.

2780

Irish Export Directory

Irish Export Board, Strand Rd, Sandymount, Dublin 4, Ireland. Order from 10 E 53d St, New York, NY 10022. Telephone (212) 371-3600. Telex 420012 IREXUI.

Directory. Lists 1700 Irish manufacturing companies and products they manufacture. Products are listed in English, French, German, Spanish, and Italian. Price £3.00 per copy.

2782

Iron Age

Chilton Co, Chilton Way, Radnor, PA 19089. Telephone (215) 687-8200.

Magazine published three times per month. Reports on management issues in metalworking industry. Price $50.00.

2783

Iron Age Metalworking International (IAMI)

Chilton Co, Chilton Way, Radnor, PA 19089. Telephone (215) 687-8200.

Monthly magazine. Provides information of interest to international metalworking industry. Multilingual. Price $40.00.

2784

Iron and Steel

Commission of the European Communities, Office for Official Publications of the European Communities, CP 1003, Luxembourg 1, Luxembourg. Telephone (352) 490081. Telex PUBLOF 1325.

Monthly bulletin. Covers iron and steel industries. Price $15.80 per year.

2785

Iron and Steel Castings

US Dept of Commerce, Bureau of the Census, Washington, DC 20233. Telephone (202) 449-1600.

Monthly report with annual summary. Provides data on shipments and unfilled orders of iron and steel castings by type of casting. Annual report includes information on pig iron, fluorspar, and iron and steel scrap. Price $3.35 per year.

2786

Iron and Steel International

IPC Business Press Ltd, 205 E 42nd St, New York, NY 10017. Telephone (212) 867-2080. Telex 238327.

Bimonthly magazine. Contains articles on steel manufacturing, with emphasis on plant engineering and metallurgy. Price $88.40. ISSN 0308-9142.

2787

Iron and Steel: Monthly Statistics

European Community Information Service, 2100 M St, NW, Suite 707, Washington, DC 20037. Telephone (202) 862-9500. Telex 248455.

Monthly report. Gives statistics on iron and steel industries in European Coal and Steel Community countries. Price $15.80 per year.

2789

Irrigation Age

The Webb Co, 1999 Shepard Rd, St Paul, MN 55116. Telephone (612) 690-7200.

Magazine issued nine times per year. Discusses farm and ranch irrigation. Reports on other agricultural issues. Price $8.00 per year.

2790

ISMEC

Data Courier, Inc, 620 S 5th St, Louisville, KY 40202. Telephone (502) 582-4111. Telex 204235.

Monthly journal. Cites and indexes mechanical engineering, production engineering, and engineering management literature. Price $275.00 per year.

2791

Issues in Bank Regulation

Bank Administration Inst, PO Box 500, 303 S Northwest Highway, Park Ridge, IL 60068. Telephone (312) 693-7300.

Quarterly magazine. Contains articles and news items on proposed and existing bank regulations. Includes views of bankers and bank regulators in discussions of regulatory issues. Price $20.00 per year.

2791.01

Italian Illustrators/2

Advertising Trade Publications, Inc, 10 E 39th St, New York, NY 10016. Order from Art Direction Book Co, 10 E 39th St, New York 10016, NY. Telephone (212) 889-6500.

Annual book. Compiles selected advertising illustrations from Italy. Price $39.50.

2792

Italian Trade Topics

Italian Embassy, Commercial Office, 1601 Fuller St NW, Washington, DC 20009. Telephone (202) 328-5500.

Bimonthly report. Covers Italian international trade. Free of charge.

2793

Italy: An Economic Profile

Italian Embassy, Commercial Office, 1601 Fuller St NW, Washington, DC 20009. Telephone (202) 328-5500.

Annual report. Presents economic picture of Italy. Free of charge.

2793.01

Items of Current Interest

National Credit Union Administration, 1776 G St, NW, Washington, DC 20456. Telephone (202) 357-1050.

Weekly newsletter. Discusses activities of National Credit Union Administration including personnel changes and publications. Price free of charge.

2794

Jane's Major Companies of Europe

BPC Publishing Ltd, Paulton House, 8 Sheperdess Walk, London, England N1 7LW. Order from Franklin Watts, 730 5th Ave, New York, NY 10019. Telephone (212) 751-3600.

Annual book. Covers corporations in western Europe, including financial data. Price £25.00. ISSN 0075-3041.

2795

Januz Direct Marketing Letter

Januz Marketing Communications, Inc, PO Box 1000, Lake Forest, IL 60045. Telephone (312) 295-6550.

Monthly newsletter. Presents direct mail marketing ideas, case histories, and special reports. Price $96.00 per year, $192.00 two years, $240.00 three years.

2795.01

Japan Chemical Annual

Chemical Daily Co Ltd, 19-16 Shibaura 3-Chome, Minato-Ku, Tokyo 108, Japan. Telephone (03) 437-9530.

Annual book. Provides overview of chemical industry in Japan and Far East. Includes statistical data and trends for each product. Price $25.00, free of charge for subscribers to Japan Chemical Week.

2795.02

Japan Chemical Directory

Chemical Daily Co Ltd, 19-16 Shibaura 3-Chome, Minato-Ku, Tokyo 108, Japan. Telephone (03) 437-9530.

Annual book. Lists 1600 Japanese organizations connected with chemicals and manufacturing chemical equipment. Includes traders, new products, and associations. Provides product index to manufacturers. Price available on request.

2795.03

Japan Chemical Week

Chemical Daily Co Ltd, 19-16 Shibaura 3-Chome, Minato-Ku, Tokyo 108, Japan. Telephone (03) 437-9530.

Weekly newspaper. Provides statistical data on supply and demand, and production capacities of the chemical industry in Japan and Southeastern Asia. Includes wholesale prices. Printed in English. Price $312.00 per year.

2796

Japan Company Handbook

Oriental Economist, 1-4 Hongokucho, Nihonbashi, Chuo-ku, Tokyo 103, Japan. Telephone (81) (03) 270-4111.

Annual book. Provides data on 1000 major Japanese corporations, including financial and stock information. Forecasts future growth. Price $49.00 Seamail, $65.00 Airmail.

2796.01

Japan Economic Journal

Nihon Keizai Shimbun, Inc, 1-9-5 Otemachi, Chiyoda-ku, Tokyo 100, Japan. Telephone (03) 270-0251.

Weekly journal. Reports on Japanese economic, business, and trade developments. Analyzes political news. Price $81.00 per year.

2797

Japan Economic Yearbook

Oriental Economist, 1-4 Hongokucho, Nihonbashi, Chuo-ku, Tokyo 103, Japan. Telephone (81) (03) 270-4111.

Yearbook. Presents chronology of significant Japanese economic and industrial events. Offers economic forecasts, statistics on gross national product, wages, and prices. Tables, charts, graphs. Price $32.00 seamail, $39.00 airmail.

2797.01

Japanese Breakthroughs

Prestwick International, Inc, PO Box 205, Burnt Hills, NY 12027. Telephone (518) 399-6985.

Annual publication. An English language digest of business opportunities and technological advances from Japan. Contains over 900 items. Price $39.50 US, $45.00 elsewhere.

2797.02

Japanese Economic Service

Data Resources, Inc, 29 Hartwell Ave, Lexington, MA 02173. Telephone (617) 861-0165.

Quarterly report. Provides economic forecast for Japan. Covers variables of consumption, investment, trade, prices, finance, and production. Price available on request.

2798

Japanese Economic Studies

M E Sharpe, Inc, 80 Business Park Dr, Armonk, NY 10504. Telephone (914) 273-1800.

Quarterly journal. Provides translations from Japanese economics publications. Price $127.00 per year.

2800

Japanese Newsletter

Petroleum Pub Co, PO Box 1941, Houston, TX 77001. Telephone (713) 621-0561.

Weekly newsletter. Provides Japanese translation of articles from Oil & Gas Journal. Price fluctuates according to Japanese monetary system.

2801

*Japan External Trade Organization
(JETRO) Business Information Series*
Japan Trade Center, 1221 Ave of the
Americas, New York, NY 10020. Telephone (212) 997-0400.

Series of booklets gives information for
foreign businessmen who want to do business in Japan. Covers Japanese financial
and labor practices, foreign investments,
and international trade. Free of charge.

2802

*Japan External Trade Organization
(JETRO) Marketing Series*
Japan Trade Center, 1221 Ave of the
Americas, New York, NY 10020. Telephone (212) 997-0400.

Series of irregularly issued reports. Covers
Japanese trade, import regulations, consumers, and distribution businessmen.
Free of charge.

2802.01

Japan Fact Book
Dempa Publications, Inc, 380 Madison
Ave, New York, NY 10017. Telephone
(212) 867-0900.

Annual book. Provides information on
Japan's electronics industry. Covers technology, practices, and leading firms. Price
$25.00.

2802.02

Japan International Reference Manual
Coopers & Lybrand, 1251 Ave of the
Americas, New York, NY 10020. Telephone (212) 536-2000.

Booklet. Provides information on Japan's
business practices and government regulations. Price free of charge.

2803

Japan Letter
Asia Letter Ltd, PO Box 54149, Los Angeles, CA 90054. Telephone (213) 322-4222.

Bimonthly newsletter. Covers Japanese
economic and political developments, and
regulations affecting foreign business.
Price $55.00 per year.

2803.01

Japan Stock Journal
Japan Journal, Inc, CPO Box 702, Tokyo,
Japan 100-91. Telephone 667-7651.

Weekly newspaper. Reports on Japanese
financial, business, and stock market developments. Lists stock market transactions. Price $62.95 per year air mail.

2804

Japan Trade and Industry News
Heavy & Chemical Industries News
Agency, Daiichifuji Bldg, 2-15, Kandajinbo-cho, Chiyoda-ku, Tokyo, Japan. Telephone (81) (3) 2303531.

Newsletter published twice a week. Offers
information on Japanese international industrial ventures. Price $334.00.

2805

Jenkins Mobile Industry News Letter
Jenkins Publishing Co, 306 W Main St,
Mascoutah, IL 62258. Telephone (800)
851-4424.

Monthly newsletter. Contains news, laws,
and regulations for mobile home and recreational vehicle industry. Price $36.00
per year.

2806

Jersey Business Review
Creative Research Group, Inc, 82 W
Main St, Ramsey, NJ 07446. Telephone
(201) 327-6010.

Monthly newspaper. Covers business conditions in New Jersey. Price $15.00 per
year.

2807

Jewelers' Circular-Keystone
Chilton Co, Chilton Way, Radnor, PA
19089. Telephone (215) 687-8200.

Monthly magazine. Covers jewelry industry and its outlets. Provides jewelers with
information to improve store management and merchandising. Price $16.00.

2808

Jewelry Newsletter International
Newsletters International, 2600 S
Gessner Rd, Houston, TX 77063. Telephone (713) 783-0100.

Monthly newsletter. Reports on international jewelry business in retail, wholesale, and manufacturing areas. Price
$75.00 per year.

2809

Job Corps Happenings
US Dept of Labor, Employment and
Training Administration, Washington,
DC 20213. Telephone (202) 376-6730.

Monthly newsletter. Reports on various
Job Corps activities. Free of charge.

2810

Job Openings for Economists
American Economic Assn, 1313 21st Ave
S, Nashville, TN 37212. Telephone (615)
322-2595.

Bimonthly report. Lists job vacancies for
economists. Price $12.00 per year.

2811

*Job Openings: Indicator of Occupational
Demand*
Arizona Dept of Economic Security,
Labor Market Information, Research and
Analysis, PO Box 6123, Phoenix, AZ
85005. Telephone (602) 255-3871.

Annual publication. Identifies occupational supply/demand conditions of job
openings most frequently listed with Arizona Job Service. Provides information
for Maricopa and Pima counties and balance of state. Price free of charge.

2811.01

Job Safety and Health
Bureau of National Affairs, Inc, 1231
25th St, NW, Washington, DC 20037.
Telephone (202) 452-4200.

Loose-leaf notebook, with biweekly updates. Provides guidance on job safety,
and health standards and practices, as
well as their impact on employee relations. Gives full text on laws, standards,
programs, and requirements. Index. Price
$215.00 per year.

2812

Job Safety & Health Report
Business Publishers, Inc, PO Box 1067,
Silver Spring, MD 20910. Telephone
(301) 587-6300.

Biweekly newsletter. Covers affairs of Occupational Safety and Health Administration. Price $115.00 per year.

2813

Jobson's Mining Year Book
Dun & Broadstreet (Australia) Pty, Ltd,
GPO Box 425G, Melbourne, Vic 3001,
Australia. Telephone (61) (03) 699-2500..

Annual book. Provides information on all
mining and oil exploration companies
listed on Australian stock exchanges, plus
major unlisted companies. Reviews mineral trends and gives industry statistics.
Price $55.00 (Australian).

2814

Jobson's Year Book
Dun & Broadstreet (Australia) Pty Ltd,
GPO Bx 425G, Melbourne, Vic 3001,
Australia. Telephone (61) (03) 699-2500.

Annual book. Lists all public companies on Australian and New Zealand stock exchanges plus other important companies. Gives details on directors, capital structure, and financial statements. Price $95.00 (Australian).

2815
Johannesburg Stock Exchange Monthly Bulletin
Johannesburg Stock Exchange, PO Box 1174, Johannesburg, South Africa 2000. Telephone (27) (11) 833-56580.

Monthly report. Contains statistical information on all companies listed on Johannesburg Stock Exchange including dividend information, number of shares traded, and stock prices. Price R15-00 per year (surface mail), R32-10 per year (air mail).

2816
Johnson's Investment Company Service
Johnson's Charts, Inc, 545 Elmwood Ave, Buffalo, NY 14222. Telephone (716) 884-2500.

Annual book plus quarterly updates. Charts indicate long-term trends for common stocks, corporate bonds, mutual funds, money market funds, US savings bonds, and other economic indicators. Price $175.00.

2816.01
Johnson Survey
John S Harold, Inc, 35 Mason St, Greenwich, CT 06830. Telephone (203) 869-2585.

Monthly publication. Provides data and comments on oil, gold and other stocks. Charts and tables. Price $78.00 per year.

2817
Journal of Accountancy
American Inst of Certified Public Accountants, 1211 Ave of the Americas, New York, NY 10036. Telephone (212) 575-6200.

Monthly magazine. Covers accountancy and related business subjects. Price $20.00 per year.

2817.01
Journal of Accounting and Economics
North-Holland Publishing Co, PO Box 211, 1000 AE Amsterdam, The Netherlands. Order from Elsevier/North-Holland, Inc, 52 Vanderbilt Ave, New York, NY 10017. Telephone (212) 867-9040.

Journal issued three times per year. Reports on applications of economic theory to accounting problems. Price $65.50 per year. ISSN 0165-4101.

2817.02
Journal of Accounting, Auditing and Finance
Warren, Gorham & Lamont, Inc, 210 S St, Boston, MA 02111. Telephone (800) 225-2263.

Quarterly journal. Provides articles on accounting, auditing, and financial concerns. Includes features on pension funds, executive compensation, and corporate developments. Price $42.00 per year.

2818
Journal of Accounting Research
University of Chicago, Graduate School of Business, 1101 E 58th St, Chicago, IL 60637. Telephone (312) 753-3600.

Semiannual magazine with annual supplement. Carries accounting research material. Covers related management science and operations research developments. Price $30.00 per year.

2819
Journal of Advertising
Brigham Young University, c/o H Keith Hunt, 395 JKB, Provo, UT 84602. Telephone (801) 378-2435.

Quarterly journal. Presents articles on advertising research. Discusses psychological and philosophical aspects of communication. Price $16.00 per year.

2820
Journal of Advertising Research
Advertising Research Foundation, 3 E 54th St, New York, NY 10022. Telephone (212) 751-5656.

Bimonthly magazine. Covers advertising and marketing issues. Emphasizes documented reports rather than theoretical discussion. Price $50.00 airmail, $86,00 foreign per year.

2823
Journal of Applied Management
Business Science Corp, 1700 Ygnacio Valley Rd, Suite 222, Walnut Creek, CA 94598. Telephone (415) 939-1200.

Bimonthly magazine. Written by professional mamagement consultants for owners and executives in small to medium-size corporations. Offers how-to information on business and management. Price $28.00 per copy.

2823.01
Journal of Applied Systems Analysis
University of Lancaster, Dept of Systems, Bailrigg, Lancaster, England LA1 4YR. Telephone Lancaster (STD 0524) 65201. ext 4487.

Annual journal. Presents research on the development of systems concepts and methodologies. Includes information on applications. Price $36.00. ISSN 0308-9541.

2823.02
Journal of Banking & Finance
North-Holland Publishing Co, PO Box 211, 1000 AE Amsterdam, The Netherlands. Order from Elsevier/North-Holland, Inc, 52 Vanderbilt Ave, New York, NY 10017. Telephone (212) 867-9040.

Quarterly journal. Contains research on financial institutions and markets. Price $117.00 per year. ISSN 0378-4266.

2826
Journal of Business
Seton Hall University, School of Business Administration, South Orange, NJ 07079. Telephone (628) 762-9000.

Semiannual magazine. Covers business-related subjects such as accounting, multinational corporations, management, and capital resources. Free of charge.

2827
Journal of Business
University of Chicago Press, 5801 S Ellis Ave, Chicago, IL 60637. Telephone (312) 753-3347.

Quarterly journal. Presents business-related articles on various subjects. Price $20.00 per year. ISSN 0021-9398.

2828
Journal of Business Communication
American Business Communication Assn, University of Illinois, 911 S 6th St Champaign, IL 61820. Telephone (217) 333-7891.

Quarterly journal. Covers topics relevant to research in business communication. Price $25.00 per year.

2829
Journal of Business Education
Heldref Publications, 4000 Albemarle St NW, Washington, DC 20016. Telephone (202) 362-6445.

Monthly magazine. Is for teachers of business subjects. Covers recent research and books. Price $12.00 individuals, $18.00 institutions.

2830
Journal of Business Finance and Accounting
Basil Blackwell Publisher, 108 Cowley Rd, Oxford, England OX4 1JF. Telephone Oxford (STD 0865) 7/2216.

Quarterly magazine. Covers business financing, capital investment, and corporate financial policy. Price $55.00 per year. ISSN 0306-686X.

2831
Journal of Business Law
Sweet & Maxwell/Stevens Periodicals, 11 New Fetter Ln, London, England EC4P 4EE. Order from Carswell Co Ltd, 2330 Midland Ave, Agincourt, Ont, Canada MIS 1P7. Telephone England (44) (01) 5839855. Telex 263398. Canada (416) 291-8421.

Quarterly journal. Pertains to law's connection to conduct of business. Contains articles, index, and book reviews. Special sections emphasize British, European, and overseas business law. Price $79.00 per year.

2831.01
Journal of Business Research
North-Holland Publishing Co, PO Box 211, 1000 AE Amsterdam, The Netherlands. Order from Elsevier/North-Holland, Inc, 52 Vanderbilt Ave, New York, NY 10017. Telephone (212) 867-9040.

Quarterly journal. Reports on business research and its applications. Price $44.00 per year. ISSN 0148-2963.

2831.02
Journal of Business Strategy
Warren, Gorham & Lamont, Inc, 210 S St, Boston, MA 02111. Telephone (617) 423-2020. (800) 225-2363.

Quarterly journal. Covers business management planning techniques. Provides studies of specific applications and major strategy components. Price $48.00 per year.

2832
Journal of Collective Negotiations in the Public Sector
Baywood Publishing Co, Inc, 120 Marine St, Farmingdale, NY 11735. Telephone (516) 249-2464.

Quarterly. Focuses on public sector labor relations. Covers collective bargaining procedures. Price $51.00 per year.

2833
Journal of College Placement
College Placement Council, Inc, PO Box 2263, Bethlehem, PA 18001. Telephone (215) 868-1421.

Quarterly magazine. Covers professional placement-recruitment. Price $20.00 subscription, $6.00 per copy.

2834
Journal of Commerce
Journal of Commerce Ltd, 2000 W 12th Ave, Vancouver, BC Canada V6J 2G2. Telephone (604) 731-1171. Telex 04-51158.

Weekly journal. Reports on western Canada's business news including bids and awards, incorporations, and construction activity. Price $145.00 per year.

2835
Journal of Commerce
Southam Communications Ltd, 1450 Don Mills Rd, Don Mills, Ont, Canada M3B 2X7. Order from Southam Communications Ltd, 2000 W 12th ave, Vancouver, BC Canada V6J 2G2. Telephone (604) 731-1171. Telex 04 51158.

Twice weekly newspaper. Covers business and construction in western Canada. Price available on request.

2836
Journal of Commerce and Commercial
Twin Coast Newspapers, Inc, 100 Wall St, New York, NY 10005. Telephone (212) 425-1616.

Daily newspaper. Covers commerce and general business news. Price available on request.

2837
Journal of Commerce Review
Daily Journal Publications, 210 Spring St, Los Angeles, CA 90012. Telephone (213) 624-3111.

Newspaper published daily (except weekends). Lists southern California real estate notices, business sales leads, and credit information. Includes general business news. Price $45.00 per year.

2838
Journal of Commercial Bank Lending
Robert Morris Associates, 1616 PNB Bldg, Philadelphia, PA 19107. Telephone (215) 665-2850.

Monthly magazine. Publishes articles on subjects related to commercial bank lending and credit. Price $19.50 per year.

2839
Journal of Common Market Studies
Basil Blackwell Publisher, 108 Cowley Rd, Oxford, England OX4 1JF. Telephone Oxford (STD 0865) 722146.

Quarterly magazine. Contains theoretical and analytical articles on economic and political integration in Europe and the rest of the world. Price $49.50 per year. ISSN 0021-9886.

2840
Journal of Consumer Affairs
University of Wisconsin Press, Journal Div, 114 N Murray St, Madison, WI 53715. Telephone (608) 262-5839.

Biannual magazine. Reports on consumer research and public issues that affect consumers. Includes book reviews. Price $25.00 individuals, $40.00 institutions per year. ISSN 0022-0078.

2841
Journal of Consumer Credit Management
Society of Certified Consumer Credit Executives, 7405 University Dr, St Louis, MO 63130. Telephone (314) 727-4045.

Quarterly journal. Reviews developments in credit. Price $8.00 per year.

2842
Journal of Contemporary Business
University of Washington, Graduate School of Business Administration, Mackenzie Hall, Seattle, WA 98195. Telephone (206) 543-4598.

Quarterly magazine. Presents articles on national and international business issues. Includes topics on business deregulation, corporate politics, accounting, commercial banks, and small businesses. Price $15.00 per year.

2843
Journal of Corporate Taxation
Warren, Gorham & Lamont, Inc, 210 South St, Boston, MA 02111. Telephone (617) 423-2020.

Quarterly journal. Pertains to corporate taxation. Price $48.00 per year.

2844
Journal of Dairy Research
Cambridge University Press, 32 E 57th St, New York, NY 10022. Telephone (212) 688-8885.

Magazine issued three times per year. Offers material on all aspects of dairy science. Price $128.00 per year.

2844.01
Journal of Development Economics
North-Holland Publishing Co, PO Box 211, 1000 AE Amsterdam, The Netherlands. Order from Elsevier/North-Holland, Inc, 52 Vanderbilt Ave, New York, NY 10017. Telephone (212) 867-9040.

Bimonthly journal. Contains information on economic development topics. Includes articles on specific countries. Price $167.00 per year. ISSN 0304-3878.

2844.02
Journal of Documentation
Aslib, 3 Belgrave Sq, London, England. SW1X 8PL. Telephone (44) (01) 235-5050. Telex 23667.

Journal. Covers documentation, librarianship, and information science. Presents new information management techniques. Price £44.00. ISSN 0022-0418.

2845
Journal of Econometrics
North-Holland Publishing Co, PO Box 211, 1000 AE Amsterdam, The Netherlands. Order from Elsevier/North-Holland, Inc, 52 Vanderbilt Ave, New York, NY 10017. Telephone (212) 867-9040.

Journal published nine times per year. Offers research in theoretical and applied econometrics. Price $245.50 per year. ISSN 0304-4076.

2845.01
Journal of Economic Affairs
Basil Blackwell Publisher, 108 Cowley Rd, Oxford, England OX4 1JF. Telephone Oxford (STD 0865) 722146.

Quarterly publication. Contains articles on wide range of economic issues by authors from diverse academic and professional backgrounds. Price $24.50 per year.

2845.02
Journal of Economic Behavior and Organization
North-Holland Publishing Co, PO Box 211, 1000 AE Amsterdam, The Netherlands. Order from Elsevier/North-Holland, Inc, 52 Vanderbilt Ave, New York, NY 10017. Telephone (212) 867-9040.

Quarterly journal. Contains theoretical and empirical research on economic decision, organization, and behavior. Price $78.50 per year. ISSN 0167-2681.

2845.03
Journal of Economic Dynamics and Control
North-Holland Publishing Co, PO Box 211, 1000 AE Amsterdam, The Netherlands. Order from Elsevier/North-Holland, Inc, 52 Vanderbilt Ave, New York, NY 10017. Telephone (212) 867-9040.

Quarterly journal. Contains articles on economic dynamics and control theory. Includes information on stability, differential games, and measurement. Price $78.50 per year. ISSN 0165-1889.

2846
Journal of Economic Issues
Assn for Evolutionary Economics, Dept of Economics, 343 College of Business Administration, University of Nebraska-Lincoln, Lincoln, NE 68588. Telephone (402) 472-3867/2332.

Quarterly journal. Contains articles on economic institutions from point of view of economic theory and social science disciplines. Price $20.00 per year.

2847
Journal of Economic Literature
American Economic Assn, 1313 21st Ave S, Nashville, TN 37212. Telephone (615) 322-2595.

Quarterly journal. Contains abstracts of articles from US and foreign economic periodicals. Includes book reviews, lists of new books and articles on economic topics. Price $100.00 per year (with American Economic Review), $15.00 per back copy.

2848
Journal of Economics and Business
Temple University, School of Business Administration, Philadelphia, PA 19122. Telephone (215) 787-8101.

Triannual publication. Presents economic, business, and related research. Subjects include applied economics, money and credit, international business, production and disribution, and management theory. Price $13.00 per year.

2850
Journal of Educational Technology Systems
Baywood Publishing Co, Inc, 120 Marine St, Farmingdale, NY 11735. Telephone (516) 249-2464.

Quarterly. Discusses application of computers and technology to education. Provides information on hardware and software. Notes classroom experimentation. Price $51.00 per year.

2850.01
Journal of Electronic Engineering
Dempa Publications, Inc, 380 Madison Ave, New York, NY 10017. Telephone (212) 867-0900.

Monthly journal. Covers electronic engineering industry. Reports on measuring instruments, components, semiconductors, and microprocessors. Price $65.00 per year air mail.

2851
Journal of Employment Counseling
American Personnel and Guidance Assn, 2 Skyline Place, Suite 400, 5203 Leesburg Pike, Falls Church, VA 22041. Telephone (803) 820-4700.

Quarterly journal. Offers articles on professional development of employment counselors. Price $11.00 per year.

2852
Journal of Environmental Systems
Baywood Publishing Co, Inc, 120 Marine St, Farmingdale, NY 11735. Telephone (516) 249-2464.

Quarterly. Deals with environmental management, protection, design, and related laws. Price $51.00 per year.

2853
Journal of European Industrial Training
MCB Publications, 200 Keighley Rd, Bradford, W Yorkshire, England BD9 4JQ. Telephone 0274 499821.

Five journals and three monographs per year. Reports on management training programs and industrial relations. Price $150.00 per year.

2854
Journal of Finance
American Finance Association, Graduate School of Business Administration, New York University, 100 Trinity Place, New York, NY 10006. Telephone (212) 285-6040.

Report issued five times per year. Covers academic subjects in the field of finance. Price $22.50 per year. ISSN 0022-1082.

2855
Journal of Financial & Quantitative Analysis
University of Washington, Graduate School of Business Administration, Mackenzie Hall, Seattle, WA 98195. Telephone (206) 543-4598.

Publication issued five times per year. Presents advanced research in finance. Discusses new theories and personal and corporate financial management. Price $17.50 per year individuals, $25.00 per year institutions.

2855.01
Journal of Financial Economics
North-Holland Publishing Co, PO Box 211, 1000 AE Amsterdam, The Netherlands. Order from Elsevier/North-Holland, Inc, 52 Vanderbilt Ave, New York, NY 10017. Telephone (212) 867-9040.

Quarterly journal. Contains research on financial economics, with emphasis on analytical, mathematical, and empirical analyses. Price $82.00 per year. ISSN 0304-405X.

2856
Journal of Financial Education
Illinois State University, Department of Finance, Williams Hall, Normal, IL 61761. Telephone (309) 436-6675.

Annual journal. Publishes articles related to teaching finance in universities. Price $5.00 per year individuals, $6.00 per year libraries.

2857
Journal of Financial Planning
Panel Publishers, 14 Plaza Rd, Greenvale, NY 11548. Telephone (516) 484-0006.

Quarterly magazine. Covers business and personal financial planning including estate planning, taxation, investments, securities, and insurance. Price $36.00 per year.

2858
Journal of Futures Markets
John Wiley & Sons, Inc, 605 3rd Ave, New York, NY 10158. Order from John Wiley & Sons, Inc, 1 Wiley Dr, Somerset, NJ 08773. Telephone (201) 469-4400. Telex 833 434. Cable JON WILE SMOT.

Monthly journal. Contains articles on financial futures, commodity forecasting techniques, corporate hedging strategies, tax and accounting implications of hedging, analyses of commodity trading systems, regulatory philosophies, and other topics pertinent to futures trading. Price $100.00 per year.

2859
Journal of General Management
Mercury House Business Publications Ltd, Mercury House, Waterloo Rd, London, England SE1 8UL. Telephone (44) (01) 928-3388.

Quarterly magazine. Carries material on administration amd management. Price £ 12.00 per year.

2860
Journal of Human Resources
University of Wisconsin Press, Journal Div, 114 N Murray St, Madison, WI 53715. Telephone (608) 262-4952.

Quarterly magazine. Focuses on human resources including manpower training, productivity, and employment opportunities. Price $13.00 individuals, $28.00 institutions per year. ISSN 0022-166X.

2861
Journal of Industrial Economics
Basil Blackwell Publisher, 108 Cowley Rd, Oxford, England 0X4 1JF. Telephone Oxford (STD 0865) 722146.

Quarterly. Concerns individual business and its relation to the economy including price, costs, finance, location, and productivity. Price $45.00 per year. ISSN 0022-1821.

2862
Journal of Insurance
Insurance Information Inst, 110 William St, New York, NY 10038. Telephone (212) 233-7650.

Bimonthly journal. Contains articles on property and liability insurance. Reviews recent books. Price $6.00 per year.

2863
Journal of International Business Studies
Rutgers University, Graduate School of Management, 92 New St, Newark, NJ 07102. Telephone (201) 648-5074.

Published three times a year. Studies international business. Includes annual reports, news about multinational subsidiaries, foreign exchange markets, and expatriate Americans. Price $30.00 per year, $35.00 for overseas.

2863.01
Journal of International Economics
North-Holland Publishing Co, PO Box 211, 1000 AE Amsterdam, The Netherlands. Order from Elsevier/North-Holland, Inc, 52 Vanderbilt Ave, New York, NY 10017. Telephone (212) 867-9040.

Quarterly journal. Reports on international economic research. Covers international trade theory and balance of payments analyses. Price $117.00 per year. ISSN 0022-1996.

2864
Journal of International Law & Economics
George Washington University, National Law Center, 2000 H St NW, Room B-01, Washington, DC 20052. Telephone (202) 676-7164.

Journal issued three times per year. Presents material related to international law and economics. Price $14.00 per year.

2865
Journal of Investment Finance/National Spot Market Weekly Price Bulletin
American Assn of Commodity Traders, 10 Park St, Concord, NH 03301. Telephone (603) 224-2376.

Weekly newsletter. Covers currency market developments. Lists spot and forward prices, option premiums, and striking prices. Price $10.00 per year.

2866
Journal of Management Studies
Basil Blackwell Publisher, 108 Cowley Rd, Oxford, England 0X4 1JF. Telephone Oxford (STD 0865) 722146.

Magazine published three times a year. Covers a wide range of disciplines such as advertising, financial institutions, personnel studies, marketing, management. Price $65.00 per year. ISSN 0022-2380.

2867
Journal of Marketing
American Marketing Assn, 222 S Riverside Plz, Chicago, IL 60606. Telephone (312) 648-0536.

Quarterly journal. Furnishes articles concerned with the practice and teaching of marketing. Price $12.00 per year member, $24.00 nonmember.

2868
Journal of Marketing Research
American Marketing Assn, 222 S Riverside Plz, Chicago, IL 60606. Telephone (312) 648-0536.

Quarterly magazine. Reports on fundamental research in marketing. Price $15.00 per year member, $30.00 pr year nonmember.

2868.01
Journal of Mathematical Economics
North-Holland Publishing Co, PO Box 211, 1000 AE Amsterdam, The Netherlands. Order from Elsevier/North-Holland, Inc, 52 Vanderbilt Ave, New York, NY 10017. Telephone (212) 867-9040.

Journal published three times per year. Discusses mathematical economics. Includes surveys of existing work, as well as new research. Price $82.00 per year. ISSN 0304-4068.

2868.02
Journal of Monetary Economics
North-Holland Publishing Co, PO Box 211, 1000 AE Amsterdam, The Netherlands. Order from Elsevier/North-Holland, Inc, 52 Vanderbilt Ave, New York, NY 10017. Telephone (212) 867-9040.

Bimonthly journal. Publishes research on monetary economics. Includes information on banking policies and credit markets. Price $167.00 per year. ISSN 0304-3923.

2869
Journal of Money, Credit & Banking
Ohio State University Press, 2070 Neil Ave, Columbus, OH 43210. Telephone (614) 422-6930.

Quarterly journal. Covers money and banking, credit markets, and fiscal policy. Price $20.00 per year.

2870
Journal of Non-White Concerns in Personnel and Guidance
American Personnel and Guidance Assn, 2 Skyline Place, Suite 400, 5203 Leesburg Pike, Falls Church, VA 22041. Telephone (703) 820-4700.

Quarterly magazine. Covers minority interests and experiences in counseling, psychology, guidance, and personnel. Price $10.00 per year.

2870.01
Journal of Operations & Production Management
MCB Publications, 200 Keighly Rd, Bradford, W Yorkshire, England BD9 4JQ. Telephone 0274-499821.

Journal issued three times per year. Covers operations management topics, including computer applications, performance measurement, and capacity planning. Price $84.00 per year.

2871
Journal of Organizational Communication
International Assn of Business Communicators, 870 Market St, Suite 940, San Francisco, CA 94102. Telephone (415) 433-3400.

Quarterly journal. Concentrates on concepts, trends, and case studies in business and organizational communication. Price included in membership fees.

2872
Journal of Pension Planning and Compliance
Panel Publishers, 14 Plaza Rd, Greenvale, NY 11548. Telephone (516) 484-0006.

Bimonthly magazine. Deals with ERISA plans, establishment, and administration. Notes Internal Revenue Service requirements. Price $60.00 per year.

2872.01
Journal of Philippine Development
Republic of the Philippines, National Economic and Development Authority, PO Box 1116, Manila, Philippines. Order from National Economic and Development Authority Economic Information Staff, Circulation Unit, Government Center, EDSA, Diliman, Quezon City, Philippines.

Semiannual journal. Provides technical information on Philippine economic development. Price available on request.

2872.02
Journal of Policy Modeling
North-Holland Publishing Co, PO Box 211, 1000 AE Amsterdam, The Netherlands. Order from Elsevier/North-Holland, Inc, 52 Vanderbilt Ave, New York, NY 10017. Telephone (212) 867-9040.

Journal published three times per year. Emphasizes formal modeling techniques used in economic decision making. Price $45.00 per year. ISSN 0161-8938.

2873
Journal of Political Economy
University of Chicago Press, 5801 S Ellis Ave, Chicago, IL 60637. Telephone (312) 753-3347.

Bimonthly journal. Presents papers on political science as related to economics. Price $30.00 per year. ISSN 0022-3808.

2874
Journal of Portfolio Management
Institutional Investor, Inc, 488 Madison Ave, New York, NY 10022. Telephone (212) 832-8888.

Quarterly report. Contains articles on stocks, bonds, and other aspects of investment portfolio management. Price $80.00 per year.

2875
Journal of Property Management
Inst of Real Estate Management, 430 N Michigan Ave, Chicago, IL 60611. Telephone (312) 440-8615.

Bimonthly magazine. Covers real estate management. Includes material on residential and commercial buildings, mortgage financing, and taxation. Price $15.00 per year.

2875.01
Journal of Public Economics
North-Holland Publishing Co, PO Box 211, 1000 AE Amsterdam, The Netherlands. Order from Elsevier/North-Holland, Inc, 52 Vanderbilt Ave, New York, NY 10017. Telephone (212) 867-9040.

Bimonthly journal. Contains research articles on public sector economics, with emphasis on the application of modern economic theory. Price $182.00 per year. ISSN 0047-2727.

2876
Journal of Purchasing & Materials Management
National Assn of Purchasing Management, Publication Sales Office, 49 Sheridan Ave, Albany, NY 12210. Telephone (212) 285-2550.

Quarterly magazine. Reports on purchasing and materials management subjects. Includes information on inventories, information systems, uniform commercial code requirements, and commodity trends. Price $10.00 per year.

2877
Journal of Quality Technology
American Society for Quality Control, 161 W Wisconsin Ave, Milwaukee, WI 53203. Telephone (414) 272-8575.

Quarterly report. Contains technical articles on quality control techniques. Price $16.00 per year. ISSN 0022-4065.

2878
Journal of Real Estate Taxation
Warren, Gorham & Lamont, Inc, 210 South St, Boston, MA 02111. Telephone (617) 423-2020.

Quarterly magazine. Covers real estate tax topics including accounting, depreciation, real estate investment trusts, and effects of Tax Reform Act of 1976. Price $48.00 per year.

2879

Journal of Regional Science

Regional Science Research Inst, Wentworth Bldg, 256 North Pleasant St, Amherst, MA 01002. Telephone (413) 256-8526.

Quarterly journal. Focuses on regional and urban problems and methods of analysis. Contains articles on economic development, industrial location, transportation, housing, population, migration, employment, wage levels and income, land use and value, public investment and environmental quality. Price $29.00 per year.

2880

Journal of Reprints for Antitrust Law and Economics

Federal Legal Publications, Inc, 157 Chambers St, New York, NY 10007. Telephone (212) 243-5775.

Semiannual journal. Reprints articles on antitrust law and industrial economics. Includes bibliography. Price $45.00 per year.

2881

Journal of Retailing

New York University, Inst of Retail Management, 202 Tisch Hall, Washington Sq, New York, NY 10003. Telephone (212) 598-2286.

Quarterly journal. Discusses retailing practices, problems, and research. Price $15.00 per year.

2882

Journal of Risk and Insurance

American Risk and Insurance Assn, Dr. R E Johnson, 297 Brooks Hall, The University of Georgia, Athens, GA 30602. Telephone (404) 542-4290.

Quarterly magazine. Offers scholarly reports on current research, management practices, and theoretical concepts relevant to insurance. Price $35.00 per year. ISSN 0022-4367.

2884

Journal of Small Business Management

West Virginia University, Bureau of Business Research, Morgantown, WV 26506. Telephone (304) 293-5837.

Quarterly magazine. Reports on small business management. Includes information on advertising and public relations, minority business, accounting, franchising, and Small Business Institute. Contains features and book reviews. Price $10.00 per year. ISSN 0047-2778.

2886

Journal of Systems Management

Assn for Systems Management, 24587 Bagley Rd, Cleveland, OH 44138. Telephone (216) 243-6900.

Monthly magazine. Interprets techniques in information systems management field. Price $17.50 per year.

2887

Journal of Taxation

Warren, Gorham & Lamont, Inc, 210 S St, Boston, MA 02111. Telephone (800) 225-2263.

Monthly journal. Furnishes in-depth analyses of tax developments for specialists in field. Price $60.00 per year.

2888

Journal of Technical Writing and Communication

Baywood Publishing Co, Inc, 120 Marine St, Farmingdale, NY 11735. Telephone (516) 249-2464.

Quarterly. Discusses technical writing. Considers relationship of graphic arts to technical communication. Price $45.00 per year.

2888.01

Journal of the American Society for Information Science

John Wiley & Sons, Inc, 605 3rd Ave, New York, NY 10158. Order from John Wiley & Sons, Inc, 1 Wiley Dr, Somerset, NJ 08773. Telephone (201) 469-4400. Telex 833 434. Cable JON WILE SMOT.

Bimonthly journal. Considers theory and practice in information science and related fields for international audience. Covers computer technology, operations research, librarianship, communications management, information storage and retrieval, reprography, and systems design. Price $55.00.

2889

Journal of the American Statistical Assn

American Statistica Assn, 806 15th St NW, Suite 640, Washington, DC 20005. Telephone (202) 393-3253.

Quarterly journal. Provides selected papers on theoretical and applied statistics. Book reviews. Price $45.00 per year.

2889.01

Journal of the Asset-Based Financial Services Industry

National Commercial Finance Conference, Inc, One Penn Plaza, New York, NY 10001. Telephone (212) 594-3490.

Bimonthly magazine. Covers developments in the asset-based financial services industry (commercial financing and factoring). Includes legislation, banking, and commerce trends. Price $40.00 per year.

2889.02

Journal of the Association for Computing Machinery

Assn for Computing Machinery, 1133 Ave of the Americas, New York, NY 10036. Telephone (212) 265-6300.

Quarterly journal. Offers theoretical papers in computer science. Includes research on computer organization and design, database theory, and operations research. Price $40.00 per year.

2889.03

Journal of the Electronics Industry

Dempa Publications, Inc, 380 Madison Ave, New York, NY 10017. Telephone (212) 867-0900.

Monthly journal. Reports on electronics industry. Provides information on technological advances, production and sales statistics, and trade. Price $92.00 per year air mail.

2890

Journal of the Fisheries Research Board of Canada

Supply and Services Canada, Canadian Govt Publishing Centre, Hull, Que, Canada K1A 0S9. Telephone (819) 994-3475, 2085.

Monthly magazine. Presents information on Canadian fisheries. Price $56.40 per year.

2891

Journal of the Glasgow Chamber of Commerce

Glasgow Chamber of Commerce, 30 George Sq, Glasgow, Scotland G2 1EQ. Telephone (44) (041) 2042121. Telex 77667.

Monthly journal. Contains articles on business in Scotland, specific companies, commercial law, and Chamber of Commerce news. Free to members.

2892

Journal of the Inst of Actuaries

Inst of Actuaries, Staple Inn Hall, High Holborn, London, England WC1V 7QJ. Telephone (44) (01) 242-0106.

Journal issued three times per year. Covers actuarial aspects of life assurance, pensions, investment, mortality statistics, and related matters. Price £4.00 each.

2893
Journal of the Inst of Bankers
Inst of Bankers, 10 Lombard St, London, England EC3V 9AS. Telephone (44) (01) 623-3531.

Bimonthly journal. Discusses British and international banking developments. Price £9.00 per year.

2894
Journal of the Marine Biological Association of the UK
Cambridge University Press, 32 E 57th St, New York, NY 10022. Telephone (212) 688-8885.

Quarterly journal. Presents material on all aspects of marine biology. Price $218.00 per year.

2895
Journal of the Market Research Society
Market Research Society, 15 Belgrave Sq, London, England SW1X 8PF. Telephone (44) (01) 235-4709.

Quarterly magazine. Publishes original contributions on market research. Price £15.00 per year.

2896
Journal of the Operational Research Society
Pergamon Press, Inc, Maxwell House, Fairview Park, Elmsford, NY 10523. Telephone (914) 592-7700. Telex 13-7328.

Monthly journal. Publishes articles relevant to theory, practice, history, or methodology of operations research. Emphasizes practical case studies. Price $115.00 per year.

2897
Journal of the Textile Institute
Textile Institute, 10 Blackfriars St, Manchester, England M3 5DR. Telephone (061) 834-8457.

Monthly publication. Contains scholarly papers from textile development workers, scientists, designers, managers, and economists throughout the world. Covers research and advances in technology. Price £3.50 per issue, £42.00 annual volume (back issues).

2898
Journal of Transport Economics and Policy
London School of Economics and Political Science, Houghton St, London, England WC2A 2AE. Order from University of Bath, England. Claverton Down, Bath, BA2 7AY, Telephone (44) (01) 0225-61244.

Magazine issued three times per year. Covers all means of transport. Emphasizes transport economics and policy. Price $60.00 per year.

2899
Journal of Travel Research
University of Colorado, Graduate School of Business Administration, Business Research Div, Boulder, CO 80309. Telephone (303) 492-8227.

Quarterly journal. Presents travel and tourist research. Includes information on tourist development in foreign countries, travel costs, and bibliography of recent studies. Price $45.00 per year. ISSN 0047-2875.

2900
Journal of Urban Analysis
Gordon and Breach Science Publishers, 1 Park Ave, New York, NY 10016. Telephone (212) 689-0360. Telex 620862.

Semiannual magazine. Focuses on urban planning research. Discusses refuse collection, municipal finance, housing, and welfare. Price $65.00.

2901
Journal of World Trade Law
Vincent Press, 10 Hill View Rd, Twickenham, Middx, England TW1 1H3 1EB. Telephone (44) (01) 892-5812.

Bimonthly journal. Covers legal and economic issues involved in development of world trade. Price US $75.00 per year.

2902
Junior Growth Stocks
Growth Stock Outlook, Inc, 4405 East-West Hwy, Bethesda, MD 20014. Order from PO Box 9911, Chevy Chase, MD 20015. Telephone (301) 654-5205.

Semimonthly newsletter. Recommends young companies whose stock may show good growth. Reviews new issues and company statements. Published since 1971. Price $78.00 per year.

2903
Juris Doctor
Master in Business Administration (MBA) Communications, Inc, 730 3rd Ave, New York, NY 10017. Telephone (212) 557-9240.

Monthly magazine. Treats topics relevant to legal profession. Is geared to new lawyers. Price $12.00 per year.

2904
Kansas Economic Indicators
Wichita State University, College of Business Adm, Center for Business and Economic Research, 023 Clinton Hall, Box 48, Wichita, KS 67208. Telephone (316) 689-3225.

Quarterly report with monthly supplements. Presents economic data and indicators for Kansas and Wichita, Kansas, area. Includes data on banking employment, production, and retail sales. Tables and charts. Price $10.00 per year.

2904.01
Kansas: Manufacturers & Products Directory **1980–81**
Manufacturers' News, Inc, 3 Huron St, Chicago, IL 60611. Telephone (312) 337-1084.

Annual book. Provides information on 4400 Kansas manufacturing firms by name, location, and product. Price $33.00.

2904.02
Kansas: State Industrial Directory **1981**
Manufacturers' News, Inc, 3 Huron St, Chicago, IL 60611. Telephone (312) 337-1084.

Annual book. Lists 4989 Kansas industrial firms. Identifies 26,556 executives. Price $40.00.

2905
Keesing's Contemporary Archives
Longman Group Ltd, Longman House, Burnt Mill, Harlow, Essex, England CM20 2JE. Telephone Harlow 26721. Telex 81259.

Weekly report. Summarizes developments in international politics, economics, and organizations. Covers treaties and conferences. Subject and name indexes. Price $179.00 per year. ISSN 0022-9679.

2907
Kelly's Manufacturers & Merchants Directory
Kelly's Directories Ltd, Windsor Court, E Grindstead House, E Grindstead, W Sussex, England RH19 1XB. Telephone (44) (01) 0342 26972.

Annual book. Gives listing of British manufacturers, merchants, and wholesalers, alphabetically and by product. Contains rundown of British importers and European exporting manufacturers and producers by product. Price £35.00 per copy.

2908

Kelly's Post Office London Directory
Kelly's Directories Ltd, Windsor Court, E Grinstead House, E Grinstead, W Sussex, England RH19 1XB. Telephone (44) (01) 0342 26972.

Annual book. Lists all London businesses by product, by street, and alphabetically. Contains guide to government and church buildings, and street atlas. Price £35.00 per copy.

2908.01

Kelly's Regional Directory of British Industry and Services
Kelly's Directories Ltd, Windsor Court, East Grinstead House, East Grinstead, West Sussex, England RH19 1XB. Telephone (44)(01) 0342 26972.

Eight-volume annual publication. Provides industrial information on the regions of the United Kingdom. Price £12.00 per volume.

2908.02

Kentucky: Manufacturers Directory 1981
Manufacturers' News, Inc, 3 Huron St, Chicago, IL 60611. Telephone (312) 337-1084.

Annual book. Contains information on manufacturing companies in Kentucky. Identifies products and number of employees. Price $28.00.

2908.03

Kentucky: State Industrial Directory, 1981
Manufacturers' News, Inc, 3 Huron St, Chicago, IL 60611. Telephone (312) 337-1084.

Annual book. Lists 2580 Kentucky industrial companies by name, location, and product. Price $40.00.

2909

Kess Tax Practice Report
Warren, Gorham & Lamont, Inc, 210 South St, Boston, MA 02111. Telephone (617) 423-2020.

Monthly report. Discusses tax subjects for professional tax advisors. Covers Tax Reform Act of 1976, Tax Reduction and Simplification Act of 1977, ERISA, and corporate tax. Price $56.00 per year.

2910

Key Indicators of Developing Member Countries of Asian Development Bank (ADB)
Asian Development Bank, PO Box 789, Manila, Phillippines 2800. Telephone (63) (2) 802631. Telex 7425071.

Publication. Provides tabular statistics on key economic indicators of member countries of Asian Development Bank. Free of charge.

2910.01

Key Issues Tracking (KIT)
New York Times Information Service, Inc, Mt Pleasant Office Pk, 1719A Route 10, Parsippany, NJ 07054. Telephone (201) 539-5850. Telex 136390.

Database. Covers major issues in the news and the activities of key leaders. Contains over 60,000 items from *The New York Times* and 44 other publications. Price $90.00 per hour.

2911

Keystone Coal Industry Manual
McGraw-Hill Book Co, Hightstown-Princeton Rd, Hightstown, NJ 08520. Telephone (609) 448-1700. Telex 843449.

Book. Supplies information on coal sales organizations and users. Price $110.00.

2912

Keystone News-Bulletin
McGraw-Hill Publications Co, 1221 Ave of the Americas, New York, NY 10020. Telephone (212) 997-1221. Telex TWX 7105814879 WUI 62555.

Monthly report. Provides data on coal mining, sales organizations, users, and trends. Price $96.00 per year.

2912.01

Key to Economic Science and Managerial Sciences
Martinus Nijhoff Publishers, 9-11 Lange Voorhout, The Hague, The Netherlands. Order from Kluwer Academic Publishers Group Distribution Center, PO Box 322, 3300 AH Dordrecht, The Netherlands.

Semimonthly review. Contains abstracts of books and articles on economics, finance, trade, industry, foreign aid, management, marketing, and labor. Includes annual index. Price $69.80 per year.

2912.02

Kiplinger Agricultural Letter
Kiplinger Washington Editors, Inc, 1729 H St, NW, Washington, DC 20006. Telephone (202) 887-6400.

Biweekly newsletter. Provides information on commodity prices, government policies, and federal legislation on food and agriculture. Price $36.00 per year.

2913

Kiplinger California Letter
Kiplinger Washington Editors, Inc, 1729 H St, NW, Washington, DC 20006. Telephone (202) 887-6400.

Monthly newsletter. Supplies information on business and investment in California. Notes developments in Washington that affect California. Price $32.00 per year.

2915

Kiplinger Florida Letter
Kiplinger Washington Editors, Inc, 1729 H St, NW, Washington, DC 20006. Telephone (202) 887-6400.

Monthly newsletter. Concerns money making in Florida. Notes population trends, new industries, planned roads, taxation, land prices, and tourism. Price $32.00 per year.

2916

Kiplinger Tax Letter
Kiplinger Washington Editors, Inc, 1729 H St, NW, Washington, DC 20006. Telephone (202) 887-6400.

Bimonthly newsletter. Contains business tax information and advice. Price $42.00 per year.

2916.01

Kiplinger Texas Letter
Kiplinger Washington Editors, Inc, 1729 H St, NW, Washington, DC 20006. Telephone (202) 887-6400.

Monthly newsletter. Reports on economic conditions and opportunities in Texas. Includes oil and gas news, land prices, investments, population trends, and defense topics. Price $36.00 per year.

2917

Kiplinger Washington Letter
Kiplinger Washington Editors, Inc, 1729 H St, NW, Washington, DC 20006. Telephone (202) 887-6400.

Weekly newsletter. Supplies briefings on business trends. Includes pertinent government policies and information on employment, investment, and interest rates. Price $42.00 per year.

2918

Kitchen Business
Gralla Publications, 1515 Broadway, New York, NY 10036. Telephone (212) 869-1300.

Reports on new home and remodeling sales of kitchens and baths. Price available on request.

2919
Kitchen Planning
Harcourt Brace Jovanovich Publications, 757 3rd Ave, New York, NY 10017. Order from Harcourt Brace and Jovanovich Publications, 1 1st St, Duluth, MN 55802. Telephone (218) 727-8511.

Bimonthly magazine. Discusses design of commercial and institutional kitchens. Notes related food service and equipment developments. Price $10.00 per year.

2920
Kompass Register Australia
Kompass Publishers Ltd, Windsor Court, E Grinstead House, E Grinstead, W Sussex, England RH1Q 1XD. Telephone 0342 26972.

Annual register. Contains information on Australian raw materials, manufactured goods, and services. Lists business data for leading companies. Price $80.00 per year.

2920.01
Kompass Register, Belgium & Luxembourg
Kompass Publishers Ltd, Windsor Court, E Grinstead House, E Grinstead, W Sussex, England RH19 1XD. Telephone 0342 26972.

Annual book. Provides information on raw materials, manufactured products, and services in Belgium and Luxembourg. Includes information on leading firms. Price £55.00 per copy.

2920.02
Kompass Register, Brazil
Kompass Publishers Ltd, Windsor Court, E Grinstead House, E Grinstead, W Sussex, England RH19 1XD. Telephone 0342 26972.

Annual directory. Compiles information on Brazilian raw materials, services, and manufactured goods. Includes data on major corporations. Price £55.00 per copy.

2920.03
Kompass Register, Denmark
Kompass Publishers Ltd, Windsor Court, E Grinstead House, E Grinstead, W Sussex, England RH19 1XD. Telephone 0342 26972.

Annual book. Supplies a guide to Danish raw materials, manufactured goods, and services. Gives information on major corporations. Price £55.00 per copy.

2920.04
Kompass Register, France
Kompass Publishers Ltd, Windsor Court, E Grinstead House, E Grinstead, W Sussex, England RH19 1XD. Telephone 0342 26972.

Annual book. Lists information on French raw materials, manufactured products, and services. Includes data on major corporations. Price £80.00 per copy.

2920.05
Kompass Register, Holland
Kompass Publishers Ltd, Windsor Court, E Grinstead House, E Grinstead, W Sussex, England RH19 1XD. Telephone 0342 26972.

Annual directory. Provides information on Dutch raw materials, manufactured products, and services. Reports business data for major companies. Price £55.00 per copy.

2920.06
Kompass Register, Indonesia
Kompass Publishers Ltd, Windsor Court, E Grinstead House, E Grinstead, W Sussex, England RH19 1XD. Telephone 0342 26972.

Annual book. Presents information on Indonesian raw materials, manufactured goods, and services. Lists leading corporations and basic company information. Price £45.00 per copy.

2920.07
Kompass Register, Italy
Kompass Publishers Ltd, Windsor Court, E Grinstead House, E Grinstead, W Sussex, England RH19 1XD. Telephone 0342 26972.

Annual book. Provides a directory to Italian raw materials, manufactured goods, and services. Includes information on major firms. Price £70.00 per copy.

2920.08
Kompass Register, Morocco
Kompass Publishers Ltd, Windsor Court, E Grinstead House, E Grinstead, W Sussex, England RH19 1XD. Telephone 0342 26972.

Annual book. Furnishes a directory to Moroccan raw materials, manufactured goods, and services. Includes data on major companies. Price £45.00 per copy.

2920.09
Kompass Register, Norway
Kompass Publishers Ltd, Windsor Court, E Grinstead House, E Grinstead, W Sussex, England RH19 1XD. Telephone 0342 26972.

Annual directory. Lists Norwegian raw materials, manufactured goods, and services. Presents data on leading firms. Price £55.00 per copy.

2920.10
Kompass Register, Spain
Kompass Publishers Ltd, Windsor Court, E Grinstead House, E Grinstead, W Sussex, England RH19 1XD. Telephone 0342 26972.

Annual register. Provides a directory to Spanish raw materials, manufactured goods, and services. Includes information on major companies. Price £55.00 per copy.

2920.11
Kompass Register, Sweden
Kompass Publishers Ltd, Windsor Court, E Grinstead House, E Grinstead, W Sussex, England RH19 1XD. Telephone 0342 26972.

Annual book. Lists Swedish manufactured products, services, and raw materials. Provides data on major corporations. Price £55.00 per copy.

2920.12
Kompass Register, Switzerland
Kompass Publishers Ltd, Windsor Court, E Grinstead House, E Grinstead, W Sussex, England RH19 1XD. Telephone 0342 26972.

Annual register. Provides a guide to Swiss raw materials, manufactured products, and services. Includes business data on leading Swiss firms. Price £55.00 per copy.

2920.13
Kompass Register, West Germany
Kompass Publishers Ltd, Windsor Court, E Grinstead House, E Grinstead, W Sussex, England RH19 1XD. Telephone 0342 26972.

Annual directory. Offers a guide to West German raw materials, manufactured goods, and services. Lists business information for major companies. Price £80.00 per copy.

2921
Korean Trade Directory
Korean Traders Assn, Inc, 460 Park Ave, Room 555, New York, NY 10022. Telephone (212) 421-8804. Telex KTANY 425572.

Annual book. Offers directory to South Korean trade, banks, insurance, export, and shipping companies. Price $10.00 per copy.

2922
Korean Trade News
Korean Traders Assn, Inc, 460 Park Ave, Room 555, New York, NY 10022. Telephone (212) 421-8804. Telex KTANY 425572.

Weekly newsletter on South Korean trade activities, industrial production, economic affairs, and international relations. Free of charge.

2923
LabData
Underwriters Laboratories, Inc Public Information Office, 333 Pfingsten Rd, Northbrook, IL 60062.

Provides technical information on product safety testing. Reports on new product innovations and safety requirements. Price $3.00 per year.

2924
Labor Arbitration Awards
Commerce Clearing House, Inc, 4025 W Peterson Ave, Chicago, IL 60646. Telephone (312) 583-8500.

One loose-leaf book and weekly reports. Carries texts of awards covering labor relations disputes. Price $405.00 per year.

2925
Labor Arbitration in Government
American Arbitation Assn, 140 W 51st St, New York, NY 10020. Telephone (212) 977-2000

Monthly magazine. Covers awards and recommendations concerning local and federal government employees. Price $75.00 per year.

2926
Labor Arbitration Reports
Bureau of National Affairs, Inc, 1231 25th St, NW, Washington, DC 20037. Telephone (202) 452-4200.

Loose-leaf books with weekly updates. Deals with labor arbitration and dispute settlements. Price $381.00 per year.

2927
Labor Area Summary
New York State Dept of Labor, Div of Research and Statistics, State Office Bldg Campus, Albany, NY 12240. Order from Bureau of Labor Market Information, Room 405, Div of Research and Statistics, NY State Dept of Labor, State Office Bldg Campus, Albany, NY 12240. Telephone (518) 457-3800.

Monthly newsletter. Analyzes employment and other labor developments in each of 11 major labor areas in New York State. Free of charge.

2928
Laboratory Equipment Digest
Morgan-Grampian Ltd, Morgan-Grampian House, Calderwood St, London, England SE18 6QH. Order from Morgan-Grampian Pub Co, 2 Park Ave, New York, NY 10016. Telephone England (44) (01) 855-7777. Telex 896238 MORGAN G. New York (212) 340-9700. Telex 425592 MGI UI.

Monthly magazine. Prints articles on aspects of laboratory work and technology. Price $100.00 per year.

2929
Laboratory Product News
Southam Communications Ltd, 1450 Don Mills Rd, Don Mills, Ont, Canada M3B 2X7. Telephone (416) 445-6641. Telex 06-966612.

Bimonthly publication. Gives capsule descriptions of new products and equipment for laboratories serving various scientific disciplines. Price $22.00 per year.

2930
Labor Cases
Commerce Clearing House, Inc, 4025 W Peterson Ave, Chicago, IL 60646. Telephone (312) 583-8500.

Sixty-six books. Present court decisions on labor relations, wage-hour, and allied problems. Price $27.50 per volume. ISSN 9170.

2931
Labor Force Estimates
Florida Dept of Labor and Employment Security, Bureau of Research and Analysis, Caldwell Bldg, Tallahassee, FL 32301. Telephone (904) 488-1048.

Monthly report. Presents statistics on labor force for Florida and individual areas. Covers employment, seasonally adjusted unemployment rate, and unadjusted unemployment rate. Mailing list restricted to Florida-based firms. Single copies available to public upon request. Price free of charge.

2932
Labor Law
Matthew Bender & Co, 235 E 45th St, New York, NY 10017. Telephone (212) 661-5050.

Eleven 10-volume loose-leaf sets of books with quarterly supplements. Discuss laws affecting labor-management relations. Cover union representation, collective bargaining, unfair labor practices, and Taft-Hartley Act. Price $500.00 with one year's supplement, $230.00 per year.

2933
Labor Law Developments
Matthew Bender & Co, 235 E 45th St, New York, NY 10017. Telephone (212) 661-5050.

Annual book. Contains proceedings of SWLF Labor Law Institute. Covers labor law cases, NLRB decisions, and bargaining and arbitration trends. Price $50.00

2934
Labor Law Guide
Commerce Clearing House, Inc, 4025 W Peterson Ave, Chicago, IL 60646. Telephone (312) 583-8500.

Two loose-leaf books plus weekly reports. Cover issues pertinent to labor relations, wages, and hours. Price $240.00 per year.

2935
Labor Law Journal
Commerce Clearing House, Inc, 4025 W Peterson Ave, Chicago, IL 60646. Telephone (312) 583-8500.

Monthly magazine. Covers relationships of labor, unions, management, law, and government. Price 45.00 per year.

2936
Labor Law Reports
Commerce Clearing House, Inc, 4025 W Peterson Ave, Chicago, IL 60646. Telephone (312) 583-8500.

Fifteen loose-leaf books with weekly reports. Provide coverage of federal and state laws regulating relationships of employees, unions, and management. Price $930.00 per year.

2937
Labor Law Reports—Summary
Commerce Clearing House, Inc, 4025 W Peterson Ave, Chicago, IL 60646. Telephone (312) 583-8500.

Weekly briefs. Summarizes current labor law events. Price $40.00 per year.

2938
Labor Market Information Directory
Alaska Dept of Labor, Employment Security Division, Research and Analysis Section, Box 3-7000, Juneau, AK 99801. Telephone (907) 465-2700.

Directory. Presents bibliography of publications prepared by Research and Analysis Department of Alaska's Department of Labor. Price available on request.

2939
Labor Market Information Directory
Virginia Employment Commission, 703 E Main St, PO Box 1358, Richmond, VA 23211. Telephone (804) 786-1485.

Directory. Provides guide to information on Virginia's labor market. Lists publications of Virginia Employment Commission and other relevant reports. Price available on request.

2940
Labor Market Trends
Florida Dept of Labor and Employment Security Bureau of Research and Analysis, Caldwell Bldg, Tallahassee, FL 32301. Telephone (904) 488-1048.

Monthly newsletter. Contains labor force and employment information for Florida's 16 standard metropolitan statistical areas. Analyzes economic trends and provides estimates of manufacturing hours, earnings, and labor turnover. Mailing list restricted to Florida-based firms. Single copies available to public upon request. Price free of charge.

2940.01
Labor Market Trends
West Virginia Dept of Employment Security, Labor & Economic Research, 112 California Ave, Charleston, WV 25305. Telephone (304) 348-2660.

Monthly reports. Each covers West Virginia's four standard metropolitan statistical areas. Provides analyses of labor market and forecasts, tables detailing changes in employment and unemployment, and list of new and forthcoming publications. Price free of charge.

2941
Labor News Memorandum
New York Dept of Labor, Div of Research and Statistics, State Office Bldg Campus, Albany, NY 12240. Order from Div of Research and Statistics, Room 6804, New York State Dept of Labor, 2 World Trade Center, New York, NY 10047. Telephone (212) 488-5030.

Semimonthly report. Summarizes labor information relating to New York State, and some of general interest. Free of charge.

2942
Labor Relations Guide
Prentice-Hall, Inc, Englewood Cliffs, NJ 07632. Telephone (201) 592-2000. Telex 13-5423.

Weekly loose-leaf service. Reports on labor relations. Explains labor laws and provides texts. Discusses collective bargaining with unions and occupational safety regulations. Price $267.00 per year.

2943
Labor Relations Reporter
Bureau of National Affairs, Inc, 1231 25th St, NW, Washington, DC 20037. Telephone (202) 452-4200.

Loose-leaf books with weekly updates. Cover labor laws, fair employment practices, wages and hours, arbitration and court decisions. Index. Price $1152.00 per year.

2945
Labor Unity
Amalgamated Clothing and Textile Workers Union, 15 Union Sq, New York, NY 10003. Telephone (212) 242-0700.

Monthly newspaper. Covers labor issues, wages, and benefits. Reports on activities of Amalgamated Clothing and Textile Workers Union. Price $1.50 per year.

2946
Labour Agreements Data Bank
McGill University, Industrial Relations Centre, Samuel Bronfman Bldg, 1001 Sherbrooke St W, Montreal, Que Canada H3A 1G5. Telephone (514) 392-6771.

Computerized service. Covers collective bargaining field including approximately 100 clauses found in contracts covering one-third of organized Canadian workers. Price varies.

2947
Labour & Employment Gazette
New Zealand Dept of Labour, Private Bag, Wellington 1, New Zealand.

Quarterly magazine. Covers New Zealand labor matters. Price $2.00 (NZ) per year.

2948
Labour and Society
International Inst for Labour Studies, PO Box 6, CH-1211, Geneva 22, Switzerland. Telephone (41) (022) 996111.

Quarterly journal. Contains information on social and labor problems and on International Institute for Labour Studies educational and research activities. Also in French. Price 40 Swiss francs.

2949
Labour Arbitration Cases
Canada Law Book Ltd, 240 Edward St, Aurora, Ont, L4G 3S9, Canada. Telephone (416) 859-3880.

Monthly reports plus four books per year. Reports decisions of Canadian arbitrators in labor disputes. Price $43.00 per volume.

2949.01
Labour, Capital and Society
McGill University, Centre for Developing Area Studies, 815 Sherbrooke St West, Montreal, Que, Canada H3A 2K6. Telephone (514) 392-5327.

Semiannual journal. Includes original articles in English and French, as well as book reviews, book notes, and bibliographical entries on labor issues in developing areas, especially Third World countries. Price available on request.

2950
Labour Force (Cat No 6204.0)
Australian Bureau of Statistics, Box 10, Belconnen, ACT 2616, Australia. Order from Australian Government Publishing Service, PO Box 84, Canberra, ACT 2600, Australia. Telephone (61) (062) 527911.

Annual report. Notes characteristics of various categories of Australia's labor force, including part-time and women workers. Price $1.60 (Australian).

2951
Labour Force
Statistics Canada, User Services, Publications Distribution, Ottawa, Ont, Canada K1A 0V7. Telephone (613) 992-3151.

Monthly magazine. Estimates Canadian labor force, employment, and unemployment. Includes age, sex, marital status, industry, region, and other information. Price $42.00 per year. ISSN 0380-6804.

2952
Labour Force Statistics
Organization for Economic Cooperation and Development, Publications Center, 1750 Pennsylvania Ave, NW, Washington, DC 20006. Telephone (202) 724-1857.

Quarterly supplement to yearbook. Provides employment and manpower statistics for each OECD country. Tables. Price $14.65

2953
Labour Gazette
Supply and Services Canada, Pub Centre, Printing and Pub, Ottawa, Ont, Canada K1A 0S9. Telephone (613) 238-1601.

Monthly magazine. Covers Canadian labor affairs. Price $7.00 per year.

2954
Labour Organizations in Canada
Canadian Dept of Labour, Ottawa, Ont, Canada K1A 0J2. Order from Pub Centre, Supply and Services, Ottawa, Canada K1A 0S9. Telephone (819) 997-2582.

Annual book. Provides directory to Canadian labor unions. Lists officers, publications, membership statistics, and provincial distribution of locals. English and French. Price $3.00. ISBN 0-660-01082-8.

2955
Labour Research
Labour Research Dept, 78 Blackfriars Rd, London, England SE1 8HF. Telephone (44) (01) 928 3649.

Monthly report. Discusses British labor and industrial news. Reports on union activities, labor legislation, and developments within specific industries. Tables. Price £9.00 per year.

2956
Labour Research Department Fact Service
Labour Research Dept, 78 Blackfriars Rd, London, England SE1 8HF. Telephone (44) (01) 928 3649.

Weekly newsletter. Reports on British labor issues such as wages and unemployment. Notes industrial production trends. Price £13.75 per year.

2957
Labour Standards in Canada
Canadian Dept of Labour, Ottawa, Ont, Canada K1A 0J2. Order from Pub Centre, Supply and Services, Ottawa, Ont, Canada K1A 0S9. Telephone (819) 997-2582.

Annual book. Sets forth provisions of federal and provincial labor legislation enacted during year. English and French. Price $2.40. ISBN 0-660-06-1.

2958
Labour Statistics (Cat No 6101.0)
Australian Bureau of Statistics, Box 10, Belconnen, ACT 2616, Australia. Order from Australian Government Pub Service, PO Box 84, Canberra, ACT 2600, Australia. Telephone (61) (062) 527911.

Annual report. Presents detailed statistics on Australia's prices, employment, wages and hours, and labor organizations. Tables and summaries of national and state wage cases. Price $6.95 (Australian).

2959
Lab World
North American Pub Co, 401 N Broad St, Philadelphia, PA 19108. Telephone (215) 574-9600.

Monthly magazine. Reports on clinical laboratory research and instruments. Notes new products and techniques, including computer systems. Price $18.00 per year.

2960
Land Development Law Reporter
Land Development Institute, Ltd, 1401 16th St, NW, Washington, DC 20036. Telephone (202) 232-2144.

Five-volume loose-leaf set, plus monthly reports. Covers land development and sales regulations of Office of Interstate Land Sales Registration, Federal Trade Commission, Federal Reserve Board, and Securities and Exchange Commission, plus major court decisions. Price $345.00 per year, $295.00 libraries.

2961
Land Economics
University of Wisconsin Press, Journal Div, 114 N Muray St, Madison, WI 53715. Telephone (608) 262-4952.

Quarterly magazine. Articles explore relationship between land and economy. Include land use policies, natural resources, and environment. Price $15.00 individuals, $28.00 institutions per year. ISSN 0023-7639.

2961.01
Land Use & Environment Law Review
Clark Boardman Co, Ltd, 435 Hudson St, New York, NY 10014. Telephone (212) 929-7500.

Annual book. Reviews environmental protection laws. Price $42.50 per volume. ISBN 0-87632-188-X.

2962
Land Use Digest
Urban Land Inst, 1090 Vermont Ave, NW, Washington, DC 20005. Telephone (202) 289-8500.

Monthly newsletter. Reports on significant developments in land use industry. Available only to members.

2963
Land Use Law and Zoning Digest
American Planning Assn, 1313 E 60th St, Chicago, IL 60637. Telephone (312) 947-2575.

Monthly magazine. Offers abstracts and analyses of land use issues. Includes material on legislation and court rulings. Annual index. Price $145.00 per year.

2964
Land Use Planning Abstracts
Environment Information Center (EIC), Inc, Catalog Order Dept, 292 Madison Ave, New York, NY 10017. Telephone (212) 949-9494.

Annual report. Compiles abstracts, statistics, and facts on land use, zoning, population control, and related topics. Tables, graphs, charts, and diagrams. Index. Price $85.00.

2965
Land Use Planning Report
Business Publishers, Inc, PO Box 1067, Silver Spring, MD 20910. Telephone (301) 587-6300.

Weekly report. Covers land planning. Price $157.00 per year.

2966
Lanston Letter
Aubrey G Lanston & Co, Inc, 20 Broad St, New York, NY 10005. Telephone (212) 943-1200.

Weekly newsletter. Covers general economic issues including interest rates, inflation, and government finance and economic policies. Free of charge.

2967
Laser Focus
Advanced Technology Publications, Inc, 1001 Watertown St., West Newton, MA 02165. Telephone (617) 244-2939.

Monthly magazine. Examines research on and development of lasers, fiberoptic communications, and related optical technologies. Price $33.00 per year.

2968
Laser Focus Buyer's Guide
Advanced Technology Publications, Inc, 1001 Watertown St., West Newton, MA 02165. Telephone (617) 244-2939.

Annual book. Provides directory of laser and fiberoptic products and suppliers. Includes general and technical information. Price $22.00.

2969
Laser Report
Advanced Technology Publications, Inc, 1001 Watertown St., West Newton, MA 02165. Telephone (617) 244-2939.

Monthly newsletter. Reports on market trends in opto-electronics and laser fields. Price $95.00 per year.

2969.01
Latin America & Caribbean 1981
World of Information, 21 Gold St, Saffron Walden, Essex, England CB10 1EJ. Telephone Saffron Walden 21150 (Std. 0799 21150). Telex England 817197 a/b Jaxpress G.

Annual book. Reports on commercial, economic, political, and social developments in Latin America and the Caribbean, with chapters on every country. Price $43.00. ISBN 0-904439-20-8.

2970
Latin America and the Development of the Law of the Sea
Oceana Publications, Inc, 75 Main St, Dobbs Ferry, NY 10522. Telephone (914) 693-5944.

Two loose-leaf binders. Examine contributions of Latin American countries to Law of Sea development. Include related national legislation. Price $150.00 per set. ISBN 0-379-10189-7.

2971
Latin America Annual Review, 1978
Middle East Review Co Ltd, 21 Gold St, Saffron Walden, Essex, England CB10 1EJ. Telephone Saffron Walden 21150 (STD 0799 21150). Telex Inglaterra 817268 a/b John PW G.

Annual book. Reports on political, social, and economic conditions in Latin America. Statistics. Price $17.00 per copy.

2972
Latin America Commodities Report
Latin America Newsletters Ltd, Greenhill House, 90-93 Cowcross St, London, England EC1M 6BL. Telephone (44) (01) 251-0012. Telex 261117.

Fortnightly newsletter. Provides analysis of major Latin American commodities. Includes information on pertinent government decisions. Price $200.00 per year.

2973
Latin America Economic Report
Latin America Newsletters Ltd, Greenhill House, 90-93 Cowcross St, London, England EC1M 6BL. Telephone (44) (01) 251-0012. Telex 261117.

Weekly newsletter. Provides data and analyses on Latin America's economic conditions. Price $100.00 per year.

2974
Latin American Economy-Economic Survey of Latin America
United Nations Publications, Room A-3315, New York, NY 10017. Telephone (212) 754-8302.

Report. Provides statistics and other data on the Latin American economy. Price available on request.

2974.01
Latin American Energy Report
Business Publishers, Inc, PO Box 1067, Silver Spring, MD 20910. Telephone (301) 587-6300.

Biweekly newsletter. Reports on energy developments in Latin America. Price $287.00 per year.

2975
Latin American Index
Welt Publishing Co, 1511 K St, NW, Washington, DC 20005. Telephone (202) 737-8080.

Bimonthly report. Covers political and economic developments in Latin America. Price $195.00.

2976
Latin America Political Report
Latin America Newsletters Ltd, Greenhill House, 90-93 Cowcross St, London, England EC1M 6BL. Telephone (44) (01) 251-0012. Telex 261117.

Weekly newsletter. Provides information and interpretation on political issues in Latin America. Price $100.00 per year.

2976.01
Latin American Service
Data Resources, Inc, 29 Hartwell Ave, Lexington, MA 02173. Telephone (617) 861-0165.

Quarterly report. Forecasts detailed trade and balance of payment accounts. Gives foreign debt positions, inflation rates, domestic demand and income production, wages, interest rates, and money supply for Mexico, Brazil, Venezuela, Argentina, Colombia, Peru, Chile, Bolivia, Ecuador, and Uruguay. Price available on request.

2976.02
Latin America Weekly Report
Latin American Newsletters Ltd, Greenhill House, 90–93 Cowcross St, London, England EC1M 6BL. Telephone (44)(01) 251-0012. Telex 261117.

Weekly newsletter. Covers economic and political news of South America and Caribbean area. Includes data on commodities. Price £208, $480.00 US per year.

2977
Law and Business of Licensing, 1975, base edition
Clark Boardman Co Ltd, 435 Hudson St, New York, NY 10014. Telephone (212) 929-7500.

Loose-leaf books supplemented annually. Cover legal and business aspects of licensing. Include information on antitrust problems and international topics. Price $250.00 for four volumes. ISBN 0-87632-136-8.

2978
Law and Policy of Intergovernmental Primary Commodity Agreements
Oceana Publications, Inc, 75 Main St, Dobbs Ferry, NY 10522. Telephone (914) 693-4944.

Two loose-leaf binders. Presents collection of intergovernmental agreements in areas affecting primary commodities, oil, minerals, and grains. Includes commentary. Price $200.00 per set. ISBN 0-379-00675-8.

2978.01
Lawn & Garden Marketing
Intertec Publishing Corp, 9221 Quivera Rd, PO Box 12901, Overland Park, KS 66212. Telephone (913) 888-4664. Telex 42-4156.

Magazine published 10 times per year. Offers information on lawn and garden products, markets, and merchandising practices. Price $20.00 per year.

2979
Law of Advertising
George Eric Rosden and Peter E Rosden. Matthew Bender & Co, 235 E 45th St, New York, NY 10017. Telephone (212) 661-5050.

Two-volume loose-leaf report with annual supplements. Analyzes laws that govern advertising. Includes information on consumers' remedies, corrective advertising, and medical and legal advertising. Price $140.00.

2980
Law of Associations: An Operating Legal Manual for Executives and Counsel
George D Webster. Matthew Bender & Co, 235 E 45th St, New York, NY 10017. Telephone (212) 661-5050.

Book. Covers legal and tax aspects of non-profit organization management. Includes certificates of incorporation, constitutions, bylaws, and accounting information. Price $65.00.

2981
Law of Electronic Surveillance
Clark Boardman Co Ltd, 435 Hudson St, New York, NY 10014. Telephone (212) 929-7500.

Book with annual supplements. Reviews federal and state laws on electronic surveillance. Cites all relevant court cases. Price $50.00. ISBN 0-87632-108-2.

2982
Law of Federal Oil and Gas Leases
Matthew Bender & Co, 235 E 45th St, New York, NY 10017. Telephone (212) 661-5050.

Two-volume loose-leaf report with annual cumulative supplements. Explains laws affecting oil and gas leases on federal lands. Covers statutes, regulations codes, rulings, and court cases. Price $150.00.

2983
Law of Liability Insurance
Matthew Bender & Co, 235 E 45th St, New York, NY 10017. Telephone (212) 661-5050.

Three-volume loose-leaf report with annual supplements. Discusses all aspects of liability insurance law including motor vehicle liability insurance and no-fault insurance. Analyzes revisions of General Liability Insurance Contract. Price $200.-00.

2984
Law of Oil and Gas Leases
Matthew Bender & Co, 235 E 45th St, New York, NY 10017. Telephone (212) 661-5050.

Two-volume loose-leaf report with annual cumulative supplements. Discusses oil and gas lease laws. Includes court cases and commentary. Price $170.00.

2985
Law of Pooling and Unitization—Voluntary, Compulsory
Matthew Bender & Co, 235 E 45th St, New York, NY 10017. Telephone (212) 661-5050.

Three-volume book with annual cumulative supplements. Covers legal and practical problems involved in oil and gas pooling and unitization. Price $160.00.

2986
Law of Workmen's Compensation
Matthew Bender & Co, 235 E 45th St, New York, NY 10017. Telephone (212) 661-5050.

Ten-volume loose-leaf report with semiannual supplements. Presents detailed explanation of state laws on workmen's compensation. Cites 1000 cases. Price $500.00.

2987
Law of Zoning and Planning
Clark Boardman Co Ltd, 435 Hudson St, New York, NY 10014. Telephone (212) 929-7500.

Loose-leaf books with annual supplements. Cover local and regional zoning and planning laws. Topics include residential zoning, racial restrictions, clubs, educational institutions, and grants of variance. Price $195.00. ISBN 0-87632-020-5.

2988
Law Reprints Trade Regulation Series
Bureau of National Affairs, 1231 25th St, NW, Washington, DC 20037.

Irregularly published book with microfiche. Consists of all trade regulation cases argued and denied certiorari before US Supreme Court. Price $148.00 per year.

2989
Lawyers' Arbitration Letter and Digest of Court Decisions
American Arbitration Assn, 140 W 51st St, New York, NY 10020. Telephone (212) 977-2000.

Quarterly loose-leaf report. Contains information on arbitration law developments and digests court decisions. Includes annual summary of legal and legislative actions. Price $50.00 per year.

2990
Lawyer's Register by Specialties and Fields of Law
Lawyer to Lawyer Consultation Panel, 5325 Naiman Pkwy, Solon, OH 44139. Telephone (216) 248-0135.

Annual book. Is national directory to legal profession by specialties and fields of law. Price available on request.

2991
Lawyers Title News
Lawyers Title Insurance Corp, PO Box 27567, Richmond, VA 23261. Telephone (804) 281-6700.

Bimonthly magazine. Deals with land and land use, real estate, commercial properties, and housing. Free of charge.

2992
Laxton's Building Price Book
Kelly's Directories Ltd, Windsor Court, E Grinstead House, E Grinstead, W Sussex, England RH19 1XB. Telephone (44) (01) 0342 26972.

Annual book. Provides material and labor prices for British construction work. Includes sections on major works, alterations, and small works. Lists brand and trade names. Price £15.00 per cpoy.

2993
Lead and Zinc Statistics
International Lead and Zinc Study Group, Metro House, 58 St James's St, London, SW1A 1LH England. Telephone (01) 499-9373.Telex 299819 1LZSG-G

Monthly report. Provides data on lead and zinc mine production, imports and exports. Tables. English and French. Price $125.00 per year.

2994
Lead Data
American Bureau of Metal Statistics, Inc, 420 Lexington Ave, New York, NY 10170. Telephone (212) 867-9450. Telex 14-7130.

Monthly report. Addresses production, shipment, and purchase of lead by US refineries. Includes statistics on US, Canadian, French, British, and West German lead trade. Price $200.00 per year.

2994.01
Leadership & Organization Development
MCB Publications, 200 Keighly Rd, Bradford, W Yorkshire, England BD9 4JQ. Telephone 0274-499821.

Quarterly journal. Covers management development techniques, such as team building and entrepreneurship. Price $84.00 per year.

2995
Leaders Letter
American Bankers Assn, 1120 Connecticut Ave NW, Washington, DC 20036. Telephone (202) 467-4123.

Newsletter published eight times per year. Reports on American Institute of Banking's chapter activities and programs. Includes directives on chapter administration. Free of charge.

2995.01
Legal Contents
Legal Contents, PO Box 3014, Northbrook, IL 60062. Telephone (312) 564-1006.

Fortnightly service. Contains tables of contents of the latest issues of over 340 legal periodicals. Includes subject index. Price $62.00 per year.

2996
Legal Information Bulletin
Industrial Relations Service, 170 Finchley Rd, London, England NW3 6BP. Telephone (44) (01) 794-4554.

Fortnightly report. Explains major legislation and interprets court decisions on industrial relations in Great Britain. Price £27.50 per year.

2996.01
Legal Resource Index
Information Access Corp, 404 6th Ave, Menlo Park, CA 94025. Telephone (800) 227-8431.

Monthly microfilm service, with cumulative update. Provides index to all articles and reviews in 600 legal periodicals and four major legal newspapers, as well as selected articles from over 400 general periodicals and newspapers, legal monographs, and government publications. Organized by subject, author, statute, and case. Price $1560.00 per year, American Association of Law Libraries members, $1720.00 non-members.

2997
Legislative Action Bulletin
Chamber of Commerce of Hawaii, Dillingham Transportation Bldg, 735 Bishop St, Honolulu, HI 96813. Telephone (808) 531-4111.

Weekly report. Covers Hawaiian legislative bills and issues of interest to business. Notes Chamber of Commerce positions. Price $2.00 per year.

2998
Legislative Brief
Associated Industries of New York State, Inc, 150 State St, Albany, NY 12207. Telephone (518) 465-3547.

Newsletter issued biweekly during New York State legislative session. Digests bills and legislative activity of labor, consumer, and business interest. Free of charge.

3001
Legislative Review
Labour Canada, Communications Services Directorate, Ottawa, Ont, Canada K1A 0J2. Order from Communications Services Directorate, Ottawa, Ont, Canada K1A 0J2. Telephone (819) 997-2617.

Annual report. Provides summary of amendments passed during the year covering Canadian legislation on employment standards, industrial relations, occupational health and safety, and accident compensation. Price free of charge.

3002
Legislative Series
International Labor Organization, 1750 New York Ave NW, Suite 330, Washington, DC 20006. Telephone (202) 376-2315.

Bimonthly publication and annual index. Covers national laws on labor and Social Security. Price $28.70 per year.

3003
Legislative Session Sheet
Council of State Governments, Iron Works Pike, PO Box 11910, Lexington, KY 40511. Telephone (606) 252-2291.

Monthly publication. Supplies data on current state legislative sessions, special sessions, and adjournment dates. Price $5.00 per year.

3004
Leisure Beverage "Insider"
Atcom, Inc, Atcom Bldg, 2315 Broadway, New York, NY 10024. Telephone (212) 873-3760.

Weekly newsletter. Provides information about beverage industry including beer and wine. Price $67.00 per year.

3004.01
Leisure, Recreation and Tourism Abstracts
Commonwealth Agricultural Bureaux, Central Sales Branch, Farnham House, Farnham Royal, Slough, England SL2 3BN. Telephone Farnham Common 2281. Telex 847964.

Quarterly magazine. Supplies abstracts of articles on British public policies, planning, parks and nature reserves, tourist industry, travel and accommodation, recreational facilities and social and cultural factors. Price $96.00 per year.

3005
Lending Law Forum
Lending Law Forum, Inc, PO Box 85, Rockville Centre, NY 11571.

Report issued eight times per year. Discusses laws and regulations that relate to loan transactions. Price $32.00 per year. ISSN 0098-891X.

3006
Lesly's Public Relations Handbook
Prentice-Hall, Inc, Englewood Cliffs, NJ 07632. Telephone (201) 592-2000. Telex 13-5423.

Book. Covers public relations theory and practice. Price $29.95. ISBN 013-530741-4.

3006.01
Letterheads Volumes I to III
Advertising Trade Publications, Inc, 10 E 39th St, New York, NY 10016. Order from Art Direction Book Co, 10 E 39th St, New York, NY 10016. Telephone (212) 889-6500.

Three-volume book. Contains 300 international letterheads. Includes illustrations. Price $30.00 per volume.

3007
Libradoc
International Co-operative Alliance, 11 Upper Grosvenor St, London, England W1X 9PA. Telephone (44) (01) 499-5991.

Quarterly magazine. Reports on International Working Party of Cooperative Librarians and international cooperative library developments. Occasional articles in German and French. Price free to institutions.

3008
Library Employee Relations Newsletter
Phillip Harris, 54 Margaret Avenue, Lawrence, NY 11559. Telephone (516) 371-1225.

Monthly newsletter on library personnel management and collective negotiations. Includes analyses of recent cases that have gone to arbitration. Price $48.00. ISSN 0363-8863.

3009
Licences and Exploration Information System (LEXIS).
Petroconsultants SA, 8-10 Rue Muzy, PO Box 228, 1211 Geneva 6, Switzerland. Order from Petroconsultants Ltd, Cumberland House, Fenian St, Dublin 2, Ireland. Telephone (41) (22) 36 88 11. Telex 27 763.

Information system. Gives data on worldwide oil exploration, except in North America and Communist countries. Price 135,000 francs (Swiss) for complete data bank; 6,250 francs (Swiss) quarterly update.

3010
Licensing in Foreign and Domestic Operations, 3d edition, 1972
Clark Boardman Co, Ltd, 435 Hudson St, New York, NY 10014. Telephone (212) 929-7500.

Annually revised loose-leaf book. Supplies information on licensing of industrial property rights, patents, trademarks, and copyrights. Price for four-volume set $295.00. ISBN 0-87632-075-2.

3011
Life and Business in New Zealand
Bank of New Zealand, PO Box 2392, Wellington 1, New Zealand. Telex 3344 MONARCH.

Annual pamphlet. Covers all aspects of life in New Zealand. Provides information for tourists, prospective immigrants, and investors. Includes cost of living, tax rate, and other economic statistics. Free of charge.

3012
Life and Health Insurance Handbook
Dow Jones-Irwin, Inc, 1818 Ridge Rd, Homewood, IL 60430. Telephone (312) 798-3100.

Book. Contains in-depth discussion of most aspects of life and health insurance business. Price available on request.

3013
Life Financial Reports
National Underwriter Co, 420 E 4th St, Cincinnati, OH 45202. Telephone (513) 721-2140.

Book. Reports on life insurance companies. Gives detailed financial information for over 1000 companies and notes types of policies offered. Price $19.00.

3014
Life Insurance Fact Book
American Council of Life Insurance, 1850 K St, NW, Washington, DC 20006.

Annual report. Provides analysis and statistics on the life insurance industry in the US. Single copy free. ISSN 0075-9406.

3015
Life Insurance in Canada
Wadham Publications Ltd, 109 Vanderhoof Ave, Suite 101, Toronto, Ont, Canada M4G 2J2. Telephone (416) 425-9021.

Bimonthly magazine. Reports on developments that affect Canadian life insurance industry including proposed legislation. Notes firm and personnel news. Price $7.00 per year.

3016
Life Insurance Planning
Inst for Business Planning, Inc, IPB Plaza, Englewood Cliffs, NJ 07632. Telephone (201) 592-2040.

Loose-leaf book with monthly supplements and semimonthly letters. Illustrates how life insurance can build tax sheltered capital and income. Charts, tables, and checklists. Price available on request.

3017
Life Rates & Data
National Underwriter Co, 420 E 4th St, Cincinnati, OH 45202. Telephone (513) 721-2140.

Book. Offers information on life insurance premiums, policies, and cash values. Compares policies of over 300 companies. Tables. Price $9.00.

3018
Lighting Equipment News
Maclean-Hunter Ltd, 30 Old Burlington St, London, England W1X 2AE. Telephone (44) (01) 434 2233.

Monthly newspaper. Reports on developments in lighting industry. Emphasizes safety regulations. Notes exhibitions in Great Britain and abroad. Price available on request.

3019
Linage Booster
Newspaper Advertising Bureau, Inc, 485 Lexington Ave, New York, NY 10017. Telephone (212) 557-1800.

Monthly booklet. Contains selling tips for newspaper sales personnel including upcoming promotional events, ad ideas, and listing of month's best-selling merchandise. Price $10.00 per year.

3019.01
Lindey on Entertainment, Publishing and the Arts
Clark Boardman Co Ltd, 435 Hudson St, New York, NY 10014. Telephone (212) 929-7500.

Loose-leaf books, supplemented biannually. Cover agreements and law in the communications industry, including books, newspapers, television, radio, and the music fields. Price $60.00 per volume.

3020
John Liner Letter
Shelby Publishing Corp, 555 Washington St, Wellesley, MA 02181. Telephone (617) 235-8450.

Monthly newsletter. Covers different aspect of insurance protection or risk management each month. Price $75.00 per year.

3021
Lipscombe Report
Lipscombe & Assoc, PO Box 158, Claremont, WA 6010 Australia. Telephone 386-7899. Telex 92-442.

Weekly telex report. Covers Australian oil industry developments. Price $700.00 (Australian) per year.

3021.01
Liquidity Portfolio Manager
Andrew R Mandala, PO Box 30240, Washington, DC 20014. Telephone (301) 654-5580.

Biweekly report. Discusses savings and loan association liquidity management. Price $110.00 per year.

3022
Liquidity Report
Amivest Corp, 505 Park Ave, New York, NY 10022. Telephone (212) 688-6667. Telex ITT: 422851.

Monthly service. Measures investment dollar value traded per each percent of price variation. Lists stocks alphabetically by industry and rank. Price $1000.00 per year.

3023
Liquor Control Law Reports
Commerce Clearing House, Inc, 4025 W Peterson Ave, Chicago, IL 60646. Telephone (312) 583-8500.

Nine volumes and monthly reports. Cover federal and state regulation and taxation of alcoholic beverages. Price $1030.00 per year.

3024
Liquor Handbook
Gavin-Jobson Associates, Inc, 488 Madison Ave, New York, NY 10022. Telephone (212) 758-5620.

Annual book. Looks at past record and future of liquor industry. Includes maps, charts, and tabular material. Price $20.00 per copy.

3025
List of Bulgarian Foreign Trade Organizations
Bulgarian Chamber of Commerce and Industry, 11a Stamboliiski Blvd, Sofia, Bulgaria. Telephone 87-26-31/35. Telex 374.

Annual report. Lists Bulgarian foreign trade organizations in English, French, German, and Spanish. Price free of charge.

3026
Literary Market Place (LMP)
R R Bowker Co, 1180 Ave of the Americas, New York, NY 10036. Order from R R Bowker Co, PO Box 1807, Ann Arbor, MI 48106. Telephone (212) 764-5100.

Annual directory. Covers American and Canadian book publishing, with key personnel, lists of publishers, agents, services and suppliers, manufacturers, and others. Price $29.50 paperbound. ISBN 0-8352-1324-2. ISSN 0075-9899.

3026.01
Livestock (Cat NO 7203.0)
Australian Bureau of Statistics, PO Box 10, Belconnen, ACT 2616, Australia. Order from Australian Government Pub Service, PO Box 84, Canberra, ACT 2600, Australia. Telephone (61) (062) 527911.

Annual report. Presents statistics on number of Australian pigs, poultry, cattle, and sheep classified by breed and purpose. Gives comparative figures for approximately 50 countries. Price free of charge.

3027
Livestock and Products Reports
US Dept of Agriculture, Crop Reporting Board, Economics and Statistics Service (ESS), Room 0005 S Blgd, Washington, DC 20250. Telephone (202) 447-4021.

Reports. Provide data on livestock numbers, value, and marketing. Include livestock slaughter and wool production figures. Free of charge.

3028
Livestock Farming
Morgan-Grampian Ltd, Morgan-Grampian House, Calderwood St, London, England SE18 6QH. Order from Morgan-Grampian Publishing Co, 2 Park Ave, New York, NY 10016. Telephone (44) (01) 855-7777. Telex 896238 MORGAN G. New York (212) 340-9700. Telex 425592 MGI UI.

Monthly journal. Deals with dairy, beef, and sheep farming in Great Britain. Price $30.00 per year.

3030
Livestock Market News Reports
US Dept of Agriculture, Agricultural Marketing Service, Room 2621-S, Washington, DC 20250. Telephone (202) 447-7861.

Irregular reports. Discuss livestock market and meat trade news. Include price of cattle and calves, hogs, sheep, lambs, and wholesale meats. Free of charge.

3031
Lloyds Bank Economic Bulletin
Lloyds Bank Ltd, PO Box 215, 71 Lombard St, London, England EC3P 3BS. Telephone (44) (01) 626-1500.

Monthly newsletter. Covers British economic, credit, and financial developments. Price available on request.

3032
Lloyds Bank Review
Lloyds Bank Ltd, PO Box 215, 71 Lombard St, London, England EC3P 3BS. Telephone (44) (01) 626-1500.

Quarterly report. Discusses general economic and financial issues. Price available on request.

3032.01
Lloyd's European Loading List
Lloyd's of London Press Ltd, Sheepen Pl, Colchester, Essex, England CO3 3LP. Telephone 0206 69222. Telex 987321.

Weekly booklet. Contains information on ships loading at European ports. Provides road haulage details. Price $280.00 per year.

3032.02
Lloyd's Law Reports
Lloyd's of London Press Ltd, Sheepen Pl, Colchester, Essex, England CO3 3LP. Telephone 0206 69222. Telex 987321.

Monthly report. Discusses maritime and insurance cases heard in British courts. Includes details of important US decisions involving shipping and aviation. Price $225.00 per year.

3032.03
Lloyd's List
Lloyd's of London Press Ltd, Sheepen Pl, Colchester, Essex, England CO3 3LP. Telephone 0206 69222. Telex 987321.

Daily newspaper. Contains shipping, insurance, transportation, energy, and finance news. Price $570.00 per year.

3033
Lloyd's Loading List, UK Edition
Lloyd's of London Press Ltd, Sheepen Pl, Colchester, Essex, England CO3 3LP. Telephone 0206 69222. Telex 987321.

Weekly booklet. Provides details of ships loading in Great Britain ports. Includes information on road haulage. Price $390.00 per year.

3033.01
Lloyd's Maritime & Commercial Law Quarterly
Lloyd's of London Press, Sheepen Pl, Colchester, Essex, England CO3 3LP. Telephone 0206 69222. Telex 987321.

Quarterly report. Reviews important maritime and commercial law developments. Includes texts of international conventions. Price $95.00 per year.

3033.02
Lloyd's Maritime Law Newsletter
Lloyd's of London Press, Sheepen Pl, Colchester, Essex, England CO3 3LP. Telephone 0206 69222. Telex 987321.

Fortnightly newsletter. Discusses international developments in maritime law. Price $206.00 per year.

3033.03
Lloyd's Monthly List of Laid Up Vessels
Lloyd's of London Press, Sheepen Pl, Colchester, Essex, England CO3 3LP. Telephone 0206 69222. Telex 987321.

Monthly booklet. Provides data on ships laid up throughout world. Includes details of vessels involved in oil storage schemes. Price $195.00 per year.

3033.04
Lloyd's Ship Manager
Lloyd's of London Press, Sheepen Pl, Colchester, Essex, England CO3 3LP. Telephone 0206 69222. Telex 987321.

Monthly magazine. Contains articles on ship operations, safety, and equipment. Price $77.00 per year.

3033.05
Lloyd's Shipping Economist
Lloyd's of London Press, Ltd, Sheepen Pl, Colchester, Essex, England CO3 3LP. Telephone 0206 69222. Telex 987321.

Monthly magazine. Offers analyses of world shipping orders, marine casualties, operating costs, sales, and purchases. Tables. Price $455.00 per year.

3033.06
Lloyd's Shipping Index
Lloyd's of London Press Ltd, Colchester, Essex, England CO3 3LP. Telephone 0206 69222. Telex 987321.

Daily report. Lists 21,000 vessels in commercial service. Includes information on ownership, flag, tonnage, current voyage, and position. Price $760.00 per year.

3033.07
Lloyd's Voyage Record
Lloyd's of London Press Ltd, Sheepen Pl, Colchester, Essex, England CO3 3LP. Telephone 0206 69222. Telex 987321.

Weekly report. Lists in chronological order reported arrivals and departures of 21,000 vessels. Price $945.00 per year.

3034
Lloyd's Weekly Casualty Reports
Lloyd's of London Press Ltd, Sheepen Pl, Colchester, Essex, England CO3 3LP. Telephone 0206 69222. Telex 987321.

Weekly booklet. Reprints all the marine, non-marine and aviation casualties published in Lloyd's List. Also includes details of fires, explosions, labor disputes, port conditions, dangers to navigation, hovercraft and air cushion vehicle casualties. Price $235.00 per year.

3035
Lobbying Reports
Plus Publications, Inc, 2626 Pennsylvania Ave NW, Washington, DC 20037. Telephone (202) 333-5444.

Semimonthly report. Reviews federal and state activity affecting lobbying profession. Topics include financial disclosure legislation and conflict of interest proposals. Price $137.00 per year.

3036
Local Area Personal Income 1973–1978
US Dept of Commerce, Bureau of Economic Analysis, Washington, DC 20230. Order from Superintendent of Documents, US Government Printing Office, Washington, DC 20402. Telephone (202) 783-3238.

Books. Contain personal income data by type of income and by major industries, population, and per capita income for various geographic areas. Price $42.75 for nine volumes.

3037
Local Financial Returns, Scotland
Her Majesty's Stationery Office, PO Box 569, London, England SE1 9NH. Telephone (44) (01) 928 1321.

Annual publication. Covers Scottish local financial returns. Price 75 per year.

3038
Local Government Financial Statistics, England and Wales
Her Majesty's Stationery Office, PO Box 569, London, England SE1 9NH. Telephone (44) (01) 928 1321.

Annual report. Gives local government financial statistics for Great Britain and Wales. Price £2.00 per year.

3039
Local Government Law
Matthew Bender & Co, 235 E 45th St, New York, NY 10017. Telephone (212) 661-5050.

Loose-leaf volumes with semiannual updates. Cover legislation affecting local governments. Price $350.00 for seven volumes; $139.50 for update.

3040
Lodging Hospitality
Penton/IPC, 614 Superior Ave W, Cleveland, OH 44113. Order from Penton/IPC, 1111 Chester Ave, Cleveland, OH 44114. Telephone (216) 696-7000.

Monthly magazine. Discusses hotel, motel, motor inn, and resort management. Price $24.00 per year.

3040.01
London Classification of Business Studies
Aslib, 3 Belgrave Sq, London, England. SW1X 8PL. Telephone (44) (01) 235-5050. Telex 23667.

Book. Provides 4000 indexing terms for business material. Includes library classification scheme. Price £22.50. ISBN 0-85142-124-5.

3041
London Shop Surveys
Newman Books, Ltd, 48 Poland St, London, England W1V 4PP. Telephone (44) (01) 439-0335.

Annual book. Surveys retail shops in London and head offices of multiple firms. Gives diagram maps of shopping areas. Price £14.50.

3042
Long Island Business Newsweekly and Reference Series
Long Island Commercial Review, Inc, 303 Sunnyside Blvd, Plainview, NY 11803. Telephone (516) 349-8200.

Weekly report. Provides information on Long Island business and economic conditions. Includes reports on insurance, security services, and banking. Price $49.00 per year.

3043
Long Island Economic Trends
Nassau-Suffolk Regional Planning Board, Veterans Memorial Hwy, Hauppauge, Long Island, New York, NY 11787. Telephone (516) 724-1919.

Monthly bulletin and quarterly supplements. Presents statistical data on Long Island, NY, employment, construction, personal income, retail sales, and other economic trends. Quarterly supplements evaluate economic developments. Free of charge.

3044
Long Range Planning
Pergamon Press, Inc, Maxwell House, Fairview Park, Elmsford, NY 10523. Telephone (914) 592-7700. Telex 13-7328.

Bimonthly magazine. Deals with development of long-range plans in economic, corporate, marketing, and computer and management science areas. Price $110.00 per year.

3045
Long Term Care
McGraw-Hill Publications Co, 1221 Ave of the Americas, New York, NY 10020. Order from McGraw-Hill Publications Co, 457 National Press Bldg, Washington, DC 20045. Telephone (202) 624-7558. Telex TWX 7105814879 WUI 62555.

Weekly bulletin. Discusses issues pertaining to nursing homes, extended care facilities, and home health agencies. Emphasizes government regulations and legislative developments. Price $187.00 per year.

3046
Looking Ahead and Projection Highlights
National Planning Assn, 1606 New Hampshire Ave, NW, Washington, DC 20009. Telephone (202) 265-7685.

Quarterly report. Presents research on varied economic and political topics, both domestic and foreign. Price $10,00 per year, $2.50 per copy.

3046.01
Los Angeles Business Journal
Cordovan Corp, 5314 Bingle Rd, Houston, TX 77092. Order from Los Angeles Business Journal, 611 S Catalina, Los Angeles, CA 90005. Telephone (213) 385-9050.

Weekly newspaper. Contains feature articles on various segments of Los Angeles business. Price $24.00 per year.

3047
Louisiana Business Review
Louisiana State University, College of Business Administration, Div of Research, 3139 CEBA, Baton Rouge, LA 70803. Telephone (504) 388-6645.

Quarterly report. Discusses Louisiana's economic conditions and business activities. Notes business law changes. Price free of charge.

3047.01
Louisiana Economic Indicators
Louisiana State University, College of Business Administration, Div of Research, 3139 CEBA, Baton Rouge, LA 70803. Telephone (504) 388-6645.

Monthly report. Provides Louisiana's employment, tourist traffic, construction, and other economic figures. Tables. Price free of charge.

3048
Louisiana Economy
Louisiana Tech University, Div of Administration and Business Research, PO Box 5796 Tech Station, Ruston, LA 71210. Telephone (318) 257-0211.

Quarterly report. Discusses Louisiana's economy and industry including housing, income, employment, and population. Tables. Free of charge.

3048.01
Louisiana: Manufacturers Directory, 1981
Manufacturers' News, Inc, 3 Huron St, Chicago, IL 60611. Telephone (312) 337-1084.

Biennial book. Names 2000 Louisiana firms by location and product. Notes parent companies and number of employees. Price $33.00.

3048.02
Louisiana: State Industrial Directory, 1981
Manufacturers' News, Inc, 3 Huron St, Chicago, IL 60611. Telephone (312) 337-1084.

Annual book. Contains information on industrial companies in Louisiana. Indicates county, city, and product. Price $30.00.

3049
LP/Gas
Harcourt Brace Jovanovich Publications, 757 3rd Ave, New York, NY 10017. Order from Harcourt Brace and Jovanovich Publications, 1 E 1st St, Duluth, MN 55802. Telephone (218) 727-8511.

Monthly magazine. Covers liquefied petroleum gas industry. Reports on distribution and wholesale and retail sales. Price $6.00 per year.

3050
LP-Gas Industry Market Facts
National LP-Gas Association, 1301 W 22nd St, Oak Brook, IL 60521. Telephone (312) 986-4800.

Annual report. Has statistics on production, sales, shipment, and other aspects of the LP-gas industry. Price available on request.

3051
Lynch International Investment Survey
Lynch-Bowes, Inc, 120 Broadway, Suite 1749, New York, NY 10271. Telephone (212) 962-2592.

Weekly newsletter. Covers world monetary and economic picture with emphasis on investments in natural resources, especially precious metals. Price $160.00 per year.

3052
Machine Design
Penton/IPC, 614 Superior Ave W, Cleveland, OH 44113. Order from Penton/IPC, 1111 Chester Ave, Cleveland, OH 44114. Telephone (216) 696-7000.

Semimonthly magazine. Focuses on machine design and design engineering. Price $42.00.

3053
Machinery & Production Engineering
Findlay Publications Ltd, 10 Letchworth Dr, Bromley, Kent, England BR2 9BE. Order from Machpress Ltd, 1 Copers Cope Rd, Beckenham, Kent, England, BR3 1NB. Telephone (44) (01) 650-4877.

Weekly publication. Pertains to marketing of machine tools in Great Britain and elsewhere. Price £32.00 per year.

3054
Mackenzie Valley Pipeline Assessment
Supply and Services Canada, Publishing Centre, Printing and Publishing, Ottawa, Ont, Canada K1A 0S9. Telephone (613) 238-1601.

Report. Discusses environmental and socioeconomic effects of proposed Canadian Arctic gas pipeline on Northwest Territories and Yukon area. Tables, graphs, and maps. Price $3.60 per copy.

3056
Madison Avenue
Madison Avenue Magazine, Inc, 369 Lexington Ave, New York, NY 10017. Telephone (212) 682-5250.

Monthly magazine. Deals with national advertising in various media. Price $30.00 per year.

3056.01
Magazine Index
Information Access Corp, 404 6th Ave, Menlo Park, CA 94025. Telephone (800) 227-8431.

Monthly microfilm service, with two loose-leaf supplements. Provides author, title, and subject indexes to 375 US magazines. Covers articles, news, product evaluations, editorials, poetry, recipes, reviews, and biographies. Price $1480.00 per year.

3056.02
Magazine Industry Market Place: The Directory of American Periodical Publishing
RR Bowker Co, 1180 Avenue of the Americas, New York, NY 10036. Order from RR Bowker Co, PO Box 1807, Ann Arbor, MI 48106. Telephone (212) 764-5100.

Annual directory. Gives information on 2150 selected periodicals, magazine publishers and other magazine industry firms, and support organizations and services. Price $35.00. ISBN 0-8352-1292-0. ISSN 0000-0434.

3057
Magazine of Bank Administration
Bank Administration Inst, PO Box 500, 303 S Northwest Hwy, Park Ridge, IL 60068. Telephone (312) 693-7300.

Monthly magazine. Includes articles on accounting, administration, bank building and organization, credit cards, automation, payment systems, bank security, personnel, and taxes. Price $16.00 per year.

3058
Magazines for Libraries
R R Bowker Co, 1180 Ave of the Americas, New York, NY 10036. Order from R R Bowker Co, PO Box 1807, Ann Arbor, MI 48106. Telephone (212) 764-5100.

Book. Serves as guide to magazine selection for librarians. Gives descriptive and critical annotations for more than 6500 periodicals. Price $37.50. ISBN 0-8352-0921-0.

3059
Mail Order Business Directory, **1981 edition**
B Klein Publication, Inc, PO Box 8503, Coral Springs, FL 33065. Telephone (305) 752-1708.

Book. Gives roster of 7000 most active mail order houses, especially those distributing catalogs. Indicates 500 largest firms. Price $55.00.

3060
Maine Business Indicators
Maine National Bank, 400 Congress St, Portland, ME PO Box 919, 04104. Telephone (207) 775-1000.

Bimonthly newsletter. Discusses trends that affect Maine's economy and business. Indicates manufacturing production, retail sales, construction employment, and other economic data. Tables. Free of charge.

3061
Main Economics Indicators
Organization for Economic Coorperation and Development, Publications Center, 1750 Pennsylvania Ave NW, Washington, DC 20006. Telephone (202) 724-1857.

Monthly report. Gives international indicators of economic activity. Price $74.-15.

3061.01
Maine: State Industrial Directory **1981**
Manufacturers' News, Inc, 3 Huron St, Chicago, IL 60611. Telephone (312) 337-1084.

Annual book. Lists 1500 Maine industrial firms by location and product. Price $20.00.

3061.02
Maine, Vermont, New Hampshire: Directory of Manufacturers **1979**
Manufacturers' News, Inc, 3 Huron St, Chicago, IL 60611. Telephone (312) 337-1084.

Biennial book. Provides information on manufacturing fi rms in Maine, Vermont, and New Hampshire by name, location, and product. Price $39.50.

3062
Mainly Marketing
Schoonmaker Associates, Drawer M, Coram, NY 11727. Telephone (516) 473-8741.

Monthly newsletter. Presents surveys and material relevant to marketing of technical products in the electronics field. Price $144.00 per year. ISSN 0464-591X.

3063
Major Mass Market Merchandisers
Salesman's Guide, Inc, 1140 Broadway, New York, NY 10001. Telephone (212) 684-2985.

Directory. Lists discount, variety, drug, supermarket, and off-price stores. Notes buyers of men's, women's, and children's wear and accessories. Price $60.00.

3064
Major Programs
US Dept of Labor, Bureau of Labor Statistics, 441 G St, NW, Washington, DC 20212. Telephone (202) 523-1221.

Annual report. Summarizes activities of Bureau of Labor Statistics. Indicates frequency with which data is made available, main publications, and principal uses of data. Describes other bureau information services. Free of charge.

3065
Major Tax Planning—University of Southern California Law Center Annual Institute on Federal Taxation.
Matthew Bender & Co, 235 E 45th St, New York, NY 10017. Telephone (212) 661-5050.

Annual book. Covers tax planning issues with emphasis on new legislation. Is based on University of Southern California Law Center Annual Inst on Federal Taxation. Price $50.00.

3066
Malpractice Lifeline
Malpractice Lifeline, Inc, 1240 Meadow Rd, Suite 207, Northbrook, IL 60062. Telephone (312) 272-3116.

Semimonthly newsletter. Reviews medical malpractice news and cases. Notes effect of malpractice legislation. Price $45.00 per year.

3067
Manage
National Management Assn, 2210 Arbor Blvd, Dayton, OH 45439. Telephone (513) 294-0421.

Quartly magazine. Contains articles on current business management topics, including labor productivity, human resources, MBO, communications, effective supervisions, meeting planning, and delegation. Price $5.00 per year.

3068
Management
Modern Productions Ltd, First Floor, Midland House, 73 Great North Road, PO Box 3159, Auckland, New Zealand. Telephone (64) (09) 768808.

Monthly magazine. Carries news of New Zealand Inst of Management, plus articles about New Zealand companies and general managment. Price $20.00 (New Zealand) per year.

3069
Management Accounting
National Assn of Accountants, 919 3rd Ave, New York, NY 10022. Telephone (212) 754-9768.

Monthly magazine. Covers management accounting topics such, as profit determinants, inflation, management information systems, small business, and budget procedures. Price $2.00 plus postage.

3070
Management Advisory Services Guidelines Series
American Inst of Certified Public Accountants, 1211 Ave of the Americas, New York, NY 10036. Telephone (212) 575-6200.

Seven loose-leaf books. Discuss management advisory services subjects. Cover administration of engagements, preparation of financial forecasts, use of computer-based application systems, and professional standards. Prices vary, $3.50–$6.00 per guideline.

3071
Management Advisory Services Manual, 1977
Canadian Inst of Chartered Accountants, 250 Bloor St E, Toronto, Ont, Canada M4W 1G5. Telephone (416) 962-1242.

Two loose-leaf books. Manual for accountants, auditors, management specialists, and business students on the undertaking, organizing, and administering of consulting engagements. Price $90.00.

3072
Management Aids
US Small Business Administration, 1030 15th St NW, Suite 250, Washington, DC 20417. Telephone (202) 655-4000. Order from US Small Business Administration, PO Box 15434, Fort Worth, TX 76119.

Pamphlets. Discusses problems financing, pricing, solid waste management, and advertising. Free of charge.

3073
Management Briefings
American Management Associations, 135 W 50th St, New York, NY 10020. Telephone (212) 586-8100.

Series of reports. Cover day-to-day management problems encountered in all types of industrial organizations. Price $7.50 per copy.

3074
Management Briefs
Howard University, School of Business and Public Administration, PO Box 748, Washington DC 20059. Telephone (202) 636-7187.

Monthly essays. Is geared to minority business owner or manager. Price available on request.

3075
Management Compensation in Canada, 1980, and The Remuneration of Chief Executive Officers in Canada, **1980**
H V Chapman Consulting & Compensation Ltd, Box 8, 24th Fl, One Dunas St W, Toronto, Ont, Canada M5G 1Z3. Telephone (416) 598-1700.

Annual books, three volumes. Present for key management positions the latest figures on annual salary, total cash bonus, and car allowances. Report on salaries, bonuses, total compensation, and company cars for chief executive officers only in second volume. Price $450.00, $282.00, and $245.00, respectively.

3076
Management Contents
Management Contents, 3014, Northbrook, IL 60062. Telephone (312)564-1006.

Biweekly service issued 26 times per year. Contains tables of contents of latest issues of business and management periodicals. Price $68.00 per year.

3077
Management Decision
MCB Publications, 200 Keighley Rd, Bradford, W Yorkshire, England, BD9 4JQ. Telephone 0274 499821.

Three journals and three monographs per year. Digest reports on such topics as management training, industrial relations, marketing, and corporate planning. Price $170.00 per year.

3079
Management Focus
Peat, Marwick, Mitchell & Co, 345 Park Ave, New York, NY 10022. Telephone (212) 758-9700.

Bimonthly magazine. Discusses current topics of interest to management. Free of charge.

3081
Management Information Manual
Samson Publications Ltd, 12-14 Hill Rise, Richmond, Surrey, England TW10 6UA. Telephone (44) (01) 948-4251.

Loose-leaf book. Contains information on law, finance, taxation, communications, travel, property, government, manpower, education, and leisure in Great Britain. Price $60.00 per year. ISBN 0-905713-00-1.

3082
Management of an Accounting Practice Handbook
American Inst of Certified Public Accountants, 1211 Ave of the Americas, New York, NY 10036. Telephone (212) 575-6200.

Loose-leaf book. Offers information on accounting practice management. Includes topics on financial administration, personnel, partnerships, and information systems. Price $150.00 per three volumes.

3083
Management of Foreign Exchange Risk
Euromoney Publications Ltd, Nestor House, Playhouse Yard, London, England EC4V 5EX. Telephone (44) (01) 236-7111. Telex 8812246 Eurmon G.

Book. Covers hedging options and techniques, use of various facilities, management controls, and Forex forecasts and factors determining their movements. Price $70.00. ISSN 0 903121 069.

3086
Management Review
American Management Assns, 135 W 50th St, New York, NY 10020. Telephone (212) 586-8100.

Monthly periodical. Covers developments in the field of management. Price $24.00 per year (available to members only).

3087
Management Review and Digest
British Inst of Management, Parker St, London, England WC2B 5PT. Telephone (44) (01) 405-3456.

Quarterly magazine. Contains articles, features, and reports on management subjects. Includes book reviews and news of current research. Price £5.00 per year. ISSN 0307-3580.

3088
Management Science
Inst of Management Sciences, 146 Westminster St, Providence, RI 02903. Telephone (401) 274-2525.

Monthly magazine. Serves management science field. Includes application of management theory. Price $50.00 per year.

3089
Management/Scope
Lawrence-Leiter and Co, 427 W 12th St, Kansas City, MO 64105. Telephone (816) 474-8340.

Quarterly newsletter. Discusses management topics including employee communications and performance appraisal.

3090
Management Services
Inst of Management Services, 1 Cecil St, London Rd, Enfield, Middlesex, England EN2 6DD. Telephone (44) (01) 363-7452.

Monthly magazine. Is directed at members and management. Considers topics such as work study, organization and methods, systems development, and allied management services. Price £18.72 per year.

3091
Management Today
Haymarket Publishing, Ltd, 76 Dean Street, London W1, England. Telephone (44) (01) 734-7124. Telex HAYMRLG 23918.

Monthly magazine. Reports on industry and business management. Emphasizes Great Britain but includes articles on Europe, US, and other countries. Price £20.00 per year. ISSN 0025-1925.

3092
Management World
Administrative Management Society, Maryland Ave, Willow Grove, PA 19090. Telephone (215) 659-4300.

Monthly magazine. Covers problems and developments in all fields of management. Price $18.00 per year.

3093
Managerial Finance
MCB Publications, 200 Keighly Rd, Bradford, W Yorkshire, England BD9 4JZ. Telephone 0274-43823.

Journal issued three times per year. Covers topics relevant to finance and management in western Europe. Price $47.00 per year.

3094
Managerial Law
MCB Publications, 200 Keighly Rd, Bradford, W Yorkshire, England BD9 4JZ. Telephone 0274-43823.

Continuously published looseleaf sheets. Concern legal aspects of day-to-day management of businesses in Great Britain. Price $90.00 per year.

3095
Managerial Planning
Planning Executives Inst, PO Box 70, Oxford, OH 45056. Telephone (513) 523-4185.

Bimonthly magazine. Presents technical research and current trends in areas of strategic, operational and financial planning. Includes topics on budgeting and accounting techniques. Price $18.00 per year.

3095.01
Managing Housing Letter
Community Development Services Inc, 399 National Press Bldg, Washington, DC 20045. Telephone (202) 638-6113.

Monthly report. Covers news and advice for public, private, and subsidized housing managers. Price $60.00 per year.

3095.02
Managing: People & Organizations
HBJ Newsletters, Inc, 757 3rd Ave, New York, NY 10017. Telephone (212) 888-3335.

Semimonthly newsletter. Addresses itself to business management techniques, including financial planning, investments, and marketing. Price $72.00 per year.

3095.03
Managing the Leisure Facility
Billboard Publications, Inc, PO Box 24970, Nashville, TN 37202. Telephone (615) 748-8127.

Bimonthly magazine. Reports on the operational aspects of mass entertainment facilities, such as arenas, stadiums, amusement parks, fairs, movie theaters, and race tracks. Price $2.95 per copy.

3096
Manchester Business School Review
Manchester Business School, Booth St, Manchester, England M15 6PB. Telephone (44) (061) 273 8228. Telex 668354.

Magazine issued three times per year. Contains articles related to business and management, particularly in Great Britain. Price £4.50.

3097
Manitoba Business Review
Canadian Dept of Industry and Commerce, 815-155 Carlton St, Winnipeg, Man, Canada R3C 3H8. Telephone (204) 944-2470, 944-2464. Telex 07-587833.

Quarterly magazine. Covers business activities in Manitoba including government programs. Free of charge. ISSN O380-6561.

3098
Manpower and Vocational Education Weekly
Capitol Publications, Inc, Suite G-12, 2430 Pennsylvania Ave, NW, Washington, DC 20037. Telephone (202) 452-1600.

Weekly newsletter. Reports on federal efforts to train people for jobs, with special emphasis on Comprehensive Employment and Training Act developments. Notes federal vocational education activities. Price $147.00 per year.

3100
Manpower Planning
Human Resources West, Inc, 681 Market St, Suite 976, San Francisco, CA 94105. Telephone (415) 397-5036.

Monthly newsletter. Focuses in each issue on one manpower planning issue, such as human resource accounting, or demand forecasting. Price $48.00 per year. ISSN 0364-7358.

3101
Manpower Review
Arizona Dept of Economic Security, Manpower Information and Analysis Section, PO Box 6123, Phoenix, AZ 85005. Telephone (602) 271-3871.

Annual report. Provides statistical analysis of Arizona's manpower developments. Free of charge.

3102
Manual of Classification
Patent and Trademark Office, Washington, DC 20231. Order from Superintendent of Documents, Government Printing Office, Washington, DC 20402. Telephone (202) 783-3238.

Loose-leaf book. Lists numbers and descriptive titles of classes and subclasses used in subject classification of US patents. Price $60.00.

3103
Manual of Oil and Gas Terms, Annotated
Matthew Bender & Co, 235 E 45th St, New York, NY 10017. Telephone (212) 661-5050.

Book. Supplies definitions of 1500 technical oil and gas terms. Price $45.00.

3104
Manual of Patent Examining Procedure
Patent and Trademark Office, Washington, DC 20231. Order from Superintendent of Documents, Government Printing Office, Washington, DC 20402. Telephone (202) 783-3238.

Loose-leaf book. Provides guide to US patent examining practice and procedure for Patent Examining Corps. Includes quarterly revisions. Price $39.00.

3105
Manual of Patent Office Practice
Supply and Services Canada, Pub Centre, Printing and Pub, Ottawa, Ont, Canada K1A 0S9. Telephone (613) 238-1601.

Loose-leaf book plus update service. Serves as guide to Canadian Patent Office practices. Bilingual. Price $42.00.

3106
Manufactured Housing Newsletter
Shepard D Robinson, 410 Grove Ave, Barrington, IL 60010. Telephone (312) 381-4312.

Semimonthly newsletter. Covers the manufactured housing industry including modular, prefabricated, and mobile homes. Price $48.00 per year.

3107
Manufacturers' Agent
Manufacturers' Agents Assn, 13A W St Reigate, Surrey, England RH2 9BL. Telephone Reigate 43492. Telex 895 4665.

Monthly newsletter. Has information pertinent to manufacturers' representatives in Great Britain and abroad. Price £10.00 per year.

3108
Manufacturers' Agents' Guide, 1976 edition
Manufacturers' Agent Publishing Co, Inc, 663 5th Ave, New York, NY 10022. Telephone (212) 682-0326.

Biennial book. Lists more than 11,500 manufacturers who distribute through agents, classified by industry. Price $27.-00.

3109
Manufacturers' Export Sales and Orders of Durable Goods
US Dept of Commerce, Bureau of the Census, Washington, DC 20233. Telephone (202) 449-1600.

Monthly report. Presents data on estimated value of manufacturers' export sales and new and unfilled orders of durable goods, including primary metals, electrical and nonelectrical machinery, motor vehicles and parts (sales data only), aircraft parts, and other transportation equipment. Price $3.00 per year.

3110
Manufacturers' Shipments, Inventories, and Orders
US Dept of Commerce, Bureau of the Census, Washington, DC 20233. Telephone (202) 449-1600.

Monthly report. Presents data on value of manufacturers' shipments, inventories, and orders. Includes seasonally adjusted data, preliminary data for current month, and revised data for previous 12 months. Price $3.60 per year.

3111
Manufacturers' Shipments, Inventories, and Orders, **1967-78 (Revised) M3-1.6**
US Dept of Commerce, Bureau of the Census, Washington, DC 20233. Telephone (202) 449-1600.

Monthly report. Revises data in monthly report, M3-1, Manufacturers' Shipments, Inventories, and Orders. Reflects shipments and inventory data to most recent levels available from 1972 Census of Manufactures and 1973 Annual Survey of Manufactures. Price $2.00.

3112
Manufacturing Chemist Aerosol Review
Morgan-Grampian Ltd, Morgan-Grampian House, Calderwood St, London, England SE18 6QH. Order from Morgan-Grampian Pub Co, 2 Park Ave, New York, NY 10016. Telephone England (44) (01) 855-7777. Telex 896238 MORGAN G. New York (212) 340-9700. Telex 425592 MGI UI.

Annual book. Serves as guide to aerosol products in Great Britain including marketing and production trends, suppliers of materials and equipment. Price $11.00 plus postage and handling.

3113
Manufacturing Chemist & Aerosol News
Morgan-Grampian Ltd, Morgan-Grampian House, Calderwood St, London, England SE18 6QH. Order from Morgan-Grampian Pub Co, 2 Park Ave, New York, NY 10016. Telephone England (44) (01) 855-7777. Telex 896238 MORGAN G. New York (212) 340-9700. Telex 425592 MGI UI.

Monthly magazine. Serves fine chemicals industries, particularly in pharmaceutical and toiletries fields. Contains special aerosols section. Price $95.00 per year.

3114
Manufacturing Directory of Idaho
University of Idaho, Center for Business Development and Research, Moscow, ID 83843. Telephone (208) 885-6611.

Book. Lists 1104 Idaho manufacturers alphabetically, geographically, SIC code, and product. Includes brief product descriptions. Price $22.50.

3115
Manufacturing Engineering
Society of Manufacturing Engineers, One SME Dr, PO Box 930, Dearborn, MI 48128. Telephone (313) 271-1500.

Monthly report. Covers trade news and developments in manufacturing technology and management. Price $22.00 per year. ISSN 0361-0853.

3116
Manufacturing Establishments, Details of Operations by Industry Class (Cat No 8203.0)
Australian Bureau of Statistics, PO Box 10, Belconnen, ACT 2616, Australia. Order from Australian Government Pub Service, PO Box 84, Canberra, ACT 2600, Australia. Telephone (61) (062) 527911.

Annual report. Gives results of census of Australian manufacturing establishments, employment, wages, expenses, and fixed capital expenditures. Tables by industry class. Price $3.05 (Australian).

3116.01
Manufacturing Industries of Canada: National and Provincial Areas
Statistics Canada, User Services, Publications Distribution, Ottawa, Ont, Canada K1A OV7. Telephone (613) 992-3151.

Annual review. Provides principal manufacturing statistics for Canada and its provinces by industry and industry group. Price $18.00. ISSN 0382-4144.

3117
Manufacturing Industries of Canada, Sub-provincial Areas
Statistics Canada, User Services, Publications Distribution, Ottawa, Ont, Canada K1A 0V7. Telephone (613) 992-3151.

Annual report. Supplies statistics on Canadian manufacturing industries for economic regions, metropolitan areas, and selected municipalities. Price $24.00. ISSN 0382-4012.

3119
Manufacturing Investment Statistics
Conference Board, Inc, 845 3rd Ave, New York, NY 10022. Telephone (212) 759-0900.

Quarterly report. Furnishes data on capital appropriations for new plants and equipment for 1000 largest manufacturing corporations. Price available on request.

3120
Marine Engineering/Log
Simmons-Boardman Pub Corp, 350 Broadway, New York, NY 10013. Telephone (212) 966-7700.

Monthly magazine. Reports on marine engineering for those involved with merchant and naval ships, offshore drilling rigs, and other commercial craft. Price $10.00 per year.

3121
Marine Policy
IPC Business Press Ltd, 205 E 42nd St, New York, NY 10017. Telephone (212) 889-0700. Telex 421710.

Quarterly magazine. Deals with uses for coastal and ocean waters and with national and international ocean regulations. Price $164.10 airmail. ISSN 0308-597X.

3122
Maritime and Construction Aspects of Ocean Thermal Energy Conversion (OTEC) Plant Ships
US Maritime Adm, Commerce Bldg, 14th & E St NW, Washington, DC 20230. Order from National Technical Information Service, 5285 Port Royal Rd, Springfield, VA 22161. Telephone (703) 487-4650.

Publication. Covers maritime and construction aspects of ocean thermal energy conversion plant ships. Price $12.00.

3124
Maritime Research Center Newsletter
Maritime Research, Inc, 11 Broadway, New York, NY 10004. Telephone (212) 269-3061.

Weekly newsletter. Lists international maritime charter fixtures by commodity, trade routes, and dates. Price $160.00 per year.

3125
Market Absorption of Apartments
US Dept of Commerce, Bureau of the Census, Washington, DC 20233. Telephone (202) 449-1600.

Quarterly report. Supplies statistics on rate at which nonsubsidized and unfurnished privately financed apartments are rented. Covers buildings with five or more units. Includes data on apartments completed during year. Price $2.80 per year.

3125.01
Market Builder Magazine
Research and Review Service of America, Inc, PO Box 1727, Indianapolis, IN 46206. Telephone (317) 297-4360.

Monthly magazine. Features subjects that influence the life insurance industry. Price $12.00 per year.

3126
Market Chronicle
Market Chronicle, 45 John St, Suite 911, New York, NY 10038. Telephone (212) 233-5200.

Weekly newspaper. Covers over 5000 over-the-counter stock prices. Contains articles on stock and bonds. Price $40.00.

3127
Marketing
Inst of Marketing, Moor Hall, Cookham, Maidenhead, Berkshire, England SL6 9QH. Telephone Bourne End (062 85) 24922.

Weekly journal. Gives news and trends within specific industries and case histories with special emphasis on the UK. Furnishes Institute of Marketing news. Price $57.00 per year air mail.

3127.01
Marketing & Media Decisions
Decisions Publications, Inc, 342 Madison Ave, New York, NY 10017. Telephone (212) 953-1888.

Monthly magazine. Interprets trends in marketing and media as they affect national advertisers and agencies. Price $36.00 per year.

3127.02
Marketing Bestsellers
North American Publishing Co, 401 N Broad St, Philadelphia, PA 19108. Telephone (215) 574-9600.

Monthly magazine. Covers mass market paperback and magazine industry. Includes paperback book reviews, list of bestselling paperbacks, and news of book tie-ins to movies and television programs. Price $9.00 per year.

3127.03
Marketing Communications
United Business Publications, Inc, 475 Park Ave S, New York, NY 10016. Telephone (212) 725-2300.

Monthly magazine. Discusses marketing communications ideas and applications. Price $13.50 per year.

3128
Marketing Economics Institute (MEI) Marketing Economics Guide, 1980–81
Marketing Economics Inst Ltd, 441 Lexington Ave, New York, NY 10017. Telephone (212) 687-5090.

Loose-leaf book. Gives information to help develop effective marketing strategy. Price $15.50.

3129
Marketing Economics Key Plants,
1979–80
Marketing Economics Inst Ltd, 441 Lexington Ave, New York, NY 10017. Telephone (212) 687-5090.

Biennial directory. Lists 40,000 plants that have more than 100 employees. Is aimed at sales people seeking industrial markets. Price $80.00 per copy. ISBN 0-914078-23-2. ISSN 0098-1397.

3130
Marketing for Sales Executives
Research Inst of America, Inc, 589 5th Ave, New York, NY 10017. Telephone (212) 755-8900.

Biweekly newsletter. Deals with marketing news for high-level management. Provides sales advice. Price $36.00 per year.

3130.01
Marketing Ideas
Predicasts, Inc, 11001 Cedar Ave, Cleveland, OH 44106. Telephone (216) 795-3000.

Weekly newsletter. Reports on marketing trends, advertising news, and market research. Price $132.00 per year.

3130.02
Marketing in Europe
Economist Intelligence Unit Ltd, Spencer House, 27 St James's Pl, London, England SW1A 1NT. Order from Economist Intelligence Unit Ltd, 75 Rockefeller Plz, New York, NY 10019. Telephone (212) 541-5730. Telex 148393.

Monthly journal. Reports on consumer markets in Europe, with emphasis on the original six EEC countries. Price $310.00 per year.

3131
Marketing Information Guide
Hoke Communications, Inc, 224 7th St, Garden City, NY 11535. Telephone (516) 746-6700.

Bimonthly bibliography lists books, articles, and other sources of information on marketing. Is indexed by subject and geographical area. Price $30.00 per year.

3132
Marketing Letter
Alexander Hamilton Inst, 1633 Broadway, New York, NY 10019. Telephone (212) 397-3580.

Monthly letter. Reports on sales and marketing techniques, new trends that affect marketing and international marketing terminology. Price $63.00 per year.

3133
Marketing News
American Marketing Assn, 222 S Riverside Plz, Chicago, IL 60606. Telephone (312) 648-0536.

Biweekly newspaper. Covers activities of American Marketing Association and other marketing news. Price included with membership, $20.00 per year nonmember.

3135
Marketing Science Institute Newsletter
Marketing Science Inst, 14 Story St, Cambridge, MA 02138. Telephone (617) 491-2060.

Newsletter issued three times per year. Pertains to research and activities of Marketing Science Institute in marketing sciences. Free of charge.

3136
Marketing Times
Sales and Marketing Executives International, Inc, 380 Lexington Ave, New York, NY 10168. Telephone (212) 986-9300.

Bimonthly magazine. Covers variety of marketing topics such as new product research and product performance. Price $10.00 per year.

3137
Market Research Abstracts
Market Research Society, 15 Belgrave Sq, London, England SW1X 8PF. Telephone (44) (01) 235-4709.

Biannual information service. Abstracts from 40 journals cover marketing and advertising research. Price £25.00.

3138
Market Research Handbook
Supply and Services Canada, Canadian Govt Publishing Centre, Hull, Que, Canada K1A 0S9. Telephone (819) 994,3475, 2085.

Annual book. Provides information on Canadian markets. Includes statistics on population growth, income distribution, and changes in consumer consumption patterns. Bilingual. Price $30.00.

3139
Market Research Society (MRS)
Newsletter
Market Research Society, 15 Belgrave Sq, London, England SW1X 8PF. Telephone (44) (01) 235-4709.

Monthly newsletter. Carries news of Market Research Society activities. Price £ 36.00 per year.

3140
Market Research Society, **Yearbook**
Market Research Society, 15 Belgrave Sq, London, England SW1X 8PF. Telephone (01) 235-4709.

Annual book. Lists members of Market Research Society, plus companies practicing market research in Great Britain that have at least one society full member on staff. Price £20.00.

3141
Market Rhythm
Investors Pub Co, PO Box 36171, Grosse Pointe Farms, MI 48236. Telephone (313) 821-3738.

Book. Describes methods of recording, measuring, and analyzing stock and commodity market trends. Evaluates short- and long-term changes. Price $100.00.

3142
Market Share Reports
US Dept of Commerce, Industry and Trade Adm, Bureau of Export Development, Washington, DC 20230. Order from National Technical Information Service, 5285 Port Royal Rd, Springfield, VA 22161. Telephone (202) 377-2000.

Annual pamphlet. Provides product-by-product comparison of exports from the US and competing industrial nations. Includes a five-year analysis of the international export market. Price $4.75 each country series, $3.25 each commodities series.

3143
Markets of the World
Chart Analysis Ltd, 194-200 Bishopsgate, London, England EC2M 4PE. Telephone (44) (01) 283-4476. Telex 883356.

Weekly report. Summarizes financial news of 16 stock markets. Offers technical comments and charts of each market index. Price £100.00 per year.

3144

Marple's Business Newsletter

Marple's Business Newsletter, Inc, 444 Coleman Bldg, Seattle, WA 98104. Telephone (206) 622-0155.

Biweekly newsletter. Covers business conditions and economic outlook in Pacific Northwest. Price $42.00 per year.

3144.01

Mart

Morgan-Grampian Ltd, Morgan-Grampian House, Calderwood St, London, England SE18 6QH. Telephone (44) (01) 855-7777. Telex 896238. Order from Morgan-Grampian Publishing Co, 2 Park Ave, New York, NY 10016. Telephone (212) 340-9700. Telex 425592 MGI UI.

Monthly publication. Serves retailers of consumer electronics, major appliances and electric housewares. Price $18.00 per year.

3145

Maryland Banking Quarterly

Maryland Bankers Assn, Maryland National Bank Bldg, PO Box 822, Baltimore, MD 21203. Telephone (301) 752-6638.

Quarterly magazine. Discusses banking and bank regulations, particularly in Maryland. Includes articles on local industries. Price $5.00 per year.

3146

Maryland Magazine

Maryland Dept of Economic and Community Development, 2525 Riva Rd, Annapolis, MD 21401. Telephone (301) 269-3507.

Quarterly magazine. Contains articles and photographs about Maryland. Price $6.50.

3146.01

Maryland: Manufacturers Directory,
1979–80

Manufacturers' News, Inc, 3 Huron St, Chicago, IL 60611. Telephone (312) 337-1084.

Biennial book. Lists Maryland manufacturing firms and identifies executives. Price $25.00.

3146.02

Maryland: State Industrial Directory,
1980

Manufacturers' News, Inc, 3 Huron St, Chicago, IL 60611. Telephone (312) 337-1084.

Annual book. Lists 4000 Maryland industrial firms by name, location, and product. Includes information on District of Columbia. Price $35.00.

3147

Maryland Statistical Abstract, **1978 edition**

Maryland Dept of Economic and Community Development, 2525 Riva Rd, Annapolis, MD 21401. Telephone (301) 269-2051.

Statistical record. Presents data on population, business, agriculture, natural resources, and other aspects of life in Maryland. Price $15.00.

3148

Massachusetts Business & Economic Report

University of Massachusetts, School of Business Administration, Amherst, MA 01003. Telephone (413) 549-4930.

Quarterly report. Considers Massachusetts economic conditions and business trends. Contains business and economic indicators and economic forecast. Tables and charts. Price free of charge.

3149

Massachusetts CPA Review

Massachusetts Society of Certified Public Accountants, Inc, 3 Center Plz, Boston, MA 02108. Telephone (617) 227-0196.

Bimonthly report. Presents information on accounting, auditing, and tax topics. Notes Massachusetts tax changes. Price free of charge to members, $15.00 per year non-members.

3149.01

Massachusetts: Directory of Manufacturers, **1981–82**

Manufacturers' News, Inc, 3 Huron St, Chicago, IL 60611. Telephone (312) 337-1084.

Annual book. Lists 8500 manufacturing firms in Massachusetts by name, location, and product. Price $49.50.

3149.02

Massachusetts: Manufacturers Directory, **1980**

Manufacturers' News, Inc, 3 Huron St, Chicago, IL 60611. Telephone (312) 337-1084.

Annual book. Provides information on 11,000 Massachusetts manufacturing firms by name, location, and product. Price $39.00.

3149.03

Massachusetts: Service Directory, **1979–80**

Manufacturers' News, Inc, 3 Huron St, Chicago, IL 60611. Telephone (312) 337-1084.

Biennial book. Contains information on 6000 service firms in Massachusetts. Price $38.00.

3149.04

Massachusetts: State Industrial Directory, **1981**

Manufacturers' News, Inc, 3 Huron St, Chicago, IL 60611. Telephone (312) 337-1084.

Annual book. Lists 10,000 industrial firms in Massachusetts and identifies executives. Price $60.00.

3150

Masters in Business Administration (MBA)

Masters in Business Administration (MBA) Communications, Inc, 730 3rd Ave, New York, NY 10017 Telephone (212) 557-9240.

Monthly magazine. Contains articles about career opportunities for those holding Masters in Business Administration, and features of general interest. Price $12.00 per year.

3151

Matekon

M E Sharpe, Inc, 80 Business Park Dr, Armonk, NY 10504. Telephone (914) 273-1800.

Quarterly journal. Offers translations of pieces on mathematical economics in USSR and Eastern Europe. Price $127.00 per year.

3152

Material Handling Engineering

Penton/IPC, 614 Superior Ave W, Cleveland, OH 44113. Telephone (216) 696-0300.

Monthly magazine. Discusses material handling systems, product design, control and application, and industrial packaging. Price $24.00.

3153

Materials Engineering

Penton/IPC, 614 Superior Ave W, Cleveland, OH 44113. Order from Penton/IPC, 1111 Chester Ave, Cleveland, OH 44114. Telephone (216) 696-7000.

Monthly magazine. Reports on materials production, evaluation, and selection. Price $24.00.

3154
Materials Handbook: An Encyclopedia for Purchasing Managers, Engineers, Executives, and Foremen, **1971 edition**
George B Brady, McGraw-Hill Book Co, Hightstown-Princeton Rd, Hightstown, NJ 08520. Telephone (609) 448-1700. Telex 843449.

Book. Lists and describes materials and their applications. Price available on request.

3154.01
Mathematical Programming/Mathematical Programming Studies
North-Holland Publishing Co, PO Box 211, 1000 AE Amsterdam, The Netherlands. Order from Elsevier/North-Holland, Inc, 52 Vanderbilt Ave, New York, NY 10017. Telephone (212) 867-9040.

Bimonthly journal, plus two additional volumes. Covers theoretical, computational, and applicational aspects of mathematical programming. Price $203.00 per year. ISSN 0025-5610 and 0303-3929.

3154.02
Mathematical Social Sciences
North-Holland Publishing Co, PO Box 211, 1000 AE Amsterdam, The Netherlands. Order from Elsevier/North-Holland, Inc, 52 Vanderbilt Ave, New York, NY 10017. Telephone (212) 867-9040.

Quarterly journal. Contains research papers, news items, calendar of meetings, and book reviews in the mathematical social sciences. Price $86.25 per year. ISSN 0165-4896.

3154.03
Matthews' CATV
Publicorp Communications, Inc, Box/CP 1029, Pointe Claire, Que, H9S 4H9, Canada. Telephone (514) 695-0289.

Index issued three times per year. Covers 630 Canadian licensed cable television systems. Notes program information, converter services, and production equipment. Price $40.00 per year.

3155
Matthews' List
Publicorp Communications, Inc, Box/CP 1029, Pointe Claire, Que, Canada H9S 4H9. Telephone (514) 695-0289.

Index issued three times per year. Lists information for Canada's communications industry. Includes news deadlines, personnel, and addresses. Price $85.00 per year.

3156
Matthews' List of CATV's
Publicorp Development Communications, Inc, PO Box 1172, Pointe Claire, Que, Canada H9S 4H9. Telephone (519) 538-1211.

Newsletter issued three times per year. Shows areas served by Canadian cable TV companies, chief executive officers, and programming and business details. Price $28.75 per year.

3157
Mattresses, Foundations, and Sleep Furniture
US Dept of Commerce, Bureau of the Census, Washington, DC 20233. Telephone (202) 449-1600.

Monthly report and annual summary. Supplies data on quantity and value of manufacturers' shipments of mattresses, foundations and dual purpose sleep furniture. Includes seasonally adjusted figures. Price $4.25 per year.

3158
MBH Weekly Commodity Future Trading Letter
MBH Commodity Advisors, Inc, Box 353, Winnetka, IL 60093. Telephone (800) 323-5486.

Weekly newsletter. Reviews commodity market trends. Offers advice on specific commodities. Graphs and charts. Price $415.00 per year.

3158.01
McCarthy Information Services
Financial Times Business Information Ltd, Bracken House, 10 Cannon St, London, England, EC4P 4BY. Order from McCarthy Information Ltd, Manor House, Ash Walk, Warminster, Wiltshire, England BA12 8PY. Telephone (44) (01) 0985-215151.

Information sheets. Provides extracts of news and comments from the world's business press, with separate page for each company or industry about which an article has been written. Price available on request.

3159
McGill University Industrial Relations Centre Review
McGill University, Industrial Relations Centre, Samuel Bronfman Bldg, 1001 Sherbrooke St W, Montreal, Que, Canada H3A 1G5. Telephone (514) 392-3077.

Newsletter published three times per year. Gives information on industrial relations in US and Canada. Announces forthcoming conferences and seminars. Features interviews with experts. Price available on request.

3160
McGraw-Hill Dictionary of Modern Economics: A Handbook of Terms and Organizations, **2d edition, 1973**
McGraw-Hill Book Co, Hightstown-Princeton Rd, Hightstown, NJ 08520. Telephone (609) 448-1700. Telex 843449.

Book. Dictionary containing definitions of terms and descriptions of organizations. Price $22.95.

3161
Measurement and Evaluation in Guidance
American Personnel and Guidance Assn, 2 Skyline Place, Suite 400, 5203 Leesburg Pike, Falls Church, VA 22041. Telephone (703) 820-4700.

Quarterly magazine. Reports on measurement and evaluation topics for guidance counselors. Price $12.00 per year.

3163
Meat Producer and Exporter
Australian Meat and Live-stock Corp, GPO Box 4129, Sydney, NSW 2001, Australia. Telephone (02) 267-9488. Telex AA 22887.

Monthly magazine. Discusses Australian Meat production and markets. Covers Australian Meat and Live-stock Corp activities. Price free of charge.

3164
Meat **(Cat No 7206.0)**
Australian Bureau of Statistics, PO Box 10, Belconnen, ACT 2616, Australia. Order from Australian Government Publishing Service, PO Box 84, Canberra, ACT 2600, Australia. Telephone (062) 527911.

Annual report. Presents statistical information on Australian meat industry including number and gross value of live-stock slaughtered and quantity of meat produced. Price free of charge.

3164.01
Meat, Poultry and Seafood Digest
Intertec Publishing Corp, 9221 Quivera Rd, PO Box 12901, Overland Park, KS 66212. Telephone (913) 888-4664. Telex 42-4156.

Monthly magazine. Covers meat, poultry, and seafood industry. Reports on new products, equipment, and processes. Price $24.00 per year.

3164.02
Mechanical & Electrical Cost Data
R S Means Co, Inc, 100 Construction Plz, Kingston, MA 02364. Telephone (617) 747-1270.

Annual book. Provides unit and systems prices for labor, equipment, and materials used in wide range of mechanical and electrical construction. Price $29.50.

3165
Media and Methods
North American Pub Co, 401 N Broad St, Philadelphia, PA 19108. Telephone (215) 574-9600.

Magazine issued nine times per year. Reports on audiovisual aids and other new educational approaches. Is aimed at junior and senior high school and college teachers. Price $18.00 per year.

3166
Media '81
Thomson Publications (Australia) Pty Ltd, 47 Chippen St, PO Box 65, Chippendale, NSW 2008, Australia. Telephone 699-6731. Telex TPAS AA22226.

Published two times a year. Contains information about the Australian newspaper, radio, television, consumer, and advertisement in business publications. Price $30.00 (Australian) per year.

3167
Media Expenditure Analysis Ltd (MEAL)
Media Expenditure Analysis Ltd, 110 St Martin's Ln, London, England, WC2N 4BH. Telephone (44) (01) 240-1903.

Monthly reports. Provides data on brand name advertising broken down by product. Includes microfilm library. Price available on request.

3168
Media Fax
Terminus Media, Inc, 1819 Peachtree Rd NE, Atlanta, GA 30309. Telephone (404) 351-8351.

Directory published annually with continuous updates provided throughout the year. Lists all advertising media in metropolitan Atlanta, GA, including newspapers, periodicals, radio, television, and outdoor advertising. Specifies prices, format, frequency, and distribution. Price $50.00 per year.

3169
Media/General (M/G) Financial Weekly Market Digest
Media General Financial Services, Inc, PO Box C-32333, Richmond, VA 23293. Telephone (804) 649-6569.

Weekly newspaper. Charts activity of some 3450 stocks for up to five years, including bonds and mutual funds. Price $98.00 per year.

3170
Media Guide International: Airline/Inflight Magazines Edition
Directories International, 1718 Sherman Ave, Evanston, IL 60201. Telephone (312) 491-0019.

Annual book. Furnishes advertising rates and data for world's airline and in-flight magazines. Price $25.00 per copy.

3171
Media Guide International: Business/Professional Publications Edition
Directories International, 1718 Sherman Ave, Evanston, IL 60201. Telephone (312) 491-0019.

Four-volume annual book. Provides advertising rates and data for more than 8000 business, professional, and trade publications. Covers 90 countries. Offers regional issues for Europe, Asia, Australia, and USSR, Latin America, Middle East, and Africa. Price $220.00 per year. ISBN 0-912794.

3172
Media Guide International: Newspapers/Newsmagazines Edition
Directories International, 1718 Sherman Ave, Evanston, IL 60201. Telephone (312) 491-0019.

Annual book. Supplies data and advertising rates for newspapers and news magazines in 110 countries. Arranges editions by continent and includes special section and multicontinental media, and advertising tax information for each country. Price $65.00 per copy. ISBN 0-912794.

3173
Media Industry Newsletter
Media Industry Newsletter, 75 E 55nd St, New York, NY 10022. Telephone (212) 751-2670.

Weekly newsletter. Reports on all aspects of the media community. Price $96.00 per year.

3174
Media International
Alain Charles Pub Ltd, 27 Wilfred St, London, England SW1E 6PR. Telephone (44) (01) 828-6107. Telex 28905.

Monthly magazine. Covers international advertising and marketing. Price $40.00 per year.

3175
Media Law Reporter
Bureau of National Affairs, Inc, 1231 25th St, NW, Washington, DC 20037. Telephone (202) 452-4200.

Loose-leaf books plus weekly updates. Furnish text of federal and state court decisions that affect newspapers, magazines, television, and radio. Price $307.00 per year.

3176
Media Records Blue Book
Media Records, Inc, 370 7th Ave, New York, NY 10001. Telephone (212) 736-7490.

Quarterly report. Contains information on newspaper advertising industry, including linage and total dollar investment by brand, market, newspaper, and other data. Price $2500.00 per year.

3177
Media Records Green Book
Media Records, Inc, 370 7th Ave, New York, NY 10001. Telephone (212) 736-7490.

Quarterly report. Covers national investments in newspaper advertising by brand, market, newspaper, and other data in 90 cities. Price $3100.00 per year.

3178
Media Reporter
Brennan Publications, 148 Birchover Way, Allestree, Derby, England. Telephone 0332-551884.

Quarterly publication. Covers professional journalistic standards, journalism education and training, and media studies in Great Britain and other parts of world. Notes pertinent conferences and books. Price £1.00 per copy (postage extra). ISSN 0309-0256.

3179
Medical & Healthcare Marketplace Guide, 3rd edition, 1981
International Bio-Medical Information Service, Inc, PO Box 756, Miami, FL 33156. Telephone (305) 665-4856.

Book. Contains data on over 2000 US-based manufacturers and dealers connected with medical field. Includes drug, medical electronic equipment, and dental supply companies. Tables. Price $200.00. ISSN 0146-8022.

3180
Medical Economics
Medical Economics Co, 680 Kinderkamack Rd, Oradell, NJ 07649. Telephone (201) 262-3030.

Fortnightly report. Publishes articles on office-based medical practices. Discusses personal and financial affairs of physicians. Price $39.00 per year.

3181
Medical Marketing & Media
Technomic Publishing Co, Inc, 265 Post Rd W, Westport, CT 06880. Telephone (203) 226-1151.

Monthly magazine. Reports on medical and health care marketplace. Includes information on government regulations, stock market and advertising. Price $25.00 per year.

3181.01
Medical Meetings
United Business Publications, Inc, 475 Park Ave S, New York, NY 10016. Telephone (212) 725-2300.

Magazine published seven times per year. Analyzes cities, resorts, and medical centers suitable for medical meetings. Price $14.75 per year.

3182
Medical School Rounds
International Bio-Medical Information Service, Inc, PO Box 756, Miami, FL 33156. Telephone (305) 665-4856.

Monthly newsletter. Reports on medical technology being developed at medical schools, institutions, and research centers throughout world. Price $100.00 per year. ISSN 0095-0998.

3183
Medical World News
McGraw-Hill Publications Co, 1221 Ave of the Americas, New York, NY 10020. Telephone (212) 997-1221. Telex TWX 7105814879 WUI 6255.

Biweekly magazine. Covers significant events in the fields of science and practice of medicine. Price $28.00 per year.

3184
Medicare-Medicaid Guide
Commerce Clearing House, Inc, 4025 W Peterson Ave, Chicago, IL 60646. Telephone (312) 583-8500.

Four loose-leaf books plus biweekly reports. Supply guide to laws, regulations, intermediary letters, and policy decisions regarding Medicare and Medicaid. Price $395.00 per year.

3185
Medicare Report
National Features Syndicate, Inc, 1 National Press Bldg, Washington, DC 20045. Telephone (202) 393-2100.

Newsletter. Discusses Medicare and related health care industry issues. Price $68.00 per year.

3186
Meeting News
Gralla Publications, 1515 Broadway, New York, NY 10036. Telephone (212) 869-1300.

Monthly magazine. Covers convention, trade show, and professional meeting planning. Price available on request.

3187
Meetings & Incentive Travel
Southam Communications Ltd, 1450 Don Mills Rd, Don Mills, Ont, Canada M3B 2X7. Telephone (416) 445-6641. Telex 06 966612.

Bimonthly magazine. Provides information on running of meetings and conventions in Canada. Price $22.00 per year.

3188
Meetings, Conferences & Conventions: A Financial Post Guide
Financial Post, 481 University Ave, Toronto, Ont, Canada M5W 1A7. Telephone (416) 596-5649.

Annual magazine. Reviews meetings, conventions, and conferences of interest to Canadian investment world. Free with Financial Post Magazine subscription.

3188.01
Memorandum by the Chief Secretary to the Treasury Appropriation Accounts
Her Majesty's Stationery Office, PO Box 569, London, England SE1 9NH. Telephone (44) (01) 928-1321.

Three-volume annual book. Gives details of expenditures incurred by British Government departments during the previous financial year. Price £29.00.

3189
Men's Apparel
US Dept of Commerce, Bureau of the Census, Washington, DC 20233. Telephone (202) 449-1600.

Monthly report. Supplies figures on cuttings of selected men's garments including suits, coats, trousers, shirts, pajamas, undershorts, and sweaters. Price $3.00 per year.

3189.01
Men's Wear
Northwood Publications Ltd, Elm House, 10–16 Elm St, London, England WC1X OBP. Order from Subscription Manager, 23–29 Emerald St, London, England WC1N 3QJ. Telephone (44) (01) 404-5531. Telex 21746.

Weekly publication. Covers men's and boys's clothing in Britain at retail level. Price £25.00 United Kingdom, £50.00 overseas.

3189.02
Men's Wear
Yaffa Publishing Group, 432-436 Elizabeth St, Surry Hills, NSW 2001, Australia. Order from Yaffa Publishing Group, GPO Box 606, Sydney, NSW 2001, Australia. Telephone (61) (02) 699-7861. Telex 21887.

Monthly magazine. Covers mens apparel industry in Australia. Includes buying guide. Price $30.00 (Australian) per year.

3190
Mercantile Gazette of New Zealand
Mercantile Gazette of New Zealand Ltd, Box 20-034, Christchurch 5, New Zealand. Telephone (64) (3) 583-219.

Biweekly magazine. Reports on bankruptcy records, company registrations and directorships, cartel securities, and commercial topics for New Zealand. Price $19.000 (New Zealand) per year.

3192

Merchandising Inventories

Statistics Canada, User Services, Publications Distribution, Ottawa, Ont, Canada K1A 0V7. Telephone (613) 992-3151.

Monthly report. Presents statistics on Canadian inventories and stocks/sales ratios by type of trade, department, and kind of business. Notes quarterly percentage changes for independent retailers. Price $30.00 per year. ISSN 0380-7177.

3194

Merchant Marine Data Sheet

US Maritime Adm, Commerce Bldg, 14th & E St NW, Washington, DC 20230.

Monthly data sheet on US Merchant Marine. Price available on request.

3195

Mergers & Acquisitions

Information for Industry, The Hay Group, 229 S 18th St, Phila, PA 19103. Telephone (215) 875-2330.

Quarterly journal. Publishes articles on the merger/acquisition/divestiture process, plus rosters listing such activity for each quarter. Price $48.00 per year.

3196

Metal and Engineering Industry Yearbook

Peter Isaacson Publications, 46-49 Porter St, Prahran, Vic 3181, Australia. Telephone (61) (03) 518431. Telex 30880.

Annual book. Reports on metal, engineering, and plastic products in Australia. Supplies special sections on industrial relations and government regulations. Lists products, services, companies, and brand names. Price $28.00 plus postage.

3196.01

Metals Daily

Llewellyn King, 300 National Press Bldg, Washington, DC 20045. Telephone (202) 638-4302.

Newsletter published every business day. Covers major policy, economic, and technological issues pertaining to the steel industry, as well as to competitive metals, ancillary industries, and essential metallic steelmaking raw materials. Price $400.00 per year, $425.00 overseas.

3197

Metals Week

McGraw-Hill Publications Co, 1221 Ave of the Americas, New York, NY 10020. Telephone (212) 997-1221. Telex TWX 7105814879. WUI 62555.

Weekly newsletter. Provides price and market information for nonferrous metals. Price $397.00 per year.

3198

Metals Week Insider Report

McGraw-Hill Publications Co, 1221 Ave of the Americas, New York, NY 10020. Telephone (212) 997-1221. Telex TWX 7105814879 WUL 62555.

Daily report. Provides information on government rulings or corporate activity that may affect metals prices. Summarizes metals-oriented developments. Price $2850.00 per year.

3199

Metals Week Price Handbook

McGraw-Hill Book Co, Hightstown-Princeton Rd, Hightstown, NJ 08520. Telephone (609) 448-1700. Telex 843449.

Handbook. Provides information on international nonferrous metals prices and markets. Price $72.00.

3200

Metalworking Directory

Dun & Bradstreet, Box 3224, Church Street Station, New York, NY 10008. Telephone (212) 285-7346.

Annual book. Contains marketing facts on all US metal producing and metalworking plants with 20 or more employees. Includes approximately 39,000 plants. Price available on request. Available to Dun & Bradstreet subscribers only.

3201

Metalworking Machinery

US Dept of Commerce, Bureau of the Census, Washington, DC 20233. Telephone (202) 449-1600.

Quarterly report with annual summary. Contains information on shipments of all metalworking machinery, with separate data for numerically controlled machines. Indicates value of export shipments. Price $1.50 per year.

3202

Metalworking Production

Morgan-Grampian Ltd, Morgan-Grampian House, Calderwood St, London, England SE18 6QH. Order from Morgan-Grampian Pub Co, 2 Park Ave, New York, NY 10016. Telephone England (44) (01) 855-7777. Telex 896238 MORGAN G. New York (212) 340-9700. Telex 425592 MGI UI.

Monthly magazine. Provides information on developments in production technology and management for engineers. Price $85.00 per year.

3203

Metalworking Production Machine Tools Survey

Morgan-Grampian Ltd, Morgan-Grampian House, Calderwood St, London, England SE18 6QH. Order from Morgan-Grampian Pub Co, 2 Park Ave, New York, NY 10016. Telephone England (44) (01) 855-7777. Telex 896238 MORGAN G. New York (212) 340-9700. Telex 425592 MGI UI.

Book published every five years. Furnishes details on age and distribution of over 200 types of machine tools. Price $20.00.

3204

Methods-Time Measurement (MTM) Journal

Methods-Time Measurement Assn for Standards and Research, 16-01 Broadway, Fair Lawn, NJ 07410. Telephone (201) 791-7720.

Quarterly journal. Is dedicated to technical aspects of methods-time measurement. Price $8.00 per year.

3204.01

Metric Standards

National Standards Assn, Inc, 5161 River Rd, Washington, DC 20016. Telephone (301) 951-1310. Telex 89-8452.

Book, with semiannual updates. Lists Metric National Aerospace Standards. Includes planned metrication projects. Price $120.00 per year, $110.00 per annual revision service.

3204.02

Metro California Media

Harold D Hansen, Box 327, Washington Depot, CT 06794. Telephone (203) 868-0200.

Annual directory. Provides media information for 19 standard metropolitan statistical areas in California. Includes data on newspapers, magazines, and radio and television stations. Identifies key people and positions. Price $59.00 per year.

3205

Metropolitan

Bobit Publishing Co, 2500 Artesia Blvd, Redondo Beach, CA 90278. Telephone (213) 376-8788.

Bimonthly magazine. Provides information on public transportation, mass transit, rail, bus, and air transport operations. Price $9.00 per year.

3206
Metropolitan Toronto Board of Trade Journal
Toronto Board of Trade, PO Box 60, 3 First Canadian Place, Toronto, Ont, Canada M5X 1C1. Telephone (416) 366-6811.

Monthly magazine. Discusses Canadian and Ontario business, political, economic, and cultural developments. Notes activities of Toronto Board of Trade. Price $1.50 per copy.

3206.01
Mexican-American Review
American Chamber of Commerce of Mexico, AC, Lucerna 78, Mexico 6, DF, Mexico. Telephone 566-08-66. Telex 1771300.

Monthly magazine. Reports on business trends and economic developments in Mexico. Includes information on tourism and foreign trade. Price $20.00 per year.

3206.02
Mexico and Central America Regional Report
Latin American Newsletters Ltd, Greenhill House, 90–93 Cowcross St, London, England EC1M 6BL. Telephone (44) (01) 251-0012. Telex 261117.

Monthly newsletter. Summarizes major political developments. Price £40, $90.00 US per year.

3207
Mexletter
Mexletter SA, Hamburgo 159, Mexico 6 D F, Mexico. Telephone 5-33-08-33.

Monthly journal. Reports on economic and financial conditions in Mexico. Price $20.00.

3208
Miami Business Journal
Cordovan Corp, 5314 Bingle Rd, Houston, TX 77092. Order from Miami Business Journal, 100 Douglas Rd, NW, Miami, FL 33135. Telephone (305) 541-4510.

Weekly newspaper. Contains feature articles on various segments of Miami/Fort Lauderdale business. Price $24.00 per year.

3208.01
Michigan: Harris Michigan Industrial Directory, 1980–81
Manufacturers' News, Inc, 3 Huron St, Chicago, IL 60611. Telephone (312) 337-1084.

Annual book. Contains information on 15,000 manufacturing firms in Michigan by location and product. Price $59.50.

3209
Michigan Manufacturer & Financial Record
Manufacturer Publishing,Co, 8543 Puritan Ave, Detroit, MI 48238. Telephone (313) 864-9388.

Monthly report. Provides news of Michigan industries. Covers banks, engineering and construction, automobile industry, and related economic developments. Price $7.50 per year.

3209.01
Michigan: Manufacturers Directory 1980
Manufacturers' News, Inc, 3 Huron St, Chicago, IL 60611. Telephone (312) 337-1084.

Annual book. Provides information on 16,000 Michigan manufacturing companies. Notes location and product. Price $95.00.

3209.02
Michigan Plant Location Directory 1980–81
Michigan Dept of Commerce (MI), PO Box 30225, Lansing, MI 48909. Telephone (517) 373-3530.

Yearly directory. Provides regional analysis of sites and facilities available in Michigan for industrial location. Furnishes index by communities and maps. Free of charge.

3210
Michigan State Industrial Directory, 1981
Manufacturer's News, Inc, 3 Huron St, Chicago, IL 60611. Telephone (312) 337-1084.

Annual book. Lists 14,500 industrial companies in Michigan. Identifies executives, location, and products. Price $70.-00.

3211
Michigan Statistical Abstract, 1980
Michigan State University, Division of Research, 5-J Berkey Hall, E Lansing, MI 48824. Telephone (517) 355-7560.

Yearly book. Offers comprehensive statistics on state of Michigan and its local areas. Price $10.95.

3212
Micrographics Newsletter
Microfilm Pub, Inc, PO Box 313, Wykagyl Station, New Rochelle, NY 10804. Telephone (914) 235-5246.

Semimonthly newsletter plus supplementary reports. Supplies information on people, products, companies, and applications of interest to microfilm users and suppliers. Price $88.00 per year. ISSN 0026-2749.

3213
Microinfo
Microinfo Ltd, PO Box 3, Newman Lane, Alton, Hampshire, England GU34 2PG. Telephone Alton 84300. Telex 858431.

Newsletter. Offers information on microfilm applications and markets relevant to both management and technical systems. Price available on request.

3214
Microprocessors
IPC Business Press Ltd, 205 E 42nd St, New York, NY 10017. Telephone (212) 889-0700. Telex 4721710.

Bimonthly magazine. Covers microprocessor field, including material on hardware, software, and applications. Price $124.80. ISSN 0308-5953.

3215
Midas
Cowan Investment Survey Pty Ltd, 405 Bourke St, Melbourne, Vic 3000, Australia.

Weekly newsletter. Offers anti-inflation investment advice for Australia. Recommends specific Australian stocks. Comments on world economic trends and their effect on Australian economy. Price $144.00 (Australian) per year.

3215.01
Mid-Atlantic Journal of Business
Seton Hall University, Division of Research, The Graduate School of Business, S Orange, NJ 07079. Telephone (628) 762-9000.

Biannual publication. Discusses business and economics from theoretical and practical standpoints. Price $4.00 per year.

3216
Middle East
IC Publications, Ltd, 122 E 42nd St, Suite 1121, New York, NY 10017. Telephone (212) 867-5159 Telex 425442.

Monthly journal. Reports on Middle East political, economic, and business news. Price $50.00 per year.

3217
Middle East and North Africa
Europa Publications Ltd, 18 Bedford Sq, London, WC1B 3JN, England. Telephone (44) (01) 580-8236.

Annual book. Gives vital statistics on 24 countries in Middle East and North Africa. Covers such topics as population, employment, finance, trade, government, and religion. Includes information on major personalities in region. Price $80.-00.

3218
Middle East Industry & Transport
IC Publications Ltd, 122 E 42nd St, Suite 1121, New York, NY 10017. Telephone (212) 867-5159. Telex 425442.

Bimonthly magazine. Contains news of transport, freight, and port activities in Middle East. Price $40.00 per year.

3219
Middle East Newsletter
International Communications, 110 E 59th St, New York, NY 10022. Telephone (212) 867-5159.

Fortnightly newsletter. Analyzes Middle Eastern business, political, financial, and international developments. Published in New York. Price $295.00 per year.

3219.01
Middle East Review 1981
World of Information, 21 Gold St, Saffron Walden, Essex, England CB10 1EJ. Telephone Saffron walden 21150 (Std. 0799 21150). Telex England 817197 a/b Jaxpress G.

Annual book. Reviews commercial, economic, political, and social developments in the Middle East. Includes chapters on every Arabic-speaking country. Price $43.00. ISBN 0-904439-17-8.

3220
Middle East Transport
International Communications, 110 E 59th St, New York, NY 10022. Telephone (212) 867-5159.

Monthly magazine. Contains news of transport, freight, and port activities in Middle East. Price $25.00 per year.

3221
Middle East Travel
IC Publications, Ltd, 122 E 42th St, Suite 1121, New York, NY 10017. Telephone (212) 867-5159. Telex 425442.

Monthly magazine. Pertains to travel, tourism, and accommodations in the Middle East. Price $40.00 per year.

3222
Middle East Week
Samsom Publications Ltd, 12-14 Hill Rise, Richmond, Surrey, England TW10 6UA. Telephone (44) (01) 948-4251.

Weekly newsletter. Reports on business opportunities, politics, and economics in Middle East. Price $125.00 per year. ISSN 0306-6908.

3223
Middle East Yearbook
International Communications, 110 E 59th St, New York, NY 10022. Telephone (212) 867-5159.

Annual book. Provides data on Middle Eastern nations. Indicates population, agriculture, minerals, oil, and gas. Maps. Price $25.00.

3224
Middle Market Directory
Dun & Bradstreet, Box 3224, Church Street Station, New York, NY 10008. Telephone (212) 285-7346.

Annual book. Lists all US businesses with net worth of $500,000 or more. Includes about 31,000 companies. Price available on request. Available to Dun & Bradstreet subscribers only.

3225
Mideast Business Exchange
News Circle, 2007 Wilshire Blvd, Suite 900, PO Box 74667, Los Angeles, CA 90057. Telephone (213) 483-5111. Telex 67-4835.

Monthly magazine. Reports on Middle East's economic conditions, trade opportunities, and business. Supplies travel information. Price $25.00 per year.

3226
Mideast Markets
Chase World Information Corp, 1 World Trade Center, Suite 4627, New York, NY 10048. Telephone (212) 552-3378. Telex RCA 235444. WU: 141489.

Biweekly newsletter. Reports news developments relevant to companies doing business in the Middle East and North Africa, including investment regulations, policies and practices, construction and shipping. Price $375.00 per year.

3227
Midland Bank Review
Midland Bank Ltd, PO Box 2, Griffin House Silver Street Head, Sheffield, England S1 3GG. Telephone Sheffield 20999 Extension 8608.

Quarterly report. Deals with banking and economic issues in Great Britain including money market, credit, and International Monetary Fund. Free of charge.

3228
Midwest Stock Exchange Guide
Commerce Clearing House, Inc, 4025 W Peterson Ave, Chicago, IL 60646. Telephone (312) 583-8500.

Loose-leaf book and monthly reports. Gives directory, officers, governors, directors, members, constitution, and rules of Midwest Stock Exchange. Price $130.00 per year.

3228.01
Mil-Hdbk-5C Handbook
National Standards Associations, Inc, 5161 River Rd, Washington, DC 20016. Telephone (301) 951-1310. Telex 89-8452.

Two loose-leaf books. Contains sanctioned design for alloys and fasteners used in aircraft and aerospace structures. Price $95.00.

3228.02
Military and Federal Standards and Specifications
National Standards Associations, Inc, 5161 River Rd, Washimgton, DC 20016. Telephone (301) 951-1310. Telex 89-8452.

Microfiche, with weekly revision service. Contains standards for civilian, military, and federal products. Price $6000.00 per year.

3229
Military Research Letter
Callahan Publications, PO Box 3751, Washington, DC 20007. Telephone (703) 356-1925.

Semimonthly newsletter. Provides information on contracting opportunities for military research, development, testing, and evaluation. Price $120.00 per year.

3229.01
Milling, Feed & Fertilizer
Turret Press Ltd, 4 Local Board Rd, Watford, Herts, England WD1 2JS. Telephone Watford (0923) 46199.

Monthly journal. Provides data on flour and animal feed milling. Price £36.70 per year, $85.00 US per year.

3230
Million Dollar Directory
Dun & Bradstreet, Box 3224, Church Street Station, New York, NY 10008. Telephone (212) 285-7346.

Annual directory. Lists all US businesses with net worth of $1 million or more. Notes officers and directors and interlocking affiliations. Price available on request. Available to Dun & Bradstreet subscribers only.

3231
Mineral Facts and Problems
US Bureau of Mines, Publications Distribution Branch, 4800 Forbes Ave, Pittsburgh, PA 15213. Telephone (412) 621-4500.

Report issued every five years. Provides information on metals, minerals, and fuels. Covers industry patterns, technology, reserves, consumption trends, environmental considerations, and related topics. Price available on request.

3232
Mineral Industry Surveys
US Bureau of Mines, Publications Distribution Branch, 4800 Forbes Ave, Pittsburgh, PA 15213. Telephone (412) 621-4500.

Irregular reports. Provides statistical and economic data on minerals and fuels. Covers trends in production, distribution, inventories, and consumption. Price available on request.

3233
Minerals Week
Business Publisher, PO Box 1067, Silver Spring, MD 20910. Telephone (301) 587-6300.

Weekly newsletter. Covers international non-fuel minerals developments. Price $217.00 per year.

3234
Mine Safety and Health Reporter
Bureau of National Affairs, Inc, 1231 25th St, NW, Washington, DC 20037. Telephone (202) 452-4200.

Loose-leaf books, with biweekly updates. Cover new mine safety and health regulations. Include standards, enforcement, litigation, statues and orders, and programs. Provide full text of decisions. Reference file. Price $492.00 per year.

3235
Mingay's Electrical Supplies Guide
Thomson Publications (Australia) Pty Ltd, 47 Chippen St, PO Box 65, Chippendale, NSW 2008, Australia. Telephone 699-6731. Telex TPAS AA22226.

Semiannual pamphlet. Provides guide to Australian electrical supplies and related products. Includes model numbers, illustrations, and suggested retail prices. Price $6.00 (Australian) per year.

3236
Mingay's Price Service—Appliance Edition
Thomson Publications (Australia) Pty Ltd, 47 Chippen St, PO Box 65, Chippendale, NSW 2008, Australia. Telephone 699-6731. Telex TPAS AA22226.

Semiannual book. Provides information on Australian domestic appliances and recommended prices. Price $75.00 (Australian) per year.

3237
Mingay's Price Service—Radio/TV Edition
Thomson Publications (Australia) Pty Ltd, 47 Chippen St, PO Box 65, Chippendale, NSW 2008, Australia. Telephone 699-6731. Telex TPAS AA22226.

Semiannual book. Lists Australian radio and television receivers, sound equipment, and allied products. Includes brand name directory. Price $48.00 (Australian) per year.

3238
Mingay's Retailer & Merchandiser
Thomson Publications (Australia) Pty Ltd, 47 Chippen St, PO Box 65, Chippendale, NSW 2008, Australia. Telephone 699-6731. Telex TPAS AA22226.

Monthly magazine. Discusses new Australian retail products with emphasis on appliances. Price $52.00 (Australian) per year.

3239
Mining and Petroleum Legislation of Latin America and the Caribbean
Oceana Publications, Inc, 75 Main St, Dobbs Ferry, NY 10522. Telephone (914) 693-1320.

Loose-leaf service in one binder plus supplement. Summarizes mining and petroleum laws for 24 Latin American and Caribbean member states of the Organization of American States. Price $74.00 per binder. ISBN 0-379-20381-2.

3239.01
Mining Lease Reports
Petroleum Information Corp, PO Box 2612, 1375 Delaware, Denver, CO 80201. Telephone (303) 825-2181.

Monthly reports. Provides information on leasing of federal and state lands for coal, uranium, sodium, and geothermal resources. Covers Montana, North Dakota, South Dakota, Wyoming, Utah, Colorado, New Mexico, and Oklahoma. Price available on request.

3240
Minnesota
Minnesota Dept of Economic Development, 480 Cedar St, St Paul, MN 55101. Telephone (612) 296-5025.

Magazine issued 10 times per year. Provides information on major business and industry trends in Minnesota. Notes available industrial buildings, world trade opportunities, and new industry. Price free of charge.

3240.01
Minnesota: Manufacturers Directory, 1979–80
Manufacturers' News, Inc, 3 E Huron St, Chicago, IL 60611. Telephone (312) 337-1084.

Biennial book. Contains information on 5000 manufacturing firms in Minnesota. Identifies products, executives, and number of employees. Price $35.00.

3240.02
Minnesota: State Industrial Directory, 1980
Manufacturers' News, Inc, 3 E Huron St, Chicago, IL 60611. Telephone (312) 337-1084.

Annual book. Lists 5508 industrial firms in Minnesota and 35,048 executives. Indicates location, products, and number of employees. Price $50.00.

3241
Minority Business Information Institute (MBII) Newsletter
Minority Business Information Inst, 295 Madison Ave, New York, NY 10017. Telephone (212) 889-8220.

Quarterly newsletter. Pertains to minority business enterprises. Includes information on aid programs, educational courses, and seminars. Free of charge.

3242
Mintel
Mintel Publications Ltd, 20 Buckingham St, London, England WC2N 6EE. Telephone (44) (01) 839-1542.
Monthly report. Covers marketing of consumer goods in Britain. Notes new products and contains original market research. Price $560.00 per year.

3243
Miscellaneous Petroleum and Coal Products Industries
Statistics Canada, User Services, Publications Distribution, Ottawa, Ont, Canada K1A 0V7. Telephone (613) 992-3151.
Annual report. Contains Canadian petroleum and coal products industry statistics. Includes number of companies, employees, wages, cost of fuel and materials, and value of shipments and inventories. Price $5.40. ISSN 0384-4757.

3244
Missile/Ordnance Letter
Callahan Publications, PO Box 3751, Washington, DC 20007. Telephone (703) 356-1925.
Semimonthly newsletter. Covers contracting opportunities for missiles, weapon systems, military ordnance, and hardware. Price $120.00 per year.

3245
Mississippi Manufacturers Directory
Mississippi Research and Development Ctr, PO Drawer 2470, Jackson, MS 39205. Telephone (601) 982-6466.
Annual directory. Offers guide to Mississippi's manufacturers. Price $25.00.

3245.01
Mississippi: Manufacturers Directory
1980
Manufacturers' News, Inc, 3 E Huron St, Chicago, IL 60611. Telephone (312) 337-1084.
Annual book. Identifies 4500 manufacturing firms in Mississippi by location and product. Price $35.00.

3246
Mississippi Metalworking Services Directory
Mississippi Research and Development Ctr, PO Drawer 2470, Jackson, MS 39205. Telephone (601) 982-6466.
Biennial directory. Offers list of Mississippi establishments that furnish metalworking services. Free of charge.

3246.01
Mississippi: State Industrial Directory,
1981
Manufacturers' News, Inc, 3 E Huron St, Chicago, IL 60611. Telephone (312) 337-1084.
Annual book. Provides information on 2271 industrial firms in Mississippi. Indicates executives, products, and number of employees. Price $35.00.

3247
Missouri
Missouri Div of Commerce and Industrial Development, PO Box 118, Jefferson City, MO 65102. Telephone (314) 751-4241.
Book. Pertains to Missouri's labor, taxes, energy, transportation, financing, and quality of life. Price free of charge.

3248
Missouri Corporate Planner
Missouri Div of Commerce and Industrial Development, PO Box 118, Jefferson City, MO 65102. Telephone (314) 751-4241.
Booklet. Discusses factors affecting business in Missouri. Free of charge.

3249
Missouri Directory of Manufacturing and Mining
Missouri Div of Commerce and Industrial Development, PO Box 118, Jefferson City, MO 65102. Order from Informative Data Co, 4401 Hampton Ave, St Louis, MO 63109. Telephone (314) 751-4241.
Directory. Offers complete listing of all Missouri manufacturers. Price $42.00.

3249.01
Missouri: Manufacturing & Mining Directories 1980
Manufacturers' News, Inc, 3 E Huron St, Chicago, IL 60611. Telephone (312) 337-1084.
Annual book. Identifies 8800 manufacturing and mining firms in Missouri by name, location, and product. Price $55.00.

3250
Missouri's New and Expanding Manufacturers
Missouri Div of Commerce and Industrial Development, PO Box 118, Jefferson City, MO 65102. Telephone (314) 751-4241.
Annual report. Covers new and expanding manufacturers, new jobs, and investment by manufacturers in Missouri. Free of charge.

3250.01
Missouri: State Industrial Directory,
1981
Manufacturers' News, Inc, 3 E Huron St, Chicago, IL 60611. Telephone (312) 337-1084.
Annual book. Contains information on 7040 industrial companies in Missouri. Lists products, executives, and number of employees. Price $50.00.

3251
Model Retailer
Boynton & Associates, Clifton House, Clifton, VA 22024. Telephone (703) 830-1000.
Monthly magazine. Contains information on model hobby stores. Discusses new products, store management, and industry developments. Includes summaries from model airplane and railroad magazines about specific products. Price $32.00 per year.

3252
Modern Africa
Johnston International Pub Corp, 386 Park Ave S, New York, NY 10016. Telephone (212) 689-0120. Telex 66811 Jonst.
Bimonthly magazine. Covers business developments in Sub-Sahara Africa including agricultural, construction, and mining trends. Price $40.00 per year $65.00 two years.

3253
Modern Asia
Johnston International Pub Corp, 386 Park Ave S, New York, NY 10016. Telephone (212) 689-0120. Telex 66811 Jonst.
Monthly magazine. Reports on significant Asian business news with emphasis on Southeast Asia. Price $50.00 per year $80.00 per two years.

3254
Modern Banking Forms
Warren, Gorham & Lamont, Inc, 210 S St, Boston, MA 02111. Telephone (617) 423-2020.

Two loose-leaf books. Give annotated bank forms. Cover all aspects of banking operations. Price $96.00.

3255
Modern Business Reports
Alexander Hamilton Inst, 1633 Broadway, New York, NY 10019. Telephone (212) 397-3580.

Monthly report. Discusses business management techniques and trends, new markets, and employee relations. Is aimed at business executives. Price $61.00 per year.

3255.01
Modern Cleaning & Maintenance
Yaffa Publishing Group, 432–436 Elizabeth St, Surry Hills, NSW 2010, Australia. Order from Yaffa Publishing Group, GPO Box 606, Sydney, NSW 2001, Australia. Telephone (61)(02) 699-7861. Telex 21887.

Bimonthly magazine. Covers cleaning and building maintenance industry in Australia. Notes refuse disposal developments. Price 18.00 (Australian) per year.

3256
Modern Materials Handling
Cahners Pub Co, Inc, 221 Columbus Ave, Boston, MA 02116. Telephone (617) 536-7780.

Monthly magazine. Contains articles on materials handling equipment. Includes reports on cost-cutting methods and equipment purchasing. Price available on request.

3257
Modern Office Procedures
Penton-IPC, 614 Superior Ave W, Cleveland, OH 44113. Order from Penton-IPC, 1111 Chester Ave, Cleveland, OH 44114. Telephone (216) 6C6-7000.

Monthly magazine. Discusses office systems, information processing, and work environments. Price $24.00 per year.

3258
Modern Paint & Coatings
Communication Channels, Inc, 6285 Barfield Rd, Atlanta, GA 30328. Telephone (404) 256-9800.

Monthly magazine. Provides information on paint technology, production techniques, marketing, and management for personnel in the paint, varnish, lacquer, and allied synthetic coatings industry. Price $21.00 per year.

3259
Modern Plant Operation & Maintenance
US Industrial Publications, Inc, 209 Dunn Ave, Stamford, CT 06905. Telephone (203) 322-7676.

Quarterly publication. Contains information on operation and maintenance of modern plants. Price $4.00 per year.

3260
Modern Plastics
McGraw-Hill Publications Co, 1221 Ave of the Americas, New York, NY 10020. Telephone (212) 997-1221. Telex TWX 7105814879 WUI 62555.

Monthly journal. Promotes industrial use of plastics. Analyzes developments in materials, processes, design, and markets. Price $22.50 per year.

3261
Modern Plastics Encyclopedia
McGraw-Hill Book Co, Hightstown-Princeton Rd, Hightstown, NJ 08520. Telephone (609) 448-1700. Telex 843449.

Book. Provides information on plastics. Offers buyers guide. Cross indexes products with manufacturers. Deals with resins, additives, and equipment. Charts. Price $32.95.

3262
Modern Plastics International Report
McGraw-Hill Publications Co, 1221 Ave of the Americas, New York, NY 10020. Telephone (212) 997-1221. Telex TWX 7105814879 WUI 62555.

Monthly journal. Discusses plastics activity outside US and Canada, particularly machinery, processing, and materials development. Price $66.00 per year.

3263
Modern Publicity
Cassell & Co Ltd, 35 Red Lion Sq, London, England WC1R 4SG. Telephone (44) (01) 831-6100. Telex Casmac 28648G.

Annual book. Contains international survey of best advertising and communications graphic designs. Price £15.00. ISBN 0289-70785-4.

3264
Modern Purchasing
Maclean-Hunter Ltd, 30 Old Burlington St, London, England W1X 2AE. Telephone (44) (01) 434-2233.

Publication. Features articles on industrial purchasing in Great Britain. Price available on request.

3265
Modern Railroads
Cahners Pub Co, Inc, 221 Columbus Ave, Boston, MA 02116. Telephone (617) 536-7780.

Monthly magazine. Provides articles on all aspects of railroad and rail transit operations in North America. Price $30.00 per year.

3266
Modern Trust Forms and Checklists
Warren, Gorham & Lamont, Inc, 210 South St, Boston, MA 02111. Telephone (617) 423-2020.

Loose-leaf book. Provides trust and estate checklists. Annual supplement includes new and revised checklists reflecting changes in trust law and practice. Price $48.50.

3266.01
Monday Morning Report
American Business Men's Research Foundation, 1208 Michigan National Tower, Lansing, MI 48933. Telephone (517) 487-9276.

Semimonthly newsletter. Covers issues, events, and opinions about alcohol abuse. Price $12.00 per year.

3267
Money
Time, Inc, Time & Life Bldg, New York, NY 10020. Order from Money, Time-Life Bldg, 541 N Fairbanks Ct, Chicago, IL 60611. Telephone (212) 586-1212.

Monthly magazine. Reports on personal finance. Includes topics on stock market trends, estate planning, taxes and tax shelters, and consumer affairs. Price $14.95 per year.

3268
MONEY BEGETS MONEY: A Guide to Personal Finance
Gary Zimmerman, GPO Box 114, Brooklyn, NY 11202. Telephone (212) 854-4494.

Book. Covers personal finance subjects. Price $95.00. ISBN 0-916202-01-1.

3269
Money Management
Financial Times, Business Information Ltd, Bracken House, 10 Cannon St, London, England EC4P 4BY. Order from: Financial Times, Ltd, 75 Rockefeller Plz, New York, NY 10019. Telephone (44) (01) 248-8000. Telex 886341-2.

Monthly periodical. Presents features and surveys on insurance, finance, mortgages, taxation, and investment. Includes comparative statistics. Price $50.00 per year.

3270
Money Management and Unitholder
Financial Times Business Publishing Ltd, Greystoke Place, Fetter Lane, London EC4A 1ND, England. Telephone (01) 405-6969.

Monthly magazine. Covers personal financial planning for professional financial advisers, including taxes, investments, insurance, mortgages, and pensions. Provides monthly performance tables for unit trusts, insurance bond funds, and offshore funds. Price £21.50 per year (second class mail), £39.00 per year (overseas airmail).

3271
Money Manager
Bond Buyer, 1 State St Plz, New York, NY 10004. Telephone (212) 943-8207. Telex 12-9233.

Weekly newspaper. Interprets international financial and economic news. Covers money markets, government, municipal, and corporate bond markets, and stock market. Price $176.00 per year.

3272
Money Reporter, **Canadian Edition**
Marpep Publishing Ltd, Suite 700, 133 Richmond St W, Toronto, Ont, Canada M5H 3M8. Telephone (416) 869-1177.

Weekly report. Provides news and advice on fixed income investments in Canada, including annuities and pensions. Price $95.00 per year.

3273
Money Reporter, **US Edition**
Marpep Publishing Ltd, Suite 700, 133 Richmond St W, Toronto, Ont, Canada M5H 3M8. Telephone (416) 869-1177.

Weekly report. Covers fixed income investments in the United States, including annuities, pensions, and Keogh plans. Price $95.00 per year.

3274
Money Tree
Avco Financial Services, 620 Newport Center Dr, PO Box 2210, Newport Beach, CA 92660. Telephone (714) 644-5800.

Bimonthly employee magazine. Discusses activities and personnel of Avco Financial Services. Offers information on countries where Avco has branches. Free of charge.

3275
Monitor
Associated Industries of New York State, Inc, 150 State St, Albany, NY 12207. Telephone (518) 465-3547.

Quarterly newsletter. Covers industry in New York State. Free of charge.

3276
Montana Business Quarterly
University of Montana, Bureau of Business and Economic Research, Missoula, MT 59812. Telephone (406) 243-5113.

Quarterly magazine. Reports on Montana business, economic, and political subjects. Price $6.00 per year.

3276.01
Montana: Manufacturers Directory
1976–77
Manufacturers' News, Inc, 3 E Huron St, Chicago, Il 60611. Telephone (312) 337-1084.

Triennial book. Identifies manufacturing firms in Montana by name, location, and product. Price $18.00.

3276.02
Montana: State Industrial Directory,
1981
Manufacturers' News, Inc, 3 E Huron St, Chicago, IL 60611. Telephone (312) 337-1084.

Annual book. Contains information on 750 Montana industrial companies. Identifies executives, products, and number of employees. Price $25.00.

3277
Monthly Abstract of Statistics
New Zealand Dept of Statistics, Mulgrave St, Private Bag, Wellington, New Zealand. Telephone (64) (4) 729119.

Monthly report. Provides abstracts of statistics pertinent to New Zealand. Price $30.00 (New Zealand) per year.

3278
Monthly Bulletin of Agricultural Economics and Statistics
Food and Agriculture Organization of the United Nations, Via delle Terme di Caracalla, Rome, Italy 00100. Order from UNIPUB, 345 Park Ave S, New York, NY 10016. Telephone 5797. Telex 61181.

Monthly report. Provides data on world food and agricultural conditions. Analyzes influential factors. Price $10.00 per year.

3279
Monthly Bulletin of Business Activity
Ministry of Economic Development, Victoria, BC, Canada V8V 4R9. Telephone (604) 387-6701.

Monthly bulletin. Presents articles on business activity in British Columbia. Statistics and graphs. Price available on request. ISSN 0524-5370.

3280
Monthly Bulletin of Canadian Upper Air Data
Supply and Services Canada, Publishing Centre, Printing and Publishing, Ottawa, Ont, Canada K1A 0S9. Telephone (613) 238-1601.

Monthly report. Furnishes upper air data for Canada. Price $6.00 per year.

3281
Monthly Bulletin of Construction Indices
Her Majesty's Stationery Office, PO Box 569, London, England SE1 9NH. Telephone (44) (01) 928 1321.

Monthly report. Covers British construction indices. Price available on request.

3283
Monthly Bulletin of Statistics
United Nations Publications, Room A-3315, New York, NY 10017. Telephone (212) 754-8302.

Monthly report. Supplies statistics from 170 countries on 60 subjects including population, food, trade, production, finance, and national income. English and French editions. Price $84.00.

3285
Monthly Catalog of US Government Publications
Superintendent of Documents, Government Printing Office, Washington, DC 20402. Telephone (202) 783-3238.

Monthly list of recently issued government publications. Annual cumulative index available. Price $80.00 per year. ISSN 0362-6830.

3286
Monthly Commodity Price Bulletin
United Nations Conference on Trade and Development (UNCTAD), Palais des Nations, 1211 Geneva 10, Switzerland. Telephone (41) (22) 346011. Telex 28 96 96.
Monthly report. Contains price indexes and series of average prices for 38 primary commodities exported by developing countries. Tables. Price available on request.

3288
Monthly Digest Annual Supplement
Central Statistical Office, Her Majesty's Stationery Office, PO Box 569, London, England SE1 9NH. Telephone (44) (01) 928-1321.
Annual book. Supplements Monthly digest by providing definitions and explanatory notes for each section and index of sources. Price £1.25 per year. ISBN 0 11 724263 2.

3289
Monthly Digest of Statistics
Her Majesty's Stationery Office, PO Box 569, London, England SE1 9NH. Telephone (44) (01) 928 1321.
Monthly report. Offers digest of statistics on Great Britain. Price £3.55 monthly.

3290
Monthly Digest of Tax Articles
Newkirk Products, Inc, 55 Grant Ave, Albany, NY 12206. Telephone (518) 489-5546.
Monthly magazine. Condenses articles on taxation from more than 200 professional journals and law reviews. Summarizes recent court and Internal Revenue Service rulings. Price $24.00 per year.

3290.01
Monthly External Trade Bulletin
European Community Information Service, 2100 M St, NW, Suite 707, Washington, DC 20037. Telephone (202) 862-9500. Telex 248455.
Monthly report. Gives detail on trade with countries outside the European Economic Community (Common Market). Price $63.00 per year.

3291
Monthly Labor Review
US Dept of Labor, Bureau of Labor Statistics, 441 G St NW, Washington, DC 20212. Telephone (202) 523-1221.
Monthly report. Reviews labor issues including employment, wages, collective bargaining, industrial relations, labor law, and foreign developments. Contains statistics and book reviews. Price $18.00 per year.

3292
Monthly Letter
Banque Canadienne National, 500 Pl d'Armes, Montreal, Que, Canada H2Y 2W3. Telephone (514) 281-2409.
Monthly newsletter. Contains one article per issue on wide-ranging economic and social subjects. French and English editions. Free of charge. ISSN 0381-5560.

3293
Monthly New Issues and Placings Service
Extel Statistical Services Ltd, 37-45 Paul St, London, England EC2A 4PB. Telephone (44) (01) 253-3400. Telex 262687.
Monthly card service. Analyzes issues and placings of stocks, shares, and loans on British and Irish stock exchanges. Covers dividends, options, acquisitions, conversions, consolidations, and liquidation distributions. Price £175.00 per year.

3294
Monthly Price Review
Urner Barry Publications, Inc, PO Box 389, Toms River, NJ 08753. Telephone (201) 240-5330.
Monthly report. Contains monthly wholesale price ranges for eggs, margarine, butter, chickens, and turkeys. Tables and graphs. Price $35.00 per year.

3295
Monthly Radiation Summary
Supply and Services Canada, Publishing Centre, Printing and Publishing, Ottawa, Ont, Canada K1A 0S9. Telephone (613) 238-1601.
Monthly magazine concerned with radiation. English and French. Price $4.00 per year.

3296
Monthly Record of Meteorological Observations in Canada
Supply and Services Canada, Publishing Centre, Printing and Publishing, Ottawa, Ont, Canada K1A 0S9. Telephone (613) 238-1601.

Monthly report. Records Canadian meteorological observations. Bilingual. Price $3.75 per year.

3297
Monthly Review of Business Statistics, Cat No 1304.0
Australian Bureau of Statistics, Box 10, Belconnen, ACT 2616, Australia. Order from Australian Government Publishing Service, PO Box 84, Canberra, ACT 2600, Australia. Telephone (61) (062) 527911.
Monthly report. Provides Australian business statistics including data on population, employment, trade, prices and wages, building, transport, communication, balance of payments, national accounts, and finance. Price $30.00 (Australian) per year.

3298
Monthly Statement of United States Currency and Coin
US Dept of the Treasury, Bureau of Government Financial Operations, Pennsylvania Ave and Madison Pl, NW, Washington, DC 20226. Order from Superintendent of Documents, Government Printing Office, Washington, DC 20402. Telephone (202) 566-2000.
Publication. Covers data on US currency and coins. Price available on request.

3302
Monthly Summary of Business Conditions in the United Kingdom
Williams and Glyns Bank Ltd, Economics Office, 7 Copthall Ave, London, England EC2R 7HB. Telephone (44) (01) 588-8161.
Monthly report. Reviews major trends affecting British economy. Includes European interest rates. Free of charge.

3303
Monthly Tax Features
Tax Foundation, Inc, 1875 Connecticut Ave, NW, Washington, DC 20009. Telephone (202) 328-4500.
Monthly newsletter. Reports on US fiscal developments. Includes topics on inflation, wages for government employees, and tax policy.

3304
Monthly Tax Report
Laventhol & Horwath, 1845 Walnut St, Philadelphia, PA 19103. Telephone (215) 491-1600.
Monthly newsletter. Reports on tax-related topics including income and estate taxes. Free of charge.

3304.01
Monthly Treasury Statement of Receipts and Outlays of the US Govt
US Dept of the Treasury, Bureau of Government Financial Operations, Pennsylvania Ave and Madison Pl NW, Washington, DC 20226. Order from Superintendent of Documents, Government Printing Office, Washington, DC 20402. Telephone (202) 566-2000.

Publication. Includes a daily statement of the US Treasury and a monthly statement of the public debt of the US. Price available on request; subscription only.

3305
Monthly Truck Tonnage Report
American Trucking Assn, Inc, 1616 P St, NW, Washington, DC 20036. Telephone (202) 797-5351.

Monthly report. Discusses intercity truck tonnage. Shows unadjusted and adjusted tonnage by region, percentage changes, and compares tonnage index with industrial production, retail sales, and wholesale and consumer prices. Tables. Free of charge.

3306
Montreal Stock Exchange Daily Official News Sheet
Montreal Stock Exchange, 800 Victoria Sq, PO Box 61, Montreal, Que, Canada H4Z 1A9. Telephone 871-2451. Telex 055-60586.

Daily newsletter. Contains data on companies listed on Montreal Stock Exchange. Price $161.78 per year.

3307
Montreal Stock Exchange Monthly Review
Montreal Stock Exchange, 800 Victoria Sq, PO Box 61, Montreal, Que, Canada H4Z 1A9. Telephone 871-2451. Telex 055-60586.

Monthly report. Contains information about companies listed on Montreal Stock Exchange. English and French. Price $22.00 per year.

3308
Moody's Bank and Finance Manual and News Reports
Moody's Investors Service, Inc, 99 Church St, New York, NY 10007. Telephone (212) 267-8800.

Two books plus twice-weekly reports. Give ratings and other information about banks, insurance companies, mutual funds, closed-end investment companies, mortgage and finance companies, and real estate investment trusts. Price $350.00 per year.

3309
Moody's Bond Record
Moody's Investors Service, Inc, 99 Church St, New York, NY 10007. Telephone (212) 267-8800.

Monthly report. Gives rates for over 25,-000 bond issues, including US, corporate, municipal, and convertible bonds, commercial paper, and industrial development revenue bond. Price $80.00 per year.

3310
Moody's Bond Survey
Moody's Investors Service, Inc, 99 Church St, New York, NY 10007. Telephone (212) 267-8800.

Weekly loose-leaf newsletter. Covers factors that may affect bond values. Gives ratings and rationale for fixed-income market. Price $475.00 per year.

3311
Moody's Commercial Paper Reports
Moody's Investors Service, Inc, 99 Church St, New York, NY 10007. Telephone (212) 267-8800.

Semiannual report. Gives ratings and facts about companies including operating information and financial statements.

3312
Moody's Dividend Record
Moody's Investors Service, Inc, 99 Church St, New York, NY 10007. Telephone (212) 267-8800.

Semiweekly loose-leaf newsletter. Gives information about dividends on approximately 11,000 issues including common and preferred stocks, nonpaying issues, income bonds, mutual funds, and foreign securities. Price $110.00 per year.

3313
Moody's Handbook of Common Stocks
Moody's Investors Service, Inc, 99 Church St, New York, NY 10007. Telephone (212) 267-8800.

Quarterly book. Contains information on over 900 stock issues. Describes companies' business, operations, 10-year statistical history, and classification. Price $90.00 per year.

3314
Moody's Industrial Manual and News Reports
Moody's Investors Services, Inc, 99 Church St, New York, NY 10007. Telephone (212) 267-8800.

Two-volume manual plus twice-weekly reports. Gives ratings for and details on all firms listed on New York and American stock exchanges, plus those listed on regional exchanges. Price $350.00 per year.

3314.01
Moody's Investors Fact Sheets
Moody's Investors Service, Inc, 99 Church St, New York, NY 10007. Telephone (212) 267-8800.

Quarterly loose-leaf fact sheets and supplement. Provide financial, operating, and corporate data for over 4000 firms. Supplement contains company rankings, key stock ratios, income statement, and balance sheet statistics for comparison of companies within the same industry. Price $800.00 per year.

3315
Moody's Municipal and Government Manual and News Reports
Moody's Investors Service, Inc, 99 Church St, New York, NY 10007. Telephone (212) 267-8800

Two books plus twice weekly reports. Cover 15,000 municipalities that have long-term debts of over $1 million. Include federal and state agencies. Ratings. Price $440.00 per year.

3316
Moody's Municipal Credit Reports
Moody's Investors Service, Inc, 99 Church St, New York, NY 10007. Telephone (212) 267-8800.

Report. Presents facts on which Moody's bases its ratings. Price available on request.

3316.01
Moody's Municipal Credit Reports On Line
Moody's Investors Service, Inc, 99 Church St, New York, NY 10007. Telephone (212) 267-8800.

Timesharing network. Provides full text of available Moody reports and index searches by name, state, Moody's rating, sale amount, report date, and bond type. Price varies.

3317
Moody's Over-the-Counter (OTC)
Industrial Manual and News Reports
Moody's Investors Service, Inc, 99 Church St, New York, NY 10007. Telephone (212) 267-8800.

Manual plus weekly loose-leaf reports. Offers ratings for and details on 3200 firms not listed on major exchanges. Price $320.00 per year.

3318
Moody's Public Utility Manual and News Reports
Moody's Investors Service, Inc, 99 Church St, New York, NY 10007. Telephone (212) 267-8800.

Book plus twice weekly loose-leaf reports. Gives vital data on more than 550 public and private utilities. Ratings. Price $300.00 per year.

3319
Moody's Transportation Manual & News Reports
Moody's Investors Service, Inc, 99 Church St, New York, NY 10007. Telephone (212) 267-8800.

Book plus twice-weekly loose-leaf reports. Covers domestic transportation companies. Includes maps and details of ownership and operation. Price $280.00 per year.

3319.01
More Facts
Missouri Div of Commerce and Industrial Development, PO Box 118, Jefferson City, MO 65102. Telephone (314) 751-4241.

Book. Pertains to Missouri's labor, taxes, energy, transportation, financing, and quality of life. Price free of charge.

3319.02
Mortgage and Real Estate Executives Report
Warren, Gorham & Lamont, Inc, 210 S St, Boston, MA 02111. Telephone (800) 225-2263.

Semimonthly report. Discusses real estate and mortgage trends. Notes regulatory developments. Price $68.00 per year.

3320
Mortgage Backed Securities Reports
Andrew R Mandala, PO Box 30240,, Washington, DC 20014. Telephone (301) 654-5580.

Weekly newsletter. Reports on mortgage-backed securities. Provides secondary market price quotations. Tables. Price $110.00 per year.

3321
Mortgage Banker
Mortgage Bankers Assn of America, 1125 15th St, NW, Washington, DC 20005. Telephone (202) 861-6557.

Monthly magazine. Reports on various phases of mortgage market. Price $20.00 per year.

3322
Mortgage Commentary
Andrew R Mandala, PO Box 30240, Washington, DC 20014. Telephone (301) 654-5580.

Weekly newsletter. Contains material of interest to institutional mortgage investors. Price $110.00 per year.

3322.01
Mortgage Securities Manual & Pricing Guide
Andrew R Mandala, PO Box 30240, Washington, DC 20014. Telephone (301) 654-5580.

Binder, with monthly supplements. Provides historical data on the Government National Mortgage Association. Price $150.00 per year.

3323
Motel/Hotel "Insider"
Atcom, Inc, Atcom Bldg, 2315 Broadway, New York, NY 10024. Telephone (212) 873-3760.

Weekly newsletter. Covers lodging industry. Includes articles on travel, management, and energy conservation. Price $57.00 per year.

3324
Motor
Motor, 224 W 57th St, New York, NY 10019. Telephone (212) 262-8631.

Monthly magazine. Offers technical articles on automotive service and repair, management, merchandising, promotion, and customer relations. Price $12.00 per month.

3325
Motor/Age
Chilton Co, Chilton Way, Radnor, PA 19089. Telephone (215) 687-8200.

Monthly magazine. Provides technical and merchandising information about service and repair of automobiles and trucks. Price $12.00.

3325.01
Motor Business
Economist Intelligence Unit Ltd, Spencer House, 27 St James's Pl, London, England SW1A 1NT. Order from Economist Intelligence Unit Ltd, 75 Rockefeller Plz, New York, NY 10019. Telephone (212) 541-5730. Telex 148393.

Quarterly journal. Covers trends in world's automotive industry. Includes charts, statistics, and commentary on sales levels. Price $295.00 per year.

3326
Motor Carrier Annual Report
American Trucking Assn, Inc, 1616 P St, NW, Washington, DC 20036. Telephone (202) 797-5351.

Annual report. Based on annual reports submitted to the ICC from Class I and II carriers. Contains balance sheet, income statement, detailed operating expenses, tonnage, and mileage statistics. Provides financial ratios and other data. Price $175.00 per year.

3327
Motor Carrier Statistical Summary
American Trucking Assn, Inc, 1616 P St, NW, Washington, DC 20036. Telephone (202) 797-5351.

Quarterly and annual report. Presents financial and operating statistics for motor carriers. Shows breakdown of intercity tonnage and mileage for Class I and II carriers by commodity group and type of carriage. Tables. Free of charge.

3328
Motor Report International
Samsom Publications Ltd, 12-14 Hill Rise, Richmond, Surrey, England TW10 6UA. Telephone (44) (01) 948-4251.

Semimonthly newsletter. Furnishes facts and comment on automotive and allied industries in United Kingdom and abroad. Price $125.00 per year. ISSN 0306-6274.

3329
Motor Truck
Wadham Publications Ltd, 109 Vanderhoof Ave, Suite 101, Toronto, Ont, Canada M4G 2J2. Telephone (416) 425-9021.

Monthly magazine. Covers developments in Canada's trucking industry. Notes government regulations, maintenance procedures, and new equipment. Price available on request.

3331
Multicast
Paul Kagan Assoc, Inc, 100 Merrick Rd, Rockville Centre, NY 11570. Telephone (516) 764-5516.

Semimonthly newsletter. Reports on Multipoint Distribution Service (MDS), FCC regulated, closed-circuit, microwave common carriers. Analyzes government decisions and FCC actions. Price $215.00 per year.

3332
Multi-Housing News
Gralla Publications, 1515 Broadway, New York, NY 10036. Telephone (212) 869-1300.

Publications. Report on multihousing construction field. Price available on request.

3333
Multinational Business
Economist Intelligence Unit Ltd, Spencer House, 27 St. James's Pl, London, England SW1A 1NT. Order from Economist Intelligence Unit Ltd, 75 Rockefeller Plz, New York, NY 10019. Telephone (212) 541-5730 Telex 148393.

Quarterly report. Discusses multinational corporate enterprises. Notes relations with governments. Price $210.00 per year.

3334
Multinational Corporations
Gower Publishing Co Ltd, 1 Westmead, Farnborough, Hampshire, England GU14 7RU. Telephone Farnborough (0252) 519221. Telex 858623.

Book. Provides information sources on multinational corporations. Includes over 500 books, 1000 research reports, papers and brochures, and 2000 periodical articles in 10 languages. Price $98.00. ISBN 92 9026 001 7.

3335
Multinational Executive Travel
Companion
Guides to Multinational Business, Inc, Harvard Sq, Box 92, Cambridge, MA 02138. Telephone (617) 868-2288.

Book. Provides information on 160 countries for business travelers. Lists government and business offices. Notes transportation, hotels, and restaurants. Price $40.00.

3336
Multinational Marketing and
Employment Directory
World Trade Academy Press, Inc, 50 E 42nd St, New York, NY 10017. Telephone (212) 697-4999.

Annual directory. Lists 7500 US corporations operating in US and abroad. Indicates main headquarters, foreign operations, and products and services. Price $100.00.

3337
Multinational Service
Europe Publications, 46 Ave Albert Elisabeth, Brussels, Belgium 1040. Telephone (32) (2) 7361193. Telex 23920 agra b.

Semimonthly newsletter. Covers multinational business activities. Price $429.00 per year.

3338
Municipal Bond Selector
Standard & Poor's Corp, 25 Broadway, New York, NY 10004. Telephone (212) 248-2525.

Bimonthly report. Gives quality ratings and statistical information for about 6500 municipal bonds. Groups bonds according to issuing states and divides them into general obligation bonds and revenue bonds. Price $160.00 per year.

3338.01
Municipal Finance Journal
Panel Publishers, 14 Plaza Rd, Greenvale, NY 11548. Telephone (516) 484-0006.

Quarterly journal. Covers municipal bond finance developments. Price $48.00 per year. ISSN 0199-6134.

3339
Municipal Index
Morgan-Grampian Ltd, Morgan-Grampian House, Calderwood St, London, England SE18 6QH. Order from Morgan-Grampian Publishing Co, Berkshire Common, Pittsfield, MA 01201. Telephone (212) 499-2550. Telex 425592 MGI UI.

Annual directory. Serves as purchasing guide for local government officials in US. Contains listing of county officials in places with over 10000 population. Price $50.00

3341
Municipal Yearbook
International City Management Assn, 1140 Connecticut Ave, NW, Washington, DC 20036. Telephone (202) 293-2200.

Annual report. Covers developments in US and Canadian municipal government. Includes listings of municipal officers and leagues. Price $19.50.

3342
Munn's Encyclopedia of Banking and
Finance, 8th Edition
Bankers Pub Co, 210 South St, Boston, MA 02111. Telephone (617) 426-4495.

Book. Contains 4000 alphabetically arranged entries on banking and finance, with illustrative examples and statistical tables. Includes technical terms, federal regulations, business laws, and abbreviations of listed securities. Price $49.75. ISBN 0-87267-019-8.

3343
Music Trades International
Turret Press Ltd, 4 Local Board Rd, Watford, Herts, England WD1 2JS. Order from Trade Papers Ltd, 4 Local Board Rd, Watford, Herts, England WD1 2JS. Telephone Watford (0923) 46199.

Monthly magazine. Covers worldwide music industry. Price £43.00 per year.

3345
Mutual Fund Fact Book
Investment Company Inst, 1775 K St NW, Washington, DC 20006. Telephone (202) 293-7700.

Annual book. Presents data on US mutual fund industry including trends in sales, assets, distributions, accumulations, and withdrawal plans. Tables and charts. Price $1.00 per copy.

3346
Mutual Fund Performance
Review
Computer Directions Advisors, Inc, 8750 Georgia Ave, Silver Spring, MD 20910. Telephone (301) 565-9544.

Monthly report. Contains information on 400 major open-end mutual funds. Notes indiviual fund performance, performance ranking, and marketing cycles. Price $350.00 per year.

3347

Mutual Funds Almanac, **8th edition, 1977**

Hirsch Organization, Inc, 6 Deer Trail, Old Tappan, NJ 07675. Telephone (201) 664-3400.

Annual book. Provides directory to over 600 mutual funds. Looks at 10-year performance. Statistics, tables, charts, and graphs. Price $20.00.

3348

Mutual Funds Forum

Investment Company Inst, 1775 K St, NW, Washington, DC 20006. Telephone (202) 293-7700.

Quarterly newsletter. Contains articles of interest to mutual fund industry. Reports on activities of Investment Company Institute. Price $6.00 per year.

3349

Mutual Funds Guide

Commerce Clearing House, Inc, 4025 W Peterson Ave, Chicago, IL 60646. Telephone (312) 583-8500.

Two loose-leaf books and fortnightly reports. Provide explanation of federal and state legal requirements for formation, operation, and management of mutual funds. Price $250.00 per year.

3351

Mutual Insurance Bulletin

National Assn of Mutual Insurance Companies, 3707 Woodview Terrace, PO Box 68700, Indianapolis, IN 46268. Telephone (317) 875-5250.

Monthly magazine. Reports on developments that affect mutual insurance companies. Discusses such insurance-related topics as arson. Covers activities of National Association of Mutual Insurance Companies. Price $6.00 per year.

3352

Mutual Savings Bank Guide to Federal Income Tax Law

National Assn of Mutual Savings Banks, 200 Park Ave, New York, NY 10017. Telephone (212) 973-5432.

Book with annual supplement service. Provides guide to federal income tax law covering mutual savings banks. Price $135.50 each. Annual supplement service $35.00.

3353

Mutual Savings Bank Report

Federal Reserve Bank of Boston, Boston, MA 02106. Telephone (617) 973-3397.

Monthly report. Provides statistical summary of activities of sample New England mutual savings banks. Covers mortgage loans, deposit flows, and savings rates. Free of charge.

3354

Nacha Quarterly Update

American Bankers Assn, 1120 Connecticut Ave NW, Washington, DC 20036. Telephone (202) 467-4123.

Quarterly newsletter. Discusses automated clearinghouse issues. Price $10.00 per year.

3356

National Aeronautics and Space Administration (NASA) Activities

National Aeronautics and Space Administration, Washington, DC 20546. Order from Superintendent of Documents, US Government Printing Office, Washington, DC 20402. Telephone (202) 755-8348.

Monthly report. Covers NASA technological and personnel activities. Notes satellite, rocket, and rocket fuel developments. Lists contracts awarded and patents pending. Price $14.50 per year.

3356.01

National Aerospace Standards

National Standards Assn, Inc, 5161 River Rd, Washington, DC 20016. Telephone (301) 951-1310. Telex 89-8452.

Eight-volume set. Provides 2500 National Aerospace Standards for component parts, machines, and tools. Price $325.00 per year.

3357

National Association of Bank Women (NABW) Journal

National Assn of Bank Women, 500 N Michigan ave, Suite 1400, Chicago, IL 60611. Telephone (312) 661-1700.

Bimonthly magazine. Contains general banking and management-oriented articles of significance to women in banking industry. Price $10.00 per year.

3358

National Association of Insurance Commissioners (NAIC) Malpractice Claims

National Assn of Insurance Commissioners, 633 W Wisconsin Ave, Suite 1015, Milwaukee, WI 53203. Telephone (414) 271-4464.

Quarterly report. Provides information on malpractice claims and legislation. Price $28.00 per year.

3359

National Assn of Mutual Savings Banks' Annual Report

National Assn of Mutual Savings Banks, 200 Park Ave, New York, NY 10017. Telephone (212) 973-5432.

Annual book. Reports on mutual savings banks' deposit and investment activity. Discusses housing, mortgage, and legislative developments that affect banks. Charts and tables. Free of charge.

3360

National Assoc of Realtors' Who's Who

National Assn of Realtors, 430 N Michigan Ave, Chicago, IL 60611. Telephone (312) 440-8008. Telex 02 53742.

Annual book. Lists National Association of Realtors member board and state association presidents, elected secretaries, and executive officers. Price $50.00.

3361

National Assn of Securities Dealers (NASD) Manual

Commerce Clearing House, Inc, 4025 W Peterson Ave, Chicago, IL 60646. Telephone (312) 583-8500.

Loose-leaf book and monthly reports. Covers National Assn of Securities Dealers member, activities, and rules of fair practice, and pertinent Securities and Exchange Commission controls. Price $130.00 per year.

3362

National Association of Small Business Investment Companies (NASBIC) News

National Assn of Small Business Investment Companies, 618 Washington Bldg, Washington, DC 20005. Telephone (202) 638-3411.

Semimonthly newsletter. Reports on legislative developments and activities of Small Business Administration, and other government agencies, that affect small business investment companies. Price $100.00 per year.

3363

National Atlas of Canada

Supply and Services Canada, Pub Centre, Printing and Pub, Ottawa, Ont, Canada K1A 0S9. Telephone (613) 238-1601.

Book. Provides maps showing Canada's national domain, natural resources, climate, and development. Price $67.20.

3364
National Bank of Australasia, National Bank Monthly Summary
National Bank of Australasia Ltd, 500 Bourke St, Melbourne, Vic 3000, Australia. Telephone (61) (3) 630471. Telex 30241.

Monthly report. Covers Australian economic, business, finance, and industrial trends. Provides article expressing National Bank of Australasia's opinion. Free of charge. ISSN 0314.

3364.01
National Bank of Canada, Economic Review
National Bank of Canada, 500 Place d'Armes, Montreal, Que, Canada H2Y 2W3.

Bimonthly report. Contains one article which focuses on Canadian or international economic topics. Includes information on Canadian business conditions. Price free of charge. ISSN 0227-2865.

3365
National Business Review
Fourth Estate Group, PO Box 9344, Wellington, New Zealand. Telephone (64) (4) 859-019.

Weekly tabloid. Covers New Zealand business and economic news, trends, and developments. Price $30.00 per year.

3367
National Contract Management Assn (NCMA) Journal
National Contract Management Assn, 6728 Old McLean Village Dr, McLean, VA 22101. Telephone (703) 442-0137.

Semiannual book. Offers material on contract management subjects. Price $10.00 per year.

3368
National Contract Management Assn (NCMA) Magazine.
National Contract Management Assn, 6728 Old McLean Village Dr, McLean, VA 22101. Telephone (703) 442-0137.

Monthly magazine. Covers contract management issues. Price $15.00 per year.

3369
National Credit Union Administration (NCUA) Annual Report
National Credit Union Administration, 1776 G St, NW, Washington, DC 20456. Telephone (202) 357-1050.

Annual report. Presents data on finances and operations of federal credit unions. Discusses activities of National Credit Union Administration. Tables and charts. Free of charge.

3371
National Credit Union Administration (NCUA) Quarterly
National Credit Union Administration, 2025 M St, NW, Washington, DC 20456. Telephone (202) 254-9800.

Quarterly magazine. Discusses activities of various credit unions. Report on financial counseling and loan management topics. Provides financial data for credit unions. Free of charge.

3372
National Electrical Manufacturers Association Standards Publications
National Standards Associations, Inc, 5161 River Rd, Washington, DC 20016. Telephone (301) 951-1310. Telex 89-8452.

Microfiche, with weekly revisions. Provides standards used in the design, selection, procurement, and inspection of industrial electrical components and equipment. Price $690.00 per year.

3373
National Electronic Injury Surveillance System NEISS Data Highlights
US National Injury Information Clearinghouse, US Consumer Product Safety Commission, 5401 Westbard Ave, Room 625, Washington, DC 20207. Telephone (301) 492-6424.

Quarterly newsletter. Provides data on injuries from various products, including electric appliances, recreational equipment, heating appliances, and toys. Charts. Free of charge.

3373.01
National Exploration Daily
Petroleum Information Corp. PO Box 2612, 1375 Delaware, Denver, CO 80201. Telephone (303) 825-2181.

Daily report. Covers oil and gas exploration in US and Canada. Notes new discoveries and wildcat wells. Price $390.00 per year.

3374
National Fact Book of the Mutual Savings Bank Industry
National Assn of Mutual Savings Banks, 200 Park Ave, New York, NY 10017. Telephone (212) 973-5432.

Annual book. Provides facts about mutual savings banks including deposit, asset, mortgage holding, and other financial information. Tables and charts. Free of charge.

3375
National Federation of Independent Business (NFIB) Quarterly Economic Report for Small Business
National Federation of Independent Business, 150 W 20th Ave, San Mateo, CA 94403. Telephone (415) 341-7441.

Quarterly report. Provides data on small business earnings, inventories, employment, and economic expectations. Tables and charts. Free of charge.

3376
National Food Review
US Dept of Agriculture, ESS Publications, Room 0054-S, Washington, DC 20250. Order from Superintendent of Documents, US Government Printing Office, Washington, DC 20402. Telephone (202) 783-3238.

Quarterly. Covers latest USDA policy and research in areas of nutrition, food safety and quality, food marketing, and food assistance. Price $5.50 per year domestic, $6.90 per year foreign.

3377
National Forecast
National Securities & Research Corp, 605 3rd Ave, New York, NY 10016. Telephone (212) 661-3000.

Annual report. Presents general economic and stock market forecasts. Examines outlook for different groups of stocks. Graphs, charts, and tables. Free of charge.

3377.01
National Geothermal Service
Petroleum Information Corp, PO Box 2612, 1375 Delaware, Denver, CO 80201. Telephone (303) 825-2181.

Weekly report. Covers geothermal energy news. Notes research, drilling progress, and well completions. Price $420.00 per year.

3377.02
National Hardware Wholesalers Guide
Southern Hardware, 1760 Peachtree Rd, NW, Atlanta, GA 30357. Telephone (404) 874-4462.

Annual directory. Lists hardware manufacturers. Notes home office and regional sales personnel. Price available on request.

3378

National Health Insurance Reports

Plus Publications, Inc, 2626 Pennsylvania Ave, NW, Washington, DC 20037. Telephone (202) 333-5444.

Fortnightly report. Covers federal legislation and programs affecting health care. Includes material on pending national health insurance legislation, health maintenance organizations, and professional standards review. Price $97.00 per year.

3379

National Hog Farmer

The Webb Co, 1999 Shepard Rd, St Paul, MN 55116. Telephone (612) 690-7200.

Monthly magazine. Pertains to hog raising issues including feeds, diseases, and finances. Price available on request.

3379.01

National Home Center News

Lebhar-Friedman Publications, Inc, 425 Park Ave, New York, NY 10022. Telephone (212) 371-9400.

Fortnightly report. Covers news of home center, lumber, and building supply industries. Price $7.00 per year.

3380

National Hospital Economic Activity

American Hospital Assn, 840 N Lake Shore Dr, Chicago, IL 60611. Telephone (312) 280-6000.

Monthly report. Provides hospital statistical data. Covers admissions, inpatient and outpatient revenues, and operating margins. Price $150.00 per year.

3381

National Income & Expenditure Accounts

Statistics Canada, User Services, Publications Distribution, Ottawa, Ont, Canada K1A 0V7. Telephone (613) 992-3151.

Quarterly magazine. Provides data on Canadian gross national product and components, sources and disposition of personal income and gross saving, government revenue and expenditure, transactions of residents with nonresidents, gross national expenditure, and implicit price indexes. Price $28.80 per year. ISSN 0318-708X.

3382

National Income and Expenditure Blue Book 2

Her Majesty's Stationery Office, PO Box 569, London, England SE1 9NH. Telephone (44) (01) 928 1321.

Annual book. Details British national accounts that measure economic performance. Sections include industry, government, corporations, and personal sector. Price £10.50 per year.

3383

National Income and Product Accounts

US Dept of Commerce, Bureau of Economic Analysis, Washington, DC 20230. Order from Budget Office, Bureau of Economic Analysis, Washington, DC 20230. Telephone (202) 523-0691.

Information service, revised quarterly. Presents data on national income and product accounts. Price $150.00.

3385

National Information Center for Educational Media (NICEM) Newsletter

Univ of Southern California, University Park, Los Angeles, CA 90007. Telephone (800) 421-8711 in California (213) 743-6681.

Quarterly newsletter. Provides information on nonbook educational matter with emphasis on National Information Center for Educational Media services. Free of charge.

3386

National Injury Information Clearinghouse, Statistical Data from National Electronic Injury Surveillance System

US National Injury Information Clearinghouse, US Consumer Product Safety Commission, 5401 Westbard Ave, Room 625, Washington, DC 20207. Telephone (301) 492-6424.

Report. Reports on product-related injuries. Covers electric appliances, home furnishings, toys and recreational equipment. Charts. Free of charge.

3387

National Institute of Economic & Social Research Annual Report

National Inst of Economic and Social Research, 2 Dean Trench St Smith Sq, London, England SW1P 3HE. Telephone (44) (01) 222-7665.

Annual report. Reviews economic and social research projects, conferences, books, and other activities of National Institute of Economic and Social Research. Price free of charge.

3388

National Investor Relations Institute (IR) Update

National Investor Relations Inst, 1730 K St, NW, Suite 307, Washington, DC 20006. Telephone (202) 861-0630.

Monthly newsletter. Deals with issues affecting corporate investor relations. Includes information on SEC and other governmental regulations, dividends, and taxation. Price $125.00 per year.

3389

National Jeweler

Gralla Publications, 1515 Broadway, New York, NY 10036. Telephone (212) 869-1300.

Tabloid. Presents news of jewelry world for retailers, wholesalers, and suppliers. Price available on request.

3390

National Labor Relations Board (NLRB) Case Handling Manual

Commerce Clearing House, Inc, 4025 W Peterson Ave, Chicago, IL 60646. Telephone (312) 583-8500.

Loose-leaf book plus periodic reports. Gives text of procedural and operational guidelines for National Labor Relations Board regional office staffs. Price $95.00 per year.

3391

National Labor Relations Board (NLRB) Case Handling Manual

US National Labor Relations Board, 1717 Pennsylvania Ave NW, Washington, DC 20570. Order from Superintendent of Documents, US Government Printing Office, Washington, DC 20402. Telephone (202) 655-4000.

Three-part loose-leaf manual. Provides General Counsel procedural and operational guidelines to National Labor Relations Board regional offices in processing of cases. Covers unfair labor practices, representation, compliance proceedings, and settlement agreements. Price $26.50.

3392

National Labor Relations Board (NLRB) Decisions

Commerce Clearing House, Inc, 4025 W Peterson Ave, Chicago, IL 60646. Telephone (312) 583-8500.

Twenty-three books. Provide digests of National Labor Relations Board decisions. Price $27.00 per volume. ISSN 9130.

3393
National Mediation Board Annual Report
US National Mediation Board, 1425 K St, NW, Washington, DC 20572. Order from Superintendent of Documents, US Government Printing Office, Washington, DC 20402. Telephone (202) 523-5995.

Annual book. Summarizes activities of National Mediation Board in administration of Railway Labor Act. Includes report of National Railroad Adjustment Board. Lists neutral arbitrators and referees appointed. Price $4.00.

3394
National Mediation Board Reports of Emergency Boards
US National Mediation Board, 1425 K St. NW, Washington, DC 20572. Order from Superintendent of Documents, US Government Printing Office, Washington, DC 20402. Telephone (202) 523-6995.

Irregularly issued booklet. Contains reports of emergency boards established by Executive Order under Section 10 of Railway Labor Act to investigate labor disputes. Contains reports that are presented to US president. Free of charge.

3395
National Monthly Bond Summary
National Quotation Bureau, 116 Nassau St, New York, NY 10038. Telephone (212) 349-1800.

Monthly report. Contains bid and price statistics over the previous six months. Price available on request.

3396
National Monthly Stock Summary
National Quotation Bureau, 116 Nassau St, New York, NY 10038. Telephone (212) 349-1800.

Monthly report. Gives stock bid and price statistics during the previous six months. Price available on request.

3396.01
National Newspaper Index
Information Access Corp, 404 Sixth Ave, Menlo Park, CA 94025. Telephone (800) 227-8431.

Monthly microfilm service. Provides indexes to the Christian Science Monitor, The New York Times, and The Wall Street Journal. Includes cumulative indexes. Price $1880.00 per year.

3397
National Office Machine Dealers Assn (NOMDA) Spokesman
National Office Machine Dealers Assn, 1510 Jarvis Ave, Elk Grove Village, IL 60007. Telephone (312) 593-3270.

Monthly magazine. reports on office machine industry with emphasis on dealers' problems. Notes new products and manufacturing developments. Price $70.00 per year.

3398
National Office Products Assn (NOPA) Industry Report
National Office Products Assn, 301 N Fairfax St, Alexandria, VA 22314. Telephone (703) 549-9040.

Biweekly newsletter. Reports on office products industry. Discusses activities of National Office Products Association. Price $36.00 per year.

3401
National Public Accountant
National Society of Public Accountants, 1010 North Fairfax St, Alexandria, VA 22314. Telephone (703) 549-6400.

Monthly magazine. Discusses general accounting topics. Notes new accounting and tax legislation, as well as new techniques, such as computer systems. Price $12.00 per year.

3402
National Radio Publicity Directory
Peter/Glenn Publications, 17 E 48th St, New York, NY 10017. Telephone (212) 688-7940.

Annual directory, with six month update. Lists radio stations publicity contacts, including college stations, network programs, and syndicated talk shows. Provides travel information for major cities. Price $75.00 per year.

3402.01
National Real Estate Investor
Communication Channels, Inc, 6285 Barfield Rd, Atlanta, GA 30328. Telephone (404) 256-9800.

Monthly magazine. Reports national news and trends of income-producing real estate construction, development, financing, investment, and management. Price $38.00 per year.

3403
National Roster of Realtors
National Assn of Realtors, 430 N Michigan Ave, Chicago, IL 60611. Order from Stamats Pub Co, Inc, 427 6th Ave SE, Cedar Rapids, IA 52406. Telephone (319) 364-6167. Telex 02-53742.

Annual book. Offers roster of National Assn of Realtors' member boards, state associations, realtors' names and addresses, and directors and executive staff of the association. Price $45.00.

3404
National Safety News
National Safety Council, 444 N Michigan Ave, Chicago, IL 60611. Telephone (312) 527-4800. Telex 25-3141.

Monthly magazine. Discusses general safety topics. Presents news of National Safety Council and Occupational Safety and Health Administration. Price $17.00 members, $21.25 nonmembers.

3406
National Ski Areas Assn (NSAA) Economic Analysis of North American Ski Areas (1979–80 season)
University of Colorado, Graduate School of Business Administration, Business Research Div, Boulder, CO 80309. Telephone (303) 492-8227.

Report. Surveys North America's ski area operations. Notes physical and economic characteristics. Tabulates financial data. Based on reports from National Ski Areas Assn's members. Price $35.00.

3407
National Tax Journal
National Tax Assn, Tax Inst of America, 21 E State St, Columbus, OH 43215. Telephone (614) 224-8352.

Quarterly report. Articles on tax research. Price $25.00 per year. ISSN 0028-0283.

3408
National Trade and Professional Associations of the United States and Canada and Labor Unions
Columbia Books, Inc, Publishers, 734 15th St, NW, Suite 601, Washington, DC 20005. Telephone (202) 737-3777.

Annual directory. Describes national trade, labor, and professional associations in the US and Canada. Price $25.00. ISBN 0-910416-27-3.

3409

National Transportation Safety Board Service

Hawkins Publishing Co, Inc, 933 N Kenmore St, Suite 220, Arlington, VA 22201. Telephone (703) 525-9090.

Loose-leaf, indexed digest. Analyzes decisions of the National Transportation Safety Board and its predecessor, the Civil Aeronautics Board. Deals with aviation safety enforcement. Price $155.00.

3410

National Travel Survey

Her Majesty's Stationery Office, PO Box 569, London, England SE1 9NH. Telephone (44) (01) 928 1321.

Report on British national travel survey. Price available on request.

3411

National Underwriter

National Underwriter Co, 420 E 4th St, Cincinnati, OH 45202. Telephone (513) 721-2140.

Weekly newspaper. Covers insurance industry trends, including property, casualty, life, and health insurance. Price $12.75 per year.

3412

National Underwriter: Life and Health Insurance Edition

National Underwriter Co, 420 E 4th St, Cincinnati, OH 45202. Telephone (513) 721-2140.

Weekly newspaper. Covers news and trends in the life and health insurance industry. Price $12.75. ISSN 0028-033X.

3413

National Westminster Bank Quarterly Review

National Westminster Bank Ltd, 41 Lothbury, London, England EC2P 2BP. Telephone (44) (01) 606-6060.

Quarterly magazine. Features articles on British economic, business, and labor issues; includes international economic topics. Price free of charge.

3413.01

National Wildcat Monthly

Petroleum Information Corp, PO Box 2612, 1375 Delaware, Denver, CO 80201. Telephone (303) 825-2181.

Monthly report. Supplies information on new oil and gas discoveries in the US. Lists operator, well name, location, and producing information. Price $300.00 per year.

3414

Nation's Business

Chamber of Commerce of the US, 1615 H St, NW, Washington, DC 20062. Telephone (202) 659-6231.

Monthly magazine. Forecasts, analyzes, and interprets trends and developments in business and government. Price $18.75 per year.

3414.01

Nation's Restaurant News

Lebhar-Friedman Publications, Inc, 425 Park Ave, New York, NY 10022. Telephone (212) 371-9400.

Fortnightly report. Discusses trends in food-service and restaurant industries. Price $15.00 per year.

3415

Nationwide Directory of Sporting Goods Buyers

Salesman's Guide, Inc, 1140 Broadway, New York, NY 10001. Telephone (212) 684-2985.

Book with three supplements. Lists top retail stores with buyers' names for all types of sporting goods, athletic apparel, and footwear. Price $80.00.

3416

Nationwide Men's and Boy's Wear

Salesman's Guide, Inc, 1140 Broadway, New York, NY 10001. Telephone (212) 684-2985.

Book with three supplements, Lists department, clothing, and specialty stores, together with the names of buyers and merchandise managers of mens' and boys apparel and accessories departments. Price $65.00.

3417

Nationwide Women's and Children's Wear

Salesman's Guide, Inc, 1140 Broadway, New York, NY 10001. Telephone (212) 684-2985.

Book with three supplements. Lists top department, family clothing, and specialty stores. Notes the names of buyers and merchandise managers of women's and children's apparel and accessories departments. Price $65.00.

3418

Natural Gas/Fuel Forecast

McGraw-Hill Publications Co, 1221 Ave of the Americas, New York, NY 10020. Telephone (212) 997-6375. Telex TWX 7105814879. WUI 62555.

Information service. Contains current figures on natural gas consumption and curtailment. Provides alternate fuel-buying plans of 5500 major US energy consumers. Price $1200.00 per year.

3419

Natural Resources (Mexican)

Commerce Clearing House, Inc, 4025 W Peterson Ave, Chicago, IL 60646. Telephone (312) 583-8500.

Monthly loose-leaf report on Mexico's natural resources. Price $54.50 per year (prices subject to change with Mexican currency fluctuations).

3420

Naval Stores Market News Reports

US Dept of Agriculture, Agricultural Marketing Service, Room 523-Annex, Washington, DC 20250. Telephone (202) 447-2265.

Series of reports. Covers gum naval stores markets. Includes prices and sales of pine gum, gum rosin, crude gum, and turpentine. Free of charge.

3421

NCUA Review

National Credit Union Administration, 1776 G St, NW, Washington, DC 20456. Telephone (202) 357-1050.

Bimonthly publication. Discusses policies, regulations, and developments affecting credit unions. Price free of charge.

3422

Near East Business

Johnston Industrial Pub Corp, 386 Park Ave S, New York, NY 10016. Telephone (212) 689-0120. Telex 666811 Jonst.

Magazine issued nine times a year. Reports on business developments in Iran and the Middle East. Price $45.00 per year, $70.00 per two years.

3423

Nebraska Journal of Economics and Business

University of Nebraska-Lincoln, Bureau of Business Research, 200 CBA, Lincoln, NE 68588. Telephone (402) 472-2334.

Quarterly journal. Presents articles on economics and business research, including consumer prices and government employment. Price $5.00 per year.

3423.01
Nebraska: Manufacturers Directory,
1980–81
Manufacturers' News, Inc, 3 E Huron St, Chicago, IL 60611. Telephone (312) 337-1084.

Biennial book. Lists 2700 Nebraska manufacturing companies by name, location, and product. Price $19.00.

3424
Nebraska Now
Nebraska Dept of Economic Development, Box 94666, 301 Centennial Mall S, Lincoln, NE 68509. Telephone (402) 471-3111.

Monthly newsletter. Reports on Nebraska's industry and tourism. Notes community development and cultural events. Free of charge.

3425
Nebraska: State Industrial Directory,
1981
Manufacturers' News, Inc, 3 E Huron St, Chicago, IL 60611. Telephone (312) 337-1084.

Annual book. Provides information on 2501 Nebraska industrial firms and their executives. Price $25.00.

3426
Nebraska Statistical Handbook
Nebraska Dept of Economic Development, Box 94666, 301 Centennial Mall S, Lincoln, NE 68509. Telephone (402) 471-3111.

Book. Supplies demographic, social, economic, and physical statistics on Nebraska. Price $4.00.

3427
Neighborhood & Rehab Report
Community Development Services, Inc, 399 National Press Bldg, Washington, DC 20045. Telephone (202) 638-6113.

Monthly newsletter. Covers urban reinvestment, including neighborhood revitalization. Price $60.00 per year.

3428
Nelson's Directory of Securities Research Information
Fairchild Publications Inc, 7 E 12th St, New York, NY 10003. Telephone (212) 741-4280.

Annual book with semiannual updates. Supplies guide to stockbrokers and dealers. Provides information on research management personnel and 1500 securities analysts in various fields of specialization. Price $85.00 per year.

3429
Netherlands-American Trade
Netherlands Chamber of Commerce in US, Inc, 1 Rockefeller Plz, New York, NY 10020. Telephone (212) 265-6460. Telex 425-587.

Magazine published eleven times a year. Comments on Dutch industries and products exported to US. Price $12.50 for two years.

3430
Network Rates & Data
Standard Rate & Data Service, Inc, 5201 Old Orchard Rd, Skokie, IL 60077. Telephone (312) 470-3100.

Bimonthly book. Provides information on television and AM radio network stations and rates in metropolitan areas. Price $20.00 per year.

3430.01
Nevada: Industrial Directory, **1981**
Manufacturers' News, Inc, 3 E Huron St, Chicago, IL 60611. Telephone (312) 337-1084.

Biennial book. Lists Nevada manufacturers, wholesalers, and public warehouses. Price $8.00.

3431
Nevada Review of Business & Economics
University of Nevada, Reno, Bureau of Business and Economic Research, Reno, NV 89557. Telephone (702) 784-6877.

Quarterly report. Discusses Nevada economic topics. Provides economic statistics for Nevada and the US. Price free of charge to US residents.

3431.01
Nevada: State Industrial Directory, **1980**
Manufacturers' News, Inc, 3 E Huron St, Chicago, IL 60611. Telephone (312) 337-1084.

Biennial book. Identifies 500 Nevada industrial firms by name, location, and product. Price $15.00.

3432
New African
IC Publications Ltd, 122 E 42nd St, Suite 1121, New York, NY 10017. Telephone (212) 867-5159. Telex 425442.

Monthly magazine that analyzes African economic, business, and political developments. Price $50.00 per year.

3433
New African Development Yearbook
International Communications, 110 E 59th St, New York, NY 10022. Telephone (212) 867-5159.

Annual book. Contains information on every African country, including population, agriculture, minerals, oil, and gas. Maps. Price $25.00.

3434
New Business Report
Executive Communications, Inc, 400 E 54th St, New York, NY 10022. Telephone (212) 421-3713.

Monthly newsletter. Provides new business leads, sales tips, and other solicitation strategies for advertising agency top executives and new business specialists. Price $50.00 per year.

3435
New Consultants, **3rd edition**
Gale Research Co, Book Tower, Detroit, MI 48226. Telephone (313) 961-2242.

Four-issue ring binder supplement to Consultants and Consulting Organizations Directory, 5th edition. Gives information on new business, industrial, and governmental consulting firms and individuals. Price $160.00. ISBN 0351-5.

3436
New DP Index
Peter Isaacson Publications, 46-49 Porter St, Prahran, Vic 3181, Australia. Telephone (61) (03) 518431. Telex 30880.

Annual book. Provides information on the installation, operation, and maintenance of computer equipment. Price $25.00 each.

3437
New Earnings Survey
Her Majesty's Stationery Office, PO Box 569, London, England SE1 9NH. Telephone (44) (01) 214 6159. Telex 915564.

Six-part series published between October and April. Provides statistics on earnings from British employment by industry, occupation, and region. Price £7.90 for each part.

3438
New Encyclopedia Britannica, **15th edition**
Encyclopedia Britannica Corp, 425 N Michigan Ave, Chicago, IL 60611. Telephone (312) 321-7308.

Thirty-volume encyclopedia of general knowledge divided into three sections. Includes the one-volume Propaedia, an outline of knowledge; the ten-volume Micropaedia with brief articles that also serve as an index; and the nineteen-volume Macropaedia with almost 5000 in-depth articles. Price available on request.

3439
New England Business Magazine
New England Business Magazine, 31 Milk St, Boston, MA 02109. Telephone (603) 482-7040.

Magazine issued 20 times per year. Reports on business and economic developments in New England. Notes industrial expansion, acquisitions, and personnel changes. Price $18.00 per year.

3440
New England Economic Indicators
Federal Reserve Bank of Boston, Boston, MA 02106. Telephone (617) 973-3397.

Monthly report. Contains statistical information and analysis of New England's economic performance in relation to national production, employment, consumption, construction, finance, and other indicators. Free of charge.

3441
New England Economic Review
Federal Reserve Bank of Boston, Boston, MA 02106. Telephone (617) 973-3397.

Bimonthly magazine. Contains articles on national and regional economic problems, monetary policy, and financial developments. Focuses on Federal Reserve Bank of Boston area. Free of charge.

3442
New Englander
Yankee, Inc, Dublin, NH 03444. Telephone (603) 563-8111.

Monthly magazine. Discusses business, economic, and social developments in New England. Notes industrial expansion and acquisitions. Price $12.00 per year.

3443
New England Journal of Business and Economics
University of Rhode Island, Research Ctr in Business and Economics, Kingston, RI 02881. Telephone (401) 792-2549.

Biannual journal. Presents papers on business and economic research, particularly those relevant to New England. Free of charge.

3443.01
New England: Manufacturers Directory, **1980**
Manufacturers' News, Inc, 3 E Huron St, Chicago, IL 60611. Telephone (312) 337-1084.

Book published every 18 months. Provides information on 23,000 manufacturing firms in Maine, Connecticut, Vermont, and Massachusetts. Lists executives and number of employees. Price $84.00.

3444
New Equipment Digest
Penton/IPC, 614 Superior Ave W, Cleveland, OH 44113. Order from Penton/IPC, 1111 Chester Ave, Cleveland, OH 44114. Telephone (216) 696-7000.

Monthly magazine. Pertains to new manufacturing equipment, including material handling, plant maintenance, and safety equipment. Price $24.00 per year.

3445
New Equipment News
Canadian Engineering Publications Ltd, 32 Front St W, Suite 501, Toronto, Ont, Canada M5J 2H9. Telephone (416) 869-1735.

Monthly tabloid. Reports on Canada's original new industrial products, equipment, materials, and methods. Price $22.00 per year. ISSN 0028-4971.

3445.01
New From Europe
Prestwick International, Inc, PO Box 205, Burnt Hills, NY 12027. Telephone (518) 399-6985.

Monthly report. Gives information on new products from Western Europe available for license, franchise, purchase for resale, or acquisition. Includes new process data. Price $275.00 per year.

3446
New From Japan
Prestwick International, Inc, PO Box 205, Burnt Hills, NY 12027. Telephone (518) 399-6985.

Monthly report. Gives information on new products from Japan available for license, franchise, purchase for resale, or acquisition. Includes new process data. Price $275.00 per year.

3447
New Governmental Advisory Organizations, **2nd edition**
Gale Research Co, Book Tower, Detroit, MI 48226. Telephone (313) 961-2242.

Semiannual loose-leaf supplement to Encyclopedia of Governmental Advisory Organizations. Reports on newly established US federal advisory groups. Price $135.00. ISBN 0252-7.

3448
New Hampshire: State Industrial Directory, **1980–81**
Manufacturers' News, Inc, 3 E Huron St, Chicago, IL 60611. Telephone (312) 337-1084.

Biennial book. Contains information on 900 industrial companies in New Hampshire. Notes executives. Price $20.00.

3449
New International Realities
National Planning Assn, 1606 New Hampshire Ave, NW, Washington, DC 20009. Telephone (202) 265-7685.

Report published three times per year. Discusses current international political and economic trends. Forecasts future developments. Price $5.00 per year, $1.75 per copy.

3450
New Jersey Business
New Jersey Manufacturers Assn, 50 Park Pl, Newark, NJ 07101. Telephone (201) 623-8359.

Monthly magazine. Reports on New Jersey business and industrial topics. Notes activities of New Jersey Business and Industry Assn. Price $6.00 per year.

3450.01
New Jersey: Directory of Manufacturers **1981–82**
Manufacturers' News, Inc, 3 E Huron St, Chicago, IL 60611. Telephone (312) 337-1084.

Biennial book. Lists 12,000 manufacturing firms in New Jersey by name, location, and product. Price $59.50.

3451

New Jersey Economic Outlook

New Jersey Office of Economic Policy, 142 W State St, Trenton, NJ 08625. Telephone (609) 292-1890.

Annual report. Analyzes New Jersey's economy. Projects economic development for the state and nation for the coming year. Free of charge.

3452

New Jersey Economic Policy Council Annual Report

New Jersey Office of Economic Policy, 142 W State St, Trenton, NJ 08625. Telephone (609) 292-1890.

Annual report. Contains statistical tables on New Jersey's economy and demography. Reviews legislation and economic development. Recommands economic policy changes including taxation and incentives. Free of charge.

3453

New Jersey International Report

New Jersey Office of International Trade, 744 Broad St, Room 1709, Newark, NJ 07102. Telephone (201) 648-3518.

Monthly report. Covers foreign business opportunities for New Jersey businesses. Available to New Jersey businesses free of charge.

3453.01

New Jersey: State Industrial Directory, 1980

Manufacturers' News, Inc, 3 E Huron St, Chicago, IL 60611. Telephone (312) 337-1084.

Annual book. Covers 14,500 industrial firms in New Jersey. Indicates location and products. Price $90.00.

3454

New Mexico Business

University of New Mexico, Bureau of Business and Economic Research, Inst for Applied Research Services, Albuquerque, NM 87131. Telephone (505) 277-2216.

Monthly report. Covers New Mexico's economy. Tables. Price $12.00 per year.

3455

New Mexico: Manufacturing & Mining Directory '81

Manufacturers' News, Inc, 3 E Huron St, Chicago, IL 60611. Telephone (312) 337-1084.

Biennial book. Contains information on 700 manufacturing and mining firms in New Mexico. Notes executives and number of employees. Price $35.00.

3455.01

New Mexico: State Industrial Directory, 1981

Manufacturers' News, Inc, 3 E Huron St, Chicago, IL 60611. Telephone (312) 337-1084.

Annual book. Provides information on 1000 industrial companies in New Mexico. Identifies executives and lists number of employees. Price $25.00.

3456

New Motor Vehicle Sales

Statistics Canada, User Services, Publications Distribution, Ottawa, Ont, Canada K1A 0V7. Telephone (613) 992-3151.

Monthly report. Supplies data on number and value of new Canadian passenger cars, trucks, and buses sold, by provinces and by source of origin. Monthly and cumulative tables. Price $30.00 per year. ISSN 0705-5595.

3457

New One-Family Houses Sold and For Sale

US Dept of Commerce, Bureau of the Census, Washington, DC 20233. Telephone (202) 449-1600.

Monthly report. Provides information on new, privately owned, one-family homes sold and for sale. Notes ratio of homes for sale to homes sold and the median number of months on the market. Price $5.25 per year.

3457.01

New Plants

Conway Publications, Inc, Peachtree Air Terminal, 1954 Airport Rd, Atlanta, GA 30341. Telephone (404) 458-6026.

Annual computer printout. Summarizes new plant announcements, including company name, SIC, amount of investment, anticipated work force, square footage under roof, and site acres. Arranged by country, state, and city. Price $95.00.

3457.02

New Product Card Index

IMS World Publications Ltd, York House, 37 Queen Sq, London, England WCIN 3BE. Telephone (44) (01) 242-0112. Telex 263298.

Continuous card index system. Contains information on new pharmaceutical products. Notes trade name, therapeutic class, composition, medical indications, and other data. Price $950.00 per year.

3458

New Product—New Business Digest

General Electric Co, Business Growth Services, 120 Erie Blvd, Room 591, Schenectady, NY 12305. Telephone (518) 385-2577.

Monthly digest. Describes over 500 new product and business programs available by purchase or license. Notes industrial research developments. Price $45.00.

3458.01

New Products & Processes From Western Europe

Prestwick International, Inc, PO Box 205, Burnt Hills, NY 12027. Telephone (518) 399-6985.

Annual publication. A digest of business opportunities and technological advances from Western Europe, contains over 600 items. Price $45.00.

3459

New Research Centers

Gale Research Co, Book Tower, Detroit, MI 48226. Telephone (313) 961-2242.

Loose-leaf supplement to Research Centers Directory, 5th edition. Contains information on new university-related and nonprofit research organizations. Price $140.00. ISBN 0451-1.

3460

New Residential Construction in Selected Standard Metropolitan Statistical Areas

US Dept of Commerce, Bureau of the Census, Washington, DC 20233. Telephone (202) 449-1600.

Quarterly report. Provides estimates on number of new, privately owned residential housing units authorized, under construction, and completed for 13 metropolitan statistical areas. Price $2.00 per year.

3461
News & Views
Council of Better Business Bureaus, Inc,
1150 17th St, NW, Washington, DC
20036. Telephone (202) 862-1200.

Quarterly newsletter. Reports on Better
Business Bureaus activities. Emphasizes
consumer protection and information.
Notes proposed consumer protection
laws. Price available on request.

3461.01
News & Views
Arthur Young & Co, 277 Park Ave, New
York, NY 10017. Telephone (212) 922-
2000.

Journal issued irregularly. Reports on developments in financing, tax planning,
and accounting procedures for the real estate industry. Price free of charge.

3462
*News and Views from the American
Arbitration Association*
American Arbitration Assn, 140 W 51st
St, New York, NY 10020. Telephone
(212) 977-2000.

Quarterly report. Discusses arbitration
news and activities of American Arbitration Assn. Free to members.

3462.01
Newsbank Library
Newsbank, Inc, 58 Pine St, New Canaan,
CT 06840. Telephone (203) 966-1100.

Microfiche plus monthly, quarterly, and
annual cumulative indexes. Provides local
news stories from 160 US newspapers.
Covers social, political, and economic
topics. Price $1596.00 per year.

3463
News for Investors
Investor Responsibility Research Ctr,
Inc, 1522 K St, NW, Suite 806, Washing-
ton, DC 20005. Telephone (202) 833-
3727.

Monthly newsletter. Provides information on shareholder resolutions. Identifies
proponents of resolutions and reports on
issues affecting corporations. Notes relevant SEC rules. Price $145.00.

3464
News from the Hill
Legislative Research International, PO
Box 1511, Washington, DC 20013. Tele-
phone (202) 293-1455.

Monthly bulletin. Reports on new US legislative developments relating to international business. Price $48.00 per year.

3465
News Front/Business Trends
Ward Publications, Box 380, Petaluma,
CA 94952. Telephone (707) 762-0737.

Bimonthly newsletter. Covers management trends. Gives computerized company analyses. Abstracts management articles from more than 500 publications.
Price $10.00 per year.

3465.01
News Front/Business Trends Databank
Ward Publications, Box 380, Petaluma,
CA 94952. Telephone (707) 762-0737.

Computer printout and tape. Supplies one
to five years of data, and up to 40 fields of
figures, percents, and ratios per year, to-
talling 200 data fields per public company
and 12 fields per private company. Price
$470 and up.

3465.02
News Front/Business Trends Directory
News Front/Business Trends, Ward Pub-
lications, Box 380, Petaluma, CA 94952.
Telephone (707) 762-0737.

Directory. Lists 50,000 leading US corporations. Provides ranked lists by three
digit SIC industries, lists by geographic
location, and by most profitable industries. Price $95.00.

3465.03
Newsletter
International Export Assn, PO Box 1,
Bourne, Lincolnshire, England. Tele-
phone 07782 3528.

Bimonthly report. Discusses international
trading opportunities. Notes the services
of the International Export Association
and its member activities. Price £40.00
per year (includes membership in the association).

3466
Newsletter on Newsletters
Newsletter Clearinghouse, 44 W Market
St, Rhinebeck, NY 12572. Telephone
(914) 876-2081.

Semimonthly newsletter. Discusses new
developments in newsletter field. Gives
case histories and tips on promotion,
graphics, and editorial content. Price
$54.00 per year.

3467
Newsletter Yearbook/Directory
Newsletter Clearinghouse, 44 W Market
St, Rhinebeck, NY 12572. Telephone
(914) 876-2081.

Annual directory to 2000 newsletters is
arranged by subject. Includes bibliography and highlights of conferences. Lists
award winners. Price $35.00.

3468
Newspaper Circulation Analysis
Standard Rate & Data Service, Inc, 5201
Old Orchard Rd, Skokie, IL 60077. Tele-
phone (312) 470-3100.

Annual book. Provides adjusted circulation and market data for daily and Sunday
newspapers. Includes rates and ranking
tables. Price $35.00 per year.

3470
Newspaper Rates & Data
Standard Rate & Data Service, Inc, 5201
Old Orchard Rd, Skokie, IL 60077. Tele-
phone (312) 470-3100.

Monthly book. Contains advertising rates
and related information for 1600 newspapers and newspaper groups. Includes religious, black, and specialized papers. Price
$111.00 per year.

3471
News Summary
Main Lafrentz & Co, 380 Park Ave, New
York, NY 10017. Telephone (212) 867-
9100.

Newsletter issued five times per year. Reports on tax and accounting matters.
Notes pending legislation and regulatory
changes. Free of charge.

3472
New Surveys
Statistics Canada, User Services, Publica-
tions Distribution, Ottawa, Ont, Canada
K1A 0V7 Telephone (613) 992-3151.

Quarterly report. Discusses new Canadian government surveys and major revisions of existing surveys. Contains brief
abstracts of surveys reported to Statistics
Canada. Price $24.00 per year. ISSN
0381-4432.

3473
New Trade Names
Gale Research Co, Book Tower, Detroit,
MI 48226. Telephone (313) 961-2242.

Supplements to Trade Names Dictionary.
Contain new trade names and information about manufacturers. Price $115.00
for both supplements. ISBN 0693-X.

3474

*New York City Business Fact Book.
Part 1: Business and Manufacturing*

New York Dept of Commerce, 99 Washington Ave, Albany, NY 12245. Telephone (518) 474-8670.

Booklet published every five years. Presents statistical tables on New York City's manufacturing, wholesale, and retail trade, and selected services. Includes data on gas and electric utilities, climate, newspapers, water supply, and other topics. Free of charge.

3475

New York City Business Fact Book. Part 2: Population and Housing

New York Dept of Commerce, 99 Washington Ave, Albany, NY 12245. Telephone (518) 474-8670.

Booklet published every 10 years. Provides statistical profile of New York City's people, jobs, and housing. Free of charge.

3476

New York Estates, Wills, Trusts

Commerce Clearing House, Inc, 4025 W Peterson Ave, Chicago, IL 60646. Telephone (312) 583-8500.

Publication covers estates, wills, and trusts in New York State. Price $365.00 per year.

3476.01

*New York: Manufacturers Directory,
1980–81*

Manufacturers' News, Inc, 3 E Huron St, Chicago, IL 60611. Telephone (312) 337-1084.

Annual book. Covers 16,000 manufacturing firms in New York. Identifies key executives. Price $39.00.

3477

*New York Mercantile Exchange
Statistical Yearbook*

New York Mercantile Exchange, 4 World Trade Ctr, New York, NY 10048. Telephone (212) 938-2222.

Biennial book. Contains annual summaries of New York Mercantile Exchange trading and industry statistics, future prices, and related information. Price $20.00.

3478

New York No-Fault Arbitration Reports

American Arbitration Assn, 140 W 51st St, New York, NY 10020. Telephone (212) 977-2000.

Bimonthly report. Summarizes selected decisions of arbitrators under New York's no-fault automobile insurance law. Price $60.00 per year.

3479

New York Publicity Outlets

Harold D Hansen, Box 327, Washington Depot, CT 06794. Telephone (203) 868-0200.

Annual directory providing information on the media in metropolitan New York area. Includes data on newspapers, magazines, radio and television stations, and identifies key people and positions. Price $55.00 per year.

3480

New York State Banker

New York State Bankers Assn, 485 Lexington Ave, New York, NY 10017. Telephone (212) 949-1178.

Semimonthly newsletter. Reports on commercial banking industry and related legislative developments. Discusses New York State Bankers Assn activities. Price $10.00 per year.

3481

*New York State Business Fact Book.
Part 1: Business and Manufacturing*

New York Dept of Commerce, 99 Washington Ave, Albany, NY 12245. Telephone (518) 474-8670.

Booklet published every five years. Issues statistics on New York State's business and industry. Focuses on manufacturing, wholesale, and retail trades. Free of charge.

3482

*New York State Business Fact Book.
Part 2: Population and Housing*

New York Dept of Commerce, 99 Washington Ave, Albany, NY 12245. Telephone (518) 474-8670.

Booklet issued every 10 years. Gives statistical data on New York State's population, work force, and housing. Free of charge.

3483

*New York State Dept of Labor Annual
Planning Report*

New York Dept of Labor, Div of Research and Statistics, State Office Bldg Campus, Albany, NY 12240. Order from Bureau of Labor Market Information, Room 405, Div of Research and Statistics, New York State Dept of Labor, State Office Bldg Campus, Albany, NY 12240. Telephone (518) 457-3800.

Annual report. Presents information on New York State's labor force and employment trends for employment program planners. Free of charge.

3483.01

New York: State Industrial Directory
1980

Manufacturers' News, Inc, 3 E Huron St, Chicago, IL 60611. Telephone (312) 337-1084.

Annual book. Covers 25,000 industrial firms in New York. Lists 250,000 executives. Price $95.00.

3484

*New York Stock Exchange (NYSE) Fact
Book*

New York Stock Exchange, 11 Wall St, New York, NY 10005. Telephone (212) 623-2089.

Annual book. Gives statistics on New York Stock Exchange members, listed issues, market activity, shares, and other data. Price $2.50 plus postage.

3485

*New York Stock Exchange (NYSE)
Guide*

Commerce Clearing House, Inc, 4025 W Peterson Ave, Chicago, IL 60646. Telephone (312) 583-8500.

Three loose-leaf books and monthly reports. Contain directory, constitution, and rules of New York Stock Exchange, plus Securities and Exchange Commission requirements. Price $195.00 per year.

3486

*New York Stock Exchange (NYSE)
Statistical Highlights*

New York Stock Exchange, 11 Wall St, New York, NY 10005. Telephone (212) 623-7603.

Monthly report. Compiles current stock market and financial statistics, including record highs and lows. Price $4.00.

3487

New York Times

New York Times, 229 W 43rd St, New York, NY 10036. Telephone (212) 556-1234.

Daily newspaper. Contains articles on business, financial, and economic news, along with general news coverage. Includes securities price statistics. Price $150.00 per year.

3488
New York Times Index
Microfilming Corp of America, 1620 Hawkins Ave, PO Box 10, Sanford, NC 27330. Telephone (800) 334-7501, in NC (919) 775-3451.

Semimonthly index, with quarterly and annual cumulations. Is index by subject to articles appearing in the New York Times. Price $345.00 per year full service, $210.00 per year semimonthly paper-bound issue, $225.00 per year annual hard-bound volume. Backfile volumes, 1851-1980, available with prices on request.

3489
New York University Annual Conference on Labor
Matthew Bender & Co, 235 E 45th St, New York, NY 10017. Telephone (212) 661-5050.

Book. Records proceedings of annual New York University Conference on Labor. Discusses labor-management relations. Price $40.00 for annual volume.

3490
New York University Annual Institute on Federal Taxation
Matthew Bender & Co, 235 E 45th St, New York, NY 10017. Telephone (212) 661-5050.

Annual two-volume set of books. Contains lectures on tax techniques given at New York University Institute on Federal Taxation. Price $95.00.

3491
New Zealand Agricultural Statistics
New Zealand Dept of Statistics, Private Bag, Wellington, New Zealand. Telephone (64) (4) 729119.

Annual report on New Zealand's agricultural statistics. Price $4.50 (New Zealand).

3493
New Zealand Balance of Payments
New Zealand Dept of Statistics, Private Bag, Wellington, New Zealand. Telephone (64) (4) 729119.

Annual report on New Zealand's balance of payments. Price $1.20 (New Zealand).

3494
New Zealand Building and Construction Statistics
New Zealand Dept of Statistics, Private Bag, Wellington, New Zealand. Telephone (64) (4) 729119.

Annual report on New Zealand's construction and building statistics. Price $1.10 (New Zealand).

3495
New Zealand Business Who's Who
Fourth Estate Group, PO Box 9344, Wellington, New Zealand. Order from Fourth Estate Group, PO Box 9143, Wellington, New Zealand. Telephone (64) (4) 859-019.

Annual book. Provides information on 10,000 New Zealand companies, executives, products and services, and marketing. Furnishes index of subsidiaries. Price $40.00 (New Zealand).

3496
New Zealand Census of Building and Construction
New Zealand Dept of Statistics, Private Bag, Wellington, New Zealand. Telephone (64) (4) 729119.

Report issued every five years. Presents information on building and construction in New Zealand. Price $1.00 (New Zealand).

3497
New Zealand Commerce
New Zealand Chambers of Commerce, Box 1071, Wellington, New Zealand. Telephone (64) (4) 723376.

Monthly magazine. Reports on New Zealand's business and trade, and on activities of the New Zealand Chamber of Commerce. Price $15.00 (New Zealand) per year.

3498
New Zealand Company Directory and Executive
Mercantile Gazette of New Zealand, Box 20-034, Christchurch 5, New Zealand. Telephone (64) (3) 583219.

Monthly magazine. Covers business and political background of New Zealand companies. Contains annual reports. Price $12.00 (New Zealand) per year.

3499
New Zealand Data Processing
Fourth Estate Group, PO Box 9344, Wellington, New Zealand. Telephone (64) (4) 859-019.

Monthly information service. Reports on developments in New Zealand's computer industry. Notes pertinent overseas developments. Price $10.00 (New Zealand) per year.

3500
New Zealand Economist
Berl Publications Ltd, PO Box 10-010, Wellington, New Zealand. Telephone (64) (4) 725563.

Monthly magazine. Reviews New Zealand's economic and business conditions. Price $20.00 (New Zealand) per year.

3501
New Zealand Exports
New Zealand Dept of Statistics, Private Bag, Wellington, New Zealand. Telephone (64) (4) 729119.

Annual book. Offers statistics on New Zealand's exports, organized by country and by item. Price $5.50 (New Zealand).

3502
New Zealand External Trade, Country Analyses
New Zealand Dept of Statistics, Private Bag, Wellington, New Zealand. Telephone (64) (4) 729119.

Quarterly report. Covers New Zealand's external trade. Furnishes analyses by country. Price $2.00 (New Zealand) per copy.

3503
New Zealand Financial Times
G R Allen, PO Box 1367, Wellington, New Zealand.

Monthly magazine. Specializes in finance and investment in New Zealand. Offers advice on personal investment problems. Analyzes company balance sheets. Price $1.50 (New Zealand) per copy.

3504
New Zealand Imports
New Zealand Dept of Statistics, Private Bag, Wellington, New Zealand. Telephone (64) (4) 729119.

Annual book. Provides data on New Zealand's imports. Shows commodities and countries of origin. Price $5.50 (New Zealand).

3505
New Zealand Incomes and Income Tax
New Zealand Dept of Statistics, Private Bag, Wellington, New Zealand. Telephone (64) (4) 729119.

Annual report on New Zealand's incomes and income tax. Price $2.50 (New Zealand).

3506
New Zealand Income Tax Law and Practice
C C H Australia Ltd, PO Box 230, North Ryde, NSW 2113, Australia. Telephone 583-8500.
Two-volume report issued every three weeks. Explains New Zealand's income tax laws. Provides full text of Income Tax Act and Land Tax Act. Price $240.00 (Australian) per year.

3507
New Zealand Industrial Production
New Zealand Dept of Statistics, Private Bag, Wellington, New Zealand. Telephone (64) (4) 729119.
Annual report on New Zealand's industrial production. Price $4.00 (New Zealand).

3508
New Zealand Insurance Statistics
New Zealand Dept of Statistics, Private Bag, Wellington, New Zealand. Telephone (64) (4) 729119.
Annual report. Offers insurance statistics for New Zealand. Price $1.20 (New Zealand).

3509
New Zealand Master Tax Guide
Commerce Clearing House, Inc, 4025 W Peterson Ave, Chicago, IL 60646. Telephone (312) 236-2350.
Book. Covers New Zealand's income tax. Price $18.00.

3510
New Zealand National Income and Expenditure
New Zealand Dept of Statistics, Private Bag, Wellington, New Zealand. Telephone (64) (4) 729119.
Annual report. Contains statistical data on New Zealand's national income and expenditures. Price $1.00 (New Zealand).

3511
New Zealand Official Yearbook
New Zealand Dept of Statistics, Private Bag, Wellington, New Zealand. Telephone (64) (4) 729119.
Annual book. Contains statistical information on New Zealand. Price $6.50 (New Zealand).

3512
New Zealand Prices, Wages and Labour
New Zealand Dept of Statistics, Private Bag, Wellington, New Zealand. Telephone (64) (4) 729119.
Annual statistical report on New Zealand's prices, wages, and labor. Price $2.00 (New Zealand).

3513
New Zealand Report and Analysis of External Trade
New Zealand Dept of Statistics, Private Bag, Wellington, New Zealand. Telephone (64) (4) 729119.
Annual report and analysis of New Zealand's external trade. Price $2.00 (New Zealand).

3513.01
New Zealand Trade Report
Chaunter Publications Ltd, PO Box 17-159, Wellington, New Zealand. Telephone (4) 766-432.
Weekly newsletter. Reports on New Zealand's political and commercial developments for domestic and overseas subscribers. Price $80.00 per year (New Zealand), $95.00 US per year overseas.

3514
New Zealand Transport
New Zealand Dept of Statistics, Private Bag, Wellington, New Zealand. Telephone (64) (4) 729119.
Annual report. Offers statistical information on New Zealand's transport. Price $2.50 (New Zealand).

3515
New Zealand Vital Statistics
New Zealand Dept of Statistics, Private Bag, Wellington, New Zealand. Telephone (64) (4) 729119.
Annual report containing New Zealand's vital statistics. Price $2.00 (New Zealand).

3516
Nielsen Newscast
A C Nielsen Co, Media Research Group, Nielsen Plz, Northbrook, IL 60062. Telephone (312) 498-6300.
Quarterly report on television audience research. Free to qualified subscribers.

3516.01
Nielsen Reporter
A C Nielsen Co, Media Research Group, Nielsen Plz, Northbrook, IL 60062. Telephone (319) 242-4505.

Report issued three times per year. Covers coupon, consumer promotions, and related activities. Price free of charge.

3517
Nielsen Researcher
A C Nielsen Co, Media Research Group, Nielsen Plz, Northbrook, IL 60062. Telephone (312) 498-6300.
Quarterly magazine. Concerns marketing of consumer food and drug products. Free to qualified subscribers.

3517.01
Nigeria Newsletter
I C Publications Ltd, 122 E 42nd St, Suite 1121, New York, NY 10017. Telephone (212) 867-5159. Telex 425442.
Biweekly newsletter. Examines political and economic developments in Nigeria. Covers commerce, oil, and trade. Price $395.00 per year.

3518
Nigerian Trade Summary
Nigerian Consulate General, 575 Lexington Ave, New York, NY 10022. Telephone (212) PL 2-1670.
Quarterly summary of information on Nigerian trade. Price 50 Kobo.

3519
Nigeria Trade Journal
Nigerian Consulate General, 575 Lexington Ave, New York, NY 10022. Telephone (212) PL 2-1670.
Quarterly magazine covering Nigerian trade. Price $3.50.

3522
1975 Handbook on Women Workers
US Dept of Labor, Women's Bureau, 200 Constitution Ave, NW, Room S3005, Washington, DC 20210. Order from Superintendent of Documents, US Government Printing Office, Washington, DC 20402. Telephone (202) 783-3238.
Book. Provides data on women workers in US. Price available on request.

3525
1977 Michigan Economic and Population Statistics
Michigan Dept of Commerce (MI), PO Box 30225, Lansing, MI 48909. Telephone (517) 373-3530.
Yearly book. Offers statistics on Michigan's economy and population. Provides comparisons with other states to assist firms considering locating in Michigan. Maps. Free of charge.

3527
Ninth District Quarterly Review
Federal Reserve Bank of Minneapolis, 250 Marquette Ave, Minneapolis, MN 55480. Telephone (612) 340-2386.

Quarterly report. Presents economic research aimed at improving policymaking by Federal Reserve System. Includes review of 9th Federal Reserve District's economy. Free of charge.

3528
Noise Control Report
Business Publishers, Inc, PO Box 1067, Silver Spring, MD 20910. Telephone (301) 587-6300.

Biweekly newsletter. Covers developments in field of noise abatement and control. Includes regulations, court decisions, and policy statements. Price $115.00 per year.

3529
Noise Regulation Reporter
Bureau of National Affairs, Inc, 1231 25th St, NW, Washington, DC 20037. Telephone (202) 452-4200.

Loose-leaf books with biweekly update. Cover noise abatement and control regulations, legislation, developments, and corrective methods. Includes current reports, reference file, text of laws, and glossary. Price $244.00 per year.

3530
Non-Destructive Testing (NDT) International
IPC Business Press Ltd, 205 E 42nd St, New York, NY 10017. Telephone (212) 889-0700. Telex 421710.

Bimonthly magazine. Reports on nondestructive testing techniques and applications for engineering products in various fields, including ultrasonics, microwaves, and vibration analysis. Price $117.00. ISSN 0308-9126.

3531
Nonferrous Castings
US Dept of Commerce, Bureau of the Census, Washington, DC 20233. Telephone (202) 449-1600.

Monthly report with annual summary. Presents information on nonferrous castings shipments. Indicates unfilled orders for sale. Price $3.30 per year.

3532
Non-Ferrous Metal Data
American Bureau of Metal Statistics, Inc, 420 Lexington Ave, New York, NY 10170. Telephone (212) 867-9450. Telex 14-7130.

Annual book. Furnishes global data on copper, lead, zinc, and other non-ferrous metals. Tables on production, consumption, and trade. Price $15.00 per copy.

3532.01
Nonwovens Industry
Household & Personal Products Industry, Box 555, 26 Lake St, Ramsey, NJ 07446. Telephone (201) 825-2552.

Monthly magazine. Covers nonwoven fabric industry. Reports on manufacturing, converting, and marketing developments. Price $18.00 per year.

3533
North
Supply and Services Canada, Canadian Govt Publishing Centre, Hull Que, Canada K1A 0S9. Telephone (819) 994-3475.

Quarterly journal. Offers information and comment on all aspects of life in Canada's North. Bilingual. Price $7.50 per year.

3534
North Carolina Industrial Data File
North Carolina Dept of Commerce, 430 N Salisbury St, Raleigh, NC 27611. Telephone (919) 733-4151.

Series of reports. Covers North Carolina's transportation, taxes, environmental regulation, manpower, industrial financing, legislation, energy, industrial training, and history. Price available on request.

3534.01
North Carolina: Manufacturers Directory **1981–82**
Manufacturers' News, Inc, 3 E Huron St, Chicago, IL 60611. Telephone (312) 337-1084.

Biennial book. Provides information on 8000 North Carolina manufacturing firms by name, location, and product. Notes executives. Price $39.00.

3535
North Carolina Review of Business and Economics
University of North Carolina at Greensboro, School of Business and Economics, Ctr for Applied Research, Greensboro, NC 27412. Telephone (919) 379-5430.

Quarterly report. Discusses North Carolina's general business and economics. Includes North Carolina's economic data. Price free of charge. ISSN 0098-8731.

3535.01
North Carolina: State Industrial Directory, **1980**
Manufacturers' News, Inc, 3 E Huron St, Chicago, IL 60611. Telephone (312) 337-1084.

Annual book. Lists 6700 North Carolina industrial firms. Notes location and products. Price $60.00.

3536
North Dakota Crop and Livestock Statistics
US Dept of Agriculture Crop Reporting Board, Economics and Statistics Service (ESS), Room 0005 S Bldg, US Dept of Agriculture, Washington, DC 20250. Order from North Dakota Crop and Livestock Reporting Service, 345 Federal Bldg, US Post Office, PO Box 3166, Fargo, ND 58102. Telephone (701) 237-5771 ext 5306.

Annual report. Gives statistical data about agriculture in North Dakota, including crop and livestock summaries, grain and stock estimates, farm labor and wage rates, prices, income, and milk and dairy products. Free of charge.

3536.01
North Dakota: Manufacturing Directory, **1980–81**
Manufacturers' News, Inc, 3 E Huron St, Chicago, IL 60611. Telephone (312) 337-1084.

Biennial book. Covers 900 North Dakota manufacturing firms. Indicates products and executives. Price $13.00.

3536.02
North Dakota: State Industrial Directory, **1981**
Manufacturers' News, Inc, 3 E Huron St, Chicago, IL 60611. Telephone (312) 337-1084.

Annual book. Contains information on 903 industrial firms in North Dakota. Identifies 5412 executives. Price $15.00.

3537
Northern Coastal California—Economic Trends in the Seventies
Security Pacific National Bank, PO Box 2097, Terminal Annex, Los Angeles, CA 90051. Telephone (213) 613-5402.

Report. Analyzes economic outlook for 16 northern coastal California counties. Price free of charge.

3538
Northern Ireland Digest of Statistics
Her Majesty's Stationery Office, PO Box 569, London, England SE1 9NH. Telephone (44) (01) 928 1321.

Semiannual service. Contains statistics from all government departments for Northern Ireland. Price £3.75 semiannually.

3539
Northern Miner
Northern Miner Press Ltd, 77 River St, Toronto, Ont, Canada M5A 3P2. Telephone (416) 368-3481. Telex 065-24190.

Weekly newspaper. Reports on Canadian mining industry, including company activities, government policies, labor issues, and metal markets. Price $28.00 per year. ISSN 0029-3164.

3540
Northern Perspectives
Canadian Arctic Resources Committee, 46 Elgin St, Room 11, Ottawa, Ont, Canada K1P 5K6. Telephone (613) 236-7379.

Report. Deals with development of Canadian north. Price available on request. ISSN 0380-5522.

3541
Northern Reporter
Capital Communications Ltd, Suite 705, Burnside Bldg, 151 Slater St, Ottawa, Ont, Canada K1P 5H3. Telephone (613) 235-9183. Telex 053-3601.

Quarterly newsletter. Discusses scientific, engineering, social, and economic developments in northern Canada. Price $50.00 per year.

3542
Northern Territory Statistical Summary (Cat No 1306.7)
Australian Bureau of Statistics, Box 10, Belconnen, ACT 2616, Australia. Order from Australian Government Publishing Service, PO Box 84, Canberra, ACT 2600, Australia. Telephone (61) (062) 527911.

Annual report. Presents vital statistics on Australia's Northern Territory. Includes list of representatives, officials, and aboriginal reserves. Price $5.30 (Australian).

3543
North Sea Letter
Financial Times Business Information Ltd, Bracken House, 10 Cannon St, London, England EC4P 4BY. Order from Financial Times Ltd, 75 Rockefeller Plz, New York, NY 10019. Telephone (44) (01) 248-8000. Telex 886341-2.

Weekly newsletter. Discusses North Sea oil and gas. Treats political issues, exploration, production, and offshore news. Price $540.00 per year.

3544
North Sea Petroleum: An Investment and Marketing Opportunity. . . How Big . . . How Soon . . . How to Participate
William C Uhl, McGraw-Hill Book Co, Hightstown-Princeton Rd, Hightstown, NJ 08520. Telephone (609) 448-1700. Telex 843449.

Data-based book. Analyzes North Sea oil commercial opportunities and development. Price $295.00. ISBN 0-07-065734-3.

3545
Northwestern Banker
Northwestern Banker Co, 306 15th St, Des Moines, IA 50309. Telephone (515) 244-8163.

Monthly report. Deals primarily with commercial banking topics. Includes information on investment, national, and state banking. Price available on request.

3546
Northwest Investment Review
Willamette Management Assoc, Inc, 534 SW 3rd Ave, Suite 400, Portland, OR 97204. Telephone (503) 224-6004.

Weekly report. Supplies information on Northwest publicly traded securities. Includes corporate news, earnings report, and earnings estimates. Price $150.00 per year.

3547
Northwest Stock Guide
Willamette Management Assoc, Inc, 534 SW 3rd Ave, Suite 400, Portland, OR 97204. Telephone (503) 224-6004.

Quarterly report. Evaluates assets and resources of Northwest corporations and considers investment potential. Presents stock prices, assets, and revenues. Price $10.00 per year.

3548
Norwegian American Commerce
Norwegian American Chamber of Commerce, Inc, 800 3rd Ave, New York, NY 10022. Telephone (212) 421-9210. Telex 423347.

Quarterly magazine. Features articles on Norwegian industry and products for export. Emphasizes oil drilling. Notes Norwegian-US trade issues. Free of charge.

3549
Noticias
National Foreign Trade Council, 10 Rockefeller Plz, New York, NY 10020. Telephone (212) 58 1-6420.

Weekly newsletter. Summarizes Latin American news dealing with political, economic, and social developments that affect US trade and foreign investment. Price $60.00 per year members only.

3551
NOW Machine
Dow Jones & Co, Inc, 22 Cortlandt St, New York, NY 10007. Telephone (212) 285-5000.

Continuous information service. Reports on business and financial developments, including stock prices and activity, European gold and money markets, and government bond prices. Price available on request.

3552
Nuclearfuel
McGraw-Hill Publications Co, 1221 Ave of the Americas, New York, NY 10020. Telephone (212) 997-3194. Telex TWX 7105814879. WUI 62555.

Biweekly service. Reports on nuclear fuel cycle developments, such as uranium production and pricing, fuel fabrication, reprocessing, and waste management. Price $490.00 per year US and Canada, $590.00 elsewhere.

3553
Nuclear Law Bulletin
Organization for Economic Cooperation and Development, Publications Ctr, 1750 Pennsylvania Ave NW, Washington, DC 20006. Telephone (202) 724-1857.

Quarterly report on international nuclear laws. Price $14.90. ISSN 0304-341X.

3554

Nuclear Regulation Reports

Commerce Clearing House, Inc, 4025 W Peterson Ave, Chicago, IL 60646. Telephone (312) 236-2350.

Two loose-leaf books plus weekly reports. Analyze laws and regulations pertaining to use and development of nuclear energy. Price $480.00 per year.

3554.01

Nuclear Waste News

Business Publishers, Inc, PO Box 1067, Silver Spring, MD 20910. Telephone (301) 587-6300.

Biweekly newsletter. Provides information on radioactive waste management developments. Price $187.00 per year.

3555

Nucleonics Week

McGraw-Hill Publications Co, 1221 Ave of the Americas, New York, NY 10020. Telephone (212) 997-1221. Telex TWX 7105814879. WUI 62555.

Weekly newsletter. Reports on development, use, and regulation of nuclear power throughout the world. Price $670.00 (US and Canada), $810.00 elsewhere per year.

3556

Number of Road Vehicles, New Registrations

Her Majesty's Stationery Office, PO Box 569, London, England SE1 9NH. Telephone (44) (01) 928 1321.

Monthly report. Supplies data on number of road vehicles and new registrations in Great Britain. Price £7.75 per year.

3557

Nursing Administration Quarterly

Aspen Systems Corp, 1600 Research Blvd, Rockville, MD 20850. Telephone (800) 638-8437.

Quarterly magazine. Reports on nursing care management. Covers staffing, scheduling, and book reviews. Price $34.00 per year.

3558

Nursing Management, 2nd edition

Aspen Systems Corp, 1600 Research Blvd, Rockville, MD 20850. Telephone (800) 638-8437.

Book. Provides guide to nursing management techniques. Topics include patient care and operational and human resources management. Price $19.95.

3558.01

Nutrition Action

Center for Science in the Public Interest, 1755 S St, NW, Washington, DC 20009. Telephone Telephone (202) 332-9110.

Monthly magazine. Discusses local and national food and nutrition policies, with special emphasis on consumer action. Covers food labeling, additives, dietary standards, and merchandising. Price $15.00 per year.

3559

Occupational Hazards

Penton-IPC, 614 Superior Ave W, Cleveland, OH 44113. Telephone (216) 696-0300.

Monthly magazine. Features information on occupational health, industrial safety, and plant protection. Price $24.00.

3560

Occupational Health and Safety Letter

Environews, Inc, 1097 National Press Bldg, Washington, DC 20045. Telephone (202) 347-3868.

Semimonthly newsletter. Concerns employment health and safety standards and enforcement, and related subjects. Price $110.00 per year.

3561

Occupational Noise Legislation

Labour Canada, PR Branch, 340 Laurier Ave W, Ottawa, Ont, Canada K1A 0J2. Order from Publications Div, Labour Canada, Ottawa, K1A 0J2. Canada K1A0J2. Telephone (819) 997-2031.

Annual book. Describes legislation concerning industrial noise in Canada. Free of charge.

3562

Occupational Outlook Handbook, **1980–81 edition**

US Dept of Labor, Bureau of Labor Statistics, 441 G St, NW, Washington, DC 20212. Telephone (202) 523-1221.

Biennial book. Covers employment outlook, nature of work, training, entry requirements, line of advancement, location of jobs, earnings, and working conditions for 850 occupations and 30 major industries, including farming. Price $8.00.

3563

Occupational Outlook Quarterly

US Dept of Labor, Bureau of Labor Statistics, 441 G St, NW, Washington, DC 20212. Telephone (202) 523-1221.

Quarterly report. Provides current information on employment trends and outlook. Supplements Occupational Outlook Handbook. Price $6.00 per year.

3564

Occupational Safety and Health Act (OSHA) Compliance Letter

Bureau of Business Practice, 24 Rope Ferry Rd, Waterford, CT 06386. Telephone (203) 442-4365.

Semimonthly loose-leaf newsletter. Covers changes in Occupational Safety and Health Administration rules, and includes information about how to improve health and safety standards. Price $39.60 per year.

3565

Occupational Safety and Health Act (OSHA) Report

Man and Manager, Inc, 799 Broadway, New York, NY 10003. Telephone (212) 677-0640.

Monthly newsletter. Covers executives' responsibilities under the Federal Occupational Safety and Health Act. Annual index. Price $48.00 per year.

3566

Occupational Safety and Health Decisions

Commerce Clearing House, Inc, 4025 W Peterson Ave, Chicago, IL 60646. Telephone (312) 236-2350.

Five books. Cover safety and health decisions from Occupational Safety and Health Review Commission and Mining Appeals Boards, as well as from federal and state courts. Price $25.00 per volume. ISSN 9040.

3567

Occupational Safety and Health Reporter

Bureau of National Affairs, Inc, 1231 25th St, NW, Washington, DC 20037. Telephone (202) 452-4200.

Five-volume loose-leaf books plus weekly reports. Offer standards, regulations, enforcement proceedings, and research on occupational safety and health. Include current reports, reference file, and decisions binder. Price $338.00 per year.

3568

Ocean Construction & Engineering Report

Sheffer Co, PO Box 19909, Houston, TX 77024. Telephone (713) 781-2713.

Weekly report. Supplies information on ocean construction projects, including oil platforms, sea floor mining, port construction, and shipyard activities. Price $170.00 per year.

3569
Ocean Construction Locator
Sheffer Co, PO Box 19909, Houston, TX 77024. Telephone (713) 781-2713.

Bimonthly report. Provides details on offshore oil construction projects. Lists fixed platforms and pipelines planned and under construction. Notes operator, contractor, water depth, specifications, and construction barges under contract. Price $245.00 per year.

3570
Ocean Development and International Law
Crane, Russak & Co, Inc, 3 East 44th St, New York, NY 10017. Telephone (212) 867-1490. Telex 423921.

Quarterly magazine. Reports on ocean use and regulation from international law viewpoint. Considers policy alternatives and compares national policies. Price $56.00 per year.

3570.01
Oceanic Abstracts
Data Courier, Inc, 620 S 5th St, Louisville, KY 40202. Telephone (502) 582-4111. Telex 204235.

Bimonthly journal. Abstracts and indexes marine literature. Covers marine biology, marine resources, pollution, and shipping. Price $495.00 per year.

3571
Ocean Oil Weekly Report
Petroleum Pub Co, PO Box 1941, Houston, TX 77001. Telephone (713) 621-0561.

Weekly newsletter. Reports on offshore oil developments throughout world. Price $110.00 per year.

3572
Ocean Resources Engineering
Harcourt Brace Jovanovich Publications, 757 3rd Ave, New York, NY 10017. Order from Harcourt Brace Jovanovich Publications, PO Box 1589, Dallas, TX 75221. Telephone (214) 631-6520.

Quarterly report. Provides information on ocean resources development, including offshore and gas exploration, drilling, production, refining, pipelines, and construction. Price $5.00 per year.

3573
O'Dwyer's Directory of Corporate Communications
J R O'Dwyer Co, Inc, 271 Madison Ave, New York, NY 10016. Telephone (212) 679-2471.

Annual directory. Identifies public and investor relations directors for 2300 major US corporations and 300 trade associations. Price $60.00.

3573.01
O'Dwyer's Directory of Public Relations Executives
J R O'Dwyer Co, Inc, 271 Madison Ave, New York, NY 10016. Telephone (212) 679-2471.

Book. Gives biographies of 3100 public relations executives. Price $50.00.

3574
O'Dwyer's Directory of Public Relations Firms
J R O'Dwyer Co, Inc, 271 Madison Ave, New York, NY 10016. Telephone (212) 679-2471.

Annual directory. Lists more than 1100 public relations firms in US. Notes firms' locations, special fields, and executives. Identifies 50 largest firms. Price $50.00.

3575
O'Dwyer's Newsletter
J R O'Dwyer Co, Inc, 271 Madison Ave, New York, NY 10016. Telephone (212) 679-2471.

Weekly newsletter. Reports on public relations personnel and account changes, successful techniques, pertinent books, and other related news. Price $80.00 per year.

3575.01
OECD Import-Export Microtables
Organization for Economic Cooperation and Development, Publications Center, 1750 Pennsylvania Ave, NW, Washington, DC 20006. Telephone (202) 724-1857.

Microfiche sets. Provide foreign trade statistics for each OECD member country. Give statistics in value and quantity by SITC number to five-digits, broken down by trading partner. Covers 1977, 1978, and 1979. Price $250.00 per year.

3576
Of Consuming Interest
Federal-State Reports, Inc, 5203 Leesburg Pike, #1201, Falls Church, VA 22041. Telephone (703) 379-0222.

Biweekly newsletter. Informs consumer professionals about federal and state legislation, regulatory, and consumer activist efforts. Provides relevant government documents. Price $99.00 per year.

3577
Office Administration Handbook
Dartnell Corp, 4660 Ravenswood Ave, Chicago, IL 60640. Telephone (312) 561-4000.

Book. Covers all aspects of office administration. Price $48.50. ISBN 0-85013-030-1.

3578
Office Automation Reporting Service
International Data Corp, 214 3rd Ave, Waltham MA 02254. Telephone (617) 890-3700.

Monthly newsletters, plus news bulletins and special reports. Focus on automated office, with data processing (DP) and communications perspective. Price available on request.

3578.01
Office Equipment and Products
Dempa Publications, Inc, 380 Madison Ave, New York, NY 10017. Telephone (212) 867-0900.

Bimonthly journal. Reports on Japan's office equipment and products industry. Lists import and export figures. Notes new products. Price $35.00 per year.

3579
Office Equipment News
Mercury House Business Publications Ltd, Mercury House, Waterloo Rd, London, England SE1 8UL. Telephone (44) (01) 928-3388.

Monthly magazine. Reports on new office equipment products and services. Analyzes particular company problems. Free of charge.

3579.01
Office Equipment News
Modern Productions Ltd, First Floor, Midland House, 73 Great N Rd, PO Box 2040, Auckland, New Zealand. Telephone (09) 768-809.

Magazine issued 11 times a year. Provides information on trends and developments in business equipment, systems and services, supplies, and furnishings. Price available on request.

3579.02
Officemation Management
Management Information Corp, 140 Barclay Ctr, Cherry Hill, NJ 08034. Telephone (609) 428-1020.

Monthly report. Provides techniques for managing the automated office and selecting automation systems. Price $245.00 per year, $135.00 renewed subscription.

3579.03
Officemation Product Reports
Management Information Corp, 140 Barclay Ctr, Cherry Hill, NJ 08034. Telephone (609) 428-1020.

Monthly report. Evaluates office automation systems, such as word processing, electronic mail, and records management. Price $245.00 per year, $135.00 renewed subscription.

3580
Office Products News
United Technical Publications, Inc, 645 Stewart Ave, Garden City, NY 11530. Telephone (516) 222-2500.

Monthly magazine. Reports on office productivity and cost savings. Free of charge.

3581
Office Salary Survey
Administrative Management Society, Maryland Ave, Willow Grove, PA 19090. Telephone (215) 659-4300.

Annual report on clerical and data processing employee salaries in the US and Canada. Price $75.00 (included in membership in Society).

3581.01
Office Systems Reports
Auerbach Publishers, Inc, 6560 N Park Dr, Pennsauken, NJ 08109. Telephone (609) 662-2070. Telex 831 464.

Book, updated monthly. Covers automated office equipment field. Provides independent product evaluations and user reactions, detailed comparison, specification charts, and updated price data. Price $325.00.

3582
Office World News
United Technical Publications, Inc, 645 Stewart Ave, Garden City, NY 11530. Telephone (516) 222-2500.

Semiannual magazine. Provides news on office systems, products, supplies, and machines. Free of charge.

3583
Official Congressional Directory
Superintendent of Documents, US Government Printing Office, Washington, DC 20402. Telephone (202) 783-3238.

Annual book. Lists members of Congress and gives biographical data. Includes congressional committee members, congressional and federal agency staffers, and US and foreign diplomats. Price available on request.

3584
Official Directory of Industrial and Commercial Traffic Executives
Traffic Service Corp, 1435 G St NW, Suite 815, Washington, DC 20005. Telephone (202) 783-7325.

Annual directory. Lists 24,000 US and Canadian industrial and commercial traffic, transportation, and distribution executives and their firms. Notes officials of related federal and state agencies. Price $37.50 per year.

3585
Official Industrial Directory for Puerto Rico
Dun & Bradstreet, Box 3224, Church St Station, New York, NY 10008. Telephone (212) 285-7346.

Annual directory. Lists 9000 manufacturers and exporters in Puerto Rico. Price available on request. Available to Dun & Bradstreet subscribers only.

3585.01
Official Journal of the European Communities
European Community Information Service, 2100 M St, NW, Suite 707, Washington, DC 20037. Telephone (202) 862-9500. Telex 248455.

Daily publication with monthly index. Reports on all EEC transactions. Price $173.00 per year, $42.00 per year for index.

3585.02
Official Railway Guide, Freight Service Edition
National Railway Publication Co, 424 W 33rd St, New York, NY 10001. Telephone (212) 563-7300.

Bimonthly guide. Provides US, Canadian, and Mexican rail freight schedules, mileages, and connections. Includes maps and personnel listings. Price $58.00 per year.

3585.03
Official Railway Guide, Passenger Travel Edition
National Railway Publication Co., 424 W 33rd St, New York, NY 10001. Telephone (212) 563-7300.

Monthly guide. Contains passenger railroad timetables for US, Canada, and Mexico. Includes information on fares and ticket offices. Price $37.00 per year.

3586
Official Records of the Organization of American States
Organization of American States, 17th St and Constitution Ave NW, Washington, DC 20006. Order from OAS General Secretariat, Dept of Publications, 6840 Industrial Rd, Springfield, VA 22151. Telephone (703) 941-1617.

Irregular publication. Reports on all OAS developments, including inter-American treaties and conventions, and records of the General Assembly, councils, and specialized conferences and organizations. Price $80.00.

3587
Official Year Book of Australia (Cat No 1301.0)
Australian Bureau of Statistics, PO Box 10, Belconnen, ACT 2616 Publishing, Australia. Order from Australian Government Pub Service, PO Box 84, Canberra, ACT 2600, Australia. Telephone (61) (062) 527911.

Annual book. Provides statistical review of Australian economic and social conditions. Discusses history, geography, and government. Price $16.80 (Australian).

3589
Offset Printer
Maclean-Hunter Ltd, 30 Old Burlington St, London, England W1X 2AE. Telephone (44) (01) 434-2233.

Magazine. Deals with offset printing in Great Britain. Offers technical guidance, news, and product information on lithography. Surveys special product groups, such as presses and cameras. Price available on request.

3590
Offshore
Petroleum Pub Co, PO Box 1941, Houston, TX 77001. Telephone (713) 621-0561.

Monthly magazine. Covers offshore oil and gas operations, including production methods, North Sea developments, and marine construction and transportation. Price $9.00 per year.

3591
Offshore Rig Location Report
Sheffer Co, PO Box 19909, Houston, TX 77024. Telephone (713) 781-2713.

Monthly report. Provides information on status of offshore drilling rigs in US and international waters. Notes current construction. Price $285.00 per year.

3592
Offshore Rig Newsletter
Sheffer Co, PO Box 19909, Houston, TX 77024. Telephone (713) 781-2713.

Monthly newsletter. Discusses offshore drilling, industry developments. Considers rig costs and performance, labor issues, and new contracts. Price $115.00 per year.

3593
Ohio CPA Journal
Ohio Society of Certified Public Accountants, PO Box 306, Dublin, OH 43017. Telephone (614) 764-2727.

Quarterly magazine. Covers accounting and management topics. Price $5.00 per year, $1.50 per copy.

3593.01
Ohio Developer
State of Ohio, Department of Economic and Community Development, PO Box 1001, Columbus, OH 43216. Telephone (614) 466-7772.

Quarterly newsletter. Reports on Ohio economic and business developments. Price available on request.

3593.02
Ohio: Industrial Directory, **1981**
Manufacturers' News, Inc, 3 E Huron St, Chicago, IL 60611. Telephone (312) 337-1084.

Annual book. Lists 17,000 Ohio firms. Indicates executives, number of employees, and approximate sales. Price $69.50.

3593.03
Ohio: Manufacturers Guide, **1981**
Manufacturers' News, Inc, 3 E Huron St, Chicago, IL 60611. Telephone (312) 337-1084.

Annual book. Provides information on 13,497 Ohio manufacturing firms by name, county, city, and product. Proce $75.00.

3594
Oil and Gas Bulletin
Quentin Cameron, PO Box 376, Hamilton Central, Qld 4007, Australia. Telephone (61) (07) 2681217.

Fortnightly newsletter about oil exploration and investment in Australia. Price $95.00 (Australian) per year.

3595
Oil & Gas Journal
Petroleum Pub Co, PO Box 1941, Houston, TX 77001. Telephone (713) 621-0561.

Weekly magazine. Reports on oil and gas developments. Includes information on technology, economics, finance, drilling, pipelining, and refining. Price $17.00 per year.

3596
Oil and Gas Law
Matthew Bender & Co, 235 E 45th St, New York, NY 10017. Telephone (212) 661-5050.

Annually updated loose-leaf books. Discuss creation, existence, and transfer of property rights in oil and gas industries. Price $550.00 for seven volumes.

3597
Oil and Gas Law: **Abridged Edition**
Matthew Bender & Co, 235 E 45th St, New York, NY 10017. Telephone (212) 661-5050.

Loose-leaf book with supplements issued as needed. Presents brief discussion of oil and gas laws. Covers property interests, conveyancing, leases, pooling and unitization, and drilling provisions. Price $60.00.

3598
Oil and Gas Lease Reports
Petroleum Information Corp, PO Box 2612, 1375 Delaware, Denver, CO 80201. Telephone (303) 825-2181.

Monthly reports. Cover oil and gas leases in Montana, Idaho, Wyoming, Nevada, Utah, Colorado, Arizona, and New Mexico. Prices available on request.

3598.01
Oil & Gas Price Regulation Analyst
Executive Enterprises Publications Co, Inc, 33 W 60th St, New York, NY 10023. Telephone (212) 489-2670.

Monthly newsletter. Advises oil and gas executives on current energy laws and regulations. Gives in-depth analysis of key issues. Price $96.00 per year.

3599
Oil and Gas Reporter
Matthew Bender & Co, 235 E 45th St, New York, NY 10017. Telephone (212) 661-5050.

Monthly loose-leaf reports. Discuss all oil and gas decisions in US state and federal courts and in Canada. Price $100.00 per volume (three volumes per year).

3600
Oil and Gas Quarterly
Matthew Bender & Co, 235 E 45th St, New York, NY 10017. Telephone (212) 661-5050.

Quarterly review. Provides information on tax developments related to oil and gas industries. Price $90.00 per year.

3600.01
Oil & Gas Taxes-Natural Resources
Prentice-Hall, Inc, Englewood Cliffs, NJ 07632. Telephone (201) 592-2000. Telex 13-5423.

Monthly loose-leaf service. Covers all aspects of federal income taxation of oil, gas, and mineral and timber production. Price $291.00 per year.

3601
Oil and Gas, The North Sea Exploitation
Oceana Publications, Inc, 75 Main St, Dobbs Ferry, NY 10522. Telephone (914) 693-5944.

Loose-leaf service. Covers laws of North Sea coastal countries relating to exploration and exploitation of oil and gas in coastal waters, as developed within framework of international law. Price $75.00. ISBN 0-379-10251-X.

3602
Oil and Natural Gas Resources of Canada, 1976
Supply and Services Canada, Publishing Ctr, Printing and Publishing, Ottawa, Ont Canada K1A 0S9. Telephone (613) 238-1601.

Report on oil and natural gas resources of Canada, by region. Offers comparisons with other resources. Discusses Alberta oil sands. Price $3.60 per copy.

3603
Oil Daily
The Oil Daily, 850 3rd Ave, New York, NY 10022. Telephone (212) 593-2100.
Daily newspaper. Covers oil industry in depth. Includes charts that reflect prices. Price $257.00 per year.

3604
Oil, Gas & Petrochem Equipment
Petroleum Pub Co, PO Box 1941, Houston, TX 77001. Telephone (713) 621-0561.
Monthly newsletter. Discusses oil, gas, and petrochemical equipment developments. Covers energy conservation, refining, and offshore and drilling equipment. Free of charge.

3605
Oil in California
Petroleum Information Corp, PO Box 2612, 1375 Delaware, Denver, CO 80201. Telephone (303) 825-2181.
Monthly report. Summarizes oil and gas activity in California and Nevada. Covers drilling activity, land and leasing information, and completion statistics. Price $264.00 per year.

3605.01
Oil in Texas
Petroleum Information Corp, PO Box 2612, 1375 Delaware, Denver, CO 80201. Telephone (303) 825-2181.
Monthly report. Reviews oil and gas activity in Texas and offshore areas. Covers current status and completion data on new field wildcats. Price $264.00 per year.

3605.02
Oil in the Mid-Continent
Petroleum Information Corp, PO Box 2612, 1375 Delaware, Denver, CO 80201. Telephone (303) 825-2181.
Monthly newsletter. Discusses oil and gas activity in the mid-continent region. Supplies leasing information and regional statistics. Price $264.00 per year.

3605.03
Oil in the Rockies
Petroleum Information Corp, PO Box 2612, 1375 Delaware, Denver, CO 80201. Telephone (303) 825-2181.
Monthly report. Covers oil and gas activity in the Rocky Mountain states. Reviews lease sales and includes regional statistics. Price $264.00 per year.

3606
Oilman
Maclean-Hunter Ltd, 30 Old Burlington St, London, England W1X 2AE. Telephone (44) (01) 434-2233.
Weekly magazine. Reports on Great Britain's oil and gas industry. Notes facilities and services in localized areas throughout world. Price available on request.

3607
Oil Pipe Line Transport
Statistics Canada, User Services, Publications Distribution, Ottawa, Ont, Canada K1A 0V7. Telephone (613) 992-3151.
Annual report. Presents Canadian oil pipeline transport information, by provinces. Includes data on receipts and deliveries, barrel-miles, pipeline mileage, and finances. Price $7.20. ISSN 0410-5591.

3608
Oil Pipe Line Transport
Supply and Services Canada, Publishing Ctr, Printing and Publishing, Ottawa, Ont, Canada K1A 0S9. Telephone (613) 238-1601.
Monthly magazine. Covers barrels of oil carried by gathering and trunk lines in Canada. Notes receipts and revenues and barrel-miles revenues. Bilingual. Price $3.00 per year.

3609
Oils and Fats
Statistics Canada, User Services, Publications Distribution, Ottawa, Ont, Canada K1A 0V7. Telephone (613) 992-3151.
Monthly report. Provides statistics on Canadian production, stock and consumption of oils and fats, crushings of vegetable oil seed, and production of oil and oil meal. Includes monthly and cumulative data. Price $18.00 per year. ISSN 0527-5911.

3611
Oklahoma Annual Planning Report
Oklahoma Employment Security Commission, Research and Planning Div, Will Rogers Bldg, Oklahoma City, OK 73105. Telephone (405) 521-3738.
Annual report. Gives population and labor force data for Oklahoma and selected geographic areas, plus other demographic and socioeconomic data. Free of charge.

3613
Oklahoma Business
Business Publications, Inc, 212 Mid-Continent Bldg, Tulsa, OK 74103. Telephone (918) 587-2401.
Monthly magazine. Discusses Oklahoma business and economic subjects. Notes proceedings of state legislature. Focuses on activities of specific companies. Price $10.00 per year.

3614
Oklahoma Business Bulletin
University of Oklahoma, Ctr for Economic and Management Research, College of Business Administration, 307 West Brooks St, Room 4, Norman, OK 73019. Telephone (405) 325-2931.
Monthly report. Surveys business conditions in Oklahoma and provides continuing economic data. Price $3.00 per year.

3615
Oklahoma Directory of Manufacturers and Products
Oklahoma Dept of Industrial Development, PO Box 53424, Oklahoma City, OK 73105. Telephone (405) 521-2401.
Biannual book. Provides guide to Oklahoma's manufacturing firms, alphabetically by location and by product. Lists mineral producers and exporters. Price $20.00.

3616
Oklahoma Economic Indicators
Oklahoma Employment Security Commission, Research and Planning Div, Will Rogers Bldg, Oklahoma City, OK 73105. Telephone (405) 521-3735.
Monthly report. Contains 16 leading indicators of Oklahoma business conditions in chart and table form. Free of charge.

3617
Oklahoma Labor Market
Oklahoma Employment Security Commission, Research and Planning Div, Will Rogers Bldg, Oklahoma City, OK 73105. Telephone (405) 521-3738.
Monthly reports. Cover Oklahoma's labor conditions and selected national economic indicators. Free of charge.

3617.01
Oklahoma: Manufacturers & Products Directory, **1980**
Manufacturers' News, Inc, 3 E Huron St, Chicago, IL 60611. Telephone (312) 337-1084.

Biennial book. Identifies 2600 Oklahoma manufacturing companies and their products. Indicates executives and number of employees. Price $29.00.

3618
Oklahoma Now!
Oklahoma Dept of Industrial Development, PO Box 53424, Oklahoma City, OK 73152. Telephone (405) 521-2401.

Bimonthly news magazine. Reports on Oklahoma's economic activity. Notes new plants and expanding industries. Price free of charge.

3618.01
Oklahoma: State Industrial Directory, 1981
Manufacturers' News, Inc, 3 E Huron St, Chicago, IL 60611. Telephone (312) 337-1084.

Annual book. Covers industrial firms in Oklahoma. Notes location and products. Price $37.00.

3618.02
Oliver Jones Report
Andrew R Mandala, PO Box 30240, Washington, DC 20014. Telephone (301) 654-5580.

Biweekly newsletter. Reports on mortgages, finance, and banking. Price $225.00 per year.

3619
Omega
Pergamon Press Ltd, Maxwell House, Fairview Park, Elmsford, NY 10523. Telephone (914) 592-7700. Telex 13-7328.

Bimonthly magazine. Reports on recent developments in manpower planning, management control, corporate planning, information systems, and other management science topics. Price $130.00 per year.

3619.01
Omnibus
Business Council of New York State, Inc, 150 State St, Albany, NY 12207. Telephone (518) 465-3547.

Monthly report. Covers activities of Business Council. Notes government news of interest to business. Free of charge to members.

3619.02
Online
Online, Inc, 11 Tannery Lane, Weston, CT 06883. Telephone (203) 227-8466.

Quarterly magazine. Covers on-line information systems. Includes: search services and new technologies. Price $52.00 per year.

3619.03
Online Bibliographic Databases: An International Directory
Aslib, 3 Belgrave Sq, London, England. SW1X 8PL. Telephone (44) (01) 235-5050. Telex 23667.

Book. Lists on–line bibliographic databases. Provides access to over 65 million references. Price £24.00. ISBN 0-85142-138-5.

3619.04
On-line Database
Railroad Research Information Service, Transportation Research Board, National Academy of Sciences, 2101 Constitution Ave, NW, Washington, DC 20418. Telephone (202) 389-6611. Telex 710-822-9589.

Database service. Contains information on railroad research activities. Covers equipment, economics, and government policy. Price available on request.

3619.05
On-Line Search Service, 1981
Derwent Publications Ltd, Rochdale House, 128 Theobalds Rd, London, England. WC1X 8RP. Telephone (44) (01) 242-5823. Telex 267487.

Data base. Provides information on patents issued in 24 countries. Price available on request.

3619.06
On-line Terminal Guide and Directory, 1979–80
On-line, Inc, 11 Tannery Lane, Weston, CT 06883. Telephone (203) 227-8466.

Biennial directory. Lists computer terminal sales and service offices. Includes charts listing terminal characteristics. Price $12.50.

3620
Ontario Business News
Ministry of Industry and Tourism, Queen's Park, Toronto Ont, Canada M7A 2E1. Telephone (416) 965-1576.

Bimonthly magazine. Reports on Ontario business developments. Covers new production techniques, new products, financial news, and activities of Ministry of Industry and Tourism. Free of charge. ISSN 0701-8533.

3621
Ontario Corporation Manual
Richard DeBoo Ltd, 70 Richmond St, Toronto, Ont, Canada M5C 2M8. Telephone (416) 367-0714.

Three loose-leaf books. Supply information on statutes and regulations affecting corporations in Ontario, Canada. Includes material on securities and one-man corporations and credit unions. Price $125.00 per year.

3622
Ontario Corporations Law Guide
CCH Canadian Ltd, 6 Garamond Ct, Don Mills, Ont, Canada M3C 1Z5. Telephone (416) 429-2992.

Loose-leaf book plus monthly updates. Covers Ontario Business Corporations Act and related regulations. Price $155.00 per year.

3623
Ontario Real Estate Law Guide
CCH Canadian Ltd, 6 Garamond Ct, Don Mills, Ont, Canada M3C 1Z5. Telephone (416) 429-2992.

Two loose-leaf books and monthly reports. Explain various Ontario statutes and regulations relating to real estate transactions. Price $185.00 per year.

3625
Ontario Securities Commission Weekly Bulletin
Ontario Securities Commission, 10 Wellesley St E, Toronto, Ont, Canada M7A 2H7. Telephone (416) 963-0259.

Weekly publication. Lists Canadian stock transactions, cease trading orders, company prospectuses and reports. Defines Ontario Securities Commission policies. Price $175.00 per year. ISSN 0030-3100.

3626
Ontario Statute Citator
Canada Law Book Ltd, 240 Edward St, Aurora, Ont, L4G 3S9, Canada. Telephone (416) 859-3880.

Two loose-leaf books plus periodic updates and weekly bulletin that reports progress of government bills. List acts in Revised Statutes of Ontario, 1970. Include texts of amendments and digests of court cases. Price $63.00 per year, $38.00 additional for binders and contents.

3627

Operating and Traffic Statistics

Assn of American Railroads, Economics and Finance Dept, American Railroads Bldg, Washington, DC 20036. Telephone (202) 293-4068.

Annual report. Offers statistics on freight train, passenger train, and yard service performance for individual Class I railroad. Includes data on motive power and car equipment. Price $5.00 per year, including Property Investment, Condensed Income Account, Railroad Revenues, Expenses and Income and Statistics of Railroads of Class I in the United States.

3628

Operation of the Trade Agreements Program

US International Trade Commission, Washington, DC 20436. Telephone (202) 523-0161.

Publication. Covers operation of Trade Agreement Program. Free of charge.

3629

Operations Research

Operations Research Society of America, 428 E Preston St, Baltimore, MD 21202. Telephone (301) 528-4146.

Bimonthly journal. Contains articles on applications of operation research. Price $65.00 per year. ISSN 0030-364X.

3629.01

Operations Research Letters

North-Holland Publishing Co, PO Box 211, 1000 AE Amsterdam, The Netherlands. Order from Elsevier/North-Holland, Inc, 52 Vanderbilt Ave, New York, NY 10017. Telephone (212) 867-9040.

Bimonthly journal. Provides original contributions on all aspects of operations research and the management and decision sciences. Price $81.00 per year.

3630

Operations Research/Management Science

Executive Sciences Inst, Inc, PO Drawer M, Whippany, NJ 07981. Telephone (201) 887-1233.

Monthly digest service. Covers international literature on operations research and managerial methods. Price $98.00 per year.

3632

Optics and Laser Technology

IPC Business Press Ltd, 205 E 42nd St, New York, NY 10017. Telephone (212) 889-0700. Telex 421710.

Bimonthly magazine. Discusses new research and applications in optics and laser fields. Notes new products, techniques, and components. Price $124.80. ISSN 0030-3992.

3633

Optimum/A Forum for Management

Supply and Services Canada, Canadian Govt Publishing Centre, Hull, Que, Canada K1A 0S9. Telephone (819) 994-3475, 2085.

Quarterly journal. Provides English/-French forum for views on management of Canadian government, universities, corporations, and industrial associations. Price $8.40 per year.

3634

Orange County Business

James C Killingsworth, PO Box 1816, Newport Beach, CA 92663. Telephone (714) 833-8511.

Bimonthly magazine. Covers Orange County, California, business news, including employment, industry, real estate, construction, banking, and transportation developments. Price $7.00 per year.

3635

Orange County Illustrated

James C Killingsworth, PO Box 1816, Newport Beach, CA 92663. Telephone (714) 833-8511.

Monthly magazine. Covers cultural, entertainment, sports, and leisure activities in Orange County, California. Includes restaurant listings. Price $10.00 per year.

3636

Orange Rockland Westchester Business Review

Greentree Publishing Co, PO Box 9, New City, NY 10956. Telephone (914) 638-1414.

Monthly newspaper. Provides business, credit, area development, education, and government information for Orange, Rockland, and Westchester counties, New York. Price $4.50 per year.

3637

Oregon: Manufacturers Directory, 1980-81

Manufacturers' News, Inc, 3 E Huron St, Chicago, IL 60611. Telephone (312) 337-1084.

Biennial book. Lists 5000 Oregon manufacturing companies by name, location, and product. Notes executives and number of employees. Price $40.00.

3638

Oregon: State Industrial Directory, **1980**

Manufacturers' News, Inc, 3 E Huron St, Chicago, IL 60611. Telephone (312) 337-1084.

Annual book. Identifies 6000 Oregon industrial companies and 29,000 executives. Notes location and products. Price $37.-00.

3639

Oregon Progress Newsletter

Oregon Dept of Economic Development, 317 SW Alder St, 9th floor, Portland, OR 97204. Telephone (503) 229-5535.

Quarterly newsletter Reports on Oregon's current economic indicators, new industries, and industrial expansion. Free of charge.

3640

Organization Dynamics

American Management Assns, 135 W 50th St, New York, NY 10020. Telephone (212) 586-8100.

Quarterly journal. Covers behavioral science theory and practice. Price $24.50.

3641

Organization for Economic Cooperation and Development (OECD) Economic Outlook

Organization for Economic Cooperation and Development, Publications Ctr, 1750 Pennsylvania Ave, NW, Washington, DC 20006. Telephone (202) 724-1857.

Biannual report. Presents economic forecasts for OECD nations. Discusses world trade, inflation, and balance of payments. Deals with oil crisis adjustments and manufacturing. Price $21.50.

3642

Organization for Economic Cooperation and Development (OECD) Economic Surveys—1981 Series

Organization for Economic Cooperation and Development, Publications Ctr, 1750 Pennsylvania Ave NW, Washington, DC 20006. Telephone (202) 724-1857.

Annual surveys. Provide detailed information about economic trends and prospects for each OECD country. Price $3.50 each, $60.00 for series.

3643

Organization for Economic Cooperation and Development (OECD) Financial Statistics

Organization for Economic Cooperation and Development, Publications Ctr, 1750 Pennsylvania Ave, NW, Washington, DC 20006. Telephone (202) 724-1857.

Annual service with monthly supplements. Offers statistical and descriptive data on international financial market and domestic financial markets of European countries, US, Canada, and Japan. Price $84.00.

3644
Organization for Economic Cooperation and Development (OECD) Observer
Organization for Economic Cooperation and Development, Publications Ctr, 1750 Pennsylvania Ave, NW, Washington, DC 20006. Telephone (202) 724-1857.

Bimonthly magazine. Reports selectively on entire range of OECD's work including coverage of new OECD publications. Price $13.85.

3645
Organization of American States (OAS) Chronicle
Organization of American States, 17th St and Constitution Ave, NW, Washington, DC 20006. Telephone (202) 381-8877.

Monthly magazine. Reports on major inter-American events. Includes text of significant official documents. Price $6.00 per year.

3646
Organization of the Government of Canada
Supply and Services Canada, Publishing Ctr, Printing and Publishing, Ottawa, Ont, Canada K1A 0S9. Telephone (613) 238-1601.

Book. Shows changes in Canadian federal structure. Charts. Price $21.00.

3647
Oriental Bloc
Commission of the European Communities, Office for Official Publications of the European Communities, CP 1003, Luxembourg 1, Luxembourg. Telephone (352) 490081. Telex PUBLOF 1325.

Bimonthly publication. Contains material on the Orient. Free of charge.

3648
Oriental Economist
Oriental Economist, 1-4 Hongokucho, Nihonbashi, Chuo-ku, Tokyo 103, Japan. Telephone (81) (03) 270-4111.

Monthly magazine. Reports on Japanese business, economics, and politics. Tables. Price $60.00 seamail, $78.00 airmail per year.

3649
Ottawa Commercial Report
Capital Communications, Ltd, Suite 705, Burnside Bldg, 151 Slater St, Ottawa, Ont, Canada K1P 5H3. Telephone (613) 235-9183. Telex 053-3601.

Monthly newsletter giving information on potential business opportunities for Canadian companies with and through the Canadian government. Price $60.00 per year.

3650
Ottawa Letter
CCH Canadian Ltd, 6 Garamond Ct, Don Mills, Ont, Canada M3C 1Z5. Telephone (416) 429-2992.

Loose-leaf book plus weekly updates. Gives news and commentary on Canadian federal government items of interest to business. Includes progress reports on bills in Parliament. Price $125.00 per year.

3651
Ottawa R&D Report
Capital Communications Ltd, Suite 306, 77 Metcalfe St, Ottawa, Ont, Canada K1P 5L6. Telephone (613) 235-9183. Telex 053-3601.

Monthly newsletter on Canadian science policy developments, including legislation and research and development. Includes Canadian R & D Directory. Price $150.00 per year.

3651.01
Outlook
California Society of Certified Public Accountants, 1000 Welch Rd, Palo Alto, CA 94304. Telephone (415) 321-9545.

Quarterly magazine. Covers accounting topics for California CPAS. Includes feature articles, news, columns, and classified and display advertising. Price $5.00 per year.

3652
Outlook
Chilton Co, Chilton Way, Radnor, PA 19089. Telephone (215) 687-8200.

Monthly newsletter. Pertains to electronic component products, people, and markets. Price available on request.

3653
Outlook
Standard & Poor's Corp, 25 Broadway, New York, NY 10004. Telephone (212) 248-2525.

Weekly newsletter. Offers comment on stock market investments. Recommends stocks for capital gain and income. Price $145.00 per year.

3653.01
Outlook and Situation Reports
US Dept of Agriculture, ESS Publications, Room 0054-S Washington, DC. Telephone (202) 447-7255.

Individual reports, issued four to five times per year. Analyzes supply and demand, price and outlook for cotton, wool, dairy, fats and oils, feed, fruit, livestock, meat, poultry, eggs, rice, sugar and sweeteners, tobacco, vegetables, and wheat. Also covers agricultural finance, fertilizer, agricultural exports, world agriculture, farm real estate market, and price spreads for farm foods. Price free of charge.

3654
Outlook for US Agricultural Exports
US Dept of Agriculture, ESS Publications, Room 0054-S, Washington, DC 20250. Telephone (202) 447-7255.

Quarterly report. Presents short-term outlook for US agricultural exports and imports. Free of charge.

3655
Overseas Assignment Directory Service
Knowledge Industry Publications, 701 Westchester Ave, White Plains, NY 10604. Telephone (914) 694-8686.

Annual loose-leaf book. Addresses itself to US businessmen operating abroad. Supplies basic information on about 43 countries. Monthly updates. Price $325.00 per year including updates.

3656
Overseas Business Reports
US Dept of Commerce, International Trade Administration, Washington, DC 20230. Telephone (202) 377-1470.

Approximately 50 reports per year. Furnishes information on overseas business conditions. Price available on request.

3657
Overseas Development Institute (ODI) Review
Overseas Development Inst, 10-11 Percy St, London, England W1P 0JB. Telephone (44) (01) 580-7683.

Semiannual journal. Analyzes economic and social issues in developing countries. Notes their relationships with developed world. Discusses protectionism, aid, technology, and international monetary and trade systems. Price $15.00 per year.

3659

Overseas Investment and Business in New Zealand

Bank of New Zealand, PO Box 2392, Wellington 1, New Zealand. Telex 3344 MONARCH.

Pamphlet on foreign investment in New Zealand. Free of charge.

3660

Overseas Trade Analysed in Terms of Industries

Her Majesty's Stationery Office, PO Box 569, London, England SE1 9NH. Telephone (44) (01) 928 1321.

Annual report. Analyzes British overseas trade by industry. Price £4.00 per year.

3661

Overseas Trade, Part 1: Exports and Imports **(Cat No 5409.0)**

Australian Bureau of Statistics, PO Box 10, Belconnen, ACT 2616, Australia. Order from Australian Government Publishing Service, PO Box 84, Canberra, ACT 2600, Australia. Telephone (61) (062) 527911.

Annual report. Presents table of Australian imports and exports for approximately 10,000 commodities. Index. Price $19.00 (Australian).

3662

Overseas Trade, Part 2: Comparative and Summary Tables **(Cat No 5410.0)**

Australian Bureau of Statistics, PO Box 10, Belconnen, ACT 2616, Australia. Order from Australian Government Publishing Service, PO Box 84, Canberra, ACT 2600, Australia. Telephone (61) (062) 527911.

Annual report. Comparative time series table range from three to ten years of Australian imports and exports, classified by country and industrial group. Price $4.50 (Australian).

3663

Overseas Trade (Preliminary), Part 1— Exports **(Cat No 5407.0)**

Australian Bureau of Statistics, PO Box 10, Belconnen, ACT 2616, Australia. Order from Australian Government Publishing Service, PO Box 84, Canberra, ACT 2600, Australia. Telephone (61) (062) 527911.

Annual report. Gives value, quantity, and detailed description of commodites exported from Australia to various countries. Price $5.00 (Australian).

3664

Overseas Trade (Preliminary), Part 2— Imports **(Cat No 5408.0)**

Australian Bureau of Statistics, PO Box 10, Belconnen, ACT 2616, Australia. Order from Australian Government Publishing Service, PO Box 84, Canberra, ACT 2600, Australia. Telephone (61) (062) 527911.

Annual report. Furnishes quantity, value, and country of origin for approximately 8000 Australian import commodities. Index. Price $11.50 (Autralian).

3665

Overseas Trade Statistics of the United Kingdom

Her Majesty's Stationery Office, PO Box 569, London, England SE1 9NH. Telephone (44) (01) 928 1321.

Monthly report. Provides statement of imports and exports by commodity and country. Price £11.00 monthly.

3669

Over-the-Counter Stock Reports

Standard & Poor's Corp, 25 Broadway, New York, NY 10004. Telephone (212) 248-2525.

Daily and weekly loose-leaf reports. Cover issues traded over the counter and on regional exchanges. Describe company activities. Assess financial results. Price $525.00 per year daily, $395.00 per year weekly.

3670

Owen's Commerce & Travel and International Register

Owen's Commerce & Travel Ltd, 100 Belsize Lane, London, NW3 5BB England. Telephone (44) (01) 794-0975.

Annual book. Provides basic business and travel information for 50 countries in Africa, Near and Middle East, Southeast Asia and Far East, Cyprus, Gibraltar, and Malta. Price $54.00. ISBN 0-900576-12-X.

3671

Owner Operator

Chilton Co, Chilton Way, Radnor, PA 19089. Telephone (215) 687-8200.

Bimonthly magazine. Carries information about ownership and operation of heavy-duty trucks and tractors. Price $8.00.

3672

Oxford Agrarian Studies

University of Oxford, Inst of Agricultural Economics, Dartington House, Little Clarendon St, Oxford, England. Telephone (44) 52921.

Annual magazine. Discusses international agricultural subjects such as farm labor migration, land reform, and economics of specific crops. Price £5.50 per year.

3673

Oxford Bulletin of Economics & Statistics

Basil Blackwell Publisher, 108 Cowley Rd, Oxford, England OX4 1JF. Telephone (44) (STD 0865) 722146.

Quarterly bulletin publishes research work in applied economics. Price $49.50 per year. ISSN 0305-9049.

3674

Oxford Economic Papers

Oxford University Press, Subscription Dept, Press Rd, Neasden, London, England NW100DD. Also available from 200 Madison Ave, New York, NY 10016. Telephone (44) (01) 450-8080.

Journal issued three times per year. Presents papers on economic theory, history, and scientific method, as well as on international economy and developing nations. Price $39.00 (US) per year. ISSN 0030-7653.

3675

Ozone Data for the World

Supply and Services Canada, Pub Ctr, Printing and Pub, Ottawa, Ont, Canada K1A 0S9. Telephone (613) 238-1601.

Bimonthly report. Provides international ozone data. Price $1.25 per year.

3676

Pacific Banker and Business

Pacific Banker and Business, 109 W Mercer St C#19081, Seattle, WA 98119. Telephone (206) 623-1888.

Monthly magazine containing news about financial communities in Alaska, Arizona, California, Hawaii, Idaho, Montana, Nevada, Oregon, Utah, and Washington. Discusses banking, marketing, and economics. Price $15.00 per year.

3677

Pacific Business News

Crossroads Press, Inc, PO Box 833, Honolulu, HI 96808. Telephone (808) 521-0021.

Weekly newspaper. Covers Hawaii business and professional items, including real estate transactions and new corporations. Price $27.00 per year.

3678
Pacific Coast Stock Exchange Guide
Commerce Clearing House, Inc, 4025 W Peterson Ave, Chicago, IL 60646. Telephone (312) 236-2350.

One loose-leaf book plus monthly reports. Contains directory, constitution, and rules of Pacific Coast Stock Exchange. Price $85.00 per year.

3679
Pacific Computer Weekly
Peter Isaacson Publications, 46-49 Porter St, Prahran, Vic 3181, Australia. Telephone (61) (03) 518431. Telex 30880.

Fortnightly newspaper directed at sophisticated computer users in Australia, New Zealand, and other Pacific areas. Covers general news and specialized areas. Price $20.00 per year.

3680
Packaged Software Reports
Management Information Corp, 140 Barclay Ctr, Cherry Hill, NJ 08034. Telephone (609) 428-1020.

Monthly report. Evaluates application software packages designed for small business systems. Price $245.00 per year; $135.00 (renewed subscription).

3681
Package Engineering
Cahners Pub Co, Inc, 221 Columbus Ave, Boston, MA 02116. Telephone (617) 536-7780.

Monthly magazine. Contains articles on the engineering and efficiency of packaging operations. Covers packaging machinery, containers, materials, and supplies. Has Annual Buyers Guide. Price $30.00 per year.

3682
Package Printing
North American Pub Co, 401 N Broad St, Philadelphia, PA 19108. Telephone (215) 574-9600.

Monthly magazine. Covers package printing and diecutting fields. Discusses gravure and flexographic inks, corrugated containers, and coating trends. Price $16.00 per year.

3683
Packaging
Wheatland Journals Ltd, 177 Hagden Lane, Watford, England WD1 8LW. Telephone Watford 47311.

Monthly magazine. Reports on packaging industry trends, including handling, adhesive systems, and pallets. Price £24.30 per year.

3684
Packaging News
Maclean-Hunter Ltd, 30 Old Burlington St, London, England W1X 2AE. Telephone (44) (01) 434-2233.

Newspaper. Concentrates on news of packaging industry. Includes information on machinery, equipment, and materials. Price available on request.

3685
Packaging News
Yaffa Pub Group, GPO Box 606, Yaffa Publishing Group, 432-436 Elizabeth St, Surry Hills, Australia. Order from Sydney, NSW 2001, Australia. Telephone (61) (02) 699-7861. Telex 21887.

Monthly newspaper. Discusses Australian packaging industry. Includes information on government regulations and new equipment. Price $30.00 (Australian) per year.

3687
Paint Manufacture
Turret Press Ltd, 4 Local Board Rd, Watford, Herts, England WD1 2JS. Order from Wheatland Journal, Inc, 4 Local Board Rd, Watford, Herts, England WD1 2JS. Telephone (0923) 46199.

Monthly magazine covering paint manufacturing industry. Price $74.75 per year.

3688
Paint, Varnish, and Lacquer
US Dept of Commerce, Bureau of the Census, Washington, DC 20233. Telephone (202) 449-1600.

Monthly report. Gives value of factory sales and quantity of production of paint, varnish, and lacquer products, industrial product finishings, and special coatings. Price $3.00 per year.

3689
Palmetto Economics
Clemson University Cooperative Extension Service, Dept of Agricultural Economics and Rural Sociology, Clemson, SC 29631. Telephone (803) 656-3475.

Periodic newsletter of the Cooperative Extension Service Division of agriculture econmics. Price free of charge.

3690
Paper and Packaging Bulletin
Economist Intelligence Unit Ltd, Spencer House, 27 St James's Pl, London, England SW1A 1NT. Order from Economist Intelligence Unit Ltd, 75 Rockefeller Plz, New York, NY 10019. Telephone (212) 541-5730. Telex 148393.

Quarterly journal. Reports on paper industry and packaging materials. Includes charts and tables. Price $265.00 per year.

3692
Paper Merchant Performance
National Paper Trade Assn, 420 Lexington Ave, New York, NY 10170. Telephone (212) 682-2570.

Annual report. Provides financial information on industrial and printing paper merchants in the US. Price $100.00.

3693
Paper Sales
Harcourt Brace Jovanovich Publications, 757 3rd Ave, New York, NY 10017. Order from Harcourt Brace Jovanovich Publications, 1 E 1st St, Duluth, MN 55802. Telephone (218) 727-8511.

Monthly report. Offers information relevant to paper wholesalers, including sales suggestions. Price $5.00 per year.

3694
Paper Trade Journal
Vance Pub Corp, 133 E 58th St, New York, NY 10022. Telephone (212) 755-5400.

Semimonthly journal. Covers paper industry news and developments. Price $10.00 per year.

3695
Paper Year Book
Harcourt Brace Jovanovich Publications, 757 3rd Ave, New York, NY 10017. Order from Harcourt Brace Jovanovich Publications, 1 E 1st St, Duluth, MN 55802. Telephone (218) 727-8511.

Yearbook. Lists wholesale paper products and manufacturers. Notes market information and sales techniques. Charts and tables. Price $40.00.

3696

Partnership Desk Book

Inst for Business Planning, Inc, IPB Plz, Englewood Cliffs, NJ 07632. Telephone (201) 592-2040.

Book. Offers information on setting up, maintaining, and dissolving partnerships. Emphasizes tax advantages. Price $39.50. ISBN 0-87624-427-4.

3697

Partnerships and Taxes: A Practical Guide

Panel Publishers, 14 Plaza Rd, Greenvale, NY 11548. Telephone (516) 484-0006.

Loose-leaf book with quarterly updates. Discusses partnership issues, including taxes, income allocation, and family partnerships. Price $98.00. ISBN 0-916592-16-2.

3698

Patent and Trademark Review

Clark Boardman Co Ltd, 435 Hudson St, New York, NY 10014. Telephone (212) 929-7530.

Monthly magazine. Contains text of new international patent and trademark laws and rules. Notes proposed legislation and related legal developments. Price $20.00 per year.

3699

Patent Attorneys and Agents Registered to Practice Before the US Patent Office

Patent and Trademark Office, Washington, DC 20231. Order from Superintendent of Documents, US Government Printing Office, Washington, DC 20402. Telephone (202) 783-3238.

Directory. Lists patent attorneys and agents registered to practice before US Patent and Trademark Office, alphabetically and geographically. Price $8.00.

3700

Patent Fraud and Inequitable Conduct

Clark Boardman Co Ltd, 435 Hudson St, New York, NY 10014. Telephone (212) 929-7500.

Loose-leaf book with annual revisions. Discusses US laws and court cases that determine patent fraud. Price $67.50. ISBN 0-87632-085-X.

3701

Patent Invalidity: A Statistical and Substantive Analysis

Clark Boardman Co Ltd, 435 Hudson St, New York, NY 10014. Telephone (212) 929-7500.

Loose-leaf book with annual revisions. Describes history and operation of US patent system. Analyzes 150 patents held invalid by courts. Price $67.50. ISBN 0-87632-127-9.

3703

Patent Office Record/Canada

Supply and Services Canada, Canadian Govt Publishing Centre, Hull, Que, Canada K1A 0S9. Telephone (819) 994-3475, 2085.

Weekly magazine. Issues reports from Canada's Patent Office. Bilingual. Price $39.00 per year.

3704

Patent Official Gazette

Patent and Trademark Office, Washington, DC 20231. Order from Superintendent of Documents, US Government Printing Office, Washington, DC 20402. Telephone (202) 783-3238.

Weekly magazine. Supplies abstracts of US patents granted and selected figure of drawings. Includes index of patents, list of patents available for license or sale, and information about changes in patent rules or classification. Price $300.00 per year.

3705

Patents and Trademarks

Oceana Publications, Inc, 75 Main St, Dobbs Ferry, NY 10522. Telephone (914) 693-5944.

Two loose-leaf binders. Provide information on patent and trademark law and practices in 65 countries. Price $110.00, $45.00 subscription service.

3706

Patents Throughout the World

Clark Boardman Co, Ltd, 435 Hudson St, New York, NY 10014. Telephone (212) 929-7500.

Loose-leaf book supplemented three times per year. Includes patent laws of 143 countries, summary tables, and texts of international conventions. Price $67.50 per volume. ISBN 0-87632-125-2.

3707

Payment Systems Action Report

Payment Systems, Inc, 100 Peachtree St, Atlanta, GA 30303. Telephone (404) 525-1593.

Weekly newsletter. Covers bank credit cards and other banking and payment systems, including electronic fund transfer systems. Price $325.00 per year.

3708

Payment Systems Newsletter

Payment Systems, Inc, 100 Peachtree St, Atlanta, GA 30303. Telephone (404) 525-1593.

Monthly newsletter. Covers commercial banks, thrift institutions, electronic fund transfer systems and various payment methods. Presents national and state news. Price $125.00 per year.

3709

Pay Planning

Inst for Business Planning, Inc, IPB Plz, Englewood Cliffs, NJ 07632. Telephone (201) 592-2040.

Two loose-leaf books with monthly supplements and semimonthly letters. Cover all aspects of employee compensation, including pension plans, profit sharing, and life insurance plans. Discuss ERISA compliance. Price available on request.

3710

Payroll Guide

Prentice-Hall, Inc, Englewood Cliffs, NJ 07632. Telephone (201) 592-2000. Telex 13-5423.

Biweekly loose-leaf service. Contains explanation of federal, state, and local payroll tax laws and other payroll regulations. Supplies sections on unemployment, disability, and wage and hour laws. Price $204.00 per year.

3711

Payroll Management Guide

Commerce Clearing House, Inc, 4025 W Peterson Ave, Chicago, IL 60646. Telephone (312) 236-2350.

Two loose-leaf books plus weekly reports. Give guidance on federal and state tax deductions, Social Security-Medicare taxes, and federal wage-hour controls. Price $155.00 per year.

3712

Pay TV Newsletter

Paul Kagan Assoc, Inc, 100 Merrick Rd, Rockville Centre, NY 11570. Telephone (516) 764-5516.

Semimonthly newsletter. Offers data on developments in pay television field. Includes semiannual census of all pay-cable and apartment systems, as well as monthly list of motion pictures available for pay television distribution. Price $250.00 per year.

3714

Pen & Ledger

National Assn of Minority CPA Firms, 1625 I St, NW, Suite 914, Washington, DC 20006. Telephone (202) 659-4153.

Quarterly newsletter. Discusses legislative and regulatory changes that affect minority certified public accounting firms. Reports on activities of National Association of Minority CPA firms. Free of charge.

3716

Pennsylvania CPA Spokesman

Pennsylvania Inst of Certified Public Accountants, 1100 Lewis Tower Bldg, 225 S 15 St, Philadelphia, PA 19102. Telephone (215) 735-2635.

Quarterly magazine. Deals with accounting topics, including corporate accounting and recent federal and Pennsylvania tax legislation. Price $2.00 per year.

3716.01

Pennsylvania: Directory of Manufacturers, 1980

Manufacturers' News, Inc, 3 E Huron St, Chicago, IL 60611. Telephone (312) 337-1084.

Annual book. Lists 15,000 manufacturing firms in Pennsylvania by name, location, and product. Notes number of employees. Price $79.50.

3717

Pennsylvania Industrial Directory

Pennsylvania Department of Commerce, 415 S Office Bldg, Harrisburg, PA 17120. Order from Bureau of Management Services, State Book Store, PO Box 1365, Harrisburg, PA 17125. Telephone (717) 783-1132.

Annual directory. Pertains to large and small industries in Pennsylvania. Price $15.00 per copy.

3717.02

Pennsylvania: State Industrial Directory, 1980

Manufacturers' News, Inc, 3 E Huron St, Chicago, IL 60611. Telephone (312) 337-1084.

Annual book. Serves as guide to 25,000 industrial companies in Pennsylvania. Identifies 100,000 executives and notes products. Price $90.00.

3718

Pennsylvania Statistical Abstract

Pennsylvania Department of Commerce, 415 S Office Bldg, Harrisburg, PA 17120. Order from Bureau of Management Services, State Book Store, PO Box 1365, Harrisburg, PA 17125. Telephone (717) 783-1132.

Annual book. Provides data on industry and all aspects of life in Pennsylvania. Price $5.00 per copy.

3719

Pension Actuary

American Society of Pension Actuaries, 1700 K St NW, Suite 404, Washington, DC 20006. Telephone (202) 785-4366.

Monthly newsletter. Contains information about pensions, including Social Security and Employee Retirement Income Security Act. Price $10.00 per year.

3720

Pension and Profit Sharing

Prentice-Hall, Inc, Englewood Cliffs, NJ 07632. Telephone (201) 592-2000. Telex 13-5423.

Weekly loose-leaf service. Provides information on pension and profit-sharing plans, including Social Security, individual retirement plans, and taxation. Price $390.00 per year.

3721

Pension and Profit Sharing Forms

Prentice-Hall, Inc, Englewood Cliffs, NJ 07632. Telephone (201) 592-2000. Telex 13-5423.

Monthly loose-leaf service. Contains plans, clauses and guides for profit-sharing, pension plans and trust agreements. Price $204.00 per year.

3722

Pension and Profit Sharing Guide

Prentice-Hall, Inc, Englewood Cliffs, NJ 07632. Telephone (201) 592-2000. Telex 13-5423.

Weekly loose-leaf service plus updates. Contains data on pension and profit-sharing plans for business executives. Price $312.00 per year.

3723

Pension and Profit Sharing Plans

Matthew Bender & Co, 235 E 45th St, New York, NY 10017. Telephone (212) 661-5050.

Five-volume set of books. Carries material on pension and profit-sharing plans, and analyzes ERISA provisions. Includes sample plans. Price $250.00.

3724

Pension Plan Guide

Commerce Clearing House, Inc, 4025 W Peterson Ave, Chicago, IL 60646. Telephone (312) 236-2350.

Five loose-leaf books plus weekly reports. Cover legal and practical requirements for pension plans, profit-sharing, employee benefits, and executive compensation under Employee Retirement Income Security Act. Price $275.00 per year.

3725

Pension Plan Guide Summary

Commerce Clearing House, Inc, 4025 W Peterson Ave, Chicago, IL 60646. Telephone (312) 583-8500.

Weekly newsletter. Summarizes current events relevant to pension plans and employee benefits. Price $40.00 per year.

3726

Pension Plans Service

Research and Review Service of America, Inc, PO Box 1727, Indianapolis, IN 46206. Telephone (317) 297-4360.

Loose-leaf book with monthly updates. Provides news relevant to pension plans. Covers pending legislation and current laws. Price $55.00, $72.00 for updates.

3726.01

Pension Pulse Beats

Insurance Field Co, Inc, PO Box 18441, 4325 Old Shepherdsville Rd, Louisville, KY 40218. Telephone (502) 459-7910.

Bimonthly newsletter. Reports significant events and trends in the pension field. Price $120.00 per year.

3727

Pension Reporter

Bureau of National Affairs, Inc, 1231 25th St, NW, Washington, DC 20037. Telephone (202) 452-4200.

Loose-leaf books with weekly updates. Cover pension and employee trust fund developments at federal, state, and local levels. Emphasize information emanating from federal departments, Congress, and tax courts. Price $288.00 per year.

3728
Pension Review Board Reports
Supply and Services Canada, Publishing Ctr, Printing and Publishing, Ottawa, Ont, Canada K1A 0S9. Telephone (613) 238-1601.

Quarterly magazine. Reports on Canada's Pension Review Board activities. Bilingual. Price $4.00 per year.

3729
Pensions & Investment Age
Crain Communications, Inc, 740 Rush St, Chicago, IL 60611. Telephone (312) 649-5227.

Semimonthly newspaper. Presents news related to pension funds. Discusses court cases and legislation. Notes various investment opportunities. Price $40.00 per year.

3730
Pensions Directory
Institutional Investors, Inc, 488 Madison Ave, New York, NY 10022. Telephone (212) 832-8888.

Annual newsletter. Lists corporate and state pension funds and profit-sharing funds. Price available on request.

3731
Pension Tables for Actuaries
American Society of Pension Actuaries, 1700 K St, NW, Suite 404, Washington, DC 20006. Telephone (202) 785-4366.

Four loose-leaf books. Contain statistical tables for actuarial use in connection with valuation of small- and medium-sized retirement plans. Price $395.00 (plus $10.00 for shipping); $25.00 per year additional for annual updates.

3732
Pension World
Communication Channels, Inc, 6285 Barfield Rd, Atlanta, GA 30328. Telephone (404) 256-9800.

Monthly magazine. Reports on employee benefit plans, such as investing pension funds, and administering or designing plans. Price $34.00 per year.

3733
People and Taxes
Public Citizen's Tax Reform Research Group, PO Box 14198, Washington, DC 20044.

Monthly newspaper. Explains tax issues. Notes legislation, tax reform, and property taxes. Price $12.00 per year businesses and institutions, $7.50 individuals.

3734
Performance Fund Selector Report
P A McDonald, 1856 Loudon Heights Rd, Charleston, WV 25314. Telephone (304) 345-8947.

Monthly loose-leaf reports. Offer advice on mutual fund investments. Include model portfolio. Price $35.00 per year.

3735
Performance Guide Publications.
Mutual Funds, Timing, Managed
Accounts
Performance Guide Publications, Inc, PO Box 2604, Palos Verdes Peninsula, CA 90274.

Monthly newsletter. Provides timing advice, timing indicators and ranks the relative performance of all active mutual funds. Price $50.00 per year.

3736
Personal Finance Letter
McGraw-Hill Publications Co, 1221 Ave of the Americas, New York, NY 10020. Telephone (212) 997-6375. Telex TWX 7105814879. WUI 62555.

Biweekly newsletter. Discusses personal finance topics, including tax planning, tax shelter, real estate, and estate planning. Price $49.00 per year.

3737
Personal Income, Population, Per Capita
Personal Income
US Dept of Commerce, Bureau of Economic Analysis, Washington, DC 20230. Order from Regional Economic Measurement Div, Bureau of Economic Analysis, Washington, DC 20230. Telephone (202) 523-0966.

Information service. Provides data on personal income, population, and per capita personal income for states, countries, and standard metropolitan statistical areas. Price $50.00.

3738
Personnel
American Management Assns, 135 W 50th St, New York, NY 10020. Telephone (212) 586-8100.

Bimonthly magazine. Covers developments and trends in the field of personnel management. Price $24.00 per year.

3739
Personnel Administrator
American Society for Personnel Administration, 30 Park Dr, Berea, OH 44017. Telephone (216) 826-4790.

Monthly magazine. Covers new developments in personnel and industrial relations. Price $26.00 per year.

3740
Personnel Advisory Bulletin
Bureau of Business Practice, 24 Rope Ferry Rd, Waterford, CT 06386. Telephone (203) 442-4365.

Semimonthly loose-leaf newsletter. Covers latest techniques of hiring, testing, interviewing, and employment. Price $36.00 per year.

3740.01
Personnel Alert
Advanced Personnel Systems, 756 Lois Ave, Sunnyvale, CA 94087. Telephone (408) 736-2433.

Bimonthly newsletter. Contains abstracts of the most significant new articles and books on personnel management from over 100 management journals and new book lists. Price $18.00 per year. ISSN 0162-105X.

3741
Personnel and Guidance Journal
American Personnel and Guidance Assn, 2 Skyline Place, Suite 400, 5203 Leesburg Pike, Falls Church, VA 22041. Telephone (703) 820-4700.

Monthly journal. Contains material relevant to personnel and school guidance counselors. Price $25.00 per year.

3741.01
Personnel Consultant
National Assn of Personnel Consultants, 1012 14th St, NW, Washington, DC 20005. Telephone (202) 638-1721.

Magazine published 10 times each year. Offers suggestions for private employment agencies and counselors. Notes National Employment Association activities. Price $37.50 per year.

3742
Personnel Guide
Commerce Clearing House, Inc, 4025 W Peterson Ave, Chicago, IL 60646. Telephone (312) 583-8500.

One loose-leaf with biweekly reports. Examine specific on-the-job problems and solutions to employer-employee relationships. Price $180.00 per year.

3743
Personnel Information Letter
Arthur Young & Co, 277 Park Ave, New York, NY 10017. Telephone (212) 922-4724.

Irregularly published newsletter. Contains information on new legislation and other developments affecting hiring, compensation, and personnel practices in United Kingdom. Free of charge.

3744
Personnel Journal
AC Croft, Inc, P.O. Bob 2440, Costa Mesa, CA 92627. Telephone (714) 646-5007

Monthly magazine. Discusses personnel management and industrial relations. Includes items on legislation, compensation and benefits recruitment, management, retirement, training, equal employment compliance, and human resource development. Price $28.00 per year.

3745
Personnel Management
Inst of Personnel Management, Central House, Upper Woburn Place, London, England WC1H 0HX. Telephone (44) (01) 387-2844.

Monthly magazine. Focuses on British personnel practices, new techniques, and recent legislation and economic trends. Price £20.00 per year £24.00 airmail per year.

3746
Personnel Management Abstracts
University of Michigan, Graduate School of Business Administration, Ann Arbor, MI 48109. Telephone (313) 763-0121.

Quarterly magazine. Abstracts articles from academic and trade journals that deal with management of people and organizational behavior. Author, subject, and title index. Price $55.00 per year. Annual accumulating issue included.

3747
Personnel Management—
Communications
Prentice-Hall, Inc, Englewood Cliffs, NJ 07632. Telephone (201) 592-2000.

Biweekly loose-leaf service. Discusses employers' communication with employees. Topics include work hours, employee benefits, and safety. Price $261.00 per year.

3747.01
Personnel Management Policies and
Practices
Prentice-Hall, Inc, Englewood Cliffs, NJ 07632. Telephone (201) 592-2000. Telex 13-5423.

Biweekly loose-leaf service. Discusses personnel practices, including hiring, training, promotions, and absenteeism. Price $261.00 per year.

3748
Personnel News & Views
National Retail Merchants Assn, 100 W 31st St, New York, NY 10001. Telephone (212) 244-6780.

Quarterly magazine. Covers topics related to retail store personnel, such as interviewing techniques, sales training programs, and minority hiring. Price $15.00 per year.

3750
Personnel Psychology
Personnel Psychology, Inc, PO Box 6965, College Station, Durham, NC 27708.

Quarterly magazine. Contains research reports on personnel problems in industry and government. Reviews books. Price $32.00 per year.

3751
Personnel Review
Teakfield Ltd, 1 Westmead, Farnborough, Hampshire, England GU14 7RU. Telephone (44) (0252) 41196. Telex 858193.

Quarterly journal. Discusses theory, research, and practice of personnel administration and industrial relations. Price $26.25.

3752
Perspective Canada II
Statistics Canada, User Services, Publications Distribution, Ottawa, Ont, Canada K1A 0V7. Telephone (613) 992-3151.

Irregular report. Presents statistics on Canadian social conditions such as health, education, and cultural affairs. Tables and charts. Price $11.10.

3753
Perspective on Aging
National Council on the Aging, Inc, 1828 L St, NW, Suite 504, Washington, DC 20036. Telephone (202) 223-6250.

Bimonthly magazine. Discusses aging. Reports on related executive decisions, legislation, and specific programs. Price single copies $3.50, otherwise membership benefit.

3753.01
Perspectives Canada III
Supply and Services Canada, Canadian Govt Publishing Centre, Hull, Que, Canada K1A OS9. Telephone (819) 994-3475, 2085.

Book. Presents statistics on Canadian social trends. Includes information on health, education, and income. Tables and charts. Price $11.95.

3753.02
Peter Dag Investment Letter
Peter Dag Investment Letter, 65 Lakefront Dr, Akron, OH 44319. Telephone (216) 644-2782.

Newsletter published every three weeks. Offers investment advice. Covers the stock market, interest rates, and economic trends. Provides forecasts. Price $115.00 per year.

3754
Petrochemical News
William F Bland Co, PO Box 1421, Stamford, CT 06904. Telephone (203) 359-1125. Telex 965-952.

Weekly newsletter. Covers worldwide petrochemical business, including new ventures, mergers, acquisitions, expansion, licensing, market outlooks, new products, and government actions. Price $250.00 per year.

3755
Petrochemical Scan
McGraw-Hill Publications Co, 1221 Ave of the Americas, New York, NY 10020. Telephone (212) 997-6375. Telex TWX 7105814879. WUI 62555.

Weekly service. Provides information on international sales and price levels of petrochemical feedstocks. Price $500.00 per year.

3756
Petrochemical Series
United Nations Industrial Development Organization, Vienna International Centre, PO Box 300, A-1400, Vienna, Austria. Telephone 26310. Telex 135612.

Series of reports on Brazilian synthetic polymer industry, petrochemicals in developing countries, plastics, and production and marketing of acrylic sheet in developing countries. Symbols: ID/SER.J/1-G. Price $.75.

3757
Petrochemical Service
Data Resources, Inc, 29 Hartwell Ave, Lexington, MA 02173. Telephone (617) 861-0165.

Quarterly report. Provides forecasts of US petrochemical production by process, price, consumption, capacity, and manufacturing costs. Price available on request.

3758
Petroleum Economist
Petroleum Press Bureau Ltd, 107 Charterhouse St, London, EC1M 6AA, England. Telephone (44) (01) 251 3501. Telex 27161.

Monthly magazine. Deals with economic and political implications of oil and energy developments. Provides oil production, prices, and shares tables. English, Japanese editions. Price $96.00.

3759
Petroleum Engineer International
Harcourt Brace Jovanovich Publications, 757 3rd Ave, New York, NY 10017. Order from Harcourt Brace Jovanovich Publications, PO Box 1589, Dallas, TX 75221. Telephone (214) 631-6520.

Monthly magazine. Provides technical and economic information on offshore and onshore oil and gas exploration, drilling, and production. Price $12.00 per year.

3760
Petroleum Independent
Independent Petroleum Assn of America, 1101 16th St, NW, Washington, DC 20036. Telephone (202) 857-4770.

Bimonthly magazine. Reports activities of the Independent Petroleum Association of America. Price $10.00 per two years.

3761
Petroleum Outlook
John S Herold, Inc, 35 Mason St, Greenwich, CT 06830. Telephone (203) 869-2585.

Monthly report interprets economic developments in petroleum industry. Charts and tables. Price $65.00 per year.

3762
Petroleum Refineries
Statistics Canada, User Services, Publications Distribution, Ottawa, Ont, Canada K1A 0V7. Telephone (613) 992-3151.

Annual report. Presents historical summary and current figures on Canadian petroleum refineries. Covers number of plants, employees, wages, fuels and materials used, and gross selling value of products. Price $5.40. ISSN 0068-7162.

3763
Mideast Markets
Financial Times Business Information Ltd, Bracken House, 10 Cannon St, London, England EC4P 4BY. Order from Financial Times Ltd, 75 Rockefeller Plz, New York, NY 10019. Telephone (44) (01) 248-8000. Telex 886341-2.

Fortnightly report on oil money. Reviews internal and external OPEC expenditures. Discusses banking and financial moves. Notes new energy developments. Price $490.00 per year.

3764
Pets/Supplies/Marketing
Harcourt Brace Jovanovich Publications, 757 3rd Ave, New York, NY 10017. Order from Harcourt Brace Jovanovich Publications, 1 E 1st St, Duluth, MN 55802. Telephone (218) 727-8511.

Monthly magazine. Discusses pets and pet supplies. Notes merchandising trends. Price $15.00 per year.

3764.01
Pharmaceutical Marketletter
IMS World Publications Ltd, York House, 37 Queen Sq, London, England WCIN 3BE. Telephone (44) (01) 242-0112. Telex 263298.

Weekly newsletter. Contains pharmaceutical industry news. Reports on marketing trends, new legislation, and new products. Price $365.00 per year.

3764.02
Pharmaceutical News Index
Data Courier, Inc, 620 S 5th St, Louisville, KY 40202. Telephone (502) 582-4111. Telex 204235.

Loose-leaf service, with 12 issues. Cites and indexes six drug industry publications. Notes research developments, government regulations, and personnel. Price $455.00 per year.

3764.03
Pharma Prospects
PJB Publications Ltd, 18a Hill St, Richmond, Surrey, England TW9 1TN. Telephone (44) (01) 940-8849. Telex 8951042.

Two annual loose-leaf volumes, and eleven monthly updates. Provide coverage of research and development of pharmaceutical products in over 25 countries. Include compounds originating from noncommercial establishments. Cummulative index. Price £1250.00 per year.

3765
Philadelphia-Baltimore-Washington Stock Exchange Guide
Commerce Clearing House, Inc, 4025 W Peterson Ave, Chicago, IL 60646. Telephone (312) 583-8500.

Loose-leaf book and monthly reports. Carries directory, constitution, and rules of Philadelphia-Baltimore-Washington Stock Exchange. Price $130.00 per year.

3765.01
Philippine Development
Republic of the Philippines, National Economic and Development Authority, PO Box 1116, Manila, Philippines. Order from National Economic and Development Authority Economic Information Staff, Circulation Unit, Government Center, EDSA, Diliman, Quezon City, Philippines.

Fortnightly magazine. Discusses Philippine government policies on economic development. Price $18.00 per year.

3765.02
Philippine Economic Indicators
Republic of the Philippines, National Economic and Development Authority, PO Box 1116, Manila, Philippines. Order from National Economic and Development Authority Economic Information Staff, Circulation Unit, Government Center, EDSA, Diliman, Quezon City, Philippines.

Monthly report. Supplies Philippine economic indicators. Price $13.20 per year.

3765.03
Philippine Letter
Asia Letter Ltd, PO Box 54149, Los Angeles, CA 90054. Telephone (213) 322-4222.

Bimonthly newsletter. Provides commentary and analyses of economic, political, and social trends and developments of special interest to foreign businessmen dealing in the Philippines. Price $48.00 per year.

3765.04
Philippine Statistical Yearbook

Republic of the Philippines, National Economic and Development Authority, PO Box 1116, Manila, Philippines. Order from National Economic and Development Authority Economic Information Staff, Circulation Unit, Government Center, EDSA, Diliman, Quezon City, Philippines.

Annual book. Provides statistical information on the Philippine economy. Price $25.00.

3765.05
Phoenix Business Journal

Cordovan Corp, 5314 Bingle Rd, Houston, TX 77092. Order from Phoenix Business Journal, 1817 North 3rd St, Phoenix, AZ 85004. Telephone (602) 271-4712.

Weekly newspaper. Contains feature articles on various segments of Phoenix business. Price $24.00 per year.

3766
Photographic Trade News

PTN Pub Corp, 250 Fulton Ave, Hempstead, NY 11550. Telephone (516) 489-1300.

Semimonthly magazine. Covers photographic industry news and trends. Discusses new products and successful retail techniques. Price $6.00 per year.

3767
Photographis

Advertising Trade Publications, Inc, 19 W 44th St, New York, NY 10036. Telephone (212) YU6-4930.

Annual book. Reproduces photographs used in advertising, annual reports, book jackets, editorial photography, magazine and record covers, packaging, calendars, and television. Price $37.50.

3768
Physician's Management

Harcourt Brace Jovanovich Publications, 757 3rd Ave, New York, NY 10017. Order from Harcourt Brace Jovanovich Publications, 1 E 1st St, Duluth, MN 55802. Telephone (218) 727-8511.

Monthly magazine. Focuses on physicians' practice management and personal finances. Price $18.00 per year.

3769
Pick's Currency Yearbook

Pick Pub Corp, 21 W St, New York, NY 10006. Telephone (212) 425-0591.

Yearbook. Provides monetary information, including exchange rates and foreign exchange controls, free and black market gold prices, and Eurocurrency market conditions. Tables. Price $180.00. ISBN 0-87551-275-5. ISSN 0079-2063.

3770
Pick World Currency Report

Pick Pub Corp, 21 W St, New York, NY 10006. Telephone (212) 425-0591.

Monthly report. Reviews currency rates, international monetary developments, and gold and silver markets. Lists metal and diamond prices. Charts. Price $400.00 per year. ISBN 0-87551-181-3. ISSN 0048-4113.

3771
Pig-irons and Steel: Basis Prices

Commission of the European Communities, Office for Official Publications of the European Communities, CP 1003, Luxembourg 1, Luxembourg. Telephone (352) 490081. Telex PUBLOF 1325.

Annual report, with supplements. Covers pig iron and steel prices. Price $227.50 per year.

3772
Pipeline & Gas Journal

Harcourt Brace Jovanovich Publications, 757 3rd Ave, New York, NY 10017. Order from Harcourt Brace Jovanovich Publications, PO Box 1589, Dallas, TX 75221. Telephone (214) 631-6520.

Monthly magazine. Discusses supply, transportation, distribution, and pipelining of natural gas, liquefied natural gas, SNG, and crude oil products. Price $6.00 per year.

3773
PI Reports

Petroleum Information Corp, PO Box 2612, 1375 Delaware, Denver, CO 80201. Telephone (303) 825-2181.

Series of reports. Supplies data on US petroleum industry by region. Notes drilling in progress and classifies wells. Price available on request.

3774
Pittsburgh Business Review

University of Pittsburgh, Graduate School of Business, Bureau of Business Research, Pittsburgh, PA 15213. Telephone (412) 624-6284.

Quarterly magazine. Covers business subjects such as marketing, accounting, and finance. Is aimed at middle- and upper-level managers. Free of charge.

3776
Plan Administrator's Compliance Manual

Prentice-Hall, Inc, Englewood Cliffs, NJ 07632. Telephone (201) 592-2000. Telex 13-5423.

Monthly loose-leaf service. Provides information needed to comply with ERISA reporting and disclosure requirements. Reflects law and regulation changes. Price $258.00.

3777
Planned Savings

Wootten Publications Ltd, 150/152 Caledonian Rd, London, England N1 9RD. Telephone (44) (01) 278-6854.

Monthly report. Discusses personal investment topics. Considers British taxes and legislation. Reviews bonds, trusts, and other investments. Price £22.00 per year.

3777.01
Planning Ideas

Predicasts, Inc, 11001 Cedar Ave, Cleveland, OH 44106. Telephone (216) 795-3000.

Weekly newsletter. Discusses corporate planning developments. Includes information on growth opportunities, management, and external environment. Price $132.00 per year.

3778
Plant Engineering

Technical Publishing Co, 1301 S Grove Ave, Barrington, IL 60010. Telephone (312) 381-1840.

Biweekly magazine. Discusses plant engineering techniques. Covers manufacturing and process industries and related nonmanufacturing industries. Price $40.00 per year.

3779
Plant Engineering Directory and Specifications Catalog
Technical Publishing Co, 1301 S Grove Ave, Barrington, IL 60010. Telephone (312) 381-1840.

Annual directory. Contains technical data on plant engineering, manufacturers' product catalog, product directory, and local sales office information. Price $35.00 per copy.

3780
Plant Location
Simmons-Boardman Pub Corp, 350 Broadway, New York, NY 10013. Telephone (212) 966-7700.

Annual book. Gives information on site location for plants. Price $15.00 per year.

3781
Plastic Bottles
US Dept of Commerce, Bureau of the Census, Washington, DC 20233. Telephone (202) 449-1600.

Monthly report with annual summary. Contains data on shipments and production of blow-molded plastics bottles, by type and weight of bottles, and by type of resin. Price $3.00 per year.

3782
Plastics Industry Europe
Plastics Industry Europe, 31 Alington Grove, Wallington, Surrey, England, SM6 9NH. Telephone (44) (01) 647-4194.

Semimonthly newsletter. Covers developments in the European plastics industry. Notes technical trends, prices, markets, and company news. Price £96.00 per year.

3782.01
Plastics Industry News
Institute of Polymer Industry, Inc, Central PO Box No 1176, Tokyo 100-91, Japan.

Monthly journal. Covers plastics industry in Japan. Reports on developments in polymers. Price $56.00 per year.

3783
Plastics World
Cahners Pub Co, Inc, 221 Columbus Ave, Boston, MA 02116. Telephone (617) 536-7780.

Monthly magazine. Contains articles on adaptation of systems, materials, and equipment to increase efficiency in plastics processing. With annual Buyers Guide. Price available on request.

3783.01
Platt's Bunkerwire
McGraw-Hill Publications Co, 1221 Ave of the Americas, New York, NY 10020. Telephone (212) 997-4452. Telex TWX 7105814879 WUI 62555.

Weekly telex report. Provides information on marine fuel prices in major international ports. Summarizes supply conditions. Price $575.00 per year.

3783.02
Platt's LP Gaswire
McGraw-Hill Publications Co, 1221 Ave of the Americas, New York, NY 10020. Telephone (212) 997-4452. Telex TWX 7105814879 WUI 62555.

Weekly telex report. Reports on liquefied petroleum gas spot prices, and supply and demand data. Notes product availability and contracts. Price $825.00 per year.

3783.03
Platt's OHA Digest
McGraw-Hill Publications Co, 1221 Ave of the Americas, New York, NY 10020. Telephone (212) 997-3016. Telex TWX 7105814879 WUI 62555.

Weekly newsletter. Covers all key decisions by US Energy Department's Office of Hearings and Appeals. Price $397.00 per year.

3784
Platt's Oilgram Legislative Service
McGraw-Hill Book Co, Hightstown-Princeton Rd, Hightstown, NJ 08520. Telephone (609) 448-1700. Telex 843449.

Semimonthly newsletter. Analyzes congressional energy-related legislative developments. Lists votes. Price available on request.

3784.01
Platt's Oilgram Marketscan
McGraw-Hill Publications Co, 1221 Ave of the Americas, New York, NY 10020. Telephone (212) 997-6375. Telex TWX 7105814879 WUI 62555.

Daily telex reports. Covers activities of major oil markets. Notes current prices. Price $900.00 per year.

3785
Platt's Oilgram News
McGraw-Hill Publications Co, 1221 Ave of the Americas, New York, NY 10020. Telephone (212) 997-6375. Telex TWX 7105814879. WUI 62555.

Daily report. Provides information on petroleum industry and related news in US and abroad. Price $677.00 per year.

3785.01
Platt's Oilgram News/Wire
McGraw-Hill Publications Co, 1221 Ave of the Americas, New York, NY 10020. Telephone (212) 997-4452. Telex TWX 7105814879 WUI 62555.

Daily telex report. Compiles international petroleum news. Notes pertinent economic and political developments. Price $2375.00 per year.

3786
Platt's Oilgram Price Report
McGraw-Hill Publications Co, 1221 Ave of the Americas, New York, NY 10020. Telephone (212) 997-6375. Telex TWX 7105814879. WUI 62555.

Daily report. Provides international crude oil and petroleum products prices. Price $677.00 per year.

3786.01
Platt's Oil Marketing Bulletin
McGraw-Hill Publications Co, 1221 Ave of the Americas, New York, NY 10020. Telephone (212) 997-6375. Telex TWX 7105814879 WUI 62555.

Weekly service. Covers petroleum marketing trends. Includes US government news that affects marketing. Price $269.00 per year.

3787
Platt's Oil Price Handbook
McGraw-Hill Book Co, Hightstown-Princeton Rd, Hightstown, NJ 08520. Telephone (609) 448-1700. Telex 843449.

Book. Provides data on international crude oil and oil products prices. Price $85.00.

3787.01
Platt's Oil Regulation Report.
McGraw-Hill Publications Co, 1221 Ave of the Americas, New York, NY 10020. Telephone (212) 997-6375. Telex TWX 7105814879. WUI 62555.

Semimonthly newsletter. Analyzes US energy regulation, including price controls on crude oil and government incentives for manufacturing more industrial fuel oil. Price $257.00 per year.

3787.02
Platt's Petrochemical Scan
McGraw-Hill Publications Co, 1221 Ave of the Americas, New York, NY 10020. Telephone (212) 997-6375. Telex TWX 7105814879 WUI 62555.

Weekly telex report. Covers current prices for petrochemicals. Price $845.00 per year.

3787.03
Platt's Polymerscan
McGraw-Hill Publications Co, 1221 Ave of the Americas, New York, NY 10020. Telephone (212) 997-4452. Telex TWX 7105814879 WUI 62555.

Weekly telex report. Provides information on spot prices in bulk polymers. Notes price ranges, major deals, and emerging trends. Price $750.00 per year.

3788
Playthings
Geyer-McAllister Publications, Inc, 51 Madison Ave, New York, NY 10010. Telephone (212) 689-4411.

Monthly magazine. Emphasizes news and merchandising information on toys, hobbies, and crafts. Price $14.00 per year.

3788.01
Plug-Compatible Peripherals Reports
Auerbach Publishers, Inc, 6560 N Park Dr, Pennsauken, NJ 08109. Telephone (609) 662-2070. Telex 831 464.

Book, updated monthly. Covers peripherals marketed by independent manufacturers, that are plug-compatible with most widely used mainframes. Provides selection criteria, price data, maintenance information, and performance evaluations. Price $325.00.

3789
Plumbing Fixtures
US Dept of Commerce, Bureau of the Census, Washington, DC 20233. Telephone (202) 449-1600.

Quarterly report with annual summary. Presents statistics on shipments, production, and stocks of plumbing fixtures, including plastic bathtubs and shower stalls. Price $.25 per issue; subscription price available on request.

3790
Pocket Digest of New Zealand Statistics
New Zealand Dept of Statistics, Private Bag, Wellington, New Zealand. Telephone (64) (4) 729119.

Annual book. Digests statistics on New Zealand. Price $1.20 (New Zealand).

3790.01
Pocket List of Railroad Officials
National Railway Publication Co, 424 W 33rd St, New York, NY 10001. Telephone (212) 563-7300.

Quarterly book. Lists names, titles, addresses, and phone numbers of 20,000 railroad officials throughout the world. Price $18.00 per year.

3791
Point and Figure Digest
Canadian Analyst Ltd, 32 Front St W, Toronto, Ont, Canada M5J 1C5. Telephone (416) 363-4431.

Quarterly book. Charts indicate price variations for 750 Canadian and US stocks and market indices. Price $88.00.

3792
Point and Figure Summary
Canadian Analyst Ltd, 32 Front St W, Toronto, Ont, Canada M5J 1C5. Telephone (416) 363-4431.

Weekly service. Indicates price changes for 750 US and Canadian stocks. Reviews technical market indicators. Price $144.00 per year.

3793
Policy, Form & Manual Analysis Service
Rough Notes Co, Inc, 1200 N Meridian St, Indianapolis, IN 46204. Telephone (317) 634-1541.

Monthly service. Provides information on over 400 current insurance policies. Price $99.95 first year, $36.00 renewals.

3794
Policy Holder Insurance Journal
P H Press Ltd, Waterloo Rd, Stockport, Cheshire, England SK1 3BN. Telephone (44) (061) 480-2083.

Weekly magazine. Reports on British legislation, new policies, and other insurance industry news. Price £28.00 per year.

3795
Policy Publications Review
IPC Business Press Ltd, 205 E 42nd St, New York, NY 10017. Telephone (212) 889-0700. Telex 421710.

Bimonthly magazine gives information on reports, surveys, and special publications issued by governments and international agencies relevant to management, research, and education. Price $52.00 per year. ISSN 0307-4757.

3796
Policy Statistics Service
National Underwriter Co, 420 E 4th St, Cincinnati, OH 45202. Telephone (513) 721-2140.

Four loose-leaf books and monthly updates. Provide data on life insurance policies of over 60 companies, including dividend and surrender value information. Tables. Price $96.00 per year.

3797
Politics and Money
Politics and Money Pub Co, 14 S Hill Park Gardens, London, England NW3. Telephone (44) (01) 435-0214.

Monthly booklet. Analyzes relationship between politics and economics through articles focusing on US and aboard. Price $14.50 per year.

3798
Polk's Daily Bank Information Service
R L Polk & Co, 2001 Elm Hill Pike, PO Box 1340, Nashville, TN 37202. Telephone (615) 889-3350.

Daily newsletter. Issues information on new banks and branches, liquidations, mergers, appointments, promotions, resignations, and other banking changes. Price $260.00 per year.

3799
Polk's World Bank Directory
R L Polk & Co, 2001 Elm Hill Pike, PO Box 1340, Nashville, TN 37202. Telephone (615) 242-1694.

Semiannual directory with updates. Lists banks of the world. Includes financial statistics and other information. Price $67.50 per issue.

3800
Polk's World Bank Directory
International Edition
R L Polk & Co, 2001 Elm Hill Pike, PO Box 1340, Nashville, TN 37202. Telephone (615) 889-3350.

Annual book. Provides material on banks and branches in South America, Africa, Asia, Australia, Oceania, and Europe. Includes information from North American edition on Canada, Mexico, and Middle America. Price $40.50.

3801
Polk's World Bank Directory North American Edition
R L Polk & Co, 2001 Elm Hill Pike, PO Box 1340, Nashville, TN 37202. Telephone (615) 889-3350.

Biannual book with three supplements. Reports on banks and branches in US, Canada, Mexico, and middle America. Includes sections on bank holding, financing, and leasing companies. Price $67.50 per copy.

3802
Pollution
Microinfo Ltd, PO Box 3, Newman Lane, Alton, Hampshire, England GU34 2PG. Telephone Alton. Telex 858431.

Newsletter. Concerns technical aspects of pollution and environment. Price available on request.

3803
Pollution Abstracts
Data Courier, Inc, 620 S 5th St, Louisville, KY 40202. Telephone (502) 582-4111. Telex 204235.

Bimonthly journal. Provides abstracts for literature on enviromental pollution and research. Covers air pollution, water pollution, and solid wastes. Price $295.00 per year.

3804
Pollution Control Guide
Commerce Clearing House, Inc, 4025 W Peterson Ave, Chicago, IL 60646. Telephone (312) 583-8500.

Seven loose-leaf books and weekly reports. Present Environmental Protection Agency's requirements and policy on air and water pollution and solid waste disposal. Price $755.00 per year.

3805
Pollution Engineering
Technical Publishing Co, 1301 S Grove Ave, Barrington, IL 60010. Telephone (312) 381-1840.

Monthly magazine. Discusses pollution control engineering subjects. Covers air, water, solid waste, and noise. Notes current legislation, government enforcement practices, and new technology. Price $18.00 per year.

3807
Polymer
IPC Business Press Ltd, 205 E 42nd St, New York, NY 10017. Telephone (212) 889-0700. Telex 421710.

Monthly magazine. Contains original research on polymers and biopolymers. Covers synthesis of plastics, fibers and elastomers, and applications. Price $390.-00. ISSN 0032-3861.

3809
Population and Vital Statistics Report
United Nations Publications, Room A-3315, New York, NY 10017. Telephone (212) 754-8302.

Quarterly report. Supplies statistics on births, deaths, and infant mortality for all countries based on latest census returns. Price $12.00.

3810
Population Projections
Her Majesty's Stationery Office, PO Box 569, London, England SE1 9NH. Telephone (44) (01) 928 1321.

Annual report. Offers forecasts on British population trends. Price £4.00 per year.

3811
Population Trends
Her Majesty's Stationery Office, PO Box 569, London, England SE1 9NH. Telephone (44) (01) 928 1321.

Quarterly report on British population trends. Price £3.00 per year.

3812
Potentials in Marketing
Lakewood Publications, Inc, 731 Hennepin Ave, Minneapolis, MN 55403. Telephone (612) 333-0471.

Magazine issued nine times per year. Covers marketing tools such as premium and incentive products, awards, training aids, meeting and convention sites, and advertising. Price $10.00 per year.

3813
Poultry Market News Reports
US Dept of Agriculture, Agricultural Marketing Service, Room 2620-S, Washington, DC 20250. Telephone (202) 447-6911.

Intermittent reports. Cover poultry and egg market developments. Note cold storage holdings and shipments. Free of charge.

3814
Powell Alert
Reserve Research Ltd, 50 Broad St, New York, NY 10004. Telephone (212) 943-3621.

Biweekly newsletter. Contains information and commentary on current trends in the economy, international affairs, and individual financial planning. Price $72.00 per year.

3815
Powell Gold Industry Guide & International Mining Analyst
Reserve Research Ltd, 50 Broad St, New York, NY 10004. Telephone (212) 943-3620.

Book. Assesses gold and other mining stocks. Price $35.00.

3816
Powell Monetary Analyst
Reserve Research Ltd, 50 Broad St, New York, NY 10004. Telephone (212) 943-3620.

Biweekly newsletter. Contains advice about investment opportunities in gold and other mining industries. Price $185.00 per year. ISSN 0146-7190.

3817
Power
McGraw-Hill Publications Co, 1221 Ave of the Americas, New York, NY 10020. Telephone (212) 997-1221. Telex TWX 7105814879. WUI 62555.

Monthly magazine. Covers engineering topics, including power generation and plant energy systems, energy conservation, environmental issues, and steam generation. Price $11.00 per year.

3818
Power—Electric Utility Generation Planbook
McGraw-Hill Book Co, Hightstown-Princeton Rd, Hightstown, NJ 08520. Telephone (609) 448-1700. Telex 843449.

Annual book. Contains information on design of electric utility generating plants and systems. Serves engineers and consultants. Price $10.00.

3819
Power Engineering
Technical Publishing Co, 1301 S Grove Ave, Barrington, IL 60010. Telephone (312) 381-1840.

Monthly magazine. Reports on power generation industry, including nuclear power, coal, and other energy sources. Emphasizes engineering aspects. Price $30.00 per year.

3820
Power Transmission Design
Penton/IPC, 614 Superior Ave, Cleveland, OH 44113. Telephone (216) 696-0300.

Monthly magazine. Discusses mechanical power transmission systems and products. Price $24.00.

3821
Practical Accountant
The Practical Accountant, 964 3rd Ave, New York, NY 10155. Telephone (212) 935-9210.

Monthly magazine. Contains articles on accounting and auditing techniques, tax audits, and estate planning. Price $36.00 per year.

3822
Practical Guide to LP/Gas Utilization
Harcourt Brace Jovanovich Publications, 757 3rd Ave, New York, NY 10017. Order from Harcourt Brace Jovanovich Publications, 1 1st St, Duluth, MN 55802. Telephone (218) 727-8511.

Biennial report. Covers basic principles of liquefied petroleum gas use, including equipment, controls, and appliances. Price $25.00 per copy.

3822.01
Practical Solar
Business Publishers, PO Box 1067, Silver Springs, MD 20910. Telephone (301) 587-6300.

Monthly newsletter. Discusses marketing and installation of solar energy systems. Price $67.00 per year.

3823
Practice Administration Manual
Canadian Inst of Chartered Accountants, 250 Bloor St E, Toronto, Ont, Canada M4W 1G5. Telephone (416) 962-1242.

Book. Provides guide to internal office administrative systems. Covers partnerships, quality control, tax services, and management consulting services. Includes forms. Price $20.00.

3824
PR Blue Book International
PR Pub Co, Inc, PO Box 600, Exeter, NH 03833. Telephone (603) 778-0514.

Book. Lists and describes public relations firms throughout the world. Price available on request.

3825
Precision Metal
Penton/IPC, 614 Superior Ave W, Cleveland, OH 44113. Telephone (216) 696-0300.

Monthly magazine. Deals with precision metal processes. Price $24.00.

3826
Predi-Briefs
Predicasts, Inc, 200 University Circle Research Ctr, 11001 Cedar Ave, Cleveland, OH 44106. Telephone (216) 795-3000.

Thirty-two sets of abstracts. Offers product, market, and other business information for different industries. Information is culled from journals, newspapers, and government reports worldwide. Price $108.00 per year for set.

3828
Predicasts Basebook
Predicasts, Inc, 200 University Circle Research Ctr, 11001 Cedar Ave, Cleveland, OH 44106. Telephone (216) 795-3000.

Annual book. Contains US economic, industrial, and product statistics, including population, gross national product, production, and employment data. Price $325.00 per year.

3828.01
Predicasts F&S Index Europe
Predicasts, Inc, 11001 Cedar Ave, Cleveland, OH 44106. Telephone (216) 795-3000.

Monthly report, with quarterly cumulatives. Contains brief summaries of articles on European business, economies, and industries. Price $295.00 per year.

3828.02
Predicasts F&S Index Europe Annual
Predicasts, Inc, 11001 Cedar Ave, Cleveland, OH 44106. Telephone (216) 795-3000.

Annual index. Provides brief summaries of articles covering European industrial, economic, financial, and political news. Price $195.00.

3828.03
Predicasts F & S Index International
Predicasts, Inc, 200 University Circle Research Center, 11001 Cedar Ave, Cleveland, OH 44106. Telephone (216) 795-3000.

Monthly report, with quarterly cumulatives. Contains abstracts of articles from international publications on business, economic, industrial, and corporate news, arranged by subject, price, and country (the US and Europe excluded). Price $295.00 per year.

3828.04
Predicasts F & S Index International Annual
Predicasts, Inc, 200 University Circle Research Center, 11001 Cedar Ave, Cleveland, OH 44106. Telephone (216) 795-3000.

Annual book. Provides abstracts of articles covering international (the US and Europe excluded) industrial, economic, financial, and political information. Price $195.00.

3828.05
Predicasts F & S Index of Corporate Change
Predicasts, Inc, 200 University Circle Research Center, 11001 Cedar Ave, Cleveland, OH 44106. Telephone (216) 795-3000.

Quarterly report, plus cumulative annual. Provides an index to US corporate mergers and acquisitions. Notes corporate bankruptcies, foreign operations, and other activities. Price $195.00 per year.

3828.06
Predicasts F & S Index United States
Predicasts, Inc, 200 University Circle Research Center, 11001 Cedar Ave, Cleveland, OH 44106. Telephone (216) 795-3000.

Weekly report, with monthly and quarterly cumulatives. Provides abstracts of articles on US business information, including mergers, investments, legislation, and new products. Price $325.00 per year.

3828.07
Predicasts F & S Index United States Annual
Predicasts, Inc, 200 University Circle Research Center, 11001 Cedar Ave, Cleveland, OH 44106. Telephone (216) 795-3000.

Annual book. Provides abstracts of articles from major business and financial publications on US corporate and business subjects. Topics include acquisitions, research, and investment. Price $195.00.

3828.08
Predicasts Forecasts
Predicasts, Inc, 200 University Circle Research Ctr, 11001 Cedar Ave, Cleveland, OH 44106. Telephone (216) 795-3000.

Quarterly. Statistical information service. Abstracts business and financial forecasts for specific US industrial products and general economy. Presents composite data for economic, construction, energy, and other indicators. Price $535.00 per year.

3828.09
Predicasts Overview of Markets & Technology (PROMT)
Predicasts, Inc, 200 University Circle Research Cntr, 11001 Cedar Ave, Cleveland, OH 44106. Telephone (216) 795-3000.

Monthly set of abstracts provides worldwide news of developments in all industries. Indexing is by product, company, and country. Price $725.00 per year.

3829
Predicasts Source Directory
Predicasts, Inc, 200 University Circle Research Ctr, 11001 Cedar Ave, Cleveland, OH 44106. Telephone (216) 795-3000.

Annual book with three quarterly supplements. Gives bibliographic information on business information sources, including newspapers, trade journals, government publications, and bank letters. Price $100.00 per year plus three quarterly supplements.

3830
Predicasts Terminal System
Predicasts, Inc, 200 University Circle Research Ctr, 11001 Cedar Ave, Cleveland OH 44106. Telephone (216) 795-3000.

On-line computerized information service. Provides direct access to data contained in a wide range of Predicasts digest, index and statistical publications. Price available on request.

3831
Preliminary Annual Area Reports
US Bureau of Mines, Publications Distribution Branch, 4800 Forbes Ave, Pittsburgh, PA 15213. Telephone (412) 621-4500.

Annual reports. Contain data on US mineral production by states. Price available on request.

3832
Preliminary Annual Data on Commodities
US Bureau of Mines, Publications Distribution Branch, 4800 Forbes Ave, Pittsburgh, PA 15213. Telephone (412) 621-4500.

Annual reports. Supply data on US mineral commodity production, trade, consumption, and related areas. Price available on request.

3833
Premium, Incentive and Travel Buyers
Salesman's Guide, Inc, 1140 Broadway, New York, NY 10001. Telephone (212) 684-2985.

Directory with quarterly supplements. Contains register of over 16,000 buyers of premium and incentive merchandise and travel incentive programs. Price $110.00.

3834
Premium/Incentive Business
Gralla Publications, 1515 Broadway, New York, NY 10036. Telephone (212) 869-1300.

Publication. Deals with premium and incentive sales and buying. Price available on request.

3835
Prentice-Hall Federal Tax Handbook
Prentice-Hall, Inc, Englewood Cliffs, NJ 07632. Telephone (201) 592-2000. Telex 13-5423.

Annual book. Explains federal tax law, including 1977 changes. Charts, tables, lists, and indexes. Price $9.50.

3835.01
Prepared Sites
Conway Publications, Inc, Peachtree Air Terminal, 1954 Airport Rd, Atlanta, GA 30341. Telephone (404) 458-6026.

Computer print-out. Index of office, industrial parks, and large-scale planned unit developments offering planning sites ready for use. Arranged by state and city. Price $400.00.

3836
Prescription Drug Industry Factbook
Pharmaceutical Manufacturers Assn, 1155 5th St, NW, Washington, DC 20005. Telephone (202) 463-2060.

Book. Contains statistics on sales and other aspects of the drug industry. Price $1.50 per copy.

3837
Prestel
Prestel Headquarters, Post Office Telecommunications, Telephone House, Temple Ave, London, England, EC4Y OHL. Telephone (44) (01) 583-9811. Telex 261040.

Computer access service. Links television sets to computers so that viewers can obtain selected information. Price available on request.

3838
Price Index Numbers for Current Cost Accounting
Her Majesty's Stationery Office, PO Box 569, London, England SE1 9NH. Telephone (44) (01) 928 1321.

Quarterly indices designed to assist British companies experimenting with current cost accounting. Give tabulations for over 200 indices, with last five years at monthly intervals. Price available on request.

3839
Price Index of New One-Family Houses Sold
US Dept of Commerce, Bureau of the Census, Washington, DC 20233. Telephone (202) 449-1600.

Quarterly report. Supplies price index data on new one-family houses sold, by physical characteristics of house, including floor area, number of stores, location, and type of foundation. Price $2.50 per year.

3841
Primary Industry Newsletter
Ronald Anderson & Assoc, 90-92 Langridge St, Collingwood, Vic 3066, Australia. Telephone (61) (03) 4173140, Telex AA36701.

Weekly newsletter. Furnishes analyses and opinion on conditions in Australia. Price $87.00 (Australian) per 50 issues.

3842
Primary Industry Survey
Ronald Anderson & Assoc, 90-92 Langridge St, Collingwood, Vic 3066, Australia. Telephone (61) (03) 4173140. Telex AA36701.

Monthly report. Analyzes rural industry in Australia. Price $50.00 (Australian) per year.

3843
Primary Iron and Steel
Statistics Canada, User Services, Publications Distribution, Ottawa, Ont, Canada K1A 0V7. Telephone (613) 992-3151.

Monthly report. Presents data on Canadian primary iron and steel. Includes furnace charges, production and shipments of pig iron and ferro-alloy, and steel ingots and castings. Shows production and disposition of rolled steel products. Price $30.00 per year. ISSN 0380-7851.

3844
Principal International Businesses
Dun & Bradstreet, Box 3224, Church St Station, New York, NY 10008. Telephone (212) 285-7346.

Annual book. Serves as world marketing directory to over 49,000 of world's leading enterprises in 133 countries. Gives addresses, sales volume, number of employees, and lines of business. Prices available on request to Dun & Bradstreet subscribers only.

3847
Print
Print, 6400 Goldsboro Rd, Washington, DC 20034. Telephone (301) 229-2225.

Bimonthly magazine. Covers current trends in graphic design in advertising and promotion, editorial design, corporate graphics, television, film and environment. Price $26.00 per year.

3848
Printing and Publishing
Superintendent of Documents, US Government Printing Office, Washington, DC 20402. Telephone (202) 783-3238.

Quarterly report. Covers trends and basic statistics in the US printing and publishing industry. Price available on request.

3849
Printing Impressions
North American Pub Co, 401 N Broad St, Philadelphia, PA 19108. Telephone (215) 574-9600.

Monthly magazine. Covers printing and allied graphic arts, including phototypesetting equipment; newspaper, book, and periodical publishing; and printing trades machinery. Price $18.00 per year.

3850
Print Media Production Data
Standard Rate & Data Service, Inc, 5201 Old Orchard Rd, Skokie, IL 60077. Telephone (312) 470-3100.

Quarterly book. Contains advertising information for daily newspapers and business, consumer, and farm publications. Price $68.00 per year.

3851
Private and Public Investment in Canada. Outlook
Statistics Canada, User Services, Publications Distribution, Ottawa, Ont, Canada K1A 0V7. Telephone (613) 992-3151.

Annual report. Provides estimates on Canadian public and private intended capital and repair expenditures for forthcoming year. Covers construction, machinery, and equipment costs. Evaluates expenditures for two previous years. Includes national, provincial, and metropolitan data. Price $7.20. ISSN 0318-2274.

3852
Private Foundations Reports
Commerce Clearing House, Inc, 4025 W Peterson Ave, Chicago, IL 60646. Telephone (312) 583-8500.

Two loose-leaf books plus fortnightly reports. Discuss federal tax law requirements of tax-exempt status for private foundations. Price $335.00 per year.

3854
Private Investors Abroad
Matthew Bender & Co, 235 E 45th St, New York, NY 10017. Telephone (212) 661-5050.

Annual book. Analyzes private investment opportunities abroad. Discusses international business transaction methods. Price $45.00.

3855
Private Placements and Restricted Securities
Clark Boardman Co Ltd, 435 Hudson St, New York, NY 10014. Telephone (212) 929-7500.

Loose-leaf book with annual revisions. Reviews Securities and Exchange Commission and court rulings in which security offerings qualify for private placement exemptions. Explains procedures for offering securities privately. Price $125.00 two looseleaf volumes. ISBN 0-87632-078-7.

3856
Probe
Probe, Inc, 78 Randall Ave, Rockville Centre, NY 11570. Telephone (516) 536-8050.

Newsletter issued 22 times per year. Presents US life insurance industry trends, forecasts, opinions, and views. Price $35.00 per year.

3857
Problems of Economics
M E Sharpe, Inc, 80 Business Park Dr, Armonk, NY 10504. Telephone (914) 273-1800.

Monthly journal. Supplies translations of articles on current Soviet economic policy in areas such as city planning, production, family budgets, and agriculture. Price $193.00 per year.

3857.01
Proceedings of the NAIC
National Assn of Insurance Commissioners, 350 Bishops Way, Brookfield, WI 53005. Telephone (414) 784-9540.

Semiannual book. Contains proceedings of the National Association of Insurance Commissioners, 1871–1977. Price $37.00 per volume.

3858
Proceedings of the 1972 National Operations and Automation Conference —"The Common Denominator— Management"
American Bankers Assn, 1120 Connecticut Ave NW, Washington, DC 20036. Telephone (202) 467-4123.

Book. Covers bank management's use of information systems, data processing, accounting systems, and check processing. Price $15.00.

3859
Process and Chemical Engineering
Thomson Publications (Australia) Pty Ltd, 47 Chippen St, PO Box 65, Chippendale, NSW 2008, Australia. Telephone (61) 699-6731. Telex TPAS AA22226.

Monthly magazine. Covers process and chemical engineering subjects, including food and drink processing, plastics, and pollution and corrosion control. Emphasizes Australian developments. Price $43.00 (Australian) per year.

3860
Process Engineering
Morgan-Grampian Ltd, Morgan-Grampian House, Calderwood St, London, England SE18 6QH. Order from Morgan-Grampian Pub Co, 2 Park Ave, New York, NY 10016. Telephone England: (44) (01) 8557777. Telex 896238 MORGAN G. New York: (212) 340-9700. Telex 425592 MGI UI.

Monthly magazine. Provides practical solutions to problems of engineers in chemical and process industries. Price $100.00 per year.

3861
Procurement Weekly
Inst of Purchasing and Supply, York House, Westminster Bridge Rd, London, England SE1 7UT. Telephone (44) (01) 9281851.

Weekly magazine. Reports current British industrial news. Includes detailed price monitor. Price £15.50 per year.

3862
Producer News
Insurance Field Co, Inc, PO Box 18441, 4325 Old Shepherdsville Rd, Louisville, Ky 40218. Telephone (502) 459-7910.

Monthly newsletter. Reports specific insurance news for the independent general insurance agent. Price $12.00 per year.

3862.01
Producer Prices and Price Indexes
US Dept of Labor, Bureau of Labor Statistics, 441 G St, NW, Washington, DC 20212. Telephone (202) 523-1221.

Monthly report, plus annual supplement. Provides data on wholesale price movements. Includes summary indexes for groups of products and commodities. Price $17.00 per year.

3863
Product Design & Development
Chilton Co, Chilton Way, Radnor, PA 19089. Telephone (215) 687-8200.

Monthly magazine. Discusses durable products for design engineers, including fasteners and supports and mechanical and power components. Price $35.00.

3864
Production
Bramson Pub Co, Box 101, Bloomfield Hills, MI 48013. Telephone (313) 647-8400.

Monthly report. Covers news about manufacturing production operations. Price $12.00. ISSN 0032-9819.

3865
Production & Inventory Control Handbook
American Production and Inventory Control Society, Inc, Watergate Bldg, Suite 504, 2600 Virginia Ave, NW, Washington, DC 20037. Telephone (202) 333-1660.

Book. Supplies information on production and inventory control, including manpower planning, transportation, and computer-based systems. Price $46.95.

3866
Production and Inventory Management
American Production and Inventory Control Society, Inc, Watergate Bldg, Suite 504, 2600 Virginia Ave, NW, Washington, DC 20037. Telephone (202) 333-1660.

Quarterly magazine. Features material on production and inventory control. Reports on research and development, evaluates techniques, and discusses their applications. Tables. Price $20.00 per year.

3866.01
Production and Stocks of Eggs and Poultry
Statistics Canada, User Services, Publications Distribution, Ottawa, Ont, Canada K1A OV7. Telephone (613) 992-3151.

Monthly report. Presents estimates of Canadian and provincial egg and poultry production. Price $30.00 per year. ISSN 0708-4897.

3867
Production Engineering
Penton/IPC, 614 Superior Ave W, Cleveland, OH 44113. Order from Penton-/IPC, 1111 Chester Ave, Cleveland, OH 44114. Telephone (216) 696-7000.

Monthly magazine. Discusses production engineering in manufacturing industries. Price $24.00.

3868
Production Handbook, **3rd edition, 1972**
Ronald Press, Div of John Wiley & Sons, Inc, 605 3rd Ave, New York, NY 10158. Telephone (212) 850-6000.

Book. Theory and practice of manufacturing operations. Price $45.95. ISBN 0-471-06651-6.

3871
Production, Shipments and Stocks on Hand of Sawmills East of the Rockies
Statistics Canada, User Services, Publications Distribution, Ottawa, Ont, Canada K1A 0V7. Telephone (613) 992-3151.

Monthly report. Contains data on Canadian sawed lumber by kinds of wood for provinces east of Rockies. Includes number of operating mills. Price $30.00 per year. ISSN 0380-464X.

3872
Production, Shipments and Stocks on Hand of Sawmills in British Columbia
Statistics Canada, User Services, Publications Distribution, Ottawa, Ont, Canada K1A 0V7. Telephone (613) 992-3151.

Monthly report. Provides statistics on British Columbian production, shipment, and stock of sawed lumber by kinds of wood. Notes active mills. Price $30.00 per year. ISSN 0708-3513.

3873
Product Liability
Oceana Publications, Inc, 75 Main St, Dobbs Ferry, NY 10522. Telephone (914) 693-1320.

Loose-leaf service in one binder. Covers product liability regulations on a country-by-country basis. Price $100.00 per binder. ISBN 0-379-20705-2.

3874
Product Liability International
Lloyd's of London Press, Sheepen Pl, Colchester, Essex, England CO3 3LP. Telephone 0206 69222. Telex 987321.

Monthly magazine. Discusses insurance and related legal and political developments. Includes legal case notes. Price $157.00 per year.

3874.01
Product Liability Legislation for Client and Counsel
Federal-State Reports, Inc, 5203 Leesburg Pike, #1201, Falls Church, VA 22041. Telephone (703) 379-0222.

Loose-leaf report, with periodic updates. Provides complete and current information about new product liability laws on state and federal levels. Price $165.00 per year.

3875
Product Marketing
Charleson Publications, 124 E 40th St, New York, NY 10016. Telephone (212) 953-0940.

Monthly magazine. Provides news and industry information for marketing/management executives and retailers. Focuses on cosmetics, toiletries, fragrances, and proprietary drugs. Price $20.00 per year.

3876
Product Safety & Liability Reporter
Bureau of National Affairs, Inc, 1231 25th St NW, Washington, DC 20037. Telephone (202) 452-4200.

Three loose-leaf books plus weekly reports. Act as guide to compliance with Consumer Product Safety Act. Include current reports and reference file, calendar, and index. Price $323.00 per year.

3877
Product Safety News
Institute for Product Safety, Inc, 1410 Duke University Rd, Durham, NC 27701. Telephone (919) 489-2357.

Monthly newsletter. Reviews and abstracts articles in technical, medical, and industrial fields that relate to product liability. Price $90.00 per year.

3878
Products Liability
Matthew Bender & Co, 235 E 45th St, New York, NY 10017. Telephone (212) 661-5050.

Loose-leaf volumes supplemented three times per year. Discuss laws pertaining to product liability, including Consumer Products Safety Act. Price $520.00 for eight volumes; $276.00 for update.

3879
Products Liability Reports
Commerce Clearing House, Inc, 4025 W Peterson Ave, Chicago, IL 60646. Telephone (312) 583-8500.

Two loose-leaf books plus fortnightly reports. Discuss liability rules and court decisions involving product-caused injuries. Charts. Price $260.00 per year.

3880
Products Shipped by Canadian Manufacturers
Statistics Canada, User Services, Publications Distribution, Ottawa, Ont, Canada K1A 0V7. Telephone (613) 992-3151.

Annual report. Offers data on Canadian and provincial shipments of manufactured products. Notes value and quantities. Price $9.6. ISSN 0575-9455.

3881
Product Standards Index
Institute for Product Safety, 1410 Duke University Rd, Durham, NC 27701. Telephone (919) 489-2357.

Book. Offers index to 2000 products grouped into major categories and 5000 selected standards that relate to product safety and performance. Price $29.95.

3882
Professional Accounting in 30 Countries
American Inst of Certified Public Accountants, 1211 Ave of the Americas, New York, NY 10036. Telephone (212) 575-6200.

Book. Discusses and compares accounting and auditing standards, reporting practices, and professional requirements in 30 countries. Price $38.50.

3883
Professional Builder
Cahners Pub Co, Inc, 221 Columbus Ave, Boston, MA 02116. Telephone (617) 536-7780.

Monthly magazine. Covers housing and light construction. Price $30.00 per year.

3884
Professional Corporation Guide
Prentice-Hall, Inc, Englewood Cliffs, NJ 07632. Telephone (201) 592-2000. Telex 13-5423.

Loose-leaf report. Provides information on professional corporations. Considers tax matters, employee benefit plans, and pertinent legislation. Price $183.00 per year.

3885
Professional Corporations and Associations
Matthew Bender & Co, 235 E 45th St, New York, NY 10017. Telephone (212) 661-5050.

Six-volume set of books. Discusses formation and operation of professional corporations and associations. Covers taxation, accounting, pension plans, and insurance. Price $300.00.

3886
Professional Corporations Handbook
Commerce Clearing House, Inc, 4025 W Peterson Ave, Chicago, IL 60646. Telephone (312) 583-8500.

Two loose-leaf books plus monthly reports. Cover federal and state rules applicable to establishment and operation of a professional corporation. Price $180.00 per year.

3887
Professional Engagement Manual
Canadian Inst of Chartered Accountants, 250 Bloor St E, Toronto, Ont, Canada M4W 1G5. Telephone (416) 962-1242.

Book. Covers all aspects of professional engagements for public accounting firms, including audit and accounting engagements and financial statements. Price $65.00.

3888
Professional Furniture Merchant
Gralla Publications, 1515 Broadway, New York, NY 10036. Telephone (212) 869-1300.

Monthly magazine. Presents articles on furniture merchandising and trends. Price $20.00.

3889
Professional Photographic Equipment Directory & Buying Guide, **1976 edition**
PTN Pub Corp, 250 Fulton Ave, Hempstead, NY 11550. Telephone (516) 489-1300.

Annual book. Provides guide to professional photographic equipment and services. Price $10.00.

3890
Professional Standards Review Organization (PSRO) Letter
McGraw-Hill Publications Co, 1221 Ave of the Americas, New York, NY 10020. Telephone (212) 997-1221. Telex TWX 7105814879. WUI 62555.

Semimonthly report. Covers government developments that relate to professional standards review organizations. Price $247.00 per year.

3891
Profile—A Continuing Study of Oil and Gas Programs
Resource Programs, Inc, 521 5th Ave, New York, NY 10175. Telephone (212) 986-7510.

Loose-leaf book. Gives facts about oil and gas drilling programs offered to public. Charts and graphs. Price $400.00.

3892
Profits
Howard University, School of Business and Public Administration, PO Box 748, Washington, DC 20059. Telephone (202) 636-7187.

Monthly periodical. Covers minority business assistance programs in private and public sector and Institute for Minority Business Education news. Price available on request.

3893
Profit Sharing Design Manual
Prentice-Hall, Inc, Englewood Cliffs, NJ 07632. Telephone (201) 592-2000. Telex 13-5423.

Quarterly loose-leaf report. Provides details on profit-sharing, individual retirement, and stock ownership plans. Includes worksheets and accounting forms. Price $114.00 per year.

3894
Progress in Planning
Pergamon Press Inc, Maxwell House, Fairview Park, Elmsford, NY 10523. Telephone (914) 592-7700. Telex 13-7328.
Bimonthly magazine. Presents in-depth research papers on various aspects of planning. Covers interdisciplinary areas such as sociology, economics, environment, transportation, and urban growth. Price $65.00 per year.

3895
Progressive Architecture
Penton/IPC, 614 Superior Ave W, Cleveland, OH 44113. Order from Reinhold Publishing Div, Penton/IPC, 600 Summer St, Stamford, CT 06904. Telephone (203) 348-7531.
Monthly magazine. Covers architectural and interior design. Price $15.00 professional, $30.00 nonprofessional.

3896
Progressive Grocer
Progressive Grocer Pub Co, 708 3rd Ave, New York, NY 10017. Telephone (212) 490-1000.
Monthly publication. Covers news and trends in the grocery business. Price $30.00 per year. ISSN 0033-0787.

3896.01
Progressive Grocer Marketing Guidebook, **1981**
Progressive Grocer Publishing Co, 708 3rd Ave, New York, NY 10017. Telephone (212) 490-1000.
Annual publication. An encyclopedia covering 79 markets for the retail and wholesale food industry. Gives profile of major US chains, wholesalers, and convenience stores. Price $159.00. ISBN 0-911790-20-9.

3896.02
Progressive Grocer Market Scope, **1980**
Progressive Grocer Publishing Co, 708 3rd Ave, New York, NY 10017. Telephone (212) 490-1000.

Annual publication. Contains share-of-market analyses for each of 263 metropolitan areas showing major grocery retailers and wholesalers, percentage of food store sales, number of outlets served by buying offices and county-by-county demographics. Price $105.00. ISBN 0-911790-00-4.

3897
Progress Wales
Development Corp for Wales, Pearl Assurance House, Greyfriars Rd, Cardiff, CF1 3AG, Wales. Telephone (44) (222) 371641. Telex 497190.
Quarterly magazine. Covers industrial and commercial developments in Wales. Price free of charge. ISSN 0019-8854.

3898
Property
Chaunter Publications Ltd, PO Box 17-159, Wellington, New Zealand. Telephone (4) 766-432.
Fortnightly newsletter. Covers the property business in New Zealand for real estate agencies, development companies, and architects. Price $35.00 per year. ISSN 0110-0793.

3899
Property and Liability Insurance Handbook
Dow Jones-Irwin Inc, 1818 Ridge Rd, Homewood, IL 60430. Telephone (312) 798-3100.
Book. Covers all major areas of property and liability insurance business. Price $14.65. ISBN 0-256-00302-5.

3900
Property Investment and Condensed Income Account
Assn of American Railroads, Economics and Finance Dept, American Railroads Bldg, Washington, DC 20036. Telephone (202) 293-4068.
Annual report. Provides statistical data on investment in transportation property. Notes net railway operating income, rate of return, and net income of individual Class I railroads. Price $5.00 per year, including Operating Traffic Statistics, Railroad Revenues, Expenses and Income, and Statistics of Railroads of Class I in the United States.

3901
Property Journal
British Property Federation, 35 Catherine Pl, London, England SW1E 6DY. Telephone (44) (01) 8280111.

Quarterly magazine. Reports on British property law. Includes articles on housing, construction, and property taxes. Price £2.50 per year. ISSN 0033-1309.

3902
Property Taxes
Prentice-Hall, Inc, Englewood Cliffs, NJ 07632. Telephone (201) 592-2000. Telex 13-5423.
Weekly loose-leaf service. Contains full text of all state property taxes, plus decisions, interpretations, and rulings. Price $612.00 per year.

3903
Proposed Foreign Aid Program, Summary Presentation to Congress
US Agency for International Development, Washington, DC 20523. Order from National Technical Information Services, 3285 Port Royal Rd, Springfield, VA 22161. Telephone (703) 557-4650.
Publication. Summarizes US Agency for International Development's proposed foreign aid program, as presented to Congress. Prices available on request.

3904
Protection
Alan Osborne & Assocs, Ltd, Unit 5, Seager Bldgs, Brookmill Rd, London, England SE8. Telephone (44) (01) 692-7991.
Monthly magazine. Focuses on occupational safety. Features articles on construction safety, eye protection, hearing conservation, and protective clothing. Price $29.00.

3906
Provincial Bank of Canada, Economic Review
Provincial Bank of Canada, 221 James St, Montreal, Que, Canada H2Y 1M7. Telephone (514) 281-3471.
Bimonthly report. Focuses on one Canadian economic or financial topic, per issue, such as balance of payments, agriculture, or housing. Free of charge. ISSN 0319-8685.

3908
Provincial Results (Underwriting)
Stone and Cox Ltd, 100 Simcoe St, 2nd Floor, Toronto, Ont, Canada M5H 3G2. Telephone (416) 593-1310.
Annual book. Contains charts for each Canadian province on direct insurance premiums written and ratio of loss incurred for each class of insurance. Price $40.00 per year. ISBN 0-919468-35-7.

3909
Provincial Taxation Services
Richard De Boo Ltd, 70 Richmond St, Toronto, Ont, Canada M5C 2M8. Telephone (416) 367-0714.

Five volume loose-leaf service. Provides information on Canadian provincial tax statutes and regulations. Includes material on federal-provincial fiscal agreements, income, corporate and other taxes. Revised and supplemental pages issued regularly. Price $89.00 per year for each volume.

3910
Provincial Tax Reports
CCH Canadian Ltd, 6 Garamond Ct, Don Mills, Ont, Canada M3C 1Z5. Telephone (416) 429-2992.

Eight loose-leaf books plus monthly updates. Cover every aspect of taxation for each Canadian province. Price $625.00 for eight volumes.

3911
PR Planner—Europe
Media Information Ltd, Hale House, Green Lanes, London, England N13 5TP. Telephone (44) (01) 882-0155.

Loose-leaf directory updated every other month. Contains information about newspapers and journals of 14 European countries. Price £103.00 per year.

3912
PR Planner—UK
Media Information Ltd, Hale House, Green Lanes, London, England N13 5TP. Telephone (44) (01) 882-0155.

Loose-leaf directory updated every three and six weeks. Provides information about magazines, newspapers, and journals in Great Britain. Price £62.00.

3913
PR Reporter
PR Pub Co, Inc, PO Box 600, Exeter, NH 03833. Telephone (603) 778-0514.

Weekly newsletter. Discusses public relations news and research. Reviews new ideas, pertinent articles, and books. Price $100.00 per year.

3914
PSM Retail Manual
Harcourt Brace Jovanovich Publications, 757 3rd Ave, New York, NY 10017. Order from Harcourt Brace Jovanovich Publications, 1 E 1st St, Duluth, MN 55802. Telephone (218) 727-8511.

Annual book. Provides details on how to plan, open, and operate a pet shop. Price $24.95.

3915
PTS Abstract Service
Predicasts, Inc, 200 University Circle Research Ctr, 11001 Cedar Ave, Cleveland, OH 44106. Telephone (216) 795-3000.

Computerized information service with weekly and monthly updates. Digests articles from international journals on new products, foreign trade, environment, manufacturing production, and other business information. Price available on request.

3916
PTS Index Services
Predicasts, Inc, 200 University Circle Research Ctr, 11001 Cedar Ave, Cleveland, OH 44106. Telephone (216) 795-3000.

Computerized information service with weekly and monthly updates. Contains brief comments on articles relevent to business research from over 2500 international newspapers, trade journals, government plans, bank letters, and reports. Covers products, services, industries throughout the world. Price available on request.

3917
PTS Federal Index—File 48
Predicasts, Inc, 200 University Circle Research Ctr, 11001 Cedar Ave, Cleveland, OH 44106. Telephone (216) 795-3000.

Computerized information service updated monthly. Provides brief comments on proposed federal legislation, court decisions, and other government activity from Federal Register, Congressional Record, Commerce Business Daily, Washington Post, and presidential documents. Price available on request.

3919
PTS Statistical Services
Predicasts, Inc, 200 University Circle Research Ctr, 11001 Cedar Ave, Cleveland, OH 44106. Telephone (216) 795-3000.

Computerized information service with monthly updates and quarterly revisions. Contains historical and projected data on demography, economics, industries, and product markets for US and rest of world. Price available on request.

3920
Pubblicita in Italia (Advertising in Italy)
Advertising Trade Publications, Inc, 10 E 39th St, New York, NY 10016. Order from Art Direction Book Co, 10 E 39th St, New York, NY 10016. Telephone (212) 889-6500.

Annual book. Presents collection of Italian advertising art. Includes posters, editorial design, brochures, calendars, cinematography, and television. Price $49.50.

3920.01
Public Administration and Development
John Wiley & Sons Inc, 605 3rd Ave, New York, NY 10158. Order from John Wiley & Sons, Inc, 1 Wiley Dr, Somerset, NJ 08773. Telephone (201) 469-4400. Telex 833 434. Cable JON WILE SMOT.

Quarterly journal. Reports, reviews, and assesses public administration practices in developing Third World countries. Focuses on practices with widespread application. Contains book and article reviews. Price $58.75 per year.

3921
Public Affairs Information Service Bulletin
Public Affairs Information Service, Inc, 11 W 40th St, New York, NY 10018.

Semimonthly bulletin. Contains list of books, publications, and articles relating to business, economic and social conditions, public administration, and international relations. Price $180.00 per year. ISSN 0033-3409.

3921.01
Public Affairs Information Service Foreign Language Index
Public Affairs Information Service, Inc, 11 W 40th St, New York, NY 10018.

Quarterly publication. Contains list of books, publications, and articles relating to business, economic and social conditions, public administration, and international relations. Covers material published in French, German, Italian, Portuguese, and Spanish. Price $175.00 per year. ISSN 0048 5810.

3922
Public Affairs Report
Chamber of Commerce of the US, 1615 H St, NW, Washington, DC 20062. Telephone (202) 659-6231.

Monthly newsletter. Covers public affairs activities for businesses, chambers of commerce, and trade and professional associations. Available to members only.

3923
Publications by the Faculty of the Harvard Business School
Harvard University, Graduate School of Business Administration, Division of Reseacrh, Soldiers Field, Boston, MA 02163. Telephone (617) 495-6852.

Annual bibliography. Lists books and articles published by Harvard Business School faculty in previous year. Price free of charge.

3923.01
Public Expenditure White Papers
Her Majesty's Stationery Office, PO Box 569, London, England SE1 9NH. Telephone (44) (01) 928-1321.

Annual book. Presents British Government's expenditure plans. Shows corresponding figures for the last five years. Price £6.25.

3924
Public Finance Quarterly
Sage Publications, Inc, 275 S Beverly Dr, Beverly Hills, CA 90212. Telephone (213) 274-8003.

Quarterly journal. Deals with raising of public revenues and other aspects of public sector of economy. Price $22.00 per year.

3925
Publicist
Public Relations Aids, Inc, 221 Park Ave S, New York, NY 10003. Telephone (212) 673-6363.

Bimonthly publication. Gives detailed case histories of national publicity campaigns and studies of public relations techniques. Is aimed at public relations professionals. Price $15.00 per year.

3926
Public Periodic Releases
US Federal Reserve System, Board of Governors, Washington, DC 20551. Order from Publication Services, Div of Administrative Services, Board of Governors of the Federal Reserve System, Washington, DC 20551. Telephone (202) 452-3245.

Weekly, semimonthly, and monthly releases. Include the following Federal Reserve bulletins: Aggregate Reserves and Member Bank Deposits; Applications and Reports Received or Acted on and Assets and Liabilities of All Commercial Banks in the US. Changes in State Member Banks; Commercial and Industrial Loans Outstanding by Industry; Deposits, Reserves, andBorrowingsofMemberBanks.

3927
Public Personnel Administration— Labor-Management Relations
Prentice-Hall, Inc, Englewood Cliffs, NJ 07632. Telephone (201) 592-2000. Telex 13-5423.

Biweekly loose-leaf report. Discusses collective bargaining with public employees. Includes annotated public employment relations laws and regulations. Price $327.00 per year.

3928
Public Personnel Administration— Policies and Practices for Personnel
Prentice-Hall, Inc, Englewood Cliffs, NJ 07632. Telephone (201) 592-2000. Telex 13-5423.

Biweekly loose-leaf report. Deals with public personnel problems and trends, including wages, hours, and employee benefits. Price $285.00 per year.

3929
Public Personnel Management
International Personnel Management Assn, 1313 E 60th St, Chicago, IL 60637. Telephone (312) 647-2570.

Bimonthly report. Covers a wide range of topics in the public personnel management field. Price $15.00 per year. ISSN 0091-0260.

3930
Public Productivity Review
National Center for Public Productivity, John Jay College of Criminal Justice, 445 W 59th St, New York, NY 10019. Telephone (212) 489-3552.

Quarterly report plus special issues. Contains articles on efficiency and effectiveness, management, and organization in such areas as law enforcement, education, and state and local governments. Price $15.00 per year.

3931
Public Relations Journal
Public Relations Society of America, 845 3rd Ave, New York, NY 10022. Telephone (212) 826-1750.

Monthly report. Covers developments in public relations and related areas. Price $20.00 per year. ISSN 0033-3670.

3932
Public Relations News
Denny Griswold, 127 E 80th St, New York, NY 10021. Telephone (212) 879-7090.

Weekly loose-leaf reports. Discuss new techniques, literature, and personnel and on account changes in public relations field. Provide case studies of successful public relations programs. Price $127.75 per year, $157.75 foreign.

3933
Public Relations Quarterly
Newsletter Clearinghouse, 44 W Market St, Rhinebeck, NY 12572. Telephone (914) 876-2081.

Quarterly magazine. Reviews professional public relations and affairs. Includes column on social sciences. Price $12.00.

3934
Public Relations Register
Public Relations Society of America, Inc, 845 3rd Ave, New York, NY 10022. Telephone (212) 826-1750.

Annual book. Directory of society members. Price $60.00.

3935
Public Sector
Corpus Information Services, Ltd, 1450 Don Mills Rd, Don Mills, Ont, Canada M3B 2X7. Telephone (416) 445-7101. Telex 06-966612.

Weekly newsletter. Covers all activities of Canadian federal, provincial, and territorial governments. Price $247.00 (Canadian) per year.

3936
Public Service Staff Relations Board Reports
Supply and Services Canada, Publishing Ctr, Printing and Publishing, Ottawa, Ont, Canada K1A 0S9. Telephone (613) 238-1601.

Loose-leaf volume with update service. Reports on Canadian Public Service Staff Relations Board. Bilingual. Price $36.00.

3937

Public Transit Report

Business Publishers, Inc, PO Box 1067, Silver Spring, MD 20910. Telephone (301) 587-6300.

Biweekly report. Carries mass transportation news. Price $115.00 per year.

3938

Publishers and Distributors of the United States

RR Bowker Co, 1180 Avenue of the Americas, New York, NY 10036. Order from RR Bowker Co, PO Box 1807, Ann Arbor, MI 48106. Telephone (212) 764-5100.

Annual directory. Lists editorial and ordering addresses for some 14,000 US publishers and distributors. ISBN index. Price $8.95. ISBN 0-8352-1299-8. ISSN 0000-0620.

3940

Publishers' Trade List Annual

R R Bowker Co, 1180 Ave of the Americas, New York, NY 10036. Order from R R Bowker Co, PO Box 1807, Ann Arbor, MI 48106. Telephone (212) 764-5100.

Six-volume annual directory. Contains trade lists of more than 1700 publishers. Price $59.00 for six volumes. ISBN 0-8352-1289-0. ISSN 0079-7855.

3941

Publishers Weekly

R R Bowker Co, 1180 Ave of the Americas, New York, NY 10036. Order from R R Bowker Co, PO Box 13746, Philadelphia, PA 19101. Telephone (212) 764-5100.

Weekly magazine. Includes articles, editorials, forecasts, and book lists on every aspect of book publishing and selling. Price $38.00 per year. ISSN 0000-0019.

3942

Publishing and Bookselling, **5th edition**

Frank A Mumby and Ian Norrie, R R Bowker Co, 1180 Ave of the Americas, New York, NY 10036. Order from R R Bowker, Co, PO Box 1807, Ann Arbor, MI 48106. Telephone (212) 764-5100.

Book. Traces 2000 years of publishing and bookselling in Great Britain, especially 1870 to 1970. Discusses contemporary issues as well. Price $37.50. ISBN 0-224-00827-7.

3943

Puerto Rico Business Review

Government Development Bank for Puerto Rico, Box 42001, San Juan, PR 00940. Telephone (809) 726-2525.

Monthly journal. Reviews economic, financial, and business developments in Puerto Rico. Charts and tables. Free of charge.

3943.01

Puerto Rico: Official Industrial & Trade Directory, **1980**

Manufacturers' News, Inc, 3 E Huron St, Chicago, Il 60611. Telephone (312) 337-1084.

Annual book. Lists 5000 industrial firms in Puerto Rico. Includes companies involved in trade. Price $60.00.

3944

Puerto Rico Tax Reports

Commerce Clearing House, Inc, 4025 W Peterson Ave, Chicago, IL 60646. Telephone (312) 583-8500.

Loose-leaf book and monthly reports. Covers new developments in Puerto Rico's taxes. Price $205.00 per year.

3945

Pulp & Paper

Miller Freeman Publications, 500 Howard St, San Francisco, CA 94105. Telephone (415) 397-1881.

Monthly report. Covers developments and gives statistics on the US and Canadian pulp and paper industry. Price $30.00 per year.

3946

Pulp & Paper Canada

Southam Communications Ltd, 1450 Don Mills Rd, Don Mills, Ont, Canada M3B 2X7. Telephone (416) 445-6641. Telex 06-9666612.

Monthly magazine. Features news of Canadian pulp and paper industry. Price $31.00 per year.

3947

Pulp and Paper Quarterly Statistics

Organization for Economic Cooperation and Development, Publications Ctr, 1750 Pennsylvania Ave, NW, Washington, DC 20006. Telephone (202) 724-1857.

Quarterly report. Presents statistics on pulp, paperboard, and paper production, consumption, and trade. Price $16.70. ISSN 0335-377X.

3948

Pulp, Paper, and Board

US Dept of Commerce, Bureau of the Census, Washington, DC 20233. Telephone (202) 449-1600.

Monthly report and annual summary. Presents data on pulp, paper, and board production, consumption, and inventories. Includes information on fibrous materials used in pulp, paper, and board manufacture, and on pulp imports from Canada. Price $4.10 per year.

3948.01

Purchase Prices of the Means of Production

European Community Information Service, 2100 M St, NW, Suite 707, Washington DC 20037. Telephone (202) 862-9500. Telex 248455.

Quarterly bulletin. Reports purchase prices of means of production in European Economic Community (Common Market) countries. Price $31.50.

3949

Purchasing

Cahners Pub Co, Inc, 221 Columbus Ave, Boston, MA 02116. Telephone (617) 536-7780.

Semimonthly magazine. Contains articles on news and trends in industrial purchasing. Price available on request.

3950

Purchasing & Supply

Inst of Purchasing & Supply, York House, Westminster Bridge Rd, London, England SE1 7UT. Telephone (44) (01) 928-1851.

Monthly magazine. Reports British industry and government purchasing news, including procurement price monitor. Price £15.50 per year. ISSN 0309-7242.

3951

Purchasing Executive's Bulletin

Bureau of Business Practice, 24 Rope Ferry Rd, Waterford, CT 06386. Telephone (203) 442-4365.

Semimonthly newsletter covering latest developments in the purchasing field. Price $30.00 per year.

3952

Purchasing Handbook, **1973**

McGraw-Hill Book Co, Hightstown-Princeton Rd, Hightstown, NJ 08520. Telephone (609) 448-1700. Telex 843449.

Book. Covers theory and practice of materials purchasing and management. Price $34.50. ISBN 0-07-001068-4.

3953
Purchasing Managers Report on Business
National Assn of Purchasing Management, Publication Sales Office, 49 Sheridan Ave, Albany, NY 12210. Telephone (212) 285-2550.

Monthly report. Discusses business trends, especially purchasing developments. Notes inventories of purchased materials and commodity supplies and prices. Price $50.00 per year members, $100.00 per year, nonmember.

3954
Purchasing People in Major Corporations
National Minority Business Campaign, 1201 12th Ave N, Minneapolis, MN 55411. Telephone (612) 377-2402.

Annual booklet for minority businessmen. Lists 750 US corporations and provides name of minority vendor program coordinator. Price $4.00.

3955
Purchasing World
Technical Publishing Co, 1301 S Grove Ave, Barrington, IL 60010. Telephone (312) 381-1840.

Monthly magazine. Discusses trends in markets, commodities, prices, and products for industrial purchasing executive. Offers metalworking and chemical process industries editions. Price $30.00 per year.

3956
Quality Control and Applied Statistics
Executive Sciences Inst, Inc, PO Drawer M, Whippany, NJ 07981. Telephone (201) 887-1233.

Monthly digest service. Covers international statistical process control, quality control, managerial applications, mathematical statistics, and probability theory. Includes tables, graphs, and annual indexes by author and subject. Price $108.00 per year.

3958
Quarterly Bulletin of Port Statistics
Her Majesty's Stationery Office, PO Box 569, London, England SE1 9NH. Order from National Ports Council, 1-19 New Oxford St, London, England WC1A 1DZ. Telephone (44) (01) 928 1321.

Quarterly report. Supplies statistical data on British ports. Price £20.00 per year.

3959
Quarterly Bulletin of Statistics for Asia and the Pacific
United Nations Publications, Room A-3315, New York, NY 10017. Telephone (212) 754-8302.

Quarterly report. Provides statistics on Asia and Pacific areas. Covers population, manpower, production, transportation, trade, prices, wages, and finance. Price available on request.

3960
Quarterly Canadian Forecast
Conference Board in Canada, Suite 100, 25 McArthur Rd, Ottawa, Ont, Canada K1L 6R3. Telephone (613) 746-1261.

Quarterly report. Presents technical material on Canadian business outlook for four to six quarters into future. Is intended for use by professional economic personnel. Price available on request.

3961
Quarterly Canadian Forecast (QCF) Historical Supplement
Conference Board in Canada, Suite 100, 25 McArthur Rd, Ottawa, Ont, Canada K1L 6R3. Telephone (613) 746-1261.

Annual report. Furnishes historical data back to early 1950s. Provides same indicators as Quarterly Canadian Forecast. Price available on request.

3962
Economic Report
Security Pacific National Bank, PO Box 2097, Terminal Annex, Los Angeles, CA 90051. Telephone (213) 613-5373

Quarterly report. Focuses on US, California, and international economic outlook. Price free of charge.

3962.01
Quarterly Economic Reviews Service
Economist Intelligence Unit Ltd, Spencer House, 27 St James's Pl, London, England SW1A 1NT. Order from Economist Intelligence Unit Ltd, 75 Rockefeller Plz, New York, NY 10019. Telephone (212) 541-5730. Telex 148393.

Series of 76 quarterly reports. Covers political, economic, and business conditions in over 160 countries. Includes forecasts. Price $4358.00 per year, for entire series.

3962.02
Quarterly Energy Reviews
Economist Intelligence Unit Ltd, Spencer House, 27 St James's Pl, London England SW1A 1NT Order from Economist Intelligence Unit Ltd, 75 Rockefeller Plz, New York, NY 10019. Telephone (212) 541-5730. Telex 148393.

Series of seven regional reviews, published quarterly. Covers developments in energy production, consumption, prices, and trade. Price $851.00 per year.

3963
Quarterly Estimates of the Canadian Balance of International Payments
Statistics Canada, User Services, Publications Distribution, Ottawa, Ont, Canada K1A 0V7. Telephone (613) 992-3151.

Quarterly report. Summarizes capital transactions between Canada and other countries. Examines Canada's reserve position for two preceding years and current year. Price $28.80 per year. ISSN 0410-5788.

3963.01
Quarterly Estimates of Population for Canada and the Provinces
Statistics Canada, User Services, Publications Distribution, Ottawa, Ont, Canada K1A 0V7. Telephone (613) 992-3151.

Quarterly report. Estimates the Canadian and provincial population. Price $12.00 per year.

3964
Quarterly Journal of Economics
John Wiley and Sons, Inc, 605 3rd Ave, New York, NY 10158. Telephone (212) 850-6515. Telex 12-7063.

Quarterly magazine. Covers new developments in science of economics, including economic theory, methodology, and current policy issues. Price $20.00.

3965
Quarterly National Accounts
Organization for Economic Cooperation and Development, Publications Ctr, 1750 Pennsylvania Ave, NW, Washington, DC 20006. Telephone (202) 724-1857.

Quarterly report. Covers national finance of the US and nine other OECD countries. Price $16.80.

3966
Quarterly Oil Statistics
Organization for Economic Cooperation and Development, Publications Ctr, 1750 Pennsylvania Ave, NW, Washington, DC 20006. Telephone (202) 724-1857.

Quarterly report. Provides oil production, trade, refinery intake and output, consumption, and stock data. Price $60.45.

3967
Quarterly Predictions of National Income & Expenditure
New Zealand Inst of Economic Research, Box 3479, Wellington, New Zealand. Telephone (64) (4) 721880.

Quarterly journal. Offers predictions on New Zealand's national income and expenditure. Price $12.50 per copy.

3968
Quarterly Provincial Forecast
Conference Board in Canada, Suite 100, 25 McArthur Rd, Ottawa, Ont, Canada K1L 6R3. Telephone (613) 746-1261.

Quarterly booklet. Analyzes economic trends in each Canadian province. Provides short-term projections of key provincial economic indicators. Price available on request.

3971
Quarterly Review of Marketing
Inst of Marketing, Moor Hall, Cookham, Maidenhead, Berkshire, England SL6 9QH. Telephone (44) (062 85) 24922.

Quarterly report on marketing, with special emphasis on Great Britain. Price £ 31.00 per year. ISSN 0307-7667.

3971.01
Quarterly Review of the Rural Economy
Australian Government Publishing Service, Publishing Branch, PO Box 84, Canberra, ACT 2600, Australia. Telephone (062) 95 4411. Telex AA62013.

Quarterly report. Reviews Australia's agricultural economy. Price available on request.

3974
Quarterly Summary of Australian Statistics, **June 1976, last edition**
Australian Bureau of Statistics, Box 17 GPO, Canberra, ACT 2600, Australia. Order from Australian Government Pub Service, PO Box 84, Canberra, ACT 2600, Australia. Telephone (61) (062) 527911.

Quarterly summary. Offers vital statistics on Australia's population, employment, building, transport, economy, and other areas. Free of charge.

3975
Quarterly Summary of Business Statistics, New York State
New York Dept of Commerce, 99 Washington Ave, Albany, NY 12245. Telephone (518) 474-8670.

Quarterly report. Measures performance of New York State's economy, and various areas within state, through use of statistical tables. Free of charge.

3976
Quarterly Summary of Pacific Northwest Industries
Seattle First National Bank, 1001 4th Ave, PO Box 3586, Seattle, WA 98124. Telephone (206) 583-3200.

Quarterly report. Provides information on Pacific Northwest industrial developments and economic conditions. Highlights specific industries such as fishing, aerospace, and agriculture. Free of charge.

3977
Quarterly Survey of Business Opinion
New Zealand Inst of Economic Research, Box 3479, Wellington, New Zealand. Telephone (64) (4) 721880.

Quarterly report. Surveys business opinion in New Zealand. Price $7.50 per copy.

3978
Quarterly Trade Statistics of the United Kingdom
Her Majesty's Stationery Office, PO Box 569, London, England SE1 9NH. Telephone (44) (01) 928 1321.

Quarterly report. Contains statistics on British trade activity. Price available on request.

3979
Quebec Corporation Manual
Richard De Boo Ltd, 70 Richmond St, Toronto, Ont, Canada M5C 2M8. Telephone (416) 367-0714.

Three loose-leaf binders. Contain statutes and regulations affecting corporations in Quebec, Canada. Include material on private corporations and mining companies. Price $125.00.

3980
Queen's Regulations and Orders for the Canadian Forces
Supply and Services Canada, Publishing Ctr, Printing and Publishing, Ottawa, Ont, Canada K1A 0S9. Telephone (613) 238-1601.

Loose-leaf report with update service. Consists of regulations and orders for Canadian forces. Price $18.00.

3981
Quick Frozen Foods
Harcourt Brace Jovanovich Publications, 757 3rd Ave, New York, NY 10017. Order from Harcourt Brace Jovanovich Publications, 1 E 1st St, Duluth, MN 55802. Telephone (218) 727-8511.

Monthly magazine. Reports on frozen foods industry. Notes equipment, packaging, and distribution. Price $15.00 per year.

3982
Quick Frozen Foods Directory of Frozen Food Processors
Harcourt Brace Jovanovich Publications, 757 3rd Ave, New York, NY 10017. Order from Harcourt Brace Jovanovich Publications, 1 E 1st St, Duluth, MN 55802. Telephone (218) 727-8511.

Annual directory. Supplies roster of frozen foods processors and products. Includes material on refrigerated warehouses, refrigerated transportation lines, and freezing equipment. Price $30.00.

3983
Race Relations & Industry
OD Parke Gibson International, Inc, 475 5th Ave, New York, NY 10017. Telephone (212) 889-5557.

Monthly newsletter. Discusses equal opportunity programs and minority group problems. Notes conditions in government and military. Race Relations and the Law, a newsletter, is published as a supplement. Price $100.00 per year, including supplements. ISSN 0033-7315.

3984
Radiation Report
Trends Pub, Inc, 233 National Press Bldg, Washington, DC 20045. Telephone (202) 393-0031.

Bimonthly report. Discusses radiation applications and safety topics. Indicates research articles and book on radiation. Price $120.00 per year.

3985
Radio Aids to Marine Navigation/Pacific
Supply and Services Canada, Publishing Ctr, Printing and Publishing, Ottawa, Ont, Canada K1A 0S9. Telephone (613) 238-1601.

Quarterly report. Covers marine navigation radio aids for Pacific. Price $2.50 per year.

3986
Radio & Electric Retailing
Turret Press Ltd, 4 Local Board Rd, Watford, Herts, England WD1 2JS. Order from Trade Papers Ltd, 4 Local Board Rd, Watford, Herts, England WD1 2JS. Telephone (0923) 46199.

Monthly magazine. Offers news on retailing of radio and electric products. Price $41.00 per year.

3987
Radio Equipment List
Supply and Services Canada, Publishing Ctr, Printing and Publishing, Ottawa, Ont, Canada K1A 0S9. Telephone (613) 238-1601.

Loose-leaf report with update service. Lists radio equipment. Bilingual. Price $6.00; updates $4.00.

3989
Ragan Report
Lawrence Ragan Communications, Inc, 407 S Dearborn St, Chicago, IL 60605. Telephone (312) 922-8245.

Weekly report. Surveys ideas and methods in organizational communications. Includes communications programs, editorial skills, writing, photography, typography, and design. Price $79.00 per year.

3989.01
Rail News Update
Assn of American Railroads, Economics and Finance Dept, American Railroads Bldg, Washington, DC 20036. Order from Assn of American Railroads, Office of Information and Public Affairs, American Railroads Bldg, Washington, DC 20036. Telephone (202) 293-4200.

Biweekly newsletter. Reports on news and issues affecting railroads. Price free of charge.

3990
Railroad Mileage by States
Assn of American Railroads, Economics and Finance Dept, American Railroads Bldg, Washington, DC 20036. Telephone (202) 293-4063.

Triennial report. Summarizes mileage operated by individual railroads in each state and in District of Columbia. Free of charge.

3990.01
Railroad Research Bulletin
Railroad Research Information Service, Transportation Research Board, National Academy of Sciences, 2101 Constitution Ave, NW, Washington, DC 20418. Telephone (202) 389-6611. Telex 710-822-9589.

Semiannual report. Contains new references to railroad research projects. Includes information on equipment, economics, and government policy. Price $40.00 per year.

3991
Railroad Retirement Board Annual Report
US Railroad Retirement Board, 844 Rush St, Chicago, IL 60611. Order from Superintendent of Documents, US Government Printing Office, Washington, DC 20402. Telephone (202) 783-3238.

Annual book. Reports on US Railroad Retirement Board operations. Summarizes retirement-survivor and unemployment-sickness benefit operations, legislation and legal rulings. Tables. Price $1.55.

3992
Railroad Retirement Board Quarterly Review
US Railroad Retirement Board, 844 Rush St, Chicago, IL 60611. Telephone (312) 751-4500.

Quarterly report. Analyzes retirement-survivor and unemployment-sickness benefit operations, legislation and legal rulings. Notes Railroad Retirement Board activities. Tables. Price single copies free.

3993
Railroad Revenues, Expenses and Income
Assn of American Railroads, Economics and Finance Dept, American Railroads Bldg, Washington, DC 20036. Telephone (202) 293-4068.

Quarterly report. Tabulates revenues, expenses, and net railway operating income of individual Class I railroad. Summarizes income account of all Class I railroads combined. Price $5.00 per year including Operating, Traffic Statistics, Property Investment, Condensed Income Account and Statistics of Railroads of Class I in the United States.

3994
Railway Accidents
Her Majesty's Stationery Office, PO Box 569, London, England SE1 9NH. Telephone (44) (01) 928 1321.

Annual report. Covers British railway accidents. Price £3.55 per year.

3995
Railway Age
Simmons-Boardman Pub Corp, 350 Broadway, New York, NY 10013. Telephone (212) 966-7700.

Fortnightly magazine. Reports on issues of importance to railway industry in US. Price $9.00 per year.

3996
Railway Carloadings
Statistics Canada, User Services, Publications Distribution, Ottawa, Ont, Canada K1A 0V7. Telephone (613) 992-3151.

Monthly magazine. Reports on cars and tons of revenue freight loaded in Canada by commodity for Class 1 and 2 railways. Gives regional information. Price $18.00 per year. ISSN 0380-6308.

3997
Railway Freight Traffic
Statistics Canada, User Services, Publications Distribution, Ottawa, Ont, Canada K1A 0V7. Telephone (613) 992-3151.

Quarterly report. Supplies Canadian revenue commodity data in tons for Class 1 and 2 railways. Indicates origin; terminations; receipts from, and deliveries to US connections. Includes provincial statistics. Price $12.00 per year. ISSN 0317-3445.

3998
Railway Operating Statistics
Statistics Canada, User Services, Publications Distribution, Ottawa, Ont, Canada K1A 0V7. Telephone (613) 992-3151.

Monthly report. Provides statistical review of Canadian railway finances, traffic, and operations for six major railways. Contains current and cumulative data. Price $30.00 per year. ISSN 0318-5964.

3999

Railway Transport Service Bulletin

Statistics Canada, User Services, Publications Distribution, Ottawa, Ont, Canada K1A 0V7. Telephone (613) 992-3151.

Monthly service. Presents early release of Canadian railway statistics. Covers finances, operations, traffic, and carloadings. Price $18.00 per year. ISSN 0700-2211.

3999.01

R & D Abstracts

Her Majesty's Stationery Office, PO Box 569, London, England SE1 9NH. Telephone (44) (01) 928-1321.

Semimonthly report. Contains abstracts of British and foreign research and development reports. Covers most fields of science and technology. Price £6.00 each.

3999.02

R & D Management Digest

Lomond Publications, Inc. PO Box 56, Mt. Airy, MD 21771. Telephone (301) 829-1496.

Monthly publication. Provides summary of new literature, events, and opportunities for research and development executives. Contains news, education and training, and literature sections. Includes science policy issues, announcements of professional meetings, and interdisciplinary reports. Price $28.00 per year.

3999.03

R & D (Research and Development) Management

Basil Blackwell Publisher, 108 Cowley Rd, Oxford, England 0X4 1JF. Telephone (44) (STD 0865) 722146.

Quarterly magazine. Covers research on resource management, including both scientist and administrator. Price $79.50 per year. ISSN 0033-6807.

4000

Rand McNally Commercial Atlas & Marketing Guide

Rand McNally & Co, 8255 N Central Park, Skokie, IL 60076. Telephone (312) 673-9100.

Annual book. Provides geographic and economic information for each state, county, and zip code area within US. Maps and charts. Price $135.00 per copy.

4001

Rand McNally International Bankers Directory

Rand McNally & Co, PO Box 7600, Chicago, IL 60680. Telephone (312) 673-9100.

Semiannual directory with updates. Describes US and some foreign banks. Price available on request.

4002

Random Lengths

Random Lengths Publications, Inc, Box 867, Eugene, OR 97440. Telephone (503) 686-9925.

Weekly newsletter. Reports on lumber and plywood, including prices and marketing. Price $110.00.

4002.01

Random Lengths Export

Random Lengths Publications, Inc, Box 867, Eugene, OR 97440. Telephone (503) 686-9925.

Biweekly newsletter. Reports on overseas markets for North American forest products. Price $60.00 per year, $75.00 overseas.

4003

Random Lengths Yearbook

Random Lengths Publications, Inc, Box 867, Eugene, OR 97440. Telephone (503) 686-9925.

Annual book. Contains charts and graphs on lumber and related products, with prices, seasonal trends, yearly market summaries, production statistics, and export volumes. Price $18.50 per year.

4004

Rates and Rateable Values in England and Wales

Her Majesty's Stationery Office, PO Box 569, London, England SE1 9NH. Telephone (44) (01) 928 1321.

Annual report. Offers information on rates and rateable values in England and Wales. Price £1.50 per year.

4005

Rates and Rateable Values in Scotland

Her Majesty's Stationery Office, PO Box 569, London, England SE1 9NH. Telephone (44) (01) 928 1321.

Annual publication. Presents data on rates and rateable values in Scotland. Price £1.00 per year.

4006

Rate Service Newsletter

Ebasco Services Inc, 2 Rector St, New York, NY 10006. Telephone (212) 785-2200.

Monthly newsletter. Covers topics pertaining to utility rates. Includes summary of increases and decreases for gas and electric utilities. Price $50.00 per year.

4007

Ratio Index Services

Standard & Poor's Corp, 25 Broadway, New York, NY 10004. Telephone (212) 248-2525.

Weekly, monthly, and quarterly reports. Provide statistical reports on Standard & Poor's indexes, including Industry Group Indexes and Relative Strength, Industry Group Market Values, and Market Value of Component Stocks in "500" Indexes. Price available on request.

4009

Readers' Guide to Periodical Literature

H W Wilson, Co, 950 University Ave, Bronx, NY 10452. Telephone (212) 588-8400.

Semimonthly index with quarterly and bound annual cumulations. Provides author and subject index to 180 leading general interest periodicals. Price $62.00 per year US and Canada, $75.00 foreign.

4010

Real Estate Appraisal Terminology, **2nd edition**

Ballinger Pub Co, 17 Dunster St, Harvard Square, Cambridge, MA 02138. Telephone (617) 492-0670.

Book. Defines real estate terms and provides information useful in the real estate business. Price $15.50. ISBN 0-88410-597-0.

4011

Real Estate Appraiser and Analyst

Society of Real Estate Appraisers, 645 N Michigan Ave, Chicago, IL 60611. Telephone (312) 346-7422.

Bimonthly journal. Features articles on real estate appraisal. Focuses on both theory and practice. Price $25.00 per year.

4012

Real Estate Financing Desk Book, **3rd edition**

Inst for Business Planning, Inc, IBP Plz, Dept 7102-81, Englewood Cliffs, NJ 07632. Telephone (201) 592-2040.

Book. Covers real estate financing. Lists money lenders and advises on financing different kinds of property. Includes glossary of real estate financing terms. Price $29.95. ISBN 0-87624-493-2.

4013
Real Estate Forum
Real Estate Forum, Inc, 30 E 42 St, New York, NY 10017. Telephone (212) MU 2-6987.

Monthly magazine. Covers national and international real estate industry. Price $35.00 per year.

4014
Real Estate "Insider"
ATCOM, Inc, Atcom Bldg, 2315 Broadway, New York, NY 10024. Telephone (212) 873-3760.

Weekly newsletter. Carries material on real estate industry. Price $57.00 per year.

4015
Real Estate Investing Letter
HBJ Newsletter, Inc, 757 Thrid Ave, New York, NY 10017. Telephone (212) 888-3335.

Monthly newsletter. Covers real estate investments, including tax stategies, depreciation, and real estate syndication. Price $72.00 per year.

4018
Real Estate Investment Trust (REIT) Fact Book
National Assn of Real Estate Investment Trusts, Inc, 1101 17th St, NW, Washington, DC 20036. Telephone (202) 785-8717.

Book. Offers facts about real estate investment trust industry, including lending procedures and liability management. Tables. Price $5.00.

4019
Real Estate Investment Trust (REIT) Industry Statistics
National Assn of Real Estate Investment Trusts, Inc, 1101 17th St, NW, Washington, DC 20036. Telephone (202) 785-8717.

Quarterly report and annual survey. Provides industrywide statistics on real estate investment trust. Price available to members only.

4020
Real Estate Journal
Real Estate Inst of New South Wales, PO Box A624, Sydney South, NSW 2000, Australia. Telephone (61) (2) 616311.

Monthly magazine. Offers articles on real estate in New South Wales. Price $1.50 per copy.

4021
Real Estate Law Journal
Warren, Gorham & Lamont, Inc, 210 S St, Boston, MA 02111. Telephone (617) 423-2020.

Quarterly magazine. Covers real estate law topics. Includes information on financing, taxation, federal and state legislation, and court cases. Price $48.00 per year.

4022
Real Estate Law Report
Warren, Gorham & Lamont, Inc, 210 S St, Boston, MA 02111. Telephone (617) 423-2020.

Monthly report. Contains information on real estate law topics. Covers court cases and state and federal legislation. Price $56.00 per year.

4023
Real Estate News
Real Estate News, 720 S Dearborn St, Chicago, IL 60605. Telephone (312) 922-7220.

Weekly magazine. Provides articles about real estate marketing trends. Contains listings of investment opportunities and classified advertising. Price $15.00 per year.

4023.01
Real Estate Newsletter
Coopers & Lybrand, 1251 Ave of the Americas, New York, NY 10020. Order from Manager of Publications, PO Box 682, Times Sq Station, New York, NY 10108. Telephone (212) 489-1100.

Periodic newsletter. Reports on real estate industry developments. Notes trends in housing and tax-shelter programs. Price free of charge.

4023.02
Real Estate Perspectives
Realtors National Marketing Institute of the National Assn of Realtors, 430 N Michigan Ave, Chicago, IL 60611. Telephone (312) 440-8540.

Quarterly journal in three editions: commercial-investment, management, residential sales. Provides articles related to real estate industry.

4024
Real Estate Review
Warren, Gorham & Lamont, Inc, 210 S St, Boston, MA 02111. Telephone (617) 423-2020.

Quarterly magazine. Provides information on real estate techniques and related topics. Price $38.00 per year.

4025
Real Estate Sales Handbook, **8th edition**
National Assn of Realtors, 430 N Michigan Ave, Chicago, IL 60611. Telephone (312) 440-8009 or 8528. Telex 02 53742.

Handbook. Discusses real estate sales methods. Offers advice on advertising and negotiations. Includes tables on rent proration, housing depreciation, and mortgage. Price $7.90.

4025.01
Real Estate Syndication Reporter
Questor Assoc, Real Estate Syndication Reporter, 115 Sansome St, San Francisco, CA 94104. Telephone (415) 433-0300.

Quarterly report. Offers financial data on public real estate investment programs sponsored by syndication firms. Includes monthly Real Estate Syndication Reporter, Newsletter and annual report. Price $450.00 per year.

4025.02
Real Estate Syndication Reporter Newsletter
Questor Assoc, Real Estate Syndication Reporter, 115 Sansome St, San Francisco, CA 94104. Telephone (415) 433-0300.

Monthly newsletter. Reports on developments affecting the real estate syndication industry. Notes financing techniques and tax-saving devices used by firms. Price $99.00 per year.

4026
Real Estate Tax Ideas
Warren, Gorham & Lamont, Inc, 210 S St, Boston, MA 02111. Telephone (617) 423-2020.

Monthly report. Offers suggestions on real estate tax advantages. Discusses court cases and Internal Revenue Service rulings. Price $48.00 per year.

4027
Real Estate Tax Shelter Desk Book, **2nd edition**
Inst for Business Planning, Inc, IPB Plaza, Dept. 7102-81. Englewood Cliffs, NJ 07632. Telephone (201) 592-2040.

Book. Discusses real estate tax shelters with reference to Tax Reform Law of 1976. Notes tax advantages of depreciation, sale-leasebacks, and various accounting methods. Price $39.50 ISBN 0-87624-502-5.

4028
Real Estate Today
Realtors National Marketing Institute of the National Assn of Realtors, 430 N Michigan Avenue, Chicago, IL 60611. Telephone (312) 440-8540.

Monthly magazine. Provides articles related to real estate industry. Price $18.-00. ISSN 0034-0804.

4029
Realtor
Washington Board of Realtors, Inc, 1511 K St, NW, Washington, DC 20005. Telephone (202) 628-4646.

Monthly magazine. Reports on Washington, DC, metropolitan area real estate news. Includes information on mortgage availability. Notes individual county developments. Price $10.00 per year.

4030
Realty
Realty, 80-34 Jamaica Ave, Woodhaven, NY 11421. Telephone (212) 296-2233.

Biweekly newspaper. Covers real estate news for New York metropolitan area and US. Deals with financing, leasing, construction, and regulation. Price $10.00 per year.

4031
Realty Bluebook
Professional Pub Corp, 122 Paul Dr, San Rafael, CA 94903. Telephone (415) 472-1964.

Annual book. Contains real estate and mortgage tables, checklists, financing, and tax information, and clauses for sales and exchange agreements, options, and leases. Price Paperback $14.00, Hardcover $19.-00.

4032
Realty Roundup
Real Estate Forum, Inc, 30 E 42 St, New York, NY 10017. Telephone (212) MU 2-6987.

Weekly newsletter. Covers various aspects of real estate, including mortgage banking and shopping centers. Price $115.00 per year.

4033
Realty Stock Review
Audit Investment Research, Inc, 230 Park Ave, New York, NY 10017. Telephone (212) 661-1710.

Semimonthly report. Analyzes securities of real estate investment trusts and companies. Tables. Price $164.00 per year.

4033.01
Recent Additions to Baker Library
Harvard University, Graduate School of Business Administration, Baker Library, Soldiers Field, Boston, MA 02163. Telephone (617) 495-6403.

Monthly publication. Lists new books and pamphlets acquired by Baker Library (Harvard Business School). Includes titles arranged by subject and Library of Congress classification numbers. Price $14.00 per year.

4034
Record of New Issues
Maclean Hunter Ltd, 30 Old Burlington St, London, England W1X 2AE. Order from Financial Post Corp Service, 481 University Ave, Toronto, Ont, Canada M5W 1A7. Telephone (416) 596-5585.

Annual report with updates. Provides information on new issues of securities. Price $6.00 per copy.

4036
Record of Valuation Day Prices
Maclean Hunter Ltd, 30 Old Burlington St, London, England W1X 2AE. Order from Financial Post Corp Service, 481 University Ave, Toronto, Ont, Canada M5W 1A7. Telephone (416) 596-5585.

Report. Provides up-to-date information on current securities prices. Price $4.00 per copy.

4037
Record of Warrants
Maclean Hunter Ltd, 30 Old Burlington St, London, England W1X 2AE. Order from Financial Post Corp Service, 481 University Ave, Toronto, Ont, Canada M5W 1A7. Telephone (416) 596-5585.

Annual report with updates. Provides information on warrants. Price $8.00 per copy.

4038
Recruiting Trends
Enterprise Publications, 20 N Wacker Dr, Chicago, IL 60606. Telephone (312) 332-3571.

Monthly loose-leaf newsletter. Discusses executive recruitment. Includes college recruiting, affirmative action, and equal opportunity employment measures. Price $55.00 per year.

4039
Reference Book of Corporate Managements
Dun & Bradstreet, Box 3224, Church St Station, New York, NY 10008. Telephone (212) 285-7346.

Annual book. Contains biographical sketches of about 30,000 executives in more than 2400 large companies of investor and general business interest. Prices on request. Available to Dun & Bradstreet subscribers only.

4040
Reference Book of Manufacturers
Dun & Bradstreet, Box 3224, Church St Station, New York, NY 10008. Telephone (212) 285-7346.

Biannual book. Offers 355,000 listings of manufacturers, with sales, credit, and purchasing data on each. Prices on request. Available to Dun & Bradstreet subscribers only.

4041
Reference Book of Transportation
Dun & Bradstreet, Box 3224, Church St Station, New York, NY 10008. Telephone (212) 285-7346.

Book. Provides credit and marketing facts on Class I, II, and III motor carriers, as well as air, rail, water, and bus carriers. Includes freight forwarding and pipeline companies. Prices on request. Available to Dun & Bradstreet subscribers only.

4042
Reference Manual on Population and Housing Statistics from the Census Bureau, 1977
US Dept of Commerce, Bureau of the Census, Washington, DC 20233. Order from Subscriber Services Section (Publications), Bureau of the Census, Washington, DC 20233. Telephone (202) 449-1600.

Book. Describes principles relevant to Bureau of Census population and housing data. Includes reference charts and list of related publications. Price $2.00.

4043
Refined Petroleum Products
Statistics Canada, User Services, Publications Distributions, Ottawa, Ont, Canada K1A 0V7. Telephone (613) 992-3151.

Monthly report. Tabulates crude oil received by Canadian refineries. Notes refinery operations, shipments, and inventories. Price $42.00 per year. ISSN 0380-8629.

4044
Refractories
US Dept of Commerce, Bureau of the Census, Washington, DC 20233. Telephone (202) 449-1600.

Quarterly report with annual summary. Contains data on shipments of clay and nonclay refractories by kind. Price $1.25 per year.

4045
Regency International Directory
Regency International Publications Ltd, Newstone House, 127 Sandgate Rd, Folkestone, Kent, England CT20 2BL. Telephone (44) 54691 (STD 0303).

Annual directory. Lists private investigators, private detectives, debt collection agents, bailiffs, and members of worldwide associations. Price $30.00.

4046
Regional Employment by Industry, 1940–1970.
US Dept of Commerce, Bureau of Economic Analysis, Washington, DC 20230. Order from Superintendent of Documents, US Government Printing Office, Washington, DC 20402. Telephone (202) 783-3238.

Book. Offers estimates of employment as measured by place of residence and industry for various geographical areas. Price $9.05.

4047
Regional Science and Urban Economics
North-Holland Publishing Co, PO Box 211, 1000 AE Amsterdam, The Netherlands. Order from Elsevier/North-Holland, Inc, 52 Vanderbilt Ave, New York, NY 10017. Telephone (212) 867-9040.

Quarterly journal. Contains theoretical articles on regional science and urban economics. Focuses on immediate or potential uses for regional and urban planning. Price $117.00 per year. ISSN 0166-0462.

4049
Regional Studies
Pergamon Press, Inc, Maxwell House, Fairview Park, Elmsford, NY 10523. Telephone (914) 592-7700. Telex 13-7328.

Quarterly journal. Presents papers on regional planning, particularly its economic aspects. Includes book reviews. Price $75.00 per year.

4049.01
Regional Trends
Her Majesty's Stationery Office, PO Box 569, London, England SE1 9NH. Telephone (44) (01) 928-1321.

Annual abstract. Presents statistics for 8 standard regions of England, Scotland, Wales, and Northern Ireland. Covers such subjects as population, social services, employment, and transportation, with regional profiles highlighting the data for each region. Price available on request.

4050
Registered Bond Interest Record
Standard & Poor's Corp, 25 Broadway, New York, NY 10004. Telephone (212) 248-2525.

Weekly report. Contains list of payments, stock exchange rulings, and 10-day calendar for more than 6300 bond issues. Price $975.00 per year.

4051
Register of Corporations, Directors and Executives
Standard & Poor's Corp, 25 Broadway, New York, NY 10004. Telephone (212) 248-2525.

Three-volume directory. Provides listing of 37,000 private and public companies, 405,000 executives by function, plus principal products. Biography volume gives brief accounts of 72,000 executives. Indexes. Price available on request.

4051.01
Register of Members
Institute of Public Relations, 1 Great James St, London, England WCIN 3DA. Telephone (44) (01) 405-5505.

Annual directory. Provides detailed listing of Institute of Public Relations 2500 members. Includes trade classification indices. Price £9.00.

4052
Register of Reporting Labor Organizations
US Dept of Labor, Labor-Management Services Administration, Washington, DC 20216. Order from Superintendent of Documents, US Government Printing Office, Washington, DC 20402. Telephone (202) 254-6510.

Book. Identifies labor unions that filed reports in accordance with requirements of the Labor-Management Reporting and Disclosure Act. Price available on request.

4054
Registrar's Service
Extel Statistical Service Ltd, 37-45 Paul St, London, England EC2A 4PB. Telephone (44) (01) 253-3400. Telex 262687.

Annual card service with weekly updating. Shows transfer requirements for all securities quoted on British and Irish stock exchanges. Price £140.00 per year.

4055
Registry of Manhattan Office Spaces
Robert F R Ballard, McGraw-Hill Book Co, Hightstown-Princeton Rd, Hightstown, NJ 08520. Telephone (609) 448-1700. Telex 843449.

Data-based book. Supplies register of 400 largest office buildings in Manhattan. Provides information on floor plans and tenants, nearby transportation, hotel and dining facilities. Maps. Price $75.00 ISBN 0-07-003485-0.

4056
Registry of Ships
Her Majesty's Stationery Office, PO Box 569, London, England SE1 9NH. Telephone (44) (01) 928 1321.

Monthly supplement to British Mercantile Navy List. Provides information on steam, sailing, and motor vessels. Price £ 49.32 per year.

4057

Regulations for Transportation of Dangerous Commodities by Rail

Supply and Services Canada, Canadian Govt Publishing Centre, Hull, Que, Canada K1A 0S9. Telephone (819) 994-3475, 2085.

Book, plus update service. Provides Canadian regulations for transporting dangerous commodities by rail. Price $42.00.

4058

Regulatory News Release

Reports, Inc, 700 Orange St, Wilmington, DE 19801. Telephone (302) 656-2209.

Weekly newsletter. Contains news of Federal government regulatory agency actions which affect credit unions. Price $250.00 per year.

4059

Rehabilitation Counseling Bulletin

American Personnel and Guidance Assn, 2 Skyline Place, Suite 400, 5203 Leesburg Pike, Falls Church, VA 22041. Telephone (703) 820-4700.

Magazine issued five times per year. Reports on new rehabilitation research, techniques, and developments. Price $12.50 per year.

4060

Renegotiation/Management Letter

Callahan Publications, PO Box 3751, Washington, DC 20007. Telephone (703) 356-1925.

Semi-monthly newsletter on renegotiation of defense and space contracts, contract procedures, and modern management practices. Price $120.00 per year.

4061

Rental Compilation

Associated Equipment Distributors, 615 W 22 St, Oak Brook, IL 60521. Telephone (312) 654-0650.

Annual book. Provides nationally averaged rental rates for more than 1100 sizes and types of construction equipment. Price $20.00.

4061.01

Rental House & Condo Investor

HBJ Newsletters, Inc, 757 3rd Ave, New York, NY 10017. Telephone (212) 888-3335.

Semimonthly newsletter. Directed to investors in rental houses, duplexes, and condominiums. Price $87.00 per year.

4062

Rent All

Harcourt Brace Jovanovich Publications, 757 3rd Ave, New York, NY 10017. Order from Harcourt Brace Jovanovich Publications, 1 E 1st St, Duluth, MN 55802. Telephone (218) 727-8511.

Monthly magazine. Reports on rental equipment industry, including party supplies, lawn and garden equipment, tools, and campers. Price $15.00 per year.

4062.01

Repair and Remodeling Cost Data

R S Means Co, Inc, 100 Construction Plz, Kingston, MA 02364. Telephone (617) 747-1270.

Annual book. Provides unit costs and building systems prices for repair, remodeling, or renovation of existing structures. Price $32.00.

4062.02

Reporter's Report

Lawrence Ragan Communications, Inc, 407 S Dearborn, Chicago, IL 60605. Telephone (312) 922-8245.

Semimonthly newsletter. Provides editors of house organs with story and photo ideas, and tips on reporting and writing. Price $75.00 per year.

4063

Reporting on Governments

Reporting on Governments, Inc, 80 Park Ave, New York, NY 10016. Telephone (212) 687-6889.

Weekly newsletter. Provides information about credit and bond markets, as well as economic conditions in US. Price $195.00 per year.

4064

Report of the Commissioners of Her Majesty's (HM) Customs and Excise

Her Majesty's Stationery Office, PO Box 569, London, England SE1 9NH. Telephone (44) (01) 928 1321.

Annual report. Contains information on British customs and excise taxes. Price £ 7.10 per year.

4065

Report of the Commissioners of Her Majesty's (HM) Inland Revenue

Her Majesty's Stationery Office, PO Box 569, London, England SE1 9NH. Telephone (44) (01) 928 1321.

Annual report. Provides data on British inland revenue. Price £2.50 per year.

4066

Report of the New Zealand Dept of Trade and Industry

Government Printing Office, Private Bag, Wellington 1, New Zealand. Telephone (64) (4) 737320.

Annual pamphlet. Reviews New Zealand's economy, with emphasis on industries and exports. Price varies annually.

4068

Report on Company Contributions

Conference Board, Inc, 845 3rd Ave, New York, NY 10022. Telephone (212) 759-0900.

Report on survey of contributions practices of selected companies. Price available on request.

4069

Report on Credit Unions

Reports, Inc, 700 Orange St, Wilmington, DE 19801. Telephone (302) 656-2209.

Monthly newsletter. Contains information on credit unions, and includes such topics as credit cards and interest rates. Price $30.00 per year. ISSN 0482-2803.

4070

Report on Livestock Surveys

Statistics Canada, User Services, Publications Distribution, Ottawa, Ont, Canada K1A 0V7. Telephone (613) 992-3151.

Quarterly report. Estimates number of pigs on Canadian farms each quarter, number of cattle and sheep semiannually. Price $19.20 per year. ISSN 0709-6526.

4071

Report on Livestock Surveys: Pigs

Statistics Canada, Publications Distribution, Ottawa, Ont, Canada K1A 0T6. Telephone (613) 992-2959.

Quarterly report. Estimates number of pigs on Canadian farms. Price $1.40 per year. ISSN 0318-7896.

4072

Report on Production Trends

Queensland Dept of Primary Industries, Marketing Services Branch, William St, Brisbane, Qld 4000, Australia.

Monthly report. Covers trends in major industries in Queensland, Australia. Free of charge.

4074

Report on the Census of Production

Her Majesty's Stationery Office, PO Box 569, London, England SE1 9NH. Telephone (44) (01) 928 1321.

Annual reports. Provide statistical data on production in Great Britain. Prices available on request.

4074.01
Reports Index
Business Surveys Ltd, PO Box 21, Dorking, Surrey, England RH5 4EE. Telephone 01-0306-887857.

Bimonthly magazine. Notes subject, source, and price of business reports available within the United Kingdom. Price $222.00 per year.

4075
Reports of Cases Before the Court
Commission of the European Communities, Office for Official Publications of the European Communities, CP 1003, Luxembourg 1, Luxembourg. Telephone (352) 490081. Telex PUBLOF 1325.

Irregular report. Covers cases before Court of Justice of the European Communities. Gives opinions and judgments handed down by Court. Price $78.80 per year.

4078
Republic of Ireland Reference Book
Dun & Bradstreet, Box 3224, Church St Station, New York, NY 10008. Telephone (212) 285-7346.

Annual book. Lists approximately 6000 business establishments in Irish Republic. Gives proprietors and associates, primary line of business, and credit appraisal. Prices on request. Available to Dun & Bradstreet subscribers only.

4078.01
Re Report
Inst for International Research Ltd, 70 Warren St, London, England W1P 5PA. Telephone (44) (01) 388-2663. Telex 263504.

Biweekly report. Covers international reinsurance market. Price $295.00 per year.

4079
Research and Development (R & D) Contracts Monthly
Government Data Publications, 422 Washington Bldg, Washington, DC 20005. Telephone (202) 966-6379.

Monthly magazine. Provides information on government research and development, design, engineering, and prototype production contracts. Indicates awardee, agency, and type of research. Price $60.00 per year.

4080
Research and Development Directory
Government Data Publications, 422 Washington Bldg, Washington, DC 20005. Telephone (202) 966-6379.

Annual book. Reports on government research and development contracts awarded during past year. Indicates awardee, agency, and nature of work. Price $15.00.

4082
Research and Development Projects
US Dept of Labor, Employment and Training Administration, Washington, DC 20213. Telephone (202) 376-6730.

Annual book. Summarizes research projects funded by the Office of Research and Development of the Department of Labor Employment and Training Administration. Discusses training and apprenticeship, employer practices, worker attitudes, labor market, and programs for unemployed. Free of charge.

4084
Research Bulletin: Wage Developments Resulting from Major Collective Bargaining Settlements
Labour Canada, PR Branch, 340 Laurier Ave W, Ottawa, Ont, Canada K1A 0J2. Order from Publications Div, Labour Canada, Ottawa, Ont, Canada K1A 0J2. Telephone (819) 997-2031.

Quarterly report plus annual consolidation. Presents data on settlements in Canadian labor disputes involving 500 or more employees. Gives annual increases in base rates of pay. Free of charge.

4085
Research Centers Directory, 6th edition
Gale Research Co, Book Tower, Detroit, MI 48226. Telephone (313) 961-2242.

Book. Provides guide to university-related and other nonprofit research organizations, arranged by subject. Price $160.00. ISBN 0453-8.

4087
Research Disclosure
Industrial Opportunities Ltd, 13-14 Homewell, Havant, Hampshire, England P09 1EF. Telephone (44) (0705)486262-3.

Monthly journal. Reports on inventions as alternative or addition to patenting. Price $40.00 per year.

4088
Research Index
Business Surveys Ltd, PO Box 21, Dorking, Surrey, England RH5 4EE. Telephone 0306-887857.

Fortnightly magazine. Indexes articles of financial and industrial interest from more than 100 periodicals and British press. Special index on specific companies. Price $198.00 per year. ISSN 0034-5296.

4089
Research Institute of American (RIA) Tax Guide
Research Inst of America (RIA), Inc, 589 5th Ave, New York, NY 10017. Telephone (212) 755-8900.

Loose-leaf book with regular updates. Covers all aspects of federal taxation of businesses and individuals. Includes examples, analyses, and recommended solutions to tax problems. Price $35.00 per year.

4090
Research Management
Industrial Research Inst, 265 Post Rd W, Westport, CT 06880. Telephone (203) 226-6356.

Bimonthly magazine on research and development management. Discusses personnel, planning, organization, and communications. Reviews current literature. Price $21.00 per year individual, $32.00 per year institutions.

4091
Research on Transport Economics
Organization for Economic Cooperation and Development, Publications Ctr, 1750 Pennsylvania Ave, NW, Washington, DC 20006. Telephone (202) 724-1857.

Semiannual bulletin. Contains subject index and an index of organizations mentioned. Price $45.00.

4091.01
Research Programs in the Medical Sciences
R R Bowker Co, 1180 Avenue of the Americas, New York, NY 10036. Order from R R Bowker Co, PO Box 1807, Ann Arbor, MI 48106. Telephone (212) 764-5100.

Directory. Provides information on over 5100 manufacturing and industrial service companies, government, academic, nonprofit organizations, and independent institutes belonging to 1600 parent organizations engaged in medical sciences research. Price $79.95. ISBN 0-8352-1293-9. ISSN 0197-0372.

4091.02
Research Reports
American Inst for Economic Research, Great Barrington, MA 01230. Telephone (413) 528-1216.

Weekly report. Discusses economic topics, including the impact of current events on the US economy and statistical indicators of business cycle changes. Includes monthly Economic Education Bulletin and membership in AIER. Price $35.00 per year.

4092
Research Reports
Business International Corp, 1 Dag Hammarskjold Plz, New York, NY 10017. Telephone (212) 750-6300.

Reports issued at varying intervals. Provide analysis of world markets and/or new international management techniques in Europe, Middle East, Africa, Asia, and Western Hemisphere. Price varies.

4093
Research Reports
The Conference Board, Inc, 845 3rd Ave, New York, NY 10022. Telephone (212) 759-0900.

Quarterly list. Contains Conference Board reports and information bulletins by number and title. Price available on request.

4094
Research Reports Supported by Office of Water Research and Technology
US Dept of the Interior, Washington, DC 20240. Order from National Technical Information Service, US Dept of Commerce, 5825 Port Royal Rd, Springfield, VA 22161. Telephone (202) 343-8435.

Semiannual report. Lists research programs supported by Office of Water Research and Technology. Includes Title I, Title II, desalination, and other reports. Price $3.50 (microfiche).

4095
Research Review
American Trucking Assn, Inc, 1616 P St, NW, Washington, DC 20036. Telephone (202) 797-5351.

Monthly report. Reviews trucking and other freight transport news, including taxation, highway construction, and government regulation. Tables. Free of charge.

4096
Residential Alterations and Repairs
US Dept of Commerce, Bureau of the Census, Washington, DC 20233. Telephone (202) 449-1600.

Quarterly report with two-part annual report. Provides estimates of expenditures by residential property owners for maintenance and repairs, additions, alterations, and major replacements. Price $1.90 per year.

4096.01
Resort Timesharing Law Reporter
Land Development Institute, Ltd, 1401 16th St, NW, Washington, DC 20036. Telephone (202) 232-2144.

Monthly newsletter. Reports on federal, state, and local regulation of resort timesharing, with document service. Price $48.00 per year, $36.00 libraries.

4096.02
Resources and Energy
North-Holland Publishing Co, PO Box 211, 1000 AE Amsterdam, The Netherlands. Order from Elsevier/North-Holland, Inc, 52 Vanderbilt Ave, New York, NY 10017. Telephone (212) 867-9040.

Quarterly journal. Contains studies on the allocation of natural resources. Focuses on energy topics. Price $76.00 per year. ISSN 0165-0572.

4097
Resources Policy
IPC Business Press Ltd, 205 E 42nd St, New York, NY 10017. Telephone (212) 889-0700. Telex 421710.

Quarterly magazine on nonrenewable resources. Focuses on political and economic implications, conservation, production, and consumption. Price $124.80 per year. ISSN 0301-4207.

4098
Restaurant Buyers Guide
Urner Barry Publications, Inc, PO Box 389, Toms River, NJ 08753. Telephone (201) 240-5330.

Weekly report. Provides market prices for beef, ham, bacon, lamb, poultry, fresh fish, fresh and frozen fruits and vegetables, butter, cheese, eggs, and other food items. Price $53.00 per year.

4099
Restaurant Hospitality
Penton/IPC, 614 Superior Ave W, Cleveland, OH 44113. Order from Penton/IPC, 1111 Chester Ave, Cleveland, OH 44114. Telephone (216) 696-7000.

Monthly magazines. Features reports on restaurant-related topics. Emphasizes restaurant chains and large commercial food services. Price $24.00 per year.

4100
Restaurant Statistics
Statistics Canada, User Services, Publications Distribution, Ottawa, Ont, Canada K1A 0V7. Telephone (613) 992-3151.

Monthly report. Estimates receipts of Canadian chain and independent restaurants. Includes provincial data. Price $18.00 per year. ISSN 0008-2627.

4100.01
Results of the Business Surveys Carried Out Among Managements in the Community
Commission of the European Communities, Office for Official Publications of the European Communities, CP 1003, Luxembourg 1, Luxembourg. Telephone (352) 490081. Telex PUBLOF 1325.

Monthly report. Covers business surveys of European Community. Price $70.00 per year.

4101
Results of the 1972 National Automation Survey
American Bankers Assn, 1120 Connecticut Ave NW, Washington, DC 20036. Telephone (202) 467-4123.

Book. Presents results of survey on extent of computerized automation in banking industry. Price $35.00.

4102
Retail Accounting Manual—Revised
National Retail Merchants Assn, 100 W 31st St, New York, NY 10001. Telephone (212) 244-6780.

Loose-leaf book. Provides chart of accounts suitable for multiunit companies and single unit retail stores. Emphasizes merchandise accounting and management reporting. Price $40.75.

4102.01
Retail Business
Economist Intelligence Unit Ltd, Spencer House, 27 St James's Pl, London, England SW1A 1NT Order from Economist Intelligence Unit Ltd, 75 Rockefeller Plz, New York, NY 10019. Telephone (212) 541-5730. Telex 148393.

Monthly journal. Covers retail trade in Great Britain. Includes information on consumer goods market research, distribution patterns, and sales trends. Price $295.00 per year.

4103
Retail Control
National Retail Merchants Assn, 100 W 31st St, New York, NY 10001. Telephone (212) 244-6780.

Monthly magazine. Presents articles on department store operations, financial management, inventory control, and computer use. Price $15.00 per year.

4104
Retail Credit Federation Membership Directory
The Consumer Credit Assn of the United Kingdom, 192A Nantwich Rd, Crewe, Cheshire, England CW2 6BP. Telephone (44) 0270 213399.

Annual book. Provides directory of members of Great Britain's Retail Credit Federation. Price £2.25.

4105
Retailing Today
Robert Kahn and Assoc, PO Box 249, Lafayette, CA 94549. Telephone (415) 254-4434.

Monthly newsletter. Discusses retail trade trends and research on retailing. Suggests ways executives can improve ethical standards. Price $24.00 per year.

4106
Retail Intelligence
Mintel Publications Ltd, 20 Buckingham St, London, England WC2N 6EE. Telephone (44) (01) 839-1542.

Quarterly report. Covers trends in retail trade, studies on retailers, and general aspects of retailing in the United Kingdom. Price $525.00 per year.

4107
Retail Memo
Newspaper Advertising Bureau, Inc, 485 Lexington Ave, New York, NY 10017. Telephone (212) 557-1800.

Weekly report. Digests retail news for retail advertising salespeople. Price $13.50 per year.

4108
Retail Operations News Bulletin
National Retail Merchants Assn, 100 W 31st St, New York, NY 10001. Telephone (212) 244-6780.

Quarterly magazine. Reports on retail store operations, including security, maintenance, and delivery. Price $14.50.

4109
Retail Roundup
Coopers & Lybrand, 1251 Ave of the Americas, New York, NY 10020. Order from Manager of Publications, PO Box 682, Times Sq Station, New York, NY 10108. Telephone (212) 489-1100.

Periodic newsletter. Discusses current developments in accounting and auditing, taxes, and computer auditing. Price free of charge.

4110
Retail Sales
Retail Council of Canada, Suite 212, 214 King St, W Toronto, Ont, Canada M5H 1K4. Telephone (416) 598-4684.

Monthly report. Gives retail sales statistics for Canada and provinces. Price $15.00 per year members, $30.00 per year nonmembers.

4111
Retail Sales of Goods (Cat No 8503.0)
Australian Bureau of Statistics, PO Box 10, Belconnen, ACT 2616, Australia. Order from Australian Government Publishing Service, PO Box 84, Canberra, ACT 2600, Australia. Telephone (61) (062) 527911.

Quarterly report. Gives value of retail sales in each Australian state for various commodity groups. Shows value and sales according to broad commodity groupings at current and 1968–69 prices. Price free of charge.

4112
Retail Services Labor Report
Bureau of National Affairs, Inc, 1231 25th St, NW, Washington, DC 20037. Telephone (202) 452-4200.

Loose-leaf book with weekly updates. Covers labor-management relations in retail and service industries. Notes legislative and union developments. Price $365.00 per year.

4113
Retail Trade
Her Majesty's Stationery Office, PO Box 569, London, England SE1 9NH. Telephone (44) (01) 928 1321.

Monthly report on retail trade in Great Britain. Price £7.75 per year.

4114
Retail Trade
Statistics Canada, User Services, Publications Distribution, Ottawa, Ont, Canada K1A 0V7. Telephone (613) 992-3151.

Monthly magazine. Reports on Canadian total retail sales by province and kind of business for chain and independent stores. Contains seasonally adjusted sales data. Price $42.00 per year. ISSN 0380-6146.

4115
Retail Trade Developments in Great Britain 4th edition
Gower Publishing Co Ltd, 1 Westmead, Farnborough, Hampshire, England GU14 7RU. Telephone Farnborough (0252) 519221. Telex 858623.

Book. Presents overview of retailing in Great Britain. Profiles largest retailing groups and surveys developments in 10 regions and 36 city centers. Price $68.50. ISSN 0 566 02152 8.

4116
Retail Trade International, **1980**
Euromonitor Publications Ltd, 18 Doughty St, London, England WC1N 2PN. Telephone (44) (01) 242-0042.

Biennial book. Furnishes results of survey of retail trade in 28 countries. Statistics. Price $420.00.

4117
Retail Wages
Retail Council of Canada, Suite 212, 214 King St, W Toronto, Ont, Canada M5H 1K4. Telephone (416) 598-4684.

Monthly report. Gives statistics on wages in Canada by trade, city, and province. Price $11.00 per year members, $22.00 per year nonmembers.

4119
Review & Digest Bulletin
Canadian Export Assn, Suite 1020, 1080 Beaver Hall Hill, Montreal, Canada H2Z 1T7. Telephone (514) 866-4481. Telex 055-60687.

Monthly newsletter. Summarizes information and opinion from publications, reports, and other papers of interest to Canadian exporters. Subscription includes Export News Bulletin. Price $25.00 per year, which covers 24 issues (Export News and Review and Digest subscriptions cannot be split). ISSN 0319-3233.

4120
Review of Business
St. John's University, Business Research Inst, Room 203, St. John Hall, Jamaica, NY 11439. Telephone (212) 969-8000, ext. 420.

Quarterly journal. Reports on business and economic topics. Includes information on research and methods of analysis. Price free of charge.

4120.01
Review of Economics and Statistics
North-Holland Publishing Co, PO Box 211, 1000 AE Amsterdam, The Netherlands. Order from Elsevier/North-Holland, Inc, 52 Vanderbilt Ave, New York, NY 10017. Telephone (212) 867-9040.

Quarterly report. Contains articles on economics, with emphasis on theoretical, empirical, and statistical analyses. Price $63.00 per year. ISSN 0034-6535.

4121
Review of Economic Studies
Longman Group Ltd, Longman House, Burnt Mill, Harlow, Essex, England CM20 2JE. Telephone (44) 26721. Telex 81259.

Report issued three times per year. Reviews theoretical and applied economics research. Emphasizes development and testing of theory and econometric articles. Price $67.00 per year. ISSN 0034-6527.

4123
Review of Income and Wealth
International Assn for Research in Income and Wealth, Box 1962, Yale Station, New Haven, CT 06520.

Quarterly review. Furnishes articles on personal and family income, government finance in specific countries, and tax policies. Price $40.00 per year.

4123.01
Review of Industrial Management and Textile Science
Clemson University, College of Industrial Management & Textile Science, Sirrine Hall, Clemson, SC 29631. Telephone (803) 656-3177.

Semiannual book. Presents articles on industrial management and new textile methods and research. Price $6.00 per year.

4124
Review of International Cooperation
International Co-operative Alliance, 11 Upper Grosvenor St, London, England W1X 9PA. Telephone (44) (01) 499-5991.

Quarterly report. Serves as official organ of International Cooperative Alliance. Discusses cooperative developments within specific countries. Reviews recent books. English, French and Spanish editions. Price £4.50 per year. ISSN 0034-6608.

4125
Review of Marketing and Agricultural Economics
New South Wales Dept of Agriculture, Div of Marketing and Economics, PO Box K220, Haymarket Sydney, NSW 2000, Australia. Telephone (61) (02) 217666.

Published three times per year. Published applied research into agricultural economics and marketing focusing on Australia. Book reviews. Price free of charge.

4126
Review of Optometry
Chilton Co, Chilton Way, Radnor, PA 19089. Telephone (215) 687-8200.

Monthly report. Presents articles on ophthalmic optics. Covers technical developments and fashion trends. Price $15.00.

4127
Review of Regional Economics and Business
University of Oklahoma, Center for Economic and Management Research, College of Business Administration, 307 West Brooks St, Room 4, Norman, OK 73019. Telephone (405) 325-2931.

Semiannual report. Discusses Southwest business and economic developments. Considers population and industry trends and changes in government regulation. Price $4.00 per year.

4128
Review of Securities Regulation
Standard & Poor's Corp, 25 Broadway, New York, NY 10004. Telephone (212) 248-2525.

Semimonthly report. Analyzes developments concerned with securities regulation. Price $200.00 per year.

4129
Review of Social Economy
Assn for Social Economics, c/o William R Waters, De Paul University, 25 E Jackson Blvd, Chicago, IL 60604. Telephone (312) 321-7781.

Trimonthly report. Reviews aspects of social economics. Price $20.00 per year.

4130
Rewarding Executive Talent: Salary and Benefit Practices by Industry and Position
McGraw-Hill Book Co, Hightstown-Princeton Rd, Hightstown, NJ 08520. Telephone (609) 448-1700. Telex 834449.

Data-based report. Covers methods of rewarding competent executives. Shows compensation trends and current job market conditions. Price $95.00 per year. ISBN 0-07-033421-8.

4131
RHM Convertible Survey
RHM Assoc, Inc, 417 Northern Blvd, Great Neck, NY 11021. Telephone (516) 487-8811.

Weekly report. Offers convertible bond and convertible preferred stock investment advice. Tables and charts. Price $125.00 per year, for six months, $72.00.

4132
RHM Survey of Warrants. Options and Low-Price Stocks
RHM Assoc, Inc, 417 Northern Blvd, Great Neck, NY 11021. Telephone (516) 487-8811.

Weekly report. Provides investment advice on warrants, call and put options, and low-price stocks. Tables and charts. Price $120.00 per year, $68.00 for six months.

4133
Rhode Island: State Industrial Directory 1981–82
Manufacturers' News, Inc, 3 E Huron St, Chicago, Il 60611. Telephone (312) 337-1084.

Annual book. Contains information on Rhode Island industrial companies, including location and products. Price $20.00.

4134
Risk Management
Risk and Insurance Management Society, Inc, 205 E 42 St, New York, NY 10017. Telephone (212) 286-9378.

Monthly magazine. Features articles and news on risk and insurance management, and employee benefits administration. Price $21.00 per year.

4135
Road Accidents
Her Majesty's Stationery Office, PO Box 569, London, England SE1 9NH. Telephone (44) (01) 928 1321.

Annual report on British road accidents. Price £4.50 per year.

4137
Road Transport Service Bulletin
Statistics Canada, User Services, Publications Distribution, Ottawa, Ont, Canada K1A 0V7. Telephone (613) 992-3151.

Report issued 10 times each year. Provides statistical summary information on the Canadian road transport industry. Price $18.00 per year. ISSN 0702-8121.

4138
Robert's Dictionary of Industrial Relations, **1971 edition**
Harold S Roberts, Bureau of National Affairs, Inc, 1231 25th St, NW Washington, DC, 20037. Telephone (202) 452-4276.

Book. Provides comprehensive definitions of special terms used in labor-mamgement relations. Price $20.00. ISBN 0-87179-135-8.

4139
Rocky Mountain Journal
Rocky Mountain Journal, 1590 S Federal, Denver, CO 80219. Telephone (303) 934-2411.

Weekly newspaper. Delivers Denver area business and financial news, as well as regional energy news. Lists real estate transactions in six metropolitan counties. Includes new corporations, oil and gas well starts, bankruptcies, OTC stocks, building permits, liquor licenses, and foreclosures. Price $25.00 per year.

4140
Rocky Mountain Mineral Law Institute
Matthew Bender & Co, 235 E 45th St, New York, NY 10017. Telephone (212) 661-5050.

Annual book on proceedings of Rocky Mountain Mineral Law Institute. Features articles on mining, oil, gas, water, and public lands. Price $60.00 per year.

4141
Roofing Siding Insulation.
Incorporating Solar Contractor
Harcourt Brace Jovanovich Publications, 757 3rd Ave, New York, NY 10017. Order from Harcourt Brace Jovanovich Publications, 1 E 1st St, Duluth, MN 55802. Telephone (218) 727-8511.

Monthly magazine. Contains information on roofing, siding, insulation, and solar energy systems. Price $9.00 per year.

4142
Rough Notes
Rough Notes Co, Inc, 1200 Meridian St, Indianapolis, IN 46204. Telephone (317) 634-1541.

Monthly magazine. Covers property and casualty insurance agency business. Price $8.00 per year.

4143
Rountree Report
Rountree Pub Co, Inc, 117 Brixton Rd, Garden City, NY 11530. Telephone Unlisted.

Fortnighty report. Digests news of new products being offered by numerous companies. Notes other company developments. Price $60.00 per year foreign.

4144
Routes Yearbook
Maclean-Hunter Ltd, 30 Old Burlington St, London, England W1X 2AE. Telephone (44) (01) 434-2233.

Annual book. Lists major operators in air freight, containerships, trainferry, and continental shipping services. Notes charter brokers and depots. Price available on request.

4145
Royal Bank of Canada. Monthly Letter
Royal Bank of Canada, Royal Bank of Canada Bldg, Box 6001, Montreal, Canada H3C 3A9. Telephone (514) 874-2110.

Monthly newsletter. Contains one essay per issue in field of social sciences, psychology, arts, or humanities. English and French. Free of charge.

4146
Royal Institution of Chartered Surveyors Year Book
(Thomas) Skinner Directories, Windsor Court, E Grinstead House, E Grinstead, W Sussex, England RH19 1XE. Order from IPC Business Press Ltd New York, 205 E 42nd St, New York, NY 10017. Telephone (212) 867-2080.

Yearbook. Offers guide to chartered surveyors in Great Britain. Price £14.00 per year. ISBN 611-00618-9.

4147
Royal Mint Annual Report
Royal Mint, Tower Hill, London, England EC3N 4DR. Order from Her Majesty's Stationery Office, 49 High Holborn, London, England EC1V 6HP.

Annual book. Reports on activities of British Royal Mint. Price £3.50. ISBN 011887002S.

4148
Rubber Industry Facts
Rubber Manufacturers Assn, 1901 Pennsylvania Ave, NW, Washington, DC 20006. Telephone (202) 785-2602.

Annual report. Gives US and world statistics on production and other aspects of the rubber industry. Price available on request.

4149
Rubber: Supply and Distribution for the United States
US Dept of Commerce, Bureau of the Census, Washington, DC 20233. Telephone (202) 449-1600.

Annual report. Provides statistics on rubber supply and distribution for US, 1972 to the present. Covers synthetic, natural, reclaimed, and styrene-butadiene rubber. Price $.25.

4149.01
Rubber Trends
Economist Intelligence Unit Ltd, Spencer House, 27 St James's Pl, London, England SW1A 1NT. Order from Economist Intelligence Unit Ltd, 75 Rockefeller Plz, New York, NY 10019. Telephone (212) 541-5730. Telex 148393.

Quarterly journal. Analyzes and evaluates the rubber market, and notes industrial trends. Price $265.00 per year.

4150
Rubber World
Hartman Communications, Inc, 77 N Miller Rd, P O Box 5417, Akron, OH 44313. Telephone (216) 867-4401.

Monthly report. Covers developments and gives statistics for the rubber industry. Price $14.00 per year.

4151
Rubio's Mexican Financial Journal
Victor M Rubio y Cia, SA, Paseo de la Reforma 292-601, Mexico, DF, Mexico. Telephone 528-8815.

Fortnightly newsletter. Analyzes business and stock market conditions in Mexico. Price available on request.

4151.01
Rules and Regulations
US Securities & Exchange Commission, Washington, DC 20549. Order from Superintendent of Documents, Government Printing Office, Washington, DC 20402. Telephone (202) 755-4833.

Contains texts of Securities and Exchange Commission's rules. Price $8.25.

4152
Rules and Regulations and Statements of Procedure of the National Labor Relations Board
US National Labor Relations Board, 1717 Pennsylvania Ave, NW, Washington, DC 20570. Order from Superintendent of Documents, US Government Printing Office, Washington, DC 20402. Telephone (202) 655-4000.

Loose-leaf report issued at irregular intervals. Contains National Labor Relations Board rules, regulations, and statements of procedure. Price $10.00.

4153
Rundt's Weekly Intelligence
S J Rundt and Assoc, Inc, 130 E 63rd St, New York, NY 10021. Telephone (212) 838-0141.

Weekly newsletter. Examines world trade markets and currencies. Notes international economic conditions. Price $565.00 per year.

4154
Rural Industries Ref. No. 10.29, 1969–70 final edition
Australian Bureau of Statistics, Box 17 GPO, Canberra, ACT 2600, Australia. Order from Australian Government Pub Service, PO Box 84, Canberra, Act, Australia 2600. Telephone (61) (062) 527911.

Annual bulletin. Pertains to Australian rural land settlement, agriculture, dairies, poultry and bee-farming. Statistics. Price $2.00 (Australian).

4156
Safe Deposit Handbook
American Bankers Assn, 1120 Connecticut Ave NW, Washington, DC 20036. Telephone (202) 467-4123.

Book. Describes effective safe deposit operations. Price $5.00.

4157
Safe Driver
National Safety Council, 444 N Michigan Ave, Chicago, IL 60611. Telephone (312) 527-4800. Telex 25-3141.

Monthly magazine. Gives safe driving advice. Discusses typical driving conditions. Issues truck, bus and passenger car editions. Price $2.50 members, $3.15 nonmembers.

4158
Safety Management
Bureau of Business Practice, 24 Rope Ferry Rd, Waterford, CT 06386. Telephone (203) 442-4365.

Monthly magazine. Gives case histories that demonstrate how companies can avoid violations of Occupational Safety and Health Administration regulations. Price $27.00 per year.

4159
Safety Perspective Securite
Labour Canada, PR Branch, 340 Laurier Ave W, Ottawa, Ont, Canada, K1A 0J2. Order from Publications Div, Labour Canada, Ottawa, Ont, Canada K1A 0J2. Telephone (819) 997-2031.

Bimonthly periodical. Covers on-the-job accident prevention programs in Canada. English and French. Free of charge.

4161
Safety Science Abstracts Journal
Cambridge Scientific Abstracts, 6611 Kenilworth Ave, Suite 437, Riverdale, MD 20840. Telephone (301) 951-13272.

Magazine with 10 issues per year. Offers indexed abstracts from periodicals, books, reports, and patents on safety research, legislation, testing, and standards in numerous areas. Price $230.00 per year.

4162
Safe Worker
National Safety Council, 444 N Michigan Ave, Chicago, IL 60611. Telephone (312) 527-4800. Telex 25-3141.

Monthly magazine. Focuses on industrial hazards, with reminders about dangerous materials, protective equipment, and machine guards. Is intended for workers. Price $2.50 members, $3.15 nonmembers.

4163
Salary Survey
American Society for Personnel Administration, 30 Park Dr, Berea, OH 44017. Telephone (216) 826-4790.

Annual survey. Reports data on personnel and industrial relations salaries by position title and suggested typical organizational reporting relationship. Shows salary by industry, geographic location, and organization's financial status. Price $95.00 for nonparticipants.

4164
Salary Survey
College Placement Council, Inc, PO Box 2263, Bethlehem, PA 18001. Telephone (215) 868-1421.

Five reports per year analyzing beginning salaries offered college graduates. Price $60.00, price varies for individual reports.

4165
Sales & Marketing Management
Sales & Marketing Management, Sales Builders Div, 633 3rd Ave, New York, NY 10017 Telephone (212) 986-4800.

Magazine issued 16 times per year. Presents articles on sales and marketing operations. Includes information on packaging, advertising and distribution of products. Price $25.00 per year.

4166
Sales and Marketing Management Survey of Buying Power (Part I)
Ken Reiss, Publisher, 633 3rd Ave, New York, NY 10017. Telephone (212) 986-4800.

Annual magazine. Gives demographic sales data with breakdowns by population, households, and retail sales. Price $55.00.

4167
Sales and Marketing Management Survey of Buying Power (Part II)
Ken Reiss, Publisher, 633 3rd Ave, New York, NY 10017. Telephone (212) 986-4800.

Annual magazine. Projects for 1981 population, households, retail sales, and other demographic data for newspaper and TV markets. Price $25.00.

4168
Sales and Marketing Management Survey of Industrial Purchasing Power
Ken Reiss, Publisher, 633 3rd Ave, New York, NY 10017. Telephone (212) 986-4800.

Annual magazine. Gives data on value of industrial shipments in counties having at least one plant with 20 or more employees. Price $25.00.

4169
Sales and Marketing Management
Survey of Selling Costs
Ken Reiss, Publisher, 633 3rd Ave, New York, NY 10017. Telephone (212) 986-4800.

Annual magazine. Surveys basic selling costs in 80 metropolitan markets. Includes compensation information; cost of sales meetings, training, and transportation. Price $25.00.

4172
Sales Management and Sales
Engineering
Institute of Sales Management, Concorde House, 24 Warwick New Rd, Royal Leamington Spa, Warwickshire, England CV32 5JH. Telephone (0926) 37621. Telex 311746.

Monthly magazine. Covers sales management and sales engineering techniques, new products, companies, and planned construction in Great Britain, plus news of the Institute of Sales Engineers. Price £20.00.

4174
Sales Manager's Bulletin
Bureau of Business Practice, 24 Rope Ferry Rd, Waterford, CT 06386. Telephone (203) 442-4365.

Semimonthly loose-leaf newsletter. Covers techniques of conducting sales campaigns, including managing a sales force, conducting market-research, and improving customer relations. Price $72.00 per year.

4175
Salesman's Opportunity Magazine
Opportunity Press, Inc, Suite 1405, 6 N Michigan Ave, Chicago, IL 60602. Telephone (312) 346-4790. Telex 25-6138.

Monthly magazine. Emphasizes direct sales and individually owned business opportunities. Notes new products and sales tips. Is aimed at salesmen. Price $8.00 per year.

4176
Sales Prospector
Prospector Research Services, Inc, 751 Main St, PO Box 518, Waltham, Boston, MA 02154. Telephone (617) 899-1271.

Monthly report. Contains market research on sales prospects in US and Canada. Price $82.00 per year.

4177
Sales Taxes
Prentice-Hall, Inc, Englewood Cliffs, NJ 07632. Telephone (201) 592-2000. Telex 13-5423.

Weekly loose-leaf service. Covers all state and local sales, use, receipts, and similar taxes. Price $453.00 per year.

4178
Sales Tax Guide—Canada, **30th edition**
CCH Canadian Ltd, 6 Garamond Ct, Don Mills, Ont, Canada M3C 1Z5. Telephone (416) 429-2992.

Book. Presents sales tax data for Canada. Price $22.00 paperbound, $27.00 hardbound.

4179
San Diego Business Journal
Cordovan Corp, 5314 Bingle Rd, Houston, TX 77092. Order from San Diego Business Journal, 3444 Camino Del Rio North, San Diego, CA 92108. Telephone (714) 283-2271.

Weekly newspaper. Contains feature articles on various segments of San Diego business. Price $24.00 per year.

4180
San Francisco Business Journal
Cordovan Corp, 5314 Bingle Rd, Houston, TX 77092. Order from San Francisco Business Journal, 745 Stevenson St, San Francisco, CA 94103. Telephone (415) 552-7690.

Weekly newspaper. Contains feature articles on various segments of San Francisco/Oakland business. Price $24.00 per year.

4181
Saskatchewan Economic Review
Saskatchewan Bureau of Statistics, T.C. Douglas Bldg, 3475 Albert St, Regina, Sask, Canada, S4S 6X6. Telephone (306) 565-6327.

Annual report. Provides commentary and statistics on Canadian and Saskatchewan economy. Includes tables, maps, and economic indicators. Free of charge.

4182
Saskatchewan Monthly Statistical
Review
Saskatchewan Bureau of Statistics, T.C. Douglas Bldg, 3475 Albert St, Regina, Sask, Canada S4S 6X6. Telephone (306) 565-6327.

Monthly report. Contains statistical data on Saskatchewan, Canada, in such areas as employment, agriculture, natural resources, production, and sales. Free of charge.

4183
Saskatchewan's Financial and
Economic Position
Dept of Finance, Investment and Financial Services Bureau, 117 Legislative Bldg, Regina, Sask, Canada S4S 0B3. Telephone (306) 565-6751.

Annual report. Evaluates Saskatchewan's economy and government finances. Provides data on manufacturing and agricultural production, personal income, and public utilities. Free of charge.

4183.01
Satellite News
Phillips Publishing, Inc, 7315 Wisconsin Ave, Bethesda, MD 20014. Telephone (301) 986-0666.

Biweekly newsletter. Covers management technology and regulation of the satellite industry. Price $167.00 per year.

4183.02
Saudi Arabia Newsletter
IC Publications Ltd, 122 E 42nd St, Suite 1121, New York, NY 10017. Telephone (212) 867-5159. Telex 425442.

Biweekly newsletter. Reports on commercial prospects, trade contacts, and government regulations in Saudi Arabia. Price $395.00 per year.

4184
Savings and Home Financing Source
Book
US Federal Home Loan Bank Board, 1700 G St, NW, Washington, DC 20552. Telephone (202) 377-6752.

Annual book. Presents historical data on financial, housing, and related activities of US Federal Home Loan Bank Board and other government and private organizations. Price available on request.

4185
Savings and Loan Fact Book
US League of Savings Assns, 111 E Wacker Dr, Chicago, IL 60601. Telephone (312) 644-3100.

Annual book. Contains historical data on savings and loan business, including housing activity, consumer savings, mortgage lending, savings association operations, and government agency activity. Charts and tables. Single copy orders free of charge.

4186
Savings and Loan Investor
Savings and Loan Investor, PO Box 7163, Long Beach, CA 90807. Telephone (213) 427-1905.

Semimonthly report on savings and loan associations. Includes buy/sell/hold recommendations and earnings-per-share estimates. Graphs and charts. Price $100.00 per year.

4186.01
Savings and Loan Letter
Coopers & Lybrand, 1251 Ave of the Americas, New York, NY 10020. Order from Manager of Publications, PO Box 682, Times Sq Station, New York, NY 10108. Telephone (212) 489-1100.

Periodic newsletter. Covers news of savings and loan industry. Price free of charge.

4187
Savings and Loan News
US League of Savings Assns, 111 E Wacker Dr, Chicago, IL 60601. Telephone (312) 644-3100.

Monthly magazine. Discusses economic, political, and operating developments affecting savings and loan associations. Price $14.00 per year.

4187.01
Savings & Loan Reporter
Andrew R Mandala, PO Box 30240, Washington, DC 20014. Telephone (301) 654-5580.

Weekly newsletter. Comments on developments affecting the savings and loan industry. Price $110.00 per year.

4188
Savings Association News
Savings Assn League of New York State, 700 White Plains Rd, Scarsdale, NY 10583. Telephone (914) 472-3500.

Monthly newspaper. Discusses savings and loan association business. Covers promotions, branching activity, and legislative and regulatory changes. Price $150.00 per year.

4189
Savings Bank Journal
National Assn of Mutual Savings Banks, 200 Park Ave, New York, NY 10017. Telephone (212) 973-5432.

Monthly magazine. Addresses itself to issues of interest to mutual savings banks, including mortgage trends, state and national legislation, and new technology such as electronic funds transfer systems. Price $23.00 per year.

4190
Savings Market
Wootten Publications Ltd, 150/152 Caledonian Rd, London, England N1 9RD. Telephone (44) (01) 278-6854.

Quarterly magazine. Provides information on British unit trusts, unit linked bonds, growth and income bonds, life insurance, and pension plans. Includes performance figures. Price 15.00 per year. ISSN 0308-1729.

4190.01
SAVVY
Savvy, PO Box 2495, Boulder, CO 80321.

Monthly magazine. Discusses management issues from a woman's viewpoint. Offers investment advice. Price $12.00 per year.

4191
SCAN
Advertising Checking Bureau, Inc, 165 N Canal St, Chicago IL 60606. Telephone (312) 648-0500.

Monthly digest. Offers condensations of recent articles on sales, advertising, and merchandising. Price $4.00 per year.

4191.01
Schechter Report/Labs
Capitol Publications, Inc, Suite G-12, 2430 Pennsylvania Ave, NW, Washington, DC 20037. Telephone (202) 452-1600.

Biweekly newsletter. Reports on federal laws and regulations which affect laboratories and blood banks. Covers Medicare and Medicaid reimbursement. Price $140.00 per year.

4192
School Bus Fleet
Bobit Pub Co, 2500 Artesia Blvd, Redondo Beach, CA 90278. Telephone (213) 376-8788.

Bimonthly magazine. Covers school bus transportation. Includes information on primary and secondary schools, private schools, colleges, and schools for the handicapped. Price $9.00 per year.

4193
School Counselor
American Personnel and Guidance Assn, 2 Skyline Place, Suite 400, 5203 Leesburg Pike, Falls Church, VA 22041. Telephone (703) 820-4700.

Magazine issued five times per year. Presents material on school guidance counseling. Price $15.00 per year members, $17.50 per year nonmembers.

4195
School Product News
Penton/IPC, 614 Superior Ave, W, Cleveland, OH 44113. Order from Penton/IPC, 1111 Chester Ave, Cleveland, OH 44114. Telephone (216) 696-7000.

Monthly magazine. Presents information on school products for public and private schools, colleges, and universities. Price $24.00.

4196
Science and Public Policy
IPC Business Press Ltd, 205 E 42nd St, New York, NY 10017. Telephone (212) 889-0700. Telex 421710.

Bimonthly magazine. Discusses national science and technology policies. Examines roles of science and technology in government, industry and business. Price $144.40 per year. ISSN 0302-3427.

4197
Science Research Abstracts Journal, Parts A & B
Cambridge Scientific Abstracts, 6611 Kenilworth Ave, Suite 437, Riverdale, MD 20840. Telephone (301) 951-1327.

Journal issued 10 times per year. Contains indexed abstracts of scientific and technical literature on superconductivity, magnetohydrodynamics and plasmas, theoretical physics, laser and electro-optic reviews, quantum electronics and unconventional energy sources. Price $245.00 per year.

4198
Science Research Abstracts Journal, Part B: Laser and Electro-Optic Reviews; Quantum Electronics; Unconventional Energy Sources
Cambridge Scientific Abstracts, Inc, 6611 Kenilworth Ave, Suite 437, Riverdale, MD 20840. Telephone (301) 864-5752.

Magazine with 10 issues per year. Contains indexed abstracts from worldwide sources on lasers and electro-optics, quantum electronics, and unconventional energy sources. Price $175.00 per year.

4199

Scientific and Technical Books and Serials in Print 1977
R R Bowker Co, 1180 Ave of the Americas, New York, NY 10036. Order from R R Bowker Co, PO Box 1807, Ann Arbor, MI 48106. Telephone (212) 764-5100.

Book. Provides bibliographic and ordering information for titles in physical and biological sciences, engineering, and technology. Includes biographies as well as author, title, and subject index. Price $52.50. ISBN 0-8352-1022-7. ISSN 0000-0248.

4200

Scientific, Engineering and Medical Societies Publications in Print 1978–1979
R R Bowker Co, 1180 Ave of the Americas, New York, MY 10036. Order from R R Bowker Co, PO Box 1807, Ann Arbor, MI 48106. Telephone (212) 764-5100.

Book. Supplies bibliographic data on print and nonprint materials from 365 US scientific and engineering societies and related organizations. Author and key word index. Price $35.00. ISBN 0-8352-1212-2.

4201

Scientific, Engineering, Technical Manpower Comments
Scientific Manpower Commission, 1776 Massachusetts Ave NW, Washington, DC 20036. Telephone (202) 223-6995.

Monthly magazine. Contains information on developments affecting recruitment, training, and use of scientific, engineering, and technical manpower. Notes supply and demand, new publications, and federal agency activities. Price $30.00 per year.

4202

Scientific Information Notes
Trends Publishing, Inc, 233 National Press Bldg, Washington, DC 20045. Telephone (202) 393-0031.

Quarterly book. Discusses sources for scientific and technical information, including information centers and service. Covers periodicals and other publications. Price $75.00 per year.

4203

Scottish Abstract of Statistics
Her Majesty's Stationery Office, PO Box 569, London, England SE1 9NH. Telephone (44) (01) 928 1321.

Annual service. Provides significant statistics from all government departments for Scotland. Price £8.50 per year.

4204

Scottish Bankers Magazine
William Blackwood & Sons Ltd, 32 Thistle St, Edinburgh, Scotland EH2 1HA. Telephone (44) (031) 225-3411.

Quarterly magazine. Covers Scottish banking topics. Price £1.20 per year.

4205

Scottish Economic Bulletin
Her Majesty's Stationery Office, PO Box 569, London, England SE1 9NH. Telephone (44) (01) 928 1321.

Semiannual service. Provides statistical data on the Scottish economy. Price £4.00 semiannually.

4206

Scottish National Register of Classified Trades
Sell's Publications Ltd, Sell's House, 39 E St, Epsom Surrey, England KT17 1BQ. Telephone Epsom 26376. Telex 21792 A/B Mono K LDN.

Directory. Contains a register of 13,000 Scottish firms, listed under 3000 trade headings. Price £12.00.

4207

Scottish Sea Fisheries Statistical Tables
Her Majesty's Stationery Office, PO Box 569, London, England SE1 9NH. Telephone (44) (01) 928 1321.

Annual report. Carries statistical tables on Scottish sea fisheries. Price £4.50 per year.

4208

Scott's Industrial Directory. Atlantic Manufacturers
Scott's Industrial Directories, PO Box 365, Oakville, Ont, Canada L6J 5M5. Telephone (416) 845-8881.

Biennial directory. Lists manufacturers, identifying their executives and products and classifying them by type of product. Covers the Canadian Atlantic provinces. Price $57.75 per copy.

4209

Scott's Industrial Directory. Ontario Manufacturers
Scott's Industrial Directories, PO Box 365, Oakville, Ont, Canada L6J 5M5. Telephone (416) 845-8881.

Book issued every 18 months. Supplies a directory to 15,500 Ontario manufacturers, noting their products, executives, and other company information. Classifies manufacturers by type of product. Price $98.50 per copy.

4210

Scott's Industrial Directory. Quebec Manufacturers
Scott's Industrial Directories, PO Box 365, Oakville, Ont, Canada L6J 5M5. Telephone (416) 845-8881.

Directory issued every 18 months. Furnishes a registry to Quebec manufacturers. Classifies the manufacturers, by type of product and provides other information on firms. French and English. Price $98.50 per copy.

4211

Scott's Industrial Directory. Western Manufacturers
Scott's Industrial Directories, PO Box 365, Oakville, Ont, Canada L6J 5M5. Telephone (416) 845-8881.

Biennial book. Provides a list of manufacturers in Canada's western provinces, classifying manufacturers by product. Notes other company information. Price $98.50 per copy.

4211.01

Screen Printing
Signs of the Times Publishing Co, 407 Gilbert Ave, Cincinnati, OH 45202. Telephone (513) 421-2050.

Monthly magazine. Covers aspects of screen printing industry, including textile and garments, decals, ceramics, electronics, and other industrial types. Price $15.00 per year. ISSN 0036-9594.

4212

Scrip World Pharmaceutical News
PJB Publications Ltd, 18a Hill St, Richmond, Surrey, England TW9 1TN. Telephone (44) (01) 940-8849. Telex 8951042

Twice weekly newsletter. Discusses European and international drug industry developments. Reviews financial growth of companies and government regulation. Price £275.00 per year.

4212.01

SDC Search Service
System Development Corp, 2500 Colorado Ave, Santa Monica, CA 90406. Telephone (213) 820-4111.

On-line retrieval service. Provides access to information on research, applications, business, and other literature-related subjects. Price available on request.

4213

Seafirst Magazine

Seattle First National Bank, 1001 4th Ave, PO Box 3586, Seattle, WA 98124. Telephone (206) 583-3200.

Bimonthly magazine. Reports on Seafirst Corporation programs and services. Outlines regional industrial activities and corporate feature stories. Price free of charge.

4214

Sea Fisheries Statistical Tables

Her Majesty's Stationery Office, PO Box 569, London, England SE1 9NH. Telephone (44) (01) 928 1321.

Annual publication. Provides data on British sea fisheries. Statistical tables. Price £3.75 per year.

4215

Seafood Price—Current

Urner Barry Publications, Inc, PO Box 389, Toms River, NJ 08753. Telephone (201) 240-5330.

Biweekly report. Lists wholesale price ranges for fresh and frozen fish and shellfish. Evaluates the seafood market. Price $75.00 per year.

4216

Seasonally Adjusted Indicators (Cat No 1308.0)

Australian Bureau of Statistics, PO Box 10, Belconnen, ACT 2616, Australia. Order from Australian Government Publishing Service, PO Box 84, Canberra, ACT 2600, Australia. Telephone (062) 52 7911.

Annual report. Presents original and seasonally adjusted data on Australia's economy in tabular and graphic forms. Price $9.00. (Australian).

4217

Seatrade

Seatrade Publications Ltd, Fairfax House, Colchester, England C01 1RJ. Telephone 0206 45121. Telex 98517 Disop G.

Monthly magazine. Covers subjects related to the shipping business. Price, UK £22.50, North America/Mexico US $85.00, Europe/North Africa/Mid East US $65.00, Australasia/Japan US $110.00, rest of world US $90.00.

4218

Seattle Business Journal

Cordovan Corp, 5314 Bingle Rd, Houston, TX 77092. Order from Seattle Business Journal, 9725 3rd Ave, NE, Suite 301, Seattle, WA 98115. Telephone (206) 522-9310.

Weekly newspaper. Contains feature articles on various segments of Seattle business. Price $24.00 per year.

4219

SEC Compliance—Financial Reporting and Forms

Prentice-Hall, Inc, Englewood Cliffs, NJ 07632. Telephone (201) 592-2000. Telex 13-5423.

Monthly loose-leaf service. Explains SEC's financial reporting rules. Notes current developments and provides forms. Price $432.00 per year.

4220

Secondary Market Reporter

Andrew R Mandala, PO Box 30240, Washington, DC 20014. Telephone (301) 654-5580.

Weekly newsletter. Reports on mortgage-backed securities. Price $110.00 per year.

4221

Secured Transactions Guide

Commerce Clearing House, Inc, 4025 W Peterson Ave, Chicago, IL 60646. Telephone (312) 583-8500.

Four loose-leaf books and weekly reports. Cover laws and regulations that protect sellers and lenders through the establishment of security interests. Price $390.00 per year.

4222

Securities and Exchange Commission (SEC) Accounting Report

Warren, Gorham & Lamont, Inc, 210 S St, Boston, MA 02111. Telephone (617) 423-2020.

Monthly report. Covers the Securities and Exchange Commission's accounting requirements and changes. Price $68.00 per year.

4223

Securities and Exchange Commission (SEC) Accounting Rules

Commerce Clearing House, Inc, 4025 W Peterson Ave, Chicago, IL 60646. Telephone (312) 583-8500.

Loose-leaf book, plus periodic reports. Contains accounting regulations and reports of the Securities and Exchange Commission. Released as revisions become official. Price $120.00 per year.

4224

Securities & Exchange Commission Annual Report to Congress

US Securities & Exchange Commission, Washington, DC 20549. Telephone (202) 755-4833.

Annual report. Gives the text of the Securities and Exchange Commission's report to Congress. Price $4.50.

4225

Securities & Exchange Commission Decisions & Reports

US Securities & Exchange Commisson, Washington, DC 20549. Telephone (202) 755-4833.

Book series. Contains the Securities and Exchange Commission's decisions and reports. 1964–1972. Price available on request.

4226

Securities & Exchange Commission (SEC) Disclosure Reports

Disclosure, Inc, 4827 Rugby Ave, Bethesda, MD 20014. Telephone (301) 951-0100.

Annual reports on microfilm. Contains financial disclosure reports for the NYSE, AMEX, and OTC companies. Has 24X magnification. Price $7.50 per document.

4227

Securities & Exchange Commission Docket

US Securities & Exchange Commission, Washington, DC 20549. Order from Superintendent of Documents, Government Printing Office, Washington, DC 20402. Telephone (202) 755-4833.

Weekly report. Contains the text of the Securities and Exchange Commission's releases for the Securities Act of 1933, Securities Exchange Act of 1934, Public Utility Holding Company Act, Trust Indenture Act, Investment Advisers Act, Investment Company Act, Accounting, Staff Accounting Bulletins, Corporate Reorganization, and Litigation. Price $79.00 per year in US, $98.75 elsewhere.

4228
Securities & Exchange Commission
News Digest
US Securities & Exchange Commission, Washington, DC 20549. Order from Superintendent of Documents, Government Printing Office, Washington, DC 20402. Telephone (202) 755-4833.

Daily newsletter. Reports on the Securities and Exchange Commission's activities, including trading suspension, hearings, Holding Company Act releases and Securities Act registrations. Price $100.00 per year in US, $125.00 elsewhere.

4229
Securities & Exchange Commission
Official Summary
US Securities & Exchange Commission, Washington, DC 20549. Order from Superintendent of Documents, Government Printing Office, Washington, DC 20402. Telephone (202) 755-4833.

Monthly report. Summarizes security transactions and holdings reported by insiders according to provisions of federal securities laws. Price $50.00 per year US, $62.50 elsewhere.

4230
Securities & Exchange Commission
(SEC) Quarterly
American Institute of Certified Public Accountants, 1211 Ave of the Americas, New York, NY 10036. Telephone (212) 575-6200.

Information service (four cassettes). Reports on the Securities and Exchange Commission's actions and changes in accounting rules and reporting requirements. Notes pertinent court cases. Price $65.00 per year.

4231
Securities & Exchange Commission
Statistical Bulletin
US Securities & Exchange Commission, Washington, DC 20549. Order from Superintendent of Documents, Government Printing Office, Washington, DC 20402. Telephone (202) 755-4833.

Monthly report. Presents data on new securities offerings, registrations, volume and value of trading on exchanges, over-the-counter volume, and related information. Price $15.00 per year in US, $18.75 elsewhere.

4232
Securities and Federal Corporate Law,
1972, base edition
Clark Boardman Co Ltd, 435 Hudson St, New York, NY 10014. Telephone (212) 929-7500.

Annually updated loose-leaf books. Deal with securities regulation. Price $215.00 for loose-leaf volumes plus binder containing monthly update service report. ISBN 0-87632-086-8.

4233
Securities Law Review
Clark Boardman Co Ltd, 435 Hudson St, New York, NY 10014. Telephone (212) 929-7500.

Annual book. Reviews securities regulations. Price $52.50 per volume. ISBN 0-87632-178-3.

4234
Securities Regulation
Prentice-Hall, Inc, Englewood Cliffs, NJ 07632. Telephone (201) 592-2000. Telex 13-5423.

Biweekly loose-leaf service. Explains all laws administered by the Securities and Exchange Commission. Includes state security laws. Price $426.00 per year.

4235
Securities Regulation & Law Report
Bureau of National Affairs, Inc, 1231 25th St NW, Washington, DC 20037. Telephone (202) 452-4200.

Loose-leaf books, with weekly updates. Provide news on developments in securities regulation and the financial disclosure field. Supply the text of proposed and enacted legislation. Price $364.00 per year.

4236
Securities Regulation Law Journal
Warren, Gorham & Lamont, Inc, 210 S St, Boston, MA 02111. Telephone (617) 423-2020.

Quarterly magazine. Concerns regulation of the securities industry. Price $56.00 per year.

4236.01
Securities Update
Coopers & Lybrand, 1251 Ave of the Americas, New York, NY 10020. Order from Manager of Publications, PO Box 682, Times Sq Station, New York, NY 10108. Telephone (212) 489-1100.

Periodic newsletter. Discusses developments in securities industry. Price free of charge.

4237
Securities Week
McGraw-Hill Publications Co, 1221 Ave of the Americas, New York, NY 10020. Telephone (212) 997-3144. Telex TWX 7105814879 WUI 62555.

Weekly newsletter. Reports on the US and foreign securities industry, government regulation of capital markets, and market developments. Price $610.00, $635.00 foreign per year.

4238
Security Charts
United Business Service Co, 210 Newbury St, Boston, MA 02116. Telephone (617) 267-8855.

Monthly set of charts. Supplies weekly price ranges, relative market performance, volumes, earnings, and dividends for 1105 stocks. Industry group charts and commentary. Price $67.00 per year.

4239
Security Dealers Directory
Standard & Poor's Corp, 25 Broadway, New York, NY 10004. Telephone (212) 248-2525.

Semiannual book. Lists brokerage and investment banking houses in the US and Canada, with their executive rosters and other data. Price $89.00 per copy, $185.00 per year.

4240
Security Distributing & Marketing
(SDM)
Cashners Publishing Co, 5 S Wabash, Chicago, IL 60603. Telephone (312) 372-6880.

Monthly magazine. Covers marketing and installation of security products. Includes technical information. Price $24.00 per year. Product directory $20.00 per issue.

4240.01
Security/Fire Equipment Manufacturers'
Directory
Marketing Development, 402 Border Rd, Concord, MA 01742. Telephone (617) 369-5382.

Book. Lists 680 security/fire equipment manufacturers. Includes addresses, telephone numbers, key officers, type of product, employment, and projected sales levels. Price $65.00.

4241
Security Industry & Product News
PTN Publishing Corp, 250 Fulton Ave, Hempstead, NY 11550. Telephone (516) 489-1300.

Bimonthly magazine. Reports on new products and services for the security industry. Price $5.00 per year.

4242
Security Letter
Security Letter, Inc, 475 5th Ave, New York, NY 10017. Telephone (212) 725-1073.

Semimonthly newsletter. Discusses corporate security issues, including management techniques, fire prevention, insurance, and occupational safety. Price $95.00 per year.

4243
Security Management
Bureau of Business Practice, 24 Rope Ferry Rd, Waterford, CT 06386. Telephone (203) 442-4365.

Twice-monthly report. Covers such management problems as drugs, vandalism, riots, gambling, and plant security. Price $36.00 per year.

4244
Security Pacific National Bank
International Trade Data Bank
Security Pacific National Bank, PO Box 2097, Terminal Annex, Los Angeles, CA 90051. Telephone (213) 613-5414.

Computer printouts. Give detailed information on the volume of imports and exports between all US customs districts and various trade centers of the world. Price $100.00 and up per report.

4245
Security Pacific National Bank Monthly
Summary of Business Conditons,
Central Valley Counties of California
Security Pacific National Bank, PO Box 2097, Terminal Annex, Los Angeles, CA 90051. Order from Security Pacific National Bank, PO Box 1691, Fresno, CA 93717. Telephone (213) 613-5402.

Monthly newsletter. Reviews economic conditions in 17 Central Valley California counties. Features the prices of agricultural products. Price free of charge.

4246
Security Pacific National Bank Monthly
Summary of Business Conditions,
Southern California
Security Pacific National Bank, PO Box 2097, Terminal Annex, Los Angeles, CA 90051. Telephone (213) 613-5402.

Monthly newsletter. Reviews economic conditions in 10 southern California counties. Price free of charge.

4247
Security Pacific National Bank Monthly
Summary of Business Conditions,
Northern Coastal Counties of California
Security Pacific National Bank, PO Box 2097, Terminal Annex, Los Angeles, CA 90051. Order from Security Pacific National Bank, PO Box 7636, San Francisco, CA 94120. Telephone (213) 613-5402.

Monthly newsletter. Reviews economic conditions in 16 northern coastal California counties. Price free of charge.

4248
Security Pacific National Bank (SPNB)
California Databank
Security Pacific National Bank, PO Box 2097, Terminal Annex, Los Angeles, CA 90051. Telephone (213) 613-5381.

Computer printouts. Offer economic data for California cities, counties, and metropolitan areas. Provide on-line service to subscribers. Statistics. Price $10.00 per time-series.

4249
Security Transactions with Non-residents
Statistics Canada, User Services, Publications Distribution, Ottawa, Ont, Canada K1A 0V7. Telephone (613) 992-3151.

Monthly report. Provides data on security transactions between Canadian residents and foreign residents by types of securities. Price $30.00 per year.

4250
Security World
Cahners Publishing Co, 5 S Wabash, Chicago, Il 60603. Telephone (312) 372-6880

Monthly magazine. Reports on topics of interest to users of security products, including professional security administrators and governmental security agencies. Price $24.00 per year. Product directory $20.00 per issue.

4252
Selected Business Ventures
General Electric Co, Business Growth Services, 120 Erie Blvd, Room 591, Schenectady, NY 12305. Telephone (518) 385-2577.

Monthly newsletters. Describe products and processes available for license or acquisition from mechanical, electronic, chemical, measuring and testing, consumer, and materials (forming and production) fields. Price $175.00 per year for first category, $250.00 per year second category, $50.00 per year each additional category (up to 6).

4253
Selected Interest and Exchange Rates
US Federal Reserve System, Board of Governors, Washington, DC 20551. Order from Publication Services, Div of Adm Services, Board of Governors of the Federal Reserve System, Washington DC 20551. Telephone (202) 452-3245.

Weekly publication. Depicts spot and forward exchange rates, Eurodollar and foreign money market rates, bond yields, stock indexes, and gold prices. Series of charts. Price $20.00 per year.

4254
Selected Water Resources Abstracts
(SWRA)
US Dept of the Interior, Washington, DC 20240. Order from US Dept of Commerce, National Technical Information Service, 5825 Port Royal Rd, Springfield, VA 22161. Telephone (202) 487-4630.

Semimonthly magazine. Contains abstracts of articles on water resources. Price $100.00 per year.

4255
Select Information Exchange (SIE)
Guide to Business & Investment Books,
1974 edition
Select Information Exchange, 2095 Broadway, New York, NY 10023. Telephone (212) 874-6408.

Book. Serves as a source finder for 8000 books offering business and investment advice in the US and abroad. Price $12.-95.

4256
Selling New & Newspaper Advertising
Worksheet
Newspaper Advertising Bureau, Inc, 485 Lexington Ave, New York, NY 10017. Telephone (212) 557-1800.

Monthly newspaper. Reports on retailing and advertising. Price $7.00 per year.

4257
Selling Today
United Commercial Travellers' Assn Section of Assn of Scientific Technical and Managerial Staffs, ASTMS, Bexton Lane, Knutsford, Cheshire, England WA16 9DA. Telephone Knutsford 4136.

Monthly trade union newspaper. Reports on employment conditions for salespeople in Great Britain and the Republic of Ireland. Price £10.00 per year.

4258
Sell's British Exporters
Sell's Publications Ltd, Sell's House, 39 E St, Epsom Surrey, England KT17 1BQ. Telephone Epsom 26376. Telex 21792 A/B Mono K LDN.

Book. Contains an alphabetical list of exporting firms and their overseas agents, and a list of export products and services. Price £12.00.

4259
Sell's Building Index
Sell's Publication Ltd, Sell's House, 39 E St, Epsom Surrey, England KT17 1BQ. Telephone Epsom 26376. Telex 21792 A/B Mono K LDN.

Book. Provides a directory to firms, products, and services in the building and construction industries in Great Britain. Price £15.00.

4260
Sell's Directory
Sell's Publications Ltd, Sell's House 39 E St, Epsom Surrey, England KT17 1BQ. Telephone Epsom 26376. Telex 21792 A/B Mono K LDN.

Book. Provides data on over 65,000 firms listed alphabetically with name, trade, address and telephone number. Also includes over 25,000 trade classifications and a trade names index, both cross referenced to the alphabetical listing. Price £20.00.

4261
Sentinel
Supply and Services Canada, Publishing Centre, Printing and Publishing, Ottawa, Ont, Canada K1A 0S9. Telephone (613) 238-1601.

Monthly report. Offers news and information regarding the Canadian armed forces. Price $4.20 per year.

4262
Serial Number Field Guide
Associated Equipment Distributors, 615 W 22nd St, Oak Brook, IL 60521. Telephone (312) 654-0650.

Annual book. Provides the original year of manufacture for more than 200 leading makes of construction equipment. Price $20.00 per copy.

4263
Serial Number Location Guide for Construction Equipment
Associated Equipment Distributors, 615 W 22nd St, Oak Brook, IL 60521. Telephone (312) 654-0650.

Annual book. Lists serial number locations for construction equipment. Gives profiles of various types of machinery as an aid in tracking that which has been stolen. Price $4.00 per copy.

4264
SER Network News
SER-Jobs for Progress, Inc, 8585 N Stemmons Freeway, Suite 401, Dallas, TX 75247. Telephone (214) 631-3999.

Newsletter. Summarizes activities of 150 SER affiliates which provide employment and training services to Hispanic Americans. Price available upon request.

4265
SER News
SER-Jobs for Progress, Inc, 9841 Airport Blvd, Suite 1020, Los Angeles, CA 90045. Telephone (213) 649-1511.

Monthly magazine. Is a supplement to the SER Newsletter. Contains articles about the employment and training of Spanish-speaking Americans. Price available on request.

4266
SER Newsletter
SER-Jobs for Progress, Inc, SER Jobs for Progress, Inc, 8585 N Stemmons Freeway, Suite 401, Dallas, TX 75247. Telephone (214) 631-3999.

Monthly newsletter. Covers manpower issues affecting Spanish-speaking Americans. Price available on request.

4267
Services and Software Information Program
International Data Corp, 214 3rd Ave, Waltham, MA 02254. Telephone (617) 890-3700. Telex 92-3401.

Continuous information service. Provides computer software vendors with market forecasts, competitive analysis, and reports on latest industry trends. Price available on request.

4268
Service to Business & Industry
Brooklyn Public Library, Grand Army Plz, Brooklyn, NY 11238. Telephone (212) 780-7759.

Monthly (September to June) pamphlet. Provides brief descriptions and bibliographic data about books and other publications of interest to people in business. Includes such topics as women in business, relocation, energy, and technical careers. Price $5.00 per year.

4270
Service World International
Cahners Publishing Company, Inc, 221 Columbus Ave, Boston, MA 02116. Telephone (617) 536-7780.

Monthly magazine. Covers food service, lodging, transportation, and related industries serving world tourism. Price $15.00 per year.

4270.01
SER Women's Update
SER-Jobs for Progress, Inc, 8585 N Stemmons Frway, Suite 401, Dallas, TX 75247. Telephone (214) 631-3999.

Monthly factsheet. Reports on employment and training issues related to Hispanic women in the labor force. Price available on request.

4271
Sewage Treatment Construction Grants Manual
Bureau of National Affairs, Inc, 1231 25th St NW, Washington, DC 20037. Telephone (202) 452-4200.

Two loose-leaf volumes, with updates, monthly, loose-leaf. Pertain to federal construction grants dealing with sewage treatment in accordance with Title II of the Federal Water Pollution Control Act. Include an index, copies of relevant forms, the text of acts, and Environmental Protection Agency guidelines. Price $205.00 per year.

4272
Share-Owners
Financial Times Business Information Ltd, Bracken House, 10 Cannon St, London, England EC4P 4BY. Order from Financial Times Ltd, 75 Rockefeller Plz, New York, NY 10019. Telephone (44) (01) 248-8000. Telex 886341-2.

Publication. Presents statistics on the ownership of shares. Price available on request.

4273
Sheets, Pillowcases, and Towels
US Dept of Commerce, Bureau of the Census, Washington, DC 20233. Telephone (202) 449-1600.

Quarterly report, with annual summary. Provides statistics on the production and shipment of sheets, pillowcases, and towels. Price $1.25 per year.

4275
Shipping and Trade News
Tokyo News Service Ltd, Tsukiji Hamarikyu Bldg, 3-3, Tsukiji 5-chome, Chuo-ku, Tokyo 104, Japan. Telephone (03) 542-8521. Telex 252-3285 STNEWS J.

Daily newspaper. Reports on Japanese and international shipping and foreign trade developments. Lists ship arrivals and departures in Japan. Price US $572.00 per year.

4281
Shoes and Slippers
US Dept of Commerce, Bureau of the Census, Washington, DC 20233. Telephone (202) 449-1600.

Monthly report, with annual summary. Provides figures on footwear production by kind of footwear. Includes data on shipments of shoes and slippers. Price $3.30 per year.

4282
Shop
Southam Communications Ltd, 1450 Don Mills Rd, Don Mills, Ont, Canada M3B 2X7. Telephone (416) 445-6641. Telex 06-966612.

Monthly publication. Deals with used and new machinery for manufacturing industries, utilities, and municipalities. Price $33.00 per year.

4283
Shopping Center Newsletter
National Research Bureau, Inc, 424 N 3rd St, Burlington, IA 52601. Telephone (319) 752-5415.

Monthly newsletter. Covers shopping center activity. Price $30.00 per year.

4283.01
Shopping Center World
Communication Channels, Inc, 6285 Barfield Rd, Atlanta, GA 30328. Telephone (404) 256-9800.

Monthly magazine. Covers all aspects of shopping center development and management. Price $30.00 per year.

4284
Short Courses and Seminars
Development Publications Ltd, Box 84, Station A, Willowdale, Ont, Canada M2N 5S7. Telephone (416) 636-2230.

Semiannual book. Presents a schedule of short business and management courses given in Canada. Includes such subjects as accounting, industrial relations, computers, and communications. Price $3.00 per copy.

4285
Significant Provisions of State Unemployment Insurance Laws
US Dept of Labor, Employment & Training Adm, Washington, DC 20213. Telephone (202) 376-6730.

Semiannual report. Contains important provisions of state unemployment insurance laws. Indicates comparative benefits, coverage, and taxes. Tables. Price free of charge.

4286
Signs of the Times
Signs of the Times Publishing Co, 407 Gilbert Ave, Cincinnati, Ohio 45202. Telephone (513) 421-2050.

Monthly magazine. Provides information about sign and outdoor advertising industries. Price $18.00 per year.

4287
Silver Data
American Bureau of Metal Statistics, Inc, 420 Lexington Ave, New York, NY 10170. Telephone (212) 867-9450. Telex 14-7130.

Monthly report. Consists of silver refining statistics for the US and other countries. Price $75.00 per year.

4289
Sino-British Trade
Sino-British Trade Council, 25 Queen Anne's Gate, London, England SW1H 9BU. Telephones: (44) (01) 222-8785, (44) (01) 222-9600.

Monthly report. Pertains to British trade with China. Price £20.00 per year, £25.00 per year foreign.

4289.01
Site Report
Conway Publications, Inc, Peachtree Air Terminal, 1954 Airport Rd, Atlanta, GA 30341. Telephone (404) 458-6026.

Bimonthly loose-leaf newsletter. Covers new projects in predevelopment, permit, or construction stages. Includes site studies and pending projects. Arranged by states. Price $250.00 per year.

4290
Site Selection Handbook
Conway Publications, Inc, Peachtree Air Terminal, 1954 Airport Rd, Atlanta, GA 30341. Telephone (404) 458-6026.

Four annual publications. Focuses each book on a different aspect of new facility location planning. Price free to subscribers of Industrial Development. Single issue $15.00; four volumes $45.00. ISSN 0080-9810.

4292
Walter Skinner's Mining International Year Book
Financial Times Business Information Ltd, Bracken House, 10 Cannon St, London, England EC4P 4BY. Order from Financial Times, Ltd, 75 Rockefeller Plz, New York, NY 10019. Telephone (44) (01) 248-8000. Telex 886341-2.

Annual book. Covers worldwide mining industries. Price available on request.

4293
Walter Skinner's North Sea and Europe Offshore Year Book and Buyer's Guide
Financial Times Business Information Ltd, Bracken House, 10 Cannon St, London, England EC4P 4BY. Order from Financial Times Ltd, 75 Rockefeller Plz, New York, NY 10019. Telephone (44) (91) 248-8000. Telex 886341-2.

Annual book. Covers North Sea and European offshore oil. Price available on request.

4294
Walter Skinner's Oil and Gas International Year Book
Financial Times Business Information Ltd, Bracken House, 10 Cannon St, London, England EC4P 4BY. Order from Financial Times Ltd, 75 Rockefeller Plz, New York, NY 10019. Telephone (44) (01) 248-8000. Telex 886341-2.

Annual book. Reviews the international oil and gas situation. Price available on request.

4295
Walter Skinner's Who's Who in World Oil and Gas
Financial Times Business Information Ltd, Bracken House, 10 Cannon St, London, England EC4P 4BY. Order from Financial Times Ltd, 75 Rockefeller Plz, New York, NY 10019. Telephone (44) (01) 248-8000. Telex 886341-2.

Publication. Presents data on key figures in the global oil and gas industry. Price available on request.

4296
Sloan Management Review
Massachusetts Inst of Technology, Alfred P Sloan School of Management, Cambridge, MA 02139. Telephone (617) 253-7170.

Journal published four times per year. Contains articles on management techniques. Price $24.00, $36.00 Foreign per year.

4297
Sludge Newsletter
Business Publishers, Inc, PO Box 1067, Silver Spring, MD 20910. Telephone (301) 587-6300.

Biweekly newsletter. Contains information on pollution control residuals management. Price $95.00 per year.

4298
Small Business Administration Annual Report
US Small Business Administration, 1030 15th St, NW, Suite 250, Washington, DC 20417. Telephone (202) 655-4000. Order from Supt. of Documents, Government Printing Office, Washinton, DC 20402.

Annual report. Covers the activities of the Small Business Administration. Price available on request.

4299
Small Business Bibliographies
US Small Business Adm, 1030 15th St NW, Suite 250, Washington, DC 20417. Telephone (202) 655-4000.

Pamphlets. Supply reference sources for individual types of businesses. Include information on retailing, mail order selling, inventory management, marketing, and other topics. Price free of charge.

4300
Small Business Computer News
Management Information Corp, 140 Barclay Center, Cherry Hill, NJ 08034. Telephone (609) 428-1020.

Monthly report. Evaluates business micro and minicomputers. Price $245.00 per year; $135.00 renewal.

4301
Small Business Management Series
US Small Business Adm, 1030 15th St, NW, Suite 250, Washington, DC 20417. Order from Superintendent of Documents, Government Printing Office, Washington, DC 20402. Telephone (202) 783-3238.

Pamphlets. Discuss small business management topics, including communications, finance, accounting, public relations, and personnel management. Price available on request.

4301.01
Small Business Report
Small Business Report, 497 Lighthouse Ave, Monterey, CA 93940. Telephone (408) 649-1691.

Monthly magazine. Reports on small business topics. Includes information on employee benefits, tax rulings, and marketing. Price $56.00 per year.

4302
Small Business Reporter
Bank of America, Small Business Reporter, Dept 3120, PO Box 37000, San Francisco, CA 94137. Telephone (415) 622-2491.

Series. Includes reports on specific types of small business and on principles and practices of business management. Reports on retail operations cover investment requirements and operations ratios. Publication index. Price free of charge.

4302.01
Small Business Tax Control
Capitol Publications, Inc, Suite G-12, 2430 Pennsylvania Ave, NW, Washington, DC 20037. Telephone (202) 452-1600.

Loose-leaf service with monthly bulletin. Provides tax-saving ideas for small businesses. Notes tax law changes. Price $76.00 per year.

4303
Smaller Manufacturer
Smaller Manufacturers Council, 339 Blvd of the Allies, Pittsburgh, PA 15222. Telephone (412) 391-1624.

Monthly magazine. Presents reports on small business and on subjects of interest to their owners. Price $1.50 per copy.

4304
Small Industry Bulletin for Asia and the Pacific
United Nations Publications, United Nations Plaza, Rm A-3315, New York, NY 10017. Telephone (212) 754-8302.

Report. Covers Asian and Far Eastern industries. Price available on request.

4307
Smart Money
Editor, Hirsch Organization, Inc, 6 Deer Trail, Old Tappan, NJ 07675. Telephone (201) 664-3400.

Monthly newsletter. Covers stock market conditions and outlook. Graphs. Price $85.00 per year, $45.00 for six months.

4308
Snack Food
Harcourt Brace Jovanovich Publications, 757 3rd Ave, New York, NY 10017. Order from Harcourt Brace and Jovanovich Publications, 1 E 1st St, Duluth, MN 55802. Telephone (218) 727-8511.

Monthly magazine. Covers the snack food industry news. Price $15.00 per year.

4309
Snack Food Blue Book
Harcourt Brace Jovanovich Publications, 757 3rd Ave, New York, NY 10017. Order from Harcourt Brace and Jovanovich Publications, 1 E 1st St, Duluth, MN 55802. Telephone (218) 727-8511.

Annual book. Lists US and foreign snack food manufacturers, distributors, and associations. Provides market data. Price $45.00 per copy.

4311
Social and Economic Trends in Northern Ireland
Her Majesty's Stationery Office, PO Box 569, London, England SE1 9NH. Telephone (44) (01) 928 1321.
Annual service. Offers statistics on social and economic trends in Northern Ireland. Price £3.00 per year.

4312
Social and Labour Bulletin
International Labour Organization, 1750 New York Ave, NW, Suite 330, Washington, DC 20006. Telephone (202) 376-2315.
Quarterly report. Concerns current national and international events pertaining to the social aspects of the labor field. Covers legislation, collective agreements, and work environment. Price $23.00 per year.

4313
Social Indicators (Cat No 4101.0)
Australian Bureau of Statistics, PO Box 10, Belcannen, ACT, 2616, Australia. Order from Australian Government Publishing Service, PO Box 84, Canberra, ACT 2600, Australia. Telephone (062) 52 7911.
Annual report. Presents significant Australian social statistics. Includes such topics as population, health, education, and criminal justice. Price $5.45 (Australian).

4313.01
Social Policy and Administration
Basil Blackwell Publisher, 108 Cowley Rd, Oxford, England OX4 1JF. Telephone Oxford (STD 0865) 722146.
Journal published three times a year. Covers the social sciences, especially social policy and issues affecting local and national governments. Price $44.50 per year. ISSN 0037-7643.

4314
Social Sciences Citation Index
Inst for Scientific Information, 3501 Market St, University City Science Center, Philadelphia, Pa 19104. Telephone (215) 386-0100.
Index issued in two triannual issues and one annual cumulation. Lists articles and authors' citations appearing in journals covering the social sciences and related fields. Price $1800.00 per year.

4315
Social Sciences Index
H W Wilson Co, 950 University Ave, Bronx, NY 10452. Telephone (212) 588-8400.
Quarterly index to 261 prominent periodicals representing the various disciplines of the social sciences. Price available on request.

4316
Social Security Explained
Commerce Clearing House, Inc, 4025 W Peterson Ave, Chicago, IL 60646. Telephone (312) 583-8500.
Book. Provides background and current interpretations of Social Security and Medicare legislation. Benefit and wage tax tables. Price $6.00.

4317
Social Security Beneficiaries in Metropolitan Areas
US Social Security Adm, Office of Research and Statistics, Washington, DC 20201. Telephone (202) 953-3600.
Annual report. Supplies data on Social Security cash benefits paid to beneficiaries living in metropolitan areas as of end of 1975. Indicates age, race, and sex of beneficiaries. Price free of charge.

4318
Social Security Bulletin
US Social Security Adm, Office of Research and Statistics, Washington, DC 20201. Order from Superintendent of Documents, US Government Printing Office, Washington, DC 20402. Telephone (202) 953-3600.
Monthly magazine. Publishes articles on the US Social Security system, including benefits and finance. Price $16.00 per year.

4319
Social Security Statistics
Her Majesty's Stationery Office, PO Box 569, London, England SE1 9NH. Telephone (44) (01) 583 9876, extension 6215.
Annual report. Presents statistics on the British Social Security. Price £7.00 per year.

4320
Social Statistics
Commission of the European Communities, Office for Official Publications of the European Communities, CP 1003, Luxembourg 1, Luxembourg. Telephone (352) 490081. Telex PUBLOF 1325.

Irregular report. Provides social statistics for the European community. Price $36.20 per year.

4321
Social Trends
Her Majesty's Stationery Office, PO Box 569, London, England SE1 9NH. Telephone (44) (01) 928 1321.
Annual publication. Illustrates distributions and trends in British society. Covers such areas as population, employment, personal income, and health. Tables and charts. Price £12.90 per year.

4323
Society of Actuaries Year Book
Society of Actuaries, 208 S LaSalle St, Chicago, IL 60604. Telephone (312) 236-3833.
Book. Lists society members. Price available on request.

4324
Socio-Economic Planning Sciences
Pergamon Press, Inc, Maxwell House, Fairview Park, Elmsford, NY 10523. Telephone (914) 592-7700. Telex 13-7328.
Bimonthly magazine. Presents information on socioeconomic planning subjects. Price $90.00 per year.

4325
Software—Practice & Experience
John Wiley & Sons, Inc, 605 3rd Ave, New York, NY 10158. Telephone (212) 850-6418.
Monthly publication. Publishes papers on system software and application software for use in batch, multiaccess, interactive and real time environments. Price $195.00 per year.

4326
Solar Age
Solar Vision, Inc, Church Hill, Harrisville, NH 03450. Telephone (603) 827-3347.
Monthly magazine. Discusses solar energy applications. Includes information on engineering, architectural designs, and construction details. Price $18.00 per year.

4326.01
Solar Energy Digest
Solar Energy Digest, PO Box 17776, San Diego, CA 92117. Telephone (714) 277-2980.

Monthly newsletter. Reports on solar energy developments. Notes meetings and seminars. Price $35.00 per year.

4326.02
Solar Energy Intelligence Report
Business Publishers, PO Box 1067, Silver Spring, MD 20910. Telephone (301) 587-6300.

Weekly newsletter. Provides information on solar energy developments. Price $127.00 per year.

4326.03
Solar Engineering Magazine
Solar Engineering Publishers, Inc, 2636 Walnut Hill Lane, Suite 257, Dallas, TX 75229. Telephone (214) 350-1370.

Monthly magazine. Reports on the solar energy industry. Focuses on technical developments. Price available on request.

4326.04
Solar Heating and Cooling Magazine
Solar Energy Industries Assn, Suite 800, 1001 Connecticut Ave, NW, Washington, DC 20036. Telephone (202) 293-2981.

Monthly journal. Covers solar heating and cooling news. Price $20.00 per year.

4327
Solidarity
United Automobile, Aerospace, and Agricultural Implement Workers of America, 8000 E Jefferson Ave, Detroit, MI 48214. Telephone (313) 926-5291.

Magazine issued every three months. Discusses the United Automobile, Aerospace and Agricultural Implement Workers of America's issues and policies. Reports on general labor developments. Price $5.00 per year.

4328
Solid State Abstracts Journal
Cambridge Scientific Abstracts, 6611 Kenilworth Ave, Suite 437, Riverdale, MD 20840. Telephone (301) 951-1327.

Magazine, ten issues per year. Supplies indexed abstracts from over 8500 periodicals, reports, dissertations, and patents on solid-state physics, chemistry, metallurgy, measurements, and thin films. Price $370.00 per year.

4328.01
Solid Waste Reference Service
Business Publishers, Inc, PO Box 1067, Silver Spring, MD 20910. Telephone (301) 587-6300.

Annual service. Provides text of new solid waste regulations as they are issued. Price $157.00 per year.

4329
Solid Waste Report
Business Publishers, Inc, PO Box 1067, Silver Spring, MD 20910. Telephone (301) 587-6300.

Biweekly newsletter. Surveys the solid waste management field. Price $127.00 per year.

4329.01
Solid Wastes Management
Communication Channels, Inc, 6285 Barfield Rd, Atlanta, GA 30328. Telephone (404) 256-9800.

Monthly magazine. Discusses processing and disposing of solid, liquid, and hazardous wastes. Notes developments in landfilling, recycling, equipment, and legislation. Price $18.00 per year.

4330
Sophisticated Investor
Select Information Exchange, 2095 Broadway, New York, NY 10023. Telephone (212) 874-6408.

Irregularly issued catalog. Provides a directory to nearly 900 periodicals and services concerned with business and investment in the US and abroad. Price $1.00. ISSN 0085-6335.

4331
Sounding Board
The Vancouver Board of Trade, 1177 W Hastings St, 5th Floor, Vancouver, British Columbia, Canada V6E 2K3. Telephone (604) 681-2111.

Newsletter. Reports on activities of the Vancouver, British Columbia, Board of Trade. Includes a directory of members' products and services. Price included in membership dues. Individual copies available on request.

4332
Sound of the Economy
Citibank, Economics Dept, 399 Park Ave, New York, NY 10022. Telephone (212) 559-4022.

Monthly service. Discusses current business, economic, and political trends. Includes such topics as interest rates, government spending, corporate profits, and unemployment. Price $124.00 per year (cassette and transcript).

4333
Source Book of Health Insurance Data
Health Insurance Inst, 1850 K St NW Washington, DC 20006.

Annual report. Covers trends and gives statistics on the health insurance industry. Price free of charge. ISSN 0073-148X.

4334
Source Guide for Borrowing Capital
Capital Publishing Corp, Box 348, Wellesley Hills, MA 02181. Telephone (617) 235-5405.

Book. Discusses how smaller businesses can raise capital through debt financing or long-term borrowing from the government or private sector. Lists federal and state financing programs and 200 finance and leasing companies. Price $49.50. ISBN 0-914470-09-4.

4334.01
Sources of Asian/Pacific Economic Information
Gower Publishing Co Ltd, 1 Westmead, Farnborough, Hampshire, England GUI4 7RU. Telephone Farnborough (0252) 519221. Telex 858623.

Two-volume directory. Serves as guide to the principal sources of economic data on Asia and individual Asian/Pacific countries. Price $160.00.

4335
Sources of European Economic Information, 3rd edition
Gower Publishing Co, Ltd, 1 Westmead, Farnborough, Hampshire, England GU14 7RU. Telephone Farnborough (0252) 519221. Telex 858623.

Directory. Acts as a guide to over 2000 sources from 17 different countries. Indexes all entries by country and subject. Price $89.00. ISBN 0 566 02150 1.

4336.01
Sources of World Financial and Banking Information
Gower Publishing Co Ltd, 1 Westmead, Farnborough, Hampshire, England GUI4 7RU. Telephone Farnborough (0252) 519221. Telex 858623.

Directory. Identifies, lists, and analyzes over 5000 sources of financial and banking data from over 150 different countries. Price $135.00. ISBN 0 566 02159 5.

4337

South Africa Yearbook

South African Consulate General, Suite 1200, 425 Park Ave, New York, NY 10022. Telephone (212) 838-1700. Telex 233290.

Annual book. Provides information on the South African government and economic and social conditions. Covers population, foreign relations, manufacturing, mining, and culture. Price $45.00 per copy. ISBN 0 621 03272 7. ISSN 0302 0681.

4339

South African Market Guide

Dun & Bradstreet, Box 3224, Church St Station, New York, NY 10008. Telephone (212) 285-7346.

Annual book. Contains data on 47,000 businesses in South Africa. Gives estimated net worth and composite credit appraisal. Price available on request, to Dun & Bradstreet subscribers only.

4340

Southam Building Guide

Southam Communications Ltd, 1450 Don Mills Rd, Don Mills, Ont, Canada M3B 2X7. Telephone (416) 445-6641. Telex 06-966612.

Bimonthly publication. Gives information on the Canadian construction industry. Statistics. Price $22.00 per year.

4341

Southam Building Reports

Southam Communications Ltd, 1450 Don Mills Rd, Don Mills, Ont, Canada M3B 2X7. Telephone (416) 445-6641. Telex 06-966612.

Daily report. Supplies advance information on contemplated building projects in Canada. Price available on request.

4342

South Bay Economic Review

Copley Newspapers, 7776 Ivanhoe Ave, PO Box 1530, La Jolla, CA 92038. Order from South Bay Daily Breeze, 5215 Torrance Blvd, Torrance, CA 92509 Telephone (714) 454-0391.

Quarterly report. Reviews business and economic news of southwest Los Angeles County. Retail sales tables. Price free of charge.

4342.01

South Carolina: Industrial Directory, **1981**

Manufacturers' News, Inc, 3 E Huron St, Chicago, IL 60611. Telephone (312) 337-1084.

Annual book. Provides information on 3300 South Carolina industrial firms listed by name, location, and product. Price $34.00.

4342.02

South Carolina: State Industrial Directory, **1980**

Manufacturers' News, Inc, 3 E Huron St, Chicago, Il 60611. Telephone (312) 337-1084.

Annual book. Lists 2500 South Carolina industrial companies and 13,500 executives. Indicates county, city, product, and number of employees. Price $30.00.

4343

South Dakota Business Review

University of South Dakota, School of Business, Business Research Bureau, Vermillion, SD 57069. Telephone (605) 677-5287.

Quarterly report. Discusses economic and business subjects, with emphasis on South Dakota. Provides data on South Dakota's gross sales, employment, and other economic indicators. Tables. Price free of charge.

4344

South Dakota Crop and Livestock Reporter

US Dept of Agriculture, Crop Reporting Board, Economics and Statistics Service (ESS), Room 0005 S Bldg, Washington, DC 20250. Order from South Dakota Dept of Agriculture, Statistical Reporting Service, Consolidated Mailing Services, PO Drawer V, Sioux Falls, SD 57101. Telephone (605) 336-2980 ext 235.

Biweekly report. Provides information on South Dakota grain, crop plantings and production, livestock, livestock products, milk and egg production, and agricultural prices. Price free of charge.

4345

South Dakota: Manufacturers & Processors Directory, **1980**

Manufacturer's News, Inc, 3 E Huron St, Chicago, Il 60611. Telephone (312) 337-1084.

Biennial book. Covers 1000 South Dakota manufacturing and processing companies. Indicates location, products, and executives. Price $13.00.

4345.01

South Dakota Manufacturers Directory, **1981 Edition**

South Dakota Dept of Economic & Tourism Development, South Dakota Idea, 221 S Central, Pierre, SD 57501. Telephone (605) 773-5032.

Biennial book. Lists South Dakota's manufacturers and processors alphabetically by location and industry. Price $8.00.

4345.02

South Dakota: State Industrial Directory, **1981**

Manufacturers' News, Inc, 3 E Huron St, Chicago, Il 60611. Telephone (312) 337-1084.

Annual book. Contains information on 850 industrial firms in South Dakota. Notes 5109 executives. Price $22.00.

4346

Southeast Asia's Economy in the 1970's

Asian Development Bank, PO Box 789, Manila, Phillippines 2800. Order from Longman Group Ltd, 74 Grosvenor St, London, England. Telephone (206) 543-8870.

Publication. Analyzes Southeast Asia's economy in the 1970s. Price £8.00.

4347

Southern California—Economic Trends in the Seventies

Security Pacific National Bank, PO Box 2097, Terminal Annex, Los Angeles, CA 90051. Telephone (213) 613-5402.

Magazine. Analyzes the economic trends in 10 southern California counties. Price free of charge.

4347.01

Southern Cone Regional Report

Latin American Newsletters Ltd, Greenhill House, 90–93 Cowcross St, London, England EC1M 6BL. Telephone (44) (01) 251-0012. Telex 261117.

Newsletter irregularly issued. Covers economic changes and political decisions in South American nations. Price £140 $315.00 US per year.

4348
Southern Economic Journal
Southern Economic Assn, University of North Carolina at Chapel Hill, Hanes Hall 019-A, Chapel Hill, NC 27514. Telephone (919) 966-5261.

Quarterly journal. Presents articles on economic and business research. Reviews books and lists new ones. Price $35.00 per year, $40.00 per year foreign.

4348.01
Southern Hardware
Southern Hardware, 1760 Peachtree Rd, NW, Atlanta, GA 30357. Telephone (404) 874-4462.

Monthly magazine. Reports on Southern hardware market. Notes new products and conventions. Price $40.00 per year.

4349
Southern Journal of Agricultural Economics
Southern Agricultural Economics Assn, c/o H Evan Drummond, Sec-Treas, FRE, McCarty Hall, University of Florida, Gainesville, FL 32611. Telephone (904) 392-1848.

Semiannual magazine. Contains articles relevant to farming and agricultural economy in the southern parts of the US. Price $10.00 per year.

4349.01
South—The Third World Magazine
Third World Foundation, New Zealand House, 80 Haymarket, London, England SW1Y 4TS. Telephone (44) (01) 839-6167. Telex 8814201 Trimed G.

Monthly magazine. Covers international issues from the viewpoint of Third World countries. Analyzes economic, political, and social developments. Price $22.00 per year.

4350
Soviet and Eastern European Foreign Trade
M E Sharpe, Inc, 80 Business Park Dr, Armonk, NY 10504. Telephone (914) 273-1800.

Quarterly journal. Surveys internal and external economic relations of COMECON members through translations from Soviet and Eastern European sources. Price $127.00 per year.

4351
Soviet-Eastern Europe-China Business & Trade
Welt Publishing Co, 1511 K St, NW, Washington, DC 20005. Telephone (202) 737-8080.

Bimonthly report. Discusses business developments and opportunities in the USSR, China and Eastern Europe. Includes developments in agriculture, manufacturing and foreign trade. Business calendar. Price $295.00 per year.

4352
Space Letter
Callahan Publications, PO Box 3751, Washington, DC 20007. Telephone (703) 783-3238.

Semimonthly newsletter. Details contract opportunities, marketing data, research, and development connected with the National Aeronautics and Space Administration. Notes military and commercial space ventures. Price $120.00 per year.

4353
Spain-US
Spain-US Chamber of Commerce, Inc, 500 5th Ave, New York, NY 10110. Telephone (212) 354-7848.

Bimonthly magazine. Covers Spain-US trade, foreign investment, tourism, legislation, and business opportunities. Price $15.00 per year.

4353.01
Specialist
Chilton Co, Chilton Way, Radnor, PA 19089. Telephone (215) 687-8200.

Magazine issued six times per year. Covers the sale and distribution of vehicles and components to truck fleets, independent truckers, wholesalers, warehouse distributors, and car fleets. Price $10.00 per year.

4354
Specialized Monthly Reports
11722 Sorrento Valley Rd, Suite I, San Diego, CA 92121. Telephone (714) 755-1327.

Information service. Provides monthly mathematical and statistical analyses of stocks to meet clients' specifications. Price $540.00 Per year.

4355
Special Libraries Directory of Greater New York, **15th edition**
Special Libraries Assn, 235 Park Ave S, New York, NY 10003. Order from R L Enequist, College of Insurance Library, 123 William St, New York, NY 10038. Telephone (212) 777-8136.

Directory. Lists more than 1000 special libraries in the greater New York City area. Indicates personnel and size of holdings. Includes subject index, index of libraries, and index of librarians. Price $25.00.

4356
Special Report
National Office Products Assn, 301 N Fairfax St, Alexandria, VA 22314. Telephone (703) 549-9040.

Bimonthly report. Covers new market trends and management topics in the office products industry. Price $30.00 per year.

4357
Special Telex Service (STS)
International Reports, Inc, 200 Park Ave S, New York, NY 10003. Telephone (212) 477-0003. Telex RCA 223139 ITT 422963 WU 147101.

Immediate report, as warranted. Provides advice on international currency emergencies, expected exchange rate changes, and foreign exchange risks. Price $585.00 per year.

4358
Specialty Salesman
Communication Channels, Inc, 6285 Barfield Rd, Atlanta, GA 30328. Telephone (404) 256-9800.

Monthly magazine. Covers facets of sales techniques for direct salespersons who work for themselves. Price $10.00 per year.

4359
Specialty Salesman & Business Opportunities
Specialty Salesman Magazine, Div of Communication Channels Inc, 6285 Barfield Rd, Atlanta, GA 30328. Telephone (404) 256-9800.

Monthly magazine. Contains articles about business opportunities in direct selling. Price $10.00 per year.

4359.01
Spectrum
Canadian Imperial Bank of Commerce, Commerce Ct W, Toronto, Ont, Canada M5L 1A2. Telephone (416) 862-4132.

Quarterly journal. Publishes opinion articles on Canadian agriculture, credit, capital, and tourism. Issued in French as Tribune. Price free of charge.

4359.02
Spectrum Convertibles Holdings Survey of Convertible Bonds and Convertible Preferred Stocks
Computer Directions Advisors, Inc, 8750 Georgia Ave, Silver Spring, MD 20910. Telephone (301) 565-9544.

Quarterly report. Lists by convertible issue the quarterly holdings and changes of all institutions with equity assets exceeding $100 million. Price $250.00 per year.

4360
Spectrum One: Investment Company Stock Holdings Survey
Computer Directions Advisors, Inc, 8750 Georgia Ave, Silver Spring, MD 20910. Telephone (301) 565-9544.

Quarterly report. Lists by common stock the holdings and transactions of all investment companies. Price $150.00 per year.

4360.01
Spectrum Two—Investment Company Portfolios
Computer Directions Advisors, Inc, 8750 Georgia Ave, Silver Spring, MD 20910. Telephone (301) 565-9544.

Quarterly report. Lists by investment company the holdings and transactions of funds with assets exceeding $25 million. Price $150.00 per year.

4361
Spectrum Three: Bank Stock Holdings Survey
Computer Directions Advisors, Inc, 8750 Georgia Ave, Silver Spring, MD 20910. Telephone (301) 589-6767.

Quarterly report. Lists the quarterly holdings and transactions of all federally chartered banks (and selected state banks). Price $200.00 per year.

4361.01
Spectrum Three—Institutional Stock Holdings Survey
Computer Directions Advisors, Inc, 8750 Georgia Ave, Silver Spring, MD 20910. Telephone (301) 565-9544.

Quarterly report. Lists by common stock the holdings and changes of all institutions with equity assets exceeding $100 million. Price $575.00 per year.

4361.02
Spectrum Four—Institutional Portfolios
Computer Directions Advisors, Inc, 8750 Georgia Ave, Silver Spring, MD 20910. Telephone (301) 565-9544.

Quarterly report. Lists by institution the holdings and changes of all institutions with equity assets exceeding $100 million. Price $575.00 per year.

4361.03
Spectrum Five—Five Percent Ownership Based on 13D, 13G and 14D-1 Filings
Computer Directions Advisors, Inc, 8750 Georgia Ave, Silver Spring, MD 20910. Telephone (301) 565-9544.

Monthly report. Lists by common stock all beneficial owners of 5 percent or more of the outstanding shares of any publicly held American corporation. Price $280.00 per year.

4361.04
Spectrum Six—Insider Ownership Based on Forms 3 and 4
Computer Directions Advisors, Inc, 8750 Georgia Ave, Silver Spring, MD 20910. Telephone (301) 565-9544.

Semiannual report. Lists by common stock and convertible issue the holdings and changes of all officers, directors, and 10 percent principal stockholders of companies whose securities are registered with the Securities and Exchange Commission. Price $95.00 per year.

4361.05
Speechwriter's Newsletter
Lawrence Ragan Communications, Inc, 407 S Dearborn, Chicago, IL 60605. Telephone (312) 922-8245.

Semimonthly newsletter. Provides information for professional speechwriters on effective writing, handling speakers bureaus, locating information, and using props and audiovisual equipment. Price $82.00 per year.

4362
Spencer's Retirement Plan Service
Charles D Spencer & Assocs, Inc, 222 W Adams St, Chicago, IL 60606. Telephone (312) 236-2615.

Three loose-leaf books, plus monthly reports. Cover retirement, pension, and profit-sharing plans, including the Keogh plan, tax-sheltered annuities, and individual retirement accounts. Price $130.00 per year.

4363
Spirits Bulletin
Her Majesty's Stationery Office, PO Box 569, London, England SE1 9NH. Order from Bill of Entry Service, HM Customs and Excise, King's Beam House, Mark Lane, London, England EC3 7HE. Telephone (44) (01) 928 1321.

Monthly report. Deals with alcoholic beverages. Price £7.19 per year.

4364
Sporting Goods Business
Gralla Publications, 1515 Broadway, New York, NY 10036. Telephone (212) 869-1300.

Publication. Provides news for sporting good retailers on industry-related topics. Price available on request.

4364.01
Sporting Goods Market
National Sporting Goods Assn, 717 N Michigan Ave, Chicago, IL 60611. Telephone (312) 944-0205.

Annual research report based on consumer survey of 40,000 US families. Presents statistics on retail sales for sporting goods and recreational equipment. Indicates the type of outlets and geographic region, annual family income, and education of customers. Price $85.00.

4365
Sportswear Graphics
Signs of the Times Publishing Co, 407 Gilbert Ave, Cincinnati, OH 45202. Telephone (513) 421-2050.

Monthly newspaper. Provides information for people involved in the merchandising, production, and selling of imprinted jackets, tote bags, T-shirts, and related items. Price $15.00 per year. ISSN 0199-5278.

4365.01
Spotlite
Sunshine Enterprises Ltd, PO Box 2873, St Thomas, USVI 00801.

Monthly report. Provides coverage of Puerto Rican financial, economic, and political news. Includes statistics. Price $75.00 per year.

4366

Spot Radio Rates & Data

Standard Rate & Data Service, Inc, 5201 Old Orchard Rd, Skokie, IL 60077. Telephone (312) 470-3100.

Monthly book. Contains information on 4500 AM and 2700 FM radio stations. Includes rates, station representatives, and market estimates. Price $123.00 per year.

4367

Spot Radio Small Markets Edition

Standard Rate & Data Service, Inc, 5201 Old Orchard Rd, Skokie, IL 60077. Telephone (312) 470-3100.

Semiannual book. Presents profiles of all radio stations in areas with population of 25,000 or less. Notes spot rate schedules. Price $39.00 per year.

4368

Spot Television Rates & Data

Standard Rate & Data Service, Inc, 5201 Old Orchard Rd, Skokie, IL 60077. Telephone (312) 470-3100.

Monthly book. Contains information on television stations and regional networks. Provides rates and market evaluation. Price $110.00 per year.

4368.02

SRI Microfiche Library

Congressional Information Service, Inc, 4520 E-W Highway, Suite 800, Washington, DC 20014. Telephone (301) 654-1550.

Microfiche file, with monthly updates. Contains economic, social, and demographic data published by private institutions and state agencies. Price $5000.00 per year.

4369

Staff Papers

International Monetary Fund, 19th & H Sts, NW, Washington, DC 20431. Telephone (202) 393-6362.

Magazine published three times per year. Contains studies by the International Monetary Fund's staff on monetary and financial problems such as balance of payments and exchange rates. Price $7.00 per year.

4370

Standard Corporation Records

Standard & Poor's Corp, 25 Broadway, New York, NY 10004. Telephone (212) 248-3469.

Seven volumes. Provide detailed business and financial information. Price $1060.00 per year.

4371

Standard Directory of Advertisers

National Register Publishing Co, Inc, 5201 Old Orchard Rd, Skokie, IL 60077. Telephone (312) 470-3100.

Annual directory. Offers a register of 17,-000 corporations responsible for 95% of US advertising. Notes their sales volume, advertising budgets, and agencies. Nine yearly supplements. Price $153.00 per copy. ISBN 0-87217-000-4.

4372

Standard Directory of Advertising Agencies

National Register Publishing Co, Inc, 5201 Old Orchard Rd, Skokie, IL 60077. Telephone (312) 470-3100.

Book published three times per year. Provides a directory to 4400 advertising agencies. Catalogs agencies' gross billings by media, annual billings, and clients. Supplies periodic supplements that carry agency news. Price $52.00 per copy, three issues $127.00. ISBN 0-87217-003-9.

4373

Standard Federal Tax Reports

Commerce Clearing House, Inc, 4025 W Peterson Ave, Chicago, IL 60646. Telephone (312) 583-8500.

Fifteen loose-leaf books, plus weekly reports. Cover federal income tax federal laws, regulations, court decisions, and rulings. Price $675.00 per year.

4374

Standard Industrial Classification Manual, 1972

US Dept of Commerce, Bureau of the Census, Washington, DC 20233. Order from Superintendent of Documents, US Government Printing Office, Washington, DC 20402. Telephone (202) 783-3238.

Manual. Defines industries in accordance with the composition and structure of the US economy. Includes conversion tables for 1972 and 1967 standard industrial classification codes. Price $8.80.

4375

Standard New York Stock Exchange (NYSE) Stock Reports

Standard & Poor's Corp, 25 Broadway, New York, NY 10004. Telephone (212) 248-3469.

Daily and weekly loose-leaf reports. Profile companies listed on the New York Stock Exchange. Forecast sales and earnings. Price and volume charts. Price $610.00 per year daily, $495.00 per year weekly.

4376

Standard—Northeast's Insurance Weekly

Standard Publishing, 1073 Hancock St, Quincy, MA 02169. Telephone (617) 773-7702.

Weekly newspaper. Provides national and regional news on the insurance industry for those who produce and sell insurance. Price $13.00 per year, $23.00 for two years.

4377

Standard Periodical Directory

Oxbridge Inc, 40 E 34th St, New York, NY 10016. Telephone (212) 689-8524.

Provides the name, address, circulation, and other data for 65,000 US and Canadian periodicals. Price $120.00.

4378

Standard Research Consultants (SRC) Quarterly Reports

Standard Research Consultants, 26 Broadway, New York, NY 10004. Telephone (212) 558-6660.

Quarterly loose-leaf report. Discusses court cases dealing with tax valuation matters, mergers and acquisitions. Price free of charge.

4378.01

Standards and Specifications Information Bulletin

National Standards Assn, Inc, 5161 River Rd, Washington, DC 20016. Telephone (301) 951-1310. Telex 89-8452.

Weekly report. Lists new or revised documents on standards and specifications. Covers aerospace, military, federal, and other standards. Price $70.00 per year.

4379

Standard Specifications for Diesel Merchant Ship Construction

US Maritime Adm, Commerce Bldg, 14th & E Sts, NW, Washington, DC 20230. Order from National Technical Information Service, 5285 Port Royal Rd, Springfield, VA 22161. Telephone (703) 487-4650.

Publication. Presents the specifications for diesel merchant ships. Price $15.00.

4380

Standard Specifications for Tanker Construction

US Maritime Adm, Commerce Bldg, 14th & E Sts, NW, Washington, DC 20230. Order from National Technical Information Service, 5285 Port Royal Rd, Springfield, VA 22161. Telephone (703) 487-4650.

Publication. Contains standard specifications for tanker construction in accordance with provisions of the Merchant Marine Act of 1970. Price $16.25.

4381

Starting a Business in Hawaii

Hawaii State Dept of Planning & Economic Development, PO Box 2359, Honolulu, HI 96804. Telephone (808) 548-4620.

Publication. Summarizes state, county, and federal regulations and tax rules concerning the starting of business and professional enterprises. Price free of charge.

4382

Starting and Managing Series

US Small Business Admn, 1030 15th St, NW, Suite 250, Washington, DC 20417. Order from Superintendent of Documents, Government Printing Office, Washington, DC 20402. Telephone (202) 783-3238.

Pamphlets. Offer suggestions for starting and managing various types of small businesses. Price available on request.

4383

State Administrative Officials (Classified by Functions)

Council of State Governments, Iron Works Pike, PO Box 11910, Lexington, KY 40578. Telephone (606) 252-2291.

Directory. Lists names, addresses, and telephone numbers of major state administrative officials who are classified by their function. Price $10.00.

4383.01

State and Area Forecasting Service

Data Resources, Inc, 29 Hartwell Ave, Lexington, MA 02173. Telephone (617) 861-0165.

Quarterly and annual reports. Contain state-by-state forecasts of employment, income, mortgage rates, prices, population, and banking in the US. Price available on request.

4384

State and County Administrator

Security World Publishing Co, Inc, 2639 S La Cienega Blvd, Los Angeles, CA 90034. Order from PO Box 272, Culver City, CA 90230. Telephone (213) 836-5000.

Monthly magazine. Publishes articles concerned with efficient government administration. Is geared to officials. Price $10.00 per year.

4386

State and Local Taxes

Prentice-Hall, Inc, Englewood Cliffs, NJ 07632. Telephone (201) 592-2000. Telex 13-5423.

Weekly loose-leaf service. Contains the full text of all state and some local taxes. Includes court decisions, rulings, and interpretations. Price $162.00-$204.00 (depending on the state).

4387

State Banking Law Service

American Bankers Assn, 1120 Connecticut Ave NW, Washington, DC 20036. Telephone (202) 467-4123.

Loose-leaf report, with annual updates. Analyzes state laws affecting state and national banks. Includes information on reserve requirements, branching, remote electronic facilities, and director and officer indemnification. Price $95.00.

4388

State Corporate Income Tax Forms

Commerce Clearing House, Inc, 4025 W Peterson Ave, Chicago, IL 60646. Telephone (312) 583-8500.

Loose-leaf book and periodic reports. Provides facsimile reproductions of state corporate income and franchise tax forms, plus general forms applicable to corporate returns. Price $170.00 per year.

4389

State Elective Officials and the Legislatures

Council of State Governments, Iron Works Pike, PO Box 11910, Lexington, KY 40578. Telephone (606) 252-2291.

Annual book. Lists names, addresses, and political affiliations of US state legislators and statewide elected officials. Price $10.-00.

4389.01

State Executive Directory

Carroll Publishing Co, 1058 Thomas Jefferson St, NW, Washington, DC 20007. Telephone (202) 333-8620.

Directory published three times per year. Identifies state government offices and personnel. Supplies phone numbers and titles. Price $84.00 per year.

4390

Statefiche

Environment Information Center (EIC), Inc, Catalog Order Dept, 292 Madison Ave, New York, NY 10017. Telephone (212) 949-9494.

Information service. Supplies microfiche of environmental laws and regulations of all US states. Organizes collection alphabetically by state and subject within state. Price available on request.

4391

State Government

Council of State Governments, Iron Works Pike, PO Box 11910, Lexington, KY 40578. Telephone (606) 252-2291.

Quarterly journal. Discusses state governmental problems. Highlights innovations and trends. Price $12.00 (annual index published).

4392

State Government News

Council of State Governments, Iron Works Pike, PO Box 11910, Lexington, KY 40578. Telephone (606) 252-2291.

Monthly newsletter. Presents material on developments in all states, plus an annual summary of legislative action. Price $12.00 (annual index published).

4392.01

State Government Research Checklist

Council of State Governments, Iron Works Pike, PO Box 11910, Lexington, KY 40578. Telephone (606) 252-2291.

Bimonthly newsletter. Lists reports by legislative research agencies, other state committees, and independent organizations of interest to states. Price $12.00 per year.

4393

State Headlines

Council of State Governments, Iron Works Pike, PO Box 11910, Lexington, KY 40578. Telephone (606) 252-2291.

Biweekly publication. Reports on state government news. Price $12.00 per year.

4394
State Income Taxes
Prentice-Hall, Inc, Englewood Cliffs, NJ 07632. Telephone (201) 592-2000. Telex 13-5423.
Weekly loose-leaf service. Explains individual and corporate income tax laws of all states, cities, and localities. Points out new rulings and relevant court cases. Price $711.00 per year.

4395
State Legislative Leadership, Committees and Staff (RM-664)
Council of State Governments, Iron Works Pike, PO Box 11910, Lexington, KY 40578. Telephone (606) 252-2291.
Book. Provides names, addresses, telephone numbers, and organizational patterns of state legislative leaders, committees and chairpersons, principal legislative staff officers, and staff members. Price $13.00.

4396
State Legislative Reporting Service
Commerce Clearing House Inc, 4025 W Peterson Ave, Chicago, IL 60646. Telephone (312) 583-8500.
Periodic reports on subjects of subscriber's choice. Cover state legislation, including texts of bills, interim reports, and texts of laws. Price minimum contract: $9000.00 for 2 years, covering at least 10 states.

4398
Statement of the Assets and Liabilities of the Chartered Banks of Canada
Supply and Services Canada, Publishing Centre, Printing and Publishing, Ottawa, Ont, Canada K1A 0S9. Telephone (613) 238-1601.
Monthly magazine. Publishes the assets and liabilities of chartered banks of Canada. Bilingual. Price $1.75 per year.

4400
Statements on International Accounting Standards
American Inst of Certified Public Accountants, 1211 Ave of the Americas, New York, NY 10036. Telephone (212) 575-6200.
Thirteen-pamphlet series. Presents basic international accounting standards prepared by the International Accounting Standards Committee. Covers finanical statements, depreciation accounting, inventory valuation, and disclosure of accounting policies. Price $2.25 per statement.

4401
State Motor Carrier Guide
Commerce Clearing House, Inc, 4025 W Peterson Ave, Chicago, IL 60646. Telephone (312) 583-8500.
Two loose-leaf books and biweekly reports. Cover the regulation of motor carriers by all states. Include statutes, regulations, court, and commission decisions. Price $440.00 per year.

4402
State of Food and Agriculture
Food and Agriculture Organization of the United Nations, Via delle Terme di Caracalla, Rome, Italy 00100. Order from UNIPUB, 345 Park Ave S, New York, NY 10016. Telephone 5797. Telex 61181.
Annual report. Reviews developments in the food and agricultural situation throughout the world. Provides forecasts and detailed studies on special subjects. Price $21.75.

4403
State of Hawaii Data Book, 1980 Edition.
Hawaii State Dept of Planning & Economic Development, PO Box 2359, Honolulu, HI 96804. Telephone (808) 548-4620.
Annual book. Contains close to 500 statistical tables on Hawaii's population, economy, environment, and related topics. Price $10.00.

4404
State-Owned Energy Enterprises
International Review Service, 15 Washington Pl, New York, NY 10003. Telephone (212) 751-0833.
Report issued six times per year. Focuses on state-owned petroleum, atomic, and other energy enterprises. Notes deals between state-owned companies and state-owned deals with private firms. Covers discoveries, commercial activities, policies, and legislation. Price $500.00 per year.

4405
State Personal Income Tax Forms
Commerce Clearing House, Inc, 4025 W Peterson Ave, Chicago, IL 60646. Telephone (312) 583-8500.
Two loose-leaf books, plus periodic reports. Issue state forms for personal resident and nonresident income tax, including individual and partnership forms. Price $185.00 per year.

4405.01
State Regulation Report: Toxic Substances & Hazardous Waste
Business Publishers, Inc, PO Box 1067, Silver Spring, MD 20910. Telephone (301) 587-6300.
Biweekly newsletter. Covers state regulations on toxic substances and hazardous waste management. Price $137.00 per year.

4406
State Sales Guides
Dun & Bradstreet, Box 3224, Church St Station, New York, NY 10008. Telephone (212) 285-7346.
Book. Gives information on companies, by individual states and some large cities, for traveling salespersons. Price, available on request, to Dun & Bradstreet subscribers only.

4407
State Slate: A Guide to Legislative Procedures and Lawmakers
Federal-State Reports, Inc, 5203 Leesburg Pike, #1201, Falls Church, VA 22041. Telephone (703) 379-0222.
Loose-leaf book, with periodic updates. Provides information on legislation in all 50 states. Lists members of legislatures, committee assignments, party affiliation, addresses, and phone numbers. Price $135.00 per year.

4408
Statesman's Year-Book, 1980–81 edition
St Martin's Press, Inc, 175 5th Ave, New York, NY 10010. Telephone (212) 674-5151.
Annual book. Covers international organizations and historical and current economic, political and social data about every constituted government in the world. Maps and bibliographies. Price $30.00.

4409
State Tax Cases Reports
Commerce Clearing House, Inc, 4025 W Peterson Ave, Chicago, IL 60646. Telephone (312) 583-8500.
Loose-leaf book, plus monthly reports. Covers the general principles of state and local taxation as developed from controlling case law. Price $155.00 per year.

4410
State Tax Guide
Commerce Clearing House, Inc, 4025 W Peterson Ave, Chicago, IL 60646. Telephone (312) 583-8500.

Loose-leaf book, plus biweekly reports. Gives facts about the taxes of all states. Includes State Tax Review. Price $340.00 per year.

4412
State Tax Handbook

Commerce Clearing House, Inc, 4025 W Peterson Ave, Chicago, IL 60646. Telephone (312) 583-8500.

Book. Gives the tax systems for all states and the District of Columbia in chart form. Provides rates and due dates. Price $8.50.

4413
State Tax Reports

Commerce Clearing House, Inc, 4025 W Peterson Ave, Chicago, IL 60646. Telephone (312) 583-8500.

Loose-leaf books, plus monthly and weekly reports. Cover state and local taxation. Issue basic books and updates for each state. Price varies with the number of states selected.

4414
State Tax Review

Commerce Clearing House, Inc, 4025 W Peterson Ave, Chicago, IL 60646. Telephone (312) 583-8500.

Weekly publication. Reviews tax trends in all states, including pending legislation and new laws. Offers comparative analyses of data. Price $5.00 per year.

4415
State Trademark Statutes

US Trademark Assn, 6 E 45th St, New York, NY 10017. Order from Law-Arts Publishers, Inc, 453 Greenwich St, New York, NY 10013. Telephone (212) 986-5880.

Loose-leaf book, with periodic updates. Contains complete texts of trademark statutes of American states, Puerto Rico, and the Virgin Islands. Price $63.00.

4416
Statex Service

Stock Exchange Research Pty Ltd, 20 Bond St, Sydney, 2000, Australia. Telephone (61) (02) 231-0066.

Annual service, with monthly updates. Provides a 10-year computer summary of financial information for leading Australian stocks. Includes comparative analyses of industry groups and component stocks. Price $2300.00 (Australian) per year.

4417
Stationery & Office Supplies

Stokes & Lindley-Jones Ltd, Alverstoke House, 21 Montpelier Row, Blackheath, London, England SE3 0SR. Telephone (44) (01) 852-9865.

Biannual report. Deals with stationery and office supplies available for export from Great Britain. Price £25.00 for three years to qualified subscribers.

4418
Statistical Abstract of Arizona

University of Arizona, College of Business & Public Adm, Div of Economic and Business Research, BPA Bldg, Tucson, AZ 85721. Telephone (602) 884-1426.

Book. Provides data on Arizona. Covers the state's population, government, natural resources, economic conditions, and communications systems. Over 500 tables and maps. Price $5.00.

4419
Statistical Abstract of Ireland

Central Statistics Office, Earlsfort Ter, Dublin 2, Ireland. Order from Government Publications Sales Office, GPO Arcade, Dublin 1, Ireland.

Annual publication. Measures social and economic facts. Includes data on agriculture, industrial production, and commerce. Price £2.40 per year.

4420
Statistical Abstract of Oklahoma

University of Oklahoma, Center for Economic and Management Research, College of Business Adm, 307 West Brooks St, Rm 4, Norman, OK 73019. Telephone (405) 325-2931.

Biennial book. Supplies data on the social and economic conditions in Oklahoma. Tables and maps. Price $15.00.

4421
Statistical Abstract of the United States

Bureau of the Census, US Dept of Commerce, Washington, DC 20233. Order from Superintendent of Documents, US Government Printing Office, Washington, DC 20420. Telephone (202) 783-3238.

Annual report. Contains tables of economic, industrial, political, and social statistics for the US as a whole as well as some areas and regions. Includes lists of publications. Price $9.00.

4422
Statistical Abstract of Utah

University of Utah, Dept of Economics, Salt Lake City, UT 84112. Telephone (801) 581-6333.

Triennial book. Presents data on Utah's business conditions. Over 200 tables and charts. Price $10.00.

4423
Statistical Analysis of the World's Merchant Fleets

US Maritime Adm, Commerce Bldg, 14th & E Sts, NW, Washington, DC 20230. Order from Superintendent of Documents, US Government Printing Office, Washington, DC 20402. Telephone (202) 783-3238.

Book. Presents data on the world's merchant fleets. Shows age, size, speed, and draft for combination passenger and cargo ships, bulk carriers, tankers, and freighters. Tables. Price $5.00 per copy.

4424
Statistical and Economic Information Bulletin for Africa

United Nations Economic Commission for Africa, Africa Hall, PO Box 3001, Addis Ababa, Ethiopia. Telephone 47200.

Monthly report. Supplies African public finance and intra-African trade statistics. Includes information on African trade and economic trends. Tables. English and French. Price free of charge.

4425
Statistical Bulletin

Conference Board, Inc, 845 3rd Ave, New York, NY 10022. Telephone (212) 759-0900.

Monthly report. Notes current status of leading business indicators, GNP projections, and principal Conference Board statistical series. Price available on request.

4426
Statistical Bulletin

Metropolitan Life Insurance Co, 1 Madison Ave, New York, NY 10010. Telephone (212) 578-5673.

Quarterly bulletin. Contains statistics on mortality, health, population, accidents, and longevity in the US. Price free of charge.

4428
Statistical Indicator Reports

Statistical Indicator Assoc, North Egremont, MA 01252. Telephone (413) 528-3280.

Weekly report. Analyzes 50 economic indicators, including stock prices, retail sales, unemployment, and interest rates. Tables and charts. Price $195.00 per year.

4429
Statistical Indicators of Short Term Economic Changes in ECE Countries
United Nations Publications, Rm A-3315, New York, NY 10017. Telephone (212) 754-8302.

Monthly report. Contains main economic indicators for Europe and the US. Derives the statistics presented from 32 countries. Price $21.00 per year.

4430
Statistical News
Her Majesty's Stationery Office, PO Box 569, London, England SE1 0NH. Telephone (44) (01) 928 1321.

Quarterly magazine. Provides details of statistical developments from all British government departments. Includes articles on current developments and a list of new surveys. Price £966. ISBN 0 11 723293 9. ISSN 0017 3630.

4432
Statistical Office of the European Communities. Basic Statistics
Commission of the European Communities, Office for Official Publications of the European Communities, CP 1003, Luxembourg 1, Luxembourg. Telephone (352) 490081. Telex PUBLOF 1325.

Publication. Presents statistics on the European community. Price 100 Belgian francs.

4433
Statistical Office of the European Communities Balances of Payments Geographical Breakdown
Commission of the European Communities, Office for Official Publications of the European Communities, CP 1003, Luxembourg 1, Luxembourg. Telephone (352) 490081. Telex PUBLOF 1325.

Annual book. Reports on the European community's balance of payments. Price $28.00.

4433.01
Statistical Office of the European Communities. Basic Statistics of the Community, **18th edition, 1975**
Commission of the European Communities, Office for Official Publications of the European Communities, CP 1003, Luxembourg 1, Luxembourg. Telephone (352) 490081. Telex PUBLOF 1325.

Publication. Offers statistical information on the European community. Price $5.80.

4434
Statistical Office of the European Communities. Monthly External Trade Bulletin
Commission of the European Communities, Office for Official Publications of the European Communities, CP 1003, Luxembourg 1, Luxembourg. Telephone (352) 490081. Telex PUBLOF 1325.

Monthly report. Contains statistical data on European community's foreign trade. Price $63.00 per year.

4435
Statistical Office of the European Communities. National Accounts ESA
Commission of the European Communities, Office for Official Publications of the European Communities, CP 1003, Luxembourg 1, Luxembourg. Telephone (352) 490081. Telex PUBLOF 1325.

Annual book. Presents statistics on the European community's national accounts. Price $24.70.

4436
Statistical Profile of Iowa
Iowa Development Commission, 250 Jewett Bldg, Des Moines, IA 50309. Telephone (515) 281-3925.

Annual book. Provides statistical information on Iowa, including the state's population and retail sales. Price free of charge.

4437
Statistical Quarterly
Alaska Dept of Labor, Employment Security Div, Research & Analysis Section, Box 3-7000, Juneau, AK 99801. Telephone (907) 465-2700.

Quarterly report. Provides statistics on employment in Alaska. Divides material by the nonagricultural employment section and local employment center and unemployment insurance section. Price available on request.

4438
Statistical Reference Index
Congressional Information Service, Inc, 4520 E-W Highway, Suite 800, Washington, DC 20014. Telephone (301) 654-1550.

Service composed of monthly, quarterly, and annual indexes and abstracts. Serves as guide to economic, social, and demographic data published by private institutions and state agencies. Price $865.00 per year.

4439
Statistical Releases (Agricultural Credit Conditions Survey)
Federal Reserve Bank of Minneapolis, 250 Marquette Ave, Minneapolis, MN 55480. Telephone (612) 340-2341.

Quarterly report. Includes a survey of agricultural credit conditions in the Ninth Federal Reserve District. Price free of charge.

4440
Statistical Review of Farming in Northern Ireland
Her Majesty's Stationery Office, PO Box 569, London, England SE1 9NH. Telephone (44) (01) 928 1321.

Annual report. Provides a statistical review of farming in Northern Ireland. Price free of charge.

4441
Statistical Review of Government in Utah
Utah Foundation, 308 Continental Bank Bldg, Salt Lake City, UT 84101. Telephone (801) 364-1837.

Annual report. Provides statistical data on Utah's economy and government. Includes information on government finance, welfare, taxes, employment, and income. Tables. Price $6.00 per copy.

4441.01
Statistical Review of Live-stock and Meat Industries
Australian Meat and Live-stock Corp, GPO Box 4129, Sydney, NSW 2001, Australia. Telephone (02) 267-9488. Telex AA 22887.

Annual report. Summarizes Australian and world meat and livestock production and exports. Price free of charge.

4442
Statistical Service
Standard & Poor's Corp, 25 Broadway, New York, NY 10014. Telephone (212) 248-3469.

Statistical series. Contains business, government, and investment information, ranging from agriculture to financial trends. Price $265.00.

4443
Statistical Trends in Broadcasting
John Blair & Co, 717 5th Ave, New York, NY 10022. Telephone (212) 752-0400.

Annual report. Contains financial statistics on television and radio stations. Price available on request.

4444
Statistical Yearbook
United Nations Publications, Rm A-3315, New York, NY 10017. Telephone (212) 754-8302.

Yearbook. Compiles international statistics on population, manpower, agriculture, mineral and manufacturing production, trade, and other economic and social subjects. Price $50.00.

4445
Statistical Yearbook for Asia and the Pacific
United Nations Publications, Rm A-3315, New York, NY 10017. Telephone (212) 754-8302.

Annual book. Is a cumulation of economic and other statistics. Price $34.00.

4446
Statistician
Longman Group Ltd, Longman House, Burnt Mill, Harlow, England Essex CM20 2JE. Telephone Harlow (0279) 26721. Telex 81259.

Quarterly journal. Contains articles on applied statistics. Focuses on established uses and new applications. Price $31.00 per year.

4447
Statisticians and Others in Allied Professions
American Statistical Assn, 806 15th St NW, Suite 640, Washington, DC 20005. Telephone (202) 393-3253.

Triennial book. Lists members of ASA, the Institute of Mathematical Studies, and the Biometric Society. Price available on request.

4448
Statistics—Africa
Gale Research Co, Book Tower, Detroit, MI 48226. Telephone (313) 961-2242.

Book. Presents a guide to published and other sources of statistics on each country of Africa and adjacent islands. Index of titles and organizations. Price $98.00. ISBN 900246-05-7.

4449
Statistics—America
Gale Research Co, Book Tower, Detroit, MI 48226. Telephone (313) 961-2242.

Book. Provides sources for market research on North, Central, and South America. Gives each country's central statistical office and principal libraries and annotated entries on major statistical publications. Price $160.00. ISBN 900246-13-8.

4450
Statistics—Asia & Australasia
CBD Research Ltd, 154 High St, Beckenham, Kent, England BR3 1EA. Telephone (01) 650-7745.

Book. Describes sources of statistical data on Asia and Australasia. Price $35.00. ISBN 900246-16-2.

4451
Statistics Canada Daily
Statistics Canada, User Services, Publications Distribution, Ottawa, Ont, Canada K1A 0V7. Telephone (613) 992-3151.

Daily service. Provides a summary of information from Statistics Canada reports and newly released publications. Price $144.00 per year. ISSN 0380-612X.

4452
Statistics—Europe
Gale Research Co, Book Tower, Detroit, MI 48226. Telephone (313) 961-2242.

Book. Presents a guide to sources for social, economic, and market research on Europe. Gives details on statistical officers and libraries and bibliographic information on major statistical publications. Price $62.00. ISBN 900246-18-9.

4453
Statistics of Foreign Trade, Monthly Bulletin
Organization for Economic Cooperation and Development, Publications Center, 1750 Pennsylvania Ave, NW, Washington, DC 20006. Telephone (202) 724-1857.

Monthly statistical report. Covers international trade. Price $45.00.

4453.01
Statistics of Foreign Trade, Series B: Annual Tables by Reporting Country
Organization for Economic Cooperation and Development, Publications Center, 1750 Pennsylvania Ave NW, Washington, DC 20006. Telephone (202) 724-1857.

Publication issued five times per year. Gives statistics for each OECD country and groups of countries. Contains tables showing foreign trade flows with 46 countries, or geographic zones for 300 products or product groups. Price $30.00 per year, $42.10 airmail.

4453.02
Statistics of Foreign Trade, Series C: Annual Tables by Commodity
Organization for Economic Cooperation and Development, Publications Center, 1750 Pennsylvania Ave, NW, Washington, DC 20006. Telephone (202) 724-1857.

Two volume set. Provides 1979 export and import data on trade of EEC, OECD Europe, and OECD member countries. Detailed statistics by SITC code to four-digit, SITC Group figures in value and quantity, section and division figures in value. Price $30.00, $42.10 airmail.

4454
Statistics of Railroads of Class I in the United States
Assn of American Railroads, Economics and Finance Dept, American Railroads Bldg, Washington, DC 20036. Telephone (202) 293-4068.

Annual report. Presents selected financial, operating, equipment, employment, and traffic statistics for a series of years for Class I railroads. Price $5.00 per year including Operating, Traffic Statistics, Property Investment, Condensed Income Account and Railroad Revenue, Expenses and Income.

4455
Statistics of Trade through United Kingdom Ports
Her Majesty's Stationery Office, PO Box 569, London, England SE1 9NH. Telephone (44) (01) 928 1321.

Quarterly service. Provides statistics on commodities and countries by ports of British overseas trade. Price £33.50 per year.

4456
Statistics of World Trade in Steel
United Nations Publications, Rm A-3315, New York, NY 10017. Telephone (212) 754-8302.

Report. Contains statistics on the export and import of steel worldwide. Price available on request.

4458
Statistics on Work Stoppages
New York Dept of Labor, Div of Research and Statistics, State Office Bldg Campus, Albany, NY 12240. Order from Div of Research and Statistics, Rm 6804, New York State Dept of Labor, 2 World Trade Center, New York, NY 10047. Telephone (212) 488-5030.

Annual report. Describes major New York State work stoppages. Gives data on the number of strikes in New York State and the number of workers involved and workdays idle. Price free of charge.

4459
Statistics Sources, 4th edition, 1974
Gale Research Co, Book Tower, Detroit, MI 48226. Telephone (313) 961-2242.

Book. Contains sources of statistics on industrial, business, financial, and other topics for the US and foreign countries. Price $110.00. ISBN 0396-5.

4460
Steel Mill Products, 1977.
US Dept of Commerce, Bureau of Census, Washington, DC 20233. Telephone (202) 449-1600.

Annual report. Presents statistics on the quantity and value of shipments of steel mill products in the US. Includes summary tables. Price $.50.

4461
Steel Service
Data Resources, Inc, 29 Hartwell Ave, Lexington, MA 02173. Telephone (617) 861-0165.

Quarterly and annual reports. Forecast steel mill product shipments and prices, trade and production by type of furnace, scrap prices, iron ore prices, and steel production costs. Price available on request.

4462
Steel Shipping Drums and Pails
US Dept of Commerce, Bureau of the Census, Washington, DC 20233. Telephone (202) 449-1600.

Monthly report, with annual summary. Contains information on shipments of steel pails and drums by diameter and type of interior. Price $3.50 per year.

4463
Stimulus
Stimulus Publishing Co Ltd, 67 Yonge St, Suite 906, Toronto, Ont, Canada M5E 1J8. Telephone (416) 368-1764.

Six issues per year. Present information about the Canadian advertising media. Include such subjects as newspapers, magazines, business publications, television, radio, and outdoor advertising. Price $20.00 per year. ISSN 0039-1574.

4464
Stock Exchange Information Service
Halevi & Co, Economic Counselling Ltd, 54 Haneviim St, Jerusalem, Israel 95141. Telephone (972) (02) 225577. Telex 26238 Hal I1.

Monthly newsletter published 10 times per year. Reports on companies registered on the Israeli stock exchange and their activities. English and Hebrew. Price $200.00 per year.

4465
Stock Exchange Official Year Book
Thomas Skinner Directories, Stuart House, 41-43 Perrymount Rd, Haywards Heath, West Sussex, England RH16 3BS.

Yearbook. Supplies information on the London Stock Exchange. Price £30 per year. ISBN 611 00629 4.

4466
Stock Guide
Standard & Poor's Corp, 25 Broadway, New York, NY 10014. Telephone (212) 248-3469.

Service. Gives statistical summary of investment data on over 5100 common and preferred stocks, listed and over-the-counter. Price $55.00.

4467
Stock Market Research Library
Securities Research Co, Div of United Business Service Co, 208 Newbury St, Boston, MA 02116. Telephone (617) 267-8860.

Monthly charts, quarterly graphs and wall chart. Present a record of prices, volume, earnings, and dividends for 1105 stocks. Price $98.00 complete annual service.

4468
Stock Photo and Assignment Source Book
R R Bowker Co, 1180 Ave of the Americas, New York, NY 10036. Order from R R Bowker Co, PO Box 1807, Ann Arbor, MI 48106. Telephone (212) 764-5100.

Book. Provides 4000 sources for obtaining stock photos for magazines, newspapers, and books. Subject and name indexes and reproductions of forms used in obtaining photos. Price $19.95. ISBN 0-8352-0879-6.

4469
Stock Summary
Standard & Poor's Corp, 25 Broadway, New York, NY 10004. Telephone (212) 248-3469.

Monthly report. Gives earnings and dividends ranking, price-earnings ratio and institutional holdings for listed and over-the-counter stocks. Price $24.00 per year.

4470
Stock Trader's Almanac, 11th edition, 1978
Hirsch Organization, Inc, 6 Deer Trail, Old Tappan, NJ 07675. Telephone (201) 664-3400.

Annual book. Presents a memo calendar book with stock tips and information for the year. Tables, charts, graphs, and statistics. Price $20.75.

4471
Stock Transfer Guide
Commerce Clearing House, Inc, 4025 W Peterson Ave, Chicago, IL 60646. Telephone (312) 583-8500.

Three loose-leaf books and monthly reports. Provide quick access to technical rules involved in stock transfers. Price $280.00 per year.

4472
Stock Values & Dividends for Tax Purposes
Commerce Clearing House, Inc, 4025 W Peterson Ave, Chicago, IL 60646. Telephone (312) 583-8500.

Annual book. Presents information on stock values and dividends. Price $6.00. ISSN 5918.

4473
Stone and Cox General Insurance Register
Stone and Cox Ltd, 100 Simcoe St, 2nd Floor, Toronto, Ont, Canada M5H 3G2. Telephone (416) 593-1310.

Annual book. Lists property and casualty insurance agencies in Ontario and the Maritime Provinces and insurances adjusting offices throughout Canada. Includes the financial statements of 300 insurance companies. Price $15.00 per year. ISBN 0-919 468-72-1.

4474
Stone and Cox Life Insurance Tables
Stone and Cox Ltd, 100 Simcoe St, 2nd Floor, Toronto, Ont, Canada M5H 3G2. Telephone (416) 593-1310.

Annual publication. Provides information on life insurance companies, particularly for Canada. Tables on premium rates, values, dividends, net costs, and other financial data. Price $14.75. ISBN 0-919468-58-6.

4475
Storage Handling Distribution
Turret Press Ltd, 4 Local Board Rd, Watford, Herts, England WD1 2JS. Order from Trade Papers Ltd, 4 Local Board Rd, Watford, Herts, England. WD1 2JS. Telephone Watford (0923) 46199.

Monthly magazine. Supplies information on the distribution and handling of materials. Offers a buyer's guide for handling materials. Price $62.00 per year.

4476
Stores
National Retail Merchants Assn, 100 W 31st St, New York, NY 10001. Telephone (212) 244-6780.

Monthly magazine. Focuses on retail issues in the areas of merchandising, operations, credit, store design, information systems, and related topics. Price $10.00 per year.

4477
Stores of the World Directory
Newman Books Ltd, 48 Poland St, London, England W1V 4PP. Telephone (44) (01) 439-0335.

Annual directory. Lists retail trade buyers in 119 countries for department stores, supermarkets, and other stores. Notes trade associations and government agencies. Price £24.00.

4478
Stores, Shops, Supermarkets: Retail Directory
Newman Books Ltd, 48 Poland St, London, England W1V 4PP. Telephone (44) (01) 439-0335.

Annual directory. Offers a guide to retail stores, including department stores, supermarkets, and discount stores in Great Britain. Local maps. Price £23.00.

4478.01
Strategic Management Journal
John Wiley & Sons, Inc, 605 3rd Ave, New York, NY 10158. Order from John Wiley & Sons, Inc, 1 Wiley Dr, Somerset, NJ 08773. Telephone (201) 469-4400. Telex 833 434. Cable JON WILE SMOT.

Quarterly two-volume journal. Publishes original reports and papers on all aspects of strategic management. Notes both theory and practice. Price $59.00 per year.

4479
Strike Preparation Manual
American Society for Personnel Administration, 30 Park Dr, Berea, OH, 44017. Telephone (216) 826-4790.

Pamphlet. Discusses problems affecting a company facing a strike. Covers negotiations, strike settlement, and work resumption. Price $2.00.

4480
Strikes and Lockouts in Canada 1979
Labour Canada, Communications Services Directorate, Ottawa, Ont, Canada K1A OJ2. Order from Canadian Government, Publishing Centre, Supply and Services Canada, 45 Sacre Coeur Blvd, Hull, Que, Canada K1A 0S9. Telephone (819) 997-2617.

Annual book. Includes statistics on strikes and lockouts in Canada, including employees involved, time lost in person-days, and listing of the main work stoppages. Bilingual. Price $4.00.

4481
Structure and Prospects of the World Coffee Economy
Jos de Vries, World Bank, 1818 H St, NW, Washington, DC 20433. Telephone (202) 393-6360.

Mimeographed publication. Analyzes the relationship among supply, demand, and price of coffee. Includes an econometric model and projections. Statistics. Price free of charge.

4482
Subchapter S: Planning & Operation
Panel Publishers, 14 Plaza Rd, Greenvale, NY 11548. Telephone (516) 484-0006.

Loose-leaf book with quarterly supplements. Discusses the effect of the Tax Reform Act of 1976 on the use of Subchapter S as a tax planning device. Includes information on stock ownership and dividends, fringe benefits, estate planning, corporate liquidations. Price $98.00. ISBN 0-916592-12-X.

4484
Subject Directory of Special Libraries and Information Centers. Vol. 1: Business and Law Libraries, Including Military and Transportation Libraries
Gale Research Co, Book Tower, Detroit, MI 48226. Telephone (313) 961-2242.

Book. Provides a directory of libraries and information centers in the US and Canada that specialize in business and law publications. Includes descriptions of collections. Price $80.00. ISBN 0-8103-0283-7.

4485
Subject Guide to Books in Print
R R Bowker Co, 1180 Ave of the Americas, New York, NY 10036. Order from R R Bowker Co, PO Box 1807, Ann Arbor, MI 48106. Telephone (212) 764-5100.

Two-volume annual book. Lists 470,000 titles under subject headings. Contains bibliographic information. Price $79.50 for two-volume set. ISBN 0-8352-1380-0. ISSN 0000-0159.

4486
Successful Estate Planning Ideas & Methods
Prentice-Hall, Inc, Englewood Cliffs, NJ 07632. Telephone (201) 592-2000. Telex 13-5423.

Semimonthly loose-leaf service. Provides information on estate planning. Includes such topics as trust and estate management, insurance, and taxes. Price $240.00 per year.

4487
Successful Meetings
Bill Communications, Inc, 633 3rd Ave, New York, NY 10017. Telephone (212) 986-4800.

Monthly magazine. Covers association meetings, seminars, and expositions around the world. Price $37.50 per year.

4488
Successful Personal Money Management 1977
McGraw-Hill Book Co, Hightstown-Princeton Rd, Hightstown, NJ 08520. Telephone (609) 448-1700. Telex 843449.

Book. Covers aspects of personal financial planning, including estate planning, tax management, and retirement. Price $19.-95. ISBN 0-07-044750-0.

4489
Success Unlimited
Success Unlimited, Inc, 401 N Wabash, Chicago, IL 60611. Telephone (312) 828-9500.

Monthly magazine. Discusses successful salespersons and sales techniques. Includes tax information and book reviews. Price $14.00 per year.

4490
Suggested State Legislation **1980**
Council of State Governments, Iron Works Pike, PO Box 11910, Lexington, KY 40578. Telephone (606) 252-2291.

Annual report. Contains proposed 1980 state legislative acts in draft statute form. Includes such subjects as senior citizens, criminal justice, and taxation. Price $10.00 per year.

4491
Summary of All Decisions and Orders Issued by the Canadian Transport Commission
Supply and Services Canada, Publishing Centre, Printing and Publishing, Ottawa, Ont, Canada K1A 0S9. Telephone (613) 238-1601.

Irregular report. Summarizes the decisions and orders of the Canadian Transport Commission. Bilingual. Price $8.00 per year.

4492
Summary of External Trade
Statistics Canada, User Services, Publications Distribution, Ottawa, Ont, Canada K1A 0V7. Telephone (613) 992-3151.

Monthly report. Presents two-year quarterly totals of Canadian exports and imports, seasonally adjusted, by seven geographic areas and commodity groups. Includes cumulative totals. Price $36.00 per year. ISSN 0318-2347.

4493
Summary of Labor Arbitration Awards
American Arbitration Assn, 140 W 51st St, New York, NY 10020. Telephone (212) 977-2000.

Monthly report. Reviews private sector labor arbitration awards. Price $75.00 per year.

4494
Summary of US Export Administration Regulations
US Dept of Commerce, International Trade Administration, Washington, DC 20230. Order from Office of Export Administration, Room 1617, Washington, DC 20230. Telephone (202) 377-2000.

Report. Summarizes US export control rules. Price available on request.

4495
Summary of US Export and Import Merchandise Trade
US Dept of Commerce, Bureau of Census, Washington, DC 20233. Telephone (202) 449-1600.

Monthly report. Provides US export and import data for each month of the current and preceding calendar years. Includes summaries of petroleum imports. Price $14.90 per year.

4496
Superintendent of Documents Price Lists
Superintendent of Documents, Government Printing Office, Washington, DC 20402. Telephone (202) 783-3238.

Publication. Provides separate listings for government publications by subject areas. Price available on request.

4497
Supermarket Business
Fieldmark Media, 25 W 43rd St, New York, NY 10036. Telephone (212) 354-5169.

Report. Covers supermarket and grocery industries. Price available on request.

4498
Supermarket News
Fairchild Publications, Inc, 7 E 12th St, New York, NY 10003. Telephone (212) 741-4224.

Weekly newspaper. Covers news of the supermarket trade. Price $24.00 per year. ISSN 0039-5803.

4499
Supervision
National Research Bureau, Inc, 424 N 3rd St, Burlington, IA 52601. Telephone (319) 752-5415.

Monthly magazine. Covers managerial supervision topics. Price $20.00 per year. ISSN 0039-5854.

4500
Supervisor's Production Planner
Dartnell Corp, 4660 Ravenswood Ave, Chicago, IL 60640. Telephone (312) 561-4000.

Monthly booklet. Presents a memo calendar to help supervisors with production planning. Incudes an article on supervision and a chart to record absences. Price $1.18 each.

4501
Supervisory Management
American Management Assns, 135 W 50th St, New York, NY 10020. Telephone (212) 586-8100.

Monthly magazine. Covers development and trends in management supervision. Price $16.00.

4502
Supervisory Management
Inst of Supervisory Management, 22 Bore St, Lichfield, Staffs, England WS13 6LP. Telephone Lichfield 51346.

Quarterly magazine. Pertains to problems facing British industrial superivsors, new supervisory techniques, new products and processes, and activities of the Institute of Supervisory Management. Price £6.00 per year.

4505.01
Supplier Price Index
Distilled Spirits Council of the US, Inc, 1300 Penn Bldg, Washington, DC 20004. Telephone (202) 628-3544.

Quarterly report. Indicates supplier to wholesaler price trends for various types of distilled spirits. Price $50.00 per year.

4506
Survey of Bank Officers Salaries
Bank Adm Inst, PO Box 500, 303 S NW Hwy, Park Ridge, IL 60068. Telephone (312) 693-7300.

Biennial book. Surveys bank officer salaries by size of bank, geographic location, and functional classifications. Price $10.-00.

4507
Survey of Bank Personnel Policies and Practices
Bank Adm Inst, PO Box 500, 303 S NorthWest Hwy, Park Ridge, IL 60068. Telephone (312) 693-7300.

Biennial report. Evaluates bank personnel policies. Contains data on the ratios of personnel to deposits, wages and salaries, training, turnover, and fringe benefits. Price $20.00.

4508
Survey of Business
University of Tennessee, Center for Business and Economic Research, College of Business Administration, 100 Glocker Business Adm Bldg, Knoxville, TN 37916. Telephone (615) 974-5441.

Quarterly magazine. Reports on national and Tennessee economic and business developments. Price free of charge.

4509
Survey of Business Attitudes
Conference Board in Canada, Suite 100, 25 McArthur Rd, Ottawa, Ont, Canada K1L 6R3. Telephone (613) 746-1261.

Quarterly booklet. Gives the results and an analysis of a survey of senior business executives on economic conditions in Canada. Price available on request.

4510
Survey of Buying Power
Sales & Marketing Management, Sales Builders Div, 633 3rd Ave, New York, NY 10017. Telephone (212) 986-4800.

Annual survey magazine. Provides estimates of population, income, and retail sales for US states, metropolitan areas, counties, cities and for Canadian provinces and metropolitan areas. Price $55.00.

4511
Survey of Buying Power Data Service
Sales & Marketing Management, Sales Builders Div, 633 3rd Ave, New York, NY 10017. Telephone (212) 986-4800.

Annual loose-leaf service published in three sections. Provides economic and demographic data for US. Summarizes retail sales. Price $239.95 per year.

4511.01
Survey of Buying Power Forecasting Service
Sales & Marketing Management, Sales Builders Div, 633 3rd Ave, New York, NY 10017. Telephone (212) 986-4800.

Annual loose-leaf service. Provides forecasts on US population, income, retail sales, and buying power for states, regions, and metropolitan markets. Price $429.95 per year.

4512
Survey of Buying Power—Part II
Sales & Marketing Management, Inc, 633 3rd Ave, New York, NY 10017. Telephone (212) 986-4800.

Annual survey issue. Provides merchandise line sales by metropolitan markets. Includes population and income projections. Price $25.00 per year.

4513
Survey of Consumer Buying Intentions
Conference Board in Canada, Suite 100, 25 McArthur Rd, Ottawa, Ont, Canada K1L 6R3. Order from Survey of Consumer Buying Intentions, Suite 1800, 333 River Rd, Ottawa, Ont, Canada K1L 8B9. Telephone (613) 746-1261.

Quarterly booklet. Surveys Canadian consumer attitudes and buying plans. Price available on request.

4514
Survey of Current Business
US Dept of Commerce, 14th St between Constitution Ave and E St, NW, Washington, DC 20230. Order from Superintendent of Documents, US Government Printing Office, Washington, DC 20402. Telephone (202) 783-3238.

Magazine. Reports on US economic conditions. Contains information on corporate profits, gross national product, employment, plant and equipment expenditures, and US international transactions. Price $35.00 per year.

4515
Survey of Economic Conditions in Africa
United Nations Publications, Rm A-3315, New York, NY 10017. Telephone (212) 754-8302.

Report. Covers current economic situation in Africa. Price available on request.

4516
Survey of Industrial Purchasing Power
Sales & Marketing Management, Inc, 633 3rd Ave, New York, NY 10017. Telephone (212) 986-4800.

Annual survey issue. Provides data on the number of US manufacturing plants and the value of shipments by industrial sector and by county. Price $25.00.

4516.01
Survey of Minority-Owned Business Enterprises, 1977, MB77
US Dept of Commerce, Bureau of Census, Washington, DC 20233. Telephone (202) 449-1600.

Five reports. Presents information on black-owned businesses for 1977 with comparable data for 1972. Price available on request.

4517
Survey of Personal Incomes
Her Majesty's Stationery Office, PO Box 569, London, England SE1 9NH. Telephone (44) (01) 928 1321.

Annual report. Surveys personal income in Great Britain. Price £5.25.

4517.01
Survey of Predecessor and Defunct Companies
Maclean-Hunter Ltd, 30 Old Burlington St, London W1X 2AE, England. Order from Financial Post Corp Service, 481 University Ave, Toronto, Ont, Canada M5W 1A7. Telephone (416) 596-5585.

Report on predecessor and defunct companies in Canada. Price $20.00 per copy.

4518
Survey of Selling Costs
Sales & Marketing Management, Sales Builders Div, 633 3rd Ave, New York, NY 10017. Telephone (212) 986-4800.

Annual survey issue. Provides selling costs index and cost-per-call estimates for 80 metropolitan markets. Notes sales meetings and sales training rates and facilities in major cities. Price $25.00.

4519
Survey of Significant New Products Introduced by New York Stock Exchange (NYSE) Listed Companies
Marketing Development, 402 Border Rd, Concord, MA 01742. Telephone (617) 369-5382.

Annual book. Surveys new industrial products introduced by companies listed on the New York Stock Exchange. Price $350.00.

4520
Survey Reports
American Management Assns, 135 W 50th, New York, NY 10020. Telephone (212) 586-8100.

Series of reports. Provide the results of a survey of managers on management questions. Tables and charts. Price $10.00 per copy.

4521

Surveys of African Economies

International Monetary Fund, 19th & H Sts, NW, Washington, DC 20431. Telephone (202) 393-6362.

Books. Present details on the economies of 32 African countries, including monetary, fiscal, exchange control, and trading systems for each country. English and French editions. Price $5.00 per volume.

4522

Swiss-American Chamber of Commerce, Yearbook

Consulate General of Switzerland, 444 Madison Ave, New York, NY 10022. Order from American-Swiss Assn, Inc, 60 E 42nd St, New York, NY 10017. Telephone (212) 986-5442.

Annual book. Presents economic data on Swiss-US trade, tourism, investment, prices, migration, and currency. Notes treaties and conventions and offers a directory to US companies in Switzerland and Swiss companies in the US. Price $100.00 per copy.

4523

Swiss Export Directory, **1978/80 13th edition**

Consulate General of Switzerland, 444 Madison Ave, New York, NY 10022. Telephone (212) 758-2560.

Periodically revised book. Supplies information on over 10,000 Swiss export products, trademarks, 7000 export firms, and service enterprises. Indicates products in English, German, and French. Price $30.00 per copy.

4524

Syracuse Journal of International Law & Commerce

Syracuse University, College of Law, Syracuse, NY 13210. Telephone (315) 423-2056.

Semiannual reports. Provides an international law forum. Focuses on public and private international law and commerce. Price $8.50 per year, $10.50 per year foreign.

4525

Systemation Letter

Systemation, North America, 14 Inverness Drive E, Bldg 8H, Penthouse, Englewood, CO 80110. Telephone (303) 770-1682.

Monthly newsletter. Offers information and suggestions for management systems analysts. Includes such topics as installation of new systems, terminals, and files. Price $24.00 per year.

4526

System of National Accounts—National Income and Expenditure Accounts

Statistics Canada, User Services, Publications Distribution, Ottawa, Ont, Canada K1A 0V7. Telephone (613) 992-3151.

Annual service. Provides data on Canadian income and expenditure data and covers industrial distribution of gross domestic product and geographic distribution of personal income. Includes a review of economic developments. Summary tables. Price $9.60. ISSN 0703-0037.

4527

Systems Auditability & Control

Canadian Institute of Chartered Accountants, 250 Bloor St E, Toronto, Ont, Canada M4W 1G5. Telephone (416) 962-1242.

Three-volume set of books. Covers data processing control and audit practices. Informs auditors about computer-based information systems. Tables. Price $30.00.

4528

Tape Subscriptions to IFS, DOT, BOP, and GFS

International Monetary Fund, 19th & H Sts, NW, Washington, DC 20431. Telephone (202) 393-6362.

Monthly magnetic tape service and corresponding book. Offers subscriptions to International Financial Statistics, Direction of Trade, Balance of Payments Yearbook, and Government Finance Statistics Yearbook. Price $1000.00 per year.

4529

Target Twenty

Chilton Co, Chilton Way, Radnor, PA 19089. Telephone (215) 687-8200.

Monthly newsletter. Furnishes an overview of the food and beverage market. Discusses advertising, market research, and industry trends. Price available on request.

4530

Tariff Brief

Cramb Tariff Services ACT Pty Ltd, PO Box 179, Civic Sq, ACT 2608, Australia. Telephone (61) (062) 48 7055.

Biweekly newsletter. Presents new information on tariffs, customs, and trade in Australia. Price $85.00 per year.

4531

Tariff Insight

Cramb Tariff Services ACT Pty Ltd, PO Box 179, Civic Sq, ACT 2608, Australia. Telephone (61) (062) 48 7055.

Monthly newsletter. Analyzes major developments relevant to tariffs and customs in Australia. Price $70.00 per year.

4532

Tariff Schedules of the US Annotated

US International Trade Commission, Washington, DC 20436. Order from US Government Printing Office, Washington, DC 20402. Telephone (202) 523-0161.

Periodically issued loose-leaf report, with supplements. Contains legal text of US tariff schedules. Supplies statistical information on customs, firms, and modifications after August 1963 and before January 1978. Price $19.00.

4533

Tax Action Coordinator

Research Inst of America, Inc, 589 5th Ave, New York, NY 10017. Telephone (212) 755-8900.

Seven loose-leaf books, with monthly supplements. Discuss tax implications of business and personal transactions. Include numerous sample tax forms with instructions for completing them. Price available on request.

4534

Tax Adviser

American Inst of Certified Public Accountants, 1211 Ave of the Americas, New York, NY 10036. Telephone (212) 575-6200.

Monthly magazine. Offers tax news, interpretations, advice, and legal decisions. Price $45.00 per year.

4535

Tax and Trade Guide Series

Arthur Andersen & Co, 69 W Washington, Chicago, IL 60602. Telephone (312) 580-0069.

Series of twenty guides direct attention to running a business in a particular country. Price free of charge.

4536
Taxation
Arthur Young & Co, 277 Park Ave, New York, NY 10017. Telephone (212) 922-4724.

Newsletter. Covers tax developments affecting Canadian companies, including shareholders of private corporations and distribution of surpluses. Price free of charge.

4537
Taxation
Taxation Publishing Co Ltd, 98 Park St, London, England W1Y 4BR. Telephone (44) (01) 629-7888.

Weekly newsletter. Reports on changes in British tax practices. Includes information on personal and corporate taxes, capital gains taxes, back duty, value added taxes, and capital transfer taxes. Price £19.50 per year.

4538
Taxation for Accountants
Warren, Gorham & Lamont, Inc, 210 S St, Boston, MA 02111. Telephone (800) 225-2263.

Monthly magazine. Concentrates on tax information for accountants who are not specialists in the field. Price $36.00 per year.

4539
Taxation for Lawyers
Warren, Gorham & Lamont, Inc, 210 S St, Boston, MA 02111. Telephone (800) 225-2263.

Bimonthly journal. Provides information about taxation for attorneys who do not specialize in the field. Price $24.00 per year.

4541
Taxation Publications
Arthur Young & Co, 277 Park Ave, New York, NY 10017. Telephone (212) 922-2000.

Series of reports. Examines rules affecting taxation of individuals and businesses in various countries. Price free of charge.

4543
Tax Correspondent
Management Services Assoc, Inc, PO Box 3750, Austin, TX 78764. Telephone (512) 327-2680.

Report issued 14 times per year. Analyzes Texas school tax news and other Texas school finance developments. Discusses related legislative action and court cases. Price $25.00 per year.

4544
Tax Court Memorandum Decisions
Commerce Clearing House, Inc. 4025 W Peterson Ave, Chicago, IL 60646. Telephone (312) 583-8500.

Annual books. Provide the full texts of Tax Court Memorandum Decisions. Price $27.50 per volume.

4545
Tax Court Reports
Commerce Clearing House, Inc, 4025 W Peterson Ave, Chicago, IL 60646. Telephone (312) 583-8500.

Three loose-leaf books, plus weekly reports. Provide information on new tax court petitions and docket developments. Include the full text of decisions. Price $345.00 per year.

4546
Tax Desk Book for the Closely-Held Corporation
Inst for Business Planning, Inc, IPB Plaza, Dept. 7102-81, Englewood Cliffs, NJ 07632. Telephone (201) 592-2040.

Book. Provides tax advice for the closely-held corporation, including information on acquisitions, trusts, and stock options. Price $29.95. ISBN 0-87624-540-8.

4546.01
Tax Digests
Institute of Chartered Accountants in England and Wales, PO Box 433, Chartered Accountants' Hall, Moorgate Place, London, England EC2P 2BJ. Telephone (44) (01) 628 7060.

Periodic digests. Deal with specific British taxation topics. Updated to cover changes in tax law. Price £25.00.

4547
Taxes
Commerce Clearing House, Inc, 4025 W Peterson Ave, Chicago, IL 60646. Telephone (312) 583-8500.

Monthly magazine. Publishes articles on legal, accounting, and economic aspects of federal and state taxes. Price $45.00 per year.

4548
Taxes of Hawaii
Crossroads Press, Inc, PO Box 833, Honolulu, HI 96808. Telephone (808) 521-0021.

Annual book. Considers Hawaii's taxes and their relation to federal income taxes. Includes information on Department of Taxation regulations. Price $13.95 plus $1.50 postage.

4549
Taxes of the State of Mexico
Commerce Clearing House, 4025 W Peterson Ave, Chicago, IL 60646. Telephone (312) 583-8500.

Two loose-leaf volumes. Discusses Mexico's taxes. Price $260.00 per year.

4550
Taxes on Parade
Commerce Clearing House, Inc, 4025 W Peterson Ave, Chicago, IL 60646. Telephone (312) 583-8500.

Weekly reports. Cover the latest federal tax developments. Price $40.00 per year.

4551
Tax Executive
Tax Executives Inst, 425 13 St, NW, Washington, DC 20004. Telephone (202) 783-7761. Telex 89687.

Quarterly magazine. Discusses corporate tax issues. Considers national and international tax philosophies and practices and reviews books. Price $10.00 per year. ISSN 0040-0025.

4551.01
Tax Exempt News
Capitol Publications, Inc, Suite G-12, 2430 Pennsylvania Ave, NW, Washington, DC 20037. Telephone (202) 452-1600.

Monthly newsletter. Covers regulations and legislation which affect tax exempt institutions. Price $87.00 per year.

4552
Tax-Exempt Organizations
Prentice-Hall, Inc, Englewood Cliffs, NJ 07632. Telephone (201) 592-2000. Telex 13-5423.

Monthly loose-leaf service. Reports on developments affecting tax-exempt organizations. Suggests how such organizations can avoid taxes and penalties. Charts, checklists, and forms. Price $246.00 per year.

4553
Tax Facts on Life Insurance
National Underwriter Co, 420 E 4th St, Cincinnati, OH 45202. Telephone (513) 721-2140.

Annual book. Contains life insurance-related tax information. Includes sections on estate and gift taxes and a review of the Tax Reform Act of 1976. Price $3.50.

4553.01
Tax, Financial and Estate Planning for the Owner of a Closely-Held Corporation
Panel Publishers, 14 Plaza Rd, Greenvale, NY 11548. Telephone (516) 484-0006.

Monthly newsletter. Discusses tax, financial, and estate planning for the owner of a closely-held corporation. Emphasizes tax-planning tactics. Price $48.00 per year.

4553.02
Tax-Free Trade Zones of the World
Matthew Bender & Co, 235 E 45th St, New York, NY 10017. Telephone (212) 661-5050.

Two-volume loose-leaf book. Provides information on 356 tax-free trade zones, free ports, and similar areas. Price $150.-00.

4553.03
Tax Haven & Investment Report
Inst for International Research Ltd, 70 Warren St, London, England W1P 5PA. Telephone (44) (01) 388-2663. Telex 263504.

Monthly report. Discusses how to use tax-minimization and investment opportunities. Price $145.00 per year.

4554
Tax Havens of the World
Matthew Bender & Co, 235 E 45th St, New York, NY 10017. Telephone (212) 661-5050.

Loose-leaf books. Provide information on the best areas for investment. Examine 28 countries. Quarterly replacement pages. Price $175.00 for two volumes; $100.00 per year.

4555
Tax Ideas
Prentice-Hall, Inc, Englewood Cliffs, NJ 07632. Telephone (201) 592-2000. Telex 13-5423.

Semimonthly loose-leaf service. Shows tax factors affecting a wide range of business and personal transactions. Price $249.00 per year.

4556
Tax Law Review
Warren, Gorham & Lamont, Inc, 210 South St, Boston, MA 02111. Telephone (617) 423-2020.

Quarterly magazine. Reviews legal tax issues. Price $36.00 per year.

4557
Tax Laws of the World
Foreign Tax Law Assoc, Inc, PO Box 340, Alachua, FL 32616.

Forty-one loose-leaf binders, supplemented weekly. Contain personal and corporate income tax laws for over 100 countries. Include some tax forms and commentaries. Price $950.00, annual renewal $600.00

4557.01
Tax Legislation Update
Arthur Young & Co, 277 Park Ave, New York, NY 10017. Telephone (212) 922-2000.

Bimonthly report. Discusses status of tax legislation before Congress. Price free of charge.

4558
Tax Letter Service
Research and Review Service of America, Inc, PO Box 1727, Indianapolis, IN 46206. Telephone (317) 297-4360.

Monthly newsletter. Pertains to taxes and financial planning. Is designed for insurance agents. Includes articles on estate planning and business insurance. Price available on request.

4559
Tax Management Compensation Planning Journal
Bureau of National Affairs, Inc, 1231 25th St, NW, Washington, DC 20037. Telephone (202) 452-4200.

Monthly journal. Reviews planning approaches and significant developments in the field of executive compensation and employee benefits. Includes the text of actual plans, articles by experts, and analyses. Index. Price $121.00 per year.

4560
Tax Management International Journal
Bureau of National Affairs, Inc, 1231 25th St, NW, Washington, DC 20037. Telephone (202) 452-4200.

Monthly journal. Reviews current international tax, fiscal, and economic developments affecting multinational businesses. Bibliography and index. Price $120.00 per year.

4561
Tax Management Program
Bureau of National Affairs, Inc, 1231 25th St, NW, Washington, DC 20037. Telephone (202) 452-4200.

Three series of portfolios revised periodically. Offer an in-depth analysis of the particular tax problem in each portfolio. Cover US and foreign income, estates, gifts, and trusts. Price available on request.

4562
Tax Newsletter
Main Lafrentz & Co, 380 Park Ave, New York, NY 10017. Telephone (212) 867-9100.

Quarterly newsletter. Covers tax subjects. Includes information on tax law interpretation. Price free of charge.

4564
Tax Planning International
Finax Publications Ltd, 31 Curzon St, London, England W1Y 7AE. Telephone (44) (01) 499-8241. Telex 262570.

Monthly newsletter. Reports on corporate and personal taxation in selected countries. Notes new tax laws and proposed legislation. Price $125.00 per year.

4565
Tax Planning Review
Commerce Clearing House, Inc, 4025 W Peterson Ave, Chicago, IL 60646. Telephone (312) 583-8500.

Loose-leaf book, plus monthly newsletter. Discusses tax-saving opportunities in business and management transactions. Price $65.00 per year.

4565.01
Tax Planning Tips From the Tax Advisor, **1981**
American Inst of Certified Public Accountants, 1211 Ave of the Americas, New York, NY 10036. Telephone (212) 575-6200.

Book. Discusses Internal Revenue Code provisions and Internal Revenue Service procedures. Covers corporate estates and trusts, transfer and employment taxes. Price $16.50.

4566
Tax Practice Management
American Inst of Certified Public Accountants, 1211 Ave of the Americas, New York, NY 10036. Telephone (212) 575-6200.

Loose-leaf book. Covers tax practice management subjects. Includes such topics as tax and estate planning, processing and filing tax returns, and Internal Revenue Service audits. Worksheets, forms, and checklists. Price $42.50.

4567
Tax Practitioners Forum
Panel Publishers, 14 Plz Rd, Greenvale, NY 11548. Telephone (516) 484-0006.

Monthly magazine. Discusses current tax cases, Internal Revenue Service rulings and legislation. Is based on data from the Tax Practitioner's Forum proceedings, C W Post College, and Long Island University. Price $60.00 per year.

4568
Tax Research Techniques
Ray M Sommerfeld and G Fred Streuling, American Inst of Certified Public Accountants, 1211 Ave of the Americas, New York, NY 10036. Telephone (212) 575-6200.

Book report. Provides information on tax research techniques. Discusses the Internal Revenue Code, administrative and judicial interpretations, and computer-assisted tax research. Price $8.50.

4569
Tax Review
Tax Foundation, Inc, 1875 Connecticut Ave, NW, Washington, DC 20009. Telephone (202) 328-4500.

Monthly newsletter. Contains one article per issue on government finance and administration. Considers the relationship between taxation and the US economy.

4570
Tax Sheltered Investments
Clark Boardman Co Ltd, 435 Hudson St, New York, NY 10014. Telephone (212) 929-7500.

Loose-leaf book periodically revised. Discusses laws affecting tax-sheltered investments, with emphasis on the Tax Reform Act of 1976. Covers real estate investments, oil and gas investments, equipment leasing, cattle feeding and breeding, farm land, and motion pictures. Price $110.00 for two loose-leaf volumes. ISBN 0-87632-093-0.

4571
Tax Shelter Opportunities in Real Estate
Executive Reports Corp, Englewood Cliffs, NJ 07632. Telephone (201) 592-2000. Telex 13-5423.

Guide with monthly supplements. Discusses uses of real estate in providing tax-sheltered income. Price $186.00 per year. ISBN 0-13-885269-3.

4572
Tax Shelters in Executive Compensation
Executive Reports Corp, Englewood Cliffs, NJ 07632. Telephone (201) 592-2000. Telex 13-5423.

Guide with monthly supplements. Covers compensation plans with built-in tax shelters and tax breaks. Notes fringe benefits plans. Price $179.40 per year. ISBN 0-13-886721-6.

4572.01
Tax Systems of Western Europe
Gower Publishing Co Ltd, 1 Westmead, Farnborough, Hampshire, England, GUI4 7RU. Telephone Farnborough (0252) 519221. Telex 858623.

Book. Summarizes tax situation in 23 European countries. Price $30.00. ISBN 0 566 02183 8.

4573
Tax Treaties
Commerce Clearing House, Inc, 4025 W Peterson Ave, Chicago, IL 60646. Telephone (312) 583-8500.

Two loose-leaf books and monthly reports. Cover treaties concluded between the US and foreign countries on income and estate taxes. Price $170.00 per year.

4574
Tax Treaties
Prentice-Hall, Inc, Englewood Cliffs, NJ 07632. Telephone (201) 592-2000. Telex 13-5423.

Monthly loose-leaf service. Contains the full text of every treaty, supplementary treaty, or protocol relating to income, estate, and gift taxes. Annotated summaries. Price $165.00 per year.

4575
Technical Bulletin
Arthur Young & Co, 277 Park Ave, New York, NY 10017. Telephone (212) 922-4724.

Irregularly published newsletter. Comments on accounting statements made by government agencies, accountancy bodies, and stock exchanges. Price free of charge.

4576
Technical Practice Aids
American Inst of Certified Public Accountants, 1211 Ave of the Americas, New York, NY 10036. Nonmembers order from Commerce Clearing House, Inc, 4025 W Peterson Ave, Chicago, IL 60646. Telephone (212) 575-6200.

Loose-leaf service. Provides a technical guide to accounting and auditing procedures. Includes information relating to financial statement presentation, assets, liabilities, deferred credits, revenue, and expenses. Price $64.00.

4578
Technical Survey
Predicasts, Inc, 200 University Circle Research Center, 11001 Cedar Ave, Cleveland, OH 44106. Telephone (216) 795-3000.

Weekly newsletter. Presents abstracts pertaining to technological research in 24 industrial areas. Price $132.00 per year.

4579
Technical Trends
Merrill Analysis, Inc, Box 228, Chappaqua, NY 10514. Telephone (914) 238-3641.

Weekly report. Gives a graphic summary of stock market barometers. Includes an analysis of selected growth companies. Price $60.00 per year.

4580
Technological Forecasting and Social Change
North-Holland Publishing Co, PO Box 211, 1000 AE Amsterdam, The Netherlands. Order from Elsevier/North-Holland, Inc, 52 Vanderbilt Ave, New York, NY 10017. Telephone (212) 867-9040.

Monthly journal. Discusses methodology and practice of technological forecasting as a planning tool. Analyzes role of social and behavioral aspects in integrative planning. Price $150.00 per year. ISSN 0040-1625.

4581
Technology Forecasts and Technology Surveys
Technology Forecasts and Technology Surveys, Suite 208, 205 S Beverly Dr, Beverly Hills, CA 90212. Telephone (213) 273-3486.

Monthly newsletter. Reports on new products and related technological developments. Surveys research in specific industries. Price $85.00 per year.

4581.01
Technology Growth Markets and Opportunities
Creative Strategies International, 4340 Stevens Creek Blvd, Suite 275, San Jose, California 95129. Telephone (408) 249-7550.

Bimonthly report. Focuses on trends and opportunities in developing technological markets. Includes information on computers, electronics, and communications. Price $495.00 per year.

4582
Technology Transfer Action
Technology News Center, Inc, PO Box 2549, Rancho Palo Verdes, CA 90274. Telephone (213) 377-8485.

Monthly report. Discusses technology transfer and diffusion topics. Covers marketing, adaptive engineering, financing, and world trade information. Price $70.00 per year.

4582.01
Telecom Insider
International Data Corp 214 3rd Ave, Waltham, MA 02254. Telephone (617) 890-3700. Telex 92-3401.

Monthly periodical. Covers all aspects of telecommunications, including voice, data, and electronic messages. Price available on request.

4583
Telecommunications Policy
IPC Business Press Ltd, 205 E 42nd St, New York, NY 10017. Telephone (212) 889-0700. Telex 421710.

Quarterly magazine. Discusses issues relating to control and management of telecommunications and information systems. Emphasizes implication for business, and social and political impact. Price $124.80 per year. ISSN 0308-5961.

4584
Telecommunications Reports
Telecommunications Publishing Co, 1293 National Press Bldg, Washington, DC 20045. Telephone (202) 347-2654.

Weekly newsletter. Reports on telecommunications industry developments. Includes information about telephones, cable television, data communications services and satellites. Quarterly index. Price $188.00 per year.

4585
Telephone Engineer & Management
Harcourt Brace Jovanovich Publications, 757 3rd Ave, New York, NY 10017. Order from Harcourt Brace and Jovanovich Publications, 1 E 1st St, Duluth, MN 55802. Telephone (218) 727-8511.

Semimonthly magazine. Discusses telephone industry issues, including equipment and management. Price $9.50 per year.

4586
Telephone Engineer & Management Directory
Harcourt Brace Jovanovich Publications, 757 3rd Ave, New York, NY 10017. Order from Harcourt Brace and Jovanovich Publications, 1 E 1st St, Duluth, MN 55802. Telephone (218) 727-8511.

Annual directory. Lists products and services used by US and foreign telephone companies for installation, operation, and maintenance. Statistics show the international growth of telephone systems and their rates. Price $30.00 per copy.

4586.01
Telephone Marketing Report
Januz Marketing Communications, Inc, PO Box 1000, Lake Forest, IL 60045. Telephone (312) 295-6550.

Semimonthly newsletter. Gives advice on improving effectiveness of telephone sales and marketing. Notes ways to reduce telephone costs. Price $96.00 per year, $192.00 two years, $240.00 three years. ISSN 0270-9635.

4586.02
Telephone News
Phillips Publishing, Inc, 7315 Wisconsin Ave, Bethesda, MD 20014. Telephone (301) 986-0666.

Biweekly newsletter. Covers the telecommunications industry, with special emphasis on news about and changes confronting voice telephone companies, interconnects, other common carriers, and equipment manufacturers as well as governmental action affecting the industry. Price $127.00 per year.

4587
Telephone Tickler
Underwriter Printing & Publishing Co, 50 East Palisade Ave, PO Box 9806, Englewood, NJ 07631. Telephone (201) 569-8808.

Annual book. Lists names, addresses, and telephone numbers of insurance companies, agents, brokers, and related suppliers in the New York metropolitan area. Price $6.00.

4588
Television Digest with Consumer Electronics
Television Digest, Inc, 1836 Jefferson Pl NW, Washington, DC 20036. Telephone (202) 872-9200.

Weekly report. Supplies information on television broadcasting and equipment and related consumer electronics equipment industry news. Notes Federal Trade Commission and congressional developments. Tables. Price $198.00 per year.

4589
Television Factbook, **1980**
Television Digest, Inc, 1836 Jefferson Pl, NW, Washington, DC 20036. Telephone (202) 872-9200.

Two-volume book. Provides information on US commercial television stations, cable systems, and key personnel. Price $137.50.

4590
Tenders
Thomson Publications (Australia) Pty Ltd, 47 Chippen St, PO Box 65, Chippendale, NSW 2008, Australia. Telephone 699-6731. Telex TPAS AA22226.

Weekly newspaper. Lists Australian federal, state, and local government tenders. Includes private commerce tenders. Price $110.00 (Australian) per year.

4591
1040 Preparation
Commerce Clearing House, Inc, 4025 W Peterson Ave, Chicago, IL 60646. Telephone (312) 583-8500.

Annual book. Provides assistance in preparing income tax Form 1040. Price $16.-50. ISSN 5373.

4592
Tennessee Business and Industrial Review
Tennessee Department of Economic & Community Development, 1007 Andrew Jackson Bldg, Nashville, TN 37219. Telephone (615) 741-1888. Telex 555196 ECD-NAS.

Monthly newsletter. Discusses new industry and industrial expansion in Tennessee. Notes management changes. Price available on request.

4593
Tennessee: Directory of Manufacturers **1981**
Manufacturers' News, Inc, 3 E Huron St, Chicago, IL 60611. Telephone (312) 337-1084.

Biennial book. Covers 4500 manufacturing firms in Tennessee by name, location, and product. Notes executives and number of employees. Price $32.00.

4593.01
Tennessee: State Industrial Directory, **1981**
Manufacturers' News, Inc, 3 E Huron St, Chicago, Il 60611. Telephone (312) 337-1084.

Annual book. Lists 4901 industrial companies in Tennessee by name, location, and product. Identifies executives. Price $40.00.

4594
Tennessee Statistical Abstract, **1980 edition**
University of Tennessee, Center for Business and Economic Research, College of Business Adm, 100 Glocker Business Adm Bldg, Knoxville, TN 37916. Telephone (615) 974-5441.

Trienniel book. Supplies current and historical data on Tennessee economic, social, and political structure. Covers the labor force, population, banking, education, and recreation. Tables, graphs, and maps. Price $18.00.

4595
Texas Banking Red Book
Bankers Digest, Inc, 1208 Mercantile Securities Bldg, Dallas, TX 75201. Telephone (214) 747-4522.

Annual book. Serves as a directory to officers and directors of Texas banks. Includes year-end statements for all Texas banks. Price $14.50 per year.

4596
Texas Business Review
University of Texas at Austin, Bureau of Business Research, PO Box 7459, Austin, TX 78712. Telephone (512) 471-1616.

Bimonthly report. Translates scholarly research into business information. Reviews various aspects of the business world. Price $15.00 per year. ISSN 0040-4209.

4596.01
Texas Facts
Texas Industrial Commission, Capitol Station, Box 12728, Austin, TX 78711. Telephone (512) 472-5059.

Irregular report. Compares Texas with other states by economic areas of taxes and financing, labor and training, markets and transportation, plus general economic overview. Price free of charge.

4597
Texas Ideas Newsletter
Texas Industrial Commission, Capitol Station, Box 12728, Austin, TX 78711. Telephone (512) 475-5551.

Monthly newsletter. Reports on Texas industrial development news and notes the activities of the Texas Industrial Commission. Lists new and expanded businesses. Price free of charge.

4597.01
Texas Industrial Update
Texas Industrial Commission, Capitol Station, Box 12728, Austin, TX 78711. Telephone (512) 472-5059.

Monthly newsletter. Reports on Texas economic development news. Notes activities of the Texas Industrial Commission. Lists industrial revenue bond activity. Price free of charge.

4597.02
Texas: Manufacturers Directory, **1980**
Manufacturers' News, Inc, 3 E Huron St, Chicago, Il 60611. Telephone (312) 337-1084.

Annual book. Identifies 12,000 manufacturing companies in Texas and their executives. Price $68.00.

4597.03
Texas Means Business
Texas Industrial Commission, Capitol Station, Box 12728, Austin, TX 78711. Telephone (512) 472-5059.

Annual report. Describes economic climate in Texas, with emphasis on the state tax structure. Compares other state tax structures and business incentives. Price free of charge.

4598
Textbook for Employee Benefit Plan Trustees, Administrators & Advisors
International Foundation of Employee Benefit Plans, 18700 W Bluemound Rd, Box 69, Brookfield, WI 53005. Telephone (414) 786-6700.

Book. Contains proceedings of the 1979 Annual Educational Conference of the International Foundation of Employee Benefit Plans, 1976. Includes such topics as ERISA administration, health care costs, and funding requirements. Price $27.00. ISBN 0-89154-125-X.

4599
Textile Institute and Industry
Textile Institute, 10 Blackfriars St, Manchester, England M3 5DR. Telephone (061) 834-8457.

Monthly magazine. Covers every sector of textile activity throughout the world. Includes articles on fashion and design. Price £3.00 per issue, £36.00 per annual volume, back issues.

4600
Textile Journal Annual Buying Guide
Yaffa Publishing Group, GPO Box 606, Yaffa Publishing Group, 432-436 Elizabeth St, Surry Hills, Australia. Order from Sydney, NSW 2001, Australia. Telephone (61) (02) 699-7861. Telex 21887.

Annual magazine. Lists major Australian textile companies. Notes their executives, products, and offices. Price $12.00 (Australian) per year.

4601
Textile Journal/Australia
Yaffa Publishing Group, GPO Box 606, Yaffa Publishing Group, 432-436 Elizabeth St, Surry Hills, Australia. Order from Sydney, NSW 2001, Australia. Telephone (61) (02) 699-7861. Telex 21887.

Bimonthly magazine. Discusses the Australian textile industry. Notes new equipment and processes. Price $30.00 (Australian) per year.

4602
Textile Organon
Textile Economics Bureau, Inc, 489 5th Ave, New York, NY 10017. Telephone (212) 661-5166.

Monthly report. Covers developments and gives statistics on the US and world synthetic fiber industries. Price $28.00 per year.

4603
Textile World
McGraw-Hill Publications Co, 1221 Ave of the Americas, New York, NY 10020. Telephone (212) 997-1221. Telex TWX 7105814879 WUI 62555.

Monthly magazine. Reports on new textile equipment, methods, and plant management techniques. Price $30.00 US and Canada per year.

4604
Textile World—Fact File Buyers' Guide
McGraw-Hill Publications Co, 1221 Ave of the Americas, New York, NY 10020. Telephone (212) 997-1221. Telex TWX 7105814879 WUI 62555.

Annual magazine. Lists over 3300 textile supplier companies and 2000 different products. Notes textile production and marketing trends. Price available on request.

4605
Thapar's First International Import & Export Directory of the World
Publishing & Distributing Co Ltd, Mitre House, 177 Regent St, London, England W1R 7FB. Telephone (44) (01) 734-6534, 6535.

Book. Provides a guide to international imports and exports. Price $60.00.

4606
Thesaurus of Industrial Development Terms
United Nations Industrial Development Organization, Vienna International Centre, PO Box 300, A-1400, Vienna, Austria. Telephone 26310. Telex 135612.

Book. Provides key indexing words to serve UNIDO's Industrial Information System. Price $7.00 per volume.

4606.01
Third World Quarterly
Third World Foundation, New Zealand House, 80 Haymarket, London, England SW1Y 4TS. Telephone (44) (01) 839-6167. Telex 8814201 Trimed G.

Quarterly journal. Presents research on Third World economic and social topics. Price $30.00 per year.

4607
33 Metal Producing
McGraw-Hill Publications Co, 1221 Ave of the Americas, New York, NY 10020. Telephone (212) 997-1221. Telex TWX 7105814879 WUI 62555.

Monthly magazine. Discusses metal mill technology, production, and engineering. Includes information on pollution control. Price $35.00 per year US and Canada; $45.00 (foreign).

4608
This Week
Barnett Banks of Florida, Inc, 100 Laura St, PO Box 40789, Jacksonville, FL 32231. Telephone (904) 791-7443.

Weekly newsletter. Supplies information on national and Florida economic trends. Contains data on money markets, municipal bonds, banking and certificates of deposit. Tables and charts. Price $36.00 per year.

4609
This Week from the Capital
Associated Industries of New York State, Inc, 150 State St, Albany, NY 12207. Telephone (518) 465-3547.

Newsletter issued weekly during the New York State legislative session. Reports on bills and legislative activity of business, consumer, and labor interests. Price free of charge.

4610
Thomas Grocery Register
Thomas Publishing Co, 1 Penn Plz, 250 W 34thSt, New York, NY 10001. Telephone (212) 695-0500.

Three-volume set. Provides directory of food industry manufacturers and distributors. Lists chains, wholesalers, brokers, exporters, warehouses, food and nonfood products, services and brand names. Price $75.00.

4611
Thomas Register of American Manufacturers
Thomas Publishing Co, 1 Penn Plz, 250 W 34th, New York, NY 10001. Telephone (212) 695-0500.

Annual set of 16 volumes. Provides listing of over 100,000 US manufacturers, their products and services, brand names, and catalogues. Price $120.00.

4612
Thom's Commercial Directory
Thom's Directories Ltd, 38 Merrion Sq, Dublin 2, Ireland. Telephone (353) (01) 76-74-81.

Annual book. Lists businesses, professions, trades and manufacturers for 155 towns in the Republic of Ireland. Includes a directory of companies and biographical information on professional, business, and educational leaders. Price £15.00 per year.

4613
Thomson's Liquor Guide
Thomson Publications (Australia) Pty Ltd, 47 Chippen St, PO Box 65, Chippendale, NSW 2008, Australia. Telephone 699-6731. Telex TPAS AA22226.

Monthly book. Contains recommended Australian price lists for beer, wines, and spirits. Provides price change information in a semimonthly bulletin. Price $108.00 (Australian) per year.

4615
Thorndike Encyclopedia of Banking and Financial Tables
David Thorndike, Warren, Gorham & Lamont, Inc, 210 S St, Boston, MA 02111. Telephone (617) 423-2020.

Book. Provides data frequently used in the banking business. Statistical tables. Price $60.00. ISBN 0-88262-062-2.

4616
Three Banks Review
Williams and Glyns Bank Ltd, Limited Economics Office, 7 Copthall Ave, London, England EC2R 7HB. Telephone (44) (01) 588-8161.

Quarterly report. Discusses economic, business, and banking subjects. Price free of charge.

4617
Thruput
American Bankers Assn, 1120 Connecticut Ave NW, Washington, DC 20036. Telephone (202) 467-4123.

Monthly newsletter. Discusses data processing developments related to the banking industry. Price $18.00 per year.

4618
Timber Tax Journal
Forest Industries Committee on Timber Valuation and Taxation, 1250 Connecticut Ave, Washington, DC 20036. Telephone (202) 223-2314.

Annual book. Pertains to timber taxation. Emphasizes the effects of capital gains taxation on timber growth and wood production and includes case histories and a survey of state forest laws. Price $25.95. ISBN 0-914272-19-5.

4619
Time
Time, Inc, Time & Life Bldg, New York, NY 10020. Order from Time, Inc, 541 N Fairbanks Ct, Chicago, IL 60611. Telephone (212) 586-1212.

Weekly magazine. Covers international and US political developments, economic conditions, medical, educational, and energy issues. Includes books, theater, and motion picture reviews. Price $26.00 per year.

4620
Time Rates of Wages and Hours of Work
Her Majesty's Stationery Office, PO Box 569, London, England SE1 9NH. Telephone (44) (01) 928 1321.

Annual report. Covers the time rates of wages and hours of work for Great Britain. Price £12.20. ISBN 0 11 361098 X.

4621
Times Atlas of the World: Revised Comprehensive Edition, 1980
Times Books, 3 Park Ave, New York, NY 10016. Telephone (212) 725-2050.

Book. Contains detailed maps of countries of the world. Price $125.00. ISBN 0-8129-0906-2.

4622
Times 1000
Times Books, 16 Golden Sq, London, England W1R 4BN. Order from Times Designs, Inc, 201 E 42 St, New York, NY 10017. Telephone London (44) (01) 434-3767; New York (212) 986-9230. Telex New York 125912.

Annual book. Provides information on leading industrial and financial firms in Great Britain, the Republic of Ireland, Europe, the US, Canada, South Africa, Australia, and Japan. Tables. Price £ 13.00 per year.

4623
Tin News
Malayan Tin Bureau, 2000 K St, NW, Washington, DC 20006. Telephone (202) 331-7550.

Monthly newsletter. Discusses the tin industry. Focuses on Malaysian mining, world tin markets, new uses of tin. Tables indicate Malaysian production, mining techniques, international production, consumption, and other data. Price free of charge.

4624
TIPS—Technical Information Periodicals Service
General Electric Co, Business Growth Services, 120 Erie Blvd, Room 591, Schenectady, NY 12305. Telephone (518) 385-2577.

Monthly listing of 150 abstracts of manufacturing productivity-oriented articles from over 100 industrial publications. Price $390.00 per year (reprints free).

4625
Titanium Ingot, Mill Products, and Castings
US Dept of Commerce, Bureau of the Census, Washington, DC 20233. Telephone (202) 449-1600.

Monthly report, with annual summary. Presents information on net shipments of titanium mill products by shape. Includes data on the production and consumption of ingots and shipments of mill products and castings for the preceding 24 months. Price $3.25 per year.

4626
Title News
American Land Title Assn, 1828 L St, NW, Washington, DC 20036. Telephone (202) 296-3671.

Monthly magazine. Covers land title issues. Price $20.00 per year.

4627
Tobacco Barometer
Tobacco Merchants Assn of the US, Statler Hilton, 7th Ave & 33rd St, New York, NY 10001. Telephone (212) 239-4435.

Monthly report. Supplies information on the production and sales of cigarettes, cigars, and little cigars. Notes other industry developments. Tables. Price $25.00 per year.

4628
Tobacco Market News Reports
US Dept of Agriculture, Agricultural Marketing Service, Room 523-Annex, Washington, DC 20250. Telephone (202) 447-2265.

Irregularly published reports. Provide tobacco market price and sales information. Indicate stocks. Price free of charge.

4629
Tobacco Merchants Assn (TMA) Guide to Tobacco Taxes
Tobacco Merchants Assn of the US, Statler Hilton, 7th Ave & 33rd St, New York, NY 10001. Telephone (212) 239-4435.

Report, with quarterly updates. Summarizes state tobacco product tax laws. Includes local tax information. Price $20.00.

4630
Tobacco Reporter
Harcourt Brace Jovanovich Publications, 757 3rd Ave, New York, NY 10017. Order from Harcourt Brace and Jovanovich Publications, 1 E 1st St, Duluth, MN 55802. Telephone (218) 727-8511.

Monthly magazine. Discusses the tobacco industry, including information about exports and imports, processing, and equipment. Price $15.00 per year.

4632
Tolley's Corporation Tax 1977/78
Tolley Publishing Co Ltd, 44a High St, Croydon, Surrey, England CR9 1UU. Telephone (44) (01) 686-9144.

Book. Provides reference material on corporate tax in Great Britain. Price £2.50. ISBN 0-510-49354-8.

4633
Tolley's Employment Handbook 1977
Tolley Publishing Co Ltd, 44a High St, Croydon, Surrey, England CR9 1UU. Telephone (44) (01) 686-9144.

Book. Summarizes and analyzes Great Britain's Employment Protection Act and other legislation affecting employment. Price £5.00. ISBN 0-510-49352-1.

4634
Tolley's Income Tax 1977/78
Tolley Publishing Co Ltd, 44a High St, Croydon, Surrey, England CR9 1UU. Telephone (44) (01) 686-9144.

Book. Provides reference material on income and capital gains taxes in Great Britain. Price £5.00. ISBN 0-510-49353-X.

4635
Tolley's Taxation in the Channel Islands and Isle of Man 1977
Tolley Publishing Co Ltd, 44a High St, Croydon, Surrey, England CR9 1UU. Telephone (44) (01) 686-9144.

Guide. Covers taxation in Jersey, Guernsey, and the Isle of Man. Price £3.00. ISBN 0-510-49363-7.

4636
Tolley's Taxation in the Republic of Ireland 1977/78
Tolley Publishing Co Ltd, 44a High St, Croydon, Surrey, England CR9 1UU. Telephone (44) (01) 686-9144.

Book. Covers the Republic of Ireland's Finance Act and the capital gains, corporation, and value added taxes. Price £4.-50. ISBN 0-510-49364-5.

4637
Top Executive Compensation
Conference Board, Inc, 845 3rd Ave, New York, NY 10022. Telephone (212) 759-0900.

Report on compensation for top executives in selected companies. Price $45.00.

4638
Topicator
Thompson Bureau, 5395 S Miller St, Littleton, CO 80123. Telephone (303) 973-2337.

Monthly service. Provides an index to advertising, communications, and marketing periodicals. Price $85.00 per year.

4639
Topics in Health Care Financing
Aspen Systems Corp, 1600 Research Blvd, Rockville, MD 20850. Telephone (800) 638-8437.

Quarterly magazine. Discusses health care financial management. Includes such topics as improving profitability and cost containment. Price $43.50 per year.

4640
Toronto Stock Exchange—Company Manual
Toronto Stock Exchange, 234 Bay St, Toronto, Ont, Canada M5J 1R1. Telephone (416) 868-5100.

Annual book. Compiled for companies whose shares are listed on the Toronto Stock Exchange. Elaborates on all areas covering requirements for and maintaining a listing. Price $20.00, plus annual sustaining fee.

4640.01
Toronto Stock Exchange—Daily Record
Toronto Stock Exchange, 234 Bay St, Toronto, Ont, Canada M5J 1R1. Telephone (416) 868-5100.

Daily report. Shows volume traded and price range for equities, options, and futures. Price $170.00 per year.

4640.02
Toronto Stock Exchange—Management of Change in the Canadian Securities Industry
Toronto Stock Exchange, 234 Bay St, Toronto, Ont, Canada M5J 1R1. Telephone (416) 868-5100.

Series of eight papers. Examines Canadian securities market and its major participants. Price $20.00 per set, $3.00 individual papers one to seven, $5.00 eighth paper.

4640.03
Toronto Stock Exchange—Members' Manual
Toronto Stock Exchange, 234 Bay St, Toronto, Ont, Canada M5J 1R1. Telephone (416) 868-5100.

Annual book. Contains complete set of by-laws and policies of Toronto Stock Exchange, plus financial and audit requirements for member firms. Includes Toronto Stock Exchange Act (1969), listing of officials, officers of member firms, and telephone numbers. Price $35.00, plus annual sustaining fee.

4641
Toronto Stock Exchange Review
The Toronto Stock Exchange, 234 Bay St, Toronto, Ont, Canada M5J 1R1. Telephone (416) 868-5100.

Monthly report. Summarizes trading in all listed stocks, options, and futures. Shows monthly and annual price ranges, earnings, price/earnings ratios, yields, newly listed securities. Price $36.00 per year.

4641.01
Toronto Stock Exchange—"300" Stock Price Indexes Manual
Toronto Stock Exchange, 234 Bay St, Toronto, Ont, Canada M5J 1R1. Telephone (416) 868-5100.

Annual book. Contains charts and historical values for January 1956 to the present, updated annually. Shows index-related statistics for all indexes. Price $45.00.

4641.02
Toronto Stock Exchange—"300" Total Return Indexes Manual
Toronto Stock Exchange, 234 Bay St, Toronto, Ont, Canada M5J 1R1. Telephone (416) 868-5100.

Annual book. Provides charts and historical values for January 1956 through December 1979 (with 1980 data in an addendum) reflecting the reinvestment of dividends, as well as price performance. Price $30.00.

4642
Toronto Stock Exchange Weekly Summary
The Toronto Stock Exchange, 234 Bay St, Toronto, Ont, Canada M5J 1R1. Telephone (416) 868-5100.

Weekly report. Gives news affecting the Toronto Stock Exchange and listed companies. Includes statistical summary, dividend changes, and most actively traded issues. Price $23.00 per year.

4643
Total Information Package for 1980-82
National Information Center for Educational Media, Univ of Southern California, University Park, Los Angeles, CA 90007. Telephone (800) 421-8711, California (213) 743-6681.

Book or microfiche, with quarterly updates. Provides indexes to educational audio-visual aids in fields such as psychology, environmental, vocational and technical education, health, safety, and special education. Price available on request.

4643.01
Toxic Materials News
Business Publishers, PO Box 1067, Silver Spring, MD 20910. Telephone (301) 587-6300.

Weekly newsletter. Discusses toxic substances control regulations. Price $217.00 per year.

4643.02
Toxic Materials Reference Service
Business Publishers, Inc, PO Box 1067, Silver Spring, MD 20910. Telephone (301) 587-6300.

Annual service. Provides text of toxic substances control regulations as they are issued. Price $257.00 per year.

4643.03

Toxic Materials Transport

Business Publishers, PO Box 1067, Silver Spring, MD 20910. Telephone (301) 587-6300.

Biweekly newsletter. Discusses transportation of hazardous materials. Price $97.00 per year.

4643.04

Toxic Substances Journal

Executive Enterprises Publications Co, Inc, 33 W 60th St, New York, NY 10023. Telephone (212) 489-2670.

Quarterly journal. Explains toxic laws and regulations, methods for meeting regulatory standards, and consequences of noncompliance. Aids in development of future strategies. Price $48.00 per year.

4644

Toxic Substances Sourcebook

Environment Information Center (EIC), Inc, Catalog Order Dept, 292 Madison Ave, New York, NY 10017. Telephone (212) 949-9494.

Book. Identifies chemicals dangerous to the environment. Provides abstracts of key reports. Tables, charts, book and film listings, an index, and a bibliography. Price $95.00.

4645

Toys Hobbies & Crafts

Harcourt Brace Jovanovich Publications, 757 3rd Ave, New York, NY 10017. Order from Harcourt Brace and Jovanovich Publications, 1 E 1st St, Duluth, MN 55802. Telephone (218) 727-8511.

Monthly magazine, with annual directory. Focuses on toys, hobbies, and crafts. Considers manufacturing and retail developments. Price $7.00 per year.

4645.01

Toys Magazine

Hong Kong Trade Development Council, 548 5th Ave, New York, NY 10036. Telephone (212) 582-6610.

Annual magazine. Covers toy industry of Hong Kong. Lists companies and products manufactured for export. Price available on request.

4646

Tractors, Except Garden Tractors

US Dept of Commerce, Bureau of the Census, Washington, DC 20233. Telephone (202) 449-1600.

Monthly report, with annual summary. Provides statistics on total production, quantity, and value of shipments of wheel tractors (except contractors' off-highway and garden type). Price $.25 per issue.

4646.01

Trade and Credit: Problems and Resolutions in the Middle East and North Africa, in Asia and the Pacific and in Latin America

Chase Trade Information Corp, 1 World Trade Center, 78th Floor, New York, NY 10048. Telephone (212) 432-8072. Telex RCA 235444.

Three updated reports. Each provides individual economic and trade coverage of the Middle East and North Africa, Asia the Pacific, and Latin America. Includes incentives for foreign investments, free trade zones, import and exchange regulations, and port information. Price $260.00 each.

4647

Trade and Economic Development

International Review Service, 15 Washington Pl, New York, NY 10003. Telephone (212) 751-0833.

Monthly report. Covers trade, finance, agreements, acquisitions, restrictions, and new projects. Reports United Nations sessions on economic problems, multinational corporations, and ECO political news. Price $250.00 per year.

4649

Trade and Industry Bulletin

Ministry of Economic Development, Vic, BC, Canada V8V 4R9. Telephone (604) 387-6701.

Monthly report. Covers import and export opportunities in British Columbia. Gives dates of special international events. Price free of charge. ISSN 0382-1919.

4650

Trade and Regulated Industries— Occupational Employment Statistics

Alaska Dept of Labor, Employment Security Div, Research & Analysis Section, Box 3-7000. Juneau, AK 99801. Telephone (907) 465-2700.

Report. Presents statistics on employment in Alaska's wholesale and retail trades and on employment in the state's regulated industries. Price available on request.

4651

Trade and Securities: Statistics

Standard & Poor's Corp, 345 Hudson St, New York, NY 10014. Telephone (212) 924-6400.

Loose-leaf book, with monthly updates. Provides current statistical information for finance, securities, production, labor, commodities, and trade. Includes statistics on specific industries, namely automobile, chemical, and textile. Price $155.00 per year.

4653

Trade Cases

Commerce Clearing House, Inc, 4025 W Peterson Ave, Chicago, IL 60646. Telephone (312) 583-8500.

Annual books. Contain court decisions on trade, price, and antitrust laws. Price $47.50 per volume.

4654

Trade Directories of the World

Croner Publications, Inc, 211-03 Jamaica Ave, Queens Village, NY 11428. Telephone (212) 464-0866.

Loose-leaf directory, plus monthly supplements. Lists approximately 3000 trade, industrial and professional directories. Includes import/export directories. Price $55.00 per year.

4654.01

Trade Financing

Euromoney Publications Ltd, Nestor House, Playhouse Yard, London, England EC4V 5EX. Telephone (44) (01) 236-7111 Telex 8812246 Eurmon G

Book. Discusses new techniques and instruments of trade financing and their best use. Price $90.00.

4655

Trade Letter and Business Barometer

Vancouver Board of Trade, 1177 W Hastings St, 5th Floor, Vancouver, BC, Canada V6E 2K3. Telephone (604) 681-2111.

Monthly newsletter. Supplies data on British Columbia's economy, including employment, bank debits, retail sales, and building permits. Notes overseas business opportunities. Tables and statistics. Price included in membership fees. Individual copies available on request.

4656

Trade Levels Option Report

Trade Levels, Inc, 301 E Colorado Blvd, Suite 400, Pasadena, CA 91101. Telephone (213) 449-3339.

Weekly newsletter. Analyzes puts and calls on CBOE, AMEX, Philadelphia, Pacific, and Midwest options exchanges. Contains option screening lists for purchase and short sales. Price $10.00 for five weeks.

4657
Trade Levels Report
Trade Levels, Inc, 301 E Colorado Blvd, Suite 400, Pasadena, CA 91101. Telephone (213) 449-3339.

Weekly newsletter. Offers a technical analysis of approximately 5000 common stocks listed on the NYSE, AMEX, and NASDAQ. Forecasts charts and stock screening lists. Price $10.00 for five weeks.

4658
Trade Lists
US Dept of Commerce, Industry and Trade Adm, Bureau of Trade Regulation, Washington, DC 20230. Order from US Dept of Commerce, Industry and Trade Adm, EID/ECLS, Rm 1033, Washington, DC 20230. Telephone (202) 377-2000.

Pamphlet issued every three years. Lists distributors, manufacturers, and agents of a wide range of products. Price $3.00.

4658.01
Trademark Alert
TCR Service, Inc, 140 Sylvan Ave, Englewood Cliffs, NJ 07632. Telephone (201) 461-7475.

Book, published as information becomes available. Contains information on federal trademark applications. Price $500.00 per year.

4659
Trademark Official Gazette
Patent and Trademark Office, Washington, DC 20231. Order from Superintendent of Documents, Government Printing Office, Washington, DC 20402. Telephone (202) 783-3238.

Weekly magazine. Contains an illustration of each US trademark published for opposition, a list of trademarks registered, a classified list of registered trademarks, and Patent Office notices. Price $88.40 per year.

4660
Trademark Protection and Practice
Matthew Bender & Co, 235 E 45h St, New York, NY 10017. Telephone (212) 661-5050.

Two loose-leaf books, with annual supplements. Cover laws affecting trademark protection and practice. Include such topics as opposition, cancellation, and infringement. Price $130.00.

4661
Trademark Register of the US
Patent Searching Service, 422 Washington Bldg, Washington, DC 20045.

Annual register of US trademarks. Price $54.00. ISBN 0082-5786.

4662
Trademark Reporter
US Trademark Assn, 6 E 45th St, New York, NY 10017. Telephone (212) 986-5880.

Bimonthly magazine. Covers US and international trademark developments, landmark cases, and US Patent and Trademark Office activities. Includes book reviews. Price included in membership to the United States Trademark Association.

4662.01
Trademark Research Service
TCR Service, Inc, 140 Sylvan Ave, Englewood Cliffs, NJ 07632. Telephone (201) 461-7475.

Computer service. Provides information on trademarks and infringements. Includes Patent Office, intrastate, common law, and other searches. Prices available on request.

4663
Trade Marks Journal
Supply and Services Canada, Canadian Govt Publishing Centre, Hull, Que, Canada K1A 0S9. Telephone (819) 994-3475, 2085.

Weekly magazine. Contains information on Canadian trademarks. Bilingual. Price $30.00 per year.

4663.01
Trademarks/7
Advertising Trade Publications, Inc, 10 E 39th St, New York, NY 10016. Order from Art Direction Book Co, 10 E 39th St, New York, NY 10016. Telephone (212) 889-6500.

Annual book. Compiles 1100 trademarks, logos, and corporate symbols. Price $16.-50.

4664
Trademarks Throughout the World, **3rd edition**
Clark Boardman Co Ltd, 435 Hudson St, New York, NY 10014. Telephone (212) 929-7500.

Loose-leaf book, supplemented three times annually. Digests trademark laws of 147 countries. Includes the texts of international conventions. Summary tables. Price $92.50, annual supplements $37.50 per year. ISBN 0-87632-126-0.

4665
Trade Names Dictionary, **1st edition**
Gale Research Co, Book Tower, Detroit, MI 48226. Telephone (313) 961-2242.

Two books. List 106,000 trade and brand names. Contain information on manufacturers, importers, marketers, and distributors. Price $160.00 per set. ISBN 0692-1.

4668
Trade Practice Rules
US Federal Trade Commisson, Washington, DC 20580. Telephone (202) 523-3598.

Series of reports. Contain the Federal Trade Commission's trade practice rules for various industries, including frozen foods, groceries, household furniture, and hosiery. Price free of charge.

4669
Trade Promotions Guide
Her Majesty's Stationery Office, PO Box 569, London, England SE1 9NH. Telephone (44) (01) 928-1321.

Quarterly magazine. Lists overseas and British fairs and conferences, overseas store promotions, and other British Department of Trade activities by product. Price available on request.

4670
Trader
Chart Analysis Ltd, 194-200 Bishopsgate, London, England EC2M 4PE. Telephone (44) (01) 283-4476. Telex 883356.

Weekly service. Provides data on 100 leading stocks and market indicators. Gives buy, hold, or sell recommendation for each stock. Charts. Price £100 per year.

4671
Trade Regulation Reports
Commerce Clearing House, Inc, 4025 W Peterson Ave, Chicago, IL 60646. Telephone (312) 583-8500.

Five loose-leaf books, plus weekly reports. Give information on antitrust regulations, trade practice, fair packaging and labeling, fair trade, and price discrimination laws. Price $665.00 per year.

4672
Trade Regulation Rules
US Federal Trade Commission, Washington, DC 20580. Telephone (202) 523-3598.

Series of reports. Provides Federal Trade Commission trade regulations for specific products. Covers deceptive advertising and labeling practices. Price free of charge.

4673
Trade Report
Consulate General of Nigeria, 575 Lexington Ave, New York, NY 10022. Telephone (212) 752-1670.

Annual report. Covers Nigerian trade. Price free of charge.

4673.01
Traders Hotline
Zweig Securities Advisory Service, Inc, 747 3rd Ave, New York, NY 10017. Telephone (212) 753-7710.

Semimonthly newsletter. Offers advice on short-term stock market timing. Includes telephone hotline reports three times a week. Price $150.00 per year.

4674
Trade Secrets
Matthew Bender & Co, 235 E 45th St, New York, NY 10017. Telephone (212) 661-5050.

Two loose-leaf books, with annual supplements. Provide a guide to the protection and use of trade secrets. Emphasize the protection of computer software. Cite statutes, regulations, and cases. Price $140.00.

4675
Trade Secrets and Know-How
Throughout the World, Revised edition, 1977
Clark Boardman, Co Ltd, 435 Hudson St, New York, NY 10014. Telephone (212) 929-7500.

Annually updated loose-leaf books. Cover trade secrets and law in industrial nations. Feature common market law. Price $295.00 for five loose-leaf volumes. ISBN 0-87632-128-7.

4676
Trade Statistics of Ireland
Central Statistics Office, Earlsfort Terrace, Dublin 2, Ireland. Order from Government Publications Sales Office, GPO Arcade, Dublin 1, Ireland.

Monthly information service. Covers the import and export of individual commodities. Price £4.50 per year.

4677
Trade Union Handbook, 2nd edition
Gower Publishing Co Ltd, 1 Westmead, Farnborough, Hampshire, England GU14 7RU. Telephone Farnborough (0252) 519221. Telex 858623.

Directory. Offers information on the structure, membership, policy and personnel of British trade unions. Price $42.-00. ISBN 0 566 02208 7.

4678
Trade Union Information
Commission of the European Communities, Office for Official Publications of the European Communities, CP 1003, Luxembourg 1, Luxembourg. Order from Commission of the European Communities, DG X, 200, rue de la Loi B-1040 Brussels, Belgium. Telephone (352) 490081. Telex PUBLOF 1325.

Fortnightly publication. Reports on trade unions in the European community. Price free of charge.

4679
Trade Union Information
Irish Congress of Trade Unions Research Service, 19 Raglan Rd, Ballsbridge, Dublin 4, Ireland. Telephone (353) (01) 68-06-41.

Monthly magazine. Discusses the Republic of Ireland's labor force and labor union issues. Explains legislative changes and evaluates industrial developments. Price 15 pence per copy.

4680
Trading Cycles
R E Andrews and Assoc, 25743 N Hogan Dr, Valencia, CA 91355. Telephone (805) 259-3742.

Monthly newsletter. Carries buy-sell instructions for long-term investors. Indicates topping signals and major lows of various stock market cycles. Price $50.00 per year.

4681
Traffic Management
Cahners Publishing Co, Inc, 221 Columbus Ave, Boston, MA 02116. Telephone (617) 536-7780.

Monthly magazine. Contains articles on traffic and physical distribution, including reports on efficient and economical distribution methods. Price available on request.

4682
Traffic Safety
National Safety Council, 444 N Michigan Ave, Chicago, IL 60611. Telephone (312) 527-4800. Telex 25-3141.

Bimonthly magazine. Covers all phases of highway safety, including legislation, court developments, and driver education. Notes current research. Price $10.50 members, $13.00 nonmembers.

4683
Traffic Topics
National Retail Merchants Assn, 100 W 31st St, New York, NY 10001. Telephone (212) 244-6780.

Monthly report. Discusses traffic operations in retail stores, including transportation information. Presents successful procedures used by particular stores. Price $14.50 per year.

4684
Training
Lakewood Publications, Inc, 731 Hennepin Ave, Minneapolis, MN 55403. Telephone (612) 333-0471.

Monthly magazine. Features articles on training and human resources development. Notes methods, systems, case studies, and related products. Price $24.00 per year.

4684.01
Training and Development Alert
Advanced Personnel Systems, 756 Lois Ave, Sunnyvale, CA 94087. Telephone (408) 736-2433.

Bimonthly newsletter. Contains abstracts of new articles and books on training and development from over 100 journals and new book lists. Price $30.00 per year. ISSN 0192-0596.

4685
Training and Development Journal
American Society for Training and Development, Inc, Box 5307, Madison, WI 53705. Telephone (608) 274-3440.

Monthly magazine. Specializes in reports on training, adult education, human resource development, and the individual in the work world. Price $30.00 per year.

4686

Training for Industry Series

United Nations Industrial Development Organization, Vienna International Centre, PO Box 300, A-1400, Vienna, Austria. Telephone 26310. Telex 135612.

Series of reports. Covers the training of economic administrators for industrial development, managerial and technical requirements in selected industries, and Lodz textile seminars. Symbols: ID/-SER.D/1, IDISER.D/2 and IDISER.D/3/1-8. Price No. 1, $2.00; No. 2, $2.50; others $1.00.

4687

Transcontinental and Regional Air Carrier Operations

Statistics Canada, User Services, Publications Distribution, Ottawa, Ont, Canada K1A 0V7. Telephone (613) 992-3151.

Monthly report. Provides information on the activities of Canadian transcontinental and regional air carriers. Includes data on passengers, miles and hours flown, goods and mail carried, and finances. Price $36.00 per year. ISSN 0380-5263.

4687.01

Transdex

Bell & Howell Micro Photo Division, Old Mansfield Rd, Wooster, OH 44691. Telephone (216) 264-6666. Telex 98-6496.

Ongoing service, with monthly reports. Offers indexed translations into English of articles from the Joint Publication Research Service covering a broad range of subject matter, including social, political and economic topics. Price available on request.

4688

Transfer Payments by Major Source

US Dept of Commerce, Bureau of Economic Analysis, Washington, DC 20230. Order from Regional Economic Measurement Div, Bureau of Economic Analysis, Washington, DC 20230. Telephone (202) 523-0966.

Information service. Gives data on transfer payments by major source for states, counties, and Standard Metropolitan Statistical Areas. Price $1000.00.

4689

Translation & Translators: An International Directory and Guide

R.R. Bowker Co, 1180 Avenue of the Americas, New York, NY 10036. Order from R.R. Bowker Co, PO Box 1807, Ann Arbor, MI 48106. Telephone (212) 764-5100.

Directory. Lists approximately 3000 translators and interpreters, representing 73 languages in 65 countries with English as either the source or target language. Covers other information on the translation field, including a translator's and interpreters' market place. Price $35.00. ISBN 0-8352-1158-4.

4690

Transnational Economic & Monetary Law: Transactions and Contracts

Oceana Publications, Inc, 75 Main St, Dobbs Ferry, NY 10522. Telephone (914) 693-5944.

Loose-leaf service in five binders. Discusses international law governing transnational economic and monetary transactions. Includes information on GATT, IMF, EEC, and UNCTAD. Price $375.00 per set. ISBN 0-379-10215-3.

4691

Transport and Communication Bulletin for Asia and the Pacific

United Nations Publications, United Nations Plaza, Room A-3315, New York, NY 10017. Telephone (212) 754-1234.

Report. Provides statistics and other information on transportation and communications in Asia and Far East. Price available on request.

4691.01

Transportation Arkansas

Arkansas Dept of Economic Development, One Capitol Mall, Little Rock, AR 72201. Telephone (501) 371-2431.

Booklet. Describes transportation facilities and services. Includes air, water, highway, and other maps. Price free of charge.

4692

Transportation Business Report

Whaley-Eaton Corp, 1141 National Press Bldg, Washington, DC 20004. Telephone (800) 553-2345.

Biweekly newsletter. Covers news and trends in the transportation industry. Price $46.00 per year.

4693

Transportation Planning and Technology

Gordon and Breach Science Publishers, 1 Park Ave, New York, NY 10016. Telephone (212) 689-0360. Telex 620862.

Quarterly magazine. Presents transportation research papers. Includes such topics as transport demand models, land use forecasting models, noise and air pollution, and technology. Price $68.75.

4694

Transportation Service

Data Resources, Inc, 29 Hartwell Ave, Lexington, MA 02173. Telephone (617) 861-0165.

Report. Forecasts freight movement by 100 commodity groups for five transportation modes, cost components and rates for three transportation modes, sales, demand, and imports for rail and truck equipment. Price available on request.

4696

Transport Laws of the World

Oceana Publications, Inc, 75 Main St, Dobbs Ferry, NY 10522. Telephone (914) 693-5944.

Loose-leaf service in four binders. Covers international laws and provides information on road, rail, inland waterway, air, container, and combined transport. Price $300.00 per set. ISBN 0-379-10195-5.

4698

Transport Statistics, Great Britain 1964-74

Her Majesty's Stationery Office, PO Box 569, London, England SE1 9NH. Telephone (44) (01) 928 1321.

Annual service. Gives 10-year statistics on British transportation. Price £7.00.

4699

Trans-Tasman

Trans-Tasman News Service Ltd, PO Box 377, Wellington, New Zealand.

Weekly newsletter. Covers affairs in Australia and New Zealand, including such topics as economic changes, federal budget, oil drilling, commerce, radio stations, and aviation. Price $70.00 per year. ISSN 0049-4380.

4700

Travel Agency

Maclean-Hunter Ltd, 30 Old Burlington St, London, England W1X 2AE. Telephone (44) (01) 434-2233.

Monthly magazine. Covers travel trade for British agents. Price available on request.

4701
Travel between Canada and Other Countries
Statistics Canada, User Services, Publications Distribution, Ottawa, Ont, Canada K1A 0V7. Telephone (613) 992-3151.

Quarterly report. Presents statistics on nonresidents entering Canada by country of residence and Canadian residents returning from trips abroad. Notes modes of transport for Canadian–US travel. Price $36.00 per year. ISSN 0380-2094.

4702
Travel Trade Directory
Morgan-Grampian Ltd, Morgan-Grampian House, Calderwood St, London, England SE18 6QH. Order from Morgan-Grampian Publishing Co, 2 Park Ave, New York, NY 10016. Telephone England (44) (01) 855-7777. Telex 896238 MORGAN G. New York (212) 340-9700. Telex 425592 MGI UI.

Annual directory. Serves as a guide to the British travel industry. Includes agents, airlines, hotels, and resorts. Price $13.00.

4703
Travel Trade Gazette Europe
Morgan-Grampian Ltd, Morgan-Grampian House, Calderwood St, London, England SE18 6QH. Order from Morgan-Grampian Publishing Co, 2 Park Ave, New York, NY 10016. Telephone England (44) (01) 855-7777. Telex 896238 MORGAN G. New York (212) 340-9700. Telex 425592 MGI UI.

Biweekly newspaper. Covers events in the travel industry in Europe and Scandanavia. Is aimed at the travel agency sales staff. Price $50.00 per year.

4704
Travel Trade Gazette United Kingdom & Ireland
Morgan-Grampian Ltd, Morgan-Grampian House, Calderwood St, London, England SE18 6QH. Order from Morgan-Grampian Publishing Co, 2 Park Ave, New York, NY 10016. Telephone England (44) (01) 855-7777. Telex 896238 MORGAN G. New York (212) 340-9700. Telex 425592 MGI UI.

Weekly newspaper. Covers events in the travel industry in Great Britain and Ireland. Is geared to travel agency sales staff. Price $50.00 per year.

4705
Travelweek
Peter Isaacson Publications, 46-49 Porter St, Prahran, Vic 3181, Australia. Telephone (61) (03) 51 8431. Telex 30880.

Biweekly newspaper. Pertains to the travel industry. Offers advice to agents and notes the activities of associations. Price $20.00 per year.

4706
Travel Weekly
Ziff-Davis Publishing Co, 1156 15th St, NW, Washington, DC 20005. Order from Ziff-Davis Publishing Co, One Park Ave, New York NY 10016. Telephone (212) 725-3680.

Semiweekly newspaper. Covers travel industry news and trends. Includes articles on air and rail travel, travel packages and agencies, hotels, and other related aspects of the industry. Price available on request.

4707
Treasury Board Pay Manual
Supply and Services Canada, Publishing Centre, Printing and Publishing, Ottawa, Ont, Canada K1A 0S9. Telephone (613) 238-1601.

Loose-leaf volume, plus update service. Publishes the Treasury Board's pay manual for Canada. Bilingual. Price $24.00.

4708
Treasury Bulletin
US Dept of the Treasury, Pennsylvania Ave and Madison Pl, NW, Washington, DC 20226. Order from Superintendent of Documents, Government Printing Office, Washington, DC 20402. Telephone (202) 566-2000.

Monthly report. Contains financial and statistical tables related to federal fiscal operations. Includes other monetary data. Price available on request (subscription only).

4709
Treasury Combined Statement of Receipts, Expenditures, and Balances of the US Govt
US Dept of the Treasury, Bureau of Government Financial Operations. Pennsylvania Ave and Madison Pl, NW, Washington, DC 20226. Order from Superintendent of Documents, Government Printing Office, Washington, DC 20402. Telephone (202) 566-2000.

Annual report. Provides a statement of combined US federal government receipts, expenditures, and balances. Price available on request.

4710
Trendline Service: Current Market Perspectives
Standard & Poor's Corp, 25 Broadway, New York, NY 10004. Telephone (212) 248-2525.

Monthly publication. Provides information on over 1500 issues for a four-year time span. Charts and statistics. Price $102.00 per year.

4711
Trendline Service: Daily Action Stock Charts
Standard & Poor's Corp, 25 Broadway, New York, NY 10004. Telephone (212) 248-2525.

Weekly service. Provides daily plotted market behavior charts on over 700 NYSE and AMEX stocks showing 12 months of price action. Price $326.00 per year for weekly listing, $102.00 per year for monthly listing.

4713
Trendline Service: OTC Chart Manual
Standard & Poor's Corp, 25 Broadway, New York, NY 10004. Telephone (212) 248-2525.

Bimonthly publication. Presents charts on unlisted stocks. Price $84.00 per year.

4714
Trend of Business in Hotels (Canada)
Laventhol & Horwath, 1845 Walnut St, Philadelphia, PA 19103. Telephone (215) 491-1600.

Monthly newsletter. Gives statistics on and analyses of the hotel business in Canada. Price free of charge.

4715
Trend of Business in the Lodging Industry
Laventhol & Horwath, 1845 Walnut St, Philadelphia, PA 19103. Telephone (215) 491-1600.

Monthly newsletter. Gives statistics on and analyses of the hotel and motel business. Price free of charge.

4716
Trends
Rural Bank of New South Wales, Box 41, GPO Sydney, NSW 2001, Australia.

Magazine published three times per year. Discusses worldwide developments in commerce, industry, and agriculture affecting the Australian economy. Price free of charge.

4717
Trends in International Banking and Capital Markets
Financial Times Business Information Ltd, Bracken House, 10 Cannon St, London, England EC4P 4BY. Order from Financial Times Ltd, 75 Rockefeller Plz, New York, NY 10019. Telephone (44) (01) 248-8000. Telex 886341-2.

Loose-leaf report. Presents information on current developments in international banking and money markets. Tables, charts, and statistics. Price $240.00 per year.

4718
Trends in the Hotel Industry, **44th edition**
Pannell Kerr Forster, 420 Lexington Ave, New York, NY 10170. Telephone (212) 867-8000. Telex 12-6580.

Annual review of income and expenses, occupancy rates, and operating statistics for hotels and motels. US and international editions. Tables and charts. Price $25.00 per copy.

4719
Trinc's Blue Book of the Trucking Industry
Trinc Transportation Consultants, Div of Dun and Bradstreet, 475 L'Enfant Plz, SW, Suite 4200, PO Box 23549, Washington, DC 23091. Telephone (202) 484-3410.

Annual book. Provides trucking industry statistics. Covers commodities carried and territory served, management and control information, and financial statements for Class I and II motor carriers. Price $145.00 per year.

4721
Trinc's Red Book of the Trucking Industry
Trinc Transportation Consultants, Div of Dun and Bradstreet, 475 L'Enfant Plz, SW, Suite 4200, PO Box 23549, Washington, DC 20024. Telephone (202) 484-3410.

Annual book, with quarterly supplements. Presents selected revenue, income, expense, and traffic data for 3000 Class I and Class II motor carriers. Price $135.00 per year.

4722
Tropical Agriculture
IPC Business Press Ltd, 205 E 42nd St, New York, NY 10017. Telephone (212) 889-0700. Telex 421710.

Quarterly magazine. Discusses all aspects of agriculture in the tropics, including soil and livestock science, ecology, and economic issues. Price $91.00 per year. ISSN 0041-3216.

4722.01
Truck & Off-Highway Industries
Chilton Co, Chilton Way, Radnor, PA 19089. Telephone (215) 687-8200.

Magazine published nine times per year. Covers the manufacturing of trucks, buses, construction equipment, tractors, trailers, and industrial vehicles. Price $20.00 per year.

4723
Truck "Insider"
Atcom, Inc, Atcom Bldg, 2315 Broadway, New York, NY 10024. Telephone (212) 873-3760.

Weekly newsletter. Contains information relevant to the truck retail, renting and leasing industry. Price $57.00 per year.

4725
Truck Trailers. **M37L**
US Dept of Commerce, Bureau of the Census, Washington, DC 20233. Telephone (202) 655-4000.

Monthly report, with annual summary. Shows the quantity and value of shipments of truck trailers by type of trailer. Price $3.30 per year.

4726
Trust Assets of Insured Commercial Banks
United States Federal Deposit Insurance Corp, Washington, DC 20429. Telephone (202) 389-4221.

Annual report. Presents data on the trust assets of all insured commercial banks. Indicates the type of account, asset distribution, and size of trust department; ranks the 300 largest trust departments. Price free of charge.

4727
Trust Audit Manual
Bank Adm Inst, PO Box 500, 303 S. Northwest Hwy, Park Ridge, IL 60068. Telephone (312) 693-7300.

Book. Discusses audit procedures for trust departments. Covers internal controls, administrative audits, and statutory and regulatory requirements. Price $20.-00.

4728
Trustee
American Hospital Publishing, Inc, 211 E Chicago Ave, Chicago, IL 60611. Telephone (312) 951-1100.

Monthly magazine. Reports on hospital issues, with emphasis on the trustee's role. Price $12.00 per year.

4729
Trust Letter
American Bankers Assn, 1120 Connecticut Ave NW, Washington, DC 20036. Telephone (202) 467-4123.

Newsletter issued 18 times per year. Provides news on leglislation and regulation affecting the trust business. Price $15.00 per year.

4730
Trust Management Update
American Bankers Assn, 1120 Connecticut Ave NW, Washington, DC 20036. Telephone (202) 467-4123.

Monthly newsletter. Provides updates on nonlegislative issues affecting trust bankers. Price $15.00 per year.

4730.01
Trusts and Estates
Communication Channels, Inc, 6285 Barfield Rd, Atlanta, GA 30328. Telephone (404) 256-9800.

Monthly magazine. Provides financial information for bank trust officers, lawyers, accountants, and insurance personnel who work in estate planning and administration. Price $42.00 per year.

4731
Try Us: National Minority Business Directory
National Minority Business Campaign, 1201 12th Ave, N, Minneapolis, MN 55411. Telephone (612) 377-2402.

Annual directory. Lists 4600 minority-owned firms alphabetically and by product or service. Provides a brief description of each company. Price $15.00 plus $1.50 postage and handling.

4732

Tube Topics

Metal Tube Packaging Council of North America, 118 E 61st St, New York, NY 10021. Telephone (212) 935-1290.

Bimonthly newsletter. Provides information on the collapsible metal tube industry. Notes new products and packaging ideas. Price free of charge.

4733

Tungsten Statistics

United Nations Conference on Trade and Development (UNCTAD), Palais des Nations, 1211 Geneva 10, Switzerland. Telephone (41) (22) 34 60 11. Telex 28 96 96.

Quarterly booklet. Supplies statistical data on tungsten ore and concentrate prices, production, consumption, trade, and stocks. Price $5.00 each copy.

4734

Tunnels & Tunnelling

Morgan-Grampian Ltd, Morgan-Grampian House, Calderwood St, London, England SE18 6QH. Order from Morgan-Grampian Publishing Co, 2 Park Ave, New York, NY 10016. Telephone England (44) (01) 855-7777. Telex 896238 MORGAN G. New York (212) 340-9700. Telex 425592 MGI UI.

Bimonthly magazine. Covers tunnelling in the civil engineering and mining industries. Price $45.00 per year.

4734.01

TV Facts

Facts on File, Inc, 460 Park Ave S, New York, NY 10016. Telephone (212) 265-2011.

Book. Provides comprehensive information on television industry, including advertising revenues, cost of commercials, and prime time scheduling since 1950.

4735

TV Publicity Outlets-Nationwide

Harold D Hansen, Box 327, Washington Depot, CT 06794. Telephone (203) 868-0200.

Quarterly television directory. Contains information on personnel, program content; network affiliations, and publicity material acceptable to show's contact. Price $89.50 per year.

4735.01

TV World

Alain Charles Publishing Ltd, 27 Wilfred St, London, England SW1E 6PR. Telephone (44) (01) 828-6107. Telex 28905.

Monthly magazine. Covers worldwide developments in buying and selling television programs. Price $36.00 per year.

4736

Twentieth Century Petroleum Statistics

DeGolyer and MacNaughton, 1 Energy Sq, 4925 Greenville Ave, Dallas, TX Telephone (214) 368-6391.

Annual report. Gives country-by-country statistics of oil production, refining, and other aspects of the oil industry. Price available on request.

4737

Ulrich's International Periodicals Directory

R R Bowker Co, 1180 Ave of the Americas, New York, NY 10036. Order from R R Bowker Co, PO Box 1807, Ann Arbor, MI 48106. Telephone (212) 764-5100.

Annual book. Gives information on 62,-000 periodicals, arranged according to subject. Bibliography. Price $69.50. ISBN 0-8352-1297-1. ISSN 0000-0175.

4738

Ultrasonics

IPC Business Press Ltd, 205 E 42nd St, New York, NY 10017. Telephone (212) 889-0700. Telex 421710.

Bimonthly magazine. Reports on ultrasound—noting new research, products, and equipments. Price $130.00. ISSN 0041-624X.

4739

Unasylva: An International Journal of Forestry and Forest Products

Food and Agriculture Organization of the United Nations, Via delle Terme di Caracalla, Rome, Italy 00100. Order from UNIPUB, 345 Parks Ave S, New York, NY 10016. Telephone (39) (06) 5797. Telex 61181.

Quarterly report. Covers forest planning, administration, products, and wildlife. Price $10.00 per year.

4740

Underwater Information Bulletin

IPC Business Press Ltd, 205 E 42nd St, New York, NY 10017. Telephone (212) 889-0700. Telex 421710.

Bimonthly magazine. Provides information on marine and freshwater underwater technology. Includes such topics as pollution, marine biology, and biological and nonbiological resources. Price $187.20 per year. ISSN 0302-3478.

4741

Underwater Letter

Callahan Publications, PO Box 3751, Washington, DC 20007. Telephone (703) 356-1925.

Semimonthly newsletter. Covers contracting opportunities in underwater defense and oceanography. Price $120.00 per year.

4741.01

Underwriters Laboratories Standards for Safety

National Standards Associations, Inc, 5161 River Rd, Washington, DC 20016. Telephone (301) 951-1310. Telex 89-8452.

Microfiche, with weekly revisions. Provides specifications for construction and performance of systems, devices, materials, and appliances submitted to Underwriters Laboratories. Price $1640.00 per year.

4742

Underwriting Results in Canada

Stone and Cox Ltd, 100 Simcoe St, 2nd Floor, Toronto, Ont, Canada M5H 3G2. Telephone (416) 593-1310.

Annual book. Provides data on the total Canadian insurance business, including premiums written, commissions, and growth rate for each insurer. Shows five-year trends. Charts. Price $35.00 per year. ISBN 0-919468-47-0.

4742.01

UNDOC: Current Index

United Nations Publications, United Nations Plaza, Room A-3315, New York, NY 10017. Telephone (212) 754-8302.

Monthly index. Lists, describes, and indexes by subject all unrestricted documents and publications of the United Nations and International Court of Justice. Price $96.00.

4743

Unemployment Insurance Fund, Evaluation of the New York State

New York Dept of Labor, Div of Research and Statistics, State Office Bldg Campus, Albany, NY 12240. Telephone (518) 457-1130.

Annual report. Appraises the New York State Unemployment Insurance Fund in relation to prospective liabilities. Gives data on employment, coverage, benefits, and contribution rates. Price free of charge.

4744

Unemployment Insurance Reports

Commerce Clearing House, Inc, 4025 W Peterson Ave, Chicago, IL 60646. Telephone (312) 583-8500.

Fourteen volumes and weekly reports. Cover federal and state Social Security, unemployment insurance, and disability benefit laws. Price $720.00 per year.

4745

Unemployment Insurance Statistics

US Dept of Labor, Employment & Training Adm, Washington, DC 20213. Telephone (202) 376-6730.

Monthly report. Provides data on state and federal unemployment insurance programs. Covers benefit payments, employer contributions, appeals decisions, and disqualifications. Tables. Price free of charge.

4745.01

Unemployment: Monthly Bulletin

European Community Information Service, 2100 M St, NW, Suite 707, Washington, DC 20037. Telephone (202) 862-9500. Telex 248455.

Monthly bulletin. Reports unemployment in European Communities member countries. Price $12.60.

4746

Unfilled Job Openings Report

Alaska Dept of Labor, Employment Security Div, Research & Analysis Section, Box 3-7000, Juneau, AK 99801. Telephone (907) 465-2700.

Report. Supplies data that analyzes unfilled job openings in the Anchorage area. Statistical tables. Price available on request.

4747

Uniform Classification of Accounts for Class 1 Common Carriers by Railways

Supply and Services Canada, Publishing Centre, Printing and Publishing, Ottawa, Ont, Canada K1A 0S9. Telephone (613) 238-1601.

Loose-leaf report, with update service. Provides uniform classification of accounts for Canadian Class I common carriers by railways. Price $6.00; binder $3.00.

4748

Uniform Classification of Accounts for Gas Pipe Line Companies

Supply and Services Canada, Publishing Centre, Printing and Publishing, Ottawa, Ont, Canada K1A 0S9. Telephone (613) 238-1601.

Loose-leaf report, with update service. Offers uniform classification of accounts for Canadian gas pipeline companies. Price $3.50; binder $3.00.

4749

Uniform Classification of Accounts for Oil Pipe Line Companies

Supply and Services Canada, Publishing Centre, Printing and Publishing, Ottawa, Ont, Canada K1A 0S9. Telephone (613) 238-1601.

Loose-leaf report, with update service. Supplies uniform classification of accounts for Canadian oil pipeline companies. Price $3.50; binder $3.00.

4750

Uniform Commercial Code Law Journal

Warren, Gorham & Lamont, Inc, 210 S St, Boston, MA 02111. Telephone (617) 423-2020.

Quarterly magazine. Discusses Uniform Commercial Code developments in such areas as commercial lending, consumer credit sales, and negotiable instruments. Reviews court decisions and legislative and administrative news. Price $54.00 per year.

4751

Uniform Commercial Code Law Letter

Warren, Gorham & Lamont, Inc, 210 S St, Boston, MA 02111. Telephone (617) 423-2020.

Monthly newsletter. Analyzes federal and state court decisions affecting business under the Uniform Commercial Code. Notes Truth-in-Lending developments and corporate and banking techniques. Price $68.00 per year.

4752

Union Labor Report

Bureau of National Affairs, Inc, 1231 25th St, NW, Washington, DC 20037. Telephone (202) 452-4200.

Periodic loose-leaf reports. Discuss topics relating to the labor union, including administration, organization, strikes, job safety and health, equal employment opportunity, and collective bargaining. Price $275.00 per year.

4753

Union-Tribune Annual Review of San Diego Business Activity

Copley Newspapers, 7776 Ivanhoe Ave, PO Box 1530, La Jolla, CA 92038. Telephone (714) 454-0391.

Annual report. Reviews San Diego's business activity and economic conditions. Includes indicators on population, employment, prices, income distribution, and data for individual cities. Tables and charts. Price $10.00.

4754

Union-Tribune Index

Copley Newspapers, 7776 Ivanhoe Ave, PO Box 1530, La Jolla, CA 92038. Telephone (714) 454-0391.

Monthly newsletter. Summarizes San Diego County's business activity. Includes data on per capita income, employment, department store sales, and bank deposits. Tables. Price free of charge.

4754.01

Unit

Dr Dvorkovitz & Assoc, PO Box 1748, Ormond Beach, FL 32074. Telephone (904) 677-7047.

Newsletter published 10 times per year. Reports on new product development in all industries. Covers technology licensing agreements. Price $20.00 per year.

4755

United Business & Investment Report

United Business Service Co, 210 Newbury St, Boston, MA 02116. Telephone (617) 267-8855.

Weekly newsletter. Evaluates stock market and other investment trends. Notes related federal developments. Tables. Price $135.00 per year.

4755.01

United Kingdom & International Point & Figure Library

Chart Analysis Ltd, 37–39 St Andrew's Hill, London, England EC4V 5DD. Telephone (44) (01) 236-5211.

Biweekly information service. Covers British and international stock markets. Charts. Price $700.00 per year.

4756

United Kingdom Balance of Payments "Pink Books"

Her Majesty's Stationery Office, PO Box 569, London, England SE1 9NH. Telephone (44) (01) 928 1321.

Annual book of British balance of payments statistics. Provides information on transactions with the EEC and British assets and liabilities. Gives data for 11 years. Price £7.00 per year.

4757
United Kingdom-Guide to Key British Enterprises I
Dun & Bradstreet, Box 3224, Church St Station, New York, NY 10008. Telephone (212) 285-7346.

Annual book. Provides detailed data on 10,000 companies, representing one-third of the British labor force and richest available markets. Price available on request to Dun & Bradstreet subscribers only.

4758
United Kingdom-Guide to Key British Enterprises II
Dun & Bradstreet, Box 3224, Church St Station, New York, NY 10008. Telephone (212) 285-7346.

Annual book. Contains information on 11,000 middle sector British companies. Price available on request, to Dun & Bradstreet subscribers only.

4759
United Kingdom Kompass Register
Kompass Register Ltd, Winston Court, East Grinstead House, E Grinstead, West Sussex, England RH19 1XD. Telephone 0342 26972.

Annual register. Gives information on British raw materials, manufactured products, and services. Includes business data for over 33,000 public and private companies. Price £60.00 per copy.

4760
United Kingdom Mineral Statistics
Her Majesty's Stationery Office, PO Box 569, London, England SE1 9NH. Telephone (44) (01) 928 1321.

Annual service. Provides statistics on minerals, employment, and other topics related to the British mining industry. Price £13.00.

4760.01
United Kingdom, News Contact Directory
Kelly's Directories Ltd, IPC Media Publications, Windsor Court, E Grinstead House, E Grinstead, W Sussex, England RH19 1XA. Telephone (44) (01) 0342 26972

Annual book. Provides guide for British journalists, public relations officers, and related fields. Price £25.00 per copy.

4761
United Kingdom Point & Figure Library
Chart Analysis Ltd, 194-200 Bishopsgate, London, England EC2M 4PE. Telephone (44) (01) 283-4476. Telex 883356.

Weekly service. Contains data related to British stocks. Covers several years of price data. Over 800 charts. Price £250 per year.

4762
United Kingdom Trade Names
Kompass Publishers Ltd, Windsor Court, East Grinstead House, E Grinstead, West Sussex, England RH19 1XD. Telephone 0342 26972.

Directory. Lists British trade names. Provides brief product description and company names and addresses and includes all industries except these: food, drink, tobacco, and pharmaceutical. Price £35.00 per copy.

4763
United Mine Workers Journal
United Mine Workers of America, 900 15 St, NW, Washington, DC 20005. Telephone (202) 638-0530.

Semimonthly magazine. Reports on coal mining and the activities of the United Mine Workers. Covers safety issues and labor contracts. Price $5.00 per year.

4764
United Mutual Fund Selector
United Business Service Co, 210 Newbury St, Boston, MA 02116. Telephone (617) 267-8855.

Semimonthly report. Evaluates mutual funds, including bond and municipal bond funds. Notes industry developments. Tables and charts. Price $63.00 per year.

4764.01
United Nations Chronicle
United Nations Publications, United Nations Plaza, Room A-3315, New York, NY 10017. Telephone (212) 754-8302.

Monthly publication. Reports on all United Nations activities. English, French, and Spanish editions. Price $11.-00.

4765
United Nations Conference on Trade and Development (UNCTAD) Guide to Publications
United Nations Conference on Trade & Development (UNCTAD), Palais des Nations, 1211 Geneva 10, Switzerland. Telephone (41) (22) 28 96 96. Telex 22 212.

Annual report. Provides a selective list of reports and studies from the United Nations Conference on Trade and Development. Free of charge on request.

4766
United Nations Conference on Trade and Development (UNCTAD) Monthly Bulletin
United Nations Conference on Trade and Development (UNCTAD), Palais des Nations, 1211 Geneva 10, Switzerland. Telephone (41) (22) 34 60 11. Telex 28 9696.

Monthly bulletin. Discusses the activities of the United Nations Conference on Trade and Development. Notes meetings and lists reports and studies. Price free of charge.

4767.01
United Nations Industrial Development Organization (UNIDO) Guides to Information Sources UNIDO/LIB/SER.D/Rev.1— Information Sources on Bioconversion of Agricultural Wastes
United Nations Industrial Development Organization, UNIDO, Vienna International Centre, PO Box 300, A-1400 Vienna, Austria. Telephone 26310. Telex 135612.

Publication. Reports on information sources on bioconversion of agricultural wastes worldwide. Price $4.00.

4767.02
United Nations Industrial Development Organization (UNIDO) Guides to Information Sources. UNIDO/LIB/ SER.D/Rev.1—Information Sources on Industrial Maintenance and Repair
United Nations Industrial Development Organization, UNIDO, Vienna International Centre, PO Box 300, A-1400 Vienna, Austria. Telephone 26310. Telex 135612.

Publication. Contains information sources on industrial maintenance and repair worldwide. Price $4.00.

4767.03

United Nations Industrial Development Organization (UNIDO) Guides to Information Sources. UNIDO/LIB/SER.D/Rev.1—Informational Sources on Industrial Training

United Nations Industrial Development Organization, UNIDO, Vienna International Centre, PO Box 300, A-1400 Vienna, Austria. Telephone 26310. Telex 135612.

Publication. Provides information sources on industrial training worldwide. Price $4.00.

4767.04

United Nations Industrial Development Organization (UNIDO) Guides to Information Sources. UNIDO/LIB/SER.D/Rev.1— Information Sources on Non-conventional Sources of Energy

United Nations Industrial Development Organization, UNIDO, Vienna International Centre, PO Box 300, A-1400 Vienna, Austria. Telephone 26310. Telex 135612.

Publication. Provides information sources on non-conventional sources of energy worldwide. Price $4.00.

4767.05

United Nations Industrial Development Organization (UNIDO) Guides to Information Sources. UNIDO/LIB/SER.D/Rev.1—Information Sources on the Beer and Wine Industry

United Nations Industrial Development Organization, UNIDO, Vienna International Centre, PO Box 300, A-1400 Vienna, Austria. Telephone 26310. Telex 135612.

Publication. Supplies information sources on the beer and wine industry worldwide. Price $4.00.

4767.06

United Nations Industrial Development Organization (UNIDO) Guides to Information Sources. UNIDO/LIB/SER.D/Rev.1— Information Sources on the Coffee, Cocoa, Tea and Spices Industry

United Nations Industrial Development Organization, UNIDO, Vienna International Centre, PO Box 300, A-1400 Vienna, Austria. Telephone 26310. Telex 135612.

Publication. Contains sources of information for the coffee, tea, cocoa, and spices industry worldwide. Price $4.00.

4767.07

United Nations Industrial Development Organization (UNIDO) Guides to Information Sources. UNIDO/LIB/SER.D/1/Rev.1— Information Sources on the Dairy Product Manufacturing Industry

United Nations Industrial Development Organization; UNIDO, Vienna International Centre, PO Box 300, A-1400 Vienna, Austria. Telephone 26310. Telex 135612.

Publication. Lists sources of information for the dairy product manufacturing industry worldwide. Price $4.00.

4767.08

United Nations Industrial Development Organization (UNIDO) Guides to Information Sources. UNIDO/LIB/SER.D/Rev.1—Information Sources on the Electronics Industry

United Nations Industrial Development Organization, UNIDO, Vienna International Centre, PO Box 300, A-1400 Vienna, Austria. Telephone 26310. Telex 135612.

Publication. Contains information sources on the electronics industry worldwide. Price $4.00.

4767.09

United Nations Industrial Development Organization (UNIDO) Guides to Information Sources. UNIDO/LIB/SER.D/Rev.1— Information Sources on the Iron and Steel Industry

United Nations Industrial Development Organization, UNIDO, Vienna International Centre, PO Box 300, A-1400 Vienna, Austria. Telephone 26310. Telex 135612.

Publication. Reports on sources of information on the iron and steel industry worldwide. Price $4.00.

4767.10

United Nations Industrial Development Organization (UNIDO) Guides to Information Sources. UNIDO/LIB/SER.D/1/Rev.1—Information Sources on the Machine Tool Industry

United Nations Industrial Development Organization, UNIDO, Vienna International Centre, PO Box 300, A-1400 Vienna, Austria. Telephone 26310. Telex 135612.

Publication. Reports on information sources for the machine tool industry worldwide. Price $4.00.

4767.11

United Nations Industrial Development Organization (UNIDO) Guides to Information Sources. UNIDO/LIB/SER.D/Rev.1— Information Sources on the Natural and Synthetic Rubber Industry

United Nations Industrial Development Organization, UNIDO, Vienna International Centre, PO Box 300, A-1400 Vienna, Austria. Telephone 26310. Telex 135612.

Publication. Supplies information sources on the natural and synthetic rubber industry worldwide. Price $4.00.

4767.12

United Nations Industrial Development Organization (UNIDO) Guides to Information Sources. UNIDO/LIB/SER.D/Rev.1—Information Sources on the Packaging Industry

United Nations Industrial Development Organization, UNIDO, Vienna International Centre, PO Box 300, A-1400 Vienna, Austria Telephone 26310. Telex 135612.

Publication. Contains information sources on the packaging industry worldwide. Price $4.00.

4767.13

United Nations Industrial Development Organization (UNIDO) Guides to Information Sources. UNIDO/LIB/SER.D/Rev.1—Information Sources on the Petrochemical Industry

United Nations Industrial Development Organization, UNIDO, Vienna International Centre, PO Box 300, A-1400 Vienna, Austria. Telephone 26310. Telex 135612.

Publication. Reports on sources of information for the petrochemical industry worldwide. Price $4.00.

4767.14

United Nations Industrial Development Organization (UNIDO) Guides to Information Sources. UNIDO/LIB/SER.D/1/Rev.1—Information Sources on the Soap and Detergent Industry

United Nations Industrial Development Organization, UNIDO, Vienna International Centre, PO Box 300, A-1400 Vienna, Austria. Telephone 26310. Telex 135612.

Publication. Lists information sources on the soap and detergent industry worldwide. Price $4.00.

4767.15
United Nations Industrial Development Organization (UNIDO) Guides to Information Sources.
UNIDO/LIB/SER.D /Rev.1—
Information Sources on the Utilization of Agricultural Residues for the Production of Panels, Pulp and Paper
United Nations Industrial Development Organization, UNIDO, Vienna International Centre, PO Box 300, A-1400 Vienna, Austria. Telephone 26310. Telex 135612.

Publication. Reports on information sources on the utilization of agricultural residues for the production of panels, pulp, and paper worldwide. Price $4.00.

4767.16
United Nations Industrial Development Organization (UNIDO) Guides to Information Sources. UNIDO/LIB/ SER.D/Rev.1—Information Sources on Woodworking Machinery
United Nations Industrial Development Organization, UNIDO, Vienna International Centre, PO Box 300, A-1400 Vienna, Austria. Telephone 26310. Telex 135612.

Publication. Reports on information sources on woodworking machinery worldwide. Price $4.00.

4768
United Nations Industrial Development Organization (UNIDO) Guides to Information Sources.
UNIDO/LIB/SER.D/1/Rev.1—
Information Sources on the Meat Processing Industry
United Nations Industrial Development Organization, PO Box 300, A-1400 Vienna, Austria. Telephone (43) (222) 26310. Telex 135612.

Publication. Reports on reference sources providing information about the meat processing industry. Price $4.00.

4769
United Nations Industrial Development Organization (UNIDO) Guides to Information Sources.
UNIDO/LIB/SER.D/2—Information Sources on the Cement and Concrete Industry
United Nations Industrial Development Organization, PO Box 300, A-1400 Vienna, Austria. Telephone (43) (222) 43 500. Telex 75612.

Publication. Reports on sources providing information about the cement and concrete industry. Price $4.00.

4770
United Nations Industrial Development Organization (UNIDO) Guides to Information Sources.
UNIDO/LIB/SER.D/3 and Corr.—
Information Sources on the Leather and Leather Goods Industry
United Nations Industrial Development Organization, PO Box 300, A-1400 Vienna, Austria. Telephone (43) (222) 43 500. Telex 75612.

Publication. Reports on sources providing information about the leather and leather goods industry. Price $4.00.

4771
United Nations Industrial Development Organization (UNIDO) Guides to Information Sources.
UNIDO/LIB/SER.D/4—Information Sources on the Furniture and Joinery Industry
United Nations Industrial Development Organization, PO Box 300, A-1400 Vienna, Austria. Telephone (43) (222) 43 500. Telex 75612.

Publication. Reports on reference sources providing information about the furniture and joinery industry. Price $4.00.

4772
United Nations Industrial Development Organization (UNIDO) Guides to Information Sources.
UNIDO/LIB/SER.D/5—Information Sources on the Foundry Industry
United Nations Industrial Development Organization, PO Box 300, A-1400 Vienna, Austria. Telephone (43) (222) 43 500. Telex 75612.

Publication. Reports on reference sources providing information related to the foundry industry. Price $4.00.

4773
United Nations Industrial Development Organization (UNIDO) Guides to Information Sources.
UNIDO/LIB/SER.D/6—Information Sources on the Industrial Quality Control
United Nations Industrial Development Organization, PO Box 300, A-1400 Vienna, Austria. Telephone (43) (222) 43 500. Telex 75612.

Publication. Reports on reference sources providing information about industrial quality control. Price free of charge.

4774
United Nations Industrial Development Organization (UNIDO) Guides to Information Sources.
UNIDO/LIB/SER.D/7—Information Sources on the Vegetable Oil Processing Industry
United Nations Industrial Development Organization, PO Box 300, A-1400, Vienna, Austria. Telephone (43) (222) 43 500. Telex 75612.

Publication. Provides information on source material for the vegetable oil processing industry. Price $4.00.

4775
United Nations Industrial Development Organization (UNIDO) Guides to Information Sources.
UNIDO/LIB/SER.D/8—Information Sources on the Agricultural Implements and Machinery Industry
United Nations Industrial Development Organization, PO Box 300, A-1400, Vienna, Austria. Telephone (43) (222) 43 500. Telex 75612.

Publication. Reports on reference sources for the agricultural implements and machinery industry. Price $4.00.

4776
United Nations Industrial Development Organization (UNIDO) Guides to Information Sources.
UNIDO/LIB/SER.D/9—Information Sources on the Building Board Industry Based on Wood and Other Fibrous Materials
United Nations Industrial Development Organization, PO Box 300, A-1400, Vienna, Austria. Telephone (43) (222) 43 500. Telex 75612.

Publication. Reports on sources providing information about the building board industry based on wood and other fibrous materials. Price $4.00.

4777
United Nations Industrial Development Organization (UNIDO) Guides to Information Sources.
UNIDO/LIB/SER.D/10—Information Sources on the Pesticides Industry
United Nations Industrial Development Organization, PO Box 300, A-1400, Vienna, Austria. Telephone (43) (222) 43 500. Telex 75612.

Publication. Reports on information available about the pesticide industry. Price $4.00.

4778

United Nations Industrial Development Organization (UNIDO) Guides to Information Sources.
UNIDO/LIB/SER.D/11—Information Sources on the Pulp and Paper Industry
United Nations Industrial Development Organization, PO Box 300, A-1400, Vienna, Austria. Telephone (43) (222) 43 500. Telex 75612.

Publication. Reports on sources providing information about the pulp and paper industry. Price $4.00.

4779

United Nations Industrial Development Organization (UNIDO) Guides to Information Sources.
UNIDO/LIB/SER.D/12—Information Sources on the Clothing Industry
United Nations Industrial Development Organization, PO Box 300, A-1400, Vienna, Austria. Telephone (43) (222) 43 500. Telex 75612.

Publication. Supplies reference material for the clothing industry. Price $4.00.

4780

United Nations Industrial Development Organization (UNIDO) Guides to Information Sources.
UNIDO/LIB/SER.D/13—Information Sources on the Animal Feed Industry
United Nations Industrial Development Organization, PO Box 300, A-1400, Vienna, Austria. Telephone (43) (222) 43 500. Telex 75612.

Publication. Provides source material for the animal feed industry. Price $4.00.

4781

United Nations Industrial Development Organization (UNIDO) Guides to Information Sources.
UNIDO/LIB/SER.D/14—Information Sources on the Graphics Industry
United Nations Industrial Development Organization, PO Box 300, A-1400, Vienna, Austria. Telephone (43) (222) 43 500. Telex 75612.

Publication. Reports on information sources for the printing and graphics industry. Price $4.00.

4782

United Nations Industrial Development Organization (UNIDO) Guides to Information Sources.
UNIDO/LIB/SER.D/15—Information Sources on the Non-alcoholic Beverage Industry
United Nations Industrial Development Organization, PO Box 300, A-1400, Vienna, Austria. Telephone (43) (222) 43 500. Telex 75612.

Publication. Provides a guide to information sources for the nonalcoholic beverage industry. Price $4.00.

4783

United Nations Industrial Development Organization (UNIDO) Guides to Information Sources.
UNIDO/LIB/SER.D/16—Information Sources on the Glass Industry
United Nations Industrial Development Organization, PO Box 300, A-1400, Vienna, Austria. Telephone (43) (222) 43 500. Telex 75612.

Publication. Provides reference sources for the glass industry. Price $4.00.

4784

United Nations Industrial Development Organization (UNIDO) Guides to Information Sources.
UNIDO/LIB/SER.D/17—Information Sources on the Ceramics Industry
United Nations Industrial Development Organization, PO Box 300, A-1400, Vienna, Austria. Telephone (43) (222) 43 500. Telex 75612.

Publication. Provides information sources for the ceramics industry. Price $4.00.

4785

United Nations Industrial Development Organization (UNIDO) Guides to Information Sources.
UNIDO/LIB/SER.D/18—Information Sources on the Paint and Varnish Industry
United Nations Industrial Development Organization, PO Box 300, A-1400, Vienna, Austria. Telephone (43) (222) 43 500. Telex 75612.

Publication. Provides information sources for the paint and varnish industry. Price $4.00.

4786

United Nations Industrial Development Organization (UNIDO) Guides to Information Sources.
UNIDO/LIB/SER.D/19—Information Sources on the Canning Industry
United Nations Industrial Development Organization, PO Box 300, A-1400, Vienna, Austria. Telephone (43) (222) 43 500. Telex 75612.

Publication. Presents information sources for the canning industry. Price $4.00.

4787

United Nations Industrial Development Organization (UNIDO) Guides to Information Sources.
UNIDO/LIB/SER.D/20—Information Sources on the Pharmaceutical Industry
United Nations Industrial Development Organization, PO Box 300, A-1400, Vienna, Austria. Telephone (43) (222) 43 500. Telex 75612.

Publication. Provides information sources for the pharmaceutical industry. Price $4.00.

4788

United Nations Industrial Development Organization (UNIDO) Guides to Information Sources.
UNIDO/LIB/SER.D/21—Information Sources on the Fertilizer Industry
United Nations Industrial Development Organization, PO Box 300, A-1400, Vienna, Austria. Telephone (43) (222) 500. Telex 75612.

Publication. Provides reference material for the fertilizer industry. Price $4.00.

4789

United Nations Industrial Development Organization (UNIDO) Newsletter
United Nations Industrial Development Organization, PO Box 300, A-1400, Vienna, Austria. Telephone (43) (222) 43 500. Telex 75612.

Monthly report. Brings industrial information to readers in the developing countries. Encourages exchange of information among the developing countries. English, Arabic, French, Russian, and Spanish editions. Price free of charge.

4790

United Nations Institute for Training and Research (UNITAR) Important for the Future

United Nations Inst for Training & Research, 801 UN Plz, New York, NY 10017. Telephone (212) 754-8618.

Journal issued five times per year. Presents articles on energy and natural resources. Price $12.00 per year.

4793

United States Airborne Exports and General Imports

US Dept of Commerce, Bureau of the Census, Washington, DC 20233. Telephone (202) 449-1600.

Monthly and annual reports. Present information on the shipping weight and value of US airborne exports and imports. Indicate ports of lading and unlading. Price $14.90 per year.

4794

United States Banker

Cleworth Publishing Co, Inc, 1 River Rd, Cos Cob, CT 06807. Telephone (203) 661-5000.

Monthly magazine. Reports on all financial institutions, including banking, investments, and insurance. Price $18.00 per year.

4794.01

United States-Belgium Trade Directory, 1980–81 edition

Belgian-American Chamber of Commerce in the United States, Inc, 50 Rockefeller Plz, New York, NY 10020. Telephone (212) 247-7613. Telex 232872 BACC UR.

Special report. Lists Belgian-American Chamber of Commerce membership, Belgian investments in US, US importers of Belgian products, US exporters to Belgium, US firms in Belgium, and Belgian and professional associations and Chambers of Commerce. Also includes articles on Belgian trade, finance and businesses. Price $28.00.

4794.02

United States-Brazil Business Listing

Brazilian–American Chamber of Commerce, Inc, 22 W 48th St, New York, NY 10036. Telephone (212) 575-9030.

Directory. Provides names and addresses of 1000 firms, subsidiaries, and affiliates operating in or having interest in the US and Brazil. Notes products and activities. Price $20.00.

4794.03

US Census Report

Business Publishers, Inc, PO Box 1067, Silver Spring, MD 20910. Telephone (301) 587-6300.

Biweekly newspaper. Covers US Census Bureau news. Focuses on implications for business and government. Price $115.00 per year.

4794.04

United States Customs and International Trade Guide

Matthew Bender & Co, 235 E 45th St, New York, NY 10017. Telephone (212) 661-5050.

Four-volume loose-leaf book with semiannual updates. Gives information on customs and trade law. Includes examples, lists, forms, and charts. Price $200.00 plus additional charge for revisions.

4795

United States Developments

Arthur Young & Co, 277 Park Ave, New York, NY 10017. Telephone (212) 922-4724.

Irregularly published newsletter. Covers US accounting and auditing developments, including those of the American Institute of CPAs and Securities and Exchange Commission. Price free of charge.

4796

United States Direct Investment Abroad 1966

US Dept of Commerce, Bureau of Economic Analysis, Washington, DC 20230. Order from Superintendent of Documents, US Government Printing Office, Washington, DC 20402. Telephone (202) 783-3238.

Book. Provides a breakdown by industry and area for the value of investments abroad, plus balance of payments transactions, foreign share of earnings, and reinvestment. Price $5.15.

4796.01

United States Economic Service

Data Resources, Inc, 29 Hartwell Ave, Lexington, MA 02173. Telephone (617) 861-0165.

Monthly and quarterly reports. Provide forecasts for 1000 US economic variables, including national income accounts, consumption, investment, prices, and foreign trade. Price available on request.

4797

United States Excise Tax Guide

Commerce Clearing House, Inc, 4025 W Peterson Ave, Chicago, IL 60646. Telephone (312) 583-8500.

Book. Covers excise tax law changes. Rate tables, lists of forms, and checklists of taxable and nontaxable items. Price $6.00.

4798

United States Exports—Commodity by Country.

US Dept of Commerce, Bureau of the Census, Washington, DC 20233. Telephone (202) 449-1600.

Monthly information service. Presents statistics on the quantity and value of individual commodities exported from the US by country of destination. Price $80.00 per year.

4800

United States Export Weekly

Bureau of National Affairs, Inc, 1231 25th St, NW, Washington, DC 20037. Telephone (202) 452-4200.

Loose-leaf books, with weekly updates. Cover official actions having impact on the US export market. Are geared to attorneys involved with the export trade. Topical index, text of laws, and calendars. Price $282.00 per year.

4801

United States Federal Deposit Insurance Corp. Bank Operating Statistics

United States Federal Deposit Insurance Corp, Washington, DC 20429. Telephone (202) 389-4221.

Annual service. Presents data on bank operations based on reports submitted by all insured commercial banks. Price free or charge.

4802

United States General Imports Schedule A—Commodity by Country

US Dept of Commerce, Bureau of the Census, Washington, DC 20233. Telephone (202) 449-1600.

Monthly report. Provides information of US general imports for the current month and cumulative for the current year. Indicates country of origin. Price $63.00 per year.

4803
United States Government Manual
Superintendent of Documents, Government Printing Office, Washington, DC 20402. Telephone (202) 783-3238.

Annual book. Lists and describes government agencies, including aims and programs. Price available on request.

4804
United States Housing Markets
Advance Mortgage Corp, Publication Dept, 406 City National Bank Bldg, Detroit, MI 48232. Telephone (313) 963-9441.

Quarterly survey, pre-publication releases, and special reports. Contain statistics and summaries of trends for local housing markets, including housing starts, employment trends, vacancy rates, and sales activity. Price $105.00 per year.

4806
United States Industrial Directory
Cahners Publishing Co, Inc, 221 Columbus Ave, Boston, MA 02116. Telephone (617) 536-7780.

Annual directory (in four volumes). Lists industrial suppliers, products, trade names, and catalogs for all US industries. Price available on request.

4807
United States Industrial Outlook
US Dept of Commerce, International Trade Administration, Washington, DC 20230. Order from Supt of Documents, US Govt Printing Office, Washington, DC 20230. Telephone (202) 783-3238.

Report. Gives an overview of US industrial conditions. Price $10.00 per copy.

4808
United States-Italy Trade Directory
Italy-America Chamber of Commerce, Inc, 350 5th Ave, New York, NY 10118. Telephone (212) 279-5520.

Annual book. Covers US-Italian trade. Includes lists of US importers of Italian commodities, US companies with business interests in Italy, and government regulations affecting trade. Price $50.00.

4810
United States Maps
US Dept of Commerce, Bureau of the Census, Washington, DC 20233. Telephone (202) 449-1600.

Series of maps. Show per capita retail sales by US county. Price $2.50.

4811
United States Master Tax Guide
Commerce Clearing House, Inc, 4025 W Peterson Ave, Chicago, IL 60646. Telephone (312) 583-8500.

Book. Covers federal income taxes for individuals, partnerships, corporations, estates, and trusts. Rate tables and checklists. Price $9.00.

4812
US News and World Report
US News and World Report, PO Box 2629, Boulder, CO 06830.

Weekly magazine. Provide news and analysis of national and international political and economic developments. Price $31.00 per year.

4813
United States Ocean Shipping Technology Forecast and Assessment, Final Report
US Maritime Adm, Commerce Bldg, 14th & E Sts, NW, Washington, DC 20230. Order from National Technical Information Service, 5285 Port Royal Rd, Springfield, VA 22161. Telephone (703) 557-4650.

Final report of the Maritime Administration on US ocean shipping technology forecast and assessment. Price $50.50.

4813.01
United States Oil and Gas Production News
Petroleum Information Corp, PO Box 2612, 1375 Delaware, Denver, CO 80201. Telephone (303) 825-2181.

Monthly report. Contains oil and gas production statistics for US by state. Notes legislative developments and new production techniques. Price available on request.

4813.02
United States Oil Week
Capitol Publications, Inc, Suite G-12, 2430 Pennsylvania Ave, W, Washington, DC 20037. Telephone (202) 452-1600.

Weekly newsletter. Provides information on federal regulatory actions and laws which affect the oil industry. Shows gasoline and distillate prices. Price $146.00 per year.

4814
United States Patents Quarterly
Bureau of National Affairs, Inc, 1231 25th St, NW, Washington, DC 20037. Telephone (202) 452-4200.

Loose-leaf books, with weekly updates, annual digests and quarterly bound volumes. Set forth published decisions on patents, trademarks, and copyrights. Price $416.00 per year.

4815
United States Rail News
Business Publishers, Inc, PO Box 1067, Silver Spring, MD 20910. Telephone (301) 587-6300.

Biweekly newsletter. Contains railroad industry news. Price $145.00 per year.

4816
United States Research and Development (R&D)
Government Data Publications, 422 Washington Bldg, Washington, DC 20005. Telephone (202) 966-6379.

Monthly magazine. Reports on research and development subjects. Covers contracts, trends, new products, techniques, and meetings. Price $60.00 per year.

4817
United States Supreme Court Bulletin
Commerce Clearing House, Inc, 4025 W Peterson Ave, Chicago, IL 60646. Telephone (312) 583-8500.

Loose-leaf book, plus daily reports while the US Supreme Court is in session. Gives texts of opinions and actions of the Court. Price $310.00 per year.

4818
United States Taxation of International Operations
Prentice-Hall, Inc, Englewood Cliffs, NJ 07632. Telephone (201) 592-2000. Telex 13-5423.

Biweekly loose-leaf service. Analyzes US tax laws for foreign corporations, nonresident aliens, and foreign income. Forms and checklists. Price $249.00 per year.

4819
United States Tax Cases
Commerce Clearing House, Inc, 4025 W Peterson Ave, Chicago, IL 60646. Telephone (312) 583-8500.
Two books annually. Give the full texts of pertinent court decisions on income, excise, estate, and gift taxes. Price $27.50 per volume. ISSN 9640.

4820
United States Tax Week
Matthew Bender & Co, 235 E 45th St, New York, NY 10017. Telephone (212) 661-5050.
Weekly loose-leaf magazine. Covers federal tax rulings, interpretations, and trends. Price $155.00 per year.

4821
United States Trade—Puerto Rico and US Possessions. FT800
US Dept of Commerce, Bureau of the Census, Washington, DC 20233. Telephone (202) 449-1600.
Monthly report. Supplies information on the net quantity and value of commodities shipped between the US and Puerto Rico and US possessions. Shows the methods of transportation. Price $16.30 per year.

4822
United States Waterborne Exports and General Imports
US Dept of Commerce, Bureau of the Census, Washington, DC 20233. Telephone (202) 449-1600.
Monthly and annual reports. Contain data on the shipping weight and value of US waterborne exports and imports. Includes information on Department of Defense-controlled cargo and note the amount carried on US flag vessels. Price $14.90 per year.

4823
University of Baltimore Business Review
University of Baltimore, 1420 N Charles St, Baltimore, MD 21201. Telephone (301) 727-6350.
Quarterly report. Discusses business and economic conditions in the Baltimore metropolitan area. Price available on request.

4825
Unquoted Companies Service
Extel Statistical Services Ltd, 37-45 Paul St, London, England EC2A 4PB. Telephone (44) (01) 253-3400. Telex 262687.

Annual card service, with regular updating. Provides financial and other information on some 2400 companies that are not quoted on the British and Irish stock exchanges. Price £1,550.00 per year.

4826
Update
Chilton Co, Chilton Way, Radnor, PA 19089. Telephone (215) 687-8200.
Monthly newsletter. Carries instrumentation and control industry news. Price $25.00.

4827
Update
Federal Reserve Bank of Atlanta, Research Dept, PO Box 1731, Atlanta, GA 30301. Telephone (404) 586-8788.
Monthly booklet. Reports on business conditions in the Sixth Federal Reserve District. Tables provide employment, income, and banking data. Price free of charge.

4828
Uranium Information
Petroleum Information Corp, PO Box 2612, 1375 Delaware, Denver, CO 80201. Telephone (303) 825-2181.
Weekly report. Covers uranium mining claims in the Rocky Mountains. Includes regional news and government regulations. Price $2640.00 per year.

4828.01
Uranium Information Western
Petroleum Information Corp, PO Box 2612, 1375 Delaware, Denver, CO 80201. Telephone (303) 825-2181.
Bimonthly report. Covers mining claims recorded in the Bureau of Land Management for Arizona, Nevada, California, Idaho, Washington, Oregon, and Alaska. Price $3300.00 per year.

4829
Urban Affairs Reports
Commerce Clearing House, Inc, 4025 W Peterson Ave, Chicago, IL 60646. Telephone (312) 583-8500.
Three loose-leaf books and weekly reports. Give information about federal aid programs of interest to state and local governments. Includes programs for housing, urban and rural development, transporation, and pollution control. Price $890.00 per year.

4830
Urban and Community Economic Development
American Bankers Assn, 1120 Connecticut Ave NW, Washington, DC 20036. Telephone (202) 467-4123.
Monthly newsletter. Surveys the banking community's involvement in local government, social organizations, business development, and public service programs. Price $18.00 per year.

4832
Urban Land
Urban Land Inst, 1090 Vermont Ave, NW, Washington, DC 20005. Telephone (202) 289-8500.
Monthly magazine. Contains information on urban land development. Available only to members.

4833
Urban Studies
Longman Group Ltd, Longman House, Burnt Mill, Harlow, Essex, England CM20 2JE. Telephone Harlow 26721. Telex 81259.
Report issued three times per year. Discusses urban affairs and regional planning. Includes book reviews and list of recent publications. Price $38.00 per year. ISSN 0042-0980.

4833.01
Urner Barry's Price-Current
Urner Barry Publications, Inc, PO Box 389, Toms River, NJ 08753. Telephone (201) 240-5330.
Daily report. Supplies wholesale prices for variety of commodities, including eggs, poultry, beef, cheese, and milk. Price $158.00 per year.

4834
Utah Construction Report
University of Utah, Dept of Economics, Salt Lake City, UT 84112. Telephone (801) 581-6333.
Quarterly book. Contains monthly and year-to-date statistics on permit-authorized construction in Utah. Price free of charge.

4835
Utah Economic & Business Review
University of Utah, Dept of Economics, Salt Lake City, UT 84112. Telephone (801) 581-6333.

Monthly book. Discusses Utah's economy and business, ecompassing population, income, employment, and tax information. Price free of charge.

4835.01
Utah: Manufacturers Directory, **1979–80**
Manufacturers' News, Inc, 3 E Huron St, Chicago, Il 60611. Telephone (312) 337-1084.

Biennial book. Provides information on manufacturing firms in Utah. Indicates location, products, and number of employees. Price $16.00.

4835.02
Utah: State Industrial Directory, **1980–81**
Manufacturers' News, Inc, 3 E Huron St, Chicago, Il 60611. Telephone (312) 337-1084.

Biennial book. Covers 2100 industrial companies in Utah. Notes location, products, and executives. Price $15.00.

4836
Utilities Law Reports
Commerce Clearing House, Inc, 4025 W Peterson Ave, Chicago, IL 60646. Telephone (312) 583-8500.

Three loose-leaf books and weekly reports. Pertain to court and commission decisions on public utility regulation. Include federal statutes and regulations. Price $730.00 per year.

4837
Utility Investment Statistics
Conference Board, Inc, 845 3rd Ave, New York, NY 10022. Telephone (212) 759-0900.

Quarterly report. Examines capital appropriations of investor-owned gas and electric utility firms for new plants and equipment. Price available on request.

4838
Valuation
American Society of Appraisers, Dulles International Airport, PO Box 17265, Washington, DC 20041. Telephone (703) 620-3838.

Semiannual journal. Publishes articles relevant to appraisals in areas such as real estate, utilities, fine arts, natural resources, and other properties and rights. Price $8.00 for two issues.

4839
Value Line Convertible Strategist
Arnold Bernhard & Co, Inc, 711 3rd Ave, New York, NY 10017. Telephone (212) 687-3965.

Weekly loose-leaf newsletter. Supplies investment information, including material on convertibles and warrants. Price $195.00 per year.

4840
Value Line Investment Survey
Arnold Bernhard & Co, Inc, 711 3rd Ave, New York, NY 10017. Telephone (212) 687-3965.

Weekly loose-leaf booklet. Covers the business activities of corporations in a variety of industries. Charts and graphs. Price $330.00 per year.

4841
Value Line OTC Special Situations Service
Arnold Bernhard & Co, Inc, 711 3rd Ave, New York, NY 10017. Telephone (212) 687-3965.

Bimonthly loose-leaf newsletter. Contains information for investors on stocks and business trends. Price $300.00 per year.

4842
Vancouver Stock Exchange Annual Report
Vancouver Stock Exchange, 536 Howe St, Vancouver, BC, Canada V6C 2E1. Telephone (604) 689-3334.

Annual report. Provides information on Vancouver Stock Exchange. Covers transactions, trading figures, listing changes, agency offerings, and other trading information. Price $30.00 per year.

4843
Vancouver Stock Exchange Review
Vancouver Stock Exchange, 536 Howe St, Vancouver, BC, Canada V6C 2E1. Telephone (604) 689-3334.

Monthly report. Covers the activities of the Vancouver Stock Exchange. Includes transactions, trading figures, listing changes, outstanding stock options, agency offerings, and dividend declarations. Price $27.00 per year.

4844
Vending Times
Vending Times, Inc, 211 E 43rd St, New York, NY 10036. Telephone (212) 697-3868.

Monthly magazine. Discusses vending and food service topics. Price $15.00 per year.

4845
Venezuela Up-To-Date
Embassy of Venezuela, 2437 California St, NW, Washington, DC 20008. Telephone (202) 797-3800.

Quarterly magazine. Covers economic political and cultural developments in Venezuela. Price free of charge.

4846
Venture Capital Journal
Capital Publishing Corp, Box 348, Wellesley Hills, MA 02181. Telephone (617) 235-5405.

Monthly loose-leaf magazine. Covers the venture capital field. Offers information on investments, trends, and companies. Price $365.00 per year.

4847
Verified Directory of Manufacturers' Representatives, **1981-82**
Manufacturers' Agent Publishing Co, Inc, 663 5th Ave, New York, NY 10022. Telephone (212) 682-0326.

Biennial directory. Lists 16,000 manufacturers' agents in the United States, Puerto Rico, and Canada. Notes sales territory covered and product lines carried. Price $52.90.

4847.01
Vermont: State Industrial Directory, **1981**
Manufacturers' News, Inc, 3 E Huron St, Chicago, IL 60611. Telephone (312) 337-1084.

Annual book. Contains information on 1500 industrial firms in Vermont and 3000 executives. Price $20.00.

4848
Vessel Entrances and Clearances
US Dept of Commerce, Bureau of the Census, Washington, DC 20233. Telephone (202) 449-1600.

Annual report. Provides statistics on the number and net registered tonnage of vessels entering and clearing the US customs area. Indicates ports of entry, and presents separate data for US and foreign flag vessels. Price $14.90 per year.

4849

Vickers Guide to Bank Trust Guide
Vickers Assoc, Inc, 226 New York Ave, Huntington, NY 11743. Telephone (516) 432-7710.

Quarterly loose-leaf report. Monitors common stock holdings and transactions of major US banks. Notes bank activity in preferred stocks and convertible debt. Price $240.00 per year.

4850

Vickers Guide to College Endowment Portfolios
Vickers Assoc, Inc, 226 New York Ave, Huntington, NY 11743. Telephone (516) 432-7710.

Loose-leaf binder with periodic updates. Lists common stock holdings and transactions of college endowments. Includes the portfolios of the largest endowments and a college endowment directory. Price $155.00 per year.

4851

Vickers Guide to Insurance Company Portfolios—Common Stocks
Vickers Assoc, Inc, 226 New York Ave, Huntington, NY 11743. Telephone (516) 432-7710.

Quarterly loose-leaf report. Lists common stock holdings and transactions by US and Canadian insurance companies. Price $220.00 per year.

4852

Vickers Guide to Insurance Company Portfolios—Corporate Bonds
Vickers Assoc, Inc, 226 New York Ave, Huntington, NY 11743. Telephone (516) 432-7710.

Loose-leaf binder in three preliminary cumulative and one final edition. Contains information on corporate bond holdings and transactions of insurance companies. Price $265.00 per year.

4853

Vickers Guide to Investment Company Portfolios
Vickers Assoc, Inc, 226 New York Ave, Huntington, NY 11743. Telephone (516) 432-7710.

Loose-leaf report issued seven times per year. Supplies information on US and Canadian investment companies' and mutual funds' stock holdings and transactions. Covers common and preferred stocks, bonds, convertible preferreds, and convertible bonds. Price $399.00 per year.

4853.01

Vickers Traders Guide
Vickers Assoc, Inc, 226 New York Ave, Huntington, NY 11743. Telephone (516) 432-7710.

Two annual books with three preliminary cumulative editions. List every holding of every institution reporting common stocks. Price $920.00 per year.

4854

Videocassette & CATV Newsletter
Martin Roberts & Assoc, Inc, PO Box 5254, Beverly Hills, CA 90210. Telephone (213) 273-0381.

Monthly newsletter. Covers the electronic audiovisual industry, including videocassettes, CATV, satellites, and video recordings. Price $42.00 per year. ISSN 0049-6243.

4854.01

Videography
United Business Publications, Inc, 475 Park Ave S, New York, NY 10016. Telephone (212) 725-2300.

Monthly magazine. Reports on video developments. Contains information on cable systems. Price $12.00 per year.

4855

VideoNews
Phillips Publishing, Inc, 7315 Wisconsin Ave, Bethesda, MD 20014. Telephone (301) 986-0666.

Biweekly newsletter. Reports on video equipment, video discs, and cable and pay television. Price $147.00 per year. ISSN 0145-9023.

4856

Video Systems
Intertec Publishing Corp, 9221 Quivera Rd, PO Box 12901, Overland Park, KS 66212. Telephone (913) 888-4664. Telex 42-4156.

Monthly magazine. Reports on video production management and techniques. Includes information on advertising, teleproduction studios, and distributors. Price $20.00 per year.

4857

Viewpoint
Main Lafrentz & Co, 380 Park Ave, New York, NY 10017. Telephone (212) 867-9100.

Magazine issued three times per year. Covers accounting, business, pension, and tax matters. Price free of charge.

4857.01

Views
Arthur Young & Co, 277 Park Ave, New York, NY 10017. Telephone (212) 922-2000.

Newsletter issued irregularly. Covers developments in accounting, taxation, and business management. Price free of charge.

4858

Virginia Accountant Quarterly
Virginia Society of Certified Public Accountants, Suite 1010, 700 E Main Bldg, Richmond, VA 23219. Telephone (804) 643-1489.

Quarterly magazine. Reviews accounting procedures and tax issues. Notes changes in Virginia tax laws. Price $12.00 per year.

4858.01

Virginia: Industrial Directory, **1980–81**
Manufacturers' News, Inc, 3 E Huron St, Chicago, IL 60611. Telephone (312) 337-1084.

Biennial book. Contains information on 4000 industrial companies in Virginia. Notes executives and number of employees. Price $28.00.

4858.02

Virginia: State Industrial Directory, **1981**
Manufacturers' News, Inc, 3 E Huron St, Chicago, IL 60611. Telephone (312) 337-1084.

Annual book. Lists 5100 Virginia industrial companies by name, location, and product. Identifies executives. Price $60.-00.

4859

Visa Information Guide
Peter Isaacson Publications, 46-49 Porter St, Prahran, Vic 3181, Australia. Telephone (61) (03) 51 8431. Telex 30880.

Annual loose-leaf. Covers visa and health requirements for every country in the world for holders of Australian, New Zealand, United Kingdom, and US passports. July and November updates. Price $30.00 per copy.

4860

Vision—The Inter-American Magazine
Vision, Inc, 13 E 75th, New York, NY 10021. Telephone (212) 744-9126.

Published 24 times a year. Contains articles on business in Latin America. Price $44.00 per year.

4861
Visual Flight Rules Chart Supplement (VFR)
Supply and Services Canada, Publishing Centre, Printing and Publishing, Ottawa, Ont, Canada K1A 0S9. Telephone (613) 238-1601.

Quarterly report. Provides chart supplement for Canadian flight rules. Price $5.50 per year.

4862
Visual Merchandising
Signs of the Times Publishing Co, 407 Gilbert Ave, Cincinnati, OH 45202. Telephone (513) 421-2050.

Monthly magazine. Pertains to visual retail merchandising. Features material about store management, design, and equipment. Price $15.00 per year. ISSN 0094-4610.

4862.01
VNR Dictionary of Business and Finance
Van Nostrand Reinhold Co, 135 W 50th St, New York, NY 10020. Telephone (212) 265-8700.

Book. Contains definitions of over 4500 terms drawn from all areas of business and finance, with examples of modern usage. Price $18.95.

4862.02
VNR Investor's Dictionary
Van Nostrand Reinhold Co, 135 W 50th St, New York, NY 10020. Telephone (212) 265-8700.

Book. Contains over 2200 definitions of terms drawn from all investment areas, with examples of modern usage. Price $16.95.

4863
Vocational Guidance Quarterly
National Vocational Guidance Assn, Suite 400, 5203 Leesburg Pike, Falls Church, VA 22041. Telephone (703) 820-4700

Quarterly journal. Discusses theories, applications, and research in the career education and vocational guidance fields. Evaluates current literature. Price $10.00 per year.

4864
Voice of Business
Chamber of Commerce of Hawaii, Dillingham Transportation Bldg, 735 Bishop St, Honolulu, HI 96813. Telephone (808) 531-4111.

Semimonthly newspaper. Reports on the activities of the Chamber of Commerce of Hawaii and its members. Price $6.00 per year.

4865
Voice of Small Business
National Small Business Assn, 1604 K St, NW, Washington, DC 20006. Telephone (202) 296-7400.

Monthly newsletter. Covers issues relevant to small businesses, including government aid programs, minimum wage, legislation and occupational safety laws. Price $40.00.

4866
Voice of the Federal Reserve Bank of Dallas Review
Federal Reserve Bank of Dallas, Station K, Dallas, TX 75222. Telephone (214) 651-6111.

Monthly review of the activities of the Federal Reserve Bank of Dallas. Includes articles on agriculture, banking, and business in the southwest. Price free of charge.

4867
Volume Retail Merchandising
Canadian Engineering Publications Ltd, 32 Front St W, Suite 501, Toronto, Ont, Canada M5J 2H9. Telephone (416) 869-1735.

Monthly tabloid. Deals with Canadian retail business, especially new products, trends, merchandising, and profits. Price $24.00 per year.

4868
Volunteer Leader
American Hospital Publishing, Inc, 211 E Chicago Ave, Chicago, IL 60611. Telephone (312) 951-1100.

Quarterly magazine. Focuses on volunteer hospital programs. Discusses operations, recruitment, training, and placement and covers in-service and community outreach programs. Price $6.00 per year. ISSN 0005-1861.

4868.01
Wage Developments Resulting from Major Collective Bargaining Settlements
Labour Canada, Communications Services Directorate, Ottawa, Ont, Canada K1A 0J2. Order from Communications Services Directorate, Ottawa, Ont, Canada K1A 0J2. Telephone (819) 997-2617.

Quarterly report. Contains data on base rate increases from major Canadian labor bargaining settlements for that period. Notes trend in base rates for all major agreements in force. Bilingual. Price free of charge.

4869
Wage-Hour Guide
Prentice-Hall, Inc, Englewood Cliffs, NJ 07632. Telephone (201) 592-2000. Telex 13-5423.

Biweekly loose-leaf service. Covers wage-hour and related laws, including child labor restrictions, the equal pay law, and overtime rules. Price $261.00 per year.

4871
Wage Rates for Selected Occupations
Alaska Dept of Labor, Employment Security Div, Research & Analysis Section, Box 3-7000, Juneau, AK 99801. Telephone (907) 465-2700.

Report. Presents statistics on wage rates for Anchorage, Fairbanks, and southeast Alaska. Price available on request.

4872
Wage Rates, Salaries & Hours of Labour
Canadian Dept of Labour, Ottawa, Ont, Canada K1A 0J2. Order from Publishing Centre, Supply and Services, Ottawa, Canada K1A 0S9. Telephone (819) 997-2582.

Series of annual booklets. Provide wage rates, salaries and hours of labor in various industries for Canada and 26 areas. English and French. Price varies. ISBN varies.

4873
Wales in Figures
Lloyds Bank Ltd, PO Box 215, 71 Lombard St, London, England EC3P 3BS. Telephone (44) (01) 626-1500.

Annual pamphlet. Gives vital statistics on Wales's industrial production, agriculture, forestry and fishing, manpower, transport, education, and public expenditure. Welsh and English versions. Price free of charge.

4874
Walker's Manual of Western Corporations
Walker's Manual, Inc, 5855 Naples Plz, Suite 101, Long Beach, CA 90803. Telephone (213) 434-3468.

Annual two-volume book with monthly supplements. Contains descriptions of nearly all publicly owned companies in 13 US western states. Includes up to 10 years of financial and related operating data, including officers, directors, and shareholdings of each. Price $182.00, $270.00 including supplements.

4875
Wallaces' Farmer
Wallace-Homestead Co, 1912 Grand Ave, Des Moines, IA 50305. Telephone (515) 243-6181.

Semimonthly magazine. Reports on Iowa agricultural news. Notes livestock prices. Price $12.00 per year.

4876
Wall Street Advisor
Wall Street Advisor, PO Box 2591, Ormond Beach, FL 32074. Telephone (800) 824-5120.

Semimonthly newsletter. Surveys the stock investment market. Presents a technical review and digest of professional opinion. Tables and charts. Price $100.00 per year.

4877
Wall Street Irregular
National Corporate Sciences, Inc, 370 E 76th St, New York, NY 10021. Telephone (212) 249-1964.

Report issued 6–10 times a year. Discusses in each report one stock issued by a medium-size company, the company's products, and its financial statement. Follow-up reports. Price $39.00 per year.

4878
Wall Street Journal
Dow Jones & Co, Inc, 22 Cortlandt St, New York, NY 10007. Telephone (212) 285-5000.

Daily newspaper. Contains news articles on business and finance and includes statistics on securities, commodities, and exchange rates. Price available on request.

4879
Wall Street Journal Index
Dow Jones & Co, Inc, 22 Cortlandt St, New York, NY 10007. Telephone (212) 285-5000.

Monthly index for retrieval of articles published in the Wall Street Journal. Price $90.00 per year.

4880
Wall Street Letter
Institutional Investor Systems, Inc, 488 Madison Ave, New York, NY 10022. Telephone (212) 832-8888.

Weekly report. Covers news and trends in the securities trade, including new regulations and changes in brokerage businesses on Wall Street. Price $395.00 per year.

4881
Wall Street Review of Books
Redgrave Publishing Co, 430 Manville Rd, Pleasantville, NY 10570. Telephone (914) 769-3629.

Semiannual journal. Reviews trade and professional books in economics, business, finance, and banking. Aims at the field of economics and securities. Price $17.00 per year.

4881.01
Wardley-cards
Extel Statistical Service Ltd, 37-45 Paul St, London, England EC2A 4PB. Telephone (44) (01) 253-3400. Telex 262687.

Loose-leaf service, with weekly updates. Supplies information on all companies quoted in Hong Kong. Price $340.00 per year.

4882
Ward's Automotive Yearbook
Ward's Communications, Inc, 28 W Adams St, Detroit, MI 48226. Telephone (313) 962-4433.

Annual book. Covers developments and gives statistics for the US and Canadian car and truck industries. Lists motor vehicle manufacturers. Contains directory of suppliers and product guide. Price $60.00 per year.

4883
Warranty Watch
Federal-State Reports, Inc, 5203 Leesburg Pike, #1201, Falls Church, VA 22041. Telephone (703) 379-0222.

Loose-leaf binder, plus newsletter. Provides documentation on Magnuson-Moss Warranty Act. Newsletter notes new FTC issuances. Price $150.00 per year.

4884
Washington Banktrends
International Banktrends, Inc, 910 16th St NW, Washington, DC 20006. Order from Washington Banktrends, Inc, 910 16th St, NW, Washington, DC 20006. Telephone (202) 466-7490.

Weekly newsletter. Digests information pertinent to commercial banks, savings institutions, credit unions and other financial organizations on financial trends. Price $100.00 per year.

4886
Washington Environmental Protection Report
Callahan Publications, PO Box 3751, Washington, DC 20007. Telephone (703) 356-1925.

Semimonthly newsletter. Covers contracting opportunities, legislation, research and development, and regulations in programs to preserve and restore the environment. Price $120.00 per year.

4887
Washington Financial Reports
Bureau of National Affairs, Inc, 1231 25th St, NW, Washington, DC 20037. Telephone (202) 452-4200.

Loose-leaf books, with weekly updates. Cover federal developments affecting banks, savings and loan associations, holding companies, and credit unions. Text, an agency blotter, and a quarterly index. Price $375.00 per year.

4887.01
Washington Health Record
McGraw-Hill Publications Co, 1221 Ave of the Americas, New York, NY 10020. Telephone (212) 997-7558. Telex TWX 7105814879 WUI 62555.

Weekly newsletter. Lists new regulations that affect health care industry. Reports on bills and Congressional activity. Notes health-related meetings, publications, and articles. Price $157.00 per year.

4887.02
Washington Information Directory, 1980-81
Congressional Quarterly, Inc, 1414 22nd St, NW, Washington, DC 20037. Telephone (202) 296-6800.

Annual directory. Serves as guide to information sources in Congress, the executive branch, and private associations. Includes subject and agency indexes. Price $25.00.

4888
Washington International Business Report
International Business-Government Counsellors, Inc, 1625 Eye St, NW, Washington, DC 20006. Telephone (202) 872-8181. Telex 440511.

Biweekly report. Covers US government policy affecting foreign trade and investment, foreign investment in the US, and multinational corporations. Price $216.00 per year.

4888.01
Washington: Manufacturers Register, 1980–81
Manufacturers' News, Inc, 3 E Huron St, Chicago, IL 60611. Telephone (312) 337-1084.

Biennial book. Contains information on 4000 manufacturing firms in the state of Washington. Notes location, product, executives, and number of employees. Price $49.00.

4888.02
Washington Manufacturers Register, 1980–81
Times Mirror Press, 1115 S Boyle Ave, Los Angeles, CA 90023. Telephone (213) 265-6767.

Biennial book. Lists 4400 manufacturers in the state of Washington. Notes number of employees, plant and branch locations, and products. Price $42.50.

4888.03
Washington Notes
US League of Savings Assns, 111 E Wacker Dr, Chicago, IL 60601. Telephone (312) 644-3100.

Weekly newsletter. Provides update on legislative and regulatory activity with implications for the savings and loan business. Price $120.00 per year.

4889
Washington Report
Chamber of Commerce of the US, 1615 H St, NW, Washington, DC 20062. Telephone (202) 659-6231.

Fortnightly newsletter. Interprets legislative, economic, and business trends and developments. Price $12.50 per year.

4890
Washington Report
National Forest Products Assn, 1619 Massachusetts Ave NW, Washington, DC 20036. Telephone (202) 797-5800.

Quarterly report. Covers all government activities affecting land, timber, environment, and wood products. Price free to association members.

4891
Washington Report on Health Legislation
McGraw-Hill Publications Co, 1221 Ave of the Americas, New York, NY 10020. Telephone (212) 997-1221. Telex 7105814879 WUI 62555.

Weekly newsletter. Reports on US health care legislative developments. Discusses the language, aims, and expected impact of pertinent bills. Price $327.00 per year.

4892
Washington Report on Medicine & Health
McGraw-Hill Publications Co, 1221 Ave of the Americas, New York, NY 10020. Telephone (212) 997-1221. Telex 7105814879 WUI 62555.

Weekly newsletter. Discusses federal rulings and legislative trends affecting health care. Price $157.00 per year.

4893
Washington State Economy: Review and Outlook
Washington Dept of Commerce & Economic Development, Research Div, General Adm Bldg, Olympia, WA 98504. Telephone (206) 753-5600.

Annual report. Reviews the state of Washington's economy. Considers the future outlook. Price free of charge.

4894
Washington State Foreign Trade Trends
Washington Dept of Commerce & Economic Development, Research Div, Genl Adm Bldg, Olympia, WA 98504. Order from Office of Foreign Trade, 312 First Ave N, Seattle, WA 98109 Telephone (206) 464-7077.

Bimonthly report. Covers developments in the foreign trade of Washington State. Price free of charge.

4894.01
Washington: State Industrial Directory, 1981
Manufacturers' News, Inc, 3 E Huron St, Chicago, IL 60611. Telephone (312) 337-1084.

Annual book. Covers 5127 industrial firms in the state of Washington. Indicates location, products, executives, and number of employees. Price $45.00.

4895
Washington State Labor Market Information Directory
Washington Employment Security Dept, Research and Statistics Branch, Olympia, WA 98504. Telephone (206) 753-5224.

Annual directory. Lists publications reporting on Washington State's labor market trends, employment, and wages. Price free of charge.

4897
Washington Weekly Report
Independent Bankers Assn of America, Sauk Centre, MN 56378. Telephone (612) 352-6546.

Weekly report. Reviews congressional and other federal government actions affecting banks. Carries material on current state banking issues and weekly economic indicators. Price free to members of IBAA, $20.00 to nonmembers.

4898
Water & Pollution Control
Southam Communications Ltd, 1450 Don Mills Rd, Don Mills, Ont, Canada M3B 2X7. Telephone (416) 445-6641. Telex 06-966612.

Monthly magazine. Covers water, waste, and industrial pollution. Price $33.00 per year.

4899
Water Pollution Control
Bureau of National Affairs, Inc, 1231 25th St, NW, Washington, DC 20037. Telephone (202) 452-4200.

Loose-leaf books, with biweekly updates. Cover water pollution control requirements, including permits, compliance and enforcement, standards, and effluent guidelines by industry and construction grants. Reference file. Price $215.00 per year.

4900
Water Resources Thesaurus
US Dept of the Interior, Washington, DC 20240. Order from National Technical Information Service, US Dept of Commerce, 5825 Port Royal Rd, Springfield, VA 22161. Telephone (202) 487-4650.

Book. Provides the vocabulary for indexing and retrieving literature on water resources research and development. Price available on request.

4901

Water Transport Service Bulletin

Statistics Canada, User Services, Publications Distribution, Ottawa, Ont, Canada K1A 0V7. Telephone (613) 992-3151.

Monthly report. Presents a statistical summary of Canadian shipping and port activity. Notes major commodities loaded and unloaded and container movements. Price $18.00 per year. ISSN 0380-0350.

4903

Weekly Bond Buyer

Bond Buyer, 1 State St Plz, New York, NY 10004. Telephone (212) 943-8200. Telex 12-9233.

Weekly newspaper. Contains municipal bond news, including proposed issues and bond sales results. Tables and charts. Price $200.00 per year.

4904

Weekly Carloading Statement

Assn of American Railroads, Car Service Div, American Railroads, Bldg, Washington, DC 20036. Telephone (202) 293-5012.

Weekly statistical and graphical analysis of railroad revenue freight arranged by districts. Serves as an economic indicator. Price $20.00 per year.

4906

Weekly Government Abstracts.
Administration

US Dept of Commerce, National Technical Information Service, 5285 Port Royal Rd, Springfield, VA 22161. Telephone (804) 557-4600.

Weekly newsletter. Provides information on government-conducted or -sponsored research projects on administration, management information systems, personnel management, and labor relations. Price $45.00 per year.

4907

Weekly government Abstracts.
Agriculture & Food

US Dept of Commerce, National Technical Information Service, 5285 Port Royal Rd, Springfield, VA 22161. Telephone (804) 557-4600.

Weekly newsletter. Reviews government-conducted or -sponsored research projects on agricultural engineering, agricultural economics, food technology, veterinary medicine, and related topics. Price $45.00 per year.

4908

Weekly Government Abstracts. Behavior & Society

US Dept of Commerce, National Technical Information Service, 5285 Port Royal Rd, Springfield, VA 22161. Telephone (804) 557-4600.

Weekly newsletter. Supplies material on government-conducted or -sponsored research on psychology and society. Includes information on job training, education, law, and the humanities. Price $45.00 per year.

4909

Weekly Government Abstracts.
Biomedical Technology &
Engineering

US Dept of Commerce, National Technical Information Service, 5285 Port Royal Rd, Springfield, VA 22161. Telephone (804) 557-4600.

Weekly newsletter. Contains information on government-sponsored or -conducted biomedical technology and engineering research. Covers instruments, prosthetics, life-support systems, and space biology. Price $45.00 per year.

4910

Weekly Government Abstracts. Building Technology

US Dept of Commerce, National Technical Information Service, 5285 Port Royal Rd, Springfield, VA 22161. Telephone (804) 557-4600.

Weekly newsletter. Provides data on government-conducted or -sponsored building technology research projects. Includes information on design, management, materials, and equipment. Price $45.00 per year.

4911

Weekly Government Abstracts. Business & Economics

US Dept of Commerce, National Technical Information Service, 5285 Port Royal Rd, Springfield, VA 22161. Telephone (804) 557-4600.

Weekly newsletter. Covers business and economics research conducted or sponsored by the government. Includes such topics as manufacturing and production, marketing, consumer affairs, banking and finance, and minority business. Price $45.00 per year.

4912

Weekly Government Abstracts.
Chemistry

US Dept of Commerce, National Technical Information Service, 5285 Port Royal Rd, Springfield, VA 22161. Telephone (804) 557-4600.

Weekly newsletter. Carries material on government-conducted or -sponsored chemical research activities. Includes such subjects as chemical process engineering; industrial, polymer, photo and radiation, and theoretical chemistry. Price $45.00 per year.

4913

Weekly Government Abstracts. Civil & Structural Engineering

US Dept of Commerce, National Technical Information Service, 5285 Port Royal Rd, Springfield, VA 22161. Telephone (804) 557-4600.

Weekly newsletter. Reports on civil and structural engineering research sponsored or conducted by the government. Covers highway engineering, flood control, construction equipment and materials, and soil and rock mechanics. Price $45.00 per year.

4914

Weekly Government Abstracts.
Communication

US Dept of Commerce, National Technical Information Service, 5285 Port Royal Rd, Springfield, VA 22161. Telephone (804) 557-4600.

Weekly newsletter. Provides information on communications research conducted or sponsored by the government. Includes data on common carriers and satellites, policies and regulations, and radio and television equipment. Price $45.00 per year.

4915

Weekly Government Abstracts.
Computers, Control & Information Theory

US Dept of Commerce, National Technical Information Service, 5285 Port Royal Rd, Springfield, VA 22161. Telephone (804) 557-4600.

Weekly newsletter. Carries material on computers, control systems, and information theory research conducted or sponsored by the government. Discusses hardware, software, and pattern recognition. Price $45.00 per year.

4916
Weekly Government Abstracts.
Electrotechnology
US Dept of Commerce, National Technical Information Service, 5285 Port Royal Rd, Springfield, VA 22161. Telephone (804) 557-4600.

Weekly newsletter. Reports on government-conducted or -sponsored electrotechnology research programs. Includes information on antennas, circuits, electron tubes, components, and semiconductors. Price $45.00 per year.

4917
Weekly Government Abstracts. Energy
US Dept of Commerce, National Technical Information Service, 5285 Port Royal Rd, Springfield, VA 22161. Telephone (804) 557-4600.

Weekly newsletter. Presents data on government-conducted or -sponsored energy research projects. Includes such topics as energy use, supply and demand, sources, fuel conversion processes, power and heat generation, engines, and fuels. Price $45.00 per year.

4918
Weekly Government Abstracts.
Environmental Pollution & Control
US Dept of Commerce, National Technical Information Service, 5285 Port Royal Rd, Springfield, VA 22161. Telephone (804) 557-4600.

Weekly newsletter. Discusses environmental pollution and control research conducted or sponsored by the government. Covers air, noise, solid waste, water pollution, radiation, and environmental health and safety. Price $60.00 per year.

4919
Weekly Government Abstracts.
Government Inventions for Licensing
US Dept of Commerce, National Technical Information Service, 5285 Port Royal Rd, Springfield, VA 22161. Telephone (804) 557-4600.

Weekly newsletter. Reports on government inventions available for licensing. Covers mechanical devices and fields of nuclear technology, biology and medicine, metallurgy, and electrotechnology. Price $165.00 per year.

4920
Weekly Government Abstracts. Health
Planning
US Dept of Commerce, National Technical Information Service, 5285 Port Royal Rd, Springfield, VA 22161. Telephone (804) 557-4600.

Weekly newsletter. Reports on government-conducted or -sponsored health planning research. Covers health services and facilities, costs, manpower requirements and training, and government and private agency activities. Price $50.00 per year.

4921
Weekly Government Abstracts.
Industrial & Mechanical Engineering
US Dept of Commerce, National Technical Information Service, 5285 Port Royal Rd, Springfield, VA 22161. Telephone (804) 557-4600.

Weekly newsletter. Covers industrial and mechanical engineering research conducted or sponsored by the government. Includes information on quality control, plant design and maintenance, environmental engineering, and machinery and tools. Price $45.00 per year.

4922
Weekly Government Abstracts. Library
& Information Sciences
US Dept of Commerce, National Technical Information Service, 5285 Port Royal Rd, Springfield, VA 22161. Telephone (804) 557-4600.

Weekly newsletter. Carries material on government-conducted or -sponsored library and information science research. Reports on systems, marketing, and personnel. Price $30.00 per year.

4923
Weekly Government Abstracts. Materials
Sciences
US Dept of Commerce, National Technical Information Service, 5285 Port Royal Rd, Springfield, VA 22161. Telephone (804) 557-4600.

Weekly newsletter. Reports on materials science research programs conducted or sponsored by the government. Includes such topics as ablation, adhesives, ceramics, elastomers, plastics, alloys, wood, and paper products. Price $45.00 per year.

4924
Weekly Government Abstracts. Medicine
& Biology
US Dept of Commerce, National Technical Information Service, 5285 Port Royal Rd, Springfield, VA 22161. Telephone (804) 557-4600.

Weekly newsletter. Supplies information on government-conducted or -sponsored medical and biological research. Covers dentistry, nutrition, occupational and physical therapy, pharmacology, and psychiatry. Price $45.00 per year.

4925
Weekly Government Abstracts. NASA
Earth Resources Survey Program
US Dept of Commerce, National Technical Information Service, 5285 Port Royal Rd, Springfield, VA 22161. Telephone (804) 557-4600.

Weekly newsletter. Contains information on NASA's Earth Resources Survey Program research. Pertains to Skylab's and earth resources satellites' feedback on earth's soil, water, and vegetation. Price $45.00 per year.

4926
Weekly Government Abstracts. Natural
Resources
US Dept of Commerce, National Technical Information Service, 5285 Port Royal Rd, Springfield, VA 22161. Telephone (804) 557-4600.

Weekly newsletter. Supplies data on natural resources research projects conducted or sponsored by the government. Covers mineral industries, soil conservation, forestry, and geology. Price $45.00 per year.

4927
Weekly Government Abstracts. Ocean
Technology & Engineering
US Dept of Commerce, National Technical Information Service, 5285 Port Royal Rd, Springfield, VA 22161. Telephone (804) 557-4600.

Weekly newsletter. Covers government-conducted or -sponsored ocean technology and engineering research. Includes information on oceanography, hydrography, underwater construction, and port engineering. Price $45.00 per year.

4928
Weekly Government Abstracts. Physics
US Dept of Commerce, National Technical Information Service, 5285 Port Royal Rd, Springfield, VA 22161. Telephone (804) 557-4600.

Weekly newsletter. Reports on physics research projects sponsored or conducted by the government. Includes such topics as optics and lasers, solid-state physics, nuclear physics, thermodynamics, and quantum mechanics. Price $45.00 per year.

4929
Weekly Government Abstracts.
Problem-Solving Information for State
& Local Governments
US Dept of Commerce, National Technical Information Service, 5285 Port Royal Rd, Springfield, VA 22161. Telephone (804) 557-4600.

Weekly newsletter. Carries government-conducted or -sponsored research reports on problem-solving for state and local governments. Includes such topics as finance, human resources, transportation, energy, and community development. Price $60.00 per year.

4930
Weekly Government Abstracts. Transportation
US Dept of Commerce, National Technical Information Service, 5285 Port Royal Rd, Springfield, VA 22161. Telephone (804) 557-4600.

Weekly newsletter. Reports on transportation research conducted or sponsored by the government. Covers air, pipeline, surface, and subsurface transportation. Price $45.00 per year.

4931
Weekly Government Abstracts. Urban Technology
US Dept of Commerce, National Technical Information Service, 5285 Port Royal Rd, Springfield, VA 22161. Telephone (804) 557-4600.

Weekly newsletter. Carries material on urban technology research conducted or sponsored by the government. Includes such subjects as urban administration, housing, sanitation, health services, pollution control, and traffic. Price $45.00 per year.

4932
Weekly Insider Report
Stock Research Corp, 50 Broadway, New York, NY 10004. Telephone (212) 482-8300.

Weekly report. Supplies information on the stock transactions of 500 or more shares by corporate officers, directors, and 10% holders who buy or sell shares in their own companies. Price $60.00 per year.

4933
Weekly Insiders Dairy and Egg Letter
Urner Barry Publications, Inc, PO Box 389, Toms River, NJ 08753. Telephone (201) 240-5330.

Weekly newsletter. Contains butter and egg wholesale and retail prices, storage stocks of frozen and shell eggs, and butter and production figures. Tables and graphs. Price $60.00 per year.

4934
Weekly Insiders Poultry Report
Urner Barry Publications, Inc, PO Box 389, Toms River, NJ 08753. Telephone (201) 240-5330.

Weekly report. Presents data on poultry wholesale and retail prices, chicken slaughters, and poultry storage holdings. Includes one to five-year comparisons. Tables and graphs. Price $60.00 per year.

4935
Weekly Insiders Turkey Letter
Urner Barry Publications, Inc, PO Box 389, Toms River, NJ 08753. Telephone (201) 240-5330.

Weekly newsletter. Indicates turkey wholesale and retail prices, storage stocks, and consumption. Tables and graphs. Price $60.00 per year.

4935.01
Weekly Marketing Notes
New South Wales Dept of Agriculture, Div of Marketing and Economics, PO Box K220, Haymarket, Sydney, NSW 2000, Australia. Telephone (02) 2176666.

Weekly newsletter. Covers agriculture markets in New South Wales, Australia. Free of charge.

4936
Weekly Market Review
Queensland Dept of Primary Industries, Marketing Services Branch, William St, Brisbane, Qld 4000, Australia.

Weekly report. Covers prices and market trends in the fruit and vegetable industry in Queensland, Australia. Price free of charge.

4938
Weekly Regulatory Monitor
Washington Monitor, 499 National Press Bldg, Washington, DC 20045. Telephone (202) 347-7757.

Weekly report. Covers proposed federal rules, regulations, and other regulatory activity. Price $300.00 per year.

4939
Weekly Roundup of World Production and Trade
US Dept of Agriculture, Foreign Agricultural Service, Information Service Staff, Rm 5918 S, Washington, DC 20250. Telephone (202) 447-7937.

Weekly report. Discusses international agricultural production and trade developments. Provides data on various commodities. Price free of charge.

4940
Weekly Summary of NLRB Cases
US National Labor Relations Board, 1717 Pennsylvania Ave, NW, Washington, DC 20570. Telephone (202) 655-4000.

Weekly report. Summarizes all published decisions of the National Labor Relations Board. Lists decisions of the board's administrative law judges. Price free of charge.

4940.01
Weekly Television Digest with Consumer Electronics
Television Digest, Inc, 1836 Jefferson Pl, NW, Washington, DC 20036. Telephone (202) 872-9200.

Weekly report. Covers broadcasting and consumer electronics developments. Notes Federal Communications Commission decisions. Price $321.00 per year.

4941
Weekly Truck Tonnage Report
American Trucking Assn, Inc, 1616 P St, NW, Washington, DC 20036. Telephone (202) 797-5351.

Weekly report. Supplies data on the outbound truck tonnage originated through terminals from 49 US production areas. Tables. Price free of charge.

4942
Weekly Underwriter
Underwriter Printing & Publishing Co, 50 East Palisade Ave, PO Box 9806, Englewood, NJ 07631. Telephone (201) 569-8808.

Weekly newspaper. Reports on insurance industry news. Includes information on government intervention, corporate risk management, and pertinent court decisions. Price $12.00 per year.

4943
Weekly Weather and Crop Bulletin
US Dept of Agriculture, NOAA/USDA Joint Agricultural Weather Facility, USDA S Bldg, Room 3526, Washington, DC 20250. Telephone (202) 655-4000.

Weekly report. Summarizes weather conditions and their effects on crops and farm activity by states. Notes international weather. Price $13.00 US, $18.00 foreign.

4944
Welding and Metal Fabrication
IPC Business Press Ltd, 205 E 42nd St, New York, NY 10017. Telephone (212) 889-0700. Telex 421710.

Ten-issue-per-year magazine. Covers the metal fabrication and welding industries. Notes research, equipment, and new processes. Price $65.00. ISSN 0043-2245.

4945
Welding Design & Fabrication
Penton/IPC, 614 Superior Ave W, Cleveland, OH 44113. Telephone (216) 696-0300.

Monthly magazine. Reports on welding-fabricating methods and equipment. Price $24.00.

4946
Welding Distributor
Penton/IPC, 614 Superior Ave W, Cleveland, OH 44113. Telephone (216) 696-0300.

Bimonthly magazine. Discusses the distribution of welding/fabricating equipment and supplies. Price $12.00 per year.

4947
Wells Fargo Bank Business Review
Wells Fargo Bank, Public Relations Dept, PO Box 44000, San Francisco, CA 94144. Telephone (415) 396-2350.

Bimonthly report. Published six times a year. Contains information on US and California business and economic trends. Price free of charge.

4948
Welsh Economic Trends
Her Majesty's Stationery Office, PO Box 569, London, England SE1 9NH. Telephone (44) (01) 928 1321.

Annual service. Provides statistical data on economic trends in Wales. Price £7.75.

4948.01
West African Farming & Food Processing
Alain Charles Publishing Ltd, 27 Wilfred St, London, England SW1E 6PR. Telephone (44) (01) 828-6107. Telex 28905.

Publication. Covers agricultural news for ministries, farms, and small holdings in region of West Africa. Price $25.00 per year.

4949
West African Technical Review
Alain Charles Publishing Ltd, 27 Wilfred St, London, England SW1E 6PR. Telephone (44) (01) 828-6107. Telex 28905.

Monthly report. Discusses West African industrial and technological management subjects. Price $50.00 per year.

4950
Western Australian Manufacturers Directory
Australian Dept of Industrial Development & Decentralisation, Superannuation Bldg, 32 St George's Ter, Perth, WA 6000, Australia. Telephone (61) (92) 25 0471.

Annual directory. Covers western Australia's manufacturers. Price free of charge.

4951
Western Massachusetts Commercial News
Lazar Stambovsky, 333 Bridge St, Springfield, MA 01103. Telephone (413) 736-7006.

Weekly newsletter. Reports on western Massachusett's business development. Includes real estate, construction, and financial news. Price $37.00 per year.

4952
West European Living Costs 1977
Confederation of British Industry, Centre Point, 103 New Oxford St, London, England WC1A 1DU. Telephone (44) (01) 379-7400. Telex 21332.

Report. Provides information on the cost of accommodations, clothing, consumer goods, entertainment, food, salaries, services, office services, postal charges, taxation, and transportation for 13 west European countries. Price £18.00 each.

4953
Westgate Commodities Letter
Financial Weekly, Westgate House, 9 Holborn, London, England, EC1N 2NE. Telephone (44) (01) 404-0733. Telex 881-2431.

Fortnightly newsletter. Provides information on commodities. Price £100.00 per year.

4953.01
Westgate Tax Planner's Letter
Financial Weekly, Westgate House, 9 Holborn, London, England EC1N 2NE. Telephone (44) (01) 404-0733. Telex 881 2431.

Monthly newsletter. Discusses tax planning. Price £ 80.00 per year.

4954
West Virginia CPA
West Virginia Society of CPA's, Box 1142, Charleston, WV 25324. Telephone (304) 342-5461.

Quarterly newsletter. Discusses general accounting topics and the activities of the West Virginia Society of CPA's. Notes changes in West Virginia's accounting laws. Price free of charge to members, advertisers and libraries.

4955
West Virginia Economic Profile
Governer's Office of Economic and Community Development, 1900 Washington St E, Charleston, WV 25305. Telephone (304) 348-2234.

Annual book. Reports on West Virginia's industry and economy. Discusses natural resources, taxes, labor force, and transportation. Tables, charts, and maps. Price free of charge.

4956
West Virginia Industrial Wage Survey
Governer's Office of Economic and Community Development, 1900 Washington St, East Charleston, WV 25305. Telephone (304) 348-2234.

Biannual report. Contains hourly wage data for 36 industrial occupations in West Virginia. Includes monthly salary information for nine occupations. Price free of charge.

4957
West Virginia Manufacturing Directory
Governer's Office of Economic and Community Development, 1900 Washington St, East Charleston, WV 25305. Telephone (304) 348-2234.

Directory. Provides information on 1800 West Virginia manufacturing firms. Price $15.00 per copy.

4957.01
West Virginia: State Industrial Directory, **1980–81**
Manufacturers' News, Inc, 3 E Huron St, Chicago, IL 60611. Telephone (312) 337-1084.

Biennial book. Provides information on 2000 industrial firms in West Virginia. Notes location, products, and executives. Price $25.00.

4958
Whaley-Eaton American Letter
Whaley-Eaton Corp, 1141 National Press Bldg, Washington, DC 20004. Telephone (800) 553-2345.

Weekly newsletter. Covers economic news and trends in the US. Includes articles on US government policies affecting business and investment. Price $66.00 per year.

4959

Whaley-Eaton Foreign Letter

Whaley-Eaton Corp, 1141 National Press Bldg, Washington, DC 20004. Telephone (800) 553-2345.

Weekly newsletter. Covers news and trends in countries throughout the world. Includes coverage of US government policies on trade and investment. Price $66.00 per year.

4960

What's Ahead in Personnel

Enterprise Publications, 20 N Wacker Dr, Chicago, IL 60606. Telephone (312) 332-3571.

Fortnightly newsletter. Reports on trends, government actions and regulations, career opportunities, and other areas of interest in the personnel field. Price $58.00 per year.

4961

What's New in Business

Morgan-Grampian Ltd, Morgan-Grampian House, Calderwood St, London, England SE18 6QH. Telephone (44) (01) 855-7777. Telex 896238. Order from Morgan-Grampian Publishing Co, 2 Park Ave, New York, NY 10016. Telephone (212) 340-9700. Telex 425592 MGI UI.

Monthly magazine. Reports on new products, services and equipment for the building industry. Price $80.00 per year.

4961.01

What's New in Electronics

Morgan-Grampian Ltd, Morgan-Grampian House, Calderwood St, London England SE18 6QH. Telephone (414) (01) 855-7777. Telex 896238. Order from Morgan-Grampian Publishing Co, 2 Park Ave, New York, NY 10016. Telephone (212) 340-9700. Telex 425592 MGI UI.

Bimonthly magazine covering new products in components, computers, hardware, instrumentation, production, semiconductors, and subassemblies. Price $30.00 per year.

4962

What's New in Farming

Morgan-Grampian Ltd, Morgan-Grampian House, Calderwood St, London, England SE18 6QH. Order from Morgan-Grampian Publishing Co, 2 Park Ave, New York, NY 10016. Telephone England (44) (01) 855-7777. Telex 896238 MORGAN G. New York (212) 340-9700. Telex 425592 MGI UI.

Monthly magazine. Covers the latest developments in techniques, products, and equipment for farmers. Price $80.00 per year.

4963

What's New in Home Economics

North American Publishing Co, 401 N Broad St, Philadelphia, PA 19108. Telephone (215) 574-9600.

Newsletter issued 15 times per year. Reports on home economics teaching methods, products, and ideas. Includes information for home economists in business. Price $29.00 per year.

4963.01

What's New In Industry

Morgan-Grampian Ltd, Morgan-Grampian House, Calderwood St, London, England SE18 6QH. Telephone (44) (01) 855-7777. Telex 896238 MORGAN G. Order from Morgan-Grampian Publishing Co, 2 Park Ave, New York, NY 10016. Telephone (212) 340-9700. Telex 425592 MGI UI.

Monthly magazine. Gives detailed information in a wide variety of industrial products, components, and services. Price $100.00 per year.

4964

Wheat Market Report

International Wheat Council, Haymarket House 28, Haymarket, London, England SW1Y 4SS. Telephone (44) (01) 930-4128. Telex 916128 Interwheat.

Monthly report. Contains data on wheat production, trade, prices, ocean freight rates, and supply and demand. Tables. Price free of charge.

4966

Wheat Statistics (Cat No 7307.0)

Australian Bureau of Statistics, PO Box 10, Belconnen, ACT 2616, Australia. Order from Australian Government Publishing Service, PO Box 84, Canberra, ACT 2600, Australia. Telephone (61) (062) 52 7911.

Annual report. Gives statistical data on wheat holdings, quantity, and production in Australia. Includes home and export prices. Price free of charge.

4967

White Collar Management

Man & Manager, Inc, 799 Broadway, New York, NY 10003. Telephone (212) 677-0640.

Semimonthly newsletter. Reports on labor-related case histories from government and regulatory agencies, courts, and other sources. Annual index. Price $52.00 per year.

4968

White Collar Report

Bureau of National Affairs, Inc, 1231 25th St, NW, Washington, DC 20037. Telephone (202) 452-4200.

Loose-leaf books, with weekly updates. Deal with labor-management relations in clerical, technical, sales, scientific, and professional fields. Note legislative and court decisions and union activity. Price $350.00 per year.

4969

White Mercantile Gazette

White Mercantile Agency, 240 Queen St, Brisbane, Qld 4000, Australia. Telephone (61) (07) 221-1122.

Weekly magazine. Concerns credit in Queensland, Australia. Price $60.00 (Australian) per year.

4969.01

White's Air Directory and Who's Who in New Zealand Aviation

Modern Productions Ltd, 1st Floor, Midland House, 73 Great N Rd, PO Box 2040, Auckland, New Zealand. Telephone (09) 768-809.

Book. Covers aviation and allied industries in New Zealand and the South Pacific. Includes listings of airport authorities, scheduled and unscheduled airlines, aeronautical manufacturers, and training facilities. Price available on request.

4970

Who Distributes What and Where: An International Directory of Publishers, Imprints, Agents and Distributors

RR Bowker Co, 1180 Avenue of the Americas, New York, NY 10036. Order from RR Bowker Co, PO Box 1807, Ann Arbor, MI 48106. Telephone (212) 764-5100.

Directory. Lists over 5000 publishers with foreign or domestic representatives, those with foreign branches or who serves as agents, representatives, or distributors for other countries. Price $35.00. ISBN 0-8352-1230-0. ISSN 0000-0426.

4971
Wholesale Trade
Statistics Canada, User Services, Publications Distribution, Ottawa, Ont, Canada K1A 0V7. Telephone (613) 992-3151.

Monthly magazine. Reports on Canadian estimated dollar sales and inventories (at cost) of wholesalers by business group. Cumulative figures. Price $18.00 per year. ISSN 0380-7894.

4972
Who Owns Whom: Australasia & Far East
Who Owns Whom Ltd, 6-8 Bonhill St, London EC2A 4BU, England. Telephone (44) (01) 628-3691.

One-volume annual book. Provides details on the developing companies of the Pacific. Offers a special section on foreign investment in Japanese companies. Price $138.00.

4973
Who Owns Whom: Continental Europe
Who Owns Whom Ltd, 6-8 Bonhill St, London, EC2A 4BU, England. Telephone (44) (01) 628-3691.

Two-volume annual book. Provides a directory to company ownership throughout the European Economic Community and other European nations. Price $221.-00.

4974
Who Owns Whom: North America
Who Owns Whom Ltd, 6-8 Bonhill St, London EC2A 4BU, England. Telephone (44) (01) 628-3691.

One-volume annual book. Serves as a directory to the structure of US multinational subsidiaries and provides an alphabetical listing of foreign parent companies. Price $149.00.

4975
Who Owns Whom: United Kingdom & Republic of Ireland
Who Owns Whom Ltd, 6-8 Bonhill St, London, EC2A 4BU, England. Telephone (44) (01) 628-3691.

Two-volume annual book with quarterly supplements. Covers 6500 parent companies and their subsidiaries in Great Britain and the Irish Republic. Features foreign investment listings and members of consortiums in special sections. Price $194.00 per year.

4975.01
Who's Pegging Where
Lipscombe & Assoc, PO Box 158, Claremont, WA 6010, Australia. Telephone 386-7899. Telex 92-442.

Weekly newsletter. Focuses on mineral prospecting in western Australia. Price $240.00 (Australian) per year.

4975.02
Who's Who **1980–81, 132nd Edition**
St Martin's Press, Inc, 175 5th Ave, New York, NY 10010. Telephone (212) 674-5151.

Annual book. Covers living persons of note worldwide. Includes up-to-date biographical data on 28,000 distinguished people. Price $99.50.

4976
Who's Who Among Professional Insurance Agents
Underwriter Printing & Publishing Co, 50 East Palisade Ave, PO Box 9806, Englewood, NJ 07631. Telephone (201) 569-8808.

Annual book. Provides biographies of insurance agents and information on insurance agencies. Price $35.00.

4977
Who's Who in America
Marquis Publications, 200 E Ohio St, Rm 5604, Chicago, IL 60611. Telephone (312) 787-2008.

Biennial book. Contains more than 73,500 biographical sketches of outstanding American men and women. Price $89.50. ISBN 0-8379-0141-3.

4978
Who's Who in American Law
Marquis Publications, 200 E Ohio St, Rm 5604, Chicago, IL 60611. Telephone (312) 787-2008.

Biennial book. Contains more than 20,000 biographical sketches of lawyers, judges, law school deans and professors, state and federal prosecutors, and justice department officials. Price $57.50. ISBN 0-8379-3502-4.

4979
Who's Who in Association Management
American Society of Association Executives, 1575 Eye St, NW, Washington, DC 20005. Telephone (202) 626-ASAE.

Annual directory to 5500 members of the American Society of Association Executives. Price $50.00 per copy.

4980
Who's Who in Banking
Taplinger Publishing Co, 200 Park Ave S, New York, NY 10013. Telephone (212) 533-6110.

Book. Lists important figures in US banking and finance. Includes biographical information. Price available on request.

4982
Who's Who in Consulting, **2nd edition**
Gale Research Co, Book Tower, Detroit, MI 48226. Telephone (313) 961-2242.

Book. Provides biographical details on over 7500 people who work as business, industrial, and governmental consultants. Price $110.00. ISBN 0360-4.

4983
Who's Who in Engineering, **4th edition —1980**
American Assoc of Engineering Societies, Inc, 345 E 47th St, New York, NY 10017. Telephone (212) 644-7840.

Directory. Lists biographies, business addresses and titles of 13,000 prominent engineers in all fields. Notes recipients of national awards. Index to engineers by specialty and geographic locations. Price $75.00.

4984
Who's Who in Finance, **2nd edition**
Gower Publishing Co Ltd, 1 Westmead, Farnborough, Hampshire, England GU14 7RU. Telephone Farnborough (0252) 519221. Telex 858623.

Publication. Serves as a directory to major figures in the financial world. Price $43.-00. ISSN 0 7161 0241 2.

4985
Who's Who in Finance and Industry
Marquis Publications, 200 E Ohio St, Rm 5604, Chicago, IL 60611. Telephone (312) 787-2008.

Biennial book. Gives information about top executives from America's largest corporations, plus data on leaders of small- and medium-size firms. Price $62.50. ISBN 0-8379-0322-X.

4986

Who's Who in Government
Chamber of Commerce of Hawaii, Dillingham Transportation Bldg, 735 Bishop St, Honolulu, HI 96813. Telephone (808) 531-4111.

Biennial report. Supplies data on Hawaiian federal, state, and county elected officials. Price $2.00.

4988

Who's Who in Insurance
Underwriter Printing & Publishing Co, 50 East Palisade Ave, PO Box 9806, Englewood, NJ 07631. Telephone (201) 569-8808.

Annual book. Supplies biographies of 5000 insurance officials, brokers, agents, and buyers. Price $40.00.

4989

Who's Who in Public Relations (International), **5th edition**
PR Publishing Co, Inc, PO Box 600, Exeter, NH 03833. Telephone (603) 778-0514.

Directory. Lists 5500 international public relations leaders. Includes personal and business information. Price $45.00. ISBN 0-914016-25-3.

4990

Who's Who in Risk Management
Underwriter Printing & Publishing Co, 50 East Palisade Ave, PO Box 9806, Englewood, NJ 07631. Telephone (201) 569-8808.

Yearly book. Contains biographies of insurance buyers for large business and industrial firms. Price $35.00 per year.

4991

Who's Who in Saudi Arabia
Europa Publications Ltd, 18 Bedford Sq, London, WC1B 3JN, England. Telephone (44) (01) 580-8236.

Book. Provides biographical data on people currently prominent in Saudi Arabia. Covers numerous fields of endeavor. Price $45.00.

4992

Who's Who in the East
Marquis Publications, 200 E Ohio St, Rm 5604, Chicago, IL 60611. Telephone (312) 787-2008.

Biennial book. Provides biographical sketches of outstanding men and women of the eastern part of the US. Price $62.50. ISBN 0-8379-0618-0.

4993

Who's Who in the Midwest
Marquis Publications, 200 E Ohio St, Rm 5604, Chicago, IL 60611. Telephone (312) 787-2008.

Biennial book. Offers concise biographies of outstanding men and women of the midwestern part of the US. Price $57.50. ISBN 0-8379-0717-9.

4994

Who's Who in the Securities Industry
Economist Publishing Co, 12 E Grand Ave, Chicago, IL 60611. Telephone (312) 944-1204.

Annual report. Contains biographical information on outstanding figures in the securities industry. Price available on request.

4995

Who's Who in the South and Southwest
Marquis Publications, 200 E Ohio St, Rm 5604, Chicago, IL 60611. Telephone (312) 787-2008.

Biennial book. Supplies biographical sketches of men and women of the southern and southwestern parts of the US. Price $57.50. ISBN 0-8379-0817-5.

4996

Who's Who in the West
Marquis Publications, 200 E Ohio St, Rm 5604, Chicago, IL 60611. Telephone (312) 787-2008.

Biennial book. Furnishes brief biographies of outstanding men and women of the western part of the US. Price $57.50. ISBN 0-8379-0917-1.

4997

Who's Who in the World
Marquis Publications, 200 E Ohio St, Rm 5604, Chicago, IL 60611. Telephone (312) 787-2008.

Biennial book. Contains biographical sketches of men and women with outstanding accomplishments in many fields throughout the world. Price $59.50. ISBN 0-8379-1105-2.

4998

Who's Who of American Women
Marquis Publications, 200 E Ohio St, Rm 5604, Chicago, IL 60611. Telephone (312) 787-2008.

Biennial book. Presents more than 21,000 biographical sketches of outstanding American women. Price $62.50. ISBN 0-8379-0412-9.

4999

Who's Who (United Kingdom)
St Martin's Press, Inc, 175 5th Ave, New York, NY 10010. Telephone (212) 674-5151.

Annual book. Covers living persons of note in Great Britain. Includes biographical data. Price $67.50.

5000

Who Writes What
National Underwriter Co, 420 E 4th St, Cincinnati, OH 45202. Telephone (513) 721-2140.

Book. Reviews life and health insurance policies offered by different companies. Supplies information on which companies handle hard-to-place lines. Price $7.50.

5001

Wiesenberger Financial Services
Warren, Gorham & Lamont, Inc, 210 S. St, Boston, MA 02111. Telephone (617) 423-2020.

Annual book, with quarterly and monthly reports. Provides financial information on open and closed-end mutual funds. Offers short- and long-term statistics and performance evaluations. Price $145.00 per year.

5002

Willings Press Guide
Thomas Skinner Directories, Windsor Court, E Grinstead House, Sussex, England RH19 1XE. Order from IPC Business Press Ltd New York, 205 E 42nd St, New York, NY 10017.

Annual book. Lists United Kingdom and major European periodicals and newspapers. Price £55.00. ISBN 611 00648 0.

5003

Wills, Estates and Trusts
Prentice-Hall, Inc, Englewood Cliffs, NJ 07632. Telephone (201) 592-2000. Telex 13-5423.

Loose-leaf report. Discusses wills, estates, and trusts. Contains the text of relevant state laws. Price $282.00 per year for 1 state, each additional state $39.00.

5004

Wills Trusts Forms
Prentice-Hall, Inc, Englewood Cliffs, NJ 07632. Telephone (201) 592-2000. Telex 13-5423.

Loose-leaf report. Provides forms for wills and trusts that have alternative and additional provisions and clauses. Offers new forms and ideas in monthly supplements. Price $204.00 per year.

5005
Wine Bulletin
Her Majesty's Stationery Office, PO Box 569, London, England SE1 9NH. Order from Bill of Entry Service, HM Customs and Excise, King's Beam House, Mark Lane, London, England EC3 7HE. Telephone (44) (01) 928 1321.

Monthly report on wines. Price £9.78 per year.

5006
Wine Marketing Handbook
Gavin-Jobson Assoc, Inc, 488 Madison Ave, New York, NY 10022. Telephone (212) 758-5620.

Annual book. Discusses trends in the wine industry, focusing on 25-44 age market. Price $12.00.

5007
Wisconsin CPA
Wisconsin Inst of Certified Public Accountants, Rm 400, 600 E Mason St, Milwaukee, WI 53202. Telephone (414) 272-2136.

Quarterly magazine. Discusses accounting techniques. Notes the activities of the Wisconsin Institute of Certified Public Accountants and reports on federal tax changes and those for Wisconsin. Price $5.00 per year nonmembers.

5008
Wisconsin Industrial Product News
SIC Publishing Corp, 8705 N Port Washington Rd, Milwaukee, WI 53217. Telephone (414) 351-1365.

Monthly newsletter. Gives information on industrial equipment, services, and processes for Wisconsin buyers and sellers. Price free of charge.

5008.01
Wisconsin: Manufacturers Directory,
1981
Manufacturers' News, Inc, 3 E Huron St, Chicago, IL 60611. Telephone (312) 337-1084.

Annual book. Lists 6500 manufacturing firms in Wisconsin and 20,000 executives. Indicates location and products. Price $50.00.

5008.02
Wisconsin: State Industrial Directory,
1981
Manufacturers' News, Inc, 3 E Huron St, Chicago, IL 60611. Telephone (312) 337-1084.

Annual book. Contains information on 4500 industrial companies in Wisconsin and 27,109 executives. Lists firms by name, county, city, and product. Price $50.00.

5009
Without Prejudice
Ontario Insurance Adjusters Assn, c/o Don McCrea, 153 Arnold Ave, Thornhill, Ont, Canada L4J 1B8. Telephone (416) 889-2234.

Monthly magazine. Reports on Canadian legislation and court cases that affect the insurance industry. Price $12.00 per year.

5010
Woman CPA
American Woman's Society of Certified Public Accountants and American Society of Women Accountants, Circulation Dept, The Woman CPA, PO Box 944, Cincinnati, OH 45201. Telephone (513) 385-3998.

Magazine. Presents articles related to women in the accounting field—including public and private practice, education, development in data processing and international arenas, and tax issues. Price $6.00 per year.

5011
Woman Executive's Bulletin
Bureau of Business Practice, 24 Rope Ferry Rd, Waterford, CT 06386. Telephone (203) 442-4365.

Semimonthly newsletter. Describes strategies to counteract the barriers women in business face. Contains a special department on managerial procedures. Price $24.00 per year.

5013
Women in Business
American Business Women's Assn, 9100 Ward Pkway, PO Box 8728, Kansas City, MO 64114. Telephone (816) 361-6621.

Magazine issued six times per year. Provides information about legislation, finance, business technology, communications, taxes, and association news for the working woman. Price $8.00 per year. ISSN 0043-7441.

5014
Women in the Labour Force: Facts &
Figures
Canadian Dept of Labour, Ottawa, Ont, Canada K1A 0J2. Order from Publishing Centre, Supply and Services, Ottawa, Canada K1A 0S9. Telephone (819) 997-2582.

Annual booklet. Carries statistics on women's employment in Canada. Price free of charge.

5015
Women's, Misses', and Juniors' Apparel
US Dept of Commerce, Bureau of the Census, Washington, DC 20233. Telephone (202) 449-1600.

Monthly report. Supplies data on cuttings of selected women's, misses' and juniors' garments, such as coats, suits, dresses, blouses, skirts, slips, and sweaters. Price $1.75 per year.

5016
Women's Work
Women's Work, 1302 18th St, NW, Suite 203, Washington, DC 20036. Telephone (202) 223-6274.

Bimonthly magazine. Discusses career opportunities for women. Notes employment trends in major cities and includes interviews and book reviews. Price $9.00 per year individuals, $18.00 per year institutions.

5017
Wood Pulp and Fiber Statistics
American Paper Inst, 260 Madison Ave, New York, NY 10016. Telephone (202) 340-0600.

Annual report. Provides statistics on the US and world wood pulp and fiber industries. Price available on request.

5018
Wool, Australia (Cat No 7212.0)
Australian Bureau of Statistics, PO Box 10, Belconnen, ACT 2616, Australia. Order from Australian Government Publishing Service, PO Box 84, Canberra, ACT 2600, Australia. Telephone (61) (062) 52 7911.

Annual report. Supplies statistical information on Australian rural holdings classified by size of sheep flocks and other categories. Notes wool yields. Price free of charge.

5020
Word Processing Information Systems
Geyer-McAllister Publications, Inc, 51 Madison Ave, New York, NY 10010. Telephone (212) 689-4411.

Magazine issued nine times per year. Lists manufacturers, equipment, and services for word processing professionals. Price $16.00 per year.

5021
Work and People
Dept of Science & Technology, Human Relations Branch, PO Box 449, Woden, A.C.T. 2606, Australia. Order from Australian Government Publishing Service, PO Box 84, Canberra, ACT 2600, Australia. Telephone 95 4711. Telex 62013.

Magazine issued three times a year. Discusses personnel management and employee participation in Australia and overseas. Emphasizes labor conditions. Price $6.90 (Australian) per year.

5022
Workforce
Specialist Newsletters Pty Ltd, PO Box 430, Milsons Point, Sydney, NSW 2061, Australia. Telephone (61) (02) 922 3255.

Weekly newsletter. Addresses itself to industrial relations in Australia. Price $120.00 per year.

5023
Working Conditions in Canadian Industry, 1978 and 1979
Labour Canada, Communications Services Directorate, Ottawa, Ont, Canada K1A 0J2. Order from Communications Services Directorate, Labour Canada, Ottawa, Ont, Canada K1A 0J2. Telephone (819) 997-2617.

Annual publication. Includes data on hours of work, paid holidays, vacations and other benefits, by province and industry. Bilingual. Price $2.50.

5024
Working Papers in Baker Library: A Quarterly Checklist
Harvard University, Graduate School of Business Adm, Baker Library, Soldiers Field, Boston, MA 02163. Telephone (617) 495-6405.

Quarterly checklist of working papers received by Baker Library (Harvard Business School) on business and economics from about 50 institutions. Price $7.50.

5025
Working Woman
Hal Publications, Inc, 1180 Avenue of the Americas, New York, NY 10036. Telephone (212) 944-5250.

Monthly magazine. Offers career advice for women. Appraises job market and provides information on personal finances. Price $9.00 per year.

5026
Worklife Magazine
US Dept of Labor, Employment & Training Adm, Washington, DC 20213. Telephone (202) 376-6730.

Monthly magazine. Discusses the activities of the Department of Labor's Employment and Training Administration. Reports on US labor trends. Price $15.30 per year.

5027
Workmen's Compensation for Occupational Injuries and Death (Desk Edition)
Arthur Larson, Matthew Bender & Co, 235 E 45th St, New York, NY 10017. Telephone (212) 661-5050.

Two-volume loose-leaf report, with annual supplements. Contains a brief discussion of workmen's compensation laws regarding occupational injuries and deaths. Price $140.00.

5028
Workmen's Compensation Law Reports
Commerce Clearing House, Inc, 4025 W Peterson Ave, Chicago, IL 60646. Telephone (312) 583-8500.

Loose-leaf book, plus fortnightly reports. Covers phases of workmen's compensation and occupational safety and health laws. Price $380.00 per year.

5029
Work Related Abstracts
Information Coordinators, Inc, 1435-37 Randolph St, Detroit, MI 48226. Telephone (313) 962-9720.

Monthly abstracts from over 250 business, labor, and professional periodicals or labor issues, such as union representation, management, wages, and recent legislation. Price $335.00 per year.

5030
Works Management
Findlay Publications Ltd, 10 Letchworth Dr, Bromley, Kent, England BR2 9BE. Order from Machpress Ltd, 1 Copers Cope Rd, Beckenham, Kent, England BR3 1NB. Telephone (44) (01) 650-4877.

Monthly magazine. Deals with works management issues. Price £22.00 UK, £30.00 US.

5031
Work Stoppages
Labour Canada, PR Branch, 340 Laurier Ave W, Ottawa, Ont, Canada K1A 0J2. Order from Publications Div, Labour Canada, Ottawa, Ont, Canada K1A 0J2. Telephone (819) 997-2031.

Monthly bulletin. Compiles news of labor strikes in Canada. Gives the number of strikes, workers involved, and man-days lost by nonagricultural workers. Price free of charge.

5032
Work Stoppages in New York State
New York State Dept of Labor, Div of Research and Statistics, State Office Bldg Campus, Albany, NY 12240. Order from the Div of Research and Statistics, Rm 6804, New York State Dept of Labor, 2 World Trade Center, New York, NY 10047. Telephone (212) 488-5030.

Monthly report. Lists the parties to New York State work stoppages, number of workers affected, location, and date. Price free of charge.

5033
Work Study
Sawell Publications Ltd, 127 Stanstead Rd, London, England SE23 1JE. Telephone (44) (01) 699-6792.

Monthly magazine. Provides technical articles about the work study field. Price $17.00.

5034
World Accounting Report
Financial Times Business Information Ltd, Bracken House, 10 Cannon St, London, England EC4P 4BY. Order from Financial Times Ltd, 75 Rockefeller Plz, New York, NY 10019. Telephone (44) (01) 248-8000. Telex 886341-2.

Monthly report. Surveys developments in world accounting. Includes proposed standards, corporate law changes, stock exchange rules, and auditing procedures. Price $260.00 per year.

5035
World Advertising Expenditures
International Advertising Assn, 475 5th Ave, New York, NY 10017. Order from Starch INRA Hooper, 420 Lexington Ave, New York, NY 10017. Telephone (212) 684-1583.

Biennial book. Covers advertising expenditures for 100 countries. Offers breakdowns for 75 major markets by media. Price $35.00.

5036
World Agricultural Economics & Rural Sociology Abstracts
Commonwealth Agricultural Bureaux, Central Sales Branch, Farnham House, Farnham Royal, Slough, England SL2 3BN. Telephone Farnham Common 2281. Telex 847964.

Monthly magazine. Contains abstracts of articles on agricultural policy, products, and marketing; international trade, finance, and credit; and rural sociology. Price $324.00 per year.

5037
World Agricultural Report
Ronald Anderson & Assoc, 90-92 Langridge St, Collingwood, Vic 3066, Australia. Telephone (61) (03) 4173140. Telex AA36701.

Fortnightly report. Contains agricultural news and analyses from around the world of interest to Australian agriculture. Price $50.00 (Australian) per year.

5038
World Agricultural Situation
US Dept of Agriculture, ESS Publications, Room 0054-S, Washington, DC 20250. Telephone (202) 447-7255.

Report published three times per year. Evaluates world agriculture for the current year. Includes regional reports that provide data by country on output, use, trade, and policy developments. Price free of charge.

5038.01
World Agricultural Supply and Demand Estimates
US Dept of Agriculture, ESS Publications, Room 0054-S, Washington, DC 20250. Telephone (202) 447-7255.

Monthly reports. Update USDA forecasts of supply-demand balance for major farm commodities. Cover current marketing season and may include one season ahead. Tables. Price free of charge.

5039
World Air Transport Statistics
International Air Transport Assn, IBM Bldg, 5 Pl Ville Marie, Montreal 2, Que, Canada. International Air Transport Assn, Public Relations, 1000 Sherbrook St West, Montreal Quebec H3A, Canada.

Annual report. Contains statistics on operations of air carriers in the association. Price $25.00.

5040
World Aluminum Abstracts
Aluminum Assn, Inc, 818 Connecticut Ave, NW, Washington, DC 20006. Telephone (202) 862-5100.

Monthly journal. Guides the user to technical literature on aluminum. Computerized subject and author indexes. Price $90.00 per year.

5041
World Animal Review
Food and Agriculture Organization of the United Nations, Via delle Terme di Caracalla, Rome, Italy 00100. Order from UNIPUB, 345 Parks Ave S, New York, NY 10016. Telephone (39) (6) 5797. Telex 61181.

Quarterly report. Focuses on livestock production, health, and products. Price $10.00 per year.

5041.01
World Automotive Market
Johnston International Publishing Corp, 386 Park Ave S, New York, NY 10016. Telephone (212) 689-0120.

Annual report. Covers yearly car production in 78 countries, world motor census as of January 1, and US exports of autos, parts, accessories, and service equipment. Price $15.00.

5042
World Aviation Directory
Ziff-Davis Publishing Co, 1156 15th St NW, Washington, DC 20005. Telephone (202) 293-3400.

Semiannual book. Lists aviation companies and personnel, air carriers, manufacturers, support services, government agencies affecting the aviation and aerospace industry, and international organizations. Price $60.00 per issue.

5043
World Bank Annual Report, 1980
World Bank, 1818 H St, NW, Washington, DC 20433. Telephone (202) 393-6360.

Annual report. Summarizes the activities of the World Bank and International Development Association. Reviews economic trends in developing countries, capital flow, and external public debt. Tables. Price free of charge.

5044
World Bank Atlas, 15th edition
World Bank, 1818 H St, NW, Washington, DC 20433. Telephone (202) 393-6360.

Annual atlas. Estimates the population, gross national product, and average annual growth rates for 187 countries and territories. Tables and maps. Price free of charge.

5045
World Banking Survey
Financial Times Business Information Ltd, Bracken House, 10 Cannon St, London, England EC4P 4BY. Order from Financial Times Ltd, 75 Rockefeller Plz, New York, NY 10019. Telephone (44) (01) 248-8000. Telex 886341-2.

Annual publication. Gives balance sheet figures for over 500 major clearing banks throughout the world. Includes articles. Price $20.00.

5046
Worldbusiness Perspectives
Conference Board, Inc, 845 3rd Ave, New York, NY 10022. Telephone (212) 759-0900.

Bimonthly publication. Present topics of international economic interest. Charts. Price available on request.

5046.01
World Business Weekly
Financial Times, Business Information Ltd, Bracken House, 10 Cannon St, London, England EC4P 4BY. Telephone (44) (01) 248-8000.

Weekly magazine. Covers business and economic developments throughout the world. Covers such subjects as international banking, real estate, insurance, aerospace, and advertising. Price $98.00 per year.

5047
Worldcasts
Predicasts, Inc, 200 University Circle Research Center, 11001 Cedar Ave, Cleveland, OH 44106. Telephone (216) 795-3000.

Abstracts of published international forecasts. Present industrial and economic predictions for all countries. Contain composite forecast data on population, steel ingot production, fiber consumption, and other areas, for 50 countries. Price $1200.00 for all worldcasts.

5048
World Commodity Report
Financial Times Business Information Ltd, Bracken House, 10 Cannon St, London, England EC4P 4BY. Order from Financial Times Ltd, 75 Rockefeller Plz, New York, NY 10019. Telephone (44) (01) 248-8000. Telex 886341-2.

Weekly report. Analyzes developments in international commodity markets. Cover metals, grains, produce, fibers, and other commodities. Price $395.00 per year.

5049
World Council of Credit Unions Annual Report
World Council of Credit Unions, PO Box 391, Madison, WI 53701. Telephone (608) 238-7391. Telex 910-296-2725 WNA MUT MDN.

Annual report. Provides a source for data on international credit unions and contemporary credit union leaders. Statistical tables. Price free of charge.

5050
World Council of Credit Unions Newsletter
World Council of Credit Unions, PO Box 391, Madison, WI 53701. Telephone (608) 238-7391. Telex 910-296-2725 WNA MUT MDN.

Monthly newsletter. Covers international credit union trends. Notes meetings and personnel changes. Price free of charge.

5051
World Council of Credit Unions Technical Bulletin
World Council of Credit Unions, PO Box 431, Madison, WI 53701. Telephone (608) 241-1211. Telex 910-296-7391 WNA MUT MDN.

Quarterly report. Discusses credit union management subjects, with emphasis on developing nations. Price free of charge.

5053
World Currency Charts, **8th edition**
American International Investment Corp, 351 California St, San Francisco, CA 94104. Telephone (415) 956-2121.

Boo' Compares 147 world currencies against US dollars. Price contribution requested.

5054
World Debt Tables
World Bank, 1818 H St, NW, Washington, DC 20433. Telephone (202) 393-6360.

Mimeographed publication. Revises data on the public debt of 86 developing countries. Debt tables of the World Bank 1976 Annual Report. Price free of charge.

5055
World Development
Pergamon Press, Inc, Maxwell House, Fairview Park, Elmsford, NY 10523. Telephone (914) 592-7700. Telex 13-7328.

Monthly magazine. Reports on international development topics. Price $150.00 per year.

5057
World Directory of Marketing Communications Periodicals
International Advertising Assn, 475 5th Ave, New York, NY 10017. Telephone (212) 684-1583.

Directory. Provides a guide to 350 publications in 34 countries relevant to the marketing field. Contains in the Introduction a code for interpreting listings in English, French, German, and Spanish. Price $8.00 per copy.

5058
World Directory of Multinational Enterprises
Facts on File, Inc, 460 Park Ave S, New York, NY 10016. Telephone (212) 265-2011.

Two-volume directory. Provides information on multinational enterprises. Lists subsidiaries, merger histories, product profit tables, and percentages of sales by product line. Price $195.00. ISBN 0-87196-440-6 and 0-87196-441-4.

5058.01
World Directory of Pharmaceutical Manufacturers
IMS World Publications Ltd, York House, 37 Queen Sq, London, England WC1N 3BE. Telephone (44) (01) 242-0112. Telex 263298.

Directory. Presents information on more than 2000 pharmaceutical companies in 33 countries. Lists five leading drug products for each company. Price $145.00.

5059
World Economic and Social Indicators
World Bank, 1818 H St, NW, Washington, DC 20433. Telephone (202) 393-6360.

Monthly mimeographed publication. Presents global economic indicators by income group, gross national product, national savings, and investment. Tables. Price free of charge.

5060
World Economic Service
Europe Information Service, 46 Ave, Albert Elisabeth, Brussels, Belgium 1040. Telephone (32) (2) 736.11.93. Telex Eurinf 26005b.

Semimonthly report. Covers the world economic conditions and agreements, industrial commodities, and Europe in a world framework. Price $330.00 per year.

5061
World Economic Survey
United Nations Dept of International Economic and Social Affairs, Rm A-3315, New York, NY 10017. Telephone (212) 754-8302.

Annual report. Covers world economic trends. Price varies.

5062
World Economy
Basil Blackwell Publisher, 108 Cowley Rd, Oxford, England OX4 1JF. Telephone Oxford (STD 0865) 722146.

Quarterly publication. Discusses world economic issues and problems as they affect corporate decisions, and national and international policies. Price $35.00 per year.

5062.01
World Economy
North-Holland Publishing Co, PO Box 211, 1000 AE Amsterdam, The Netherlands. Order from Elsevier/North-Holland, Inc, 52 Vanderbilt Ave, New York, NY 10017. Telephone (212) 867-9040.

Quarterly journal. Analyzes world economic problems. Price $65.75 per year. ISSN 0378-5920.

5063
World Energy Supplies
United Nations Publications, Rm A-3315, New York, NY 10017. Telephone (212) 754-8302.

Report. Provides data on available energy worldwide. Price available on request.

5063.01
World Environmental Directory
Business Publishers, Inc, PO Box 1067, Silver Spring, MD 20910. Telephone (301) 587-6300.

Biannual directory. Provides information on pollution control agencies and equipment manufacturers. Price $67.00.

5064
World Farming
Intertec Publishing Corp, 9221 Quivera Rd, PO Box 12901, Overland Park, KS 66212. Telephone (913) 888-4664. Telex 42-4156.

Bimonthly magazine. Reports on farming topics. Includes information on livestock, crop production, and equipment. Price available on request.

5065
World Guide to Abbreviations of Organizations, 5th edition
Gale Research Co, Book Tower, Detroit, MI 48226. Telephone (313) 961-2242.

Book. Gives the full name behind initials and abbreviations used for companies, international agencies, and government departments throughout the world. Price $100.00. ISBN 2015-0.

5066
World Guide to Scientific Associations and Learned Societies
R R Bowker Co, 1180 Ave of the Americas, New York, NY 10036. Order from R R Bowker Co, PO Box 1807, Ann Arbor, MI 48106. Telephone (212) 764-5100.

Directory. Provides current data on 12,000 groups, from over 130 countries, concerned with research, medicine, and education. Price $62.50. ISBN 3-7940-1213-5.

5067
World Guide to Trade Associations
R R Bowker Co, 1180 Ave of the Americas, New York, NY 10036. Order from R R Bowker Co, PO Box 1807, Ann Arbor, MI 48106. Telephone (212) 764-5100.

Book. Provides information on 26,000 trade- and industry-related organizations in 153 countries. Lists chambers of commerce, artisan guilds, trade unions, and employers' and employees' groups in the US and abroad. Subject index. Preface and headings in English and German; entries in language of country of origin. Price $72.50. ISBN 3-7940-1032-9.

5067.01
World Health Environmental Surveys
IMS World Publications Ltd, York House, 37 Queen Sq, London, England WCIN 3BE. Telephone (44) (01) 242-0112. Telex 263298.

Book. Surveys health situation and pharmaceutical policies in 60 countries. Reports on health statistics, medical services, and health economics. Price $300.00.

5067.02
World Index of Economic Forecasts, 2nd edition
Gower Publishing Co Ltd, 1 Westmead, Farnborough, Hampshire, England GU14 7RU. Telephone Farnborough (0252) 519221. Telex 858623.

Index. Contains details of forecasting groups in over 40 different countries together with their coverage, method, and published output. Includes a new section covering forecasts derived from industrial survey work. Price available on request.

5068
World Insurance Report
Financial Times Business Information Ltd, Bracken House, 10 Cannon St, London, England EC4P 4BY. Order from Financial Times Ltd, 75 Rockefeller Plz, New York, NY 10019. Telephone (44) (01) 248-8000. Telex 886341-2.

Fortnightly report. Reviews international property and liability insurance and reinsurance issues. Covers laws affecting insurance and people in insurance. Price $530.00 per year.

5068.01
World Law of Competition
Matthew Bender & Co, 235 E 45th St, New York, NY 10017. Telephone (212) 661-5050.

Two-volume loose-leaf book with periodic replacement pages as needed. Covers the law of competition in North America and Western Europe. Notes pricing practices, distribution practices, and unfair trade practices. Price $125.00 per volume plus additional charge for revisions.

5068.02
World License Review
IMS World Publications Ltd, York House, 37 Queen Sq, London, England WC1N 3BE. Telephone (44) (01) 242-0112. Telex 263298.

Annual survey. Reports on corporate drug licensing activity. Lists joint venture agreements and product launches. Price $750.00.

5069
World Marketing
Dun & Bradstreet, Box 3224, Church St Station, New York, NY 10008. Telephone (212) 285-7346.

Semimonthly report. Focuses on overseas marketing developments and trade possiblities throughout the world. Price available on request to Dun & Bradstreet subscribers only.

5070
World Markets Intelligence Report
Microinfo Ltd, PO Box 3, Newman Lane, Alton, Hampshire, England GU34 2PG. Telephone Alton 84300. Telex 858431.

Newsletter. Reviews new market survey data for raw materials and manufactured products of all kinds. Price available on request.

5071
World Money Outlook
Barclays Bank, Group Economic Intelligence Unit, 54 Lombard St, London, England EC3P 3AH. Telephone (44) (01) 283-8989.

Biannual pamphlet. Carries the views of economists of the Societe Financiere Europeenne concerning the financial position and outlook of each member's country. Price free of charge.

5072
World of Learning
Europa Publications Ltd, 18 Bedford Sq, London, WC1B 3JN, England. Telephone (44) (01) 580-8236.

Two-volume annual book. Contains detailed information on over 24,000 colleges, universities, art and music schools, libraries, societies, research institutes, museums, and art galleries as well as the personnel of these places. Price $125.00.

5072.01
World of Logotypes, Volumes I & II
Advertising Trade Publications, Inc, 10 E 39th St, New York, NY 10016. Order from Art Direction Book Co, 10 E 39th St, New York, NY 10016. Telephone (212) 889-6500.

Two-volume book. Contains 3000 logotypes and corporate symbols. Price $26.50 each.

5073
World of Work Report
Work in America Inst, Inc, 700 White Plains Rd, Scarsdale, NY 10583. Telephone (914) 472-9600. Order from Van Nostrand Reinhold, Inc, 7625 Empire Dr, Florence, KY 41042. Telephone (606) 525-6600.

Monthly newsletter. Reports on new trends and experiments in the organization of work. Covers productivity, manpower training, and labor relations and includes US and foreign case studies. Price $48.00 per year for US, Canada, Mexico, $60.00 for foreign. ISSN 0361-6959.

5073.01
World Patents Abstracts, **1981**
Derwent Publications Ltd, Rochdale House, 128 Theobalds Rd, London, England WC1X 8RP. Telephone (44) (01) 242-5823. Telex 267487.

Series of weekly booklets. Provides abstracts of all patents by country and by subject. Price available on request.

5073.02
World Patents Index, **1981**
Derwent Publications Ltd, Rochdale House, 128 Theobalds Rd, London, England WC1X 8RP. Telephone (44) (01) 242-5823. Telex 267487.

Series of indexes. Provides bibliographic data and titles for all patents issued in 26 countries. Price available on request.

5073.03
World Pharmaceutical Introductions
IMS World Publications Ltd, York House, 37 Queen Sq, London, England WCIN 3BE. Telephone (44) (01) 242-0112. Telex 263298.

Quarterly loose-leaf report. Covers new drugs in 26 countries. Reports on research developments. Price $600.00 per year.

5074
World Production and Reserve Statistics
Petroconsultants SA, 8-10 Rue Muzy, PO Box 228, 1211 Geneva 6, Switzerland. Telephone 36 88 11. Telex 27 763 PETRO CH.

Information service. Presents historical and current data on crude oil production and reserves in 53 countries and on natural gas in 12, excluding the Communist bloc. Charts and graphs. Price 1000.00 Swiss francs.

5075
World Products
Dun & Bradstreet, Box 3224, Church St Station, New York, NY 10008. Telephone (212) 285-7346.

Monthly report. Provides information on new products available from overseas suppliers. Price available on request to Dun & Bradstreet subscribers only.

5076
World Report
Employment Conditions Abroad Ltd, Devonshire House, 13 Devonshire St, London, England W1N 1FS. Telephone (44) (01) 637-7604. Telex 299751 Eureca G.

Monthly report. Deals with employment throughout the world. Includes information on legislation, cost of living, and industrial relations. Price $45.00 per year.

5077
World Reporter
World Council of Credit Unions, PO Box 391, Madison, WI 53701. Telephone (608) 238-7391. Telex 910-296-2725 WNA MUT MDN.

Tabloid. Covers credit union subjects, the cooperative philosophy, and the international credit union movement. Illustrated. Price free of charge.

5078
World's Fair
World's Fair Ltd, PO Box 57, Union St, Oldham, Lanc, England OL1 1DY. Telephone (44) (061) 624 3687. Telex 667352.

Weekly newspaper. Reports on British amusement parks, carnivals, and coin-operated amusement equipment. Notes international developments. Price $27.00 per year.

5078.01
World Shipping Laws
Oceana Publications, Inc, 75 Main St, Dobbs Ferry, NY 10522. Telephone (914) 693-1320.

Loose-leaf service in three binders. Covers international shipping laws, rules and regulations. Price $80.00 per binder. ISBN 0-379-10164-3.

5078.02
World's Largest Industrial Enterprises
Gower Publishing Co Ltd, 1 Westmead, Farnborough, Hampshire, England, GUI4 7RU. Telephone Farnborough (0252) 519221. Telex 858623.

Directory. Gives detailed analyses on the structure, growth, performance and international involvement of over 800 largest companies in the world. Price $67.50. ISBN 0 566 00422 4.

5079
World's Monetary Stocks of Gold, Silver and Coins—On a Calendar Year Basis
US Dept of the Treasury, Bureau of the Mint, 15th & Pennsylvania Ave, NW, Washington, DC 20220. Telephone (202) 566-2000.

Book. Carries data on the world's monetary stocks of gold, silver, and coins on a calendar-year basis. Price available on request.

5079.01
World Solar Markets
Financial Times Business Information Ltd, Bracken House, 10 Cannon St, London, England EC4P 4BY. Order from Financial Times Ltd, 75 Rockefeller Plz, New York, NY 10019. Telephone 01-248-8000. Telex 886341-2.

Monthly report. Monitors development of solar energy usage and output of solar plants throughout the world. Price available on request.

5080
World Tables 1980
World Bank, 1818 H St, NW, Washington, DC 20433. Order from John Hopkins University Press, Baltimore, MD 21218. Telephone Baltimore (301) 338-7875; Washington (202) 393-6360.

Book. Contains basic economic data from the World Bank files on individual countries. Supplies economic indicators and demographic and social data. Technical notes, glossary, translations, and index. Price $22.50 (hardbound); $8.95 (paperbound). ISBN 0-8018-1886-9 (hardbound); ISBN 0-8018-1898-2 (paperbound).

5081
World Tax Series—Germany
Commerce Clearing House, Inc, 4025 W Peterson Ave, Chicago, IL 60646. Telephone (312) 583-8500.

Two loose-leaf books and monthly reports. Analyze West German's tax system. Price $290.00 per year.

5082
World Trade Annual
Walker & Company, 720 5th Ave, New York, NY 10019. Telephone (212) 265-3632.

Five-volume annual book. Offers statistics and detailed information on various aspects of the world trade situations. Price $250.00 per year.

5083

World Trade Centers Association (WTCA) News

World Trade Centers Assn, Inc, 1 World Trade Center, Suite 55 W, New York, NY 10048. Telephone (212) 466-8287.

Monthly newsletter. Covers Association news, trade fairs and missions, and other items affecting world trade centers. Price free of charge to association members.

5083.01

World Trade Information Center

World Trade Information Center, 1 World Trade Center, Suite 86001, New York, NY 10048. Telephone (212) 466-3069.

Service. Handles trade information requests through data collection. Has direct access to major on-line data bases, worldwide individual and organization contacts, and customized reports and surveys. Price varies.

5084

World Travel Directory

Ziff-Davis Publishing Co, 1156 15th St, NW, Washington, DC 20005. Order from Ziff-Davis Publishing Co, One Park Ave, New York, NY 10016. Telephone (212) 725-3680.

Annual book. Provides a directory of retail and wholesale travel agencies. Lists and describes travel packages. Price available on request.

5084.01

World Video Report

Microinfo Ltd, PO Box 3, Newman Lane, Alton, Hampshire, England GU34 2PG. Telephone Alton 84300. Telex 858431.

Newsletter. Concerns business and consumer applications and markets for video-based products and publishing systems. Price available on request.

5085

World Who's Who in Science

Marquis Publications, 200 E Ohio St, Rm 5604, Chicago, IL 60611. Telephone (312) 787-2008.

Book. Presents more than 32,000 sketches of scientists from antiquity to 1968. Price $60.00. ISBN 0-8379-1001-3.

5086

Worldwide Directory of Computer Companies

Marquis Publications, 200 E Ohio St, Rm 5604, Chicago, IL 60611. Telephone (312) 787-2008.

Directory. Lists more than 4000 firms in the computer industry, including those that provide hardware, software, equipment, and services. Price $44.50. ISBN 0-87876-33-4.

5087

Worldwide Directory of Federal Libraries

Marquis Publications, 200 E Ohio St, Rm 5604, Chicago, IL 60611. Telephone (312) 787-2008.

Directory. Provides information about US federally operated libraries throughout the world. Price $29.50. ISBN 0-87876-029-6.

5088

Worldwide Guide to Medical Electronics Marketing Representation, 1977

International Bio-Medical Information Service, Inc, PO Box 756, Miami, FL 33156. Telephone (305) 665-4856.

Book. Lists over 400 medical electronics marketing organizations throughout the world, excluding the US. Furnishes demographic and medical data for 100 nations. Indexes. Price $195.00 US, $200.00 elsewhere. ISSN 0146-8014.

5089

Woven Fabrics: Production, Inventories, and Unfilled Orders

US Dept of Commerce, Bureau of the Census, Washington, DC 20233. Telephone (202) 449-1600.

Monthly report. Contains data on production, inventories, and unfilled orders of woven fabrics by class of fabrics. Price $3.00 per year.

5089.01

Wright Investors Service

Wright Investment Publications, Wright Investors' Service, Park City Plz, 10 Middle St, Bridgeport, CT 06604. Telephone (203) 333-6666.

Series of weekly and quarterly services. Provides investment analyses of stocks. Includes comprehensive data on selected stocks, including 250 companies selected for institutional investment. Price $1250.00 per year.

5089.02

Wyoming: Directory of Manufacturing and Mining, 1980

Manufacturers' News, Inc, 3 E Huron St, Chicago, IL 60611. Telephone (312) 337-1084.

Annual book. Covers manufacturing and mining companies in Wyoming. Notes executives, products, and number of employees. Price $15.00.

5090

Yearbook, 1974-1978

Commission of the European Communities, Office for Official Publications of the European Communities, CP 1003, Luxembourg 1, Luxembourg. Telephone (352) 490081. Telex PUBLOF 1325.

Yearbook on the European community. Price free of charge.

5090.01

Yearbook of Agricultural Statistics

Commission of the European Communities, Office for Official Publications of the European Communities, CP 1003, Luxembourg 1, Luxembourg. Telephone (352) 490081. Telex PUBLOF 1325.

Annual book. Contains agricultural statistics for the European community. Price $17.80.

5090.02

Yearbook of Industrial Statistics

United Nations Statistical Office, United Nations, New York, NY 10017. Telephone (212) 754-5543.

Annual book. Contains general industrial statistics for individual countries and commodity production data. Price $35.-00.

5091

Yearbook of Industrial Statistics, 1975. Volume I-, General Industrial Statistics

United Nations Publications, Rm LX 2300, New York, NY 10017. Telephone (212) 754-1234.

Yearbook. Presents industrial activity statistics for 101 countries. International tables on index numbers of industrial employment and production. Price $32.00.

5092

Yearbook of Industrial Statistics, 1975. Volume II-, Commodity Production Data 1966-1975

United Nations Publications, Rm LX 2300, New York, NY 10017. Telephone (212) 754-1234.

Yearbook. Supplies internationally comparable data on the production of 527 industrial commodities for 200 countries. Price $32.00.

5093
Yearbook of International Organizations
Union of International Associations, 1 rue aux Laines, Brussels, Belgium 1000.

Book. Gives basic information on international organizations in a wide range of fields. Price $80.00.

5094
Yearbook of International Trade Statistics **1979**
United Nations Publications, United Nations Plaza, Room A-3315, New York, NY 10017. Telephone (212) 754-8302.

Two-volume annual book. Provides a compilation of trade statistics. Price $70.-00.

5095
Year Book of Labour Statistics
International Labour Organization, 1750 New York Ave, NW, Suite 330, Washington, DC 20006. Telephone (202) 376-2315.

Annual book. Summarizes principal labor statistics in 190 countries in such areas as population, employment, wages, labor productivity, and hours worked. Trilingual: English, French, and Spanish. Price $57.00.

5096
Yearbook of National Accounts Statistics
United Nations Statistical Office, UN Publications, United Nations Plaza, Rm LX 2300, New York, NY 10017. Telephone (212) 754-5650.

Three books. Give national income, gross national product, and other national statistics by country over a 12-year period. Regional statistics. Price varies.

5096.01
Yearbook of Procurement Articles
Federal Publications, Inc, 1120 20th St, NW, Washington, DC 20036. Telephone (202) 337-7000.

Annual book plus 12-volume index. Reproduces articles on government procurement published in journals during the previous year. Price $120.00 for yearbook, $95.00 for index.

5097
Yearbook of Railroad Facts
Assn of American Railroads, Economics and Finance Dept, American Railroads Bldg, Washington, DC 20036. Telephone (202) 293-4054.

Yearbook. Summarizes railroad operations during the preceding and prior years. Price free of charge.

5098
Yearbooks of Fishery Statistics
Food and Agriculture Organization of the United Nations, Via delle Terme di Caracalla, Rome, Italy 00100. Order from UNIPUB, 345 Park Ave S, New York, NY 10016. Telephone (39) (6) 5797. Telex 61181.

Yearbooks. Contain data on production and foreign trade in fishery and related products. Tables of imports and exports. Price $63.00.

5099
Yearbooks of Forest Products Statistics
Food and Agriculture Organization of the United Nations, Via delle Terme di Caracalla, Rome, Italy 00100. Order from UNIPUB, 345 Park Ave S, New York, NY 10016. Telephone (39) (6) 5797. Telex 61181.

Yearbooks. Provide data on production, trade, and consumption for roundwood, sawnwood, sleepers, plywood, wood pulp, paper, paperboard, and fiberboard. Uses material from over 100 countries during the two years preceding publication. Price $40.50.

5100
Year-End Summary of the Electric Power Situation
Edison Electric Inst, 1111 19th St, NW, Washington, DC 20036. Telephone (202) 828-7400.

Annual report. Presents a survey of the US electric power supply, expansion of generating facilities, and manufacture of heavy electric power equipment. Price $7.00.

5101
You and the Law
Research Inst of America, Inc, 589 5th Ave, New York, NY 10017. Telephone (212) 755-8900.

Biweekly newsletter. Provides a guide to current legal developments affecting business executives. Price $36.00 per year.

5102
Arthur Young Client Memorandums
Arthur Young & Co, 277 Park Ave, New York, NY 10017. Telephone (212) 922-4724.

Memorandums. Deal with accounting, auditing, financial reporting, and tax matters. Price free of charge.

5103
Arthur Young Journal
Arthur Young & Co, 277 Park Ave, New York, NY 10017. Telephone (212) 922-4724.

Magazine issued three times per year. Covers business, accounting, auditing, and management topics. Price free of charge.

5104
Arthur Young Views
Arthur Young & Co, 277 Park Ave, New York, NY 10017. Telephone (212) 922-4724.

Monthly newsletter. Provides information on recent developments in accounting and auditing, financial reporting, taxation, and management issues. Price free of charge.

5105
Zero-Base Digest
Tufty Communications, 986 National Press Bldg, Washington, DC 20045. Telephone (202) 347-8998.

Monthly report. Covers zero-base budgeting and planning. Discusses attempts to implement such at the federal, state, and local level and in industry. Price $120.00 per year.

5106
Zinc Data
American Bureau of Metal Statistics, Inc, 420 Lexington Ave, New York, NY 10170. Telephone (212) 867-9450. Telex 14-7130.

Monthly report. Tenders statistics on zinc production, shipments, and smelters in the US and other countries. Trade figures. Price $200.00 per year.

5107
Zosen
Tokyo News Service Ltd, Tsukiji Hamarikyu Bldg, 3-3, Tsukiji 5-chome, Chuo-ku, Tokyo 104, Japan. Telephone (03) 542-8521. Telex 252-3285 STNEWS J.

Monthly magazine. Discusses shipbuilding, shipping, and related industries. Emphasizes Japanese developments and reviews the tanker and iron and steel markets. Price US $60.00 per year.

5108
Zweig Forecast
Zweig Securities Advisory Service, Inc, 747 3rd Ave, New York, NY 10017. Telephone (212) 753-7710.

Newsletter published 18 times per year. Evaluates stock market trends and offers stock and other investment advice. Tables. Price $165.00 per year.